I0605115

On Trial in the Welsh Press

On Trial in the Welsh Press

Latter-day Saint Missionaries Declare and Defend the Faith, 1840–1860

Translated and Edited by

Ronald D. Dennis

Published by the Religious Studies Center, Brigham Young University, Provo, Utah.

http://rsc.byu.edu

Printed in the United States of America by Sheridan Books.

ISBN: 978-1-9503-0447-9
Jacket design by Carmen Durland Cole.

Library of Congress Cataloging-in-Publication Data

Names: Dennis, Ronald D., 1940– translator, editor.
Title: On trial in the Welsh press : Latter-day Saint missionaries declare and defend the faith, 1840–1860 / translated and edited by Ronald D. Dennis.
Description: Provo: Religious Studies Center at BYU, 2022. | "Published by the Religious Studies Center, Brigham Young University, Provo, Utah." | Includes index.
Identifiers: LCCN 2023937698 | ISBN 978-1-9503-0447-9

Dedicated to the following colleagues in Wales:

Wil Aaron for assistance with my research over the past several years.

Professor D. L. Davies for his frequent guidance over the past four decades.

Dr. Huw Walters for his orientation concerning Latter-day Saint Welsh publications.

The late professor Bobi Jones for allowing me to audit his classes.

The late professor Tedi Millward for his classroom instruction and personal tutoring.

My heartfelt thanks to Marilyn Davies for solving many lists of my "translation traumas" and to the following Brigham Young University team members for their superb editing and proofreading skills: Emma Ebert, Skyler Garrett, Tina Hawley, Kiersten Guymon, Abigail Huch, Devan Jensen, Sara McOmber, Robbyn Merrell, Heather Randall, and Erica Smith.

Contents

Section 2: Pamphlets

Section 3: Poems

Foreword

Aaron C. Eastley

Dan Jones enjoys wide name recognition among members of The Church of Jesus Christ of Latter-day Saints. He is legendary—but in another sense largely unknown. As newly called missionaries open *Preach My Gospel*, the Church's guide to missionary service, they are greeted on page 1 of chapter 1 by Clark Kelley Price's painting *Dan Jones Awakens Wales*. The caption reads, "Dan Jones, one of the greatest missionaries in this dispensation, preaches the gospel in Wales." The painting depicts Jones standing on a stonework platform addressing townspeople while boldly holding aloft the *Book of Mormon*. Mud and water cover the street, industrial chimneys belch smoke in the background, and the gathered onlookers range from gentle folk in fashionable attire to coal miners in their pit dirt. But *Preach My Gospel* includes only a portion of Price's original painting. Perhaps in order to serve as more of a banner atop the opening page, the bottom half of the original scene—where many of the onlookers are depicted—has been cut off.

What is missing from the picture is what is abundantly revealed in this volume: the inner workings of the spirited mid-nineteenth-century struggle for the souls of the people of Wales. Price imagines this by surrounding Jones with what appear to be earnest listeners, among whom are two particularly interesting figures, situated opposite each other in the bottom corners of the original. The first is an elderly gentleman, clearly agitated, who looks as if he might be a minister. The other is a wide-eyed miner. The ministerial figure is remonstrating with a well-dressed and serious-looking man next to him, while the miner is seemingly beckoning to a fellow. One can easily imagine the miner as a member of the minister's congregation—one in real danger of being drawn away by the message of miracles and modern-day martyrdom brought back by Jones from America to Merthyr Tydfil (a town itself named for an early Christian martyr, or "merthyr"). The minister seems about as happy under the circumstances as one might expect. Even in the silence of a painting, the tenor of his discourse to the man next to him we can readily guess. But how much more interesting would it be to have his very words? And again, to have Jones's words in reply? As Price's complete image rightly portrays, Jones was both a magnet and an agitator, and he was so, notably, both in person and in print. Beyond his proselytizing on street corners, he was an incredibly prolific writer, publishing literally thousands of pages in defense of the Restored Gospel of Jesus Christ.

Here, then, is the great value of this collection. It offers a remarkably comprehensive view of an era and area of the history of The Church of Jesus Christ of Latter-day Saints (not to mention the history of Wales) that has long effectively been under erasure. For while many today might recognize Dan Jones's name or image and know something of his success in converting his countrymen, how many can tell what he actually had to say? What was the substance of his sermons, the details of his written discourses? And what was said against him and the Church by others, inciting his responses? These particulars have been largely lost to time and curtained off from all but a relative few by that familiar but formidable barrier: language. For Jones's missionary work in Wales was, quite naturally, conducted almost entirely in Welsh. Hence, most people even in the Church that he championed have long been unable to become familiar with the particulars of it. Wonderfully, in recent years this has changed. Thanks to several previous volumes also brought to us by Ronald Dennis, we have come to appreciate that Jones's published periodicals, *Prophwyd y Jubili* and *Udgorn Seion* (*Prophet of the Jubilee* and *Zion's Trumpet*), may rightly be seen as Welsh counterparts to the well-known English language *Millennial Star*. What Parley P. Pratt, Orson Hyde, Orson Pratt, and others famously did in Liverpool beginning in 1840 was matched by the Welsh-language work of Dan Jones, John S. Davis, Daniel Daniels, Benjamin P. Evans, and William Ajax from 1846 to1862.

Yet even in Dennis's previous volumes, as in the portion of Price's painting included in *Preach My Gospel*, we find an incomplete picture. For a great deal of what Jones and his Welsh successors had to say came in response to newspaper articles and pamphlets published by the Church's many critics. The lengthy complete collections of the Welsh Latter-day Saint periodicals are still only half the story. Here in this volume, for the first time, we get the full broadside of the invective of Jones's enemies. These enemies found the claim of Church members to be latter-day saints "so presumptuous as if it had been written by the fingers of the devil, who had dipped his pen in the venom of dragons or the fiery furnace itself, and had it printed in the gates of hell." Such sentiments led one particularly persistent and virulent assailant to contend that converts to the new religion should be known not as "saints" but "Satanists." Though this detractor staged his assault from behind a mask of anonymity, the plucky Jones quickly brought things into the open: "His name—no need to ask; who does not know that it is the Rev. W. R. Davies who is the father of this name?" Davies, a Baptist minister, emerged as Jones's great antagonist in print: self-appointed spokesman for a surprisingly unified contingent of both Nonconformist and Anglican opponents who feared the missionaries' "constant assaults on believers and unbelievers in the areas of the Works, and the fact that they have beguiled many children and weak-minded people." In their likely sincere but frantic and often mean-spirited anxiety, these critics flooded the streets with lengthy printed condemnations, writing derisively of "Joe Smith," spouting the now-tired-but-then-novel theories surrounding Solomon Spaulding and the *Book of Mormon*, mocking reported healings and speaking in tongues, and engaging in relentless juvenile name-calling of the sort Davies displays above. The scene painted by Price seems apt indeed!

Having the words of their critics alongside the responses of the Welsh latter-day faithful creates a dynamic and detailed portrait of the times. This portrait is gratifyingly augmented by Dennis's interwoven commentaries, which consistently put the various "episodes" of conflict in context for us as readers. This format also allows Dennis to give either shorter or longer excerpts from the original documents in order to best tell the story of each discursive encounter. What is necessarily left out is covered by the commentaries, and what is included is analyzed. The final product, panoramic in its details, is thought-provoking and inspiring.

It is particularly so for me personally as William Harmon, my ancestor, could well have been the humble coal miner depicted in Price's painting. Born in Merthyr in 1820, William heard the gospel message preached by Jones and others in the mid-1840s and quickly joined the Church. It is fascinating and deeply moving for me to think of him doing so amid the vociferous war of words that I now know was taking place all around him. Of course, I see him not as weak-minded or childish but clear thinking and courageous. As readers of this book will quickly see, tremendous personal courage and clarity of conviction was absolutely necessary. For the contests carried on both in person and in print, reproduced and commented on in the pages that follow, were not demure or deferential discussions. They were knock-down, drag-out debates—what Dennis rightly labels classic examples of "nineteenth-century polemic." We do not often argue in this way today, unless perhaps it is in the largely anonymous environment of online exchanges. But no such distance separated miner, minister, and missionary in the 1840s.

This brings up my final thought regarding the relevance of this volume for us today. We are now in a moment, it seems clear to me, when courage and plain speaking are again particularly needful. As I complete this foreword, my thoughts echo with the words of two leaders of The Church of Jesus Christ of Latter-day Saints who just delivered messages. President Dallin H. Oaks, First Counselor in the First Presidency of the Church, on September 13, 2022, urged the Brigham Young University community to "dare to be different." This phrase was in reference to a recent article by Elder Clark G. Gilbert, commissioner of the Church Educational System, in which he asserted the tremendous potential he sees for religious institutions like BYU, "but only if they dare to continue with and strengthen their religious identity—only if they dare to be different from their peers . . . in ways that are true to [their] distinctive light." Both talks follow up on an address by Elder Jeffrey R. Holland to the faculty and staff of Brigham Young University in August of 2021, in which he urged faithful member-scholars to remember "the builders of the temple in Nauvoo, who worked with a trowel in one hand and a musket in the other." The point of this metaphor was, I believe, to confirm the need not only to do as the Apostle Peter urged and "be ready always to give an answer to every man that asketh you a reason of the hope that is in you" (1 Peter 3:15) but also to defend against the misrepresentations of those who assail us. This ought to be done in "meekness," as Peter goes on to affirm, but it must not be left undone. In this I can think of no better role models than Dan Jones and his Welsh fellows—early Latter-day Saints who would likely have found our increasingly argumentative present environment rather familiar and would—I have no doubt—eagerly have sought opportunities to add their deeply compassionate but fearless and hope-filled voices to the ongoing polemics that will certainly continue and increase in fervor until the long-awaited Second Coming of our Savior Jesus Christ.

Introduction

Religious Background of the Welsh

The Church of England was set up in 1534 by King Henry VIII and continued to be the state religion in Britain until 1689, at which point the Toleration Act permitted other churches to exist. But the so-called "Nonconformists" (those who chose not to conform with the doctrine and practices of the government-ruled church) were not allowed to hold most public offices and were still required to pay local taxes to the Church of England. Such restrictions continued to be imposed on these Nonconformists until the early 1800s.

Around the time the Latter-day Saints began proselyting in Wales, about 75 percent of the Welsh identified themselves as Nonconformists—the Baptists, Methodists, Congregationalists, Wesleyans, Independents, Unitarians, and Quakers being the principal religions of nonconformity, according to the 1851 British religious census. Members of the Church of England, known as Anglicans, were at this point in the minority in Wales.

The Welsh Nonconformists disagreed with one another regarding the mode of baptism and various points of doctrine and practice. But when the missionaries for The Church of Jesus Christ of Latter-day Saints began preaching their message in Wales in 1840, all the Nonconformists seemed to agree with one another on one thing: that they should oppose the Saints and their teachings. The Latter-day Saints were, after all, siphoning off their parishioners to strengthen their own ranks.

The opposition from the leaders of other religions in Wales came not only from their sermons but also from their parishioners and their children. At the instigation of their ministers, they shouted at the Latter-day Saint preachers on the street corners and threw pebbles at them as they walked along the streets. All were encouraged to disturb the meetings of the evil Latter-day "Satanists" and never to listen to them lest they be beguiled. Even violence was sometimes encouraged, such as the violence toward David Jeremy and Daniel Thomas as they preached the new doctrine out in the open on Sunday, 1 October 1854, near the town of Brechfa, Carmarthenshire. That day, a group of worshippers led by an innkeeper named John Davies came out of the Saron Chapel and began harassing the two missionaries, soon escalating into physical attacks. Jeremy later reported to Dan Jones that the angry mob would most certainly have killed him had it not been for the intervention of Dafydd Evans, who came by and shouted at the mob, "You'll not kill him before killing me. Leave him alone."[1] This "philanthropic friend" helped Jeremy to a nearby farmhouse, "Treolmawr," where a Mr. H. Howells took care of him and "showed every kindness he could." Jeremy recuperated and eventually married, but he was unable to father children as a result of the battering he received—from some ordinary, churchgoing citizens who had permitted themselves to become outraged over a difference in religion.

Some of the converts said that, contrary to their ministers' intentions, they were motivated by the warnings to instead learn more about the Latter-day Saints. Job Rowland, who was once a Baptist in the Dowlais congregation of Rev. W. R. Davies, wrote the following about his conversion:

> As soon as the Saints came to these areas our teachers, especially Mr. W. R. Davies, began to persecute them and hate them, saying all manner of evil against them. Mr. Davies said one time in our house that his desire was to do the same with their elders as was done to Joseph Smith, that is to kill them. That, together with many other things prompted me to look into their principles; and after having the honor of associating with the Saints, I saw that they were not the way Mr. Davies and others had described them. I saw also that their doctrine was harmonious with the doctrine in the scriptures; and when I heard their testimony, I decided immediately that it was true.

The most unrelenting opposition, however, came through the press. During the 1840s and 1850s in Wales, more than four hundred articles appeared in over twenty religious periodicals condemning "Mormonism" and all things related to it. And nearly seven hundred articles—varying in length, but nearly always denouncing the hated "Mormonites" and their teachings—were printed in fifteen newspapers during this period. The Latter-day Saints, however, did their utmost to defend and propagate their beliefs in whatever way possible. And that way was preaching in the open air, in the homes of converts, and in the long rooms of pubs, since the clergy refused the use of their own chapels for what they considered to be such a nefarious purpose. The modest building dedicated in Llanelli by Dan Jones in 1849 was the only purpose-built chapel in Wales during the nineteenth century.

Success of the Early Latter-day Saint Missionaries in Wales

North Wales

Elders Henry Royle and Frederick Cook were the first missionary pair to preach the gospel in North Wales. They were called to "go to Cly [Cloy] in Flintshire" at the 6 October 1840 conference held in Manchester, England. Their call to proselytize in such a small town was most likely a referral from twenty-three-year-old Martha Thomas who was baptized by Elder Joseph Fielding in 1839 in Manchester. That Royal and Cook had baptisms in the River Dee only two days after their arrival on 16 October 1840 and a total of thirty converts by the end of that month suggests that Martha may have been in the area explaining her new religion to family and friends.[2]

The 15 August 1848 *Millennial Star* reports 170 members in Wales as of 6 April 1841. No statistics are presented for Wales for the years of 1842, 1843, or 1844. Perhaps this absence of information could be attributed to a reorganization of boundaries that placed the branches in Wales under a different heading. For 1845, a total of 316 members in Wales is given.

South Wales

Elder John Needham appears to have been the first missionary to serve in South Wales. He wrote the following in his personal history: "In the year 1840 I went to Monmouthshire and Wales and with God's blessing was able to do great work there, for a people was quite ready to receive the Gospel, and I had a blessed, happy time with them." He reports having organized "many branches of the church in Monmouth and in Wales, getting help from other Elders and many that I ordained and sent out to preach." The *Millennial Star* has no specific report of baptisms in 1840 for Monmouth or for Wales, so perhaps Needham's converts were included in the numbers for the Herefordshire Conference.

Heartland Wales

In 1842, Elder William Henshaw, a Cornishman, was doing missionary work in Wolverhampton when he was called on a new mission by Elder Lorenzo Snow. Henshaw was to take his wife and children to the heartland of Wales to preach the restored gospel there. He had his first baptisms in Merthyr Tydfil on 19 February 1843. Henshaw had married Mary Ann Lewis eight years earlier in Breconshire. His being in Wales at that time suggests that he probably had gone there from Cornwall to work in the mines. And his having a Welsh wife, one who most likely spoke Welsh, may have influenced Lorenzo Snow to send Henshaw, a monoglot English speaker, on a mission to the heartland of industrial Wales.

In April 1845, a little over two years since his first baptisms, Henshaw reported a total of 316 members of the Church in South Wales—an increase of about twelve baptisms per month during that time period. By December 1845, nine months later, the number of members had grown to 493, a growth rate of nearly twenty baptisms per month.

Dan Jones in North Wales

Though William Henshaw had success in the Merthyr Tydfil area, Dan Jones had been preaching the entire year of 1845 in North Wales and had baptized but three converts. After one year of what must have been a period of great frustration, Dan was transferred to Merthyr Tydfil to assume the reins of the entire Welsh mission.

Dan Jones and William Henshaw Join Forces

The following chart shows the growth of the Church in Wales during the three years (1843, 1844, and 1845) that William Henshaw was by himself in South Wales, followed by the three years (1846, 1847, and 1848) that Jones and Henshaw were together in South Wales:[3]

Date of report	# of members	# of months	Increase	Average converts per month
18 Feb 1843	0			
6 Apr 1845	316	~ 26	316	~ 12
14 Dec 1845	493	~ 9	177	~ 20
1 Jan 1847	979	~ 12	486	~ 40
27 Dec 1847	1,933	~ 12	954	~ 80
31 Dec 1848	3,603	~ 12	1,670	~ 140

In a 3 December 1845 letter to Brigham Young, Dan Jones sums up the situation of the Church in Wales at that time:

> The number of the Welsh Saints are about 600 north & South; in the latter place a very worthy Bro. Henshaw has been preaching in English successfully, & converts Welsh who understand no English; another new thing under the Sun! This caps Solomons wisdom, a noble Bro. God bless him, he has a Mormon Soul, that's the secret of his success.

The Conversion of Dan Jones

Welsh-born Dan Jones first learned of The Church of Jesus Christ of Latter-day Saints at some point in the fall of 1842 as he hauled people and goods up and down the Mississippi River on the *Maid of Iowa*, a small steamboat he and his partner, Levi Moffat, had built during the summer of 1842. Thomas Sharp, the editor of the *Warsaw Signal*, penned vicious articles about the hated "Mormons," and these articles had piqued Jones's curiosity. Jones later wrote:

> For our part, we should thank this Sharp for the information we got about the Saints; for it was by reading his and others' accusations that our attention was drawn to them before we saw them, while living in that country. . . . My mind was not satisfied then until I got hold of one of the Mormons, and, once I had found him, it was not just two or three nights that we sat up to investigate the differences of opinion that existed between us about the gospel; and to my great surprise, I perceived that I was almost a full-fledged Mormon already, which when I realized it frightened me greatly; for I could foresee my popularity at an end the minute I had this despicable name; and consequently, my livelihood and my all.[4]

After a deep and thorough investigation into this new religion, Jones became a believer and was baptized on 19 January 1843 in what must have been a frigid Mississippi River, very probably in the shadow of the *Maid of Iowa*. In April of that same year, he took a load of British Latter-day Saints from St. Louis upriver to Nauvoo where he first met Joseph Smith, a meeting that promptly resulted in a close friendship between the two.

Upon learning that Jones's partner, Levi Moffit, was concerned that business would plummet because the *Maid of Iowa* had become a "Mormon" boat, Smith soon thereafter purchased Moffit's half of the boat for $1,375.[5] Thus, Smith and Jones became business partners.

A Press in Wales

In a letter written several years later, Jones quotes Smith as having said the following to him just a few days before the martyrdom:

> I have a check in the house for $1200; as soon as I can get it cashed you shall have $1100 of it, and the start for Wales, not with your fingers in your mouth but prepared to buy a Press; and do business aright.[6]

From Smith's comment, it is clear that Jones fully intended to have his own press during his mission to spread the word in Welsh to his compatriots. Furthermore, Smith's final recorded prophecy has to do with Dan's mission in Wales. The night before the Prophet was murdered, he heard gunfire outside the window of Carthage Jail, so he chose to sleep on the floor. Near him was Jones. Smith asked Jones if he was afraid to die. Jones replied, "Has that time come, think you? Engaged in such a cause I do not think that death would have many terrors." Then Smith prophesied, "You will yet see Wales, and fulfill the mission appointed you before you die."

Unfortunately, because of the confusion that resulted from the martyrdom, Dan Jones did not ever receive the $1,100 that Joseph Smith had promised to give him for his half of the steamboat. Consequently, Jones could not purchase his own press and was forced to use others' presses in Wales to get his message out. The first such hired press was that of William Bayley in Wrexham, whom Jones employed in April 1845 to print his forty-eight-page pamphlet entitled *Y Farw Wedi ei Chyfodi yn fyw! neu yr Hen Grefydd Newydd (The Dead Raised to Life! or the Ancient Religion Anew)*.

Elder Jones Preaching the Gospel

Curiously, nowhere in his first pamphlet does Jones mention the name of The Church of Jesus Christ of Latter-day Saints, nor does he ever use the word "Mormon." Despite having this Welsh-language publication to support his proselytizing, Jones managed only three baptisms during the entire year he spent in North Wales. But the story became different in December 1845 when the captain was transferred to South Wales, where his older brother John lived. John was a Congregationalist minister, and he owned a press in Rhydybont, a village near the market town of Llanybydder in Carmarthenshire. Unlike other press owners, John had no qualms about printing his brother's religious ideas during the week and preaching against them on Sunday. In April 1854, Dan had the pleasure of baptizing the three ladies in his brother's life—John's wife, Jane; their twenty-one-year-old daughter, Sarah; and their nineteen-year-old daughter, Elizabeth. Although there was a rumor that the Reverend John Jones himself had also been baptized, Dan stated in his periodical that such was not the case.[7]

Because John agreed to print the "dull and idiotic" writings of the "Mormons," his colleagues of the cloth accused him of operating a "prostitute press."[8] John's reaction to such accusations was calm: "Our work in printing their books proves nothing more than the fact that our press is made of iron and its owner is a free craftsman."[9]

While in Rhydybont, Dan became acquainted with John S. Davis, a brilliant young man who had completed an apprenticeship as a printer and had worked not only for Dan's brother but also for the editor of a Baptist periodical (*Seren Gomer*, or *Star of Gomer*) in Carmarthen. Within weeks Davis converted, and he worked side by side with Jones in all his printing activities during the next three years. And it was Davis who would later translate the Latter-day Saint scriptures into Welsh.

In December 1845, Jones printed his second pamphlet, this time on the Rhydybont press—the Welsh translation of the Proclamation of the Twelve Apostles in The Church of Jesus Christ of Latter-day Saints. A few weeks later, he printed a twenty-four-page pamphlet entitled *Reply to the Objections Which Are Most Commonly Brought throughout the Country against the Latter-day Saints, and the Doctrine Which They Profess.* He borrowed heavily from the writings of Orson Pratt, and the content was purely doctrinal.

Jones's next publication was a sixteen-page pamphlet entitled *The Scales.* It was a direct response to a thirty-two-page pamphlet which David Williams had published a few weeks earlier, entitled *The Deception of the Latter-day Saints.* This latest publication of Jones launched his career as a polemicist and revealed his remarkable gift to readily engage in verbal combat with anyone who might dare to make nasty observations about the religion he revered and wished fervently to defend.

The First Non-English Latter-day Saint Periodical

Jones's first four publications served as a prelude to *Prophet of the Jubilee*, the Welsh-language periodical Jones launched in July 1846. The curious title probably came as a result of his seeing issues of the *Prophet*, a newspaper initiated in New York on 18

May 1844 to promote the presidential campaign of Joseph Smith. Following Smith's death, the focus of the publication changed to Church events and doctrine. Dan Jones visited New York en route to his mission in the fall of 1844. He no doubt became acquainted with the *Prophet* at that time and may well have decided to use the name as part of the title of his own periodical several months later.

A number of periodical articles were published against the Latter-day Saints during the first several months that Jones was in South Wales. The editors systematically refused to print the responses Jones sent them. No wonder that a frustrated Jones wrote the following in the first issue (July 1846) of his periodical to the subscribers:

> Is everyone allowed to put out his magazine but us? Is the press locked against us? Is that the freedom of Wales in the nineteenth century? Have the monthlies been locked? We shall open our own monthly, then. Has the press been polluted by libeling us? We shall cleanse it by defending ourselves then.[10]

And defend his religion, he did! In addition to the constant use of his new periodical and numerous pamphlets, Jones traveled up and down the country preaching to all who would listen, often engaging in verbal combat by debating all comers. He would often send advance word by town criers to announce that he would be speaking at a certain time in the next town and that his objective was to baptize the entire population!

But the Nonconformist and Anglican ministers were just as angry as Jones and the missionaries he sent to various parts of Wales were relentless. These ministers were aghast and perplexed at their parishioners who left them by the scores for a religion that championed miracles, healings, angels, and even migration to another continent. The ministers gave stern warnings from their pulpits of the danger of even listening to the "Latter-day devils." They presented lectures about Joseph Smith and his "true" history of fraudulent practices, his lies, his evildoing, and his pact with the devil to get gain.

A Change of the Name and Editor for *Prophet of the Jubilee*

On 26 February 1849, the *Buena Vista* was towed out to sea from the Waterloo Dock in Liverpool. On board were 249 Welsh converts to The Church of Jesus Christ of Latter-day Saints, the first group from among the Welsh to sail to America. Their leader was Captain Dan Jones. The eighty-three other Welsh converts who wanted to be with the group on the *Buena Vista* had to wait until the following week when they sailed away on board the *Hartley*.[11]

William S. Phillips replaced Dan Jones as mission president in Wales at this time. And replacing Jones as editor of the mission periodical was the young but very able John S. Davis, who by then had purchased his own press. He had produced the final two issues of *Prophet of the Jubilee* (November and December 1848) in Carmarthen and the first two issues (January and February 1849) of the newly named *Zion's Trumpet*, also based in Carmarthen. Sometime before the printing of the March 1849 issue of the periodical, Davis had moved himself and his press to Nantygwenith Street in the area of Merthyr Tydfil known as Georgetown.

Davis produced six volumes of *Zion's Trumpet* over the next five years. The periodical appeared monthly during 1849 and 1850. During 1851 and 1852, it was published semimonthly. And two more volumes were printed on a weekly basis during 1853.

Printer John S. Davis and President William S. Phillips were released from their ecclesiastical duties at the end of 1853 and sailed together with their families to New Orleans on board *The Golconda*. Dan Jones was back in Wales on his second mission to take both their places as editor and mission president. *Zion's Trumpet* continued as a weekly publication until September 1854, at which time it was printed every other week. The 29 March 1856 issue would be the last for Dan Jones because he was being released to take a group of 707 Latter-day Saints—over five hundred of them Welsh converts—on the *S. Curling* to Boston. At this point his close friend Daniel Daniels became mission president and editor of the periodical until the end of 1857.

Benjamin P. Evans replaced Daniel Daniels in January of 1858, and once again the periodical began to appear weekly until its demise in April 1862. When Evans was released after three years as editor (1857, 1858, and 1859), the entire printing operation was transported to Liverpool, the headquarters of the Church in Britain. The press was loaded onto the steamer *Sovereign* on 24 March 1861 at Swansea and reached Liverpool three days later.[12] The move was effected in order to cut costs and increase efficiency. George Q. Cannon, president of the Church in Great Britain, became the official editor. Since he spoke no Welsh, twenty-nine-year-old William Ajax was assigned to move to Liverpool and took on the responsibility of publishing *Zion's Trumpet*. The last issue to be printed, according to William Ajax's journal entry for 9 April 1862, was the fourteenth for that year, most likely one dated 5 April 1862. For its final years of publication (1859, 1860, 1861, and part of 1862), only seventeen isolated issues of *Zion's Trumpet* are extant.

By combining calculated figures with known figures, it appears that 7,792 pages of *Zion's Trumpet* were produced during the thirteen years and three months of its existence. Adding the 580 pages of its predecessor—*Prophet of the Jubilee*—to all those of *Zion's Trumpet* brings the combined total number of pages of the Welsh-language periodical under both names to 8,372 pages—truly a remarkable accomplishment in view of its limited audience and the small number of qualified persons who could assist in its publication.

Other Publications by Dan Jones and John S. Davis

Dan Jones and John S. Davis published several other items in addition to the periodical.[13] During his first mission (1845–48), Jones published the following:

- Thirty full issues of *Prophet of the Jubilee*, 580 pages.
- Fourteen pamphlets ranging in size from 4 to 104 pages, 328 pages.
- A scriptural commentary in defense of Latter-day Saint doctrine, 288 pages.
- A hymnal containing 133 hymns, 64 pages.

During his second mission (1852–56), Jones published the following:

- Twenty-one pamphlets ranging in size from 2 to 52 pages, 274 pages total.

- Seventy-two full issues of *Zion's Trumpet*, 1,152 pages.

During John S. Davis's five years (1849–53) as editor of *Zion's Trumpet*, he published the following:

- One hundred twenty-nine issues of *Zion's Trumpet*, 2,352 pages.
- Twenty-five pamphlets ranging in size from 2 to 72 pages, 302 pages total.
- Fifteen poems ranging in size from 1 to 4 pages, 28 pages.
- Three hymnals:
  - The 1849 hymnal, containing 194 hymns, 112 pages
  - The 1851 hymnal, a second edition of the 1846 hymnal, 64 pages.
  - The 1852 hymnal, containing 575 hymns, 384 pages.
- A register book for recording membership information, 184 pages.
- A new edition of the *Testament of the Twelve Patriarchs*, 74 pages.
- Six translations from English into Welsh:
  - *The First General Epistle*, 12 pages.
  - *Lectures on Faith*, 40 pages.
  - *The Great First Cause*, 28 pages.
  - The Book of Doctrine and Covenants, 320 pages.
  - The Book of Mormon, 496 pages.
  - The Pearl of Great Price, 85 pages.

The combined efforts of Dan Jones and John Davis spanned an eleven-year period and resulted in the publication of an impressive total of 7,167 pages—2,686 by Jones and 4,481 by Davis.

Publications by Others—An Additional 4,778 Pages

During his time as editor of *Zion's Trumpet* (1856–57), Daniel Daniels published a total of 982 pages—744 pages of the periodical, 224 pages of the Welsh translation of the Orson Pratt *True Faith* series, plus a fourteen-page Welsh translation of *Marriage and Morals in Utah* by Parley P. Pratt. Benjamin P. Evans published 2,750 pages of *Zion's Trumpet* during the three years (1858–60) he was editor of *Zion's Trumpet*, and William Ajax, as managing editor, published 1,056 pages of the periodical from January 1861 until its demise in April 1862. These 4,778 pages combined with the 7,167 pages of Dan Jones and John S. Davis come to a grand total of 11,955 pages of publications during a period of just over seventeen years.

An Example of the Impact of Latter-day Saint Welsh Publications

Just how much of an impact all these pages had on the approximately one million Welsh speakers in Wales would be impossible to measure; however, there is no doubt that the publications played an extremely significant role in the growth of The Church of Jesus Christ of Latter-day Saints in mid-nineteenth-century Wales. One lay Baptist minister in Aberdare by the name of William Howells ascribed full credit for his conversion to an 1847 pamphlet by Dan Jones.[14] Characterizing himself as "too bashful" to approach any of the Latter-day Saints directly for information concerning their religion, Howell later wrote,

> A poor widow, supported with her family by the poor fare of the parish, found means to get a tract, which she gave me; which, like the little captive maid of Israel, in the house of Naaman the leper, convinced me of the poverty of my religion.[15]

Certain ministers thought the tract William Howells referred to was "an odious patchwork," "dull and idiotic," "blasphemous to the common sense of the Welsh," and "presumptuous rubbish" which had been printed on a "prostitute press" at Rhydybont. But to Howells, the pamphlet was the ambrosia-like catalyst which prompted him to seek out its author in Merthyr Tydfil and request baptism at his hands. Following a long conversation, Dan Jones baptized William Howells that same evening.

Dan Jones expressed elation in a letter to his file leader in Liverpool about the impromptu visit he received one evening in the fall of 1847:

> Last evening, I baptized a gentleman who is now, and has been, a Baptist minister for the last eighteen years. He preached to his flock last Sunday, and has an appointment for the successive Sunday. He came four miles purposely to be baptized, though he had never heard a sermon, only reading my publications; especially my last reply . . . finished him entirely, and he came in as good a spirit as anyone that I ever saw, and has just returned on his way rejoicing.[16]

Howells spread his rejoicing to family, friends, and former parishioners following his baptism. On 19 March 1849, he reported his success in a letter to Orson Spencer:

> I have in the course of the last twelve months, baptized about one hundred, which I consider a fair commencement.[17]

Howells has the distinction of being the first Latter-day Saint missionary to preach the gospel in France. He went on his first journey to France to Le Havre in July 1849, taking with him a supply of English tracts plus *L'Evangile* (*The Gospel*), a two-page leaflet in French printed on John S. Davis's press in Merthyr Tydfil. Howells returned to Wales after one month to check on his family. On his second missionary journey to France (August to October 1849), he took with him his nine-year-old daughter Ann, thinking that she could learn French quickly and assist him in communicating with the French. They were mainly in the Dinan area. His third journey (February to May 1850) was without his daughter and lasted about three months in the Boulogne area. And on his fourth and final journey (June to September 1850), Howells escorted Elder John Taylor, Curtis Bolton and John Pack to France for their missions. Howells was present on the seashore of Boulogne when Elder Taylor offered the dedicatory prayer for the preaching of the gospel in France.

William Howells began his next journey in Liverpool on 4 March 1851 on board the New Orleans–bound *Olympus*. Nearly three weeks into the voyage, on Sunday, 23 March, a storm of hurricane force threatened to sink the ship. The captain ordered his second mate to go below and tell Howells, the presiding elder of the Latter-day Saints on board, that "if the God of the Mormons can do anything to save the ship and the people, they had better be calling on him to do so." When approached, Howells immediately called about a dozen brethren to form a prayer circle and instructed that each man in the circle take a turn to pray vocally that the Lord would spare the vessel. Elder Howells prayed last, and, when he had finished, the storm suddenly abated. Sunday services were held the following day, and twenty-one of the sixty passengers who were not Latter-day Saints requested to be baptized. Before the end of the journey, a total of fifty had been converted and baptized. Howells rejoiced at this increase, in much the same way over three years earlier he had rejoiced after reading a pamphlet that had propelled him toward baptism, a baptism that was administered by Dan Jones, the author of the pamphlet.

From Obscurity to Prominence

Most of the few articles about the Latter-day Saints in the newspapers and periodicals in Wales during the first half of the 1840s were of a general and negative nature. But Rev. W. R. Davies, having lost at least two of his parishioners to the proselytizing of Elder William Henshaw, was very specific in his attacks on the Latter-day Saints in the *Baptist*. Using such noms de plume as "Tobit" and "T. ab Ieuan" while referring to Elder Henshaw with such monikers as "Quack H-n-s-h-w" and "the dolt Billy," Davies mocked Henshaw's efforts to heal the sick. And he even went so far as to send for publication in the July 1844 issue of the *Baptist* an "epistle" signed by George Rees, "an apostle of the Saints in Abersychan." The Latter-day Saints believed that Davies was actually the author of what they claimed to be a forged letter, but the editor of the *Baptist* refused to print any of the Saints' letters in his periodical.

This battle ceased to be one-sided, however, with the arrival of Dan Jones in South Wales in December 1845. Within six months Jones had launched his own monthly periodical, *Prophet of the Jubilee*, and took obvious pleasure in combatting the opposition of Rev. W. R. Davies and his colleagues of the cloth. With his own publication, Jones was finally able to answer whatever charges and accusations were leveled against the religion he dearly cherished. Over the next two and a half years (July 1846 to December 1848), his periodical and pamphlets combined with his proselytizing, and that of a small cadre of members-turned-missionaries, to result in a staggering three thousand convert baptisms—an average of one hundred new members per month.

Why Latter-day Saint Publications Were Ignored for So Long

Since the mid-nineteenth century, only a modicum of attention has been given to the amazing success of the Latter-day Saint missionary effort in Wales. A number of letters in English by Dan Jones, William Phillips, and Daniel Daniels were printed in the *Millennial Star* and have some excellent information, but the vast majority of the story is told from the Latter-day Saint view in their own periodicals and pamphlets—all in Welsh!

The converts who left Wales to join the body of the Church in Utah had every intention of preserving and perpetuating their native tongue; however, their descendants failed to have the same enthusiasm for speaking their ancestral tongue in an environment in which English reigned supreme and had infinitely more practical value. Initially the gatherings and celebrations of the Welsh immigrants to Utah and Idaho were in their native tongue, but with the advent of the twentieth century, the Welsh language ceased to be used as a means of communication.

My Modified Personal Quest

A half century ago, I began writing a biography of Captain Dan Jones, my great-great grandfather, knowing only of his letters printed in various issues of the *Millennial Star*. My quest at the time was to find among his other descendants any of his papers and especially his journals which he had mentioned in one of his letters—a quest that has proven fruitless to this day. One good thing that emerged from the search is the cane that Dan Jones had made out of the first coffin of Joseph Smith.[18] And one other good thing is Dan Jones's spyglass.[19]

In 1971, I happened across an unbound volume that contained all thirty issues of *Prophwyd y Jubili (Prophet of the Jubilee)*. I learned from its owner that the editor of this small periodical had been my ancestor, Dan Jones. Eventually I persuaded the owner to sell it to me, and at that point my quest became one of getting all 580 pages of it translated into English. I set about to find some speakers of Welsh in Utah, where I lived, but after taking one look at the literary brand of Welsh used in the periodical, they all sadly informed me that their ability in Welsh did not go past the conversational level.

Having professional translators perform the task far exceeded my means as an assistant professor of Portuguese at Brigham Young University. Consequently, I decided to take on the task of learning Welsh myself in order to do the translating. The accomplishment of this goal was made possible by my receiving a six-month sabbatical leave from BYU, during which I took my wife and five children to live in Aberystwyth, Wales. I immersed myself in the language and made considerable progress. Subsequent summer visits to Wales on my own eventually brought me to the level of being able to translate the periodical myself. I did, however, obtain the help of some student assistants whom I hired to solve my numerous "translation traumas."

Thinking it a pity for readers of the translation not to be able to experience the "flavor" of the original volume, I decided to publish it as a "facsimile translation"—i.e., a matching, to the extent possible, of the page-by-page arrangement and the typesetting of the original. I increased the size of the pages of the book by about 30 percent so that readers would not need a magnifying glass to navigate their way through it. I also added a section titled "Annotated Contents" to explain the various items throughout and put them into the historical context of the 1840s. Twenty-five years after beginning my quest to share *Prophet of the Jubilee* with the aficionados of Latter-day

Saint history, I experienced the immense satisfaction of holding its English "facsimile translation" in my hand.[20]

Also, to add to the body of knowledge about the history of the Latter-day Saints in Wales, I have prepared "facsimile translations" of all ten of the extant volumes of *Udgorn Seion* (*Zion's Trumpet*) from 1849 through 1857.[21]

Using the same translation approach for Dan Jones's thirty-five pamphlets and John S. Davis's twenty-one pamphlets and fifteen poems, I put together a book entitled *Defending the Faith: Early Welsh Missionary Publications.*[22]

My Most Recent Quest

Having published the foregoing, my new quest became that of identifying all the articles that opposed the Latter-day Saints in the periodicals and newspapers during the 1840s and 1850s. This goal became possible when the National Library of Wales posted online the digitization of nineteenth-century Welsh-language periodicals. And when the British Newspaper Archive appeared online, the digitized copies of the nineteenth-century Welsh newspapers became accessible.

Use of the search tool for these amazing resources brought to light over five hundred periodical articles, the vast majority in Welsh, and nearly seven hundred newspaper articles, the vast majority in English. These are all mentioned in the chronological commentary. The respective translations and transcriptions of all these can now be accessed on JSTOR.

My Objective

This book provides historical context and the publication history of The Church of Jesus Christ of Latter-day Saints in the Principality of Wales during the 1840s and 1850s—the Church's beginnings, its growth, and its progress amid the constant opposition and allegations from other religious persons and organizations that felt threatened by the doctrine and proselytizing of Latter-day Saint missionaries.

Nearly a Half Century of Gathering

I began collecting material for this book in 1976 during a six-month sabbatical leave from Brigham Young University. I lived with my family in the seaside town of Borth, located about eight miles north of the National Library of Wales in Aberystywyth, mid-Wales. My purpose was twofold: to acquire proficiency in reading nineteenth-century Welsh and to identify all the publications of Dan Jones, John S. Davis, and other "defenders of the faith." My findings were published by the Brigham Young University Religious Studies Center in 1988 with the title *Welsh Mormon Writings from 1844 to 1862: A Historical Bibliography.*

Latter-day Saint Periodicals and Pamphlets

The first non-English Latter-day Saint periodical was published by Dan Jones in Welsh beginning in July 1846 and continuing through December 1848, during his first mission in his native land. This monthly publication, *Prophwyd y Jubili* (*Prophet of the Jubilee*), provided an instrument for Jones not only to communicate with Welsh converts to the Church but also to defend his adopted religion from the heavy stream of vicious opposition that issued forth from the various Nonconformist religions in Wales—the Baptists, the Methodists, the Congregationalists, the Wesleyans, the Independents, and the Unitarians—as well as from the Anglicans. The entire thirty issues (580 pages) of *Prophet of the Jubilee* were published in an English "facsimile translation" in 1997 by the Brigham Young University Religious Studies Center. (My definition of "facsimile translation" is a translated document typeset to make it look as much like the original as possible, including the original pagination.)

In 1849, the periodical was renamed *Udgorn Seion* (*Zion's Trumpet*) and was published until April 1862. All ten of its extant volumes (1849–57) have been published as facsimile translations by the Brigham Young University Religious Studies Center. Also, the thirty-five pamphlets by Dan Jones and the thirty-six pamphlets and poems by John S. Davis were published in 2003 as facsimile translations in one volume entitled *Defending the Faith: Early Welsh Missionary Publications*, again published by the Brigham Young University Religious Studies Center.

Early Methodology

To research the oppositional literature stimulated by the proselytizing and publishing efforts of the Welsh Latter-day Saints, I arranged for students in Wales to peruse nineteenth-century Welsh-language periodicals in search of articles that had anything to do with The Church of Jesus Christ of Latter-day Saints, or the "Mormons," as they were then called, by their opponents as well as by their converts. English translations were then prepared from the copies made of the nearly three hundred articles identified. Because many similar searches had already been performed for newspapers, the students did not search for newspaper articles at the time.

Recent Methodology

Many years later, digitized versions of the nineteenth-century Welsh-language periodicals were posted on the National Library of Wales website. Computer searches of these periodicals nearly doubled the number of articles previously identified. The English translations for all these articles are available on JSTOR.

Also, thanks to the recent digitization of English-language newspapers by the British Newspaper Archive, searches brought to light several hundred more articles about the nineteenth-century Welsh Latter-day Saints. The transcriptions for these articles are available on JSTOR.

Dan Jones and John S. Davis: Main Responders

Oppositional items printed during the 1840s and 1850s were published in numerous periodicals and newspapers. Essentially all of the printed responses prompted by the opposition were launched from the Latter-day Saint periodical along with several pamphlets. From January 1846 to mid-1856, the two principal responders were Captain Dan Jones and John S. Davis, the two editors of *Prophet of the Jubilee* and *Zion's Trumpet* during this period. Because of the momentous contributions Jones and Davis made through their writings to the success of the Church they represented and cherished, I have devoted the entire first chapter of this publication to acquainting the reader with these men and their work.

Items

I use the term *item* to refer to each entry of information about The Church of Jesus Christ of Latter-day Saints in the periodicals as well as in the newspapers. These items range in length from a few words to multiple pages. Items focused mainly on events and people in Wales are discussed in some detail throughout the chronological commentary. Items with little or no focus on events or people in Wales are included in this study because they constitute an important part of the information made available to the Welsh people about a religion that carried potential importance for them; however, these items receive little or no discussion in the overall commentary.

Chronological Commentary

Beginning with chapter 2, quotations and discussions are presented in chronological order for all the periodical and newspaper items as well as for the pamphlets and the poems. The basic pattern for the discussions is as follows:

- Entry headings are formatted as follows:

    Year: Day Month, *Welsh Periodical Title* (*English Periodical Title*), page number, (word count). "Article Title."
- The Welsh title for a publication that contains an item is followed by an English translation of the title, an indication that the original item is in the Welsh language.
- An English title by itself is an indication that the item was originally in English and that it has simply been transcribed. Unless otherwise indicated, emphasis such as italics is as in the original.
- An approximate word count is given in the listing for each item to provide the reader with some idea as to the item's length.
- Brief items are given in their entirety in the chronological commentary.
- Longer items are discussed in the chronological commentary with varying amounts of detail.

- All items are housed in their entirety on JSTOR, where the translations/transcriptions are grouped chronologically according to the periodical or newspaper of origin.
- Some items (as well as other documents of interest to this book's topic) are also available on the Welsh Saints Project website (http://www.welshsaints.byu.edu/). Such documents are identified in endnotes.
- Unless otherwise stated, all emphases (italics or underline) are as in the original text.

Episodes

The term *episode* refers to a group of several items that focus on one person or on one event, collected under one heading. The beginning and end of the episode are indicated in italics. All other items that are not part of an episode are chronologically ordered before and after each of the episodes. A list of the relevant episodes is given at the start of each chapter.

Pamphlets

Section 2—Pamphlets has the following:

The facsimile translations for fourteen of the nineteen identified oppositional pamphlets.

The facsimile translations of the segments of Pamphlets 9 and 13 that are focused on the Latter-day Saints.

The title pages for Pamphlets 17, 18, and 19.

Discussions for all nineteen pamphlets are in Section 1—Commentary, according to their chronological appearance.

Poems

Section 3—Poems has the following:

Nonpoetic English translations for twenty-two oppositional poems published in Wales from 1846 to 1854 in Welsh-language periodicals.

Nonpoetic English translations for four oppositional poems published as separate items in mid-nineteenth-century Wales.

A facsimile of "Saints of a Latter-day: A Rhyme for the Principality of Wales," the only English-language poem thus far identified as published in mid-nineteenth-century Wales.

JSTOR

The JSTOR online database has the English translations for all the articles originally printed in Welsh and the transcriptions for all the articles originally printed in English. If a translation is located elsewhere, it is stated in a footnote appending the relevant text. To access any of these documents, visit https://www.jstor.org/ and type "English translations for Welsh articles" into the search bar.

Notes

1. *Zion's Trumpet* 1854: 569–70.
2. Mary Ann Clements, "Martha Thomas: The Church in Wales." *Keepapitchinin* (blog). May 25, 2021, http://www.keepapitchinin.org/2021/05/25/guest-post-martha-thomas-the-church-in-wales.
3. Dates and numbers in the first two columns are from the *Millennial Star.*
4. "History of the Latter-day Saints," in Ronald D. Dennis, ed., *Defending the Faith: Early Welsh Missionary Publications* (Provo, UT: BYU Religious Studies Center, 2003), 60.
5. "Steamboat Maid of Iowa," Whitney Collection.
6. 20 December 1855 letter from Dan Jones to Thomas Bullock.
7. *Zion's Trumpet* 1854: 226–27.
8. *Seren Gomer* (*Star of Gomer*), December 1847, 375.
9. *Y Golygydd* (*Editor*), January 1846, page 2 of the wrapper.
10. *Prophet of the Jubilee* July 1846, page 2 of the wrapper.
11. See *The Call of Zion.*
12. William Ajax Journal, typescript copy, 57–59, BYU Library.
13. All these are discussed in *Welsh Mormon Writings*, published in 1988 by the Religious Studies Center at Brigham Young University.
14. Review of the Lectures of the Rev. E. Roberts—item 17 in *Welsh Mormon Writings.*
15. See 2 Kings 5:1–19.
16. *Millennial Star* 9:363.
17. *Millennial Star* 11:121.
18. A picture is in "Resources" under "Photos" at http://www.welshsaints.byu.edu/Immigrant_View.aspx?id=898.
19. A picture is in "Resources" under "Photos" at http://www.welshsaints.byu.edu/Immigrant_View.aspx?id=898.
20. A PDF file of this unique translation is at http://www.welshsaints.byu.edu/Resource_Info.aspx?id=24377.
21. PDF files for these volumes are available on the website Welsh Saints Project at http://www.welshsaints.byu.edu/Resource_Listing_new.aspx?group=General+Resources.
22. A PDF file is at https://archive.org/stream/DefendingTheFaithEarlyWelshMissionaryPublications#page/n1/mode/2up.

SECTION 1

Commentary

Chapter 1

Dan Jones and John S. Davis

There were many opponents to the Latter-day Saints and their religion during the 1840s and 1850s in Wales. These antagonists principally expressed their opposition from the pulpit, in the press, and through the disruption of meetings, which were held in buildings or as open-air gatherings where missionaries shouted out their message to all who would listen. Hundreds of newspaper and periodical articles about Latter-day Saint teachings, meetings, and proselytizing have survived in abundance and are currently available on JSTOR.

In July 1846, the growing group of Latter-day Saints in Wales were elated when the first issue of their own periodical came off the press in the village of Rhydybont, near the market town of Llanybydder in Carmarthenshire. At last, they had a monthly means of circulating their message and defending it against the assaults of their numerous adversaries. Dan Jones was the founding editor of this monthly publication, and young John S. Davis provided valuable assistance. After twenty-eight issues, John S. Davis became the editor of *Prophwyd y Jubili* (*Prophet of the Jubilee*) for its final two issues—November and December of 1848. And in January 1849, the name of the periodical was changed to *Udgorn Seion* (*Zion's Trumpet*). For the following five years, Davis served as the editor of this periodical. During this time, he also translated the Doctrine and Covenants, the Book of Mormon, and the Pearl of Great Price into Welsh.

By the beginning of 1854, Dan Jones was back on his second mission to Wales and became editor of *Zion's Trumpet* in place of John S. Davis, who left a few weeks later with a group of Latter-day Saints headed for Salt Lake City.

Because of the prominent roles Jones and Davis played in challenging the opposition through the printed word, it seems appropriate to present, in this first chapter, the details of their publishing activities over a full decade—all in defense of the religion and set of beliefs they both loved. From the mid-1840s to the mid-1850s, the attacks on the "Latter-day Satanists," as their many enemies frequently called them, were relentless and vicious. Throughout the remaining chapters of this study, a chronological array of the barrage of attacks, along with the response of Jones and Davis to many of them, will be presented.

On 19 January 1843, Dan Jones, the captain of a small riverboat, received his baptism by immersion in the Mississippi River near St. Louis, Missouri. At the time, he was living on board the *Maid of Iowa*, a steamboat he, Levi Moffat, and some partners had built the previous summer in Augusta, Iowa, just twenty miles north of Nauvoo, Illinois (the "City of Joseph"). Dan Jones's baptism into The Church of Jesus Christ of Latter-day Saints brought to a successful close his lifelong search for the true religion. He would spend over half his remaining years on this earth proselytizing in Wales to proclaim the good news of the Restoration to his compatriots.

Born in the little town of Halkyn, Denbighshire, North Wales, in 1810, just five years before Napoleon's defeat at Waterloo, Dan spent his formative years in a very religious home with a father who was an elder in the Methodist church. Dan most likely spent time in the local lead mines with his father and older brothers; the ever-present dust he inhaled in the mines as a boy was likely to have created the chronic lung affliction that plagued him until his death at age fifty-one.

While on the Mississippi River, Dan began to focus his attention toward the vicious printed attacks on Joseph Smith and the religion Joseph had founded nearly thirteen years earlier. These attacks appeared in the *Warsaw Signal*, whose editor was Thomas Sharp—an avowed enemy of "Mormonism," as the religion was often called. While Jones was in his native Wales, serving a mission for his new faith four years after his conversion, he reflected on the attacks in the *Warsaw Signal*:

> For our part, we should thank this Sharp for the information we got about the Saints; for it was by reading his and others' accusations that our attention was drawn to them before we saw them, while living in that country.

On 12 April 1843, not quite three months following his baptism in St. Louis, Dan made the personal acquaintance of Joseph Smith in Nauvoo, where Dan had taken a group of English converts up the Mississippi River from St. Louis. On May 12, exactly one month later, Dan and Joseph became business partners when Joseph presented Levi Moffat with $1,375 for Levi's half of the steamboat. The mission call to Wales that Dan Jones had received one day earlier, on 11 May 1843, was not answered until sixteen months later because Joseph gave Dan numerous assignments having to do with the *Maid of Iowa*.

The strong friendship that developed between Dan and Joseph was interrupted on 27 June 1844, when Joseph was martyred in the jail at Carthage. Dan had been with him in the jail until that same morning, when Joseph had requested that Dan report the gunshots heard during the night to Governor Ford at the Hamilton Hotel.

In 1855, while back in his native Wales on a second mission, Dan responded to a request from the Church historian by writing an account of the martyrdom from his perspective. In Dan's lengthy letter to Thomas Bullock, he recalled,

> A few days previous to being arrested [Joseph] told me "I have a check in the house for $1200; as soon as I can get it cashed you shall have $1100 of it, and the start for Wales, not with your fingers in your mouth but prepared to buy a Press; and do business aright."[2]

The phrase "buy a Press" is a clear indication that Dan intended to inform his Welsh compatriots of the true gospel of Jesus Christ using the same method by which he learned of it—through publications—but with a more positive approach. However, he did not receive the promised money because of the confusion following Joseph's death. As a result, Dan was obliged to make use of two presses during his first mission to Wales from 1845 to 1849. The first one was owned by William Bayley in Wrexham, North Wales, and the second was that of Dan's older brother John, who lived in South Wales. On the first press, Dan printed his first pamphlet, and on the second all his other publications during his first mission.

Dan spent nearly all of 1845, the first year of his mission, in North Wales where his parents still lived at that time. But during that entire year, his first pamphlet helped to convince only three persons to receive the baptism he offered them. Those who were baptized were not his family members or people he had known during his formative years.

Jones printed his second pamphlet, his Welsh translation of the *Proclamation of the Twelve Apostles*, on the press owned by his older brother, the Reverend John Jones. John was the pastor of the Congregationalist church in the village of Rhydybont, Carmarthenshire, and his press was located in his home next to the church. At the time, a young man by the name of John Sylvanus Davis was employed as a typesetter for the pastor's publications. Having learned his trade as a printer's apprentice during his youth, Davis also had the advantage of being fluent in English as well as his native Welsh.

By setting the type for the *Proclamation of the Twelve Apostles*, Davis was introduced to a religion that claimed to be the true church of God, restored through the Prophet Joseph Smith. Furthermore, Davis was able to converse with Dan Jones, who had been a friend and business partner of the Prophet of the Restoration for a year's time prior to the martyrdom. As a result, Davis converted to the new religion and was baptized on 19 April 1846.

At this point The Church of Jesus Christ of Latter-day Saints had two highly skilled publishers and polemicists to propagate its doctrines and to engage in written battles with its many opponents: twenty-three-year-old John S. Davis and thirty-six-year-old Dan Jones. Logically, these battles would have taken place in the numerous religious periodicals and newspapers, with one side responding to the other side in typical polemic fashion. Lamentably, with but few exceptions, only the side of the opponents of Dan Jones was printed.

But, as of July 1846, Dan Jones finally had a means of responding to the assaults from his enemies. That means came in the form of a periodical entitled *Prophwyd y Jubili* (*Prophet of the Jubilee*), the first non-English periodical of the Church of Jesus Christ. In the first issue, Dan explained to his subscribers the frustration he had previously experienced by not having a way to defend himself and the Church he represented:

> We had no way of keeping our characters above all invention, libel, and lies, except, like you, through the medium of the printing press. You know how we have been accused of every evil, trickery, yes, and of every foolishness. We sent, in the mildest manner, to the monthlies which accused us, letters asserting our innocence. But, were they allowed to appear? No! Were we accused in the *Times*, *Star of Gomer*, *Instructor*, *Baptist*, etc.? Yes, yes. Was space provided for us to clear ourselves? No, no! rather every poor excuse was sought.[3]

He then triumphantly declared:

> Is everyone allowed to put out his magazine but us? Is the press locked against us? Is that the freedom of Wales in the nineteenth century? Have the monthlies been locked? We shall open our own monthly, then. Has the press been polluted by libeling us? We shall cleanse it by defending ourselves, then.[4]

Under the editorship of Dan Jones, *Prophet of the Jubilee* appeared monthly from July 1846 through October 1848. John S. Davis assumed the editorship for the final two issues—November and December 1848—while Dan was preparing to escort the first group of Welsh converts to Utah. In January 1849, the name of the periodical was changed to *Zion's Trumpet*, and the editor from that date until December 1853 was John S. Davis. By then, Dan Jones was back in Wales on his second mission, and he was the editor from January 1854 until issue number 7, dated 5 April 1856, after which he returned to Utah. At that point, Daniel Daniels became editor of the periodical until the end of 1857. The periodical's final issue was in April 1862, but no complete volume is extant from 1858 until then.

Even though the issues of *Prophet of the Jubilee* and *Zion's Trumpet* were the main conduit through which the Saints were able to defend themselves against the constant opposition from other Christian religions, the Saints also made use of pamphlets. Of the thirty-five pamphlets Dan Jones published during his two missions to Wales, seven of them are directed at specific individuals who had attacked or opposed the Church of Jesus Christ in some way.[5]

- *The Scales* (1846): A sixteen-page response to *The Deception of the Latter-day Saints*, a thirty-two-page pamphlet by David Williams.
- *Defense of the Saints versus the Accusations of Thomas Jones, Merthyr, and Others* (1846): An eight-page response to Thomas Jones, an apostate who had attacked his former church.
- *Defense of the Saints, against the False Accusations of Those Who Call Themselves "Cuckoo of Ton"* (1847): A twelve-page response to an article in the Baptist periodical *Star of Gomer*.
- *"Haman" Hanging from His Own Gallows!* (1847): An eight-page response to *The Correct Image, Wherein One Can Perceive Clearly the Deceit of the Mormons*, a twelve-page pamphlet by Daniel Jones, a blind man.
- *A Review of the Lectures of the Reverend E. Roberts* (1847): A forty-two-page response to the lectures of Edward Roberts.

- *A Review of the Last Lecture* (1848): A response to another lecture by Edward Roberts.
- *A Defense of the Saints; Refutations of the False and Malicious Accusations of a Man by the Name of Rees Davies, from New Orleans, against the Saints*: a twelve-page response to Rees Davies.

Of the twenty-one pamphlets authored by John S. Davis during his five years as editor of *Zion's Trumpet*, four of them are directed at specific individuals who had lectured or published against the Church of Jesus Christ.

- *An Anti-Mormon sermon. To the Rev. T. Williams, Ebenezer, near Carmarthen* (1849) is Davis's four-page response to a lecture by Thomas Williams.
- *Observations on a Sermon about "The Latter-day Saints and Miraculous Gifts"* (1849) is Davis's eight-page response to a lecture by David Evans.
- *A Review of the Treatise of W. Jones, Bethesda* (1851) is Davis's sixteen-page response to *Principles of the Latter-day Saints Weighed on the Scales of Reason and Scriptures*, a twenty-four-page pamphlet by William Jones.
- *Treatises on Miracles, Containing a Review of the Lectures of the Rev. J. Jones, Llangollen, and the Pamphlet of the Rev. J. Davies, Llanelli, on the Same Subject* is Davis's seventy-two-page (six different pamphlets) response to his former employer, the Reverend John Jones, and also to a sixty-page pamphlet by John Davies.

Much more numerous than pamphlet responses to the opposition are the numerous and frequent articles in *Prophet of the Jubilee* and *Zion's Trumpet*.[6]

Although Dan Jones was a well-known and vociferous proponent and defender of his religious beliefs, John S. Davis for many months kept his conversion and baptism into The Church of Jesus Christ of Latter-day Saints secret. In a 28 March 1847 letter to "Dear Brother" (possibly Thomas Jeremy), Davis wrote:

> There are hardly any yet who know that I am one of the Saints. They can know slowly and peacefully. [7]

Since his baptism had occurred nearly a year earlier, Davis was obviously in no hurry for word of his conversion to become generally known. He wrote this letter from Llanelli in the "Office of the *Revivalist*," a periodical of the Independents for which he had recently been invited to work. He had also been employed for two years by the *Star of Gomer*, a Baptist periodical in the town of Carmarthen.

Davis made his debut in polemics with an article entitled "The Nature of Miracles" in the October 1846 issue of *Star of Gomer*.[8] Using the nom de plume "I. M.," Davis wrote this 2,500-word article as a response to an even longer article that had appeared two months earlier in the August 1846 issue of *Star of Gomer*.[9] The longer article was also entitled "The Nature of Miracles" by someone who called himself Gwilym ab Dewi.

For most of his article, Gwilym ab Dewi provides general information about the miracles of the New Testament. He states that he sees no need for miracles "for the purpose of proving the truth of the Christian religion" and that he believes the Christian religion without having seen a single miracle. "But," he writes, "perhaps, since Christianity has split into a number of branches, a miracle would be necessary to prove which one of these branches is founded on the witness of Christ, the evangelists, and the apostles." At this point, since The Church of Jesus Christ of Latter-day Saints claims to be the only branch of Christianity in which miracles are performed, he extends the following invitation to members of this Church:

> If Captain Jones, or any others of the prophets of these Saints, will present themselves within the confines of Abersychan or Talywain, and have it in their mind to work a Miracle, I will set before them five loaves and two fishes, at my own expense; and if they can, by giving thanks, feed five thousand, besides women and children, and take up twelve baskets of fragments, then I will think it obvious that they are built on the foundation of prophets and apostles. If they will send their announcement here, I am confident that we can have a multitude of five thousand, besides women and children, to partake of the loaves and the fish, and to be witnesses of the Miracle.[10]

Compared to other writers such as David Williams and the Reverend W. R. Davies, Gwilym ab Dewi is actually quite civil in his comments about the Latter-day Saints and their teachings. He does not lower himself to ad hominem assaults, as Williams and Davies do constantly in their writings. Instead, by using syllogistic reasoning and scriptures, Gwilym ab Dewi puts forth his arguments against the Saints' ideas about such phenomena as the working of miracles and the casting out of evil spirits, and he comes forth as being a rather polite and well-mannered person. In his August 1846 article, Gwilym writes:

> Now, if the Latter-day Saints can perform miracles, let them raise someone from the dead—let them give eyes to some blind man—ears to a deaf man—speech to a mute—and let them hold back the *Atlantic Ocean*, so that they might go through it on dry land to their new Jerusalem.[11]

"I. M." (John S. Davis), in his October 1846 article, responds:

> Here he is again very eager for a sign; and a very large, but totally pointless, sign is the one he wishes to receive, that is for us to hold back the Atlantic Ocean, and walk on dry land to America. It would be far wiser to take boats to cross over, for it would be very wearisome to walk such a long way.[12]

Amazingly, Davis was but twenty-four years old when his article appeared in the October 1846 issue of *Star of Gomer*. He had already worked for two years at this Baptist periodical in Carmarthen, his hometown, before going twenty miles to the northeast to work for the Reverend John Jones in Rhydybont.[13]

Because John S. Davis was such a central figure during some of the most impactful years of the establishment of The Church of Jesus Christ of Latter-day Saints in Wales, perhaps the following timeline will assist the reader in identifying important events in his association with the press:

John S. Davis (1822–82) Timeline

1835–42	Apprentice printer—age 13 to 20
1842–43	In Carmarthen working for the *Star of Gomer* press
1844–45	In Haverfordwest working at the *Herald*—13 December 1845 letter from John S. Davis to Joseph Potter
1845–46	In Rhydybont working for the press of the Reverend John Jones
1846	19 April—Baptized by Thomas Harries in Llanybydder, Carmarthenshire
	August—Meurig's article in *Star of Gomer*—Miracle of the pig, discussed in Chapter 3
	August—"Nature of Miracles" by Gwilym ab Dewi in *Star of Gomer*
	October—"Nature of Miracles" by John S. Davis ("I. M.") in *Star of Gomer*
	November—"Zeal without Knowledge" by John S. Davis in *Star of Gomer*
	December—Question of "Meurig" in *Star of Gomer*
1847	January—"Nature of Miracles Again" by Davis ("I. M.") in *Star of Gomer*
	28 March letter to Thomas Jeremy written from Llanelli
	March to May—In Llanelli working for the *Revivalist* press
	June to September 1848—In Carmarthen working for the *Star of Gomer* press
	June—"Speaking with Tongues" by John S. Davis in *Star of Gomer*
	August—Davis's critique of the Williams sermon—*Prophet of the Jubilee*
	September—Challenge of H. Tegai to defend Mormonism in *Star of Gomer*
	December—"Speaking with Tongues" by John S. Davis in *Prophet of the Jubilee*
1848	May—"What is to be done with the editor of *Star of Gomer*?" *Prophet of the Jubilee*
	August—"Anti-Mormon Sermon" by John S. Davis in *Prophet of the Jubilee*
	October—"Review of Mormonism" by Anti-Humbug in *Star of Gomer*

	November & December—In Carmarthen—Davis is the printer for the final two issues of *Prophet of the Jubilee* (Davis had purchased "an old Caledonian printing press, second-hand type, and fitted up an office of his own at his father's house in Tanerdy" [an area of Carmarthen])[14]
1849	January & February—In Carmarthen—Davis is the printer for the first two issues of *Zion's Trumpet* on his own press
1849–53	In Merthyr as editor of six volumes of *Zion's Trumpet* (a total of 2,352 pages) (For a list of all his publications, see *Welsh Mormon Writings*, pp. x–xi)

Davis's third article to be published in the *Star of Gomer* (January 1847) is entitled "Nature of Miracles Again" and was in response to the "Meurig" query in the December 1846 article in the *Star of Gomer*:

> To Mr. I. M., Glanteifi
>
> Sir—In your notes about the article of Mr. W. Davies, you said that the disciples of Christ could be listed, who were the workers of the true miracles, and on the same ground as the Latter-day Saints, who are nothing but the workers of false miracles; and your reason for that was because the disciples failed to cast out the evil spirit mentioned in Matthew 17:14–21; Mark 9:17–29; Luke 9:39–42. We wish to know from you whether it was a lack of power or a lack of faith that was the cause of their lack of success? If the former, why did their Teacher chastise them for failing to fulfill that which was impossible for them to do?
>
> Glan yr un Teifi[15]

In the January 1847 issue of *Star of Gomer*, Davis responds to Meurig that the disciples' "power depended on their faith," and that they failed because they "were lacking faith."[16]

Davis worked in Llanelli for the *Revivalist*, a Congregationalist periodical, for only a few weeks during April and May of 1847 before receiving an offer to return to Carmarthen to work for *Star of Gomer*. In an unpublished article among his papers, Davis explains the welcome he received from Samuel Evans, the editor:

> But permit me now to tell of the kind favor which the Editor did for me when I arrived there. A few months before that, I sent an article to the *Star*, on "Speaking with tongues."[17] But I saw no sign that it had been published. But with my entrance to the office, the first thing I saw was the article under scrutiny on the press, set to appear in the June 1847 issue. He did that, I believe, only to please "Satan."[18]

In his rather brief article titled "Speaking with Tongues" in the June 1847 issue of *Star of Gomer*, Davis presents a scripturally based discussion about this New Testament gift of the Spirit and concludes:

> This, and all other things, show clearly, then, that speaking with tongues and the interpretations were only for the edifying of the church, and that such was done when the spirit of God was resting on those who were speaking.[19]

This was Davis's fourth and also his last article to be published in *Star of Gomer*. Samuel Evans, the editor, may not have known about Davis's conversion to the Church of Jesus Christ when he approved both the October 1846 article about the nature of miracles and Davis's January 1847 follow-up article on the same topic. In March 1847, Davis clearly indicates his religious status in a letter to Thomas Jeremy: "There is no one who knows that I am one of the Saints. They can find out slowly and quietly." But by the time Evans allowed Davis's article "Speaking with Tongues" to appear in the June 1847 issue of *Star of Gomer*, Evans definitely knew about his coworker's new religion.

Reacting to Davis's June 1847 article, the Reverend Hugh Hughes, using the nom de plume "H. Tegai,"[20] issues the following challenge to Davis in the September 1847 issue of *Star of Gomer*:

> I saw in the June *Star* an article of one J. D., on "Speaking with Tongues." If J. D. wishes to come forth to defend Mormonism, let him come to the root of the debate at once, by answering, 1. Did Christ and his apostles work public miracles? If they did, 2. Do the Mormons do so in the same way? Let J. D. answer as he may, and then I shall have a word to say to him. H. T.[21]

Davis wrote a response to H. Tegai's questions and fully expected that it would be printed in *Star of Gomer*. When the response was refused publication in that periodical, Davis submitted it to Dan Jones, who was pleased to publish it in the December 1847 issue of *Prophet of the Jubilee*. Davis explains the article's trajectory in an introductory paragraph addressed to Dan Jones:

> Some questions were directed at me in the September *Star*, by one Independent Reverend from the North, and I wrote an answer for them, being sure in my mind that I would receive the same fair play that the inquirer received; but to my disappointment, I was told that it was too poor, that there was none of the "cleverness" in this article that I had shown on other occasions, and that the aforementioned Reverend would take no notice of it. The only thing I shall say is, that I did my best. Now, I set my cause before you, and begging the fair play that was denied me in the place where it should have been received.[22]

Davis has a much more argumentative tone in this article than he used in his four articles that were allowed to appear in *Star of Gomer*. Addressing the editor of the periodical, Davis responds to the accusation that he had "come forth to defend Mormonism":

> About last February when I sent you an article on "Speaking with Tongues," which appeared in the *Star* for June, little did I think that anyone would be so perceptive as to see that it was defending Mormonism; for it was nothing more than an investigation into the New Testament to know what is to be understood by "speaking with tongues."[23]

To Tegai's statement, "Let J. D. answer as he may, and then I shall have a word to say to him," Davis writes,

> This thing looks like a trap or a net; and if the words are taken "spiritually," they mean, in my opinion, that Mr. Tegai has determined beforehand what he will say; yes, even if I were to convince him of the complete opposite. But that makes no difference, for I hope, that when our friend lifts his net, that a miracle will take place (as in the time of Christ), and instead of capturing me, he will have captured the truth, and that as it is in Christ. Amen.[24]

For an understanding of the ensuing battle between John S. Davis and Samuel Evans, Davis's senior by nearly thirty years and the editor of *Star of Gomer*, five items are essential to bear in mind:

- An article by Benjamin Jones in the May 1848 issue of *Prophet of the Jubilee* entitled "What Is to Be Done with the Editor of the *Star of Gomer*?"[25]
- An article by John S. Davis in the August 1848 issue of *Prophet of the Jubilee* entitled "Anti-Mormon Sermon by T. Williams, Ebenezer."[26]
- An article by "Anti-Humbug" (Samuel Evans) in the October 1848 issue of *Star of Gomer* entitled "A Review of Mormonism, and the Rev. T. Williams."[27]
- An article by John S. Davis in the December 1848 issue of *Prophet of the Jubilee* entitled "Observations on a Sermon about 'The Latter-day Saints and Miraculous Gifts.'"[28]
- An unpublished article entitled "The Editor of *Star of Gomer*, Anti-Humbug, and J. Davis," written by John S. Davis on 6 October 1848.[29]

In the first item, Benjamin Jones from Carmarthen expresses mock concern about the state of the editor of the *Star of Gomer* in light of his recent excommunication from the Baptists and asks in feigned bewilderment, "What is to be done with the Editor of the *Star of Gomer*?" Benjamin Jones muses:

> For the sake of his soul, poor thing, he ought to get some religion yet; but which one, is the question. As the religion of the Satanists is the closest one to the Baptists, who knows whether he might obtain a place with those? . . . But what good is it to speak like this? for the Satanists are "very soon" to come to request their place with the Baptists; consequently, what good would it be for the Editor to join with the Satanists, and then be considered unworthy to be received back along with the Satanists?[30]

The second item is Davis's review of an "Anti-Mormon" sermon given by the Rev. Thomas Williams on 2 July 1848 from his pulpit at the Ebenezer Chapel of the Independents in Llangynog. John S. Davis was in attendance during the sermon and took copious notes. Four days later he had composed his critique, which was published in the August 1848 issue of *Prophet of the Jubilee*.[31] According to Davis, among the various inconsistencies in Williams's sermon was his stance concerning more than one baptism:

> But one thing you said about the Mormons baptizing more than once, requires particular attention. If it is unscriptural for the Mormons to baptize after the Baptists, it is unscriptural also for the Baptists to baptize after the Mormons, as was done with two women in Llwyni, according to the account given in a recent issue of the *Baptist*.[32]

The third item appeared in *Star of Gomer* in the October 1848 issue. The editor, now excommunicated from the Baptist faith, published a vicious, ad hominem, two-thousand-word review of Davis's article. Using the nom de plume "Anti-Humbug," Samuel Evans has nothing but praise for the Reverend Thomas Williams and his sermon. But for Davis, his former coworker, Evans has nothing but derision and ridicule, and he even—possibly intentionally—misspelled his coworker's surname, using Davies instead of Davis.[33] Here are some examples of Evans's style:

> This J. Davies indicates that he will write again. It would be as well for him to slow down, until he can write some sense, and form more decent and respectful expressions for his fellow creatures. Seeing some ignorant and selfish dwarf of a man inflate with self-importance is a scandal to humanity. . . . It is a beautiful characteristic in everyone that they know their place. Mr. Gomer, what consistency is there between a minister who preaches the faith of the Independents on the one hand, and prints the Latter-day Saints' books on the other?[34]

The fourth item is Davis's eight-page review, in the December 1848 issue of *Prophet of the Jubilee*, of a twenty-page pamphlet entitled *The Latter-day Saints and Miraculous Gifts* by the Reverend David Evans, a curate in the Anglican Church. Evans gave a sermon by the same title on 27 August 1848 in the St. David's Church in Carmarthen and had the sermon printed a few weeks later. The editor of the *Sun* reacted to David Evans's pamphlet in the December 1848 issue:

> In our time the Mormons, or the Latter-day Saints, and their beliefs, are too despicable to take any note of them; but the common folk are paying attention to them; and the apostles of this blasphemous heresy are deceiving many of the people and putting their salvation at risk. The Sermon under scrutiny is an excellent antidote to this deadly poison; but for it to have effect, it would be better for the reverend author to devise some way of bringing it off the press more cheaply, in order to disseminate it generally.[35]

Not surprisingly, John S. Davis's reaction was considerably different. In the opening paragraph of his response, Davis explains his motive for focusing on the twenty-page pamphlet:

> The name attached to the sermon is the only reason I consider making comments on it. The great task Capt. Jones has in looking after about three thousand Saints, prevents him from commenting on everything that may be published against our religion; but somehow or other, it happens most often that the books that are published against the Saints, especially Mr. Evans's sermon, have already been answered by him in various books.[36]

Although the Anglican curate accuses the leaders of The Church of Jesus Christ of Latter-day Saints of being false prophets, he presents scriptures and arguments to substantiate his statements and this conclusion. On page fifteen of his pamphlet, he throws out the following challenge:

> Let the deaf be shown whose ears have been opened through the power of the Saints. Who of them has loosened the tongue-strings of the mute, causing him to speak the praises of God?

Davis is pleased to respond:

> We answer that Mr. Evans can see a person who came to hear and speak—yes, speak the praises of God, after being baptized by the Saints, and that recently, and also in Wales.[37]

He then refers Evans to the November 1848 issue of *Prophet of the Jubilee*, which has the account of Reuben Brinkworth, who had been deaf and mute for eight years prior to the night of 22 September 1848. It was on that night that Brinkworth received his baptism into the Church of Jesus Christ and on coming up out of the water he cried out, "Thank the Lord, I can speak and hear again, as well as any of you!"[38]

Toward the end of 1848, because Dan Jones was busy organizing the emigration of over three hundred Welsh converts to sail from Liverpool to New Orleans in February, one could safely assume that he had probably assigned Davis to prepare an answer to the curate's pamphlet. And likely because Davis used *Prophet of the Jubilee* to respond, his attention was diverted from taking his own personal revenge against the excommunicated Baptist minister at the time of the minister's attack on Jones in the October 1848 article in *Star of Gomer*.

The fifth item, the 6 October 1848 letter of defense by John S. Davis, was precipitated by Samuel Evans's barrage of personalized and targeted aggression in the October 1848 *Star of Gomer* article. To be so verbally maligned to the point of being sarcastically called "the great apostle" by a colleague of several years over a difference of religious allegiance no doubt caused considerable anguish and frustration for John S. Davis, as well as a desire to defend himself and his religion. He did exactly that by writing out his frustrations to send to *Star of Gomer*. He must certainly have known that the letter would not be allowed publication in his hometown periodical. Nevertheless, his feelings were soon on display on ten sheets of paper:

> Then I sat "the great apostle down, and I gave birth" to the article by the name of "Speaking with Tongues, The New Testament, and Mormonism," [which was published in the December 1848 issue of *Prophet of the Jubilee*] being sure in my mind that I would receive the same fair play which the asker of the question received; but to my disappointment, I was told by the editor [Samuel Evans] that there was none of the "cleverness" in that article that I had shown on other occasions, and that H. Tegai had made no mention of that. That was proof, then, that the work of the Editor was not to give fair play.[39]

In contrast, Davis tells of his relationship with two other work colleagues:

> I continued in this office for another week or two after printing the September [1848] *Star*, when I left as a result of the notice I had given to the printer a month before that because of some words between us a month earlier. I left in a very peaceful and gentlemanly way, and I have every respect for the printer, and for the publisher, the Reverend H. W. Jones. It was these two who recommended writing to me in the first place, and as I left them, I can testify that they treated me in an honest and Christian-like manner.[40]

Davis also reflects on the verbal attacks aimed at him by the editor who had a few months before been expelled from the Baptist religion:

> Now, I wish for all to put common sense into operation. Is it not just envy and jealousy that have caused this excommunicated Editor to attack me in the manner described? And what have I ever done to him? Is it for revenge because I did not loan three pounds to his wise and clever wife when she asked it of me? If that is the reason, he should forgive me; for he ought to know that a "Satan" like me is as clever as she in determining to whom money should be lent. But I think that the reason for these attacks is in the temperament of the Editor.[41]

Very hurtful to Davis was the advice "Anti-Humbug" offered him in his vicious article:

> It would be wisdom for J. Davies to follow the profession that is most familiar to him, and leave teaching the people to those who have received the gift.[42]

To this offensive counsel given by the fifty-five-year-old veteran Samuel Evans, the twenty-six-year-old Davis offered the following defiant challenge:

> Now, if Anti-Humbug or Gomer wish to debate with me about Mormonism, let them declare that the columns of the *Star* are free; or if those columns are too pure, let them come and face me on the soapbox.[43]

Notes

1. "History of the Latter-day Saints," in Ronald D. Dennis, ed., *Defending the Faith: Early Welsh Missionary Publications* (Provo, UT: Religious Studies Center, Brigham Young University, 2003), 59.
2. Letter from Dan Jones to Thomas Bullock, January 20, 1855.
3. *Prophet of the Jubilee*, July 1846, wrapper, 2.
4. Ibid.
5. See Dennis, *Defending the Faith: Early Welsh Missionary Publications*, for the English translations of all the pamphlets and poetry authored by Dan Jones and John S. Davis from 1845 to 1856.
6. The English translations of the three volumes of *Prophet of the Jubilee* (1846–48) and of the ten extant volumes of *Zion's Trumpet* (1849–57) can be accessed through the Welsh Saints Project.
7. John S. Davis papers, in private hands.
8. *Star of Gomer*, October 1846, 301–303.
9. *Star of Gomer*, August 1846, 233–35.
10. Ibid., 233.
11. Ibid., 234.
12. *Star of Gomer*, October 1846, 302.
13. 6 October 1848, unpublished article in the John S. Davis papers, pg. 2. "I worked for years in the office of *Star of Gomer*. Originally, after spending two years there, I left because I was not content with my pay."
14. A biography of John S. Davis is available at the Welsh Saints Project website.
15. *Star of Gomer*, December 1846, 378. In a bit of a joke about John S. Davis being from "Glanteifi," which means "along the bank of the Tovey River," Meurig indicates his home as being on the "Bank of the same river Tovey."
16. *Star of Gomer*, January 1847, 17.

17. *Star of Gomer*, June 1847, 173–74.
18. 6 October 1848 unpublished article in the John S. Davis Papers.
19. *Star of Gomer*, June 1847, 174.
20. Tegai is the name of a fifth-century Welsh saint. There is a small village in North Wales near Bangor named after him—Llanadygai.
21. *Star of Gomer*, September 1847, 258.
22. *Prophet of the Jubilee*, December 1847, 181–85.
23. Ibid., 181.
24. Ibid., 185.
25. *Prophet of the Jubilee*, May 1848, 76.
26. *Prophet of the Jubilee*, August 1848, 118–22.
27. *Star of Gomer*, October 1848, 304–5.
28. *Prophet of the Jubilee*, December 1848, 176–83.
29. John S. Davis papers, in private hands.
30. *Prophet of the Jubilee*, May 1848, 76.
31. *Prophet of the Jubilee*, August 1848, 118–22.
32. Ibid., 121.
33. In Wales, Davies and Davis are pronounced identically.
34. *Star of Gomer*, October 1848, 305. The "minister" is a reference to the Rev. John Jones, the older brother of Dan Jones.
35. *Sun*, December 1848, 402.
36. *Prophet of the Jubilee*, December 1848, 176–83.
37. Ibid., 182.
38. *Prophet of the Jubilee*, November 1848, 163–65.
39. Unpublished 6 October 1848 letter, 4.
40. Ibid., 5.
41. Ibid., 6.
42. *Star of Gomer*, October 1848, 305.
43. Unpublished 6 October 1848 letter, 10.

Chapter 2

Episodes

2.1—Three different writers report on the woman who drowned at her baptism
2.2—Response of the press in Wales to the Martyrdom

Salient Events

- **6 April 1837.** The first Latter-day Saint missionaries set foot in England.
- **16 October 1840.** Missionaries Henry Royle and Frederick Cook arrive in the border town of Overton, Flintshire, in North Wales. By 30 October they have a branch with thirty-two baptized members.
- **"In the year 1840."** John Needham reports having organized "many branches of the church in Monmouth and in Wales." See Needham's claim to have been the first missionary to preach the gospel in South Wales on the Welsh Saints Project website.
- **6 April 1841.** The *Millennial Star* reports 170 Church members in Wales. These were probably all in North Wales and were possibly the result of the proselytizing of Henry Royle, Frederick Cook, and James Burnham around the Overton, Flintshire, area. See the Welsh Saints Project.
- **10 May 1841.** Dan Jones and two partners sign the enrollment document for the *Ripple*, one of the smallest steamboats on the Upper Mississippi. Just six months later the *Ripple* struck a rock and sank near New Boston, about sixty-five miles upriver from Nauvoo. During the summer of 1842 Dan Jones and his partner Levi Moffat built a new steamboat, the *Maid of Iowa*, on the Skunk River at Augusta, Iowa, located about seventeen miles north of Nauvoo, Illinois. It was while operating this steamboat on the Mississippi River that Jones became acquainted with Thomas Sharp's newspaper, the *Warsaw Signal*, and the scurrilous reports about Joseph Smith and the Church he had founded.

- **Fall/Winter 1842.** William Henshaw, a Cornishman, is sent from Wolverhampton by Lorenzo Snow to Merthyr Tydfil. Henshaw spoke no Welsh, but his wife did. Initially, Elder Henshaw could share his message only with speakers of English. As bilingual Welshmen believed the message of the gospel, they were then able to communicate that message to monoglot Welshmen.
- **19 January 1843.** Dan Jones is baptized in the Mississippi River. As the captain of the steamboat *Maid of Iowa*, he had noticed the articles in the *Warsaw Signal* by its editor, Thomas Sharp. Incredulous at how evil Joseph Smith and his religious doctrine were portrayed to be, Jones located some Latter-day Saint missionaries who taught him the beauties of the restored gospel. Upon believing the message, he received his baptism in the icy waters of the river he knew well, probably in the shadow of the *Maid of Iowa*, his home at the time. He became personally acquainted with Joseph Smith on 12 April 1843 when he docked his steamboat at Nauvoo, Illinois, with a group of English converts on board. Jones bonded with the Prophet almost immediately and was with him at Carthage Jail until just a few hours before the martyrdom. (See his biography, *A Steamboat for an Eldership*, at the Welsh Saints Project.)
- **19 February 1843.** William Henshaw has his first baptisms: the William R. Davis family. Born in Carmarthenshire in 1805, William R. Davis had also lived in Bristol where he was surrounded by speakers of English. At the time he became acquainted with Henshaw, Davis had set up a tailor's shop in Merthyr Tydfil. William and Rachel Davis went to the United States with Dan Jones on board the *Buena Vista* in February 1849. Their son George was serving a mission in Wales at that time. He died of cholera in July 1849.
- **September 1844.** William and Jane Perkins are baptized in Swansea. As a result of their conversion, William lost his job, and the family spent some time in the poor house. Decades later, their son Benjamin was the architect of the 1880 "Hole in the Rock Expedition" in Utah.
- **1 January 1845.** Dan Jones and his wife Jane arrive in Liverpool, having crossed the ocean in company with Wilford Woodruff and his wife. Jones was assigned to North Wales where he had spent his formative years and where his parents and some of his siblings still lived. He failed to bring any family members, former teachers, or acquaintances into the gospel during what must have been a very frustrating year of proselytizing in the area where he had spent his youth.
- **6 April 1845.** The clerk at a conference in Manchester reacts to the remarks of Dan Jones:

  > We would here remark that we are utterly incapable of doing anything like justice to the address of Captain Jones, for though delivered while struggling with disease, such was its effect upon ourselves, and we believe upon others, that we ceased to write, in order to give way to the effect produced upon our feelings.[1]

- **April 1845.** Dan Jones publishes his first pamphlet in Wrexham. He relies heavily on Parley P. Pratt's *Voice of Warning*.

- **Mid-1845.** In Rhosllanerchrugog, North Wales, Dan Jones baptizes Robert Evans, formerly a "gifted Campbellite preacher." Evans remained faithful for several years until he went to Utah. He returned to Wales aligned with the Reorganized Church of Jesus Christ of Latter-day Saints.
- **1 June 1845.** William Henshaw reports on a recent conference held in Merthyr Tydfil:

  > Dear Brother Ward. We held a conference in the Large Room, at Merthyr, according to appointment; the day was fine, and many of the Saints were present from a distance of twenty miles or more. One sister nearly seventy years of age walked forty-two miles. I spoke much on the object for which we were met, and exhorted them to continue in love and union, and the Spirit of the Lord would crown our labors with success. Elder Rees, and others, spoke on the organization of the church in an interesting manner; many strangers were present; and we feel that much good will be done here. We have baptized forty since the General Conference; the Lord is rolling on his work. This has been the best Conference held in South Wales, it lasted two days, and truly it was a time of rejoicing. The Saints are in good spirits, and are determined to spread the gospel, and very soon will many arise and cross the might deep to the Land of Zion. Yours truly, in the covenant of peace, William Henshaw.[2]

- **Summer 1845.** Dan Jones visits South Wales and is thrilled to meet other Welsh-speaking members of the Church for the first time.
- **Late 1845.** *The Latter Saints*, an anonymous twenty-four-page pamphlet, is published in Merthyr Tydfil, with contents of a general nature. It received no response from Dan Jones. (See Pamphlet 1 in Section 2.)
- **Late 1845.** *The Deception of the Latter Saints Exposed*, a thirty-two-page pamphlet by David Williams, is published in opposition to Dan Jones's first pamphlet. (See Pamphlet 2 in Section 2.)
- **3 December 1845.** Dan Jones prints four thousand copies of his second pamphlet, the Welsh translation of *Proclamation of the Twelve Apostles*, on his brother's press in Rhydybont, Carmarthenshire.
- **December 1845.** Dan Jones moves to Merthyr Tydfil and becomes president of the Church in all of Wales. During the following three-year period, over three thousand converts were baptized.

Commentary

1838: 2 November, *Welshman*, p. 4 (2,700 words).

Information about the beginnings of this new religion, The Church of Jesus Christ of Latter-day Saints, in the United States. Mention is made of the first missionaries who arrived in Preston and began converting locals. The final paragraph has an account of the strife that existed between the Latter-day Saints and their enemies in Missouri.

1838: 24 November, *Silurian*, p. 1 (240 words).

General information about the origins of the Latter-day Saints and a mention of the rumor of Joseph Smith's attempt to walk on water. The writer comments, "Of a truth, Mormonism is a superstition worthy to be classed with that of Johanna Southcott."

1838: 22 December, *Silurian*, p. 1 (150 words).

This article is taken from a piece in the *St. Louis Republican* about the Haun's Mill massacre. The writer comments, "For the honor of the State, we could have wished that such savage enormities had not attended a controversy in itself disgraceful enough. Will the actors in the tragedy be suffered, by the Courts of that district, to go unpunished?"

1839: 26 October, *Monmouthshire Merlin*, p. 4 (200 words).

A report of a visit of the Latter-day Saints to various places in Patterson, New Jersey, after which "they left the town for the woods, followed by about 500 factory girls, and held a bush meeting all that afternoon and night."

1839: November, *Cyfaill o'r Hen Wlad yn America* (*Friend of the Old Country in America*), pp. 325–27 (1,500 words).

> In the town of Palmyra, in the northern part of the State of New York, an idiot, who, is said to have been born dumb, a few years ago suddenly announced that 'one night' he was visited by an angel who commanded him to rise from his bed and follow him.

Following this introduction, the writer presents his version of the coming forth of the Book of Mormon.

1840: 2 October, *Welshman*, p. 2 (260 words).

> There are at present in the neighborhood of Gateshead two ministers of a sect called 'Latter-day Saints,' who state that they have come out 'without purse or scrip,' as a voice of warning to the people.

This comment is followed by a description of the missionaries' message.

1840: 21 November, *Monmouthshire Beacon*, p. 4 (870 words). "The Mormonites or Latter-day Saints. (Abridged from the Cheltenham Free Press.)"

This article has five sections: "Their Origin," "Their Proposed Object," "Their Tenets," "Their Book of Mormon," and "Their Progress." Nothing is said about Wales.

1841: January, *Seren Gomer* (*Star of Gomer*), pp. 6–8 (1,380 words).

The writer indicates concern about the presence of the Latter-day Saints in Cheshire and other places in England. The writer had looked at issues of the *Millennial Star*, as well as a copy of the Book of Mormon. He then presents a history of the coming forth of the Book of Mormon.

1841: February, *Cyfaill o'r Hen Wlad yn America* (*Friend of the Old Country in America*), p. 57 (160 words). "The Growth of Mormonism."

This piece contains some statistics about the Saints, taken from the *Times and Seasons*.

1841: 29 May, *Monmouthshire Beacon*, p. 3 (225 words). "Mormonite Preacher."

An account of a three-hour discussion held at the Temperance Hall in the town of Monmouth, between Mr. Cluer, a temperance lecturer, and Mr. Curtis, a "preacher among the Mormonites, or Latter-day Saints." The writer declares Mr. Cluer the winner.

1841: 31 July, *Monmouthshire Beacon*, p. 3 (200 words). "The Mormonites."

An account of the arrest of Joseph Smith and the evil nature of his followers.

1841: 14 August, *Cardiff and Merthyr Guardian*, p. 4 (140 words). "The Mormonites in America."

This article recounts the latest arrest of Joseph Smith and erroneously reports that Martin Harris had been shot through the head.

1841: 21 August, *Monmouthshire Merlin*, p. 4 (200 words). "Mormons Again."

The writer discusses the preaching of "Mr. Herringshaw" in Louth.

1841: 28 August, *Monmouthshire Beacon*, p. 3 (1,225 words). "The Latter-day Saint Swindle."

The writer relates the negative experience that a Mr. and Mrs. Margretts had after leaving their home near Cheltenham and crossing the ocean to Nauvoo. After meeting Joseph Smith and other coreligionists in Nauvoo, they realized their error in leaving England and returned. The Margretts are very likely the Margaret [Margaretz] family (Thomas, age 46, farmer; Elizabeth, age 45; and their three children) whose names are on the shipping list for the *Echo* that left Liverpool on 16 Feb 1841 and arrived at New Orleans on 16 April 1841.

1841: 28 August, *Cambrian*, p. 4 (230 words).

More about the disappointing experience of Thomas Margretts.

1841: 27 November, *Monmouthshire Beacon*, p. 2 (60 words). "The Mormonite Fanatics."

A large group of Latter-day Saints from Gloucester is on their way to Nauvoo.

1841: 27 November, *Cardiff and Merthyr Guardian*, p. 4 (60 words).

The same article appears in the *Monmouthshire Beacon* for 27 November 1841 (see previous entry).

1841: December, *Seren Gomer* (*Star of Gomer*), pp. 373–74 (1,210 words). "The Mormons."

Disturbed at the success the Latter-day Saints continued to have in some parts of England, the editor wishes to expose the "disgraceful deceit they use to beguile the innocents into believing the most shameless superstitions ever proclaimed in a Christian country." He does so by copying from the *Monmouthshire Beacon* the story of the Margretts family.[3]

1842: 19 August, *Welshman*, p. 2 (35 words).

> Joe Smith, the Mormon Prophet, has quarreled with his two disciples, Rigdon and Bennett, and they threaten to expose his chicanery. How melancholy that so many emigrants should leave England to join these miserable fanatics!

1842: 20 August, *Monmouthshire Beacon*, p. 1 (215 words). "Bankruptcy of the Mormon Impostors."

The writer discusses the "vile scheme" of Joseph Smith and the "revolting immoralities practiced by the Mormon leaders."

1842: 17 September, *Monmouthshire Beacon*, p. 3 (300 words). "Mormonism."

A few lines about a young woman who left her home in Cheltenham on her way to join with the Latter-day Saints in America. Upon arriving in London, she sent a letter to her mother asking for forgiveness and some money to return home.

1842: October, *Y Drysorfa* (*Treasury*), pp. 310–11 (780 words).

A reader asks the editor about the "religious tenets" of the Latter-day Saints. The editor responds that their history is "interwoven with everything that is loathsome, odious, and barbaric." He then provides a long response to substantiate his assertion.

1842: November, *Seren Gomer* (*Star of Gomer*), p. 351 (170 words).

The writer laments the "many thousands" who have left Britain to go to Nauvoo. One woman said that even if the ship sank, she would be taken "in the belly of some sea-monster" safely to Nauvoo.

1842: 23 December, *Welshman*, p. 2 (155 words). "Mormonism."

Some people in Kendal were "so infatuated by the dogmas of Mormonism as to refuse medical advice in cases of sickness." The writer also adds some very negative lines about "Pontiff Joe Smith."

1842: 24 December, *Silurian*, p. 1 (190 words). "Mutiny."

The writer reports the difficulties that arose between the leaders of the Latter-day Saints and Captain Pierce of the ship *Henry*, which had left Liverpool on 29 September 1842.

1843: 14 January, *Cardiff and Merthyr Guardian*, p. 4 (110 words).

The same article appears in the *Welshman* for 23 December 1842 (see previous entry), save for the final sentence.

1843: May 6, Unpublished letter by Rev. W. R. Davies.[4]

The Reverend W. R. Davies, an ordained Baptist minister for the Caersalem Chapel in Dowlais (almost contiguous with Merthyr Tydfil), was the most vociferous opponent of The Church of Jesus Christ of Latter-day Saints in Wales from May 1843 to September 1849, when he died of cholera. Elder William Henshaw had been sent from Wolverhampton by Elder Lorenzo Snow to preach the gospel in Merthyr Tydfil, the heartland of South Wales at that time. On 19 February 1843, a bilingual tailor by the name of William Rees Davis became the first to accept the gospel message from Henshaw. Three months later, in a letter dated 6 May 1843, the Reverend W. R. Davies wrote to his friend, William Jones, a draper living in Llanystumdwy, about Henshaw's initial success of twelve convert baptisms. For context, one of the converts was a woman from the Reverend's own congregation:

> I am baptizing every month, and it is quite likely that it will continue so for a while at least, but I will tell you some news. There is a new sect here. "Latter-day Saints" they call themselves. They baptize as we do, and that at night. They

> profess they can do everything the apostles could – heal the sick, cast out demons, raise the dead, speak in tongues, etc., etc. And the minister has been in the house with me, endeavoring to convince me. He is succeeding, and has baptized from 10 to 12 in the last three months. And he baptized one woman who was a member with us.

Davies then comments to his friend about the mode of baptism used by Henshaw:

> What? you say. Will he rebaptize after the *Baptist*? He will, indeed. How so, when he baptizes by immersion? etc. Oh, because no authority had been obtained from Christ by anyone in the world but him and his brothers. The Holy Ghost has commanded him to go and preach in the same way as you order some man to strike an iron for you in order to forge a shoe for an old horse in the smithy. And he had, he said, been arguing that he was not qualified. But He commanded him to go immediately.

With respect to the doctrine preached by Henshaw, Davies writes:

> He is half threatening that the end of the world will be in a year's time. But he preaches that Christ will come on the earth to reign in forty years' time and that they will be the only men who will reign with him. Which do you think? Will it be he and his company or the Sandemanians who will be higher in authority? Well, you ask, what sort of man is he? Well, he is an ignorant little English-speaking collier. One of his disciples was telling me this the other day: "Well, Davies, laugh as much as you like. I believe the thing I saw. I believe, yes, I believe my own eyes before believing anyone else. I saw someone come to him with a large swelling in his limb. He put his hand on the swelling, and it immediately went down under his hand. And he was completely cured."

Davies mentions in jest an apparent ailment his friend suffered from, followed by his invitation to Henshaw to go with him to heal a neighbor:

> It will be a good thing for you to bring your arm to him, if it is not better. But he absolutely refused to come with me to cure the cancer of a man who lived near our house. Yet he is successful despite deceiving some, as you see. And it is possible that he will get some more fools to believe him. It is easier for a man to believe anything but the truth, be it as foolish as the babbling of children. Which do you prefer, Quick or Hobgoblin's Hole? Understand that "Hobgoblin's Hole" is the name of the place where Quick lives. Is it not a very heavenly name? May a blessing be on the Quick and the Hobgoblin.

1843: 15 August, *North Wales Chronicle*, p. 4 (210 words). "The Mormons in America."

Taken from the *St. Louis Republican* piece about the latest arrest of Joseph Smith and the rescue by his followers. It says in part, "The Mormons have conducted the false prophet to Nauvoo, where they will strengthen their military position, and wait the action of the state authorities."

1843: December, *Y Diwygiwr* (*Revivalist*), pp. 370–71 (890 words). "A Letter from America."

The editor reprints a 26 July 1843 letter from John Griffiths, son of the Reverend Samuel Griffiths of Horeb Chapel in Llandysul. There is no editorial comment to the letter. It is simply John Griffiths's account of his travels to Missouri, Iowa, and Illinois. Because he heard talk when he was back home in Llandysul of there being Welsh Indians around the Missouri River, he listened carefully to a group of Native Americans he encountered as he traveled from St. Louis along the Missouri River. But he was disappointed that they spoke neither Welsh nor English. According to legend, the "Welsh Indians" were the descendants of a Prince Madoc and his group of Welsh who sailed away from Wales in 1170. They ended up off the coast of what is now South Carolina. Failing to achieve their objective of establishing a Welsh colony in America, they eventually adopted the ways of the Native Americans and became a separate, Welsh-speaking tribe. Griffiths also mentions his brief encounter with Dan Jones: "Captain Jones, the brother of Rev. Jones, Rhydybont, offered to take me on his vessel, 150 miles upriver and along the Des Moines River, but I didn't go." The "Rev. Jones, Rhydybont" is John Jones, the older brother of Dan Jones, who had recently been ordained a Congregationalist minister in Rhydybont, a village about ten miles northeast of John Griffiths's hometown of Llandysul. The press owned by Rev. Jones in Rhydybont would later be used between 1846 and 1849 to print nearly all of Dan Jones's publications in defense of his new beliefs. The "vessel" referred to is the *Maid of Iowa*, a small steamboat that Dan Jones and his partner, Levi Moffat, had built a year earlier near Augusta, Iowa, about twenty miles northeast of Nauvoo, Illinois. In his letter, Griffiths mentions nothing about Dan Jones's recent affiliation with The Church of Jesus Christ of Latter-day Saints, an affiliation that Jones had established by receiving his baptism in the Mississippi River only six months earlier. Griffiths did, however, mention his visit to Nauvoo and the nearly twenty-five thousand followers of Joseph Smith who lived there. He also tells of Joseph Smith's failure to walk on water because "some rascal" had removed one of the benches arranged about a foot beneath the water's surface so Smith could show the gathered crowd a miracle.

1843: 23 December, *Silurian*, p. 2 (270 words). "The Mormonites."

An account as to how Robert Turner of Sheffield, who was a spring-knife cutler and also an LDS priest, drowned during a baptism.

1843: 30 December, *Silurian*, p. 1 (95 words). "Mormonism in Leicester."

The writer reports on the Church's progress in Leicester as well as accounts of speaking in unknown tongues and other characteristics of this new religion.

Episode 2.1

Start: Three different writers report on the woman who drowned at her baptism

1844: January, *Seren Gomer* (*Star of Gomer*), p. 31 (235 words). "Remarkable Superstition."

A woman in Chester reportedly was forced by her husband to be baptized by the Latter-day Saints. The person performing the baptism lost his grip on the woman, and she went down the river and drowned. The writer describes the reaction of the woman's husband:

> The husband went home unconcerned, and he said that it was God's will that she drowned, and that it was caused because of the weakness of her faith, but that he was certain that she was in glory.

Her husband and the person that attempted to perform the baptism were taken to the Chester jail and charged with manslaughter.

1844: January, *Y Dysgedydd* (*Instructor*), p. 32 (250 words). "Drowning by Immersion."

A woman in Chester drowned at her baptism. The writer of this article adds some information about the woman's reason for accepting baptism:

> Her husband practically drove her insane with his insistence and tormenting that she needed to "obey;" a very frequent word in the *vocabulary* of the immersers according to all the locals. He told her that unless she *obeyed*, "she would never have peace with him."

1844: April, *Y Dysgedydd* (*Instructor*), pp. 116–17 (650 words). "Remarkable Superstition."

The writer responds to the January issue of the *Instructor* and uses the same title: "Remarkable Superstition." He expresses bewilderment as to why the previous writer would use such a title:

> I was unable to discern what the writer was thinking when he called this *Remarkable Superstition*. Immersing is what the Mormons were doing, and immersing is what the Baptists, or the Immersers, do; what, therefore, is any more superstitious in the one than in the other?

He concludes that they are both wrong and that the proper mode of baptism is by aspersion.

End: Three different writers report on the woman who drowned at her baptism

1844: March, *Y Bedyddiwr* (*Baptist*), pp. 99–100 (670 words). "A Strange Birth among the Saints."

This article is signed "Tobit by the Bridge," one of the several noms de plume used by the Baptist minister W. R. Davies in Dowlais. His introduction to this article is indicative of his basic position regarding members of The Church of Jesus Christ of Latter-day Saints:

> The foolish and mad men who call themselves "Latter-day Saints" have arrived in Pendaran. They profess to work miracles, to prophesy, to speak in unknown tongues, yea, in a word to do everything which the apostles did. I am sorry to say that a number of the dregs of society are now believers. They baptize at night, and those receiving baptism must undress for them and go to the water *stark naked*!

Davies then gives an account of the attempted healing of a woman by the laying on of hands. It turns out that the woman, a recent convert to The Church of Jesus Christ of Latter-day Saints, was actually giving birth. Since the first man to lay his hands on her to give her a blessing was unsuccessful in relieving the woman of her pain, a second brother whom Davies calls the "Chief Apostle" was sent for. This is most likely a sarcastic reference to William Henshaw, the leader of the Church in Merthyr Tydfil. Henshaw came and gave the woman a blessing, but she got worse. Finally, it was discovered that the woman had given birth, and the child had died in the bed. Davies concludes the article with some very harsh observations about the new sect:

> This will serve to show to our race what kind of animals the Latter-day Saints are. All the Saints are the chief fools around. They say they are all going before long to Joe Smith in America—that the second Zion is being built now, and that it will be heaven on earth for them before long. I shall give more of their story to you when I get a chance, if I think it will serve some purpose. I did not think there were men so stupid in Wales to believe such a heap of nonsense and presumption.

1844: April, *Y Bedyddiwr* (*Baptist*), pp. 123–24 (1,525 words). "A Strange Account of the Latter-day Saints."

In this issue of the *Baptist,* W. R. Davies (again with the nom de plume of "Tobit by the Bridge") presents an account of several failed attempts on the part of the Latter-day Saints to proselytize the Welsh who lived in and around Merthyr Tydfil. Among those gathered to hear them were Dafydd Oliver, a member of the Sion Baptist congregation, and James Wilkins, a Baptist minister. After the missionary finished his presentation, Oliver asked him for a clarification of one of his assertions, "which led to a heated and fierce debate." According to Davies, "the infallible one had to admit in the presence of those present that he had misworded the subject, that he had intended otherwise, etc." At this point, Davies says:

> [Oliver] took hold of him with invincible strength, showing him to be a satanic and presumptuous wretch, trying to blind a few of the weak-headed fools who followed him into believing that he was speaking infallibly and was a recipient of visions and revelations directly from God, when he was forced to confess before them all that he was confused like a wild bull in a snare, and he had to fall from his fallibility to his shame and arrogance.

Two more meetings of the debate took place in which Oliver, according to Davies, "gained a clear victory." And at the end of the third debate, James Wilkins asked for permission to speak, and, again according to Davies, "he showed their stupidity and arrogance, which, as he observed, was clear to everyone, and that they would not come ever again to disturb the camp of the Saints, as they were beneath the notice of every man of common sense, etc."

After failures in several other places while debating with the Baptists, the Latter-day Saints arranged for a series of debates with the Independents of the Bethesda Chapel near Merthyr Tydfil. Davies says, "An intelligent and gifted young man who was a member in Bethesda, a deacon in the Sunday School and a warrior from his youth, was selected to chase the Saints from their boundaries." Davies reports that the first debate was about miracles and that the Independents "appeared victorious in the eyes of the public." But the topic for the second debate was baptism, and "the sprinklers were slain forthwith." As for the representative for the Independents, "he fell silent, and what's more he went of his own free will with the Saints from the scene of the debate to the river and was baptized!" The irony was that among the listeners of the debate was the father of the "intelligent and gifted young man." But within a few days following the debate, the father was baptized along with another of his sons and his daughter.

Contemporary records for The Church of Jesus Christ of Latter-day Saints indicate that the name of the debater who went from the debate to the river to be baptized into the Church he had initially opposed was Abel Evans. From that time forth, Abel served as an extremely effective missionary for his new religion until 1850, when he left Wales to join with the main body of the Saints in the Rocky Mountains. On the ship he met Mary Jones, a convert from Llangynog, Carmarthenshire, and they were married in St. Louis. He was thirty-eight years old and she was twenty-three. They settled in Lehi, Utah, about thirty miles south of Salt Lake City. In 1865, Abel was called to return to Wales as a missionary. Eighteen months later, he was helping some Welsh converts to get ready to sail to America when he contracted a serious illness and died. He left three widows and fifteen children in Lehi. He was buried in the Cefncoedycymmer Cemetery, about two miles from the scene of the life-changing debate he had had twenty-two years earlier while representing the Independents.[5]

1844: April, *Y Bedyddiwr* (*Baptist*), p. 124 (500 words). "The Saints Still."

This much shorter account immediately follows the account of the debate that ended in the baptism of Abel Evans. The author of this account gives his nom de plume as simply "I" from Abersychan, but it could well be the Reverend W. R. Davies, hiding behind one of several noms de plume he used before his real identity was brought forth by Dan Jones nearly two years later. This report presents the brief story of "two *nice* boys" who were baptized by the Latter-day Saints in Abersychan. The first is quoted as having received baptism to see if was true "that they can give sight to the blind." The second boy, William, according to the reporter, had been persuaded by his brother George to be baptized. Two days following William's baptism "a disease broke out on his knee." He appeared to be healed after receiving the laying on of hands from two of his new brethren in the Church, but a short time later his condition worsened to the point of being near death. The reporter's conclusion: "What this shows is that they are nothing but heretics, wolves, false prophets and deceivers. William is unable to work until now, but he thinks that he will be totally healed when the prophet Henshaw comes to this area; this story I shall yet transmit to you."

1844: May, *Y Bedyddiwr* (*Baptist*), p. 160 (260 words). "The Saints Again."

The reporter who wrote "A Strange Account of the Latter-day Saints" in the April issue of this periodical fulfills his promise of providing an update as follows: "Oil was given to him by the Saints for the purpose of making the leg whole, but it did not appear to have any healing effect until the great prophet placed his hand on it; but it appears that neither the oil nor anything else the Saints did had left any effect." The last the reporter saw of William, his leg "was bigger than the leg of his trousers," with no sign of reverting back to his former place with the Wesleyans.

1844: June, *Y Bedyddiwr* (*Baptist*), p. 196 (440 words). "The Saints Again, Again."

W. R. Davies, using yet another nom de plume—"T. ab Ieuan"—tells of a faithful member of The Church of Jesus Christ of Latter-day Saints who was about to give birth. She called for the elders of her church to give her a blessing. They came, but, according to Davies, their "benevolent hands" and their "gibberish" had no beneficent effect on her. The midwife who was present was not allowed to assist in the birth. A doctor at the door was turned away, and the expectant mother was "three hours without being released any longer than appropriate." Finally, the doctor was invited back and was able to save the mother and her child. Davies's conclusion: "We see that there is nothing but nonsense, along with trickery of the worst kind, that are associated with this group."

1844: June, *Y Bedyddiwr* (*Baptist*), p. 192–93 (1,350 words). "The Source of the Bible."

Someone who calls himself "R. P. D." heard from a friend in Ohio, and he wished to relay the odd things his friend has sent him about the Latter-day Saints. The writer states that it was actually someone by the name of Solomon Spaulding who wrote the Book of Mormon and not Joseph Smith. He also quotes two ordinances approved by the City Council of Nauvoo. The first one states that anyone coming to the city to arrest Joseph Smith shall himself be arrested and put in jail. And the second ordinance gives to Joseph Smith a license to "sell or give spirits of any quantity he in his wisdom shall judge to be for the health, comfort, or convenience of such travelers, or other persons as shall visit his house from time to time."

1844: July, *Y Diwygiwr* (*Revivalist*), p. 213–15 (1,350 words).

The same article that appeared in the *Baptist* for June 1844, p. 192–93.

1844: July, *Y Bedyddiwr* (*Baptist*), p. 220–21 (1,165 words). "Epistle from an Apostle."

This is one of the most curious articles in opposition to The Church of Jesus Christ of Latter-day Saints ever to appear in the Welsh press. Entitled "Epistle from an Apostle," it purports to be a letter from George Rees, "an Apostle of the Saints in Abersychan" to "our dear brother Saint John Thomas, Merthyr Tydfil." Early LDS records show the baptism for a George Rees on 30 August 1843 in the Rhymney Branch and the baptism for a John Thomas on 18 February 1844 in the Penydaren Branch near Merthyr Tydfil, the only persons by those names for these records dating from 19 February 1843 to 20 April 1844.[6]

The author of the letter describes William Henshaw, the leader of all the converts to The Church of Jesus Christ of Latter-day Saints in South Wales, as a man "similar to the Apostle Paul in so many ways":

1. He is a former deist
2. He was put in jail (in Cardiff)
3. He was held by state authorities (in Newport during the Chartist riots)
4. He is able to cast out devils
5. He can work mighty miracles

The author, speaking on behalf of "a few of the Abersychan Saints" commands John Thomas to lead his brethren on a mission to the Zion Baptist Chapel in Merthyr Tydfil. He tells them to go to their "old deceitful, ungodly, and hypocritical brethren... at the time of the largest public meeting" to "leave them without excuse at the coming judgment" by working "a miracle on the old sinner who is there under the name of minister" by giving him "a new knee, as the apostle did for the lame man at the gate of the temple." Also, John Thomas is commanded to "let brother Abel [Evans] walk to Bethesda [Chapel], where he was once under the name of member, and . . . give an arm to that accursed minister." The writer adds that by performing these miracles "our religion will be established forever in Merthyr, and the gates of hell will never be able to move them." The writer also adds, "We must truly show our miracles, for otherwise we will be shameful to the world." In the postscript to the letter, the author writes, "Since we are not sure how to direct this so you will be sure to receive it, we are sending it in care of the evil and accursed man, James Wilkins, since we know that he lives near you."

In a separate letter printed immediately following the foregoing letter, the Reverend James Wilkins of the Zion Baptist Chapel of Merthyr Tydfil writes, "I received the foregoing epistle through the post on the 25th of May without any stamp on it, neither had there ever been one. It was addressed to my care to give it to John Thomas." Not knowing to which of the men by the name of John Thomas in his neighborhood he should deliver the letter, he looked at it and saw the words "Apostle" and "Saints" and "miracles." He then knew to which John Thomas he should go with the letter. He then went to John Thomas's house and found him in bed with a very repentant attitude "for ever having been so foolish as to have been ensnared and bewildered" by the Latter-day Saints. Wilkins then offers the letter to the editor of *Y Bedyddiwr* (the *Baptist*) to be printed.

At the time the Reverend James Wilkins sent his letter of explanation along with the "Epistle," which was very likely of his own composition, he had an eleven-year-old son named Henry. Six years later, Wilkins would disown Henry for converting to The Church of Jesus Christ of Latter-day Saints. Apparently, the Reverend gave his permission for his son to emigrate with a group of the Saints, for Henry's name is on the passenger list of the *Joseph Badger* which left Liverpool on 17 October 1850 and arrived in New Orleans on 23 November 1850. From St. Louis, Henry wrote a letter to his father in which Henry expressed regret for ever having left home. He claimed that he was treated poorly by those he at one time trusted. His father sent Henry's letter to be printed in the April 1851 issue of *Y Bedyddiwr* (the *Baptist*)[7] as evidence that those of his son's new faith were not the saintly Christians they pretended to be. John S. Davis, the editor of *Udgorn Seion* (*Zion's Trumpet*), responded to Henry Wilkins's report of being deceived by members of his new faith.[8] In the very next issue of *Udgorn Seion*,[9] Davis printed Henry's letter of apology to William Phillips, the leader of The Church of Jesus Christ of Latter-day Saints in Wales. The repentant lad said he had written the letter to his father in a moment of anger and because he "gave heed to all the old tales that [he] was hearing in this place." He also said he had plans to continue on to the Salt Lake Valley so that he could "gain a greater knowledge of the law, and receive [his] endowment." Phillips expressed hope that this recent letter from the Reverend Wilkins's son would be printed in the *Baptist* "so that the country [could] have further information concerning the 'Mormon Disappointment,'" the title given to Henry's first letter.

Episode 2.2

Start: Response of the press in Wales to the martyrdom

1844: August, *Y Cenhadwr Americanaidd* (*American Messenger*), p. 249 (500 words). "Joe Smith, the Mormon Prophet, Has Been Killed."

A one-sided article describing the events that led to the martyrdom:

> This corrupt man, who deceived many by his evil tricks and lies, has now met with his death by murder.

1844: 3 August, *Monmouthshire Merlin*, p. 4 (15 words).

> Joe Smith, the Mormon prophet, has been shot dead, in an attempt to escape from custody.

1844: 17 August, *Monmouthshire Merlin*, p. 1 (485 words). "Joe Smith, the Mormon Prophet."

After giving some background information about Joseph Smith and the history of the Church he founded, the writer expresses his admiration: "The Mormons, greatly to their credit, submit to the loss of their leaders in silence. Not the slightest disturbance has occurred."

1844: September 1844, *Y Bedyddiwr* (*Baptist*), pp. 293–94 (220 words). "The Mormons, or the Latter-day Saints."

The writer explains what he believes caused the death of Joseph Smith:

> Because one of the saints tried to rush the jail, which angered the guards who were restraining him, he fired a rifle at one of them and injured him; then a general commotion around the jail followed. At that time, Joe and his friends began to shoot, (they had secretly obtained some handguns), and they tried to escape through the window of the jail, when all the guards turned their rifles on them, and it is said that Joe received a hundred bullets in his body, and his brother several, until the two of them were corpses on the floor.

1844: September, *Seren Gomer* (*Star of Gomer*), p. 287 (90 words).

> We are informed from this country that Joe Smith, the Mormon prophet, and Hyrum his brother, have been murdered by the inhabitants of Illinois, who were very angry at them because of the corrupt works they were carrying on in Nauvoo, the place where they had settled. Another brother of the deceivers has been appointed as prophet in his place, and is to be the leader of the Mormon sect. We intend to give a full history of this deceiver and his sect, in a future issue.

1844: 7 September, *Monmouthshire Merlin*, p. 2 (385 words). "Joe Smith, the Mormon Prophet."

After presenting a brief history of the background of Joseph Smith and the Book of Mormon, the writer quotes from the *New York Express*:

The Mormons, greatly to their credit, submit to the loss of their leaders in silence. Not the slightest disturbance has occurred. The prophet and his brother were buried, yesterday, without parade, and in secrecy.

1844: 28 September, *Monmouthshire Beacon*, p. 4 (40 words).
Emma, Joe Smith, the Mormon prophet's wife, has had the box in which the dead body of Joe was carried from Carthage to Nauvoo, sawed into suitable strips for walking canes, and has sold them to the faithful as mementos of the prophet.

1844: 12 October, *Monmouthshire Beacon*, p. 4 (30 words).
Notwithstanding the death of the Mormon leader, Joe Smith, a number of dupes of this strange delusion left Lancashire for Nauvoo, the headquarters of the sect, last month.

End: Response of the press in Wales to the martyrdom

1844: 21 September, *Monmouthshire Merlin*, p. 3 (160 words). "Mormonism."

A few Latter-day Saints fell into a "dark and dirty pit" as they were walking at night from Rhymney to Dowlais. One man dislocated his arm, and their "holy prophet," presumably William Henshaw, broke his leg.

1844: November, *Y Dysgedydd* (*Instructor*), pp. 339–40 (815 words). "Fraud of the Book of Mormon."

The writer expresses concern at the spread of this new religion in Britain and gives some background on Joseph Smith and the gold plates he obtained.

1844: November, *Seren Gomer* (*Star of Gomer*), pp. 327–31 (3,960 words). "History of Joseph Smith, the Mormon Prophet."

The text is largely borrowed from Eber D. Howe's *Mormonism Unvailed* [*sic*] and other such sources.

1844: December, *Seren Gomer* (*Star of Gomer*), p. 381 (175 words). "Diverse Opinions about Millenarianism."

Various opinions as to when the Millennium will begin. "Some prophets from America frighten ordinary folk by asserting that the millennium and Christ's personal reign are to begin before the end of this year; and they prove their imaginings from Joe Smith's Mormon book."

1845: January, *Y Drysorfa Gynnulleidfaol* (*Congregationalist Treasury*), p. 24 (80 words). "The Mormons."

The author addresses the question of who will be the successor to Joseph Smith.

1845: 6 April, *Millennial Star*, p. 167 (29 words).
Merthyr Tydville Conference—Represented by elder William Henshaw, including 12 branches, containing 316 members, 7 elders, 10 priests, 7 teachers, 4 deacons; baptized since last general conference, 195.

It is astonishing that a Cornishman who spoke no Welsh and had no use of a press or printed materials in Welsh could in just over two years have over three hundred converts.

1845: November, *Seren Gomer* (*Star of Gomer*), p. 351 (35 words).

> Frightful persecution is being carried out against the Mormons; and it is likely that that people will be driven out of the country, and the building of their New Jerusalem will come to an end.

1845: November, *Y Diwygiwr* (*Revivalist*), p. 356 (120 words).

A cobbler asked a Latter-day Saint, who had prophesied the world would end in a week, why he was ordering a new pair of shoes.

1845: 1 November, *Monmouthshire Merlin*, p. 4 (55 words).

> The Mormon troubles had subsided, but not until an effectual demonstration had been made by the local authorities, who were prepared to put them down by force, by the strong arm of the law. Lynch law, according to the papers, had been put into requisition in the case of some Mormons near St. Louisville.

1845: 18 November, *North Wales Chronicle*, p. 3 (15 words).

> The Mormon difficulties have been arranged, the sect having agreed to emigrate next spring.

1845: 13 December, *Monmouthshire Beacon*, p. 4 (330 words).

A report of the troubles of the Church in Nauvoo, especially determining Joseph Smith's successor.

1845: 20 December, *Monmouthshire Merlin*, p. 4 (105 words).

A Latter-day Saint in Girvan, Scotland, received the gift of tongues, "alarming the whole neighborhood with the most unearthly screams and jabbering—a most decidedly unknown tongue. This she has continued to mutter, only for her own private benefit, ever since. We could recommend a lunatic asylum for such prophetesses."

1845: 26 December, *Welshman*, p. 4 (25 words).

> The Mormons have resolved to remove to the Bay of San Francisco, in California, in the spring, and have already commenced selling their property at Nauvoo.

Notes

1. *Millennial Star*, April 1845, 170.
2. *Millennial Star*, 1 July 1845, 128.
3. *Monmouthshire Beacon*, 28 August 1841, 3.
4. National Library of Wales, Cwrtmawr Collection, 71E (2).
5. A full-length biography—*Indefatigable Veteran: History and Biography of Abel Evans, a Welsh Mormon Elder*—is available on the Welsh Saints Project website.
6. Church History Library, Salt Lake City.
7. *Baptist*, April 1851, 127–28.
8. *Zion's Trumpet*, 3 May 1851, 135–37.
9. *Zion's Trumpet*, 17 May 1851, 149–51.

Chapter 3

Episodes

3.1—David Williams's attack and Dan Jones's aggressive response
3.2—Dan Jones accuses the Reverend W. R. Davies of forging a letter
3.3—The Reverend W. R. Davies claims that William Hughes's leg was not broken
3.4—Dan Jones responds to the twenty-page pamphlet published by the Reverend W. R. Davies
3.5—Thomas Jones apostatizes and then changes his mind
3.6—John S. Davis makes his debut in writing and publishing articles

Salient Events

- **January 1846.** Dan Jones, after one year in North Wales, moves to Merthyr Tydfil in South Wales and begins his first of three years as president of the Church in Wales.
- **1846.** Meetings are held in the upper room of the White Lion Inn located adjacent to the Merthyr Tydfil Parish Church. This room was known as the "Cymreigyddion Hall" (i.e., the hall of those who cherish the Welsh language). Dan Jones lives at 45 Cyfarthfa Row in Georgetown, an area of Merthyr Tydfil near the modern-day stake center.
- **1846.** *The Latter Saints*, an anonymous twenty-four-page pamphlet, is published in Merthyr Tydfil. The pamphlet has contents of a general nature and receives no response from Dan Jones. See Section 2.
- **18 January 1846.** William Hughes's leg is broken in an accident in the Cyfarthfa Mine. His claim that it was miraculously healed by special blessings he received from Dan Jones and others was hotly contested by the Rev. W. R. Davies in the March 1846 issue of the *Baptist*. See Episode 3.3.

- **March 1846.** Reverend W. R. Davies publishes *The Latter Saints*, a twenty-page pamphlet intended to show "The Deceit of the Creatures who call themselves the Latter-day Saints." See Section 2.
- **About March 1846.** Dan Jones publishes *The Scales*, his first pamphlet of a polemical nature, to counter the David Williams pamphlet published a few months earlier.[1]
- **19 April 1846.** John S. Davis is baptized in Llanybydder.
- **July 1846.** The first issue of *Prophet of the Jubilee* is published at Rhydybont. Dan Jones finally has his own monthly periodical in which he can put forth the teachings of his religion and combat W. R. Davies and others who attack him.[2]
- **July–December 1846.** In each of these six issues of *Prophet of the Jubilee*, except for the August issue, Dan Jones uses several pages to counter the accusations of Rev. W. R. Davies.
- **7 July 1846.** Daniel Jones, a blind man, is baptized in Llanybydder. He is confirmed in "Glantrenfawr," the house of Thomas Jeremy. See Episode 4.2.
- **November 1846.** Dan Jones publishes a small hymnal, the first foreign-language hymnal of the Latter-day Saints.[3]
- **December 1846.** The Reverend John Parry, from Flintshire, is baptized along with members of his family. After arriving in Utah in 1849, he was invited by Brigham Young to form a choir to sing at a conference of the Church. This choir evolved into the Mormon Tabernacle Choir. John Parry's son John was the master mason for the construction of the Logan Temple, and his nephew Edward Lloyd Parry was the master mason for the construction of the St. George Temple as well as for the Manti Temple.
- **December 1846.** Dan Jones uses eight pages of his periodical to answer various accusations, including those of Thomas Jones, an early convert who had apostatized. See Episode 3.5.

Commentary

1846: *Y Seintiau Diweddaf* (*The Latter Saints*), pamphlet, 24 pages.

The anonymous author states in his first chapter:

> It is intended in this treatise to capture a brief account of the rise of the Mormon sect, or as they call themselves "The Latter Saints." This account shows an example of the religious deceit on the one hand and of idiotic gullibility on the other, the like of which is unprecedented in this century.[4]

On the title page is the following list of contents:

1. Foreword
2. Original history of the religious denominations in the United States
3. The testimony of Joseph Smith
4. Origin and character of the Bible of the Saints
5. Linguistic instruction of the Prophet

6. The Saints being warned from the sky
7. The new temple of the Saints
8. Missouri, promised land of the Saints—War—The Saints lose the day
9. Commotion in Nauvoo—Imprisoning the Prophet—Hyrum his brother and he are killed
10. Short history of the United States
11. Reference to books about the history of the Saints

The content of the pamphlet is more focused on providing general information about The Church of Jesus Christ of Latter-day Saints than on attacking its beliefs. Compared to other writings in Wales about Joseph Smith and the Church he founded, this pamphlet is rather innocuous. No response from Dan Jones has been identified. A facsimile translation is in Section 2.

Episode 3.1

Start: David Williams's attack and Dan Jones's aggressive response

1845: April, *Y farw wedi ei chyfodi yn fyw: neu'r hen grefydd newydd. Traethawd yn dangos anghyfnewidioldeb teyrnas Dduw* (*The Dead Raised to Life: or the Old Religion Anew. Treatise Showing the Immutability of the Kingdom of God*), pamphlet, 48 pages.[5]

In this, his first printed pamphlet, Dan Jones makes use of more than two-thirds of the section titled "The Kingdom of God" from Apostle Parley P. Pratt's widely circulated pamphlet *Voice of Warning*. At times Jones translates directly; at times he paraphrases; other times he rearranges the order. Nearly always he elaborates on Pratt's line of logic. Although at least three-fourths of Jones's pamphlet is original, generally this "nonborrowed" portion is an expansion of ideas which had been set forth by Parley P. Pratt. Some of the more significant expanded concepts are the necessity of baptism, the existence of spiritual gifts in modern times, and the reality of the death and resurrection of the Savior. Curiously, not once in this pamphlet does Dan Jones mention the word "Mormon" or even "The Church of Jesus Christ of Latter-day Saints." But the various ministers of other religions apparently knew perfectly well which faith Jones represented, and they united in opposition. In a cooperative effort, the Baptists and the Independents of Merthyr Tydfil appointed one David Williams to refute Jones's pamphlet with one of their own. The title of their pamphlet went right to the point: *Deception of the Latter Saints Exposed.*

1845: December, *Twyll y Seintiau Diweddaf yn cael ei ddynoethi, mewn nodiadau byr ar draethawd a ysgrifenwyd yn ddiweddar gan Capt. D. Jones, dan yr enw, "Traethawd ar Anghyfnewidioldeb Teyrnas Dduw," etc.* (*Deception of the Latter Saints Exposed in Brief Notes on a Treatise Written Recently by Capt. D. Jones, under the Title, "Treatise Showing the Immutability of the Kingdom of God," etc.*), pamphlet, 32 pages.[6]

On 14 and 15 December 1845, Dan Jones was in Manchester for a conference and was appointed to preside over the branches and operations of The Church of Jesus Christ of Latter-day Saints in Wales, in place of William Henshaw. Jones and Henshaw traveled together from the conference to Merthyr Tydfil, where Jones would assume his new position. Awaiting him in Merthyr Tydfil was David Williams's pamphlet, *Deception of the Latter Saints*. What had been occasional skirmishes since the arrival of Henshaw in South Wales had now exploded into full-scale war, a war that brought a degree of unity to the Nonconformist churches throughout Wales. Previously their battles had been with each other over points of Christian doctrine and the meaning of various scriptures from the Bible. But now they had a common enemy—The Church of Jesus Christ of Latter-day Saints, whose missionaries declared that they represented the only true Church of the Savior on the earth, a church that had only recently been restored in its fullness through a prophet in America, the Prophet Joseph Smith.

The author of *Deception of the Latter Saints*, David Williams, was a railroad worker from Abercanaid, a town near Merthyr Tydfil. Williams declares in the preface:

> This pamphlet is not restricted to one specific denomination, and no single denomination of Christians will be answerable for its content, only so far as they agree with what it contains.

Four other railway workers, two Baptists and two Congregationalists, supported Williams with fundraising, printing, and distribution of the pamphlet.

In polemic fashion typical of the age, Williams conducts a point-by-point analysis of the assertions and claims of the pamphlet which Dan Jones had published several months earlier in North Wales. Even though Jones had not made specific mention of the religion he represented and defended, Williams had no difficulty in identifying it and arguing against it. Toward the end of the pamphlet Williams expresses particular shock at Jones's second publication entitled *Proclamation of the Twelve Apostles in The Church of Jesus Christ of Latter-day Saints. To all the kings of the earth, to the president and to the governors of the United States of America, and to the rulers and all the people of the world*:

> By the time I had glanced over the above treatise on the kingdom of God, yet another one came to my attention, one so presumptuous as if it had been written by the fingers of the devil, who had dipped his pen in the venom of dragons or in the fiery furnace itself, and had it printed in the gates of hell, and this under the name "Proclamation of the Twelve Apostles—the Saints, etc., to all the kings of the earth, etc." Oh my! for human nature to have sunk so low, and become so impudent as to assert such majestic things in a deceitful way. The above booklet, that is the Proclamation, has gone so far in its baseless assertions, that all one Welshman has to do is read it carefully to see its madness.[7]

Residents of Rhydybont were no doubt greatly surprised to learn that they were, at least according to David Williams, living in "the gates of hell." And Dan Jones no doubt welcomed the attention being focused on the church and doctrine he represented, believing correctly that giving scrutiny to the polemic would result in converts.

The David Williams pamphlet was the opening salvo of the warfare of words, both printed and spoken, between Dan Jones and those who assailed the Church and the doctrine that he cherished. Immediately upon reading Williams's vicious attack, Jones penned a letter to Wilford Woodruff asking for a letter of authorization for him "to collect what I can from the Welsh Saints . . . to enable me to bring out another pamphlet now, in answer to one now just out by the joint stock of Priests, just such another as the Mormonism Unveiled tho' in Welsh, published in this place."[8]

His request was obviously granted, because in a letter to Reuben Hedlock just a few weeks later, Jones reported the following:

> I have now the last form of my pamphlet in press, and am busily engaged working them off myself. I have also a reply ready, to a pamphlet published lately, printed in Welsh, at Merthyr, against my first pamphlet, by a clan of priests, misrepresenting us, and our good Mormon creed, most foully. This I can publish within a month, if I stay here to do it.[9]

1846: *Atebydd y Gwrthddadleuon a Ddygir yn Fwyaf Cyffredinol Drwy y Wlad yn erbyn Saint y Dyddiau Diweddaf, a'r Athrawiaeth a Broffesant* (*A Reply to the Objections Which Are Most Commonly Brought throughout the Country against the Latter-day Saints, and the Doctrine Which They Profess*), pamphlet, 24 pages.

This pamphlet is the "pamphlet in press" mentioned above. Jones imitates the format Orson Pratt used in "Dialogue between tradition, reason, and scriptus." Jones does not target any particular person or religion in this publication. The same is not true, however, in his next pamphlet, *The Scales*.

1846: *Y Glorian, yn yr hon y gwelir David yn Pwyso Williams, a Williams yn pwyso David; neu David Williams, o Abercanaid, yn gwrthddweyd ei hun, wedi ei ddal yn ei dwyll a'i brofi yn ddeistaidd* (*The Scales, in Which Are Seen David Weighing Williams, and Williams Weighing David; or David Williams, from Abercanaid, Contradicting Himself, Caught in His Deceit, and Proved Deistic*), pamphlet, 16 pages.

As indicated by the title, Dan Jones takes a scornful attitude toward David Williams as he puts him on the scales—David on one side and Williams on the other—and proceeds to point out his contradictions. Throughout the entire sixteen pages, each full of satire and derision, Jones simply follows the standard, mid-nineteenth-century techniques of the polemic. The bulk of Jones's defense centers around the signs that were to follow the believers, as mentioned in Mark 16:17–18. Williams had challenged Jones to prove that Jones was sent of God by healing all the sick of Merthyr Tydfil and by drinking something deadly without suffering any harmful effect. Jones counters with scriptural quotations concerning sign-seekers. He also counters Williams's attack on Latter-day Saint beliefs concerning additional scripture, the necessity of baptism, and Williams's vitriolic observations about the Proclamation of the Twelve Apostles. This segment is typical of Jones's style throughout the pamphlet:

> Who says that? Williams, I think, for David in the previous two lines says the complete opposite to that in this admission. . . . Which one do you believe?

> David or Williams? I believe David now. . . . Well done, Williams! Although he lost before, he wins now, and is closer to the truth than David.

End: David Williams's attack and Dan Jones's aggressive response

1846: 6 January, *North Wales Chronicle*, p. 2 (13 words).
The Mormons have nearly 2500 wagons ready for their California expedition next spring.

1846: 3 March, *North Wales Chronicle*, p. 2 (60 words).
The March of Intellect. It is said that the wagons that are to convey the Mormons to California will number 5000 and will form a line twenty-five miles long! In the front there will be a press and types, from which will be issued every morning a paper, to be sent back to inform the rear-guard what is going on in the van!

1846: March, *Y Dysgedydd* (*Instructor*), pp. 79–81 (1,620 words). "Joseph Smith."
The editor does not indicate the source of the information, but it was possibly borrowed from *Mormonism Unvailed* by Eber D. Howe. The article says nothing about events concerning the Church in Wales.

Episode 3.2

Start: Dan Jones accuses the Rev. W. R. Davies of forging a letter

Over eighteen months had passed since the Reverend W. R. Davies had attacked William Henshaw and other members of The Church of Jesus Christ of Latter-day Saints in the March, April, May, and June 1844 issues of the Baptist. And Davies may also have been behind the strange "Epistle from an Apostle" (George Rees) to John Thomas in the July 1844 issue of the Baptist. But the appearance of Dan Jones's Welsh translation of the Proclamation of the Twelve Apostles, the David Williams pamphlet *The Deception of the Latter-day Saints*, and Jones's *Reply to the Objections* were very possibly the catalyst that inspired the Reverend W. R. Davies to take pen in hand once again to launch a new assault.

1846: March 1846, *Y Bedyddiwr* (*Baptist*), p. 90 (605 words).
The Welsh translation of the supposed letter from Emma Smith, dated 20 November 1845, to the editor of the *New York Sun* in which she laments her current situation and declares, "I have never for a moment believed in what my husband called his apparitions and revelations." No response from Dan Jones about this letter has been identified. He did, however, have a thundering response concerning the following two articles.

1846: March 1846, *Y Bedyddiwr* (*Baptist*), pp. 90–91 (350 words). "To the Rev. W. R. Davies."
Supposedly written by Abel Evans and William Henshaw, this letter is actually a challenge, dated 10 January 1846, for W. R. Davies to debate "our praiseworthy

Apostle" Dan Jones on Thursday night, the fifteenth of January, at the White Lion Inn, Merthyr Tydfil. The letter is filled with numerous grammatical errors and misspellings, intended to show how uneducated the supposed writers were. The letter ends with the following:

> Not from our part do we fear you, rather we shall honor him [Dan Jones] this time as our oldest "Apostle" and "Most Respected Teacher" in Wales. Take the path that you see best to follow, and if you do not come, your absence will be proof of your heresy.

The editor of the *Baptist* explains how he overcame his reluctance to print the challenge and Davies's reply:

> Because of the presumption of these rascals who erroneously call themselves Saints, and their constant assaults on believers and unbelievers in the areas of the Works, and the fact that they have beguiled many children and weak-minded people with their disrespect for the ordinances of Heaven through their sinful imitations of them, we hereby provide space for the following pieces of correspondence which have been exchanged between the Rev. W. R. Davies, Dowlais, and them.

Regarding Davies's reply, the editor wrote:

> We must confess that the response of Mr. Davies to them is rather clumsy, but considering the limited understanding and the low morals of those who address him, perhaps it would be difficult to do better.

1846: March 1846, *Y Bedyddiwr* (*Baptist*), pp. 91–93 (1,895 words). "A Reply to the Above. To the most learned A. Evans and W. Henshaw."

The Reverend W. R. Davies claims to have received a letter from Abel Evans and William Henshaw in which they challenged him to a religious debate. Davies replies:

> I received a most learned note from you, the contents of which prove the extent of your knowledge, together with the arrogance of your hearts. . . . I understand from your letter addressed to me, that the intention is to get me to hold a "fair" with some sinful creature you call the "apostolic Captain."

Davies claims that Evans and Henshaw declared in their letter that his failure to appear would be proof of Davies's "heresy." Davies replies:

> I consider that my appearance in such a place and on such an occasion, would be proof of my foolishness.

Davies then presents a list of five reasons for his refusal:

1. The persons who address me are beneath my attention.
2. The names which you give yourselves are too low to be despised, such as "the only true church of Jesus Christ—our praiseworthy apostle Cap. D. Jones."
3. The mad and arrogant teachings which you proclaim are beneath the attention of every man of common sense.
4. I refuse your offer with scorn, since I judge that one of your purposes in holding a "fair" is to collect fools together, but mainly to try to collect money.

5. I am completely determined to refuse your offer out of true respect for the inspired advice of God through the mouth of one of his holy apostles, who advised me saying in 1 Tim. 6:5, "Perverse disputings of men of corrupt minds, and destitute of the truth: from such withdraw thyself."

In the closing paragraph of his lengthy letter, Davies writes,

> I do not ask you to forgive me for not calling you "saints," as this would be an insult to common sense, a disgrace to Christianity and a sin against God, but I call you by your proper names, sons and daughters of the devil, the enemies of all righteousness.

1846: May, *Y Bedyddiwr* (*Baptist*), pp. 193–94 (470 words). "Defense of the 'Saints.'"

In answer to the 10 January 1846 letter purportedly written by Abel Evans and William Henshaw and printed in the columns of the *Baptist* for March 1846, Evans and Henshaw sent a letter to the editor of the *Baptist* to firmly deny that they had written the original letter:

> But we testify in sobriety and truth, in the presence of God and men, that we never wrote, or caused to be written, the aforementioned letter, or any other piece of writing to this man. . . . It is easy for every man who knows anything about us to see that the letter is a fake. We do not, and neither does Capt. D. Jones claim to be an apostle, and no one in Britain, as far as we know, claims, or is given the title of apostle in our midst.

Although the editor of the *Baptist* expressed a degree of reluctance about the printing of the 10 January letter, he makes the following disclaimer immediately below the letter he printed in the May 1846 issue of his periodical:

> Whether the letter referred to is false or authentic, the writing is very much like *the writing of this letter*. They are so similar that everyone who saw them *decided* at once that it was the *same hand which wrote the two letters*.

1846: September, *Prophwyd y Jubili* (*Prophet of the Jubilee*), pp. 78–84 (4,145 words). "The Editor of the *True Baptist*."

In this lengthy article, Dan Jones responds to all five of the reasons Davies had presented in the March 1846 issue of the *Baptist*,[10] for not having a meeting with Abel Evans and William Henshaw at their request. For example, here is the first reason Davies gives for not accepting the supposed invitation:

> The persons who address me are beneath my attention. Abel and Henshaw, Oh, Excellent names! Oh, bright characters! "May my soul never become a party to their secret."

And here is Jones's response:

> His proof that they are beneath his notice is, because of their names: "Abel and Henshaw; Oh, excellent names! Oh, bright characters!" There is a specimen of new-fashioned logic, or old-fashioned from the days of Bajazett. Who has heard that Mr. Davies has ever discussed a single subject? His subject is persons; assertion is his reason, and libeling is his trade! And so here,

> because a man's parents named him "Abel," he and every other Abel, from the oldest down, are "beneath the notice" of this renowned man! . . . It is not long since Mr. Davies considered William Henshaw's character to be shining enough for him to bring him to his house, and extend an offer for him to join with him, and be a preaching assistant to him. And the next thing this gentle man offered him after he had refused his services, and shown abhorrence for his company, was to ask him if he would drink a glass of poison, to prove that Christ had spoken the truth—"If they drink any deadly thing, it will do them no harm."

Toward the end of his article, Jones takes exception to one particular assertion made by Davies:

> And it gives me great happiness to announce that only a *few* of my fellow countrymen have been ensnared by these evil creatures. . . . And of those who have been tricked by them, *many* have seen the deceit.

Jones then takes obvious delight in pointing out the glaring error in Davies's statement:

> A *few* have joined, and *many* have turned back. It is beyond common scholarship to say, when one takes *many* out of a *few*, how many will be left? Only Mr. Davies's arithmetic can answer that.

1846: April, *Y Golygydd* (*Editor*), pp. 89–90 (170 words).

Even Reverend John Jones, Dan Jones's older brother, had something to say in his own periodical, the *Editor*, about the letter supposedly written by Abel Evans and William Henshaw:

> If Abel Evans and William Henshaw wrote this letter to Mr. D., they deserve to be rebuked; but not half as much as he himself deserves for the letter he sent in reply. Ah! if only he could hide his letter from the eyes of the country. . . It is true that many heresies are preached by them; but, in the name of goodness, what is consuming Mr. Davies, and the others who write against them? Do you not know that the best way to increase a strange sect is to persecute it, thereby taking on a more unclean and libelous character than it has? Is there anyone at all around Merthyr and Dowlais, of the men who slander them, who dares attack their subjects? We beg, for the sake of the character of our literature, that our editors not release any more such persecution into their pages, and for the sake of the withering and ending of the Mormons, that no one persecute or disrespect them.[11]

Although the Reverend John Jones came to a partial defense of Evans and Henshaw and the Church they represented, and although he was perfectly willing to print the materials of their Church, there is no evidence that he ever converted. There is record, however, that his wife and two daughters were baptized by Dan Jones himself.[12]

End: Dan Jones accuses the Rev. W. R. Davies of forging a letter

Episode 3.3

Start: The Rev. W. R. Davies claims that William Hughes's leg was not broken

1846: March, *Y Bedyddiwr* (*Baptist*), pp. 111–12 (715 words). "A Miracle! A Miracle! At Last!"

This very sarcastic article is by "Quick-in-Water," a nom de plume Dan Jones declares to be that of the Reverend W. R. Davies. The "miracle" ridiculed is the healing of William Hughes's leg that was broken in a mine accident. Davies's opening sentence has reference to the relatively large number of converts (approximately four hundred) to The Church of Jesus Christ of Latter-day Saints in the Merthyr Tydfil area under the leadership of William Henshaw (during part of 1844 and all of 1845):

> The "Satanists" greatly professed many of their miracles, and they deceived an uneducated, irreligious and good-for-nothing crowd—they succeeded in charming a host of the dregs of Merthyr to follow them.

Davies then tells of the arrival of Dan Jones:

> And they were continuing with their deception quite well until the "praiseworthy apostle" came here to strengthen them in the faith, and to sell the craziest sort of pamphlet ever seen, beneath the attention of every man in his senses. This was published by some little creature sometimes called "the apostle" and other times "Captain D. Jones," it was printed by his natural brother, John Jones, Rhydybont, (Llangollen), or the Rhymni baptismal fair member. This pamphlet claims the Satanists' ability to "perform miracles, talk with fairies," etc., etc.

The "craziest sort of pamphlet ever seen" refers to the Welsh translation of *Proclamation of the Twelve Apostles in The Church of Jesus Christ of Latter-day Saints. To all the kings of the earth, to the president and to the governors of the United States of America, and to the rulers and all the people of the world.* After translating the "Proclamation" into Welsh, Dan Jones wrote a letter to his file leader, Reuben Hedlock, in which he told of printing the *Proclamation* on his brother's press in Rhydybont:

> I have now the last form of my pamphlet in press, and am busily engaged working them off myself.[13]

The final page of the *Proclamation* is titled "To the Welsh Reader," dated 1 December 1845. In the final paragraph, Jones makes this fervent appeal to his compatriots:

> I ask the Welsh to reserve their judgment on our characters for a while yet, and they will have sufficient proofs that what was published us in the True Baptist, the Star of Gomer, The Times, etc., are lies. As there are several calumnies about us and our religion, published by men who refuse to publish the rebuttal, these will appear as short treatises.

Davies, of course, was not about to reserve his judgment about people who posed such a threat to his own congregation. He readily gives his explanation about William Hughes's leg:

> William Hughes, a collier who lives in Collier's Row, Cyfarthfa, had an accident; (he is one of the Satanists), he broke the small bone in his leg at work—Dr. Davies was sent for and he put it back in place and tied it up, etc.—then he was followed in a visit by the "praiseworthy apostle" and a crowd of the Satanists, and they pulled off the bandage and the apostle placed his hand on the painful area pretending to pray; and the Satanists claimed in the strongest way that they saw the swelling lessen and disappear under his hand.

Davies further explains,

> The next day Dr. Davies called to see the man; and to his surprise he found him much worse than expected, his leg terribly swollen and very painful, etc. The doctor could not understand these things; but to his surprise, on looking at the leg he saw that some idiot had opened the bandage which he had applied the day before, and this had caused the above mentioned; and when questioned the sufferer admitted everything, and the foolish scoundrel has not gotten better to this day.

1846: May, *Y Bedyddiwr* (*Baptist*), p. 194 (125 words).

An angry letter directed at "Mr. Quick yn Dwr," written by Ed. Lewis from Cwm Gelli Dywyll, a farm in Blackwood. Lewis asks the author of the March article entitled "A Miracle! A Miracle! At Last!" to show proof for the claim that the miracle of healing William Hughes's leg was bogus. Lewis also says that some of the "Saints" of the Blackwood area went to Merthyr Tydfil to get informed about the healing and learned that the accusations were false and that Hughes did not belong to the Merthyr Tydfil parish, nor did he receive a single penny from the poor fund.

1846, June, *Y Bedyddiwr* (*Baptist*), pp. 232–33 (340 words).

A response by Roger Williams, Relieving Officer, to Ed. Lewis's letter that was printed in the May issue of *The Baptist.* Lewis claimed that Mrs. Hughes had never received "a single penny" from the Merthyr parish and that she and her husband did not belong to that parish. Williams declares in his letter that Mr. and Mrs. Hughes were, indeed, members of the Merthyr parish and that Williams had personally given Mrs. Hughes five shillings per week over a period of seven weeks.

1846: June, *Y Bedyddiwr* (*Baptist*), p. 232 (880 words). "The Saints Caught in their Own Net."

Also in the June 1846 issue of the *Baptist* is this brief paragraph with the heading "The Saints":

> One of the chief prophets of these evil men has left the above Satanic brotherhood in America, and has published a book to make public the deceit and tricks of the chief leaders, and the deceit of their deacons; it doubtless contains many of the tricks and deceit of the children of hell, and hopefully it will serve the purpose of opening the eyes of many men deceived by the satanic crowd.

This paragraph may well refer to John C. Bennett's *The History of the Saints: Or, an Expose of Joe Smith and Mormonism.*

1846: July, *Prophwyd y Jubili* (*Prophet of the Jubilee*), pp. 22–28 (4,110 words). "Fulfillment of a Prophecy."

Regarding Davies's article entitled "A Miracle! A Miracle! At last!" Jones devotes seven pages of this first issue of *Prophet of the Jubilee* to explaining the context of the miraculous healing of William Hughes's broken leg. The "prophecy" mentioned in the title refers to a prophecy given to Joseph Smith by the angel who first visited him in 1823:

> When they begin to hear that God has shown you these things, the workers of iniquity will seek your overthrow; they will proclaim and publish stories and lying accusations about you to destroy your reputation, and also will seek to take your life without cause, and as a result they will persecute those who believe in the same organization.[14]

Jones then indicates that this prophecy was being fulfilled in Wales and manifesting itself through the opposition of the Reverend W. R. Davies, a Baptist minister in the town of Dowlais:

> Let even Dowlais be ashamed in seeing a man who professes to be a servant of God climbing into their pulpits, and in a foolish and blasphemous "fair," teaching his fellow travelers towards wise judgment "not to call" those who worship the God of heaven and believe in Christ according to the scriptures "Saints, rather call them (says he) Latter-day Satanists." Oh, humanity, what shame on you! His name—no need to ask; who does not know that it is the Rev. W. R. Davies who is the father of this name?[15]

Jones ends his article in *Prophet of the Jubilee* by printing his own letter regarding William Hughes, a convert to the Church of Jesus Christ of Latter-day Saints, and the miraculous healing of his broken leg. Jones had sent this letter to the editor of the *Baptist*, but the editor had refused to print it. The greater part of the letter is the testimony of Hughes himself, a testimony which Jones most likely transcribed for him, since Hughes was illiterate—he signed the testimony with a cross. Only one of the ten other witnesses of the miracle was able to sign his name—all the others signed with a cross. And four of the witnesses had their own special paragraph:

> We testify that the above story is true, to the utmost of our knowledge. We know that William Hughes's leg was broken; we also heard the doctor say on the spot that the two bones were broken completely; and although we do not profess or believe in the faith of the Latter-day Saints, yet what we felt with our hands and saw with our eyes, we testify to it to give truth a fair chance.[16]

With specific reference to Davies's article entitled "A Miracle! A Miracle! At Last!" Jones writes:

> I confess that we have never before seen a treatise half as large as this published, especially in a periodical that professes to be religious, but not more than one statement of it was truth, in some corner or another.

End: The Reverend W. R. Davies claims that William Hughes's leg was not broken

Episode 3.4

Start: Dan Jones responds to the twenty-page pamphlet by the Reverend W. R. Davies

1846: March, *Y Seintiau Diweddaf. Sylwedd Pregeth a Draddodwyd ar y Gwyrthiau, er mwyn Goleuo y Cyffredin, a Dangos Twyll y Creaduriaid a Alwant eu hunain yn Seintiau y Dyddiau Diweddaf* (*The Latter Saints. The Substance of a Sermon Which Was Delivered on the Miracles, to Enlighten the Public, and Show the Deceit of the Creatures Who Call Themselves the Latter-day Saints*), pamphlet, 20 pages.[17]

The major part of this pamphlet focuses on miracles as they are portrayed in the New Testament. In the preface, however, Davies directs a few lines at William Henshaw:

> This ignorant, unlearned, and characterless ENGLISHMAN from *Cornwall*, after recently being put in Cardiff jail by the Welsh for evil deeds, is he the one, together with a few ignorant and characterless creatures, who possess the knowledge and secret of the kingdom of heaven?

Davies makes disparaging remarks about Dan Jones on page 16. And on page 17, Davies tells of a visit that William Henshaw had made to his home in Dowlais. Davies asked Henshaw to speak to him in Welsh to demonstrate the gift of tongues: "But instead of speaking in tongues I heard (as I knew I would) *I can't speak Welsh, sir.*" Then Davies asked Henshaw to take some poison to demonstrate that "no deadly thing will harm you." Henshaw refused, and Davies concluded that what Henshaw was teaching was nonsense.

1846: September, *Prophwyd y Jubili* (*Prophet of the Jubilee*), pp. 70–78 (5,040 words). "Review."

Dan Jones begins this review of the Reverend W. R. Davies's twenty-page pamphlet with this comment:

> We would like to see Mr. Davies, or someone else, attacking our doctrines, in order to show our errors, or else leaving us alone.[18]

After listing several of the "pious sentences of the pen and soul of the reverend minister of Caersalem, Dowlais," such as "the false Christs," "fool-headed followers," "a mockery of administering sacraments," Jones makes an appeal to his readers:

> Dear brethren, pray for this Mr. Davies, for his soul too is precious despite everything! We and he are known by our fruits. And also, we would like the reader to bear in mind that we are not attacking Mr. Davies, but we are merely men who have finally been forced to defend that way in which we worship the God of our fathers in all conscience, and we shall endeavor to be as gentle as his needless attacks on us allow us to be.[19]

In a total of twenty-eight pages, spread out over four issues of his periodical, Dan Jones meticulously dissects the many assertions made in Davies's pamphlet and declares them to be fallacious and distorted. Finally, Jones states his conclusion:

> Having searched carefully through what you see fit to call "The Substance of a Sermon," we have failed to find any substance in it; and if this is an example

of your sermons, one need not ask who sent you to preach them, for by your sermons shall ye be recognized.[20]

Here are the references for the other three segments of Dan Jones's "Review," in which he continues to unleash his wrath against the Reverend W. R. Davies while countering Davies's' teachings about miracles:

1846: October, *Prophwyd y Jubili* (*Prophet of the Jubilee*), pp. 107–09 (1,310 words). "Review."

1846: November, *Prophwyd y Jubili* (*Prophet of the Jubilee*), pp. 128–31 (2,520 words). "Review."

1846: December, *Prophwyd y Jubili* (*Prophet of the Jubilee*), pp. 156–60 (2,545 words). "Review."

1847: February, *Seren Gomer* (*Star of Gomer*), pp. 47–49 (2,990 words). "Review of the Press."

A very lengthy review of the Reverend W. R. Davies's twenty-page pamphlet, *The Substance of a Sermon*, which Davies published in March 1846. "Mathetes" is the nom de plume of the Reverend John Jones, a young Baptist minister who authored the review. He has nothing but praise for Davies's brilliant analysis of miracles. Here is one example:

> It is not the inhabitants of Merthyr and Dowlais that Mr. Davies has served in the composition of this sermon, nor one religious *denomination*, but the cause of the Savior in general. Those who buy it, read it and ponder it in such detail that the author's reasonings are carved in an *ineradicable* fashion on your minds, and so you will thoroughly understand one of the most important subjects in theology, and be able to silence the arrogant and ungodly proponents of the age.

The "arrogant and ungodly proponents of the age" is a direct reference to the Latter-day Saints about whom John Jones writes:

> The arrogant creatures that Mr. Davies calls *Satanists* in this Sermon have caused a bit of commotion in some parts of the country, especially in Merthyr and Dowlais; but God preserve me from being so stupid as to list their despicable, shameful, and unreasonable *movement* among the important revolutions of the age.

End: Dan Jones responds to the twenty-page pamphlet by the Reverend W. R. Davies

1846: July, *Prophwyd y Jubili* (*Prophet of the Jubilee*), p. 3 (wrapper)(145 words). "To Our Libelers."

In this first issue of his periodical, Dan Jones makes the following announcement and fervent appeal to all who all might be too hasty in their judgment of the religion he represents:

> Precious Souls—The *Prophet* does not intend to *settle* the account with you. Another has taken that solemn task upon Himself! You will receive from us

> only bare testimonies to the world on behalf of our characters, and fervent prayers to heaven on your behalf. Forgiveness and brotherly love once conquered the world in the apostolic age. Forgiveness and brotherly love are fast conquering it in your age too. This will conquer you also. It will turn your hatred into love, and your slander into prayers. Draw near, brethren, and look at us. Make sure you know us before you turn away. You are slandering what you do not know. We are not *perfect*. It is our plan that possesses that quality. Attack it, and we shall assist you as soon as you prove it to be trickery, or our knowledge of it unworthy.

Episode 3.5

Start: Brother Thomas Jones apostatizes and then changes his mind

1846: July, *Y Bedyddiwr* (*Baptist*), p. 250–51 (1,175 words).

In this issue of the *Baptist*, David Williams—the author of *The Deceit of the Latter Saints Exposed in Brief Notes on a Treatise Written Recently by Capt. D. Jones*, which was published six months earlier—submitted a new kind of attack on the Welsh followers of Joseph Smith. Instead of simply showing examples of their doctrine and relating stories of their supposed wrongdoing, Williams here provides the transcript of an interview with Thomas Jones, a convert who had been a member in good standing with the Saints for over three years. Williams introduces Jones to the readers as someone who was "one of the most esteemed officers" in their midst but who was now prepared to reveal the details about how he had been deceived. Jones answered each one of several questions put to him by Williams and then signed Williams's written account of the interview to authenticate its truthfulness.

Six weeks later, Thomas Jones admitted, in the presence of witnesses, that he had not been completely truthful in the interview with Williams and that he was repentant for having allowed it to be published. Thomas Jones's declaration, according to an affidavit signed by eight witnesses, was recorded by Elder Robert Evans, one of Dan Jones's three converts in North Wales, in his (Evans's) journal on 13 July 1846.

1846: September, *Y Bedyddiwr* (*Baptist*), p. 353–55 (1,330 words).

A letter to the editor written by one "Meiriadog" (a nom de plume used by John Edwards, a poet and Campbellite Baptist) in which he recounts a visit that Robert Evans made on 2 August 1846 to Llanfaircaereinion, where Meiriadog lived. Meiriadog was present when Evans gave a sermon about the restored gospel. Following the sermon, Meiriadog, Evans, and Evans's companion went to Meriadog's home for a visit. During their conversation, Meiriadog quoted from the July issue of the *Baptist* about the Thomas Jones incident, whereupon Evans produced Jones's repentant comments which Evans had recorded in his personal journal. Meiriadog requested and received permission from Evans to copy Jones's comments and then quoted them as part of a lengthy letter to the editor of the *Baptist*. Meiriadog challenged Robert Evans to a written debate through the columns of the *Baptist* and assured Evans that the editor would print their writings; Evans responded that the

Baptist printed only insults about the Church he represented and would never print any of their defenses. Meiriadog wrote this response:

> I said that the claim was a lie—I added that everything of theirs would appear as the rest, and that I would give my life for their publication. They promised to send their correspondences to me to send to the *Baptist*. Remember, Mr. Baptist, leave space for them.

With a footnote, the editor of the *Baptist* responded to Meiriadog's request for both sides of the proposed debate with Robert Evans:

> The *Baptist* is open to all to defend themselves in the face of an accusation brought against them, except when the defendants have forfeited their truthful characters; on this ground the saints are free to defend themselves as long as they bring credible and well-known witnesses to confirm their evidence. We cannot allow anything other than this because we have caught them in their own traps before. But the Saints should remember that the *Baptist* does not exist as a tool for them to spread their tales and their assertions up and down the country.

1846: October, *Y Bedyddiwr* (*Baptist*), pp. 369–70 (1,300 words).

Upon seeing Thomas Jones's about-face as described in Meiriadog's letter, a desperate and clever David Williams immediately sent another letter to the editor. This letter was printed in the October 1846 issue of the *Baptist*. Williams carefully worded his letter to make it appear that Thomas Jones had made yet another about-face since his repentant comments recorded by Robert Evans in his journal and which Evans had had Jones sign to verify their authenticity. But in the December 1846 issue of *Prophet of the Jubilee*, seeing through Williams's attempt to create a second but non-existent interview with Thomas Jones, Dan Jones argues that Williams was merely drawing further from his original interview with Thomas Jones for his "latest" derogatory observations about the falling out with the Saints.[21] Dan Jones also mentions that Thomas Jones had been excommunicated from The Church of Jesus Christ of Latter-day Saints, suggesting that revenge was probably the motive for Thomas Jones's rancor against the Church and his former colleagues.

These events prompted three of Thomas Jones's acquaintances from the Church he had denounced—William Phillips, William Henshaw, and Thomas Pugh—to send a letter of defense to the editor of *The Baptist* to clarify the confusion. And according to the editor's previous stance of refusing to publish any defense whenever the writers had "forfeited their truthful characters," the editor refused to print their letter in his periodical.

1846, December, *Prophwyd y Jubili* (*Prophet of the Jubilee*), pp. 148–56 (4,850 words). "Defense of the Saints versus the Accusations of Thomas Jones, Merthyr, and others."

The first part of this lengthy article tells of when William Phillips, William Henshaw, and Thomas Pugh went to Cardiff to see Samuel Evans, the editor of the *Baptist*. The three visitors describe the reaction of the editor:

> We implored earnestly and humbly for the opportunity to clear ourselves from the villainous filth with which we were plastered without provocation; but, as usual, the answer we received from him was a shameless refusal! Yes, poor thing, he was terrified; he turned blue, red, black and pale; he fumed and raged without a single cause except the malicious agitations of a guilty conscience until his knees and his whole body trembled worse than those of Belshazzar of long ago.[22]

The second part of this article is a copy of the letter William Phillips, William Henshaw, and Thomas Pugh had sent to the editor of the *Baptist*. The three men wrote the letter to defend themselves against the accusations the excommunicated Thomas Jones had leveled against them in his interview with David Williams. The editor of the *Baptist* refused to print the letter.

The third part of this article, written by Dan Jones, consists partly of observations about the apostate Thomas Jones.

There is also a section about David Williams, with this heading: "A Glance at that David Williams from Abercanaid, who has put his finger so deep in this salty pottage." The first sentence refers to Williams's pamphlet entitled *Deception of the Latter Saints Exposed*:

> Here is that man who published the fruit of his mixed-up brain and his dirty slander against the Saints in a small treatise lately.[23]

The second sentence refers to Dan Jones's response to Williams's pamphlet entitled *The Scales, in which are seen David weighing Williams, and Williams weighing David*:

> And here is the man who was weighed so fairly in his own scales and found wanting with respect to logic, scripture and truth; and he was proven a libelous deist through his little booklet.[24]

Jones suggests that Williams may have had something to do with converts to The Church of Jesus Christ of Latter-day Saints' losing their jobs because of religious persecution:

> We do not claim that it was he who persuaded one of his members to turn all the Saints from their work and from their homes, on the assertion that only because of their religion was that done. But this we shall say, If he was not the instigator of this shameless persecution and incomparable cruelty, this David Williams did not prevent one of his flock from doing it.

Here is another of Jones's "suggestions" regarding David Williams:

> We heard of some persecuting preacher who failed to keep his feet under him, and where do you suppose he found himself, rather, where he was found by others, upon returning from preaching one Sunday night, but in a duck pond! We shall not give the identity of that unfortunate wretch.

The article ends with a half-page affidavit signed by eight witnesses claiming they had seen Robert Evans record in his diary the contrite expressions of Thomas Jones.

1847: *Amddiffyniad y Saint versus cyhuddiadau Thomas Jones, Merthyr, ac ereill* (*A Defense of the Saints versus the Accusations of Thomas Jones, Merthyr, and Others*), pamphlet, 8 pages.

This is an eight-page pamphlet whose contents are taken directly from *Prophet of the Jubilee*, December 1846, pp. 148–56.[25]

1847: June, *Prophwyd y Jubili* (*Prophet of the Jubilee*), pp. 93–94 (805 words). "Loudmouth 'Meiriadog' from Llanfaircaereinion Forfeiting His Head to Be a Football!!"

In September 1846, after a sermon given in the town of Llanfaircaereinion by Elder Robert Evans, one of his listeners—John Edwards ("Meiriadog")—invited Evans to his home for a visit. When Meiriadog brought up the Thomas Jones incident, Robert Evans produced notes from his journal showing that Thomas Jones had confessed to lying about his lack of belief in The Church of Jesus Christ of Latter-day Saints after three years as a loyal supporter. Meiriadog then challenged Evans to a written debate and guaranteed him that both their writings would be published in the columns of the *Baptist*. Evans responded that the editor of the *Baptist* would never agree to such a debate, since the policy of the editor had always been to publish only negative information about the Church Evans represented. At this point, Meiriadog promised before witnesses "that he would allow his throat to be cut, and his head to be a *football*, if the writing of R. Evans were not allowed to appear in *The Baptist* as does the writing of others." Evans then promised to send to Meiriadog a defense of his religion to be published in the *Baptist*. Evans fulfilled his promise, and after several months of failing to see his letter printed in the *Baptist*, he sent a letter to Dan Jones. In this letter Evans wrote:

> I wrote to him [Meiriadog] a defense of that which I had promised. . . . I requested him to send it to the *Baptist* according to his strong promise. I had plenty of reason to understand that he had received it, and I expected month after month to see it in the *Baptist*; but I saw nothing! Like this, since that time, many moons came and went without a *hew* or a *mew* from the great *challenger*, or my defense!! Neither did I hear of his death, but several here and there are heard saying that *Meiriadog* has *forfeited* his head to me, much more than did John to Herod.

End: Brother Thomas Jones apostatizes and then changes his mind

1846: July, *Seren Gomer* (*Star of Gomer*), p. 215 (990 words). "The Mormons."

Most of the article is simply the Welsh translation of an article that had appeared in a New York newspaper. The newspaper article contained information about the exodus from Nauvoo, the city that the followers of Joseph Smith had built in Illinois. The editor of Star of Gomer promises an update of this story later "since various Welshmen have been so foolish as to join with them, and are now in their midst."

1846: 18 July, *Monmouthshire Merlin*, p. 1 (385 words). "The Mormon War Renewed."

About the aftermath of the expulsion from Nauvoo.

1846: August, *Y Diwygiwr* (*Revivalist*), pp. 137–43 (4,200 words). "Paraphrase of Mormonism."

A lengthy article by someone who calls himself "Nodach" Chambers. *Nodach* is a Welsh word that means "short notes" or "odds and ends." All the contents except for the opening and closing paragraphs are borrowed and translated into Welsh from various sources, and it appears that *Mormonism Unvailed* by Eber D. Howe is the most often used of all. So, perhaps the word *nodach* was used with the sources in mind.

In the opening paragraph, Chambers makes his position toward the religion he calls "Mormonism" very clear. He states his purpose as follows:

> In order to give a general, rough overview and to put the weak minded on alert, lest he be charmed by the lies and deceit of such dangerous charlatans, we are inclined to reward the reader who might be susceptible of being charmed in this manner with a little of the history of the founder of the false and deceptive religion, which is known these days by the name of Mormonism, or the Latter-day Saints.

And in the closing lines, Chambers congratulates himself for a task well done:

> It is needless for us to enlarge on this matter, since every single witness thus far brought forth assists in exposing Mormonism as hideous and repugnant deceit, and unworthy of any kind of attention except to learn of the dangers which have been exposed here.

1846: August, *Y Drysorfa Gynnulleidfaol* (*Congregationalist Treasury*), p. 2 (wrapper) (70 words). "To Our Distributors and our Subscribers."

This brief note of the editor is an explanation for why he refused to publish the correspondence he had received from Dan Jones about a "Profession of Faith" which had been printed in the June 1846 issue of the periodical. This note will be discussed in the 1847 chapter along with the republication of the "Profession of Faith" in The Baptist and Dan Jones's response in *Prophet of the Jubilee.*

1846, August, *Seren Gomer* (*Star of Comer*), p. 253 (315 words). "A Mormon Miracle."

The author, using the nom de plume of "Meurig," reports that "Latter-day Saints" had been in the neighborhoods of Talybont and Ystradmeurig "with little books to offer to the country."[26] According to Meurig, one of the listeners purchased a pamphlet "which showed how to perform [miracles]. When the man returned home, he found a little pig trespassing on his property, so he struck it with a long stick until it was lying flat on the ground. He supposed it to be the property of his neighbor. "Meurig" describes the miracle:

> So, lest anyone should suspect him, he threw it into a hidden nook. A little after he returned to his house, he heard his wife saying that she had lost a little porker, for which she paid twelve shillings the other day; so, he returned without delay to the supposed corpse, and taking hold of it, and blowing in its

> mouth, and making various grimaces, he had the pleasure of seeing it returning to life and running about as usual!

1846: 25 September, *Welshman*, p. 4 (45 words).

The large body of troops under Colonel Kearney, 3500 strong (including one thousand Saints), had reached Bent's Fort on their way to Santa Fe; at which town, it is now stated, the inhabitants are prepared to welcome the American army as friends and customers.

Episode 3.6

Start: John S. Davis makes his debut in writing and publishing articles

When John S. Davis was baptized a member of The Church of Jesus Christ of Latter-day Saints on 19 April 1846, he was unmarried and just a few weeks short of his twenty-fourth birthday. Having apprenticed as a printer and being fluent in both Welsh and English, Davis was well equipped to be of considerable assistance to Dan Jones, the leader of the Latter-day Saints in Wales who had already published a few pamphlets and two issues of a new monthly periodical. Davis was still getting acquainted with the doctrine and teachings of his new religion when an article by Gwilym ap Dewi, entitled "Nature of Miracles," appeared in the columns of the August 1846 *Star of Gomer* (a periodical published in the town of Carmarthen, where Davis had at one time been employed). Having gained a new understanding about miracles by means of his recent conversion, Davis decided to take issue with Gwilym ap Dewi about some of his ideas and write his own article on this topic.

1846: August, *Seren Gomer* (*Star of Gomer*), pp. 233–35 (2,970 words). "The Nature of Miracles."

The writer, whose nom de plume is "Gwilym ab Dewi," provides general information about the miracles of the New Testament and states that he sees no need for miracles "for the purpose of proving the truth of the Christian religion." He explains that he believes the Christian religion without having seen a single miracle. "But," he writes, "perhaps, since Christianity has split into a number of branches, a miracle would be necessary to prove which one of these branches is founded on the witness of Christ, the evangelists, and the apostles." At this point, since The Church of Jesus Christ of Latter-day Saints claims to be the only branch of Christianity in which miracles are performed, he extends the following invitation to members of this Church:

> If Captain Jones, or any others of the prophets of these Saints, will present themselves within the confines of Abersychan or Talywain, and have it in their mind to work a Miracle, I will set before them five loaves and two fishes, at my own expense; and if they can, by giving thanks, feed five thousand, besides women and children, and take up twelve baskets of fragments, then I will think it obvious that they are built on the foundation of prophets and apostles. If they will send their announcement here, I am confident that we can have a multitude of five thousand, besides women and children, to partake of the loaves and the fish, and to be witnesses of the Miracle.

Compared to other writers such as David Williams and the Reverend W. R. Davies, Gwilym ab Dewi is actually quite civil in his comments about the Latter-day Saints and their teachings. He does not lower himself to name-calling, as Williams and Davies had done constantly in their writings. Instead, using syllogistic reasoning and scriptures, he puts forth his arguments against the Saints' ideas about such phenomena as the working of miracles and the casting out of evil spirits, and he comes forth as being a rather polite and well-mannered person.

1846: October, *Seren Gomer* (*Star of Gomer*), pp. 301–03 (2,480 words). "The Nature of Miracles."

John S. Davis, using the nom de plume "I. M.," elects to engage in a polemic with Gwilym ab Dewi by using an approach similar to the one Gwilym ab Dewi used. I. M. does not identify himself as a member of The Church of Jesus Christ of Latter-day Saints, but he does defend the Church's position on several topics in his response.

Here is an example. Gwilyn ab Dewi had written:

> Now, if the Latter-day Saints can perform miracles, let them raise someone from the dead—let them give eyes to some blind man—ears to a deaf man—speech to a mute—and let them hold back the *Atlantic Ocean*, so that they might go through it on dry land to their new Jerusalem.

I. M. responds:

> Here he is again very eager for a sign; and a very large, but totally pointless, sign is the one he wishes to receive, that is for us to hold back the Atlantic Ocean, and walk on dry land to America. It would be far wiser to take boats to cross over, for it would be very wearisome to walk such a way.

Davis would defend his new religion through the press as well as from the pulpit during the following eight years before emigrating. He would also translate into Welsh and publish the Book of Mormon, the Doctrine and Covenants, and the Pearl of Great Price during an eighteen-month period. And he also would serve as the editor of *Zion's Trumpet*, the official periodical of the Church in Wales, from 1849 to 1853.

1846: November, *Seren Gomer* (*Star of Gomer*), p. 343 (820 words). "Zeal without Knowledge"

This essay is written by "Songbird of Ton."[27] Despite identifying himself only by his nom de plume, the writer is actually John S. Davis, the same whose article about miracles appeared in *Star of Gomer* for October 1846.[28] He makes clear his sympathy for the Latter-day Saints and believes they are being verbally punished by all the other Christian religions.

The writer observes:

> The Christians of these days appear to be as if they have changed from what they were in the days of the Apostles, to a worse behavior; instead of praying for everyone, they pray only for those who are of the same opinion as they themselves about religious things. They threaten all who do not lend their ears to them, as did the Pharisees of old; and if they but had the same authority that Bonner had, *the seal of the Queen on their belt*, I am certain that they would make the Latter-day Saints either stop talking or experience that which Stephen

> experienced; and that many of their "Pastors" would hold their clothes considering them as holy as Saul's in days gone by.

1846: December, *Seren Gomer* (*Star of Gomer*), p. 378 (170 words).

With reference to John Davis's article entitled "Nature of Miracles" in the October issue of *Star of Gomer*, Meurig poses a question about miracles to I. M.:

> SIR—In your notes about the article of Mr. W. Davies, you said that the disciples of Christ could be listed, who were the workers of the true miracles, and on the same ground as the Latter-day Saints, who are nothing but the workers of false miracles; and your reason for that was because the disciples failed to cast out the evil spirit mentioned in Math. 17:14–21; Mark 9:17–29; Luke 9:39–42. We wish to know from you whether it was a lack of power or a lack of faith that was the cause of their lack of success? If the former, why did their Teacher chastise them for failing to fulfill that which was impossible for them to do?

1847: January, *Seren Gomer* (*Star of Gomer*), pp. 16–17 (865 words). "'The Nature of Miracles' Again."

This article by I. M. (John S. Davis) is in response to the question posed by Meurig in the December 1846 issue of *Star of Gomer*.[29] Meurig's question is whether it was a lack of power or a lack of faith that caused the New Testament disciples to fail in their attempt to cast out the evil spirit mentioned in Matthew 17:14–21. After some comments about miracles and their nature, Davis explains that the failure of the New Testament disciples to cast out the evil spirit was because of their lack of faith.

1847: January, *Seren Gomer* (*Star of Gomer*), pp. 7–8 (2,060 words). "Notes on an Article by 'Songbird of Ton.'"

A very long response to the article entitled "Zeal without Knowledge" in the November 1846 issue of *Star of Gomer*.[30] The author of this lengthy response to John Davis's November article signs himself "Cuckoo of Ton," which is yet another nom de plume of the Reverend W. R. Davies. Cuckoo disagrees with Songbird's position about the Latter-day Saints, which was that other Christians in Wales were treating this new Christian religion in their midst in much the same fashion Paul treated the Christians in his day prior to his conversion. Cuckoo chides Songbird that he "should remember that it is zeal according to [and not 'without'] knowledge which causes us to treat such stinking rubbish with the scorn and contempt it deserves." In the article, Cuckoo also touches on the matter of William Hughes, a convert who testified that his broken leg had been healed as a direct result of a priesthood blessing given to him a year earlier in Merthyr Tydfil. Cuckoo ridicules the Church members for believing and propagating such "nonsense."

1847: *Amddiffyniad y Saint, yn ngwyneb camgyhuddiadau y rhai a alwant eu hunain yn "Gwcw y Don," yn y* Seren Gomer, *Ionawr, 1847* (*Defense of the Saints against the false accusations of those who call themselves "Cuckoo of Ton," in* Star of Gomer, *January 1847*), pamphlet, 12 pages.[31]

Dan Jones was rabid when he learned about the article by Cuckoo and immediately set about writing a defense. Instead of allowing his response to occupy space in his periodical, Jones elected to respond to Cuckoo, whom he identifies as the Reverend W. R. Davies, with the aforementioned pamphlet. Here is a sample of Jones's response:

> A strange bird is this species of cuckoo that blasphemes and reviles. The cuckoo has a delightful song; but more akin to the cursing magpie is the reviling of men who have done no harm to so much as one feather of her wings, or to anyone else, by calling them "false prophets," "praiseworthy apostle," "Joe," instead of Joseph, "arrogant sinners," without proving them so; "stinking rubbish," she calls the divine religion on which thousands of people as good as she depend for eternal life.[32]

In addition to showing how unfair Davies had been regarding the healing of William Hughes's leg in spite of numerous witnesses (four of them not members of The Church of Jesus Christ of Latter-day Saints), Jones also answers the charges that Davies brings against the Church members in his article. In true polemic fashion, Jones extrapolates on Davies's nom de plume:

> At first, we thought that it was the little cuckoo from Ton we had in our grasp, and then it turned into a profaning magpie; after that we thought perhaps the strange bird was a parrot until it became a rapacious kite.[33]

End: John S. Davis makes his debut in writing and publishing articles

1846: October, *Seren Gomer* (*Star of Gomer*), p. 309 (160 words). "A Public Debate."

One who signs himself "D. W. P." reports on the debate that was held in Towyn, Merionethshire, between G. Evans and "one of the apostles of the Latter-day Saints." The latter maintained that the "gift of miracles in its whole force and early fullness, was just as attainable to these Latter-day Saints as it was to the Saints of the apostolic age." Mr. Evans "denied this statement, and overturned it with no small dexterity."

1846: 16 October, *Welshman*, p. 4 (90 words).

About the troubles of the Latter-day Saints in Illinois.

1846: 17 October, *Silurian*, p. 1 (90 words).

About the serious difficulties of the Latter-day Saints in Nauvoo.

1846: 17 October, *Cardiff and Merthyr Guardian*, p. 2 (30 words).

All remained quiet at Nauvoo. The place was nearly deserted. Mormons were arriving at St. Louis in a state of starvation, having fled from Nauvoo without bringing with them any means of support.

1846: 20 October, *North Wales Chronicle*, p. 4 (30 words).

We learn from St. Louis that two Mormon spies had been shot by the Anti-Mormon mob at Nauvoo. This, it is feared, is the commencement of a sanguinary conflict between these factions.

1846: 23 October, *Welshman*, p. 4 (110 words).

About the difficulties of the Latter-day Saints in Nauvoo.

1846: October, *Y Cenhadwr Americanaidd* (*American Messenger*), p. 311 (80 words).

Information about the "bloody battles between the Mormons and the Anti-Mormons in the area of Nauvoo" in mid-September, which resulted in the departure of the remaining Latter-day Saints.

1846: 19 November, *Yr Amserau* (*Times*), p. 2 (165 words). "Latter-day Saints"

A sixteen-line poem by Clwydfardd,[34] the nom de plume for David Griffith who was a well-known poet at this time and later the Achdruid of Wales. The poem was sent to the *Times* by the poet's friend "G. Dinam," probably a nom de plume as well.[35]

The first four lines of the poem are as follows:

> You, Latter-day Saints,
> I shall follow whilst I live,
> If you can perform the miracles
> Which our Lord's Apostles did.

1846: December, *Y Drysorfa Gynulleidfaol* (*Congregationalist Treasury*), p. 354 (120 words).

The following lines are from an article entitled "Psalm 72:17":

> His name shall endure forever: his name shall be continued as long as the sun: and men shall be blessed in him: all nations shall call him blessed.

In a section that focuses on the phrase "His name shall endure forever," the author laments:

> It is true that there are many things in our kingdom at present which tend to create panic in the fear. The Papist streams originate from one of the main fountains of instruction of our kingdom, and many drink from these polluted streams—Mormonism spreads its wings over the ignorant and the foolish.

1846: 18 December, *Welshman*, p. 2 (30 words).

> From Santa Fe we learn that the Mormon levy had at length arrived, and would shortly set out *en route* to California, in the track of General Kearney's force.

Notes

1. See *Defending the Faith: Early Welsh Missionary Publications*, item J4.
2. The complete volume is available on the Welsh Saints Project website at http://welshsaints.byu.edu/Resources/pdf/24375.pdf.
3. See *Welsh Mormon Writings*, 35–39.
4. Anonymous, *The Latter Saints*, 1846, 5.
5. Facsimile translation is in *Defending the Faith*, item J1.
6. Facsimile translation is in Section 2. Only the second printing is extant. On the title page is "Second printing" and the date of 1846.
7. A facsimile translation of Williams's pamphlet is in Section 2. Facsimile translations of all the pamphlets of Dan Jones are in *Defending the Faith: Early Welsh Missionary Publications*.
8. Dan Jones, 2 January 1846 letter to Wilford Woodruff.
9. Dan Jones at Rhydybont, 7 February 1846 letter to Reuben Hedlock. *Millennial Star* 7:62. The "pamphlet in press" first mentioned has reference to item 3 in *Welsh Mormon Writings*, 20–23. The "reply ready" has reference to item 4 in *Welsh Mormon Writings*, 23–27. See *Defending the Faith*, items J3 and J4, for the English translations.
10. *Baptist*, March 1846, 91–93.
11. *Y Golygydd* (*Editor*), April 1846, 89–90.
12. See Swansea branch records at the Church History Library in Salt Lake City for details.
13. Dan Jones, 7 February 1846 letter to Reuben Hedlock.
14. *Prophet of the Jubilee*, July 1846, 22.
15. Ibid., 24–25.
16. Ibid., 28.
17. Facsimile translation is in Section 2.
18. *Prophet of the Jubilee*, September 1846, 70.
19. Ibid., 71.
20. *Prophet of the Jubilee*, December 1846, 159.
21. Ibid., 155.
22. Ibid., 148.
23. Ibid., 154.
24. Ibid.
25. See *Defending the Faith: Early Welsh Missionary Publications*, item J6.
26. These little books were most likely the four-page pamphlet entitled *What Is Mormonism?* See *Welsh Mormon Writings from 1844 to 1862: A Historical Bibliography* (Provo: Brigham Young University Religious Studies Center, 1988), 33–35.
27. The word *Ton* appears to be a place.
28. *Star of Gomer*, October 1846, 301–303.
29. *Star of Gomer*, December 1846, 378.
30. *Star of Gomer*, November 1846, 343.
31. *Defending the Faith*, item J9.
32. *Defense of the Saints*, pamphlet J9, 2.
33. Ibid., 9.
34. "Poet of Clwyd," a county in North Wales.
35. "Dinam" means "blameless" or "true."

Chapter 4

Episodes

4.1—Dan Jones responds to "The Profession of Faith of the Latter-day Saints"
4.2—After a blind man is baptized, he attacks the Church—Dan Jones responds
4.3—John S. Davis's article is refused publication in *Star of Gomer*
4.4—Dan Jones proves the "Hater of Deceit" to be a "Lover of Deceit"
4.5—Was the reverend's claim because of untruthfulness or a faulty memory?
4.6—The Reverend E. Roberts fails to "kill Mormonism and bury it by Christmas"
4.7—Dan Jones declares the "Proclamation of the Latter-day Saints" blasphemy
4.8—The "jabbering woman" in Newmarket is not a Latter-day Saint
4.9—Should the Baptists rebaptize a repentant Latter-day Saint, or not?
4.10—Did James Strang really perform a miracle, or was it just phosphorus?

Salient Events

- **January 1847.** John Taylor speaks at the conference held in Merthyr Tydfil on 3 and 4 January, the first Apostle to visit the Welsh Saints. It appears that summaries in Welsh were presented following the talks given in English.[1]
- **January 1847.** In *Prophet of the Jubilee,* Jones reports there are 979 members of the Church in Wales on January 1847, p. 17.
- **January 1847.** The following assignments are given to missionaries:[2]
  - John Morris to Pembrokeshire
  - Thomas Pugh, Evan Rees, David Matthews, and Thomas John to Cwmbychan
  - Hopkin Matthews to Treforris
  - Benjamin Jones to Carmarthen
  - Abel Evans to North Wales
  - John Phillips and Dafydd Rees to Cyfyng, near Ystradgynlais

- o William Hughes to Llanelli
- o William Henshaw to Garway Conference
- o Jacob Watkins and John Carver to Garway Conference
- o William Evans "and others with him" to Pontypridd
- o Ebenezer Morris to Llantrisant

- **Before April 1847.** The publication of a pamphlet entitled *The Correct Image Wherein the Deception of the Mormons or the "Latter-day Saints" Can Be Perceived Clearly*. The author of this pamphlet is Daniel Jones, the blind man who had been baptized on 7 July 1846 and who believed he had been deceived by Dan Jones.[3]
- **April 1847.** The publication of *"Haman" hanging from his own gallows! or Daniel Jones [the blind man] and his booklet proving the truth of Mormonism!!* by Dan Jones, in which he contests the allegation of the blind man.[4]
- **21 June 1847.** Dan Jones reports in his letter to Brigham Young about his publishing activities: "Making in all, without one scratch of another's pen but my own nearly one million pages."
- **July 1847.** Dan Jones reports in his periodical the publication of his 102-page *History of the Latter-day Saints*, the first comprehensive history of the Church to be published.[5]
- **2 September 1847.** The Reverend Edward Roberts presents a lecture against the Latter-day Saints in the Caersalem Chapel in Dowlais, the chapel of the Reverend W. R. Davies. See Episode 4.6.
- **October 1847.** Dan Jones publishes *A Review of the Lectures of the Rev. E. Roberts*, a forty-page pamphlet in answer to Edward Roberts.[6]
- **Early November 1847.** After reading *A Review of the Lectures of the Rev. E. Roberts*, William Howells walks four miles to converse with its author and is baptized that same night.[7]
- **December 1847.** The Merthyr Tydfil branch reports nearly six hundred members, making it the largest branch in all of Britain.[8]

Commentary

Episode 4.1

Start: Dan Responds to "The Profession of Faith of the Latter-day Saints"

1846: June, *Y Drysorfa Gynnulleidfaol* (*Congregationalist Treasury*). "The Profession of Faith of the Latter-day Saints."

This particular issue of the *Congregationalist Treasury* is missing from the online collection of the National Library of Wales, but the article it carried is mentioned in the August issue of the periodical. (See below.)

1846: August, *Y Drysorfa Gynnulleidfaol* (*Congregationalist Treasury*), wrapper, p. 2 (70 words). "To Our Distributors and our Subscribers."

> We have received correspondence from one D. Jones, about that profession of faith by the Mormons, alias the Latter-day Saints, which appeared in our June

> issue. Let it be known by that D. Jones, that it is contrary to the principles of the Treasury to publish anything that may be personal and discourteous even from the Saints. His article contains blasphemy.

This brief note of explanation came as no surprise to Dan Jones, since he had received similar treatment from the editor of *Star of Gomer* as well. But when "The Profession" reappeared in the January 1847 issue of the *Baptist*, Dan Jones decided to respond.

1847: January, *Y Bedyddiwr* (*Baptist*), pp. 11–12 (925 words). "The Profession of Faith of the Latter-day Saints."

This list of ten supposed beliefs of the Latter-day Saints was first published six months earlier in the June issue of the *Congregationalist Treasury*. The writer, "A Southerner," then submitted a copy of "The Profession" to the editor of the *Baptist*, citing two witnesses—Thomas Hopkins and Evan Davies—as his sources. This "Profession" contains ten itemized, basic beliefs of the Latter-day Saints; a detailed account, related by a Latter-day Saint, of casting out a devil; and also a description of a Latter-day Saint woman who was dead for two hours but whose spirit returned to her body.

1847: February, *Prophwyd y Jubili* (*Prophet of the Jubilee*), pp. 28–30 (1,500 words). "Defense of the Mormons."

By the time "The Profession" appeared for the second time, Dan Jones had his own periodical through which he could accomplish two objectives. He could print his response to the editor of the *Baptist*, and he could also print the letter he had sent to the uncooperative editor of the *Congregationalist Treasury*. Jones makes the following observation about the two editors who saw fit to publish "The Profession" in their respective periodicals:

> A short time ago these two "reverend" Editors and their factions were at loggerheads with each other; but now, here is an excellent way of removing the barrier between them, and mutually reconcile themselves to persecute the Saints, and that which one accuses will be verified by the other.[9]

Because the *Congregationalist Treasury* had published very little against The Church of Jesus Christ of Latter-day Saints before the June 1846 article, Dan Jones used a very conciliatory tone in his letter to the editor of that publication:

> We do not wish your correspondent and his witnesses to think that I am accusing them of deliberate misrepresentation; and yet, I am sure that either they have received a misrepresentation, or they have greatly misunderstood, and it is not impossible that that "Profession" is the fruit of the one and the other.[10]

Regarding the editor of the *Baptist*, however, Dan Jones's tone was anything but conciliatory:

> As for the Editor of the *Baptist*, we did not intend to lower ourselves any more to take notice of his odiferous rubbish; but for yet one more time, we shall take a glance at his unfairness. He had refused a defense one time, but after delivering his lies about us, he shouted that he would have nothing to do with us, and he promised to leave us in peace, but he discharged the filthy story that appeared in the next issue; then he closed his press against any defense.

And in his final paragraph, Jones pleads with his readers and fellow Latter-day Saints not to give heed to their detractors:

> Do not believe them, lest you be deprived of the truth. It is obvious that they do not want their readers to understand our principles; otherwise, they would use that which we believe from our own books. Is it we, or rather our enemies, who can explain our tenets most correctly, I wonder? If we believed the aforementioned "Profession," would there be any reason for us to deny it publicly?[11]

End: Dan Jones responds to "The Profession of Faith of the Latter-day Saints"

1847: January, *Y Tyst Apostolaidd* (*Apostolic Witness*), pp. 16–17 (595 words). "The Mormons."

The editor of this periodical explains that this modest bit of information about the Latter-day Saints would be useful to his readers. His conclusion is a warning concerning the Latter-day Saints' message:

> As they preach, the teachers of the Saints do not mention the Book of Mormon, nor the revelations of Joe Smith; but their primary purpose is to persuade men to believe that they are able to work miracles, and that there are no godly people who cannot work miracles; once they have convinced men who are sufficiently daft to believe that, they will then be able to get them to believe in the godliness of Joe very easily. But knowing the history of this superstition from its beginning to the present, is sufficient remedy against it. "Be ye not deceived."[12]

1847: 9 January, *Monmouthshire Beacon*, p. 4 (205 words).

Report of a large group assembled at the Delph (near Manchester) for a baptismal service for the Latter-day Saints. It was necessary to break the ice in the canal.

Episode 4.2

Start: After a blind man is baptized, he attacks the Church—Dan Jones responds

1846: *Millennial Star*, vol. 8, pp. 40–42. "Letter to the President."

In this 24 July letter Dan Jones presents an account of the baptism of a blind man in Llanybydder on 7 July 1846. Jones suspected the man's lack of integrity and decided to have a public baptism in an effort to frustrate any insidious plans of those who were associated with the blind man and who wanted to show the Church in a negative light. He preached a long sermon preceding the baptism:

> I showed them that our religion was true, whether the blind man got his sight or not; it was true before the blind man was heard of, that it would remain as true when he was dead and forgotten, and that it is eternally true, and I knew it.

He then describes the events following the baptism:

> While walking up to the house to be confirmed, it was amusing to hear the remarks as the crowd followed, crossing and re-crossing to peep at his eyes, to

> see whether his sight was restored; some said it was, some that he was blinder than before, and that was difficult. . . . I confirmed the man, anointed and laid hands on him, and he shouted for joy in the presence of all, and testified that while hands were on his head he could "see the candle in the candlestick on the table; that he was more than satisfied."

Later, witnesses testified to having heard Jones admit that he had agreed to the baptism as a "prepared Judas," who would then reject the Church because of the Saints' inability to heal him of his blindness.

1847: January, *Y Drych Cywir, lle y gellir canfod yn eglur Twyll Mormoniaid, neu "Seintiau y Dyddiau Diweddaf," mewn dull o Holiadau ac Atebion, rhwng Daniel a'i Gyfaill* (*The Correct Image, Wherein One Can Perceive Clearly the Deceit of the Mormons, or the "Latter-day Saints," in the Form of Questions and Answers, between Daniel and His Friend*), pamphlet, 12 pages.

The Correct Image begins with a poem of eight four-line stanzas. Here are the second and eighth stanzas:

> They travel throughout Wales,
> And bitterly they announce,
> That all are lost
> Unless they join with them.
> And now I must testify,
> That the Saints only deceive,
> If you buy this you will have the full story,
> Of the way I was charmed.

In this pamphlet, a series of questions and answers between the blind man and the Reverend Josiah Thomas Jones, the blind man recalls the incident:

> It is true that I thought and believed I would regain my sight, indeed, I believed so strongly that at one time I thought I could see, and I shouted at them to continue, that I was beginning to see.[13]

The blind man attended only two meetings with his new coreligionists following his baptism. He confesses that he was unable to "receive the Spirit" in the same way others in the meetings did. Consequently, he did not attend any more meetings and eventually concluded that the members of the Church were "lying deceivers."

1847: February, *Y Drysorfa Gynnulleidfaol* (*Congregationalist Treasury*), pp. 47–48 (975 words). "Press Review."

A writer, who calls himself "The Welshman," presents some lengthy quotes from the blind man's pamphlet about his experience with the Latter-day Saints, following a scathing introduction:

> It was impossible for Daniel to better serve his nation than by revealing the treachery of these deceitful atheists; we would advise everyone to buy it, so that they may find in the Image, an accurate portrayal of such a pack of rapacious wolves, who scatter their destructive heresies the length and breadth of Wales in general, until they charm some of the superstitious and weak-headed in our country into believing such false doctrines as are published by the Mormons.

1847: February, *"Haman" yn hongian ar ei grogbren ei hun! neu Daniel Jones (ddall) a'i lyfr yn profi gwirionedd Mormoniaeth!!* (*"Haman" Hanging from His Own Gallows! Or Daniel Jones (the Blind) Proving the Truth of Mormonism!!*) pamphlet, 8 pages.

Captain Jones's reaction to the blind man's pamphlet was an eight-page pamphlet of his own—*"Haman" hanging from his own gallows!*—describing the details of the baptism, the momentary restoration of the blind man's sight, and the testimony of various witnesses.

In a chance meeting in October 1846, Dan Jones had warned the blind man that if he continued his campaign against the Saints, the hand of God would be on him and his fate would be hotter than that of Kora, Dathan, and Abiram, the three who were swallowed up in the earth after fighting against Moses. In spite of the warning, the blind man was persuaded to publish a pamphlet about his experience and thus warn the Welsh of the Mormons' deceit.

1847: *Millennial Star*, vol. 9, p. 218.

In his report of a conference held on 25 April 1847, Dan Jones recounts the fulfillment of his October 1846 prophetic warning:

> No sooner was the reply [The Correct Image] out of press, than on the old blind man it came, hot and heavy. He cried out that he was burning up alive; his friends poured cold water on him night and day in vain! He would rush out from them to a pool that was by, and there he would roll, and wallow, and yelp until he terrified the passersby. . . . Yes, he died a monument of the displeasure of a just God for hypocrisy, is the admission of many besides Saints.[14]

1848: November, *Prophwyd y Jubili* (*Prophet of the Jubilee*), pp. 170–72. "The Blind Man and His Book."

In this letter, Thomas Jeremy reports that the twelve-page pamphlet published by the blind man had been reprinted and that "those who sell it say that its author is not yet dead!"

> It is a strange thing that men who were fashioned in the image of the truthful God should so succumb to the influences of the father of lies as to claim that he (Daniel Jones) is still alive. If he is alive, he must have taken part in the first resurrection.

Jeremy describes what happened to the blind man after receiving the stern warning from Dan Jones:

> He was taken very ill, so that he felt his intestines on fire inside him: he drank a lot of cold water to stop the supposed fire inside him, and also he ran out of the house to wallow in water in order to cool down; but all in vain. He died in this painful condition; although I was not present, I heard about him. I live about three miles from the place where he died. I have been with Mr. James Evans, the Registrar, who has registered the death of Daniel Jones, and he is willing to give a copy to anyone who wishes, if they pay 2s. 6c. and the postage.

End: After a blind man is baptized, he attacks the Church—Dan Jones responds

1847: April, *Seren Gomer* (*Star of Gomer*), p. 120 (240 words). "Persecution of the Mormons."

A borrowed article from "one of the newspapers of America." The article briefly recounts the efforts of "a great number of wretches [who] had formed an alliance to cause the Mormons to leave their country and their property." In consequence of their persecutors, the Latter-day Saints in America "are now poor and needy wanderers in the inaccessible wilds of the new world, with hundreds of them dying of fatigue and hunger!" Of the articles to appear in the Welsh press, this article is one of the very few that had a tone of compassion for the Latter-day Saints.

1847: May, *Y Drysorfa* (*Treasury*), p. 160 (380 words). "The Latter-day Saints."

This brief article appeared in the *Treasury*, a Welsh-language Calvinistic Methodist periodical published in Chester, England—not to be confused with *Y Drysorfa Gynnulleidfaol* (the *Congregationalist Treasury*), which was published in Swansea, Wales. This article is simply an account of a Latter-day Saint missionary, whom the author refers to as "a fluent and gifted speaker . . . well versed in the Scriptures," who had recently visited the town of Mold in North Wales. During a conversation with a local resident, the missionary quoted Mark 16:18, which refers to the signs that would be given to believers of the apostles' message. The resident then asked the missionary whether the members of his church had the miraculous gifts mentioned in the scripture. When the missionary responded in the affirmative the resident provided the missionary with a drink with arsenic in it and asked him to drink it as proof that the "deadly thing" would not hurt him. The article ends with this statement:

> The apostle turned a pale-blue, and without uttering a word he was off as soon as he could, showing by the haste of his departure that he was glad to see the door. There is no need to say that the ministry of the false apostle has come to an end in Mold in this visit with our friend, as he was never heard from again.

Episode 4.3

Start: John S. Davis's article is refused publication in Star of Gomer

1847: June, *Seren Gomer* (*Star of Gomer*), pp. 173–74 (1,070 words). "Speaking with Tongues."

Nowhere in this article is any reference made to The Church of Jesus Christ of Latter-day Saints. The writer discusses the Apostle Paul's ideas about speaking with tongues, brings up examples from the nineteenth chapter of the Book of Acts and from the fourteenth chapter of 1 Corinthians, and concludes the following:

> This, and all other things, show clearly, then, that speaking with tongues and the interpretations were only for the edifying of the church, and that such was done when the spirit of God was resting on those who were speaking.[15]

The article is signed "J. D." and was written by John S. Davis.[16]

1847: September, *Seren Gomer* (*Star of Gomer*), p. 258 (80 words). "Part of the Jewish Statute-book as a Path to the Christian Statute-book," by "H. Tegai."

Following the article is this postscript which is directed to "J. D.":

> P. S. I saw in the June STAR, an article by one J. D., on "Speaking with Tongues." If J. D. wishes to come forward to defend Mormonism, let him come to the root of the debate immediately, by [answering], 1. Did Christ and his apostles work public miracles? If they did, 2, Do the Mormons do so in the same way? Let J. D. answer however he wishes, and then I will have a word to say to him.

1847: December, *Prophwyd y Jubili* (*Prophet of the Jubilee*), pp. 181–85 (2,670 words). "'Speaking with Tongues' of the New Testament, and Mormonism!"

Davis wrote a response to H. Tegai's questions and fully expected that it would be printed in *Star of Gomer*. When the response was refused publication in that periodical, Davis submitted the response to Dan Jones, who was pleased to publish it in this issue of *Prophet of the Jubilee*. Davis explains the article's trajectory in an introductory paragraph addressed to Dan Jones:

> Some questions were directed at me in the September Star, by one Independent Reverend from the North, and I wrote an answer for them, being sure in my mind that I would receive the same fair play that the inquirer received; but to my disappointment, I was told that it was too poor, that there was none of the "cleverness" in this article that I had shown on other occasions, and that the aforementioned Reverend would take no notice of it. The only thing I shall say is, that I did my best. Now, I set my cause before you, and begging the fair play that was denied me in the place where it should have been received.[17]

Davis has a much more argumentative tone in this article than he used in his three articles that were allowed to appear in *Star of Gomer* for October 1846, January 1847, and June 1848. Addressing the editor of the periodical, he responds to the accusation that he had "come forth to defend Mormonism":

> About last February when I sent you an article on "Speaking with Tongues," which appeared in the Star for June, little did I think that anyone would be so perceptive as to see that it was defending Mormonism; for it was nothing more than an investigation into the New Testament to know what is to be understood by "speaking with tongues."[18]

To Tegai's statement, "Let J. D. answer as he may, and then I shall have a word to say to him," Davis writes:

> This thing looks like a trap or a net; and if the words are taken "spiritually," they mean, in my opinion, that Mr. Tegai has determined beforehand what he will say; yes, even if I were to convince him of the complete opposite. But that makes no difference, for I hope, that when our friend lifts his net, that a miracle will take place (as in the time of Christ), and instead of capturing me, he will have captured the truth, and that as it is in Christ. Amen.[19]

End: John S. Davis's article is refused publication in Star of Gomer

Episode 4.4

Start: Dan Jones proves the "Hater of Deceit" to be a "Lover of Deceit"

1847: May, *Y Diwygiwr* (*Revivalist*), pp. 144–46 (1,370 words). "The Deceiving Mormons."

The writer declares himself to be from Blackwood and signs himself "A Hater of Deceit." He says that he has been an eyewitness to failed healings of the sick, unfulfilled prophecies, and bogus speaking in tongues by members of this new religion in his area. "And since it is in secret that they introduce their destructive heresies," he writes, "I think it is high time for everyone to wake up, and strive to root out these secrets, and steadfastly proclaim them clearly."

1847: May, *Prophwyd y Jubili* (*Prophet of the Jubilee*), pp. 69–75 (3,930 words). "The 'Hater of Deceit' Proved a Lover, a Maker, and a Publisher, of 'Deceit' Himself."

In a written defense three times the size of the attack, Jones dissects each point of Hater's argument and discusses the flaws as he proceeds to make a mockery of the entire article. With the Prophet of the Jubilee as his battering ram, Jones confidently counters Hater's accusations:

> Although for any thoughtful man the writing throughout contains sufficient proofs that its author is deserving of the character we have given him, still we shall glean some of the ears of corn from his labor, to show more clearly the kind of harvest that one can expect, together with the filth of the field that produces such cabbages.[20]

1847: June, *Prophwyd y Jubili* (*Prophet of the Jubilee*), pp. 90–93 (1,760 words). "The 'Hater of Deceit' Proved a Lover, a Maker, and a Publisher, of 'Deceit' Himself."

The continuation and conclusion of the *Prophet of the Jubilee* May article. Here is his final sentence:

> Let Mr. Rees also take a few of these pills with you; yes, let all our persecutors swallow their dose so the filth may be purged from their stomachs, for their good, and bring them to love truth instead of loving lies is our desire, that's all.[21]

1847: July, *Y Diwygiwr* (*Revivalist*), pp. 212–13 (1,430 words).

The Hater of Deceit responds aggressively to Dan Jones. Unlike Hater's previous article, in this one Hater focuses his defense on the teachings and practices of "Mormonism . . . the most innocuous little thing we have ever seen." He refers to Joseph Smith as "that deceptive monster" and sounds the alarm for all Welsh people:

> Dear Wales! can you sleep while seeing your fellowmen turning away from the truth; and while seeing, perhaps, your closest relatives charmed by their lightness, to gallop towards the land of woe? Awake for the sake of your souls, and stand firm by the principles of the true religion. Show courage against the false prophets, and strive to persecute false prophesies to annihilation.

1847: September, *Prophwyd y Jubili* (*Prophet of the Jubilee*), pp. 137–141 (2,770 words). "The 'Hater of Deceit' Proving himself a False Prophet Again!!"

Dan Jones fires back at the Hater of Deceit:

> Listen, reader, to another example of our persecutor's madness, and we are surprised that he was able to get a place in any publication! "But I thank him (he says, that is, he thanks us for whipping him 'quite harshly' as he says); my only wish was to get him to oppose me," and so, poor fellow, here you are not only having got your wish like everyone else who opposes our dear religion with lies, but also hanging yourself again with your own words.[22]

Jones then rails at his accuser for not revealing his identity:

> Poor fellow, you want to get us to oppose you, do you, only to threaten and falsely accuse us. No wonder you refuse to reveal your name just like every deceiver or slanderer. Oh, evil man, hiding in his black hole like the fox, gnashing his teeth from there at those who go by; is this fair? Give your name to the world, so that they understand who deserves the whip, and who are our accusers. We are never ashamed to own our names in public under what we publish in support of the truth, as you are ashamed to own up to your ridiculous lies![23]

1847: September, *Yr Haul* (*Sun*), pp. 299–300 (510 words). "Attack of the Editor of The Revivalist on the Mormons."

Jones was not the only person to have negative opinions and comments about the Hater of Deceit. David Owen, a former Baptist minister who had converted to the Church of England a few years earlier, decided to weigh in on the fierce battle between Dan Jones and his vociferous opponent. Owen was also the editor of the Welsh-language Anglican Church periodical *Yr Haul* (The Sun) at the time he saw the vicious article by the Hater of Deceit in *The Revivalist*. Owen declares the author of the articles in *The Revivalist* to be David Rees, who was the editor of the periodical and was also a Congregationalist minister. Owen explains in his own periodical that Rees pretends to have received a letter from a correspondent in Blackwood to make himself look more important. Owen adds:

> This is not the first time for the Editor to flee to the shelter of silence for safety—he has no talents, no instruction, nor gift for public debate.

Owen opines that Rees's letter is "one of the clumsiest letters ever to appear in print," and he also declares Mormonism to be "a snake, generated by the extremes of Nonconformity" which will "certainly be poisoned to death."

Dan Jones must have enjoyed himself immensely as he read the harsh criticisms leveled against a Congregationalist minister by an Anglican vicar who had no affinity for any of the Nonconformists nor for the Latter-day Saints.

1847: September, *Y Diwygiwr* (*Revivalist*), pp. 286–87 (1,170 words). "The False Prophets—Who Are They?"

This is yet another article condemning Dan Jones and his religion, in which the author presents himself as the arbiter of the polemic between the Hater of Deceit and Dan Jones, calling himself the "Prover of Deceit." Since the article appears in the September issue of *The Revivalist*, the editor had probably not seen the September 1847 issue of the *Sun* and thus offered no response to David Owen's criticism. The Prover of Deceit ends this September article with the following:

> Now, I must end, and reveal my name. Did I say, my name? An unknown name, to be sure; for what if Mr. Hater of Deceit should get hold of me,

and take me for a "deceiver!" It could be dangerous, for often he is a sniper through the hedges.

It is very likely that Prover of Deceit and Hater of Deceit are one and the same person—i.e., David Rees, the editor of *The Revivalist*, as accused by David Owen, the editor of *The Sun*.

End: Dan Jones proves the "Hater of Deceit" to be a "Lover of Deceit"

1847: 11 June, *Welshman*, p. 3 (85 words).

Residents of Pembroke Dock are warned that Latter-day Saint missionaries are preaching in the area. Two Wesleyan Methodist ministers preached against them in the open air.

1847: July, *Catecism* (*Catechism*) [nonextant].

This publication by the Reverend W. R. Davies has not been identified by title, nor are there any details available other than those revealed by Dan Jones in his ferocious attack on the publication in the August[24] and September[25] issues of the 1847 *Prophet of the Jubilee.*

> Since I reviewed his treatise [*The Latter Saints. The Substance of a Sermon which was delivered on the miracles*, March, 1846] in such detail, and answered everything that merited attention [1846 *Prophet of the Jubilee* for September, October, November, and December], and as his Catechism is only a revamping of that, having had done to it what some ladies do to their bonnets, or the dandies to their old coats, that is to turn them and bring them out in some new fashion, we will not be expected to review his Catechism here until he offers to refute our previous review; yet, let us take note of the above accusations to see if it is he, or we who merit them at all.[26]

Here is an example of the many accusations Jones brings forth about Davies:

> This man accuses the Saints of trying to "Entice the uneducated and the unbalanced, for the purpose of attracting their money, and living in idleness at the expense of the weak-headed ones who believe them," says he. This would be considered a very weighty accusation if it came from any mouth but the soiled lips of Mr. Davies of Dowlais; yes, one who needs strong proofs before he would be believed: but it is vain to expect any sort of proof, example, or reason from him to prove it, any more than he provides for anything else; otherwise, it would long ago have been out in public. Is it Mr. Davies who brings this accusation! From how many chapels does he himself receive his salary, I wonder? Who lives in such idleness at the expense of his devotees, and electioneers so much for money, money, all the time as our accuser?... Living in idleness at the expense of others, is it? Which of them prove themselves guilty of this by building new houses, etc.? Who was the man who was off for three months without preaching once in any of his chapels, and on his return got £50 from his devotees at home![27]

1847, August, *Y Drysorfa Gynnulleidfaol* (*Congregationalist Treasury*), p. 234 (70 words).

Following an article about the Ascension of Christ is this footnote:

It is claimed by the delusional and arrogant people who call themselves Latter-day Saints, that they now receive the Spirit in its miraculous gifts, but there is as much truth in that as there is in that prophecy of theirs that the town of Abergavenny would sink on a day appointed by them, the day came and went, and the town still remains unshaken to this day.

1847: 6 August, *Welshman*, p. 4 (30 words).

It is stated in an Illinois journal, that the famous Mormon Temple at Nauvoo, has been sold for a Roman Catholic church at the large price of 75,000 dollars.

1847: 7 August, *Monmouthshire Merlin*, p. 1 (30 words).

It is stated in an Illinois journal, that the famous Mormon Temple, at Nauvoo, has been sold for a Roman Catholic church for the large price of 75,000.

1847: 21 August, *Cardiff and Merthyr Guardian*, p. 3 (85 words).

Street Oratory. Public lectures are getting frequent; and crowds of people are often in the neighborhoods of Market-square and George Town, listening to open-air orators upon Teetotalism, and upon the truths or errors of Mormonism—subjects upon which the speakers get impassioned, and sometimes quarrelsome. It is amusing, on Sunday evenings, in the neighborhood of the Dynevor's Arms, to find three speakers within hearing of each other expressing their sentiments, upon distinct subjects, at the same time; and these scenes sometimes end in very hot discussions.

1847: September, *Prophwyd y Jubili (Prophet of the Jubilee)*, p. 141–43. "To the One who Calls Himself 'The Traveler of Nantyglo, or William Williams.'"

See Chapter 5 for commentary.

Episode 4.5

Start: Was the reverend's claim because of untruthfulness or a faulty memory?

1847: September, *Y Tyst Apostolaidd* (*Apostolic Witness*), pp. 199–201 (1,970 words). "The Mormons."

This article is signed "Tobit ger y Bont" (Tobit by the Bridge), a nom de plume previously used by the Reverend W. R. Davies. By this time, Dan Jones was certainly sufficiently familiar with Davies's writings that he could recognize them, regardless of the name used, but such a high recognition was probably not the case with the general reading public. So perhaps Davies elected to use a variety of noms de plume to promote the idea that many writers were greatly concerned about the doctrines and growth of The Church of Jesus Christ of Latter-day Saints in Wales and were willing to preach against the Church from the pulpit as well as through the press.

In the opening paragraph of the article, Davies declares his wish to "place before the public my reasons for calling the creatures under observation 'Satanists of the nineteenth century' and not 'Saints of the Latter Days,' as they arrogantly call themselves." He proposes to do so on three bases:

1. "I shall prove that they are devilish men with their own mouth, by the manner in which they profess to cast out devils." Davies then uses some twisted logic to explain that the Latter-day Saints cast out devils from

people who differed from the kinds of people from whom Christ and his apostles cast out devils.

2. "Satanists of the nineteenth century," and not "Saints of the latter days." Davies explains that since the latter days had not yet arrived and since the "Saints" are really "Satanists" that they should be called "Satanists of the nineteenth century."
3. "The King of Zion has given a rule for his saints to follow without exception while in the world, namely the way in which they are to behave toward their enemies when they are persecuted and killed." Davies quotes from Dan Jones's *History of the Latter-day Saints*, published recently in Rhydybont on his brother's press, that the Latter-day Saints in Nauvoo killed some of their enemies when under attack.[28] He then quotes the Savior—"Dearly beloved, avenge not yourselves"—as proof that the Latter-day Saints sinned by defending themselves.[29]

Davies rails at Dan Jones for claiming that miracles had been wrought among the Saints and challenges him to offer proof that even one miracle has occurred. Davies ends his lengthy harangue with the following:

> I hear that they are boasting throughout the country, that many members of the Baptists in Caersalem have joined them. I myself can assure you that that is not true, except for one old woman.[30]

1848: September, *Prophwyd y Jubili* (*Prophet of the Jubilee*), p. 132 (1,020 words). "Testimony of Rees Price, Dowlais."

As proof of Davies's untruthfulness, or perhaps his faulty memory, here is the statement of Rees Price, a former parishioner of W. R. Davies. After hearing the Saints, Price began to search the scriptures for truth:

> While engaged in this careful search, in obedience to the scripture that says, "Prove all things, hold fast that which is good," news of it reached the ears of Mr. Davies, namely that I was inclined toward a judgment and in danger of joining with the Saints; because of this I was publicly disciplined, under the accusation that I had neglected my meeting attendance; but in reality, I say, that I was diligently searching for the truth. When Mr. Roberts came from Rhymney to Dowlais to lecture against the Saints, the meanness of his stories, the illogic of his allegations, his deceit, and his unfairness, convinced me more and more that the religion of the sufferers was better than the religion that caused the attackers to abuse them, to persecute them, and to falsely accuse them as these did.

Price explains the repercussions that occurred when he and his wife left the Baptists:

> Also my beloved wife, who was formerly a zealous member with Mr. Davies, Dowlais, has left him and obeyed the order of God; and she also is greatly rejoicing in the privileges of the church of God. We are more content in our family and in every other consideration than ever before, although we are subject to pointing fingers and mocking laughter along the streets, and our old brethren and our old pastor scorn us, treat us like slime, and falsely accuse us

> publicly. Poor things; let that be between them and the gracious God they kick against.

1848: December, *Prophwyd y Jubili* (*Prophet of the Jubilee*), pp. 187–88 (480 words). "Letter to the Editor."

And here is the statement of Job Rowland, a former Baptist in Davies's chapel in Dowlais, who received his baptism into The Church of Jesus Christ of Latter-day Saints on 13 January 1847—several months earlier than the date of Davies's assertion that only "one old woman" had left his congregation to become a Latter-day Saint:

> As soon as the Saints came to these areas our teachers, especially Mr. W. R. Davies, began to persecute them and hate them, saying all manner of evil against them. Mr. Davies said one time in our house that his desire was to do the same with their elders as was done to Joseph Smith, that is to kill them. That, together with many other things, prompted me to look into their principles; and after having the honor of associating with the Saints, I saw that they were not the way Mr. Davies and others had described them.

End: Was the reverend's claim because of untruthfulness or a faulty memory?

Episode 4.6

Start: The Reverend E. Roberts fails to "kill Mormonism and bury it by Christmas"

Dan Jones did not respond in *Prophet of the Jubilee*, according to his normal pattern, to the assault by Tobit ger y Bont (W. R. Davies) that appeared in the September 1847 issue of the *Apostolic Witness*.[31] The reason was very probably because of Jones's shift of attention to a highly publicized lecture on "The Deceit of Mormonism" presented in the Caersalem Chapel in Dowlais by the Reverend Edward Roberts on the second of September. Caersalem Chapel was W. R. Davies's chapel, and Davies had invited his colleague of the cloth, a Baptist minister in Rhymney, to deliver a powerful blow against the religion they both hated and persecuted.

Roberts's lecture was announced for the evening of 2 September 1847 at the Caersalem Chapel in Dowlais. Dan Jones endeavored to steal the Baptists' thunder by beginning a series of lectures of his own about the Book of Mormon on 21 August 1847 in Dowlais, about two weeks before Roberts's scheduled presentation. Handbills were circulated to announce these lectures and Jones's rebuttal to Roberts's lecture. The rebuttal was to be on the evening of 3 September 1847.

1847: October, *Seren Gomer* (*Star of Gomer*), p. 318 (1,260 words). "Lectures on Mormonism."

This report, by one who calls himself "A Listener," is a contrast to Dan Jones's reaction to Roberts's performance. The Listener writes the following:

> To give an account of the detail and excellent composition of this lecture would be too long by far in an article like this; it is enough to say that, although it lasted for a few minutes less than two hours, all the listeners

> stayed attentive till the end, showing their approval in endless cheers while the speaker continued. A better meeting was never had in Dowlais, according to the evidence of everyone who was there, except one or two Mormons who were there, and ready to chew their fingers in anger, at the terrible treatment their evil and deceitful principles received.

The Listener ends his report with an appeal:

> The fervent wish of the thousands who listened to Mr. Roberts both nights, is that he would send the skillful and necessary lectures to be printed in the Star; and hopefully he will, for the sake of stopping the weak among the people throughout all Wales from being bewitched by such rubbish.

1847: October, *Y Tyst Apostolaidd* (*Apostolic Witness*), pp. 224–25 (820 words). "Lectures on Mormonism."

Here is W. Jones's very enthusiastic reaction to the Reverend Edward Roberts's lecture:

> After the meeting was begun by Mr. W. Jones, Llansanan, Mr. E. Roberts, Rhymney was called to deliver his lecture. After that, he went ahead and delivered one of the most eloquent and well-crafted lectures we have ever heard, to a numerous crowd of listeners who were stretching their necks to listen as if for their lives; indicating at the same time, through several signs, the greatest satisfaction for that which they heard. The meeting was carried forward in a peaceful and civil manner; and everyone left after being completely satisfied, except for a few of the "Saints," who insisted that they had not been convinced, nor had they heard the truth.[32]

1847: October, *Prophwyd y Jubili* (*Prophet of the Jubilee*), pp. 151–54 (2,170 words). "Review of the Lecture of the Rev. D. Jones, Cardiff, on 'The Excellence of the Christian Religion.'"

This review is the first part of a two-part series about this lecture. The Rev. D. Jones presented his lecture immediately following the Rev. E. Roberts's lecture the night of 3 September 1847. Since Dan Jones could not be present that night, he assigned others to take notes for him. After reading the notes, Dan Jones reacted to the lecture by writing the following in his periodical:

> The first thing that came from his mouth was the cruel sentence that follows: "My brother [E. Roberts] has shown quite clearly that Mormonism is deceit, and only deceit;" when at the same time his brother had not disproved any principle that belongs to "Mormonism," but made horrible hobgoblins out of his own work, and that of others of the same taste, and torturing them alternately.[33]

Dan Jones then systematically responds to several statements made by the Reverend D. Jones. The responses were so numerous that Dan Jones extended them into the following issue of Prophet of the Jubilee.

1847: November, *Prophwyd y Jubili* (*Prophet of the Jubilee*), pp. 165–68 (2,290 words). "Review of the Lecture of the Rev. D. Jones, Cardiff, on 'The Excellence of the Christian Religion.'"

The second part of Dan Jones's response to what he considered erroneous statements made by the Rev. D. Jones.

1847: ***Adolygiad ar ddarlithoedd y Parch. E. Roberts, (Gweinidog y Bedyddwyr yn Rymni,) yn erbyn Mormoniaeth, pa rai a draddododd yn Nghaersalem, Medi yr Ail, ac yn Bethania (Capel yr Annibynwyr,) Medi y Trydydd, yn Nowlais (A Review of the Lectures of the Rev. E. Roberts, [a Baptist minister in Rhymni,] against Mormonism, Which Were Delivered in Caersalem, September the Second, and in Bethania [a Congregational chapel], September the Second, and in Bethania [a Congregational chapel], September the Third, in Dowlais*), pamphlet, 40 pages.**[34]

Dan Jones responds to the September second and the September third lectures given by Edward Roberts. Jones's forty-page pamphlet has the date of 18 October 1847 in the preface. In true polemic fashion, Jones ridicules Roberts's points of argument one by one. Jones accuses Roberts of raising money for a Baptist chapel by preaching lies. With respect to Roberts's observation about Joseph Smith's big hands, Jones replies, "You workers of Dowlais, remember to keep your hands hidden from this preacher lest you be condemned as badly as Joseph Smith."[35] Jones laments that Roberts had resorted to fantasies and stories about Mormonism instead of dealing with principles and doctrines. Over one-third of the pamphlet considers the charge that Joseph Smith had borrowed from Solomon Spaulding's manuscript in writing the Book of Mormon. This segment is essentially a translation of Benjamin Winchester's 1840 pamphlet on the same topic.[36]

Jones declares in the preface how opposition serves as a catalyst for the work to move forward:

> The bulls and the anathemas of the Pope, and the conspiracies of the papist friars regarding the life of Luther, were better for the spreading of his reformation than all the previous peace and sufferance. And the blasphemies and unfounded claims of Mr. Davies of Dowlais, and Mr. Roberts of Rhymney; yes, the public blasphemies on the streets made by their followers are better for the spread of Mormonism than the stillness to be found in some other places; and while persecution and shame, although falling on myself and my brethren, are a means of spreading the truth in my dear country—welcome persecution! Welcome pain! Welcome shame! Behold the bodies, the characters and the feelings that suffer them are happy, even though they flow from men who should know better.[37]

1847: *Millennial Star*, vol. 9, pp. 318–19. "Letter to Elder Orson Spencer."

Dan Jones begins this letter, dated 29 September 1847, with the following:

> Dear President Spencer, Having but just retreated for a few hours from the battleground, while my guns are cooling for another broadside, I will report to you the progress of the war.[38]

Jones describes the atmosphere the night of 2 September in the Caersalem Baptist Chapel in Dowlais, where the Reverend E. Roberts was about to present "the funeral sermon of Mormonism":

> The scene was truly picturesque, which presented the first of this crusade! It was in a Baptist chapel, one of their collegians being the hero. The big seat was

> crowded with reverends, etc., from far and near, and although they exacted sixpence for admission, yet the chapel was crowded with anxious listeners, who, with opened mouths, eagerly anticipated to hear the funeral sermon of Mormonism. I seated myself in front, and took notes of his topics, and were you to see the fingers and eyes that evidently marked me as a gone case, you would have thought that I had seven horns, if not as many heads, and every time that the harlequin would strike the pulpit with his paw, and cry, "Down with Mormonism!" etc., in the mist of the echo of cheers, I had time and opportunity to inspect nearly all eyes in the place.[39]

Jones then describes the scene at the end of Roberts's lecture:

> I had sent one of my placards (publishing that I should reply the following evening, and admission by buying a shilling book for sixpence, and thereby paying them sixpence for coming, which contained the history of the church, Joseph Smith, and refutations to most of those charges, etc.) to the chairman, with a request for him to read it at the close, but he refused to read it, and when one of the Saints asked him, I was replied to in the negative by one of them jumping on top of the seat in front of me, and in front of a seatful of the reverend divines, with his fist in my face, and gnashing his teeth, and in the attitude of sending me to judgment, apparently, if I said a word: and instead of allowing his hearers to come and hear both sides, as an honest man would do, behold, he published that he would deliver another lecture the following night gratis! And thus showing the white feather in his tail. However, I fulfilled my appointment, and sent reporters to his second lecture, and from that time I have been lecturing there to crowded audiences of eager hearers, almost without cessation, and many believing the gospel.[40]

1847: November, *Prophwyd y Jubili* (*Prophet of the Jubilee*), pp. 171–73 (1,380 words). "The Persecution of Dowlais, and the Good It Has Done."

Dan Jones reports to his readers:

> But, the truth is, instead of the Saints being a "blasphemy and a curse," as [the Rev. W. R.] Davies says, and instead of some leaving them in Dowlais, not so much as one has left them since this last persecution began! And furthermore, let the world understand that there has been more success and growth among the Saints, even in Dowlais, since that than ever before![41]

1848: February, *Prophwyd y Jubili* (*Prophet of the Jubilee*), pp. 23–24 (730 words). "Praise for the Review of Capt. Jones on the Lectures of the Rev. E. Roberts, Rhymni, and His supporters, against Mormonism."

As might be expected, Jones's *Review of the Lectures of the Rev. E. Roberts* fared extremely well in *Prophet of the Jubilee.* One Daniel ab Iago from Rhymney even wrote a poem in praise of the pamphlet and the author. He declares that the Review is "brilliant" and that it is well worth reading. Here are the first and fourth stanzas of the nine-stanza poem:

> He raises his head no more a Captain—joyful
> Sovereign—praiseworthy;
> Though their tempest was terrible,

A giant of strength, he beat them.
You shattered all their castles—vile things,
Without making mischief;
You revealed and pulled down
In dreadful shame their odiousness.

Daniel ab Iago explains what motivated him to compose his poem:

> An impartial consideration of the disgraceful behavior of some of the preachers of the age (especially the Baptists) towards the Latter-day Saints, compelled me to compose the above, and to offer it for your public use, and I hope it will be convincing to many of the devotees of the said persecutors, so that they are not misled by their fabricated tales. What but Satan is stirring them up so that they do not leave their innocent and conscientious neighbors in peace to worship God as they please?

1847: *Millennial Star*, vol. 9, pp. 363–64. "Extracts from Elder Dan Jones's Letters to Orson Spencer."

In this 3 November 1847 letter to Dan Jones's file leader in Liverpool, concerning the forty-page pamphlet Jones had recently published about the lectures of the Rev. E. Roberts, Jones exults:

> Last evening, I baptized a gentleman who is now, and has been, a Baptist minister for the last eighteen years: he preached to his flock last Sunday, and has an appointment for the successive Sunday. He came four miles purposely to be baptized, though he had never heard a sermon, only reading my publications; especially my last reply (of which I sent you a copy—a pamphlet of forty pages) finished him entirely, and he came in as good a spirit as anyone that I ever saw, and has just returned on his way rejoicing. He is a wealthy man of great influence, and, as he said, he feared that he was not a servant of God, because he heard every person universally praising him, whereas the scripture says, "Wo unto you when all men speak well of you."[42]

The "gentleman" of whom Dan Jones writes is William Howells, a lay Baptist preacher from Aberdare. Howells was later the first missionary of The Church of Jesus Christ of Latter-day Saints to serve in France. And within a year after his conversion, William Howells had been instrumental in bringing over one hundred relatives, former parishioners, and neighbors into the gospel family.

1849: May, *Udgorn Seion* (*Zion's Trumpet*), pp. 93–97 (2,015 words). "Letter to Brother J. Davis."

A recent convert by the name of William Howells writes this letter in answer to a question posed by John S. Davis in the April 1849 issue of Zion's Trumpet. Here is the question:

> How much good did Roberts [the Rev. Edward Roberts] of Rhymney and Davies [the Rev. W. R. Davies] of Dowlais do by preaching against the Saints? Is it possible to name anyone the Saints lost as a result? Or, is it not possible to prove that there are scores in Merthyr and Dowlais who today testify that the above two were instrumental in opening their eyes to perceive the truth of the Saints' religion?[43]

In his 10 May 1849 letter to John S. Davis, William Howells answers Davis's question by recounting the events that led to Howells's baptism by Dan Jones in early November 1847:

> Much good, I say, in many ways and means. Together with the scores in Merthyr and Dowlais who can testify that the above two were instruments in opening their eyes to perceive the truth of the Saints, there are several in Aberdare, among which, with grateful spirit, I count myself; and I can testify boldly in the day of judgment that it was the Review of brother Capt. D. Jones, on the Lecture of Roberts from Rhymney, that was the means of convincing me of the deceit of the religion that I professed, and, like Saul, which I followed with great zeal. I knew practically nothing about the Saints, or their religion, until the Rev. W. R. Davies came to Aberdare, to show their deceit; but to the surprise of my mind, the more he shouted, pounding the Bible and the pulpit, "Great deceit, infernal hypocrisy, and pitiful darkness of the Latter-day Satanists," all the greater shone the principles of the Saints, like rays of godly truth, until I was caused to begin to believe, that if these men were Satanic, that his satanic majesty had more of the godly truth of the Bible, than did the religion that I professed.[44]

1847: November, *Y Tyst Apostolaidd* (*Apostolic Witness*), p. 256 (335 words).

In a 7 October 1847 letter to the editor, The Reverend E. Roberts explains the delay in the publication of his pamphlet:

> In the issue of *The Witness* for last month, I saw the account of my Lectures on Mormonism in Dowlais. You wished for a written report of them for the Witness, but I must disappoint you in that for the time being—for my friend, Mr. W. Roberts, Blaenau, Gwent, is busy working to gather an account of the Mormons from their beginning to the present, with the intent of publishing it all in one low-priced Booklet, so that all the Welsh may come to know of them to the greatest detail.

1847: November, *Seren Gomer* (*Star of Gomer*), p. 347 (390 words). "Lectures on Mormonism."

This is also a letter from Edward Roberts explaining the delay in the publication of his pamphlet.

1847: December, *Seren Gomer* (*Star of Gomer*), pp. 374–75 (965 words). "A Lecture on Mormonism."

Dafydd Lewis describes the 2 November 1847 lecture by Edward Roberts:

> Mr. Roberts, with exceptional skill, brought this absurd patchwork to the attention of the respectable audience which was before him, showing the weakness of the system, that had no strong defense for its assertions than what was in that dull and idiotic book [a reference to Dan Jones's forty-page Review of the Lectures of the Rev. E. Roberts]; not to mention the weakness of its reasoning (?), that it was offensive to Welsh as a language, in which it was—and calumny against the common sense of the Welsh that such rubbish is being brought to their attention. Pay attention—IT WAS PRINTED ON THE RHYDYBONT PRESS; no other press could be obtained that is enough of a prostitute to give birth to such a monster!

Lewis describes those in attendance:

> The Chapel of Ebenezer was too small to hold the listeners who wished to be present; and in the audience that was inside we found our town's most respectable inhabitants from amongst all the religious denominations—Calvinists—Wesleyans—Independents—Baptists—and the Anglican Church—even priests.

And he ends his review with a sixteen-line poem by Twm o'r Nant, a well-known Welsh poet. Here are the first four lines:

> "There is only deceit and trickery,
> Going on in this business,
> Because of asking and enquiring to understand the squares,
> Like the fortune-tellers, it pays."

1848: January, *Y Tyst Apostolaidd* (*Apostolic Witness*), pp. 21–22 (855 words).

Lewis's Star of Gomer[45] article was also printed one month later in the Apostolic Witness, minus his comments on the press at Rhydybont and minus the sixteen-line poem printed at the end of the Star of Gomer version.

1848: February, *Twyll Mormoniaeth. Darlith a draddodwyd gan y Parch E. Roberts, Gweinidog y Bedyddwyr, Rhymney* (*Deceit of Mormonism. A Lecture Delivered by the Rev. E. Roberts, Minister of the Baptists, Rhymney*), pamphlet, 23 pages.

The long-awaited pamphlet, Deceit of Mormonism, was available in February 1848 for sixpence, the same price charged for admission to Roberts's first lecture. The date in the preface is 4 February 1848. The contents are a Welsh translation of materials taken from the writings of Eber D. Howe, John C. Bennett, and Henry Caswall.

On 29 November 1847, Roberts lectured once more against Dan Jones and the Latter-day Saint religion while in North Wales. No further mention was made of Roberts in *Prophet of the Jubilee* or *Zion's Trumpet* until 1850, when a note was inserted in the January Zion's Trumpet: "He [Roberts] was thrown from Rhymney to North Wales, and from North Wales to Liverpool where he now earns his living hawking tea, having been excommunicated from the Baptists for transgressions we do not wish to bring to mind."[46]

1848: *Adolygiad ar ddarlith olaf y Parch. E. Roberts, Rymni, yn erbyn "Mormoniaeth"* (*A Review of the Last Lecture of the Rev. E. Roberts, Rhymni, against "Mormonism"*), pamphlet, 12 pages.

Dan Jones's forty-page *Review of the Lectures of the Rev. E. Roberts* did little to discourage the determined Baptist minister of Rhymney. On the evening of 2 November 1847, two months following Roberts's first two lectures in Dowlais, Roberts delivered yet another lecture against the Latter-day Saints, this time at the Ebenezer Chapel in Merthyr Tydfil. Before Roberts's third lecture, Dan Jones sent a copy of his forty-page *Review* to Roberts so that the Baptist minister would have "the advantage of seeing his false ideas."[47]

The following week, on 10 November 1847, Dan Jones delivered a lecture at the White Lion Inn in Merthyr Tydfil to review Roberts's latest presentation. He enumerated and condemned over thirty of Roberts's accusations and contradictions and said it was obvious that those in attendance "loathed the slanderous, disgraceful and unwarranted attack" which Roberts had launched against the Latter-day Saints. Jones's comments are in his twelve-page pamphlet entitled *A Review of the Last Lecture of the Rev. E. Roberts, Rhymney, against "Mormonism."*[48] Jones also announces that Roberts and others can spare themselves the trouble of preparing their elegies and funeral sermons for Mormonism, and then Jones makes this prophecy: "There will be a call for the funeral sermons for Mr. Davies, from Dowlais, Roberts from Rhymney, Dafydd Lewis and the Editor of Star of Gomer, together with all her persecutors before she [The Church of Jesus Christ of Latter-day Saints] dies; yea, before there is even one sign of illness!"[49] *Review of the Last Lecture* appears to have been published in February 1848. Jones declares on page 2 of this second *Review* that he had delayed its publication because he was awaiting the appearance of a pamphlet by Roberts.

Jones also declared in his *Review of the Last Lecture* that Roberts had done nothing more than single out two minor details: (1) the use of the formal you in place of the familiar thou in addressing the reader, and (2) the use of the word debate where no official challenge to a debate had ever been issued. This nitpicking, observed Jones, hardly represented the "unusual dexterity" which Lewis claimed for Roberts.[50]

1848: April, *Y Tyst Apostolaidd* (*Apostolic Witness*), pp. 96–97 (515 words). "Deceit of Mormonism."

An unsigned review of the twenty-three-page pamphlet which the Reverend E. Roberts published following his lecture on November 2 the previous year in Rhymney. Roberts dated the preface of this twenty-three-page pamphlet as 4 February 1848 and signed it with his nom de plume "Iorwerth Glan Aled," the translation of which is "Handsome lord from the banks of the River Aled" (a river in North Wales). The writer of the review, probably William Williams, the editor of the *Apostolic Witness* at that time, observed:

> I think the publisher should have done a better job, but the author is not responsible for that. Iorwerth did his part very well; he did a considerable amount of research on the history of the Saints, as they are called, and he put the result before us in a compact, clear and very powerful manner.

The reviewer praises Roberts for shedding light on "the remarkable and superstitious proceedings and actions of the Mormons" and declares the "splendid lecture of Mr. Roberts . . . an excellent means of keeping the Saints from progressing further." Roberts had promised that he would "kill Mormonism in Rhymney on Christmas day and bury it the next."[51] The reviewer concludes:

> We would advise any of our readers who wish to know the history of this rabble to purchase the lecture of Mr. R. The name of the lecturer, together with the high approval he received from such a number of people in several places, is sufficient praise for it.

1848: May, *Seren Gomer* (*Star of Gomer*), pp. 142–43 (2020 words). "Deceit of Mormonism."

Effusive praise to the pamphlet recently published by the Rev. E. Roberts. This review of the pamphlet is much longer than the one in the *Apostolic Witness*[52] and contains several lengthy quotations from the pamphlet itself. Like the review in the

Apostolic Witness, this one in *Star of Gomer* is also unsigned, an indication that the author is most likely Samuel Evans, the editor of *Star of Gomer*. Evans's opening paragraph expresses complete confidence that the lecture, now in pamphlet form, will accomplish the stated objective of the Baptist reverend from Rhymney:

> And we have no doubt but what it fully answers the aim that the honorable and eloquent author had in mind—that is, to deal the death blow to the deceit of Mormonism.[53]

The editor's closing paragraph declares his belief that Edward Roberts has "performed an act of mercy" that will benefit all who read the pamphlet and who might otherwise have been bewitched by the deceitful "Mormons,"

> [B]y the delivering and publication of this splendid lecture, since it fully explains the whole deceit, so that, in our opinion, no Mormon could ever raise his head again having read it. We now present it confidently for the attention of our fellow countrymen, and hope that everyone will do his best to distribute it, particularly in the places where Mormonism has started to show its arrogance.[54]

1847: November, *Y Drysorfa Gynnulleidfaol* (*Congregationalist Treasury*), p. 342 (280 words).

A discussion of whether a minister—the Reverend J. Jones, Llangollen—should be allowed to print bad books.

End: The Rev. E. Roberts fails to "kill Mormonism and bury it by Christmas"

Episode 4.7

Start: Dan Jones declares the "Proclamation of the Latter-day Saints" blasphemy

1847: November, *Seren Gomer* (*Star of Gomer*), p. 341 (515 words). "Proclamation of the Latter-day Saints to their Compatriots."

This poem, authored by "One Who Would Wish to See Every Man and Woman a Saint," consists of fourteen six-line stanzas. The "narrator" of the poem pretends to be a Latter-day Saint. Here is the fourteenth stanza:

> We have secrets,
> Which no one knows but Saints,
> Of the most expert in our midst,
> Where fake miracles are wrought,
> So that we may exploit the innocent,
> And eliminate further dispute.

1847: December, *Prophwyd y Jubili* (*Prophet of the Jubilee*), pp. 189–90 (580 words). "The *Star of Gomer* and Its Religious Blasphemy!"

Dan Jones vents his outrage in the final issue of his periodical for 1847:

> What reasonable man can find worthy words to show the atrocity, the slander, and the sinfulness of that article that appeared in the *Star of Gomer* for

> November, under the title of "Proclamation of the Latter-day Saints to their Compatriots!" Was it not bad enough to publish lies about us under pseudonyms, and no names at all, and then this latest and ungodly deed of forging our names? Having the audacity to publish such slanderous rubbish in our own names!! That has really done it.[55]

End: Dan Jones declares the "Proclamation of the Latter-day Saints" blasphemy

Episode 4.8

Start: The "jabbering woman" in Newmarket is not a Latter-day Saint

1847: 4 November, *Yr Amserau* (*Times*), p. 3 (220 words).

The writer of this brief article begins with these two sentences:

> The Mormons pay frequent visits to this place [Newmarket, Flintshire]. It shows that the disciples of Joe Smith have a great liking for the place, and more of a desire to get the inhabitants of Newmarket from the reach of the destruction of the world to safe California, than to get the inhabitants of any other neighborhood in these parts.

The next two sentences had no connection to the previous sentences:

> A woman was jabbering some nonsense here on Monday night. The application of soap and water on her skin and clothes would not have been out of place, as she had great need of it.

And the only connection the writer makes with the next sentence is that the man who attacked a young girl is the woman's husband:

> The following Tuesday night this woman's husband attacked a young girl in an isolated spot about a mile-and-a-half from the village.

The remaining sentences have to do with the woman's husband and his attempt to have his way with the girl:

> Very fortunately for the girl, someone happened to come past in the meantime, and so she was spared. He was followed and caught in a tavern. It is said that he had on him several sharp weapons and plasters. He tried to put plaster on the girl's mouth to keep her from screaming, and in the struggle he missed the mark, and he put it on her cheek. He is now in the Flint jail "suffering persecution." It will be seen whether the family of miracles succeed in getting an angel to open the doors of that jail, and to lead this "saint" out.

1847: December, *Prophwyd y Jubili* (*Prophet of the Jubilee*), pp. 185–89 (2,025 words). "The 'Times' and Its Lying Slime on the Saints Again! Again!!"

In Jones's response to the "jabbering woman" account, in which no connection is established between the jailed man and the Church of Jesus Christ of Latter-day Saints, Dan Jones unleashes his understandable outrage at the editor for his obvious implication that there was a connection. Jones explains the grave injustice the editor had committed against the Latter-day Saint religion. Jones quotes the few lines the editor printed about a defense he had received from John Parry, a missionary in North Wales who was present at the time the woman was "jabbering some nonsense":

> No space can be given in *The Times* for the long letter of Mr. J. P. in defense of the Mormons, or the "Latter-day Saints;" for there would never be an end to the debate on such a subject. Our correspondent can have his article, if he calls at our office.

Adding to Dan Jones's frustration was yet another comment that appeared in the following issue of the *Times* (18 November 1847):

> William Smith, the Mormon prophet or patriarch, is now about to be tried for odious immorality.

In Jones's attempt to set the record straight by explaining that William Smith had been excommunicated two years earlier from the Church of Jesus Christ of Latter-day Saints, Jones addresses the editor as "Mr. Slanderer." But Jones's best efforts to defend his beloved religion against the constant stream of opposition did little to stem the tide. Even though the attention such attacks drew to the Church would at times have positive results, as in the case of William Howell—the minister in Aberdare who, after hearing the venom against the Church, became converted by reading one of Dan Jones's pamphlets—the hostility continued unabated.

1847: December, *Y Drysorfa* (*Treasury*), p. 391 (180 words). "Latter-day Saints."

This brief account also deals with the woman who was "jabbering some nonsense" in Newmarket, as reported by the *Times*. But the writer specifically states that she "professed the principles of the 'Latter-day Saints.'" Dan Jones makes no mention of this article in his response to the one in the *Times*, so either he was not aware of the article or he chose to ignore it.

End: The "jabbering woman" in Newmarket is not a Latter-day Saint

1847: November, *Yr Eurgrawn Wesleyaidd* (*Wesleyan Treasury*), p. 352 (270 words). "Latter-day Saints."

This brief report is of a Thomas Richard's court appearance for being drunk and disorderly while preaching on the streets of Cardiff. He confessed that the charge was accurate. The mayor ordered him not to preach until after living "three years in temperance." The final sentence is as follows: "Then the offender left the court greatly ashamed of himself." Except for the title of the article, there is no indication that Thomas Richard was a member of The Church of Jesus Christ of Latter-day Saints. Nor did Dan Jones print any reaction to the incident in *Prophet of the Jubilee*.

1847: December, *Y Dysgedydd* (*Instructor*), pp. 365–66 (940 words). "The Mormons, or the Latter-day Saints."

Using the nom de plume Eta Delta, the Reverend Evan Davies presents the "foundational topics" of this religion as they appear in the March 1847 issue of *Prophet of the Jubilee*.[56] He declares that the Saints have "a very narrow, low, and erroneous view of the entire Bible" and then concludes the following:

> In short, it appears that they are well known for insisting, challenging, arguing, maligning, and rebuking everyone who differs from them as they explain the Bible. They scorn education and scholars, and all books except their own.[57]

Finally, he laments the Saints' claims of success:

> They say they are having notable success in Merthyr Tydfil, Dowlais, Nantyglo, Tredegar, Penycae, Sirhowy, Coed-duon, Abersychan, Cwmbach, Llwyni, Rhymney, Cardiff, etc. Is this true? Are the people in South Wales so ready to reject the Bible, and accept the Book of Mormon, and the dreams of the late Joseph Smith from America? I do not think so ill of them.[58]

1847: December, *Seren Gomer* (*Star of Gomer*), pp. 375–76 (935 words). "A Warning to the Welsh—Religious and Non-religious."

The warning that the Reverend W. R. Davies sends to his compatriots is to beware of "a swarm of idle, characterless, and lazy little men . . . walking all through the different counties of Wales, pretending to preach the gospel freely." He claims that they "hawk certain old, senseless, worthless books and pamphlets full of lies" and that they are the "chief refuse of Merthyr." The men to which Davies refers, of course, are converts to The Church of Jesus Christ of Latter-day Saints endeavoring to proselytize the Welsh. Davies uses much of the article to answer charges made about him by Dan Jones in the August[59] and September[60] issues of *Prophet of the Jubilee*. Jones had accused Davies of being "off for three months without preaching once in any of his chapels, and on his return got £50 from his devotees at home." A very frustrated Davies responds as follows:

> Although it is seen by the writer that I am the man who was off. I was off more than a year ago, visiting my relations, etc. "Three months" was it? No, six weeks and three days. There are certain limits to lies in ordinary people; but concerning the lies of the "Satanists", they are like the ocean. "Received £50." Pooh, why didn't they say £500? That would be just as true.[61]

After venting his anger, Davies declares the following:

> And following my thoughts now, I shall not pay any attention to them ever again, but let them alone in peace to die in their filth.

Davies, however, did not keep his promise. The written battle between him and the Latter-day Saints continued until his death of cholera in September 1849.

Episode 4.9

Start: Should the Baptists rebaptize a repentant Latter-day Saint, or not?

1847: December, *Seren Gomer* (*Star of Gomer*), p. 368 (700 words). "Questions to the Rev. Daniel Jones, Minister of the Baptists, Felinfoel."

This open letter from the Reverend W. R. Davies to a fellow Baptist minister consists of several observations about the "Satanists," i.e., "the followers of that evil, deranged, hypocritical, and lying wretch, Joe Smith." The question that Davies poses to his colleague has to do with members of the Baptist faith who have converted to The Church of Jesus Christ of Latter-day Saints: "Does the Church of God have some way, or is it possible on the basis of the Bible, to receive these persons back into the unity and communion of the saints and the family of God?"[62]

1847: December, *Y Tyst Apostolaidd* (*Apostolic Witness*), p. 268 (700 words). "Questions to the Rev. Daniel Jones, Minister of the Baptists, Felinfoel."[63]

1848: January, *Y Tyst Apostolaidd* (*Apostolic Witness*), pp. 18–19 (1,620 words). "To Mr. William R. Davies."

Although the two letters of the Reverend W. R. Davies to the Rev. Daniel Jones are very similar,[64] the two very lengthy responses of Reverend Daniel Jones to Reverend W. R. Davies are quite different. The objective of both missives is to point out the numerous flaws of the Latter-day Saints in doctrine and procedure and to eventually answer Davies's basic question as to readmission to the Baptist faith by rebaptism for those returning after receiving baptism from the Latter-day Saints.

> My earnest and determined thought, with respect to receiving them back, is that we ought to recognize the difference between some and others.

The Reverend Daniel Jones then gives an illustration of some who might be readmitted:

> As for one who was enticed to them by his wife or her husband, after having the excuse of a transgression in the church and being excluded from communion, and went to the [Satanists] S-t-n-ts in tribulation, what I think is that there is a difference between the two to be carefully considered by the church of God.[65]

As for those who wish to leave the Latter-day Saints after being baptized by them but who had not ever been baptized by the Baptists, here are Daniel Jones's thoughts:

> Regarding those who had not been baptized prior to joining with them [the Latter-day Saints], and then leaving them and returning to the church of Christ, there is no need to doubt if their profession of faith and their life are satisfactory, whether they should, without hesitation, be baptized in the strict sense of the word, for the thing they received under the name of baptism, is nothing more than a vile forgery.[66]

1848: January, *Seren Gomer* (*Star of Gomer*), pp. 19–20 (1,685 words). "To the Rev. W. R. Davies, Dowlais."

This response from the Rev. Daniel Jones is considerably different from the one in the *Apostolic Witness* in its phraseology; however, his basic premise is that the doctrine and the people in the Church of Jesus Christ of Latter-day Saints are evil. As to Davies's fundamental question about rebaptism into the Baptist faith, the Reverend Daniel Jones words his response in the following manner:

> If someone who was baptized conventionally, and went to this wretched crew, were to return to the church of God, can he be taken back, because he was admitted to the church on profession of his own faith, etc.—I think we should be very cautious; that is how I shall be until the next Star, and I trust that I shall satisfy you then.[67]

A search in the 1848 issues of *Star of Gomer* for further clarification about the readmission and rebaptism of errant Baptists yielded no results.

1848: February, *Y Tyst Apostolaidd* (*Apostolic Witness*), p. 40 (165 words). "To Mr. W. R. Davies."

One who calls himself "A Lover of Order" poses the following question to W. R. Davies:

> If one of these men who call themselves saints, without having professed with the Baptists previously, received his baptism from the apostle, and then confesses his foolishness and their deceit, and during his repentance puts himself before the church and is received, would you immerse such a one again?

1848: March, *Y Tyst Apostolaidd* (*Apostolic Witness*), pp. 69–70 (760 words). "Answer to Lover of Order."

W. R. Davies was prompt to answer the question in the very next issue of the *Apostolic Witness*. It is entirely possible that Davies himself wrote as A Lover of Order so that he could set up his answer in the March issue of the periodical. He refers to the answer which the Reverend Daniel Jones gave to the same question in the January 1848 issue of the *Apostolic Witness*:

> In the first place, I direct you to the review of Mr. Daniel Jones, in the *Witness* for January, page 19; I am of completely the same opinion as he. Every evangelical ordinance is administered according to rules, and in consultation with the church of God, and with worthy and appointed persons; were it not so, they would not be ordinances of Christ. The low, ungodly, and arrogant manner in which the satanic fiends take upon them to administer baptism, as they do with every other thing they have, is frightening.[68]

The answer Daniel Jones gives on page 19 of his article is as follows:

> Regarding those who had not been baptized prior to joining with them, and then leaving them and returning to the church of Christ, there is no need to doubt, if their profession of faith and their life are satisfactory, whether they should, without hesitation, be baptized in the strict sense of the word, for the thing they received under the name of baptism, is nothing more than a vile forgery. Worse in my opinion than children immersing each other in the summer while playing; their imitation of baptism was a useless illusion to satisfy the conscience.

But Davies openly admits to having baptized one who had, in fact, been baptized by the vile "Mormons":

> I baptized one from them lately, in Caersalem to the Christian faith, who, said he, had been baptized in the middle of the night by a man who all those acquainted with him knew (though at the time was a priest in the Melchizedek order) that he had the same amount of grace in his heart as did Judas Iscariot.[69]

Apparently, at least according to Davies, it was permissible to "rebaptize" such a person. But in the strict sense of the word it would not be a "rebaptism" since the first experience could not be called a "baptism" because it had been performed by someone without the proper authority.

Davies then presents four reasons for condemning all baptisms performed by any members of The Church of Jesus Christ of Latter-day Saints:

1. Since they baptize at night there may not be witnesses to ascertain total immersion.
2. It cannot be a Christian baptism since they do not customarily use the names of godly persons when they baptize.
3. They give too much respect to the ordinance, claiming that they go down into the water as sinners and rise up perfectly clean.
4. The ministers are "the lowest characters in all knowledge and behavior, having not one sign of common courtesy or morality."

"In short," he concludes, "their baptism is nothing more than deceit, and the greatest infernal presumption that the heart has ever imagined. . . . it is nothing more than infernal mockery and insult to the ordinance of great Jesus."[70]

Davies's final sentence in the article has this statement:

> No one but one woman from Caersalem went to them from the beginning until now.[71]

This, of course, is the same assertion he had made in the September 1847 issue of the *Apostolic Witness*.[72] But, as pointed out in the previous chapter of this commentary, one of his former parishioners by the name of Job Rowland claimed to have received his baptism into The Church of Jesus Christ of Latter-day Saints on 13 January 1847. Rowland's mother and his two brothers, presumably from that same congregation, also converted and were passengers on the *Buena Vista* in 1849.[73]

1848: March, *Prophwyd y Jubili* (*Prophet of the Jubilee*), p. 37 (355 words). "Return of the Prodigals."

Regarding the return of faithful converts to The Church of Jesus Christ to their former religious beliefs and requesting a rebaptism, Dan Jones had a much different view from that of the Baptists. In this article, Jones reports the sad experience of Herbert Walters, "the only one from the midst of all the Saints who turned to them":

> O! if they could hear him now telling of his bitter experience, from the sufferings of a guilty conscience day and night because of what he had done. . . . He earnestly wishes for the forgiveness of the Saints for that which he did against them, and for a part in their prayers for God to forgive him and keep him in the face of all temptation ever again.[74]

1848: May, *Prophwyd y Jubili* (*Prophet of the Jubilee*), p. 76 (455 words). "What Is to Be Done with the Editor of the Star of Gomer?"

With tongue in cheek, a Latter-day Saint in the town of Carmarthen directs this question to the Reverend Daniel Jones, Felinfoel, in order to make sport of the Reverend W. R. Davies, who had asked the same Reverend Jones regarding the rebaptism of errant Baptists who had received baptism at the hands of the Latter-day Saints. Benjamin Jones, the writer, mockingly asks Daniel Jones concerning the fate of Samuel Evans, the editor of Star of Gomer, who had recently been excommunicated from the Baptist church in Carmarthen.

1848: May, *Y Bedyddiwr* (*Baptist*), p. 188 (155 words).

This is a request from Edward Williams for the editor to print the good news of the arrival of the Reverend H. W. Hughes in Maesteg (twenty-four miles to the southeast of Swansea). Williams reported that the new minister had baptized eleven in a short period of time, a number that included two "who had been very zealous with the Latter-day Saints."

The editor responds in a footnote:

> We do not consider it an honor for the church to receive anyone who has been so insane as to be with the Mormons. We would have the same doubt in receiving some from the insane asylum as in receiving them.

1848: June, *Prophwyd y Jubili* (*Prophet of the Jubilee*), pp. 88–90 (1,690 words). "The Baptists Baptize 'Satanists and Demons!!'"

After attempting to shame "that meek servant of God who preaches the gospel of peace of the Baptists in Dowlais" (i.e., the Reverend W. R. Davies) for teaching "the children of his God to shout 'Satanists and demons' after their neighbors along the streets," Dan Jones declares:

> But an even greater surprise is the readiness of the Baptists, and their great eagerness, to baptize those whom they would call "Satanists and demons!" Yes, they strive in every way, by saying puffed-up words of futility, and the appearance of humility in religious will, to entice back the occasional weak woman who is new in the faith, who had escaped once from their heresies to the way of truth; and at last the Baptist screams through its screeching trumpet the victorious news that two women who had been with the Saints have been baptized by the Baptists in Llwyni, namely two she-Satanists or she-demons, of course! Good gracious! here are the Baptists baptizing "Satanists and demons," namely those whom they themselves call such!

Jones ends his lengthy harangue at Davies and the Baptists by concluding:

> Baptizing "Satanists and demons," is it! Good heavens! who knows how long it will be before hell itself becomes all Baptists!

End: Should the Baptists rebaptize a repentant Latter-day Saint, or not?

Episode 4.10

Start: Did James Strang really perform a miracle, or was it just phosphorus?

1847: December, *Y Diwygiwr* (*Revivalist*), p. 391 (235 words). "Mormon Miracle."

This piece is taken from a brief article carried by the *Ottawa Free Trader*, and the editor declares the newspaper's "assurance of its truth." The article has to do with a "miracle" performed by James Strang, one of the many who sought to lead The Church of Jesus Christ of Latter-day Saints following the martyrdom. Strang had promised to his followers that he would show them an "uncommon gift" if they would build a house for him and his family. After the house was built, he anointed their heads with a mixture of oil and phosphorus and then took them to a dark room where their heads shone "as if with the brightness of the sun." When one of his followers accused him of deceit, Strang admitted the deceit and explained that it was all to prove that "all the miracles of Moses and Jesus Christ were accomplished the same way."

1848: January, *Prophwyd y Jubili* (*Prophet of the Jubilee*), pp. 3–6 (2,105 words). "Mormon Miracle."

In response to David Rees, the editor of *The Revivalist,* Dan Jones points out that James Strang had been excommunicated from The Church of Jesus Christ of Latter-day Saints long before his "miracle" and that he was no longer a "Mormon." Jones also takes issue with the phrase "assurance of its truth," and then presents the Welsh translation of a letter of Elder William Atholl McMaster in which McMaster describes some true miracles which had occurred in Scotland through the anointing with oil and the laying on of hands—speech was restored to one sister and sight was restored to two brothers.

1847: 5 November, *Welshman*, p. 1 (320 words).

A brief account of "the prophet Strang" and his miracle with phosphorus.

1847: 6 November, *Monmouthshire Beacon*, p. 4 (320 words). "A Mormon Miracle."

A brief account of James Strang performing a miracle with phosphorus.

1847: 13 November, *Monmouthshire Merlin*, p. 4 (120 words). "A Mormon Miracle."

A brief account of "Stacey" [Strang] and his miracle with phosphorus.

1848: January, *Y Bedyddiwr* (*Baptist*), pp. 16–17 (910 words).

Reverend W. R. Davies sent two items to be published by *The Baptist.* The first article is about the reward offered by Governor Reynolds for the apprehension of O. P. Rockwell, and the second is the Ottawa Free Trader article that has to do with James Strang and his miracle.

1848: January, *Y Drysorfa Gynnulleidfaol* (*Congregationalist Treasury*), pp. 31–32 (305 words).

A slightly different version of the *Ottawa Free Trader* article about James Strang and his miracle.

1848: February, *Y Drysorfa Gynnulleidfaol* (*Congregationalist Treasury*), pp. 37–38 (935 words).

This is the same article, with only minor variations, as is in the January 1848 issue of the *Baptist,*[75] also submitted by W. R. Davies.

End: Did James Strang really perform a miracle, or was it just phosphorus?

1847: December 24, *Cambrian* (785 words). "Latter-day Saints."

This article consists of a letter sent to the editor by one of his subscribers. It is actually the English translation of an article taken from *Yr Amserau* (*The Times*), and it features some of the Latter-day Saints in the neighborhood of Ystradgunlais. The article says that "the wife of one of the Saints became deaf in consequence of fever." Her husband declared that she was "possessed of a devil." His efforts to cast out the devil drew the attention of neighbors late at night. Three "Elders" of the couple's new church were called when one of their children sprained an ankle. The blessing pronounced by the couple's coreligionists was ineffective, as was a blessing given to one of the couple's other children who was "sick of fever." Later a child in the family fell down and sprained his ankle. The efforts of three elders were not successful to heal him. The writer offered a suggestion to his compatriots:

> Welshmen! Many are your privileges and numerous are your advantages. How long will you be blinded and seek after errors of this kind? Let us rise as one man to expose the Saints' deceit, that they may not gull the ignorant multitude any longer with their fanaticism.

Notes

1. *Prophet of the Jubilee,* January 1847, 16–18.
2. *Prophet of the Jubilee,* January 1847, 36.
3. The facsimile translation is in Section 2.
4. The facsimile translation is in *Defending the Faith: Early Welsh Missionary Publications,* item J10.
5. See *Welsh Mormon Writings,* 54–57.
6. The facsimile translation is in *Defending the Faith: Early Welsh Missionary Publications,* item J13.
7. The biography of William Howells is posted on the Welsh Saints Project.
8. *Prophet of the Jubilee,* December 1847, 192.
9. *Prophet of the Jubilee,* February 1847, 30.
10. Ibid., 28.
11. Ibid., 30.
12. *Apostolic Witness,* January 1847, 17.
13. J. T. Jones, *The Correct Image, Wherein One Can Perceive Clearly the Deceit of the Mormons, of the "Latter-day Saints," in the Form of Questions and Answers, between Daniel and His Friend,* January 1847, 8.
14. 15 July 1847, 219.
15. Translation in Section 3.
16. Davis revealed his identity in the 1847 volume of *Prophet of the Jubilee,* 181, in his response to "H. Tegai."
17. *Prophet of the Jubilee,* December 1847, 181–85.
18. Ibid., 181.
19. Ibid., 185.
20. *Prophet of the Jubilee,* May 1847, 69.
21. *Prophet of the Jubilee,* June 1847, 93.
22. *Prophet of the Jubilee,* September 1847, 138.
23. Ibid., 139.
24. *Prophet of the Jubilee,* August 1847, 120–23.
25. *Prophet of the Jubilee,* September 1847, 134–37.
26. *Prophet of the Jubilee,* August 1847, 121.
27. Ibid., 121–22.
28. Dan Jones, *History of the Latter-day Saints,* 95.
29. The facsimile translation of *History of the Latter-day Saints* is item J12 in *Defending the Saints: Early Welsh Missionary Publications.*
30. *Apostolic Witness,* September 1847, 201.
31. *Apostolic Witness,* September 1847, 199–201.
32. *Apostolic Witness,* October 1847, 225.

33. *Prophet of the Jubilee*, October 1847, 151.
34. Facsimile translation in *Defending the Faith*, item J14.
35. *Review of the Lectures of the Rev. E. Roberts*, 5.
36. *The Origin of the Spaulding Story*, Philadelphia, Brown, Bicking and Gilbert, 1840.
37. *Review of the Lectures of the Rev. E. Roberts*, [2].
38. *Millennial Star*, 9:318.
39. Ibid.
40. Ibid.
41. *Prophet of the Jubilee*, November 1847, 173.
42. *Millennial Star*, 9:364.
43. *Zion's Trumpet*, April 1849, 78.
44. A biography for William Howells is in *Supporting Saints* (Provo, UT: BYU Religious Studies Center, 1985), 43–81.
45. *Star of Gomer*, December 1847, 374–75.
46. *Zion's Trumpet*, January 1850, 32. Facsimile translation in the "Pamphlets" section.
47. Dan Jones, *A Review of the Last Lecture of the Rev. E. Roberts, Rumney, against "Mormonism,"* 1.
48. Facsimile translation in *Defending the Faith: Early Welsh Missionary Publications*, item J14.
49. Ibid., 10.
50. Ibid., 1, 8.
51. *Prophet of the Jubilee*, March 1848, 40.
52. *Apostolic Witness*, April 1848, 96–97.
53. *Star of Gomer*, May 1848, 142.
54. Ibid., 143.
55. *Prophet of the Jubilee*, December 1847, 189.
56. *Prophet of the Jubilee*, March 1847, 37–39.
57. *Instructor*, December 1847, 366.
58. Ibid.
59. *Prophet of the Jubilee*, August 1847, 120–23.
60. *Prophet of the Jubilee*, September 1847, 134–37.
61. *Star of Gomer*, December 1847, 375.
62. The same article, with minor variations, as in the *Apostolic Witness*, December 1847, 268.
63. The same article, with minor variations, as in *Star of Gomer*, December 1847, 368.
64. *Star of Gomer*, December 1847, 368, and the *Apostolic Witness*, December 1847, 268.
65. *Apostolic Witness*, January 1848, 19.
66. Ibid., 19.
67. Ibid., 19.
68. *Apostolic Witness*, March 1848, 69.
69. Ibid.
70. Ibid., 70.
71. Ibid.
72. *Apostolic Witness*, September 1847, 201.
73. *The Call of Zion: the Story of the First Welsh Mormon Emigration*, 118.
74. *Prophet of the Jubilee*, March 1848, 37.
75. *Baptist*, January 1848, 16–17.

Chapter 5

Episodes

5.1—Elder Thomas Harris spends two months in jail for stealing a dictionary
5.2—Four accounts entitled "Baptizing an Apostle" are published
5.3—Benjamin Job Davies writes letter from America—his brother receives baptism
5.4—Dan Jones attacks five periodicals—the Reverend W. R. Davies angrily responds
5.5—"Anthony Fair Play" sinks to a new low—Dan Jones is irate
5.6—Elder Abel Evans defends himself from the allegations of "A Listener"
5.7—Phillip Sykes defends the Church from charges made by the Reverend W. R. Davies
5.8—The Ivorians cause twenty-nine Latter-day Saints to be dismissed from the mine
5.9—John S. Davis explains "Spiritual Gifts" to the "Observer from the North"
5.10—John S. Davis defends against the charges of an excommunicated Baptist
5.11—John S. Davis offers proof of a miracle to the "Hater of Deceit"

Salient Events

- **January 1848.** Elder Thomas Harris is sentenced to two months in jail, without hard labor, for stealing a dictionary. See Episode 5.1.
- **January 1848.** Branches, branch presidents, and numbers of members are reported in the January 1848 issue of *Prophet of the Jubilee*, pp. 9–10:

Branch	Branch President	Number of Members
Merthyr Tydfil	W. Phillips	606
Penydarren	T. Griffiths	53
Dowlais	Alfred Clark	145
Rhymni	William Davies	58

Branch	Branch President	Number of Members
Cwmbach	John Price	33
Aberdare	J. Davies	30
Hirwaun	Daniel Davies	22
Dihewyd	J. Richards	13
Cardiff	W. Jenkins	38
Llwyni	Samuel Davies	28
Cwmbychan and Bryn	T. Pugh	63
Treboeth	J. Matthews	21
Cyfyng	Wm. Davies	17
Cwmaman	J. Griffiths	12
Pont Yates	H. Williams	39
Llanelli	Wm. Hughes	103
Carmarthen	Ben. Jones	37
Llanybydder	T. Jeremy	29
Brechfa	David Jeremy	30
Monmouthshire Conf.	W. Phillips	262
Pembrokeshire Conf.	J. Morris	40
Throughout the North	[not listed]	109
Throughout Garway	W. Henshaw	145
Total	[n/a]	1933

- **February 1848.** A letter written by Abednego Williams is printed in *Prophet of the Jubilee*, pp. 27–29. His conscience smitten, Williams writes to Dan Jones to beg forgiveness of all the Saints for having composed a nasty ballad about them, one that had become quite popular in Nantyglo and the surrounding environs. Since composing the ballad, Williams had converted to Mormonism himself and now had to hear his own words against the religion he now espoused being sung on the streets.
- **March 1848.** Dan Jones prints the account of Herbert Walters in the *Prophet of the Jubilee*, p. 37. Herbert Walters had abandoned his Church membership when he heard the lectures of the Reverend Edward Roberts in Dowlais in September 1847, but soon afterwards he was repentant for having done so and wished to be permitted to come back into the fold. Jones was happy to welcome him back along with others who were repentant for similar reasons. Jones was also happy to call the attention of the Reverend W. R. Davies to this return.
- **March 1848.** Dan Jones taunts the editors of five periodicals. See *Prophet of the Jubilee*, pp. 37–42, for Jones's high-spirited response to the *Revivalist*,

the *Star of Gomer*, the *Apostolic Witness*, the *Instructor*, and the *Baptist*, followed by his assessment of the Reverend Edward Roberts's attempt to "kill Mormonism."

- **March 1848.** Phillip Seix (Sykes) is excommunicated. See Episode 5.7.
- **March 1848.** Rees Price, the "right hand man" to the Reverend W. R. Davies, is baptized in Dowlais. See *Prophet of the Jubilee*, September 1848, pp. 131–33, for Price's detailed account of his conversion and the crass treatment he and his wife received from Reverend Davies and members of his congregation. Also see *Prophet of the Jubilee*, March 1848, pp. 45–47, for a detailed update of missionary activity in various parts of Wales.
- **April 1848.** A Latter-day Saint in Pembrokeshire receives a severe beating while simply standing at the door where a Church meeting was being held. See *Prophet of the Jubilee*, May 1848, pp. 60–61, for Elder John Morris's letter describing the incident.
- **April 1848.** The broken bones of a young boy are healed after receiving a blessing from the elders. Thomas Rees, one of the earliest converts in Merthyr Tydfil, writes about administering to his eleven-year-old son, who had broken his leg at the Cyfarthfa Colliery. The doctor who set the broken bones stated that the boy's leg had been broken in two places. The bones knitted together immediately after the father's priesthood blessing, whereupon the neighbors began to claim that the bones had not been broken. The names of three witnesses who had heard the diagnosis of the doctor are given at the end of the letter. See the account in *Prophet of the Jubilee*, pp. 61–63.
- **May 1848.** Dan Jones chides the Reverend Edward Roberts for failing, as he had promised, to "kill Mormonism and bury it the next day." See *Prophet of the Jubilee*, May 1848, pp. 77–79, for a detailed update of missionary activity in various parts of Wales.
- **July 1848.** The fifth and final segment of the *Scriptural Treasury* is published, a total of 288 pages. This reworking of Benjamin Winchester's *Synopsis of the Holy Scriptures and Concordance* did not turn out to be as popular with the Welsh Saints as Dan Jones had hoped. Six years after its publication, Robert Evans asked Dan Jones about a second edition and was informed that "hundreds of copies" of the first edition had been languishing in stock for years.[1]
- **September 1848.** A branch of Welsh Latter-day Saints is created in Minersville, Pennsylvania. See *Prophet of the Jubilee*, September 1848, pp. 138–39, for the letter of Thomas Richards about the small branch of Welsh speakers who were working in the mines to obtain money to travel to Utah and join the main body of the Church there.
- **September 1848.** It is announced that the first group of Welsh converts are to leave from Liverpool in January or February the following year.[2]
- **December 1848.** Thomas D. Giles, although blind because of a coal mining accident, is called as the president of the Monmouthshire Conference. Over the following six years, various men were called to assist him in carrying out

his responsibilities. In 1856, he crossed the plains in the Bunker handcart company. Near Fort Bridger, he became seriously ill. After holding back the company for two days, Captain Bunker ordered the camp to move on, leaving two men to bury Giles when he died. It was expected that death would come in a matter of hours. Elder Parley P. Pratt, who was headed east on the trail, came by and gave Giles a blessing in which he promised him that Giles would be instantly healed and arrive safely in the Salt Lake Valley, where he would rear a family and be permitted to live as long as he wished. These blessings were all fulfilled, and he lived another thirty-nine years. He was known as the "Blind Harpist" and made his living playing the harp and singing hymns and popular songs of the day at dances and other events. His profile and journal are on the Welsh Saints Project website.[3]

Commentary

Episode 5.1

Start: Elder Thomas Harris spends two months in jail for stealing a dictionary

1848: 1 January, *Monmouthshire Beacon*, p. 4 (55 words).

A Latter-day Saint (Thomas Harris) is arrested and taken into custody for stealing a dictionary:

> A Latter Day, or Mormon, preacher, has been taken into custody at Bronfre, near Llanayron [Llanerchaeron], on the charge of stealing a Welsh Dictionary from the Crown public house at Llandewi Aberarth. His reverence, who, we are ashamed to confess, is a printer, was preparing his sermon at the time he was apprehended with the book upon him.

1848: 1 January, *Monmouthshire Merlin*, p. 3 (55 words).

Same report as printed in the *Monmouthshire Beacon*, 1 January 1848, p. 4.

1848: January, *Prophwyd y Jubili* (*Prophet of the Jubilee*), pp. 14–16 (1,330 words). "Announcement."

Dan Jones reports that Harris had been sentenced to two months in prison on 4 January 1848 and that he had also been excommunicated from The Church of Jesus Christ of Latter-day Saints "not for intentional theft, but because of his neglect for the honor of his religion under these dangerous circumstances, which were known to him."[4] The "neglect" was that of not returning the book "the minute he realized that another man's property was in his possession" even though "he did not take the book intentionally."

1848: February, *Seren Gomer* (*Star of Gomer*), p. 64 (65 words).

A frequent critic of the Latter-day Saints, the editor of *Star of Gomer* was no doubt elated to report that an LDS elder was punished for stealing a dictionary:

One of the "Latter Saints" by the name of Thomas Harris, who was on a preaching journey through Cardiganshire, was punished in the last Tri-Monthly Court of that county for stealing a dictionary from a house where he was lodging. He said, in his defense, that the "evil one" tempted him. But he was not enough of a "prophet" to foresee the consequences.

1848: February, *Y Bedyddiwr* (*Baptist*), pp. 75–76 (510 words). "The 'Saint' Turned Thief."

The editor of the *Baptist* had also printed a number of articles portraying the Latter-day Saints as "Satanists" and here presents a number of details about the Thomas Harris incident not found in the *Star of Gomer* or the *Monmouthshire Beacon*—i.e., that Harris had worked as a printer for the Reverend J. Jones of Llangollen, that he had "learned to preach Mormonism" with Dan Jones, and that he eventually confessed that he had stolen the book after first denying it.

The prisoner confessed that he had stolen the book and that it had been in his pocket when he [the book's owner] had asked him about it. He also confessed that he had scratched out the owner's name and that he was sorry for that.

1848: May, *Prophwyd y Jubili* (*Prophet of the Jubilee*), pp. 72–74 (1,145 words). "The Saint out of Prison, and his Defense."

Dan Jones is no doubt happy to announce the release of Thomas Harris from prison. He explains:

> After Thomas Harris was released from prison, there was a further inquiry before the Council of the Glamorgan Conference, where it was unanimously permitted that he should have his church membership, on the conditions that he go through the environs where he had been preaching when the unpleasant misfortune had taken place, and to make known there, in order to remove the obstruction out of the way of the honest in heart, the truth of all the aforementioned circumstances.

Also in this issue of the *Prophet of the Jubilee* is a letter, dated 25 March 1848, written by Harris and William Evans, in which they outline the various places and persons they visited as Harris fulfilled the conditions Jones described for being readmitted to the Church of Jesus Christ of Latter-day Saints. Evans, perhaps as a witness to visits made, describes Harris's meeting with the owner of the book in question:

> After that, we went to Llanddewi Aberarth, where the owner of the book in question lived. We soon told the people what was in our message, and they then took the news to the village, where the people came together joyfully to see Thomas Harris; but no one was more pleased than Mr. Davies, the owner of the book, who gave his hand affectionately to T. H., confessing in the presence of the crowd these words: "I never believed, my dear Harris, that you had stolen the book deliberately; and whatever trouble you have had, I can say that it has not been more than has been on us as a family, because of this circumstance."[5]

Evans then describes Harris's own report concerning the book:

> Then Thomas Harris gave a report of the way he found the book in his pocket without knowing how it had come to be there. He admitted also that he was at fault for neglecting to return the book at once himself, instead of trusting another to do that, during which the tears were streaming down the cheeks of Mr. Davies, the owner of the book, out of sympathy.[6]

Jones adds to the Evans and Harris letter a postscript describing an inquiry that was held before the Council of the Glamorgan Conference, the members of which voted unanimously to welcome Harris back into the Church. During the meeting, "additional supportive testimonies of the story" were brought forth, testimonies that "demonstrated even more clearly that T. H. had no intention of stealing this book." Jones then tells of a man who, after Harris's preaching at Davies's house, "obstinately argued with" Harris. This same man appeared at the house the next morning and "was the first one to utter a word about the book, to call the attention of the family of the house to it." He said that he would "guarantee that the Saint had stolen it, and then ran to fetch the policeman with no one asking that of him." The implication is, of course, that this man had planted the dictionary in Harris's pocket, where it was found by the policeman.

Jones laments the ceaseless persecution of the "slanderous Editors of our country" against The Church of Jesus Christ of Latter-day Saints in Wales and adds:

For example, notice the filthy [periodical] *Baptist,* and its "scratched out his name," "admitted that he had stolen it," etc., etc., when there was not a syllable of truth in them.[7]

End: Elder Thomas Harris spends two months in jail for stealing a dictionary

1848: *Llyfr Cronicl Prophwydi Mormonaidd. Ychydig o hanes Gweithredoedd Twyllodrus, rhai o'r "Seintiau y Dyddiau Diweddaf." Ynghyd a Melldithion Ofnadwy Duw, ar Gau Brophwydi a'r Rhyfygus* (*A Chronicle Book of the Mormon Prophet. Some of the Deceitful Deeds of Some of the "Latter-day Saints." Together with the Frightful Curses of God, on the False and Arrogant Prophets*), pamphlet, 12 pages.

The first section of this pamphlet consists of just two pages (pp. 3 and 4) and is labeled "Mormon Deceit." The writer begins by expressing his disappointment that so many of the people in Wales have been deceived by the Latter-day Saints. He then presents a brief narrative of a failed attempt on the part of two of these "Mormon prophets" to restore life to the daughter of one of the members, who had died:

> The manner in which they attempted to do this was by filling her body with oil, and after that by blowing air into her through a tube!!!

But it was all in vain, "for they failed to breathe into this girl the breath of life, and the dead remained dead." The writer then tells of an old woman who testified that the two "Mormon prophets" had nearly destroyed her feet by anointing them with the oil used in their attempt to restore life to the girl who had died.

The third and final story is that of a Latter-day Saint shopkeeper who was about to travel to Bristol to purchase some shoes to sell in his shop. He was put in a quandary when he received a request to baptize some new disciples—should he respond to the request immediately or take care of his errand first? He knelt down and prayed for guidance, and when he arose, the box he planned to take to Bristol was full of shoes. "Thus, the prophet was able to go to baptize the disciples."

The other three sections of the pamphlet are entitled "The Judgments of God on False Prophets," "The Judgments of God on Blasphemers," and "The Judgments of God on the Breakers of the Sabbath." None of the random examples presented in these three sections about false prophets, blasphemers, and breakers of the Sabbath bear even a remote connection with The Church of Jesus Christ of Latter-day Saints or its members. If Dan Jones was ever aware of this very strange pamphlet, he makes no mention of it in any issue of his monthly periodical or in any of his own pamphlets.

1848: 22 January, *Monmouthshire Merlin*, p. 3 (220 words).

In Abersychan, a Latter-day Saint woman felt ill. After receiving a blessing from the elders, she felt "as fresh as a lark." When her husband said it was all "a fib," one of the elders shouted at him. The husband then went to the pub, taking the key to the house with him. When his wife asked him for it, he refused, "saying that as she and the saints could do such miraculous things, she had better try her hand without a key." The woman said "she would wash her hands of the saints, elders, and all, . . . a consummation which has given much satisfaction to her husband."

1848: January, *Y Bedyddiwr* (*Baptist*), pp. 16–17 (910 words).

The Reverend W. R. Davies sent two items to be reprinted in the *Baptist*. The first item was a notice was taken from the *New York American*, 10 October 1842:

> Governor Reynolds has offered a reward of six hundred dollars for the apprehension of O. P. Rockwell, the Mormon assassin of Governor Boggs, and Joseph Smith as an accessory; or three hundred dollars for each of them. Also a reward of one hundred and fifty dollars for James Bratton, charged with the murder of William Claybrook; and one hundred and fifty dollars for John Taylor, charged with the murder of L. D. Bowen.

To this brief paragraph, the Reverend W. R. Davies adds his own comments:

> Dear Welshmen, here are the founders of the pure religion for you! Here's a shining man for the eternal God to choose to set up his kingdom on earth!! A man, because he helped to kill an American governor, fleeing like Cain long ago, and the government printing handbills and offering rewards for his capture! May hell be surprised! That one Welshman could sink so low and lend an ear to listen to the followers of such a crowd!

Davies obviously treats the information given in the *New York American* as fact, without bothering to note that Governor Boggs had survived the attack. The second item he sent was an article taken from the *Ottawa Free Trader* that has to do with James Strang. (See the discussion about the *Revivalist*, December 1847, p. 391 for details. Dan Jones's very thorough treatment of the topic is found in *Prophet of the Jubilee*, January 1848, pp. 5–6.)

1848: February, *Y Drysorfa Gynnulleidfaol* (*Congregationalist Treasury*), pp. 37–38 (935 words).

This is the same article, also submitted by W. R. Davies with only minor variations, as is in the January 1848 issue (pp. 16–17) of the *Baptist*. It is surprising that a Baptist minister would have his writing printed in a Congregationalist periodical. And even more surprising is that this Congregationalist periodical would actually print a lengthy response from President Dan Jones, the leader of the Latter-day Saints in Wales, in their March 1848 issue (pp. 76–78). See the discussion further down.

1848: February, *Y Diwygiwr* (*Revivalist*), p. 68 (145 words). "Tricks of a Saint."

According to this brief account by "Dewi" [Davey], a "Saint from Neath" negotiated a contract to dig five hundred tons of ore. Thanks to the efforts of twenty workers, he completed the task but decided to keep all the money for himself. Dewi explains the "Saint's" justification for doing so:

> There was no harm in robbing some rascals who had never before had the opportunity to associate with angels, as he had done a week before that; and that the best way to practice his religion was to remove himself and the money as well and leave the poor workers to ponder about Saintliness.

1848: February, *Y Bedyddiwr* (*Baptist*), p. 76 (63 words). "Mormonizing a Woman."

This brief article reprinted from the *New York Standard* has this bit of information:

> The *New York Standard* says that Henry Cobb of Boston has recently divorced his wife Augusta because she has become a *spiritual wife* according to Mormon doctrine, and has gone to live with Brigham Young, the one who claims his right to be Joe Smith's successor. (People, you had better beware of the present-day Satanists lest they steal your wives.)

Episode 5.2

Start: Four accounts entitled "Baptizing an Apostle" are published

1848: February, *Y Tyst Apostolaidd* (*Apostolic Witness*), p. 52 (390 words). "Baptizing an Apostle."

This incident takes place "within one hundred miles of Machynlleth," in "a pool in the river which is known as Forge Pool." A salesman of pottery who was a member of The Church of Jesus Christ of Latter-day Saints, known as "Apostle, Ned the Pots," was approached by a young man who requested baptism at his hands. At midnight, a few of the local Church members gathered at the river to observe the baptism. According to the account, here is what transpired:

> After a prayer the two of them went down into the water, and, after reaching the intended depth, the young man proved that he was filled with some spirit,

> for he wrestled the apostle three times head over heels into the water and held him down each time until he was more than half drowned! The Satanists ran away, and left the apostle to work miracles; after freeing himself, he ran for his life, and in his fright and in his confusion he went out of the water to the wrong side, and climbed to a steep wooded hill, and made his way through the thorns and thicket.

The writer of the account observes:

> Of everything the Satanists have done from the beginning until this time, this is the thing most similar to a miracle of all: namely to be able to climb such a hill and work his way through such a place.

1848: February, *Y Bedyddiwr* (*Baptist*), p. 75, (385 words). "Baptizing an Apostle."

This article is very similar to one of the same title in the *Apostolic Witness* for February 1848, p. 52.

1848: May, *Seren Gomer* (*Star of Gomer*), p. 152, (175 words). "Baptism Battle."

Someone using the nom de plume "Iorwerth Gwynedd" gives his own version of the baptism in Machynlleth:

> One of the great apostles of the Saints one evening immersed some boy, three times over his head in succession, in a pool of water, "to the point that he almost lost his breath!!!" and then he let him go on his way full of the Holy Ghost in his baptism: but the poor boy in his fright, no doubt, ran up some uncommonly steep and high hill.

1848: July, *Seren Gomer* (*Star of Gomer*), pp. 203–4 (490 words). "The 'Baptism Battle.'"

Someone who calls himself "A Correspondent" provides a much more detailed and possibly a much more accurate account of the "Baptism Battle." Putting the event at "within one hundred miles of Machynlleth" is the first thing he disputes:

> It would have been just as correct for him to say, "not a hundred thousand miles from Machynlleth," or write about some event that happened, and that he knew about than to give an account completely at odds with what happened.[8]

He then explains that a young man from Forge, about a mile and a half from Machynlleth, decided to tell "Tom Ellis, the Post" that he was interested in getting baptized. Tom Ellis, according to the writer, was "one of the main apostles of the sect." Tom then talked with "Ned the Potter," and the two of them went to Forge that same night at about eleven o'clock to accompany the young man to the river. The writer then provides the details of the baptism:

> Having gone to the riverbank, which was scarcely a hundred yards from the house, the old apostle said some gibberish, and they went into the river; but before the Saint was ready to perform the ritual, the young man kicked up his feet three times, until the Saint was wet from head to toe. The old boy saw by now that the young man had intended to play a trick on him, and that the applicant had not returned to the true faith. He ran full pelt through the river

> to the other side; but he was unfortunate enough to hit the bank so that he went tumbling over twice. By then a crowd of children had hidden in an old barn nearby, and out they rushed like hunting dogs after the old Saint, and he was chased to the town quicker than he came from there. The old Potter had fled to a nearby hillside, when he saw the old Saint going down for the first time; and thus ended the Baptism Battle.[9]

End: Four accounts entitled "Baptizing an Apostle" are published

Episode 5.3

Start: Benjamin Job Davies writes letter from America—his brother receives baptism

1848: January, *Y Diwygiwr* (*Revivalist*), pp. 12–13 (1,275 words). "History of Joseph Smith in a Letter from America."

This letter is from Benjamin Job Davies in the United States to his brother Thomas Job in Wales. Davies claims to have made the personal acquaintance of Joseph Smith before his death four years earlier. He tells about the Spaulding manuscript as the source for the Book of Mormon and also mentions the apocryphal story of Smith's attempt to walk on water as well as his dressing up in a large dove costume for baptisms. Three years later, despite his brother's letter, Job converted to the church established by Smith. No response to Benjamin Job Davies's letter appeared in *Prophet of the Jubilee*.[10]

This letter appeared in print, with only minor differences, two more times during 1848: once in the April issue of the *Wesleyan Treasury* and again in the October issue of the *Instructor*. The annotated entries immediately below this entry provide information as to the differences in content of each.

1848: April, *Yr Eurgrawn Wesleyaidd* (*Wesleyan Treasury*), pp. 113–15 (1,380 words). "History of Joseph Smith, in a Letter from America."

This is the same letter that appeared in the *Revivalist* for January 1848, pp. 12–13. This version, however, has a brief note from a David Evans, Tredegar, describing his reason for transcribing the letter of Benjamin Job Davies and submitting it to *The Wesleyan Treasury*.

1848: October, *Y Dysgedydd* (*Instructor*), pp. 289–91 (1,550 words). "The Mormons. The Story of Joseph Smith, in a Letter from America."

This is the same letter that appeared in the *Revivalist* for January in the *Wesleyan Treasury* for April 1848. This version, however, has a lengthy postscript with details as to how misguided the "Mormons" are in their beliefs. The editor provides a list of certain aspects of their "false doctrine" that was meant to serve as a warning to all his readers to refrain from even talking with those who have been deceived by them.

1. They are idol worshipers since they believe that man was created in the likeness of God.
2. They do not understand the scriptures because they claim to have continual revelation.

3. They claim that there has not been a true religion in the world from the time of the apostles until the calling of Joseph Smith.
4. The "Mormons" are nothing but shameless and impudent deceivers, and many of them are more dangerous and poisonous than professed atheists.
5. Those in this country who have embraced their views are completely dark, unprincipled, and weak-minded people.

End: Benjamin Job Davies writes letter from America—his brother receives baptism

1848: March, *Seren Gomer* (*Star of Gomer*), p. 96 (55 words).

Not all the comments about members of The Church of Jesus Christ of Latter-day Saints in the religious periodicals in Wales during the 1840s and 1850s are in the form of articles. Some consist of just a few lines that are always negative with the objective of ridiculing them. Here is an example:

> Four of the "Saints" went to the Pantmawr, near Llanfynydd [near Brechfa] lately to pretend to preach; but while they were there babbling nonsense, the Musical Choir came past, and all the people ran out to listen to it, and finally the four Saints went out also, to take part in the *spree.*

Another example follows.

1848: March, *Yr Eurgrawn Wesleyaidd* (*Wesleyan Treasury*), p. 95 (85 words). "A Foolish Religion."

> Last Sunday morning, a man by the name of Frederick Weston was found in the yard of Mr. Beard, in Ovingdean, lying in his blood, having cut himself dreadfully. He was carried to the hospital, where he now lies in a sorry state. The man is thirty years old and belongs to the people known as "The Latter-day Saints." His intention, he says, in doing this was to do justice to God! Strange blindness! He did the greatest injustice to his own soul.

Episode 5.4

Start: Dan Jones attacks five periodicals—the Reverend W. R. Davies angrily responds

1848: March, *Prophwyd y Jubili* (*Prophet of the Jubilee*), pp. 37–42 (3,305 words). "What Is the Matter?"

Dan Jones includes in the March issue of his periodical a taunt of the chief opponents of his religion and their periodicals. He begins with a confident declaration of the failure of his enemies:

> The principality is on fire—its usurper is striking up for volunteers—the priests of great Babylon are on its towers blowing their horns, long and loudly, to gather all their armies to do holy sectarian battle against the Saints—their foundations are shaking—their armies are fleeing before the cannons of the truth—the giants of the principality are falling before the two-edged sword of the Spirit, and the others are enraged in the pangs of death—the devil is losing subjects in every battle—the hind parts of the great goddess are being bared—her worshipers are retreating from her temples in shame and enlisting under the banners

> of the King Jesus—the treacherous tricks of the chief leaders of the usurper are coming into full public view—his crown, and the hope of profit of his priests are about to fail!![11]

Jones then rails against the various periodicals that continually oppose the religion he represents. He declares that the *Times* has the horn that "is going to sound loudest in this massive campaign." He says that the *Revivalist* has "devoted as much as the enemies of Mormonism wanted of [its] columns to slander it." For the *Star of Gomer*, he makes a comparison: "It is like a bellows, blowing wherever there is a spark of the fire of malice, and away it goes until it sets the whole state on fire with all its might." As for the *Apostolic Witness*, Jones says, "it is marrow to thy bones, and honey to thy mouth under a pseudonym, like all false apostles and false angels, to show the length of thy filthy tongue against Mormonism forever." The *Instructor* has "cannons [which] roar to the point of startling the goatherds and the goats of Cader Idris, and driving them over the cliffs." Regarding the *Baptist*, Jones writes, "The last, and the dirtiest also, to come to our attention is Mr. *Baptist*, and its tasty stories." Regarding the Reverend Edward Roberts, the man who "promised to kill Mormonism in Rhymney on Christmas day and bury it the next," Jones says, "Of all the vain men who have been on the field against their common foe, the most stupid, the most impudent, and the most shameless, is that one who blows his strident horn from the Rhymney Valley."

1848: March, *Y Drysorfa Gynnulleidfaol* (*Congregationalist Treasury*), pp. 76–78 (1,530 words). "Dowlais Reverend and the 'Satanists.'"

This title has obvious reference to the Reverend W. R. Davies, who lived in Dowlais (a town about two miles from Merthyr Tydfil) and who was the minister of a congregation of Baptists in the Caersalem Chapel. This published letter to the editor is dated 2 February 1848 and is signed "An Observer."

"An Observer" in all likelihood is Dan Jones, Davies's favorite target during the previous two years since Jones's arrival in South Wales to assume the reins of leadership of The Church of Jesus Christ of Latter-day Saints for all of Wales. Not only had Davies preached against Jones and his religion from the pulpit, he had also authored numerous articles for a variety of religious periodicals to point out the "heresies" of the "Satanists," he had published a twenty-page pamphlet against them, he had recently invited his colleague, the Reverend Edward Roberts, to preach against them from the pulpit at Caersalem, and he had even encouraged little children to follow them in the streets and shout after them "Latter-day Satanists."

Jones had sent letters of response to earlier attacks published in the *Baptist* and *Star of Gomer*, two Baptist periodicals, but his letters were refused publication. This article in the *Congregationalist Treasury*—published in Swansea—appears to be the only writing of Jones ever to appear in any religious periodical in Wales except for *Prophet of the Jubilee* and *Zion's Trumpet*. And even more surprising is that the editor of the *Congregationalist Treasury* at that time was the Reverend Josiah Thomas Jones, the same minister whom Dan Jones accused of being the force behind the baptism of the blind man in Llanybydder about eighteen months earlier.[12] The reverend, however, placed the following disclaimer at the end of Jones's spirited response:

> We hope that none of those who receive the *Treasury* will take offense for our having published this one time an article of the foregoing nature, although it is not entirely in keeping with the principles of our publication.—Editor.

Possibly Josiah Jones softened his stance upon reading Dan Jones's opening statement in his 1,500-word letter to the editor:

> Sir,—Since your publication is free to oppose the "Satanists," it is reasonable to expect it to be free also to put out a word on their side; and because of that I am going to say a little at present.[13]

Or perhaps, as a Congregationalist minister, Josiah Thomas Jones actually relished the vicious attacks in his columns made by Dan Jones against the Baptist minister, W. R. Davies, with whose religious beliefs Josiah Jones had many issues. One is left to wonder.

Dan Jones begins his article with mock disappointment:

> It is strange how a man is disappointed. I thought that our fellow countrymen would never again have Mr. Davies's service in opposing the "Saints" when I saw the following from him in the *Star of Gomer* for December 1847: "Let me be allowed ONCE and for all, to note the following" (p. 375). "And following my thoughts now, I shall not pay any attention to them ever again, but let them alone in peace to die in their filth" (p. 376).

But Davies was certainly not going to retreat from his role as chief critic of those he referred to as the "Latter-day Satanists." Neither was Dan Jones going to pass up any opportunity to point out the inconsistencies and flaws in Davies's assaults. In this March 1848 issue of the *Congregationalist Treasury*, Jones produces a continual stream of cynical observations. Here are a few:

He refers to the *Baptist* periodical as the "*True Baptist*." During 1841, the Reverend John Jones, Dan's older brother, had published a series of articles offering scriptural evidence and discussion against baptism by immersion. These he bound and named "The Baptist." In January 1842, a group of Baptists in Cardiff, apparently offended that a Congregationalist minister would use that title in defending baptism by immersion, established a monthly periodical they named *The True Baptist*, thus delegitimizing Jones's title for his writings. After two years the word "True" was removed from the title, and the periodical was given the new name of the *Baptist*, a periodical that continued for many years.

1. He takes issue with Davies's citing of the *Christian Messenger* as proof of one of his claims about Joseph Smith. Jones responds: "I would like to know if the *Christian Messenger* is as truthful as the Bible, and if one can depend on its testimony as infallible?"
2. In a similar fashion, he objects to Davies's recommendation for anyone who doubts the truth of James Strang's "phosphorus miracle" to read the *Weekly Dispatch* for 31 October 1847: "What is this publication? Is it an inspired one, I wonder?"
3. He reacts to the letter from Benjamin Job Davies in the January issue of the *Revivalist* that contains the claim that Joseph Smith dressed as a large dove to be present at baptisms. Jones makes this sarcastic pun: "I com-

> mend the Reverend D. Rees, Llanelli, for publishing it, in order to *revive* the nineteenth century."

1848: June, *Y Drysorfa Gynnulleidfaol* (*Congregationalist Treasury*), pp. 168–70 (2,220 words). "Mormonism."

In the March (pp. 76–78) article three months earlier, the editor stated that the article of "An Observer" (most likely written by Dan Jones) was "not entirely in keeping with the principles of our publication," but he had no problem with printing the response by the Reverend W. R. Davies, a 2,200-word response that is overflowing with venom, hatred, and accusations. Davies had obtained a copy of the March 1848 *Prophet of the Jubilee* which carried Jones's blistering attack on his adversaries (p. 37–42), mentioning five periodicals by name: the *Revivalist*, the *Star of Gomer*, the *Apostolic Witness*, the *Instructor*, and the *Baptist*. Jones's blitz on his opponents enraged Davies, and he is like a man possessed as he responds to the claims of the "Observer."

Davies mentions his own February 1848 article in the *Congregationalist Treasury* and also Jones's response the following month in the same periodical:

> He [Dan Jones] did not dare to deny one of the facts noted in mine of February, but left them as they were. It is hard to struggle against truths as bright as the sun; yet it is clear that the "Observer" has not observed many things.[14]

Davies then proceeds to point out the weakness and inconsistency of the points made by Jones in his March 1848 article, except for some that he considers "not worth noticing." Here is a list of the issues that Davies either mentions, dismisses, or discusses:

1. James Strang and the "miracle of phosphorus"
2. Davies's promise that he would pay no more attention to the "Satanists"
3. The dilemma as to whether or not persons should be re-baptized by the Baptists once they have received baptism from the Saints and then wish to return to the Baptists
4. Contents of the March 1848 issue of the *Prophet of the Jubilee* that Davies had obtained and read with great bewilderment
5. Herbert Walters who had left the Saints to rejoin the Baptists and then because of great guilt returned to the Saints once again
6. Thomas Harris and the stolen dictionary
7. The excommunication of Philip Sykes from the Saints and the stealing of his money by Captain Jones
8. Daniel the blind man and the attempt to restore his sight in Llanybydder
9. The baptism of Davies's "right hand man" and of others from among Davies's congregation in Dowlais

To the assertion that Davies's "*right hand man*" had become a Latter-day Saint, he responds:

> I fear the devil of Nantyglo has taken possession of the man who wrote this brilliant story. The old Satan, father of all the Satans, could not have uttered

> more hellish lies. Remember that. It is certain that we expelled a man some time ago, and he went to them.[15]

One might fairly ask whether the expulsion occurred before or after the man's conversion. Job Rowland, the man in question and one of the Reverend Davies's former parishioners, wrote a letter to the editor of *Prophet of the Jubilee* in which he explained his reason for leaving Davies and the Baptist faith:

> But as soon as the Saints came to these areas, our teachers, especially Mr. W. R. Davies, began to persecute them and hate them, saying all manner of evil against them. Mr. Davies said one time in our house that his desire was to do the same with their elders as was done to Joseph Smith, that is to kill them. That, together with many other things prompted me to look into their principles.[16]

Davies concludes his somewhat disjointed and often confusing article with the following declaration about the Welsh converts to The Church of Jesus Christ of Latter-day Saints:

> There is not so much as one man of substance and influence as a MAN in their midst; NOT ONE in Dowlais, anyway, and they are only the objects of scorn with the irreligious; and objects of pity with every man who fears God.[17]

End: Dan Jones attacks five periodicals—the Reverend W. R. Davies angrily responds

1848: May, *Yr Eurgrawn Wesleyaidd* (*Wesleyan Treasury*), p. 147 (160 words).

A reader of the *Wesleyan Treasury* by the name of Newo Sdrawde [Owen Edwards spelled backwards], writes the following:

> Mr. Editor—I shall be highly grateful if you permit me, through means of your Golden Treasury, to express my most loving thanks that I could obtain the history of *Joe Smith*, confident of getting more of the history of his tricks, and also his virtues (if there be any), from month to month.

The writer no doubt makes reference to Benjamin Job Davies's letter about Joseph Smith that was published in the previous issue of the *Wesleyan Treasury*.

Episode 5.5

Start: "Anthony Fair Play" sinks to a new low—Dan Jones is irate

1848: May, *Y Bedyddiwr* (*Baptist*), pp. 186–87 (450 words). "Baptisms. Church of Meinciau."

Using the nom de plume "Anthony Fair Play," the writer declares his acquaintance with the goings on of the Baptist cause in the little town of Meinciau, about two miles northeast of Kidwelly. He states:

> But the most peculiar thing that I am aware of is that the Mormon rascals have sown seeds of lies, by saying far and wide that there are members of Meinciau, that the majority, but not all, have joined them.

He then explains:

> We declare that this claim is untrue, because there are only three of the members of Meinciau who have gone to the fraudulent rascals, and that one of these is like the *wandering Jew*, that is, that he had been with practically every sect of believers that are in our country, before coming to us in Meinciau; and we did not think as we received him as a member with us, that he would be with us more than a few others for long; but as long as he was with us he would grab onto some new sect.

And then he makes this astonishing declaration regarding one of the three converts:

> For as for the third, he is good for nothing but the dungheap.

1848: June, *Prophwyd y Jubili* (*Prophet of the Jubilee*), pp. 83–84 (1010 words). "False Accusations of the Baptists against the Saints Again!"

Dan Jones expresses his outrage at "Anthony Fair Play" and his assessment of the recent conversion of some members of the Baptist faith at Meinciau to The Church of Jesus Christ of Latter-day Saints. Regarding the writer's shocking conclusion about the third man, Jones responds:

> What! a man who was formed in the pure image of his God—a man who possesses an immortal soul—a man who is a member of society—a man who is a subject of the state, and his neighbor—yes, that man is "good for nothing but the dungheap!" Shame on the man who dared to publish such words before men! Who can believe a word of the man who said such a thing?

End: "Anthony Fair Play" sinks to a new low—Dan Jones is irate

Episode 5.6

Start: Elder Abel Evans defends himself from the allegations of "A Listener"

1848: 4 May, *Yr Amserau* (*Times*). "Noteworthy Miracles of the Saints."

The writer of this article calls himself "A Listener." Unfortunately, no copy of this issue of the *Times* has survived to the present, but two persons responded to it in later issues of the *Times*. The first respondent calls himself "Elias," and his article appears in the next issue (18 May, p. 7). He asks "A Listener" for the identity of the person referred to in the article as "the prophet." The second respondent signs his name as Abel Evans, and his article appears in the 15 June 1848 issue (p. 6). "A Listener" then responds to Abel Evans in the 29 June 1848 issue of *The Times*. Discussions of all three of these "response" articles follow.

1848: 18 May, *Yr Amserau* (*Times*), p. 7 (520 words). "The Spirit of Mary of the White Veil."

The author of this article is "Elias" from Tanygrisiau (near Blaenau Ffestiniog). In his opening statement, "Elias" refers to the article that had appeared in the 4 May 1848 issue, in which the author, "A Listener," expressed uncertainty as to the identity of the "prophet" who had lately been preaching in the areas of Ffestiniog.

"Elias," without identifying the "prophet" by name, compares him to "an old woman who lived in Anglesey during the last century who deceived many by saying that she was someone" known as "Mary of the White Veil." He then compares the "Spirit of Mary of the White Veil" to that of "the prophet" when he was at a special meeting that was held on Easter Sunday (23 April) at the home of David Peters, "near the village of Ffestiniog." A blessing was given by the "prophet" by the laying on of hands to Owen P. Jones, a thirty-year-old man who had received his baptism a few weeks earlier and who had lost the sight of one eye as a boy. According to the article, Jones lost the sight of the other eye as a result of the blessing and became totally blind. But according to his obituary,[18] Jones had lost his sight in a mine accident. The writer closes his article with the following advice to "the prophet":

> We think, Mr. Editor, that the prophet had best return to his own country, to his own people, and to his own followers, and let him deceive those if he can. Let him leave the innocent people of Ffestiniog alone, and let him never again put his bungling hands on their precious eyesight. How is it that men did not see the deceit and the audacity of these stupid *pretenders*?

Owen P. Jones emigrated on the *Hartley* in 1849, settled in Brigham City near the David Peters family, and was a mail carrier for many years before his death on 6 Jan 1894.

1848: 15 June, *Yr Amserau* (*Times*), p. 6 (925 words). "Defense of the Saints."

This is a response written by a Latter-day Saint missionary by the name of Abel Evans who was proselytizing in North Wales at the time. In the 4 May 1848 article in *The Times*, written by "Elias," Evans is sarcastically referred to as "the prophet." The editor of the newspaper gives the following disclaimer just before Evans's response:

> Not all ideas that appear in a publication which contains differing views are consistent with the personal opinions of the Editors; and one should not attribute to them the faults, any more than the virtues, in the style or the language of the correspondents.

Then, one by one, Evans clarifies the "miracles" mentioned by "A Listener" in his accusatory article:

1. He says that a woman from Criccieth, to whom he apparently gave a blessing by the laying on of hands, "ended up regaining her health." And he states that her name was Jane Roberts—apparently "A Listener" accused Evans of not providing her name.
2. He states that the name of the man to whom he gave a blessing in Rhosllanerchrugog was John, better known as "Jack the Tailor." Here again, "A Listener" accused him of not providing the name.
3. "A Listener" accused Evans of having claimed to place his hands on an eleven-year-old English boy "until he was so completely filled with the Spirit that he spoke in five languages right then and there." Evans denies ever having said "any such thing."
4. "A Listener" accused Evans of having claimed that "the Saints were baptizing from ten to thirty every week in Merthyr." Evans clarifies: "The Saints

were baptizing nine or ten some weeks in Merthyr, and that I had heard of their baptizing thirty in one week there."

5. Apparently "A Listener" had claimed that the "Saints had ceased to exist in Merthyr" when Evans stated that there were over six hundred Saints in the Merthyr branch. Evans reaffirms that the Merthyr branch did in fact have that many members.
6. Evans takes exception to being called "prophet" by "A Listener" and claims that it was "mocking blasphemy . . . in order to create prejudice against" him.
7. Evans also objects to the accusation of having claimed "miraculous power." He emphatically states it is God who works miracles, and not the Saints.

1848: 29 June, *Yr Amserau* (*Times*), p. 6 (240 words). "Defense of the Saints."

In this brief article, "A Listener" reacts to Abel Evans's "Defense of the Saints." He takes exception to Evans's reference to his article as a "distorted piece of writing" and also to Evans's criticism that "A Listener" did not know the names of the persons on whose heads Evans had placed his hands:

> I declare, and if I have life and health, I shall continue to declare, if need be, that I did not know the names of the persons for whom Mr. A. E. says he performed miracles until the previous issue of the *Times* came to hand.

Then he presents his evaluation of Evans's entire article:

> From start to finish, the "review" is the most slanderous declaration ever before seen. It would be too much respect for its author, a waste of *ink*, paper, and time, to go into detail about his distorted and deceitful phrases. Mr. A. E. is afraid to deny those things he said, although there are plenty of witnesses to prove that he said them. Now the Mormons are beginning to deny their miraculous power. Truly, it is time for them to do so, to their shame.

"A Listener" than avails himself of the opportunity to give Evans a piece of advice:

> For goodness' sake, Mr. Abel Evans, before putting your hands on either an English person or a Welsh person, do not blame others for reporting your stupidity, and put your hands on your own skull, for it appears to me that your head is quite senseless.

1848: 29 June, *Yr Amserau* (*Times*), p. 6 (185 words). "The 'Saints' and the Times."

Also in this issue of the *Times* is a brief and very sarcastic reaction to Evans's article by "M—th" in "V. Fawr." This writer mocks Evans's disavowal that he was ever a prophet:

> I am sorry that the old "earlier" prophet, namely the man who defended his brethren in your previous issue, has been dismissed (for he was once a prophet according to his own words).

Next the writer explains what he would do if Evans still had his prophetic powers:

> I would ask him for the proper name of one of his brethren who gave up reading *The Times* over a year ago, but without yet seeing fit to pay for the issues he had received.

End: Elder Abel Evans defends himself from the allegations of "A Listener"

1848: June, *Y Tyst Apostolaidd* (*Apostolic Witness*), pp. 138–40 (1,705 words). "Baptism for the Dead."

The writer of this article, the Reverend W. R. Davies, in addition to the topic suggested by the title, touches on several other characteristics and practices of The Church of Jesus Christ of Latter-day Saints. He begins:

> Strange are the extremes to which the children of men run in their views, in nature and religion; and of all the idiotic, superstitious religious fanatics who have ever come to the world, at least to Wales, in all of their creeds, the followers of Joe Smith surpass everyone and everything.[19]

Here is a list of issues that Davies discusses in his article:

1. The manner in which converts describe the feeling of receiving the Holy Ghost.
2. The very strange practice of baptizing for the dead.
3. The second baptism of a young couple who stole from a draper before their marriage, were both in jail for "a long term," and then received baptism again from the "Satanists."
4. Dan Jones's claim of great growth in numbers in Dowlais to the point of needing a bigger hall. Davies says the real reason for the new hall was because the owner of the tavern known as the "Dowlais Inn" no longer allowed them to meet there.
5. Davies denies the claim of Dan Jones in the March 1848 issue of *Prophet of the Jubilee* that Davies's "right hand man" had converted to the religion of "the Saints."
6. Dan Jones claimed that "several" of Davies's congregation in Dowlais had received their baptism from "the Saints." Davies vigorously disputes such a claim.

1848: June, *Y Bedyddiwr* (*Baptist*), pp. 209–11 (1,705 words).

The same article as in the *Apostolic Witness*, June 1848, pp. 138–40.

1848: June, *Yr Haul* (*Sun*), pp. 196–97 (475 words). "Dinner for One of the Preachers of the Latter-day Saints."

David Owen, the editor of the *Sun*, an Anglican periodical, had at one time been a Baptist. This account was written by "Ioan Ysgythrydd" (John, the Engraver). John relates a story of two women, residents of Kidwelly, who both converted to "the Saints' way." At one of their houses, they prepared a meal for one of the missionaries of their new religion. Before the dinner began, the lady of the house sent her husband, a member of the Anglican Church, into the garden because "she did not consider him suitable to sit down to dinner with people as pure and unsoiled as they." Here is the surprise ending:

> The husband, having considered for some time in the garden the disregard his wife was inflicting on him, ran into the house and into the parlor or the dinner room; and they were about to start; and in the twinkling of an eye, he snatched the *leg of mutton* from the dish, together with a sixpenny loaf from the table, and out he went, through the street of the town, with his plunder

> under his coat; and off he went towards his father's house, who lives about twenty miles away; and he feasted on them happily along the way.[20]

The "lady of the house" may well be Elizabeth Lewis, who emigrated in 1849 with her six children on board the *Buena Vista*.

1848: June, *Yr Haul* (*Sun*), pp. 187–89 (845 words). "The Shepherds of Epynt."

A regular feature in the *Sun* was "The Shepherds of Epynt," a conversation held among a few shepherds who tended their flocks in an area known as Mount Epynt, not far from Llandovery where the *Sun* was published each month. In the June 1848 issue, the conversation is between Idwal, a Nonconformist, and Ivor, an Anglican. Idwal expresses alarm at the high level of success of the "Mormons":

> We preach against Mormonism, write against Mormonism, and curse Mormonism constantly; but, for all of this, Mormonism succeeds despite us.[21]

Ivor agrees that "Mormonism" is a "deceitful, unreasonable, unscriptural, and blasphemous heresy" and then points out that, while large numbers of Nonconformists have converted to it, practically none of the Anglicans have done so. Idwal acknowledges that such is the case. Ivor questions the effectiveness of Nonconformity in combatting the new religion:

> There must be some significant mistake in your religious education; you must not be cultivating minds and teaching the people properly, otherwise a heresy and system of errors such as that of Joseph Smith could not trick the people away from you as it is doing at present![22]

Idwal counters weakly:

> Men will go after errors, despite everything; and the most sensible of men are enticed by heresies.[23]

At this point, Ivor presents his closing argument and places the blame for the success of "Mormonism" at the feet of the Nonconformists because they are not rooted in truth:

> That is true enough; but Mormonism is not a heresy in clothing, but a stark-naked heresy. Not a heresy with a pleasant bait on the hook, but a heresy with only the hook itself. Not a heresy appearing in the guise of the truth; but a shameless naked lie walking in the light, with its horns, its tail, its hooves, its whole deformity clear in every part of it; and this Mormon deceit, in all its unreasonableness, in all its enormity, and in all its disagreement with the Scriptures of the blessed God, has drawn scores if not hundreds of you after it! Much Mormon success is attributable to you; for you are not, for all your fuss, rooted and built in the sacred truth, and therefore you fall prey to the Spirit of Mormonism.[24]

1848: June, *Seren Gomer* (*Star of Gomer*), p. 180 (1,050 words). "Address to the Mormons, or Satanists, who misname themselves *Latter-day Saints*."

The author of this lengthy poem calls himself "A Well-Wisher to the Saints" as well as "E. D. S." at the end of the poetry following his 170-word postscript.

In Part I of the poem, consisting of fourteen stanzas of four lines each, the writer addresses the followers of Joseph Smith and explains as to how Smith has deceived them. The writer uses a number of epithets throughout to describe Smith—"wicked Joe," "great moneylender," "wicked wretch," "madman," "servant of Satan," and "thick-skinned man." Here is a sample stanza:

An arrogant, sorcerous family—always
At some work for darkness,
From them Jo is sprung—
Sore their appearance as a host will testify.

In Part II of the poem, consisting of twelve stanzas of four lines each, is a plea for the "Satanists" to "flee and run from the offensive swarm." To those who are planning to go to America to join with the main body of The Church of Jesus Christ of Latter-day Saints, the writer warns them to "watch the bright Captain, over there closely, lest he prove deceitful." The use of "Captain" is a reference to Dan Jones, their leader in Wales.

A third segment of this poem consists of twenty lines and is entitled "Joe's Address to His Puppets and His Half-Wits." The writer, in a mocking tone, has Joseph Smith bear witness of his mission and that of the Book of Mormon.

In his ending paragraph, the writer declares his intention to continue to speak out against the "bewitched people," pointing out that such is his duty to do his part to put a stop to the "godless scum which gibber under the name of preaching."

1848: July, *Yr Haul* (*Sun*), pp. 216–19 (2,135 words). "Mormonism."

The contents of this very lengthy editorial consist mainly of some philosophical considerations rather than any accounts of events in Wales. David Owen, the editor of the Anglican periodical the *Sun* and a former Baptist, writes:

> For years we have heard about Mormonism and have read some parts of the Book of Mormon; but we looked at and considered this organization as being like mist which would soon disappear, or as being like a bubble bursting on the surface of the water as soon as it was formed.[25]

But in the five years the new Church had begun proselytizing efforts around Merthyr Tydfil, more than three thousand new adepts had received their baptism. Such progress was not only astounding but also worrisome to religious leaders throughout the principality. Owen admitted that the new religion had lofty objectives:

> The Mormons profess that their efforts are to restore the Christian Church to its original purity, and do so in its teachings, in the administration of its ordinances, in its discipline, in its practices, and in everything that pertains to it; and as far as these are their intentions, they are honorable for their objectives.[26]

He further opines:

> And apart from the revelation of the Book of Mormon, there is nothing new in the Mormon System that is not already believed or professed by some Christian sect or other, since hundreds of years that have passed, without such requesting and waiting for new revelations.[27]

However, despite the positive aspects of the new religion, Owen continues to share the same view as W. R. Davies, Edward Roberts, and numerous other divines:

> It is a deceitful, blasphemous, and devilish heresy—a perfect *caricature* of Christianity![28]

1848: July, *Seren Gomer* (*Star of Gomer*), p. 221 (160 words). "The Trickery of the Saints."

This brief report is borrowed from the *Silurian,* or *South Wales General Advertiser,* published in Brecon. The writer reports that the "Saints," while preaching in the little towns of Penmarc and Llancarfan in Glamorganshire, had resorted to fabricated miracles, with one of them pretending to cure his own hand. The writer concludes: "All this work (for it cannot be called religion) appears to be shameful blasphemy; and it has only excited pity and scorn in the minds of all sensible people in these places."

Episode 5.7

Start: Phillip Sykes defends the Church from charges made by the Rev. W. R. Davies

1848: March, *Seren Gomer* (*Star of Gomer*), pp. 92–93 (400 words). "The Madness of One of the Satanists."

"T. E. J." reports that the Latter-day Saints have caused Phillip Sykes, one of their recent converts, to lose his money and his senses.

> He claimed more than once to have sinned unforgivably, and he is now in the madhouse at the expense of the parish.[29]

The writer says that he has sent this information to appear in the periodical "not to make the unfortunate wretch the object of ridicule, but as a warning to those who have not been bewitched by the accursed mob so far."

1848: March, *Prophwyd y Jubili* (*Prophet of the Jubilee*), pp. 43–45 (1,380 words). "Excommunication of Phillip Sykes, Blaina, Monmouthshire, from the Church."

Dan Jones goes to great lengths to explain the reason behind the excommunication of Phillip Sykes, a convert to The Church of Jesus Christ of Latter-day Saints who lived in the little mining town of Nantyglo. Jones says it was because of disobedience and not because Church leaders wanted to take Sykes's money:

> We have witnesses who heard him say that no one of the Saints was in his debt, but that he was in their debt. It never cost him a penny for food whenever he came this way, and the reward we have for our generosity to him is to be accused by his enemies, enemies to every good thing, of plundering his belongings, is it! But we shall not tolerate it any longer.[30]

Jones also placed a great deal of blame for Sykes's difficulties on his being afflicted with an evil spirit. Religious leaders had used the laying on of hands to cast out this evil spirit, but Sykes disobeyed their counsel and the spirit returned. Finally, Sykes's mental state deteriorated to the point that he had to be institutionalized.

1848: July, *Seren Gomer* (*Star of Gomer*), pp. 201–2 (1,685 words). "Satanists Casting Out Satan."

With this letter to the editor, the Reverend W. R. Davies continues the rage he had expressed in the articles he had published in three different periodicals—the *Baptist*, the *Apostolic Witness*, and the *Congregationalist Treasury*—the previous month. In this lengthy piece, he focuses on the report entitled "Excommunication of Phillip Sykes, Blaina, Monmouthshire, from the Church" printed in the March 1848 issue of *Prophet of the Jubilee*. Although Davies had already made a few comments about the Sykes episode in his June 1848 article in the *Congregationalist Treasury*, he had much more to add about it in this piece. He obviously takes delight in mocking the detailed account in *Prophet of the Jubilee* and showing the absurdity of the various steps the coreligionists of Sykes took to help him come to his senses. First he quotes from *Prophet of the Jubilee*:

> When his religious brethren understood what was troubling him—that it was the influence of the devil, etc., in accordance with the commands of Jesus Christ in such a circumstance (see Mark 16:18), they rebuked that evil spirit from him by the laying on of hands and the prayer of faith.[31]

Then Davies elaborates in his own words regarding the continual failure to resolve Sykes's distress:

> And in accordance with all reason and scripture, was the bedeviled creature restored to his sense forever? Oh, no, hardly! "But he went under similar influences as before." Is he, poor thing, left like that again? Oh no. "He got salvation again through the same means as before." Behold, has he now been completely purged, and has the evil one completely left him? No, no: "But again and again he was taken over by the same thing, or worse spirits, afterwards."[32]

Davies ridicules the Latter-day Saints for their unsuccessful attempts to rid Sykes of the "evil spirit," which Davies calls "the devil of Nantyglo," that had possessed him. Referring to his own success in gaining adepts to his Baptist chapel in Dowlais, Davies writes:

> We were quite hearty in Dowlais, until we saw "The Star of the Saints" [the *Prophet of the Jubilee*] that was noted; because when we saw some man or woman with more devilish signs than others, we were always talking about sending them to the Satanists to cast out the spirits. But now here we are up against the wall. What is the point sending anyone to them, lest the devil of Nantyglo be in the people?[33]

Davies ends with an earnest plea to the editor of the *Star of Gomer*:

> Now, Mr. Gomer, I ask you to give a place to this article in some corner of the *Star*, not because of worthiness of the foolishness it lays bare, but for the sake of our fellow countrymen in general, and the religion of Christ especially: perhaps its frightful blasphemy will be a warning to some innocent and ignorant persons, to keep away from the greedy wolves, and to avoid the philosophies of men and devils.[34]

1849: February, *Udgorn Seion* (*Zion's Trumpet*), pp. 31–32 (540 words). "The Testimony of Phillip Sykes, Blaenau, Monmouth."

Phillips Sykes writes to John S. Davis, the editor of the periodical, as follows:

> I wish to have space in the *Trumpet* to inform the public with respect to the lies that have been spread about me, about William Phillips, and about Capt. Jones, after I was placed in the insane asylum. I have now come out of that place, and am considered in my right mind, and am fully able to say what I know.

Not only did Sykes wish to realign himself with The Church of Jesus Christ of Latter-day Saints, but he also wished to set the record straight about the behavior of Church leaders toward him:

> At present I am not a member with the Saints, although I wish to join with them soon; but, at the same time, I would like to clear the characters of William Phillips and Capt. Jones in the face of the shameful lies told about them.

He closes his letter by removing all blame from his Church leaders and placing it on himself:

> I know that the Saints are good men, and that their religion is of God, and that they did their best for me. That which was out of place was not in the Saints, or their religion, but in me.

Davis adds a postscript to Sykes's letter with the following warning to the Reverend W. R. Davies:

> Before finishing, we would like to warn Mr. Davies that the "devil of Nantyglo" is now searching for a place to rest in dry areas; and if he is to avoid him, he should keep his interior, as it usually is, plenty *wet*.

End: Phillip Sykes defends the Church from charges made by the Rev. W. R. Davies

Episode 5.8

Start: The Ivorians cause twenty-nine Latter-day Saints to be dismissed from the mine

1847: March, *Prophwyd y Jubili* (*Prophet of the Jubilee*), pp. 49–51 (910 words). "The Ivorians Expelling Their Members because of Their Religion!!!"

Dan Jones launches a blistering accusation against the executives of the trade union.

> It is quite true that the committee of Lodge 299, Ivor Hael Lodge, Carmarthen Union, Ivorians, have expelled a party of religionists from their society, on the admission that it was because they dared to worship the God of heaven consciously according to the holy scriptures![35]

According to Jones, the catalyst behind the expulsion was Thomas Evans, a Baptist minister who took exception to the preaching of the Latter-day Saints in the hall of the Yew Tree Inn in the town of Blaina.

> [He] stood up to face them; and by doing so he showed his foolishness, bringing the reproach of the crowd on him, and causing the listeners to disregard him; and then he rushed out in shame.[36]

Jones further explains that Evans assembled a committee of a few men of influence within the trade union, called an "Ivorian inquisition" by Jones, and engineered the firing of all the members of Lodge 299 who had any connection with the Latter-day Saints. Jones furnishes the names of all the committee members and asks:

> What is the slavery of the most enslaved Negro in comparison to the Ivorite slavery of the fairest Welshman who dares to choose his own religion in his own free country?[37]

1847: September, *Prophwyd y Jubili* (*Prophet of the Jubilee*), pp. 141–44 (1,680 words). "To the One Who Calls Himself 'The Traveler of Nantyglo, or William Williams.'"

William Williams was a representative of the Ivor Hael Lodge 299 Carmarthen-based trade union located about fourteen miles to the northwest of Merthyr Tydfil. Dan Jones's first sentence is as follows:

> Sir, In a small essay of yours, you accuse *Prophet of the Jubilee* of containing an article, in which there were the "most impudent and shameless lies that man could possibly imagine.[38]

The "article" appears to refer to the one Dan Jones published in the March 1847 issue in the previous entry, but the "small essay" by William Williams has not been identified. Jones continues:

> If we were deceived in the story to which you refer, we plead, we demand, yes, humanity will force you, since you have made that accusation, to bring convincing and fair proofs that this story consists of impudent lies. A reasonable man will not consider "you are lying" as one proof of the matter in a debate. Oh no; nothing less than witnesses, or facts, will satisfy him who seeks the truth.[39]

He also points out Williams's use of such phrases as "these rogues have a mouth to swear, but no teeth to chew" and "secretive sneaks, despite scorn, slander, and reviling" do little to make a case against Jones and the religion he represents. He invites the men of Lodge 299 to defend themselves from the accusations made against them by their expelled members by sending proofs of their assertion that it is all an "impudent lie." He then assures them that their response "will have the most prominent place in the columns of the publication that you accuse."

1848: July, *Seren Gomer* (*Star of Gomer*), pp. 202–3 (1,590 words). "The Ivorians and the Saints," signed "The Traveler from Nantyglo."

This article is William William's defense on behalf of the trade union, a defense that Dan Jones had requested ten months earlier in the September 1847 issue of *Prophet of the Jubilee*. But instead of sending it directly to Dan Jones, Williams elected to send it to the editor of the *Star of Gomer* with the following greeting:

> Mr. Gomer—I beg you once again for space for what follows in your impartial *Star*, the only publication which is counted thus in our country. The True Ivorians will be most grateful to you for the favor, apart from many others who love for everyone to have the truth.

Then Williams addresses his remarks to "the editor of the *Prophet of the Jubilee*." And instead of offering some reason for the long delay, he begins with a very conciliatory tone:

> Sir: I have so much respect for you, that I fear you have done something without careful consideration; that is, accusing the Ivorians in a libelous and malicious way in your great zeal for a group of rioters who were expelled from the Lodge of Ivor Hael, the Saint David Union, near the Iron Works of Cwmcelyn and Blaina, of expelling their members (you say) because of their religion.[40]

He then explains in considerable detail that the "group of rioters" were all troublemakers who hurled threatening insults at members of the Lodge such as "If you do not believe our gospel, you shall be damned, and serve you right too" (English in original). Williams concludes that such awful behavior on the part of the "Saints" justified the actions taken against them by the Ivorians.

1848: August, *Prophwyd y Jubili* (*Prophet of the Jubilee*), pp. 115–17 (1,155 words). "The Persecution of the Saints in Cwmbychan and Bryn!—Twenty-nine Saints are turned from the mine because of their religion!!—Sectarian stewards attempt to starve about fifty wives and children of the Saints!!!"

This long title describes the action taken by the stewards of Lodge 299 of the iron works against all of their employees who were members of The Church of Jesus Christ of Latter-day Saints. This article was no doubt triggered by the article in the previous month's *Star of Gomer* by William Williams, although Dan Jones does not address Williams directly.

In his opening paragraph, Dan Jones reports that soon after twenty-nine of his coreligionists had been expelled by the stewards of Lodge 299, "the chief Steward was fired from his job by the Company." In his place was a Mr. Bidelph, who came to the works as the "chief overseer," and who Jones declared to be "much more charitable than the others mentioned."

The twenty-nine workers who had been fired because of their religion presented a petition of their grievances addressed to John Bidelph. The petition is quoted in its entirety in the article and contains details of the persecution of the stewards. Here is an example of the consequences the twenty-nine workers and their families suffered without just cause:

> And furthermore, those Stewards who turned us away from the mine have decided to drive us out of this country; they sent the Bailiff and the Policeman to turn us out of the houses, and to sell our furniture, if the rent money was not brought forward immediately, and through that depriving us and our families immediately, not only of food, but also of refuge or shelter against the fierce storms of February, and in the land of our birth.[41]

Dan Jones concludes the article with the following observation:

> Let the reader consider who is the God, and what is the kind of religion of these oppressors; and their cruelties and their wicked deeds do not prove which cause motivates them, any more obviously than they prove also the divinity of the religion and the godliness of the sufferers, and the truthfulness of the Son of God, namely, "Ye shall be hated of all men for my name's sake."[42]

The only date given in the petition is that of the month of February when the persecution was apparently at its high point. Without further information regarding this episode, one is left to conjecture about the approximate timetable of the events preceding the petition and the consequences that resulted from it. The following are some tentative conclusions:

1. The "small essay," written by William Williams after the *Prophet of the Jubilee* March 1847 article, preceded the September 1847 *Prophet of the Jubilee* article, since it was mentioned therein.
2. The only response to Dan Jones's September 1847 request to William Williams for a defense of the terrible treatment given the Latter-day Saints at the mine is the letter directed at Dan Jones that was sent ten months later to the editor of *Star of Gomer* to be printed in the July 1848 issue of his periodical.
3. The more severe treatment meted out to the "Saints" in February, combined with the dismissal of the inimical stewards, prompted the petition to Mr. Bidelph.
4. The stewards behind the severe treatment were at some point under review by their superiors before the somewhat-conciliatory letter by William Williams was printed in the July 1848 *Star of Gomer*.
5. Mr. Bidelph must have taken action against Williams and the other stewards shortly after the July 1848 *Star of Gomer* article in order for the petition to have appeared in the August 1848 *Prophet of the Jubilee*.
6. The only other article having to do with the expulsion of this group of Latter-day Saints from Lodge 299 is in the September 1848 issue of *Star of Gomer* (see next entry). But the writer, in place of offering any new information about the matter, reflects back on the annual meeting of the Ivorians held in Dowlais a year earlier and the discussion that occurred there. Referring to individuals as "an Ivorian brother," "one official," and "one old minister," he quotes them as agreeing wholeheartedly with the leaders of the Lodge who expelled the "mob of base wretches." Referring to the letter of William Williams in the *Star of Gomer* July 1848 article, this "Ivorian and Oddfellow Brother" concludes:

> I see, in the letter of the Traveler, that they tried to overturn the Lodge of Ivor Hael; but to the honor of our brothers there, they got what they deserved, that is their expulsion from the union; and it will be seen further, that they tried to persuade the public "that they are being persecuted because of their religion," when, in truth, they were rejected because of their blasphemy against religion, and their hellish arrogance, as the Traveler notes.[43]

1848: September, *Seren Gomer (Star of Gomer)*, pp. 268–69 (1,025 words). "The Ivorians and the Saints." This piece is item 6 in the above explanation.

End: The Ivorians cause twenty-nine Latter-day Saints to be dismissed from the mine

1848: August, *Seren Gomer* (*Star of Gomer*), p. 238 (160 words). "An Interpretation of the Dream of T. Hughes, Rhuthin."

A sarcastic and rather cryptic poem by "Little Davy" of Abercarn. Four years after this publication, "T. Hughes, Rhuthin" presented two lectures in the Town Hall of Rhuthin, which he later printed in two pamphlets (see Pamphlets 12 and 15 in Section 2). Here are eight of the twenty-eight lines of Little Davy's poem:

> John the angel was seen
> With the Gospel in his hand,
> Which he hid in an old cave
> On the land of distant America,
> And there it would be kept hidden
> Through the ages of the world forever,
> Had it not been for the *true godliness*
> Of the great Prophet Joe Smith!

1848: 4 August, *Yr Amserau* (*Times*), p. 3 (130 words). "Joseph Smith, the Mormon."

> We believe that Joseph Smith was shot. We understand from one of the publications in London that the full story of this wandering deceiver is at the press.

This very brief article quotes from another paper, the *Standard of Freedom.* The author then presents a few comments about the origin of the Book of Mormon.

1848: October, *Y Drysorfa Gynnulleidfaol* (*Congregationalist Treasury*), p. 306 (80 words).

Edmund Jones sends a question to someone referred to as "Caerwysion":

> Together with others, I wish for you to be so kind as to give to us through means of the *Treasury* the Lecture delivered by you lately in Glamorgan, on the beginning of the fall of Mormonism. By doing so you will do me a favor as well as the public in general.

No lecture by "Caerwysion" that fits the above description has been found as yet.

Episode 5.9

Start: John S. Davis explains "Spiritual Gifts" to the "Observer from the North"

1848: October, *Seren Gomer* (*Star of Gomer*), pp. 293–96 (5,230 words). "Spiritual Gifts."

This is the first installment of four by "Observer from the North." He begins with his concern:

> When we consider that there is a great heresy pertaining to the above topic, which has spread throughout South and North Wales; but that there are over two and a half thousand of our fellow men, yes, of our fellow nation, the Welsh, who believe (or *profess* to believe) that the spiritual gifts are enjoyed now in the church of the "*Latter-day Saints*," as they were in the churches in the age of the Apostles of old, it deserves serious consideration.[44]

The writer's objective is to show evidence that Dan Jones, the leader of The Church of Jesus Christ of Latter-day Saints in Wales, is totally misguided and that the church he represents is definitely not what Jones claims it to be. The writer announces that his focus will be on the topic of spiritual gifts as discussed by Dan Jones in his recently published *Scriptural Treasury*, a scriptural commentary of nearly three hundred pages.[45] What follows is a purely philosophical monologue of over five thousand words on the topic.

1848: November, *Seren Gomer* (*Star of Gomer*), pp. 327–29 (3,500 words). "Spiritual Gifts."

The second installment of the writings of the "Observer from the North."

1848: December, *Seren Gomer* (*Star of Gomer*), pp. 362–66 (6,100 words). "Spiritual Gifts."

The third installment of the writings of the "Observer from the North."

1849: February, *Seren Gomer* (*Star of Gomer*), pp. 42–46 (5,600 words). "Spiritual Gifts."

The fourth and final installment of the writings of the "Observer from the North." The writer indicated following the fourth installment that there would be more. Apparently the editor disagreed, as no further installments appeared in the *Star of Gomer*.

1849: April, *Udgorn Seion* (*Zion's Trumpet*), pp. 67–71 (2,100 words). "The Spiritual Gifts in the Court of the Enemy," first installment.

Since at this time Dan Jones was very busy making preparations to lead a group of converts to the United States in February, he likely did not have time to enter into a polemic with "Observer from the North." John S. Davis, however, elected to write answers to "Observer," someone he apparently knew personally, probably having worked with him at the *Star of Gomer* previously. Davis's writings to "Observer" were refused space in the *Star of Gomer*. Consequently, he published his answers to "Observer" in *Zion's Trumpet*.

He entitled his writings "The Spiritual Gifts in the Court of the Enemy," the "Court of the Enemy" being Davis's label for the *Star of Gomer* because, in his mind, the periodical was an enemy of the truth.

In this first installment, Davis declared that his publication, *Zion's Trumpet*, had insufficient space to review all of "Observer's" writings. In light of this, he explained what his approach would be:

> Therefore, let us pass over the parts where the Observer is snarling and lowering himself to misrepresentation, and let us go directly to the parts where he is as one trying to reason.[46]

Davis then adds another reason why he calls the *Star of Gomer* the "Court of the Enemy":

> The court of the *Star* is so different from other courts, that no one is allowed to bring forth anything in favor of the "Spiritual Gifts," rather everything must be against them.[47]

1849: May, *Udgorn Seion* (*Zion's Trumpet*), pp. 85–93 (3,800 words). "The Spiritual Gifts in the Court of the Enemy," second installment.

1849: June, *Udgorn Seion* (*Zion's Trumpet*), pp. 108–13 (2,520 words). "The Spiritual Gifts in the Court of the Enemy," third installment.

1849: July, *Udgorn Seion* (*Zion's Trumpet*), pp. 128–31 (1,720 words). "The Spiritual Gifts in the Court of the Enemy," fourth and final installment.

1849: July, *The Spiritual Gifts in the Court of the Enemy* (pamphlet, 24 pages). Following the printing of the fourth installment of his reply to "Observer," John S. Davis combined all four installments into a twenty-four-page pamphlet, the preface of which is dated 12 July 1849.[48]

End: John S. Davis explains "Spiritual Gifts" to the "Observer from the North"

1848: 30 September, *Monmouthshire Merlin*, p. 3 (400 words). "Extraordinary Occurrence."

The account of a young man named Reuben Brinkworth who, after having lost his hearing and his speech "in the midst of a storm of thunder and lightning," regained both hearing and speech upon being baptized a Latter-day Saint.

1848: September, *Seren Gomer* (*Star of Gomer*), pp. 264–65 (2,320 words). "Miracles."

The author of this very lengthy article gives only his nom de plume, "Iago Silin." The writer's opening statement is this:

> Strange how sin has brought down the human race to such a deep, damp swamp and the awful quicksand in which they are by nature—all open to the deceit of tricksters going out and about, and many being tricked by them.[49]

He then pinpoints the most recent generation of "tricksters:"

> And this generation will not pass without being tempted by the "Latter-day Saints," or some other Satans. These dreamers and imaginers fancy that they can turn the Almighty, who is without change or any shadow of conversion, from his own order, to operate according to their whim; but may God be truthful and the "Latter-day *Saints*" false in their words, and deceivers in their actions.[50]

After some rather extensive explication of scriptures having to do with miracles, referring to no specific modern events, the writer then closes by issuing a warning:

> Let us not listen to the performers of miracles and advocates of every baseless tradition; but rather follow the inspirational rule in everything, and pray greatly for the Lord to keep all of Wales out of the grasp of these Satanic arch-deceivers who are in our country, and out of the jaws of Capt. Jones, who is like a roaring lion walking about, seeking whomever he can to swallow.[51]

Episode 5.10

Start: John S. Davis defends against the charges of an excommunicated Baptist

1848: August, *Prophwyd y Jubili* (*Prophet of the Jubilee*), pp. 118–22 (2,520 words). "Anti-Mormon Sermon. To the Rev. T. Williams, Ebenezer, near Carmarthen."

John S. Davis was in the Ebenezer Chapel, Llangynog, on 2 July 1848 when the Reverend T. Williams presented his sermon. A few weeks later, the copious notes

Davis took appeared in the August 1848 issue of *Prophet of the Jubilee* as a harsh critique of the sermon. Davis writes:

> I am pleased to announce that you [Williams] preached better, in your manner, than I expected you could.[52]

He then points out a number of what he considers to be erroneous points in the sermon. He also takes issue with Williams's warning for his listeners not to give any heed to the preachers of The Church of Jesus Christ of Latter-day Saints, whose teachings he considered blasphemous. Davis closes with some stern counsel for members of Williams's own congregation:

> You members of Ebenezer, do you know what you are? I ask in all seriousness, do you know that you are "spirits in prison," and that the Rev. Mr. Williams is preaching to you, and that his intention is to keep you there for a long time? Oh, flee for freedom to the Mormons, "and you shall be truly free."[53]

No response from Williams to Davis has been identified; however, an excommunicated Baptist and editor of the *Star of Gomer* did have some pointed observations about Davis's article, which appeared in the October 1848 issue of his own publication.

1848: October, *Seren Gomer* (*Star of Gomer*), pp. 304–5 (1,910 words). "A Review of Mormonism, and the Rev. T. Williams."

The author, Samuel Evans, had recently been excommunicated from the Baptist faith but continued on as the editor of *Star of Gomer*. Here he presents his thoughts and opinions about Davis's article, calling it "worthless and shapeless." He also declares that "telling lies is one of the most remarkable characteristics of Mormonism." He had such a low opinion of Latter-day Saints that he even uttered this prophecy regarding Dan Jones and the group of Welsh members of the Church he would be taking to America in a few months' time:

> Having got enough money to get a ship or ships to voyage to California, their Leader will sail to Cuba and sell them as slaves, every man jack of them. That would serve them right for having so little respect for Christ's book as to give it up for the Book of Mormon.[54]

And having worked for some time as Davis's boss at the *Seren Gomer* office in Carmarthen, Evans believed that he should give him some advice:

> Seeing some ignorant and selfish dwarf of a man inflate with self-importance is a scandal to humanity. It would be wisdom for J. Davies [Davis] to follow the profession that is most familiar to him, and leave teaching the people to those who have received the gift. It is a beautiful characteristic in everyone that they know their place.[55]

End: John S. Davis defends against the charges of an excommunicated Baptist

1848: October, *Yr Haul* (*Sun*), p. 333 (180 words).

The editor warns his readers of the "Tractarians," also known as the "Puseyites," who he claims "are at work day and night spreading the deadly Roman poison in every manner and means they can." Apparently, some of the vicars of the Anglican Church were open to bringing Catholicism back to England and Wales. The editor fears that if these efforts were made "under the mantle of any kind of Sectarianism" that the Welsh "are ready to receive it." He adds: "Evidence of this is the success of the Mormons."

1848: 14 October, *Monmouthshire Beacon*, p. 4 (13 words).

The great Mormon Temple, at Nauvoo, has been purchased for a Protestant College.

1848: November, *Yr Haul* (*Sun*), pp. 354–55 (185 words). "Llandovery versus Mormonism."

This is a poem of eight stanzas of four lines each. The poet, "Anti-Mormon," could well be the *Sun*'s editor, David Owen. The opening stanza makes it clear that the people of Llandovery are ready to deal with the missionaries who preach in their town:

Mormonism is trying
To extend its dwelling place;
To Llandovery it now has gone,
But it will find no succor there.

The writer makes it clear that the people of Llandovery are self-sufficient and have no need of anything the missionaries might offer them, including speaking in tongues and working miracles. Furthermore,

Nearby is Brutus once more,
Killing evil vipers,
Of every color, and every kind,
And he will kill Mormonism.

"Brutus" is the nom de plume of the Reverend David Owen, and (if Owen is indeed the author) he obviously feels totally competent to deal effectively with any doctrine, practice, or stratagem the missionaries might introduce to his town. He makes clear his position concerning the hated "Mormons":

Therefore, I shall end now,
Shouting to the utmost,—
Of every trick that has come to the world,
Mormonism is the meanest.

1848: November, *Y Cyfaill o'r Hen Wlad yn America* (the *Friend of the Old Country in America*), p. 345 (15 words).

The Mormon temple in Nauvoo burned to the ground on the 9th of last month.

1848: November, *Y Drysorfa Gynnulleidfaol* (*Congregationalist Treasury*), p. 350 (130 words).

A brief report that "one of the Mormon priests" had been put in jail in Carmarthen for debt. The writer poses two questions:

> Why do they not work a miracle for this believer, by causing the doors of the prison to open and allow him to go free? Or why did Thomas the Blacksmith,

> their authorized prophet, not tell him that such a thing could happen to him? . . . We hope that this lesson will teach this creature, when he comes out, to think more about his calling, and not allow himself to be hoodwinked any more by the Mormon sorcerers and their crazy followers.

1848: November, *Seren Gomer* (*Star of Gomer*), p. 348 (225 words). "The Saints."

"Gwilym" reports that in the Pontypridd area, a recent visit of "their Captain" had caused "quite a commotion." The writer expresses bewilderment regarding the Latter-day Saints' baptismal services:

> They administer the ordinance of baptism sometimes, and at night as well; but what reason they have for that I do not know; they probably have some reason out of the strange book of Mormon.

The writer states that the "Saints" are not all in agreement regarding miracles, as "some assert that they can perform them, and others to the contrary." He leaves the readers to judge for themselves after reading the following account:

> A meeting of the Saints was held very recently in a house in this area. Before long after they had gathered, the room went dark, and to their surprise a shining light was seen on the mantelpiece over the fireplace. One of the gathering asked what was that light. One of the Saints answered that they were the angels of God!! "Are they really?" said the man, taking hold of them and smashing them to pieces. What were their angels, do you suppose, but rotten old white wood! This is how these deceivers bewitch the ignorant people into believing that angels of God visit them in their meetings!!

1848: 14 November, *North Wales Chronicle*, p. 1 (520 words). "A Mormon Miracle."

When asked if he could perform a miracle, Joseph Smith "declared that upon a certain day, he would walk across the broad waters of the Missouri without wetting the soles of his feet." He then asked a crowd of his followers at the edge of the Mississippi River if they had faith that he could perform the miracle. When they responded in the affirmative, he put his boots back on and walked away, saying that since they had such faith, there was no need for him to perform the miracle.

1848: 16 December, *Monmouthshire Beacon*, p. 4 (105 words).

> Destruction of the Mormon Temple at Nauvoo. The celebrated Mormon Temple, in Nauvoo, has been entirely destroyed by incendiary fire. No effort was made to stop the progress of the flames.

1848: 2 December, *Monmouthshire Merlin*, p. 3 (350 words). "Pious Fraud. Three Mormon Prophets."

An account of a Latter-day Saint missionary who overnighted somewhere and pretended to be dead when his hosts looked in on him the next morning. Soon afterward, two other missionaries came calling for him. Upon learning that he was "dead," they claimed to have power to raise the dead. The head of the house then threatened to hit the missionary lying in bed with a cudgel, at which point he leaped from the bed to avoid getting clubbed. This is among the most popular stories told by the enemies of the Latter-day Saints.

1848: 16 December, *Monmouthshire Merlin*, p. 3 (35 words).

The gang of burglars, which was captured at Cardiff by Sergeant Trewartha, (see our fourth page) was committed for trial on Thursday. James Rodd, one of the prisoners, had been a Mormon prophet.

1848: December, *Seren Gomer* (*Star of Gomer*), pp. 373–75 (430 words). "Invitation to California."

In mid-nineteenth-century Wales, the location of "California" included what is now Utah. At this time, word was circulating in Wales that Dan Jones would soon be taking a group of approximately three hundred of his fellow Welshmen to the "promised land" in America to join with the main body of the Saints in the Rocky Mountains. One who called himself "Little Wren," from a place located "Near Bogeyman's Hole," composed this poem of nine stanzas as a mocking "invitation" to all the Welsh to travel with Captain Jones and find paradise. The opening stanza sets the tone for the remaining eight:

Oh, come to California,
    Dear Welshmen, dear Welshmen,
Stand here no longer,
    Dear Welshmen;
There are heavens for us there,
We shall have land without rent or taxes,
Prepare to come without delay,
    Dear Welshmen, dear Welshmen,
Do not tarry here except for that,
    Dear Welshmen.

The following verses promise "bread without baking it," "vehicles that will run by themselves without horses," "clothes that come from the clouds," and other miraculous phenomena. The final stanza alludes to Thomas Jeremy, a Church member and wealthy farmer from Llanybydder who lived at "Glantrenfawr":

The man of Glantren is about to get under way,
    A great prophet, a great prophet,
He is zeal from his feet to the crown of his head,
    A great prophet;
He has sold his things,
Already for the journey,
May a fair wind call him to begin,
    Great prophet, great prophet,
Until he reaches the land of the Saints,
    Great prophet.

Sadly, Thomas and Sarah Jeremy would bury three of their little daughters, all of whom died of cholera, upon reaching the Missouri River.

1848: December, *Y Drysorfa Gynnulleidfaol* (*Congregationalist Treasury*), p. 367 (155 words).

In the Questions and Answers section, David Griffiths provides the answers to questions posed in the previous issue of the periodical by J. Jones, Carmarthen. One of Jones's questions was "Are the miraculous gifts imparted in the present day, as the Mormons claim?" David Griffiths's answer is as follows:

> No, they are not. First, because there is no example of such gifts with any group of believers at the present time, neither with the Mormons, except for deceit and lies for such gifts. If it were useful, we could note many of their tricks in this regard.

Griffiths adds a second reason, using Paul's words in 1 Corinthians 13:8 to substantiate his answer:

> Charity never faileth: but whether there be prophecies, they shall fail; whether there be tongues, they shall cease; whether there be knowledge, it shall vanish away.

From these words Griffiths draws this conclusion:

> All these things which are to vanish are spiritual gifts, namely those parts of the spiritual gift which the Spirit activated at that time, imparting each one individually as desired. It is better to believe Paul than to give credence to the deceitful assertions of the followers of Joseph Smith.

1848: 14 December, *Yr Amserau* (*Times*), p. 6 (285 words). "A Mormon Miracle."

Using the nom de plume "T. ab Ieuan," the writer of this article declares that he knows many who call themselves "Saints" in Monmouthshire. He says he wishes to be fair in presenting what he calls "a miracle." He tells of a person by the name of "Will from the Dune," one of the "Saints," and who claims that modern-day miracles happen. The writer presents an account of the "miraculous" incident:

> One day, the venerable gentleman got it into his head to exchange a few *rounds* with his wife, and he, Mr. Miracles, demonstrated much greater strength than his Eve; and then a neighbor woman took the wife's side, and she grabbed hold of the Saint's head, and there ensued a fierce battle between them. He put his backside against her, and she put her backside against him; and then something the most similar to a miracle in this neighborhood took place.

The writer then brings in a witness:

> Johnny Cosac (one of the Saints) said that they did many things, but that was the only miracle he was aware of—the saint used arms of the flesh against the woman sinner!

At this point the writer promises to obtain the "whole account of the mysterious deceit of the Mormons, from someone who has been in their midst, and is determined to direct it all to the *Times* very soon." One is left to wonder if perhaps a sentence or two of this brief paragraph may have been inadvertently omitted. Any follow-up article that might clarify this supposed miracle remains unidentified.

Episode 5.11

Start: John S. Davis offers proof of a miracle to the "Hater of Deceit"

1848: *Saint y Dyddiau Diweddaf a Doniau Gwyrthiol: Sef Pregeth a draddodwyd, Dydd Sul y 27ain Awst, 1848, yn Eglwys Sant Dewi, Caerfyrddin,* gan y Parch.

David Evans, Curad yr Eglwys Hono (*The Latter-day Saints and Spiritual Gifts: Namely a Sermon Delivered, Sunday the 27th of August, 1848, at the Church of Saint David, Carmarthen*, by the Rev. David Evans, the Curate of that Church), pamphlet, 20 pages.

This pamphlet lacks the vicious language that other antagonists were then using whenever they mentioned The Church of Jesus Christ of Latter-day Saints. Evans does, however, severely criticize the defense that the Church offered for a continuation of miracles from the time of Jesus Christ. He presents his ideas in a gentlemanly fashion and concludes that the members of the Church are false prophets and heretics.

1848: December, *Yr Haul* (*Sun*), p. 402 (120 words).

The editor of this Anglican periodical gives his brief assessment of the pamphlet authored by the curate David Evans:

> In our time the Mormons, or the Latter-day Saints, and their beliefs, are too despicable to take any note of them; but the common folk are paying attention to them; and the apostles of this blasphemous heresy are deceiving many of the people and putting their salvation at risk. . . . This Sermon is an excellent antidote to this deadly poison.

1848: December, *Prophwyd y Jubili* (*Prophet of the Jubilee*), pp. 176–83 (5,700 words). "Observations on a Sermon about 'The Latter-day Saints and Miraculous Gifts.'"

John S. Davis, in this eight-page response to David Evans's pamphlet, has a strongly different opinion. He writes:

> I thought when I gave my sixpence for this ten-page sermon that I was buying an original product, and one worthy of the order of priesthood; but when I saw that the most particular materials of the product had been in the skull of W. R. Davies, Dowlais, (Baptist) and a host of other heretics in the eyes of the Pure Church, I was tremendously disappointed.

Davis defends the idea that miracles continue to occur in modern times, especially in The Church of Jesus Christ of Latter-day Saints. He concludes with an invitation to anyone who wishes to have evidence of modern-day miracles to go to Newport and talk with Reuben Brinkworth, a young man who had been deaf and dumb for several years because of the effects of an electric storm while at sea, but who, following his baptism as a Latter-day Saint, had had his speech and hearing restored.

1849: January, *Seren Gomer* (*Star of Gomer*), pp. 16–17 (1,275 words). "Sermon about the Saints."

The writer, possibly the editor of the periodical, signs himself "Hater of Deceit." He firmly asserts that the printed sermon of the Reverend David Evans will "serve as a remedy for the mortal poison which [the Latter-day Saints] throw into the minds of the simpletons of this age," and he, a Baptist, recommends that his readers purchase a copy of the pamphlet by Evans, an Anglican, who, according to John S. Davis, had been brought up in a Presbyterian Academy and also had been an Independent minister.

In his pamphlet, Evans had issued the following challenge:

> Let the deaf be shown whose ears have been opened through the power of the Saints. Who of them has loosened the tongue-strings of the mute, causing him to speak the praises of God?[56]

In the *Prophet of the Jubilee*, John S. Davis had responded to the reverend's challenge:

> We answer that Mr. Evans can see a person who came to hear and speak—yes, speak the praises of God, after being baptized by the Saints, and that recently, and also in Wales. If anyone wants proof, let him go to Newport, and ask for a man, namely Reuben Brinkworth, in the house of Mr. Nash, basket maker, in Market Street; and let him read what the editor of the newspaper there, the *Merlin*, published in one of the issues for September, 1848.[57]

And in his response, the "Hater of Deceit" discounts the story about Reuben Brinkworth's hearing and speech being restored, declaring that it was merely "the effect of the electricity of which the air was so full at the time."

He then presents a brief account of a supposed event that had taken place recently in Wales. According to "Hater," a woman who had provided lodging to a man knocked lightly on his door the following morning but received no response. A short time later she and her husband went into the room and saw what they thought was a dead man. Just then two other men knocked on the door. "Hater" writes:

> As soon as they saw the woman, they said to her, "You have a dead man in the house!" The woman answered that there was; and asked how they knew that? "Oh," the two men said, "it has been revealed to us by an angel of heaven." The husband, who was, it seems, a little more cunning than his wife, had been listening silently to this, and said, "Oh, so, certainly; I see through it all now!" Then he took hold of a good cudgel, and having run up to the corpse, he held it over him in such a way that the corpse leaped out of bed, put his clothes on with the greatest of haste, and then ran down the stairs. And having joined his brothers, the prophets, the three went away without delay, without saying to the man and woman of the house so much as, "Good morning to you."[58]

"Hater" then quotes a long paragraph from *Life in the Far West*, a book by George Frederick Ruxton (1821–48), a British explorer and travel writer, who wrote articles of the same title for Blackwood's Magazine using the nom de plume La Bonté. Here is part of that paragraph:

> Joe Smith, and other prophets who had recently risen, declared that they were the chosen ones of the Lord; and their general belief was that on the Day of Judgment, he would take his place at the right hand of the throne, and that no one would be allowed to pass into the kingdom of heaven without his touch and seal. One of their main subjects is faith in "spiritual marriage." Not one woman would be allowed to go to heaven, without having first been "approved" by one of the Saints! To qualify them for this, the woman had first to be received by one of the Mormons as an "earthly wife," so that they would not approve anyone without having full knowledge about them.[59]

"Hater" concludes,

"There is a description, Mr. Gomer, that is enough to damn the character of the Mormons forever; and I have not heard that they have made any attempt to disprove it."

1849: January, *Seren Gomer* (*Star of Gomer*), p. 17 (375 words). "Greeting to the Doctor of Madness."

This poem of ten four-line stanzas, authored by "A Small Druid," is positioned in the periodical immediately after the article authored by the "Hater of Deceit." One might suspect that the article and the poem might have been penned by the same hand. The poet makes an appeal for "the Doctor" to provide a tonic for an infectious disease then rampant in South Wales that was causing the people to behave insanely—a disease that has been leading people to believe the Book of Mormon and accept the religion it propagates.

It swells their throats so they will not swallow reason,
It brings about weak-headedness; it puts them down terribly;
No Priest or Pope can raise them;
Joe Smith, with his poison, has caused it.

Other indications of the disease are these:

The signs of the Madness are believing the Book of Mormon,
Going with a false teacher, having a dunk in some river,
And speaking, like geese, quite a multitude of languages,
And performing false miracles to deceive the people.

In the ninth stanza, the "Small Druid" makes a fervent appeal:

Please, Doctor of Madness, give the people a tonic,
You will be paid for your trouble from the taxes of the poor.
You will be thanked by many, and you will get a song from me,
If you pull the Madness from the Saints' cloaks.

End: John S. Davis offers proof of a miracle to the "Hater of Deceit"

Notes

1. *Zion's Trumpet*, 23 September 1854, 509; also see *Welsh Mormon Writings*, 65–68.
2. *Prophet of the Jubilee*, September 1848, pp. 141–42.
3. Welsh Saints Project, welshsaints.byu.edu.
4. *Prophet of the Jubilee*, January 1848, 15.
5. *Prophet of the Jubilee*, May 1848, 73.
6. Ibid.
7. *Prophet of the Jubilee*, May 1848, 74.
8. *Star of Gomer*, July 1848, 203.
9. Ibid.
10. The 1987 biography of Thomas Job by Bliss J. Brimley is posted on the Welsh Saints Project.
11. *Prophet of the Jubilee*, March 1848, 37.
12. See Jones's pamphlet, *"Haman" Hanging from his Own Gallows!* 1, facsimile translation, in *Defending the Faith: Early Welsh Missionary Publications*, item J10.
13. *Congregationalist Treasury*, March 1848, 76.
14. *Congregationalist Treasury*, June 1848, 168.
15. Ibid., 169–70.

16. *Prophet of the Jubilee*, December 1848, 187.
17. *Congregationalist Treasury*, June 1848, 170.
18. *Brigham City Bugler*, Saturday, 6 January 1894.
19. *Apostolic Witness*, June 1848, 138.
20. *Sun*, June 1848, 196.
21. *Sun*, June 1848, 188.
22. Ibid.
23. Ibid.
24. Ibid.
25. *Sun*, July 1848, 216.
26. Ibid., 217.
27. Ibid., 218.
28. Ibid., 219.
29. *Star of Gomer*, March 1848, 93.
30. *Prophet of the Jubilee*, March 1848, 45.
31. Ibid., 43
32. *Star of Gomer*, July 1848, 201.
33. Ibid.
34. Ibid., 202.
35. *Prophet of the Jubilee*, March 1847, 49.
36. Ibid., 50.
37. Ibid., 51.
38. *Prophet of the Jubilee*, September 1847, 141.
39. Ibid., 142.
40. *Star of Gomer*, July 1848, 202.
41. *Prophet of the Jubilee*, August 1848, 115–16.
42. Ibid., 117.
43. *Star of Gomer*, September 1848, 269.
44. *Star of Gomer*, October 1848, 293.
45. See *Welsh Mormon Writings from 1844 to 1862: A Historical Bibliography*, 65–68, for a description of this publication.
46. *Zion's Trumpet*, April 1849, 67.
47. Ibid.
48. See *Defending the Faith: Early Welsh Missionary Publications*, item D6.
49. *Star of Gomer*, September 1848, 264.
50. Ibid.
51. Ibid., 265.
52. *Prophet of the Jubilee*, August 1848, 118.
53. Ibid., 122.
54. *Star of Gomer*, October 1848, 305.
55. Ibid.
56. *The Latter-day Saints and Spiritual Gifts: Namely a Sermon Delivered*, 15.
57. *Prophet of the Jubilee*, December 1848, 182.
58. *Star of Gomer*, January 1849, 16–17.
59. Ibid., 17.

Chapter 6

Episodes

6.1—John S. Davis responds to "The Stranger" about the "Miracle of the Cudgel"
6.2—The first group of Welsh Latter-day Saint emigrants causes a stir in the press
6.3—Five brief articles are written about the Reverend Rhys Morgan
6.4—John S. Davis responds to the Reverend D. Davis, an old friend of the family
6.5—The Reverend Thomas Price challenges John Pugh—John S. Davis intervenes
6.6—The Reverend O. Williams is questioned about the death of a "Mormon"
6.7—The story of Sarah Holder, Bayliss, and their baby is discussed in the press
6.8—Welsh Latter-day Saints arrive in Minersville, Pennsylvania
6.9—John Lloyd sets the record straight

Salient Events

- **January 1849**—When President Orson Pratt did not come from Liverpool for the year-end conference in Merthyr Tydfil, Dan Jones had no choice but to release himself and set apart his replacement, William Phillips. Because the long room in the White Lion Inn could not accommodate all who were in attendance, the long room in the nearby Railway Inn was used for the overflow. In his account of the conference, Dan Jones wrote that he spoke with his "whole strength for seven hours and a half, with but little cessation." The reason he spoke for such a long period is because he went back and forth between the two assembly rooms, speaking at each one. The most salient feature of the simultaneous meetings was the conversation Jones had with the evil spirits that had possessed three of the females present.[1]
- **January 1849**—John S. Davis assumes the editorship of *Zion's Trumpet.* Whereas Dan Jones's primary focus with *Prophet of the Jubilee* had been a vigorous defense of the Church from the attacks launched by Reverend

W. R. Davies and others, John S. Davis included far fewer of such heated defenses and much more variety, with humor, poetry and the occasional reminder of proper etiquette for Church members. He also included a four-page printed wrapper for each issue of the 1849 and 1850 volumes.[2]

- **28 January 1849**—A small chapel built by the members in the Llanelli Branch is dedicated by Dan Jones. In a letter to Orson Pratt the following day, Jones wrote: "During each meeting, it was crowded to overflowing, notwithstanding public notices had been published in every other chapel here, prohibiting any of their members attending, upon the penalty of being 'turned out of their synagogues.'"[3] Before its demolition a few years ago, this chapel was the oldest standing building in the Church built by Latter-day Saints except for the Kirtland Temple.[4]
- **February 1849**—Sixteen-year-old David John from Little Newcastle, Pembrokeshire, is baptized by Elder Daniel Williams. When he told his parents, both ardent Baptists, his father forbade him to attend Latter-day Saint meetings. When he sought advice from Elder Phillip Sykes, David was counseled to do as his father had told him until he came of age. A year later David's father granted him permission to leave home on the condition that he stay away from the Latter-day Saints until he turned twenty-one. But by the time he reached that age, he had found his way into the Baptist College at Haverfordwest and was studying for the ministry. He even preached at the Beulah Chapel near his home, where his father shed tears of joy upon hearing his son's sermons. Then on 28 January 1856, the night before his twenty-third birthday, David had a vision-filled dream in which an angel had an extensive conversation with him, explaining the reasons why he needed to realign himself with the Latter-day Saints. His doing so resulted in enormous resentment from his parents and his brother. He was disowned and disinherited, and when his father died seven weeks later, the neighbors placed the blame on David. At his father's funeral, David was called a murderer by former friends and neighbors. But David John continued faithful to his new religion until his own death in Provo, Utah, in 1908. His five-volume journal, the best ever to be written by a Welsh convert, is posted on the Brigham Young University Library's website.[5]
- **26 February 1849**—From Waterloo Dock in Liverpool, the first group of Welsh Latter-day Saint emigrants set sail on the *Buena Vista*.[6] See Episode 6.2.
- **5 March 1849**—The *Hartley* leaves Waterloo Dock in Liverpool with eighty-three passengers who, for lack of space, had not been able to depart a week earlier on the *Buena Vista*.
- **17 March 1849**—Elias Morris is baptized by John Parry Jr. in the sea near Abergele, North Wales. Three years later, Morris was put in charge of the machinery for the Deseret Sugar Manufactory on board *The Rockaway*. On 20 February 1855 in Cedar City, Utah, he and his young wife were at the bedside of Morris's younger brother, John, who lay dying. John's final request was that Morris marry his soon-to-be widow, Mary Lois Walker Morris, who was also in the room. She indicated her willingness to do according to her

husband's dying wish, but it was more than a year later that she was emotionally able to honor the strange request. One of the eight children born to Elias and Mary Lois Morris was George Q. Morris, who served as a member of the Quorum of the Twelve Apostles from 1954 to 1962.

- **17 May 1849**—The surviving *Buena Vista* passengers arrive at Council Bluffs.
- **8 June 1849**—The surviving *Hartley* passengers arrive at Council Bluffs. The number of those who died of cholera between New Orleans and Council Bluffs was at least sixty-seven—20 percent of all the Welsh passengers on the *Buena Vista* and the *Hartley*. This percentage is higher than that of the Martin and Willie handcart companies who, seven years later, would perish on the plains. On board the *Hartley* were William and Eleanor Owens and their seven children. Only twenty-four-year-old Cadwallader, twenty-year-old Margaret, and thirteen-year-old Owen would survive the cholera epidemic and reach Council Bluffs.
- **July 1849**—William Morgan is appointed by Dan Jones as president of the Welsh branch in Council Bluffs. Morgan's branch was composed of 113 members who had left Liverpool on either the *Buena Vista* or the *Hartley* four months earlier. Soon after this tragedy, Dan Jones, along with eighty-one other Welsh pioneers, joined the George A. Smith Company to cross the plains to Salt Lake City.
- **1 September 1849**—Reverend W. R. Davies dies of cholera in Merthyr Tydfil. Here is the notice that John S. Davis posted in the September 1849 *Zion's Trumpet*: "Yes, it is true that the well-known Rev. W. R. Davies, from Dowlais, has died of cholera. He died having returned home, when it was thought that the illness had left the place."[7] Davis certainly maintained decorum in avoiding any further comment on the passing of the Saints' most vociferous enemy in Wales.
- **26 October 1849**—The George A. Smith Company, with its eighty-two Welsh pioneers, arrives in Salt Lake City. Of the Welsh who had left Liverpool on board the *Buena Vista* or the *Hartley* eight months earlier, only one-fourth of them continued on to Salt Lake City that same year. The others had either succumbed to cholera or had remained in St. Louis or Council Bluffs. With their melodious singing each night, the Welsh created a great sensation with their non-Welsh fellow travelers. And when Brigham Young greeted them in Salt Lake City, he asked Father John Parry to form a choir for the next Church conference in the bowery, a choir that evolved into the famous Mormon Tabernacle Choir, later called The Tabernacle Choir at Temple Square.
- **24 November 1849**—Dan Jones leaves on the Southern Expedition. Jones was following the counsel given him by Brigham Young to travel with Parley P. Pratt in order to seek out the Welsh Indians, a group that, according to legend, had come to America centuries earlier under the leadership of a Prince Madoc. One of Jones's most earnest desires was to convert these Welsh-speaking Indians to the restored gospel and take some of them back to Wales to preach to their compatriots. Not only was he unsuccessful in

his search, but he also suffered great deprivations during the two months of travel. And it required a blessing from Parley P. Pratt to rid him of the snow blindness that afflicted him toward the end of the journey.[8]

Commentary

1849: *Cyfeiliornadau a Dichellion Saint y Dyddiau Diweddaf a Llyfr Mormon, yn cael eu dynoethi, gan y Parch W. J. Morrish* (*Heresies and Deceptions of the Latter-day Saints and the Book of Mormon, Exposed by the Rev. W. J. Morrish*), pamphlet, 24 pages.

The title of this twenty-four-page pamphlet was modified from the two "letters" which Reverend W. J. Morrish had published in English several years earlier in Ledbury. (The first letter was entitled "The Latter-day Saints and the Book of Mormon. A Few Words of Warning from a Minister to His Flock," and the second letter was entitled "The Latter-day Saints and the Book of Mormon. A Second Warning from a Minister to His Flock.") The contents, however, are unaltered in the pamphlet's Welsh translation. In the first letter, Morrish focuses mainly on the Book of Mormon and the theory that it was written by Solomon Spaulding, declaring that Joseph Smith simply forged Spaulding's manuscript into the content for a book whose origin Smith claimed to be some plates of gold given him by an angel. In the second letter, Morrish writes the following:

> Now I say *you do not know the doctrines these people really teach*, because they are too cunning to let you know the whole depth of the wickedness at once, lest you should be afraid to join them.

He then provides numerous quotes from the Book of Mormon and the Doctrine and Covenants and explains what he judges to be the heresy in the doctrine contained in them. He assures his readers that no new revelation is needed for them to be saved.

1849: 13 January, *Monmouthshire Merlin*, p. 1 (675 words). "The Land of Gold."

An article about the gold rush in California. "But the worst feature at present is, that the Mormons—several thousand strong, and about 1,000 fighting men—claim the whole region!"

Episode 6.1

Start: John S. Davis responds to "The Stranger" about the "Miracle of the Cudgel"

1849: January, *Yr Haul* (*Sun*), pp. 33–34 (1,135 words). "Miracle of the Cudgel."

The author, who calls himself "The Stranger," recounts the supposed happening of the lodger in Newport who pretended to be dead, an account slightly longer than that of the "Hater of Deceit" in the January 1849 *Star of Gomer*. He also gives evidence of having heard of the evil spirits that during the recent conference in Merthyr Tydfil had caused considerable confusion by possessing three women. John S. Davis related the incident in his report of the conference in his first issue of *Zion's Trumpet*,[9] but the account given by "The Stranger" differs noticeably:

> One of their Apostles found out last Sunday that devils had entered seventeen of the Saints, and that they had fallen from grace; and that it will be a difficult

> job to get so many villains out of the men. It is also appropriate to note that the devils dragged the pure men to Bacchus and Venus; and there is great trouble in China, Merthyr ["China" at that time was a rough neighborhood in Merthyr Tydfil], because of it.[10]

"The Stranger" praises "Davies from Dowlais" (the Baptist minister W. R. Davies) and "Iorwerth" from Rhymney (the Baptist minister Edward Roberts) for their efforts to "stand up for truth against the Mormon Bible." He also commends the Reverend William Rowlands for his recent sermon at the Merthyr Tydfil parish church, in which Rowlands defended "the Scriptures against the Mormons Bible." With his final paragraph, "The Stranger" describes how Rowlands disposed of the Mormon Bible:

> Before the end of the sermon, a small book was seen being held up in the Minister's hand; and after making it known that it was the Mormon Bible, which came up from the earth in America, he compared it with the beast John saw rising from the earth, since it spoke like a dragon, although it looked like a lamb. After the Minister had further proved that the Booklet could not be of divine authority, he said above it, "From the earth thou camest, and in the earth thou shalt be placed." And down it went.[11]

1849: April, *Udgorn Seion* (*Zion's Trumpet*), pp. 77–79 (870 words). "Miracle of the Cudgel—True or False?"

John S. Davis wrote a response to the article in the *Sun*, but the *Sun*'s editor refused to publish it. Consequently, Davis decided to provide space for it in the April issue of his own periodical. He begins the article by paying a compliment to the editor of the *Sun* for refusing to publish some of the stories against the Latter-day Saints that were "so unreasonable and contradictory." With respect to the story which the editor did agree to publish, about the "three Apostles [who] were going to a nearby town," Davis provides his own account:

> They went to the door of a house in the town and asked for lodgings for one of the three; they obtained what they wanted; the stranger went to the bed betimes and slept through the night. The woman of the house, seeing him not getting up from his bed as late as ten o'clock in the morning, went to call the stranger to get up; but alas! the Saint was dead. The woman shook the lodger; but there was no life, not a breath in the Saint.

At this point, the other two "Apostles" knocked on the door and were informed that their friend was dead. They said they could perform a miracle and raise him from the dead. The man of the house had his wife bring him a cudgel.

> He took hold of it, and started beating the dead man, shouting, "I'll give him resurrection—the cudgel's the thing." Up shot the dead man from the grave of the bed, onto his feet, and was soon standing dressed, not in a shroud, but in his clothes and his right mind.

Davis points out that for miracles in the Bible the persons involved are named, and details associated with the miracles are given. He mockingly observes:

> It is important for us to have greater knowledge of an even greater miracle which has happened as close to us as Newport. Is it not possible to obtain the names of the apostles, and the man of the house who so virtuously used the cudgel? And as for the woman, we ought to have her name with the

> testimony, so that we can be certain of the miracle. We should be informed as to the house, and how "recently" the miracle took place.

Davis also informs the editor of the *Sun* of a source that "gives an account of the beginning of the story in question, which was invented by seamen trying their skill in telling the best lie." He adds that the story had come from America to England and that it had been in Wales for three years, "continually being improved, and becoming truer and newer every day."

End: John S. Davis responds to "The Stranger" about the "Miracle of the Cudgel"

1849: 19 January, *Cambrian* (90 words).

An account of the supposed thievery of a Latter-day Saint who asked permission to preach at the home of a laborer in the town of Neath. According to the article, the man in question received not only the opportunity of preaching but also food and lodging. However, the next morning he arose early and took "from the poor man's larder sufficient food for several days."

1849: 3 February, *Monmouthshire Merlin*, p. 1 (350 words). "The California Gold Mines."

This medium-sized article includes the following: "A party of Mormons had collected large quantities of gold in the neighborhood of the Salt Lake; while on the journey one of them lost a mule with 1,280 dollars' worth of gold on its back. The animal being frightened ran off in the midst of a vast plain, and was irretrievably lost."

1849: February, *Y Bedyddiwr* (*Baptist*), p. 68 (255 words).

An account of two Latter-day Saint missionaries who selected a place near Cardiff to preach in the open air. The writer describes the missionaries as being of "the same lineage as the one of old who 'went to and fro in the earth and walked up and down on it,'" a reference to Satan.[12] The missionaries left in haste when an "old soldier" threatened them. Some children who witnessed the scene said among themselves, "What manner of man is this, that even the Latter-day Saints flee from him?"

1849: 3 February, *Monmouthshire Merlin*, p. 2 (175 words). "The Mormons in Wales."

A brief report of the Latter-day Saint conference held in Merthyr Tydfil on 31 December 1848 and on the following day and of a variety of statistics. It ends with this quote from the *Swansea Herald*:

> The thousands of Mormons in Wales appear to have great affection for, and confidence in, Captain Dan Jones, who intends returning in February to the valley of the Salt Lake in California. About 360 saints intend emigrating with him.

1849: 17 February, *Monmouthshire Merlin*, p. 3 (55 words).

> The fanatic Mormons, about 1,200 in number, first discovered the precious metal during their march, and are said to have extracted an immense quantity before it became known. Governor Mason, in his report of August last, says, from all he has learned he believes 13,000,000 dolls. worth had been extracted to that date.

1849: February, *Seren Gomer* (*Star of Gomer*), p. 62, item 1 (135 words). "The Mormons of Neath."

A more elaborate version of the account of supposed thievery printed in the *Cambrian* for 19 January 1849.

1849: February, *Seren Gomer* (*Star of Gomer*), p. 62, item 2 (440 words). "The Mormons of Pontypridd."

The account of "Dai the Blockhead," a collier who suffered a mine accident and received a blessing of healing from his fellow members of The Church of Jesus Christ of Latter-day Saints. "Little Morris," the writer, portrays the event thus:

> One of his fellow workers took him on his back to his home. Of course, a number of the brothers gathered around him soon, prohibiting the sending of any doctor to him. They rubbed Dai's back well for a little while, while the rest of the brothers prayed; then they asked him whether his back was feeling better. He answered, "Yes, very much; but please, be gentle, brothers." Having gone through the process, Dai said he could go to work the following day; but he did not go till the second day, having recovered completely!! I leave the above account to the attention and judgment of your numerous readers.

Despite the positive outcome for the injured collier, the writer continues:

> But I can say without hesitation, that I have not seen, as far as I can say, without hesitation, that I have not seen, as far as impudence and shamefulness go, anyone equal to the Mormons of Pontypridd.

The writer then proceeds to tell a few other, in his opinion, nonsensical stories of converts to this strange religion. He ends with four lines of poetry in which he expresses the hope that all these "Servants of hell" leave Wales and go to California (which at this point in Wales referred to all of the western United States).

1849: 2 February, *Cambrian* (135 words). "A Miracle in Prospect."

This article has to do with "a preacher of the Latter-day Saints" in Newcastle who negotiated with a "certain party" to miraculously make his crooked legs straight in exchange for accommodation.

> A large crowd collected to hear the preacher on Sunday who harangued his audience at considerable length. In the meantime, the kindly occupant is in daily expectation of getting up some fine morning with a pair of straight legs. We wish he may get 'em.

1849: 8 February, *Yr Amserau* (*Times*) (460 words). "Defense of the Mormons."

The writer of this defense, dated 2 February 1849, was Thomas Jeremy, a well-to-do farmer who had been baptized by Dan Jones almost three years earlier. His home in Llanybydder, named "Glantrenfawr," was used as a meeting place until he emigrated, just a few weeks after sending this defense to the editor of the *Times*. Jeremy wrote the defense in response to some erroneous statements made by an anonymous writer in the 11 January 1849 issue of the *Times* (which is unfortunately not extant). After presenting his angry defense, Jeremy then bears his testimony:

> I know that I have the true religion, which is disposed toward making everyone happy; therefore, let our false accuser repent, and call back his lying tales which he has told about us, so that he also may take hold of the one true religion.

1849: 9 February, *Cambrian* (630 words). "Mormon Dishonesty."

This article contains a letter from a reader in Tipton, Staffordshire, in which he condemns the preacher who was portrayed in the 19 January issue of the *Cambrian* as stealing food from the poor man who had extended him hospitality. The writer then repeats stories from "Mr. Caswall" about numerous robberies from a "respectable gentleman residing at Montrose," allegedly committed by the Latter-day Saints during a three-year period, and then includes the following comment about Joseph Smith:

> The prophet Joe Smith, alluding to these robberies in a sermon said that he "did not care how much was taken" from the gentleman in question, and added the following words: "The world owes me a good living; if I cannot get it otherwise, I will steal it and catch me at it if you can."

1849: 16 February, *Cambrian*, item 1 (345 words). "To the Editor of the Cambrian."

In this, the first of four articles in the 16 February 1849 issue of the *Cambrian*, a reader—"H. J." of Maesteg—responds to the article entitled "Mormon Dishonesty" printed in the previous issue. He declares that "R. L.," the writer of that article, "seemed to be in a spirit of inaccurate obscurity, inverting false conclusions from mere mock statements, without a shadow of truth pertaining to them." "H. J." also states that he had made "diligent enquiries at Neath" concerning the Latter-day Saint preacher who purportedly stole food from a poor man and declares: "I could not even be informed that a Latter-day Saint had preached in any house there on the Sunday in question." "H. J." further denounces "R. L." for concluding that the actions of one individual "reflected on the common honesty" of all the nearly seven-hundred thousand Latter-day Saints in the world (a gross overestimation on the author's part). Furthermore, since the accusation is not true,

> the conclusion he invents is still more notorious and proves that the various base accusations of "stealth" which he endeavors to establish against these people, have emanated from similar falsifiable sources.

The foregoing is a rare example of someone in Wales other than Dan Jones and John S. Davis coming to the defense of the Latter-day Saints in the press.

1849: 16 February, *Cambrian*, item 2 (95 words). "Mormonism at Woolwich."

The second of the four articles and consists of only a few lines giving the alarming report of a "considerable number of disciples" of the Latter-day Saints being "immersed in the Thames." The writer reports that a "Dr. Carlisle" had recently delivered two lectures "containing an exposition and argumentative refutation of Mormons" and that "many waverers" had "returned to the "good old way."

Episode 6.2

Start: The first group of Welsh Latter-day Saint emigrants causes a stir in the press

1849: 20 January, *Cardiff and Merthyr Guardian*, p. 3 (125 words). "Merthyr and Neighborhood. California."

> The gold seeking mania has at last invaded the mountains of Wales; and the general desire to get suddenly rich has been well applied in the service of religious fanaticism. In consequence large numbers of the operatives of this district are preparing to visit California for the double purpose of obtaining gold in abundance, and of settling in the Canaan of the Mormon prophet.

This piece most likely has reference to the group of Latter-day Saints who were preparing to gather in Swansea to take the steamer *Troubador* to Liverpool to begin their voyage to the United States.

1849: 27 January, *Monmouthshire Beacon*, p. 4 (125 words). "Emigration to California."

Other than minor differences in punctuation, the opening of this article is identical to the text that appears in the 20 January *Cardiff and Merthyr Guardian*.

1849: 16 February, *Cambrian*, item 3 (140 words). "The Saints and their New Jerusalem."

This is a brief report of the departure of "these misguided men" who had "commenced their expedition to California," having left Merthyr Tydfil on Monday, 12 February 1849. The writer says that the men's intention is not to "proceed to the gold district," but that they will "march in detachments":

> One detachment will proceed to a depot where everything has been provided for them. They will there sow wheat, set potatoes, and put everything in process for yielding a plentiful harvest to the next detachment; who will reap the labors of the others, and confer the same themselves on those succeeding them.

1849: 16 February, *Cambrian*, item 4 (540 words). "Emigration to California."

This piece contains a detailed description of the arrival of a large number of Welsh people in Swansea on 13 February 1849, nearly all of them Latter-day Saints. Their intent was to take the *Troubadour* steamer to Liverpool, "where a ship is in readiness to transport them next week to the glittering regions of California." Mention is made of the arrival of Dan Jones:

> He entered the town amidst the gaze of hundreds of spectators, and in the evening he delivered his valedictory address at the Trades Hall to a numerous audience, the majority of whom were led by curiosity to hear his doctrines which are quite novel in this town.

A description is given of the composition of the large group:

> Amongst the number who came here were several aged men varying from 70 to 90 years of age and whose "hoary locks" not only proclaimed their "lengthened years" but render it very improbable they will live to see America; yet so deluded are the poor and simple saints that they believe that everyone amongst them, however infirm and old they may be, will as surely land in California safely as they started from Wales. Their faith is most extraordinary.

Contrary to this dire prediction, all of the men did indeed live to "see America." Two women, however, were buried at sea during the voyage. And cholera, mostly along the Missouri River, would eventually claim as its victims one in five of the group.[13]

1849: February, *Y Drysorfa Gynnulleidfaol* (*Congregationalist Treasury*), pp. 53–54 (275 words).

This piece continues the discussion of California and the gold rush. The writer comments on the reaction of the "Mormons" to the fever for gold:

> It is said that the Mormons have gotten hold of an abundance of gold near the Salt Lake. All the Mormons are leaving California to search for gold on

> the shores of the Salt Lake. It is said that by the 1st of March in New York, they will have received about three million dollars, and from then on they will receive one million each month. Such an abundance of gold is certain to lower the worth of gold throughout the world. What effect will this have on the financial situation of England?[14]

1849: 16 February, *Principality*, p. 5, item 1 (150 words). "Swansea. Mormonites. Emigration to California."

This is a brief report of the large number of Latter-day Saints who arrived in Swansea to take the *Troubador* steamer for Liverpool.

> They do not go in quest of gold, but for the purpose of cultivating the land. This extraordinary expedition formed the general topic of discussion and conversation amongst all classes during the whole day. Capt. Jones is among them. He delivered a kind of valedictory discourse to his disciples at the Trades Hall in the evening.

1849: 16 February, *Principality*, p. 5, item 2 (60 words). "Merthyr. Mormonites."

> Many scores if not hundreds of this sect left this town and neighborhood the beginning of this week for the far-famed region of California. Some widows who have buried their husbands here have taken their clothes with them, expecting to meet them in that distant country! Do we really live in the 19th century?

1849: March, *Y Drysorfa* (*Treasury*), p. 96 (60 words).

Same as the *Principality* for 16 February 1849.

1849: March, *Y Bedyddiwr* (*Baptist*), p. 97 (120 words). "New Heaven."

The writer comments about the widows taking the clothes of their deceased husbands as reported in the 16 February *Principality* (see preceding entry). He expresses sarcastically, "I hope they have a fair wind to go sufficiently far from here."

1849: March, *Y Drysorfa Gynnulleidfaol* (*Congregationalist Treasury*), p. 94 (375 words). "Departure of the Mormons."

Also about the large group of Latter-day Saints that gathered in Swansea to take a steamer to Liverpool where they would set sail for America. The writer comments:

> Even though the fools promise themselves heavenly bliss in California, yet we think, in all conscience, that it would be nearly as well for them to go straight to hell.

The writer expresses his mixed feelings:

> Some spirit impels us to say, "Thank goodness, to be rid of so many fools from Wales." But at the same time, we feel sad because so many of our compatriots are being enticed to destruction by these cheats.

The writer also mentions that "one woman from Carmarthen was paying the transport costs of forty" of the group. This has reference to Elizabeth Lewis, who used her share of the sale of the "White Lion" in Kidwelly to help a large number of the emigrants to make the journey.[15]

1849: March, *Yr Haul* (*Sun*), p. 103 (50 words). "California."

A brief comment about all the people who are going to California:

> Men by the thousands are going toward California to search for gold; and good gracious, it is said that scores, if not hundreds, of people of our country

> have been charmed by the Mormons to sell their possessions and have already started off toward that land!

1849: April, *Yr Eurgrawn Wesleyaidd* (*Wesleyan Treasury*), p. 127, item 1 (85 words).

> It is said that a newspaper is being published in this distant land, on yellow paper, a sign of the gold that can be obtained there.

1849: April, *Yr Eurgrawn Wesleyaidd* (*Wesleyan Treasury*), p. 127, item 2 (85 words). "California Again."

> The "Latter-day Saints" are gathering by the hundreds to California, "the land of gold," from several parts of our country. If the day of judgment is as close as one of their preachers in Swansea said before departing, it is hardly worthwhile for him [the aforementioned preacher] and his brethren to go so far.

1849: April, *Yr Haul* (*Sun*), p. 135 (60 words).

The writer refers to California as "the land of gold, and the paradise of the Mormons." According to him, murders and pillaging are rampant there, and no inquiry is made into them.

1849: April, *Y Cyfaill yr Hen Wlad yn America* (*Friend of the Old Country in America*), pp. 123–24 (605 words). "Mormons in Wales."

In the first paragraph of this article, the writer cites the statistics given by Dan Jones at the Merthyr Tydfil conference of 31 December 1848 and 1 January 1849. These statistics appear to be taken from Jones's 6 January 1849 letter to Orson Pratt that was printed in the *Millennial Star*.[16] The writer observes,

> California fever has heated them up and has captivated them, and it is likely that thousands of them are on their way there by now.[17]

The writer then quotes a sizeable portion of the 16 February 1849 article from the *Cambrian* about the departure of the Latter-day Saints from Swansea on the *Troubadour*. He also quotes from the *Swansea Herald*: "Three hundred great ships could scarcely transport the hosts of 'saints' who are now desirous of emigrating from the isle of Britain." And, finally, he quotes the brief article from the *Principality* for 16 February 1849 about the widows taking their deceased husbands' clothes and "expecting to meet them in that distant land." He then observes:

> These facts do much more to prove the darkness and gullibility of the Welsh nation than all the reports of the Blue Books of the Commissioners of the Government.[18]

The "Blue Books" were the published findings of three English commissioners who were sent to Wales to create a government report about the state of education in the Principality. The published results in 1847 of their conclusions included comments such as the following:

> The Welsh language is a vast drawback to Wales, and a manifold barrier to the moral progress and commercial prosperity of the people. It is not easy to overestimate its evil effects. It is the language of the Cymri, and anterior to that of the ancient Britons. It dissevers the people from intercourse which would greatly advance their civilization, and bars the access of improving knowledge to their minds. As a proof of this, there is no Welsh literature worthy of the name.[19]

They were also highly critical of what they saw as the poor moral and religious attitude of Welsh people, especially the women:

> They learn anything but delicacy of thought and feeling and when they grow to womanhood and marry, they know next to nothing of the management of a house. As wives they are most slovenly and improvident, and as mothers, ignorant, and injudicious.[20]

Not one of the English commissioners could speak or understand the Welsh language, and consequently, they were able to communicate with only a very small percentage of the population of the Principality of Wales. Their report caused an immediate and lasting anger toward the English for disparaging the Welsh. So to accuse The Church of Jesus Christ of Latter-day Saints and its followers of being the greater cause of "darkness and gullibility" among the Welsh than the recently published "Blue Books" was a very serious statement indeed.

1849: April, *Y Cenhadwr Americanaidd* (*American Messenger*), p. 120 (95 words).

About the proposed "New Temple of the Mormons" to be built "near Salt Lake, in California." The report that the temple would be "600 feet high" and that it would be seen "from over 80 miles away" gives new dimensions to the frequent exaggerations made concerning The Church of Jesus Christ of Latter-day Saints during the nineteenth century. At its dedication in 1893, the highest spire of the Salt Lake Temple was only 210 feet high.

1849: June, *Y Drysorfa Gynnulleidfaol* (*Congregational Treasury*), p. 181 (180 words). "Farewell to the Saints."

In this six-stanza poem, the composer is essentially saying "good riddance" to the Saints. He maintains that their real motivation for leaving Wales was to get rich in the gold fields. The Reverend W. R. Davies composed the poem under the name "T. ab Ieuan," one of several noms de plume. Here is the final stanza:

Farewell to your dreadful deceit,
Your people have gone over the sea,
According to your wish; your desire is great,
To collect poor earthly wealth.

1848: December, *Prophwyd y Jubili* (*Prophet of the Jubilee*), p. 186 (230 words). "The Saints' Farewell."

A poem of three twelve-line stanzas composed by John S. Davis. It is obviously intended for the emigrating Saints to sing to the well-wishers on the dock as the departing ship is towed out to sea. Ironically, it would be another five years before the composer himself would be able to sing it on board a departing ship. Here is the final stanza:

Let us also bid farewell
To the Saints for a short while,
Until we see them all at home:
Our farewell is long
To them that deny the truth,
For they are not of the family of Heaven.
Let us go singing across the sea,
Without one fear in our hearts;
God by his kindness shall watch the vessel

As it rides the wave;
And may the Saints throughout this island,
Be also in His care.

1848: December, *Prophwyd y Jubili* (*Prophet of the Jubilee*), pp. 190–91 (225 words). "Who Will Go?"

A poem of six eight-line stanzas by "Noah." The composer, Noah Roberts Jones, extends a challenge intermixed with an invitation for "all supporters of dear Jesus" to accept the gospel message. He and his wife, Esther, had buried three of their four children in Wales before leaving on the *Buena Vista* in 1849. Their twelve-year-old daughter, Mary, accompanied them on the voyage to America. While headed for Council Bluffs on the *Highland Mary* on the Missouri River, Esther fell victim to the cholera that also claimed many other lives among the Welsh immigrants. Noah composed a poem of four nine-line stanzas to express his grief and sent it to his family back in Wales along with two other poems, including "Who Will Go?" John S. Davis published the grief poem under the title "Lament of the Emigrant," along with the other two.[21] Here is the first stanza:

My dear friends in the environs of Wales,
Kindly hear my lament in verse;
Lamenting still am I in sorrow
Over the loss of my dear Esther,
Whom I loved as my own soul
While she was mind;
But God called for my maiden;
Only He knows why;
She had to depart, though against my will.

1850: *Cyfarwyddiadau i'r Ymfudwyr tua Dinas y Llyn Halen* (*Directions to the Emigrants Bound for Salt Lake City*), pamphlet, 12 pages.[22]

Included in this twelve-page pamphlet is a poem of four four-line stanzas entitled "Verses," composed by "Gwilym Ddu," the nom de plume of William Lewis, who sailed on the *Buena Vista* in 1849. Lewis, together with all the Welsh Latter-day Saints, was well aware of the following dire prophecy of Samuel Evans, the editor of *Star of Gomer*:

> Having got enough money to get a ship or ships to voyage to California, their Leader will sail to Cuba and sell them as slaves, every man jack of them. That would serve them right for having so little respect for Christ's book as to give it up for the Book of Mormon.[23]

In his poem, Lewis responds to the prophecy:

Some of the sectarians insist,—that to sell us
In shame, like animals,
Across the sea, our leaders would do:
Such was the group's cry.
"The Captain," they say, "enticed,—in the area
Of Merthyr, a vast number of Wales's children,
That they might be sold,—
Yes, a shipful from among the host."
Oh! blind men, poor souls,—if they continue

In their course of an angry disposition,
When the judgment and the plague come upon them,
Their false tales will be as the wind.
Our Moses and mighty chief—is Jones,
Our supreme and heavenly teacher;
Full of the energy of holy wisdom
To lead us into the land of praise.

End: The first group of Welsh Latter-day Saint emigrants causes a stir in the press

1849: 3 March, *Monmouthshire Merlin*, p. 3 (540 words). "Pontypool. More Mormon Miracles Just Out."

The writer gives an account of two "Mormon" miracles and then explains how they had been staged to hoodwink the observers. The first miracle was that of a poor woman being offered miraculous money if she "joined their community." She agreed, and soon afterwards her cat came in "with a bag of money round its neck." The second miracle occurred when a Latter-day Saint missionary healed a growth on a man's back, but it allegedly turned out to be staged ahead of time.

1849: March, *Yr Eglwysydd* (*Churchman*), pp. 73–75 (1,040 words). "Mormonism."

William Morris, the editor of the *Churchman*, is most likely the writer of this article. He does not present any particular events casting the Church in a bad light in order to substantiate his labelling of it as heresy. He clarifies his basic position:

> We do not wish to waste the time of our readers in disproving the false doctrines of this sect. As someone said about Catholicism, so say we about these people, that the best book ever written against them is the *Bible*. Mormonism cannot stand in the light of the good book. And Mormonism understands this; that is why they insist on having another Bible, and another guide besides the word of God.[24]

Morris expresses dismay that any of his compatriots would be deceived by the "false prophets," and then discusses several scriptures that warn against the "nonsense" of the Latter-day Saint deceivers.

1849: 2 March, *Cambrian* (50 words).

> The Mormons or Latter-day Saints are making some progress in Neath, more particularly in the locality of 'The Green' where they have several followers; on Sunday week two young women underwent the rite of baptism by immersion in Neath Canal, which was performed by one of the brethren.

1849: 9 March, *Cambrian* (115 words).

A brief report of the progress made by the Latter-day Saints, "notwithstanding the extravagant doctrines they expound." At one of their open-air meetings, which were "numerously attended, but far from being decorously conducted," the following happened:

> A scene of the greatest uproar and confusion occurred in consequence of a Mr. David, the preacher on the occasion, challenging a discussion, Mr. Short, tailor, opposing; the affair was of so ludicrous a character that many of the

bystanders assailed the disputants with cries of "Bravo, Short," "Well done, Short," "Go it, Davies," etc, etc.

Episode 6.3

Start: Five brief articles are written about the Reverend Rhys Morgan

1849: 16 March, *Cambrian* (320 words). "Aberavon, Mormonism or the Latter-day Saints."

A lecture by Reverend Rhys Morgan, a Baptist minister, was scheduled in the town hall in Aberavon. But so many people showed up that the meeting had to be held in the Baptist chapel.

> He [Morgan], in a very solemn and impressive manner urged upon the audience to read, mark, learn and inwardly digest Mormonism, its absurdity and its delusive tendency. The lecturer also expressed as opinion that if his audience did thus, the doctrine of "the new lights" would be treated in its true light.

The writer ends his article with the following comment:

> It is rumored that great apostle of the saints has been sent for to reply. I think really they had better pause, for assuredly the best shots are yet in the locker.

1849: 16 March, *Principality*, p. 5 (140 words). "Aberavon. Mormonism or the Religion of the Latter-day Saints."

Another report of the lecture by Reverend Rhys Morgan. The parenthetical note at the end reads:

> (Another correspondent, who sent a notice of the meeting, says that the "Great Apostle" has been sent for to reply to Mr. Morgan's lecture.)

1849: April, *Y Bedyddiwr* (*Baptist*), p. 128 (112 words). "The Mormons."

A brief report—taken from the *Principality*—of the 14 March lecture given at the Baptist chapel by the Baptist minister Rhys Morgan "on the rise and increase of these simpletons." That the meeting was chaired by an Anglican vicar is an indication of the harmony that existed between chapel and church when opposing their common enemy.

1849: April, *Seren Gomer* (*Star of Gomer*), p. 120 (265 words). "Mormonism."

This is also a report of the Rhys Morgan lecture but with greater details than those of the *Cambrian* or the *Baptist*.

> It is thought that about 1,500 were present, and in their midst, several *Saints and Mormon Doctors.* It was proposed and seconded "that the meeting's thanks be given to the Chairman for his noble manner of presiding," and also "to the Lecturer, for his skillful and excellent manner of delivering to our ears *the history of the latter-day false religious deceivers*," with which the whole audience (except for the Saints) agreed by a show of hands. I think that this Lecture will be a *death blow* to the Saints in the Aberavon area. May it so be, says A Lover of the Truth, Aberavon.

The following request is made at the end of the article:

> We would be grateful to our friend Lleurwg [the nom de plume of the lecturer and Welsh for "Hirwaun," a town adjacent to Aberdare], if we might publish this Lecture, for the benefit of the Saints in other parts.

1849: 6 April, *Cambrian* (330 words).

No pamphlet containing Morgan's lecture has yet surfaced, but he did make his presentation a second time on March 30 in the town hall of Neath, a town just over seven miles northwest of Aberavon. A report of that lecture is given in this issue of the *Cambrian*. The writer describes the presentation:

> Mr. Morgan in a long eloquent speech delivered in Welsh, which was listened to with the greatest attention, and repeatedly cheered by the assembled hundreds, traced the rise and progress of Mormonism, their first settling in America, their disgusting manners and customs while there, the lives of their principle leaders, the fearful extent to which they carried their pernicious doctrine, until the United States government was compelled to interfere, and exterminate or rather expel them from their stronghold, Nauvoo, which was finally done after a protracted siege and great slaughter, a few years ago.

End: Five brief articles are written about the Reverend Rhys Morgan

Episode 6.4

Start: John S. Davis responds to the Reverend D. Davis, an old friend of the family

1849: April, *Udgorn Seion* (*Zion's Trumpet*), pp. 71–76 (2,540 words). "The Rev. D. Davis, Panteg, and Mormonism."

At the writing of this article, John S. Davis was twenty-six years old, still single, and had been a Latter-day Saint for three years. During most of that time, he had worked closely with Dan Jones in preparing and printing the *Prophet of the Jubilee*, twenty-eight issues of which had come off the press at Rhydybont, near the market town of Llanybydder in Carmarthenshire. Sometime before November 1848, Davis had purchased a press of his own and had set it up in Carmarthen. It was on this press that the final two issues (November and December 1848) of *Prophet of the Jubilee* were printed, and Davis's name is given as the printer. As of January 1849, the name of the periodical became *Zion's Trumpet*, and the first two issues (January and February 1849) were printed on Davis's press in Carmarthen. He had just finished printing the February 1849 issue when the Reverend D. Davis, Panteg, called on him at the printing office. That John Davis had known this Independent minister for many years is made evident in a comment in this article, which he addressed to the reverend, about his conversion to The Church of Jesus Christ of Latter-day Saints:

> After reading through the scriptures, I believed the new doctrine, and I received my baptism 'for the remission of sins.' I had been taught by you and by others, that "I should prove *all* things, and hold fast that which was good."[25]

During his visit, the reverend requested a copy of the latest issue of Davis's periodical. Upon receiving it, the reverend asked, "What if I do not agree with some things that are in it, and choose to make some comments about them, where can I publish them?" Davis told him he would have the *Trumpet* at his service. About a week later the reverend returned, and Davis asked him what he thought of the new publication. Here is Davis's account of the reverend's answer:

> He answered that he felt very sorry for us, that we were publishing such foolishness, because everything in it is devoid of reason and scripture, etc., degrading our modest gift as lower than was appropriate for a man of his advantages.[26]

Apparently, the two engaged in some rather heated debate. Davis writes:

> The discussions we had between us are too long for us to think of relating here; but we were after him like a greyhound from one place to the other, until he was forced to escape to the wilderness of the devil to seek a sign from us, to prove we were of God. We said to him at that time, that he imitated Mr. Devil extremely well. We are sorry to say that Mr. Davis was more excited than we wished him to be.[27]

Davis "begged him [the reverend] earnestly" to write to the *Trumpet* and explain his disagreements. The reverend refused. Davis writes:

> He continued to say that he would not write, and that we could give him no sign; otherwise, we would have given it to him right then and there. When we saw that he would not write anything, we told him that we would do that for him; and this we do now.[28]

Davis then inserts a long letter, dated 1 March 1848, which he had written to the Reverend D. Davis over a year earlier. Davis explains:

> Rev. Sir—I am writing to you, since I do not have the opportunity of speaking to you. I used to have a high opinion of you and tended to think that you had some opinion of me as well. At that time, I was one of the world, not having joined any kind of religion, and it appeared that you had love toward me. You were Christians, and I was one of the subjects of the kingdom of darkness; despite that we were like friends.[29]

Davis tells of his discovery of religion:

> After this quiet period, somehow I found a religion, a religion which is 'spoken against everywhere'; it is called Mormonism by some, and Satanism by others.[30]

He also tells of his desire to share his new religion with others:

> I was eager for my neighbors to hear my religion, but I failed to understand how I should preach it to them; but at last, a tenant moved from an old house my father owned, and I took the liberty, without asking anyone, to preach there. Men came to hear me. My father is a member of a certain chapel, and he was greatly condemned by the minister for giving a place for his son to speak his mind!!! Now, such a minister, perhaps, is one of the Independents, and I wish to ask you if you know who he is?[31]

That the minister in question was the Reverend D. Davis, Panteg, is confirmed by a brief letter in English he had sent to John S. Davis a few days later:

> Dear Sir—I happened to tell your father, that I was afraid his character would suffer by allowing you and your people to meet at the vacant house by Tannerdy. I did it entirely for his sake. Nothing to me. Whenever you are ready to prove to me that you get extraordinary supplies, or that you have studied a sermon, I shall be most happy to introduce your case to the friends at Penuel. Yours, D. Davis, Panteg.[32]

Davis responded immediately, asking the reverend how he can ever prove that he has "studied a sermon" or that he has gotten "extraordinary supplies" so that he can be allowed to preach at the Penuel chapel.

> I do not know how to understand this properly: perhaps some of the words are to be taken figuratively or spiritually. How am I to prove that I get "extraordinary supplies" without your hearing me speak spontaneously? and how can you hear that, *before* introducing my case to the friends at Penuel? If it is possible, how? Also, how can I prove to you that I have studied a sermon, before doing so? *After* doing so, it is easy to prove. But, if I do study a sermon, how can I then prove to you the "extraordinary supplies?"[33]

Davis ends this letter to the reverend with a bit of sarcasm:

> Now, since I cannot prove the foregoing things, without having the opportunity, I humbly ask you to do your best by me, as a man of influence, to allow me to preach in one of your chapels. I sincerely hope to hear from you soon.[34]

There is no evidence Davis was ever able to preach a sermon at the Penuel chapel.

End: John S. Davis responds to the Reverend D. Davis, an old friend of the family

1849: 13 April, *Cambrian* (190 words). "The Latter-day Saints."

In this short article, three of these "deluded but devoted men" visited the neighborhood of Mumbles and Sketty. After describing them as "very illiterate persons," the writer gives his impression of the discourse given by one of them:

> Having heard a portion of the leader's discourse we perceived that his whole mind was enveloped in fanaticism. He avowed himself with much emphasis to be endowed with the Holy Ghost—that he knew it—and that those who worshipped in churches and chapels did not possess it for if they did they would be endowed with the same miraculous power as they apostles of old possessed; of healing the sick, etc., etc. He averred that the Latter-day Saints did possess that power.

1849: April, *Seren Gomer* (*Star of Gomer*), p. 116 (400 words). "Beware of False Teachers."

In addition to the report of the Rhys Morgan lecture on p. 120 of this issue of *Star of Gomer* (see preceding entry in this chapter), the issue includes this poem of sixteen four-line stanzas, entitled "Beware of False Teachers," by "James" of Glan Camlas. Referring to the servants of the devil who wish to deceive the children of God, the poet writes:

> When they fail in their deception
> In rash enchantment and sickness,
> They welcome the refuse of the world,
> And call them all "Saints."

In his final stanza, the poet looks forward to the day when the "Saints" are eliminated:

> Farewell to the false prophets for now,
> Farewell to deception for a longer time;

> Farewell to the corrupting of the Lamb's family,
> Weeping in eternal pain.

1849: April, *Y Dysgedydd* (*Instructor*), p. 120 (340 words).

An article about the Reverend J. Jones, Dan Jones's older brother, and his recent move from Rhydybont to Merthyr Tydfil. The Reverend Jones's willingness to print his brother's periodical and his pamphlets was widely opposed, and his press was even labeled the "prostitute press" by one Dafydd Lewis in the *Star of Gomer*.[35] With such a negative reputation, it is surprising that the writer of the article includes information about the rather large sums of money raised by J. Jones's neighbors to help with his move. Even the local Anglican vicar donated £2. Included also is a statement of appreciation from the reverend's deacons.

Episode 6.5

Start: The Reverend Thomas Price challenges John Pugh—John S. Davis intervenes

1849: April, *Udgorn Seion* (*Zion's Trumpet*), pp. 80–81 (530 words). "To the Rev. Thos. Price, Aberdare."

John S. Davis directs his comments to Reverend Thomas Price, the Baptist minister in Aberdare, a town about seven miles to the west of Merthyr Tydfil. He begins:

> We saw recently a letter from you, to our brother John Pugh from Aberdare, inviting him to come to debate with the "public voices" of the Saints in Wales, about the main principles of our religion.

Davis writes that he had advised John Pugh "to leave such a public debate alone," the reason being that "it would only create ill feelings among people, and cause the light to be dimmer than ever before." As a preferable alternative, Davis suggested a written debate and even offered his periodical as a "field for the battle." He received a response from Price in time to publish it in the May issue of *Zion's Trumpet* (see next entry).

1849: May, *Udgorn Seion* (*Zion's Trumpet*), pp. 99–101 (1,305 words). "Mr. John Pugh and Thomas Price, Aberdare. To the Editor of *Zion's Trumpet*."

Dated 9 May 1849, this is Rev. Thomas Price's response to John S. Davis's letter in the April issue (see preceding entry). He begins by correcting Davis's implication that Price was "inviting" John Pugh to debate. He declares:

> I would never consider extending an invitation to debate John Pugh, or any other man of similar character.[36]

Price insists that it was John Pugh who extended a "challenge" to him for a debate. Price mockingly describes his fearful reaction at receiving Pugh's challenge:

> It would have been terrible had I died of fright on the day of battle, and had my poor wife had to press charges of *manslaughter* against Pugh and his *challenge*.[37]

Price then specifies his requirements for a "public debate" to take place in the columns of *Zion's Trumpet*. The first requirement Price demands is for Pugh's letter to him and his response to Pugh be printed in *Zion's Trumpet*. Davis responds to Price's demands in a postscript following Price's letter to him:

> We have reason to be silent from now on about our brother J. Pugh, since his course recently ended in death.[38]

Davis again extends his offer to debate Price in writing by using his periodical. Apparently, Price did not pursue the debate, since nothing resembling an exchange of ideas between him and Davis ever appeared in *Zion's Trumpet.* This John Pugh may be the same John Pugh who died in a mining accident.[39]

End: The Reverend Thomas Price challenges John Pugh—John S. Davis intervenes

Episode 6.6

Start: The Reverend O. Williams is questioned about the death of a "Mormon"

1849: May, *Seren Gomer* (*Star of Gomer*), p. 149 (295 words). "To the Rev. O. Williams, Trefforest," by "Small Iota."

> The other day, word came to this neighborhood that a man in the Trefforest area was tormented to death by the people who call themselves Latter-day Saints by giving him and causing him to take some kind of oil, until he died.

"Small Iota" then asks the following four questions:

1. Was the man who "belonged to the Saints" buried in the neighborhood lately?
2. Is it true that the man was forced to take too much oil until he suffocated?
3. Are there proofs that on the evening the man died that the Saints carried him three times to the stream?
4. Why has there not been an inquest?

1849: July, *Seren Gomer* (*Star of Gomer*), p. 214 (335 words). "Answer to the Questions of 'Small Iota.'"

Here is part of the statement offered by the Reverend O. Williams:

> Since the topic you have under scrutiny is related to those men who call themselves "Latter-day Saints," remember that it is very difficult to give a complete disclosure of that which is done by them, since there is no one of any prominence that has anything to do with their deeds, only obscurity and secrecy.

With respect to the deceased, Williams confirms that he had died and that he was buried on Sunday, but that Williams himself did not know how much oil was given to him or to what extent that may have affected his life. One can imagine that Williams's response may not have been entirely satisfactory to "Small Iota," who was very likely a Latter-day Saint himself.

End: The Reverend O. Williams is questioned about the death of a "Mormon"

Episode 6.7

Start: The story of Sarah Holder, Bayliss, and their baby is discussed in the press

1849: May, *Seren Gomer* (*Star of Gomer*), pp. 153–54 (715 words). "Superstition of the Saints."

This article contains the account of Sarah Holder, a young woman who lived in Cheltenham. A man by the name of Bayliss convinced Sarah to live with him, his wife, and their three children. Later a child was born to Sarah and Bayliss, which they claimed had lived for a time after its birth. After the child died, they placed it in a box and kept it in the house. During the trial that was held for them, a doctor testified that the child had been stillborn. Bayliss "insisted on taking it [the child's body] into his possession," but the child was taken from him by force. "Then the scoundrel raised up his hands, and asked for God's protection in the 'martyrdom' he was suffering." The writer of the *Star of Gomer* article issues a challenge to the editor of "the *Star of the Saints*," an alternate title for *Zion's Trumpet*, to explain the story of Sarah Holder and Bayliss, who the writer alleged to be members of The Church of Jesus Christ of Latter-day Saints.

1849: May, *Udgorn Seion* (*Zion's Trumpet*), wrapper, p. 2 (160 words). "To the Editor of the *Star of Gomer*."

A letter from T. Brown, Bedford, to John S. Davis about the Sarah Holder story is as follows:

> To the Editor of the *Star of Gomer*. In response to what he asked us, in his May issue, about "Superstition of the Saints," we publish the following for him from the *Weekly Times*: "Sir, in your useful paper for the 1st of April, there appeared an account of a preacher by the name of Bayliss, who lived in Cheltenham, seducing a woman named Holder, both, it seems, professing to be members of the church of the Latter-day Saints. Permit me to say that neither of them is a member of that church. She has never been a member; he was once a member, but he was excommunicated for misbehavior two years ago, from which time he has opposed, and spoken against the Saints, who consider the recent shameful deed a crime against all laws, human and divine. By placing this in the columns of your paper, you fulfill a righteous act, and you satisfy, yours respectfully, T. Brown. Bedford, April 7, 1849.

End: The story of Sarah Holder, Bayliss, and their baby is discussed in the press

1849: May, *Y Tyst Apostolaidd* (*Apostolic Witness*), p. 117 (570 words). "Questions and Answers."

Someone who calls himself "Tychicus" presents to the editor a list of six questions he would like answered. Essentially, "Tychicus" is asking the editor to explain his reasons for persecuting the Latter-day Saints and for referring to them as "Satanists" and other bad names. The editor refuses to go into detail with his answer and tells "Tychicus" that he will have to be satisfied with a general comment. In his own defense, the editor explains that his original intention was "not to say a word about the folk who call themselves 'Saints,'" but that his readers had "insisted on some discussion of them to our considerable displeasure." Furthermore, he points out that Christ had called Peter "Satan" and that "we have not heard that he corrupted anyone's morals by so doing."

After suggesting that his correspondent did not understand the meaning of "persecution," the editor proceeds to explain that the word does not mean "telling the truth about men." He declares that the Latter-day Saints "ought to be exposed as religious deceivers, but they should not be persecuted, that is, to deprive them of their freedom." In some cryptic language at the end of his response, the editor refers to "Quick"—probably the Baptist minister W. R. Davies of Dowlais, who had written extensively using a variety of noms de plume, "Quick" being one of them. The editor also refers to the "Cap."—undoubtedly a reference to Captain Dan Jones. One has cause to wonder if "Tychicus" was actually the editor himself, who had submitted the questions in order to provide himself with the opportunity to continue his attacks against the Latter-day Saints in his answers.

1849: 11 May, *Cambrian* (290 words). "Freaks of the Latter-day Saints."

The word "freaks" in the title of this article appears to indicate odd happenings to members of The Church of Jesus Christ of Latter-day Saints in Wales. This article tells of "one of them" who sprained his ankle at the Trades Hall in Swansea recently. The writer tells of the "operation" performed on him by his co-religionists:

> His bandages were torn off, his foot exposed and his body prostrate on the ground for three mortal hours. Mighty and loud were the holy invocations made during this long interval but unfortunately for the patient to no effect.

The patient's wife eventually intervened and arranged for medical aid for her husband. The writer observes:

> This circumstance we hear has since had its salutary effect and has shaken the man's faith most materially in the miraculous part of the Latter-day Saints' powers, at least.

Episode 6.8

Start: Welsh Latter-day Saints arrive in Minersville, Pennsylvania

1849: May, *Y Cyfaill o'r Hen Wlad yn America* (*Friend of the Old Country in America*), pp. 150–51 (345 words). "Mormonism in Minersville."

The writer of this article tells of the group of Latter-day Saints in this Pennsylvania mining town who were desirous of going "with all haste" to their "New Jerusalem in Upper California." And to accomplish their desire, they were putting considerable pressure on one among them who was "unburdened with an oversupply of sense" but who had "a bit of this world's goods," to help finance the journey they all wished to make. The writer describes the plight of this man:

> It is now said that these Mormons have some "drops," to give to those who listen to them for the purpose of driving out the evil spirit from them, and that the aforementioned man received an overdose which instead of driving out the evil spirit drove out the little remaining sense he had; and it almost drove out his breath of life.[40]

The writer ends his article with the following assertion:

> It is worthy of note that it is from among the "Baptized" Brethren, almost without exception, that the Mormon converts are obtained here; and it is also my understanding that it is the same in Wales and every other place where their odious and heretical doctrines flourish.[41]

1849: 8 June, *Principality*, p. 6 (25 words).

> An American correspondent of *Le Populaire* asserts that the Mormons by the extraordinary ardor of their proselytism, are making rapid, unceasing, and considerable progress.

1849: June, *Y Cyfaill o'r Hen Wlad yn America* (*Friend of the Old Country in America*), p. 181 (340 words).

Although it is true that many of the converts to The Church of Jesus Christ of ter-day Saints came from among the Baptists, or the "Baptized" Brethren, as the writer of the article in the May issue of this periodical calls them, there were also many who did not. "Phi.," also from Minersville, takes exception to the article by "A Miner" in the previous issue:

> Let "Miner" take note that not one single member from the "Baptized" brethren, or from any other denomination, here, in Wales, or any other place, has gone to them.

"Miner" then challenges "Phi." to offer evidence of his assertion:

> Now, I ask "Miner" how he can prove that it is from the "Baptized" brethren, almost without exception, that the Mormon converts are obtained, here and in Wales, and every other place? I wait, in anticipation that he will reward us with facts, and not fiction, in your next issue.

It appears that "Phi." had to wait in vain, as apparently no response from "Miner" ever appeared in the following issue or any other.

Among the Latter-day Saints in Minersville were some Welsh converts. One of these was Thomas M. Richards, who gave credit for his 1846 conversion to Dan Jones. Richards was so anxious to gather with the body of the Saints in America that he left Wales in early 1847 and went as far as Minersville, Pennsylvania. He sent a letter with news from Minersville to Dan Jones dated 15 July 1847,[42] one to John Davis in 1849,[43] one to John Davis later in 1849,[44] one to Dan Jones dated 1 May 1854,[45] and one to Dan Jones dated 20 November 1854.[46]

End: Welsh Latter-day Saints arrive in Minersville, Pennsylvania

1849: June, *Y Tyst Apostolaidd* (*Apostolic Witness*), p. 145 (140 words).

The writer tells of Reverend W. R. Davies giving a sermon and then performing nine baptisms. In the final lines, the writer is obviously very pleased to welcome back one who had spent some time among the Latter-day Saints:

> One of the baptized had been blinded and ensnared some time ago by the followers of Joe Smith, and had been baptized to those loathsome and devilish doctrines; but we believe that such a baptism was nothing more than the play of children, or an impudent joke of the things of God; in our view it was nothing but sinful frivolousness. This is the second to be baptized here lately from this deluded household.

Episode 6.9

Start: John Lloyd sets the record straight

1849: 8 June, *Cambrian* (60 words). "An Ex-Latter-day Saint."

> On Sunday week a most excellent and impressive sermon was preached at the house of Mr. David Jones of Cwmguedd, Ystradgunlais, by the Rev. John Lloyd (alias John the Blacksmith) late a Latter-day Saint, to a large and respectable congregation from the verse, "O ye, generation of vipers, who hath warned you to flee from the wrath to come?"

1849: 22 June, *Cambrian* (100 words). "To the Editor of the *Cambrian*."

An angry John Lloyd declares to the editor that the brief article of the 8 June issue was totally false:

> Sir. Having seen a paragraph in your *Cambrian* of the week before last, stating that "the Rev. John Lloyd (alias John the Blacksmith), had been preaching at a house at Cwmguedd, etc." I beg to state that the whole is a direct falsehood, probably the weak invention of some wiseacre of this neighborhood, to make dupes of the public. By giving insertion to this in your next *Cambrian,* or by using some other means of contradicting the statement alluded to, you will greatly oblige.
> Your humble servant, John Lloyd, Ystradgunlais, June 18th 1849.

Precisely what had triggered such indignation on the part of John Lloyd is unclear.

End: John Lloyd sets the record straight

1849: 16 July, *Hanes Chwech o Benboethiaid Crefyddol: Sef, Joseph Smith, Mahomet, Richard Brothers, Jemimah Wilson, Ann Lee, and Joanna Southcotte* (*History of Six Religious Fanatics: Namely, Joseph Smith, Muhammed, Richard Brothers, Jemimah Wilson, Ann Lee, and Joanna Southcott*), pamphlet, 24 pages.

In the foreword to this pamphlet, the author, Evan Lewis, declares:

> Since the deceitful Mormons suppose their honorable prophet to be someone great, I have put him alongside his brothers and sisters, so that they and all who read the book can see the similarity between the one and the other.

Only the first five pages of this pamphlet are focused on Joseph Smith, and these are simply quoted from Joseph Smith's account of his first vision and the initial spread of the Church he founded.

1849: 7 July, *Monmouthshire Merlin*, p. 3 (160 words). "Mormonist Miracles."

A follower of the "notorious Joseph Smith" claimed that "'on a true believer, poison would have no effect.'" Some of his listeners presented him with some prussic acid and urged him to take some. A policeman intervened and rescued him.

1849: 21 July, *Monmouthshire Merlin*, p. 4 (65 words).

A brief account of the Latter-day Saint preacher claiming that "a true believer might swallow poison with impunity."

1849: 21 July, *Cardiff and Merthyr Guardian*, p. 4 (65 words).

Yet another brief report of "a Mormon orator" who claimed that poison would have no effect on a true believer.

1849: July, *Y Diwygiwr* (*Revivalist*), p. 226 (185 words). "The Saints in a Dilemma."

John Pugh, a member of The Church of Jesus Christ of Latter-day Saints, had been burned in the Gwerfa coal works in Aberdare, along with several other workers. According to this article, Pugh's religious leader advised him not to receive treatment from the doctor but rather to rely on his faith along with a blessing from an "apostle," the title given sarcastically by enemies of the Latter-day Saints to their leaders even though there were no apostles in Wales at that time. The writer concludes:

> The jurors were very close to returning a verdict of manslaughter against the apostle, and the *coroner* warned him to be careful in the future not to pretend to have the ability to cure through miracles; but the apostle placed all the blame on the faith of John Pugh, and he claimed that had his skin and his bones been removed from his arm, he would have mended like putting one hand in the other.

1849: July, *Y Cenhadwr Americanaidd* (*American Messenger*), p. 212 (440 words).

Two poems appear here, the first by "Eiddil" from Minersville, and the second by "David from Monmouth," who was also from Minersville. The first consists of forty eight lines. Here is the first stanza:

> Through the mirror, I shall examine the Saints,
> The latest chaff of the scoundrel* **Joe Smith*
> Their contemptible beliefs I declare
> To be a great darkness in our Lord's world.

And here is the final stanza:

> From my heart I desire—that you should not go
> Dear ones, to join
> The saints of sins, while there is
> In you a soul uniting.

The second poem consists of sixteen lines. Here is the first stanza:

> I sing, I offer to give advice to the saints
> To pause a while;
> And my prayer today to God:
> Open the eyes of the unbelievers.

1849: July, *Y Cenhadwr Americanaidd* (*American Messenger*), p. 223 (215 words). "Mormon Miracle."

This is a brief account of the futile efforts of the Latter-day Saints in Ystradgynlais to keep a baby alive. The writer concludes:

> A miracle failed to be worked through grace and without grace. To the great disappointment of the simpletons, they had to put the child in "the pre-appointed house of all men."

1849: August, *Seren Gomer* (*Star of Gomer*), p. 248 (280 words). "A Religious Success."

This is yet another attack by Rev. W. R. Davies on those whom he called the "Latter-day Satanists." Writing as "T. ab Ieuan," he tells of a conversation he had had with a fellow minister about the effect of the cholera epidemic on the growth of the

Baptists and other Nonconformists as compared with the growth of The Church of Jesus Christ of Latter-day Saints. His friend commented:

> Yes, there isn't so much talk of progress among the "Saints" in a situation like this. When the world was lighthearted and carefree, they got their share like others, but when the cause of the soul becomes serious over and above the mind, there is not so much to attract people to them.

Davies concludes with a few observations that encapsulate the abiding hatred and the barrage of venom he had unleashed about William Henshaw and Dan Jones and their religion over the previous six years:

> The above comment of the respectable minister Mr. Williams is completely true, and so it is easy enough to conclude that Tomfoolery and Mormonism are completely synonymous things. Also, Mr. Gomer, it is only everyone's refuse and rubbish that are aborted by other denominations who join the family of Joe Smith, while it is the other denominations that win men of blameless character. Let not one of them say that they get anyone except those who could be spared with the greatest cheerfulness.

These would be the Reverend's final published words about the religion he so deeply abhorred and despised. On 1 September 1849, he fell fatally ill of the cholera then rampant in Wales.

1849: August, *Y Tyst Apostolaidd* (*Apostolic Witness*), p. 192 (235 words). "The Socinians and the Mormons in Dowlais and Merthyr."

In the eyes of their opponents, the Latter-day Saints were "Satanists" and thus did not accept the divinity of Christ, much like the Socinians. According to the writer, both groups were having great difficulty in getting people to listen to their messages and "have dwindled in these places to the point that they are beneath notice."

1849: 10 August, *Cambrian*, item 1 (85 words). "A Scene at Trades Hall."

The Latter-day Saints were holding a meeting at this hall when "a Reverend gentleman . . . thought it no harm to question the parties." The resulting confusion led to the intruder's being "most unceremoniously ejected minus of every button on his coat."

1849: 10 August, *Cambrian*, item 2 (80 words). "The Latter-day Saints."

A few lines about an evening outdoor meeting of the Latter-day Saints. Because of the calm weather, the "uncouth strains of the preacher were heard at a long distance and afforded a fertile theme for the rude jests and pleasantries of many who were amongst the large number assembled, waiting the return of the excursionists from Ilfracombe and Lynton."

1849: 15 September, *Monmouthshire Beacon*, p. 6 (23 words).

> A Mormon settlement has been formed on the Beaver Islands, in Lake Michigan. The population is already about five hundred, and rapidly increasing.

1849: September, *Y Diwygiwr* (*Revivalist*), p. 289 (315 words). "The Mormons in California."

Referring to the title, the writer states that "these religious fanatics have now come to the field against [US] President [Zachary] Taylor." He then quotes Samuel S. Snow as he rages against Taylor for declaring "a day of fasting, humility, and prayer" to "beseech God to turn away . . . the contagious scourge of cholera." Snow, who claims to be "the Prime Minister of Jesus Christ, declares: 'May God hasten the war, the famine, and the plague, and the destruction of all those who are wicked!'" That Snow was a "Millerite" and not a "Mormon" did not deter the editor of the *Revivalist* from making this incident into an attack on The Church of Jesus Christ of Latter-day Saints.

1849: October, *Y Drysorfa Gynnulleidfaol* (*Congregationalist Treasury*), p. 319 (315 words). "The Deceit of the Mormons."

This is the story of eighty-two-year-old Elinor Rees. The Latter-day Saints purportedly promised her that if she accepted baptism from them, "not only would they assure her eternal life, but they would restore to her the use of her eyes, and she would be restored to health, and she would not have to fear the cholera." But just a few days after her baptism, she died of cholera. The writer concludes:

> It is obvious that increasing their number is the Mormons' only endeavor, and they do not care what deceit or what lies are told by them in order to achieve their end, and they care not what characters, be they thieves, or whores, or drunkards, and completely unconverted and unrepentant ones at that, they get into their communion.

1849: 13 November, *North Wales Chronicle*, p. 4 (37 words).

> It was generally considered that the application of the Mormons for the admission of their territory as a distinct State into the Union, under the title of the State of Deseret, would not be entertained by Congress.

1849: 16 November, *Principality*, p. 5 (165 words). "A Mormonitish Feast."

A report of a dinner at the house of Thomas Lewis of Blaendare, a Latter-day Saint. A group of his co-religionists gathered at his house, and "Mr. John Barleycorn became a great favorite among all the company." And the "strange affair" with dances and bagpipes did not break up "till the dawn of the day, . . . when most of the male and female members had some difficulty in finding their way home."

1849: 23 November, *Principality*, p. 6 (1,165 words). "The New Mormon State."

A fairly long article from the *Daily News* which outlines the progress of the Church in Britain. The writer says of Joseph Smith:

> He drank, swore, and swindled; drove about with a lumbering wagon in a broad-brimmed hat, cracking his whip, like a courier, and could scarcely stutter an intelligible address to extort the dollars of his followers.

1849: 23 November, *Principality*, p. 7 (25 words).

> The *Shrewsbury Journal* notices the drowning of a Mormon "elder" whilst performing the ceremony of immersing a female convert. The latter narrowly escaped with life.

1849: November, *Y Bedyddiwr* (*Baptist*), p. 351 (125 words). "The Latter-day Saints."

George Thomas in Haverfordwest died from cholera after receiving baptism from his brother John. After a postmortem examination was conducted, the verdict of the jurors was "that his death had been hastened by being immersed in water at his own request." The writer concludes: "When will this people gain a little wisdom, I wonder!"

1849: November, *Seren Gomer* (*Star of Gomer*), p. 350 (230 words). "Death of a Man by Baptism."

This is a report of the death of George Thomas in Haverfordwest. This writer quotes the verdict:

> That the deceased died of cholera, and that his death was brought about by his being immersed in cold water, by John Thomas, at his own request. . . . This verdict, especially the final phrase "at his own request," is what saved this group, once again, from being taken up and put on trial for manslaughter.

1849: November, *Y Drysorfa Gynnulleidfaol* (*Congregationalist Treasury*), p. 352 (100 words). "Haverfordwest."

This is yet another brief report about the death of George Thomas as a result of being baptized by immersion and adds nothing new to what the *Baptist* and the *Star of Gomer* articles contain.

1849: November, *Y Drysorfa Gynnulleidfaol* (*Congregationalist Treasury*), p. 351 (145 words). "Mormonism in Llangadog."

Someone, perhaps the editor, tells of a recent experience:

> One Sunday morning recently when I happened to be taking a stroll, Ben the *Sausage* had placed his fat body by the wall, and was shouting out his ungodly chatter, without so much as a man listening to him.

The writer observes that poor Ben would probably not be preaching in Llangadog ever again because the people there "would not listen to one of the followers of Joe Smith, the murderer." He then makes a prediction:

> In the next issue a *specimen* will be given of two sermons preached recently near the Amman iron works, so that the country may discover their presumption and their ungodliness.

No such sermons appear in the next issue of the *Congregationalist Treasury.*

1849: November, *Y Drysorfa Gynnulleidfaol* (*Congregationalist Treasury*), p. 340 (185 words). "Verses to Mormonism."

This poem was composed by "the late J. W. Hughes." The first of the six four-line stanzas sets the stage for the other five:

> Of all people, and of all pains—I never saw
> A worse one than Saintism;
> Mormonism is a wall of peat,
> Dung of the age, it has gone to nothing.

The remaining five stanzas contain disparaging observations about Joseph Smith, false doctrine, and miracles. Hughes gives his assurance that he will become a Saint if an adept of Smith's religion can raise someone from the dead.

1849: 24 November, *Cardiff and Merthyr Guardian*, p. 4 (38 words).

> Another person has fallen a victim to Mormon baptism. An elder named Lloyd had just immersed a woman in the Severn at Shrewsbury last week, when his foot slipped, and he fell into the river and was drowned.

1849: 15 December, *Monmouthshire Merlin*, p. 4 (50 words).

> The Mormons of Deseret (Salt Lake), indulge in polygamy, and hold the doctrine that a man may have as many wives as he can support. It is said that some of the old men there have 20 wives, but that few of the young men have more than five.

1849: 18 December, *North Wales Chronicle*, p. 2 (50 words).

The same few lines that were printed in the *Monmouthshire Merlin* for 15 December.

1849: December, *Y Drysorfa* (*Treasury*), pp. 397–98 (540 words). "Latter-day Saints."

This article adds a few more details to the incident described in the *Principality* (16 November, p. 5, see previous entry in this chapter) and ends with this sarcastic observation: "This is an example of the saintliness of the 'Saints.'"

1849: December, *Seren Gomer* (*Star of Gomer*), p. 378 (165 words). "The Drowning of a Mormon Preacher."

This account is taken from a newspaper in Shrewsbury. A small group of Latter-day Saints had gathered at the river for the baptism of a convert named Ann Griffiths. A brother named Thomas Lloyd took her into the river, baptized her, and then went under water while trying to come out. The woman was rescued, but the brother drowned. Unlike most articles about The Church of Jesus Christ of Latter-day Saints, this one has only one negative phrase referring to the Church, calling it a "deluded sect."

1849: December, *Y Drysorfa* (*Treasury*), pp. 397–98 (540 words). "Latter-day Saints."

This writer of this article quotes from the *New York Tribune* and the *Millennial Star* about the progress of the Latter-day Saints in Wales. He also mentions the article from *The Principality* (16 November, p. 5) and the "happy evening" at the house of Mr. Thomas Lewis and quotes from the *Shrewsbury Journal* about the drowning of Thomas Lloyd(as related also in the *Star of Gomer* for December 1849, p. 378).

1849: December, *Y Drysorfa Gynnulleidfaol* (*Congregationalist Treasury*), p. 376 (150 words). "The Saints."

This article is reprinted from the October 17 *New York Tribune*. Given the positive nature of its contents and the phraseology, the *New York Tribune* article is likely to have been written by a Latter-day Saint. Here is a sample:

> From the time Captain Jones left Wales, over 800 have been baptized in the Church of Jesus Christ, and the sick have been healed through the power of faith, and many believe.

The writer of the *New York Tribune* article refers to reports given in the *Millennial Star* that cholera had been cured, the mute had been made to speak, and many miracles had been wrought. The writer for the *Congregationalist Treasury* ends with a statement of surprise, as if to say, "This doesn't sound like the Latter-day Saints that we know in Britain." Here is the statement:

> No one this side of the Atlantic had any idea that such wonders as these were to be seen in "the old country."

Notes

1. *Millennial Star* 11 (1849): 38–42.
2. The facsimile translation for both the 1849 and the 1850 volumes of *Zion's Trumpet* are available on the Welsh Saints Project.
3. *Millennial Star* 11 (1849): 92.
4. *Zion's Trumpet,* January 1849, 42–43.
5. https://contentdm.lib.byu.edu/digital/collection/SCMisc/id/9982
6. For the details see *The Call of Zion: The Story of the First Welsh Mormon Emigration* on the Welsh Saints Project.
7. *Zion's Trumpet*, September 1849, wrapper, 3.
8. "Captain Dan Jones and the Welsh Indians," *Dialogue: A Journal of Mormon Thought* 18, no. 4 (Winter 1985): 112–17. See also Jones's account in the 1851 volume of *Zion's Trumpet*, 197–202, 219–23, 237–41, 254–58.
9. *Zion's Trumpet,* January 1849, 15.
10. *Sun,* January 1849, 33.
11. Ibid., 34.
12. See Job 1:7.
13. See *The Call of Zion: the Story of the First Welsh Mormon Emigration* for further details.
14. *Congregationalist Treasury*, February 1849, 54.
15. See *The Call of Zion: the Story of the First Welsh Mormon Emigration* for further details.
16. *Millennial Star* 11 (1849): 38–42.
17. *Friend of the Old Country in America*, April 1849, 123.
18. Ibid., 124.
19. Jelinger C. Symons, *Reports of the Commissioners of Inquiry into the State of Education in Wales*, 3 vols. (London: William Clowes and Sons, 1847), 2:66.
20. Symons, *Reports*, 2:66.
21. See *Defending the Faith*, item P4.
22. See *Defending the Faith*, item D15.
23. *Star of Gomer*, October 1848, 305.
24. *Churchman*, March 1849, 74.
25. *Zion's Trumpet*, April 1849, 73.
26. Ibid., 72.
27. Ibid.
28. Ibid.
29. Ibid.
30. Ibid.
31. Ibid., 73.
32. Ibid., 75.
33. Ibid.
34. Ibid.
35. *Star of Gomer*, December 1847, 375.
36. *Zion's Trumpet*, May 1849, 99.
37. Ibid.
38. Ibid., 101.
39. *Revivalist,* July 1849, 226.
40. *Friend of the Old Country in America*, May 1849, 150–51.
41. Ibid., 151.
42. *Prophet of the Jubilee*, September 1848, 138–39.
43. *Zion's Trumpet,* June 1849, wrapper, 2.
44. *Zion's Trumpet*, November 1849, wrapper, 2.
45. *Zion's Trumpet*, 3 June 1854, 330–31.
46. *Zion's Trumpet*, 6 January 1855, 6–8.

Chapter 7

Episodes

7.1—John S. Davis reprimands an Independent minister and an Anglican curate
7.2—The saga of the forged letter ends in tragedy for the one who composed it
7.3—"A bit of surprise"—*Star of Gomer* publishes an impartial article
7.4—Mr. French opposes the Church, joins the Church, then leaves the Church
7.5—Four articles are published containing historical information about the Latter-day Saints
7.6—A prolonged polemic about the "similarity of the Baptists and the Saints" is published
7.7—A Unitarian ("Philalethes") debates with a Latter-day Saint (John Richards) and a former Latter-day Saint

Salient Events

- **5 January 1850**—Elder Levi Richards is appointed "to go to Wales, and give counsel and instruction to the presidency of the Welsh conferences, and everyone else that may be in their midst."[1] This appointment no doubt came as a shock to William Phillips, who had succeeded Dan Jones as president. Perhaps an even greater shock was that Elder Richards's wife, Sister Sarah Griffith Richards, was to accompany her husband. Orson Pratt, president of the Church in Great Britain, also said, "Our particular wish is for the Welsh conferences to contribute of their means toward the support of Brother Richards and his family." Neither Elder Richards nor his wife, although she was a native of Monmouthshire, could speak any Welsh. In the February 1850 issue of *Zion's Trumpet*, John S. Davis clarified: "Brother Richards has not been sent to preside instead of Elder Phillips, but to teach and confer with the presidency."[2] In the April issue of *Zion's Trumpet* is the following from John S. Davis: "Brother Dr. Levi Richards will make his home most particularly in Swansea, where the West Glamorgan District will contribute toward his needs. We hope this brother will be respected wherever he goes."[3] This last comment suggests that at least some of the Welsh Latter-day Saints may have had a difficult time in dealing with the authority that Richards enjoyed in their domain. Richards is mentioned a few other times in *Zion's Trumpet* as having spoken at conferences in Wales but never as having issued any instructions to the membership in Wales or to their presidency. At the October conference in Manchester, Richards received the sustaining vote to serve as counselor to his brother, Franklin D. Richards, in the presidency of the Church in Britain.

- **18 February 1850**—Elder Abel Evans sails on the *Josiah Bradlee*, one month after being released as counselor to William Phillips. Evans had served just one year in the Welsh mission presidency. The release came as a result of William Morgan's 2 September 1849 letter to Phillips, to which Morgan added a postscript: "Brother Jones wishes for you to send Abel Evans with the next company, if you can spare him."[4] One can only conjecture what Dan Jones may have had in mind for Evans, since they did not cross paths for another two and a half years. When they did finally meet, it was briefly, about eighty miles east of Salt Lake City. Evans was traveling in a pioneer company coming from Council Bluffs, and a group of missionaries that included Dan Jones was headed east and crossed Evans's path. Dan Jones was on his way back to Wales to serve his second mission. After this encounter, it would be at least another four years before they would both be in Utah at the same time. Evans returned to Wales on a mission in 1865, four years after Jones's death in Provo, Utah. Sadly, Evans died on 30 November 1866 following a long illness, while still serving his mission. He was buried in the Cefncoedycymmer Cemetery near Merthyr Tydfil, and the headstone placed on his grave by some of his fellow missionaries still stands. He left three wives and fifteen children back in Lehi, Utah.[5]
- **8 March 1850**—A special conference is held at the White Lion Inn in Merthyr Tydfil during which Thomas Pugh, from Aberdare, is called as a counselor to President William Phillips.[6] Pugh served until 17 January 1853 when he and his three sons sailed from Liverpool on the *Ellen Maria*. In his absence, at a special conference in Merthyr Tydfil on 12 March 1853, he was excommunicated in absentia for adultery, though he would not know that until later.
- **9 June 1850**—The second visit of the Apostle John Taylor to Wales, at a conference in Merthyr Tydfil. The membership of the Church had increased by over three thousand since his first visit in January 1847.
- **28 August 1850**—Jennette Eveline Evans is born in the area known as Clwydyfagwyr near what is now the Merthyr Tydfil Stake Center. Her parents, Thomas and Margaret Evans, converted to The Church of Jesus Christ of Latter-day Saints and sailed with their six children to America in 1856

on board the *Horizon*. Jenette later married David McKay, and their son, David O. McKay, later became the ninth President of The Church of Jesus Christ of Latter-day Saints.

- **5 October 1850**—The *Monmouthshire Merlin* reports the "Lectures against Mormonism" given by J. Williams and R. French at the Newport town hall. The reporter identifies Mr. French as "late a student at the Carmarthen Presbyterian College" and writes that the lecture of Mr. French "was declared to be one of the most argumentative and eloquent addresses ever heard on a similar subject." Three months later, the same newspaper reported that Mr. French had converted to "the very faith he had denounced" the previous week. During the next three years, Mr. French presented several lectures about the new religion he had adopted. However, he left the Church in 1854, and a lengthy report about why he had recently left the faith he had adopted three years earlier can be found in the 14 April 1854 issue of the *Monmouthshire Merlin*. See Episode 7.4.

Commentary

1850: 5 January, *Monmouthshire Beacon*, p. 6 (675 words).

> "The Mormonites," says the *Worcester Herald*, "are still preaching, as they call it, in this town, but we are glad to hear that they are put to considerable shifts to get an audience together. Last Sunday they announced that they should immerse twenty-six individuals in the miserable place which we mentioned before; but the whole affair turned out merely to be a *ruse* to attract somebody to hear their harangues."

After this introduction is an abstract of a lecture at Birmingham by Mr. John Bowes of Manchester, editor of the *Christian Magazine*, on the character and work of Joseph Smith, polygamy, missions and spiritual wives, and the Danites.

1850: 5 January, *Silurian*, p. 1 (43 words).

> Travelers from the Mormon settlements of Deseret (Salt Lake) say that money and gold dust are very abundant, that the people have agreed upon a constitution for their new state, and have established a mint for Mormon coinage. The crops were unusually abundant.

1850: January, *Y Diwygiwr* (*Revivalist*), p. 6–9 (Excerpt). "A Word to Our Subscribers."

The Reverend David Rees, minister of Capel Als in Llanelli, makes some comments about his ecclesiastical contemporaries in general—that they are "weighed and measured" by a higher standard than the average citizen of Wales. Their standing in society, he explains, often causes many of them to view themselves as being exceptional:

> There is nothing that is right in heaven or on earth except what is brought forth by their own line and measure. They are surprised and amazed as to why

> the world cannot see and recognize their superiority and bow down to worship them while ignoring everyone and everything else.[7]

Rees then admits:

> This is but a very imperfect portrayal of the antics and pronouncements of some who go around the country these days to convince the innocents that no one on earth is or ever has been like them. Neither do all of them belong to the sect that *claim* to be representatives of that heinous lunatic, Joe Smith, and deserving of more respect than the Bible.[8]

Rees then turns his focus to one of these ministers in particular, the Reverend John Jones, who on his press at Rhydybont—about thirty-five miles to the north of Llanelli—had printed the periodical and pamphlets of his brother Dan Jones from 1846 to 1848. And although John Jones was not a believer in the religion established twenty years earlier by Joseph Smith, he had stooped to aiding its propagation in Wales by printing its materials.

Finally, Rees explains that John Jones still owed Rees over £250 for materials that Rees had printed for Jones several years earlier. He even includes a bill showing the details. At this point Jones had relocated himself and his family to Aberdare near Merthyr Tydfil. He would eventually leave Wales under a cloak of secrecy a few years later with the aid of his brother Dan.

1850: 29 January, *North Wales Chronicle*, p. 3 (50 words).

> The Mormons were forming a new colony in the Pitch Valley, about 200 miles south of Salt Lake City. It is represented as remarkably fertile, and the climate as being very fine. About 100 wagons were dispatched thither with provisions and property, and from 50 to 100 families accompanied.

1850: 9 February, *Monmouthshire Beacon*, p. 4 (20 words). "Migration of 'Saints.'"

> A large number of the disciples of Mormon left Cardiff a few days since for Bristol, *en route* for California.

1850: February, *Y Bedyddiwr* (*Baptist*), p. 67 (270 words). "The Spur and Not the Bridle."

This piece is an obituary for William Powell, who had been a faithful member of the Baptists in Pontypool for several decades. The writer of the obituary praises Powell for his service as a deacon and for his ability to deliver a sermon from the pulpit. He also says Powell was not like many other preachers, who suffered from the "Speechifying Itch." The editor of the periodical inserts a footnote in which he explains in some detail the symptoms of this ailment: "lightheadedness, an itch at the root of the tongue, hallucinations of an imagination that is running wild, and an irresistible lust for talking." He points out that the physical world has its safety valves that "provide escape to secretions and church-associated troubles" and then describes one of those valves among the Welsh:

> You have Mormonism, for example, which is a kind of safety valve. . . . The speechifyers are hereby encouraged to join the Saints where they may unburden themselves "from dawn to dusk." A brother from Merthyr told me the other day that there is a Saint who customarily speechifies opposite his house

> every Sunday afternoon, spending an hour babbling on while no one is listening. The glory of these moments is that there was no one listening.[9]

1850: February, *Y Diwygiwr* (*Revivalist*), p. 68, item 1 (70 words). "The Latter Saints."

This is the first of two articles on this page of the *Revivalist.* Here is the sarcastic comment about the "Saints" in this article:

> Four of these were caught fishing, in an unlawful way, in Ammon. Three of them took off: but the other one was seized, and the following day he was fined 20 shillings. It is dangerous for the fish when the Saints fish, for one can command the other to throw the net for all the fish in the river—the Saints can work miracles.

Episode 7.1

Start: John S. Davis reprimands an Independent minister and an Anglican curate

1850: February, *Y Diwygiwr* (*Revivalist*), p. 68, item 2 (245 words). "The Saints."

Someone by the name of Evan from "Yonder Town" submits a brief account of a "great rumpus in the Saints' meeting" that was held on Saturday, 27 January, in the chapel built by the local Latter-day Saints in the town of Llanelli and dedicated by Dan Jones about a year before. David Rees, the editor of the *Revivalist,* allowed space in his periodical for this account, along with the deplorable poem that accompanied it. Here is how the writer, Evan, describes the scene:

> Nick came there, and took hold of one of them, but we did not hear if it was a male or female saint, and squeezed him until he was as flat as a board, and if David Williams and another brother had not been able to collar the old fellow, it is likely that he would have completely done away with one of this brotherhood, if he had not taken the head of the house into the bargain.

Evan then poses two questions:

> Why is Nick so fond of meeting the Saints? Does he feel that some of them are a little too forward with his majesty? Does he say, "Jesus I know, and Paul I know, but who are you?"

The editor then adds a sixteen-line poem composed by Evan that begins with yet another question: "What are the saints of Mormon religion?" In answer to this question, Evan provides fifteen very nasty, brief descriptions. Here is a sample:

> A dunghill of the dregs of the churches.
> The cattle gnats of the Pharoah all together;
> The servants of slander, abominable deists,
> The chaff of society, living maggots.

1850: March, *Yr Haul* (*Sun*), pp. 96–97 (340 words). "The Mormons."

Editor David Owen printed a different version of the recent "tremendous stir" at the Latter-day Saint chapel in Llanelli as written by "W. D.":

> One Sabbath evening recently, one of them dressed up in the guise of the evil spirit, with two horns and a big tail. Only a few of the Saints knew of his

> coming; consequently, there was quite a commotion, and many were frightened. Diabolus took advantage of this, and performed his tricks on the floor, waving his tail and stamping his feet terrifyingly.

Describing The Church as "a viper that has leaped across the heat of the fire that has been lit by the various Sects in Wales," David Owen observes:

> No wonder that godless men are joking like this, because they have not seen a much better example from the Nonconformist ministers, men from whom one would expect better things. These are turning their houses of worship into playhouses, for every bit of rubbish to make the things they deem best in them.

1850: March, *Udgorn Seion* (*Zion's Trumpet*), pp. 84–87 (1,195 words). "The 'Nick' of the Rev. D. Rees, Llanelli."

John S. Davis, the editor of *Zion's Trumpet*, devoted a few pages of his periodical to presenting additional information about the incident that transpired at the little Latter-day Saint chapel in Llanelli. He begins by quoting the article as it appeared in the *Revivalist*, including all sixteen lines of the scurrilous poem that followed. He then quotes the entire first paragraph of the account that appeared in the Anglican periodical the *Sun*. At this point, Davis appeals to his own readers in order to make sense of the two accounts, which differ greatly concerning the details of what took place:

> Now, dear readers, whom do you believe, Mr. Rees or W. D.? Neither says he was there. Mr. Rees believes everything he hears against the Saints, however unreasonable it may be.[10]

In order "to show the stupidity of Mr. Rees regarding the 'Nick' who came to the Saints' meeting in Llanelli," Davis quotes from a letter he received from Dafydd Williams, who was presiding at the meeting in question:

> I assure you that what appeared in the *Revivalist* is falsehood, without the least basis in fact. Dafydd Williams, Mynydd (formerly of Llwyni), was presiding that day; and the principal devil seen there was ONE of the PRINTERS of the *Revivalist*!! He went out in an unseemly fashion, and pulled the door behind him so violently, that the whole building reverberated![11]

In his letter of explanation to John S. Davis, Dafydd Williams wrote that he had gone in person to talk with David Rees, the editor of the *Revivalist*, and asked him to retract the "falsehood." But David Rees had flatly refused to do so, using some very abusive language to someone he considered to be far below his own station:

> Indeed, I [Rees] was not the author; I only received it, and so I took it to be the truth; and I do not think it is worth retracting it, and I would never go to that much trouble: also, since you believe in casting out devils, what harm can there be in the story? I shall never retract it, because I believe it. And you be quiet, you fool; how do you know that you are that Dafydd Williams? is there only one Dafydd Williams in Llanelli? And do you know who you are talking to, you half-witted, impertinent fool, etc.[12]

Davis elected not to print the full conversation, which Williams had written out and sent with his letter; however, Davis did make some observations from his reading of it:

> It can be seen from the letter of the Dafydd Williams who was presiding over the meeting, that this "Nick" was ONE OF THE PRINTERS of Mr. Rees after all; but is it not likely that Mr. Rees knew that his *Printer's Devil* was in the habit of wearing horns and a tail, and was able to squeeze men like boards?[13]

Davis also decided to offer some advice to Rees, who, besides being the editor of the *Revivalist*, was also an Independent minister and cared for his flock at the nearby Als Chapel:

> It would be better for our friend Mr. Rees to keep his "Nick" in the office, than to let him go out to blacken his character with the Latter-day "Satanists"; for they are not of the same species. Mr. Rees's "Nick" is better suited to go to Als Chapel to show his power: perhaps there is more avarice there to obtain a new "head of house" than there is among the Saints, should there be no one there "able to collar the old fellow."[14]

Davis closes his article with a mocking expression of gratitude for the poetry that accompanied the *Revivalist* article:

> We thank Mr. Rees for publishing the two heavenly verses of Evan from Yonder Town; no doubt they can be of help to the sheep of Als Chapel as they ford the old river Jordan which they expect to cross in death, unless they now prove that their shepherd is being led by the Spirit of N—(Nick, is it not?).[15]

Davis's final comment in the article could possibly be classified as a literary coup de grâce:

> If we could compose verses as full of true Christianity as those of Evan, we would be eager to pay him back, doubly twice over; but our muse is not used to producing such honeyed words, and so it is pointless for us to try.[16]

End: John S. Davis reprimands an Independent minister and an Anglican curate

1850: 1 February, *Cambrian* (42 words). "The Latter-day Saints and the Promised Land."

> About one hundred of the Latter Day Saints from the hills and a neighbouring county arrived at Swansea this week and embarked in the *Troubadour* for Liverpool *en route* for the Land of Promise.

1850: 30 March, *Caernarvon and Denbigh Herald*, p. 3 (48 words).

> Lately a scene occurred at St. Thomas's Churchyard, Bampton, Derbyshire, between the incumbent and a party of Mormons resolute to bury there a deceased brother. The clergyman read a formal protest against being compelled to perform the service, and the sad office was fulfilled ultimately by the curate.

1850: March, *Y Diwygiwr* (*Revivalist*), p. 100 (440 words). "Elder in a Predicament."

The Elder is "one of the Mormon brotherhood" who went inside a tavern in Llanelli and began to preach. He was approached by a disorderly woman who he declared was possessed by a devil. The writer of the account uses considerable detail in describing the elder's unsuccessful attempt to cast out the devil.

1850: April, *Y Dysgedydd* (*Instructor*), p. 120 (27 words). "Verse to the Mormons."

> Wolves and wanderers full of faults—fools,
> Failing to work miracles;
> There's no sense in the false guides,
> Nor truth in their words.

Episode 7.2

Start: The saga of the forged letter ends in tragedy for the one who composed it

1850: May, *Udgorn Seion* (*Zion's Trumpet*), pp. 139–40 (315 words). "There Is One Who Avenges."

On 26 February 1849, the *Buena Vista* had set sail from Waterloo Dock under the leadership of Dan Jones, who had just completed his four-year mission to Wales. From New Orleans he sent a long letter, dated 18 April 1849, to John S. Davis with an account of the crossing. Since the letter was too long to appear in *Zion's Trumpet*, Davis published it as a twenty-four-page pamphlet to be sold separately. In the preface of this publication, entitled *An Account of the Saints' Emigration to California* and dated 26 May 1849,[17] Davis inserted a transcription of a letter, received by him "a short time ago from one Capt. Jones, the purpose of which was to deceive the Saints." Here is Davis's description of the letter:

> It is written on paper which is used by the Oddfellows, and contains their emblem; an attempt is made to imitate the *post marks* on it, by stamping it with a seal of the Oddfellows' secretary, on which there is a word rather similar to "Llansamlet."

The letter was supposedly sent from New Orleans on 27 February 1849, just one day after the departure of Dan Jones's group from Liverpool. But John S. Davis, in his preface, declares the letter to be a forgery. The letter is addressed to Mr. W. Llewellyn, Merthyr. Here are the full contents of the letter, purportedly written by Dan Jones:

> New Orleans, Gulf of Mexico, Feb. 27, 1849—My Dear Brother in the Lord—I am pleased to be able to inform you that we have landed safely in New Orleans, after a short and comfortable voyage. There is evident care in our behalf, which is clear proof to the world of the truthfulness of our religion, despite so much talk against it by the numerous false religions of the world; and perhaps this letter will come to your hand also rather miraculously; if so, proclaim it before the public, and proclaim in Gath

> and Ashkelon about the providential care of our Heavenly Father over us. We are going from here to Nauvoo, on the banks of the Mississippi, in the state of Illinois, and from there to Council Bluffs, in the state of Missouri. An angel showed the directions to you in a dream; inform everyone of this also. Tell all the brethren that we are well and comfortable, and that we are convincing the world as we go along; and our numbers will be thousands by the time we reach the end of our journey: and before long, we shall overthrow all the kingdoms of the earth, and we shall live one thousand two hundred and sixty years after that happens. I do not have time to write much to you, for I have much to do. I am, yours affectionately, Your father in the Lord, Capt. Dan Jones.

The next letter Davis quotes is the one in the header of this entry, titled "There Is One Who Avenges." The letter is dated 17 May 1850 and is authored by John Rhys Roberts, a Latter-day Saint residing in Swansea. Here is the first paragraph of his letter:

> Dear Brother Davis—I wish to notify you of an example, in my opinion, and one that has had a great impression on the minds of the Saints in Swansea, which happened here yesterday, of the revenge of our Heavenly Father on those who persecute his children.[18]

Roberts references the letter addressed to (and in actuality forged by) W. Llewelyn sixteen months earlier, a letter supposedly from Dan Jones about the "miraculous" one-day voyage from Liverpool to New Orleans. Jones writes:

> Yesterday, in the house of the one, and under whose direction the letter was written, the person was destroyed by that which the world calls an accident.[19]

The person "destroyed" was Llewelyn. The accident came as a result of Llewelyn's having arranged for a tram full of rocks to be released from a higher point on the tracks, in order "to have a little fun." Roberts adds:

> It is surprising to report [that] his own son, who it is thought wrote the letter, was the tool in the hand of the great Being to destroy his father. By so doing, a rock shot out of the tram, and struck him dead, by splitting his head. He was laughing at the time, and by his order the tram was allowed to run free. This is the truth as to how it happened.[20]

Roberts gives his reason for sending this account:

> I write this, so that you may know; you may publish it, or not, as you think best. It may be a warning to those who continue to persecute the Saints.

End: The saga of the forged letter ends in tragedy for the one who composed it

1850: May, *Seren Gomer* (*Star of Gomer*), p. 149 (340 words). "A Remarkable Story."

A poem of eight eight-line stanzas by "Siencyn." The story has to do with one of the leaders of The Church of Jesus Christ of Latter-day Saints, who moved from

Carmarthen to the town of Llandovery. The third stanza of the poem contains the objective of "Benny Bwt," the "chief Satan":

> You only need to believe
> All these people's rule,
> The pox and the itching get better,
> The cough and the ague:
> Benny Bwt went with his bottle
> To work in his house,
> He intended to cast the devil
> From Nanny, Cwmsarnddu.
>
> And the final stanza tells of Benny's failure when the devil rebukes him:
>
> "Oh, shut up about miracles,
> I won't believe for the life of me,
> Leave alone your telling of lies
> While you're in earshot of me?"
> At this Benny cried
> "Oh! Oh! Oh, dear me!
> Now I have to yield
> To Nanny, Cwmsarnddu."

1850: 22 June, *Monmouthshire Merlin*, p. 4, item 1 (335 words). "The Latter-day Saints."

A detailed description of a recent meeting held in Cheltenham. The situation was quiet in the morning, but the meeting deteriorated towards evening:

> One of the "elders" declared that there never had been but one angel come down from heaven, and that was the one that came to Joseph Smith. The audience expressed their unbelief by hooting and hissing, and some by throwing dead cats and hands full of barley on[to] the platform. . . . The scene that followed, beggars description. Men lost their hats and coattails, and ladies the skirts of their dresses, in the general "scrimmage," and altogether it was such a scene as has not been witnessed in Cheltenham, on a Sunday evening, for many a day.

1850: 22 June, *Monmouthshire Merlin*, p. 4, item 2 (215 words). "The Baptism of Mormonites."

A detailed description of the baptism of several ladies in Pentonville, near London.

1850: June, *Y Drysorfa Gynnulleidfaol* (*Congregationalist Treasury*), p. 187 (125 words). "California."

The writer describes California as being "extremely tumultuous" and "full of stories of plundering and murders." He expresses wonderment as to how the "Saintly fools" have determined this to be their "New Jerusalem."

1850: June, *Y Dysgedydd* (*Instructor*), p. 191 (70 words).

A brief account of a Latter-day Saint meeting at a tavern near Bridgend. A woman in attendance took exception to something the preacher said and threw her shoe at him.

Episode 7.3

Start: "A bit of surprise"—Star of Gomer publishes an impartial article

1850: July, *Seren Gomer* (*Star of Gomer*), pp. 220–21 (795 words). "The Mormons."

This article quotes a long portion of the *Cincinnati Atlas* about the settlement of the Latter-day Saints in the western part of North America. In his introduction, the editor of *Seren Gomer* warns his readers to beware of the writer of the article:

> He does not choose to lay bare the wicked crimes which they committed everywhere they have lived in America, and because of which they were driven from one place to the other, like creatures unworthy to associate with reasonable and moral beings.[21]

The writer of the *Cincinnati Atlas* article is actually quite complimentary regarding the tenacity of the Latter-day Saints in overcoming the adversity suffered in Nauvoo and successfully settling in a remote place in the Rocky Mountains.

1850: July, *Udgorn Seion* (*Zion's Trumpet*), pp. 196–98, (135 words). "Mormons. From the *Star of Gomer* for July 1850."

John S. Davis elected to publish the entire article from a recent issue of the *Cincinnati Atlas* that was translated into Welsh to be printed in the July 1850 issue of *Star of Gomer*.[22] His reaction was one of great wonderment and surprise:

> The appearance of the previous piece in the *Star of Gomer* causes us a bit of surprise; for when has it ever come out with anything so impartial? But let all "be on their guard lest the editor of the aforementioned newspaper be somewhat too favorable towards these deceivers!" Let everyone have plenty of prejudice and animosity against the Saints, and then there will be no harm in reading it! Let everyone believe that it is all deceit, and then no one will be led astray! Let everyone understand that it was not "atrocious crimes" of the American Christians, to persecute the Saints, destroy their cities, kill their prophet and their brethren, ravish their women, burn their houses and their temple; rather that along with all the other evil they did was their godliness!—ED.

End: "A bit of surprise"—Star of Gomer publishes an impartial article

1850: 12 July, *Principality*, p. 2 (43 words).

> The Temple of Nauvoo erected by the Mormons in 1845, but purchased in March, 1849, by the Icarian community, was totally destroyed by a hurricane on the 27th of May. A new edifice of magnificent dimensions is to be erected in its place.

1850: 12 July, *Cambrian* (50 words).

> Ystalafera. The Latter Day Saints, after long-continued and ineffectual efforts to make themselves popular in this place, on Monday evening last had resort to roadside preaching, by which dodge they succeeded to get a crowd of women and children together; but we have not heard of any converts made.

Episode 7.4

Start: Mr. French opposes the Church, joins the Church, then leaves the Church

1850: 27 July, *Monmouthshire Merlin*, p. 3 (235 words). "Latter-day Saints."

> This body of people, who regard their common designation, "Mormons," as a term of reproach, have established a pretty considerable connection in Newport; and having procured a large tent, capable of seating several hundred persons, commenced operations beneath it on Sunday afternoon last, on the Marshes of the burgesses.

A description then follows of the two meetings held on that day at which Captain Wheelock spoke.

1850: 10 August, *Monmouthshire Merlin*, p. 3 (850 words). "The Latter-day Saints."

This lengthy article has an unusually detailed description of the "discussion" between R. Hill and Capt. Wheelock:

> For the last few days our town has been placarded with the announcement that a discussion would take place at the British School Roots, between Mr. R. Hill, a Wesleyan local preacher, and Capt. Wheelock, an elder of the Mormonite body, on Tuesday evening last. Long before the time for commencing, numbers hastened to secure seats, as it was anticipated the attendance would be large. In this there was no disappointment; for the room was crammed, and numbers listened outside.

The writer also included in his article Mr. Hill's account of the Saints' efforts to remove from a man's back a "hump," which had been there for some time. A woman addressed the gathering and declared that "for the last three years, she had every day (Sundays excepted) washed the back of the so-called hunchback, and that there was nothing the matter with it."

1850: 5 October, *Monmouthshire Merlin*, p. 3 (530 words). "Lectures against Mormonism."

Yet another account of the lectures of Mr. Williams and Mr. French at the Newport town hall. This reporter identifies Mr. French as "late a student at the Carmarthen Presbyterian College" and writes that the lecture of Mr. French "was declared to be one of the most argumentative and eloquent addresses ever heard on a similar subject."

1850: 5 October, *Monmouthshire Beacon*, p. 8 (60 words). "Lecture on Mormonism."

A brief report on the two lectures given by Messrs. J. Williams and R. A. French at the town hall in Newport. These lectures were also covered by the *Cardiff and Merthyr Guardian* of the same date.

1850: 5 October, *Cardiff and Merthyr Guardian*, p. 3 (240 words). "Lectures on Mormonism."

Two lectures—one on Joseph Smith and the other on the Book of Mormon—were delivered at the town hall in Newport. The two lecturers were Messrs. J. Williams and R. A. French.

> After the delivery of the two lectures, an animated discussion took place between a Captain Wheelock and the lecturers. It was ultimately arranged that the captain should have an opportunity afforded him to rebut the views taken by the lecturers.

The writer was particularly impressed with one of the lecturers:

> We cannot pass over this opportunity without noticing the ability displayed by Mr. French, which was highly gratifying to the company.

1850: 26 October, *Cardiff and Merthyr Guardian*, p. 3 (60 words). "Mormon Controversy."

A very large assemblage of people attended on Tuesday and Wednesday last, to hear the discussion between Captain Wheelock and Messrs. French and Williams, which was held at the large room in the Sunderland Inn, Llanarth-street, the mayor having very properly refused the use of the Town-hall. The meeting lasted a considerable time, and the room was densely crowded.

1850: 26 October, *Monmouthshire Merlin*, p. 3 (1,385 words). "Mormonism and Its Opponents."

A very long account of the debate between Captain Wheelock and Mr. French at the Sunderland Inn in Newport, Wales, on Monday evening, 21 October. The writer declares:

> Captain Wheelock, who is an American, certainly proved an acceptable orator to the recipients of the new creed in Newport. Whether his "arguments" were well grounded or not, they bore about them the stamp of originality, as the most incoherent and absurd theories frequently may.

The writer points out the benefit such debates provided for the Latter-day Saints:

> It is almost a folly to attempt anything like a discussion with such a sect, on the baseless creed thrown up. It is a decided folly to attempt to conquer and convince them, too, on the public platform. It is a waste of time, and more—it is actually a furtherance of their interests, to give them public notoriety and the supposed character of martyrs, by lashing them with the whip-cord of tenfold argument, the severity of truth, or the pungency of well-aimed sarcasm.

Captain Wheelock spoke for "about one hour and a-half" and did not leave sufficient time for French to respond. French had given thirteen points to the captain which he wished for him to address. But, according to French, Wheelock had failed to address a single one of them. It was announced that Wheelock would deliver another lecture the following evening.

1850: 2 November, *Monmouthshire Beacon*, p. 3 (65 words).

A brief report on the dispute between Captain Wheelock and Messrs. French and Williams. The dispute was also covered by the *Cardiff and Merthyr Guardian*[23] and the *Monmouthshire Merlin*.[24]

1851: 25 January, *Monmouthshire Merlin*, p. 3 (85 words). "Alleged Mormon Conversion."

> It is reported that Mr. French, who obtained some little notoriety in Newport and elsewhere recently, by forcible and eloquent denunciations of "the

> Mormon imposture," was "converted" to the very faith he had denounced, on Sunday last! We have received a letter on the subject, in which hints are thrown out that it would be prudent not to call it a "conversion," as there was some particular motive at work, which did not warrant the application of that term, in its commonly-received sense.

1851: 15 February, *Monmouthshire Beacon*, p. 5 (295 words).

On Tuesday, 11 February, R. French was slated to present a lecture on the famous poet and intellectual John Milton.

It was also stated that the lecturer would give his audience his reasons for following the tenets of the Mormon faith, against which he was some time ago engaged in lecturing, but to which he has recently become a convert.

French gave scriptural support for his decision to convert.

When asked the question how it was that he had so strangely and suddenly changed his mind on so important a question as religion, his answer was to the purpose that he did not then fully understand the Mormon "religion"—rather a singular and inconsistent reply for one who had professed to be competent to confront its warmest admirers.

The writer observes:

> Mr. French is considered to be a man of some ability, and his course of conduct seems so much the more unaccountable.

1851: 29 August, *Monmouthshire Merlin*, p. 3 (290 words). "The Bible."

Discussion was invited after a Baptist minister had made a presentation at the Newport town hall.

> A young man named French, who has recently attracted public notice, as an example of the most eccentric oscillations in religious sentiment, came forward, and made some vague and irrelevant observations upon what had transpired. . . . Having listened about a quarter-of-an-hour, the meeting became impatient at the inappropriate character of Mr. French's remarks, and a gentleman present proposed that he be requested by the chairman to confine himself to the subject named for discussion, and not to deliver a lecture upon Mormonism.

French was permitted to speak a few minutes longer, but, according to the writer, he took advantage of the opportunity "to mingle a further measure of the Mormon element with his remarks." The Reverend Allen "replied to his observations, fully exposing their flimsy and inapplicable character, and completely demolishing those portions in which there was even the appearance of argument."

The writer adds that others wished to address the meeting:

> But as it was understood that they were merely desirous of making statements likely to be personally offensive to Mr. French, their aspirations were judiciously subdued.

1853: 8 April, *Monmouthshire Merlin*, p. 4 (32 words). "Mormonism."

> A discussion between Messrs. French and Owen, and the Rev. J. Barfield and Mr. Flannigan, on Mormonism, is to take place at the Town Hall on several evenings in the ensuing week.

1853: 16 April, *Monmouthshire Beacon*, p. 8 (390 words). "Mormonism. Controversy at Newport."

The first item of this article has to do with "a series of discussions upon the tenets of the Latter-day Saints" that had "created much excitement during the past week":

> Two elders of the Church of Latter-day Saints, Mr. R. H. French and Mr. Wm. Owen defended the new faith, and the fallacy of it was exposed by the Rev. John Barfield, B. A., of Dock Street chapel, and Mr. Flannigan, Scripture reader. The feeling of the meetings went against the elders; but Mr. Edward Thomas, draper, who occupied the chair, suppressed any unseemly interruption.

A pretty "Mormon maid" had attracted French's attention, and he "deserted from his colors and his cause, and became the champion of error and the Mormons."

The writer suggests serious wrongdoing on the part of some of the male converts to The Church of Jesus Christ of Latter-day Saints:

> And occasionally, here, in Newport, Mormonite men take their departure for the valley of the saints; and soon after their departure it is discovered that they are accompanied by "spirituals" of the other sex, while their wives and other little obligations are left behind—abandoned and flung away—forlorn and unprotected—to fight the battle of life, and struggle with the world and all its difficulties, alone, and to the best of their poor ability.

After elaborating on other ways in which "Mormonism . . . yields reason to passion," the writer sums up the current status of The Church of Jesus Christ of Latter-day Saints in Newport:

> And they shirk about our byeways, and there work insidiously, so that Mormonism progresses. But Mormonism is a "delusion, a mockery, and a snare"—an outrage upon civilization, and, above all, an outrage upon Christianity. And therefore, Mormonism ought to be checked, and, if possible, crushed, extinguished, and utterly put out.

1853: 22 April, *Monmouthshire Merlin*, p. 4 (710 words). "Discussion upon Mormonism."

An account of the fourth and final discussion at the town hall in Newport. On the one side, representing The Church of Jesus Christ of Latter-day Saints, were R. French and William Owen. On the other side were Reverend J. Barfield and Mr. Flannigan. The subject for discussion was "The doctrines of the Latter-day Saints about spiritual wives and miracles."

Reverend J. Barfield opened the debate, contending, with great earnestness, and an evident reliance upon the truthfulness of his cause, that although the practice of polygamy prevailed at an early period of the world, still Moses had sought to convince the people that it was regarded with displeasure by the Almighty, by fencing it round with certain guards and prohibitions in the cases of distinguished individuals.

The two Latter-day Saints "contended that, with regard to many polygamists spoken of in the Bible, not only was there no evidence that God regarded them with displeasure, but upon some of them (Abraham and others) his blessing had signally rested."

Regarding miracles, Barfield read from the *Millennial Star* about the supposed healing by the Latter-day Saints of a blind child by the name of Selina Bounsell, but he added that it was then "well known that the child's blindness had been cured in the Taunton Eye Infirmary, under the treatment of Mr. Billet, surgeon to that institution." French disagreed and "offered to produce the parents and the child, and to meet Barfield again for a further discussion of the doctrine of miracles."

1853: 13 May, *Monmouthshire Merlin*, p. 1 (55 words). "The Alleged Mormon Miracle at Bristol."

> At a public meeting, held at the town hall, Newport, Monmouthshire, the report of which will be found in this day's *Merlin*, the following resolution was unanimously passed:—
>
> "That this meeting is of opinion that the fullest reliance may be placed upon the statements of Mr. Thomas, with reference to the alleged Mormon miracle, in the case of Selina Bounsell; and can come to no other conclusion from Mr. Thomas's statements, as well as from those of Mr. Bounsell, the father of the child, given at this meeting, than that the pretended miracle is a deliberate and complete imposture.
>
> Signed on behalf of the meeting, Edward Thomas, Chairman.

1853: 13 May, *Monmouthshire Merlin*, pp. 2–3 (5,440 words). "Investigation of a Pretended Mormon Miracle."

This report is the longest article about The Church of Jesus Christ of Latter-day Saints in any newspaper connected with Wales that has yet been identified—well over five thousand words. It is the report of a lengthy investigation held to reach a definitive answer as to whether the sight of Selina Bounsell was healed miraculously or whether it was restored by a Dr. Billet at the Taunton Eye Infirmary. The issue had arisen in a debate held three weeks earlier at the Newport town hall in a debate between Reverend J. Barfield and Mr. Flannigan on the one side and Messrs. R. French and William Owen on the other. Toward the end of the debate, Barfield read aloud an 1849 account of four-year-old Selina Bounsell being healed of her blindness, in which the writer affirmed that the restoration of her sight was a miracle. Both of Selina's parents signed the letter affirming that their daughter's sight had been miraculously restored. But Barfield stated that it was then "well known that the child's blindness had been cured in the Taunton Eye Infirmary, under the treatment of Dr. Billet, surgeon to that institution." French, then a Latter-day Saint, disagreed with that assessment and "offered to produce the parents and the child, and to meet Mr. Barfield again for a further discussion of the doctrine of miracles." And, according to French, his opponents would arrange for Dr. James Billet to be present as well. Shortly thereafter, however, when it became known that Dr. Billet would not be present and that Edward Thomas, the chairman of the recent discussion, would merely report the result of a very recent interview he had had with Dr. Billet, French sent notice that he would not be present at the investigation.

Even without the presence of French, the investigation was held as scheduled. Noting the absence of French at the outset of the meeting, Barfield again read the account of the "pretended miracle from a volume entitled 'Orson Pratt's Works,' which he had procured at the depôt of the Latter-day Saints, in this town." Barfield then read the following statement, dated 18 June 1852 and signed by Dr. Billet:

> I hereby certify that Selina Bounsell was admitted a patient of the Taunton Eye Infirmary, in 1845, under my sole care, and was discharged cured, in 1846, at which time she could see to pick up a pin or other minute objects, as well as any of the children with whom she was in the habit of playing.

18 June 1852 is almost a year before the meetings in Newport between Barfield and French. Thus, it appears that someone much earlier had been looking into Selina Bounsell's operation by Dr. Billet in Taunton, possibly in preparation for the series of debates there. Dr. Billet's sworn statement also contains this postscript:

> P.S. The following is a verbatim copy of her discharge, as taken from the books of the above institution:
>
> Selina Bounsell, congenital cataract, cured 1846.
>
> The above can be verified on oath, by a witness, if necessary.

At this point, Barfield turned the time over to the chairman, Edward Thomas, who then reported on his recent visit to Taunton to persuade Dr. Billet to travel with him to Newport for the "investigation" into the miracle which supposedly had restored sight to Selina Bounsell many years earlier. According to Thomas's report, Dr. Billet was unable, because of age, to travel from Taunton to Newport. While in Taunton, Thomas also spoke with George and Mary Rogers, two people who had been associated with Dr. Billet, and who, at Thomas's request, had signed statements to the effect that they had assisted in the operation by holding the child. Thomas also located the child's paternal grandmother, Susannah Bounsell, who put her mark to this statement: "This is to testify that I held Selina Bounsell, while Mr. Billet operated on her for the cataract, being grandmother to the child." Thomas asked the grandmother whether "she would have any objection to testify that she [Selina] was taken to the Infirmary, and sent out cured by Dr. Billet." The grandmother's response was, "Not the least; and I am sorry that my son has joined the Mormons; he is practicing a great delusion."

Just after the signed statement of George Rogers was read to the audience, a man blurted out, "That is false." At that juncture, the chairman had told the man that he would be given permission to speak in a few moments. And when the chairman told the man he could speak, the man identified himself as the father of Selina Bounsell and, referring to the statement attributed to his mother—i.e., that she was sorry that her son had joined the Mormons and that he was practicing a great delusion—he said, "I am sure what you said about my mother was false. She never would say such a thing as that." Many questions were then posed to William Bounsell. Even though he was no longer affiliated with The Church of Jesus Christ of Latter-day Saints, he declared the following: "I am sure I never heard the gospel more truly preached than by the Latter-day Saints."

After many other comments and questions involving William Bounsell and others, the writer brought his very long article to a close with the following observation:

> Mr. Barfield said he would now ask any Mormon who might be present to consider this subject well. They had proved the pretended miracle to be a mere delusion; and he would ask the Latter-day Saints if they would peril their salvation upon such a pretense, which, upon a fair and candid examination, proved to be utterly unfounded—a fiction, a delusion, and a snare.

1853: 14 May, *Monmouthshire Beacon*, pp. 7–8 (1,065 words). "Latter-day Saints and Spiritual Wives. Mormonism and Miracles."

The writer recounts how "three summers ago," Captain Wheelock had debated on the same stage with "the youth, by name 'French,'" who "combated the great captain with such courage and earnestness that he quite bewildered the captain." Because of a "Mormon maid," French subsequently joined forces with Wheelock:

> But the great captain was old and wily, and the youth juvenile and imprudent. The Elder bided his time, and alas! the youth unwarily approached too closely to the enemy's camp and there beheld a Mormon maid. Now the maid was pretty, and we fear she possessed the power of fascination. The youth admired the prettiness of the maid, and she reciprocated the kindliness of the youth, albeit the enemy of her faith. And suddenly a cloud descended upon the youth and obscured his better judgment—till, at last, French the chivalrous champion of truth and Christianity, deserted from his colors and his cause, and became the champion of error and the Mormons.

Wheelock returned to Salt Lake City, but French remained in Newport and was still preaching his new faith three years later.

The writer also reports that Reuben Brinkworth, the young man who had regained both hearing and speech upon being baptized a Latter-day Saint four years earlier, continued faithful to his new religion:

> And here, too, in Newport, one Reuben Brinkworth, one of the "rogue and vagabond" species, aided by others of the saints, practices a *gross deception*.[25]

1853: 21 May, *Monmouthshire Beacon*, p. 5 (115 words). "The Alleged Mormon Miracle at Bristol."

> At a public meeting, held at the town hall, Newport, Monmouthshire, on the 6th last, the report of which will be found in this day's *Merlin*, the following resolution was unanimously passed:—
>
> "That this meeting is of opinion that the fullest reliance may be placed upon the statements of Mr. Thomas, with reference to the alleged Mormon miracle, in the case of Selina Bounsell; and can come to no other conclusion from Mr. Thomas's statements, as well as from those of Mr. Bounsell, the father of the child, given at this meeting, than that the pretended miracle is a deliberate and complete imposture.

Signed on behalf of the meeting, Edward Thomas, Chairman."

1854: 25 February, *Udgorn Seion* (*Zion's Trumpet*), p. 124 (12 words).

The final installment of the minutes of a conference held 25 December 1853 in Merthyr Tydfil. "Brother French, Newport, gave a few remarks and a song, in English."

1854: 14 April, *Monmouthshire Merlin*, pp. 4–5 (935 words). "Lecture by Mr. French. The Russian Question and the Mormons!"

A lengthy report on why Mr. French had recently left The Church of Jesus Christ of Latter-day Saints after having converted just over three years earlier. The reporter describes French's reasoning:

> Joe Smith was undoubtedly inspired, and all he wrote or spoke, was true; but the prophets or apostles, or what they were whom the lecturer characterized as "the powers that be," in the Mormon church, did not stick to what Smith had laid down, and wanted to establish new doctrines.

The reporter concludes with the following:

> However, he didn't like to part with Mormonism on bad terms; and so repeated that there were a few good touches about it, though he didn't like it "as a whole"; and he should not wish to get the contempt of the Mormons or of any other people, for what he had done, or what he had not done; and so hoped that the great principle which should actuate the universal brotherhood of mankind, "Love one another," would let him down easily in regard to his cutting the Saints in the manner he had done.

1854: 15 April, *Monmouthshire Beacon*, p. 7 (73 words). "The Errors of Mormonism."

> At the Town Hall on Tuesday evening Mr. French, who two years back somewhat startled his friends by becoming a convert to Mormonism, having, just before his conversion, been publicly lecturing in opposition to the sect, delivered a lecture upon Russia and Turkey, and at the conclusion of the lecture recanted his adhesion to Mormonism, alleging his belief that the doctrine, as now taught, was full of error.

End: Mr. French opposes the Church, joins the Church, then leaves the Church

1850: 17 August, *Monmouthshire Merlin*, pp. 3 (220 words). "Pontypool. A Mormon Miracle Interrupted."

The account of a "Mr. H., one of the elders looked up to by the Latter-day Saints." Mr. H. supposedly told a widower that for fifty pounds he would bring the widower's wife back to life. Just then a third party came in and "declared that the old Latter-day Saint was a gammoning the poor gentleman." Mr. H. then "pitched into the intruder, and a pugilistic encounter ensuing, the dead was left to rest."

1850: August, *Y Drysorfa Gynnulleidfaol* (*Congregationalist Treasury*), pp. 250 (55 words).

The Nauvoo Temple, which was built by the followers of the wretch Joe Smith, the Latter-day Saints, but which was purchased in March 1849 by the "Icarian Community," was completely destroyed by a violent wind on the 27th of last May. But a more beautiful and larger edifice is being built in its place.

Episode 7.5

Start: Four articles are published containing historical information about Latter-day Saints

1850: August, *Yr Eglwysydd* (*Churchman*), pp. 151–53 (1,375 words). "The Mormons."

Part one of a four-part series. The content is basically a history of the establishment and growth of The Church of Jesus Christ of Latter-day Saints in the United States. It has obviously been translated from sources in English and says nothing about the presence or activities of the Latter-day Saints in Wales.

1850: September, *Yr Eglwysydd* (*Churchman*), pp. 164–66 (1,100 words). "The Mormons," part two.

1850: October, *Yr Eglwysydd* (*Churchman*), pp. 188–90 (1,205 words). "The Mormons," part 3.

1850: November, *Yr Eglwysydd* (*Churchman*), pp. 208–10 (1,190 words). "The Mormons," part four.

End: Four articles are published containing historical information about the Latter-day Saints

1850: 13 September, *Cambrian* (95 words).

This article is a brief report of an inquest into the death of Mary Ann Richards, a six-year-old girl who "died in consequence of being burnt, by her clothes taking fire in carrying hot coals from her parents' house to a public oven." Accidental death was the verdict, but the jury strongly censured her father, a Latter-day Saint, "for his interference with, and preventing for a time, the attendance of a medical gentleman."

1850: 21 September, *Monmouthshire Merlin*, p. 3 (70 words). "Emigration."

A brief account of a "saint" who had left for "the New Jerusalem" but had neglected to "pay certain debts due by him in this port" before leaving.

1850: 21 September, *Monmouthshire Merlin*, p. 4 (45 words).

There was a disgraceful riot at the Mormon chapel, Spalding, last Sunday, one of "elders" having said in his discourse, that all in Spalding, except the "Saints" of the Mormon faith, were doomed to everlasting torments. The inhabitants severely punished the Mormon for the assertion.

1850: 21 September, *North Wales Chronicle*, p. 6, item 1 (545 words). "The Mormons."

An article taken from the *Athenaeum: Journal of Literature, Science, and the Fine Arts*, published in London. Here are the first few lines of its analysis of The Church of Jesus Christ of Latter-day Saints:

> We have from time to time noticed in our columns the doings of the Mormons in America. Few incidents in modern days are more strange and interesting to the reader of history than the rise, progress, and present state of this singular sect. . . . As a creed, and as a polity, it has now taken its place on the stage of nations. The latest advices from Deseret represent it as in flouring condition.

And following a number of analytical observations about the future endeavors of this new religion, the writer concludes,

> It may be hoped—though we dare not be sanguine about it—that the diffusion of so much knowledge may help to discredit the crude impostures on which the Mormon faith is based.

1850: 21 September, *North Wales Chronicle*, p. 6, item 2 (42 words).

> An address just issued from the headquarters of the Mormons, at Great Salt Lake City, concludes thus: "Push the Salute to Zion, and persuade all good brethren to come, who have a wheelbarrow, and faith enough to roll it over the mountains."

Episode 7.6

Start: A prolonged polemic about the "similarity of the Baptists and the Saints" is published

1850: July, *Y Drysorfa Gynnulleidfaol* (*Congregationalist Treasury*), pp. 212–14 (1,550 words). "Similarity of the Baptists and the Saints."

A writer who calls himself "A Saint" touches off a debate that would end only in March 1851 and occupy the pages of three periodicals: the *Congregationalist Treasury*, *Star of Gomer*, and *Zion's Trumpet*. The anonymous writer of this first article discusses seven major points which he declares to be areas in which the Baptists and the Saints can find common ground:

1. Baptism by immersion is essential for salvation.
2. Only believers should receive baptism.
3. Miracles still occur.
4. The New Testament is not the sufficient guide to salvation.
5. Both Baptists and Saints assert infallibility.
6. The laying on of hands after baptism is essential.
7. The Millennium will include only Baptists (according to the Baptists) or only Saints (according to the Saints).

Because this article touched off a polemic that would continue over a period of nine months, the following list summarizing the path of the debate may be helpful to the reader:

1. July 1850—*Congregationalist Treasury*—the first article, by "Saint"
2. Sept. 1850—*Congregationalist Treasury*—response by "Mathetes"
3. Sept. 1850—*Star of Gomer*—reprinted response of "Mathetes" as in the *Congregationalist Treasury*
4. Sept. 1850—*Zion's Trumpet*—reaction of John S. Davis

5. Oct. 1850—*Congregationalist Treasury*—"Mormon Lies" by T. Williams
6. Dec. 1850—*Congregationalist Treasury*—"Saint" responds
7. Jan. 1851—*Congregationalist Treasury*—"Mathetes" responds (part 1)
8. Feb. 1851—*Congregationalist Treasury*—"Mathetes" responds (part 2)
9. Mar. 1851—*Congregationalist Treasury*—"Saint" responds—end of debate

1850: September, *Y Drysorfa Gynnulleidfaol* (*Congregationalist Treasury*), pp. 272–75 (3,325 words). "The Bungling Saint."

In their September 1850 issues, both the *Congregationalist Treasury* and *Star of Gomer* carry the same article that a Baptist minister by the name of John Jones wrote. Using the nom de plume "Mathetes," Jones had apparently sent a copy of his response to both editors. The editor of *Star of Gomer* was probably happy to print the outrage expressed by John Jones at anyone who would put Baptists and "Mormons" in any kind of a positive relationship. And the editor of the *Congregationalist Treasury* was no doubt delighted to cooperate in promoting anything that would poke fingers in the eyes of both the Baptists and the Mormons, not to mention the possible increase in the readership of his periodical with such an entertaining polemic. In this long and tedious article, Mathetes addresses each of the seven points presented in the July article by "Saint." He also expresses skepticism as to whether the "Saint" was actually a member of The Church of Jesus Christ of Latter-day Saints:

> The common opinion is that the Saint is some weakling of an Independent, or some phantom Methodist, striving (but failing) to hide his literary ugliness, and his moral disgrace, under a pseudonym. I hope for the best; but I fear the worst.

1850: September, *Seren Gomer* (*Star of Gomer*), pp. 261–63 (3,325 words). "The Bungling Saint."

The exact same article published in *The Congregationalist Treasury* was also published in this issue of *Star of Gomer* (see previous entry).

1850: September, *Udgorn Seion* (*Zion's Trumpet*), pp. 240–44 (465 words). "Laying on of Hands."

John S. Davis responds to the skepticism expressed by Mathetes in the September article about whether the "Saint" was a Latter-day Saint or not.

> Mr. Mathetes does not believe that one of the Saints wrote it; nevertheless, because that writer calls himself a "Saint," our instructor attacks him as if he were one of the Mormons, using the words "Satanist," "rascal," "insane," "Joe," etc., as weapons of his warfare.[26]

Davis does not indicate his opinion about whether "Saint," the author of the article entitled "Similarities of the Baptists and the Saints," was or was not a member of The Church of Jesus Christ of Latter-day Saints. But it is highly unlikely that "Saint" was actually affiliated with the Latter-day Saints, his most glaring shibboleth being his affirmation that both the Latter-day Saints and the Baptists claimed infallibility. Furthermore, all his arguments have the ring of an Independent defending himself against Baptist doctrine with hardly any mention of the Latter-day Saints.

Davis then presents a fairly long quotation from Mathetes about the practice of the laying on of hands. After admitting to the occasional use of this practice among "some of the Baptists," Mathetes declares that "it is not a general rule pertaining to the denomination." Mathetes further declares:

> On the other hand, the practice is losing ground continually; and it is hoped that it will be in the land of oblivion in a little while. Those who practice "the laying on of hands" in our midst are not, after all, like the Mormons; the Baptists do not profess to impart any blessing through the practice; but the Mormon fiends pretend to bestow the Holy Ghost, although they are as incapable of that as of extinguishing the sun.[27]

Regarding these comments, Davis observes:

> You see how much less respect the Baptists give to the "old practice" of laying on hands, than to the "old practice" of baptizing![28]

And then, as if to emphasize the extent to which Davis considered the doctrine of The Church of Jesus Christ of Latter-day Saints linked to that of the "primitive Saints," he inserted an entire article on "Spiritual Gifts" that had appeared in an issue of *Star of Gomer* nearly twenty years earlier (see next entry).

1832: April, *Seren Gomer* (*Star of Gomer*), pp. 103–5 (1,450 words). "The Thousand Years—Spiritual Gifts."

The author of this lengthy article, which John S. Davis quotes in its entirety in his September 1850 issue of *Zion's Trumpet*,[29] indicates his identity only with the initial "C." In his opening paragraph, this writer places himself at odds with the opinion of the then-prevailing Baptist theologians:

> If I caused so much discomfort to some of your readers through my announcement of the millennial doctrine, what will be the agitation they feel at that which I declare in my present writing? For I intend to assert, with boldness, the following tenets: namely, that all the miraculous gifts, that were possessed by the primitive church among the followers of the apostles and evangelists, are as much an inheritance to the church in the present day as they were in the first century, and that nothing but lack of faith only prevents the church from performing miracles today with the same measure of power and authority as it did in its earliest age.

This statement reflects the view of the Latter-day Saints precisely, and it would be safe to conclude that John S. Davis inserted this 1832 article in *Zion's Trumpet* for the express purpose of poking his editorial finger in the eye of Mathetes and his fellow Baptists. Any response from the Baptists has yet to be identified.

1850: October, *Y Drysorfa Gynnulleidfaol* (*Congregationalist Treasury*), p. 298 (2,120 words). "Mormon Lies."

T. Williams, associated with Ebenezer Baptist Chapel in Llangynog, comes right to the point in responding to the assertions of the "Saint," the author of "Similarities of the Baptists and the Saints" in the 1850 July issue of the *Congregationalist Treasury*.[30] Each of the following items contains a quoted phrase that represents Williams's position regarding each of the seven purported similarities:

1. Baptism by immersion is essential for salvation. "This is a barefaced lie."
2. Only believers should receive baptism. "It comes close to the truth."
3. Miracles still occur. "This is a hypocritical lie."
4. The New Testament is not the sufficient guide to salvation. "Another untruth."
5. Both Baptists and Saints assert infallibility. "Do not bear false witness."
6. The laying on of hands after baptism is essential. "Some do and some do not."
7. The Millennium will include only Baptists (according to the Baptists) or only Saints (according to the Saints). "Does not everyone believe the very same thing?"

1850: December, *Y Drysorfa Gynnulleidfaol* (*Congregationalist Treasury*), pp. 392–94 (2,206 words). "Similarity of the Baptists and the Saints Again."

"Saint" responds to the articles of both Mathetes and T. Williams by flexing his writing muscles:

> You know, Mr. Editor, that truth is powerful and unconquerable: its face never grows pale, its knees never knock, neither does its voice weaken nor its tongue stammer; despite being slandered by being called a bungler, liar, Satan, *cat's paw*, monkey, father of lies, Dick's donkey, Congregationalist weakling, Methodist magician, etc., by such worthies who have matriculated from Billingsgate College[31] such as Mathetes and his ilk. M. showed sense in writing to the *Star*, because in an empty ring and fighting with his own shadow, he might have a chance of winning.

"Saint" then presents an explanatory list in order to "confront the two giants of the battlefield, armed as they are with all their Baptist weaponry." Here is a list of his basic conclusions:

1. The Baptists and the Saints both believe that *baptism by full immersion* is essential for salvation.
2. The Baptists maintain that only believers should be baptized.
3. Baptists perform miracles.
4. Baptists do not believe that the New Testament as received from the early Christians is a sufficient guide.
5. Baptists claim infallibility.
6. Baptists receive people into their Churches according to the apostolic example, through the laying on of hands.

1851: January, *Y Drysorfa Gynnulleidfaol* (*Congregationalist Treasury*), pp. 21–25 (2,875 words). "The Saint Weighed in the Balance and Found Wanting."

Mathetes responds to the article of "Saint" in the December 1850 *Congregationalist Treasury*.[32] Mathetes refers to his previous article that appeared in the September issues of both the *Congregationalist Treasury* and *Star of Gomer*:

> In my last essay, I let it be understood that Saint was some kind of practitioner of infant baptism in disguise, and I rebuked him harshly for the literary and theological bungling in his leading article. But his comments in the November issue of *Treasury* do not touch upon any of the said rebukes, indicating that the discipline thus meted out was justified by the resulting display of graciousness.

Mathetes's main topic was that of baptism and whether sprinkling of infants is ever to be accepted. Toward the end of this long essay, Mathetes comments:

> Everyone (especially professors of religion) can unite in what is moral in its scope, namely, praising God, etc., even if everyone cannot unite in the direct ordinance of the special feast, which belongs to those described above.

But this comment is not the end of his long and rambling essay, since it was to be continued in the February issue of the periodical.

1851: February, *Y Drysorfa Gynnulleidfaol* (*Congregationalist Treasury*), pp. 51–55 (2,990 words). "The Saint Weighed in the Balance and Found Wanting."

This is the second part of Mathetes's response to the article of "Saint" in the December 1850 issue of the *Congregationalist Treasury*.[33] This continuation of Mathetes's essay from the January issue of the *Congregationalist Treasury* is equally as long and rambling as the first part. He reaffirms his stance regarding The Church of Jesus Christ of Latter-day Saints:

> Mathetes [referring to himself] continues to believe that Mormonism is nothing but a joke and a fraud from beginning to end; that it is just a "game" designed by unprincipled layabouts in order to live in idleness on the backs of superstitious simpletons. . . . The Mormons are made up for the most part of cunning and fraudulent snake oil salesmen, fanatical and crazy fools, along with those who have been disciplined for their wayward lifestyles by other religious denominations; these charlatans set themselves up as the top dogs, while the poor dupes are forced to bear the burden of the system which they have created. . . . I am now tired of relating "Saint's" lies and bungling, although I have not totally exhausted all his writings. Whether "Saint" is a Mormon or someone who practices infant baptism, I do not intend to write any more.[34]

The editor of the *Congregationalist Treasury* adds this comment:

> (If "Saint" so wishes, I will publish one more of his letters, but it must be short; this will end the debate. Editor)[35]

1851: March, *Y Drysorfa Gynnulleidfaol* (*Congregationalist Treasury*), pp. 73–76 (1,640 words). "Similarity of the Baptists and the Saints Again."

In this final article of this seemingly interminable polemic, "Saint" offers his "warmest thanks" to the editor of the *Congregationalist Treasury* for lending the columns of this publication to "Saint" and his opponents. He also makes many unkind comments about Mathetes's ability to engage in debate. Here is a sample:

> Without boasting, you know, Mr. Editor, that I have forgotten more doctrine and literature, etc., than Mathetes ever learned.

"Saint" concludes with a proposal:

> I propose that Mathetes and I agree together to ask the *Treasury* to print 500 or 1,000 copies of it. I shall pay half the cost, and I shall take half the books—let Mathetes bring forward the other half of the cost and receive the other half of the books, so that everyone may see which direction the scales tip.[36]

There is no evidence that Mathetes or the editor ever accepted this proposal.

End: A prolonged polemic about the "similarity of the Baptists and the Saints" is published

1850: 14 September, *Monmouthshire Beacon*, p. 6, item 1 (90 words). "Mormonism."

> People have often wondered what the word Mormon meant. It is easily explained. *Mormo*, or *Mormon*, is the Greek for humbug, or hobgoblin, and paraphrastically, for delusion or counterfeit. Little did that crafty impostor, Joe Smith, with all his craftiness, suspect the close-fitting cap he was asking for his newly-concocted imposture, when he gave his statute book the name of the *Book of Mormon*, literally the *book of humbug*. Such are sometimes the silent, unlooked-for, and mysterious incidents by which Providence brings to light the satanic inventions of revilers and gainsayers.

1850: 14 September, *Monmouthshire Beacon*, p. 6, item 2 (24 words).

> Mormon women, it is said, have commenced dressing in pantaloons. It is not stated whether the men have undergone a change in their apparel. *Burritt's Christian Citizen.*

1850: September, *Y Drysorfa Gynnulleidfaol* (*Congregationalist Treasury*), pp. 275–76 (1,140 words). "The Saints and Their Tricks Again."

The writer calls himself "A Hater of Deceit" and is most likely the editor of the periodical. Unlike many of the brief reports with accusations against the Latter-day Saints, this report is replete with details and particulars of an incident that took place in early April 1850, at a farmhouse named Penrhiwgwion located near the town of Carmarthen. The woman who lived there was visited by Latter-day Saint missionaries, and after hearing their message, she agreed to be baptized. Following her baptism, the woman was possessed by an evil spirit which the missionaries attempted to cast out. The report then presents the conversation between the evil spirit and one of the missionaries, then the writer sums up the event with an invitation:

> She had been a member of the Established Church for forty-two years, and she is now seeking fervently to regain her place, after undergoing the harsh treatment of Saintism. If anyone doubts the truth of the preceding story, we hope they will be so kind as to send to the above old woman, who lives at Penrhiwgwion, near Carmarthen, and they will find out that it is all true, and much more than this story contains.[37]

1850: September, *Y Dysgeddyd* (*Instructor*), p. 287 (20 words). "Mormon Women."

> The Mormon women have started to wear trousers (*pantaloons*). It is not said that the men wear corresponding clothes in exchange. *Burritt's Christian Citizen.*

1850: October, *Ifor Hael* (*Generous Ivor*), p. 319 (26 words). "Mormon Women."

The Mormon women have started to wear trousers. But so far, we have no information that the men are wearing corresponding clothes in exchange. What next?

1850: 19 October, *Caernarvon and Denbigh Herald*, p. 4 (185 words). "Anglesey, Llanddaniel. The fanatics who call themselves 'Latter-day Saints.'"

A detailed description of a lecture that was designed keep the residents of this "rural and secluded village" from being deluded by the "condemnable trash" of the Latter-day Saints.

1850: 19 October, *North Wales Chronicle*, p. 6 (47 words).

> Lately a hundred persons arrived in Liverpool from Bedford and the neighborhood, on their way to the Salt Lake Valley. North America, the adopted country of that singular sect the Mormons. The party consisted of small farmers, market gardeners, mechanics, and laborers, with their wives and children.

1850: 5 October, *Monmouthshire Beacon*, p. 8 (62 words). "Lecture on Mormonism."

A brief report on the two lectures given by Messrs. J. Williams and R. A. French at the town hall in Newport. Also covered by the *Cardiff and Merthyr Guardian* of the same date.

1850: 5 October, *Monmouthshire Merlin*, p. 3 (130 words). "Lectures against Mormonism."

Yet another account of the lectures of J. Williams and R. A. French at the Newport town hall. This reporter identifies French as "late a student at the Carmarthen Presbyterian College" and writes that the lecture of French "was declared to be one of the most argumentative and eloquent addresses ever heard on a similar subject."

1850: 5 October, *Monmouthshire Merlin*, p. 4 (675 words). "A Mormon Pulpit Orator."

The setting for this article is a courtroom at the end of a session. Here is the introductory paragraph:

> During the whole of the previous proceedings in court, a short, thin, and cadaverous little man, with blue coat and woolen check shirt, lank visage, staring eyes, and long, straggling, wiry locks hanging over his slanting forehead, was observed stuck up in a corner behind the magistrates' clerk, ever and soon appearing to be muttering something which, possibly, he fancied an opportunity would presently occur for his delivery. At length, just before the Rev. magistrates were leaving the bench, with the county members, two official-looking documents were thrust before the rev. gentlemen.

The "cadaverous little man" is William Williams, a Welsh miner who was in the room waiting for his opportunity to have some papers signed that he thought would authorize him to preach his religion—that of the Latter-day Saints. A long conversation between Williams and a Mr. Coles is then presented in which the writer portrays Williams in a very condescending manner.

1850: 12 October, *Cardiff and Merthyr Guardian*, p. 4 (27 words).

> Mormon women, it is said, have commenced dressing in pantaloons. It is not stated whether the men have undergone a corresponding change in their apparel.

1850: October, *Seren Gomer* (*Star of Gomer*), p. 319 (1,205 words). "The New Mormon State."

This unsigned article offers "the latest news from America" as its source. The writer sounds the alarm about the danger of admitting a "Mormon" state to the union of the United States. His first target is Joseph Smith:

> The filthy and awful life, and pitiful death, of Joe Smith, their first "prophet," did not serve to cause people to disbelieve the terrible deceit; and at the

> present moment, Mormonism, and all its false doctrines, are more acceptable and prestigious than they have ever before been.

He then gives this assessment:

> It is cunning, though not perhaps surprising, that this sect is kept up chiefly by immigrants, and most of those are Welsh and English! Very seldom, in comparison, do they proselyte to any of the Americans born in the States.

He presents further reasons the US government should not grant statehood to Utah and then concludes with further information about the religion's founder:

> Joe Smith lived in the view of the world for years in the practice of the most wicked and disgraceful depravity. There was not one ounce of secrecy or doubt about the true character and personality of the deceiver; and he never tried to hide his depravity and religious deceit. He became drunk, swore and cursed, and deceived everyone he could; driving about insanely in an old wagon, cracking his whip like an express messenger, and he hardly had enough eloquence to say a word to cheat money from his bewitched followers.

1850: October, *Y Bedyddiwr* (*Baptist*), p. 324 (100 words). "Mormonism."

The writer declares that he has discovered the meaning of the word "Mormon," and he is pleased to inform the public that the word derives from a Greek word that means "Humbug." Therefore, he concludes, the Book of Mormon can be called "The Book of Humbug."

1850: October, *Y Diwygiwr* (*Revivalist*), p. 323 (110 words). "Mormonism."

The writer declares the same message as is found in the *Baptist* about the meaning of the word "Mormon."[38] The wording varies, but the conclusion is the same—the Book of Mormon can be called "The Book of Humbug."

1850: October, *Y Drysorfa Gynnulleidfaol* (*Congregationalist Treasury*), pp. 281–88 (6,005 words). "Mormonism."

The writer of this article calls himself "Daleth." In the preface, Daleth explains his objective:

> Mr. Editor—At the request of several friends of the truth, I present the following Lecture to the attention of your numerous readers, in which the beginning, the history, and the doctrines of the Latter-day Saints are investigated.[39]

The author obviously borrows and translates the information in this article from sources published in English. One source he names specifically is Orson Pratt's *Remarkable Visions*. Another is J. B. Turner's *Rise, Progress, and Causes of Mormonism*. On the final page of the article the writer indicates that his lecture will be concluded in the next issue of the *Congregationalist Treasury*, but there is nothing in the next issue or any other issue after that.[40]

1850: October, *Y Bedyddiwr* (*Baptist*), pp. 302–5 (2,580 words). "A Lecture on False Religions."

The writer, David Lloyd Isaac, begins his very long lecture with Ephesians 4:14, in which the Apostle Paul warns men not to be "tossed to and fro, and carried about with every wind of doctrine." Isaac then presents a minute explication of how not to be "tossed to and fro," with examples of how "Mormonism" and other religions attempt to manipulate and deceive others to gain their discipleship. Just before his final paragraph, he indicates his plan: "Mormonism weighed up in the next Issue." Then he makes the following offer to the editor of the *Baptist*:

> If it is thought that a *tract* containing the part above and the remaining part of the lecture will be of service, send to me, in "Pontypool" by the 10th of October, *orders* for the number required of them, and if the orders reach a thousand copies, it will be sent to them with the *Baptist* for November. Every effort will be made to keep the price to no more than two pence. The sale has to be sufficient to pay the Printer, and that is all; and I have neither time nor inclination to go three steps after it to sell it.—D. LL. I.

Extensive searches have not shown any evidence of Isaac's "weighing up of Mormonism" or that the editor of the *Baptist* gave any thought to the author's offer concerning a tract. Just three years after solemnly issuing this warning, and ironically considering its subject matter, Isaac left his Baptist faith to affiliate himself with the Church of England. He then wrote voluminously for the *Sun*, the Anglican voice in Wales, for many years.

1850: November, *Y Diwygiwr* (*Revivalist*), p. 356 (115 words). "Counsel of an Apostate Saint."

This is a brief note from Evan Jones, a miner in Pennsylvania. Jones declares that he would be glad to hear about his brothers back in Wales and whether they were still "Saints" or not. He says he was hoping they had "turned against that deceitful and lying doctrine which was conjured up by Joe Smith." He then admits:

> With sadness I must tell you that I myself was beguiled, when in their midst, to give credence to his heresy; but with joy I notify you that I have had the honor of leaving the Satanists through being convinced of their deceit and have joined the Saints of the Bible.

1850: 6 December, *Cambrian* (23 words).

From the Swansea Petty Session minutes:

> On Wednesday, before the Mayor, Timothy Davies, a laborer and a Latter-day Saint, was charged with being drunk and disorderly. Remanded to Thursday.

Episode 7.7

Start: A Unitarian ("Philalethes") debates with a Latter-day Saint (John Richards) and a former Latter-day Saint

1850: August, *Yr Ymofynydd* (*Inquirer*), pp. 187–89 (1,985 words). "Mormonism."

The author of this article calls himself "Philalethes" (lover of truth). At the outset, the writer states his main sources: *Chambers's Miscellany* and *Rise, Progress, and Causes of Mormonism* by Professor J. B. Turner, published in New York in 1844. Then Philalethes declares the following:

> Nothing here will be reported but what seems to be on good authority. And if anyone sees, or if anyone thinks anything is wrongly reported, the *Inquirer*, unless it should change its custom, will be free to accept and publish the refutation.[41]

Philalethes quotes from his sources to present the story of Joseph Smith and some of the contents of the Book of Mormon but does not refer to the current situation in Wales regarding any of Smith's followers. He ends his article with the following:

> An attempt will be made in a future article, if permission is granted, to return to the subject, in order to continue an account left half-finished, and complete, if possible, what was left deficient.[42]

This was the first of nine articles about "Mormonism" to appear in this Unitarian periodical published in Cardiff, in addition to one additional article that was published in the Latter-day Saint periodical *Zion's Trumpet*:

1. Aug. 1850, pp. 187–89—Philalethes throws out the gauntlet, but no one responds
2. Nov. 1850, pp. 261–63—continuation of Aug. 1850 by Philalethes
3. Feb. 1851, pp. 44–46—J. Richards, a Latter-day Saint, responds to Philalethes
4. Mar. 1851, pp. 67—Philalethes responds to J. Richards
5. June 1851, pp. 139–40—J. Richards responds to Philalethes
6. July 1851, pp. 163–64—J. Richards continues his response
7. Aug. 1851, pp. 183–84—Philalethes responds with his final article
8. Oct. 1851, pp. 236–37—David Tell-the-truth, a former Latter-day Saint, criticizes J. Richards
9. 18 Oct. 1851, pp. 336–39—*Zion's Trumpet*—J. Richards to David-Tell-the-truth
10. Jan. 1852, p. 21–22—David Tell-the-truth, second letter—end of polemic

1850: November, *Yr Ymofynydd* (*Inquirer*), pp. 261–63 (1,675 words). "Mormonism—Letter 2."

Philalethes continues the August 1850 article by quoting from the same sources. In his defense, the writer declares:

> What is more important, no one has yet, as far as I know, tried to disprove the facts that I reported. Since I wrote, I have taken every opportunity that I could to research the subject further, but I have not yet discovered the least reason to doubt the truth of Professor Turner's report nor the evidence that was presented regarding the moral character of Joseph Smith and his co-workers as men totally unworthy of trust.[43]

1851: February, *Yr Ymofynydd* (*Inquirer*), pp. 44–46 (1,895 words). "A Few Notes on the Essays of 'Philalethes,' Vol. 3, pages 187, 261."

The writer of these "few notes" is John Richards, a Latter-day Saint from Trehafod in the Rhondda Valley. As could be expected, Richards questions Philalethes's line of reasoning. Here is a sample:

> See again the November Issue, page 261—"What is more important, no one has yet, as far as I know, tried to disprove the facts that I reported." What? Is

> the fact that no one has yet tried to disprove, proof that there is no disproof? I cannot perceive the weight of a feather in this. . . . Further, let it be remembered that Chambers, J. B. Turner, Caswell, and Hubert are enemies to Smith, and therefore their testimonies concerning him are unacceptable to every thinking man. The testimony of an enemy is not acceptable in a civil or religious court; why, therefore, should it be acceptable in Smith's case? Would Philalethes accept the testimony of the scribes and the Pharisees regarding Christ? No; not likely. So, neither shall I.

1851: March, *Yr Ymofynydd* (*Inquirer*), p. 67 (685 words). "Mormonism. In answer to 'J. R.'s' Essay. Previous issue, Page 44."

Among other things, Philalethes responds to Richards's exhortation for all his readers to read the Book of Mormon:

> I do not agree with J.R. urging your readers to give their three shillings for The Book of Mormon. . . . I have read all of the Book. And I believe that no intelligent man that reads it deliberately and without prejudice can but be of the same opinion as myself, as to the obvious signs of deceit and forgery that are throughout it.

1851: June, *Yr Ymofynydd* (*Inquirer*), pp. 139–40 (1,080 words). "Mormonism. Additional Notes on the Writings of Philalethes, Vol. 3."

Richards quotes the following statement from Philalethes:

> If one looks into the insolent allegations which are the basis of their *system*, it will be seen that they are extremely offensive and blasphemous.

Richards responds:

> True that they are extraordinary according to the traditions of these times, but that they are extraordinarily offensive to reason and Scripture is a matter not yet proven; there is not here yet even a single word, with proof.

1851: July, *Yr Ymofynydd* (*Inquirer*), pp. 163–64 (1,255 words). "Mormonism. Answer to Philalethes's Article, March Issue, page 67."

Richards continues his article from the previous issue of *The Inquirer*:

> You said that I did not attempt to disprove the facts that you reported, and that the facts stand hardly touched. I did not promise to disprove them, because I did not see the need for such an undertaking since the facts (if they are worthy of the name) disprove each other; I offered to note some of the contradictory assertions; and I achieved my aim.

This is Richards's final article to appear in the *Inquirer*.

1851: August, *Yr Ymofynydd* (*Inquirer*), pp. 183–84 (1,295 words). "Mormonism."

Philalethes gives a review of the ways in which he and Richards have disagreed in their exchange of ideas concerning the topic of "Mormonism." Regarding the testimony of the three main witnesses of the Book of Mormon—Oliver Cowdery, David Whitmer, and Martin Harris—Philalethes writes:

> And on this, so as not to exhaust the patience of your readers, it is enough to note that evidence of that sort *requires corroboration. Without such*

> *corroboration it collapses to the ground*—in the same way as J. R.'s assertion, page 164, that he has had proof from God, etc. I shall now desist.

This is Philalethes's final article to appear in *The Inquirer*.

1851: October, *Yr Ymofynydd* (*Inquirer*), pp. 236–37 (895 words). "Mormonism."

At this point, although the debate between Philalethes and John Richards appears to be at an end, someone who calls himself "David Tell-the-truth" sends a letter to the editor of the *Inquirer* with his assessment of the religion which Philalethes had condemned and Richards had defended. As a former member of The Church of Jesus Christ of Latter-day Saints, "David Tell-the-truth" sides with Philalethes's condemnation and takes issue with Richards's defense, and he directs his comments to Richards:

> Not on a whim, nor with malice, do I direct these few lines to you, J. R., Dinas; but from a desire to convince you. You are either a man of weak thinking or a complete deceiver. You said that in your church there were prophets, speaking with tongues, the gift of interpretation of tongues, etc., and that you have "testimony," etc. You said that you had been in their midst for some years and that you saw no disorder among them.

"David" then presents two reasons he believes he was defrauded during his time with the Latter-day Saints: failed prophecies regarding the cholera plague and the false practice of the gift of tongues and their interpretations. He ends his letter by promising the editor that he will write again. And the editor adds a brief note:

> We would not publish the above letter, had not our Correspondent given us, in *private*, his proper name.—Editor.

1851: 18 October, *Udgorn Seion* (*Zion's Trumpet*), pp. 336–39 (1,305 words). "Response to 'David Tell-the-Truth' in the 'Inquirer' for October, page 236."

Because John Richards was unsure that his letter would be published in the *Inquirer*, and because he believed his voice would be louder in a "Trumpet," he sent his response to "David Tell-the-Truth" to be printed in *Zion's Trumpet*. Speaking directly to David, Richards says:

> I leave unnoticed your condemnation of me, since you have not been placed as a judge over me, and remember the saying of the scriptures, that "with what judgment ye judge, ye shall be judged."[44]

Richards reminds David that at one time they had believed the same things. Richards then asks:

> What sin did you commit to cause you to be excommunicated?

After scolding David for being in spiritual darkness and speaking against the Church he had formerly cherished, Richards invites David to return:

> I would greatly love for him to pull his cloak down. What need is there to fear embracing the truth?

1852: January, *Yr Ymofynydd* (*Inquirer*), pp. 21–22 (1,005 words). "Mormon Deceit—Letter 2."

There is no evidence in this second letter of David Tell-the-Truth to the editor of *The Inquirer* that David had read John Richards's letter to the editor of *Zion's Trumpet* previously. Perhaps David had read the letter and had simply chosen to ignore it. In any event, in this second letter he presents several additional reasons for his separation from the Latter-day Saints. Then he adds a final rebuke:

> My fellow countrymen, did I wrong these men, in my previous letter, in saying that the greatest duty that a Mormon has is lying? No. I have only told the truth. Is it not clear that the weak are beguiled by them, to believe the things mentioned?[45]

End: A Unitarian ("Philalethes") debates with a Latter-day Saint (John Richards) and a former Latter-day Saint

1850: 2 December, *Yr Amserau* (*Times*), p. 3 (2,225 words). "Joseph Smith, the Fraud, and His Religion."

This piece is a rather lengthy article by "W. T. T." that contains information borrowed from an assortment of sources. The writer refers to the article as "Smith's ludicrous tale." He includes the condemnatory 1833 affidavit signed by fifty of the Smiths' neighbors around Palmyra, as well as the Spaulding story about the origin of the Book of Mormon. He ends the article with a challenge and a declaration:

> So, if the Mormons claim to have miraculous gifts among them, let them show that by bringing the world to believe. Thus, having experienced the Mormon "spirit," we must conclude that it is not of God, and therefore we cannot believe it without some manifestations other than those we have received. I have used too much space and time already, so I must be still and profess myself as a defender of all truth, and a full-throated hater of all deceit.

Notes

1. *Zion's Trumpet*, January 1850, 26.
2. *Zion's Trumpet*, February 1850, 57.
3. *Zion's Trumpet*, April 1850, wrapper, 2.
4. *Zion's Trumpet*, November 1849, 219.
5. See his biography, *Indefatigable Veteran: History and Biography of Abel Evans, a Welsh Mormon Elder* at the Welsh Saints Project.
6. *Zion's Trumpet*, March 1850, 81.
7. *Revivalist*, January 1850, 7.
8. Ibid.
9. *Baptist*, February 1850, 67.
10. *Zion's Trumpet*, March 1850, 86.
11. Ibid.
12. Ibid.
13. Ibid., 86–87.
14. Ibid., 87.
15. Ibid.
16. Ibid.
17. *Defending the Faith*, item D4.
18. *Zion's Trumpet*, May 1850, 139.
19. Ibid.

20. Ibid.
21. *Star of Gomer*, July 1850, 220.
22. Ibid., 220–21.
23. *Cardiff and Merthyr Guardian*, 26 October 1850, 3.
24. *Monmouthshire Merlin*, 26 October 1850, 3.
25. See *Monmouthshire Merlin*, 30 September 1848, 3, for a detailed account.
26. *Zion's Trumpet*, September 1850, 240.
27. Ibid., 240–41.
28. Ibid., 241.
29. Ibid., 241–44.
30. *Congregationalist Treasury*, July 1850, 212–14.
31. "Billingsgate" is an area of London on the Thames River. The fish market located there was sometimes referred to as "Billingsgate College" from which the fishermen graduated after learning the foul, abusive language used there.
32. *Congregationalist Treasury*, December 1850, 392–94.
33. Ibid.
34. *Congregationalist Treasury*, February 1851, 55.
35. Ibid.
36. *Congregationalist Treasury*, March 1851, 76.
37. *Congregationalist Treasury*, September 1850, 276.
38. *Baptist*, October 1850, 324.
39. *Congregationalist Treasury*, October 1850, 281.
40. About midway through the Welsh translation in the *Congregationalist Treasury*, mention is made of an "Attachment A." There is no such attachment in the periodical.
41. *Inquirer*, August 1850, 187.
42. Ibid., 189.
43. *Inquirer*, November 1850, 261.
44. *Zion's Trumpet*, October 1851, 337.
45. *Inquirer*, January 1852, 22.

Chapter 8

Episodes

8.1—Henry Wilkins writes a letter to his father in Wales and another to William Phillips
8.2—Baptist minister Dewi Elfed Jones joins the Saints, is excommunicated, and is reinstated
8.3—The *Star of Gomer* will not advertise Latter-day Saint publications—the *Star of Wales* will
8.4—William Phillips defends the Church from attacks in six different periodicals
8.5—William Jones from Bethesda writes a pamphlet, and John S. Davis responds

Salient Events

- **11 January 1851**—The first issue of the Welsh periodical *Zion's Trumpet* comes off the press as a biweekly publication. Unlike the 1849 and 1850 volumes, the individual issues have no four-page printed wrappers, and the number of pages is reduced to sixteen.
- **22 February 1851**—The first sixteen-page segment of the Welsh translation of the Doctrine and Covenants is sent out with the 22 February 1851 issue of *Zion's Trumpet.* John S. Davis had "received counsel" to translate the Doctrine and Covenants into Welsh in August 1850, and his plan was to print the translation in signatures of sixteen pages and send them out with the biweekly issues of *Zion's Trumpet.* The subscribers were to save all the signatures, and upon receiving the final signature, they could have all of them bound, thus having their own complete copy of this book of scripture. Perhaps to lighten the burden of producing thirty-two pages in print every two weeks—sixteen pages for the periodical and sixteen translated pages for the latest signature of the Doctrine and Covenants—Davis elected to

include a segment of "Testaments of the Twelve Patriarchs" for each of the first twelve weeks of his periodical (11 January through 14 June). Merely having an assistant set the type for a few pages of the 1822 Welsh translation of this Jewish work—part of the pseudepigrapha—was a much simpler task than for Davis to write or translate those pages.

- **4 March 1851**—William Howells, the lay Baptist minister who three years earlier had walked from Aberdare to Merthyr Tydfil to request baptism after reading a pamphlet by Dan Jones, embarks with his family on the *Olympus*. In his 27 April 1851 report of the voyage to President Franklin D. Richards, Howells uses idyllic language to report the terrific storm that occurred the night of 22 March:

> The evening shades of darkness caused all to retire to their berths, on each side of our extensive bedroom, about thirty yards long by eight wide, containing about 300 devotees of Morpheus [the Greek god of sleep], but this night he received little attention, for Boreas [the Greek god of the north wind and winter] by 10 p.m., caused, under a covering of darkness, one of his light artillery to go forth in sharp breezes, causing the rippling billows to increase into wild mountainous waves, that caused the ship to tremble, shake, crack, and rock from side to side, like a drunken man. The Saints being novices in sea life, the sight and circumstances were new to all. The raging and roaring of the boisterous elements, with the noise of falling and rolling tins and bottles caused not the least confusion or fear in the bosoms of those who have been truly likened to Mount Zion.[1]

Wilson G. Nowers, who had been baptized a member of the Church just two days before the departure of the *Olympus*, overheard the ship's captain instruct Mr. Hamilton, the second mate:

> You go to the captain of the Mormons and tell him from Captain Wilson that if the God of the Mormons can do anything to save the ship and the people, they had better be calling on Him to do so, for we are now sinking at the rate of a foot every hour; and if the storm continues, we shall all be at the bottom of the ocean before daylight.[2]

Nowers accompanied Hamilton to the lower deck and later wrote:

> We made our way to Elder William Howell, who had charge of the company of Saints. Finding him in his bed we aroused him and delivered our message. In response he said, in a surprisingly calm tone, "Very well. You may tell Captain Wilson that we are not going to the bottom of the ocean, for we embarked from Liverpool on a voyage for New Orleans, and we will arrive safely in that port. Our God will protect us." Mr. Hamilton returned to deliver the reply to Captain Wilson, but I remained with my brethren. The scene between decks can scarcely be described; all was confusion; trunks and packages that were not properly secured were rolling and sliding from one side to the other. Some of the passengers were crying, others praying, and again others trying to feel composed. President Howell arose, dressed himself, and called a few of the brethren

> (about 12, myself included) to his side, all of whom engaged in prayer, one after another, as directed by the President, who finally prayed himself. While he was still engaged in prayer, I noticed a material change in the motion of the ship; for instead of her rolling and pitching as she had been doing, she seemed to tremble as one suffering from the effects of a severe cold. Varied thoughts passed through my mind; I could not entertain the idea that the vessel was sinking, nor could I realize that the storm had so suddenly abated. At the close of the prayer of President Howell, all responded with a hearty Amen, and we arose from our position. President Howell then remarked, "You may all retire to your beds." I returned to the deck to find that the storm had miraculously ceased; the wind had gone down, and the waves were stilled immediately round about the ship, while in the distance the billows were still raging. The vessel trembled and seemed to quiver at the effects of so sudden a change.[3]

Nowers ends his report with this comment: "During the voyage, fifty persons were baptized, including one baptism just prior to embarking and one after the arrival of the company at New Orleans."[4] Sadly, William Howells died at Council Bluffs just six months after his arrival there.[5]

- **April 1851**—The *Baptist* prints a letter from seventeen-year-old Henry Wilkins to his father, the Reverend James Wilkins, in which Henry outlines the negligent treatment he had received from his coreligionists since embarking with them on board the *Joseph Badger* on 17 October 1850. But the 17 May 1851 *Zion's Trumpet* contains a letter in which young Henry Wilkins apologizes to William Phillips—the president of The Church of Jesus Christ of Latter-day Saints in Wales—for the earlier letter. See Episode 8.1.
- **27 April 1851**—David Bevan "Dewi Elfed" Jones, the ordained Baptist minister in Aberaman, is baptized a member of The Church of Jesus Christ of Latter-day Saints in the Cynon River. Jones not only gave his heart and soul to his new religion but also presented to William Phillips the keys for Jones's chapel, which he had raised funds to erect. Four years later, Jones was excommunicated for misuse of church funds and one year after this was reinstated. See Episode 8.2.
- **23 August 1851**—The final of twenty signatures of the Doctrine and Covenants is sent out with this issue of *Zion's Trumpet*. Since the first signature was sent out with the 22 February 1851 issue of John S. Davis's periodical, it appears that more often than not, Davis was able to send out two signatures of the Doctrine and Covenants with each issue of *Zion's Trumpet*—producing possibly as many as ninety-six published pages in a single month!
- **20 September 1851**—The first signature of the Welsh translation of the Book of Mormon is sent out with this issue of *Zion's Trumpet*. This first signature for the Book of Mormon came just four weeks after the final signature of the Welsh translation of the Doctrine and Covenants was sent out. Thirty-one weeks later, the final two signatures were sent

out with the 17 April 1852 *Zion's Trumpet*. Thus it appears that an average of two signatures of the Welsh Book of Mormon were sent out with each issue of *Zion's Trumpet*. In John S. Davis's foreword to the Welsh Book of Mormon, dated 6 April 1852 (probably in commemoration of the organization of the Church on that date twenty-two years earlier), Davis stated that the translation was "the best that could be done under disadvantages which the majority of translators do not labor under." He explained that "perspicuity and plain language" had been sought more than "any kind of adornment." Davis also declared to the antagonists of The Church of Jesus Christ in Wales, "Many of you have freely given your opinion of this book and condemned it without ever having seen it; but now after laboring so long under disadvantages, you can read it for yourselves and see whether your former opinions were correct." Two interesting sidelights to the translation are preserved in a biographical sketch of Davis in Orson F. Whitney's *History of Utah*: first, the entire translation was written with one quill pen; second, Samuel Evans, editor of the *Star of Gomer* (the Baptist periodical for which Davis had formerly worked), said that it was a "pity such valuable labor in producing so perfect a translation had been bestowed upon so worthless a work as the *Book of Mormon*."[6] Davis's foreword in Welsh and in English is posted on his profile on the Welsh Saints Project website.[7]

- **4 November 1851**—Three men accost President William Phillips and Elder Lorenzo Snow in the middle of the night. After preaching to a large crowd in the Tredegar town hall, Phillips and Snow took their lodging in an eating house. They were not too concerned when they noticed that there was no lock on the door to their room, "not thinking anything bad would happen." But during the night, three men entered their room, one with a lighted candle in his hand. They approached the bed, swearing at the two men in it. Phillips describes in the next issue of *Zion's Trumpet* what the men did, after issuing many threats:

> After that they began to drip the tallow of the candle on us, by slanting it above our heads, but we tried to hide our faces as best we could. Then they tried to set fire to the blankets, but failed completely. Brother Snow had a nightcap on his head, and they ordered him to take it off, which he did immediately, and then they tried to burn the nightcap in his hand, but they failed.[8]

The men tried to get Phillips and Snow out of bed, but the man with the candle "fell down and hit his back against the wall," and the candle went out.

> Then we sat up in the bed, and they were now vowing and swearing that they would kill us after lighting the candle. We feared lest they might harm us with a knife in the dark, but then we perceived that they had all gone out of our room.[9]

Leaning against the door, Phillips and Snow struggled to keep the men from reentering the room. The commotion awoke the lady of the house, who then persuaded the men to come down to their own room. They did so, all the while swearing they would be back. Fortunately, they did not return. Phillips ended his account thus:

> We thank God for saving us again this time: and we counsel all the elders, that if they sleep in such places, to make sure to lock the door of the room they sleep in; and if there is not a lock on it, let them sleep with one eye open.[10]

Commentary

1851: 11 January, *Udgorn Seion* (*Zion's Trumpet*), pp. 14–17 (1,355 words). "The Nature of Miracles." Addressed to "The Editor of the *Star of Gomer*."

This piece is the first part of an article written by John S. Davis that was originally published in the *Star of Gomer* in 1846.[11] The second part of this reprint is in the next issue of the 1851 *Zion's Trumpet*.[12] Davis added a postscript explaining: "Since only a few of the Saints have seen the foregoing article of ours in the *Star of Gomer*, we thought that its publication in the *Trumpet* would be useful." Another possible reason might have been Davis's need for more time to translate the Doctrine and Covenants into Welsh. See Chapter 3 for further commentary.

1851: 18 January, *Silurian*, p. 3 (125 words). "Mormon Emigration."

A report of the preparations being made "on a very extensive scale" for many Welsh Saints to leave in the spring for the Salt Lake Valley.

1851: 25 January, *Silurian*, p. 1 (25 words). "California."

> I observe also that gold abounds in the Mormon country. Eleven persons arrived at St. Louis on Saturday, from Salt Lake City, with 80,000 dollars.

1851: 8 February, *Udgorn Seion* (*Zion's Trumpet*), pp. 48–50 (850 words). "'Nature of Miracles' Again."

A reprint of an article that John S. Davis had published in the *Star of Gomer* in 1847,[13] as well as a response by "Meurig."[14] See chapter 3 for commentary.

1851: January, *Y Bedyddiwr* (*Baptist*), p. 30 (280 words). "A Description of Joe Smith."

The writer gives a brief portrayal of Joseph Smith according to "a gentleman who recently visited the city of the Mormons." The visitor had a brief interview with Joseph Smith during which the visitor placed a copy of the book of Psalms in Greek in Joseph's hands and asked him to identify the language in which it was written. According to the visitor, Joseph responded that it was a dictionary in the Egyptian language. The writer tells the reader, "The book was Greek after all—which shows that poor Joe did not know any more about secrets of this nature than he knew about the carvings of the Egyptian pyramids."

1851: January, *Seren Gomer* (*Star of Gomer*), pp. 44–45 (285 words). "Mormon Deceit."

This article is a brief report by "Gwilym ap Dewi" about Dafydd Jones, a Latter-day Saint who lived in the Abersychan area. Dafydd had injured his knee in a fall and was treated by a doctor. Some of his coreligionists convinced him to remove the medications applied by the doctor and to receive from them a blessing by the laying on of hands. The writer describes the result:

> Their mistreatment brought inflammation and putrefaction; and the poor and superstitious creature died after a few days. Here is a warning again. The writer is truly sorry that any of his fellow countrymen are so illiterate, so lightheaded, and soft, and soulless as to accept being fooled and ridden by false louts which wander about the country to eat the bread of idleness, to take money from credulous fools, bringing distress, bad weather, and shame upon innocent families and making, also, religion into a subject of gossip for drunkards and atheists. There was an inquest on the dead man, but we have not heard the verdict.[15]

1851: February, *Y Diwygiwr* (*Revivalist*), p. 66 (160 words). "Emigration of the Merthyr Mormons."

The writer laments that yet another group of "these lunatics" are making preparations to journey to "their imaginary heaven in California." He declares:

> They will be under the leadership of six of the most well-known from among their fanaticism and their foolishness, and who are now living comfortably in Aberdare! Can any of the prophets inform them how many of them will be dead on the sea, in New Orleans, or other places before reaching the end of the journey?

One of the six leaders mentioned above is William Howells, who was appointed the president of the company that crossed the sea on board the *Olympus*, which left Liverpool on 4 March 1851. In his 27 April 1851 letter sent from New Orleans to Franklin D. Richards, Howells reported that despite "the raging and roaring of the boisterous elements," all the passengers survived except for two infants. He also mentioned the conversion and baptism of fifty souls from among the crew and other non-Latter-day Saint passengers.[16]

1851: February, *Y Dysgedydd* (*Instructor*), pp. 59–60 (40 words). "Mormons."

> A Mormon preacher was taken up, recently, in Stanway, for stealing sheets, blankets, and other things. He had also charmed the wife of another man; and since the man got his wife back, he allowed the Mormon to go away unpunished.

1851: 21 February, *Cambrian* (590 words). "Disgraceful Conduct of the Latter-day Saints at Ystradgynlais."

The writer tells of Mary Philips, "a member of this deluded sect," who attempted to steal a large lump of coal. When Superintendent Vigors took Philips to the stationhouse, she told him that her brother was ill at home, and she was allowed to return home. The next morning, she filed a complaint "for attempt of rape against the officer in question." When the case was heard a few days later, it was proved "that the complainant had on various other occasions threatened several other parties with [accusations of attempted] rape." The writer concluded:

> Such are the doings of this deluded sect in this neighborhood and how often do we read of their plunging one another to eternity by refusing medical aid when required. There are in this place about twenty of the Latter-day Saints,

> the greatest number of whom are of the lower order, and outcasts of other societies which are very well known to the inhabitants of the place.

1851: March, *Y Drysorfa* (*Treasury*), p. 104 (420 words). "Latter-day Saints."

The writer expresses shock and concern that there are more than thirty thousand Latter-day Saints in Britain, according to the *Millennial Star*. Especially troubling is the number of those in Wales—nearly five thousand. The writer reacts:

> Is it possible for this to be true?—that there are nearly five thousand of these deceived ones in Wales? For the honor of our nation, we trust that this estimation is baseless.

He then relates the account of the baptism of a convert in the River Conwy.

> After the man was immersed, the officiator asked the convert whether he had seen the Holy Ghost upon coming up out of the water. Upon saying that he had not, the convert was immersed a second and then a third time. By then, the poor creature, half dead, said that he had seen something but that he did not quite know what it was; and then the Rev. Mr. Deceiver assumed that he had witnessed the correct scene, and he went away.

The writer gives the solution to avoid being deceived by those who called themselves "Mormons":

> An ounce of common sense, not to mention anything further, is sufficient security against the influence of such evil tricks.

1851: 18 April, *Monmouthshire Merlin*, p. 4 (150 words).

A reprint of a notice from "one of the newspapers published at the Mormon settlement on the Great Salt River":

> P. P. Pratt is intending to take his departure on the first of January 1851, and may be absent for some years on a foreign mission. This is, therefore, to inform his debtors that he frankly forgives all debts due to him, and calls upon all persons who have demands against him to present them for payment on or before the 25th of December next, or ever after hold their peace. . . . He would like to rest in peace, without having old debts to stare him in the face.

Episode 8.1

Start: Henry Wilkins writes a letter to his father in Wales and another to William Phillips

1851: April, *Y Bedyddiwr* (*Baptist*), pp. 127–28 (975 words). "The Disappointment of Mormonism."

The first part of this article is a 28 December 1850 letter from seventeen-year-old Henry Wilkins to his father, the Reverend James Wilkins, in which Wilkins outlines the negligent treatment he received from his coreligionists during the five-week voyage on the *Joseph Badger* from Liverpool to St. Louis, Missouri. He laments:

> Oh! My dear father, if only I had listened to you and my dear brother James when I was with you in the little room where James worked; but that's how it was—I was deceived by others.[17]

Following the letter is a note written by the boy's father, in which he explains his reason for sending it to appear in the periodical:

> If you judge that the above letter might prevent anyone from being deceived to go to California, or the earthly heaven of the Mormons, it is at your disposal.[18]

1851: 3 May, *Udgorn Seion* (*Zion's Trumpet*), pp. 135–37 (1,200 words). "'Disappointment of Mormonism'—Letter of Henry Wilkins."

John S. Davis, the editor of *Zion's Trumpet*, had been well acquainted with Henry Wilkins before his departure about five months earlier. In this article, Davis expresses bewilderment at Wilkins's letter while trying to explain the puzzling transformation the boy had undergone since his conversion to The Church of Jesus Christ of Latter-day Saints against his father's wishes.

1851: 17 May, *Udgorn Seion* (*Zion's Trumpet*), pp. 149–51 (830 words). "Henry Wilkins Again—Letter from Him to President William Phillips."

Only a few days after John S. Davis's article appeared in the 3 May 1851 issue of *Zion's Trumpet*, a letter dated 12 April 1851 and sent by Henry Wilkins from St. Louis reached the hands of his spiritual leader in Wales, President William Phillips. Davis was pleased to make this letter his lead article in the 17 May 1851 issue of *Zion's Trumpet* for all to read Wilkins's apology for the consternation his earlier letter had caused. Wilkins's letter was prompted by one which he had received from Phillips on 8 April 1851 asking about the reasons behind the 28 December 1850 letter to Wilkins's father. Wilkins explains:

> Dear Brother Phillips, the reason for my writing, and calling you and others deceivers, was that I wrote it in my anger, and because I gave heed to all the old tales that I was hearing in this place, which I have proven completely false.[19]

Wilkins excitedly declares that he will be going to the Salt Lake Valley soon, as the driver for an elderly sister by the name of Mrs. George. Davis's excitement is also evident in his ending comment:

> The foregoing is an accurate copy of the letter; and if anyone doubts, he can see the original by calling at our office. President Phillips is exhorting the Rev. James Wilkins to publish the other letter in the *Baptist*, if he deems it well, so that the country can have further information concerning the "Mormon Disappointment."[20]

There is no evidence that Henry's letter of contrition ever appeared in the columns of *The Baptist*, but one can easily imagine Davis's elation at having it on full display in the pages of *Zion's Trumpet*.

End: Henry Wilkins writes a letter to his father in Wales and another to William Phillips

1851: May, *Y Diwygiwr* (*Revivalist*), p. 162 (315 words). "Mormons."

The writer admits that although the "Mormon preachers" do not accept money for their work, they do have a way of being compensated:

> But they have their way of taking spoils in the most cruel and merciless way, namely by going on the Sabbath to totally eat their neighbors out of house and home, in swarms of locusts together.

The writer gives three examples:

1. A "poor man in Ffynonddrain" slaughtered a pig to feed his "starving family," and the preachers went there and devoured the pig.
2. A man called "Harry, the Tea, from Carmarthen" was living comfortably before he became a Saint, but his new coreligionists "were not long in eating up his living, so that he has gone very poor in his old age."
3. A farmer near Abergwily converted to the new religion, "and the Saints are going there in plundering hordes, and in all likelihood it will not be long before the full corn crib of Blaencwm, both hay and corn, and the cattle and the pigs, and everything, in some way will be driven one after the other in a strong troop down the wide open mouth of the Saints."

1851: 16 May, *Monmouthshire Merlin*, p. 3 (120 words). "Emigration from South Wales."

> A large number of the best and most efficient workmen connected with the mining and iron districts of Rhymney, Blaenavon, and Blaina are about to leave this country in the course of a very few weeks, intending to embark as emigrants for the United States. . . . Vessels are continually sailing from the various ports in South Wales with emigrants, and ere long a large body of Latter-day Saints will find their way, for the purpose of emigrating to the great Mormon city or settlement on the banks of the Great Salt Water Lake.

Episode 8.2

Start: Baptist minister Dewi Elfed Jones joins the Saints, is excommunicated, and is reinstated

David Bevan Jones, the ordained Baptist minister in Aberaman and better known by his nom de plume "Dewi Elfed Jones," was baptized a member of The Church of Jesus Christ of Latter-day Saints in the Cynon River on 27 April 1851. Following his baptism and that of four of his congregants, Jones led his new leader, William Phillips, and a large group of his new coreligionists to his chapel in Aberaman. There, he and the other four received their confirmation by the laying on of hands. Although baptism by immersion was practiced by both the Baptists and the Church of Jesus Christ, only the latter had as part of its doctrine the laying on of hands to impart the gift of the Holy Ghost. And it was this difference that had motivated Jones to part company with the Baptists.

Jones not only gave his heart and soul to his new religion but also presented to Phillips the keys to "his" chapel, a building for which Jones had raised funds to erect.

And for a brief time after, the Gwawr Chapel in Aberaman was used as a meeting-house for the Church of Jesus Christ. The courts, however, disagreed with Jones's claim of ownership, and by September of 1851, the chapel was again a Baptist chapel.

Jones and David Rees, the assistant preacher at the Gwawr Chapel, were assigned by their new leaders to preach in various places in South Wales. Crowds gathered to witness two former Baptist preachers praising Joseph Smith and the doctrine of the gospel that had been restored through him.

1851: 17 May, *Udgorn Seion* (*Zion's Trumpet*), pp. 162–63 (190 words). "The Voice of 'Zion's Trumpet.'"

Within three weeks following his baptism, Dewi Elfed Jones published a poem in *Zion's Trumpet*. Here is the first of four stanzas in praise of the Latter-day Saint periodical:

> Come, come to the escape,
> Flee to the refuge, hasten quickly
> From the ugly oppression of Babylonia,
> The day of its destruction is drawing nigh.
> See! thou canst be delivered from thine enemies,
> Stand bravely in thy part;
> Yonder on the lovely mount Zion
> Thou canst rejoice in a while.

1851: 14 May, *Yr Amserau* (*Times*).

In this nonextant issue of the *Times*, a Welsh-language newspaper published in Liverpool, a writer gives the account of "a minister with the Baptists in Aberdare becoming one of the saints." When the Reverend Thomas Price, the Baptist minister in Aberdare, saw this article, he immediately wrote a letter to the editor of the *Times* to correct the mistake: it was the Baptist minister in Aberaman, a town about two miles to the southeast of Aberdare, who had converted to The Church of Jesus Christ of Latter-day Saints. The letter of correction appears in the 28 May 1851 issue of *The Times* (see next entry).

1851: 28 May, *Yr Amserau* (*Times*) (685 words). "'Latter-day Saints' in Aberdare."

This piece is the letter of correction from the Reverend Thomas Price, the Baptist minister in the town of Aberdare, who was erroneously reported in the 14 May 1851 issue of the *Times* as having converted to The Church of Jesus Christ of Latter-day Saints a short time before. Price clarifies that the minister who had converted to the faith known as the "Latter-day Saints" was in reality Dewi Elfed Jones and that Jones's chapel was in the town of Aberaman, not Aberdare. Price emphatically states his feelings about ever being associated with the hated Latter-day Saints:

> I can assure you that for the Baptists of Aberdare it would be just as well to be linked with the *sons of perdition*, as to acknowledge the slightest relationship with the godless, unprincipled, disreputable, uneducated, worthless, lying, blasphemous, presumptuous, hateful, satanic wretches called "Latter-day Saints."

Upon seeing Price's article in the 28 May 1851 issue of the *Times*, Jones immediately wrote a response and sent it to the editor.

1851: 18 June, *Yr Amserau* (*Times*), p. 2, item 1 (70 words).

In response to this possible debate, the 18 June 1851 issue of the *Times* only included a few explanatory lines, to justify why Jones's article was not being printed. The full text is as follows:

> That the Review of the *Saint* "Dewi Elfed Jones" on the letter of the Reverend T. Price, Aberdare, is already in print, as evidenced by the copy sent to me, is sufficient reason for us to refuse space for it in the *Times*; also its contents are such as to put before us the necessity of opening up a debate that would provide perfect boredom to our readers.

The "Review" which the editor declared to be "already in print" had appeared in the 14 June 1851 issue of *Zion's Trumpet* (see next entry).[21]

1851: 14 June, *Udgorn Seion* (*Zion's Trumpet*), pp. 184–86 (1,280 words). "To the Editor of the 'Times.'"

This is Dewi Elfed Jones's response. Thomas Price, in his letter, had expressed outrage that Jones and David Rees, Jones's assistant minister, had received baptism into The Church of Jesus Christ of Latter-day Saints. Jones responds:

> It is also true that T. Price, because of this [our baptism], is incandescent with rage, frothing at the mouth, and spouting curses against the Saints until his reverend corpus is about to break and fall to shreds. No doubt his vessel will soon be so full of malice for the Saints that he will explode and his loathsome parts become as tiny fragments. Well, the sooner the better, then! His murderous blast will have no more effect on the Saints than the barking of a dog at the moon.[22]

Jones then presents four objectives that the Reverend Thomas Price had in sending his letter to the *Times*:

1. To obscure the truth that Dewi Elfed Jones and David Rees, together with many other Baptists "have turned away from the Baptists" and joined the Latter-day Saints.
2. To blacken the character of Dewi Elfed Jones.
3. To claim the membership of the Gwawr Chapel as his own.
4. To pour forth the profane reservoir of his heart upon the Saints.

Jones also poses eight very pointed questions to his former colleague and invites him to answer, which, judging from an apparent lack of response, Price elected never to do.

1851: 14 June, *Udgorn Seion* (*Zion's Trumpet*), p. 194 (330 words). "Condition of the Church in Monmouthshire."

This 6 June 1851 letter from Thomas Giles provides evidence that the conversion of Dewi Elfed Jones and David Rees had a major impact on the level of interest among members of their new religion as well as on others:

> The following Sunday, the hall of the Belle Vue Inn between Victoria and Penycae was opened, where Elders Dewi Elfed Jones and David Rees had an opportunity to give their testimony to hundreds of people. The hall was overflowing with listeners in the morning, and many were unable to get in. At two,

> it was decided to preach at the window, so that those inside, as well as those outside, could hear; there were between a thousand and fifteen hundred listening, and many more by six.

1851: 15 November, *Udgorn Seion* (*Zion's Trumpet*), pp. 369–72 (730 words). "Groans of the Reverends."

In addition to preaching his newfound gospel, Dewi Elfed Jones also attracted attention to the Church's doctrine by composing clever verses of poetry to ridicule what he considered the futile efforts of his former colleagues of the cloth to combat the Latter-day Saints. In this issue of *Zion's Trumpet*, he does so with a poem of twenty-one 4-line stanzas. He mockingly indicates that it is to be sung to the tune of "Sectarianism in Danger." Here are the first stanza and the chorus:

> Wales, Wales, awake soon,
> Lift thy voice, and do not slumber;
> Come in strength and endless energy,
> To vanquish all the Mormons.
> Oh, how sad is our heart;
> The Saints of this age,
> And their influence must be overcome.
> Oh, how sad is our heart.

1852: 8 May, *Udgorn Seion* (*Zion's Trumpet*), p. 146 (285 words). "Eisteddfod of the Saints."

A brief report of an *eisteddfod*, which is a meeting for competitions or presentations of oratory, recitation, and singing. The eisteddfod was held in Merthyr Tydfil and presided over by Dewi Elfed Jones. John S. Davis writes that he had "the honor of presenting President [William] Phillips with a handsome copy of the Book of Mormon in the Welsh language, which had a moving effect on all of those present."

1852: 30 October, *Udgorn Seion* (*Zion's Trumpet*), p. 347 (45 words). "Minutes of a Special General Conference of the Church in Wales, which was held in Merthyr, October 4, 1852."

Among the many items of business transacted at this conference was the following:

> President Phillips proposed, and seconded by President Davis, that Brother Dewi Elfed Jones meet with Brothers Davis and Morris to learn from them the way to keep accounts of the books, so that he can show that to those conferences and branches where he goes. Carried.

Being involved in handling money and keeping accounts is what eventually led to Jones's excommunication in July 1855.

1853: 26 March, *Udgorn Seion* (*Zion's Trumpet*), pp. 209–12 (930 words). "Sectarianism Ensnared."

After his conversion to Mormonism in April 1851, the ex–Baptist minister Dewi Elfed Jones became openly critical of his former colleagues. He introduces this lengthy poem with a brief explanation that his poetic gift was stirred by the comment of "one of the chief Reverends of Glamorganshire" that "the kingdom of heaven is within us."

Jones then presents a "Reverendish Exhibition" featuring the minister on an imaginary tour throughout Great Britain, giving angry speeches about the Mormons. The poem consists of thirty-three four-line stanzas, each of which is followed by a two-line chorus. Nineteen of the stanzas are in this issue of *Zion's Trumpet*, and the remaining fourteen appear in the following issue. Here are the twenty-second stanza and the chorus as an example:

O surprise of surprises, a truly remarkable sight,
That the reverend has such a huge belly,
That is full of everything imaginable;
What a wonder that he is able to take care of his stomach.
    On seeing something like this, who can blame the Mormon
    For laughing ha, ha, ha! at the Reverends?

1853: 23 April, *Udgorn Seion* (*Zion's Trumpet*), p. 273 (1,130 words). "The Presidency of the Saints in Wales."

A poem of seventeen eight-line stanzas with a final four-line stanza by Dewi Elfed Jones. The poem praises the Latter-day Saint leaders in Wales, the Welsh translations of the Book of Mormon and the Doctrine and Covenants, the periodical *Zion's Trumpet*, and the presence of the Church in Wales in general. The fourth stanza is filled with praise for William Phillips, John S. Davis, Dan Jones, Thomas Jeremy, and Daniel Daniels:

A period of joy has descended on Wales,
    With vibrant Apostles of strength in our midst;
Her own sons, ordained, are thereby at hand
    And thousands rejoice in receiving their news;
To Phillips and Davis and Jones we make hail
    While Zion is clothed in a matchless array;
And blessings like dewdrops on meadows of green
    On Jeremy and Daniels pour forth their refrain.

Jones's poetic gift was also a great benefit to John S. Davis in regard to the hymnal Davis published toward the end of 1852. Of the 575 hymns, 57 were attributed to Jones.[23]

1853: 14 May, *Udgorn Seion* (*Zion's Trumpet*), pp. 321–24 (1,025 words). "Conversation among a Member, a Reverend, a Vicar, and a Saint."

A poem of seven twenty-two-line stanzas by Dewi Elfed Jones. The Member represents all religious people in Wales who realize the need to flee from their current religion and join with the Saints for deliverance. The Reverend represents the various Nonconformist sects in Wales, all of which see the Saints as the vile enemy of truth. The Vicar represents the Anglican Church, which was once powerful in Wales, but gave way to the Nonconformists. The Saint represents The Church of Jesus Christ of Latter-day Saints, whose goal it is to rescue the people from the clutches of false religion. In the first stanza, the Member agonizes over his decision to seek refuge with the Saints. In the second stanza, the Reverend points out how foolish the Member would be to relinquish his safe place with the Nonconformists to join with the wicked Saints. In the third stanza, the Member declares that the false teachers of Nonconformity offer him nothing that can cleanse his life. In the fourth stanza, the Reverend admits that Mormonism is unassailable and that it has brought him down. In the fifth stanza, the Vicar berates the Reverend for his weak stance against the Mormons and declares his intent to persist in his efforts to combat Mormonism, although he recognizes that deceit and treachery are the foundations of the Anglican Church. In the sixth and seventh stanzas, the Saint tells the Reverend and the Vicar that their efforts to destroy Mormonism are futile and that the Saints will emerge triumphant on Mount Zion. As a sample of this poem, here is the fifth stanza with a Vicar speaking:

> Oh, fie, reverend, what a weak and infirm,
> And irritable one is your cry;
> We priests are sorry that the Mormons
> See our deceit and treachery.
> I'll staunchly fire paper bullets
> Through the fortress of their rampart;
> With my rush sword I'll put an end
> To their fate forthwith;
> With my strong arm now, as weighty as a great feather,
> I'll pursue the Saints, children of Heaven,
> And drive like some giant;
> Through the power of Our Father and the Common Prayer,
> I shall be the Vicar,
> With my thin palms in the mighty sides
> Of the Saints night and day:
> To the beast I'll give a share of the product of my weak soul,
> To the god of the darkness the banner can rise
> As high as the church belltower.
> In pain and anguish the Vicar of Merthyr,
> Has a headache which persists;
> Like a clumsy boar I shall once more
> Root around Aberdare.

1853: 2 July 1853, *Udgorn Seion* (*Zion's Trumpet*), pp. 16–19 (1,430 words). "To the Ministers of the Baptists."

Here is how Dewi Elfed Jones begins his lengthy appeal to his former Baptist colleagues:

> Beloved—After my postponement for a lengthy season, here I am again humbly summoning back your attention to the cause of my departure from your association.[24]

He then declares that he had sent private letters to some of the ministers in an attempt to clarify his reasons for having left the Baptists to join with the Latter-day Saints. He wanted to avoid negative reactions, such as this one, from former Baptist friends:

> Dewi, Dewi! O! Jones, Jones! how about that; well, well; good heavens, dear me, what has bewitched you, indeed despite that, to leave your dear old

> religion, the religion that as a young lad you professed zealously and diligently, and join with those weak-minded creatures, the old Latter-day Saints?[25]

Several similar comments follow. Apparently, Jones's explanation for having left the Baptists was denied publication in the *Baptist* and the *Star of Gomer*. Consequently, Jones decided to have the appeal published in *Zion's Trumpet* in order to reach at least some of those who were concerned about his dramatic departure from their midst.

1853: 10 September, *Udgorn Seion* (*Zion's Trumpet*), pp. 177–78 (240 words). "The Poet's Longing for Zion."

A poem of eight four-line stanzas in which Dewi Elfed Jones expresses his desire to leave Wales and make the journey to Salt Lake City. Here are the first and last stanzas:

> Every night and day I long
> To be set free from Babel,
> And receive my worthy endowment,
> Within the holy Temple of God.
> O hasten, hasten the break of dawn,
> To set me free from the great affliction,
> For the profound peace of long duration,
> After finishing the work of my Heavenly Father.

1853: 29 October, *Udgorn Seion* (*Zion's Trumpet*), pp. 277–87 (4,400 words). "To the Reverends of the Baptists Again—Their accusations against Dewi Elfed Jones and his congregation, clarified."

Although Dewi Elfed Jones, since his conversion to The Church of Jesus Christ of Latter-day Saints, had sent accounts of his reasons for leaving his post as a Baptist minister to his former colleagues with requests that the accounts be printed in the Baptist publications, they had all been refused. Consequently, he turned to John S. Davis with a request that they be allowed to appear in *Zion's Trumpet.*

Jones administered baptism by immersion, as did all the other Baptist ministers in Wales. But as a Latter-day Saint, he also administered the laying on of hands, a practice that most of his ex-colleagues rejected and even condemned as heretical. In his defense, Jones explains in a footnote the right that each Baptist minister had to some degree of flexibility within his own congregation:

> Every church has the inherent right to judge for itself about its circumstances and its discipline, in line with the rule of the Baptists' Profession of Faith, and no minister has the right to sit in judgment on the doctrine of another.

The Reverend Thomas Price, however, called for a meeting of his fellow Baptist ministers in Glamorganshire on 5 November 1850—nearly six months before receiving baptism into The Church of Jesus Christ of Latter-day Saints—to challenge Jones's well-known practice of the laying on of hands and to invite Jones to the meeting to explain and defend himself. A note was sent to Jones requesting his presence at a meeting the following day at ten o'clock. He immediately responded in writing to the invitation, saying that he would be there. According to Jones's letter to Davis, the Baptist reverends had drawn up a list of accusations against their colleague and had determined that if he acknowledged guilt with respect to even one of them that he was to be excommunicated [from the Baptists].

During the meeting the following day, the list of accusations was read out loud. Jones's request for the paper in order to make a copy of it was denied. Jones describes in his letter the ensuing scene:

> They asked me if I admitted some of them. I replied that I admitted most of them, but not all of them. "That is enough," said one of them. "Just admitting one is enough to condemn you." Things had got quite rowdy by now, and I asked permission to defend my principles. And then the chairman, D. Jones, Cardiff, sat, with his hands stretched out above the table, and his little face as white as the wall, and in his childish voice said, "Prevent the man from speaking, prevent the man from saying a word!!!!" I told him very kindly, that that was beneficial for him, and them, because I knew they were all incapable of disproving my principles.[26]

Jones's repeated requests to speak to the assembly in his own defense were vehemently denied. He describes his exit from the meeting:

> In the middle of them I raised my hand as testimony that I was leaving them; and I said, "O evil and perverse men, let my soul never ever come into your fellowship. What I have preached will stay with you, so that you will not be free of it while you live; and I shall preach even in front of the doors of your houses, and I shall not cease to preach the truth even if I had to die because of it."[27]

The others reacted by shouting, "Throw him out, go to fetch the police to throw him out," and "Out with him." And as he left, Jones asked the assembly, "Is there 'crucify him, crucify him' too?"

The rogue former Baptist minister added the following postscript in this long letter to Davis:

> The account of the cruelties which were visited upon me, from this time until many months after I joined the Saints, shall appear in a future issue, if you can spare the room for it.[28]

Davis was the editor of *Zion's Trumpet* for only another two months, during which time nothing further from Jones was printed. Nor is there any additional information about Jones's tête-à-tête with his former colleagues in any issue of *Zion's Trumpet* during all of 1854 and 1855 (after Dan Jones had reassumed editorship of the periodical). However, Dewi Elfed Jones did write more on other topics.

1853: 31 December, *Udgorn Seion* (*Zion's Trumpet*), pp. 427–31 (1,520 words).
"Selections from 'History of Henry the Eighth.'"

Dewi Elfed Jones addressed this article "To the Priests, or the Reverends of the Surplice." The "surplice" refers to the loose white linen vestment worn over a cassock by members of the clergy. Since, he points out, the vicars of the Church of England had often criticized Joseph Smith, the founder of The Church of Jesus Christ of Latter-day Saints, it would be fitting for them also to revisit the history of the first head of the Church of England, Henry VIII, and compare the two. After itemizing numerous atrocities committed by this king, Jones points out the following:

> Inasmuch as Henry left in his will six hundred pounds to the Priests, for praying his soul out of purgatory, they no doubt have much more than a full task ahead of them, even if they work very hard at it. It will be time enough for them to begin deriding and trying to disgrace the Prophet Joseph Smith, or any other of the authorized servants of God, after they have gotten Henry the Eighth, father of their freedom, out of purgatory.[29]

He then closes his article by issuing an invitation to all the Anglican priests to free themselves "from the yoke of captivity and join with the Latter-day Saints."

1854: 14 January, *Udgorn Seion* (*Zion's Trumpet*), p. 36 (90 words). "About Zion."

One of several poems by Dewi Elfed Jones in which he expresses his strong desire to gather with his family to Salt Lake City.

> Great the roar of the sea each second—By day and night,
> Fierce the swift and fiery lightning—By day and night.
> Great the poet's constant love,
> For his faithful blue-eyed sweetheart—
> Greater is my longing for Zion—By day and night.
> Land of the Temple I would go to—By day and night,
> Where the sacraments are ministered—By day and night:
> Land of the best happy family,
> Land of healthful water and meadows,
> Land I sing to every day—By day and night.

1854: 29 July, *Udgorn Seion* (*Zion's Trumpet*), p. 447 (27 words).

A notice of Dewi Elfed Jones's new assignment:

> Elder Dewi Elfed Jones, of the Presidency of the Llanelli Conference, has been assigned as President of the West Glamorgan Conference, with A. L. Jones as Scribe.

"A. L. Jones" is Aneurin L. Jones, the adult son of Jones. One year from this time, Jones would be excommunicated for embezzlement. No mention is made in *Zion's Trumpet* about any action taken against the son.

1854: 4 November, *Udgorn Seion* (*Zion's Trumpet*), pp. 559–61 (830 words). "West Glamorgan Conference Eisteddfod."

As mentioned in a previous entry,[30] the eisteddfod is a longstanding tradition in Wales, a meeting in which people are invited to enter various competitions involving poetry, singing, recitation, and the like. With the permission of the Church presidency in Wales, Dewi Elfed Jones had organized an eisteddfod to be held on Christmas Day. In this invitation for competitors, he presented the topics and prizes and other details of the event.

1855: 21 July, *Udgorn Seion* (*Zion's Trumpet*), pp. 233–35 (945 words). "To the Presidents of Conferences and Branches."

Dan Jones begins this very solemn missive by calling the attention of all leaders serving under him to the vital importance of keeping "correct and clear accounts . . .

of the Saints' contributions." Concerning those who violate the trust placed in them in this regard, Jones has this to say:

> If anyone sells himself into such sinfulness, we will not consider excommunication out of the church of God a punishment equal to the transgression until the last farthing is repaid.

Whether Dewi Elfed Jones repaid "the last farthing" before his own reinstatement less than a year later is not clear from the *Zion's Trumpet* articles about his case.

1855: 21 July, *Udgorn Seion* (*Zion's Trumpet*), pp. 235–37 (1,580 words). "Warning to the Saints!"

In this letter to Dan Jones, his counselor Daniel Daniels tells of Dewi Elfed Jones's reaction to his recent excommunication:

> I received a letter from Dewi Elfed Jones, while in Monmouthshire, complaining that he had been excommunicated from the church unjustly because of your animosity toward him, and trying to prove that he is not a debtor to the Offices, or to the Conference, except for a few pounds. I understand that he is also busy writing letters to various places, and I have seen some of them, full of lies known to me, trying to justify himself for that which I know him to be guilty of.[31]

In his letter, Daniels provides considerable detail about Jones's embezzlement of Church funds. Following Daniels's letter is a brief note confirming the accuracy of Daniels's assessment, signed by Emrys Davies and William Richards, former counselors to Dewi Elfed Jones. Two other faithful brothers, Thomas Harries and William Lewis, also confirmed the accuracy of the missing amounts of money, and made the following observation regarding the relationship Dan Jones had with Dewi Elfed Jones:

> We know that President [Dan] Jones has dealt lovingly with him, and that he has done his best to restore him from his perversity, and that he has administered an overabundance of mercy to him, and that in every circumstance he has received hatred in return; and we know that D. E. Jones bears animosity toward President Jones, and that he has said much to injure his character in his absence for some time.[32]

A scathing letter about Dewi Elfed Jones, written by Franklin D. Richards to Dan Jones, follows the letters. Richards enclosed a letter he had received from Dewi Elfed Jones along with the one Richards sent to Dan Jones with the following explanation:

> So that you may know the spirit of the man through his own speech, and that you will be better prepared to deal with him.[33]

Dan Jones adds his own brief reflection following the letters he had received on the matter:

> It is not a pleasure, but rather a grievous duty to publish the foregoing, yes, a duty forced upon us by Dewi Elfed Jones himself, by his having written letters to different places, several of which are sent to us by their recipients, loathing his malicious assertions to hide his sins by vilifying the innocent. The foregoing illumination of places where he has written in contradiction of the truth is

> required, and it is fair for the Saints to have the other side of the matter as he has given them the first side himself. Defending the truth against falsehood is the duty of every philanthropist, and here is the attempt of your editor.[34]

1856: 10 May, *Udgorn Seion* (*Zion's Trumpet*), pp. 156–57 (390 words). "Letter of Reconciliation to President Daniel Daniels."

Dewi Elfed Jones begins this 3 May 1856 letter by recalling a recent conversation with Dan Jones and other leaders:

> As you know, there was a loving and reconciling conversation that took place between me and President Jones a little before his departure, where you, President Thomas Harris, and others were present; for such an opportunity I greatly rejoice.

He then issues profuse apologies for his "awful offenses" and requests "clemency and forgiveness." His final statement includes his wish to "be delivered quickly out of Babylon to the land of 'Zion,'" a wish that would not be fulfilled for another four years.

1856: 10 May, *Udgorn Seion* (*Zion's Trumpet*), pp. 157–59 (395 words). "Hymn of Tribulation."

A poem of eight eight-line stanzas by Dewi Elfed Jones in which he expresses the great anguish he suffered after being excommunicated from the Church a little less than a year earlier.

1856: 10 May, *Udgorn Seion* (*Zion's Trumpet*), p. 159 (200 words). "To President Daniels."

Thomas Harris, President of the West Glamorgan Conference, wrote this 8 May 1856 letter to Daniel Daniels in support of Dewi Elfed Jones and his desire to be accepted back into the Church.

1856: 10 May, *Udgorn Seion* (*Zion's Trumpet*), p. 160 (320 words). "Response of President Daniels."

In this response, Daniel Daniels endorses wholeheartedly the acceptance of Dewi Elfed Jones back into the Church.

> I recommend him from my heart to the attention, goodwill, and trust of the Saints and pray for him while burying all that was, without further mention of it, so that we may be of one heart in supplicating in his behalf, that he shall have the strength to redouble his diligence until the gap caused during the time we have lost is fully made up.

1856: 24 May, *Udgorn Seion* (*Zion's Trumpet*), pp. 173–76 (700 words). "Hymn of Tribulation."

The second part of the poem published in the 10 May 1856 *Zion's Trumpet*. In the first part (see previous entry), Dewi Elfed Jones expressed his discouragement at being out of the Church for nearly a year. In a brief introduction to this second part, he asks permission of the reader to sing "Welcome Rejoicing." This second poem consists of fourteen eight-line stanzas.

1856: 19 July, *Udgorn Seion* (*Zion's Trumpet*), p. 240 (80 words).

An announcement that Elders John Jones and Dewi Elfed Jones have been appointed as traveling elders.

1856: 16 August, *Udgorn Seion* (*Zion's Trumpet*), pp. 271–72 (165 words). "To Zion."

A poem, dated 1853, of three ten-line stanzas by Aneurin L. Jones, the son of Dewi Elfed Jones. There is no evidence that Aneurin ever emigrated.

1856: 22 November, *Udgorn Seion* (*Zion's Trumpet*), pp. 378–80 (990 words). "Editors of the *Hero* Repelling the Truth, and the Truth Repelling the Editors of the *Hero*."

Dewi Elfed Jones explains that he was prompted to write to the editor of *Zion's Trumpet* because of some letters that had appeared recently in the periodical the *Welsh Hero*.[35] Dewi Elfed refers to the authors of the letters as "half Saints at some time," suggesting that they were apostate Latter-day Saints. He chides the editors of the periodical, saying that they had decided not to print his response to the erroneous information about the Latter-day Saints in their periodical for fear that "the honest and the sincere [would] have a fair chance of judging the fanatical partisanship of the *Hero* and its editors, and become enlightened about their made-up, distorted and impudent lies about the Latter-day Saints." He mockingly refers to Thomas Price, a Baptist minister, as "his immersive reverence from Aberdare" and to Price's co-editor of the periodical, a Congregational minister, as "his sprinkling reverence from Aberaman." Price was the person who had taken issue with Jones's unprecedented decision five years earlier to present the key to and ownership of the Gwawr Baptist Chapel in Aberaman to William Phillips, the leader of the Church in Wales. In a legal battle the courts had decided, despite Jones's fundraising campaign to build the chapel, that it would remain in the hands of the Baptists.

1857: 25 April, *Udgorn Seion* (*Zion's Trumpet*), pp. 129–32 (1,780 words). "A Looking Glass of Local Manufacture."

A letter, dated 8 April 1857, written by Dewi Elfed Jones to Daniel Daniels. Jones's letter is very similar in tone and content to Parley P. Pratt's "A Looking Glass, in which to examine ourselves, to see whether we be in the faith," the lead article in a previous issue of *Zion's Trumpet* (11 April 1857). Whereas Pratt wrote about the Reformation as it applies to Church members in general, Jones directed his observations specifically at the members of the Church in Wales.

1857: 13 June, *Udgorn Seion* (*Zion's Trumpet*) p. 200.

Aneurin L. Jones is mentioned as being the scribe to President Abednego S. Williams, evidence that this son of Dewi Elfed Jones was in full fellowship in the Church at this time.

1857: 27 June, *Udgorn Seion* (*Zion's Trumpet*), p. 224 (190 words). "Verses."

This poem by Dewi Elfed Jones consists of six four-line stanzas and is dated 31 May 1857. It is an elegy for his infant grandson, David John Griffiths, son of Daniel and Anna Griffiths. The death date is given as 29 April 1857.

The volumes of *Zion's Trumpet* for 1858, 1859, and 1860 are nonextant, but one would expect that Dewi Elfed Jones would have contributed poetry and articles to all of them until his departure for America on 11 May 1860 aboard the *William Tapscott*. In early August 1862, he and his wife Hannah, together with their eighteen-year-old son, Daniel, and fourteen-year-old daughter, Eleanor, journeyed across the plains with the Henry W. Miller Company. Jones's death in Logan, Utah, on 18 June 1863 meant that he spent only about eight months in the Zion he had dreamed of and written poetry about during the previous decade.[36]

End: Baptist minister Dewi Elfed Jones joins the Saints, is excommunicated, and is reinstated

1851: 7 June, *North Wales Chronicle*, p. 5, item 1 (195 words). "Latter-day Saints."

A report of a conference held in London at the Freemasons' Tavern on Great Queen Street. The writer presents a very favorable account of the events:

> The proceedings were of a singular nature, commencing with a procession of the "twelve apostles," or "fathers in Israel," accompanied by "presidents of branches," by a number of young women dressed in white, and by twelve young men wearing large blue scarfs, and carrying a Bible in the right hand, and a "Book of Mormon" in the left.

The writer also presents several statistics regarding the growth of the Church in the United Kingdom.

1851: 7 June, *North Wales Chronicle*, p. 5, item 2 (105 words). "Spread of Mormonism."

Reprinted from the *Liverpool Journal*. In addition to comments regarding the growth of the Latter-day Saints in Britain, the writer makes this rather strange comment:

> It is not generally known that the Mormons use the arguments found in the books of Roman Catholic controversy, and are now making incredibly large purchases of these books.

1851: 24 July, *North Wales Chronicle*, p. 2 (27 words).

> Some new revelations to the Mormon Church are announced; the portion of the golden plates withheld from Joe Smith having been exhibited mysteriously to Elder Orson Hyde.

1851: 21 June, *Monmouthshire Merlin*, p. 4 (15 words).

> A soldier, at Roscommon, says that Mormonism is spreading among the soldiers of his regiment.

1851: 21 June, *Cardiff and Merthyr Guardian*, p. 4 (60 words).

> From the Great Salt Lake it is stated that the Mormons had sent out two new colonies, one to Lower-end Basin, the other to Lower California. The General Assembly of the Church for the State of Deseret had transferred all

their powers to the territorial Government, and Governor Young was awaiting the arrival of the territorial officers to organize the Government.

1851: June, *Seren Gomer* (*Star of Gomer*), p. 287 (85 words). "Mormonism and Polygamy."

A brief quote from the *Christian Chronicle* that the approximately ten thousand "Mormons" who had settled on the shores of the "Salt Lake" were in a "deplorable and barbaric condition." The writer further points out:

> The thing called "spiritual marriage" is a secret point of doctrine—it appears that it is the belief of this uncivilized people; and on the validity of that corrupt point of doctrine the union of the two sexes carries on by the same rule as the animals have.

1851: June, *Y Diwygiwr* (*Revivalist*), pp. 176–77 (400 words). "Observations on the Catholic Religion and the Religion of the Bible."

This is a lengthy article by "Eta Delta," the nom de plume used by the Reverend Evan Davies. For most of the article, Davies focuses on the Catholic religion and its deficiencies. But in the final segment, he declares that Catholicism, despite all its faults, is "a thousand times superior to Mormonism." Here is his description of the Latter-day Saints:

> The most worthless men—too lazy to work, the most uneducated, the most impudent and arrogant, going across the country, and lying, promising to work miracles, and claiming that if only they can immerse men, they will be reborn after coming out of the water and will receive visions from heaven, etc.[37]

The following is his call to arms:

> And, as Nonconformists in Wales, are we overly lazy, and too ready to amuse one another, or debate one another, for meaningless things, instead of opposing the sins of the age, and work together in the kingdom of Christ? And to be sure, there ought to be *a great deal more* concern, counseling together, feeling, and keeping vigil, and praying, with a keen eye on raising up preachers, choosing students, and ministers.[38]

1851: 18 June, *Yr Amserau* (*Times*), p. 2, item 2 (1,025). "Mormon Festival."

This lengthy article has to do with a 2 March 1851 meeting held at the Freemasons' Tavern in London with over a thousand people in attendance. Other than labelling those gathered as "deceitful wretches," the detailed account does not describe anything negative about the events of that evening.

1851: 18 June, *Yr Amserau* (*Times*), p. 2, item 3 (320 words). "The Saints in Llanrwst."

Someone using the nom de plume "A Humble One" tells of three men "under the name of Saints" who two weeks earlier had come to Llanrwst to preach. He describes the first one to preach as being "so destitute of effectiveness on the crowd, in a spiritual way, as if he had been a soldier facing his enemies with a wooden sword." About the second one he declares: "If some of this kind were to come to enlighten the country, it would be the blind leading the blind." And because the third one was a "first-rate shouter," the writer "could not stand his howling" and went away.

1851: 28 June, *Silurian*, p. 1 (70 words).

> The Mormons of Salt Lake City propose to construct a railroad from the Salt Lake to San Francisco, and this proposition is highly favored by capitalists and leading men in San Francisco. The Mormons, though a fanatical, are really a wonderful people for indomitable energy, industry, and perseverance. Already they form quite a powerful nation in the very center of savage tribes, and their metropolis contains 25,000 souls.

1851: 19 July, *Monmouthshire Beacon*, p. 3 (90 words). "Sanguinary Fanaticism of the Mormons."

A report of the brutal murder of Thomas Bennett at Beaver Island. The Church of Jesus Christ of Latter-day Saints once again was blamed for the deeds of one of the apostate groups.

1851: 1 August, *Monmouthshire Merlin*, p. 2 (85 words). "Acquittal of the Mormons in Michigan."

This article is about the trial of James J. Strang on an indictment for obstructing the United States mail.

1851: 1 August, *Monmouthshire Merlin*, p. 3 (155 words). "A Mormon Prophet."

John Price, a missionary for The Church of Jesus Christ of Latter-day Saints, was summoned before the magistrates at Pembroke "to show cause why he should not be adjudged to be the father of the illegitimate child of Eliza Lewis, a single young woman, a member of his congregation."

1851: August, *Y Diwygiwr* (*Revivalist*), p. 258 (190 words). "Virtue of the Saints."

The writer gives an account of "two Saints [who] were brought up on the suspicion that they had stolen a blanket, one of which is a preacher, if not an apostle, with the Saints." According to the writer, the two Saints had spent the night with two prostitutes in Merthyr Tydfil. When the men awoke the next morning, they discovered that the two women had taken six shillings that were hidden in one of the men's shoes, whereupon the men "took possession of the blanket."

> They were obliged to return the blanket and go on their way. They had been in an important conference the previous day with their brethren. How long will the innocents of Wales continue to be hoodwinked by these dreadful knaves?

It is difficult to determine whether such stories were based on facts. The absence of names and details leads one to wonder.

Episode 8.3

Start: The Star of Gomer *will not advertise Latter-Day Saint publications—the* Star of Wales *will*

1851: 9 August, *Udgorn Seion* (*Zion's Trumpet*), p. 259 (285 words). "Prejudice of the *Star of Gomer*."

In this article, the editor of *Zion's Trumpet*, John S. Davis, pokes fun at the editor of the periodical for which Davis had worked a few years before. Upon reading on the wrapper of the *Star of Gomer* that the Baptist periodical was willing to publish "every kind of notice," Davis decided to send a list of thirty-one Latter-day Saint publications to be advertised. This list consisted of his own publications as well as those of his predecessor, Dan Jones. Davis reports:

> But the *Star* will not advertise the books of the *Saints*, despite being paid in advance. "No," says the Rev. D. Ll. Isaac, in his letter to us, "it is not appropriate for us to do so." He said that he would be glad to please us, but that it was not appropriate to advertise the books of the Saints in the *Star*. Why not, Mr. Isaac? Are you afraid for the world to see them and afterwards see your deceit? Is there a reason for the Rev. D. Ll. Isaac, such a great scholar, to be afraid to advertise a few of the books for the Saints? Does he have some "goddess" in danger, or is he rather *scorning* us? No, not *scorning*, for he says that he would like to please us, but it would not be *appropriate* to do that! The religion of Mr. Isaac must be in danger were he to advertise the books of the Saints, and thus he had best not; and with that we shall leave him in peace now with regard to this matter.

1851: 13 August, *Seren Cymru* (*Star of Wales*), p. 1 (40 words).

In this, the first issue of the first volume of the newspaper *Star of Wales*, a brief notice appears on the first page:

> To Printers: John Davis, Printer, Georgetown, Merthyr, wishes to advertise that he has a CALEDONIAN PRINTING PRESS, Double Power, Super Royal, for sale at a low price. It is guaranteed to work well, as well as if it were new.

Davis was offering his Caledonian printing press for sale because he had recently purchased a new "Columbian Printing Press, super royal," on which he intended to print the signatures of his Welsh translation of the Book of Mormon.[39]

In his prospectus for this endeavor, Davis had announced,

> The entire book will be printed with completely new letters, and on good paper, and each signature will contain more reading than the signatures of the Book of Doctrine and Covenants.[40]

1851: 30 August, *Seren Cymru* (*Star of Wales*), p. 1.

On the first page of this second issue of the first volume of the newspaper *Star of Wales* is a list of Latter-day Saint publications for sale.

1852: 8 July, *Seren Cymru* (*Star of Wales*), p. 1.

Another list of Latter-day Saint publications appears in this issue of *Star of Wales*. Not all the issues of this newspaper are extant; thus, it is possible that other lists may also have been published.

End: The Star of Gomer *will not advertise Latter-Day Saint publications—the* Star of Wales *will*

1851: 23 August, *Cardiff and Merthyr Guardian*, p. 4 (2,340 words). "The Mormons—Their Creed and Their Kingdom."

A very long article from the National Illustrated Library. The article has basic information about the beginnings of the Church, borrowed from a variety of sources.

1851: 30 August, *Monmouthshire Beacon*, p. 6 (2,340 words). "The Mormons—Their Creed and their Kingdom."

This article is the same as the 23 August article in the *Cardiff and Merthyr Guardian*.

1851: September, *Y Bedyddiwr* (*Baptist*), p. 290 (220 words). "The Domestic Gentleness of the Saints."

The writer tells of a woman who was "seriously ill" and wished for her husband to come home from work and send for a doctor. The husband refused to leave his work and declared that his wife "had refused to believe." He was sent for a second time, and again he refused to return home. One of the neighbors, however, decided to act:

> But seeing the woman about to give up the ghost, one of the neighbors ran to call the doctor who came at once and testified that if the woman had been another ten minutes without help, she would have died. It seems from the above fact that there is something in Joe Smith's religion which dries up the warm feelings of the human nature and tends to confuse families and make them unhappy. May all the young girls of the Principality be saved from such devilish wolves.

1851: 6 September, *Monmouthshire Beacon*, p. 3 (216 words). "Fruits of Mormonism."

This report provides a few details about the criminal trial of "Strong" (James Strang) for such crimes as "interrupting, forcibly, the United State mail; passing counterfeit money; and murder." The article says, "For want of proof they were finally acquitted."

1851: 27 September, *Cardiff and Merthyr Guardian*, p. 4 (105 words).

A meeting of the Church Pastoral Aid Society at the town hall in Cardiff. At the meeting, the bishop spoke about something that he had found in a journal published in Cardiff.

> In the same journal he had subsequently seen a history of Mormonism. They knew what Mormonism was—that strange infatuation which had spread in this country within a few years to an almost incredible extent. The article contained a statistical account of the number of Mormons. The meeting would hear with horror and deep regret that there were calculated to be 4,342 of those unhappy people who had embraced this delusion in Wales—South Wales principally (hear, hear). He wished to appeal to other evidence; and he was sure the meeting would see it was disinterested as far as concerned the questions between the Church and Dissent.

1851: 27 September, *Silurian*, p. 2 (285 words). "The Mormons."

This article contains several bits of information taken from the *New York Tribune* about the settling of Salt Lake City. The article is very positive in every comment about how industrious and well-organized the settlers are. John S. Davis was so impressed with this article that he elected to publish it in his own periodical for 18 October 1851.[41] Davis also adds:

> We can observe that there is no one in America, where they know best, who dares to say that the Mormons are lazy and idle men, as the occasional ignorant man in Wales suggests. If there are some here who do not work with their hands, they are not lazy, rather they are diligent in the work of God.

Episode 8.4

Start: William Phillips defends the Church from attacks in six different periodicals

1851: 20 August, *Swansea Herald*. "The Saints."[42]

This is a paragraph from a letter received by "L. John" from his brother "E. J." who had recently been in Utah. The paragraph is copied in the September issue of the *Revivalist*.[43]

1851: September, *Y Diwygiwr* (*Revivalist*), p. 290 (155 words). "The Saints."

This brief paragraph is taken from the above-mentioned 20 August 1851 issue of the *Swansea Herald* (nonextant). It is partly paraphrased and partly quoted in the *Revivalist*:

> I am sorry that so many of my compatriots are being deceived by hypocrites and allow themselves to become fools and voracious oppressors. The closest market is 1,000 miles from *Salt Lake*, and the way is such that I would not wish for anyone to travel it except such a rascal as Captain D. J., who succeeded in getting a number of Welsh to go out with him, who are now far worse off than prisoners. Among them is a respectable woman from Carmarthenshire, who sold her belongings, and who left her husband at home without a penny, going with D. J., and is now his concubine, or what is called a "spiritual wife." The president has twenty-five such women in his home. I saw these things for myself.

1851: September, *Seren Gomer* (*Star of Gomer*), pp. 427–28 (410 words). "A Letter from America."

L. John wrote a letter to the editor of the *Star of Gomer*, explaining that he had sent the brief article on "Mormonism and Polygamy" that was printed in the June issue of the *Star of Gomer* to his brother in America.[44] L. John then quotes a paragraph from his brother's letter. Part of the letter is an account of E. J.'s disillusionment with his "journey to the gold country" along with his visit to Salt Lake City. E. J. makes the following observation about the Latter-day Saints:

> I went on my way past the valley of the Great Salt Lake, into the midst of the Latter-day Saints; and it is surprising that anyone from Wales is so dimwitted as to be led to destruction by a mob of unprincipled and wicked scoundrels, who don the mantle of religion in order to deceive the ignorant. They are not, those who were bewitched to go over, any better than slaves.

Furthermore, he notes:

> In their midst there is a quite respectable woman from Carmarthenshire—she left her husband and went with the Captain D. J. and she is at present a * * * [censored in original] to him.

1851: 15 October, *Yr Amserau* (*Times*), p. 2 (875 words). "The Mormons."

A letter written by William Phillips, the leader of the Latter-day Saints in Wales, to the editor of the *Times*. Phillips makes a fervent appeal to the editor:

> Be so honest as to receive a defense as well as accusations relating to the Latter-day Saints, by providing space for the following.

Phillips may also have sent his letter of defense to the *Revivalist* and the *Star of Gomer*, but only the *Times* elected to publish the defense—a curious incident, since there is no evidence the accusations were ever published in the *Times*. Phillips identifies the supposed "spiritual wife" of Dan Jones as Mrs. Elizabeth Lewis from Kidwelly:

> We think that the "spiritual wife" is Mrs. Lewis, formerly from Kidwelly, who emigrated at the same time as Capt. Jones, leaving her husband and her sister behind to settle some legal matters, which were still unfinished at the time of the emigration; and since Mrs. Lewis had arranged for space on a ship for her family, and to prepare everything, her husband and her sister agreed to remain behind until the next emigration, in order to receive some other money that was coming to them. Her husband and her sister ended up emigrating with the first ship after her; and we understand that they have joined with the family in the Valley.[45]

Phillips then presents several quotes from the Doctrine and Covenants as evidence that members of The Church of Jesus Christ of Latter-day Saints did not practice polygamy. He concludes:

> Polygamy is something that is not tolerated in the church, and neither the president nor anyone else is to practice it. It is contrary to the confession of our faith. I have been in this church for eight years, and I have never heard such a teaching, and it is a pity that we are wrongly treated, and we are determined not to suffer more. . . . We have respect for you and your publication, as long as it contains truth, but the lies that are in it are repugnant to us, and we counsel you to prevent such writings of your correspondents lest you yourself receive grief because of them.

The editor responded with a note at the end of Phillips's article:

> There we are being "so honest" as to provide space for the above letter; and in our next issue we shall give the historical account of the beginning of the Mormons, taken from the *Welsh Woman* for the current month. Also, we intend to give translations from time to time of the principles of these men, for the purpose of exposing their frightful heresies. It is pointless for Mr. Phillips to think of frightening the editors with his empty threats; they know perfectly well concerning their rights, and they will defend the freedom of the press to publish facts, and pass judgment on them as well.

1851: October, *Y Gymraes* (*Welsh Woman*), pp. 300–7 (3,985 words). "The Mormons."

This very long article has general information about the early history of The Church of Jesus Christ of Latter-day Saints. On page 304 of the article, the writer, using the nom de plume "Eta Delta," includes the quote from the 20 August 1851 issue of the *Swansea Herald*. In the rest of the article, entitled "Liars and Deceivers of the Latter Days," he lists seven disagreements he has regarding this new religion:

1. Joseph Smith was "an evil, lazy, and lying man" and not a prophet.
2. The Book of Mormon is not scripture.
3. God does not reveal anything new to the Latter-day Saint prophet.
4. It is blasphemous for them to assume titles such as apostles, prophets, elders, etc.
5. They do not have spiritual gifts.
6. Baptism by immersion is not indispensably necessary.
7. Not only "Mormons" will be with Christ during the Millennium.

At the end of the article is this comment from "I. G.":

> We have provided space for the above article at the request of the Author, but we completely reject his views on state and religious freedom.—I. G.

The segment entitled "Liars and Deceivers of the Latter Days" is also in the November issue of the *Instructor*[46] and in the December issue of the *Revivalist*.[47]

1851: 18 October, *Udgorn Seion* (*Zion's Trumpet*), pp. 333–34 (465 words). "The 'Welsh Woman' and the Mormons."

John S. Davis presents his opinion about the lengthy article that had recently appeared in the *Welsh Woman* about Dan Jones and his "spiritual wife":

> She repeats what other people say, who have been proven false many times. We do not have patience at present to answer the tales the *Welsh Woman* tells us; let her read the various treatises, in Welsh and English, published by the Mormons, in order to know otherwise.[48]

Davis declares firmly that Jones had no such thing as a "spiritual wife"; however, the accusation was true. And just over a year later, on 1 January 1853, Davis would publish in his Welsh periodical for the same declaration about the reality of plural marriage that was published on that same date in English in the *Millennial Star*.

1851: 22 October, *Yr Amserau* (*Times*), p. 1 (1,365 words). "The Mormons."

The editor makes good on his promise in the previous issue (15 October 1851) to publish "the historical account of the beginning of the Mormons, taken from the *Welsh Woman* for the current month." The *Times* has in this issue a large portion of the *Welsh Woman* article.

1851: 29 October, *Yr Amserau* (*Times*), p. 1 (1,055 words). "The Mormons."

This issue of *The Times* contains another large portion of the *Welsh Woman* article.

1851: November, *Y Dysgedydd* (*Instructor*), pp. 341–42 (1,480 words). "Liars and Deceivers of the Latter Days."

This article is also in the October 1851 issue of the *Welsh Woman*[49] and in the December 1851 issue of the *Revivalist*.[50]

1851: December, *Y Diwygiwr* (*Revivalist*), pp. 298–300 (1,460 words). "Liars and Deceivers of the Latter Days."

This article is also in the October 1851 issue of the *Welsh Woman*[51] and in the November 1851 issue of the *Instructor*.[52]

End: William Phillips defends the Church against attacks from six different periodicals

Episode 8.5

Start: William Jones from Bethesda writes a pamphlet, and John S. Davis responds

1851: *Egwyddorion Saint y Dyddiau Diweddaf yn cael eu pwyso yn nghlorianau rhesymau ac ysgrythyrau* (*Principles of the Latter-day Saints Weighed on the Scales of Reasons and Scriptures*), pamphlet, 24 pages.

William Jones begins with this statement concerning the opinions of the Latter-day Saints:

> The remarks made in these pages are intended to review only a few of the weak-headed opinions of the Mormons, who call themselves Latter-day Saints, for they are too numerous, and too full of inconsistency.

With respect to their doctrines, he adds:

> Their doctrines are an interwoven mixture of reckless, destructive heresies, if one looks at them in the simplicity of the gospel.

He presents a list of eight of the Latter-day Saint beliefs with which he takes issue:

1. They believe that the true church left the earth following the apostolic age.
2. They believe God revealed the gospel to Joseph Smith and authorized him to reestablish the Christian church on earth.
3. They claim that they have the same commission that the apostles received from Jesus Christ.
4. They claim to have the same qualifications to make a Bible as the apostles and the holy prophets had.
5. They believe that there is to be a trial situation after death, and that all who were in the world from the apostolic age to the time the gospel was revealed to Joseph Smith will be subject to it, and that salvation will be offered to them, through the preaching of the gospel in Paradise.
6. They believe that the day of judgment will last a thousand years.
7. They believe there are two heavens, quite apart from the firmament and the starry heavens.
8. They believe, after they have gone to California, that Jesus Christ will come to meet them, and that they shall reign with him for 1,000 years, when everyone else will be destroyed.[53]

Regarding the Book of Mormon, Jones writes:

> I shall not comment on the deceit of the Book of Mormon; its fate to my mind is like the Mohammed's Koran. Humanity should blush because of it

> and deny its relationship with it; let it be buried in the land of its birth, and let its memory go to a vortex of perdition.[54]

Jones then presents numerous scriptures along with his own explanations in refuting the beliefs of the Latter-day Saints. Nowhere in his pamphlet does he simply resort to name-calling or vicious language in describing how awful they are.

1851: 6 September, *Udgorn Seion* (*Zion's Trumpet*), pp. 282–87 (2,435 words). "*Principles of the Latter-day Saints weighed on the scales of reasons and scriptures*—by William Jones, Bethesda."

A review of William Jones's pamphlet (see previous entry). John S. Davis, the editor of *Zion's Trumpet*, writes at the outset:

> One of the brethren in the North has been kind enough to send the above booklet for us to review, which we shall do with pleasure. It contains twenty-four pages, and we must confess that it is somewhat more genteel than many that preceded it in discussing the Saints.[55]

Davis is equally "genteel" in countering each of Jones's numerous claims and explanations, something Davis does in this issue of *Zion's Trumpet* as well as in the following issue.[56] Shortly thereafter, he had his two articles printed as a separate pamphlet.[57]

1851: 20 September, *Udgorn Seion* (*Zion's Trumpet*), pp. 293–303 (4,740 words). "*Principles of the Latter-day Saints weighed on the scales of reasons and scriptures*—by William Jones, Bethesda."

The conclusion of John Davis's response to William Jones.

End: William Jones from Bethesda writes a pamphlet, and John S. Davis responds

1851: 1 October, *Yr Amserau* (*Times*), p. 3 (570 words). "Brotherly Love of the Mormons in Merthyr Tydfil."

David Jones, a resident of Merthyr who lived on Tramroad, was able to observe "the cruel treatment the Latter-day Saints [gave] to one of their brethren," a tailor who lived "to the side of Tramroad, near Twynyrodyn." The writer explains that when the tailor first became ill, he received regular visits from his coreligionists, but such attention eventually diminished and even turned into cruelty, leaving the poor man destitute. The writer concludes:

> Now he has been given notice by the landlady, also a Mormon, to vacate the house; and he lives at present only through the mercy of the neighbors, without a single Mormon to give him so much as a drop of water. I hope this will be a warning, lest anyone be so foolish as to trust the mercy of these ungodly and arrogant deceivers, those who are known quite appropriately as the Latter-day *Satanists*.

No response to the account of David Jones is to be found in *Zion's Trumpet*.

1851: October, *Y Cyfaill o'r Hen Wlad yn America* (*Friend of the Old Country in America*), p. 320 (60 words). "Mormonism."

These few lines are to inform that "Mormonism these days is as different from anything taught or ordained by the Prophet Smith as are Mohammedism and Christianity."

1851: 16 October, *Seren Cymru* (*Star of Wales*), p. 5 (235 words). "Llanidloes."

> Some of the sect called "Mormons" or "Latter-day Saints" have been coming over the last several months. They hold their meetings weekly and on the Sabbath under the old Hall, continuing faithfully and assiduously to offer their Mormon balderdash to the people; but it appears that the Llanidloesians are not so weak-minded and insipid as to receive their despicable rubbish into their minds.

The writer declares that this new religion has but little hope for success in Llanidloes.

1851: 8 November, *Monmouthshire Beacon*, p. 3 (110 words).

An article taken from the *Arbroath Guide*, published in Scotland, about "the Mormonite way of paying old debts." The article claims that "a Mormon preacher" excused himself from paying a debt since he "took with him neither purse or scrip."

1851: 21 November, *Cambrian* (55 words). "Cwmtwrch."

> A lecture on the Errors of Mormonism was delivered at the Baptist Chapel Cwmtwrch on last Wednesday evening, by the Rev. J. Rhys Morgan of Aberavon. The chapel was crowded on the occasion. Admission tickets were 6d. each, the profits to be devoted to the funds for the education of young men intended for the Ministry.

1851: 29 November, *Cardiff and Merthyr Guardian*, p. 3 (620 words).

In an article about "State Education," the writer discusses the topic of national education. He asserts that the Church (i.e., the Anglican Church) "is up and doing" but that "Dissent [the Nonconformists] folds up its arms, and thinks it enough to care for the souls of the adults, without troubling itself with the education of children." He continues:

> Whatever the establishment may be doing at Lampeter or elsewhere, the fact is patent here, that the only religious bodies increasing in strength in Merthyr are the Church—and its religious antipode—Mormonism.

He draws the following conclusion:

> The progress of Mormon worship, which Dissenting preachers rail at but do not understand, is in truth the result of their indifference to day school tuition.

1851: 17 December, *Yr Amserau* (*Times*), p. 3 (125 words). "The Latter-day Saints."

This is a poem of four four-line stanzas by Dafydd Williams, Holyhead. Here are the first and fourth stanzas:

> It is readily seen that a putrid plague,
> Is the spirit of the wandering Saints;
> It is the followers of *Smith*, the son of the black devil,
> Who seek to deceive our dear nation.

Their principles are filled
With the stench of hell, that is their gift;
If they cannot truly repent,
Before long, their place will be hell.

1851: December, *Yr Eurgrawn Wesleyaidd* (*Wesleyan Treasury*), pp. 368–70 (1,580 words). "The Mormons or Latter-day Saints."

This article is basically an overview of the beginnings of The Church of Jesus Christ of Latter-day Saints, the Book of Mormon, and the resettling of Church members in Utah. The information in the article is taken from the National Illustrated Library.[58] The only information the article presents about the Latter-day Saints in Wales is the following opinion about *Zion's Trumpet* (here called by its subtitle, *Star of the Saints*):

> There is a publication pertaining to this sect, which is printed in Merthyr Tydfil, under the title "Star of the Saints," full of the most offensive, ungodly, and presumptuous views we have ever seen or heard.

Notes

1. *Millennial Star* 13 (1852): 188.
2. Wilson G. Nowers, "Reminiscences," *Church Emigration Book*, vol. 2 (1850–54), 1–7.
3. Nowers, "Reminiscences."
4. Nowers, "Reminiscences."
5. See the profile for William Howells on the Welsh Saints Project for the Nowers account.
6. Orson F. Whitney, *History of Utah*, 4 vols. (Salt Lake City: George Q. Cannon, 1904), 4:352.
7. See the profile for William Howells on the Welsh Saints Project.
8. *Zion's Trumpet*, 15 November 1851, 366.
9. Ibid., 367.
10. Ibid., 369.
11. *Star of Gomer*, October 1846, 301–3.
12. *Zion's Trumpet*, 25 January 1851, 32–35.
13. *Star of Gomer*, January 1847, 16–17.
14. *Star of Gomer*, December 1846, 378.
15. *Star of Gomer*, January 1851, 44–45.
16. See the profile for William Howells at the Welsh Saints Project.
17. *Baptist*, April 1851, 127.
18. Ibid., 128.
19. *Zion's Trumpet*, May 1851, 149.
20. Ibid., 151.
21. *Zion's Trumpet*, June 1851, 184–86.
22. Ibid., 184.
23. See *Welsh Mormon Writings*, 159–62.
24. *Zion's Trumpet*, July 1853, 16.
25. Ibid., 17.
26. *Zion's Trumpet*, October 1853, 284.
27. Ibid., 286.
28. Ibid., 287.
29. *Zion's Trumpet*, December 1853, 431.
30. *Zion's Trumpet*, 8 May 1852, 146.

31. *Zion's Trumpet*, July 1855, 235.
32. Ibid., 237.
33. Ibid.
34. Ibid., 238.
35. This particular issue of *Y Gwron Cymreig* (*Welsh Hero*) has yet to be identified.
36. For further biographical information about Dewi Elfed Jones, see D. L. Davies, "From a Seion of Lands to the Land of Zion: The Life of David Bevan Jones," in *Mormons in Early Victorian Britain*, ed. Richard L. Jensen and Malcolm R. Thorp (Salt Lake City: University of Utah Press, 1989), 118–41. See the David Bevan Jones profile on the Welsh Saints Project for a more detailed biography.
37. *Revivalist*, June 1851, 177.
38. Ibid.
39. See Document 4432 in the Church History Library, Salt Lake City.
40. *Welsh Mormon Writings*, item 58.
41. *Zion's Trumpet*, October 1851, 332–33.
42. This issue of the *Swansea Herald* is nonextant.
43. *Revivalist*, September 1851, 290.
44. *Star of Gomer*, June 1851, 287.
45. After crossing the sea and the plains in the same company, Elizabeth Lewis and Dan Jones were married by Brigham Young in November 1849.
46. *Instructor*, November 1851, 341–42.
47. *Revivalist*, December 1851, 298–300.
48. *Zion's Trumpet*, October 1851, 333.
49. *Welsh Woman*, October 1851, 304–7,
50. *Revivalist*, December 1851, 298–300.
51. *Welsh Woman*, October 1851, 304–7.
52. *Instructor*, November 1851, 341–42.
53. William Jones, *Principles of the Latter-day Saints weighed on the scales of reasons and the scriptures*, 1851, 5–6.
54. Ibid., 6.
55. *Zion's Trumpet*, September 1851, 282.
56. *Zion's Trumpet*, 20 September 1851, 293–303.
57. See *Defending the Faith: Early Welsh Missionary Publications*, item D20, for a facsimile translation.
58. *The Mormons; or Latter-Day Saints. With Memoirs of the Life and Death of Joseph Smith, the American 'Mahomet.' Illustrated with forty engravings.* London: Office of the National Illustrated Library, 326.

Chapter 9

Episodes

9.1—One vicar attacks, and another vicar agrees—John S. Davis responds
9.2—William Rowlands, another vicar, publishes a pamphlet—John S. Davis scoffs
9.3—John S. Davis faces off against his former boss, J. Jones of Llangollen
9.4—Apostate Evan Howell accuses—Eyewitness Alfred J. Wood defends
9.5—Two different writers assess the Welsh translation of the Book of Mormon
9.6—Four hundred Latter-day Saints are miraculously unharmed by a ceiling collapse in Newport
9.7—An Independent minister defends the Latter-day Saints and is attacked by a colleague
9.8—Thomas Hughes's first pamphlet receives eight rave reviews

Salient Events

- **2 March 1852**—William Phillips responds publicly to the 25 February 1852 lecture of Reverend J. Jones, Llangollen. John S. Davis responds to two other lectures presented by his former boss, Reverend J. Jones. Davis had worked as a typesetter for J. Jones a few years earlier, before and during the time Dan Jones was publishing materials in Rhydybont, Carmarthenshire. In response to J. Jones's lectures, Davis would eventually publish six lectures on the nature of miracles. (See Episode 9.3.) In the introduction to the first one, he wrote,

  > Although we are but a small "shepherd boy" alongside the Giant of Llangollen, yet we feel totally unafraid, and although we heard him proclaim in his last lecture, "It will have to be *something* before it can bring me down," yet who knows but what some sharp stones of truth from our insignificant sling, will adhere to his skull, and cause him to fall to the

> ground. God knows best concerning that; but we know this, that we are battling for God, and woe unto them that fight against him.[1]

- **17 April 1852**—The final signature of the Welsh Book of Mormon is sent out with this issue of *Zion's Trumpet*. A preface entitled "To the Welsh" has the names of William Phillips, John Davis, and Thomas Pugh, but the translation is clearly Davis's work. Here is the first paragraph of the preface:

  > Beloved Countrymen.—It is not without feelings of gratitude to God that we have the honor of presenting before you this valuable book in the Welsh language. Many of you have freely given your opinion of this book, before you ever saw it, and condemned it, but now, after laboring so long under disadvantages, you can read it for yourselves and see whether your former opinion was correct. We did not of ourselves take upon us this work but were counseled to do it by our President F. D. Richards, who is over us in the Lord. We need not praise this book any more than the Bible, for both speak for themselves, to those that love light and truth. It will suffice, therefore, to say that we know it is a good book, and a gift of God, and that whoever will believe and do according to its words shall receive eternal life, but it is in vain to think that *all* will say the same of it; for *few* are those that walk in the narrow path.[2]

- **10 May 1852**—A mine explosion in the little mining town of Cwmbach, Glamorganshire, claims the lives of sixty-seven men and boys. Of this number, nineteen were members of The Church of Jesus Christ of Latter-day Saints. Sadly, President Ebenezer Morris and his two sons, eleven-year-old John and ten-year-old David, were three of the nineteen. Morris had been sent on a mission to preside over the Cwmbach Branch. He moved there with his family and found employment in the mine. Ten months after the explosion, his widow, Mary Reese Morris, and their four surviving children went to Salt Lake City and eventually settled in Wellsville, Cache County, Utah. Because the mine in Cwmbach was known for having dubious safety regulations, the pay was a bit higher than that offered by other mines. Wanting to save up enough money to emigrate as soon as possible, David Jenkins, another victim, had been willing to take the risk. Two of his children were able to journey to Utah in 1866, fourteen years after the explosion. Two years later, these two children made it possible for David's widow, Anna Evans Jenkins, to finally accomplish her dream of going to America with the other children. They settled in Samaria, Oneida County, Idaho.[3]

- **8 July 1852**—In his periodical, the editor of the *Star of Wales* expresses his reaction to the recently published Welsh translation of the Book of Mormon:

  > We cannot be expected to give any approval whatsoever to this work, or praise the superstition of the Welsh people for supporting its publication in Welsh; and there is no composition set up as equal to the Word of God which deserves any more than the most definitive condemnation. Whatever of that, there is no danger that anyone who reads it attentively will be deceived by it, so as to become one of the Latter-day Saints; for it appears

to us to be nothing but a pack of foolish lies, composed deceitfully to imitate, to some extent, the scriptural account, and the names of persons have been changed, and many fables have been added. Whatever of that, the work has been printed well, with clear letters and excellent paper, as is all the work of Mr. Davis. The translation also is fluid and intelligible.

- **12 July 1852**—On this Monday evening, the ceiling of the Sunderland Hall in Newport, South Wales, collapsed. An estimated four hundred Latter-day Saints were gathered in this large hall when the ceiling came down on them. Miraculously no one was seriously injured except for "two or three unbelievers, who had gone thither to revile and sneer at the true followers of Joe Smith."[4] See Episode 9.6 in this chapter.
- **18 September 1852**—Lewis Bowen is baptized in Blaenavon, Wales. His minister had requested that he curb the astounding progress of the Latter-day Saints in that area by debating them. During the debate, however, Bowen stated to all present that the elders were the ones who had the truth. His father immediately disowned him and two years later sent a letter reprimanding Bowen for being in his brother's home: "You have been . . . sowing the *weeds* of Mormonism in the locality, which thing your mother and I scorn to the uttermost degree." His father added: "Because of this, we cannot conscientiously ask you to our house. For one thing, your mother is too weak to stand the sorrow you have caused her, and you have received advantages to know better than to join such presumptuous, assumptive, deceiving, and vile people." Eighty-two years later, Lewis's grandson, Albert E. Bowen, was called to the Quorum of the Twelve Apostles.[5]
- **20 September 1852**—Dan Jones, on his way back to Wales, meets up with William Morgan and other Welsh pioneers who were on the plains eighty miles east of Salt Lake City. Many of the Welsh in this company had been on the *Buena Vista* with Jones three years earlier, and it was a tear-filled reunion. Some of the tears were for joy at reuniting, and some were for sadness at remembering the many who had died of cholera on the Missouri River.
- **16 October 1852**—John S. Davis announces in print that his Welsh translation of the Pearl of Great Price is available for purchase for one shilling twopence. He says, "We do not think any of the Saints should be without a copy."[6]
- **27 December 1852**—Dan Jones, Thomas Jeremy, and Daniel Daniels arrive back in Merthyr Tydfil to serve missions. William Phillips would continue as the president of the Church in Wales throughout 1853, and John S. Davis would continue as editor of *Zion's Trumpet* all during 1853. Dan Jones would become the president of the Church in Wales at the beginning of 1854, with Jeremy and Daniels as his counselors. Jones would also become the editor of *Zion's Trumpet* at the beginning of 1854. Jones, Jeremy, and Daniels were the first Welsh missionaries to have made the journey to Utah.

Commentary

1852: January, *Y Bedyddiwr* (*Baptist*), pp. 32–33 (605 words). "Saintly Literature."

This article consists of three letters, one that the sender, "Dafydd Avan," wrote to the editor, and two that are from Emrys Davies—a recent convert to the Church—to J. Bedford, the distributor of the *Baptist* in Aberavon, near Port Talbot, regarding a debate arranged between Emrys Davies and Thomas Davies for 8 December 1851. Apparently, Bedford had agreed to "settle the rules of the debate." In his first letter, dated 3 December 1851, Emrys Davies wishes to offer some rules he considers "to be fair and reasonable." In the second, dated 6 December 1851, Davies expresses remorse that his opponent in the debate is unwell and that the debate must be postponed.

"Dafydd Avan" is possibly the nom de plume of J. Bedford, the original recipient of the Davies letters. In his letter to the editor, Avan explains that he is sending copies of the two Emrys Davies letters, which Avan had rewritten "word for word," to be printed in the *Baptist* "for the readers' amusement at the beginning of a new year." He himself finds the letters amusing because of all the grammatical and spelling errors Davies made, errors which Avan painstakingly reproduces.[7]

1852: 10 January, *Monmouthshire Beacon*, p. 5 (53 words).

> The Mormons are laboring at the Sandwich Islands, in companies of two, to convert the population (natives, foreigners, missionaries, and all) to their faith. It is not a little worthy of note, that while in England and Scotland they have made converts by thousands, in Hawaii they have met with no success whatever.

1852: 23 January, *Welshman*, p. 2 (180 words). "Mormonism."

Some statistics regarding plural marriage taken from the *New York National Police Gazette*. Here is an example:

> The pluralist wife system is in full vogue here. Governor Young is said to have 90 wives. He drove along the streets a few days ago with 16 of them in a long carriage, 14 of them having each an infant at her bosom.

1852: 24 January, *Cardiff and Merthyr Guardian*, p. 3 (600 words). "Mormonism in America."

The writer quotes the report of the Utah Territory judges relative to the proceedings of "the Mormons." He says the report is "full of disgusting details of the debauchery carried on by the leading members of that sect." The focus is mainly on plural marriage.

1852: 29 January, *Y Gwron Cymreig* (*Welsh Hero*), p. 4 (180 words). "Mormonism."

The writer quotes the *New York National Police Gazette* to reveal "a host of the most disgusting stories relating to the behavior of this sect by the Salt Lake." He declares:

> The alarming truth is that even now hosts of men are leaving Great Britain to join with the Mormons, despite all the odious reports made of them.

Episode 9.1

Start: One vicar attacks, and another vicar agrees—John S. Davis responds

1852: 30 January, *Cambrian* (845 words).

John Griffith, the vicar of Aberdare, wrote this letter entitled "The Mormons or Latter-day Saints." Having read the latest report "made to Congress by the Judges of Utah Territory," Griffith felt compelled to express his concern at the presence of such a large number of "Mormons" in Wales and especially in his town of Aberdare. The report to the United States Congress by the judges who lived in Utah declared that polygamy was "openly avowed and practiced in the territory, under the sanction and in obedience to the direct commands of the Church." Griffith condemned the "universality" of polygamy as well as its "shamelessness" and its "incestuous nature." He also declared that there should be a greater effort made throughout Wales to educate the working classes about this evil in order to stem the tide of converts to this new religion. Griffith's letter was also printed in the *Cardiff and Merthyr Guardian* and the *Monmouthshire Merlin*.

1852: 31 January, *Cardiff and Merthyr Guardian*, p. 4 (865 words). "The Mormons, or Latter-day Saints."

The same letter by John Griffith that was printed in the 30 January 1852 issue of the *Cambrian*.

1852: 6 February, *Monmouthshire Merlin*, p. 3 (865 words). "The Mormons, or Latter-day Saints."

The same letter by John Griffith that was printed in the 30 January 1852 issue of the *Cambrian* and the 31 January 1852 issue of the *Cardiff and Merthyr Guardian*.

1852: 14 February, *Cardiff and Merthyr Guardian*, p. 4 (800 words). "Mormonism. To the Editor of the Cardiff and Merthyr Guardian."

David Evans, the vicar of Aberavon—about twenty-five miles to the southwest of Aberdare—agrees wholeheartedly with his colleague John Griffith about the menace of The Church of Jesus Christ of Latter-day Saints:

> The letter on Mormonism by the Vicar of Aberdare, which appeared in your last impression, is at this time of greater importance than many, perhaps, are disposed to attach to it.

He explains further:

> Many are they who consider Mormonism and its abominations too despicable to be noticed; but when it is remembered how many thousands of our fellow-immortals have been led astray by it, some to the vortex of the foulest licentiousness—and some, after loss of goods, reputation, and peace, to utter destruction both of body and soul!—and when it is further remembered that it still continues to lead, as if by silken bands, thousands more to the same abyss of ruin, I think that the voice of scripture, equally with the voice of reason, calls loudly upon every faithful minister and disciple of the Blessed Savior to use every legitimate means to banish and drive away this monstrous heresy.

Evans then declares the vital importance of the press in combating "this evil." He indicates that the publication "best calculated to give a true picture of this 'abortion'" is a pamphlet entitled "Mormonism, an exposure of the impositions adopted by the sect called the Latter-day Saints," written by the Reverend F. B. Ashley, vicar of Wooburn, Buckinghamshire. Evans adds that he has already indicated to a friend his willingness to translate Ashley's pamphlet into Welsh. The Welsh version of the pamphlet in question was indeed published the following year (1853), but the translator was not the Reverend David Evans of Aberavon; rather, it was the Reverend G. C. F. Harries, the curate of the Merthyr Tydfil parish. (See Section 2 for more information.)

In closing, Evans expresses this wish regarding the impact of the Welsh translation of Ashley's pamphlet:

> I hope . . . that this destructive heresy will be banished from the hills to the valleys, and from the valleys to the sea, and may ere long sink like a stone into the deep and perish in the waters.

1852: 7 February, *Udgorn Seion* (*Zion's Trumpet*), p. 37 (1,610 words). "The Mormons in Utah."

Instead of responding directly to the allegations presented by John Griffith and David Evans in their articles in the *Cardiff and Merthyr Guardian*, John S. Davis elected to print in his own periodical a lengthy article that had appeared in the *New York Daily Tribune* on 13 January 1852. In this article, which favorably regards the Latter-day Saints then in Utah, the writer opens with the following statement:

> We have published the statements of Judges Brocchus and Brandeburg and Secretary Harris, accusing the Mormons of sedition as well as immorality, and stating reasons why those officials could not consistently remain in the Territory. These statements have been flatly contradicted by Mr. Bernhisel, the Delegate of Utah, on the floor of Congress, who challenges and demands the strictest investigation of the whole matter, so far as it concerns the Government of the United States.[8]

He then quotes from the *Republic* "an article on the Mormon side" which, he says, "comes from a responsible source." The unnamed writer of this article had been present for the Fourth of July celebration in Salt Lake City the previous year, and he reports that he witnessed nothing but appropriate behavior on the part of the Latter-day Saints in their support of the United States government. He also defends the Latter-day Saints concerning their reaction a few years earlier to a request for a battalion of five hundred men to fight for their country in its war with Mexico; the reaction was very positive and patriotic, the direct opposite of the resentful response the Saints had been accused of.

The writer also includes the words of praise written by John Wilson, who had passed through Utah on his way to the West Coast to assume the office of Indian Agent in California:

> A more orderly, earnest, industrious, and civil people, I have never been among than these, and it is incredible how much they have done here in the wilderness in so short a time.[9]

The writer concludes by expressing his opposition to the US government's sending an "armed expedition to reduce them to subjection":

> It does not appear that the Mormons desire to separate from us, and if they do not, they should remain and be treated fairly, according to the Constitution and laws of the Union.[10]

1852: 28 February, *Cardiff and Merthyr Guardian*, p. 3 (445 words). "Mormonism. To the Editor of the Cardiff and Merthyr Guardian."

The Reverend John Griffith, vicar of Aberdare, addresses John S. Davis's method of defending The Church of Jesus Christ of Latter-day Saints through *Zion's Trumpet*:

> Sir—The Mormon Church of these parts [has] replied to my letter on Mormonism by reissuing at Merthyr an article from the *New York Tribune*. This little pamphlet their delegate brought me on Sunday last.

Griffith points out the glaring omission of any mention of his primary objection to Davis's religion:

> There is not one word in it touching the serious crime of polygamy with which the American judges charged them. Surely this silence is very significant. Either the *New York Tribune* must know it to be true and cannot refute it; or, knowing it to be true, it did not, like a faithful Mormon, care to rebut it.

Griffith then presents some of the details surrounding the wife and child of a Latter-day Saint who formerly lived in Aberdare and who had "abandoned his wife and child now for nearly two years, and, as far as we can learn, she has heard nothing yet of him, or received anything from him." He adds:

> If it had not been for the parish and the kindness of individuals, both his wife and child would have perished of starvation.

Griffith concludes:

> When, therefore, these things can be said of them, it requires a very different kind of testimony to that which they have brought forward from the *New York Tribune* to set aside the special report of solemn judges. Testimony, indeed, it is none, as there is no pretense in it anywhere to meet the charge of immorality. The entire article turns on the civil and not on the moral administration of the community.

End: One vicar attacks and another vicar agrees—John S. Davis responds

1852: 31 January, *Silurian*, p. 1 (705 words). "Mormon Immoralities in America."

A fairly long article taken from "the report of the Judge of the Utah Territory." The article is "full of disgusting details of the debauchery carried on by the leading members of the sect."

1852: January, *Cronicl y Cymdeithasau Crefyddol* (*Chronicle of the Religious Societies*), p. 27 (650 words). "The Mormons."

The writer of this article reports that those who call themselves "Latter-day *Saints*" are now divided into seven different sects. He expresses surprise and disappointment that people who called themselves "Saints" are not more unified and then gives the following advice:

> If there is anyone in any place who wishes to become one of the Mormons, first let him sit down pensively and honestly to examine their history, and to study their principles; and then if he is convinced that they are sincere "Saints," and that they have the miraculous gifts, and that they alone are the "*one* true church," let him then profess Mormonism in a dignified and unassuming spirit.

1852: January, *Y Cenhadwr Americanaidd* (*American Messenger*), pp. 20–21 (860 words). "The Mormons. Letter from One Who Was an Eye-witness of Their Superstitions."

One who calls himself "A Welshman from Missouri" writes a lengthy letter about his fourteen-day visit to Salt Lake City. He begins his letter with observations about the land, the houses, and the preaching in the large meetinghouse where he heard Brigham Young say that "he [Young] was in the pleasures of the world for thirty years" without knowing what happiness was "until he embraced Mormonism," and then "he was a happy man." The writer continues:

> Well, if women are what make a man happy, he is sure to be one of them. He has ninety of them, according to their own assertions; and I can assure you that the Mormons do not tell lies about their leader. Some of them have two or three wives, and their leaders have more than that. They are united in their creed that a man may have as many wives as he wants, if he is able to take care of them.

He has this to say about the reception he received from the Welsh in Salt Lake City:

> I saw there several Welshmen, who were very kind to me. Wonder! Wonder! Wonder! forever, that the fair Welsh, beautiful in their appearance, have become so foolish as to believe the doctrine of this second Mohammed! Some of them have followed the example of their leaders by taking more than one wife. Yes, and even worse, some of them have taken the wives of some others as wives for themselves! May the Lord have mercy on them; but those are nearly hopeless.

Finally, the writer has a warning for his fellow Welsh:

> Beware, Welshman! lest you be caught in the snare. There are many Welsh who were wealthy when they went there, but now they are very poor. And there are scores there, yes, perhaps hundreds who have repented for the bad bargain they have made, and who wish to have the chance to escape from them—and especially the women.

After his letter was printed in the *American Messenger* in New York, the "Welshman from Missouri" sent it to his brother in Wales.

Episode 9.2

Start: William Rowlands, another vicar, publishes a pamphlet—John S. Davis scoffs

1852: *Twyll Mormoniaeth; yn nghyd a hanes bywyd a marwolaeth Joseph Smith, o America, Prophwyd Santyddol y Dyddiau Diweddaf* (*Deceit of Mormonism;*

***Together with the History of the Life and Death of Joseph Smith, from America, the Hallowed Prophet of the Latter Days*), pamphlet, 16 pages.**

This entire pamphlet by William Rowlands consists of a series of questions and answers. Most of the questions are about Joseph Smith and the church he founded. The answers come from a variety of publications listed on the final page. Here are some examples:

> Q. What did Joe have in mind by putting verses from the Bible in his own book, to mix truth and untruth together?
>
> A. Only to make the fly similar to the color of the water, in order to hook men.
>
> Q. Are men so ignorant as to believe such foolishness as this?
>
> A. Yes, and to our great surprise, the Welsh believe it.

1852: 21 February, *Udgorn Seion* (*Zion's Trumpet*), pp. 53–55 (1,037 words). "Reviewing Books."

Instead of writing a long article to answer point by point the erroneous statements made by William Rowlands, John S. Davis wrote this article. Here are his opening sentences:

> Reviewing books against the Saints has become a very tedious task for us lately, because our detractors write things for which they have been provided answers before. They are unwilling to look into our principles or our history; rather they heap up old nonsense from books of the enemies who have written before them.[11]

He then specifically refers to the pamphlet recently published by Rowlands:

> There is a pamphlet before us now, entitled "Deceit of Mormonism, together with an Account of the Life and Death of Joseph Smith," by the Rev. William Rowlands, curate, Merthyr; which shows clearly that its author has made no effort to search out anything about the principles of the Saints, or the history of Joseph Smith, except only in the books of our detractors, which had been proved false before Mr. Rowlands ever saw them.[12]

Davis then encourages Rowlands and all others who wish to have accurate information about The Church of Jesus Christ of Latter-day Saints to read the various publications available at his office. He gives his general assessment of Rowlands's pamphlet:

> It is utterly shameful that Mr. Rowlands attaches his name to so much senseless rubbish that is in his pamphlet, not to mention the barefaced lies that speckle its pages.[13]

End: William Rowland, another vicar, publishes a pamphlet—John S. Davis scoffs

1852: 5 February, *North Wales Chronicle*, p. 2 (1,070 words). "The Mormonites in America."

A rather long article full of many of the common criticisms of the members of The Church of Jesus Christ of Latter-day Saints who lived in the United States.

1852: 14 February, *Silurian*, p. 4 (620 words). "Mormon priest Drowned at a Baptism in the Trent."

A detailed account of the drowning of William Barnes, age twenty-two, in the Trent River. Barnes was there to baptize a young girl and had preached a farewell discourse in the place of meeting at Beeston, since he planned to emigrate. Considerable detail is provided about his drowning.

1852: 26 February, *Y Gwron Cymreig* (*Welsh Hero*), p. 2 (835 words). "The Mormons in California."

This letter is the same one that appears in the *American Messenger*,[14] with only slight modifications.

1852: February, *Yr Haul* (*Sun*), pp. 71–72 (110 words). "Mormonism."

> The *New York National Police Gazette* has a lot of news about the Mormons of Salt Lake, in California. One of the correspondents of this newspaper gives a frightening account of their morals. "President Young has ninety wives; he has ridden in a carriage through the town lately accompanied by sixteen of them; and fourteen of them have children on their laps. It is said that Heber C. Kimball, a member of the Tribunal council, and the second person in the Trinity, has about the same number, among which are a mother and her two daughters. One man is free to keep as many wives as the other."

1852: February, *Yr Hyfforddwr sef Misiadyr Llenyddol* (*The Guide or the Literary Monthly*), p. 32 (95 words). "The Glory of Mormonism."

This article is taken from the *London Times* and has the same information about polygamy in Utah as appeared in the *Sun* during the same month, with very similar wording.[15]

Episode 9.3

Start: John S. Davis faces off against his former boss, J. Jones of Llangollen

1852: 20 March, *Udgorn Seion* (*Zion's Trumpet*), pp. 97–98 (660 words). "Lectures on Miracles."

John S. Davis introduces this battle of words and ideas about the topic of miracles, a topic he engaged in with "J. Jones, Llangollen," a Congregationalist minister who was the older brother of Dan Jones.

> Perhaps many of our readers are aware that the Rev. J. Jones, Llangollen, has been delivering a number of lectures on the above topic in several places, and latest in Merthyr Tydfil, where we had the pleasure of listening to him, on the 25th of February, and on the 3rd and the 17th of March.

Davis was well acquainted with J. Jones, since Davis had previously been in Jones's employ as a typesetter in the village of Rhydybont near the market town of Llanybydder, located about eighteen miles north of Carmarthen. In December 1845, Dan Jones had used his brother's press to print his Welsh translation of *Proclamation of the Twelve Apostles*.[16] During the three years that followed, the press at Rhydybont would print for Dan Jones more than a dozen other pamphlets, a hymnal, a history of the Latter-day Saints, and twenty-eight issues of *Prophet of the Jubilee.* John S. Davis, twenty-three years old at the time, was baptized on 19 April 1846, just four months after becoming acquainted with Dan Jones and the Church he represented.

About three years later, with Dan Jones's departure for America in February 1849, twenty-six-year-old Davis became the printer for The Church of Jesus Christ of Latter-day Saints in Wales. Using a press he had acquired, he printed the final two numbers of *Prophet of the Jubilee* (November and December 1848) and the first two numbers of *Zion's Trumpet* (January and February 1849) in his hometown of Carmarthen. By March 1849, Davis had relocated to Merthyr Tydfil, where he continued his printing activities for the next five years.

The Reverend J. Jones also moved with his family to Merthyr Tydfil, but he no longer had his own press or his own congregation. He did, however, give public lectures, three of which John S. Davis attended and during which Davis no doubt took copious notes. To Jones's 25 February 1849 lecture, William Phillips responded a week later on 2 March in Cymreigyddion Hall, the long room above the Railway Inn where the Latter-day Saints regularly met. To Jones's 3 March lecture, Davis—more than twenty years Jones's junior—responded on 9 and 11 March in the same venue "before large congregations."

In his March 1852 issue of *Zion's Trumpet,* Davis assesses the objective of Jones's lectures:

> Mr. Jones, in his lectures, attempted to gainsay the majority of the principles of the Saints, and as he delivered them, he received every approval the world could give him; for the world loves its own.[17]

Davis then lists over twenty assertions made by Jones, assertions which "have been disproved by the Saints." Davis then announces his plan of action:

> The definite verses under scrutiny will be the next thing for the Saints to focus on, if we dare to come out, for Mr. Jones threatens to treat us roughly if we come out again to oppose him. Mr. Jones boasts that he has conquered hosts before us, and that "it must be something in order to fell him." We see that he is Goliath, and that we are little David the shepherd boy, who depends on his God, and on his sling.

Davis later wrote, in the introduction to the first of his "Treatises on Miracles," the following:

> But since Mr. Jones continues to deliver these lectures up and down the country, we deemed it appropriate, through the encouragement of hosts of brethren, to review them in a series of treatises, which can visit every corner of Wales. At the same time, we shall review the pamphlet that is called "Spiritual Gifts," by the Rev. J. Davies, Llanelli, Brecknockshire, which, in many topics agrees with Mr. Jones.

1852: *Y Doniau Gwyrthiol fel eu Darlunir yn yr Ysgrythyrau Sanctaidd, gyda Sylwadau ar Bynciau Eraill Cysylltiedig a Gwyrthiau* (*The Spiritual Gifts as They*

***Are Portrayed in the Holy Scriptures, with Observations on Other Topics Related to Miracles*), pamphlet, 60 pages.**

The pamphlet has eight chapters, the last of which is entitled "The Growth and Deceit of the Latter-day Saints." The contents of this final chapter consist mainly of information taken from English-language sources about the history of Joseph Smith and the origins of the Book of Mormon. Davies ends the pamphlet with a caution for his fellow Welsh:

> Who in Wales will be so foolish and insult his intelligence and damage his temporal and eternal well-being by joining with and supporting this kind of deceit! The latest letters published from Salt Lake, as well as the reports of the United States delegates, prove the existence there of violence and oppression, sin and corruption of the most loathsome kind. No doubt if Salt Lake were closer to us and the delivery of letters were more convenient, we would have hundreds of letters revealing the repentance from those who spent their money for that which was not bread and gave their labor for that which does not satisfy.[18]

After Davis had reviewed Davies's pamphlet, Davis's involvement in translating and publishing the Book of Mormon in Welsh slightly delayed the appearance of his treatises on the topic of miracles. The last signature of *Llyfr Mormon* (The Book of Mormon) was sent out with the 17 April 1852 *Zion's Trumpet*, and the first treatise on miracles is dated 21 May 1852; the other five are dated 3 June, 15 June, 19 June, 2 July, and 15 July 1852. Each segment of Davis's translation of the Book of Mormon into Welsh was sent out with an issue of *Zion's Trumpet* for distribution and sale. The treatises were later bound into a seventy-two-page pamphlet.[19]

1852: August, *Y Diwygiwr* (*Revivalist*), pp. 246–47. "The Spiritual Gifts as They Are Portrayed in the Holy Scriptures."

A review of Davies's pamphlet (see previous entry). After commenting on the genesis of the pamphlet and making a few observations concerning its contents, the editor of the *Revivalist* gives his endorsement:

> We enthusiastically recommend this book as very necessary and suitable for the circumstances of the present times, when there are so many of the wavering children being confused by the baseless assertions of the hare-brained impostors. We are confident that the churches will strive to spread the book among the people in general; and if, after reading it, the fools decide to be offended, plundered, deceived, defiled, and destroyed, body, soul, and circumstances by the Mormons or anyone else, they will be free to say loudly as God said, "That which dies, let it die."[20]

1852: 5 August, *Seren Cymru* (*Star of Wales*), p. 123 (605 words). "The Miraculous Gifts."

This article is another review of the Davies pamphlet. The editor declares this sixty-page booklet to be "one of the best on the topic that has ever come to our attention." With specific reference to the final chapter, "Rise and Deceit of Mormonism," he writes:

> Although we have never considered the Mormon deceit worth spending our time to write against, we respectfully believe that the author of this little booklet is worthy of praise, since he has performed a service to religion; and if the booklet happens to fall into the hands of some Mormon, or into the hands of someone who is halting between two opinions, we do not doubt but what it will be of great benefit to him, if it is read thoughtfully.

1852: 2 September, *Seren Cymru* (*Star of Wales*), p. 139 (2,015 words). "The Growth and Deceit of Mormonism."

The editor of *Star of Wales* elected to quote this entire chapter, six pages in all, from Davies's pamphlet. The primary focus of this, the pamphlet's final chapter, is the Spaulding theory of the origin of the Book of Mormon and is taken entirely from English-language sources. The facsimile translation of these six pages is in Section 2.

End: John S. Davis faces off against his former boss, J. Jones of Llangollen

1852: March, *Y Bedyddiwr* (*Baptist*), pp. 95–97 (1,540 words). "Mormonism in Its Glory."

In July 1851, a group of federal territorial appointees arrived in Salt Lake City to assume their offices in the Utah territorial government. Almost immediately they incurred the wrath of Church leaders and members with their insulting remarks about Utah society and the practice of plural marriage. About three months later, the federal appointees abruptly left Utah to return to Washington. Their lengthy report to the United States government included numerous unflattering statements about what they had observed during their brief stay in Utah. This article in the *Baptist* contains an assortment of their statements. Their report is the original source of the oft-quoted statement about Brigham Young's excursion with sixteen of his wives, fourteen of whom had babies on their laps.

1852: March, *Yr Ymofynydd* (*Inquirer*), pp. 67–68 (905 words). "The Immorality of the Mormons in America."

This article is similar to the one that appears in the *Baptist* for March 1852 (see above). The stated source is the *News of the World* for 25 January 1852, which obtained its information from the report of the federal territorial appointees after their three months in Salt Lake City. The reporter concludes:

> So goes the story in the *News of the World*. I hope it will be read and considered by many a Welshman who is possibly on the verge of being lured by their deceit and fraud, and that he can be saved from falling into such a foul ditch—such shameless immorality—such filth beyond paganism! A mother and two daughters married to the same man—no, an animal, and not a man! Pagans, blush—humanity, hide your head in tears! Is the thing believable? Is it possible? Can all this take place under the name of religion! Mormons, Mormons, hold on, slow down, consider where you stand.[21]

1852: March, *Y Diwygiwr* (*Revivalist*), p. 100, item 1 (70 words). "An Honest Saint."

This article contains the account of Elder Erasmus Snow's admission about his plural marriage, a topic he addressed at a gathering in Utah before he left on a mission:

> "Brethren," said he, "I have two wives, and what is that to anyone else?" The comment was received with smiles among the ladies, and shouts of approval by the men.

1852: March, *Y Diwygiwr* (*Revivalist*), p. 100, item 2 (175 words). "Mormonism."

This article contains the same account about Brigham Young and his excursion with sixteen of his wives as reported in the March issue of the *Baptist*.[22] The writer concludes:

> It is a lamentable truth that even now there are hosts of men leaving Great Britain to join with the Mormons despite all the repugnant revelations made about them.

1852: March, *Yr Haul* (*Sun*), p. 104 (105 words). "The Fate of a Mormon."

As a man by the name of William Barnes entered the Trent River near Beeston to baptize two converts into The Church of Jesus Christ of Latter-day Saints, he was swept away by the river and drowned. The writer concludes:

> We had intended to make a brief observation here, but we shall refrain from doing so at present.

Episode 9.4

Start: Apostate Evan Howell accuses—Eyewitness Alfred J. Wood defends

1852: 10 March, *Yr Amserau* (*Times*), p. 3 (805 words). "The Saints Again."

A 7 December 1851 letter written from St. Louis by Evan Howell (sometimes referred to as "Evan Powell" in print), a passenger on the *Ellen Maria*, which had left Liverpool on 1 February 1851 with 378 passengers. Howell was accompanied by his wife, Mary, and their infant son. He recounts their experience to discourage others from leaving Wales with the Latter-day Saints:

> I wish for you to make every effort within your power to persuade my friends and all the people there to stay where they are, instead of being hoodwinked by the Mormons, which is nothing but complete humbug, which I have been able to experience to my grief and sorrow.

He claims that of the four hundred passengers on the *Ellen Maria*, "about 200 of them have died." He tells of having to bury his wife and son with no help from his coreligionists, and he states that the Saints failed to deliver on their promises and had no respect for keeping the Sabbath.

1852: 19 March, *Welshman*, p. 3 (555 words). "Mormonism."

A shorter version of the letter that was in the *Times* for 10 March 1852.

1852: 20 March, *Cardiff and Merthyr Guardian*, p. 4 (550 words). "Copy of a Letter from a Latter-day Saint in America."

This letter is the same version of the Evan Howell letter of 7 Dec 1851 that was printed in the *Welshman* for 19 March 1852.

1852: 3 April, *Silurian*, p. 4 (405 words). "The Mormons in America."

Quoting the *Swansea Herald*, this article is a shorter version of the Evan Howell letter.

1852: 9 April, *Monmouthshire Merlin*, p. 3 (405 words). "The Mormons."

Quoting the *Swansea Herald*, this article contains part of the Evan Howell letter.

1852: 9 April, *Cambrian* (345 words). "The American Mormons."

Also has quotes from the Evan Howell letter.

1852: 10 April, *Caernarvon and Denbigh Herald*, p. 7 (550 words).

The same version of the letter that was in the *Cardiff and Merthyr Guardian* for 20 March 1852.

1852: April, *Y Drysorfa* (*Treasury*), p. 140 (415 words). "The Latter-day Saints in their 'New Jerusalem.'"

This article contains quotes from the Evan Howell letter.

1852: April, *Yr Haul* (*Sun*), pp. 136–37 (755 words). "Mormonism."

This is the Evan Howell letter with but few variations from how it appeared in the *Times*. The submitter expressed alarm at the large numbers among the Welsh who had converted to the new religion of the Latter-day Saints:

> Twenty years ago, if anyone had said that the time was at hand for wanderers to come to the door, and preach an American prophet to the people, that he had seen visions of the Almighty, had received revelations from heaven, that he had received a golden book through the hands of angels, that the followers of this sect would perform miracles and wonders, would speak in foreign tongues, and that the people would go away in their hundreds to the ends of the earth, to establish a new state and church, etc., it would have been thought that the one who said this was completely mad. But it has happened, yes, in Wales. Hundreds, if not thousands, of the Welsh have accepted this deceit.[23]

1852: April, *Yr Hyfforddwr sef Misiadyr Llenyddol* (*The Guide or the Literary Monthly*), pp. 63–64 (890 words).

The editor explains why he had chosen to print the Evan Howell letter in his periodical:

> The following letter was published in *The Times* for March 10. Since the *Guide* can reach the hands of some who do not have the opportunity to see *The Times*, we, for the sake of such, are reprinting it, hoping that it will serve as a warning to those who may be inclined to be deceived through the cunning of the Mormons. If anyone doubts the authenticity of the letter, the original can be seen by visiting Mr. J. Lewis, Mineral Agent, Victoria Iron Works.

1852: 12 June, *Udgorn Seion* (*Zion's Trumpet*), pp. 189–93 (1,780 words). "False Accusers of the Saints."

John S. Davis, the editor of *Zion's Trumpet,* received a long letter in English from Alfred J. Wood, a passenger on the *Ellen Maria*—the same ship on which Evan Howell sailed from Liverpool to New Orleans. Alfred describes his feelings upon seeing Howell's letter in the *Cardiff and Merthyr Guardian*:

> I was truly disgusted with its contents, and I fearlessly assert that it is nothing but false and exaggerated accounts, which could not emanate from any but wicked, designing apostates, infuriated by their deep-rooted hatred to the Mormons.

He then offers clarifications rebutting the various accusations made by Howell concerning his difficulties. Davis then adds that his reason for printing Wood's letter in English in his periodical was "so the Saints may show it to the persons who read the English newspapers." He also sent the Wood letter to the *Welshman* and the *Cardiff and Merthyr Guardian.* The former does not appear to have printed the letter, but the latter printed a brief letter from William S. Phillips as well as the Wood letter in its entirety.[24]

1852: 12 June, *Cardiff and Merthyr Guardian*, p. 3 (145 words in the request from W. S. Phillips; 1,695 words in Wood's letter). "The Latter-day Saints."

The editor printed the entire letter of Alfred J. Wood, preceded by the request from W. S. Phillips. Here is the request in its entirety:

> Sir—Having read in one of the numbers of your paper a letter from Evan Howell (late of Victoria) and William Davies (late of Abercarn), who reside at present in St. Louis, North America, charging the Latter-day Saints with unkindness towards them there, I desire of you if you will be so kind as to let the enclosed appear in the next number of your paper. If you will please grant this favor, I know it will be satisfactory to many of the readers of the *Cardiff Guardian,* who I am particularly acquainted with, and who are particularly acquainted with Alfred Wood. I took the trouble to copy [it] from Wood's letter, which Mr. John Davis, printer, of this place, received last Sunday morning, with whom the original may be seen, if required. Yours respectfully, W. S. Phillips, 14, Castle Street, Merthyr Tydfil. June 8th, 1852.

1853: 4 March, *North Wales Chronicle*, p. 8 (390 words). "The Mormons in America."

A quote from the *Swansea Herald* about the St. Louis 7 December 1851 letter from Evan Howell (here called "Powell"). It is strange that the *North Wales Chronicle* would publish this well-known letter a full year after its first appearance in *Yr Amserau* (the *Times*).

End: Apostate Evan Howell accuses—Eyewitness Alfred J. Wood defends

1852: March, *Cyfaill o'r Hen Wlad yn America* (*Friend of the Old Country in America*), pp. 80–82 (1,320 words). "Joe Smith and the Mormons."

Efrawc Gadarn translated this article from English into Welsh to appear in *Friend of the Old Country in America*. The English version of the article is in the June 1851 issue of *Harper's New Monthly Magazine* and contains general information about Joseph Smith and the establishment of The Church of Jesus Christ of Latter-day Saints.[25]

1852: April, *Cyfaill o'r Hen Wlad yn America* (*Friend of the Old Country in America*), pp. 113–15 (1,520 words). "Joe Smith and the Mormons."

The second part of Efrawc Gadarn's Welsh translation.

1852: 22 April, *Y Gwron Cymreig* (*Welsh Hero*), p. 2 (710 words). "Mormonism."

"Glan Aerfen" is the writer of this sizable article. He expresses surprise and alarm that so many in Wales had allowed themselves to be "allured by the untutored breezes of the Mormon foolishness." He warns his compatriots to be vigilant and resist the deceit of the Latter-day Saints, whom he describes in the following manner:

> What is the life of "the Saints" (may the saints on high forgive me for calling them such) but a filthy abomination? What are the elders of the "Saints" but the excommunicated offscourings of religion, and if the life of the "Saints" is an abomination here, what are they like on the far side of the sea!! What is Mormonism? A cunning device of the followers of Mammon to persuade the naïve to part with their possessions. An accursed scheme devised by the lustful so that they may enjoy the desires of their lascivious passions; Mormonism is a blast of hot air that shrivels all virtue.

1852: 24 April, *Silurian*, p. 4, item 1 (185 words). "A Mormon Miracle."

Taken from the *Liverpool Courier*.

> A boilermaker, who was a Mormonite, met with an accident from the nut of a screw, which flew off while he was at work, and struck him on the eye with such force as to destroy the pupil.

The injured man asked the elders for the laying on of hands to restore his sight. When they learned that his employers had recommended that he consult Dr. Neill, the eminent oculist, one of the elders said that he should do so and that "whatever he does we will bless, and God will bless it too." The writer concludes:

> The man accordingly went to Dr. Neill, but whether the pupil of his eye was restored or not, he got his vision in another way, and saw enough of Mormonism to leave it.[26]

1852: 24 April, *Silurian*, p. 4, item 2 (210 words). "The Mormon Bible."

Account of a discussion held recently in Carlisle "between a Mormonite leader and a lecturer named Porter." The lecturer read some extracts from the Book of Mormon about the barges constructed to convey a group across the Atlantic Ocean.

1852: April, *Yr Eurgrawn Wesleyaidd* (*Wesleyan Treasury*), pp. 132–33 (480 words). "The Mormons. Abridgement of the letter of one who visited their holy place in California."

This letter, considerably abridged, is the same one that appears in the *American Messenger*.[27]

1852: April, *Y Dysgedydd* (*Instructor*), p. 119 (170 words). "Impromptu Verses to the Mormons."

A poem of eight 4-line stanzas. Here is the second stanza:

> Behold ungifted black magicians—all
> Wanting to trick each soul,
> And some dark hideous swarm—lowly minstrels,
> The old Mormons, we wish they were dead.

1852: 1 May, *Caernarvon and Denbigh Herald*, p. 3 (90 words).

> Another terrible steamboat explosion, by which it is supposed 100 lives have been sacrificed, took place on April 9, at Lexington. The *New York Herald* says: "The steamer *Saluda*, bound for Council Bluffs, exploded her boilers at Lexington, on Monday, April 9. She had on board, besides other passengers, a large number of Mormon emigrants. All the officers of the boat were killed, except the first clerk and mate. About 100 lives are supposed to have been lost. The boat is a total wreck. Her boilers have been in use several years.

1852: 1 May, *Cardiff and Merthyr Guardian*, p. 2 (30 words).

> Another awful steamboat explosion took place on the 9th instant, at Lexington, Missouri. The Saluda burst her boilers, killing 100 passengers—Mormons, on their way to the Salt Lake.

1852: 14 May, *Cambrian* (50 words).

A brief announcement that Reverend William Griffiths and Reverend C. Short will be preaching their lectures on Mormonism.

1852: 21 May, *Cambrian* (90 words). "Mormonism."

A brief report of the lecture delivered by Reverend C. Short at the Mount Pleasant chapel.

1852: May, *Seren Gomer* (*Star of Gomer*), p. 238 (730 words). "The Mormons."

This article is a set of quotes from the report written by the group of federal territorial appointees who had spent about three months in Salt Lake City from July to September 1851. The editor of *Star of Gomer* elected to include the paragraphs about the dictatorial reign of Brigham Young, the murder of James Munroe, and the information about polygamy. The final paragraph consists of the editor's own conclusion:

> Here is a survey of Mormonism now in Utah, in its own territory, where it is allowed to work out its polluted and blasphemous principles unchecked; and if they do not bear the same horrible fruit in this country, that must be attributed to the hindrance put in their way by the laws of the kingdom, rather than to the natural tendency of the principles of that system of atheism,

> which is believed and professed by the people who presume to call themselves "Latter-day Saints," "in the Church of Jesus Christ," and at the same time be guilty of the most fearsome blasphemies, the bloodiest murders, and live in the most horrible adultery and incest! Perhaps some of the brotherhood in Wales will try to deny this; but it is not fitting for them to do so; because the facts are realized by respectable and credible officials, who testify to what they heard and saw. It is mournful to think that scores of our fellow nationals have been deceived and bewitched to go to the Sodom-like Utah which is portrayed above; and perhaps some of them are wallowing in the wicked filth described. We shall give more yet of their story before long.

1852: May, *Y Diwygiwr* (*Revivalist*), p. 164 (185 words).

The brief account of a boilermaker whose eye was seriously injured in an accident.[28] Rather than consult with Dr. Neill in Liverpool, as his work masters advised him to do, the boilermaker opted to request a blessing from the elders of his church. Seeing the impossibility of the boilermaker ever regaining the use of his eye, and knowing that he had been counseled by his work masters to consult with Dr. Neill, the elders said, "Very well, go to Dr. Neill, and whatever he chooses to do, he has our blessing, and God will bless him as well." The writer concludes:

> He went to Dr. Neill; but whether he received his natural eye or not, his eye was opened in another way, so that he was able to see enough of Mormonism to the point of leaving it.

1852: 8 May, *Udgorn Seion* (*Zion's Trumpet*), p. 147 (150 words). "Defense of the Mormons."

Davis was obviously very pleased to include in his periodical this highly positive report from the *Liverpool Journal* about the Latter-day Saints:

> A correspondent in Philadelphia of the *Manchester Examiner* says: "I have noticed the utterly untrue and vain accounts of the tumult of the Mormons in Salt Lake, and their unwillingness toward the federal government, etc. Many of these that are mentioned are erroneous and exaggerated, and inappropriately tend to cast undeserved insult on that deceived and misguided, but diligent, frugal and successful society; for it has clearly been shown through more recent information, and through being able to hear the two sides of the controversy, that the judges and the other officers who were sent out by the government in Washington, have behaved in an arrogant and improper manner, and are more to blame than are the Mormons. It is beyond argument that the Mormons have been highly successful, and on the whole contented and happy, in their new settlement, and their numbers are rapidly increasing."

1852: 5 June, *Silurian*, p. 1 (145 words). "Mormon 'Fashions.'"

A quote from the *Deseret News* of 10 January 1852 about "one of the ladies of Utah" who "appeared in the public assembly last Sabbath, clad in a buckskin sack beautifully ornamented with the same material." The article also mentions Captain David Evans, who "has made his appearance in the Representatives' Hall clad in his own family manufactured habiliments, worthy the imitation of a nabob."

1852: 12 June, *Cardiff and Merthyr Guardian*, p. 1 (210 words). "The Mormon Bible."

The same article as had been printed in the *Silurian* for 24 April 1852.

1852: 30 June, *Yr Amserau* (*Times*), p. 1 (125 words). "Cerrigydrudion."

A brief and rather puzzling account of a Latter-day Saint missionary's recent visit to the town of Cerrigydrudion in North Wales:

> On the 21st of this month, this area was visited by one of the "Saints." He testified as he began to address his listeners, that it was not their custom to take a topic except it be given them directly from heaven; but in order for the listeners to have the proper idea of the sermon this time, he would take one. And so the natural deduction is, that he himself would be allowed to wend his way through the service without receiving anything from above. But he did not utter a word of observation on the "text" except just to say it; he promised to visit us once again, and perhaps we will have more to report the next time.

1852: 17 June, *Y Gwron Cymreig* (*Welsh Hero*), p. 4, item 1 (315 words). "Witching and Mormoning."

The writer, "Llywarch," equates witchcraft with the persuasive power of the Latter-day Saint proselytizing. He explains the success this new religion was having among the Welsh:

> I am not the least surprised that the Mormons are receiving a welcome in Wales, for the country has not been cleansed from witching yet. And since witching and Mormoning are two things so similar to each other, and are offered by unlearned, but crafty men, to simple people who are so easily charmed and ensnared, is it any wonder that the occasional disciple is won to the Mormon cause here and there throughout the Principality?

1852: 17 June, *Y Gwron Cymreig* (*Welsh Hero*), p. 4, item 2 (435 words). "Mormonism or Saintism."

This is the second article in this issue of the *Welsh Hero*. The writer states his previous approach to dealing with this new set of beliefs:

> Mormonism is such an unnatural manifestation of human folly, such a concoction of madness and nothing but madness, that one feels that it is rather an insult to reason to debate the subject. We have felt this for a long time, and as a result have refrained from commenting on the absurd hodgepodge, lest we should lend it a significance it does not deserve.

He then presents his current stance:

> To save those who have sunk entirely into this polluted mire is out of the question; it could be that to try to restrain those who are on the verge of falling in is equally hopeless; but possibly there is yet one, here and there, the odd one—one in whom there is some grain of common sense, who is in danger—and it is possible to save him.

The writer then recommends to his readers that they read a pamphlet entitled *Joseph Smith, the Great American Impostor*, which was recently published by a Congregationalist minister named Thomas Tyson.

1852: June, *Yr Eurgrawn Wesleyaidd* (*Wesleyan Treasury*), p. 207 (160 words). "The Mormons."

A poem that consists of three eight-line stanzas. The poet opens the poem with the question, "Who are the wandering strangers of devilish, poisonous tongue?" and then provides a variety of answers throughout the remainder of the poem. Here is the final stanza:

> A fine religion to the taste of mortals,
> It gives the comforts of the here and now;
> Their hope is in the things of this world,
> Their faith in the California gold!
> They perform wondrous false miracles,
> They make the blind more blind,
> They teach hard workers to be idle,
> And send their children on the parish.

1852: June, *Yr Hyfforddwr sef Misiadyr Llenyddol* (*The Guide or the Literary Monthly*), p. 104 (60 words). "A Mormon Denies His Religion."

> One of the Saints (?) from Machynlleth, while in Llanfair lately, was asked whether he was a Saint. He denied it and said that he was one of the Dear Baptists! "I am not ashamed of the gospel of Christ," but "I am ashamed of the gospel of Joe," says the behavior of this Mormon.

Episode 9.5

Start: Two different writers assess the Welsh translation of the Book of Mormon

1852: 8 July, *Seren Cymru* (*Star of Wales*), p. 4 (175 words).

A brief review of the Welsh translation of the Book of Mormon, or *Llyfr Mormon*. The converts to The Church of Jesus Christ of Latter-day Saints in Wales were elated to finally have, in their own language, this book of what they believed to be scripture. John Davis, the editor of *Zion's Trumpet*, was the translator and publisher of *Llyfr Mormon*, and beginning on 20 September 1851, he sent out signatures—sixteen-page segments—of his translation with biweekly issues of the periodical. The more than 1,500 subscribers to the periodical and the translation project would collect the signatures and eventually have them bound. The final signature was sent to the subscribers on 17 April 1852, just thirty-one weeks following the distribution of the first one. Samuel Evans, the editor of *Star of Gomer*, a Baptist periodical for which Davis had formerly worked, said that it was a "pity such valuable labor in producing so perfect a translation had been bestowed upon so worthless a work as the Book of Mormon."[29] Evans published the following review:

> We cannot be expected to give any approval whatsoever to this work, or praise the superstition of the Welsh people for supporting its publication in Welsh; and there is no composition set up as equal to the Word of God which deserves any more than the most definitive condemnation. Whatever of that, there is no danger that anyone who reads it attentively will be deceived by it,

> so as to become one of the Latter-day Saints; for it appears to us to be nothing but a pack of foolish lies, composed deceitfully to imitate, to some extent, the scriptural account, and the names of persons have been changed, and many fables have been added. Whatever of that, the work has been printed well, with clear letters and excellent paper, as is all the work of Mr. Davis. The translation also is fluid and intelligible.

1852: 4 September, *Udgorn Seion* (*Zion's Trumpet*), pp. 285–86 (620 words). "Review of the Book of Mormon."

Upon completing his translation of the Book of Mormon into Welsh, John S. Davis sent a copy to Samuel Evans, the editor of *Star of Wales*. Evans's review appeared in the 8 July 1852 issue (see previous entry). In addition to printing the complete review in *Zion's Trumpet*, Davis made a few observations of his own:

> Now, that is the opinion of the above Editor about the Book of Mormon; and we feel grateful to him for speaking his mind; for he could not say anything that would give any more approval to the Book of Mormon, than what he said.[30]

Davis adds:

> Little do the sectarian editors and preachers know that their reviews and their sermons against the Book of Mormon speak more in its favor than their hearts ever imagined.[31]

End: Two different writers assess the Welsh translation of the Book of Mormon

1852: 15 July, *Y Gwron Cymreig* (*Welsh Hero*), p. 2, item 1 (105 words). "Mormonism."

A brief note from a subscriber to the publisher.

> Reverend Sir—I take this present opportunity to write a few lines to say that I do not wish you to send me the *Hero*. It is totally superfluous to my requirements at present, and for that reason I do not wish you to send me anything more, as mercifully, I have broken all connection between us at present, as I have been released from the law of sin. I now conclude. Briefly yours, William James, Twyncarno.

1852: 15 July, *Y Gwron Cymreig* (*Welsh Hero*), p. 2, item 2 (660 words). "Mormonism."

A letter to the editor from "J. B. D.," who wishes to report a prophecy about the destruction of Cwmbach, Aberdare. This prediction was made by a self-proclaimed prophet "sent by God, obliged to come and warn the inhabitants of the place, which is to happen 120 years hence." The writer reports a variety of this preacher's statements about Joseph Smith, Brigham Young, and the restored gospel of Jesus Christ. He concludes:

> Gentle reader, I now write this down so that you will be prepared by the time you hear the prophet, if you have not already heard him. Guard against meddling in foolishness, lest you should be so foolish as to believe false prophets.

Episode 9.6

Start: Four hundred Latter-day Saints are miraculously unharmed by a ceiling collapse in Newport

1852: 17 July, *Cardiff and Merthyr Guardian*, p. 3 (620 words). "Alarming Occurrence at Newport."

The writer presents a lengthy and detailed account of a roof collapse in Newport where the Latter-day Saints were meeting:

> Scarcely had tea been commenced, when, without a moment's warning, exactly one half of the lofty and heavy ceiling of the building fell with a sudden crash. For a moment all was blinding and suffocating dust and confusion, then succeeded the most appalling shrieks and the most terrifying clamor; and, amidst the din and horrible confusion that ensured, people rushed from all the surrounding houses, apprehending that some great calamity had occurred. Fearful screams were again heard bursting forth, presently the windows of the hall were dashed out, and the affrighted creatures within flung themselves through the broken sashes to the ground below; some were observed clinging with extreme tenacity to the window frames and sills apprehending death within, and fearful of mutilated limbs if they fell. The doors were burst open from without as well as the piles of people heaped upon one another inside permitted, and ingress being at length obtained, the sight that presented itself was enough to appall the stoutest heart—beams and rafters, whole patches of ceiling, amidst clouds of dust, lying upon scores of people; while the tea tables, affording protection to many, were crowded below with numbers crying aloud for mercy, for protection, and for a miracle to save them.

The writer then explains how the miracle came about:

> Immediate exertions were made, and in the course of an hour the wretched creatures were all extricated from the ruins, and on a minute search being instituted, not one was found missing; and, what is still more remarkable, although the beams and rafters were heavy, and some, with huge pieces of entire ceiling, fell directly upon the tables, and others in a direction that appeared to insure [ensure] inevitable death, not one single Mormon was injured, though it was estimated that two or three unbelievers, who had gone thither to revile and sneer at the true followers of Joe Smith, received injuries, which may serve their consciences as remembrances.

1852: 17 July, *Silurian*, p. 4 (600 words). "Extraordinary and Miraculous Escape of Four Hundred Latter-day Saints."

This article is another lengthy and detailed account of the roof collapse in Newport where the Latter-day Saints were meeting. The author, however, is not the same one who wrote the account printed in the *Cardiff and Merthyr Guardian*.

1852: 21 July, *Yr Amserau* (*Times*), p. 2 (280 words). "Accidents."

A much shorter account of the roof collapse in Newport. This one adds the detail that, miraculously, the only persons injured were "two or three men who went there to mock the acts of the Joe Smithites."

1852: 24 July, *Udgorn Seion* (*Zion's Trumpet*), p. 243 (44 words). "Happening."

Here is the complete article:

> In the banquet after the latest Conference in Newport, when the hall was overflowing with Saints, the ceiling fell on them, from above the platform; but we are happy to report that no one received any injury, which caused surprise through the whole town.

The articles printed by the *Cardiff and Merthyr Guardian*, the *Silurian*, and the *Times* all have much greater detail in their reports.

1852: August, *Y Bedyddiwr* (*Baptist*), p. 258 (295 words). "Mormons."

A shorter account of the roof collapse in Newport.

1852: August, *Seren Gomer* (*Star of Gomer*), p. 382 (275 words). "A Frightful Happening."

Another shorter account of the roof collapse in Newport.

End: Four hundred Latter-day Saints are miraculously unharmed by a ceiling collapse in Newport

1852: 29 July, *Y Gwron Cymreig* (*Welsh Hero*), p. 2 (910 words). "The Mormons."

The writer, using the nom de plume "Sion Callestr," condemns the "arrogance of the Mormons" and objects to "the great infallibility which they claim." He poses this question:

> Which is easier to believe, a man who has made learning and theology the chief study of his life, who has lived a life worthy of the Gospel, being of good repute, who preaches the truth, who has stayed in the same place, amongst the same people for twenty to forty years, more or less, or else to listen to ignorant strays who are unable to write two grammatically correct sentences in any language under heaven; and who blurt out the first thing that comes into their heads at street corners and at the roadside? They must be very foolish, or think that people are very foolish, when they expect their philosophy to be accepted by anyone in his right mind.

He concludes his article by expressing optimism:

> We in Wales have never heard of such a crowd of ignoramuses, with nothing but arrogance to commend them, trying to promote their beliefs, until the followers of Joe Smith climbed up to the stump. One has confidence that the country generally possesses more common sense than to be drawn into their trap.

1852: 6 August, *Monmouthshire Merlin*, p. 6 (39 words).

A letter from Hamburg states that the Mormons have established a weekly newspaper at Hamburg, and have prepared a translation of their Bible. They have

> missionaries actively employed, and seem to have money. In Norway their doctrines are spreading.

1852: 6 August, *North Wales Chronicle*, p. 7 (33 words).

This article is the same one that appears in the *Monmouthshire Merlin* for 6 August 1852, minus the final sentence.

Episode 9.7

Start: An Independent minister defends the Latter-day Saints and is attacked by a colleague

1852: *Yr Amserau Presenol* (*Present Times*), booklet, 55 pages.

This booklet by Rev. Joshua Lewis, an Independent minister, was the result of two presentations given by the author in late 1851. Some from among his audience suggested that he put the presentations into print. On pages 23 and 24, Lewis makes a few observations about The Church of Jesus Christ of Latter-day Saints:

> *Mormonism* is a manifestation of something more than the ignorance, foolishness, and superstition of those who support it. It is a clear and public manifestation of the spiritual poverty and deficiencies of the churches. Its existence and its success constitute an important and instructive fact in the civilized world; it behooves us to consider it in a wise, fair, and deliberate spirit.

Unlike other critics of the Latter-day Saints in Wales, Lewis does not issue a blanket condemnation of the converts to this new religion:

> Not *all* of the Latter-day Saints are the most ignorant and thoughtless dregs of the world and refuse of society.

He then points out:

> Men and women of respectable position in the world, and equal to their neighbors in knowledge and wisdom, are among them.

1852: August, *Y Diwygiwr* (*Revivalist*), pp. 243–46 (910 words). "The Present Times."

This article is a lengthy response to Reverend Joshua Lewis from his colleague of the cloth, Reverend Rhys Jones, who uses the nom de plume "Gwesyn" (meaning "a youth"). Gwesyn puts forth a very supercilious observation of Lewis's writing in general:

> It appears to me that it would be good for you, when you write, to have someone at your side now and then, to bring to mind that there is a world and being outside your personal existence, and that there are abundant areas besides the area of Henllan, in which there are men who think as well as you do.[32]

And Gwesyn is just as supercilious in his comments about Lewis's observations on "Mormonism":

> It is better for you to have a second look at Mormonism before reporting anything further about it. I conclude one of two things—either you have not had the opportunity to become acquainted with *real* Mormonism, and consequently

> you have formed an *ideal* of it in your own mind, which is completely contrary to the *real*, as contradictory as are substance and spirit, or else you have been blinded by the fair look which it wears on the outside, without paying any attention to its component parts.[33]

1852: September, *Y Diwygiwr* (*Revivalist*), pp. 272–75 (860 words). "The Present Times."

This article is Lewis's lengthy response to Gwesyn, in which Lewis also assumes a very condescending attitude in addressing his critic. Regarding "Mormonism," Lewis writes:

> I look on it as an important *Phenomenon* in the moral world, and as a fact overflowing with important teachings and resolute warnings. It is cause for lament that it has not been viewed in a more *philosophical* spirit.[34]

Lewis then proceeds in this "philosophical spirit" to answer the question of why any sensible person would convert to this new religion. He postulates:

> Here is a serious man, but unlearned, a holder of strong convictions; his fears about his spiritual status are awakened and causing daily torment to his soul. There is in him a thirst for the happiness and the peace which are promised to the faithful, but which he has never before experienced.[35]

Lewis then describes the impact on such an individual when he is introduced to a new way of thinking:

> In this condition, he meets a *Mormon*. He tells him that if he is but *immersed* by him, that he will be freed from his fears—that he is a child of God—that he will receive daily proofs that his prayers are heard and that he will have continual association with God—and that he will be filled with spiritual comfort. Such things cannot help but have influences on him. Those are the things he needs.[36]

Lewis points out that the promises of "comfort, of peace and rest" are "deceitful promises." And then he suggests a possible approach to the issue:

> If we wish to understand the *genius* of Mormonism, we ought to look at it as it relates to the best class of those who profess it, as well as the worst class. That is only fair. The spirit of the age toward this heresy is not only *irreligious*, but also *unphilosophical*.[37]

1852: November, *Y Diwygiwr* (*Revivalist*), pp. 339–44 (3,300 words). "'The Present Times' Again."

Gwesyn's continued response to Joshua Lewis's analysis of "Mormonism." The first part of Gwesyn's article is entitled "Philosophy" and contains no mention of "Mormonism." The second part, however, is an entirely different matter. Gwesyn exhibits bewilderment at the outset:

> I fail to account for the tenderness Mr. Lewis feels toward the Mormon deceivers. He complains because of the behavior of the age toward them, while he himself sets them out, without exception, as unprincipled deceivers. Some of his statements pertaining to them appear to me as *new*, *strange*, and *erroneous*, and *some of his arguments as defective*. . . . And if we have deciphered

> the proper meaning of the words, I think that Mormonism will never receive better praise from the mouth of its best friends than is given to it here. . . . We expect before long to see the *Millennial Star* quoting the *Revivalist* to encourage the Mormons to go forward in their deceit.[38]

Gwesyn states clearly that he views all who accept the teachings of Joseph Smith as "fools or knaves or both." In support of the position that such teachings are "a heap of blasphemies and foolishness," Gwesyn presents part of a letter written by Captain Dan Jones nearly four years earlier regarding a conference held in Merthyr Tydfil. In the letter, Jones recounts how the adversary disrupted the meeting:

> He sent a legion of evil spirits into the hall at that time, as though he was determined with one grand rally to storm our little fortress and demolish our citadel with impunity. In five minutes after their arrival, which was seen by some, three females were possessed and many more nearly as bad; however, I perceived the enemy's design, and having command of the post, I lost no time in returning him a heavy broadside with the artilleries of heaven by commanding every evil spirit in the place to depart in the name of Jesus Christ, which was responded to by all the audience with such powerful Amens! that the neighbors thought it thundered, that all the devils, except three, had run away in a fright; and the echoes opened the windows of heaven, so that the power of God was felt and seen by all others in the place, and some of our worst persecutors, having come there with evil intent, confessed that God was with us, and shouted Amen as loud as any.[39]

Dan Jones then tells of the interaction he had with the evil spirits:

> They swore that they would not depart without "Old Brigham Young, from America, and that if he would come, that they would have to obey him; but that they held an office higher than any others." I questioned one of them on whether he had ever possessed any other person in Wales. "Yes, very many!" was the reply. I asked, "Did you ever leave one unless compelled?" He replied, "No, nor will I go from here either." Then I rebuked him for telling a falsehood, inasmuch as that Brigham Young had never visited Wales, and that he had better business than to come and wait on such beings as him, at which he sneered and laughed; that echoed through the hall and alarmed many; at the same time the streets were crowded with strangers and policemen, drawn there by the noise, and shortly the whole town was in an uproar, like Ephesus of old."[40]

Following the letter, Gwesyn declares:

> Without making any further comments, I will leave to Mr. Lewis the task of persuading the readers of the *Revivalist* to believe that a religious system whose chief leaders write such lying rubbish is unfairly dealt with by the age through leaving it unobserved.[41]

End: An Independent minister defends the Latter-day Saints and is attacked by a colleague

1852: 14 August, *Caernarvon and Denbigh Herald*, p. 6 (40 words). "The Mormons on the North of Europe."

> A letter from Hamburg states that the Mormons have established a weekly newspaper at Hamburg, and have prepared a translation of their bible. They have missionaries actively employed, and seem to have money. In Norway also their doctrines are spreading.

1852: August, *Yr Hyfforddwr sef Misiadyr Llenyddol* (*The Guide or the Literary Monthly*), pp. 143–44 (345 words). "Mormon Deceit."

The review of a lecture given recently by a "Mr. Jones." Someone who attended the event sent to the editor of *The Guide or the Literary Monthly* an outline of the "excellent lecture" which consisted of three main points:

1. That man is able to determine the truth of things.
2. That the revealed will of the Son of God is easy to determine as truth.
3. That it is impossible, while being consistent with reason and revelation, to determine the truth of Mormonism.

At the end of his lecture, Mr. Jones offered to allow anyone to oppose his lecture "by reason and scripture," at which "one little Saint arose and said that he would review the lecture of Mr. Jones the following Thursday night." The editor concludes:

> But despite going to the Town Hall to hear him, I heard nothing more than a greater confirmation of the Lecture, and a greater display of the wretchedness of Mormonism than I had ever seen.[42]

1852: August, *Y Cenhadwr Americanaidd* (*American Messenger*), p. 253 (605 words). "The Fall of the Anti-Christ."

A poem of fourteen eight-line stanzas composed by William Watkins of Llewellyn, Pennsylvania. The poem is a prophecy of the eventual triumph of truth over evil. Watkins declares that the two main forces of evil then opposing truth on the earth were "Mormonism" and "Papism." Here are the two stanzas that focus on the "Mormons":

It is said that the Mormons
    Are wicked and wild people
And that they can work miracles
    As in the days of old,
Namely to cause the blind to see,
    And the lame to walk freely,
And the mute to speak
    If he has the faith.
The wicked Mormon says
    That it is appropriate for man
To have a great number of wives
    All to himself;
But reason and the scripture
    Clearly forbid it,
For Adam had only
    Eve in the garden.

The poem has equal disdain for the Catholics and predicts that both they and the "Mormons" will be put down at the Second Coming.

1852: August, *Y Diwygiwr* (*Revivalist*), p. 253 (320 words).

About "J. Jones, Llangollen," the older brother of Dan Jones, the leader of the Latter-day Saints in Wales. As a Congregationalist minister, J. Jones was as controversial in Wales as his younger brother was. This article deals with someone's request "to reconsider the appropriateness of allowing Mr. Jones, Llangollen, to preach" Christ. The writer of the response in the *Revivalist* declined to take sides in the issue.

1852: 11 September, *Silurian*, p. 3 (85 words). "The Mormons."

> The Latter-day Saints are prosecuting the propagation of their peculiar notions with characteristic industry; and, it would seem, with no want of success. Among us in Wales they have obtained not a few converts. We observe that they are now laboring energetically in spreading their doctrines in Norway and Sweden; that they have prepared an edition, in German, of the Book of Mormon; and that they have established a weekly newspaper in Hamburg, for the better advocacy of Latter-day Saintism among the dreamy Germans.

1852: September, *Yr Eurgrawn Wesleyaidd* (*Wesleyan Treasury*), pp. 316–17 (290 words). "These Three Are One."

The "Three" are the Pagan, the Catholic, and the Latter-day Saint. The writer compares the three regarding their modes of receiving communication from God, their methods of preaching, and their beliefs about the hereafter. Here is what the writer says about the three differing beliefs regarding the hereafter:

> The Pagans say that the souls of those who are dead go to other bodies; the Catholics say that they go to purgatory; and the Saints say that the departed godly people, who were erroneous in their judgments, are in some place of punishment until the morning of the resurrection.

1852: September, *Yr Eurgrawn Wesleyaidd* (*Wesleyan Treasury*), p. 327 (65 words). "Who Are Right?"

The Welsh translation for "Who Are Right?" is "Pwy sydd yn eu lle?" But this Welsh version has two possible translations: "Who Are Right?" or "Who Are in Their Place?" Here is the answer to both translations according to the periodical:

> This is a common question in our country with regard to the religious Denominations; and it was answered the other day by one of them as follows: "The 'Saints' were certain of being in their place [or "being right"] the Sunday before last, for they were preaching at the top of the place called 'Trunk of Lies.'"

1852: September, *Y Greal* (*Grail*), pp. 197–98 (315 words). "The Laying On of Hands."

This is the first part of a two-part article by "Mathetes," the nom de plume of John Jones. Mathetes explains that his article is a response to an article also entitled "The Laying On of Hands," authored by John Evans of Abercanaid and published in the

April 1852 issue of *The Baptist*.[43] Here is part of a small section in which Mathetes mentions the practice of the laying on of hands by the "Mormons":

> If the laying on of hands is anything, it is an ordinance; if it is viewed as an ordinance, it would be desirable to know by whom it was established. The practice of the apostles is the rule of the Mormons, according to their witness; and thus, according to this reasoning, this doctrine is thorough Mormonism; and the procedure of these impostors is to lay on hands, anoint with oil, work miracles, etc. May Mr. Evans cease to blaspheme "*brothers of a trade*." The proper Mormon view in the opinion of the writer is to see six or seven "reverends" placing a hand (not hands) on that which they call the "head of the preacher," in order to ordain him to baptize and break bread.[44]

Although the various Baptist ministers in nineteenth-century Wales were consistent in baptizing by immersion, they were at odds with each other concerning the practice of the laying on of hands. The ordained Baptist minister David Bevan Jones, whose nom de plume was "Dewi Elfed Jones," of the Gwawr Chapel in Aberaman, was censured by his colleague, Thomas Price, for practicing the laying on of hands. Jones eventually converted to The Church of Jesus Christ of Latter-day Saints. After President William Phillips baptized Jones by immersion in the Cynon River, Phillips confirmed Jones a member of the Church of Jesus Christ by the laying on of hands in Jones's own Baptist chapel. See Episode 8.2 for more details.

1852: 2 October, *Caernarvon and Denbigh Herald*, p. 7 (50 words). "Latter-day Saints: New Way of Getting a Congregation."

> On Sunday morning last, several persons stopped in coming out of the different chapels to read the anti-militia papers which had been posted on the walls of the Meat-market. One of the saints mounted a chair and delivered a Mormon lecture to the loungers.

1852: 30 October, *Silurian*, p. 4 (1,205 words). "The Settlement of the Mormons on the Great Salt Lake."

A lengthy quotation from *An Expedition to the Valley of the Great Salt Lake* by Howard Stansbury, published in 1852.

1852: October, *Y Bedyddiwr* (*Baptist*), pp. 320–21 (620 words).

This is a strange report about a man named Richard Duckett, who was taken before a magistrate in London. Duckett's wife had sworn out a complaint against him for threatening her life. When the magistrate asked Duckett to explain the difficulty between him and his wife, he answered: "My wife said to me a few days ago, 'If you do not receive your baptism in the church of the Latter-day Saints, your soul will be lost, and you will be damned.' I said to her, 'If you continue to annoy me about your damned religion, I will cut your throat.'" The next morning Duckett was accosted by some men who took him by force and tied him to a straw bed in a large building. There, a doctor interviewed Duckett twice, said that Duckett was not insane, and ordered his release. When Duckett appeared with his wife before the magistrate, he explained that although he had attended meetings of the Latter-day

Saints over a short period of time, he had stopped going when "he found out what kind of people he had to deal with." Then his wife "had him arrested as a lunatic." The magistrate told him:

> You are no more crazy than I am, although the circumstances you have been through have been sufficient to make you so; and the persons who caused you to be imprisoned are accountable for the consequences. I hereby nullify the warrant and release you.

1852: October, *Yr Eurgrawn Wesleyaidd* (*Wesleyan Treasury*), p. 351 (625 words). "The Perfection of Mormonism."

Using the nom de plume "Delta," the writer explains to the editor that the letter he is submitting was written by John Evans, a Latter-day Saint, to Evans's uncle. In the letter Evans declares that his work is "to preach the Eternal Gospel which has the power of everlasting life" and wishes for his uncle and his family to accept baptism. The letter is filled with erroneous grammar and spelling and lacks punctuation. Following the letter, Delta adds:

> I took care to write the above as it is in the original letter—every letter as it was written—in the hope that they may appear in the same way.

The correspondent's obvious aim is to demonstrate the ignorance and low level of sophistication of the Latter-day Saints. The unintended consequence, however, is that the very sincere desire of John Evans to benefit his relatives and share his happiness with them is also on display.

Episode 9.8

Start: Thomas Hughes's first pamphlet receives eight rave reviews

1852: *Darlithiau ar Dwyll Mormoniaeth: Darlith I* (*Lectures on the Deceit of Mormonism: Lecture 1*), pamphlet, 16 pages.

This pamphlet is the printing of the first lecture given by Thomas Hughes (using the nom de plume "T. ab Gwilym") at the Rhuthin town hall on 3 September 1852. His intent was to present a total of six lectures on the following topics:

1. Exposing the deceit of the beginning of Mormonism
2. The opinion of the Saints about God, angels, and the souls of man
3. The Spiritual Gifts—the belief and claims of the Saints about them
4. The belief of the Saints about preaching to the spirits in prison and baptism for the dead
5. The Bible is the only standard of faith and conduct of man, and there is no basis to expect new revelation.
6. The primary objective of the prophet Joseph Smith and his apostles through this deceit was to establish an earthly kingdom in America for their own benefit and worldly glory.

Hughes declared at the outset:

> After delivering the stated lectures, I am confident that I will have painted a very accurate picture of the monstrousness of Mormonism; and it is not impossible that a clear look at the corrupt system may perhaps give fright to a few saints to come to the point of shouting, "Who will deliver me from this society of suffering?"

In this first lecture, Hughes quotes substantially from the writings of Orson Pratt and then explains why Pratt is mistaken in his assertions. Hughes also borrows heavily from a seventy-page booklet by John Bowes entitled *Mormonism Exposed*.[45]

In addition to the printing of his first lecture, only the pamphlet that resulted from Hughes's second lecture has been identified. The facsimile translations for these first two are in Section 2.

1852: 11 September, *Caernarvon and Denbigh Herald*, p. 5 (750 words). "Lectures on the Mormon Delusion."

A very lengthy and laudatory review of the first lecture presented by Thomas Hughes at the town hall in Ruthin on 3 September.

1852: 17 September, *North Wales Chronicle*, p. 8 (715 words). "Lectures on the Mormon Delusion."

Nearly identical article to the one published in the *Caernarvon and Denbigh Herald* for 11 September 1852.

1852: October, *Seren Cymru* (*Star of Wales*), p. 3 (590 words). "Press Review. Lectures on the Deceit of Mormonism by Thomas Hughes (T. ab Gwilym). Isaac Clarke, Ruthin."

The editor of the *Star of Wales* was exultant in his review of Hughes's first lecture:

> The lecturer treats his topic in this lecture with unusual skill, and we are not surprised that it has received such high praise by those who heard it being delivered. It exposes all the deceit and the tricks used in the establishment of Mormonism, so that there is no further reason to hesitate about them; and we are amazed that any man in his right mind has been enticed to believe such blasphemous foolishness.

The editor adds:

> There is no doubt that these lectures will be of tremendous benefit in forestalling Mormonism, and we would counsel all to read them attentively if they wish to know the truth. . . . If everyone knew the undeniable facts which are set out in this lecture, we think that Mormonism would cease immediately.

1852: December, *Y Drysorfa* (*Treasury*), pp. 416–17 (135 words). "Lectures on the Deceit of Mormonism. Lecture I."

Another review of Thomas Hughes's first lecture. The reviewer declares:

> The irrefutable facts herein prove that Joe Smith and his co-workers in the founding of Mormonism were unprincipled and fraudulent persons, and that the "Book of Mormon" is nothing but the fruit of cunning thievery interspersed with lies. Those who believe Mormonism must have turned their backs on common sense,

> if ever they had any sense at all; for on the scheme from start to finish there are nothing but the fingerprints of impudence and knavery.

1852: December, *Y Diwygiwr* (*Revivalist*), pp. 376–77 (280 words). "Lectures on the Deceit of Mormonism by Thomas Hughes."

The reviewer observes:

> Mormonism is such a moral epidemic in the country that it will not be cured by making local superficial adjustments; for the structure has risen from general debility. The skilled doctor, most often, heals the sick and cures external injuries to the human body by giving something to the sufferer to take, and not by any outward application. Mormonism is made up of such elements, so that it cannot be killed by curing only the head. The deism, Catholicism, and the worldliness that pertain to it are incurable, except through an inner adjustment of the religious truths in the church, until it improves as a body, and then Mormonism will die in its own stench.

1853: January, *Cronicl y Cymdeithasau Crefyddol* (*Chronicle of the Religious Societies*), pp. 18–19 (650 words). "The Deceit of Mormonism, by T. Hughes (T. ab Gwilym)."

The writer, "J. R.," announces that the first lecture of Thomas Hughes on "a *revelation of the deceit of the beginning of Mormonism*" is now off the press, with five more to follow. He does not review the lecture but instead presents the strange story of someone he knew who had been baptized a Latter-day Saint. Admitting that his personal knowledge of this religion does not extend beyond North Wales, J. R. declares:

> What I have heard with my ears, and seen with my eyes, leads me to pity them rather than fear them—to pray for them rather than waste arguments on them.[46]

He says this about Joseph Smith and the religion he founded:

> But there is nothing clearer than the fact that *Joe Smith* in America intended to play Mahomet as his brother had done in Asia. The disorderly Mormon system is made up of Atheism, Muslimism, Catholicism, and a pretense of Christianity.[47]

He further observes:

> Mormonism in America has had some able and skillful defenders, such as Orson Pratt, etc., but our honest opinion is that they were paid servants selling their gift for money, and not seekers for the truth. The skill of their defense, and the madness of the principles they uphold, are completely irreconcilable on any other grounds.[48]

1853: January, *Yr Athraw at Wasanaeth yr Ysgolion Sabbathol* (*Teacher at the Service of the Sunday Schools*), pp. 21–22 (145 words). "Lectures on the Deceit of Mormonism, by Thomas Hughes, Rhuthin."

The editor declares that the pamphlet containing the first lecture of Thomas Hughes is now off the press. He sizes up the new religion of "Mormonism" as follows:

> The lecturer shows that the origin of Mormonism is from deceit, that its principles are contrary to the religion of Christ, except for a few things, which are used as bait to attract.

1853: June, *Yr Eurgrawn Wesleyaidd* (*Wesleyan Treasury*), pp. 206–8 (1,160 words). "Review. Lectures on the Deceit of Mormonism."

On 25 February 1853, Thomas Hughes gave his second lecture at the Rhuthin town hall. In this review, the writer presents several quotations from Hughes's lectures and laments the success that the Latter-day Saint missionaries had had in Britain:

> It is remarkable . . . the increase they have made among some part of the population. It appears from their statistics in January 1851 that this cunning deceit throughout the United Kingdom has been effective in enticing 30,747 into their system; and what is even more surprising and distressing is that 4,848 of that number are in Wales![49]

Of the projected six lectures and six pamphlets, apparently only the first two materialized (see next entry).

1853: *Darlithiau ar Dwyll Mormoniaeth: Darlith II* (*Lectures on the Deceit of Mormonism: Lecture 2*), pamphlet, 16 pages.

This is the printing of the second lecture given by Thomas Hughes (T. ab Gwilym) at the Rhuthin town hall on 25 February 1853. The topic for this second lecture was "the opinion of the Saints about God, angels, and the souls of man." As in the first, Hughes borrows heavily from the writings of Orson Pratt and refutes them with a great deal of sarcasm.

End: Thomas Hughes's first pamphlet receives eight rave reviews

1852: *Dirgelion Saint y Dyddiau Diweddaf, yn cael eu Dinoethi* (*Mysteries of the Saints of the Latter Days, Exposed*), pamphlet, 24 pages.

The author, Hugh Jones, had been with The Church of Jesus Christ of Latter-day Saints for two years before leaving. In his preface, dated 6 November 1852, Hugh Jones explains the reason behind his 24-page pamphlet:

> My conscience compelled me, to the extent possible, to undo whatever damage I was enabled to do by defending such an organization; and I have no way to do that except through the press.

Jones also expresses his wish for all who may read of his experience:

> I can only hope that the reading of the following pages will be a means of keeping those who may be as little children, from being led to such foolishness, and I am confident that it will be a means of opening the eyes of every honest person who may be among them, so that they may be able to flee from such a mortal sin.

Jones provides numerous details regarding his conversion and his two-year journey in his new faith. Over time, he wearied of the constant monetary collections imposed on him—for tithing, fast offerings, emigrating funds, temple funds, and the support of the district president. He had doubts about the Book of Mormon and the Doctrine and Covenants. He also questioned the comportment of some of the leaders. But it was the whisperings of the practice of polygamy in Utah that appear to have prompted him to leave the Church. For "the sake of fair play," Jones includes in his pamphlet a copy of the entire letter written by William Phillips to the editor of the *Times* and printed in the 15 October 1851 issue. In his letter Phillips states categorically:

> The polygamy of the Saints is an old story, and everyone can know that it is a lie just like its devil father.[50]

Hugh Jones writes that "Mr. Phillips is concealing the truth in order to preserve his own character." And he concludes by saying that his two-year journey with The Church of Jesus Christ of Latter-day Saints was a "departure from the [true] path" and one that he regrets.

The only mention of the name of Hugh Jones in any Latter-day Saint publication is one in the 1852 volume of *Zion's Trumpet* for 16 October, just three weeks before the preface date of *Secrets of the Saints*:

> President Simms, of the Anglesey Conference, wishes it to be known that Hugh Jones, a seller of varnish, etc., has been cut off from the Church, together with his wife.[51]

1852: 11 November, *Seren Cymru* (*Star of Wales*), p. 7 (25 words).

> The Mormons have sent one of their prophets to East India; and it is said that he is very successful in converting the Hindus.

1852: 4 December, *Silurian*, p. 4 (190 words). "The Mormons."

A quote from Lieutenant Gunnison, the associate of Captain Stansbury in the US government survey of the Great Salt Lake. Gunnison said, "The contemplation of plurality [plural marriage] is highly distasteful to the young Mormon ladies of any independence of feeling."

1852: 17 December, *Cambrian* (170 words). "Latter-day Saints Concert."

The concert was held at a small chapel in Llanelli, the only such structure built by the Latter-day Saints in Wales during the nineteenth century. According to this report, the concert consisted of "many popular airs, songs, duets, glees, etc." sung by choirs from Carmarthen and Llanelli. Also "Elder Martel excited much merriment by the recitation of a dialogue between a saint and a 'man of the world.'"[52]

Notes

1. *Defending the Faith: Early Welsh Missionary Publications*, item D21, 2.
2. For more details concerning the translation of the Book of Mormon into Welsh, see the profile for John S. Davis on the Welsh Saints Project.
3. For further information about the Morris and Jenkins families and the 1852 Cwmbach mine explosion, see the profile for Anna Evans on the Welsh Saints Project.
4. *Cardiff and Merthyr Guardian*, 17 July 1852, 3.
5. See the profile for Lewis Bowen on the Welsh Saints Project.
6. *Zion's Trumpet,* October 1852, 340.
7. These errors are not reflected in the English translation.
8. *Zion's Trumpet*, 7 February 1852, 37.
9. Ibid., 39.
10. Ibid., 40.
11. *Zion's Trumpet*, 21 February 1852, 53.

12. Ibid.
13. Ibid.
14. *American Messenger*, January 1852, 20–21.
15. *Sun*, February 1852, 71–72.
16. See *Welsh Mormon Writings*, item 2.
17. *Zion's Trumpet*, March 1852, 97.
18. John Davies, *The Miraculous Gifts as They Are Portrayed in the Holy Scriptures*, 60. See also Isaiah 55:2.
19. See *Defending the Faith: Early Welsh Missionary Publications*, item D21.
20. *Revivalist*, August 1852, 247. See also Zechariah 11:9.
21. *Inquirer*, March 1852, 68.
22. *Baptist*, March 1852, 95–97.
23. *Sun*, April 1852, 136.
24. See the *Cardiff and Merthyr Guardian*, 12 June 1852, 3.
25. *Harper's New Monthly Magazine*, June 1851, 64–66.
26. A similar account of this incident is in the *Revivalist*, May 1852, 164.
27. *American Messenger*, January 1852, 20–21.
28. A similar account of this incident is in the *Silurian*, 24 April 1852, 4, item 1.
29. Orson F. Whitney, *History of Utah*, vol. 4 (Salt Lake City: George Q. Cannon, 1892), 352.
30. *Zion's Trumpet*, 4 September 1852, 286.
31. Ibid.
32. *Revivalist*, August 1852, 243.
33. Ibid.
34. *Revivalist*, September 1852, 273.
35. Ibid.
36. Ibid.
37. Ibid., 274.
38. *Revivalist*, November 1852, 341–42.
39. *Millennial Star* 11:39, quoted in Welsh in ibid., 343.
40. Ibid.
41. Ibid.
42. *The Guide or the Literary Monthly*, August 1852, 144.
43. *Baptist*, April 1852, 109–12.
44. *Grail*, September 1852, 197.
45. John Bowes, *Mormonism Exposed, in Its Swindling and Licentious Abominations, Refuted in Its Principles, and in the Claims of Its Head, the Modern Mohammed, Joseph Smith* (London: about 1850).
46. *Chronicle of the Religious Societies*, January 1853, 18.
47. Ibid., 19.
48. Ibid.
49. *Wesleyan Treasury*, June 1853, 208.
50. Hugh Jones, *Mysteries of the Saints of the Latter Days, Exposed*, 1852, 21.
51. *Zion's Trumpet*, 16 October 1852, 340.
52. A "man of the world" indicates anyone having opinions not in agreement with those of the followers of Joseph Smith.

Chapter 10

Episodes

10.1—John Dunn Roberts answers the accusations of "H. L."
10.2—Robert Parry (known as "Robyn Ddu Eryri") spends one year and five weeks as a devout and supportive Latter-day Saint
10.3—An English source in Wales provides information about the Latter-day Saints in America
10.4—The Anglicans and Nonconformists blame each other regarding the increase of the Latter-day Saints

Salient Events

- **1 January 1853**—This issue of *Zion's Trumpet* is the first of fifty-three issues to be published during the year. At this point it had become a weekly periodical.
- **1 January 1853**—The practice of plural marriage is publicly recognized in this issue of *Zion's Trumpet*, which includes the Welsh translation of section 132 of the Doctrine and Covenants. The practice had been publicly announced in Utah four months earlier on 29 August 1852.
- **3 January 1853**—Dan Jones is called to be second counselor to President William Phillips in place of Thomas Pugh, who was released to emigrate after three years as counselor. Pugh sailed on the *Ellen Maria* two weeks later on 17 January 1853 and was excommunicated in absentia on 12 March 1853 for adultery.
- **12 March 1853**—The first of a three-day special general counsel presided over by Samuel W. Richards, the president of the Church in Britain. Richards had come in order to deal with the hard feelings that had arisen among the Welsh leaders of the Church with respect to the transgressions

of Thomas Pugh, the former second counselor in the presidency, who had emigrated a few weeks earlier. Some negative feelings that existed toward President William Phillips were also discussed. The return of Captain Dan Jones to Wales at the first of the year was extremely awkward for Phillips and John S. Davis, since Jones had been their leader for the three years preceding his departure in February 1849. Some of the other leaders had expected and even hoped that Jones would immediately replace Phillips as president and were disappointed that Jones instead became second counselor to Phillips. Pugh, the outgoing second counselor in the presidency, had previously made derogatory comments about Phillips, which made the situation even worse. Richards called for mutual forgiveness and unity, and the situation was resolved.

- **25 May 1853**—The records of the Swansea Branch show that on this date a man by the name of Robert Parry was baptized. Parry was a well-known figure in the literary world of Wales at that time and often gave public lectures on temperance and other topics. During 1850 and 1851, he had been the editor of the periodical *Y Wawr* (*Dawn*) and customarily used the nom de plume "Robyn Ddu Eryri," translated as "Black Robin of Snowdonia." He was forty-nine years old at the time of his conversion and was then hired by John S. Davis to assist in the publication of *Zion's Trumpet*. When Dan Jones reassumed the editorship of *Zion's Trumpet* in January 1854, Parry continued as a valuable employee and contributor to the periodical for about six months. Parry expressed his admiration for Jones in a 17 March 1854 letter to Thomas Jeremy: "Captain Jones, who is a kindred spirit with my heart, is not only a good man, rather I consider him to be one of the best men I have ever met."[1] Then, after a full year of intense support of the Church as a dedicated convert, Robert Parry apparently abandoned his new religion. In mid-1854, Parry went to North Wales on a missionary assignment, and his name is never again mentioned in *Zion's Trumpet*. In his memoir, published three years later, he describes his association with the Latter-day Saints as a "writing and translating job."[2] See Episode 10.2.
- **November 1853**—A forty-four-page pamphlet, titled *Exposure of Mormonism; Containing the History of Joseph Smith, Seven Degrees of the Temple, Spiritual Wifery, Together with the Ceremonies That Are Used on Acceptance into That Order*, is published in Welsh in Swansea. The author clearly intended to defame the Latter-day Saints because of their belief in plural marriage and their acceptance of the temple ceremonies associated with this practice. The author refers to himself as "The Levite," and he declares that the information for this "Exposure of Mormonism" has been gleaned from a variety of sources, including eyewitness accounts of very secret ceremonies by persons who had participated in them in the Nauvoo Temple. Unlike other similar attacks on the teachings and practices of the Latter-day Saints, this forty-four-page pamphlet prompted no response from any Latter-day Saint publications. See item 16 in Section 2.

Commentary

1853: 1 January, *Caernarvon and Denbigh Herald*, p. 3 (72 words).

A short report stating that about three hundred converts to The Church of Jesus Christ of Latter-day Saints were at that time on their way from Copenhagen to Liverpool and then on to New Orleans.

1853: 8 January, *Silurian*, p. 4 (55 words). "The Mormons."

> Three hundred Mormons, from Norway and Denmark, arrived per Lion, from Hamburg, on Tuesday night, and were forwarded by Mr. R. J. Cortis, the agent, to Liverpool, *en route* for New Orleans and the Salt Lake. Two missionaries from America have converted 2,000 persons; the remaining 1,700 follow in the spring. *Eastern Counties Herald.*

1853: 15 January, *Cardiff and Merthyr Guardian*, p. 4 (1,080 words). "Lectures on Mormonism."

A report, written by "A Correspondent of the *Birmingham Gazette*," summarizing four lectures which A. B. Hepburn, an apostate from the Church, delivered "on the delusions of the Mormons or Latter-day Saints." The writer describes Hepburn as follows:

> Mr. Hepburn is a specimen of the native intelligence and shrewdness, and we might even say genius, so often found among those in the humbler walks of life. He was himself a Mormon for ten months; but having soon penetrated the flimsy veil of hypocrisy and pretension which deludes the votaries of the sect, he separated from them, and has since devoted himself to the refutation of the doctrines and exposure of the self-styled Saints.

1853: 28 January, *Cambrian* (140 words). "Llanelly Latter-day Saints."

A notice that "about 20 members of this peculiar sect, residing in this neighborhood, departed [Wales] on Tuesday." They joined about 120 others in Swansea to embark on the *Troubadour*, a steamer that would take them to Liverpool where a chartered vessel awaited them. The writer comments:

> We believe that the poor deluded people who thus leave their native land and comfortable homes, would, when the time of departure had arrived, gladly wait behind, if the money they had deposited in their treasury was returned to them; and we shall not be surprised to hear of several preferring to remain at New Orleans or St. Louis, or some other of the American town[s], than proceed onwards; at all events this was the case with several who departed last spring.

1853: 28 January, *Monmouthshire Merlin*, p. 5, item 1 (140 words).

> On Tuesday, a large number of the followers of the Mormon creed, estimated at between 300 and 400, left this town, to commence their wearisome journey to the Salt Lake. Men, women, and children looked well and hearty, and appeared to look forward with anything but dread to the perils of their journey. It is understood they are a detachment only of those who are in course of the season to emigrate, under the care of Capt. Jones.

1853: 28 January, *Monmouthshire Merlin*, p. 5, item 2 (1,330 words). "Newport Christian Young Men's Society."

A very detailed report of a debate that did not materialize between the challenger, J. Flanigan, and the one challenged, Elder Shirtcliffe. Flanigan had left the following note with "the good lady of the house" at 1 Dolphin Street, Newport, where Shirtcliffe resided:

> Sir,—I have a *serious* charge to bring against you, this evening, at the meeting to be held in the Girls' British School-room, Llanarth-street: the subject for discussion is thus:—"Was Mohammed or Joseph Smith the greatest impostor?" Your attendance to rebut (if you can) my charge, is earnestly requested, and also to aid in explaining your views of Joseph Smith's Prophetic office, which we brand with imposition and deceit.
>
> Sir, I am yours, etc., J. Flanigan

Whether Shirtcliffe received the note or not, he did not appear that evening at the appointed place to answer Flanigan's challenge. Initially there were some in attendance who favored the return of the threepence entrance fee for the debate. Others, however, prevailed in allowing the meeting to continue in hopes that "there might be something worth the entrance fee, after all." Flanigan ended up being the final speaker of several who addressed the group about the evils of "Mormonism." During his remarks, Flanigan made mention of "his desired communications with Mr. Shirtcliffe."

> Here the lady who was just now described as making an observation, rose, and emphatically intimated that Mr. Flanigan, unlike the generality of his countrymen, was no gentleman, for he did not tell the truth. When he came with the note to her house for the Elder—and here the truth burst on the meeting, that a female Mormon was present, and many stood up to gaze upon her—he had spoken very differently, and far more meekly, than he had done tonight.

The lady then said in Shirtcliffe's defense that "he had gone to Cardiff on particular business." But when Flanigan said "that the Elder had shifted ground often before when he was wanted in controversy," the lady "walked out with undisguised contempt." Flanigan brought the meeting to a close by expressing "a hope that the children of all present, might be brought up in detestation of the vicious principles of Mormonism."

1853: January, *Y Bedyddiwr* (*Baptist*), p. 21 (65 words). "Ordination of a Minister in Aberaman near Aberdare."

In April 1851, the Reverend David Bevan Jones (Dewi Elfed Jones) had presented this chapel to The Church of Jesus Christ of Latter-day Saints following his baptism (see Episode 8.2). After much litigation, however, the courts ruled that it was still a Baptist chapel. Someone using the nom de plume "Lenox" gave great praise to the new minister, William Jones, and ended with the following triumphant reminder:

> The reader will remember that this is the chapel that for a season was in the hands of the Saints. It is now very beautifully finished and has been secured for the Baptists, and we are confident, despite all the *Satanists* of the world, that the cause will yet blossom here for Jesus Christ.

1853: January, *Y Methodist* (*Methodist*), pp. 14–17 (1,095 words). "A Mormon Miracle."

The Welsh translation of a story "told by a man by the name of Mr. Tucker, who was one of the printers who printed the Book of Mormon the first time." The story had found its way into a book published in 1842 by John C. Bennett, who had served as a counselor to Joseph Smith for over a year before being excommunicated and removed from his position.[3] The story has to do with "a farmer in one of the States" who extended hospitality to "a respectable-looking man at his gate who requested permission to pass the night under his roof." During the night, the man supposedly died, and the next morning two elders of The Church of Jesus Christ of Latter-day Saints appeared at the farmer's door. When the elders learned of the "death" of the stranger, they told the farmer that they could raise the dead man to life, explaining that they had been commissioned by the Lord to work miracles "in order to prove the truth of the Prophet Joseph Smith, and the inspiration of the books and doctrines revealed to him." The farmer then sent for his neighbors, according to instructions from the elders, and also secretly hid a "well-sharpened broad axe" under his coat. When all were assembled, the farmer asked the elders if they could raise the dead man to life even if one of his arms or legs were missing from an accident. They assured him that they could. Then he asked them if they could perform their miracle even if the dead man's head had been cut off. Again, they responded in the affirmative. The farmer then said, "So, by your leave, if it makes no difference whatever, I will proceed to cut off the head of this corpse." The climax of the story follows:

> Accordingly, he produced a huge and well-sharpened broad axe from beneath his coat, which he swung above his head, and was apparently about to bring it down upon the neck of the corpse, when, lo and behold! to the amazement of all present, the dead man started up in great agitation, and swore he would not have his head cut off for any consideration whatever![4]

The elders then confessed to having prearranged the whole incident. The story concludes as follows:

> The farmer, after giving the impostors a severe chastisement, let them depart to practice their humbuggery in some other quarter.[5]

1853: February, *Yr Haul* (*Sun*), pp. 65–68 (2,745 words). "The Origin and Growth of Mormonism."

Part one of a three-part article. All three parts consist simply of the Welsh translation of parts of *Mormonism Unvailed* [*sic*], the 1834 publication of Eber D. Howe.[6] Part two appears in the April 1853 issue of the periodical,[7] and part three appears in the June 1853 issue.[8] In order to discredit Joseph Smith's account of how he had received the golden plates, Howe presents the testimonies of several individuals who had known Smith and his family. Peter Ingersoll, an acquaintance of Smith, gives in his testimony a brief account of what he says Smith had told him about the "golden Bible":

> "As I was passing, yesterday, across the woods, after a heavy shower of rain, I found, in a hollow, some beautiful white sand, that had been washed up by

> the water. I took off my frock, and tied up several quarts of it, and then went home. On my entering the house, I found the family at the table eating dinner. They were all anxious to know the contents of my frock. At that moment, I happened to think of what I had heard about a history found in Canada, called the golden Bible; so I very gravely told them it was the golden Bible. To my surprise, they were credulous enough to believe what I said. Accordingly I told them that I had received a commandment to let no one see it, for, says I, no man can see it with the naked eye and live. However, I offered to take out the book and show it to them, but they refused to see it, and left the room." Now, said Jo, "I have got the damned fools fixed, and will carry out the fun."[9]

Strangely, the final sentence of the above quote is omitted in the Welsh translation with an asterisk inserted in its place. The footnote at the bottom of the page explains the omission:

> The part left out is the observation of Smith about the scene. It is considered inappropriate to be stated here because of its base corruption.[10]

One is left to wonder about the editor's reason for omitting this part of Ingersoll's account.

1853: 12 February, *Silurian*, p. 3 (70 words). "Extraordinary Delusion."

> Among the numerous party that has, within the last few days, left this neighborhood for the Mormon settlement, at the Salt Lake, is an old woman, 81 years of age, who is firmly impressed with the belief that she will not only reach the promised land in safety, but she will also become a young woman again. Her husband is a poor blind pauper, residing at Dyffryn, near St. Nicholas.

1853: 18 February, *Monmouthshire Merlin*, p. 4 (110 words). "Mormon Emigrants."

> About sixty Mormons (men, women, and children) lately living in Newport and Pontypool, having made up their minds to proceed to the land of promise, and join the camp in the precincts of the Salt Lake, this week left Newport per rail for Liverpool, there to embark for the territory henceforward to be their home. Among the party from this town, is a respectable widow, who has nearly run out the allotted span of human existence; and she has expressed a firm conviction, that her husband, though long since placed in a Cambrian grave, will be restored alive to her among the prophets and elders, to whom she is progressing.

1853: 26 February, *Silurian*, p. 2 (105 words). "The Mormons."

> Upwards of twenty of "the Latter-day Saints" or Mormons, from this town, and the mineral districts, left on Monday last, per South Wales Railway for Liverpool, there to embark for the Salt Lake. Amongst the number was an old man upwards of 60, (an agent in this port to an extensive coal proprietor,) who some years ago lost one of his legs by an accident; he has gone firm in the faith that when he arrives there he will no longer have any necessity for its wooden substitute, as the absent member will be restored to him in all its original vigor.

1853: 26 February, *Silurian*, p. 2 (110 words). "Mormon Emigrants."

This is the same article carried by the *Monmouthshire Merlin* for 18 February 1853.

1853: March, *Y Cenhadwr Americanaidd* (*American Messenger*), p. 91, item 1 (575 words). "The Mormons."

In this letter to the editor, J. Price Jones of Burlington, Iowa, expresses alarm that "over a thousand Welsh people have emigrated already to the Salt Lake Valley." He reports with sadness what he had seen during a recent stay in St. Louis:

> I saw several hundred Welsh people going through that city toward the valley and in their midst were scores of the fairest, most modest young women industrial Wales possessed. Poor innocents! Little did they know of the dreadful fate which awaited them—all to become despoiled slaves to the wanton passions of the loathsome Mormon leaders!

Regarding polygamy, Jones writes,

> The Mormons impudently denied for a long time that polygamy was a feature of their religion; but now they assert and defend the subject with the same impudence as they denied it before.

He refers to a book published by John W. Gunnison entitled *The Mormons, or, Latter-day Saints, in the Valley of the Great Salt Lake*:[11]

> Mormonism is probably one of the remarkable phenomena of this age in the speed of its growth. *Lieut. Gunnison*, in the work he published recently about Mormonism, says that the population increase and temporal success of the Valley are surprising. They are making a part of America's most barren wilderness bloom like a rose. They have machines for sugar and leather works, brought directly from France together with many men from that country to operate them. They have many famous public works in their midst. Their harvest has been extremely abundant.

Despite Gunnison's praise of the Latter-day Saints, Jones concludes,

> But what of that? There are elements of civil and social disturbance in their midst. Polygamy cannot but be an element which is sure to effect their downfall. They are "daylight plunderers." So many scores of the female sex of our nation have already fallen prey to their teeth, when there was no savior for them! It is not choleric hatred but a necessity to shout over the whole Welsh world, through the medium of the *Messenger*—that Mormonism is a curse on mankind, loathsome in society, and a stench in the creation.

1853: March, *Y Cenhadwr Americanaidd* (*American Messenger*), pp. 91–92, item 2 (340 words).

This article is from a correspondent of the *New York Tribune* writing from Council Bluffs, Iowa. He tells of the preparations being made for the immigrants to continue their trek to Salt Lake City:

> Missionaries here were sent from there to assist and encourage the people in their preparations for migrating, and it appears that there will be from five to six thousand going there in the spring.[12]

The writer further comments about the land that the Latter-day Saints had cultivated:

> The improvements made to the land by these Mormons will facilitate the settlement of this part of Iowa. They have cultivated a considerable amount of land, and some of that has been enclosed to a good extent; and they will sell it for what it has cost to plough the prairie and enclose it.[13]

1853: 4 March, *North Wales Chronicle*, p. 7 (58 words). "The West Indies."

> Four Mormons had arrived at Kingston from the territory of Utah, but were prevented from lecturing in that city by the mayor and attorney-general, through apprehensions of a riot. One of them, however, had lectured in Spanish Town by permission of the governor, but he was so quizzed by the wags that he could not complete his harangue.

Episode 10.1

Start: John Dunn Roberts answers the accusations of "H. L."

1853: April, *Y Bedyddiwr* (*Baptist*), p. 119 (600 words). "Mormonism."

The writer, "H. L.," provides an account of some "young boys" in the Brecon area who had received baptism from the Latter-day Saints about a year earlier, one of whom, David Davies, was taken ill and died. According to H. L., Davies suffered from extreme guilt for having converted to the new religion and instructed his mother not to allow any of them to come near him. H. L. also added:

> As much as half an hour before dying, he hit the bed intending to hit John Roberts, the one who baptized him, and he died in that way. His death has caused all the aforementioned boys to leave the Saints.

1853: 23 April, *Udgorn Seion* (*Zion's Trumpet*), pp. 270–73 (1,190 words). "Defense."

A response to H. L. from John Dunn Roberts, the person who had baptized David Davies, the young boy who subsequently died. Regarding H. L.'s assertion that young Davies, at the onset of his illness, would not allow any of the Saints to come near him, Roberts declares,

> Claiming that he did not allow any of the Saints to go near him is a baseless lie and a fabricated tale; for while he was able to go out after he was taken ill, he came most often to my house, and I went to his house; and the neighborhood where he lived are witnesses of that.[14]

As for Davies's attempt to hit Roberts just before Davies died, Roberts writes:

> Had he hit me, H. L. could call that a miracle, to be sure; for at the time the above brother died, I was about twenty miles from Brecon, which many know.[15]

In his article, Roberts also responds to H. L.'s statement that no scripture other than the Bible is necessary and that there is no further need for miracles.

End: John Dunn Roberts answers the accusations of "H. L."

1853: April, *Yr Eurgrawn Wesleyaidd* (*Wesleyan Treasury*), pp. 128–29 (365 words).

An account by a shopkeeper in Newbury, England, concerning Richard Currell, a cobbler who had converted to The Church of Jesus Christ of Latter-day Saints. In the spring of 1848, the shopkeeper was reading aloud from the *Millennial Star* to some young men about "the ordination of Richard Currell into the Mormon priesthood." One of the young men observed that Currell was a cobbler who lived in the town and was known by the name of Dusty Currell. Later, in answer to the shopkeeper's request, the young man identified Currell when Currell was looking in the window of the shop. The shopkeeper invited the cobbler into his shop and asked him if it was true that he had been arrested with others in Warwick and Leamington the previous year for raising a riot in the streets. After receiving an affirmative answer, the shopkeeper explained his motive for posing the question:

> "My reason for questioning you like this is that I recently saw the magazine of the Latter-day Saints, entitled *The Millennial Star*, in which it is said that you were *ordained* a *priest* in Leamington, and *that they cast many devils out of you*, the number being mentioned, namely a hundred and forty, I think, or something around that; and *that they saw them* coming out of you, but that they went back again as fast as they came out, and a lot faster; and I wanted to ask you if you know about the matter?" "Ho!" said he, "a *set* of d——d fools! I heard they had put something about me in the paper; but they never let me see it!" And at that, he went out of the shop.[16]

The correspondent ended his account with this comment:

> I hear that Dusty is again an official member of the religion of the Latter-day Saints and speaks in a foreign tongue in their public meetings.[17]

An account of the incident appears in the 1 August 1847 *Millennial Star*, submitted by Thomas Smith, the President of the Leamington Spa Conference.[18] Smith indicates that Richard Currell "had been proposed at the council meeting at Stratford-on-Avon, to be ordained to the office of a priest." Smith adds:

> But as soon as he had expressed his willingness to take the office, some evil spirits (devils) entered him, and declared he should not be ordained, and if he went to the conference they would go too.[19]

Four days later, in the company of a Brother and Sister Freeman, Currell started on his twenty-mile walk to Coventry to attend a conference where he was to be ordained a priest. Smith reports:

> On the road, the devils entered Brother C. several times, and four times while passing through the town of Warwick, and were as often rebuked by Elder Freeman, in the presence of many people, to whom he bore a faithful testimony. At length they arrived at Leamington Spa, in order to remain the night, but as soon as they entered the house, the devils began to rage and swear.[20]

Thomas Smith then tells of his own arrival in Leamington Spa:

> I got to the house about nine o'clock in the evening. I had scarcely got in before they began to swear at me. I rebuked them, and they came out of him; but as fast as one lot went another came, declaring Currell should not go to Coventry, each party tearing him and trying to kill him. Thus, they continued until one o'clock, when we lay down until five, when another party came swearing that we should not take him to conference, and tried to choke him. We cast out several lots until eight o'clock, when five of us started to take him with us to Coventry, 10 miles distant.[21]

The attacks continued along the way to Coventry and after they arrived for the meeting. Smith continues his report as follows:

> While we were preparing for dinner, some stronger devils took possession of Brother C. We expelled them, and in came two policemen, and took Brother Currell to the police station. I went with him, others following, amid the insults and hooting of the mob, to the station. The superintendent, on hearing the case, ordered Brother C. to be locked up for having a devil, and me for casting him out, and thus causing a disturbance.[22]

After two hours in "a filthy room along with two drunken men," Smith and Currell were released. They went to the conference where Currell was ordained a priest. But during the ordination, Currell was again possessed. And they continued to be troubled by evil spirits during the remainder of the conference. Smith was philosophical about the situation:

> Instead of these things doing us any harm it has done us good, and we feel to bless the name of God, to give him all the glory, and shout his praise among the people, and to preach the gospel with renewed energy among the sons of men.[23]

1853: 5 May, *Y Gwron Cymreig* (*Welsh Hero*), p. 4 (310 words). "Manners and Customs of the Mormon Preachers."

Two things in this article are the cause for wonder: First, the title includes the phrase "Mormon Preachers," neglecting to clarify that George Adams, the focus of the article, had been excommunicated from The Church of Jesus Christ of Latter-day Saints several years earlier in 1845. Second, the opening phrase of the article is as follows: "The *Boston Herald*, upon publishing the death of Elder George Adams, a Mormon preacher." The editor is obviously confusing two people by the name of George Adams, for the one associated with the Latter-day Saints did not die until 1880. The remainder of the article consists of a report of "Elder" George Adams and the thrashing he reportedly gave to the editor of the *Boston Herald* after the editor's "rather harsh critique" of Adams's portrayal of Richard III in the National Playhouse.

1853: 7 May, *Caernarvon and Denbigh Herald*, p. 6 (47 words).

> These deluded people the Mormons, principally from Carmarthenshire, still continue to leave their native shore in large numbers for the land of promise—the Salt Lake. Last week, nearly one hundred persons, many of them highly-respectable yeomen, left Swansea for Liverpool in the *Troubadour* steamer for embarkation.

1853: June, *Seren Gomer* (*Star of Gomer*), p. 278 (125 words). "Verses to the Latter-day Saints."

An insulting poem of four 4-line stanzas by "Iolo Gwyddolwern." Here is the first stanza:

> Latter-day Saints—there is a miracle,
> If I follow true power,
> I shall flee from the disgrace of lies,
> To better men, if I find deceit.

1853: June, *Yr Eurgrawn Wesleyaidd* (*Wesleyan Treasury*), pp. 206–8 (1,160 words). "Review. Lectures on the Deceit of Mormonism."

A review of the second pamphlet that resulted from the second lecture of Thomas Hughes given on 25 February 1853 at the Rhuthin town hall. See Episode 9.8.

1853: *Mormoniaeth, neu Draethawd ar y Sect a Elwir "Seintiau y Dyddiau Diweddaf," gan y Parch. F. B. Ashley* (*Mormonism: Or a Treatise on the Sect Called "The Latter-day Saints,"* by the Rev. F. B. Ashley), pamphlet, 34 pages.

For more particulars regarding this pamphlet, see the discussion below for *Yr Haul* (*Sun*) for June 1853 or pamphlet 17 in section 2 of this book.

1853: June, *Yr Haul* (*Sun*), pp. 230–31 (890 words). "Mormonism, or a Treatise on the Sect Called 'The Latter-day Saints,' by the Rev. F. B. Ashley."

A review of the Welsh translation of the pamphlet by this name. It is fitting that this thirty-four-page treatise was recommended by the editor of the Anglican periodical, *The Sun*, since the author, Francis B. Ashley, was an Anglican vicar in Wooburn Parish, Buckinghamshire. The writer of the review gives his name as "Hywel," but his real identity is most likely David Owen, the one-time Baptist who had become an Anglican vicar and editor of the *Sun*. In his review, Hywel praises Harries for his work in providing this "inexpensive treatise on Mormonism in the Welsh language." Hywell also recommends that Anglican vicars and "others who wish the good of their parishioners" purchase a few hundred copies of the treatise for distribution. He then warns:

> The appearance of this treatise is timely; in a month or two from now, the Mormon tribe will begin to crawl out like snakes, and other poisonous vermin, from the coal pits and underground holes and cellars of Glamorgan, and they will appear on Sundays, and fine days, in swarms across the country, along the hedgerows, on bridges, and in villages, and in the houses of lascivious women; in a word they will be teeming like the frogs in Egypt. They will climb up and come into thine House, oh Welshman, and into thy bedchamber, and upon thy bed, and upon the bed of thy wife, and thy daughter, and thy servant girl; and into the remains of thy food. Buy this treatise on Mormonism, and keep it in the house, and it will be enough of a spell to keep away the awful disease and plague.[24]

1853: 24 June, *Monmouthshire Merlin*, p. 5, item 1 (90 words). "Mormonism."

Mr. George Gaisford, of Ebbw Vale, has again addressed us on the subject of Mormonism—his principle object being to reply to statements made respecting him, in a letter recently published in the *Merlin*, at the request of Mr. John Flanegan, of Newport. Mr. Gaisford goes somewhat at length into matters brought forward in Mr. Flanegan's letter, and gives a direct contradiction to many of his statements. As, however, the matter has now assumed a simply personal character, further correspondence upon it would be destitute of public interest.

1853: 24 June, *Monmouthshire Merlin*, p. 5, item 2 (125 words). "The Latter-day Saints."

Since our last notice of the Latter-day Saints, they have attempted with double vigor to persuade the inhabitants into an acceptance of their creed. On Sunday evening last, they held a meeting on the Castle Green, which was attended by a large congregation; but none of their own sect. At the conclusion of the addresses of Messrs. Owen and Gibbs, the congregation almost unanimously hooted them from Castle Green to Flannel Street, where the so-called Saints had recourse to the assistance of the police for protection, fearing violence from the mob. Mr. Owen has at length refused to give an answer to any question put to him in public; but says he is willing to explain the principles of Mormonism in private.

1853: 25 June, *Caernarvon and Denbigh Herald*, p. 6 (34 words).

A Mormon preacher, named O'Kelly, while preaching at Spurstow, on Sunday week, said the reason of the *disease* among cattle and potatoes, was on account of the martyrdom of *Joseph Smith*, the Mormon prophet.

Episode 10.2

Start: Robert Parry (known as "Robyn Ddu Eryri") spends one year and five weeks as a devout and supportive Latter-day Saint

The 1853 conversion of the poet and lecturer Robert Parry (often known by his nom de plume "Robyn Ddu Eryri") to The Church of Jesus Christ of Latter-day Saints caused a reaction of bewilderment in the Nonconformist community. In the Latter-day Saint community, however, Parry's conversion came as a pleasant surprise. And John S. Davis most likely viewed Parry's conversion as a personal blessing—Davis recognized Parry's literary talents and soon had him assisting with the preparation and publication of the weekly periodical *Zion's Trumpet*.

1853: 11 June, *Udgorn Seion* (*Zion's Trumpet*), p. 388 (34 words).

A brief note about Robert Parry's baptism:

We are informed by a letter from Elder T. Jeremy, that the famous Mr. Robert Parry (Robyn Ddu) was baptized recently in Swansea, and that he has enlisted in the army of the Saints.

The Llanelli Branch records indicate that Parry was baptized on 25 May by William Thomas and confirmed on 29 May by Robert Evans, the branch president.

1853: 9 July, *Udgorn Seion* (*Zion's Trumpet*), p. 6 (35 words). "The Poet to Himself."

A four-line poem that Robert Parry wrote about his conversion:

> I was baptized, let it be a promise—to live henceforth,
> Without the urges of my faults;
> Through fervent godly prayer,
> From the deep pain, Robyn will come.
> Robyn Ddu, Eryri.

1853: 24 September, *Udgorn Seion* (*Zion's Trumpet*), p. 197 (5,000 words). "Definitive Proof That the Saints of the Most High Did Not Deceive nor Were They Deceived."

Robert Parry places the following scriptural quotation at the top of this twelve-page testimony, which details his conviction of the truthfulness of the doctrine of The Church of Jesus Christ of Latter-day Saints:

> I am not mad, most noble Festus; but speak forth the words of truth and soberness. Acts 26:25.

Parry had no doubt experienced considerable bewilderment from his Nonconformist friends and associates when he made the sudden decision to align himself with the Latter-day Saints. The scripture he quoted was obviously to assure his friends that he had not lost his senses.

He then proceeds to describe in great detail the reasons for his conversion. Referring to himself in the third person, Parry writes,

> Whatever opinion readers of the foregoing reasons form of their strength, perhaps some of them will think the following is quite weak; but to the writer, the following is the strongest of the lot: namely, that he, in his obedience to the Gospel, received testimony to and for himself; that he received his testimony through revelation; and that he knows that he was received into the community of the Saints, in the Church of Jesus Christ. There was scarcely any acquaintance between him and any people among the Saints, before he joined them, and not many of them are known to him to this day; nevertheless, he testifies that no money could buy him from his certain knowledge of the religion they profess: and he has seen more brotherly love between them in a few weeks than he saw in his whole life amongst other believers.[25]

Parry then promises the readers of his testimony that "through their obedience to all the conditions of the Gospel, and having its sacraments administered to them by servants sent by God, with the Latter-day Saints, that they will receive testimony themselves."[26]

Two periodicals and four newspapers reported on and reacted to the baptism of Robert Parry (see the descriptions below).

1853: 24 September, *North Wales Chronicle*, p. 3 (130 words). "Mormonism."

The writer first comments about the success of the Latter-day Saints in South Wales:

> The adherents to the doctrines of Mormonism increase rather than diminish in those districts of South Wales where they have established themselves, and of late they have received an accession of strength in several persons of middle-class station. A well-known Welsh lecturer, named Robert Parry, better known by his appellation of "Robyn Ddu," has recently joined the ranks of Mormonism.

The writer then reports on the large numbers of converts leaving Wales:

> An extensive exodus has taken place during the summer, and numbers have found their way over to the waters of the Salt Lake. Large bodies of these people have left Glamorganshire, Carmarthenshire, and the hill country of Monmouth for America, and numbers will leave their native land next spring for their Elysium. Miracles are reputed to have been performed by the elders of the sect, all of which are faithfully believed.

1853: October, *Yr Haul* (*Sun*), p. 363 (220 words). "Robyn Ddu Eryri."

The editor pokes fun at the Independents for their treatment of Robert Parry, who had recently converted to The Church of Jesus Christ of Latter-day Saints. During 1850 and 1851, Parry was the editor of the periodical *Y Wawr* (the *Dawn*) and was a well-known speaker on temperance in Wales. The writer points out:

> When Robyn was a *de facto* member among the Independents, and lecturing in favor of temperance, many of the chapels of the Independents were closed against him. He was denied the use of the chapel of the Independents in Cardiff to preach or to lecture; but when Robyn was in Cardiff editing *The Dawn*, being neither member nor preacher, or even associated with the Independents or anyone else, he was invited by the Independents in Cardiff to deliver a lecture in their chapel in order to collect money to pay the debt of the chapel.

1853: 7 October, *Cambrian* (75 words). "Cwmtwrch."

A brief report on a sermon given by Robert Parry (Robyn Ddu Eryri) at the George the Fourth pub in Cwmtwrch, a village located about fifteen miles north of Swansea. At first the audience was just a few people, but it eventually increased to about thirty. The writer refers to Parry as "the great orator" and observes that the Latter-day Saints are "but very few in the neighborhood."

1853: 15 October, *Caernarvon and Denbigh Herald*, p. 3 (40 words).

> On Friday week last, the celebrated Robert Parry (Robin [*sic*] Ddu) delivered a sermon on Mormonism, in Swansea. From thirty to forty persons went to hear the great orator. The Latter-day Saints number but very few in the neighborhood.

1853: 15 October, *Silurian*, p. 2 (100 words).

> Mormonism is increasing rather than diminishing in those districts of South Wales where it has established itself, and of late it has received an accession of strength in several persons of the middle class. A well-known Welsh lecturer, named Robert Parry, better known by his appellation of "Robin [*sic*] Ddu," has recently joined the ranks, and is now holding forth to the deluded people. An exodus has taken place during the summer, and numbers have found their way over to the Salt Lake. Large bodies of these misguided people have left Glamorganshire, Carmarthenshire, and the hill country of Monmouth for America, and numbers will leave next spring.

1853: November, *Y Cyfaill o'r Hen Wlad yn America* (*Friend of the Old Country in America*), p. 445 (190 words). "Mormonism in Wales."

> The well-known Welsh orator Robert Parry, or Robyn Ddu, has enlisted himself under the Mormon banner, and is now preaching zealously to the deceived people.

The writer expresses alarm at the large number of Welsh from South Wales who had become Latter-day Saints and ends his article with the following:

> It is to the credit of the Americans that not many of them have swelled the armies of the Mormon Prophet, while the shame of Wales is greater through this their foolishness than anything the Blue Books could place on them.

The "Blue Books" refers to the 1847 reports of the English commissioners about the state of education in Wales. The Blue Books caused great resentment among the Welsh for the manner in which the Welsh were disparaged in the reports.

1854: 15 July, *Udgorn Seion* (*Zion's Trumpet*), pp. 417–19 (125 words). "Letter from President Jeremy."

In this 22 March 1854 letter to Dan Jones, Thomas Jeremy quotes from a 17 March 1854 letter he had received from Robert Parry:

> I shall tell you a little secret: Captain Jones, who is a kindred spirit with my heart—is not only a good man, rather I consider him to be one of the best men I have ever met. If I considered him unworthy of the respect I have for him, I would have concluded these lines without mentioning his name, any more than to say that he sends you his regards. But as I told you, he is one of the best I have seen; it is not necessary to say that I am sincere in my statement—I can swear to you and prove that he is such, and with pleasure, trust, and Christian love I can put my name in writing by this statement.

Just two months later, Robert Parry sent a letter directly to Dan Jones from North Wales. In the letter, Parry expresses his love for The Church of Jesus Christ of Latter-day Saints.

1854: 8 July, *Udgorn Seion* (*Zion's Trumpet*), pp. 402–3 (380 words). "Letter from Elder Robert Parry."

This letter to Dan Jones is dated 20 May 1854, just a few days short of Parry's one-year anniversary as a member of The Church of Jesus Christ of Latter-day Saints.

Parry was in North Wales when he wrote the letter, and he sends greetings from several faithful followers in that area. He adds:

> I told them in response to some questions, that our church is superior to all others, not only in the various spiritual gifts, but also in the effects that are caused by them, such as godly men, unity, charity, and doing good with generosity, that I have seen more brotherly love in this church, during six months, than in the seventeen years I belonged to the Independents.

1854: 22 July, *Udgorn Seion* (*Zion's Trumpet*), p. 433 (28 words). "East Glamorgan Conference."

The minutes for this conference, held on 2 July 1854 in Merthyr Tydfil, contain the following entry:

> Elder Robert Parry was permitted to go to North Wales to preach the gospel, according to his own desire. He was released from this Conference by unanimous vote.

The foregoing entry is the final mention of Robert Parry in *Zion's Trumpet.*

After a full year of intense activity and support of the Church as a dedicated convert, Robert Parry apparently abandoned his new religion. Three years later, he published *Teithiau a Barddoniaeth Robyn Ddu Eryri* (Travels and Poetry of Robyn Ddu Eryri), in which he describes his association with the Latter-day Saints as a "writing and translating job." He avoids mentioning that he was baptized by them and that he preached their doctrine as an ordained elder, nor does he mention the reason behind the falling out he obviously had with them.

In the *Biographical Dictionary of Wales* is the following assessment by Parry's biographer:

> [Robert Parry] failed to master any craft or trade and spent years of his life wandering from place to place in Wales and England; he once visited the United States, but did not stay long. He was at different times, a schoolmaster, a lawyer's clerk, a preacher, a lecturer on temperance, an advocate of Mormonism, and, between 1850 and 1852, editor of *Y Wawr* [*The Dawn*], a periodical published in Cardiff. He was best known as a speaker on temperance; many doubted his sincerity, in view of his own conduct.[27]

End: Robert Parry (known as "Robyn Ddu Eryri") spends one year and five weeks as a devout and supportive Latter-day Saint

1853: 2 July, *Caernarvon and Denbigh Herald*, p. 4 (145 words).

Another story of a "Mormon" rising from the dead—in this case, "200 of these disciples of Mormon had met in a school-room in order to witness the resurrection of a corpse."

1853: 9 July, *Cardiff and Merthyr Guardian*, p. 2 (245 words).

Brigham Young addresses a congregation of saints and denounces the disobedient. Here is a sample of what he says:

> Now, you nasty apostates, clear out, or judgment will be put to the line, and righteousness to the plummet. (Voices generally—"Go it, go it!") If you say it is right, raise your hands. (All hands up.)

1853: 16 July, *Monmouthshire Beacon*, p. 8 (360 words). "Mormonism."

The writer shows surprise about how gullible the converts to The Church of Jesus Christ of Latter-day Saints are. He tells of an "aged widow" who expected to meet her dead husband in Salt Lake City "in perfect health." He also writes of a man who claimed to have sufficient faith to remove a mountain in his neighborhood. And he describes the experience of a crippled man who was healed and convinced he could fly, but while the man was flying to Salt Lake City, he was shot out of the sky.

1853: 23 July, *Cardiff and Merthyr Guardian*, p. 3 (78 words).

> Intelligence by the Overland Mail states that the Mormons are making a desperate effort just now for the conversion of India to the creed of Joe Smith. Thirteen "ministers" arrived from the city of the Salt Lake, via California, a month or six weeks ago, and their "high priest" has lately got one of the newspapers to publish his manifesto. They seem likely, however, to proceed with some difficulty, as their gift of tongues does not include Bengalee.

1853: August, *Seren Gomer* (*Star of Gomer*), p. 382 (215 words). "Dissention in the Mormon Camp."

The writer reports on Brigham Young's attempts to get the pioneers to continue their journey from Council Bluffs to the Salt Lake Valley, some of whom, "to the great discomfort of President Brigham Young," asked for "proof." The writer counsels:

> We think it would be wiser for them to ask for "proof" before leaving their homes. We hope, however, that this will be a warning to others. We understand that the gentleman, president, on the 27th of last June, addressed "the true Saints" with raging and ferocious eloquence, commanding the skeptics to get on their way to California; and he appealed to his listeners to drive away the dissenters by the power of arms—for which work he asked for divine help. Whether this law was put completely into action or not, we do not yet know.

1853: 6 August, *Cardiff and Merthyr Guardian*, p. 3 (360 words). "Mormonism."

The same article as in the *Monmouthshire Beacon* for 16 July 1853.

1853: 13 August, *Monmouthshire Beacon*, p. 6 (265 words).

> A murderous attack was made upon a body of Mormons in Beaver Island on the 13th of July.

For readers in Wales, the followers of James Strang continued to be confused with The Church of Jesus Christ of Latter-day Saints.

1853: 10 September, *North Wales Chronicle*, p. 2 (60 words). "Mormonism."

> One of the disciples of Joe Smith, the Mormon prophet, sporting the *sobriquet* of Captain Jones, or Rev. Capt. Jones, we are not certain as to his precise classification, delivered a lecture or sermon in support of the above delusion,

in the Waterloo Rooms, in this city [Bangor], on Monday evening. The audience consisted of about twenty people of both sexes.

1853: 24 September, *North Wales Chronicle*, p. 3 (130 words). "Mormonism."

The adherents to the doctrines of Mormonism increase rather than diminish in those districts of South Wales where they have established themselves, and of late they have received an accession of strength in several persons of middle-class station. A well-known Welsh lecturer, named Robert Parry, better known by his appellation of "Robyn Ddu," has recently joined the ranks of Mormonism. An extensive exodus has taken place during the summer, and numbers have found their way over to the waters of the Salt Lake. Large bodies of these people have left Glamorganshire, Carmarthenshire, and the hill country of Monmouth for America, and numbers will leave their native land next spring for their Elysium. Miracles are reputed to have been performed by the elders of the sect, all of which are faithfully believed.

1853: 8 October, *Udgorn Seion* (*Zion's Trumpet*), pp. 229–32 (1,270 words). "The Cause of the Various Sects."

John S. Davis inserted this article which had been printed nearly a decade earlier in the February 1844 issue of *Star of Gomer*. He offered no commentary or observations; rather, he allowed the article to speak for itself.

The author of the article identifies himself as "A Lame Welshman"; his objective is to show by scriptural evidence that there can be only one "Christian" religion. For, he explains, if a religion differs in any way, though the difference be minor, from the doctrine established by the Savior, it then ceases to be a Christian religion and must be called by some other name. Several denominations considered themselves to be Christian: the Baptists, the Methodists, the Congregationalists, and numerous other similar religions, despite their differences, referred to one another as Christian, for they all claimed to believe in Christ and follow His teachings. Also, they were all in agreement that The Church of Jesus Christ of Latter-day Saints was heretical and undeserving of being called Christian. They took great offense whenever the Latter-day Saints referred to themselves as constituting the only true and authentic church established by the Savior according to his doctrine.

Davis's apparent objective in printing the article is to demonstrate the contradiction of the various "Christian" religions, which assumed this title among themselves while at the same time asserting the existence of only one "true" church of Christ and vociferously claiming that The Church of Jesus Christ of Latter-day Saints was definitely not that church.

1853: 15 October, *Udgorn Seion* (*Zion's Trumpet*), pp. 250–53 (1,300 words). "Signs of the Last Days."

As he had done only a week before, John S. Davis elected to insert an article from the *Star of Gomer* in this issue of his periodical. The article, which appeared in the January 1827 issue of the *Star of Gomer*, was written by "R. from the North" and focuses on the topic of signs of the last days. By including this article, Davis again shows that the Baptists had the right idea but that their interpretation of the scriptures was faulty. Davis quotes the following from R. from the North:

> There is no scriptural basis for calling anyone Christian except those who profess the faith and willingly agree to keep everything commanded by Christ; and woe betide the world when men put light in place of darkness, and sweet for bitter; and shout that there is delight and peace, when destruction is near and at the doors.[28]

By using this quote without commentary, Davis implies that the term *Christian* can be applied to only The Church of Jesus Christ of Latter-day Saints—the only church that implements the teachings of the Savior in the way they were intended.

1853: 8 October, *Cardiff and Merthyr Guardian*, p. 2 (200 words).

An account of a priest administering last rites to a dying woman. The priest said:

> After I had finished prayer, one of her family (who is a Mormonite and also a preacher with them) seemed very desirous to argue with me, on the fitness of men to be priests, according to the order of Moses and Aaron, and such other views as they hold. But I said, "Sir, this is not a fitting place to have controversy. My duties are with the dying, and the only priesthood I can now talk of is after the order of Melchizedek, He, who is our great High Priest; and if you are a Christian man, you will be more anxious to pray to that great High Priest to hear our prayers, and save the soul of this poor dying woman." This put an end to the wished-for controversy, and in a few moments after, the poor woman died.

1853: 26 November, *North Wales Chronicle*, p. 6 (60 words). "Amenities of Yankee Journalism."

> The *New York Tribune*, in an elaborate article on the Mormons, defends bigamy out-and-out. This is rather odd for a "reform paper."—*Lowell Journal and Courier*. "The *Lowell Journal and Courier*, in an unelaborate article on progress, tells a lie out-and-out. This is not at all odd for a paper that needs reforming."—*New York Tribune*.

Episode 10.3

Start: An English source in Wales provides information about the Latter-day Saints in America

1853: October, *Welsh Calvinistic Methodist Record*, pp. 225–29, item 1 (2,875 words). "Mormonism. The Parentage and More Private Life of Joe Smith."

The following introduction precedes this first of three articles on the topic of Mormonism:

> As the abettors of "the last and lowest" religious imposture are displaying renewed activity in various parts of Wales, we will lay before our readers in this and two or three succeeding numbers a few facts respecting the false prophet and his sect.

1853: December, *Welsh Calvinistic Methodist Record*, pp. 269–74, item 2 (2,960 words). "Mormonism. Alleged Discovery of the Book of Mormon."

Here is a portion of the opening paragraph for this second article:

> "Evil men and seducers," wrote Paul to Timothy, "shall wax worse and worse, deceiving and being deceived." A more impressive illustration of the truth contained in these words cannot be taken out of modern history than that supplied by the career of the impostor Joe Smith. Being a dissolute character, his idle habits led him to resort to the most unscrupulous shifts for the purpose of securing the means of sensual gratification. He therefore found it necessary to add lying to idleness and drunkenness.

1854: February, *Welsh Calvinistic Methodist Record*, pp. 27–32, item 3 (2,915 words). "Mormonism. Advance of the Sect up to the Death of Smith."

Here is a portion of the opening paragraph for this third and final article:

> In this portion of the history of the Mormons, we shall see the growth of the love of power in the mind of the false prophet, leading to the practice of deceit on a larger scale and with more audacity as well as more tact than ever.

All three articles in this Carmarthen-based, English-language periodical consist of quotations from various English-language sources; however, aside from the editor's reflections as quoted above, these articles contain nothing pertinent to Wales or to the Welsh.

End: An English source in Wales provides information about the Latter-day Saints in America

1853: November, *Dynoethiad Mormoniaeth; yn cynwys Hanes Joseph Smith, Saith Gradd y Deml, Gwreigiaeth Ysbrydol, yn nghyda'r Seremoniau a arferir ar Dderbyniad i'r Urdd hono. O Enau Tystion Profedig.* (*Exposure of Mormonism; Containing the History of Joseph Smith, Seven Degrees of the Temple, Spiritual Wifery, Together with the Ceremonies That Are Used on Acceptance into That Order. From the Mouths of Proven Witnesses*), pamphlet, 44 pages.

In his foreword, dated November 1853, "The Levite" gives his place of residence as Ystradgynlais (though no other identifying information) and describes his motive for producing this pamphlet:

> The current situation of our compatriots in their relationship with Mormonism is sufficient reason for calling attention to the subject. No matter how stupid and foolish this religion is, how senseless its followers are, and how low and contemptuous are the one and the other in the opinion of the best men of the world, since there are souls being enticed by them, it is good to try to do something to head off the calamity. And we cannot think of anything better than to present an open description of the life and religion of the Mormons before our friends, from the mouths of credible witnesses, and allow them to judge for themselves. We have selected that which is seen on the following pages from several English-language books published in America, with a wide circulation—read by a host

> of Mormons, who dare not refute their veracity. We have made extensive use of a critical article in the *British and Foreign Evangelical Review* of one of the books referred to above.

The historical information about Joseph Smith contained in pages 5–17 appears to have been borrowed from the writings of Eber D. Howe and a variety of other sources. Publications by John Van Dusen, an excommunicated Latter-day Saint, are the source for pages 17–35. He and his wife had participated in the ceremonies performed in the Nauvoo Temple during its brief use in late 1845 and early 1846. They published their recollections, along with some possible embellishments of their experience, and sold them for a substantial amount of money in New York. The commentary in pages 35–41 is inserted to answer the question "What are the religious tenets of the Mormons?" Several passages from the Doctrine and Covenants are used to provide information about Latter-day Saint teachings. Pages 41–44 contain the oft-used tale of the missionary who pretended to be dead after spending the night at the home of a kind family. The next morning, two of his colleagues claimed they could raise him from the dead, at which point the head of the house raised the missionary from his bed by threatening to cut off the missionary's head with a knife.

No response to this pamphlet is to be found in *Zion's Trumpet* or in a separate publication. Nor has any commentary in religious or secular publications from other enemies of The Church of Jesus Christ of Latter-day Saints been identified.

Episode 10.4

Start: The Anglicans and Nonconformists blame each other regarding the increase of the Latter-day Saints

1853: 12 November, *Silurian*, p. 4 (540 words about the Latter-day Saints).

A long and very sarcastic letter dated 25 October 1853 and written by David Rees, editor of the Congregationalist periodical the *Revivalist*. The letter, which was directed to the Anglican bishop of Llandaff, was written in answer to the bishop's lecture given recently in the Cardiff town hall and entitled "What to do about the Nonconformists?" Neither the Baptists nor any of the other Nonconformists were in "conformity" with the Catholic beliefs or those of the Church of England. Nonconformity had largely supplanted the Church of England throughout Wales by the mid-eighteenth century, and the Welsh became a "chapel-going" people. Those who remained members of the Church of England went to "church." Thus, the Anglican bishop of Llandaff posed the question as to what the Anglicans were to do with the Nonconformists. David Rees, a Congregationalist, answered the bishop's question with one of his own:

> Pray, what, my Lord, can there be in you, or in your creed, or in your sect, to fit you to take our places on the field of contest, in order to counteract the evils that are said to be now overwhelming, or are about to overspread the country? What particular adaptation is there in your social position, in your religious

> formulas, or in your general habits and arrangements, as a body corporate, to meet the exigency of the case, and to cast out those sturdy devils which are said to be about to defeat the united armies of Dissent?

Rees counseled the bishop:

> Of a truth, my Lord, I would advise you to stand aloof, lest they should answer you as a similar tribe answered the sons of Sceva, "Jesus we know, and the Dissenters we know, but who are ye?" and prevail against you.

Rees pointedly asked the bishop, "What can you do to cast out Mormonism?" Then Rees went on to compare this new religion to that of the Anglicans:

> Are the Mormons not your offspring? Do they not bear your image? Have they not a baptismal regeneration like you? Do they not anoint the sick like you? Have they no confirmation like you? Have they no apostolical succession like you? Do they not claim the exclusive right of preaching like you? Can they not remit sins like you? Have they not holy orders like you? Have they not the right to confer the Holy Ghost like you? The common prayer book contains everything the Saints profess to receive from the book of Mormon. Is it supposable that these Satans can be cast out by Satans of precisely the same nature? Whom could you, my Lord, depute from your ranks to encounter that terrible heresy—the denial of the existence of the devil? Your chief instructor through the press is, I am told, an heretic on this point. You have not heard that any minister or editor of the orthodox sects is so presumptuous as to inculcate such a heresy; but, if I am misinformed, Brutus is not a fit person to be entrusted with the task of establishing the doctrine of the entity of his Satanic Majesty. It is no wonder if there are few on the Hills wicked enough to follow Brutus in this heresy.

The negative comments about "Brutus" are directed at David Owen, the editor of the Anglican periodical the *Sun*. David Owen had used his nom de plume, Brutus, since the time he was an ordained Baptist minister in his twenties and was responsible for four chapels in North Wales. But when he appealed for financial aid from the Unitarian Association, claiming that his congregations had accepted Unitarian beliefs, he was expelled from the Baptists and became an Independent. Then in 1835, at age forty, he was given the editorship of the *Sun* and became an Anglican.

In the December 1853 issue of his periodical, Owen presents a seven-page rebuttal to the attacks which David Rees had leveled against the bishop of Llandaff through the *Revivalist*.[29] Regarding Rees's comparison of the Anglicans to the "Mormons," Owen elected not to defend the Anglicans against such offensive charges; rather, he opted to counterattack the Nonconformists. To do so, he quoted from an article by "Eta Delta" (Evan Davies) in the June 1851 issue of the *Revivalist*:[30]

> As Nonconformists and other Dissenters in Wales, we have cause to lament, to humble ourselves, and to repent, especially before God, for the apathetic and stagnant condition of the churches in our midst, and because of the darkness and ignorance of the country in general. We have no room to boast or take comfort; rather to be ashamed, to weep, and to fear greatly! Despite all the houses of worship, the schools, ministers, preachers, deacons, Sabbath School teachers, all the hundreds of manifold congregations, and thousands of religious

> communicants or those who profess religion—yet many are seen turning to Catholicism, yes, different kinds of Catholicism! And worse, and even more contemptible than the Catholics are the Mormons. . . . It is my understanding that there are hundreds of Welsh who have accepted Mormonism, to their worldly and eternal ruin![31]

Owen also quotes from another article by Eta Delta in the December 1851 issue of the *Revivalist*:[32]

> It is intensely lamentable that our Nation is so blind, unconcerned about the truth, and religiously unfeeling. It is said that our *Magistrates* grant licenses to them to preach the gospel, as if they [the Mormons] were proper Christians![33]

There is no evidence in John S. Davis's published writings that he was even aware of this dispute between Brutus and David Rees. But there is also the possibility that he was, indeed, very much aware of the dispute and decided to enjoy the quarrel while ignoring it in his publications.

1853: 16 November, *Yr Amserau* (*Times*), p. 2 (540 words in the segments about the Latter-day Saints).

This article is a Welsh translation of David Rees's letter published in the *Silurian*, 12 November 1853.

1853: November, *Y Diwygiwr* (*Revivalist*), pp. 350–54 (540 words in the segments about the Latter-day Saints).

This article is another Welsh version of David Rees's letter that appears in the *Silurian*, 12 November 1853. Since David Rees was the editor of the *Revivalist* at the time, it is entirely possible that he wrote the English version to be printed in the *Silurian*, an English-language publication, as well as the Welsh version for his own Welsh-language publication.

End: The Anglicans and Nonconformists blame each other regarding the increase of the Latter-day Saints

1853: 7 December, *Yr Amserau* (*Times*), p. 3 (130 words).

A brief story taken from the *Deseret News*, the newspaper published in Salt Lake City, Utah. Here is the story:

> A woman was walking along, and a man looked at her and followed her. The woman said, "Why are you following me?" "Because I have fallen in love with you," was the response. The woman asked, "What is the reason you have fallen in love with me? My sister is much prettier than I. She is coming after me; go and love her." The man turned back and saw a woman coming who was far uglier than the first. After being greatly disappointed, he went back again to the first and asked her why she had lied. The woman answered, "You also lied; for if you loved me, why did you go to the other woman?" The man was confused. It is easy for us to believe this.

Although this story does not specifically mention The Church of Jesus Christ of Latter-day Saints, by inference the story depicts members of the Church negatively.

1853: 24 December, *Caernarvon and Denbigh Herald*, p. 10 (21 words).
The Mormons intend to surround Great Salt Lake City with a wall, to protect themselves from the attacks of the Indians.

1853: 31 December, *Caernarvon and Denbigh Herald*, p. 7 (165 words).
An account of the massacre of Captain Gunnison and some of his exploring party by several Indians on Sevier River.

Notes

1. *Zion's Trumpet*, 15 July 1854, 418.
2. Robyn Ddu Eryri, *Teithiau a Barddoniaeth Robyn Ddu Eryri (Travels and Poetry of Robyn Ddu Eryri)*, 1857.
3. John C. Bennett, *History of the Saints: An Exposé of Joe Smith and Mormonism* (Boston: Leland & Whiting, 1842), 176–79.
4. *Methodist*, January 1853, 17.
5. Ibid.
6. Eber D. Howe, *Mormonism Unvailed* [*sic*] (Painesville, OH: self-pub., 1834).
7. *Sun*, April 1853, 142–45.
8. *Sun*, June 1853, 207–9.
9. Howe, *Mormonism Unvailed* [*sic*], 235–36; *Sun*, February 1853, 67 (translation).
10. *Sun*, February 1853, 67.
11. John W. Gunnison, *The Mormons, or, Latter-day Saints, in the Valley of the Great Salt Lake* (Philadelphia: J. B. Lippincott, 1852).
12. *American Messenger*, March 1853, 91.
13. Ibid.
14. *Zion's Trumpet*, 23 April 1853, 271.
15. Ibid.
16. *Wesleyan Treasury*, April 1853, 129.
17. Ibid.
18. *Millennial Star*, August 1847, 231–33.
19. Ibid., 232.
20. Ibid.
21. Ibid.
22. Ibid.
23. Ibid.
24. *Sun*, June 1853, 231.
25. *Zion's Trumpet*, 24 September 1853, 209.
26. Ibid.
27. Edward Morgan Humphreys, "Parry, Robert (Robyn Ddu Eryri; 1804–1892), poet," in *Dictionary of Welsh Biography* (online).
28. *Zion's Trumpet*, 15 October 1853, 253.
29. *Sun*, December 1853, 421–27.
30. *Revivalist*, June 1851, 176–77.
31. Ibid., 176.
32. *Revivalist*, December 1851, 298–300.
33. Ibid., 299.

Chapter 11

Episodes

11.1—A false rumor is printed that Dan Jones's brother was baptized, but Jones debunks it
11.2—Rees Davies accuses the Saints from New Orleans, and Dan Jones defends from Merthyr

Salient Events

- **1 January 1854**. Dan Jones replaces William Phillips as president of the Church in Wales. He selects two old friends, Thomas Jeremy and Daniel Daniels, as his counselors. Jones also replaces his protégé, John S. Davis, as the editor of *Zion's Trumpet*.
- **4 February 1854**. The *Golconda* leaves Liverpool with 464 Welsh and English converts on board. Among the 264 Welsh are William Phillips and John S. Davis and their families. Three persons who had intended to be on board were Hannah Daniels Job and two of her daughters—six-year-old Mary and four-month-old Ann. Hannah's husband Thomas had convinced her to make the journey and had already paid the money for their passage. But as the time for departure drew near, Hannah changed her mind and declared to Thomas that she and the children would remain in Wales. She took the children to Carmarthen to live with her parents after their house had been sold. Thomas went one last time to the home of his in-laws hoping to persuade his wife to change her mind. When he saw six-year-old Mary and two-year-old Elizabeth in front of their grandparents' house, he attempted to take them both with him. But Mary ran from him, and he was able to get only Elizabeth. With her in his arms, he managed to get to the steamer in Carmarthen Bay that would take them to Liverpool to board the *Golconda*. Once they had crossed the

ocean and the plains and had arrived in Salt Lake City, Thomas sent letters to Hannah back in Wales, still trying to convince her to bring Mary and Ann to join him. Two years later, she decided to make the journey. On 19 April 1856, she sailed on the *S. Curling*, but only Mary was with her, as Ann had died nearly two years earlier. Her happiness at seeing Thomas in Salt Lake was brief. When he informed her that he had married a second wife the year before and already had a child with her, Hannah opted for divorce. Three months later, she married Albert Miles, a widower with three children, and eventually bore him eight more children. Years later, a granddaughter asked her whether she was happy with her decision to part company with Thomas Job. She confessed that she was sorry not to have stayed with him. Some years later, Thomas converted to the Reorganized Church of Jesus Christ of Latter-day Saints and became that Church's most successful missionary in Utah and Idaho.[1]

- **25 March 1854**. On this date, Dan Jones is happy to print in *Zion's Trumpet* a letter from Thomas Jones, a new convert living in Carmarthen.[2] Thomas Jones tells of his conversion:

> I was 40 years a member with the Baptists; and when I heard about the Saints, I decided to oppose them as far as I was able. I intended to cut off the head of the Saints with their own sword; and for that purpose, I reviewed their books: but the more I searched their doctrinal principles, the more I went along with them, believing the truth, and I received my baptism.[3]

He also tells of the "bitter treatment" he received from his family, but he is especially pleased to relate the following success:

> One whom I baptized is the brother who is known as "the Reverend David Davies," Porth Cawl, a minister with the Independents. He received a witness and much persecution for proclaiming that [witness]. Saturday night, the 19th of this month, I baptized the Reverend John James, a minister of the Baptists, in Cefncoedycymmer, together with a young preacher who belonged to the same house of worship.[4]

- **29 March 1854**. The *Swansea Herald* reports that the Reverend J. Jones of Llangollen had been baptized by Dan Jones, his younger brother. The latter vehemently denies that any such baptism of his older brother ever took place and scolds those behind the false rumor. The Swansea Branch records show a baptism for Sarah Jones, the reverend's daughter on 12 April 1854, and for his wife, Jane, and his other daughter, Elizabeth, four days later on 16 April 1854. However, the record does not show a baptism for the reverend himself. That he may have been considering going to Utah is implied in a 19 September 1854 letter written by Dan Jones to Brigham Young. See Episode 11.1.
- **8 July 1854**. A statistical report in this issue of *Zion's Trumpet*[5] for the first six months of 1854 shows the total number of members in Wales at the time was 4,318. Emigration, along with excommunications, would certainly be part of the cause of the decrease from previous numbers. Also included in the statistics are 248 excommunications, 50 deaths, and 236 emigrants.

Conference	Branches	Baptisms	Members	President
East Glamorgan	32	160	1,887	D. Jones
West Glamorgan	18	38	462	R. Evans
Monmouthshire	19	86	578	T. D. Giles
Breconshire	7	15	151	T. Morgan
Llanelli	10	24	288	D. E. Jones
Carmarthen	6	7	157	Thos. Jones
North Pembroke	4	0	57	David Rees
South Pembroke	13	8	210	John Price
Cardiganshire	5	11	113	J. Evans
Merionethshire	6	2	76	J. Davies
Flintshire	5	8	115	John Jones
Denbighshire	6	13	125	John Parry
Conway Valley	5	6	99	R. Roberts

- **15 July 1854**. A 30 November 1853 letter from Job Rowlands to his brother Ephraim is printed in *Zion's Trumpet*.[6] Job had been a member of the Caersalem Baptist chapel in Dowlais, where the Reverend W. R. Davies presided. It was Davies's comments about Dan Jones that had prompted Rowlands and his family members to leave Davies's congregation and receive baptism at the hands of the Latter-day Saints: "Mr. Davies said one time in our house that his desire was to do the same with their elders as was done to Joseph Smith, that is to kill them." Rowlands, his mother, and two of his brothers had emigrated in 1849 on board the *Buena Vista*. This letter is typical of a number of other such letters that had appeared in *Zion's Trumpet*. It begins with Rowland's acknowledgement of having received Ephraim's letter dated 28 September 1854, an indication of the two-month period generally required for letters between Utah and Wales. Rowlands tells Ephraim that he could expect to emigrate from Wales in the spring of 1855, an indication that family members already in Utah were working to send financial assistance to those in Wales who wished to emigrate. Rowlands then reports his "wealth at present": "a fine house worth three or four hundred dollars, two cows, two yoke of oxen, two mules, one horse, three wagons, three pigs, and twenty-three acres of land." Such reports motivated relatives back in Wales to make the journey to Utah so they too could be landowners, an absolute impossibility for them in their homeland, where their highest hope was to rent land. At the end of his letter, Rowlands sends regards to his sister and her husband, hoping that they had changed their minds about the Church, as well as his regards to other relatives and friends.
- **24 July 1854.** Thomas John, a forty-year-old passenger on the *Buena Vista* five years earlier, puts his "X" on a letter of this date directed to Dan Jones. He tells of the difficulty he had been experiencing to "have any peace of

conscience, until I recognized my faults against you, so I beg for your forgiveness." Following this letter in the *Zion's Trumpet* issue is a brief note by Thomas Jeremy in which he vouches for John, declaring him to be "truly repentant" for all he had done against Jones. In his answer, Jones declares: "It is said that there is joy among the angels of God for *every* sinner who repents, and we ourselves feel joy in reporting that we can forgive Thomas John in light of his repentance, *even though* his sins were as scarlet."[7]

- **3 August 1854.** The *Welsh Hero* prints correspondence written by Rees Davies, a young Welshman in New Orleans, to his father in Wales. In his letters, Davies makes many scurrilous accusations against the Latter-day Saints who had arrived in New Orleans on 18 March 1854 on board the *Golconda*. One of his accounts involved an eighteen-year-old girl named Margaret Williams asking him to "take her somewhere away from the Mormons." He claims to have taken her to a Mrs. Hughes, where she stayed on as a nursemaid. The following day, he says he went to her previous home "to fetch her clothes" and that "the Mormons were ready to kill me." Dan Jones responded to these and other claims by publishing a twelve-page pamphlet entitled *Defense of the Saints*.[8] See Episode 11.2.
- **12 August 1854.** Beginning on this date, *Zion's Trumpet* is published every other week until the final issue of 1857, then weekly until its demise in April 1862. Only seventeen issues printed during 1858–61 have survived: three from 1858, five from 1859, six from 1860, and three from 1861. Evidence from these issues strongly suggests that a complete volume was published for each of these years, but none of these volumes are extant in complete form.[9]
- **26 August 1854.** *Zion's Trumpet* prints the report of Daniel Spencer, counselor to President Samuel W. Richards, after he gave a "second examination to several accusations brought against President D. Jones." The examination, at the "wish of John Jones and others," was to determine whether Dan Jones had abused his office in any way. After a "patient hearing lasting many hours, of all that could be raked together against him," President Spencer reports that "I am happy to be able to say that they completely failed to prove any accusation or transgression in him of a single law of God or man; rather through it all, the behavior of Elder D. Jones appears to be very satisfactory to me and in the eyes of the Lord; yet suspicious men, blinded with envy, have falsely accused him!"[10]
- **28 August 1854.** Thomas Jeremy writes a letter to Dan Jones. Jeremy had been a firm and faithful friend to Jones since Jeremy's baptism in Llanybydder, Carmarthenshire, more than eight years earlier on 3 March 1846. (It was in Jeremy's house in Glantrenfawr that meetings were held and where a blessing of healing was given to Daniel Jones, the blind man who shouted out during the blessing that "he had come to see the candle in the candlestick on the table."[11]) In his letter, Jeremy congratulates Jones on the vindication he had recently received from President Spencer. Jeremy also confirms his fidelity to his longtime friend: "It is a comfort to me that I have done my best by you and have agreed with you in all things, and my

unshakeable determination is to strive to carry your counsels into action, according to the power and the wisdom the Lord gives me." And most certainly the beleaguered Jones was comforted by his friend's letter, since he printed it in *Zion's Trumpet* the following October.[12]

- **9 September 1854**. *Zion's Trumpet* is printed in Swansea for the first time. In his announcement of the change, Dan Jones sounds jubilant and hopeful that the change will provide an improvement in his health:

  > After lengthy preparations, at long last we are able to date our *Trumpet* from Swansea! Whether it sounds more loudly or with a clearer voice, let the hearing of its users be the judge. At least we are confident that the customary clean air of the sea will clear the voice of its *Trumpeter*, and probably his friends will join with him in wishing that the giver of lives will strengthen his constitution, so as to arouse the sleepy inhabitants of our country to flee from the imminent destruction, to the safe place, before it pours out upon them. Not without feelings besides those we are describing—not without fond memories, and not without pondering over the religious feasts we enjoyed in Merthyr and its environs can we leave, nor shall we forget our dear coworkers in the vineyard of our Jesus, our desire for their benefit will be no less than our *Trumpet blast* to comfort them, and it will not be long, we trust, before we have the great pleasure of joining hand and voice in unison to convey the praises of our God, until it echoes from the borders of beloved Zion.[13]

Several weeks before the move to Swansea and the reduction of *Zion's Trumpet* to a biweekly publication, Jones's right-hand man Robert Parry (Robin Ddu Eryri) had left South Wales on a mission to North Wales and is never again mentioned in the periodical. Such a loss may have constituted, to some extent, at least, the decision to reduce *Zion's Trumpet*'s frequency from weekly to biweekly.

- **23 September 1854**. R. Evans asks if there are plans for a second printing of the *Scriptural Treasury*, a 288-page book of scriptural commentary published six years earlier in 1848. A surprised Dan Jones replies that hundreds of the first printing had been on hand for years and urges all the missionaries and leaders in Wales to get a copy.[14]
- **1 October 1854.** Two Latter-day Saint elders, David Jeremy and Daniel Francis, are viciously attacked by an angry mob as they preach in the area of the Saron Chapel, near the town of Brechfa, Carmarthenshire.[15]
- **4 November 1854.** The first *eisteddfod* specifically for Latter-day Saints, organized by Dewi Elfed Jones with permission from the Welsh presidency, is announced in *Zion's Trumpet* (see Episode 8.2). The eisteddfod is a long-standing tradition in Wales in which people are invited to enter various competitions, such as poetry, singing, recitation, and the like. In this invitation for competitors, Jones presents the topics, prizes, and other details of the event, to be held on Christmas Day. The tradition of the Welsh eisteddfod was carried on in Utah for a time, as well as in Malad City, Idaho, where the number of Welsh settlers was substantial.

Commentary

1854: 20 January, *Monmouthshire Merlin*, p. 2 (180 words). "The Great Salt Lake." A brief description of the area and the settlers.

1854: 4 February, *Cardiff and Merthyr Guardian*, p. 3 (100 words). "The Latter-day Saints."

> Mormonism still retains its hold on a considerable number of the working men of this place, and large numbers are wistfully turning their longing eyes to that holy land which borders on the Great Salt Lake. One part of the Merthyr Mormonites took their departure for this Western Canaan on Friday last; and many others were anxious to have gone. This is another of the signs of the times, which we commend to the serious consideration of the religious world, for the existence of such infatuation surely indicates that there is "something rotten in the state of Denmark."

1854: 4 February, *Monmouthshire Beacon*, p. 8 (80 words). "The Mormons."

> On Saturday morning last, about 250 men, women, and children, from the neighboring hills passed through Newport, *en route* to Liverpool, there to embark for the Mormon's Land of promise—the valley of the Great Salt Lake. By Mr. Mann's report upon the various forms of religious worship at present existing in this country, it is stated that there are at least 30,000 persons in England belonging to the Mormon community, and that 20,000 have already departed.

1854: 4 February, *Monmouthshire Beacon*, p. 4 (130 words). "A Freight of Mormonites."

> On Sunday morning last, the Newport up train arrived at the Abergavenny station, when the unusual number of carriages attached caused no little excitement to the parties collected at the station. It appeared that the carriages contained between 200 and 300 of those deluded fanatics called Latter-day Saints, who were proceeding to Liverpool, from whence they take their departure for the Salt Lake River [sic], to join the wolves in sheep's clothing; who inform them that upon their arrival at their place of destination, they will not only lead a heavenly life, but that their deceased relatives will be restored to them and live together as they formerly did. Nearly the whole of these deluded creatures are natives of Glamorgan and Monmouthshire.

1854: 4 February, *Silurian*, p. 2 (55 words). "Emigration of Mormons."

> About 300 of these infatuated people, disciples of Joe Smith, known by the title of Mormons, or Latter-day Saints, from this neighborhood and Merthyr, left Cardiff, on Friday evening, by South Wales Railway for Liverpool, from which port they intended to sail on Wednesday last, in several ships, for the Salt Lake.

1854: 4 February, *Caernarvon and Denbigh Herald*, p. 6 (70 words). "Aberystwyth. Latter-day Saints."

> The *Zephyr* steamer took, on Friday last, about 20 persons, converts to Mormonism, to Liverpool, intending to emigrate to the Salt Lake City. They were all from the neighborhood of Llanarth in this county, with the exception

of one from this town, who had been in service at Llanarth, and married one of the Saints. There were old women about 80 years of age among the emigrants.

1854: 18 February, *Silurian*, p. 3 (38 words).

In a tract distributed by the Mormon preachers, the following question and answer occur.—"What shall be the reward of those who have forsaken their wives for righteousness' sake?—A hundred-fold of wives here and wives everlasting hereafter."[16]

1854: 4 March, *Caernarvon and Denbigh Herald*, p. 7 (220 words).

Reprinted from the *Leeds Mercury*. J. M. Browne of Northallerton sends an extract of a letter received from his brother in St. Louis, dated 15 Jan 1854. The brother tells of his "delusion" after four years with the "Mormons."

1854: 25 March, *Udgorn Seion* (*Zion's Trumpet*), pp. 190–91.

Thomas Jones, the author of this letter to Dan Jones, tells of his conversion:

> I was forty years a member with the Baptists; and when I heard about the Saints, I decided to oppose them as far as I was able. I intended to cut off the head of the Saints with their own sword; and for that purpose, I reviewed their books. But the more I searched their doctrinal principles, the more I went along with them believing the truth, and I received my baptism.[17]

Despite receiving considerable persecution from his family and his "old religious friends," Jones began to preach his new beliefs. He reports:

> I had the privilege of baptizing several; and since it happened that I baptized some well-known men, perhaps you will permit me to name them, so that the reading of their names may lead other men, like them, to consider and perceive a little of the value of the religion of the Son of God.[18]

He tells of baptizing the Reverend John James, a Baptist minister in Cefncoedycymmer, "together with a young preacher who belonged to the same house of worship." He also tells of a meeting held the morning after the baptisms:

> Brother J. James met with the people, in the Chapel of the Baptists, the next morning, for the purpose of terminating their obligation with one another; and a host came together in the afternoon, to witness the confirmation of the two brothers.[19]

He also tells of the baptism of "a young student enrolled in the school [in Carmarthen] where preachers are taught by men":

> He was confirmed at the water's edge; he gave himself to earnest prayer; and within forty-eight hours, he had a clear witness; but, because he spoke of what the Lord had done to his soul, he was turned out of the school, the chapel, and the house of his father![20]

These conversions may have been the cause of the alarm expressed by the author of an article in the July 1854 issue of the *Churchman* (see entry later in this chapter).

Episode 11.1

Start: A false rumor is printed that Dan Jones's brother was baptized, but Jones debunks it

1854: 15 April, *Udgorn Seion* (*Zion's Trumpet*), pp. 226–27 (365 words). "Refutation to a False Accusation."

The editor of *Zion's Trumpet* at this time was Dan Jones, back in Wales on his second mission. Here he is taking issue with an announcement that had appeared in the 29 March 1854 issue of the *Swansea Herald*. Jones quotes the following from that publication:

> That the people of Aberdare marvel because of a circumstance that took place lately—the Rev. Mr. Jones, better known by the name of "Jones, Llangollen," was immersed by one of the "Apostles of the Latter-day Saints." What next?[21]

Jones responds to this allegation regarding his older brother, John Jones:

> We answer that it is totally untrue—completely unfounded, without reason, without even any excuse for it; rather it was evil malice that caused anyone to believe or publish such a thing. . . . Had he acted according to our counsel he would have been baptized years ago, or had he known what was best for his own good.[22]

Though John Jones had not been baptized, he had allowed Dan Jones to use his press to print materials in support of The Church of Jesus Christ of Latter-day Saints (to which Dan had converted only three years earlier) during the time John Jones was living in the village of Rhydybont in the county of Carmarthenshire. These materials included twenty-eight issues of *Prophet of the Jubilee*, the periodical for which Dan Jones was editor from July 1846 to October 1848.

John Jones's family had been baptized right around the time of this printing. The Swansea Branch records for 1854 show the baptisms for Sarah Jones on 12 April and for Elizabeth Jones and Jane Jones on 16 April. Sarah and Elizabeth were John Jones's daughters, and Jane Jones was his wife. These three women sailed on the *Chimborazo* the following year, but they ended up in Ohio instead of Utah. John Jones joined them in Ohio, where he died in 1856. That his intention may at one time have been to settle in Utah is implied in Dan Jones's 19 September 1854 letter to Brigham Young (original English spelling has been preserved):

> I am happy to be able to introduce two of my Brotheren to Zion, hopeing [sic] that if they feel as they ought and as others do, they will be of service in the upbuilding of Zion. The Elder is called a scientific character and classed among the "literati" of Wales, of many years experience as Coal (Master) Iron manufacturing and is said to be some thing of a mineralogist, &c. But you will be able to analyse him soon no doubt and make him usefull I hope. The other is a Botanist and has had several years experience in some of the principal Gardens of England, one reason why he did not like to reside at Manti in preference to G.S.L. City, but I presume he will be subject to your counsels should you deem him worthy of them.[23]

The first of the two "Brotheren" mentioned is John, Dan's older brother by nine years, and the other is Edward, Dan's older brother by seven years. Edward Jones had left Wales in February 1854 on the *Golconda* with his wife and three children and ended up in Ephraim, Utah. His family would live there until their deaths.

End: A false rumor is printed that Dan Jones's brother was baptized, but Jones debunks it

1854: 8 April, *Udgorn Seion* (*Zion's Trumpet*), pp. 201–4 (1,380 words). "The Mormons."

Dan Jones quotes an entire article from what he calls "some little paper that is called *Press*," apparently published in Aberystwyth, Cardiganshire. Here is the article:

> These pitiful people are rushing from their country in droves toward the vicinity of the Salt Lake. To swell the ranks, on the 28th of last month, several were seen starting from this town on board a steamboat to Liverpool, with the intention of heading toward the imaginary Canaan across the ocean. In their midst was an old woman, 87 years old, who professed her strong confidence of seeing her old husband (who was buried years ago) after landing there, and presenting him with warm stockings, which, to prove the truth of her faith, she had gone to the trouble of knitting, to warm the feet of one who had become cold so long ago. I can hardly praise the behavior of these people, for if they believe the truth of their religion, they should, before being worthy of Canaan, strive more than they have done on behalf of their fellow men, in order to enlighten them about the desirability of the blessed place, instead of turning their backs at once and leaving them so destitute in the old wilderness. Alas and alack! we have been surprised over and over again that anyone in the enlightened land of the Sunday schools would give credence to such a concoction of unscriptural nonsense! It shows that we have a great work yet to do, to enlighten and establish the country in the simple and priceless principles of true Christianity.[24]

Jones responds to this vicious attack with an equally vicious counterattack in his own periodical:

> It [the above article] is a mirror, then, in which he is seen from his crown to his sole, and in it one can detect the unclean, lying stench of the atrocious pit of his stomach.[25]

Not being personally acquainted with the editor of "*Press*," nor with anyone in that area of Wales, Jones is left to draw his conclusions simply from the content of the article:

> His story was formed from libelous materials, woven and entwined together, every thread of it, from the coarse hemp of slander—Mr. Editor, the weaver, and the *Press* from Aberystwyth is the loom that weaves it. . . . If this is the kind of editors the Sunday schools of Cardiganshire turn out, may the God of truth keep the literature of our country out of the reach of the ruinous stench of their breath.[26]

1854: 28 April, *Cardiff and Merthyr Guardian*, p. 4 (95 words).

Reprinted from the *Baton Rouge Advocate*:

> The *John Simonds*, a three-decker steamer, running to St. Louis, passed our landing yesterday with about 800 emigrants on board, all bound for the Mormon settlement at Utah. They are composed, we were told, nearly exclusively of English and Welsh converts to the Mormon religion and morality (or immorality), under the guidance of one of the Latter-day Saints, who has been on a missionary tour to Great Britain. About half, or more than half, the number were women, mostly young and buxom-looking lasses. What were their views of spiritual matrimony we did not ascertain.

1854: 29 April, *Silurian*, p. 2 (115 words).

> The new number of the *Edinburgh Review* has a good long article on those strange people the Mormons. It appears they have had more converts in England than elsewhere, and that the places in which they have gained the greatest number have been Manchester and Merthyr Tydfil. The reviewer shows it is not want of education that makes men Mormons, and [he] also hints that many victims of this imposture might have been saved had our popular teachers taught their hearers to draw the line of separation between the religion of the Old Testament and that of the [N]ew. There is some truth in these remarks, and the whole article is well worthy [of] perusal.

1854: 5 May, *Monmouthshire Merlin*, p. 6 (95 words).

Reprinted from the *Baton Rouge Advocate*:

> The *John Simmonds*, a three-decker steamer, running to St. Louis passed our landing yesterday with about 800 emigrants on board, all bound for the Mormon settlement at Utah. They are composed, we were told, nearly exclusively of English and Welsh converts to the Mormon religion and morality (or immorality), under the guidance of one of the Latter-day Saints, who has been on a missionary tour to Great Britain. About half, or more than one half, the number were women, mostly young and buxom-looking lasses. What were their views of spiritual matrimony we did not ascertain.

1854: 13 May, *North Wales Chronicle*, p. 5 (125 words).

> Aberystwyth. On Thursday last a lecture was delivered, by the Rev. William Williams, in Zoar Chapel, Aberystwyth; the subject being the "false doctrines of Mormonism, and their Salt Lake Valley." Several of the Mormonites came there for the purpose of having a debate on the subject, which Mr. Williams would not allow. Among the Saints was the noted Robin Ddu who visited this town a few years ago, and who lectured then on total abstinence, being then a member with the Independents, but who has been since converted to the Mormonial faith. On Tuesday, the 9th inst., the Saints held their meeting at the Assembly Rooms, for the purpose of disproving Mr. Williams's lecture, which they did in some unimportant parts, but left the leading facts untouched.

1854: 3 June, *Silurian*, p. 2 (70 words).

A brief report of Samuel Richards's appearance before a private committee on emigration in the House of Commons. Richards made a favorable impression on the committee:

> Mr. Richards gave his evidence in a straightforward manner, and earned and received the thanks of the committee in consequence. The impression seemed to be, that however objectionable Mormonism may be, still there was one thing they did decently and well, and that is carry their converts decently, and properly, and healthfully across the Atlantic. It is a pity only Mormonites may go out in these Mormon ships.

1854: 24 June, *Silurian*, p. 3 (25 words).

> The death of Clarissa, wife of John Smith, and mother of the Mormon imposter Joe Smith, is announced by the *Deseret News*. She was aged 63.

Obviously, Clarissa and John Smith were not Joseph Smith Jr.'s parents, but they were his aunt and uncle on his father's side. Both Clarissa and John passed away in the first half of 1854.

1854: 16 June, *Monmouthshire Merlin*, p. 6 (95 words).

> Lieutenant Gunnison states that, when he was in Utah, the three members of the Mormonite Presidency had no less than eighty-two wives between them, and that one of the three was called an old bachelor, "because he had only a baker's dozen." And Captain Stansbury describes the numerous family of the president (Brigham Young) as mingling freely in the balls, parties, and other social amusements of the place. Utah is now in the transition-state of a "Territory," containing somewhat above 30,000 inhabitants. During the fourteen years from 1837 to 1851, 17,000 Mormons had emigrated from England.

1854: 23 June, *Monmouthshire Merlin*, p. 2 (95 words).

A review of *The Great Highway: A Story of the World's Struggles*, a three-volume book recently published in London by S. W. Fullom. The writer makes some observations about what Fullom had to say about the Latter-day Saints:

> The author gives us a lengthened description of those deluded, but many of them deluding men called Latter-day Saints. He exposes their proceedings; and shows how the leaders of the movement make capital out of the ignorance, superstition, and degradation of the unenlightened masses. Mormonism tells a deplorable tale! It tells us, that nothing but audacity was wanting, to enable a man of some greatness, it must be confessed, though the greatness of a fiend, to set himself up as the founder of a religion, which now numbers above two millions of adherents.

1854: July, *Yr Eglwysydd* (*Churchman*), pp. 75–77 (1,105 words). "Mormonism."

The unnamed author draws on numerous English-language sources for the greater part of his writing. In his introduction, he expresses alarm at the growth of The Church of Jesus Christ of Latter-day Saints in Wales and especially that preachers numbered among the converts:

> As there were false prophets enticing the Israelites astray, so there are false teachers in our midst who are leading a host of learned and sensible men to all sorts of false religion and absurdity. Of the recent heresies or schisms, one of the most notable is Mormonism. However repugnant and despicable the doctrines contained in this deceitful system may be, many hundreds of Welsh people, yes, and *several Non-conformist preachers in Wales* have embraced them! We will give herein some of the story of "The Book of Mormon," or the *new bible* of the Latter-day Saints.[27]

The writer's concern may well have originated from preacher conversion in the area, details of which can be found in Thomas Jones's letter to Dan Jones that had been printed in *Zion's Trumpet* a few months earlier (see previous entry in this chapter).[28]

1854: 1 July, *Wrexham Advertiser*, p. 3 (40 words). "An Immoral Religion."

> In a tract distributed by the Mormon preachers, the following question and answer occur.—"What shall be the reward of those who have forsaken their

wives for righteousness' sake?—A hundred-fold of wives here and wives everlasting hereafter."[29]

1854: 3 August, *Y Gwron Cymreig* (*Welsh Hero*), p. 4, item 1 (85 words). "Mormons Leaving Abergele Last Year."

A poem of three four-line stanzas by "A Welshman." Here is the first stanza:

Fleeing from Abergele—flew,
Some swam in the guise of saints,
Who can say after they have moved further
That they will not sail after them?

Episode 11.2

Start: Rees Davies accuses the Saints from New Orleans, and Dan Jones defends from Merthyr

1854: 3 August, *Y Gwron Cymreig* (*Welsh Hero*), p. 4, item 2 (965 words). "Letters from America."

The first letter is dated 26 March 1854 and was sent from New Orleans by the writer, Rees Davies, to his father who lived in Cardiganshire. Upon seeing the letter, a member of The Church of Jesus Christ of Latter-day Saints expressed doubt to Davies's father about the claims made therein. Here is a list of the claims:

1. The Latter-day Saints marry the young little girls to the oldest old men.
2. If they are not willing, two of the elders take hold of the girl and put her in bed with the one who loves her most.
3. Many women run away from them here [in the United States].
4. Those who run away and are caught are tied up until the boat leaves New Orleans.
5. One girl named Margaret approached Rees Davies and asked him to take her away from the Latter-day Saints.
6. When Davies went to retrieve the girl's clothes from her home, the Latter-day Saints were ready to kill him.
7. Old Esther [Jones] was ready to come back to Wales if she could.

Because the Church member challenged the truthfulness of these claims, Rees Davies's father agreed to write a letter to his son in New Orleans to give him a chance to re-state his claims where necessary. The son wrote a reply, dated 10 June 1854, in which he expressed anger that anyone would doubt his claims. And in this second letter, he made the following additional claims:

1. He told Margaret about his father's letter.
2. The Latter-day Saints wrote home to her mother but would not allow Margaret to see the letter.
3. They would not allow Margaret to write a letter to her mother.
4. Margaret asked Davies to write to her mother and tell her that she was very sorry that she did not act on her advice to remain in Wales.
5. The Latter-day Saints took nearly all of Margaret's clothes.
6. They tied Margaret to the bed post to prevent her from going with Davies.

7. When Margaret was leaving the boat with Davies, three other girls were trying to run away.
8. The Latter-day Saints were holding the three girls, carrying them back to the boat, and tying them hand and foot.

Following this second letter is a paragraph in English, presumably by Rees Davies also, about "a young girl of 15 . . . a native of South Wales," who had previously arrived in New Orleans. Davies had learned the following from this girl's sister:

> On the Atlantic coming over, the leader of the Mormons wanted the young woman to marry an old shoemaker with one leg, but she refused. For three days they tried to coax her to marry, but she would not. On the 4th day, the chief compelled her to marry the wooden-leg shoemaker, and the villain even with his own hands laid her in bed against her will with the old clump. So much for the Mormon religion.

Davies ends this paragraph in English with a request:

> Show this to my uncle, Rev. H. Davies, Cenarth, and he can send it to be published.

This odd request makes one wonder whether perhaps Davies's intention with his two letters, filled with rather astonishing accusations, may have been to get them into print in Wales to negatively affect the Latter-day Saint proselytizing activities among his compatriots.

1854: September, *Yr Haul* (*The Sun*), p. 301 (360 words). "Mormonism."

Merely a shortened version of Rees Davies's first letter, dated 26 March 1854.

1854: October, *Yr Haul* (*The Sun*), p. 337 (460 words). "Mormonism."

The same letter that Rees Davies wrote, dated 10 June 1854, though in this article, the letter is misdated 20 June 1854.

1854: *Amddiffyniad y Saint; sef, gwrth-brofion o gamgyhuddiadau maleis-ddrwg dyn o'r enw Rees Davies, o New Orleans, yn erbyn y Saint* (*A defense of the Saints; refutations of the false and malicious accusations of a man by the name of Rees Davies, from New Orleans, against the Saints*), pamphlet, 12 pages.[30]

Dan Jones faced serious challenges and disadvantages in defending his religion against attacks made by Rees Davies, a fellow Welshman, not of the same faith, writing from the other side of the Atlantic. In his twelve-page refutation of Davies's claims, Jones appeals to the common sense of his readers and states that he is certain that such actions would not be allowed among the men of good standing on board the ship, many of whom Jones had known for years. He points out the inconsistencies of Davies's accusations and includes evidence gleaned from letters sent back to relatives in Wales by passengers on the *Golconda* that suggests the accusations were false.

Much of Jones's defense centers around Margaret Williams, an eighteen-year-old girl from Aberystwyth who purportedly had asked Rees Davies to help her escape from the "Mormons" and to write to her mother and tell her that she (Margaret) was sorry for not following her mother's counsel to remain in Wales.

Davies's account is contradicted by Margaret's letter as printed in Jones's pamphlet. She writes:

> I wish for you, my dear mother, not to worry about me, as if I were going to destruction by going to the land of America, for many have gone before me; they are doing well, and they are sending assistance to their parents, and perhaps I shall be able to do the same for you, before the end of our lives.[31]

One of Davies's numerous claims was that "Old Esther was ready to come back to Wales if she could." This has reference to Esther Jones, listed on the shipping list as being eighty-four years old. Margaret writes the following in her letter about Esther:

> Esther Jones from Rhiwbren Fawr is hale and hearty and sends her regards, grieving that you are not here with her.[32]

Margaret's letter is dated 17 March 1854, one day before the arrival of the *Golconda* in New Orleans. But lest Jones's readers think that Margaret had finished writing her letter before all of Davies's claims were made, Jones adds the following in a postscript to his pamphlet: "We understand that the letter [by Margaret Williams] was finished the day R. D. [Rees Davies] says [in his 26 March 1854 that] she escaped, or after that."

End: Rees Davies accuses the Saints from New Orleans, and Dan Jones defends from Merthyr

1854: September, *Y Cyfaill o'r Hen Wlad yn America* (*Friend of the Old Country in America*), p. 359 (90 words). "Mormonism as It Is."

> The Mormon law on polygamy reads as follows: "If any man espouse a virgin, and desire to espouse another, and the first give her consent, and if he espouse the second, and they are virgins, and have vowed to no other man, then is he justified; he cannot commit adultery for they are given unto him; for he cannot commit adultery with that that belongeth unto him and to no one else."[33] There is another article (that follows) to take the virgin if the previous spouse refuses to give her consent.

The practice of polygamy in The Church of Jesus Christ of Latter-day Saints had been announced to the Welsh through the 1 January 1853 issue of *Zion's Trumpet*.[34]

1854: September, *Y Tywysydd a'r Gymraes neu Cylchgrawn i Feibion a Merched Cymru* (*The Instructor and the Welsh Woman or the Periodical for the Boys and Girls of Wales*), p. 182 (645 words).

A long poem of twelve eight-line stanzas. The poem is entitled "Song" and has this brief explanation at the beginning: "In the manner of a conversation between Mother and Son on the day of the Son's departure to the Salt Valley, he being one of the Latter-day Saints." The mother speaks in the first stanza:

> Oh! David why do you now leave
>   Your mother to grieve for you so;
> Who studied your dearest face,
>   Who nursed you upon her lap?
> Oh, don't break my aching heart,
>   Don't load so my spirit with grief;
> Why not be content to stay home
>   As always in times hitherto?

The son responds:

Sweet mother, is this the last time
    I'll ever behold your face?
Such a thought is just like a spear
    Piercing my very heart;
But I must set forth whatever the pain—
    So farewell, farewell my mother:
You'll never be far from my mind—
    I'll always retain you there.

The mother says (second-to-last stanza):

There is no need of a Vale of Salt
    Nor California land
For a Latter-day Saint,
    To voyage forth
To gain a fuller share
    Of all salvation's joy—
For Jesus who was crucified
    Encompasses the world.

The son (final stanza):

Perfect joy abides but there
    Where sickness is not known;
Within the Valley's happy bounds
    No winter, only Summer comes;
And there our dear prophet lives,
    His loving spirit stays,
With *Book of Mormon* close at hand—
    My parents both, farewell!

1854: 22 September, *Monmouthshire Merlin*, p. 6, item 1 (1,280 words). "Spirit of the Press. Mormonism."

An abridgment of an article in the *Times* (published in London). Here are two quotes that indicate the flavor of the article:

> We do not propose that a man should be persecuted because he is a Mormonite; but we submit to the good sense of the country that he should not be entitled to call himself a "Protestant Dissenter," and as such to claim rights and privileges which were intended for others. Let a man, by all means, be a Mormonite, if he is silly enough, or wicked enough, to credit so monstrous a tissue of absurdities as the creed involves; but, at least, let not the Parliament of England stamp the mystic twaddle which he calls his Bible, with its *imprimatur*. Let us not, in other words, sacrifice the feelings and opinions of a million rational beings, to the distempered ravings of a single blockhead or knave.

1854: 22 September, *Monmouthshire Merlin*, p. 6, item 2 (2,660 words). "Middlesex Sessions, Wednesday, Sept. 13."

A very long account of the trial of Andrew Hepburn for having "willfully and maliciously disturbed a certain number of persons, who had assembled for the purpose of religious worship in a place duly registered according to the statute."

1854: 23 September, *Silurian*, p. 4 (580 words). "A Visit to a Mormon Prophet."

A brief account of Henry Caswall's visit to Joseph Smith.

1854: 30 September, *North Wales Chronicle*, p. 7 (210 words). "Isolation of the Mormon Settlement."

A quotation from Benjamin G. Ferris's *Utah and the Mormons*, in which he indicates all the many disadvantages of the Great Basin, the Latter-day Saints' chosen settling place.

1854: 6 October, *Monmouthshire Merlin*, p. 3 (45 words). "Return of the Mormons Eastward."

From the *New York Herald*:

> A Western paper says that a few days since, a train, composed of nine wagons and 50 persons, crossed the Missouri eastwardly in search of a new home. They had left the Salt Lake City on account of the oppression and immorality of their church.

1854: 6 October, *Cambrian* (120 words). "To the Editor of the Cambrian."

A brief letter supposedly sent by one Ichabod Roberts who claims to have been severely criticized in the previous issue. Here is the letter:

> Sir, In your newspaper, called the *Cambrian*, last week you inserted some letters against the Mormonites and the Peace Society, and one of them stabs at me, I suppose, because I delivered an oration on peace at our last gathering. I should like to lay my hands on that man anywhere and in any place, and I demand on you to deliver up that person to me. The workings of the Spirit is on the Mormonites and the men of peace and we will defy the powers of darkness to work evil against us.
>
> Yours obediently, Ichabod Roberts
>
> (It would be unlawful to comply with Mr. Roberts demand to *deliver up*; and his intemperate application can receive no courtesy from us. Editor.)

Blatant is the irony of a man who speaks on peace and yet wishes to "lay his hands" on the one who would dare to criticize him. One just might believe that the editor was using the nom de plume Ichabod Roberts and was himself the writer of the article.

1854: November, *Y Bedyddiwr* (*Baptist*), p. 352 (50 words).

A very brief notice of the death of "William Richards." This probably has reference to Willard Richards, who had been serving as counselor to Brigham Young in the First Presidency. Here is the notice in full:

> We have learned that a Mormon Elder by the name of William [Willard] Richards died lately in the town of the Great Salt Lake and has left *twenty* widowed women to mourn his loss! If this is not a shame to mankind, we do not know what is.

1854: November, *Yr Eglwysydd* (*Churchman*), pp. 125–27 (1,060 words). "Mormonism."

An article probably written by the editor William Morris, who was an Anglican bookseller in Holywell. In his opening paragraph, the author tells of an encounter he had with two members of The Church of Jesus Christ of Latter-day Saints:

> As the Scriptures say that the man who went from Jerusalem to Jericho fell among thieves, so too did I fall on my journey one day, if not among thieves, certainly among false teachers, namely some of the apostles of the Latter-day Saints. And, if they failed to strip me of my religion, wound my feelings, and leave me half dead, it was not a lack of sufficient impudence to try to do so that was the cause, but a lack of skill and ability, for they attacked me with all their might and cunning as soon as I fell into their midst.[35]

Morris then uses the form of a conversation to describe the "attacks" he received. The first such attack has to do with authority:

> *Mormon:* How do you know that your ministers have authority from God to preach the gospel?
>
> *Churchman:* I know that from the complete devotion many of them have for the work of the ministry, and that they have received their authority from those who were authorized successively from Christ to send ministers into the vineyard.
>
> *Mormon:* Successive authority is what you have; I have restored authority.[36]

The conversation also includes differing opinions on gifts of the Spirit, modern-day revelation, and living prophets. The author ends the conversation by presenting the following reminder to his opponent:

> You and I will have to appear before the Omniscient Judge to give an accounting for that which we do at present. And remember that all false intents, although hidden to men, are exposed and open to His eyes, and will be brought forth plainly visible before the whole world.[37]

1854: 10 November, *Cardiff and Merthyr Guardian*, p. 3 (60 words). "To the Mormons."

> We advise all sane and rational people to read a little book, entitled "Utah and the Mormons"—six-months' residence in the Great Salt Lake City, by Benjamin G. Ferris, late Secretary of Utah Territory. It is published by Low, Son, and Co., London. If this work does not abate the low Welsh fever, no other remedy can avail.

1854: 2 December, *Silurian*, p. 4 (155 words). "A Luckless Mormon Journey."

> A letter from Berlin of the 20th [of November] says: "At the commencement of the present year the king of Prussia procured through his Minister Plenipotentiary at Washington, and through the Chevalier Bunsen, at that time minister at London, a complete collection of all the publications concerning the Mormons in the United States and in England. The Mormons considered this measure as likely to be favorable to the propagation of their religion in Prussia, and, in consequence, they determined on sending to Berlin a deputation to compliment his Majesty. This deputation arrived, a few days ago, by the railway from Stettin; but no sooner had the persons composing it quitted the carriages, than a detachment of soldiers who were in waiting at the station, marched them off to the director of police. That functionary subjected them to a lengthened interrogatory—after which they received orders to leave Berlin in twenty-four hours. The next morning they left the capital."

1854: 9 December, *Caernarvon and Denbigh Herald*, p. 2 (70 words).

The King of Prussia having ordered a collection of the books of the Mormons, the Latter-day Saints jumped to the conclusion that he must be about to favor their views. So a deputation set out from Stettin to wait upon the Monarch to "compliment" him; but when the train arrived at Berlin, the Mormons were arrested by the police, interrogated at great length, and ordered to leave the city in twenty-four hours.

Notes

1. The source of the foregoing information is *The Book of Thomas Job* by Bliss Brimley, available on his profile at the Welsh Saints Project.
2. *Zion's Trumpet*, 25 March 1854, 190–92.
3. Ibid., 190.
4. Ibid., 191.
5. *Zion's Trumpet*, 8 July 1854, 403.
6. *Zion's Trumpet*, 15 July 1854, 419–20.
7. *Zion's Trumpet*, 29 July 1854, 451–52, emphasis in original.
8. For a facsimile translation of Jones's pamphlet. see *Defending the Faith: Early Welsh Missionary Publications*, item J20.
9. For greater detail concerning *Zion's Trumpet* and its predecessor, *Prophet of the Jubilee*, see *Welsh Mormon Writings from 1844 to 1862*, 27–32 and 72–79. Complete facsimile translations of all surviving volumes of *Zion's Trumpet* are posted at the Welsh Saints Project.
10. *Zion's Trumpet*, 26 August 1854, 480–84.
11. *"Haman" Hanging from His Own Gallows! Or Daniel Jones (the Blind) Proving the Truth of Mormonism!!* in *Defending the Faith*, Item J10, p. 4.
12. *Zion's Trumpet*, 7 October 1854, 531–32.
13. *Zion's Trumpet*, 9 September 1854, 493–94, emphasis in original.
14. See *Welsh Mormon Writings*, 65–68.
15. For more details, see *Zion's Trumpet*, 18 November 1854, 569–73; see also this book's preface.
16. Also printed in the *Wrexham Advertiser* for 1 July 1854, p. 3.
17. *Zion's Trumpet*, 25 March 1854, 190.
18. Ibid., 191.
19. Ibid.
20. Ibid., 191–92.
21. *Zion's Trumpet*, 15 April 1854, 226.
22. Ibid., 227.
23. Dan Jones to Brigham Young, 19 September 1854, Church History Library, Salt Lake City, original spelling preserved.
24. *Zion's Trumpet*, 8 April 1854, 201.
25. Ibid., 202.
26. Ibid., 202–3.
27. *Churchman*, July 1854, 75, emphasis in original.
28. *Zion's Trumpet*, 25 March 1854, 190–92.
29. Also printed in the *Silurian*, 18 February 1854, 3.
30. *Defending the Faith: Early Welsh Missionary Publications*, item J20.
31. Dan Jones, *A Defense of the Saints*, 11.
32. Jones, *A Defense of the Saints*, 12.
33. Doctrine and Covenants 132:61.
34. *Zion's Trumpet*, 1 January 1853, 5–16. See entry in chapter 10.
35. *Churchman*, November 1854, 125.
36. Ibid., 125–26.
37. Ibid., 127.

Chapter 12

Episodes

12.1—John E. Davis tells of his disillusionment after traveling to Salt Lake City and back
12.2—Dan Jones debates with Andrew Balfour Hepburn and Reverend Short
12.3—The *Edinburgh Review* prints six installments about "Mormonism"
12.4—Dan Jones exposes an *exposé* in sixteen pages

Salient Events

- **12 January 1855**. The *Cardiff and Merthyr Guardian* prints a 7 November 1854 letter from John E. Davis to his friend Charles Vachell, the mayor of Cardiff. At the time he wrote the letter, Davis was in San Francisco on his way back to Wales after some frustrating and disappointing months in Utah as a convert to The Church of Jesus Christ of Latter-day Saints. He states that he looks forward to revealing the reasons for his negative experience. Upon his return to Cardiff, Davis proceeds to carrying out his intent with lectures, newspaper articles, and also a forty-eight-page pamphlet, which he published in May 1856, titled *Mormonism Unveiled; or a Peep into the Principles & Practices of the Latter-day Saints.*[1] Also see Episode 12.1.
- **20 January 1855**. The Wales statistical report in *Zion's Trumpet* for the final six months of 1854 shows the total number of members at the time was 4,240. Also mentioned are 309 excommunications, 36 deaths, and 74 emigrants.

Conference	Branches	Baptisms	Members	President
East Glamorgan	34	206	1,1802	R. Evans
West Glamorgan	19	47	483	D. E. Jones

Monmouthshire	19	46	556	T. D. Giles
Breconshire	7	10	141	T. Morgans
Llanelli	11	30	338	Ben. Jones
Carmarthen	7	13	155	T. Jenkins
North Pembroke	4	1	52	T. Evans
South Pembroke	13	13	197	T. Price
Cardiganshire	5	6	108	B. Evans
Merionethsire	6	4	72	J. Davies
Flintshire	5	10	121	D. Davies
Denbighshire	5	7	114	John Parry
Anglesey and Conway	6	6	98	Rd. Roberts
Total	141	399	4,240	n/a

- **28 January 1855**. This issue of *Zion's Trumpet* announces that the *Guide to Zion* is off the press and available in sufficient quantity for that year's emigrants. The sixteen pages include twelve headings that have detailed amounts of advice and counsel regarding journeying to and integrating into the Saints' community in the Salt Lake Valley.[2] Under the first heading, "Preparation of Emigrants before Departing from Wales," are three general instructions:
    - First, pay your rightful debts to everyone.
    - Second, strive to be free in your consciences by warning all your fellowmen you can.
    - Third, search for history, names, births, marriages, and deaths of your ancestors as far as you can.

  Other headings include the following:
    - Female preparations for this class
    - Household furniture, etc.
    - To those who are going with the £13 company
    - To the "Emigrating Society" class
    - To various craftsmen
    - General advice while in Liverpool
    - General counsel on the sea
    - What things to buy in St. Louis
    - Choosing horned animals
    - Instructions for driving oxen
    - Directions to camp, watch, etc.

Jones's "Instructions for driving oxen" occupy four pages in this sixteen-page pamphlet. Here is a brief, entertaining segment:

> Hold the yoke with the left hand, and the bow in the right hand, and then go to the furthest ox first, very quietly, saying, *sook*, *sook*, until you get the bow around his neck and the yoke on his shoulders; and if he moves or treads on your toes, it is better for you to bite your tongue

than scream at that time, as you do not know when you will have such a chance again.

- **9 February 1855**. In this issue of the *Cardiff and Merthyr Guardian*, the writer reports that someone by the name of Hepburn had been presenting a series of lectures at the Temperance Hall "Upon the Horrid Doctrines of the so-called Latter-day Saints." Andrew Balfour Hepburn had joined The Church of Jesus Christ of Latter-day Saints in Scotland over a decade earlier, but he had left the Church after ten months and began lecturing against its doctrines and practices. This newspaper article appears to be the first indication that Hepburn had made his way down to Wales. In addition to giving lectures, Hepburn also challenged Dan Jones to a public debate. Jones's refusal in the April 14 issue of *Zion's Trumpet* to "wrangle with the corrupt man" is puzzling, since during his first mission, he was often the one to invite others to debate the teachings of the Latter-day Saints. However, he also explains that the main reason for his refusal was that he was following "the counsel of our head President in the matter."[3] While in Swansea, Hepburn collaborated with the Reverend Charles Short to publish in English a forty-eight-page pamphlet entitled *Mormonism Exploded; or, the Religion of the Latter-day Saints Proved to Be a System of Imposture, Blasphemy, and Immorality*.[4] See Episode 12.2.
- **17 April 1855**. The *Chimborazo* departs from Liverpool with 446 Latter-day Saint emigrants on board, over two hundred of them Welsh. The leader of the Welsh emigrants was Thomas Jeremy, who had been released as first counselor to Dan Jones after just over a year of service. Also with Jeremy were three members of Reverend J. Jones's family—the reverend's wife Jane (listed, incorrectly, as a widow on the shipping list) and their two daughters, Sarah, age twenty-two, and Elizabeth, age twenty. These three had been baptized a year earlier in Swansea by Dan Jones, the brother-in-law to Jane and uncle to Sarah and Elizabeth (see Chapter 11). Instead of crossing the plains to Utah, however, the three women traveled to Ohio to join the Reverend J. Jones there. He had left Wales earlier, possibly to escape the results of some business dealings that had gone awry. Although Jane was not a widow during the crossing of the *Chimborazo*, she became one on 18 November 1856, when the reverend died in Cincinnati. A brief obituary has the following information:

  > Lately in Cincinnati, North America, John Jones [of] "Llangollen." Mr. Jones left two beautiful and faithful daughters to mourn his loss; also, a grieving widow who rightfully and naturally feels devastated. The three of them, had the welcome opportunity with every consideration of watching death pull down a house of dust. And it is very likely that two of the sons, also somewhere, would be glad to have the same opportunity. Whether they are in Wales or in this country, no one here knows except for the family members themselves. What the reason may be for this secrecy is not known. The two daughters are carrying forward the millinery business which provides a comfortable living for them and their mother.[5]

- **June 1855**. The first of six installments entitled "Mormonism" appears in *Y Bedyddiwr* (*Baptist*). All six are translated from the English-language periodical the *Edinburgh Review*. The only installment to have any content related to events in Wales is the one printed in the November issue, in which a battle between Dan Jones and the evil spirits is mentioned. In a 6 January 1849 letter to his leader, Orson Pratt, Jones describes his conversation with these unwanted visitors, who had appeared at a conference held a few days earlier at the White Lion Inn in Merthyr Tydfil. See Episode 12.3.
- **21 July 1855**. This issue of *Zion's Trumpet* announces that Dewi Elfed Jones has been mishandling Church funds. (As a point of interest, the former Baptist minister had been confirmed a member of The Church of Jesus Christ of Latter-day Saints by William S. Phillips while Jones was seated in the special minister's seat in his own chapel.) See Episode 8.2.
- **27 October 1855**. The first part of a two-part article by Dan Jones appears in *Zion's Trumpet*, discussing a novel entitled *Female Life Among the Mormons; a Narrative of Many Years' Personal Experience by the Wife of a Mormon Elder, Recently from Utah*.[6] Segments of this novel, translated into Welsh, had recently appeared in several issues of *Yr Amserau* (*Times*), issues that unfortunately are now nonextant. As Jones critiques these novel segments, he employs some of his greatest outrage ever. At the outset of his article, he writes:

  > Even though we have read everything that we could lay our hands on of the filth of the scum of authors and editors in every language we understand for over a dozen years, having to hold our nose tightly many times, while we analyzed the malodorous entrails of their anti-Mormon *bug bears* searching for a crumb of truth, we confess that this dirty bag is the filthiest of all.[7]

  After discussing and discrediting many of "the endless stream of lies" in the novel, Jones concludes:

  > The editor of the *Times* proves himself totally unfit to edit any publication, and unworthy of the trust of the public by lowering himself with this shameless stream of lies, and not a single man or woman who possesses a grain of true religion will ever believe him again, we should think, whenever he delivers his opinion about any religion of his fellowmen.[8]

  Eighteen months later, four additional segments of *Female Life* were printed in *Y Dysgedydd* (*Instructor*) in March, April, May, and June 1857. No response appeared in the 1857 *Zion's Trumpet*, which by then was under the editorship of Daniel Daniels. See Episode 12.4 and Episode 14.1.

Commentary

1855: 5 January, *Monmouthshire Merlin*, p. 8 (1,630 words). "Mormonism."

Taken from the *Chicago Tribune*, this unsigned letter is from a person who had become a Latter-day Saint four years earlier and had been living in Salt Lake City for eighteen months. The writer addresses a friend who had opposed his conversion to

The Church of Jesus Christ of Latter-day Saints. He tells of the many positive aspects of the Latter-day Saint society in Salt Lake City and even defends the practice of plural marriage as he describes his own experience with three wives. He describes several of the advantages:

> In Deseret there are no libertines, with their paramours, no houses of prostitution, no cases of seduction, or those which disturb the peace of families in the States, under your laws. Here, every woman can have what God intended she should—a husband—and every man that wants to, may have a wife. And the woman that is the wife of a man who has one or more other wives, is more fortunate than if she were the only one, for in case of plurality the duties of the house are divided.

1855: 6 January, *Silurian*, p. 3 (25 words).

> John Mear, aged fifty-four, Mormon preacher, was charged with stealing a pair of shoes, the property of William Taylor, at Builth, on the 7th December.

1855: 19 January, *Monmouthshire Merlin*, p. 6, item 1 (80 words).

> A military governor has been appointed over the Mormons. Lieutenant-Colonel Steptoe, of the United States army, has received the appointment, with the understanding however that he shall leave the army. It is doubtful (says a letter from New York) whether he will accept the appointment on such terms. The Mormons are strong enough to give this country great trouble and will, no doubt, do so. The men are well drilled, and having bold determined leaders, will be put down with difficulty.

1855: 20 January, *North Wales Chronicle*, p. 3 (80 words). "The Mormonites."

The same article as in the *Monmouthshire Merlin* for 19 January 1855 (see previous entry).

1855: 19 January, *Monmouthshire Merlin*, p. 6, item 2 (25 words).

> Some shameless missionaries of the Mormons are laboring most sedulously amongst the ignorant populations of several districts in Gloucestershire, particularly urging their brutal doctrines of polygamy.

Episode 12.1

Start: John E. Davis tells of his disillusionment after traveling to Salt Lake City and back

1855: 12 January, *Cardiff and Merthyr Guardian*, p. 3 (275 words). "The Mormons and Their Disciples."

The editor received a request from C. Vachell that a letter be printed in his newspaper. The letter is from John E. Davis (not to be confused with John S. Davis, the one-time editor of *Zion's Trumpet*). John E. Davis was a former resident of Cardiff who was on his way back home after a negative experience in Salt Lake City. Here is the letter:

> San Francisco, Nov. 7th, 1854. Sir—I have taken the liberty of sending this note to you, hoping you may not think me too presumptuous in sending to you. I have crossed the continent of North America to Salt Lake; and I did

> not find Mormonism as it was represented in England. I thought of sending to you from Salt Lake, but all letters were opened by the Mormon authorities previous to their being sent away. I have enjoyed excellent health for a man of my years, considering the many difficulties I have to contend with. I return you my sincere thanks for the many favors I have received from your hands. I am sorry to say my sight is no better than when I left. I am coming to England in the ship *William*. We are going to bring home guano from Peru. I expect to be in England about May, if God spares me so long. I remain, yours respectfully, John Davis, Late from No. 12, Herbert Street, Cardiff.

1855: 13 January, *Silurian*, p. 3 (275 words). "The Mormons."

This is the same letter that appears in the *Cardiff and Merthyr Guardian* for 12 January 1855 (see previous entry).

1855: 19 January, *Cardiff and Merthyr Guardian*, p. 3 (90 words). "To the Editor of the *Cardiff and Merthyr Guardian*."

> Sir—Having observed a letter in your last, sent to Mr. C. Vachell, from one John [E.] Davis, late of Herbert Street, Cardiff, containing charges derogatory to the character of the Mormons in the Great Salt Lake Valley, I shall be prepared next week to bring forward facts to disprove the assertions contained in the said letter, and beg the public will suspend their judgment in the meantime. I remain, Sir, yours most respectfully, Samuel Evans. 6, Great Frederick Street, Cardiff, January 17th, 1855.

1855: 26 January, *Cardiff and Merthyr Guardian*, p. 3 (530 words). "Mormons and Their Disciples."

As promised the week before, Samuel Evans presents his letter to the public in order to "bring forward facts to disprove the assertions" made in the John E. Davis letter. Evans first addresses Davis's assertion that in Utah "all letters were opened by the Mormon authorities previous to their being sent away" by pointing out the absurdity of such a claim, since there were forty thousand inhabitants in Utah at the time, with elected officials who were "under the control and supervision of the United States' authorities." Next, Evans responds to Davis's assertion that "he did not find Mormonism as it was represented in England" by quoting three other former Cardiff residents who had gone to Salt Lake City. The first, John Lewis, had written the following to his aged parent: "Utah is the best place in the world for those that will keep in the Commandments of God." The next, James Ellis, had written, "Utah is a place where the people are taught how to live, and where children see no bad habits, but are taught righteously and in the fear of the Lord." Thirdly, Mrs. Hannah Thomas had written, "When we arrived here there were hundreds that were ready to greet us as brothers and sisters in the new and everlasting covenant."

1855: 27 January, *Silurian*, p. 3 (595 words). "To the Editor of the *Silurian*."

This version of Samuel Evans's response to John E. Davis is very similar to the letter which appears in the *Cardiff and Merthyr Guardian* for 26 January 1855 (see previous entry); however, there are numerous spelling, punctuation, and grammatical errors.

The editor of the *Silurian* also includes a brief note following Evans's letter:

> Believing that discussion always serves the cause of truth, we readily insert the letter of Mr. Evans, but he does not appear to comprehend that the public must naturally attach greater weight to the evidence of a man who has *witnessed* what he testifies, than to the statements of one, who, writing from Cardiff, professes to give an account of the state of affairs at a distance of more than five thousand miles. Editor.

1856: 16 February, *Cardiff and Merthyr Guardian*, p. 5 (1,975 words). "The Cardiff Mormonites."

A second letter from John E. Davis is reprinted here alongside a lengthy article with general information about The Church of Jesus Christ of Latter-day Saints and, more specifically, the establishment and growth of the Latter-day Saints in Cardiff. Here is the letter:

> Sir—after a boisterous passage of nearly fifteen months, thank God I have arrived safe in England, by the ship *William* (Captain McPhea). My object in sending this note is, in the first place, because I consider it my duty from the favors you have bestowed on me previously. Secondly, knowing it is about the time that parties leave Wales for the Mormon country, I wish you to caution them against any false delusion they might be laboring under. I have lived amongst them nine months, and the supposed Zion I found to be a city of the Sultan. Virtue or good deeds are never placed in the balance of justice. Should this caution be insufficient, be kind enough to tell them to take care of their money, as it is very scarce in Salt Lake Valley. Laboring men, if they can get employment, which is difficult, cannot get money except under peculiar circumstances, but must take anything their employers think proper to give—say, flour, potatoes, lumber, etc. I myself have lived for weeks on bread and potatoes only, at the same time fully employed, and can state without fear of contradiction that many others have done the same. I hope, if it please God, soon to be in Cardiff, and shall then be able to fully explain to you and others the false delusions thousands have labored under. Hundreds at this present moment would leave this talked-of Zion, but are without means to do so. I left, myself, in the dead of the night, and travelled on foot 1400 miles, at times with great privations. Nothing but Divine Providence has brought me here, and I will explain to the world the supposed Zion. My eyesight is no better after the Mormon Prophet laying hands on me. I am waiting here to see Doctor Alexander, whom I trust will relieve me.
>
> I remain, Sir, your humble Servant,
>
> John Davis
>
> C. Vachell, Esq., Crockherbtown, Cardiff
>
> P.S.—Sir, I beg to add that I lived under your brother, 12, Herbert-street, Cardiff.

1856: 23 February, *Monmouthshire Merlin*, p. 3 (370 words). "The Latter-day Saints."

The editor of the *Monmouthshire Merlin* described the text as "a copy of a letter received by the Mayor of Cardiff, from an inhabitant of the town, who emigrated to the city of Utah, in the great Salt Lake Valley, and which we have been kindly permitted to publish." After this brief introduction, the editor prints the same letter (by John E. Davis to C. Vachell) as appeared the previous week in the *Cardiff and Merthyr Guardian* for 16 February 1856 (see previous entry).

1856: 1 March, *Monmouthshire Beacon*, p. 7 (410 words). "Cardiff. Mormon Delusions."

This is the same letter as quoted in the *Cardiff and Merthyr Guardian* for 16 February 1856 (see previous entry).

1856: *Mormonism Unveiled; or a Peep into the Principles & Practices of the Latter-day Saints*, pamphlet, 48 pages.[9]

The author states his purpose in the preface:

> The following pages are intended to shew [*sic*] the detestable proceedings of the Disciples of Joseph Smith, the founder of the sect of the Mormons, and the delusion and sufferings of the victims of the leaders of the self-styled Latter-day Saints, at the city of the Salt Lake, Utah. They are not written with an attempt at language, but with a view to depict faithfully what the writer saw and heard, during a nine months' residence among them. It is "a plain unvarnished tale" and the only object in its publication is, if possible, to deter others from being duped by the inducements held out by these specious deceivers; who have so far beguiled an immense number of unthinking, credulous, and enthusiastic people, as to be enabled to live in luxurious indolence on the earnings extorted from their infatuated followers, and to give full scope to their demoralizing and unprincipled propensities. It is unnecessary to make any further remarks, the facts speak plainly for themselves.

An article reviewing and quoting from the first edition of this pamphlet appears in the 24 May 1856 issue of the *Cardiff and Merthyr Guardian* (see next entry).

1856: 24 May, *Cardiff and Merthyr Guardian*, p. 8 (4,800 words). "A Visit to the Salt Lake by a Cardiff Resident."

A very lengthy article in which the writer comments on and quotes from *Mormonism Unveiled; or a Peep into the Principles & Practices of the Latter-day Saints*, by John E. Davis. The writer introduces the topic thus: "A pamphlet was last week published by Mr. Hugh Bird, of Duke Street, in this town, containing 'A short account of a journey from Cardiff to the Salt Lake,' by John E. Davis, who has just returned from the Mormon settlement, and who, previous to his departure, resided at 12, Herbert Street, Cardiff."

1856: 31 May, *Cardiff and Merthyr Guardian*, p. 8 (515 words). "A Visit to the Salt Lake by a Cardiff Resident."

The conclusion of the article from the previous week (see previous entry).

1858: 22 May, *Caernarvon and Denbigh Herald*, p. 3 (375 words). "Lecture on Mormonism.

Some three years following his return to Wales, John E. Davis continued to lecture against the people he was once aligned with and whom he learned to despise. This lecture took place on Friday evening, 21 May, at the Athenaeum in Llanelli and was reported on in the *Caernarvon and Denbigh Herald* the day after. Davis's principal focus in this lecture was the practice of plural marriage among the Latter-day Saints. The following exchange took place after the lecture concluded:

> The Rev. D. Rees, in moving the thanks of the meeting to the chairman, remarked, that inasmuch as the Mormons believed in the plurality of wives, he should like to know their reason for not carrying out their principal in this country? Upon this Mr. David Davies, the president of the Llanelli District of Saints, arose and said that the law of God and that of Victoria did not agree on the point, and therefore they were prohibited in this country, from having more than one wife, but in Zion they would be enabled to give perfect obedience to God's commandments. Mr. Rees maintained that if the saints were thoroughly convinced that a plurality of wives was taught in the Bible, they ought to act consistently with that principle in this country even if they were martyred for so doing. The saint in reply quoted a passage of Scripture, which as proceeding from 'Satan" to our Savior, was anything but armor proof.

End: John E. Davis tells of his disillusionment after traveling to Salt Lake City and back

Episode 12.2

Start: Dan Jones debates with Andrew Balfour Hepburn and Rev. Charles Short

1855: 9 February, *Cardiff and Merthyr Guardian*, p. 3 (240 words). "Mormonism."

The writer reports that Andrew Balfour Hepburn had been presenting a series of lectures at the Temperance Hall "Upon the Horrid Doctrines of the so-called Latter-day Saints." Here is a list of the topics:

1. The Origin of *Joe Smith*, the Yankee Smith, and his Book of Mormon proved unscriptural.
2. The money system, and how the people are robbed; three Baptisms for the Living and one for the Dead, and the price of each; the Peopling of other Worlds in Eternity.
3. The Casting out of 319 Devils from one woman; their Pretended Miracles proved False; their Unknown Tongue a Delusion.
4. The Election in Heaven between Jesus Christ and the Devil; the Origin of God and his Wives in Heaven; the Mysteries of the Mormon Temple in America.
5. The Seduction of Young Females from this Country to the Salt Lake Valley. To *this lecture* no females will be admitted.

The writer then comments,

> This is a revolting catalogue of blasphemy and absurdity; and if Mr. Hepburn's facts are authentic, he is doing good service to the cause of truth in unveiling this modern libel upon the name of religion. We are happy to find, however, that the delusion in this district is dying away, that the Saints are rapidly decreasing in number, and that Mormonism has lost its hold upon the minds of the people.

1855: 30 March, *Cambrian* (1,020 words). "Lectures on Mormonism."

The writer expresses alarm at the exodus of so many Welshmen to "the Salt Lakes of America" where "doctrines the most blasphemous are promulgated, and scenes the most atrocious perpetrated." He then reports on the first of three lectures given recently at the Swansea Town Hall by Andrew Balfour Hepburn, a person who had spent ten months as a member of The Church of Jesus Christ of Latter-day Saints. Hepburn declared that it was "his duty to show that the creed of the Mormons was a bundle of lies and absurdities." The author also reported:

> The people of this country knew but little or nothing of Mormonism—they must go to America where Mormonism was rampant, to see its principles carried out—there young girls of the tender age of eleven years had been made prostitutes to those professing themselves the apostles of Jesus Christ.

The writer ended by promising his readers details of the second and third lectures in future issues of the *Cambrian,* but these have not been identified and may not have been published.

1855: 14 April, *Udgorn Seion* (*Zion's Trumpet*), pp. 113–19 (2,680 words). "Religious Persecution and Its Effect."

Dan Jones responds to the attacks of Andrew Balfour Hepburn in a rather surprising manner, especially when compared to previous responses to previous opponents. Jones prefaces his new approach by quoting Paul as a reminder to his readers of what faithful followers of the Savior can expect:

> All that will live godly in Christ Jesus shall suffer persecution.[10]

After three pages discussing persecution of the righteous all through the Christian era, Jones poses the question that he assumes his readers are asking at this point:

> "If they are telling lies about you, why do you not go to their presence to prove them wrong?" says someone.[11]

He then answers the question by again quoting Paul:

> Perverse disputings of men of corrupt minds, and destitute of the truth, from such withdraw thyself.[12]

Finally, Jones comes to what is most likely his primary motivation for this new and uncharacteristic approach to dealing with Hepburn, whose name he has not yet even mentioned in his article:

> You shall have more of our reasons for not lowering ourselves to wrangle with the corrupt man in our *defense* against the vilification, and we have pleasure in reporting that we act according to the counsel of our head President in the matter, and similar to the way we deal with him is the way all our Brethren have dealt with him in other places, but we know that so far the result of his lecturing here has been to open the eyes of honest men to search into our religion; every day we were told of some who had been to his lectures until they became sick of him, and believed that the Saints had true religion long before Reverends and laymen were seen to encourage such a character to falsely accuse the religion of their innocent neighbors.[13]

In the final paragraph of the article, Jones comes close to naming Hepburn but instead gives only the initial of his surname:

> May our friend Mr. H—— (there! We came close to sullying our mouth by naming him, but we restrained!) well, we were about to say may he carry out his favorite task, as the prodigal of old carried *husks to the pig trough*, until he comes to possess humanity.[14]

1855: 28 April, *Udgorn Seion* (*Zion's Trumpet*), pp. 136–39 (1,280 words). "The Debate in Swansea."

In this editorial, Dan Jones explains and defends his reasons for not dealing with Hepburn, again without mentioning his name.

> We consider our religion too important and honorable to be derided by such a disreputable character as our challenger has proven to be, and before this, all reasonable men with whom we have conversed on the topic, without *excepting his own chief supporters*, have acknowledged that we have proceeded honorably and in wisdom for our religion by practicing *silent contempt*.[15]

Jones quotes from a handbill he had circulated around Swansea:

> We would not dare to refuse to defend one and all of our principles in the face of one and all of the "Revered ministers of the gospel" in Swansea, who support the challenger, the Holy Scriptures according to the King James I translation; with our own authorized books to be the only standard, claiming the same right to test the assertions of our gainsayer according to the same standard.[16]

The handbill had prompted the Reverend Charles Short to challenge Jones to debate him on the following statements, which Jones includes for context:

- Mormonism is false in its origin.
- Blasphemous in its opinions.
- Immoral in its practices.[17]

Here is Jones's response:

> We refused the above because of their lack of clarity, and because it was obvious to us that the purpose was to use the group of proofs which we refused to quarrel over previously, namely, the slime and false accusations of enemies.[18]

Prior to the printing of this article, but during the time that Jones was dealing with the opposition of Hepburn and Short, he was also assisting his counselor, Thomas Jeremy, in preparing a group of about two hundred Church members to travel on board the *Troubador* to Liverpool, from which point they would begin their journey to Salt Lake City. Jeremy was released from the Wales presidency and would travel with the group from Liverpool to Philadelphia and then on to join the main body of the Saints in the Rocky Mountains. Jones was also to travel with the group to Liverpool, where he would take care of getting them on board the *Chimborazo*. After seeing the group off, he returned to Swansea and continued negotiations for an official debate with Short, which also took place before the printing of this article.

Jones describes the meeting he had with Short and his committee after arriving back in Swansea:

> Upon our return, we met with Mr. Short and his Committee, Monday, April 23rd, and to our surprise we understood from Mr. Short that his messengers had informed him that we had promised to debate the aforementioned topics,

> and two of them, who were present, summoned the impudence to assert that they had understood as much! This caused a considerable change in things.[19]

Jones had prepared the following topics for the debate between him and Short, topics which Short's four delegates had agreed to three weeks earlier prior to Jones's departure for Liverpool:

1. Are faith, repentance, and baptism for the remission of sins essential for salvation?
2. Are the preachers of the Baptists "ministers of the gospel?"
3. Are apostles and prophets, together with the gifts of the Holy Ghost essential to the existence of the church of Christ on the earth?
4. Are the doctrines, ordinances, and organization of the church of the Baptists in accordance with the New Testament plan?
5. Do the scriptures contain prophecies of the discovery of a sacred oracle, and are such fulfilled in the coming of the Book of Mormon?
6. Do the scriptures approve of polygamy?
7. The Trinity. Are the Father and Son separate persons?[20]

Jones describes Short's reaction:

> We read the following basic principles in the presence of Mr. Short, but he did not stay to hear them all; he went away in haste despite all we and his friends could do to persuade him to stay, away he went, and the last word we heard from him was, "Perhaps you wish to have the Urim and Thummim on your nose before you see!"[21]

Following Short's abrupt departure, Jones continued to read the topics to the members of Short's committee:

> But it was in vain; after his exit, his Committee followed, saying they had no right to accept the offer. Two of us said definitely that we refused the first statements at the start, and offered further proofs of the same thing; despite all that, and although we informed them that we would proclaim all that to the world, they rushed out, leaving us in the room.[22]

Because Short refused to participate in a debate, Jones printed his plan of action in *Zion's Trumpet*:

> Lectures will be delivered on the topics offered as subjects for debate to our gainsayers, in the Saints Hall, Orange Road, Swansea, starting Friday night, April 27, 29, 30, May 1, 3, 6 and 7, beginning at half past seven in the evening, consecutively, as they are listed. Entrance by tickets 3c. each, or 1s. for all the lectures. Sundays at 6 o'clock in the evening, free.[23]

1855: May, *Mormonism Exploded: Or, the Religion of the Latter-day Saints Proved to Be a System of Imposture, Blasphemy, and Immorality; with the Autobiography and Portrait of the Author*, pamphlet, 48 pages.[24]

The author, Andrew Balfour Hepburn, was a weaver by trade and had converted to The Church of Jesus Christ of Latter-day Saints in 1844 while living in Biggar, a small town located twenty-seven miles southwest of Edinburgh. Ten months after his baptism, he began presenting lectures against the Church. He claims in his autobiography that he had convinced many to leave the Church. In 1850, he went to England to continue his lectures, and in 1854, he was in Merthyr Tydfil, where he claims to have been "the means of rescuing six of the Mormon 'saints' from the errors of the church." In Swansea, he was assisted by the Reverend Charles Short of the Mount Pleasant Baptist chapel in preparing and publishing this forty-eight-page pamphlet.

Reverend Charles Short appeared as editor on the title page, as he assisted Hepburn in writing and publishing the pamphlet. Short also included a preface with his own statement on the pamphlet's topic:

> The purpose of the following little book is to give a clear, condensed, and popular exposition of the leading features of Mormonism. There is nothing precisely of this character already in existence, that I am aware of. The larger books already published on this subject, are too voluminous and expensive for circulation among the masses of the people; and the smaller ones are too meagre and incomplete, and some of them too ill-arranged, to give the reader a full and general idea of Mormonism. Besides, it is a *growing* system; its doctrine of a daily revelation is constantly adding something to an already accumulated heap of impostures, absurdities, and impieties. There is no apology needed, therefore, for this attempt to expose the origin and development of one of the most successful frauds of modern times.

He also explains his role in the production of the pamphlet:

> Mr. Hepburn is not only in name, but in *fact*, the principal author of the following pages. He has supplied me with the books, materials, and references, and I have reduced them to the shape and order in which they appear. . . . My hope was, I should be able to comprise, in about fifty pages, all the most essential matter of the Mormon system; but this has proved to be impossible. Another *part*, of the same size and price as this, will follow almost immediately, and will contain, I hope, so complete a view and exposure of the system, as to prove an antidote to the virulent moral poison of Mormonism.

Evidence has yet to surface that a second part was ever published. One possible explanation is that the market for an English-language pamphlet costing sixpence was severely limited in the Principality of Wales, where monoglot Welshmen far outnumbered the bilinguals and even more those whose only language was English.

Following a nine-page autobiography of Hepburn are the following chapters:

1. Joe Smith's Account of the Origin of the Book of Mormon
2. The Fraud Exposed
3. The Book of Mormon; Its Claims, Contradictions, and Absurdities
4. Smith as Prophet, Seer, and "Revelator"

For the first chapter, Short quotes briefly from the *Millennial Star* and from two publications of Orson Pratt. But in the other three chapters, the quotes are from *History of the Saints* by John C. Bennett, the counselor to Joseph Smith who turned on the Church following his excommunication.

1855: 12 May, *Udgorn Seion* (*Zion's Trumpet*), pp. 154–57 (1,170 words). "Counter Proofs of the 'Anti-Mormon' Accusations!!"

Unwilling to simply let the contention between him and Charles Short fade away, Dan Jones provides the complete text of a recently circulated handbill. Jones's handbill fills three full pages of his periodical, offering his defense that he had not backed away from a debate with Short. He refers to three different issues of the *Swansea Herald*—April 5, April 11, and April 25—in which Short had presented his version of Jones's unwillingness to debate him. Jones refutes these accusations and includes statements from various witnesses to support his position.

His opening statement is as follows:

> Mr. Short has accused me of a lie, stating that I denied receiving his challenge to debate the three topics named by him. In response I offer the following testimonies from among several that I have by me.[25]

1855: 26 May, *Udgorn Seion* (*Zion's Trumpet*), pp. 171–72 (450 words). "The Debate in Swansea."

In this article, Dan Jones gives his final printed word concerning the altercation he and the Reverend Charles Short had engaged in over the past several weeks. For those who wished to have more information about his disagreement with Short, he suggests:

> Let anyone who desires greater details concerning this matter have a look at our defense in the "Herald" for May 10th.[26]

Apparently, the same local newspaper—the *Swansea Herald*—that in three previous numbers had provided space for Short to present his position had also allowed Jones to present his.

Continuing in this article in his own periodical, Jones summarized the series of lectures he had announced in the 12 May issue (see previous entry):

> The lectures that have been delivered in the Saints' Hall here by us and our revered brethren Wheelock and Ross, concerning the principles about which our challenger refused to debate, have stimulated great interest in this place, and have caused hosts of people to search for the truth for themselves; and in fulfillment of the words of God that all things would work together for the good of those who love God, we are pleased to say that several people believe, and some have been baptized, and others promise to be baptized shortly; and far from the tales of our enemies disheartening the Saints, the effect is the complete opposite; the few who neglected their duties earlier, who were lukewarm, are more zealous, faithful and spiritual than before, and all indications promise very great success shortly for the work of our God. He who owns us and our dear religion that is being smeared will be glorified through it all—may our brothers and sisters pray with us.[27]

No further mention is made of Short or Hepburn in *Zion's Trumpet*.

1855: 16 June, *Silurian*, p. 2 (20 words). "Mormonism."

> We understand that Mr. Hepburn, the Anti-Mormon lecturer, will deliver an address tonight, (Friday) in the Cardiff Arms Park.

1855: 29 September, *Merthyr Telegraph*, p. 3 (90 words). "Tredegar. Mormonism."

> A course of four lectures has been delivered by Mr. P. Hepburn, of Scotland, during the past week in the Town Hall, at this place, upon the delinquencies of Mormonism. As the lecturer stated that he had himself belonged to that

> community he pretended to be well able to "shew up" their nefarious practices. For ourselves, we look with considerable suspicion on the sincerity of these ignorant and idle itinerant lecturers who foist themselves on the weaker portion of the public by pretending to be influenced by *public good.*

End: Dan Jones debates with Andrew Balfour Hepburn and Reverend Charles Short

1855: 10 February, *Caernarvon and Denbigh Herald*, p. 10 (940 words). "The Mormons at Utah."

A former resident of Manchester, who signs his name as "Tell Truth," writes this letter, dated 30 November 1854, from Salt Lake City. Many people are mentioned in the letter, but no names are given. The writer presents his assessment of the state of affairs in Salt Lake City:

> Things are as different here from what they are represented in England as darkness from light. People dare not say their souls are their own; in other words, they dare not give their opinion upon anything in opposition to what the authorities say. If they do, it is at the risk of their lives; in fact, I am writing this at the risk of my life, which would be forfeited if they found me out.

The writer paints a very negative picture of how the English are treated upon their arrival in Salt Lake City. He advises all English converts to The Church of Jesus Christ of Latter-day Saints to stay in England. The letter, reprinted from the *Manchester Guardian*, bears few if any marks of authenticity.

1855: 16 February, *Cambrian* (140 words). "The Mormonites."

About the proselytizing efforts of the Latter-day Saints.

> The emissaries of the Mormonites are most active in various parts of South Wales in spreading the doctrines of the Latter-day Saints, and among the laboring and ignorant population they are particularly zealous in urging the advisability of polygamy.

The writer laments that this religion has had success not only among the poorer classes but also among some of the "wealthier people" of South Wales.

1855: 17 February, *Caernarvon and Denbigh Herald*, p. 10 (140 words). "The Mormonites in the West."

> For some time past there has been a small colony of Mormons in Taunton, and their practices have rendered them so offensive that they have on more than one occasion been attacked by mobs. These attacks have at last become so serious that the matter was brought before the magistrates a few days since. A large crown of persons, it appears, assembled round the meeting house of the Mormons, and broke the windows and did other damage, which rendered it necessary to call in the assistance of the police, when several of the offending parties were apprehended. The magistrate said that, however objectionable the doctrines of the Mormons might be—and no one felt stronger on the subject than himself—they must be protected by the law, and he therefore inflicted a small fine upon the offenders.

1855: 24 February, *Monmouthshire Beacon*, p. 2 (140 words). "The Mormonites in the West."

The same article as in the *Caernarvon and Denbigh Herald* for 17 February 1855 (see previous entry).

1855: March, *Y Cyfaill o'r Hen Wlad yn America* (*Friend of the Old Country in America*), p. 123 (50 words). "Mormonism Fails to Hold Light."

The writer reports with great satisfaction:

> One of the Mormons in London, convinced of the errors of Mormonism, by one of the small pamphlets of the Treatise Society, was the means of convincing *a hundred* of his previous friends by the same means. They had to leave this neighborhood, Bermondsey Street.

The pamphlet mentioned has not been identified.

1855: 3 March, *Caernarvon and Denbigh Herald*, p. 4 (40 words).

> Mr. J. T. Hammack calls attention, through the *Times*, to the proceedings of the Mormons, who are striving to supply their harems in America with young women from England; and they appear to be but too successful.

1855: 10 March, *Silurian*, p. 3 (120 words). "The Latter-day Saints."

> A considerable number of people assembled on the beach, opposite the Traveler's Rest, on Sunday morning last for the purpose of witnessing the somewhat novel spectacle of baptism by immersion in the sea, conducted by some of the elders of the Latter-day Saints, or Mormons. The ceremony, by a singular freak, did not take place when the tide was at its height, but the converts, by way, we presume, of testing their faith, had to wade through the mud to the water, which had receded as far as the weirs at low water mark. After several persons had been immersed, addresses were delivered to the assembled crowd, in support of the doctrines and tenets of this peculiar sect.

1855: 7 April, *Monmouthshire Beacon*, p. 6 (825 words). "Horrible Mormon Revelations."

An 1854 letter from an unnamed "young lady" whose father resides in Islington. In 1852, she had crossed the plains with the "sugar company." She tells how horrible the crossing was and also how horrible Salt Lake City and the people were:

> On the 1st of June, 1854, we quitted the "City of Abominations," for such it truly is to all intents and purposes, and arrived at this place, K——, on the 15th of August.

1855: 12 April, *Monmouthshire Merlin*, p. 5 (200 words). "Railway Accident."

> On Sunday morning last, a number of Latter-day Saints, or Mormons, left Blaenavon by rail, to attend a gathering of the sect at Newport. They had previously made arrangements with the railway company to have a special train from Newport in the evening, which was provided for them, and everything on their return journey went on very well until they arrived at Pontypool, where an extra carriage was attached to the train for the accommodation of some members of the Wesleyan connection of some members of the Wesleyan connection, who had been attending an anniversary of the Wesleyan Sunday School

at Pontypool. With this addition, the train consisted of three carriages, and proceeded towards Blaenavon, but on arriving at the Varteg Incline, the cranks of the engine broke, and a delay of about half an hour occurred while a pilot engine was being sent for to Pontypool. Some of the Mormons assert that the engine broke down in consequence of the addition which was made to the train at Pontypool, while others say it was done at the bidding of one of the elders, who had been called upon by an unbeliever to perform a miracle.

1855: 13 April, *Monmouthshire Merlin*, p. 3 (55 words). "The Mormons."

A large number of these deluded people left Swansea, on Wednesday afternoon last, by the Blarney from Liverpool, en route to the Salt Lakes of America. The party seemed to consist chiefly of small farmers from Carmarthenshire and the neighborhood of Swansea, with their wives and daughters, many of the latter being apparently respectable females.

1855: 20 April, *Monmouthshire Merlin*, p. 3 (36 words).

Jersey. About 80 unfortunate people left this island by the Sir Francis Drake steamer last week for Plymouth thence to proceed across the Atlantic, on their way to the Mormon settlement on the "Great Salt Lake."

1855: May, *Y Cyfaill o'r Hen Wlad yn America* (*Friend of the Old Country in America*), p. 184 (815 words). "The Latter-day Saints."

The writer, B. W., declares at the outset:

Perhaps there is no other current topic of such importance, in connection with the nation of the Welsh, as is *Mormonism*, whether they dwell in the hills of Wales or in the midst of the broad valleys of the United States is of no import; for it brings a special connection with the one and the other, and thus it merits the attention of the public in general.

The writer then states that the purpose of the article was to provide some warning to his fellow nation "lest they be deceived by the enticements of these false latter-day prophets." He then presents his arguments against the practice of polygamy and issues an invitation to any of the Saints who "wish to reason on fair ground" to enter into a debate with him. And in the final paragraph, he gives his assessment of the lamentable situation of his fellow Welshmen who have gone to Salt Lake City:

If time permitted, we could comment on several other topics in connection with Mormonism. Nevertheless, my fellow nation can plainly see that the *Salt Lake* and environs are no paradise. No, there are thousands there this day who lament having been persuaded to leave the land of their birth and who wait fretfully to see the day dawn in which they will be able to escape the clutches of their cruel betrayers.

1855: May, *Seren Gomer* (*Star of Gomer*), pp. 222–24 (105 words).

Focuses on the scripture 1 Corinthians 15:29, which has to do with the baptism of the dead. The only connection the article has with The Church of Jesus Christ of Latter-day Saints is in a very sarcastic footnote:

Yesterday, as I was conversing with a friend about your questions, Mr. Crwt, I heard that the "Latter-day Saints" baptize for the dead. If that is true, it just

> adds to the list of amusing things. And that people, in a religious consideration, are not worthy of Christian commiseration, for they deny the Testament of our Lord Jesus Christ, as the only religious standard; therefore, they are beyond the boundary, in the same wilderness with the Muslims, Hindus, etc., and if they do not return, let them go to the Salt Lake Valley, or the valley of the *other* lake, to their own place.[28]

1855: 11 May, *Cambrian* (345 words). "Pocket Picking in the Saints' Hall, Orange Street."

> On Tuesday evening last Mr. Murray, French polisher, and his wife, were led by curiosity to enter the hall, perhaps being anxious to hear the peculiar tenets held and practiced by these fanatics. We know not whether the preacher was descanting upon the first great principle of human nature "protect thyself" (*ergo* thy pockets) or whether he was enforcing with equal warmth the commandment "Thou shalt not steal," but true it is that after Mrs. Murray had been in the hall for about 20 minutes she discovered that her pocket had been picked of five shillings and a penny; thus proving that whilst Captain Dan Jones or one of his satellites was talking, one of his audience (setting at defiance every principle of morality or common honesty) was *acting* and leisurely helping himself to the contents of his neighbor's pocket.

The writer sees this incident as a "literal translation" of the scripture in Matthew 21:13, which he quotes as "Ye have turned my Father's house into a den of thieves."

1855: June, *Y Cyfaill o'r Hen Wlad yn America* (*Friend of the Old Country in America*), p. 240 (70 words). "Mormon Colony."

A brief notice of the arrival of the ship the *Siddons* in Philadelphia. Unlike most articles with any mention of "Mormons," this one has nothing negative about them. It even has a positive comment about the arrivals:

> The ship *Siddons* reached Philadelphia lately, from Liverpool, with 425 Mormon immigrants on their journey, as evidenced by the directions on their chests, to "Salt Lake City." They were composed of British families, English and Welsh, and they had a healthy look to them. We saw 250 of the same religion headed to the same place, after starting from Swansea, at the beginning of last April.

Episode 12.3

Start: The Edinburgh Review prints six installments about "Mormonism"

1855: June, *Y Bedyddiwr* (*Baptist*), pp. 170–74 (3,050 words). "Mormonism."

This article, appearing in six parts, was originally printed in English in the *Edinburg Review*, then translated into Welsh to appear in the *Baptist*. The source and some further information appears in a footnote in this first installment:

> The following observations on Mormonism are a Review on a great number of Mormon Books which appeared lately in the *Edinburgh Review*.[29]

1855: July, *Y Bedyddiwr* (*Baptist*), pp. 194–98 (3,255 words). "Mormonism," the second installment.

1855: September, *Y Bedyddiwr* (*Baptist*), pp. 260–63 (2,250 words). "Mormonism," the third installment.

1855: October, *Y Bedyddiwr* (*Baptist*), pp. 293–96 (3,030 words). "Mormonism," the fourth installment.

1855: November, *Y Bedyddiwr* (*Baptist*), pp. 326–29 (2,840 words). "Mormonism," the fifth installment.

This is the only installment that has any content that specifically relates to Wales—a modified quote from a 6 January 1849 letter of Dan Jones to Orson Pratt about evil spirits that caused a great commotion in a conference held a few days earlier in Merthyr Tydfil:

> But there are scenes much more abominable taking place in the casting out of evil spirits. Daniel [*sic*] Jones, who at present is one of the three "Presidents of the Church in Wales," describes the following event in which he was acting as conjurer: "All during this time the evil spirits were causing the greatest disturbance by calling out, 'Old Captain, have you come to trouble us? Damned old Captain, we will hold you a battle.' Many other expressions used would be indecent to utter and others useless, I suppose. Some spoke English through one that knew no English herself. Others spoke in tongues, praying for a reinforcement of evil spirits, and chiding some dreadfully by names, such as *Borona*, *Menta*, *Philo*. They swore that they would not depart, *unless old Brigham Young would come from America to them*."[30]

1855: December, *Y Bedyddiwr* (*Baptist*), pp. 354–58 (3,360 words). "Mormonism," the sixth installment.

At the end of this sixth installment is an indication that the series is to be continued in the next issue of the *Baptist*. A thorough search has failed to reveal any further installments.

End: The *Edinburgh Review prints six installments about "Mormonism"*

1855: 29 June, *Cambrian* (42 words).

A brief report from the Swansea Petty Sessions records:

> Monday (before J. T. Jenkins, Esq., Mayor) James George, horse jobber, of Norton; John Cutliffe, an Elder of the Latter-day Saints Church; [and others] were severally charged with drunken and disorderly conduct in the public streets and were each fined 5s. and costs.

1855: 2 June, *North Wales Chronicle*, p. 2 (170 words). "Mormons on Slavery."

> Brigham Young, the High Priest of the Mormons at the Great Salt Lake, has recently issued a manifesto, in which he replies to charges brought against the Mormons by the people of the United States. He states that the charge against the Mormons of being hostile to American slavery is a calumny. His words are:

"The seed of Ham, which is the seed of Cain descending through Ham, will, according to the curse put upon him, serve his brethren, and be a 'servant of servants' to his fellow-creatures, until God removes the curse, and no power can hinder it. But the conduct of the whites towards the slaves will, in many cases, send both slave and master to hell. The blacks should be used like servants, and not like brutes; but they must serve. It is their privilege to live so as to enjoy many of the blessings which attend obedience to the first principles of the gospel, though they are not entitled to the priesthood."

1855: July, *Yr Eurgrawn Wesleyaidd* (*Wesleyan Treasury*), p. 251 (100 words).
"Mormon Wife."

A short time ago a lady in Frostburg, [Maryland, in] America, was taken up on the accusation of being in possession of five husbands, all them alive, but living in different parts of the country. When the Judge asked her the reason for such behavior, she said that the old things have gone by, and the rites have changed; "for," said she, "in every age of the world men have had more than one wife, and from now on the women will have more than one husband; for in those days one woman will take hold of seven men."[31]

The reporter of this information does not state that the woman was a member of The Church of Jesus Christ of Latter-day Saints, but the title implies that she was. Accuracy and responsible verification of the facts were generally not allowed to get in the way of casting the Latter-day Saints in a bad light at every opportunity in this and many other publications.

1855: 6 July, *Cambrian* (90 words).

An "apology" from the editor that was requested with regard to the brief report given in the newspaper for the previous week:

We are requested by some three or four members of the Church of Jesus Christ of Latter-day Saints to contradict the statement made in our last to the effect that John Cutliffe, the man charged on Monday week with drunken and disorderly conduct in the public streets, belongs to the Church. As we wish to give fair play to everyone, we willingly recall our statement; but may add that some three or four police officers can testify that the defendant himself admitted whilst drunk that he did belong to this body.

1855: 21 July, *Wrexham Advertiser*, p. 4 (175 words).

An anonymous letter preceded by the following comment of the editor:

Ruthin. The following is an extract of a letter from a respectable man residing at St. Louis, Missouri, America, a native of Ruthin. It is hoped it will have the effect of cautioning others from being entrapped by the devices and snares of a hypocritical and deceiving set of pretenders who, from the tenor of this letter, add robbery and peculation to deceit and falsehood.

Here is the letter:

St. Louis 6th June, 1855. Dear Mother—I have a man and his wife just arrived here with the Mormons from Abergele; his name is Richard Morgan Stevens. They are cousins to Mr. Prichard, late gardener at Llanbedr Hall, near Ruthin.

> They came here in a very destitute condition. They had all their things taken from them by the Mormon ministers. There are hundreds of them about here in the same condition, and many dying for want of food and lodgings. They are acquainted with Edward Roberts's two sons, of Borthy. They wish the truth of their condition to be made public in Wales, to prevent others from being deceived.

On the shipping list of the *Chimborazo*, which landed in Philadelphia on 21 May 1855, there is a couple from Abergele by the name of Richard Stephens (age thirty-seven), a tailor, and Anne Stephens (age forty). The writer may have confused the cities of St. Louis and Philadelphia.

1855: 18 July, *Caernarvon and Denbigh Herald*, p. 3 (175 words).

The same letter as appears in the *Wrexham Advertiser* for 21 July 1855 (see previous entry).

1855: 28 July, *Monmouthshire Merlin*, p. 2 (600 words). "Mormonism as It Is."

The account of a "Mrs. Parsons" in London who, along with her husband, had become a Latter-day Saint about ten years earlier. While her husband was off serving missions, Mrs. Parsons went with her two children to St. Louis where he later caught up with her. He went on ahead to Atchison, Kansas, where she later caught up with him. Upon learning that he had two other wives, Mrs. Parsons begged him to leave them and take care of her. When he refused to do so, she decided to take the children and leave. A "generous citizen" was kind enough to "secure a place for her in the Home of the Friendless, and provided a temporary retreat for her children." This account is taken from the *St. Louis News.*

1855: August, *Yr Eurgrawn Wesleyaidd* (*Wesleyan Treasury*), pp. 272–76 (3,890 words). "Mormonism, or the Tenets of the Latter-day Saints Exposed and Refuted."

In his opening paragraph, the writer observes:

> Mormonism has created quite a commotion in Wales during the last few years. A large number of our compatriots have fallen victim to this religious falsehood. Neither the pulpit nor the press have done their part to deliver our nation from the seductive doctrine of Joe Smith.[32]

He then refutes the general attitude of the English toward the Welsh and offers an explanation:

> Some of the English accuse us of being ignorant as a nation, and extremely ready to accept every kind of heresy. But it was not in Wales that Mormonism had its start, rather in America, among the English; and from there it spread to England, and then to Wales.[33]

By the mid-nineteenth century, the Welsh had become a Nonconformist nation with regard to religion, the bulk of them having put aside the Anglican Church in favor of Nonconformity. This transformation may well have been the writer's reason for saying, "It may be that we are as free from deadly heresy as any people." But he then softens his stance a bit except for his exclusion of two camps:

> The truth in its main points is believed and taught by all the denominations in general, except those who deny the divinity of Christ and the Mormons.[34]

The writer aligns himself with many other preachers and editors in Wales by classifying the "Mormons" with non-Christian heathens in general. He then declares what he believes to be the basic objection to the religion founded by Joseph Smith:

> The immorality of the Mormons is in their *behavior* instead of in their standard works; but since *continual* revelation is going on, is it possible that some inspiration descends to *teach* immorality of the worst kind?[35]

The lengthy article that follows is presented under ten headings:

1. Opening observations
2. Rise of the Mormon deceit
3. The rapid spread of the Mormon deceit
4. Reasons for resisting Mormonism
5. Every man in his right senses must completely refuse the Book of Mormon
6. Internal and external proofs show that the Book of Mormon contains lies and heresies
7. Not one single book exists that co-testifies in favor of the Book of Mormon
8. We fully reject the Book of Mormon because Joseph Smith was a man of indecent morals
9. Joe Smith and his followers allow polygamy
10. Mormonism adds to the word of God

1855: August, *Yr Eurgrawn* (*Treasury*), p. 284 (65 words).

A brief notice concerning the families of Brigham Young and his counselor Heber C. Kimball:

> *Latter-day Saints.* Brigham Young, the leader of the Mormons, is building two great and splendid houses next to the one he currently lives in, in Salt Lake City, to have space for his growing family. He is now rejoicing in the possession of from fifty to sixty wives, and from forty to fifty children. Elder Kimball, one of the Mormon apostles, has between sixty and seventy wives.

1855: 11 August, *Monmouthshire Merlin*, p. 5 (12 words).

The Mormons at the Salt Lake are likely to suffer from famine.

1855: 11 August, *Usk Observer*, p. 6 (260 words).

"An officer belonging to Colonel Steptoe's command, now stationed at Salt Lake City, in a letter to the *Providence Journal*," writes of the condition of the Latter-day Saint women:

> Their condition is infinitely worse than that of the slaves of the South. . . . Their case is peculiarly hard, separated by hundreds of miles of plain and dessert from the outside world brought here by false inducements, degraded and oppressed, with no hope of succor—they are in great, very great numbers, entirely disaffected. They abhor the very thought of polygamy, the very name of Mormonism. This is the simple truth.

1855: 15 August, *Monmouthshire Merlin*, p. 3 (87 words).

> From Utah territory a week's later advices have been received. The Mormons in the valley of the Great Salt Lake were anticipating a famine. All the crops were being devoured by insects, and flour was very scarce, at the price of six dollars per 100 lbs. A person, of the name of Young, who has commenced lectures among the Mormons, advises his brethren to take short excursions throughout the country. With their families. This Mormon acknowledges to the possession of ninety wives, and a multitude of children.

1855: 18 August, *Wrexham Advertiser*, p. 3 (36 words).

> The Mormons in the valley of the Great Salt Lake are anticipating a famine. All the crops were being devoured by insects, and flour was very scarce at the price of 6 dollars per 100 lbs.

1855: 18 August, *Monmouthshire Merlin*, p. 3 (785 words). "Prospect of Famine amongst the Mormons."

An article reprinted from the *New York Herald* about the dire circumstances faced by the residents of Utah. The writer predicts that "it is quite possible that the kingdom and the institution of Mormondom will be extinguished or expelled from our western territories within a few years, by causes and instruments which have never entered into the calculations of saints, philosophers, or politicians." In this long article, the writer also presents considerable background and commentary on the practice of polygamy among the Latter-day Saints.

1855: 18 August, *Silurian*, p. 7 (1,255 words).

This is the same article as appears in the *Monmouthshire Merlin* for the same date (see above entry), with three additional paragraphs.

1855: 18 August, *Caernarvon and Denbigh Herald*, p. 10 (90 words). "Mormon Emigration."

> From a statement contained in the weekly organ of these fanatical people, and which now openly espouses the principle of polygamy, it seems that in the half-year between November 1854 and April 1855, the number of Mormonites who left the port of Liverpool for the United States, en route for the Salt Lake, was 3,626, of whom 2,291 were English, 401 Scotch, 287 Welsh, etc. The total number of the Scandinavian mission is said to have been 533, of whom 409 were Danes, 71 Swedes, and 53 Norwegians.

1855: 18 August, *Monmouthshire Merlin*, p. 6 (205 words). "California."

The writer begins his article with information about Colonel Steptoe's arrival in California with his troops and the preparations being made by the Latter-day Saints to fortify their city. He observes:

> These wretches are the very scum and refuse of the earth, and the Government ought to burn the town about their ears.

He also comments about the arrival of Orson Hyde "accompanied by fifteen wives!"

1855: 18 August, *Monmouthshire Merlin*, p. 5 (105 words). "Progress of Mormonism."

> Twenty-five years ago, the "Prophet" Joseph Smith organized the Mormon Church with six members. At the present time, the Church in Utah Territory contains three presidents, seven apostles, 2026 "seventies," 715 high priests, 994 elders, 514 priests, 471 teachers, 227 deacons besides the usual ratio of persons in training for the ministry, but not yet ordained, and 489 missionaries abroad. During the six months ending with the beginning of April last, 965 children were born in the territory of Utah, 278 persons died, 479 were baptized in the Mormon faith, and 86 were excommunicated from the Church. [Reprinted from] *New York Paper.*

1855: 18 August, *North Wales Chronicle*, p. 6, item 1 (105 words). "Progress of Mormonism."

This is the exact same article as appeared in the *Monmouthshire Merlin* for the same date (see previous entry).

1855: 18 August, *North Wales Chronicle*, p. 6, item 2 (230 words). "The Mormons Again."

> The Mormons in the valley of the Great Salt Lake were anticipating a famine. The crickets, grasshoppers, and locusts devoured everything in the fields and gardens, and, in spite of active and unceasing efforts to counteract their deprecations, there was little hope of the crops arriving at maturity. Add to this calamity the ravages of the Indians—who seem to have again broken from the control of the whites—and it will be admitted that the Latter-day Saints are in a bad way; to say nothing of flour selling at six dollars per hundred, and very scarce at that price. In view of this state of things, Brigham Young, who had just returned from a jaunt through the country, delivered an address, wherein he advised the faithful to take short excursions with their families, taking care, however, to leave the babies at home. Young acknowledges to the possession of ninety wives, and of children a multitude, and he believes it would promote their health and cheer them up to camp out. The ravages of the insects and the total destruction of the crops suggest the probability of the Mormons abandoning their settlements at the Great Salt Lake City. Supplies cannot be procured nearer than San Bernardino, which is 800 miles distant, and the excursions recommended by the governor may be but the preliminary to a general movement.

1855: 25 August, *Monmouthshire Beacon*, p. 3 (230 words). "Progress of Mormonism."

This is the same article that appeared a week earlier under the same title in the *Monmouthshire Merlin*.[36]

1855: September, *Y Bedyddiwr* (*Baptist*), pp. 287–88 (1,060 words). "The Likely Destruction of the Mormons."

A detailed description of the predicted doom of the Latter-day Saints in Utah and elsewhere. The opening paragraph sets the stage:

> According to the latest accounts which have come to us from Utah, it is quite likely that the Mormon kingdom and settlement will be utterly destroyed, or they will be exiled from our western territories within a very few years, by causes and means which have never before come to the imagination of saints, philosophers, or rulers.[37]

The writer then explains that grasshoppers and crickets have devasted the recent crops, leaving the land desolate, and that despite the intervention of the seagulls, the future looks bleak. Here is his final statement:

> Consequently, being cut off from receiving any outside assistance or deliverance, there is but one choice left for the Mormons, after the destruction of their crops over one harvest, but to emigrate to look for bread, or to starve to death if they do not.[38]

1855: September, *Yr Eurgrawn* (*Treasury*), pp. 319–20 (310 words). "Heinousness of Mormonism."

This article, taken from the *Cambridge Chronicle*, contains the Welsh translation of a letter sent from Salt Lake City by a "woman who had embraced Mormon deceit and had gone to the abode of Mormonism in America." The letter contains no specific details and bears all the markings of a fictitious creation. Here is a sample of its contents:

> You dare not speak your mind; you are surrounded by spies who carry every word that may resemble dissatisfaction; you do not know whom you can trust; in short, you distrust everyone, and everyone distrusts you. A human life is of no worth here; cutting throats is spoken of with as little concern as cutting fingernails; truly, if it is thought that you are separating yourself from their principles, it is considered a kindness to kill you, so that your soul will be saved.[39]

The supposed writer declares her fear and a plea:

> Here I have become so fearful that I cannot take pleasure in anything; in the midst of all the wickedness and evil that are here, my every wish is for life to cease. Think of me, and pray for me.[40]

1855: September, *Yr Haul* (*Sun*), p. 299, item 1 (75 words). "The Mormons."

> The *New York Herald* says that the Mormons in the Salt Lake Valley are being threatened with a frightful famine. It appears that crickets, locusts, and grasshoppers have destroyed and are destroying the country's entire crop. It is said that the Mormon settlement there will be completely broken, and in all likelihood, thousands will starve to death. What will Brigham Young do with his wives? It is said that he has about ninety of them.

1855: September, *Yr Haul* (*Sun*), p. 299, item 2 (60 words). "Success of Mormonism."

> Twenty-five years after the thing called the Mormon Church was formed by the Prophet Joseph Smith, presently there are 3 main officials in the territory of Utah; 7 apostles; 2026 seventies; 715 high priests; 994 elders; 514 priests;

471 teachers; 227 deacons; and 48 missionaries in various countries. Is it not very strange that this strange deceit has succeeded?

1855: 1 September, *Monmouthshire Merlin*, p. 2 (95 words). "Explosion of Fire Damp."

We regret to state that on Monday morning, at nine o'clock, a fearful explosion of fire damp took place in the New Colliery, at this place, by which five men were dreadfully burnt. It is supposed that the ignition took place through one of the men having secured the gauze of his lamp too loosely. Three of the unfortunate men are Mormons, and rumors are rife of the cures which the "Mormon oil," administered by the "Elders," will produce in this lamentable case. The men were all much injured.

1855: 8 September, *North Wales Chronicle*, p. 6 (35 words). "A Mormon 'Saint' and his Wives."

Orson Hyde, one of the Mormon saints, was lately in St. Louis, for the purpose, it is said, of marrying twelve more wives, to whom he is affianced!

1855: 15 September, *Monmouthshire Beacon*, p. 6 (35 words).

The same article as appeared in the *North Wales Chronicle* for 8 September 1855 (see previous entry).

1855: 15 September, *North Wales Chronicle*, p. 6 (40 words).

News from Great Salt Lake City to the 1st of July has come to hand. The grasshoppers had destroyed the third crop of grain, and starvation or an abandonment of the settlements were the alternatives presented to the Mormons.

1855: 15 September, *Merthyr Telegraph*, p. 4 (40 words).

The same article as appears in the *North Wales Chronicle* for the same date (see previous entry).

1855: 22 September, *Silurian*, p. 2 (65 words).

A young man, named John Dudman, of Bath, aged twenty, Mormon preacher, who had for several days been in the neighborhood of Plymouth, propagating the doctrines of the notorious Joe Smith, has been accidentally drowned in the River Lynher, whilst in the act of bathing. Deceased was accompanied to the river by a person named Gartrell, whom he urged to bathe with him.

1855: 29 September, *Silurian*, p. 5 (65 words).

Coedycymmer—The first anniversary of the Baptist Chapel, at this place, took place on Sunday last, when the Revs. J. Evans, Abercannaid, R. Roberts, Tabernacle E. Evans, Caersalem, J. Lloyd, Ebenezer, and J. Jones, Zion, delivered highly appropriate sermons on the occasion. On Monday evening, the latter gentleman delivered a lecture on 'Mormonism,' which made such havoc in that congregation, the Rev. R. Jenkyn presiding.

1855: 29 September, *Merthyr Telegraph* p. 2 (65 words). "Chapel Anniversary."

The same information as appears in the *Silurian* for 29 September 1855 (see previous entry).

1855: October, *Y Dysgedydd* (*Instructor*), p. 404 (100 words). "The Mormons."

The Mormons in Salt Lake City are afflicted greatly by locusts, crickets, and a kind of destructive fleas. This is the third year that the locusts have destroyed their crops. At present the land of promise is not before the Mormons; rather they must starve or flee for their lives. Can it be that the senseless and deceitful wretches will come to see their error when the famine comes upon them? Until now they have scorned reason and the gospel; but it is likely that the locusts will bring the wisest of them to their senses.

1855: 6 October, *North Wales Chronicle*, p. 7 (240 words). "Revolt of the Mormon Wives."

While the Government troops were at the holy city of Great Salt Lake, these soldiers appropriated every opportunity to take the wives and daughters of the saints out walking and riding—especially sleigh-riding—and the havoc which they thus made among the beauties of the principality may be partly conjectured from the announcement that they carried off with them an indefinite number of the Mormons fair ones, "for better or for worse"—"sink or swim, survive or perish"—en route for California. This is momentous news, and very significant withal. It shows that the Mormon women are ripe for rebellion, and that a detachment of the regular army is a greater terror to the patriarchs of the Mormon Jerusalem than Indians, or drought, or grasshoppers. It indicates the way, too, for the extinction of the peculiar institutions of Utah. The astonishing results of the expedition of Colonel Steptoe in this view do most distinctly suggest the future policy of the Government touching this next of Mormons. It is to send out to the Great Salt Lake a fresh detachment of young and good-looking soldiers, and at the end of two or three months order them off to California, and replace them by a new detachment at Salt Lake City, and so on, till those Turks of the desert are reduced by feminine desertions to the standard Christian regulation of one wife apiece. [Reprinted from the] *New York Herald.*

1855: 6 October, *Wrexham Advertiser*, p. 2 (240 words).

This is the same article as appears in the *North Wales Chronicle* for 6 October 1855 (see previous entry).

1855: 27 October, *North Wales Chronicle*, p. 6 (530 words). "Mormonism at the Salt Lake."

A letter, reprinted from the *Edinburgh News* two weeks before, written by "a Mormonite" who signs himself "One of the Deluded." He tells of his extremely negative experience in making the journey to Salt Lake City: all his belongings were taken from him, Brigham Young would do nothing for him, he was threatened by the "destroying angels," thousands would gladly make their escape if they could, and women are terribly degraded.

1855: 17 November, *North Wales Chronicle*, p. 5 (95 words). "A Desperate Mormon."

I have never yet talked so rough in these mountains as I did in the United States when they killed Joseph (Smith). I there said boldly and aloud, "If ever

> a man should lay his hands on me, and say, on account of my religion, 'You are my prisoner,' the Lord Almighty helping me, I would send that man to eternity." I feel so now. Let mobbers keep their hands off me, or I will send them where they belong. I am always prepared for such an emergency. —Brigham Young.

1855: 8 December, *North Wales Chronicle*, p. 4 (1,340 words). "The Mormons."

A long article from the *New York Herald* that presents many details about Salt Lake City.

Episode 12.4

Start: Dan Jones exposes an exposé in sixteen pages

1855: Pre-October, *Yr Amserau* (*Times*), nonextant.

Sometime before 27 October 1855, a Welsh translation of segments of an 1855 anonymous novel about polygamy in The Church of Jesus Christ of Latter-day Saints appeared in the *Times*. Unfortunately, the issues of the *Times* containing these segments are missing from the National Library of Wales's newspaper collection, and research has failed to unearth them elsewhere. The novel in question is *Female Life Among the Mormons; a Narrative of Many Years' Personal Experience by the Wife of a Mormon Elder, recently from Utah*, published by J. C. Derby in New York in 1855. *The Times*'s printing of the segments evidently came to the attention of Dan Jones, who unleashed a vitriolic critique of them in two separate issues of *Zion's Trumpet*—a critique that began on 27 October 1855 and extends to 10 November 1855 (see next entries).

1855: 27 October, *Udgorn Seion* (*Zion's Trumpet*), pp. 337–44 (3,460 words). "The *Times* with Its Carcass in Its Mouth!" Part 1.

Jones states angrily at the outset of his article:

> Even though we have read everything that we could lay our hands on of the filth of the scum of authors and editors in every language we understand for over a dozen years, having to hold our nose tightly many times, while we analyzed the malodorous entrails of their anti-Mormon *bug bears* searching for a crumb of truth, we confess that this dirty bag is the filthiest of all.[41]

He declares the book to be "entirely fictitious"[42] and points out numerous historical inaccuracies in support of his position. Here are a few assertions made by *Female Life*'s author with which Jones takes issue and provides corrections:

- Joseph Smith is killed while riding horseback with a woman behind him—he was assassinated while in prison.
- Joseph Smith is described as having "piercing black eyes"—he had light-colored eyes.
- The Saints traveled to Nauvoo from New York—it was from Missouri.
- It was one month after the Martyrdom that the Saints left Nauvoo—it was in fact two years.

1855: 10 November, *Udgorn Seion* (*Zion's Trumpet*), pp. 353–61 (3,730 words). "The *Times* with Its Carcass in Its Mouth!" Part 2.

After sixteen pages of outrage across two issues, Jones concludes:

The editor of the *Times* proves himself totally unfit to edit any publication and unworthy of the trust of the public by lowering himself with this shameless stream of lies, and not a single man or woman who possesses a grain of true religion will ever believe him again, we should think, whenever he delivers his opinion about any religion of his fellowmen.[43]

End: Dan Jones exposes an exposé in sixteen pages

1855: 3 November, *Monmouthshire Beacon*, p. 6 (530 words). "Mormonism at the Salt Lake."

The same article as appeared in the *North Wales Chronicle* for 27 October 1855 (see previous entry).

1855: 1 December, *Monmouthshire Merlin*, p. 6 (315 words). "Disturbance of a Mormon Congregation."

A *Worcester Chronicle* account of a Latter-day Saint meeting in Worcester about polygamy. When discussion was invited from those in attendance, many questions were asked that prompted the leader to have the gathering "take shelter in a hymn."

> This, however, was not allowed by the audience, who drowned the music with shouts, stamps, catcalls, hisses, and the firing of a cracker, which reprehensible proceeding filled the female portion of the audience with alarm. Shortly after this, and when order had been somewhat restored, the gas was suddenly turned out, and then arose a din almost deafening. A rush was made for the door, a very narrow aperture, causing the upsetting of benches and forms, and this, together with shrieks and screams of women, who were being terribly crushed, and some of whom had little children in their arms; and the cries of boys and girls, and shouts for candles, completed a scene such as might be fit for Pandemonium, but not at all to be expected in a licensed place of worship.

The sequel to all of the above is also included:

> On Tuesday, at the meeting of the town council, Mr. Watkins called attention to "a nest of infamy" in Carden Street, where the Latter-day Saints assembled and promulgated doctrines more calculated to injure the morals of the rising generation than anything since the creation of the world. The mayor said he could not interfere in matters of opinion.

1855: 1 December, *Caernarvon and Denbigh Herald*, p. 10 (50 words). "Renewed Disturbance of a Mormon Congregation at Worcester."

This is the same article, with only a few differences, as appeared in the *Monmouthshire Merlin* for 1 December 1855, p. 6.

1855: 29 December, *Caernarvon and Denbigh Herald*, p. 3 (50 words). "The Mormonites."

> At the forthcoming Dover sessions the question will be brought forward for the Recorder's decision, whether Mormonites are protestant dissenters. This arises from the charge recently preferred against a young man for disturbing public worship in a Mormonite meeting house, when the magistrates held the offender to bail.

Notes

1. This English-language pamphlet is available online at archive.org.
2. For the English translation of this pamphlet see *Defending the Faith: Early Welsh Missionary Publications*, Item J27.
3. *Zion's Trumpet*, 14 April 1855, 116.
4. Hepburn's pamphlet is posted online at archive.org.
5. The *Revivalist*, 22 January 1857, 31.
6. *Zion's Trumpet*, 27 October 1855, 337–44, 353–61.
7. Ibid., 337, emphasis in original.
8. Ibid., 360.
9. The second edition of this is available online at archive.org.
10. 2 Timothy 3:12, in *Zion's Trumpet*, 14 April 1855, 113.
11. Ibid., 116.
12. 1 Timothy 6:5, in ibid.
13. Ibid.
14. Ibid., 119.
15. *Zion's Trumpet*, 28 April 1855, 136–37, emphasis in original.
16. Ibid., 137.
17. Ibid.
18. Ibid.
19. Ibid.
20. Ibid.
21. Ibid.
22. Ibid., 138.
23. Ibid., 139.
24. It is available online at archive.org.
25. *Zion's Trumpet*, 12 May 1855, 154.
26. *Zion's Trumpet*, 26 May 1855, 172.
27. Ibid.
28. *Star of Gomer*, May 1855, 223.
29. The *Baptist*, June 1855, 170.
30. The *Baptist*, November 1855, 329. See also Dan Jones to Orson Pratt, 6 January 1849, *Millennial Star* 11:39.
31. See Isaiah 4:1.
32. *Wesleyan Treasury*, August 1855, 272.
33. Ibid.
34. Ibid.
35. Ibid.
36. *Monmouthshire Merlin*, 18 August 1855, 5.
37. *Baptist*, September 1855, 287.
38. Ibid., 288.
39. *Treasury*, September 1855, 319–20.
40. Ibid., 320.
41. *Zion's Trumpet*, 27 October 1855, 337.
42. Ibid., 341.
43. *Zion's Trumpet*, 10 November 1855, 360.

Chapter 13

Episodes

13.1—Joseph Hodgetts retrieves part of his family from the *Enoch Train*
13.2—W. Parrott lectures against his former religion
13.3—William Webb accuses Thomas and Pamela Hewlett of stealing his sister
13.4—Reverend J. Jones of Llangollen dies in Cincinnati

Salient Events

- **5 January 1856.** *Zion's Trumpet* prints a letter written by Thomas Job from Salt Lake City. Dated 27 August 1855, the letter is addressed to Daniel Daniels, the uncle of Thomas's wife, Hannah. Just over one year earlier, Thomas had left Wales for Utah, taking his two-year-old daughter, Elizabeth, with him. At that time, his wife had been unwilling to make the journey, but she later changed her mind. Thomas indicates in his letter that he would gladly pay Hannah's way as well as the way for various other relatives. See the full account of the Job family in the Salient Events section of chapter 11.
- **28 January 1856.** David John from Little Newcastle, Pembrokeshire, has a dream in which an angel instructs him to realign himself with the Latter-day Saints (he had been baptized seven years earlier, at the age of sixteen). The poem he composed shortly after this life-changing dream is printed in the 1 March 1856 issue of *Zion's Trumpet*. Here are the first two stanzas of his poem, entitled "Feeling of a Young Saint":

  I lost all my former friends,
  When I joined with the Saints;
  Nevertheless, I have gained,
  And it is a wondrous honor to me.
  If I have lost the smiles of my dear mother,

And of my many relatives old and young;
I have received an even more valuable treasure
That Jesus pure has promised.[1]

See the Salient Event for February 1849 for more information about David John. While he and his family were crossing the plains in 1861, his daughter Annie died at eight months old. The approximate location of her grave was discovered later, the account of which is available online.[2]

- **2 February 1856.** The *Zion's Trumpet*'s statistical report for Wales for the final six months of 1855 shows the total number of members at that time to be 3,785. Also mentioned are 590 excommunications, 54 deaths, and 219 emigrants. Undoubtedly Dan Jones and other church leaders were concerned that there were 71 more excommunications than there were baptisms during this period. One must bear in mind, however, that during this era, members were often excommunicated for relatively minor offenses, such as nonattendance at meetings and consumption of alcohol.

Conference	Branches	Baptisms	Members	President
East Glamorgan	27	232	1,632	Robert Evans
West Glamorgan	17	53	421	Thomas Harris
Monmouthshire	20	68	465	Thomas D. Giles
Breconshire	7	21	145	Thomas Morgan
Llanelli	11	50	327	Benjamin Jones
Carmarthen	7	21	126	Thomas Jenkins
North Pembroke	4	3	32	Thomas D. Evans
South Pembroke	10	25	175	John Price
Cardiganshire	5	3	80	John Richards
Merionethshire	6	4	71	John Davies
Flintshire	4	8	106	Lewis Davies
Denbighshire	5	7	114	John Parry
Anglesey and Conway	6	6	98	William Lewis
Total	129	519	3,789	n/a

- **23–26 February 1856.** A four-day conference is held in Merthyr Tydfil at the White Lion Inn. In attendance were the presidency of the Church in Great Britain: Franklin D. Richards, Daniel Spencer, and Cyrus H. Wheelock. The following paragraph provides some idea as to the conditions of this conference, the final one at which Dan Jones would preside:

  > President Jones made some preliminary remarks to bring the numerous congregation to order, requesting the Saints to make room for one another, and for those who were on the steps and on the road wishing to have a place to listen somehow. He requested those who did not understand English to be patient since it was in that language the brethren would speak.[3]

Jones occasionally summarized in Welsh the messages of English speakers for the benefit of those in attendance who did not speak English; many of the speakers encouraged the monoglot Welsh to learn English. Jones also announced that "half the number of those who give five pounds to the P. E. Fund will receive their passage to the Valley this year if they have been faithful Saints for over six years, and the other half will be given passage next year." In looking back on the travels of Daniel Daniels and himself, Jones was pleased to report that "there was never a contrary word or action, rather cooperation in love always." On the final day of the conference, Daniels was set apart as president of the Church in Wales in place of Jones. Daniels's counselors were Israel Evans and Benjamin Ashby, two Americans who spoke no Welsh. No doubt Jones was happy not to have a repeat of what occurred at the conference held in the same location seven years earlier, when he was to be released from the same office: the leaders from Liverpool had not been in attendance, despite promising to come, and Jones had had to release himself and set apart his replacements.

- **15 March 1856.** In this issue of *Zion's Trumpet,* Dan Jones reaffirms his belief that a Welshman by the name of Prince Madoc had discovered America some three hundred years before Columbus's arrival. Jones declares his determination to continue the search that he had begun on the Southern Expedition with Parley P. Pratt seven years earlier and also pleas for additional information that anyone might have:

  > Despite how much others may doubt the story that Madawg ab Owen Gwynedd [Madog ab Owain Gwynedd] discovered America before Columbus, we have gathered satisfactory proofs of the fact in our searches across the continent for the "Welsh Indians" during the past twenty years, and since we are determined to re-initiate at the end of this month a search with no turning back, if they are living on land, we beseech those who may have a more correct or more extensive story than that given by "Powell" or the "Triads" about the departure of Madawg from this country or by his descendants on the other side of the sea, to assist us in our venture; not their money, we do not ask that, rather for accounts which will help us to accomplish the objective which has cost us several hundred already.[4]

There is no evidence during the remaining six years of Jones's life that he was able to pursue his passion of searching for the Welsh Indians. That he was beset with financial difficulties and many health issues during this period possibly explains his lack of action.

- **29 March 1856.** Dan Jones declares in *Zion's Trumpet* that this issue would be his last as its editor, as he had been assigned to take a large group of emigrants to America, and that his good friend Daniel Daniels would take over the editorship.[5] The following is a brief summary of Jones's history with the Welsh periodical (see Chapters 3 and 6 for more details):
  - **July 1846.** Jones founds the *Prophet of the Jubilee.* Published monthly for two and a half years, this was the first non-English publication for The Church of Jesus Christ of Latter-day Saints.

- o **January 1849.** The periodical is renamed *Zion's Trumpet*, and its base of operations moves to Merthyr Tydfil under the editorship of John S. Davis, who serves as editor for the next five years. Davis also publishes Welsh translations for the Book of Mormon, the Doctrine and Covenants, and the Pearl of Great Price.
- o **January 1854.** Jones, back in Wales as a missionary, becomes the editor of *Zion's Trumpet* and serves until March 1856.

- **5 April 1856.** The *Caernarvon and Denbigh Herald* becomes the first newspaper in Wales to report the excitement on the ship *Enoch Train* that occurred just hours after its departure from Liverpool on 23 March 1856. The story had first appeared in the *Worcestershire Chronicle* only three days after Joseph Hodgetts had chased down the *Enoch Train* just minutes before it entered the open sea. His objective was to persuade his wife and children to return home to Worcester with him. While Hodgetts had been away on business, Ann Hodgetts had taken £314 from the bank and then had gone with her children to board the ship in Liverpool. The story, with varying amounts of detail, also appeared in the *North Wales Chronicle*, the *Cardiff and Merthyr Guardian*, the *Usk Observer*, and the *Monmouthshire Merlin*. See Episode 13.1.
- **12 April 1856.** On page 121 in this issue of *Zion's Trumpet*, Daniel Daniels expresses his trepidation at having accepted not only the responsibility of the editorship of the periodical but also that of the presidency of the Church in Wales:

> We are far from being so conceited as to claim the same skill in a war as that of an old soldier who has been in the battle fighting with the family of the devil as if for life and having done so from the first time the banner of Jesus waved over the hills of Gwalia until now. . . . Here we are poor weaklings and too grossly inexperienced, you conference presidents included, after having been set in our places to do the best we can. . . . Dear fellow soldiers, please complete the deficiency of your president and editor who is at present unskilled, by keeping the divine armor shiny, and your swords sharp, and wage war to the sound of the *Trumpet*, through which we shall seek to blow only that which is most interesting and useful.[6]

Daniels fails to mention yet another worry he most likely had: having two American counselors, Israel Evans and Benjamin Ashby, who did not speak any Welsh. Evans, however, expressed his joy at having received his new assignment:

> I have wanted to visit Wales ever since I was a child, for this is the land of birth of my forebears, although they are not in the land of the living at present. . . . My heart jumped for joy when President Franklin said to me—"Brother Israel—I want you and Brother Ashby to go to Wales to labor, and to learn the Welsh language, which will be an eternal blessing to you."[7]

No doubt Daniels appreciated Evans's enthusiasm for his new calling; however, there is no evidence that either Evans or Ashby ever learned Welsh while serving in Wales.

- **19 April 1856.** The *S. Curling* leaves Liverpool with 707 Latter-day Saint passengers, 560 of them Welsh, under the leadership of Dan Jones. After a journey of just five weeks, the ship docked at Boston where they boarded a train for Iowa City, the terminus of the railroad at that time. In Iowa City, a handcart company was formed with 232 members, nearly all of them Welsh, under the leadership of Edward Bunker, a veteran of the "Mormon Battalion." Bunker later wrote in his journal:

> I had for my counselors Brothers Grant, a Scotchman, and tailor by trade, and MacDonald, a cabinet maker, neither of whom had much experience in handling teams. Both were returned missionaries. The Welsh people had had no experience and very few of them could speak English. This made my burden very heavy. I had the mule team to drive and had to instruct the teamsters about yoking the oxen.[8]

The Saints who traveled in handcart companies across the plains showed great courage, faith, and ingenuity on their journeys. To better understand their experiences were like, see accounts such as those concerning John Parry Jr., Ann Morris Butler, Priscilla Merriman Evans, Thomas D. Giles, and Robert David Roberts.[9]

The Edward Bunker Handcart Company reached Salt Lake City on 2 October 1856, five and a half months after the *S. Curling* had sailed from Liverpool.

- **3 May 1856.** Dewi Elfed Jones writes a letter to Daniel Daniels in which he expresses his great remorse for the wrongdoing that had resulted in his excommunication in 1855. Letters had appeared in the 21 July 1855 *Zion's Trumpet* revealing that Jones's misuse of Church funds had been the reason for excommunicating him (see Episode 8.2). The postscript of his letter is a long poem of contrition entitled "Hymn of Tribulation." Next is a letter by Thomas Harris, one who had spoken out against Jones nearly a year earlier, but who now speaks in favor of his reinstatement. The final word on the subject is a letter by Daniel Daniels:

> I recommend him from my heart to the attention, goodwill, and trust of the Saints and pray for him while burying all that was, without further mention of it, so that we may be of one heart in supplicating in his behalf, that he shall have the strength to redouble his diligence until the gap caused during the time we have lost is fully made up.[10]

Jones emigrated in 1860 on the *William Tapscott* and died three years later in Logan, Utah, at the age of fifty-six.

- **3 May 1856.** A writer for the *North Wales Chronicle* tells of receiving a long letter from William Saunders Parrott in which he had written of his experience among the Latter-day Saints. After spending a period of time "enchanted with the system," Parrott decided not only to end his association with his new Church but also to warn others by giving lectures to reveal "the fallacies and absurdities of the Mormon belief." Other newspapers in Wales reported on his lectures. See Episode 13.2.

- **7 June 1856.** The *Monmouthshire Beacon* prints an article about Mary Ann Webb, "the daughter of a laboring man living in the Baptist chapel yard, who is himself a devoted Latter-day Saint." Ten months later, in the 11 April 1857 issue of the same newspaper, another article about Webb appeared. These articles provide information about Webb's decision to take residence in the nearby home of Thomas and Pamela Hewlett, also Latter-day Saints. Although Webb's father, who was also a Latter-day Saint, supported her going to stay with the Hewletts, her mother strongly disapproved. Ann left Liverpool on the *George Washington* in March 1857 and eventually made her way to Salt Lake City. Two days later Thomas Hewlett accused William Webb of "putting dirt in his house," and an altercation broke out. A lawsuit resulted. See Episode 13.3.
- **30 August 1856.** *Zion's Trumpet* prints a letter from Daniel Daniels's wife, Mary. Mary had learned of her husband's new calling from John S. Davis, who had seen an issue of the *Millennial Star* with the change in the leadership in Wales. Writing from Salt Lake City on 27 June 1856, she expressed her feelings of disappointment:

  > This news was not sweet to me at first, but, as you said in your letter, "that the will of the Lord be done, and his counsel be respected," is my wish, although it may not always be in accordance with the feelings of human nature."[11]

- **3 September 1856.** Dan Jones and fifteen others depart from Florence, Nebraska, on their way to Salt Lake City. At the end of the 1856 immigration season, Franklin D. Richards and several other immigration agents and returning missionaries remained in Florence to close the accounts. Members of this "express company" then made their way to Salt Lake City, arriving on 4 October 1856. They met with Brigham Young and informed him concerning the companies still out on the plains. Plans were implemented immediately to go rescue the Martin and Willie handcart companies.
- **6 December 1856.** Israel Evans and Benjamin Ashby are released as counselors to Daniel Daniels. William Miller and James Taylor are appointed to be the new counselors to Daniels. One is left to wonder as to the reason for the continuation of non-Welsh speakers occupying these important positions.

Commentary

1856: January, *Y Cyfaill o'r Hen Wlad yn America* (*Friend of the Old Country in America*), pp. 42–43 (190 words). "Mormon Numbers."

Taken from the *Deseret News*, this article contains information on several Church demographics: the number of Latter-day Saint missionaries serving in various parts of the world, the newspapers and periodicals then being published by the Church, and the languages into which the Book of Mormon had been translated.

1856: 19 January, *Cardiff and Merthyr Guardian*, p. 8 (305 words). "A Female Mormon Tyrant."

This brief article, taken from *Putnam's New York Magazine*, is an interview of a "tidy English woman, from Bath, of some native refinement of manner." During the interview, another woman comes into the room who is revealed to be another wife of the woman's husband. The reporter learns of the great unhappiness of the "woman from Bath" because of this polygamous relationship. He ends the article: "She could not even have the privilege of a cup of tea without asking the jade's permission, so effectually had the intruder usurped all authority in this humble abode. My heart wept for her."

1856: 23 February, *Monmouthshire Beacon*, p. 6 (445 words). "A Mormon Elder in Siam. A King with 1000 Wives."

A quote from the *Millennial Star*—here is the first part of it:

> A Letter from Salt Lake City, dated Oct. 31st, gives a detailed account of the Great Mormon Conference which took place there on the 6th, 7th, and 8th of the month. The proceedings were of no general interest. Several returned missionaries gave accounts of their journeyings and works in foreign lands. One Elder Luddington had been on a rather unsuccessful mission to Siam, having only baptized the captain of one of the ships he sailed in, and his wife. Considerable sensation was observed among his Mormon auditory when he informed them that the first King has one thousand wives, and the second five hundred. He stated that each king has fifty dancing girls, selected for their faultless forms and beauty.

1856: 23 February, *Cardiff and Merthyr Guardian*, p. 8 (745 words). "The Cardiff Mormonites."

A continuation of the article published the previous week. The writer, possibly in an attempt to show some fairness after the dismal picture portrayed of a polygamous wife in the previous issue,[12] prints a letter from Ann Ellis, a former resident of Cardiff currently living in Utah. In this letter to her sister Jane, Ann expresses contentment with her new life in America:

> We are doing very well: we shall have about 300 bushels of potatoes, and we have planted some corn, and a great many other things. We have got plenty of everything except wheat. James is getting very good wages all the summer—from three to four dollars a-day.

Ann also explains how she has fared with regard to the practice of polygamy:

> You wished me to answer some questions for you: James has no other woman than myself yet; and when we have got more property—that is, when we are in a way to maintain her without injuring ourselves—then it will be my duty to look out for another woman for him,—that is my duty, and not his.

1856: 15 March, *Caernarvon and Denbigh Herald*, p. 10 (160 words). "Report of the Proceedings of the Yorkshire Welsh Society."

The writer of the report places the blame for the weakening Anglican Church in Wales on the leaders who appointed almost exclusively English monoglot clergy to preside in Wales—thus they did not connect with the people, many of whom did not speak any English. In a section of the report entitled "Present State of the Church in Wales," the writer says:

> The Welsh have become a nation of Dissenters; and whilst the chapels of the latter are thronged with worshippers, the churches are deserted, or nearly so.

He then quotes from the minute book of a member of the committee—notes made during this person's visit to the diocese of St. David. He tells of the low attendance in various parish churches because so much is done in English in comparison to Welsh.

> During my sojourn in this diocese I everywhere encountered the disciples of Mormon, who appeared to be making the greatest efforts to propagate their tenets amongst the peasantry. They were well versed in both Welsh and English. They preached in the lanes and highways and the corners of the streets, and distributed their tracts from house to house; and no attempt, as far as I could learn, was being made by the diocesan or his clergy, to arrest the onward movement of these heretics. Indeed, the English prelate is regarded by the mass of the population as a perfect cipher in the country, utterly disqualified to be of any service to the cause of true religion amongst them.

1856: 15 March, *North Wales Chronicle*, p. 3 (340 words). "Mormonism."

The same article as in the *Cardiff and Merthyr Guardian* for 19 January 1856 (see previous entry).

Episode 13.1

Start: Joseph Hodgetts retrieves part of his family from the Enoch Train

1856: 26 March, *Worcestershire Chronicle*, p. 2 (1,340 words). "Mormonism Illustrated—Chase Extraordinary."

This lengthy article has the most complete account of Ann Hodgetts and her attempted escape from her husband to take her children to Salt Lake City.[13] A short summary is as follows:

In 1850, Joseph and Ann Hodgetts were living with their family at Spring Hill in the city of Worcester. In December of that year, their nineteen-year-old son, Benjamin, converted to The Church of Jesus Christ of Latter-day Saints, and in 1852, he went to Salt Lake City. By 1856, he was back in England as a missionary. He convinced Ann to leave Joseph and take her other children to Liverpool to sail for the United States. While Joseph was away on business, Ann withdrew £314 from the bank and set off with her children for Liverpool, where they boarded the *Enoch Train* headed for Boston. Before leaving, however, she had her seventeen-year-old daughter, Maria, write a letter of explanation to leave for Joseph. Upon reading the letter, Joseph set out for Liverpool, where he hired a tugboat to pursue the ship that had only hours before been towed out toward the open sea. He was able to board the ship and immediately demanded that the captain bring forth his wife and children. After pleading with Ann for some time, he finally convinced her to return home with him. The younger children accompanied them, but fifteen-year-old Emily and seventeen-year-old Maria insisted on continuing their journey. After reaching Boston, Maria received word from home that her mother was in poor health and needed her help. So she returned to England and assisted her mother for two years until Ann's death. The following year, Maria married and had a large family. She died in England in 1894 at age fifty-six. Emily crossed the plains in the Hodgetts wagon company, which was led by her twenty-five-year-old brother Benjamin. Benjamin died four years later at age twenty-nine. In 1860, Emily married John Lowder, and they eventually settled in southern Utah. Emily gave birth to nine children and lived to be 102.

1856: 29 March, *Usk Observer*, p. 3 (125 words). "The Mormon Exodus."

> An extraordinary scene was witnessed a few days ago at the New-street railway station, Birmingham. A fine ship, the *Enoch Train,* having been chartered to convey a cargo of Mormons to the United States, *en route* to their settlement in Utah territory, three hundred men and women, boys and girls, formed the contingent supplied by the Birmingham district. They left by the half-past ten train. All seemed to belong to the working classes, and the proportion of the sexes was about equal. Many hundreds of their relatives and fellow saints assembled at the station to bid them farewell; and, in spite of the efforts of an instrumental band to cheer the spirits of the females, some very affecting scenes were witnessed. There will be 900 on board.

1856: 5 April, *Caernarvon and Denbigh Herald*, p. 10 (245 words). "Mormonism Illustrated."

A condensed version of the article in the *Worcestershire Chronicle* for 26 March 1856 (see previous entry) entitled "Chase Extraordinary."

1856: 5 April, *Merthyr Telegraph*, p. 4 (65 words). "The Mormons."

> A fine ship, the *Enoch Train*, having been chartered to convey a cargo of Mormons to the United States *en route* to their settlement in Utah territory, 300 men and woman [sic] and boys and girls left Birmingham for the purpose on the 19th, to join the rest of the contingent at Liverpool. There are altogether 900 on board the *Enoch Train*, which sailed on Monday.

1856: 5 April, *Wrexham Advertiser*, p. 3 (65 words).

The same article that appeared in the *Merthyr Telegraph* for 5 April 1856 (see previous entry).

1856: 5 April, *North Wales Chronicle*, p. 5 (390 words). "Extraordinary Elopement."

A shorter version of the article in the *Worcester Chronicle* for 26 March 1856 (see previous entry).

1856: 12 April, *Cardiff and Merthyr Guardian*, p. 2 (390 words).

The same article as in the *North Wales Chronicle* for 5 April 1856 (see previous entry).

1856: 12 April, *Usk Observer*, p. 4, item 1 (390 words). "Extraordinary Elopement."

The same article as in the *North Wales Chronicle* for 5 April 1856 (see previous entry).

1856: 12 April, *Usk Observer*, p. 4, item 2 (60 words). "A Greater and a Greater Still!"

> The *Worcester Chronicle* tells a story of a very unseemly woman, who, taking her children with her, ran away from her husband, and embarked for America, to join the Mormons. The woman was, no doubt, something of a fool; but what shall we say of the husband who, following the fair one bound for the Salt Lake, brought her back again?

1856: 3 May, *Caernarvon and Denbigh Herald*, p. 3 (815 words). "The Recent Mormon Elopement."

The same article as printed in the *Worcestershire Chronicle* for 23 April 1856 (see previous entry), except for two differences. The first is that the title in the *Worcestershire Chronicle* reads "Mormonism Exemplified. The Late Elopement." The second difference is that the editor of the *Caernarvon and Denbigh Herald* has corrected some of the spelling and punctuation that were reproduced from the original letter as printed in the *Worcestershire Chronicle* version.

Here first is the editor's introduction, then the letter Maria wrote with Ann's guidance:

> When Mr. Hodgetts came home and found that his wife and family had "flitted" to the Salt Lake, he also found a letter for him written by his daughters telling him that they were off to the Mormon settlement, and endeavoring to put him on a false scent in case he should pursue them. The whole epistle is so illustrative of the sort of morality likely to be produced by Mormonite teachings that we (*Worcestershire Chronicle*) think we shall do well to insert it.

It runs verbatim as follows:

> Spring Hill, Worcester, March 13, 1856. My dear Father—By the request of my mother I take my pen to write the following lines to you. We are gone to the Valley you told Mother in my hearing either to quit Mormonism up or go to the Valley. So we have chosen going to the Valley, for it is God's will. All the money in the world would not have enticed me to go, if we were not sure that Mormonism was not true. But we know it is true and will stand for ever and ever. Mother says she has left a good home and a good husband and the comforts of life to go and look for a livelihood and had enough to live upon. But she would rather live poor and obey the commandments of the Lord than she would live in luxury and disobey them. These words are from her own lips she is telling me what to say. All her grief has been ever since she knew Mormonism that she could not make you obey it. All that grieves her is that she has to leave you behind. But it shall be our earnest prayer to God that in some future time you will obey the gospel of the true and living God. We have

taken the three hundred pounds out of the bank, which you know is very little to go such a journey with five children. Tis a hard task for her, but tis with a pure motive to gain salvation and to keep God's commandments. Ben is not gone with us. He is somewhere about. But where I know not. Mother hopes you will endeavor to see Ben and reason with him, and she is sure he will do all in his power to help you. This is not Ben's doing, for he would not go with us. We shall leave England on Thursday morning 20 instant on board a steam vessel from Southampton. It will be useless you spending your money to follow us, for we never intend coming back. No, never, if it costs us our lives. Suffer what we may, we WILL go. I have left the books all right. The rent leaf and all accounts are in the large green book on the table. Mother wishes you to get someone to gather your money in. Then you will be able to pay for the house being now built when you have all your money up. Mother says she did not leave you because she disliked you, but she went because the commandments of the Lord called her away and nothing else, I can assure you. I will write to you every month and let you know how we all get along. Mother has taken no more than I have told you. She has not left you in debt one farthing. So if any bills should be brought you, pay them not, for there is nothing owing. Mother and all the children send their love to you. Mother wishes me to say you have very often complained to keep your children to do nothing. But you will not have that to complain of again. There was no peace for her, she says, nor of us children when you were near us. So we all determined to stay no longer. We are gone by ourselves and of course we shall have to earn our bread before we eat it. You have many times told mother to go. Mother says she has taken all the expense and trouble off your hands. So now you can live a gentleman's life. If you should ever make up your mind to come to Salt Lake, we shall be most happy to receive you, and you will find mother and your family the same as you left them. Mother wishes to say she has not left you for the sake of man or men, but just to do the will of God our father, for he has declared to gather his people. But we feel it our duty to comply with the will of the Lord. I must conclude with all our prayers in your behalf that you may obey the gospel of the living God. From your affectionate wife and daughter, Ann & Maria Hodgetts.

1856: 10 May, *Monmouthshire Merlin*, p. 6 (860 words).

The same letter written by Maria Hodgetts to her father as it had appeared the previous week in the *Caernarvon and Denbigh Herald* for 3 May 1856 (see previous entry). After a brief outline as to what had transpired with the Hodgetts family, the editor comments: "The epistle is illustrative of the sort of morality likely to be produced by Mormon teachings."

End: Joseph Hodgetts retrieves part of his family from the Enoch Train

1856: April, *Seren Gomer* (*Star of Gomer*), pp. 189–90 (245 words). "A Letter from California."

The letter is dated 23 November 1855, from "Bottle Hill." Although the name of the writer is not given, the letter is addressed to "My dear Uncle Hugh and family."

Here is the portion that has to do with the writer's visit to Salt Lake City:

> I have been in Salt Lake City also, and I saw the order of the Latter-day Saints in their Zion. I have seen many orders during my life, but this one goes beyond them all. I saw old, white-haired men who had five or six wives, some a dozen, most of them young girls from sixteen to twenty years old! They are permitted to have as many wives as they wish, for it is considered a duty in order to raise up a holy nation and to build Zion. There are hundreds of women who would give the hair off their heads for the freedom to leave this place. Their lives, however, are in peril if they try to accomplish such a venture, for a word from the Prophet Brigham is all it would require for the life of any man there. The city has about six thousand inhabitants and is built on a very beautiful spot on the edge of a valley twenty miles wide and over a hundred and fifty miles long. The surrounding mountains are high and steep, and they are covered in some places with snow all year. Water runs from the mountains to the city, and it is carried through the streets in gutters. I saw many Welsh people there, some with very poor lives. The women have been bewitched and are forced to work like dogs and live in a state of licentiousness.[14]

Such reports about Salt Lake City did not seem to be a serious deterrent to members of The Church of Jesus Christ of Latter-day Saints in Wales whose earnest desire was to join their fellow Saints in their gathering place.

1856: 12 April, *Monmouthshire Beacon*, p. 6 (70 words). "Mormon Conference."

> The Latter-day Saints held a grand conference at the Sunderland Arms Assembly Room on Sunday last, when a number of "elders," "saints," "brothers," etc., held a "great talk," the subject being, of course, the delights of Mormonism, and the advantages of a sea-trip to the other side of the Atlantic—where Mormon settlements do most abound. England and Wales can well afford to spare the deluded creatures.

1856: 18 April, *Cambrian* (70 words). "The Mormons."

[Some words are illegible and are marked with underscores in the transcription.]

> A large number of these deluded fanatics left our port on Wednesday by the *Troubadour* for Liverpool en route for the Salt Lakes. They consisted chiefly of the very —— class of society from the surrounding hills. Some of their relatives and friends were assembled on the quay to bid them adieu, and many shed tears —— separation. Society at large, however, —— deplore their departure.

The *Troubadour* was the steamer that transported passengers from Swansea to the Liverpool docks where they would board ships that would carry them across the ocean to various points of destination. The ship that the "deluded fanatics" boarded in Liverpool was the *S. Curling*, and their destination was Boston. From there they went by train to its terminus in Iowa City, Iowa. And from Iowa City they would push handcarts to Salt Lake City, a distance of nearly 1,200 miles. This particular crossing had over five hundred converts from Wales under the presidency of Captain Dan Jones.

1856: 19 April, *Monmouthshire Beacon*, p. 7 (140 words). "Flight of Mormons."

A report of the arrival of a large group of men, women, and children in Monmouth on their way to Utah.

> About 250 started on Monday morning from the Abergavenny station on their journey to Liverpool. We wish them a pleasant journey across the Atlantic to join their fanatic brothers and sisters.

1856: 19 April, *Usk Observer*, p. 1 (120 words). "Abergavenny. Departure for the Salt Lake."

> On Saturday and Sunday last, a large number of men, women and children, arrived in this town from the "Hills." It was at first represented that they were miners and colliers emigrating to America, but on Sunday afternoon all conjectures were put an end to by a member of the fraternity holding forth on the delightful prospects of their safe arrival at the Salt Lake, and to feast their eyes with a view of Brigham Young and his beautiful pair of spectacles, which were discovered by Joe Smith in the rock, when he found the tables which now forms the Book of Mormon. About 250 started on Monday morning from the Abergavenny station to Liverpool.

1856: 26 April, *Cardiff and Merthyr Guardian*, p. 7 (725 words). "More Victims to Mormonism. A Prophet Checkmated."

An account taken from the *Hereford Journal* about Elder Reece, a Latter-day Saint missionary, who gained the confidence of an elderly woman who owned a shop. According to the writer, the missionary convinced the woman that by going to America "she would be blessed with unfading youth, would have her sight restored, and, being joined again to her deceased but risen husband, would be fruitful and multiply." But her neighbors convinced her to remain in Britain. The writer concludes:

> Since then there has been great wavering among the flock in St. Martin's Street and many have resolved not to leave the shores of old England, to become the victims of an abominable delusion.

1856: 26 April, *Cardiff and Merthyr Guardian*, p. 8 (640 words). "An Evening Party at Utah."

The author of this account was Cornelia Ferris, wife of Benjamin Gilbert Ferris, who had been appointed as secretary of the Territory of Utah in 1852. Cornelia Ferris describes the entry of various apostles with their wives. Parley P. Pratt brought four wives with him and introduced each one as Mrs. Pratt. The writer expresses her reaction:

> The thought came over me, with what scorn these people, who are here first and foremost, would be banished from society at home. . . . One thing was peculiar—it was only the first wives that tried to make themselves familiar

with me. Dancing continued fast and furious till a late hour. Each man danced with two women at a time, and took the lead in all the *chassés* promenades, so it seems that even in their amusements, women take a subordinate position.

1856: 10 May, *Cardiff and Merthyr Guardian*, p. 8 (205 words). "Mormon Dupes."

The early cheap up train from Bristol to Worcester on Monday morning was laden with Mormonites on their way to Liverpool en route for the Salt Lake. At Worcester no less than sixty-eight others, of whom at least one-third were children under five years of age, were waiting to join them. They were almost all clad in smock frocks, and were evidently country folk of the most ignorant class. One old man, who said he was eighty-two years of age, and stone blind, with a wallet on his back, told one of the railway porters with the gravest possible countenance that he had "faith," and was going off in the full expectation of having his sight restored. One woman, faint of heart, was going to run away at the last moment, but the elder caught her by the arm, and compelled her to return. The "prophet" who had the chief oversight of the "saints," having seen them all safely in the carriages (himself much too knowing to go along), went round and gave them the kiss of peace, not forgetting to make a collection for himself, which he did so successfully that he carried away a double handful of copper and silver."—[reprinted from the] *Worcester Chronicle.*

1856: 17 May, *Cardiff and Merthyr Guardian*, p. 2 (550 words). "The Emigration of the Mormon Prophet Reece and his Deluded Victims."

Referring back to the 26 April issue of this newspaper (see previous entry), the writer was sad to report that the elderly woman who had been convinced by her neighbors to remain in Britain instead of leaving with the Latter-day Saints had changed her mind once again and had left with Elder Reece and other converts. Another of Reece's "victims" was a woman who, without telling her husband, left with their three children for America.

1856: 17 May, *Wrexham Advertiser*, p. 2 (60 words).

A correspondent of the *Bristol Times* states that on his withdrawal from the Mormon body he was publicly anathematized in the following language: "May his eyes sink in their sockets; his flesh rot and fall from his bones; may he wish to die, but not be able; may his right arm wither; may he beg his bread, but none be given him."

Episode 13.2

Start: W. S. Parrott lectures against his former religion

1856: 3 May, *North Wales Chronicle*, p. 4 (500 words). "Life among the Mormons."

The writer tells of receiving a long letter from a Mr. Parrott in which he had told of his experience among the Latter-day Saints. After spending a period of time "enchanted with the system," Parrott decided to end his association with his new church. He claims to have been anathematized in the following language:

> May his eyes sink in their sockets; his flesh fall from his bones; may he wish to die, and not be able; may his right arm wither; may he beg his bread, but none be given him.

Parrott also states:

> The real object of the American Mormon leaders, called priests, in their mission to the United Kingdom, is under the mask of religion, to recruit men, women, and children, for the purpose of raising an army to carry the Book of Mormon, by the sword and fire, into the present peaceful States of America, of which army Brigham Young, like a second Mohammed, is to be the king.

1856: 17 May, *Cardiff and Merthyr Guardian*, p. 7 (500 words). "Life among the Mormons."

Except for a few minor differences, this is the same article that appeared in the *North Wales Chronicle* for 3 May 1856 (see previous entry), quoting from the *Pembrokeshire Herald.*

1856: 14 November, *Cambrian* (155 words). "Mormonism."

A brief report of a series of three lectures given by a "W. Parrott of Bristol" about "the fallacies and absurdities of the Mormon belief." The report writer gives the following background about Parrott:

> Mr. Parrott was at one time a believer in the Mormon faith but being convinced of its absurdity has now the manliness to denounce it throughout the length and breadth of the land, especially in the Principality, which alas is considered one of the strongholds of this sect.

1856: 6 December, *Cardiff and Merthyr Guardian*, p. 3 (670 words). "Mormonism."

The writer says the following about W. S. Parrott, a former Latter-day Saint who had given two lectures about his experience at the Temperance Hall:

> The lecturer is evidently an uneducated man, murders the Queen's English very frequently, and speaks what may be termed an American dialect; but these drawbacks are much more than counterbalanced by the abundance of his facts, the intimacy of his acquaintance with the secret workings of Mormonism, and the authority which attaches itself to the revelations of personal experience.

The next evening the chairman suggested the following:

> [That Parrott] describe the means used to allure persons to join the Mormons the way in which he was induced to become one of their number, his experience in that position, the general conduct of Mormons in this country, and the fate which awaited the deluded victims after leaving this country.

The writer observes:

> In adopting this course, the lecturer introduced a good deal of irrelevant matter; but in the main, his speech fixed the attention of his hearers and was the means of conveying a large amount of very peculiar, and apparently, trustworthy information. He revealed the existence of an amount of blasphemy, debauchery, and knavery, that was quite revolting to hear, and would have been quite incredible in itself, but that the books of the Mormons themselves were cited in support

> of his assertions, and that his own experience, and that of "old John [S.] Davis," confirmed the accusations. We could have wished that Mr. Parrott had been a man of greater ability, and one more competent to deal with the doctrinal errors of the sect.

At the end of Parrott's lectures, "invitations were given to Mormons . . . to step forward and discuss the points advanced or to refute the accusations made."

> One or two parties accepted the challenge and attempted to show, but very ineffectually, that he had misrepresented their doctrinal views; but no attempt was made to disprove the moral enormities charged against the sect.

1857: 31 October, *Cardiff and Merthyr Guardian*, p. 8 (255 words). "Mormonism in Bath."

A good description of W. S. Parrott's procedures to oppose anything and everything having to do with the Latter-day Saints:

> In the course of the last six months we have had frequent occasion to advert to Mr. Parrott, the indefatigable antagonist of Mormonism. After giving himself to this work in Bristol, London, and Wales, he arrived here in May, a stranger and uninvited, and found the system in full and vigorous operation. The chapel was well attended, the congregation consisting chiefly of infatuated young woman [sic] from 12 to 20 years of age; who, moreover, were then engaged in attempts to entrap others of their sex by means of tract distribution. Mr. Parrott immediately began his labors by holding public meetings in the Old Market and on the Quay. He next waited on the Mayor, Bishop Carr, and the other clergy, the magistrates, and the gentry, daily bringing the subject before them. A large public meeting in the Guildhall, at which Bishop Carr presided, was the consequence. Mr. Parrott likewise held meetings in the High Common, the Bear Inn field, the parochial schoolrooms, and the Riding School. These meetings were attended by thousands. He has also visited from house to house, exposing the system. Some thousands of books and tracts have, besides, been dispersed by him; and, the public press aiding his efforts, it is most gratifying to state that since Mr. Parrott commenced his labors Mormonism in Bath has not obtained a single new convert; while some have seceded, and are now laboring to expose the imposture. Nor less influential have the newspaper reports proved in the neighboring villages. *Bath Paper.*

End: W. S. Parrott lectures against his former religion

1856: 24 May, *North Wales Chronicle*, p. 3 (75 words). "Departure of the Mormons for Utah."

> On Wednesday morning at half-past six, a party of Mormons, comprising several families, in all 152 men, women, and children, under the care of Elders Squires and Broderick, left London by the London and North-Western Railway for Liverpool, thence to embark with other parties going with them

from different parts of the country for Boston, whence they will proceed by the new northern route for the promised land.

Episode 13.3

Start: William Webb accuses Thomas and Pamela Hewlett of stealing his sister

1856: 7 June, *Monmouthshire Beacon*, p. 8 (435 words). "The Mormons."

About Mary Ann, a young woman who has shown signs of fondness for a "prophet" in the neighborhood. Her father, a convert to The Church of Jesus Christ of Latter-day Saints, has no objection to her daughter's acceptance of an invitation from the "prophet" to live with him and his wife. Mary Ann's mother, however, strenuously objected to these new arrangements and went one night to her daughter's new residence in an effort to persuade her to return home with her. Here is the final paragraph of the article:

> But of no avail. The mother returned without having accomplished her purpose. The next day she was taken very ill; and some friends then succeeded in prevailing upon her daughter to return. She has since been living at home, but still expresses her determination to leave for the Salt Lake, whenever the prophet shall require her to do so.

1856: 14 June, *Cardiff and Merthyr Guardian*, p. 6 (435 words). "The Mormons."

The same article as appeared in the *Monmouthshire Beacon* for 7 June 1856 (see previous entry).

1856: 2 August, *Monmouthshire Beacon*, p. 8 (720 words). "Mormonism Exposed."

The article begins with the following account:

> Four Mormon preachers, on Monday night last, held a public service in the open air Over Monnow, where a number of working men listened attentively to an address on Latter-day Saintism. And we were sorry to find that several uneducated people of this town have been initiated into the Mormon delusion. The principles of Mormonism are deeply rooted in sensuality; therefore, many find in that creed liberty and facilities to satiate their base desires—the secret of their amazing success.

The writer then explains that the Book of Mormon originated from a "forgotten manuscript of poor Solomon Spaulding." Next he mentions the failure of the elders to heal two women who were suffering from cholera. He then laments:

> Some of our intelligent readers will be astonished to learn that an inhabitant of Monmouth, a married man and a Mormon disciple, has publicly averred his adhesion to the doctrine of plurality of wives!

Toward the end of his article, the writer reports:

> On the same evening, a disturbance took place at the house of Thomas Hewlett, shoemaker, living at the bottom of Monnow Street, whither the preachers retired after the open-air service, followed by a large mob. He has

> rendered himself obnoxious to the neighborhood in consequence of his profession of the Mormon belief and the part he took in harboring the young woman who was induced by a Mormon prophet to leave her home in the Baptist-chapel yard, as recently detailed in this paper.

The writer then promises that readers of the newspaper "will be presented with the whole particulars of the attack upon misguided people" when the whole matter is "brought before the magistrates."

1857: 11 April, *Monmouthshire Beacon*, p. 4 (1,150 words). "The Mormons."

Like her father, but unlike her mother, a young woman by the name of Mary Ann Webb had become a Latter-day Saint. At the invitation of Thomas Hewlett and his wife, also Latter-day Saints, Webb moved to their home from her parents' home, perhaps to escape the scorn her mother had for her daughter's new religion. The writer opines:

> The fact that a plurality of wives is allowed among the followers of Joe Smith, and the suspicion that Miss Webb was about to be drawn into some snare of the kind, caused much indignation among the neighbors, and they have many times gone with the relatives to demand the restitution of the deluded girl. Sometimes they succeeded; but she returned, and is now not forthcoming. From the excited state of feeling on both sides, arose the present case.

A few months later Webb's brother, William, pressed charges against Thomas Hewlett for assaulting him. Hewlett later testified that someone had thrown "two bucketfuls of sludge" under his door. Because Webb had left for America, Hewlett thought that her brother William was the culprit.

The article gives considerable detail about the trial, during which William explained that he had gone to Hewlett's house to confront him for spreading the word that William was the culprit. The verdict handed down was that "both cases should be dismissed, on payment by each party of its own expenses, which amounted to 3s. 6d."

Mary Ann Webb left on the *George Washington* for Boston with a group of Latter-day Saints emigrants on 28 March 1857. However, it was not until May 1860 that Thomas and Pamela Hewlett left on the *William Tapscott* for America. Thus they had another three years dealing with neighbors to whom Thomas referred to as "the oldest enemies I have in town."

End: William Webb accuses Thomas and Pamela Hewlett of stealing his sister

1856: 14 June, *Wrexham Advertiser*, p. 2 (191 words). "Mormon Emigration from Preston."

> The emigration of the inhabitants of our town, under the auspices of the Mormonites, is more extensive than we were led to imagine. We find it is not unusual for husbands to return home at night and find wife, daughter, and children fled, the house stripped and a pretty long list of debts incurred on the eve of departure, left unpaid. Tradesmen, too, in seeking after debtors, are astonished to find those who promised to pay, off to the land of promise. A hard

case has recently come under our notice. A laboring man took his wages home on the Saturday evening, returned to his work, which detained him until a late hour. When he had finished his labor he again returned home, but found his wife and family had fled, and his home stripped. Subsequently he ascertained that, instead of applying his wages to their proper use, they had run greatly in debt, and allowed their money to accumulate, to assist them in their flight. They sailed from Liverpool on the 23rd ult., with a large number of others from various places, in the *Horizon*, bound for Boston.—*Preston Guardian*.

1856: 14 June, *Monmouthshire Merlin*, p. 3 (55 words). "Garndiffaith."

On May 30th, Mr. Allen, of Newport, delivered lectures on "The Advantages of Education," "The Errors of Mormonism," and "The Benevolence of Oddfellows, M. U." His addresses were listened to with much attention and satisfaction, with the exception of occasional and somewhat rude interruptions on the part of a Mormonite who was present.

1856: 21 June, *Wrexham Advertiser*, p. 3 (40 words).

The Mormons at Preston are busy in making converts of the wives and daughters of laboring men. This emigration of the weaker, but not better, halves is said to be unprecedented. A shipload sailed from Liverpool a short time since.

1856: 21 June, *Merthyr Telegraph*, p. 3 (55 words). "Preachers' License."

Two Mormon preachers, who gave their names Abednego Williams, and Israel Evans, residing in Garden Street, applied for license to preach at the White Lion. Having taken the oaths of abjuration, of allegiance, and of supremacy, and made the declaration against popery according to the 52 Geo. III., the licenses were granted.

1856: 28 June, *Merthyr Telegraph*, p. 1 (100 words). "Mormonism Again!! Truth Will Prevail!"

The Latter-day Saints will hold their Half Yearly Conference in the Cymreigyddion Hall, White Lion Inn, Merthyr, on Sunday, the 29th June, 1856, when Presidents Daniel Daniels, Israel Evans, and others from the Salt Lake Valley, with several Presidents of Conferences will address the Audience. Meeting to commence at Half-past Ten, a.m., Half-past Two, and Half-past Six, p.m. *Come and hear and judge for yourselves!* On the following Monday there will be a Tea Party and Concert.—Tea on the Tables at Three o'clock, Concert to commence at Seven. Tickets, One Shilling Each.

1856: 28 June, *Cardiff and Merthyr Guardian*, p. 6 (275 words). "To the Editor of the Cardiff and Merthyr Guardian."

The writer begins his letter with this observation:

I have seen in your paper various letters and other credible statements as to the detestable proceedings of the ignorant fanatics called Mormons. Were you occasionally to take notice of the "*Abode of Love*," (*Agapemone*) where, on a smaller scale, but much nearer home, somewhat similar acts of insanity

> are being perpetrated, you might enlighten your readers as to what is carrying on near their own doors.

The writer then presents some recent happenings, which he considers deplorable, among the Agapemonites.

1856: July, *Y Cyfaill o'r Hen Wlad yn America* (*Friend of the Old Country in America*), p. 285 (150 words). "Mormonism."

The writer reacts to the passing of "eight hundred Mormon immigrants" who had recently gone through Buffalo. He laments that "the majority of them" were Welsh and expressed his concern over "the virtuous young women from the hills and areas of Wales who may become the seventh or the eighth wives to adulterers of this shameful and insufferable sect." The writer then recommends that his readers read *Female Life Among the Mormons* for an understanding of the treatment of women in Utah.

1856: 12 July, *Usk Observer*, p. 3 (140 words).

> The Hon. James J. Strang, commonly called "King Strang," the leader and prophet of the Mormons located on Beaver Islands, has been shot by two of his follower[s], and received injuries from which he is not likely to recover. Strang was a ruling spirit among the Mormons, a large number of whom are Welsh, who are located on and have control of the six islands in the northern part and near the outlet of Lake Michigan, called Beaver Islands, and since 1853 he has represented Newago county, which is composed of those islands, in the lower branch of the Michigan legislature. He has been the means, in times past, of causing considerable disturbance in the regions adjacent to where he resides, and robbery, murder, and piracy are crimes which have been freely attributed to him and his followers.

1856: 12 July, *Wrexham Advertiser*, p. 2 (165 words). "The Mormons in America."

Very similar to the article in the 12 July 1856 *Usk Observer* (see previous entry).

1856: 12 July, *Wrexham Advertiser*, p. 3 (560 words). "Polygamy in Mormondom."

A letter from "a Mormon elder who has just escaped from the Mormon territory." The letter contains a description of the practice of plural marriage in Utah and numerous examples of its many ills.

1856: 19 July, *Cardiff and Merthyr Guardian*, p. 8, item 1 (1,280 words). "The Mormons."

This 19 July 1856 article is a follow-up to to a statement in the the 17 May 1856 issue of the *Cardiff and Merthyr Guardian* (see previous entry) about LDS emigrants:

> The *New York Herald* contains some further particulars of the case of the Mormon emigrants from Hereford, to which we have previously called attention. It will be recollected that the husband of the woman Jarvis (who, accompanied by her three children, had eloped from Hereford with a Mormon "elder,") had followed her to New York, and obtained a warrant for the recovery of his children. It appears that Jarvis had armed himself with the authority of the following letter from the Secretary of State:

Foreign Office, May 9, 1856. "I am directed by the Earl of Clarendon to instruct you to give all proper assistance to a person named Samuel Jarvis, of Hereford, who proceeds by steamer to New York, in pursuit of his wife, who, having joined the Mormonites, has clandestinely left him, and has embarked at Liverpool on board a sailing vessel, for New York, taking Jarvis's three children with her. I am, Sir, your most obedient humble servant, E. Hammond."

The article has the *New York Herald's* account of the proceedings before the New York authorities on the writ of habeas corpus obtained by Jarvis. Here is the opening paragraph of the writer's report:

The Court room was densely crowded. The applicant, a decent-looking, little hen-pecked husband, was present. The mother, a tall, good looking and healthy specimen of an English woman, was also in court. She is, apparently, some years younger than the husband, and has been, in part, instigated to this extraordinary step towards moral and religious degradation by her brother and another man, who accompany her in her wanderings. The children—two girls and a boy—are fine little creatures, "half sunshine, half tears," as if now and again conscious of their unhappy situation.

Apparently, the court ruled in favor of Mrs. Jarvis, as the following names are listed as having crossed the plains in the Edward Martin Handcart company: Amelia Ann Jarvis, age thirty-five, Amelia Jane Jarvis, age twelve, Agnes Elizabeth Jarvis, age eight, and Frederic Jarvis, age five. Mrs. Jarvis died in Laramie, Wyoming, in 1887.

1856: 19 July, *Cardiff and Merthyr Guardian*, p. 8, item 2 (140 words).

The Hon. James J. Strang, commonly called "King Strang," the leader and prophet of the Mormons located on Beaver Islands, has been shot by two of his followers, and received injuries from which he was not likely to recover. Strang was the ruling spirit upon the Mormons, a large number of whom are Welsh, or are located on and have control of the six islands in the northern part and near the outlet of Lake Michigan, called Beaver Islands, and since 1853 he has represented Newago county, which is composed of those islands, in the lower branch of the Michigan Legislature. He has been the means, in times past, of causing considerable disturbance in the regions adjacent to where he resides, and robbery, murder, and piracy are crimes which have been freely attributed to him and his followers.

1856: 25 July, *Cambrian* (90 words). "A Latter-day Saint in Trouble."

Wm. Phillips and Sarah Phillips, his wife, were summoned by George Watts, a Latter-day Saint, with having made use of threats towards him, and against whom he applied for sureties of the peace. From the statement made by Watts it appeared that both the defendants had made use of the most dreadful oaths and threats towards him, from which he was in bodily fear he would have some harm done to him. Ordered to find sureties to keep the peace for three months.

Whether George Watts felt threatened because of his religion or because of some other dispute is not clear.

1856: 26 July, *Cardiff and Merthyr Guardian*, p. 3 (355 words). "The Mormons."

This account, reprinted from the *Detroit Advertiser*, gives an account of the arrest by the sheriff of Mackinaw, and his posse, of a number of Latter-day Saints at Beaver Island, who were accused of setting fire to some houses, committing thefts and other depredations on other portions of the island.

1856: 26 July, *Wrexham Advertiser*, p. 3 (225 words). "An Irish Mormon."

Among the many thousands of Mormons who come to this country, we do not believe there has been anyone who belonged to Ireland. The elders do not obtain any converts among the Irish, nor do their doctrines find favor. A well-known Irish gentleman in New York has in vain tried to detect an Irish man or woman among the Mormons who have entered Castle Garden. On Saturday last 700 Mormons were landed at the depot from the ship Thornton, most of them having been sent out at the expense of the Mormon Emigrant Fund. He saw among them English, Scotch, Welsh, Jerseymen, Danes, and Swedes in great numbers, and at last he thought he detected a solitary Paddy. Walking up to him he asked him his name. "John Daly, sir," he replied. "Are you an Irishman?" "Truth, I am the same, yer honor." Assuming a tone of rebuke, he continued, "Are you a Mormon, too?" With an air of exquisite drollery he whispered, "Faith, I am not; but you see, I wanted me passage." "Have you any money?" "Nivir a hap'ny." "Then you had better go with them to the West, to St. Louis, and leave them there." "Indade, sir, I've been wid 'em too long already, and I'm thinking I'll lave 'em and be off at wanst." *New York Paper.*

1856: 26 July, *Merthyr Telegraph*, p. 3 (325 words). "Utah and the Mormons."

A lecture was delivered on Thursday evening, the 17th inst., in the long room of the Talbot Inn, Tredegar, upon the Geography of the Great Salt Lake Country and the State of Religion and Morals amongst the Inhabitants, by Elder J. Evans, from the Salt Lake Valley, and one of the first settlers therein. A general invitation was given for all who were desirous to learn the truth concerning these singular and far-off people, to come and hear for themselves. The admission fee was threepence, and the audience numbered about forty. According to the elder's statement he had been [with] the Mormons about 22 years, although he did not seem to your correspondent to be quite so old as even that. He had preached, prayed, fought, and in short done almost everything that man could do for the promotion of Mormonism. He was no fatalist, he did not believe in the do-nothing system, he even believed in the necessity of fighting as much as he did in the virtue of praying for the prosperity of the church of God. He said that it was nine years ago, the 24th of the present month, since they had first entered those regions. The extent of their territory from north to south, and from east to west, is about 350 miles, whilst the population is from 77,000 to 80,000. That their houses and other buildings are chiefly composed of sun-dried bricks. He also stated that three-fourths of the salt lake water is pure salt, and that it was from this supply they obtained all they used. The country throughout was eminently healthy, and was suitable for all that chose to make

> themselves useful. Much (said the speaker) had been said against the authority exercised by its just and godly rulers, but in Utah was the very acme of liberty, *for every man there was permitted to take as many wives as he was able to support!* (emphasis in original)

1856: 2 August, *Monmouthshire Beacon*, p. 7 (300 words). "The Mormons and Their Wives."

The writer begins thus:

> The *Cleveland Herald*, an American journal, has recently published some letters from Salt Lake, exposing the tyrannous conduct of the Mormons over their wives, and, moreover, showing the depraved condition of the sect.

Additional details are then given concerning the treatment of women in Utah.

1856: 9 August, *Cardiff and Merthyr Guardian*, p. 3 (335 words). "Mormon Morals."

Quotes about polygamy from the *Deseret News*. Here is one by Brigham Young:

> God never introduced the patriarchal order of marriage with a view to please man in his carnal desires, nor to punish females for anything which they had done; but he introduced it for the express purpose of raising up to his name a royal priesthood, a peculiar people.

Here is another from Jedediah Grant:

> You cannot alter it; you cannot alter it; you cannot revoke this eternal law. If a man has 50 wives, and the 50th is the best, and does the most good, she will get the greatest reward, in spite of all the grunting on the part of the first ones.

1856: 9 August, *North Wales Chronicle*, p. 5 (335 words). "Mormon Morals."

The same article as in the *Cardiff and Merthyr Guardian* for 9 August 1856 (see previous entry).

1856: 9 August, *Usk Observer*, p. 2 (335 words). "Mormon Morals."

The same article as in the *Cardiff and Merthyr Guardian* for 9 August 1856 (see previous entry).

1856: 9 August, *Merthyr Telegraph*, p. 2, item 1(165 words). "The Mormons."

> Open-air meetings are held in some part of the town or neighborhood of Merthyr every Sunday evening, by parties who formerly belonged to the Mormons, but who are now intent upon exposing their "abominations and wickedness." One of the latest pieces of intelligence of the Mormon doings in Utah is the following: John Strong, a blacksmith of long standing, in Allhollows'-lane, Kendal, with his wife, and a numerous family, left Kendal for Utah, on the Salt Lake, in the spring of last year, at which place of abominations his eldest son, brought up to the same business as his father, had been settled a few years. Intelligence has arrived in Kendal that Strong has been short for refusing to give his wife and daughter up to the embraces of the high priest! Strong was a leader and priest of the Mormon connection in Kendal for some years previous to his departure therefrom, and no advice or admonition could break his faith in the detestable infatuation.

1856: 9 August, *Merthyr Telegraph*, p. 2, item 2 (215 words). "A Mormon Apostle Nearly Drowned."

> On Sunday last, several of the Latter-day Saints of this place were to be baptized, and in order to have the Holy ordinance performed with decency and to the exclusion of the rabble, the apostles R—T—and W—J—who are well known as miners at the Plymouth iron works, were followed up about six o'clock in the morning to the Clynmil pond, and after the ceremony was over the two brethren apostles contested as to which of them would be able to give proof of the strongest faith, upon which brother R—T—said that he could walk upon the water without any inconvenience, to the astonishment of all present, as our Savior did of old; and in order to prove his assertion he plunged into the deep, but unfortunately his faith failed him, and he sank twice to the bottom, and when he was nearly drowned (for he had been left there long enough to test his faith) was rescued by a second party from a watery grave, and in a state of great exhaustion. It is a great pity that the human race are so degraded as to be led astray by a set of deluded people to desecrate the Sabbath day. *A Correspondent.*

1856: 9 August, *Wrexham Advertiser*, p. 2 (120 words). "The Mormons."

> John Strong, a blacksmith, of long standing, in Allhallows' Lane, Kendal, with his wife and a numerous family, left Kendal for Utah, on the Salt Lake, in the spring of last year, at which place of abomination his eldest son, brought up to the same business as his father, had been settled a few years. Intelligence has arrived at Kendal, that Strong has been shot for refusing to give his wife and daughter up to the embraces of the high priest! Strong was a leader and priest of the Mormon connection in Kendal for some years previous to his departure therefrom, and no advice or admonition could break his faith in the detestable infatuation.—*Carlisle Patriot.*

1856: 16 August, *Cardiff and Merthyr Guardian*, p. 5 (245 words). "Women in Mormondom."

Several negative quotes from "a Mormon elder, just escaped from the Mormon territory" are printed about the practice of plural marriage, including the following:

> The majority of these poor women are compelled to work for their daily bread, and many are forced to seek charity of strangers. One of the wives of the chief apostles gained her livelihood by washing for the boarders of a public house in town. Indeed, it is not uncommon for those "lords of creation" to send their wives out for wood, and any day you can see women chopping logs and driving cattle to the mountains.

1856: 16 August, *Caernarvon and Denbigh Herald*, p. 9 (135 words). "The Mormon Delusion."

> The Fort Des Moines (Iowa) papers give some details of the passage of a band of Mormon emigrants through that place. In the broiling sun, these poor creatures, the majority of whom are women, moved along slowly in Indian file, dragging behind them in little carts the necessaries for the journey, sometimes two women dragging the cart, at other times a man and woman together. The

company was from Europe, and mostly consisted of English people, who had left their comfortable homes, their early associations of all the attachments which render the English such unwilling emigrants, and here, with a journey of more than a thousand miles before them, of which two hundred would be through a perfect desert, without shade or water, these miserable deluded people were trudging forward.

1856: 23 August, *Usk Observer*, p. 2 (430 words).

Various quotes from the *Deseret News* about the famine and scarcity of food in Utah.

1856: 30 August, *Usk Observer*, p. 2 (135 words). "The Mormons."

A history has been published in German of the Mormons, or Latter-day Saints, in North America, from which it appears that America contains 68,700 of that sect, of whom 38,000 are in Utah, 5,000 in New York, 4,000 in California, 5,000 in Nova Scotia and Canada, and 9,000 in South America and the islands. Europe contains 39,000, of whom 32,900 are in Great Britain and Ireland, 5,000 in Scandinavia, 1,000 in Germany and Switzerland, 500 in France, and 500 in the rest of Europe. In Asia there are said to be 1,000 in Australia and Polynesia, 2,400, in Africa 100, on travel 1,800. There are, besides, 8,500 Schismatics, including Strangites, Rigdonites, and Wightites. The numbers amount in the aggregate to 116,500, and it is supposed that the whole sect cannot exceed 126,000.

1856: 30 August, *Wrexham Advertiser*, p. 2 (110 words).

Mormonism is making much progress in Denmark. Jutland is the great hotbed of Mormon proselytism; and, as they eventually make up caravans or parties of four or five hundred together, to emigrate to America, in order to settle on the banks of the Great Salt Lake, the result will have the effect of ultimately depopulating the province to a great degree, and depriving its agriculture of many industrious hands. It is especially to this point that a petition to the King, just sent in from the town of Aalborg, and signed by upwards of two hundred of the principal inhabitants, lays much stress, and calls the attention of the government.

1856: September, *Yr Haul* (*Sun*), pp. 291–92 (295 words). "Mormonism."

Some of the Mormon preachers have recently been very busy in the Cardigan area spreading the poisonous seeds of their beliefs.[15]

The writer then describes how a young student from St. David's College was able to confront the Latter-day Saint preachers and disprove "their unfounded assertions, with verses from the Holy Scripture, so much so that they had nothing to say in answer to his questions." He then concludes:

It is everyone's duty to put a stop to deceit on every occasion, in whatever form it may be, but the fact that so many of our countrymen have been enticed to the Salt Lake Valley by the Mormon deceivers, and the treatment they have received there, make it imperative that we show the country what Mormonism really is.[16]

1856: 6 September, *Merthyr Telegraph*, p. 4 (50 words).

Mormonism is making such progress in Denmark that several petitions have been sent in to the Government from different parts of the kingdom, praying that a stop may be put to the nuisance. Jutland is the part where the great hotbed of Mormon proselytism is to be found.

1856: 20 September, *Usk Observer*, p. 3 (335 words). "The Mormons in Denmark."

Someone writing from Denmark reports the events of a meeting held by a group of Latter-day Saints in a Copenhagen hotel. A Jewish person proclaimed that he was ready to renounce Judaism and "embrace the worship of the Latter-day Saints." He was immediately accepted and invited to "take his place on the platform amongst his new fellow believers." He then got up and "proposed the abolition of polygamy." This proposition touched off "an angry discussion" between the Latter-day Saints and the new convert:

> "If we abolish polygamy," cried a jovial butcher, "we shall never make any more proselytes, for that is the bait at which people bite." "If polygamy be abolished," shouted a shriveled tailor, "I will abandon Mormonism at once. I only adopted it in order to be able to marry as often as I liked." These declarations were received with shouts of derision from the spectators in the galleries. At length the Mormons became exasperated, and rushing on the Jew, they beat him savagely, and even trampled him under foot. This led to a regular fight between the polygamists and their adversaries, and the windows, lamps, and chairs were smashed to provide missiles. After a while a body of police came in, arrested the leaders in the row, and cleared the room. One of the Mormon priests, on being arrested, pompously summoned the police to release him, on the ground that he was "inviolable," but to his intense disgust he was locked up.

1856: 20 September, *Wrexham Advertiser*, p. 2 (22 words).

The Mormons of the great Salt Lake City are threatened with famine. Their crops have been destroyed by drought, grasshoppers and worms.

1856: 20 September, *Wrexham Advertiser*, p. 3 (495 words). "The Mormons."

The account of a lecture presented by one who had been with the Latter-day Saints for the previous eight years. In his presentation, the speaker outlined his reasons for leaving his former religion, the main reason being what he described as the "immoral conduct" of Elder Cyrus Wheelock.

1856: 27 September, *Cardiff and Merthyr Guardian*, p. 5 (95 words). "The Mormons."

The rapid rise of this sect is truly marvelous. A few years have sufficed to enable them to erect cities, construct a vast social system, and perform acts of novel import to the human race. Under the title of "The Mormons or Latter-day Saints," a book has just appeared that is full of extraordinary revelations. It gives the History, Present Condition, and Future Prospects of Mormonism; and is illustrated with fifty original Portraits and Views of the leading Mormons and their Settlements. This work will be read with great interest. Price 3s. 6d.

1856: 27 September, *Merthyr Telegraph*, p. 2 (950 words). "Mormonism Again!"—"Angels' visits"—"Few and far between."

Here is the writer's brief introduction to this lengthy article:

> We are rather at a loss whether to laugh heartily at the absurdities of Mormonism or look stern, and lament, that in an age of progress, such as the present, men *will* be such arrant dupes. Well; in this narration we will treat them gently, for to oppose "Saints," is to encourage them to persevere in levying tribute from the poor misguided working man, who, too often, is looked upon as a capital bit of prey for the wary "liver on his wits."

The writer then presents two accounts of "miracles" among the Latter-day Saints. The first has to do with the reaction of a group of Latter-day Saint miners after learning that their leaders had requested additional contributions from the faithful. One of the miners suggested that they ask for light from above in place of their candles, which, according to the rules of the mine, they had to purchase with their own money. The writer reported the result:

> The candles were blown out on the instant, and the men waited anxiously for some time, expecting the appearance of gas lights, argand lamps, or such like, but as none came, the candles were again lighted, and with strong, but expressive language, they worked away in rather a desponding state of mind, half inclined to adopt extremely heterodox opinions.

The next account is about a man whom the writer calls "Smith" and who lives in Twynyrodyn, a small town adjacent to Merthyr Tydfil. Smith had been "ailing for nine years with a complication of disorders, the chief of which was asthma." But as he lay in bed one Sunday morning, "by his bedside knelt an Angel, clothed in a *black* surplice!!" The angel conversed with Smith in Welsh for a while and then asked him if he had any anointing oil. When Smith answered in the negative the angel told him he must send for some. The writer ends his account:

> Directions were also given how to apply the "wonderful remedy for the cure of all disorders"; and, with a few words of comfort, the mysterious visitor departed, or rather disappeared, leaving Smith "no ways alarmed, but most hopeful that he would soon be sound again." When the family returned, the surprising news was told them; the oil was obtained—leading members flocked to the room; nine times was the oil applied, and now, so *they* say, the sick man is himself again—free from any ail, and vigorous in mind.

1856: 4 October, *Cardiff and Merthyr Guardian*, p. 2 (635 words). "The Mormons."

Quotes from the *Deseret News* about the drought in Utah and several other items.

1856: 11 October, *Monmouthshire Beacon*, p. 7 (25 words).

> Some of the "great guns" of the Mormon church have, according to announcement, been holding forth here on the propriety of polygamy—the horrid creatures!

1856: 11 October, *Usk Observer*, p. 1 (395 words). "Abersychan. Storms."

Thomas Genevar, a Latter-day Saint who worked at the Abersychan Iron works, provides details of his miraculous escape from being killed by a train. He concluded: "Is this not a miracle, who could be thus saved but a *Latter-day Saint?*" The writer of the article concludes with a sarcastic remark:

> He now believes that he has been reserved for some great work among the adopted. Although he is nearly seventy years old, he is confident of reaching Western Zion, and that he will have to tread the Golden pavement of the Great Temple.

1856: 18 October, *Wrexham Advertiser*, p. 2 (245 words). "The Mormons and the Law of the States."

A report that the Supreme Court of Utah had determined that polygamy was as illegal in the territory of Utah as it was in the States. The writer predicts that as Utah, "now possessing the license of isolation, comes into contact with the advancing population of the States, the theocracy is doomed."

1856: 25 October, *North Wales Chronicle*, p. 8 (605 words). "Mormonism."

An anonymous reader requests that the editor insert extracts of two letters "to bring to light another instance of the treacherous and cruel conduct of the Mormonites." The first letter, addressed to "Dear Brother," is dated 26 June 1856 from St. Louis and is signed by a "broken hearted sister, A. S." She explains,

> I am sorry to say that my dear husband is dead. He had been ill all last fall, and did but very little work. He fretted very much of his ever having left home, and never enjoyed himself, but still wished to return; and the doctor said he had killed himself with fretting, and taking but little food.

This same "A. S." sent a second letter, addressed to "Dear Friend," dated 27 July 1856. She writes:

> I have to inform you that my dear husband died five weeks ago, and so I am bereaved of a comfortable home. I am left lonesome on the wide continent of America. I feel myself weak in body and mind, and depend now on your feelings towards me. If you will assist me, you will not lose your reward.

The lack of specifics causes one to wonder at their authenticity.

1856: 25 October, *Merthyr Telegraph*, p. 2 (1,385 words). "The Latter-day Saints."

The sub-heading for this long article is "Mormonism is Greek for humbug—Knavery.—*Welshness.*" The introduction follows:

> Mormonism is not yet dead, though in a sickly condition. The last bulletin we had was ominous, leaving little hope amongst the faithful of its ever rising from its prostrate state, and assuring the unbelievers, of all classes, that the leprous taint is passing away to its fitting resting place—obscurity.

The writer then relates "another instance of the gross superstition existing lately amongst the brethren," an instance related to him by an unnamed former Latter-day Saint from Pembrokeshire. This anonymous person tells of an experience he had soon after his conversion, when he was invited by an elder to be present at the casting out of a devil from a sister named Dolly. The elder commanded the unclean spirit to come out of Dolly, but to no avail. The new convert continues:

> The next part of the farce, for such I know it was now, though then I was as great a goose as any of them, was for the elder to exclaim, with his hands uplifted towards the ceiling—"Thou wicked and unclean spirit, by the power of the holy priesthood in me conferred, I command thee to tell me thy name?" The answer to this was, "Dolly," (Dolly was the name of the sister) "now hark ye," said the elder to me, "how cunning he is, trying to deceive us by making use of the sister's name for his own." What was to be done?—we thought it was no use going on this way, for the unclean spirit would not budge an inch. Well, another trial—so my friend, the elder, in a loud voice said, "I command thee to tell me where thou comest from?" "Where do I come from," said a voice, apparently Dolly's, "why, from Sardis mountain." This was another puzzler, for Sardis mountain was not only the place where Dolly was born, but in olden times, it was a noted quarter for ghosts, witches, and such like things, so the answer of the evil spirit confounded us again. Never say die, said the elder, but this is an awkward customer to move, beats all I ever heard of. "Now then, hark ye" said he, and with increased vehemence of manner, and fierce countenance, he cried out, "Where, spirit is thy abiding home?" "Sardis mountain," (Dolly's residence) was the reply as before; so seeing we were not to be successful, we came away. . . . If there was a devil in Dolly when we visited her, he still remained when we left, for all our efforts were fruitless.

In his final paragraph, the writer predicts that "Mormonism" will soon be annihilated, "leaving but a recollection to remain as a moral and a lesson to the world."

1856: November, *Y Bedyddiwr* (*Baptist*), pp. 350–51 (350 words). "The Mormons in the Salt Lake Valley."

The writer ponders the various "false religions" of the world and the different ways which God has of dealing with them. Some are allowed to remain on the earth a short time while others "continue for a long time." He makes this observation with respect to The Church of Jesus Christ of Latter-day Saints:

> The continuation of blasphemous Mormonism is not as brief as some of us would wish; but, in all human likelihood, it will not be long before the beginning of worries that they are likely to become extinct as a body of believers.[17]

In support of his prediction he refers to the *Times* [of London] and presents the following argument:

> The Editor of the *Times* says that the Supreme Court of Utah has decided that the original law of the country is compelling the territory to be subject to the general law of America; and since the named law is the Constitution for the States, the general law of America nullifies all the acts of the Mormon Senate. Consequently, polygamy will be as unlawful in the Salt Lake Valley as it is in any other part of the United States; and the aforementioned decision abolishes every law that Brigham Young has enacted.[18]

The writer concludes:

> If they oppose the law, we will see the history of the Mormons in Nauvoo being carried out the second time, but in a much more frightful way, and without a desert to flee into, where they could have refuge over their heads.[19]

1856: 8 November, *Caernarvon and Denbigh Herald*, p. 5 (105 words). "Machynlleth."

> A lecture was delivered at the Town Hall on Sunday last by J. R. Franklin, of London, who has just arrived from the Salt Lake. The subject was "Mormonism or the doctrines of the Latter-day Saints." The lecturer proved to the entire satisfaction of all present, that Joseph Smith and B. Young were false prophets, and that the Mormon city resembled Pandemonium. The lecture lasted two hours. There was no interruption of any kind, and the audience went home much pleased with the proceedings. The lecturer has thrown out a challenge to any champion of the Mormon faith for a public discussion.

1856: 8 November, *Usk Observer*, p. 2 (920 words). "The Experience of a Mormon Emigrant from England to the Salt Lake."

An unsigned letter written from Sugar Grove, Iowa, purportedly by a husband and wife from Manchester to their children. The mother laments:

> I fainted by the way several times; and not only we but many others fainted for want of food. The women and children cried for bread, but the leaders would not give them anything to eat, and would not allow them to ride. When we got seventy miles west of Iowa City, we could not go any further; so we stopped at a farmhouse, where we are at present.

Having acquired information about their adopted religion that differed from what they had been told in England, the couple advised their children to cease their support of The Church of Jesus Christ of Latter-day Saints and join them in Iowa and become landowners. The lack of specific information about the couple and their children back in England arouses suspicion that their letter may be inauthentic.

1856: 8 November, *Wrexham Advertiser*, p. 3 (200 words). "The Mormons and the 'Gentiles.'"

A brief assessment of the adversarial relationship between the Latter-day Saints and those in their midst who are not affiliated with their Church. The writer predicts "trouble ahead with this community."

1856: December, *Methodist*, p. 291 (155 words). "The Latter-day Saints."

The writer quotes from a work "published recently in German" about the number of members of The Church of Jesus Christ of Latter-day Saints throughout the world.

Episode 13.4

Start: Reverend J. Jones of Llangollen dies in Cincinnati

1856: December, *Y Cyfaill o'r Hen Wlad yn America* (*Friend of the Old Country in America*), p. 476 (210 words).

An obituary for Dan Jones's older brother, the Reverend John Jones:

> November 18th, In Cincinnati, Ohio, Mr. John Jones, Llangollen. He was ill for three weeks with the *Intermittent Fever*, which together with the goiter on his throat, caused his death. He left behind a widow and two daughters to mourn his loss.

The writer also makes a brief mention of the death of Dan Jones:

> P.S. A report reached our ears today that his [John's] brother, namely Captain Jones, the famous Mormon, has died, near Salt Lake.

The report is false, however, as Dan Jones did not die until 3 January 1862, and he did so in Provo, Utah.

1857: January, *Y Diwygiwr* (*Revivalist*), p. 31 (205 words).

Another obituary for John Jones of Llangollen that has a few additional details.

End: Reverend J. Jones of Llangollen dies in Cincinnati

1856: 13 December, *Cardiff and Merthyr Guardian*, p. 7 (1,575 words). "Society among the Mormons."

From the *New York Times*. The article has considerable detail about Bill Hickman, the Danite band, and the attack on the United States deputy surveyor, Joseph Troskolawski.

1856: 13 December, *North Wales Chronicle*, p. 4 (780 words). "Troubles of Polygamists."

Some quotes from the *Deseret News* about the challenges of the practice of plural marriage among the Latter-day Saints in Utah. Jedediah Grant laments,

> And we have women here who like anything but the celestial law of God; and if they could break asunder the cable of the church of Christ, there is scarcely a mother in Israel but would do it this day. And they talk it to their husbands, to their daughters, and say they have not seen a week's happiness since they became acquainted with that law, or since their husbands took a second wife. They want to break up the church of God, and to break it from their husbands, and from their family connections.

Brigham Young is also quoted concerning his plan for women who are having difficulty dealing with plural marriage.

1856: 20 December, *Cardiff and Merthyr Guardian*, p. 2 (780 words). "Troubles of Polygamists."

The same article as in the *North Wales Chronicle* for 13 December 1856 (see previous entry).

Notes

1. See Salient Events in Chapter 6 for more information about David John. For the account of the discovery of the approximate location of the grave of his eight-month-old daughter, Annie, who died in 1861 while crossing the plains, see Randy Brown, "The Death of Annie John," Welsh Saints Project, the profile of David John.
2. Ibid.
3. *Zion's Trumpet*, 1 March 1856, 74–79.
4. *Zion's Trumpet*, 15 March 1856, 95–96.
5. *Zion's Trumpet*, 29 March 1856, 107.
6. *Zion's Trumpet*, 12 April 1856, 121.
7. *Zion's Trumpet*, 26 April 1856, 139.
8. Edward Bunker, autobiography, 1894, pp. 22–23, Church History Biographical Database.
9. See the profiles for John Parry Jr., Elizabeth Ann Morris, Priscilla Merriman, Thomas Davis Giles, and Robert David Roberts on the Welsh Saints Project.
10. *Zion's Trumpet*, 10 May 1856, 160.
11. *Zion's Trumpet*, 30 August 1856, 284.
12. *Cardiff and Merthyr Guardian*, 19 February 1856, 8.
13. *Worcestershire Chronicle*, 26 March 1856, 2.
14. *Star of Gomer*, April 1856, 189–90.
15. The *Sun*, September 1856, 291.
16. Ibid., 292.
17. The *Baptist*, November 1856, 350.
18. Ibid., 350.
19. Ibid., 351.

Chapter 14

Episodes

14.1—The *Instructor* publishes four installments of "Female Life among the Mormons"
14.2—Daniel Daniels responds to John Davies's absurd claims
14.3—Daniel Daniels scolds the editor of the *Leader* for his accusations
14.4—Various reports are printed of the sixth annual conference of the Latter-day Saints held in London
14.5—*Cambrian* makes accusations—Daniel Daniels answers
14.6—Various writers react to the Deseret Alphabet

Salient Events

- **10 January 1857**. *Zion's Trumpet* prints a quote from the *Millennial Star* with some sad news for those who were counting on assistance from the Perpetual Emigrating Fund to take them to Salt Lake City during 1857:

  > This Office will not send any P. E. Fund emigrants to Utah during the year 1857. All the funds that the Company can command will be exhausted in discharging the heavy liabilities, incurred in sending out over two thousand souls, in the year 1856. The Saints will bear in mind that two thousand persons cannot be sent to Utah without incurring an expense of about eighteen thousand pounds sterling. It will probably require nearly two years from the present time for the P. E. Fund Company to discharge the debts contracted by last season's operations.[1]

- **24 January 1857**. *Zion's Trumpet* prints a statistical report for Wales for the final six months of 1856. It shows the total number of members at 3,010. Also mentioned are 270 excommunications, 87 deaths, and 528 emigrants. The emigrants for 1856 included many seasoned veterans in leadership positions throughout Wales. The large numbers of excommunications and deaths further diminished the branches and left The Church of Jesus Christ of Latter-day Saints in Wales in a greatly weakened condition. The days of the wondrous growth of the Church during the late 1840s and early 1850s would never be repeated.

Conference	Branches	Baptisms	Members	President
Brecon	7	9	132	J. Thomas
Monmouth	13	34	377	B. Evans
East Glamorgan	27	168	276	A. Williams
West Glamorgan	18	38	370	Thos. Harris
Llanelli	6	12	195	Dd. Davies
Carmarthen	6	6	80	Wm. Jones
Pembrokeshire	10	26	168	E. D. Miles
Cardiganshire	5	5	75	Thos. Jones
Merionethshire	4	10	57	J. Treharne
Flintshire	6	13	105	Thomas Rees
Denbighshire	4	6	89	Gr. Roberts
Conway Valley and Anglesey	5	11	84	Wm. Ajax
Total	111	338	3,010	n/a

- **27 June 1857**. *Zion's Trumpet* prints a second letter from Mary Daniels, Daniel Daniels's wife (see Salient Events in previous chapter). Mary must have wondered at the fairness of the extension of her husband's mission. After all, he had returned to Wales on his initial mission in September 1852 in the company of Dan Jones and Thomas Jeremy. Jeremy had been released from his mission in April 1855 to accompany a group of Welsh on the *Chimborazo*. Jones had been released from his mission in March 1856 to accompany a group of Welsh Saints on the *S. Curling*. And who could say how much longer her husband's extension would be? In this her second letter, dated 30 March 1857, she wrote:

> My dear husband—I was thinking you would be released to return to the bosom of the Church, and to your dear family, this year; but by now I have been brought to understand through the *Mormon* that you have been appointed to stay in Wales another year. Although my fondest wish is to get to see you, yet, through the power of the Holy Ghost, I shall be content, and I pray daily for the will of God to be done in relation to your important mission.[2]

As it turned out, Daniels was released both as President of the Church in Wales and editor of *Zion's Trumpet* at the end of 1857.

- **25 July 1857**. The editor of the *Usk Observer* prints a letter from a passenger on the 1855 crossing of the *S. Curling*, written to his brother in Abergavenny, in which he gives an account of his travels from Liverpool to Nephi City, his current residence. Despite the death of his wife and numerous hardships associated with the journey, the writer remains very positive about the total experience.[3] Furthermore, he strongly encourages his brother to follow after him. A week later, in the 1 August 1857 issue of *Usk Observer*, the repentant editor explains why he had printed a letter that contained only positive information about The Church of Jesus Christ of Latter-day Saints (see below entry).

- **15 August 1857**. The *Cardiff and Merthyr Guardian* of this date carries an article entitled "Remarkable Letter from an Escaped Mormon." The "escaped Mormon" is John Davies, a young man who left Britain with his family on board the *S. Curling* in April 1856. After his father died along the way, John and his mother and siblings continued on to Salt Lake City. The following year, John decided to travel back to Florence, Nebraska. In his letter to his brother Thomas in Wales, John tells of the great difficulty he had in getting out of Salt Lake City and making his way west. Some of his assertions are outlandish, such as claiming that he was armed with six revolvers and that he—at age twenty—had given his mother $500 before he left. In the next issue of *Zion's Trumpet*, Daniel Daniels takes issue with most of what Davies had written, and he chastises the newspaper for publishing such "blatant and contradictory lies."[4] See Episode 14.2.
- **15 August 1857**. In this issue of *Zion's Trumpet*, Daniel Daniels defends his religion against the attacks of the *Leader* (*Yr Arweinydd*), a newspaper published in Pwllheli, North Wales. Unfortunately, no copies of the newspaper are extant. Daniels begins with this observation about the editor of the *Leader*:

> He gives some unsavory accusations against the Saints, mocking their God in a very unusual way.[5]

Daniels then proceeds to list and address the various accusations. See Episode 14.3.

- **12 September 1857**. The sixth annual conference of The Church of Jesus Christ of Latter-day Saints is held in London at the Adelaide Gallery, Lower Arcade, Strand. This event triggered articles in the *Monmouthshire Beacon*, the *North Wales Chronicle*, the *Usk Observer*, the *Caernarvon and Denbigh Herald*, the *Chepstow Weekly Advertiser*, the *Cardiff and Merthyr Guardian*, and the *Star of Wales*. Attendance was estimated at about one thousand, and the reaction in all of the articles that appeared in the Welsh press was one of great disdain and even worry as to the growth of this religion in Britain. See Episode 14.4 for more details.
- **19 September 1857**. On this date two newspapers—the *Chepstow Weekly Advertiser*—and the *Caernarvon and Denbigh Herald*—carry the same article about the new "Deseret Alphabet" with this prophecy: "So the *Deseret News* will probably hereafter be a profound mystery, at least in part, to all but the initiated." See Episode 14.6.
- **26 September 1857.** This issue of *Zion's Trumpet* carries Daniel Daniels's 165-word reaction to a report in the *Cambrian* of some Latter-day Saint preachers in Llansamlet, who were "pelted with cabbages, potatoes, apples,

etc." by "200 or 300 people." Daniels asks the editor of the *Cambrian* to "show where his Bible supports and praises persecutors and maligners." See Episode 14.5.

- **26 September 1857.** Also in this issue of *Zion's Trumpet* is Daniel Daniels's 2,170-word review of a pamphlet entitled *Heresies and Deceptions of the Latter-day Saints, and the Book of Mormon, Exposed,* written by the Reverend W. J. Morrish. Daniels responds to the "renewed commotion" that had been reported to exist among some of the Church members in North Wales because of this pamphlet, which had been published eight years earlier. To address these concerns, Daniels agrees to "show as much of its [the pamphlet's] inconsistency" in the limited space of *Zion's Trumpet* as he can. In typical polemical fashion, he refutes a number of the so-called heresies and deceptions that the Anglican vicar puts forth in his publication. In doing so, Daniels shows himself to be a first-rate polemicist on the same level as his predecessors, Dan Jones and John S. Davis. A facsimile translation of Morrish's publication is in the pamphlet section.
- **26 September 1857.** The *Usk Observer* for this date carries an article entitled "Expedition against the Mormons." This is the first of numerous articles in many Welsh newspapers about the conflict between The Church of Jesus Christ of Latter-day Saints and the United States Government, often referred to as the "Utah War."
- **10 October 1857.** This issue of *Zion's Trumpet* includes the following announcement: "In view of the difficulties which are now threatening the Saints, we deem it wisdom to stop all emigration to the States and Utah for the present." This information is followed by an optimistic prediction: "We anticipate that it will not be long until the way will again be opened so that you can go home."[6] It appears that the next ship to sail from Liverpool with Welsh Latter-day Saint emigrants was the *William Tapscott* on 11 April 1859.

Commentary

1857: 24 January, *Cardiff and Merthyr Guardian*, p. 8 (455 words). "Mormon Polygamy."

Statistics of Latter-day Saint polygamy as reported by a correspondent of the *San Francisco Herald.* He gives a list of leaders and the number of wives each one has. His final paragraph is as follows:

> To which add 68 for the number then living of Governor [Brigham] Young's wives, and you have the whole number of women thus represented by the members of the Legislature, officers of the same, and his Excellency, amounting to 420; or, in other words, 40 men and 420 wives. These, Mr. Editor, are sober truths, and in what they will end is for the dark and doleful future.

1857: 24 January, *Usk Observer*, p. 2 (95 words). "Mormon Polygamy."

A greatly scaled-down version of the information in the 24 January 1857 issue of the *Cardiff and Merthyr Guardian* (see previous entry).

1857: 24 January, *Caernarvon and Denbigh Herald*, p. 10 (95 words). "Mormon Polygamy."

Same article as in the *Usk Observer* for 24 January (see previous entry).

1857: 31 January, *Chepstow Weekly Advertiser*, p. 3 (285 words). "Mormon Life in Hull."

In the town of Hull, a "young married female of respectability" was deserted by her husband of four years because she would not become a Latter-day Saint along with him. She went to the workhouse to claim relief, but since her position was not sufficiently dire, "the relieving officers were considering whether to grant her any relief or not." The magistrate issued an order to apprehend her husband, but he "had left the town."

1857: February, *Y Drysorfa* (*Treasury*), pp. 58–59 (320 words). "The Present Situation of Mormonism."

> The goal of the Mormons in going to Utah, no doubt, was to establish an independent government; but it was not long after they moved there that the American Government gained possession of California; and now the Mormons are being squeezed by the growing population of America from the East and from the West.[7]

The writer then explains why he has reason to hope concerning the Latter-day Saints:

> Those who leave them with loathing give deplorable accounts of their morals; and those who remain with them are beginning to see the need for a reform. . . . There is a kind of pressure from within and from without on this fanatical, deceived, and unrefined people, which is certain to end in their reform soon.[8]

1857: 14 February, *Chepstow Weekly Advertiser*, p. 3 (20 words).

Letters from the American plains report numerous deaths and great suffering among the Mormon emigrant teams, from want and cold.

1857: 14 February, *Cardiff and Merthyr Guardian*, p. 3 (745 words). "News for Mormon converts."

A letter by William Hartle to his brother in Leeds. William had sailed on the *Horizon* from Liverpool to Boston a few months earlier with his wife Elizabeth, their four sons (John, Samuel, William, and Ephraim), William's father (John), his mother (Lydia), and his sister (Mary). They started across the plains in the Martin handcart company. Only William and his son John survived to reach Utah. William's letter must certainly have given pause to his coreligionists in Britain as they contemplated a similar journey.

1857: 28 February, *Wrexham Advertiser*, p. 3 (270 words). "Mormons Perishing on the Plains."

A correspondent of the *Missouri Republican* gives a dire account of the handcart companies that had encountered heavy snows on their way to Salt Lake City the previous year:

> They were very badly clothed, and in consequence of the hardships many of them were dying; in one camp they buried fifteen in one day. The mode of burial, since they cannot dig the frozen ground, is to lay the bodies in heaps, and pile over them willows and heaps of stones. Governor Brigham Young, learning something of their condition dispatched some men and provisions to

> their relief; but these were met by the mail party returning to the city again, having been turned back by the violence of the storms they encountered. What the poor creatures will do, or what will become of them, is "hard to tell."

1857: 28 February, *Merthyr Telegraph*, p. 2 (280 words). "A Mormon Madman."

A report of a wealthy man in Denmark who became a Latter-day Saint but was frustrated that his wife would not abandon her belief in the Lutheran religion. According to the account, the man claimed that an angel had "charged him in the name of God to convert her to the faith of the Mormons." Upon her refusal the man reportedly stabbed his wife to death.

Episode 14.1

Start: The Instructor publishes four installments of Female Life among the Mormons

1857: March, *Y Dysgedydd* (*Instructor*), pp. 105–10 (5,145 words). "The Mormons—the Migration of the Mormons, under the leadership of Jo Smith, toward the Salt Lake," part 1 of 4.

1857: April, *Y Dysgedydd* (*Instructor*), pp. 139–43 (3,645 words). "The Mormons—the Migration of the Mormons, under the leadership of Jo Smith, toward the Salt Lake," part 2 of 4.

1857: May, *Y Dysgedydd* (*Instructor*), pp. 185–87 (2,450 words). "The Mormons—the Migration of the Mormons, under the leadership of Jo Smith, toward the Salt Lake," part 3 of 4.

1857: June, *Y Dysgedydd* (*Instructor*), pp. 223–25 (1,455 words). "The Mormons—the Migration of the Mormons, under the leadership of Jo Smith, toward the Salt Lake," part 4 of 4.

Except for the two opening paragraphs in the March 1857 issue, all the installments consist of the Welsh translations of various segments of *Female Life Among the Mormons; a Narrative of Many Years' Personal Experience. By the Wife of a Mormon Elder, Recently from Utah.* The segments selected from the *Instructor* for translation into Welsh represent but a fraction of the forty-eight chapters (449 pages) of the original English of this anonymous novel, which was written to portray The Church of Jesus Christ of Latter-day Saints in the most negative light possible. In his opening paragraph, the editor explains why he had elected to present to his readers the selections from the unnamed novel:

> We do not intend to say anything at present about the religious disease of the human mind, of which Mormonism is the lowest and most corrupt form, except insofar as it is essential in order to throw light on something so irresponsible, that such an unclean and odious form of religion should have been accepted by anyone on whom the slightest ray of general knowledge has shone. But Mormonism remains a fact in the year one thousand eight hundred and fifty-seven and counts its disciples in the thousands! Some maintain that God, in a judgment, has allowed men to fall into firm error, to believe lies, to give credence to heretical spirits, to deceive, and to be deceived.[9]

In his second paragraph, the editor provides further justification for his decision and labels the followers of Joseph Smith as follows:

> Poor, ignorant, little people, only one step above the animal which is destroyed—for whom their Mormonism is more of a misfortune than a sin, and they themselves objects more to be pitied than condemned.[10]

End: The Instructor *publishes four installments of* Female Life among the Mormons

1857: 7 March, *Merthyr Telegraph*, p. 3 (110 words). "Sufferings of Mormon Emigrants."

> The *Boston Puritan* says: "We have dreadful accounts of the sufferings among the Mormon emigrants by the handcart train which is now in the mountains. The train contained 350 souls; one-seventh are already dead; and they are dying at the rate of fifteen per day. There are some 600 more behind, of which we have heard nothing. We hope that they stopped at Laramie. It is impossible for them to get through this fall. The Mormons estimate that there are no less than 1,500 of their brethren yet to come in, and the snow is reported to be not less than a foot deep in the mountains."

1857: 7 March, *Caernarvon and Denbigh Herald*, p. 9 (85 words).

> The *New York Tribune* states that malignant smallpox broke out among a part of emigrants *en route* through Utah territory to California. The medical men, on making a rigid investigation, discovered that a child had picked up a bead filled with smallpox *virus*, the ends being stopped with cotton. The theory was that it must have been placed there by Mormons, in the hope that they would thus implant the seeds of that dreadful disease among the Indians, whom they have been unable to make tools of.

1857: 14 March, *Chepstow Weekly Advertiser*, p. 3 (21 words).

> The Mormons at Great Salt Lake City are threatened with famine. Their crops have been destroyed by drought, grasshoppers, and worms.

1857: 21 March, *Merthyr Telegraph*, p. 3 (375 words). "Letter from the Salt Lake."

Rees Llewellyn, "a person well known in the neighborhood of Pentrebach," reports on his journey in a handcart company to Salt Lake City. Despite the many difficulties he and his wife had experienced, he wrote:

> But for all I am quite happy here, and send my best respects to you my dear mother, and all my friends. . . . I have very little to say of the country. It is healthy, and the atmosphere is here much clearer than in the old country. It is a good country for the Mormons; but there are many living here that do not belong to them; whilst there are some of the worst men on the face of the earth here, I know there are a few of the best men. As the net cast into the sea, brings all kinds of fish, so you may depend on my word there are some sharks here.

1857: 25 March, *Yr Amserau* (*Times*), p. 3 (570 words). "Saintism in the South."

The writer, identifying himself as "An Enemy of Deceit," observes:

> These fanatical people have been very successful in Wales during recent years, but by now the majority of them have emigrated to their *earthly heaven*, although a few of them are to be seen here and there.

The writer is accurate with respect to all three of his above observations. Historical facts are as follows:

- During the previous decade, approximately 7,000 Welsh had converted to The Church of Jesus Christ of Latter-day Saints. Ministers of other religious were greatly perturbed as they watched members of their own congregations abandon their pews and adopt the Latter-day Saint message.
- In 1849 the first group—approximately 330—of the Welsh converts emigrated to their "earthly heaven." Each year after this initial departure, smaller groups of the Welsh went on several ships along with English and Scottish converts. And in April 1856, over five hundred Welsh Saints sailed on board the *S. Curling*, with Salt Lake City as their final destination.
- When this *Times* article was published in 1857, the Latter-day Saint presence in Wales was considerably diminished, as many leaders and stalwarts in the faith had been among the large *S. Curling* party.

The writer then tells of a miner who had converted to The Church of Jesus Christ and who had decided to forsake the use of tobacco "to have money to throw into the treasury of the saints." Also "he withheld permission for his wife to use tea, telling her that it was harmful." The miner was successful in giving up his pipe, but chewing tobacco presented a much great challenge. The writer explains how the miner succeeded in abandoning his habit:

> He went up a small stream and selected a smooth stone, and he kept it in his mouth during the day, moving it as slowly as Atlas moved the world long ago. It was not much smaller at night than it was in the morning, and it did not cost him anything. He met a friend one morning who, when he saw something large in his mouth, asked if he had gone back to chewing. He answered in the negative and explained that it was a stone that he had. His friend wanted him to use a *marble*, but his answer was that he was afraid that he would swallow it.

The writer offers the following advice to the miner:

> Our counsel to the above friend is to use everything that is proper for him as a man, and to stop denying permission for his wife to use anything that is for her good. Let him not be deceived by the saints, and let him not listen to their promises of happiness in Salt Lake. . . . We can assure him that many from South Wales have had to *pay dearly* for their journey to Salt Lake. This is the secret for the success of saintism in this country, namely their promises for happiness across the ocean; and after reaching the promised land they will experience the disappointment, but then it is too late to turn back. Let them inquire of those who have returned from there, and they will hear what kind of happy place the *land of promise* of the Saints really is.

1857: 28 March, *Chepstow Weekly Advertiser*, pp. 2–3 (170 words). "A Mormon Worthy."

> Mr. David Wilkins of New York, already happy in the possession of two better halves, who were sisters, fell in love with a pretty Scotch girl. This beauty,

however, had an aged mother, whom she refused to leave. David thereupon, with the consent of Brigham, overcame the difficulty by marrying both mother and daughter. But last spring, finding that with the enormous rates for provisions and breadstuffs he could not support four wives without making large inroads into his pile of the needful, he gave the two sisters notice that he had supported them long enough, and that they must find accommodation elsewhere. Accordingly, they had to leave him, and now support themselves by washing for some of the Gentiles. Again, you will find at Springville, on Utah Lake, Mr. Aaron Johnson (its bishop) serving the Lord by supporting as his spirituals *five sisters, his own nieces,* and the report is that he has engaged to marry the sixth as soon as she reaches her teens. *New York Tribune.*

1857: 4 April, *Chepstow Weekly Advertiser*, p. 3 (90 words).

The Mormon prophet, Young, recently denounced a man named Gideon, who had spoken against polygamy, in this wise: "Who is this Gideon that has come amongst you? He used to sell tape in St. Louis, and now he is here to blaspheme the Lord, and to destroy the house of Israel. And what should ye, children of the covenant, do in return for this evil work? Out with the bowie knives ye wore like breastpieces at Nauvoo, and, in the name of God and the prophet, give him h——ll!"

1857: 11 April, *Chepstow Weekly Advertiser*, p. 1 (50 words). "Mormon Exodus."

About 150 persons from Gloucester, Cheltenham, and Bristol, left Worcester on Tuesday last, for the Salt Lake, via Liverpool. The party contained persons of all ages, from decrepit old men and women down to infants in arms; and what was a significant fact, there were more females than males.

1857: 11 April, *Wrexham Advertiser*, p. 2 (37 words).

The Mormons are greatly incensed at the prospect of having a large military force stationed in Utah, and, according to the tenor of the latest advices, were prepared to show a forcible resistance to the federal troops.

1857: 11 April, *Wrexham Advertiser*, p. 3 (82 words).

We have no doubt that there is positive information in this city that Brigham Young and his crew have burned the United States archives, court records, etc., in Utah territory; that they have demanded the appointment of one or two schedules of federal officers, both headed by Brigham Young for governor, with the avowal of the purpose of driving any other out of the territory by force of arms. The truth is, the Mormons are already practically in a state of rebellion.

1857: 18 April, *Wrexham Advertiser*, p. 2 (395 words). "The Governorship of Utah."

An article taken from the *New York Times* with regard to the future of Utah in which the writer states the importance of replacing Brigham Young as governor. He predicts:

The Mormons are an active, enterprising people, and are more closely to be watched on that account. When they shall have established themselves in the most desirable parts of the territory of Utah, they will be masters of a region, extending from the thirty-seventh degree of north latitude, and from the eastern base of Sierra Nevada to the summits of the Rocky Mountains—a domain

> more extensive than California, and as healthy and well adapted to the physical development of the human race as any in the world. . . . By prompt action, the vast territory of Utah may be rescued from worse than anarchy, a better class of population may be attracted to its fertile fields, and a source of annoyance for years to come, if not bloodshed, may be averted.

1857: 25 April, *North Wales Chronicle*, p. 3 (305 words). "Rebellion in Utah."

An article taken from the *New York Herald* in which the writer expresses concern about Utah in light of a recent act of rebellion in Salt Lake City. He writes:

> In January last a party of Mormons, of high standing in the church, under the advice of Brigham Young, broke into the offices of the United States District Judge, and Clerk of the Supreme Court, and carried away by force all the papers and books belonging to the Supreme Court. The reason they gave for this outrage was, that Congress would not admit them as a state, and that they did not intend to tolerate any United States offices in the territory.

He ends his report with the following recommendation:

> One of the very best men in the country should be sent to Salt Lake City, with a sufficient force of United States troops to enforce respect; and an end should be put, once and forever, by fair means or foul, to the series of outrages of which this violation of the records of the Supreme Court of Utah is the last.

1857: 25 April, *Usk Observer*, p. 2 (305 words). "Rebellion in Utah."

The same article as in the *North Wales Chronicle* for 25 April 1857 (see previous entry).

1857: 2 May, *Chepstow Weekly Advertiser*, p. 3 (85 words). "English Mormons."

> On Tuesday afternoon one of the continental steamers brought about 560, in all, men, women, and children, to Grimsby, *en route* to Liverpool, thence to the Salt Lake. The majority of them looked in a healthy condition, and seemed to enjoy their transmigrating life. So far as intoxicating liquors are concerned, they are said to be total abstainers; and it is also asserted that out of that vast number there is not one who smokes or chews tobacco. *Eastern Counties Herald.*

1857: 2 May, *Wrexham Advertiser*, p. 3 (200 words). "The Mormons in Utah."

A report of the recent action taken by the Buchanan administration regarding Utah:

> It is proposed to send to Utah a military force of 2,000 men, officered by persons of character, and who have families; and judges and executive officers of worth and high standing, who have families, are to be appointed in place of Brigham Young and his satellites. The measure will, it is believed, afford ample protection to the territorial functionaries, and at the same time impart an enlightened and purer tone to the morals of the community.

1857: 2 May, *Seren Cymru* (*Star of Wales*), p. 169 (900 words). "The Mormons in America."

> The accounts received from the Mormon territory in Salt Lake are enough to cause every lover of mankind worry and shame, because of the filth and immorality which flourish in their midst. It is not without cause that they are spoken and written about; and the ministers of the gospel and the teachers of

> our Sabbath schools should raise their voices loudly against them, exposing their atrocious abomination, so that more of our fellow nation will not be seduced to emigrate to their ungodly Sodom. So that our readers may have a glimpse at the villainy that is carried on by them, we set before them an excerpt of a letter which was sent by a Baptist Minister to his brother in Wales.

The letter contains the minister's assessment of the practice of plural marriage in Salt Lake City. He expresses shock at learning of the success of the proselytizing efforts of the Latter-day Saints in Wales:

> And the thing that surprised me more than anything else was to learn from a Mormon traveler that there were many Welsh among them. O! where are you, friends of religion and mankind? The light of life is in your hands to fill the small Principality with the light of Christ; how is it that you have not done so? Mormonism cannot dwell in the light; therefore, there must be some places remarkably dark, even in Wales, where this monstrous deceit finds quiet to prosper.

The minister then describes the experience of the Latter-day Saint women:

> The poor creatures! they suffer frightful tribulations on their journey to Utah as they cross a desert from six to seven hundred miles wide; and when they arrive there those who possess the slightest degree of moral feeling in their bosoms will be so terribly disappointed upon seeing themselves not in paradise, as their deceivers had promised, but in the Great Sodom of the West, where adultery is the law of the land, and where a woman whom God had made to be honored, loved, and respected, as a diadem to crown his fair creation has been cast down from her nobility to the deep mire of affliction and humiliation.

The writer for the *Star of Wales* concludes:

> This is dreadful blasphemy! The abomination of Mormonism is worse than that of Muslimism, and that of the worst system of paganism.

1857: 2 May, *Caernarvon and Denbigh Herald*, p. 6 (1,305 words). "The Esoteric Doctrines of Mormonism."

A *New York Tribune* correspondent's letter, dated October 1856, from Salt Lake City. The letter is about polygamy, and the very long response points out the "aspects and atrocities of this practice." A little story at the end is as follows:

> The second wives, or spirituals, are not supported by their husbands; on the contrary, there are numerous cases on record in which the women support the men, going out even in the field to work. The light in which the women are looked upon in this country is illustrated by the following incident: When the first handcart train entered the city, foremost in the line were noticed three buxom Welsh girls, who had drawn their handcart some 1500 miles. Wishing the next day after their arrival to see a Mormon with whom I had some business to transact, I inquired of one of his spirituals where I could find him. She answered me, with an ironical smile on her lips: "He has gone to engage as spirituals those three Welsh girls who were in the lead of the handcart train. He thinks they would be very useful in hauling his winter's wood from the canoes, they make such an excellent team."

1857: 2 May, *Monmouthshire Beacon*, p. 6 (85 words). "English Mormons."

> On Tuesday afternoon one of the continental steamers brought about 560, in all, men, women, and children, to Grimsby, *en route* to Liverpool, thence to the Salt Lake. The majority of them looked in a healthy condition, and seemed to enjoy their transmigrating life. So far as intoxicating liquors are concerned, they are said to be total abstainers; and it is also asserted that out of this vast number there is not one who smokes or chews tobacco.—*Eastern Counties Herald.*

1857: 9 May, *North Wales Chronicle*, p. 4 (24 words).

A dispatch from Boston, dated April 20, says: "Eight hundred and fifty Mormons arrived here today from Liverpool, in the packet ship *George Washington*."

1857: 9 May, *Caernarvon and Denbigh Herald*, p. 6 (265 words). "The Mormons."

> The official report of Judge Drummond, of the Supreme Court of the territory of Utah, to the Hon. Jeremiah S. Black, Attorney-General of the United States, Washington City, D. C.

This very long report is followed by a "leading article" that appeared in the *Times*, giving credence to every detail of the Drummond report and condemning the Latter-day Saints. Here is a sample:

> Mormonism, if conceived in America, is propagated and supported in England, nor do we know of any sign of our times more bewildering than the success of this shocking imposture among a civilized and instructed population. Witchcraft is a mere nothing by the side of this living and moving monstrosity.

1857: 9 May, *Cardiff and Merthyr Guardian*, p. 7 (500 words). "The Mormons."

This official report of Judge Drummond appeared also in the *Caernarvon and Denbigh Herald* for 9 May 1857 (see previous entry) and is followed by an analysis and commentary taken from the *New York Express*.

1857: 13 May, *Yr Amserau* (*Times*), p. 3 (925 words). "Freaks of Popular Sovereignty Among the Mormons—Resignation of W. W. Drummond, Chief Justice of Utah."

The Welsh translation of a lengthy article that had appeared in the *Orleans Courier* for 3 April 1857. The introductory paragraph of the article is the editor's account of a visit he received from William W. Drummond:

> We had the gratification yesterday morning of a call from Judge W. W. Drummond, of Chicago, late Chief Justice of Utah Territory. He was in that condition of fine health and spirits in which we always rejoice to see good, sturdy, manly democrats. He entertained us for a considerable time with an account of his personal and judicial experience among the Saints, and of their manners, habits, history, notions and purposes. Although we were disgusted with this set of miserable fanatics from accounts which had already reached us, some relations given by Judge Drummond, in addition to those contained in his letter to Attorney-General Black, added many revolting shades to the picture.

The "revolting shades" to which the editor refers include details about the following positions the Latter-day Saints took:

- Their hatred for those who were not of their faith.
- Their hatred for the United States.
- Their unquestioned obedience to all instructions given by Brigham Young.

- Their unfair and often cruel treatment of the American Indians.
- Their practice of plural marriage.

The final portion of the article consists of the 30 March 1857 letter of Judge Drummond to the Attorney General of the United States, in which he sets forth the many reasons for his resignation.

1857: 16 May, *Wrexham Advertiser*, p. 4 (53 words). "Mormonism."

The apostles of Mormonism are again busy seeking to make converts of the Rhos colliers and are exhorting them to emigrate to that delightful spot, the Salt Lake Valley. What their success has been we do not know; but those who are capable of being thus deluded we can very well spare.

1857: 16 May, *Merthyr Telegraph*, p. 2, item 1 (195 words). "Clubs in Public Houses."

We give the working men of Merthyr Tydfil credit for entertaining, and, to some extent, adopting, the advice from time to time given them. As regards ourselves *we* have rarely originated plans, or devised methods whereby the homes of industry might be made happier; but in pointing out what others have suggested, and co-operating where assistance was needed, we have endeavored, however humbly, to do our part, and benefit them and theirs. One instance we may, perhaps, be suffered to mention: the influence once held over great numbers of the artisans of this neighborhood by the Mormons. What is the condition of the Mormon faith now? Hopefully we prophesied its decline in our district; energetically were efforts made by thoughtful, earnest men to effect that decline. Now we see the result. Great numbers used to meet at the White Lion—lately only *eleven* met. Formerly the Penydarren branch was strong—now it has dwindled into insignificance. A little while ago they numbered many in Georgetown—they are now but *three*; and these, with a few from Penydarren, and eleven at Mill Street, form the total strength of a foolish body of men!

1857: 16 May, *Merthyr Telegraph*, p. 2, item 2 (65 words). "Merthyr Police Court."

Monday. (Before J. C. Fowler, Esqr.) Mormonism. John Morgan applied for a license to preach the gospel according to Mormonism. He took the oath of adjuration, the oath of allegiance, the oath of supremacy, and subscribed to the declaration of being a Christian Protestant and a believer of the Old and New Testament Scriptures, as translated and used in protestant churches.

1857: 16 May, *North Wales Chronicle*, p. 4 (940 words). "The Mormons in Utah."

Taken from the *Deseret News*, this article contains Brigham Young's message to the Utah Legislature, numerous observations about the Saints, and general encouragement to the inhabitants of Utah. Here is the final portion of the message, an exhortation from President Jedediah Grant:

This people are asleep, and I will vouch that there are many of them who do not pray; or if they do, three prayers, "would freeze hell over," as a Methodist minister once said. I want you to pray with the Holy Ghost upon you. It is your duty to keep clean. I have given the teachers a new set of questions to ask the people. I say to them, ask the people to keep clean. Do you wash your bodies once in each week, when circumstances will permit? Do you keep your dwellings, outhouses, and door yards clean? The first work of the reformation with some should be to clear the filth away from their premises. How would some like to have President Young to visit them, and go through their buildings, examine their rooms, bedding, etc.? Many houses stink so bad that a clean man could not live in them. Some men were raised in stink, and so were their fathers before them. I would not attempt to bless anybody in such places. You may inquire why I talk so. Can you talk in a better style about dirt, nastiness, and filth? If you can, I cannot, and at the same time make people feel enough upon the subject to put away their filth and be clean. If you want me to speak smoother, do better, and keep cleaner. Were I to talk about God, Heaven, angels, or anything good, I could talk in a more refined style, but I have to talk about things as they do exist among us.

1857: 16 May, *Chepstow Weekly Advertiser*, p. 4 (67 words). "A Yankee Vatican." The Mormons regard Brigham Young as the successor of Joe Smith, and Joe Smith as the viceregent of Heaven. It would be an interesting question to propound to a rapping spirit, whether Mormonism will, or not, ever become a great ecclesiastical organization, and, if it does, whether the United States will not one of these days have to conclude a Concordat with Utah? *Punch.*

1857: 16 May, *Cardiff and Merthyr Guardian*, p. 3 (1,340 words). "The Mormons."

From the *Times.* A very long article with a final reaction to Judge Drummond's report:

> Unhappily, the whole case touches us nearly. Mormonism, if conceived in America, is propagated and supported in England, nor do we know of any sign of our times more bewildering than the success of this shocking imposture among a civilized and instructed population. Witchcraft is a mere nothing by the side of this living and moving monstrosity.

1857: 16 May, *Cardiff and Merthyr Guardian*, p. 5 (40 words). "The Mormons." By the City of Washington, Captain W. Wylie, which arrived at Liverpool on Wednesday morning, we are informed that serious dissensions are reported to have broken out among the Mormons, both at San Bernardino and Salt Lake.

1857: 16 May, *Caernarvon and Denbigh Herald*, p. 4 (265 words). "Slave Dealers."

In this correspondence of the *New York Tribune,* the Latter-day Saints are called "slave dealers." Children "are suffered to grow up in ignorance and vice. Without the hallowed influence of home to restrain them, they are vicious, profane, and obscene." The writer points out the "most profane and indecent language" that is heard in the tabernacle and corrupts the "urchins." He also mentions four hundred Indian children who are "held in bondage under the pretense of apprenticeship." They are "purchased from the Indians (who steal them from the neighboring tribes) for sums varying from twenty dollars to forty dollars. This traffic is thus encouraged by Mormons, and in fact sanctioned by their laws."

1857: 23 May, *Cardiff and Merthyr Guardian*, p. 5 (65 words). "Mormon Tracts." These pestilential productions are still being forced into the houses of the working population of this town, and we therefore again beg to caution the heads of families on the subject, earnestly hoping that our fellow-townsmen, of all ranks, will use their utmost endeavors to stop these systematic attempts to circulate the vile and profligate delusions in which the Mormon impostors trade.

1857: 30 May, *Cardiff and Merthyr Guardian*, p. 6 (35 words). "Mormonism."

George Daken Thomas, Georgetown, subscribed to the usual declaration of being a Christian, and took the usual oaths of abjuration and supremacy, to enable him to follow his profession as a Mormon preacher!

1857: 30 May, *Merthyr Telegraph*, p. 3 (35 words). "Mormonism."

The Rev. George Dukir Thomas, Georgetown, subscribed to the usual declaration of being a Christian, and took the usual oaths of adjuration and supremacy, to enable him to follow his profession as a Mormon preacher.

1857: June, *Seren Gomer* (*Star of Gomer*), p. 284 (140 words).

A brief report to the effect that Judge Drummond has resigned his office for two reasons. The first reason is that "the Mormons believe that their allegiance to the Church, as they call themselves, is above their allegiance to the United States." The second reason is as follows:

Because Brigham Young and the Church pervert the jurors, burn the letters of the legal courts, kill officials and put the blame on the Indians, and that Brigham, as governor of the territory, pardons the criminals after they are given a just sentence by the courts.

1857: 6 June, *Wrexham Advertiser*, p. 2 (170 words). "The Mormon Iniquity."

The last accounts from the Great Salt Lake represent matters in that quarter as being most unsettled, and contain a narrative of startling facts, showing that unmitigated treason, murder, arson, robbery, and forcible debauch are every day incidents of Mormon life, and that not an effort is made to check the perpetration of any of these terrible crimes. . . . Women are becoming scarce in the territory, and the Mormons consequently are resorting to more children to replenish their harems; while the most fiendish oppression is resorted to for the purpose of forcing reluctant females to become the "spirituals" of Mormon Turks.

1857: 6 June, *Cardiff and Merthyr Guardian*, p. 3 (55 words). "The Mormons."

By the *Europa*, which arrived at Liverpool on Sunday, we learn that the rumor of Brigham Young having had to flee from Utah is incorrect. He still remains at the Mormon settlement, at Salmon River. For some unknown cause the Mormons at Bernardino and the surrounding settlements had been summoned to Salt Lake City.

1857: 6 June, *Monmouthshire Beacon*, p. 4 (85 words).

The state of things in the Mormon territory grows worse and worse, and every law of decency and nature is now violated in that wretched place. The forcible debaucheries are too horrible to be told, and as women are becoming scarce, it seems the merest children are seized to replenish the harems. President Buchanan must put these monsters down with the strong arm of the sword, and we hear he will do so. General Walker is reported at his last gasp as usual.

1857: 6 June, *Monmouthshire Beacon*, p. 6 (170 words). "Extensive Robbery by a Mormon."

On Monday last a number of Mormons left Mansfield, Nottinghamshire, for Liverpool, *en route* for Utah. Among them was a man named Robert Wright, who was one of the executive officers of an Odd Fellows' lodge held at the Angel

> Inn, the funds of which were kept in a strong box, locked with three locks, each key being in the possession of a different member, one of whom was Wright. Among the papers and money was a cheque for £218, ready drawn and signed. After Wright had left the town on Monday, some of the members caused the box to be broken open, when it was discovered the cheque was missing. It was subsequently found that the cheque was cashed so far back as the 13th of April. The police started in pursuit of Wright, and arrested him and his family on their way to the station at Sheffield, *en route* for Liverpool. A portion of the money was found upon the prisoner, who was taken before the magistrates and remanded.

1857: 6 June, *Monmouthshire Beacon*, p. 8 (310 words).

A series of negative reports about Utah:

> The news from Utah is becoming anxious; at one time Brigham Young is said to have taken flight—then that the greatest atrocities have been committed to retain his power. . . . The last accounts from the Great Salt Lake contain a narrative of startling facts, showing that unmitigated treason, murder, arson, robbery, and forcible debauch, are everyday incidents of Mormon life, and that not an effort is made to check the perpetration of any of these terrible crimes.

1857: 6 June, *Caernarvon and Denbigh Herald*, p. 9 (210 words).

Some information about Brigham Young's not having to flee from Utah. He was "at Great Salt Lake City, organizing a secret expedition to somewhere in the north, for some purpose unknown to the Gentile world. This fact is corroborated by a dispatch from St. Louis." Furthermore, "women were becoming scarce in the territory, and the Mormons consequently are resorting to mere children to replenish their harems; while the most fiendish oppression is resorted to for the purpose of forcing reluctant females to become the "spirituals" of Mormon Turks."

1857: 13 June, *Caernarvon and Denbigh Herald*, p. 4 (175 words). "The Mormons."

More unconfirmed information about Brigham Young and his "proposed expedition to the north." Also, "the Mormons are about commencing a settlement near Council Bluffs for an outpost or receiving station."

1857: 13 June, *North Wales Chronicle*, p. 4 (60 words).

> We learn from Washington that major B. M'Culloch has declined the governorship of Utah territory. It is stated a Westernman has been selected for the post. It is furthermore stated that the government has determined upon adopting vigorous measures as regards the Mormons. A large military force is to be dispatched thither, probably under command of General Harney.

1857: 13 June, *Chepstow Weekly Advertiser*, p. 1 (50 words).

> Open air preaching is now practiced in Bristol and Clifton, both by Clergy of the Establishment and by Nonconformists. It is hoped by this means to counteract the designs of the Mormons, who are constantly forcing their pestiferous trash on domestic servants and others who will receive them.

1857: 13 June, *Chepstow Weekly Advertiser*, p. 4 (180 words). "The Mormons and the United States Government."

It is stated that the Government has determined upon adopting vigorous measures as regards the Mormons. A large military force is to be dispatched thither, probably under command of General Harney. The movements of Brigham Young had attracted some attention since the receipt of the report that he had fled from Utah. Now that it has been ascertained that there is no truth in this report, his proposed expedition to the north forms the interesting feature of Mormon intelligence. It was stated, on reliable authority, that the Mormons are about commencing a settlement near Council Bluffs for an outpost or receiving station. The leading men of the new settlement are to be Eastern men, who have not been initiated into the real mysteries of Mormonism, and who will, therefore, be better fitted for taking charge of young disciples and giving them their first lessons in the new faith. It is more than probable that the founding of this settlement is the real cause of Brigham's "secret expedition to somewhere in the North."

1857: 13 June, *Caernarvon and Denbigh Herald*, p. 6 (35 words).

The Mormons in Merthyr are laboring to obtain proselytes with a zeal worthy of a better cause. During the past fortnight four young men in Merthyr have obtained licenses to officiate as Mormon preachers.

1857: 13 June, *Seren Cymru* (*Star of Wales*), p. 219 (340 words).

"An Observer" writes that Roger Daniel, a Latter-day Saint from Sirhowy, had been persuaded by his coreligionists "to starve himself, and carry every halfpenny he could get to them":

> Nor did they allow him to eat anything but bread and water; but he failed to continue with his work in a little while, because of physical weakness. He was again persuaded that he did not need a doctor, that they would cure him; and he, poor thing, believed every word they said, as though they were reading the Bible to him.

The writer further describes the cruelty of the Latter-day Saints to Roger Daniel and blames them for his eventual death. The writer then addresses his compatriots:

> Oh, people of Wales! how long will you be tricked by these rapacious wolf-hounds, who swarm like locusts all over the world, to trick and cheat innocent men, and slander everyone but themselves? I think these are the voracious dogs mentioned in the Bible.

1857: 13 June, *Monmouthshire Beacon*, p. 4 (160 words).

America sends us intelligence of some importance. The Mormons are to be driven out of Utah root and branch, and a large army is now on its way to Salt Lake, under the able command of General Harney. It is reported that Brigham Young, the Mormon chief, is in treaty with the Indians for a grant of land on which to form a new settlement somewhere on the banks of the Red River. This looks like giving up possession of his old quarters without fighting, and indeed there can be no doubt that discretion would be the better part of valor in his case, being without soldiers or money to pay them with. There is news of General Walker, who at the last accounts was surrounded on all sides and driven up in a corner, but he has been so often in similar straits that we should not be surprised at his managing to extricate himself from this dilemma.

1857: 13 June, *Usk Observer*, p. 2, item 1 (330 words). "The Mormons in Utah."

The announcement of the arrival of Governor Drummond in Utah followed by several dire predictions of the outcome.

1857: 13 June, *Usk Observer*, p. 2, item 2 (275 words).

> Utah, another territory, is likely to give us more trouble. We have the anomaly of the age to deal with there—Mormonism—the strangest form of heathenism that has ever been found growing up in the neighborhood of civilization.

Possible plans then being devised by the American government are then to deal with "one of the most serious struggles in which it has ever been engaged."

1857: 20 June, *Usk Observer*, p. 2 (46 words).

> A Mormon preacher at Southampton said in his sermon a Sunday or two ago: "Shall I tell you, my brethren, when the comet shall come and strike this earth? When Brigham Young chooses to say the word, then will the comet come and strike the earth."

1857: 20 June, *North Wales Chronicle*, p. 3 (46 words).

The same article as in the *Usk Observer* for 20 June 1857 (see previous entry).

1857: 20 June, *Wrexham Advertiser*, p. 2 (46 words).

The same article as in the *Usk Observer* for 20 June 1857, p. 2 and the *North Wales Chronicle* for 20 June 1857 (see previous entry).

1857: 20 June, *Caernarvon and Denbigh Herald*, p. 10, item 2 (46 words).

The same article as in the *Usk Observer* for 20 June 1857, p. 2 and the *North Wales Chronicle* for 20 June 1857 (see previous entry).

1857: 20 June, *North Wales Chronicle*, p. 6 (52 words).

> The news from the United States is of considerable importance in a political sense. In the first place there is the Mormon difficulty. Then the news from Utah is certainly of war, for Mr. Brigham Young, the successor of the Prophet, is reported to be driving all Nonconformists out of the State.

1857: 20 June, *Monmouthshire Beacon*, p. 7 (100 words).

> The American papers record the death of Orson [Parley] Pratt, the famous Mormon elder. He seduced the wife of a man named M'Lean, in San Francisco, and was conveying her and her children into Utah, where she was to live with him as his ninth wife. M'Lean followed the fugitives and shot Pratt dead at Van Buren, in Arkansas. The deceased was a man of considerable ability, and had traveled as a missionary through Great Britain, Denmark, Sweden, and Germany. He was next in influence to Brigham Young, and was one of the original followers of Joe Smith, the Mormon founder.

1857: 20 June, *Usk Observer*, p. 3 (100 words).

The same article as in *Monmouthshire Beacon* for 20 June 1857, p. 7 and the *Caernarvon and Denbigh Herald* for 20 June 1857 (see previous entries).

1857: 20 June, *Caernarvon and Denbigh Herald*, p. 9, item 1 (100 words).

The same article as in *Monmouthshire Beacon* for 20 June 1857 and *Usk Observer* for 20 June 1857 (see previous entries).

1857: 20 June, *Cardiff and Merthyr Guardian*, p. 7 (100 words).

The same article as in *Monmouthshire Beacon* for 20 June 1857 and *Usk Observer* for 20 June 1857 (see previous entries).

1857: 20 June, *Caernarvon and Denbigh Herald*, p. 9, item 2 (29 words).

> It is reported that the schism in the Mormon Church at the Great Salt Lake has assumed a formidable character. Brigham Young is afraid to show himself in public.

1857: 20 June, *Caernarvon and Denbigh Herald*, p. 10, item 1 (14 words).

> The number of Mormons in England, according to return of last year, is 22,400.

1857: 20 June, *Chepstow Weekly Advertiser*, p. 3, item 1 (65 words).

> The news from America is not very satisfactory. The Mormon difficulty seems growing upon the Government, and indeed they seem scarcely competent to grapple with it. Brigham Young, the successor of the false prophet Joe Smith, seems to feel his power to be on the increase, for he is now threatening banishment to all who do not give in their adherence to his strange doctrines.

1857: 20 June, *Chepstow Weekly Advertiser*, p. 3, item 2 (95 words). "Mormonism Vindicated."

> Elder J. Bond, from the Great Salt Lake City, delivered a lecture in the Victoria Room, Newcastle, on Tuesday, in refutation of the charges made against Mormonism. He defended polygamy on Scriptural grounds—contrasted Moses and Brigham Young at the expense of Moses—contrasted civilized and savage life at the expense of civilization—and spoke of the "peculiar institutions" of Utah in language which the *Newcastle Chronicle* declines to print. At the close, he seems to have been driven by something more than "moral suasion" into arrangements for a public discussion. *Gateshead Observer*.

1857: 20 June, *Chepstow Weekly Advertiser*, p. 4 (845 words). "Mormon Leader."

A detailed report about Parley P. Pratt's assassination and the events that led up to it.

1857: 24 June, *Yr Amserau* (*Times*), p. 3, item 1 (260 words). "Murder of Orson Pratt."

The editor has obviously confused which of the two Pratt brothers—Orson and Parley—was murdered. The writer refers to Pratt as "the most highly educated and gifted Mormon of all," but he also claims that the wife of his murderer was "charmed and degraded by him."

1857: 24 June, *Yr Amserau* (*Times*), p. 3, item 2 (50 words). "The Mormons."

About the passing of Jedediah M. Grant, a counselor to Brigham Young:

> These people have lost one of the great lights, one J. M. Grant, and the notice of his death ends in the following manner: "He is gone now, leaving seven mourning widows and several children, four of which are under eight years of age, to mourn their irretrievable loss."

1857: 27 June, *North Wales Chronicle*, p. 4 (195 words). "The Mormons."

Reports and details of the tension between Brigham Young and the United States government.

1857: 27 June, *Usk Observer*, p. 3, item 1 (195 words).

The same as the article in the *North Wales Chronicle* for 27 June 1857 (see previous entry) with only a few minor differences.

1857: 27 June, *Usk Observer*, p. 3, item 2 (375 words).

A description of Brigham Young along with some observations about his lack of intellect by someone who had attended one of his presentations.

1857: 27 June, *Monmouthshire Beacon*, p. 3 (45 words).

> According to a report from the Great Salt Lake, the schism in the Mormon church had assumed a formidable character. Brigham Young was said to have deserted the Tabernacle and remained shut up in his own house, guarded night and day by his friends.

1857: 27 June, *Cardiff and Merthyr Guardian*, p. 5 (60 words).

> But it is from Utah that we have the most stirring news. Brigham Young has for some time been bidding defiance to the United States Government, but the General in command of the United States forces is to offer an asylum to all in the Mormon State wishing to get out of it, and many will assuredly avail themselves it.

1857: 27 June, *Seren Cymru* (*Star of Wales*), p. 241, item 1 (235 words). "Landing of Mormons in America."

The first of two articles in this issue of the *Star of Wales*, both of which are designed to cast members of The Church of Jesus Christ of Latter-day Saints in a bad light. In this one, taken from the *Boston Courier*, the writer tells of the arrival of the ship *George Washington* from Liverpool and quotes the captain as making the following claim:

> There were many families who had considerable goods. The captain estimated that the travelers had about £20,000 of gold on the ship; and he said that he knew that many persons possessed £1,000 each. . . . There were many women who had left their husbands so that they could go to dwell in the land of the Saints. When the captain asked one woman what had caused her to leave her husband, she answered that she had done so for the sake of Christ; he had promised that if anyone were to leave father, mother, and husband for his sake, they would receive so much in this world and they would receive eternal life in the world to come.

1857: 27 June, *Seren Cymru* (*Star of Wales*), p. 241, item 2 (320 words). "A Mormon Robbery."

The second article in this issue of *Star of Wales* has to do with a man by the name of Wright who was arrested in Sheffield, along with his wife, for stealing money and property from Colonel Cook for whom Wright had worked. The writer indicates that the Wrights were "Mormons" and that they had worked with two other members of the same faith whose names were Hollis and Bentley. Having determined that Wright had sent luggage from Mansfield to Liverpool in the name of Ann Jones, Palethorpe [a detective] sent a telegram to the authorities in Liverpool ordering them to hold the luggage. He and his assistant went by train immediately to Liverpool, hired a boat, and chased after the ship on which Ann Jones had just set sail. Palethorpe was able to board the ship, search Ann Jones, and locate a bag of gold coins worth £150.

On the passenger list of the *Tuscarora*, which sailed from Liverpool on 30 May 1857, are the names of Robert Wright, age twenty-six; Ann Wright, age twenty-four; George Wright, age four; and Sarah Wright, age one. Beneath their names is the name of Ann Jones, age twenty-five, "Spinster." The amount paid—£15, 10 shillings, and then £20, 10 shillings—is crossed out with a double line, and the note below that reads "Transfd to Ann Jones below, advice of Mr. Cook".[11]

1857: 27 June, *Caernarvon and Denbigh Herald*, p. 9 (575 words).

An article taken from the *Daily News* about the affairs in Utah, which "seem to be rapidly approaching a crisis." Brigham Young has at last determined to drive "all heathen gentiles" out "from the Canaan of the saints." More details are given about the sad state of affairs. "It is said that there are not less than forty thousand women in Utah, who are held in the most degrading state of concubinage, utterly helpless either to fly from their wrongs or to redress them. Among them are many of superior education, who now recall the recollection of their distant English, Scotch, or Welsh homes, where they were virtuously brought up, where they first loved and became wives and mothers."

1857: July, *Seren Gomer* (*Star of Gomer*), p. 323 (110 words). "The Things of Zion."

A brief and very negative report of the situation in Salt Lake City. Here is the complete assessment:

> The things of the Zion of the Great Salt Lake are getting darker and darker; from within all signs are committed in the same space, burning and tearing down houses, robberies, murders, and as for adultery, there is no sin there by that name—spiritual wifery is that name; and because women are scarce, the lascivious degenerates force young girls into their harems. It is said that Brigham Young has bargained with the Pa Uta Indians to flee to the north. Outside this salty paradise, United States soldiers are gathering under the command of General Harney, with full purpose of putting things in order.

1857: July, *Y Cyfaill o'r Hen Wlad yn America* (*Friend of the Old Country in America*), p. 286, item 1 (68 words). "The Shooting of One of the 'Mormon Apostles.'"

The first of three articles in this issue having to do with The Church of Jesus Christ of Latter-day Saints. Here is the entire article:

> Recently in Utah, Parley P. Pratt, a brother of Orson Pratt, a native of England and one of the "Mormon Apostles," while traveling with the wife of one Hector McLean, from New Orleans, was overtaken by her husband and was shot to death. The wife is complaining bitterly about her husband and sympathizing with the apostle, but the country in general approves of the deed of the husband.

1857: July, *Y Cyfaill o'r Hen Wlad yn America* (*Friend of the Old Country in America*), p. 286, item 2 (109 words). "Mormon Immigrants."

The second of three articles to appear in this issue. Here is the entire article:

> The *Baltimore Sun* for the 4th reports: That the train from Philadelphia on the day before had brought there over five hundred Mormons on their way

> to Salt Lake. They were mainly Norwegian. They were under the direction of a "high priest" by the name of Mathias Crowley [*sic*], who is a strong and healthy-looking man. He is about five and a half feet tall, of light complexion, with red hair. His face was almost all hair. He wore a beard similar to those of the old patriarchs. There are many craftsmen among the immigrants. There was one handsome man who bragged of having six wives already, and twenty-one children!

1857: July, *Y Cyfaill o'r Hen Wlad yn America* (*Friend of the Old Country in America*), pp. 286–87, item 3 (220 words). "Utah and Mormonism."

The final article of three to appear in this issue. It is a brief assessment of "the condition of things in Utah," as the writer sees them. He states that Brigham Young has "far too much power" and that "the more the principles of Mormonism come to light in their deeds, as is happening daily in Utah, the more repugnant it appears." But he expresses a certain degree of hope:

> The aim of the government, as soon as the new Governor arrives there, is to make known the protection offered to whoever wishes to return to the States. It is expected that the women in general will accept the offer. After that, the circumstances must reveal.

1857: July, *Y Dysgedydd* (*Instructor*), p. 279 (15 words).

> A great disagreement has broken out between the Mormons in San Bernardino and Salt Lake.

1857: July, *Yr Haul* (*Sun*), p. 221 (175 words). "Mormonism."

The writer declares,

> There is no limit to the gullibility of men; otherwise, Mormonism would not be able to catch so many in its snares and get them to bow under the yoke, thus making a man less than a man in order to follow it. Mormonism, as a system of religion, is unreasonable, inconsistent, deceitful, superstitious, impudent, and corrupt to the extreme degree.

He is glad to report the following:

> It is now said that the North American Government has begun a serious undertaking with regard to the Mormons in California by sending troops there to oust that great corrupt beast known by the name of Brigham Young, together with bringing the people to some sort of order.

1857: 4 July, *Cardiff and Merthyr Guardian*, p. 3 (580 words). "The Mormonites in Utah."

The writer of this *New York Times* article begins: "Affairs in Utah, the Mormon territory, seem to be rapidly approaching a crisis." He sees only bleak prospects of the Latter-day Saints in Utah and offers considerable speculation as to what Brigham Young will do about the crisis.

1857: 4 July, *Usk Observer*, p. 4 (65 words).

> With regard to the Mormons, the New York papers say, "Colonel Cummings will receive this week a commission from the President as successor to Brigham Young in the government of the Mormon territory General Harney is already moving troops across the plains to support the Governor in taking possession

> of his new office, should it be necessary, and vindicate the authority of the federal government."

1857: 11 July, *Seren Cymru (Star of Wales)*, p. 257 (110 words). "Llanidloes."

The writer, Dafydd Risiart, reports that no one in this town was listening to the "Satanists" as they preached in the old market hall. He explains:

> No one of this wandering, unprincipled tribe dares present himself here, because the Sunday Schools are too numerous, and their adherents too knowledgeable to be tricked by such rogues as these vagabonds.

1857: 11 July, *Seren Cymru (Star of Wales)*, pp. 260–61 (110 words). "Shooting of a Mormon Leader."

A report of the death of Parley P. Pratt.

1857: 11 July, *Chepstow Weekly Advertiser*, p. 3 (30 words).

> The difficulties of the United States with the Mormons, and with Mexico, however, continue. United States troops have been dispatched to Utah, to enforce American laws among the Mormons.

1857: 11 July, *Monmouthshire Beacon*, p. 8 (75 words).

> The last mail from New York states that General Scott had been summoned to Washington to perfect arrangements for the dispatch of troops to Utah; the troops were already in motion for the Mormon territory, but it is said that no attempt will be made to interfere with the religious or social arrangements of the Mormons, the only purpose of the Government being to secure the enforcement of the laws of the United States.

1857: 18 July, *Cardiff and Merthyr Guardian*, p. 5 (130 words). "The Mormons at Bath."

> The disclosures which have recently been made with regard to this sect have caused considerable excitement amongst some of the lower orders of this city. A few evenings since a large number of persons congregated outside the Mormon chapel, Westgate buildings, and on the appearance of the elders, who had been conducting the service, they were hooted by the mob along the Lower Borough walls and down Southgate street. Not content with this demonstration, they pelted the Mormon leaders with stones, one of whom received a severe wound in the head, and they were obliged to run for protection to the Widcome police station. The mob continued outside hooting and yelling, and it was feared that an attempt would be made to force the station.

1857: 18 July, *North Wales Chronicle*, p. 6 (480 words). "The Rebellious Saints."

Developments relating to the United States troops being sent to Utah in order to bring "Young and his subjects to their senses."

1857: 18 July, *Usk Observer*, p. 2 (480 words). "The Rebellious Saints."

The same article as in the *North Wales Chronicle* for 18 July 1857 (see previous entry).

1857: 25 July, *Usk Observer*, p. 1 (1,835 words). "Mormonism."

A letter from a Saint who sailed on the *S. Curling* in 1855, writing now to his brother in Abergavenny. The writer gives an account of his travels from Liverpool to Nephi City, his current residence. Despite the death of his wife and numerous hardships associated with the journey, the writer remains very positive about the total experience. He also strongly encourages his brother to follow after him:

> I think yourself, wife, and family will believe me (it would be no benefit to me to tell you untruths, or endeavor to lead you into errors, and God knows it never was in my head to do any such thing) when I testify to you all, in the name of God, that the doctrine taught by the Latter-day Saints is truth, and the only plan of salvation that ever was or ever will be offered to the human family; and I do exhort your wife and children, as one who loves their souls, to embrace it; and be sure to remain steadfast yourself; and all of you come to these valleys as soon as the Lord shall open a way for you.

1857: 25 July, *Cardiff and Merthyr Guardian*, p. 8 (780 words). "Troubles of Polygamists."

A report from the *Deseret News* about discourses of Jedediah Grant and Brigham Young, who wished to grant liberty to the whiners from among their wives to leave and go somewhere else.

1857: 25 July, *Chepstow Weekly Advertiser*, p. 3 (95 words).

> The *Millennial Star*, the organ of the Mormons, in noticing the murder of Parley P. Pratt, one of the Twelve Apostles of Jesus Christ of Latter-day Saints, thus commences to lament his death: "Another martyr has fallen!—another faithful servant of God has sealed his pure and heavenly testimony to the truth of the Book of Mormon with his blood." Our readers will recollect that the apostle was murdered by a man whose wife he had seduced. If they had begun their chant thus: "Another rascal has fallen," it would have been more suited to the occasion.

1857: August, *Yr Eurgrawn Wesleyaidd* (*Wesleyan Treasury*), p. 280 (140 words).

A report of the intention of the United States government to send troops to Utah in order to "uphold the authority of Colonel Cummings." Also mentioned is the death of Parley P. Pratt.

1857: August, *Y Dysgedydd* (*Instructor*), p. 319 (45 words).

A report that most likely has reference to the death of Parley P. Pratt.

> The Mormons have lost one of their great luminaries, about whom it can be said, "He is gone at present, leaving behind him seven inconsolable widows, and several children, four of which are under the age of eight, to mourn their irretrievable loss."

1857: 1 August, *Wrexham Advertiser*, p. 2 (65 words).

> Since the 1st of January last there have arrived in the United States by different vessels upwards of two thousand one hundred emigrants who had espoused the Mormon faith in the old country, and were *en route* to Utah Territory, in the Great Salt Lake basin. These Mormons were composed mostly of Welsh and English, with a sprinkling of Danes and Norwegians, and a few Germans.

1857: 1 August, *Usk Observer*, p. 1 (460 words). "The Mormons."

A repentant explanation from the editor as to why a week earlier he had printed a letter (see 25 July 1857 entry for this publication above) that contained only positive information about The Church of Jesus Christ of Latter-day Saints.

> The letters which have reached this country from the proselytes to this absurd and erring faith, hold out inducements to the friends of the converts to join them at the Salt Lake, and become regenerated. A specimen of one of these letters we inserted last week, to show up the fallacy of their creed, which appears to be so demoralizing and dangerous, that none but the most illiterate of the community can possibly be led to place reliance in it.

The editor also suggests censorship of negative letters sent from Utah:

> Letters written by the Mormons to their friends in this country, pass through the hands of the Prophets, and are inspected by them. If they are found to contain any statement unfavorable to the cause they are suppressed.

He ends with a warning:

> The illiterate portion of the community should avoid the snare laid to entrap them, or they will too soon prove they have become the dupe of a Mokanna—a humbug—a delusion.

1857: 1 August, *Usk Observer*, p. 3, item 1 (210 words).

> The Mormons who are somewhat numerous in the district of Vestra Sallerup, near Malmoe, in Sweden, have built in the village of the former name a house and chapel. On the 25th June they assembled in the chapel for some grand ceremony of their form of worship, and when they were so engaged a band of peasants, armed with thick sticks, some of them with guns also, marched on the chapel, and summoned them to disperse. The Mormons refused, on which the peasants expelled them by force, and drove them from the village. As some of the Mormons were armed with guns, and made use of them, several of the combatants on both sides were wounded. The peasants having driven the Mormons to a tan-pit, dipped several of them in it, and then let them go. At Burlof, the local authorities have decided that any person who may lend his house to the Mormons for their meetings, or may take any of that sect into his service, or even receive them into his house, shall be fined 25 rixdalers. Several inhabitants of the district who had embraced Mormonism have abandoned it, to return to the Lutheran religion.

1857: 1 August, *Usk Observer*, p. 3, item 2 (65 words).

> Since the 1st of January last there have arrived in the United States by four different vessels upwards of two thousand one hundred emigrants who had espoused the Mormon faith in the old country, and were *en route* to Utah Territory, in the Great Salt Lake basin. These Mormons were composed mostly of Welsh and English, with a sprinkling of Danes and Norwegians, and a few Germans.

1857: 1 August, *North Wales Chronicle*, p. 4 (400 words). "Anti-Mormon Riot in Birmingham."

Following a lecture of Dr. Brindley about "the abominations of Joseph Smith's followers," some of his listeners went to a chapel where a large number of Latter-day Saints were meeting. The writer describes the scene that resulted:

> The aisles and unoccupied seats were speedily filled, and then a running fire of comment on the sermon was commenced and carried on by the intruders

> for some five or ten minutes. It is stated that much of the language used was of the lowest and most disgraceful kind. At last Aubrey abruptly closed his discourse, and dismissed his congregation. It was with great difficulty that they forced their way through the crowds in the chapel yard and street. The females were hustled, insulted and bespattered in mud; the men had their hats knocked off and were struck on every side.

The police were sent for, and they were able to restore order to some extent. But when the constables left, "the door of the chapel was burst open, the crowd rushed in, the front windows were smashed, and Bibles and several other books stolen. The interior of the chapel was a scene of utmost riot." Here is the scene that followed:

> A body of police arrived at this moment, and dispersed the mob, or in all probability there would have been very serious results, as hints of an intention to burn the chapel were freely circulated. No other disturbance took place that night, but on Monday morning the chapel doors were again burst; lockfast closets entered and ransacked, and a large number of school and music hooks were torn in pieces and strewn about the yard. Except when a policeman made his appearance, the crowd remained in possession of the building during the day. In the evening, showers of stones were hurled through the smashed windows. Yesterday, however, the police took active measures to prevent a repetition of these scenes. *Manchester Guardian.*

1857: 8 August, *Wrexham Advertiser*, p. 2, item 1 (210 words). "The Mormons in Sweden."

The same article as in the *Usk Observer* for 1 August 1857, item 1 (see previous entry).

1857: 8 August, *Wrexham Advertiser*, p. 2, item 2 (40 words).

> A Birmingham mob attacked a Mormon congregation on Sunday evening, maltreating both women and men, and destroying property in the interior of the chapel. The mob had been excited by a lecture against Mormonism delivered on the Sunday by Dr. Brindley.

1857: 8 August, *Monmouthshire Beacon*, p. 4 (75 words).

> Turning our eyes again to Utah, we find those abominable pests to humanity, the Mormons carrying matters with a high hand, and the feeling of these misguided zealots will be seen in an original letter we publish in another part of our paper. President Buchanan has fallen on troublous times, but we believe him equal to the emergency; and it will be remembered that a great man is greatest in the hour of danger.

1857: 8 August, *Chepstow Weekly Advertiser*, p. 3 (32 words).

> Owing to a preaching crusade against Mormons and Mormonism, by Dr. Brindley, in Birmingham, the Latter-day Saints in that town are mobbed in the streets and in their own places of worship.

Episode 14.2

Start: Daniel Daniels responds to John Davies's absurd claims

1857: 15 August, *Cardiff and Merthyr Guardian*, p. 6 (1,275 words). "Remarkable Letter from an Escaped Mormon."

In his introduction to this letter, the editor indicates that it had previously appeared in the *Swansea Herald*. John Davies, the writer of the letter and a former resident of the Maesteg neighborhood, had left Wales two years earlier with his parents to journey to Salt Lake City, a city which he describes as follows:

> The walls about the city are 15 feet high, and surrounded by a deep ditch. The city is entered by four gates, which are all guarded by night. Those gates or entrances are so narrow that only one wagon can pass at a time.

Davies tells of some of the obligations of any male resident of the city:

> The next thing he has to do is to give a tenth of what he gets, and the tenth day in every year, and must keep from two to ten wives; and the man who refuses to obey these laws must quit the place, and in doing so is in danger of losing his life every moment—as they would sooner kill him than that he should be the means of conveying to the States, or elsewhere, information of their proceedings.

He then claims to have witnessed many murders:

> Great numbers have been shot whilst attempting to leave. I myself have seen scores of persons shot down in the streets, and a few days before I made my escape, I witnessed three persons being killed only because they were preparing to go away.

Some of the details Davies provides of his escape and Patrick Lynch's efforts to take him back to Salt Lake City are a test of the reader's credulity:

> This man fired a shot from a revolver—the ball whizzed by me. They then rode up and inquired my name, which I gave, when they said I must go back with them to the city; and upon my refusing to obey their command, they said they would "blow my d—— brains out." One of them seized a revolver—he had one on each side of his horse. I then took a revolver from my belt, and told him to fire if he wished. I was armed with six revolvers—four in my belt and one in each of my boots, and also a rifle.

Davies's account becomes even more spectacular as he reaches Fort Bridger:

> The number of our pursuers had by this time increased to twenty, and we were again compelled to take refuge in the woods. We traveled the whole of that night, and were fortunate in meeting with a party of friendly Indians, and partook of some Buffalo meat with them. On the day following we came up with a train of wagons, called "Mrs. Babbit's train," 28 in number. I was engaged to drive one of the wagons drawn by six mules. We had some trouble with a party of Indians, known as the Crow tribe, numbering about 1,000 horsemen, armed with rifles, bows and arrows, etc. We had about 600 shots in our camp, and killed about thirty of the Indians, losing five of our own men.

Davies ends his letter by reporting his safe arrival in Florence and expressing hope that his mother and siblings would join him:

> I am desirous that mother and the children should quit the Salt Lake and join me here, as if they do, I will buy some land, which I can get for a dollar and a quarter. I left 500 dollars with mother to keep until she may be enabled to leave. I am employed here as superintendent in a brickyard, at 30 dollars per month, board and lodgings inclusive.

1857: 29 August, *Udgorn Seion* (*Zion's Trumpet*), p. 286–88 (820 words).

Daniel Daniels, then the editor of *Zion's Trumpet*, indicates that he had read John Davies's account in the *Welsh Herald* (*Yr Herald Cymraeg*), a weekly Welsh-language newspaper published in Caernarvon. No issues of this newspaper appear to have survived from this time period.

Daniels begins his response to Davies's letter:

> Until last week we could not believe that Welsh Editors could be so obtuse in their anti-Mormon zeal as to put the blatant and contradictory lies which they claim have all come from one John Davies.

Regarding Davies's description of Salt Lake City, Daniels writes:

> Although we have been in the Salt Lake Valley ourselves, and although our beloved family is there, we did not learn about the walls, the narrow gates, or the moat around Salt Lake City before reading this "interesting" account, as it is called by the *Welsh Herald*, which smacks its lips after consuming the carcass.

To the editor of the *Welsh Herald*, Daniels poses the following questions:

- Where did the poor lad get the means to purchase "six revolvers and one rifle?"
- What kind of boots did he have to hold two revolvers and to enable him to be so nimble?
- How did his sneaky friends escape on foot from men on horseback?
- What trees were they in? We do not know about them. Surprising that three armed men failed to kill one. Even more surprising, that one of the three, after getting J. Davies on the ground, did nothing but cut his belt with a knife, taking four revolvers, instead of cutting his throat and taking everything!
- Where else can one find the story that Mrs. Babbit's company defeated a thousand Indian warriors? A thousand!!
- Where did the poor boy get the 500 dollars to leave to his mother?

1857: 5 September, *Seren Cymru* (*Star of Wales*), p. 341 (1,210 words). "Letter from a Mormon Refugee."

A slightly shorter version of the letter that appeared in the *Cardiff and Merthyr Guardian* for 15 August 1857 (see previous entry).

1857: 24 October, *Caernarvon and Denbigh Herald*, p. 4 (920 words). "An Escape from Salt Lake."

A considerably shorter version of the letter that appeared in the *Cardiff and Merthyr Guardian* for 15 August 1857 (see previous entry).

1857: 14 November, *Wrexham Advertiser*, p. 2 (935 words). "Narrow Escape from the Mormon Murderers at Salt Lake."

Except for the differences in the editor's introduction, this is the same article as in the *Caernarvon and Denbigh Herald* for 24 October 1857 (see previous entry).

End: Daniel Daniels responds to John Davies's absurd claims

Episode 14.3

Start: Daniel Daniels scolds the editor of the Leader *for his accusations*

1857: 15 August, *Udgorn Seion* (*Zion's Trumpet*), pp. 257–61 (1,660 words). "A Nut or Two for the *Leader* to Chew on."

Daniel Daniels defends his religion against the attacks of the *Leader* (*Yr Arweinydd*), a newspaper published in Pwllheli, North Wales. Unfortunately, the newspaper is not extant. Daniels begins with this observation about the editor of *The Leader*: "He gives some savory accusations against the Saints, mocking their God in a very unusual way."[12] He then proceeds to list and address each of the following accusations:

- With regard to his first accusation, namely, "that 'Mormonism' does not have established beliefs, but that its principles and its doctrines are open to being changed according to whim, and according to the special purposes of church leaders."
- That "it is a mixture of paganism, Judaism, Christianity, Mohammedanism, idol worship, and atheism." As part of his argument to disprove this accusation, Daniels reprints John Richards's rather long poem, "Great God of the Sectarians," which first appeared in *Zion's Trumpet* in the 25 January 1851 issue.[13]
- That their "ideas have changed considerably with respect to the Godhood from the beginning of [their] organization."
- That they "are reaching to obtain in the end the crown of Godhood for their own heads." Daniels agrees with this "accusation" and cites the verses of Philippians 2:5–6 to confirm the accuracy of the goal. He also tells the editor that "in order to prove and establish these topics," he is sending a copy of Dan Jones's pamphlet entitled "Who is the God of the Saints?"[14] Daniels explains a second reason for sending the pamphlet: "So that we will not take up too much of our space in answering you, since the treatise explains its topic, and disproves your false accusations."
- Daniels mocks the editor of the *Leader* for accusing the Latter-day Saints of practicing polygamy as if it were a recent development: "Hasten to the patent office with your remarkable discovery, and stop saying what you do not know." He also suggests "that you get a new name for the *Leader*, namely *The Follower*."

He ends his answer to the editor of the *Leader* with an appeal to the subscribers of *Zion's Trumpet*: "Whenever our readers see some piece in any publication touching on 'Mormonism,' do us the kindness of sending it here."[15]

End: Daniel Daniels scolds the editor of the Leader *for his accusations*

1857: 15 August, *Cardiff and Merthyr Guardian*, p. 6 (400 words).

The same article as in the *North Wales Chronicle* for 1 August 1857 (see previous entry).

1857: 15 August, *North Wales Chronicle*, p. 6 (80 words).

> Sir Benjamin Hall added that it had been found necessary to put a stop to preaching in the parks, as advantage had been taken of the permission for Mormons, Infidels, and advocates of all sorts of dangerous and immoral doctrines to promulgate them. He might add that many states contained in a memorial lately addressed to the Government by the friends of preaching, setting forth that the Sunday bands gave rise to scenes of drunkenness, were wholly unfounded.

1857: 15 August, *Caernarvon and Denbigh Herald*, p. 10 (555 words). "Mormon Blasphemy."

The opening comments by the editor to the quotation of parts of a sermon given by Orson Hyde in defense of polygamy:

> The Mormon elders are going far, by their extreme ignorance and gross sensuality, to break up the community they have formed in Utah. Even the most callous cannot but realize disgust at hearing words such as these which follow.

1857: 22 August, *Seren Cymru* (*Star of Wales*), p. 320, item 1 (60 words). "The Mormons."

This, the first of two brief articles in this issue of the *Star of Wales*, simply reports the following:

> Since the 1st of last January, in four different ships, more than two thousand one hundred immigrants who had embraced the Mormon faith in the old country, arrived in the United States, and they went ahead to the Utah territory. These Mormons were composed chiefly of English and Welsh, together with a few Danes, Norwegians, and Germans.

1857: 22 August, *Seren Cymru* (*Star of Wales*), p. 320, item 2 (155 words). "The Mormons in Birmingham."

This second of two articles in this issue of the *Star of Wales* has to do with a powerful lecture on the "Abomination of Mormonism," delivered to a large congregation in Birmingham by a "Dr. Brindley" from Leamington. The listeners were so stirred up by what they heard that they "went straightway to the nearby chapel of the Mormons, where President Aubrey was preaching at the time":

> Every empty space was filled immediately, and some began to make observations on the sermon, so that Aubrey was obligated to end in the middle, and the "Saints" had to flee for their lives through the crowd. The greatest scorn was shown them; and it was said that they would have set the chapel on fire had not the police not come to the place. They attacked the chapel again on Monday; they broke the windows and the doors, and they tore their books into shreds.

1857: 29 August, *Chepstow Weekly Advertiser*, p. 4 (1,890 words). "Adventures of a Mormon."

The editor introduces quotations from this lengthy letter, which was first printed in the *Edinburgh News*, by pointing out that they are taken from "a private letter, dated Western Missouri, July 11, 1857." The *Edinburgh News* had "purposely suppressed the names mentioned" in the letter and added that the writer "was about fifteen years a member of the Mormon body, and an active propagandist; but has at length abandoned that body, having seen the villainy of its leaders, and the misery of their dupes."

The writer begins the letter by describing the extreme hardships suffered by many who crossed the plains in the Martin handcart company and the manner in which hundreds lost their lives in the process. He points out:

> It is the policy of the Church to leave the weak, the infirm, and the old by the way, that they may have no paupers to support.

Upon arriving in Salt Lake City, the writer was not inclined at first to be rebaptized. But he changed his mind when he was told the following by the teachers who visited him:

> They said I should shut my eyes and open my mouth, and swallow everything; at least it amounted to that.

He then provides several examples of very harsh treatment given to some of the disobedient by the "Danites":

> Some have their houses pulled down, some their horses, oxen, and other property stolen. Good honest people! And all this is done under the name of religion!

The editor adds this note at the end of the article:

> He then describes how he got back to the States with nothing left but his "pluck," which we should say was considerable.

1857: September, *Yr Haul* (*Sun*), pp. 270–74 (665 words). "Mormonism."

In the editor's first few paragraphs, he presents a reaction to this new religion that is typical of its various opponents from among the Nonconformists as well as from the Anglicans which he represents:

> It is a great surprise that hundreds in Wales have embraced this religious deceit; yes, a deceit that immediately attacks the revealed religion of the Old and the New Testaments.[16]

He takes particular exception to the Latter-day Saints' teaching about God:

> What does Mormonism teach us? It teaches us that the eternal blessed God is not Spirit, but a corporeal being who has a body like a man's body! This religion must be deceitful, since it, united with the pagans, lowers the immortal and invisible Great King to the level of mortal men, the dust of the earth![17]

And he is incredulous at the success of this new religion:

> It is so sad to think that a polluted religion such as this one could have acceptance in the last part of the nineteenth century! Who would think that there could be men so superstitious and ignorant as to receive such dreadful and frightful deceit as their religion.[18]

The remainder of the article is quoted from *Y Cymro Americanaidd* (*The American Welshman*), a Welsh-language periodical published at that time in New York. The quotation consists of the Welsh translation of parts of a pamphlet, by John (Increase) and Maria Van Duesen, entitled "Mormonism Laid Bare, the Seventh Degree of the Temple."[19]

The Van Duesen's had participated in the Nauvoo Temple endowment ceremony in 1846, and soon afterward they apostatized from The Church of Jesus Christ of

Latter-day Saints and began publishing pamphlets in an attempt to expose the deceit of the Latter-day Saints and to generate income for themselves.

1857: 5 September, *Seren Cymru* (*Star of Wales*), p. 344 (120 words).

A brief paragraph about the Latter-day Saints in Utah:

> Not only are they threatened by the soldiers of the United States, who are on their way to Utah, but it is affirmed that great hosts of the Indians are attacking their possessions and stealing and destroying their cattle and their horses; there is frightful contention and division among the Saints themselves.

The writer concludes that Brigham Young has been searching for a new home for his followers and that they will eventually migrate "further to the north and to the west."

1857: 11 September, the *Cambrian* (970 words). "The City of the Mormons."

A detailed depiction of Salt Lake City taken from the *New York Tribune.*

1857: 12 September, *Wrexham Advertiser*, p. 2 (60 words).

> The *Bund* says: It is positively stated that an extensive baptism of Mormons lately took place at night in the lake of Zurich. The police did not interfere to prevent the ceremony, but the people who had assembled in crowds attacked the new converts, and drove them away with blows from sticks. The Mormon priest, it is said, was particularly ill-treated.

1857: 12 September, *Chepstow Weekly Advertiser*, p. 2 (540 words). "News from Mormon Land."

A group of about twenty people had "escaped" and had gone to San Francisco where they reported their negative experiences of living in Salt Lake City.

> They say one-half the population of Salt Lake will leave, if the United States Government sends a military force sufficient to protect them from the punishments inflicted upon apostates.

The party told of numerous "atrocious practices," such as the advocation of "open and avowed murder of all who have and are becoming obnoxious," the increasing murders and robberies by the "Destroying Angels," and the "Earthly Hell" of polygamy.

> Here are warnings enough, one would think, to prevent deluded women from throwing themselves into the fangs of these lecherous, incestuous murderers. One blushes to hear that many of these wretched victims are English and most Welsh.

1857: 12 September, *Merthyr Telegraph*, p. 3 (540 words). "California."

The same article as appears in the *Chepstow Weekly Advertiser* for 12 September 1857 (see previous entry).

1857: 12 September, *Chepstow Weekly Advertiser*, p. 4, item 1 (930 words). "The *Times* on the Mormons."

A reflective article on the current condition of The Church of Jesus Christ of Latter-day Saints. The writer's opening statement is as follows:

> It said that Mr. Buchanan is resolved to put down Mormonism—at any rate, to break up the community at Utah. There will be great difficulties, owing to the weakness of the Federal Government, half of whose force is reported to have deserted already. But the new President is a resolute man when he has undertaken a thing, and we hope the days of this abomination are counted.

The writer laments that possibly as many as nine-tenths of Latter-day Saints are "English, Scotch, and Welsh":

> How is this? Who is responsible for this? What have our orthodox parish priests been doing, and what have our orthodox Dissenting ministers been doing, that their own congregations have been the feeders of such an enormity as this?

Concluding that fanaticism was the cause, the writer delves into a philosophical and historical explanation of the success of this new religion.

1857: 12 September, *North Wales Chronicle*, p. 3, item 1 (335 words). "An Escape from Utah."

Joseph Routledge had taken his wife, Alice, and their baby daughter, Elizabeth, on the *Golconda* in January 1853 to New Orleans, and from there to Salt Lake City. In his 11 July 1857 letter to his parents, he tells of the very negative experience he had during his four-year stay in Utah:

> It is not very pleasant to be forced to serve God whether you will or not, and even, if you won't, to have your throat cut, which was the threat used towards us because we would not stay to become serfs to Brigham.

He declares:

> You see they got us out there under the cloak of religion; but I was not there long before I found out that it was nothing more than a political scheme to gain power and a usurpation.

Episode 14.4

Start: Various reports are printed of the sixth annual conference of the Latter-day Saints held in London

1857: 12 September, *Monmouthshire Beacon*, p. 5 (90 words).

> The annual Mormon conference in London is a disgrace to the age. This miserable delusion so far from abating, seems really to be taking a firmer hold on the public mind, and the fact that one thousand persons of both sexes can be brought together to testify to its success in the metropolis of the civilized world, is a phenomenon not easily account[ed] for. The assembly is said to have been composed chiefly of elders and saints, but we should imagine the far great number was made up of egregious dupes.

1857: 12 September, *North Wales Chronicle*, p. 3, item 2 (600 words). "Mormon Conference in London."

An account of the proceedings of a recent conference held in London. Here is the opening paragraph:

> This sect held its sixth annual conference on Sunday, at the Adelaide Gallery, Lower Arcade, Strand. It was presided over by "two of the apostles," Brothers Orson Pratt and Ezra Benson. About 600 persons were present in the morning, about 1,000 in the afternoon, and upwards of 1,000 in the evening, most of whom judging from appearances, were Latter-day Saints, or Mormons. The proceedings consisted chiefly of addresses.

Reports from a number of conference presidents are then summarized in the article. Here are the final lines of the article:

> The proceedings of the afternoon were pleasantly varied by refreshments, such as ginger beer and other cooling drinks. The proceedings of the evening consisted chiefly of a rapid review of the origin and history of Mormonism down to the present time, by Mr. Orson Pratt. Collections were made after each meeting.

1857: 12 September, *Usk Observer*, p. 2, item 1 (600 words). "Mormon Conference in London."

The same article as in *North Wales Chronicle* for 12 September 1857 (see previous entry, item 2).

1857: 12 September, *Caernarvon and Denbigh Herald*, p. 2, Supplement (600 words). "Mormon Conference in London."

The same article as in *North Wales Chronicle* for 12 September 1857 (see previous entry, item 2).

1857: 12 September, *North Wales Chronicle*, p. 3, item 3 (1,070 words). "Another Mormon Meeting."

Following the account of the conference held at the Adelaide Gallery in London is the account of a "social meeting" held the following night at the Teetotal Hall, Broadway, Westminster. Here is the opening paragraph:

> Last night the Mormon Conference was brought to a close by a social meeting at the Teetotal Hall, Broadway, Westminster. The proceedings were certainly of such a character as were never witnessed in a "conference" before. The attendance was not very numerous, but it comprised all the leading members of the Conference. At the outset, the assemblage sang, in a loud strain, one of their favorite hymns, led on by Elder Bernard, to the tune of "The Low-backed Car." The purport of this song was the long looked-for day when they would all get to Zion Utah. It seemed to be rather a painful effort to Brother Bernard, and it was decidedly so to those of the audience who happened not [to] be Mormons.

The writer then reports on a number of songs sung, recitations given, and discourses presented. Here, as an example of the writer's very condescending tone throughout the entire article, is the final paragraph:

> Ezra Benson, another Apostle from the Salt Lake Valley, addressed the audience in his shirt sleeves. His speech was full of Yankee humor, rather coarse, but it told well with the saints. He said he felt "fust rate." He referred to the subject of marriage, and to his own wives and children whom he had left in Utah, and said he believed that all his wives would not apostatize, and that, he would not be likely to undergo the misery of remaining single in heaven. He described Brigham Young as the best and holiest man in the world, and said he did not wonder at the sisters falling in love with him. Every good man, he said, ought to have more than one wife. He said he would advise the editors who abused them to consult their works, and they would find everything "as right as taturs." He indulged in a variety of jokes of the same class. The proceedings terminated shortly after ten o'clock. (We omit to record some of the more improper sayings and doings of the evening.)

1857: 12 September, *Usk Observer*, p. 2, item 2 (1,070 words). "Another Meeting."

Same as the article in *North Wales Chronicle* for 12 September 1857 (see previous entry, item 3).

1857: 12 September, *Chepstow Weekly Advertiser*, p. 4, item 2 (1,075 words).

The writer provides only sketchy information regarding the Sunday meeting of this conference held at the Adelaide Gallery. However, his report of the Monday meeting held at the Teetotal Hall, Broadway, Westminster, has considerable overlap with the *North Wales Chronicle* article (see previous entry) and contains many word-for-word segments.

1857: 19 September, p. 3 *Cardiff and Merthyr Guardian* (320 words). "A Mormon Meeting."

This report does not cover the conference held at the Adelaide Gallery, Lower Arcade, Strand. Rather, it is a shorter account of the meeting held the following evening at the Teetotal Hall, Broadway, Westminster.

1857: 3 October, *Seren Cymru* (*Star of Wales*), p. 380 (230 words). "Mormon Conference."

A shorter account than the one in *North Wales Chronicle* for 12 September 1857 (see previous entry, item 2).

End: Various reports are printed of the sixth annual conference of the Latter-day Saints held in London

Episode 14.5

Start: The *Cambrian makes accusations—Daniel Daniels answers*

1857: 18 September, *Cambrian* (85 words). "The Mormons."

> This fanatical sect have of late been holding forth in various localities contiguous to our town, and they seem to have attained something like a "stronghold" in Llansamlet. On Sunday last (the 13th), however, they so disgusted their hearers with their profane and preposterous "sermons" and their assertions in reference to the impostor Joe Smith, that they were pelted with cabbages, potatoes, apples, etc., and were compelled to beat a precipitate retreat followed by the hootings and jeers of 200 or 300 people. [Llansamlet is a town just above Swansea]

1857: 26 September, *Cardiff and Merthyr Guardian*, p. 6 (85 words). "The Mormons."

The same article as in the *Cambrian* for 18 September 1857.

1857: 26 September, *Udgorn Seion* (*Zion's Trumpet*), p. 314 (165 words). "Religious Persecution."

After presenting the Welsh translation of the 18 September 1857 article in the *Cambrian*, Daniel Daniels responds:

> Here is another example of the boastful "Christianity" of the nineteenth century! Can the slanderous asp, the *Cambrian*, show where his Bible supports

and praises persecutors and maligners, and we ask from which sections are the persecutors and the persecuted—the one who strikes and the one who turns the other cheek? Stronger preachers than the Saints will come, soon, when perhaps the *cabbage*, the potato, or any other bits and pieces will not be so plentiful!

End: The Cambrian *makes accusations—Daniel Daniels answers*

1857: 19 September, *North Wales Chronicle*, p. 4, item 1 (350 words). "The Mormons' Land of Plenty."

Here are the first few lines of this paragraph taken from the *Saturday Review*:

> The Mormons promise a land of plenty. They address the senses. They hold out to the small farmer, and to the starving, scrambling, petty tradesman, the assurance of plenty to eat and drink; and they point to the Bible for confirmation of the fact that God's chosen people have always had the blessings as well as the promises of the present world. . . . Theirs is the reverse of spiritual religion. It is of the earth, earthy; and the earth is with them the mother of abundance, and of all sorts of riches and mere animal enjoyments—flocks and herds, feasts and concubines. . . . This is the sort of language which tells on the pining, hard-working laborer, either in field or factory; and this is what wins to the Mormon cause. *Saturday Review.*

1857: 19 September, *North Wales Chronicle*, p. 4, item 2 (715 words). "The Mormon 'Deceit' in America."

The writer compares the defiance of the Latter-day Saints in Salt Lake City—toward the United States military expedition sent to subdue them—to the current troubles the British were then experiencing with the rebels in Delhi.

Episode 14.6

Start: Various writers react to the Deseret Alphabet

1857: 19 September, *Chepstow Weekly Advertiser*, p. 4 (115 words). "Mormon Secretiveness."

The following articles have reference to the Deseret Alphabet, which Brigham Young had asked George D. Watt to devise in order to facilitate the learning of English. Considerable effort and expense were invested in the project during the early years of the settling of Utah.

> The new "Deseret Alphabet" is completed, and a fount of pica type has been cast in St. Louis. Specimens of the type are published in the St. Louis papers, but they are unproducible [*sic*] in types that common people use. The type founders have supplied the Mormons with molds and other apparatus for re-casting their old metal. So the *Deseret News* will probably hereafter be a profound mystery, at least in part, to all but the initiated. The new characters are 41 in number, and bear a striking resemblance to those of the Ethiopic alphabet. The ukases of Brother Brigham will hereafter be a sealed letter, literally, to Gentile eyes. *New York Paper.*

1857: 19 September, *Caernarvon and Denbigh Herald*, p. 6 (115 words). "Mormon Secretiveness."

The same article as in *Chepstow Weekly Advertiser* for 19 September 1857 (see previous entry).

1857: 26 September, *Usk Observer*, p. 4 (235 words). "Mormon Intelligence."

The Mormons have invented a new alphabet. They are to have a newspaper of their own, set up in type that they only can read. The Mormons are a separate type of people, and as such we see no harm in their having a separate type to themselves. On the contrary, we are rejoiced that the good, honest type which is generally used for the purposes of civilization, will not be defiled by their foul fingers. In truth, we possessed no type that could have suited their base purposes. "Bougeois," for a set of dissolute reprobates that have not a good *Bourgeois* amongst them, would have been far too respectable. "Minion" would have been about the most congenial representative of a minion race like them. We fervently hope that the Mormon characters are such as cannot possibly be met with in any other part of the world—characters of so base a cast that no respectable printer would think of admitting them into his establishment. It should be with Englishmen a great source of congratulation that a people, that has not a single thought in common with us, should have adopted a distinctive medium for giving shape to their thoughts on paper. It is a safeguard, for which we should be grateful, as there will be less danger of our simple-minded cooks and housemaids being for the future corrupted by their dangerous doctrines.

1857: 3 October, *Seren Cymru* (*Star of Wales*), p. 381 (75 words). "New Plan of the Mormons to Keep their Deeds Secret."

The Mormons have devised a new alphabet, and their new letters have been made for printing. They intend to print the newspaper which is published by them in Utah with these new letters; and thus it will be a secret to all except for those who are taught by them. Their new alphabet has forty-one letters which are very similar to the Ethiopian letters.

End: Various writers react to the Deseret Alphabet

1857: 19 September, *Cardiff and Merthyr Guardian*, p. 5 (140 words).

While Birmingham is about to hold its conference on all social subjects, London has had its meeting on the prospects of Mormonism, or rather has had a series of meetings. There were few Apostles on the ground, and as to disciples their name is Legion. Human ignorance is boundless, and all who are dissatisfied with their present condition listen eagerly to those who point to something else. Joe Smith, like his predecessor Mahomet, knew how to take advantage of the weaknesses of humanity; and it cannot be denied that he has brought together, and so far, kept together, what the auctioneers would call "a miscellaneous lot." It is said that the President of the United States has resolved on rooting the Mormons out of Utah, and certainly they will get little sympathy from this side of the water.

1857: 19 September, *Cardiff and Merthyr Guardian*, p. 6, item 1 (30 words). "Mormon Polygamy."

> Thirteen members of the council of the Utah territory have no less than 171 wives, of whom fifty-seven constitute the seraglio of the President of the Council.

1857: 19 September, *Cardiff and Merthyr Guardian*, p. 6, item 2 (85 words). "The Mormons."

> By the Royal mail steamship *Arabia*, which arrived at Liverpool, on Sunday last, we learn that the military expedition for Utah had been ordered to proceed to its destination. Dr. Forny had accepted the appointment of superintendent of Indian affairs in Utah. General Harney or Colonel Johnson would have the command of the force. Ten companies had been dispatched to Kansas to replace those ordered to Utah. The *New York Times* states that one-third of the force selected for the expedition had deserted.

1857: 26 September, *Udgorn Seion* (*Zion's Trumpet*), pp. 308–13 (2,170 words). "Review of the Treatise, Heresies and Deceptions of the Latter-day Saints, and the Book of Mormon, Exposed, by the Reverend W. J. Morrish, translated from the English by David Roberts, from Caernarvon."

Daniel Daniels responds to the "renewed commotion" that had been reported to exist among some of the Church members in North Wales because of this twenty-four-page pamphlet published eight years earlier. To address these concerns, Daniels has agreed to "show as much of its inconsistency" in the limited space of *Zion's Trumpet* as he can. In typical polemical fashion, he refutes a number of the so-called heresies and deceptions that the Anglican vicar puts forth in his publication. In doing so, Daniels shows himself to be a first-rate polemicist on the same level as his predecessors Dan Jones and John Davis.

1857: 26 September, *Usk Observer*, p. 2 (165 words).

> The Mormonite delusion, I fear, is spreading. A map of London has been divided into sections: each of these sections has been sent to one or other of the "Branches of the Church." In each "Branch" a society is organized, with a president, secretary, and treasurer, to superintend the distribution of tracts; to see that every house in their several districts, as indicated on their sections of the map, is visited; and to raise funds. They hold meetings and report progress in the "Branches," and every six weeks delegates from all the branches meet and receive instructions from the president of all the tract societies, who is also assisted by a general secretary and treasurer. Now, when we consider that there are about 2,000 Mormons in London alone, and that nearly every one of these "Brethren and Sisters," as they are called, is doing something to spread their peculiar doctrines, have we not sufficient cause for alarm, and ought not our clergy to stir themselves up?

1857: 26 September, *Usk Observer*, p. 3 (285 words). "Expedition against the Mormons."

> A letter from New York says:—About 1,500 men, a large proportion cavalry, are on their way to Utah, and one from Salt Lake Valley says,—A part of

Californians which passed Salt Lake City on the 1st of July, and arrived here yesterday, brings the intelligence that the Mormons, when they learned they were about to receive a visit from a large number of troops, became very much excited, and forthwith instituted a regular system of drills and other warlike preparations. Besides pushing onward their defenses around the city with more than ordinary vigor, they are also engaged with a strong force in fortifying Fort Bridger, an old trading post in the Mountains, near the head of one of the branches of Green River, about one hundred miles this side of Salt Lake. It is also stated that they intend occupying some of the passes between that point and their city. There are several of these passes, which, as military positions, are said to be almost as defensible as Gibraltar. One of them is a gorge or canyon (as it is called) eighteen miles in length, so very tortuous and narrow, with the escarpments on each side so lofty and precipitous, that an army once shut into and threating it might be easily cut to pieces by a comparatively inferior force occupying the adjoining heights. Should there be no way of turning these defiles, the army will be under the necessity of operating at great disadvantage in penetrating them in the face of fixed batteries. Whether the Mormons will have the temerity to attempt to arrest the march of our troops at Bridger's Fort or any other point remains to be seen.

1857: October, *Y Dysgedydd* (*Instructor*), p. 399 (42 words). "The Mormons."

There is a group of Mormons that numbers about 400, who arrived in Peoria, Illinois, who have become disgusted with the story they hear from Salt Lake, and they are likely to disperse and settle wherever they can purchase homes.

1857: 2 October, *Cambrian* (100 words). "The Mormons Again."

On Monday evening last the Rev. Williams delivered a lecture at Waunarlwydd on the absurdities and blasphemies of the faith of this fanatical sect. The creed of the book of Mormon was shown to be a delusion and a snare invented by the crafty devices of man to entrap the simple minded. A Mr. John Davies, president of the West Glamorganshire conference of the Latter-day Saints addressed the meeting in which he attempted but in vain to confute the arguments and statements of the lecturer. Davies was loudly hissed and hooted, and the proceedings terminated very uproariously.

1857: 3 October, *Wrexham Advertiser*, p. 2 (37 words).

The Mormons are greatly incensed at the prospect of having a large military force stationed in Utah, and, according to the tenor of the latest advices, were prepared to show a forcible resistance to the federal troops.

1857: 3 October, *Seren Cymru* (*Star of Wales*), p. 380 (230 words). "Mormon Conference."

The conference was one held on 7 September 1857 at the Adelaide Gallery in London. Elders Orson Pratt and Ezra Benson gave a presentation on the topic of polygamy:

Women are encouraged not to marry anyone except Mormons; otherwise, when they awake on judgment day, they will find themselves without men, and they will be alone for eternity. . . . Ezra Benson also referred to the topic

> of marriage, and to his own wives and children whom he left in Utah; and he said that he believed that not all his wives would apostatize, and for that reason he would not have to suffer the misfortune of being without a wife in heaven.

Surprisingly, the writer summarized the events and messages of the conference without offering a single criticism or negative remark.

1857: 3 October, *Chepstow Weekly Advertiser*, p. 3 (16 words).

> Mormon theatricals at Salt Lake are opened with prayer, and the actors dismissed with a benediction.

1857: 3 October, *North Wales Chronicle*, p. 4 (175 words). "The Mormon Campaign."

> Newspapers from Salt Lake City report a public speech of Brigham Young, in which he uttered the following threats: "Now, let me tell you one thing; I shall take it as a witness that God designs to cut the thread between us and the world when an army undertakes to make their appearances in this territory to chastise me or to destroy my life from the earth. I lay it down that right is—or at least should be—might with Heaven, with its servants and with all its people on the earth. As for the rest, we will wait a little while to see, but I shall take a hostile movement by our enemies as an evidence that it is time for the thread to be cut. I think that we will find 300 who will lap water, and we can wipe out Midianites. Brother Heber said that he could turn out his women, and they would whip them. I ask no odds of the wicked, the best way they can fix it.

1857: 10 October, *Monmouthshire Beacon*, p. 5 (125 words).

> The Mormons, it is quite evident, are a great source of trouble to President Buchanan, and Brigham Young seems to be a man of action, for he has suspended relations with the American government, closed the Mormon chapels in New York, and bids the great ruler at Washington open defiance.

1857: 17 October, *Seren Cymru* (*Star of Wales*), p. 404, item 1 (180 words). "Fugitives from the Mormons."

A letter has been received from Lawrence, Kansas, reporting the arrival of a hundred persons who "had escaped from the Mormons in order to obtain deliverance from the injustices of the government of Brigham Young." The writer adds:

> They said that about one thousand had left the area of Salt Lake at about the same time—some to the states, about four hundred to Oregon, and themselves to Kansas—and that there were many others who were still there who would flee if they could; but that there were also many there who were firm in their faith of the corrupt principles of this deceiver and prepared if necessary to give their lives for him.

1857: 17 October, *Seren Cymru* (*Star of Wales*), p. 404, item 2 (31 words).

> The large number of 740 new Mormon missionaries [a clear exaggeration] arrived in England from the Utah territory. It appears that they wish to make a special effort to win disciples in this country.

1857: 24 October, *North Wales Chronicle*, p. 6 (20 words).

> America. It is stated that the Mormons had fortified Fort Bridger, intending to defend it against the United States troops.

1857: 24 October, *Caernarvon and Denbigh Herald*, p. 9 (33 words).
Our advices from Salt Lake state that the Mormons were fortifying the fort and bridges, with the intention of contesting the progress of the United States troops now on the way to Utah.

1857: 24 October, *Cardiff and Merthyr Guardian*, p. 3 (33 words).
The same article as in the *Caernarvon and Denbigh Herald* for 24 October 1857 (see previous entry).

1857: 31 October, *Cardiff and Merthyr Guardian*, p. 7 (18 words).
The Mormon newspaper, published in New York, has suspended, after an existence of two years and seven months.

1857: 31 October, *Chepstow Weekly Advertiser*, p. 3 (25 words).
The Mormons have been fortifying Fort Bridger, with the intention of contesting the progress of the United States troops now on their way to Utah.

1857: 7 November, *Chepstow Weekly Advertiser*, p. 3 (20 words).
The chief Siamese Ambassador acknowledges to the luxury of no fewer than fifty-eight wives. He is called "the Eastern Mormon."

1857: 14 November, *Seren Cymru* (*Star of Wales*), p. 444 (73 words).
There were several officials in the service of the government who had been chased away from the great city of Salt Lake by the Saints, who had placed themselves in a defense position against any attacks from the outside. Some of the top officials of the Saints assert that by now they are sufficiently powerful to challenge the strongest army of the United States!

1857: 14 November, *Usk Observer*, p. 3 (135 words).
Heber C. Kimball, one of the most prominent of the Mormon elders, has lately delivered a discourse at Salt Lake City, in which he takes strong ground against the government of the United States, and expresses the determination of the Mormons to resist the troops to the last extremity. Brigham Young also made a speech in the same vein. In view of the anticipated difficulty with the Mormons, an unfortunate occurrence took place on the Great Plains. A drover, without any provocation, killed a woman and a child belonging to a tribe of Indians which has hitherto refused to join the Mormons against the government, and also fired at the chief. It is feared that this may have the effect of creating a hostile feeling, which will end in alliance of the tribe with Brigham Young.

1857: 14 November, *Monmouthshire Beacon*, p. 6 (110 words).
The *St. Louis Republican* publishes a discourse delivered by Heber C. Kimball, at Salt Lake City, August 30th, in which strong grounds are taken against the United States Government, and a determination is expressed to resist their troops to the last extremity. The "Mormon Children" are called upon to arm themselves and people generally are exhorted to lay up grain and otherwise prepare for the conflict. During the discourse, Kimball says: "We are the Kingdom of God and the State of the Deseret, and will have Brigham Young for Governor just so long as he lives." Young made a speech equally bold in its declarations of hostility against the United States.

1857: 21 November, *North Wales Chronicle*, p. 5 (96 words). "Mormonism Exposed."

A lecture was delivered on Tuesday by the Rev. John Brindley, LL. D., at the British Institution, Cowper Street, City Road, on the subject of Mormonism, the object of which was to refute the pretensions of Mormonism, and expose the abominable practices of the self-styled Latter-day Saints. Mr. Joseph Payne occupied the chair. The Rev. lecturer, who traced the Mormon imposture to its source, and ably set before his audience the iniquitous doings of its professors, was well received. At the close of the lecture a vote of thanks to Mr. Brindley was unanimously awarded. *Star.*

1857: 21 November, *North Wales Chronicle*, p. 6 (130 words). "The Mormons Getting Ready for War."

The Mormons, according to a letter from Omaha City, in the *New York Times*, are on the march; and only ten or twelve days since, on the Loupa Fork of the Platte River, near the mouth of Beaver, and known as Beaver settlement of Mormons, about one hundred miles from Omaha City. Some renegade Mormons or seceders from the Mormon Church, fleeing from the Danites of Salt Lake, had reached that settlement, bringing the news that a large force of the Mormon militia, under Brigham Young and Heber C. Kimball, were preparing to leave Salt Lake City, with provision and ammunition for a six weeks' campaign in the mountains to the eastward, and thus stop, if possible, the progress of the United States' Corps.

1857: 21 November, *Cardiff and Merthyr Guardian*, p. 6 (18 words).

It is stated that there are no less than 33 Mormon meeting houses in London and the suburbs.

1857: 21 November, *Caernarvon and Denbigh Herald*, p. 4 (68 words).

The Mormons were to leave Carson Valley on the 25th of October. Brigham Young has ordered a secret cavalry company to organize from the Saints in Carson Valley, armed and equipped with one year's provisions and clothing. It is said to be their intention, should matters go too serious, to seek a refuge in the Russian possessions, where they have already driven the stakes for a new Zion.

1857: 28 November, *Cardiff and Merthyr Guardian*, p. 6 (88 words).

The Mormons are on the march, and only ten or twelve days since, on the Loupa Fork of the Platte river, near the mouth of Beaver, and known as Beaver settlement of Mormons about one hundred miles inland from Omaha city. A large force of the Mormon militia, under Brigham Young and Heber C. Kimball, are preparing to leave Salt Lake City, with provision and ammunition for a six-weeks' campaign in the mountains to the eastward, and thus stop, if possible, the progress of the United States Corps.

1857: 28 November, *Monmouthshire Beacon*, p. 8 (130 words).

The military expedition against the Mormons has been postponed. A military officer sent across the Rocky Mountains to report on the state of affairs found the Mormons bent on resistance; and, as the only road into their valley from the Missouri country is a deep and rugged pass fifty miles long, he was of opinion that they resist great odds without much difficulty. It is also reported that the Mormon militia, under Brigham Young and Heber Kimball, had marched from Salt Lake City to meet the advancing United States troops at a pass in the mountains known as the Steeple Rocks, "with an almost certainty of 'wiping out' the force sent against them." Should they fail in defeating the invaders, the Mormons would found a new Zion in Russian territory.

1857: 28 November, *Caernarvon and Denbigh Herald*, p. 9 (183 words).

The opening sentences are as follows:

> The government has received intelligence from the military post at Leavenworth to the effect that the Mormons are calling in their people and making preparations to resist the troops now on their way to Utah, under the command of Col. Johnston. There is no doubt of the truth of this report.

The remainder of the article has a few more sentences about the impending Utah War.

1857: 28 November, *Caernarvon and Denbigh Herald*, p. 10 (77 words).

A report on Colonel Johnston's current position and a forecast that the expedition will not reach Salt Lake City this season.

1857: 28 November, *Seren Cymru* (*Star of Wales*), p. 452 (1,270 words). "The Great Temple of the Latter-day Saints in the Valley of the Salt Lake, Utah."

This lengthy article is taken from *Y Drych a'r Gwiliedydd* (the *Mirror and the Sentinel*), a Welsh-language newspaper then being published in New York. In the opening paragraph, the writer expresses concern that the Latter-day Saints are increasing so rapidly in number and that so many Welsh are among them:

> The Mormon matter is creating quite a stir amongst the populace these days, for many reasons. The moral and civilized class feel for the reputation of our country and nation; and they are worried by the constant reports that the Mormons are increasing so rapidly. Also, many a Welshman is compelled to bow his head, as he reads about the emigration ships, that nearly every one contains some number of Welsh. That was the nature of the recent news from Boston, about some ship that came there fairly recently, when it was said that all the Saints were English or Welsh.

The writer then presents detailed information about the building of the temple and the tabernacle in Salt Lake City as well as the large homes being built for Church leaders, their numerous wives, and their children. He ends his article with this comment:

> And the feast is released by a blessing with clasped hands; and often the prophets will be so drunk that they can hardly stand on their feet while talking.

1857: 28 November, *Seren Cymru* (*Star of Wales*), p. 464, item 1 (90 words).

> The news from the Mormon settlement is extremely hostile and uncertain. The latest stories report that the strong force of the Mormon soldiers, under Brigham Young and Heber C. Kimball, is ready to leave Salt Lake City, with military resources for six weeks; it is said that their aim is to keep the United States soldiers from coming to the city. Another account is given that the aim

> of the Mormons is, if things get too hot for them, to move to Russian territories and build their New Jerusalem there.

1857: 28 November, *Seren Cymru* (*Star of Wales*), p. 464, item 2 (155 words).

From *Y Drych a'r Gwiliedydd* (*The Mirror and the Sentinel*). Here is the lead statement:

> News has been received that recently the Mormons have attacked the soldiers of the United States, in the borders of the 'holy city,' and have defeated them, and have killed 1,400 of them. We do not know to what extent we can rely on the foregoing report, since there are many who doubt it. Nevertheless, it is generally believed that all the Saints are armed and determined to defend their rights. The news from St. Louis, on the 21st, say that the military expedition against Utah has arrived at Fort Laramie by the 24th of September. Also, at the same time there were eight regiments with large cannons. The arrival of Captain Cook at the fort was expected at any day in the lead of six regiments. They intend to exact full revenge on them for opposing the laws of the United States. All success to Uncle Sam, we say.

1857: 28 November, *Chepstow Weekly Advertiser*, p. 4 (580 words). "The Mormon Church Militant."

The writer of this *Times* article compares Johnston's Army, then on their way to subdue the rebels in Salt Lake City, to several armies in the Old Testament who were defeated by the Israelites. He then compares the Latter-day Saints to the Puritans:

> They are fighters, at least they appear to be prepared to fight and make a bold stand. We should not quarrel with them for being able to fight, if it was for a good cause, but death in the cause of concubinage is a strange martyrdom. The Puritan was savage and relentless, but his severe morals redeem him. He fought cruelly, but it was for a stern creed and an ascetic standard of life. A sensualized Puritan is an abomination and a monster. Such a monster is Mormonism.

1857: 5 December, *Caernarvon and Denbigh Herald*, p. 2, item 1 (205 words).

More official dispatches about the progress of Colonel Johnston.

1857: 5 December, *Caernarvon and Denbigh Herald*, p. 2, item 2 (95 words).

> From Carson Valley we learn that the Mormons had departed in a body for SLC. They numbered nearly 1,000 souls, of whom only 350 were men. Their departure left the remaining inhabitants partly unprotected from the ravages of hostile Indians, and an application had been made to the Governor of California for assistance. The emigration across the plains was very large, and we have an account of one party from Missouri and Arkansas, numbering over 100 persons, having been massacred by the Indians.

1857: 5 December, *Usk Observer*, p. 2 (30 words).

> The Mormons are reported by the New York papers to have committed their first overt act of treason against the federal authorities by the seizure of the provision trains.

1857: 5 December, *North Wales Chronicle*, p. 4 (520 words). "The Expedition against the Mormons."

The first paragraph is as follows:

> The War Department today received some highly interesting official dispatches, including a proclamation of Brigham Young, declaring martial law in Utah.

1857: 5 December, *North Wales Chronicle*, p. 6 (725 words). "The Mormons and the United States. Brigham Young's Declaration of War."

This declaration is dated 15 September 1857. Following the declaration is Colonel Alexander's reply:

> Colonel Alexander, in reply, states to Brigham Young that the troops were there by order of the President, and would be disposed of as the commanding General saw proper.

1857: 5 December, *Monmouthshire Beacon*, p. 4 (165 words).

The latest report of the military campaign against Salt Lake City:

> The Mormons are victorious so far. It is now quite evident that the martial prowess of these misguided people has been much underrated, and their Yankee foes will have a dangerous enemy to encounter.

The report then says that President Buchanan has given orders to abandon his winter campaign.

1857: 12 December, *Seren Cymru* (*Star of Wales*), p. 452 (455 words).

The editor again copies an article from *Y Drych a'r Gwiliedydd* (*The Mirror and the Sentinel*). The writer tells of Brigham Young's careful planning to stop the advance of the large number of soldiers headed for Salt Lake City as well as his invitation to the Native Americans to join Young's people in this "holy war."

1857: 12 December, *Chepstow Weekly Advertiser*, p. 4 (555 words). "Prospect of the Mormon 'Saints.'"

The first part of the article is as follows:

> The military expedition sent against "the Saints" of Utah (says the *Times* correspondent) may be pronounced a failure. It will not reach Zion on the Salt Lake this winter, as it is understood it has gone into quarters at some station short of the holy city, with the loss of 75 wagons loaded with stores, on which a roving and armed body of Mormons pounced suddenly, finding the train marching without a guard, plundered it of what suited them, and burnt the rest, the wagons inclusive. It was a bold stroke, and a clear act of rebellion; but, as a military operation, it was very neatly executed. It was not supposed, probably, that so audacious an act of defiance of the Federal troops would be attempted.

Further analysis is provided about the efforts of the United States government to take control of Utah, as well as about the relationship between the Latter-day Saints and the Indians.

1857: 12 December, *Usk Observer*, p. 2 (295 words).

Here are the first two sentences:

> It would seem that Brigham Young has assumed the powers of an independent sovereign, and formally declared war against the United States. His reasons for this high-handed course, or rather the reasons assigned by the telegraphic reports, are rather contradictory, and will not be accepted by the government as entirely satisfactory.

The remainder of the article consists of musings as to Brigham Young's method of dealing with this difficult situation and what the government's reaction ought to be.

1857: 19 December, *Caernarvon and Denbigh Herald*, p. 9 (19 words).

> Brigham Young, the Mormon leader, has claimed the independence of Utah, and thrown off allegiance to the United States.

1857: 19 December, *North Wales Chronicle*, p. 4 (150 words). "The Mormon Expedition."

> A gentleman [who] just arrived from Leavenworth states that before he left a rumor had reached that city, and obtained credence among the officers at the fort, that the Mormons had raised forces and blockaded all the avenues to Salt Lake City by the route taken by the United States forces, in many cases rendering the canyons impassable, by means of rocks and other impediments. Brigham Young declares that it is not the design of the Mormons to shed blood, unless provoked to do so by a similar action on the part of the Government. It is believed that they will endeavor to possess themselves of the horses, mules, and stores of the expedition, in order to a removal early in the spring. From the exposed position now occupied by the advance, this will be a comparatively easy task, unless the army shall fall back upon Fort Laramie.

1857: 26 December, *Caernarvon and Denbigh Herald*, p. 4, item 1 (27 words).

> There has been a skirmish between Colonel Alexander's forces and the Mormons. A large force is sent against the latter, and a protracted war is considered inevitable.

1857: 26 December, *Caernarvon and Denbigh Herald*, p. 4, item 2 (64 words).

> The Mormons are to be signally chastised for their defiance of the Sovereign Authority, and an increase of the army is demanded for the purpose. Meanwhile we hear that Brigham Young intends coming to close quarters at once. He will fight the United States troops while he can, before reinforcements have arrived, and after destroying the Mormon possessions in Utah leave for another country.

1857: 26 December, *Caernarvon and Denbigh Herald*, p. 9 (1,040 words). "Utah—the Mormons."

A very long review of the relationship of Brigham Young and the United States government, the current status, predictions, etc.

1857: 26 December, *Monmouthshire Beacon*, p. 5 (115 words).

> Further intelligence from the Utah expedition states that, on the 3rd of November, Colonel Cook's command was 150 miles west of Fort Laramie, proceeding as fast as possible towards the winter quarters fixed upon by

Colonel Johnson, on the Honey Fork of Green River. A rumor prevailed that Brigham Young intended to fight the troops this winter, while there was a chance for an equal, or rather for an unequal conflict, and that before reinforcements could be sent out in the spring, he would destroy all the Mormon possessions in Utah, and proceed to some other locality. Various Indian tribes had offered their services to the Federal Government in the suppression of the Mormon rebellion.

1857: 26 December, *Monmouthshire Beacon*, p. 6 (63 words).

Decided measures are called for against the Mormons, and the formation of four new regiments is urged. A territorial government for Arizona, and construction of a railroad to the Pacific, are recommended. Other portions of the message possess only local importance. . . . The Mormons are giving more trouble to the Federal troops. Some of them in a skirmish had been taken prisoners.

1857: 26 December, *North Wales Chronicle*, p. 6 (80 words). "The Mormons' Expedition."

Further advices had been received from the Utah expedition. Six hundred cattle had been run off by them in sight of Colonel Alexander's command. It was expected that the three divisions of the army under Colonels Johnston, Alexander, and Cook would soon be concentrated, and Governor Cummins and the other territorial officers were determined to enter Salt Lake City, if possible. A skirmish had taken place, in which three or four of the Mormons were taken prisoners.

1857: 26 December, *Usk Observer*, p. 4 (45 words). "A Death Blow to Mormonism."

President Buchanan had better not throw away powder and shot upon the Mormons. Let him send them fashion books. The necessity of crinoline will destroy polygamy. It will render Brigham Young himself unable to support more wives than one.

1857: 26 December, *Wrexham Advertiser*, p. 2 (225 words). "More Trouble with the Mormons."

A communication dated St. Louis, 8th December, says: An express passed through this city yesterday for Washington, with dispatches from Colonel Johnston. The *Republican* received letters this morning from the army to November 3. The Mormons had run off six hundred cattle in sight of Colonel Alexander's camp, near Ham's Fork, Green River. At the date of the letter it was supposed that Colonel Johnston had concentrated his force with Alexander's and that in a fortnight from that time Colonel Cook's command would be with them. They expected to winter on Henry's Fort, Green River. There was a good deal of suffering for want of provisions and clothing, and the horses were giving out for want of forage. Governor Cumming and the other territorial officers were determined to get into Salt Lake City if possible. The Mormons were determined on resistance to either the military or civil officers. A skirmish had taken place between Colonel Alexander's troops and the Mormons and three or four of the latter were captured. Colonel Hoffman, from Fort Laramie, last of October, arrived here on Sunday night, but he brings no news of the Utah expedition. The *Democrat* learns that news has been received at Fort Leavenworth from Major's and Russell's trains, that the government animals were dying in great numbers on the plains.

Notes

1. *Zion's Trumpet*, 10 January 1857, 10.
2. *Zion's Trumpet*, 27 June 1857, 209.
3. *Usk Observer*, 25 July 1857, 1.
4. *Zion's Trumpet*, 29 August 1857, 286–88.
5. *Zion's Trumpet*, 15 August 1857, 257.
6. *Zion's Trumpet*, 10 October 1857, 331.
7. The *Treasury*, February 1857, 58.
8. Ibid., 58–59.
9. The *Instructor*, June 1857, 105.
10. Ibid.
11. See the Saints by Sea website at saintsbysea.lib.byu.edu.
12. *Zion's Trumpet*, 15 August 1857, 257.
13. *Zion's Trumpet*, 25 January 1851, 35–36.
14. *Defending the Faith: Early Welsh Missionary Publications*, item J15.
15. Ibid., 263.
16. *Sun*, September 1857, 270.
17. Ibid.
18. Ibid.
19. The portion quoted in the *Sun* comprises pages 27–35 of Pamphlet #16 in the pamphlet section of this study.

Chapter 15

Episodes

15.1—Several accounts of Frederick Loba and his years with the Latter-day Saints are printed
15.2—Dr. Brindley of Leamington gives a lecture in the Wrexham Music Hall
15.3—"Handy Helps to Useful Knowledge" includes chapters about the Latter-day Saints
15.4—Henrietta Polydore is returned to her father in England
15.5—The *Instructor* prints seven long articles entitled "Mormonism"

Salient Events

- **1 January 1858.** Daniel Daniels is replaced as mission president and editor of *Zion's Trumpet* by Benjamin Evans. Daniels had served five years as a missionary in his native land, the final twenty-one months of which he served in the two aforementioned callings. The following information about further reorganization of the Welsh mission appears on the final page of the 1857 volume of *Zion's Trumpet*:

  Appointments of Elders to Preside over the Welsh Conferences, from January 1, 1858: Over the mission, President—Benjamin Evans; Counselors, John Davies, David John

Conferences	President
East Glamorgan	John Davies
Monmouth	William Ajax
Cardiff	Edward D. Miles
West Glamorgan	Thomas Rees

Llanelli	David Davies
Pembrokeshire	Edward Burgwyne
Cardiganshire	John Treharr
Denbighshire	Hugh Evans
Flintshire	Edwin Price

Pastor over the Northern Conferences—Thomas Jones

The Monmouthshire and Brecon Conferences will be joined under the name of the former.

The Carmarthen and Merioneth Conferences will be dissolved, and their branches will be aligned as follows:—Carmarthen and Saint Clears in the Llanelli Conference, and Brechfa, Pencader, Llansawel, Dinas Mawddwy and Machynlleth in the Cardiganshire Conference: Harlech and Ffestiniog in the Caernarfon Conference, which from now on will be known by the name of Conway Valley and Anglesey Conference.

We are deprived of the labor of our faithful brother, Joseph Griffiths, in the presiding circle, because of his illness.

The diligent and tireless labors of Pastor J. E. Jones are known to God and his children. More will yet be said about him.[1]

- **19 February 1858.** Daniel Daniels leaves Liverpool on board the *Empire*, reaching New York in just twenty-eight days. Upon arriving at Salt Lake City on 21 June 1858 with other members of the John W. Berry handcart company, Daniels finds the city deserted. Due to Johnston's forces advancing, Salt Lake City residents had gone south. A few years later, Daniels settles in Malad City, Idaho, where he dies in 1879.
- **26 May 1858.** *Potter's Electric News* runs an article entitled "Mormon 'Experiences'" (borrowed from the 1 May 1858 *New York Times*) about Frederic Loba from Switzerland, a convert to The Church of Jesus Christ of Latter-day Saints. After three years of being "in the midst of a wicked and degraded people," Loba secretly "escaped" from Salt Lake City and later related his experiences to a reporter for the *New York Times*. See Episode 15.1.
- **5 June 1858.** This date's *Wrexham Advertiser* has an announcement for a lecture to be presented on Monday, 21 June, by Dr. Brindley of Leamington in the Wrexham Music Hall on the topic of "'Mormonism,' its Follies, its Frauds, and its Vices, with a detailed account of doings at the Salt Lake, as related by those who have escaped therefrom." Brindley's lecture a year earlier in Birmingham had caused a mob to attack "a Mormon congregation . . . maltreating both women and men, and destroying property in the interior of the chapel."[2] There appears to have been no such consequence resulting from this latest lecture, as "there were not many present."[3] See Episode 15.2.
- **3 July 1858.** The *Merthyr Telegraph* carries an article entitled "Flight of the Mormons." Beginning just over nine months earlier, with the article "Expedition against the Mormons" in the 26 September 1857 issue of the *Usk Observer*, the vast majority of the published articles in Wales had to do

with the conflict between the United States government and the followers of Brigham Young in Utah. Since only three issues of the 1858 *Zion's Trumpet* are extant, it is difficult to get a sense of the impact the Utah War had on the progress of the Latter-day Saints in Wales during this period. However, this *Merthyr Telegraph* article provides some perspective from critics (see entry later in this chapter).

- **21 August 1858.** This issue of the *Cardiff and Merthyr Guardian* contains the first chapter of a series entitled "Mormons." A new chapter appears in each of the following six issues, for a total of seven chapters. These chapters are all taken from a source entitled "Handy Helps to Useful Knowledge." See Episode 15.3.
- **25 September 1858.** An article titled "An English Girl Rescued from the Mormons" appears in this issue of the *Caernarvon and Denbigh Herald.* The girl mentioned is named Henrietta, the twelve-year-old daughter of Henry and Henrietta Polydore of Gloucester. In 1854, the girl's mother had taken her to Salt Lake City without her father's permission. Henry Polydore then enlisted the help of the government of Great Britain and eventually succeeded in having his daughter brought back to his home in Gloucester in 1858. See Episode 15.4.
- **December 1858.** The *Instructor* prints a lengthy article entitled "Mormonism." Between January and September 1859, six additional articles under the same title appear in this periodical. See Episode 15.5.

Commentary

1858: January, *Seren Gomer* (*Star of Gomer*), p. 44 (110 words).

A brief notice about the testimony of Brigham Young in which he testified against the authority of the government to send soldiers to the Utah Territory.

1858: 2 January, *North Wales Chronicle*, p. 6 (1,035 words). "The Americans and the Mormons."

A report of Brigham Young's defiance of the US army that was advancing to take control of Salt Lake City. The report includes a letter from the wife of one of the Latter-day Saint soldiers in which she praises the Saints' efforts to "never let the Gentiles come into the valleys."

1858: 6 January, *Potter's Electric News*, p. 4 (920 words). "The City of the Mormons."

An abbreviated version of a much longer article published on 28 November 1857 in the *Star of Wales* (see previous chapter).

1858: 9 January, *North Wales Chronicle*, p. 3 (93 words).

A weekly mail route is established between Washington and the troops serving in Utah.

1858: 9 January, *North Wales Chronicle*, p. 6 (920 words). "The City of the Mormons."

Another abbreviated version of a much longer article published on 28 November 1857 in the *Star of Wales* (see previous chapter).

1858: 9 January, *Wrexham Advertiser*, p. 2 (390 words). "The Mormon Hegira."

Colonel Alexander is camped 143 miles from Salt Lake City until spring. The Latter-day Saints may relocate to Sonora, the most northwest province of Mexico.

1858: 9 January, *North Wales Chronicle*, p. 3 (93 words).

Further "important arrangements are expected to be made concerning the Mormon expedition." Even the British government is cooperating:

> The government is officially advised of the arrival in New York of two boxes of firearms, a present from the British government in return for the arms sent thither in August last.

1858: 16 January, *Cardiff and Merthyr Guardian*, p. 5 (32 words).

> Dr. Mackay, who is now in America, has a new work in the press upon the Mormons—their present Condition and Future Prospects. Very interesting letters from him arrive by every mail.

1858: 16 January, *Merthyr Telegraph*, p. 4 (32 words).

The same article published on 16 January 1858 in the *Cardiff and Merthyr Guardian* (see previous entry).

1858: 16 January, *Cardiff and Merthyr Guardian*, p. 7 (340 words). "Brigham Young and Ignatius Loyola—A Curious Parallel."

The writer shows "points of resemblance between Young and Loyola as developed in their respective systems" and reveals some of the "Mysteries of Mormonism," claiming that in secret ceremonies that all Latter-day Saints are required to swear "eternal enmity to the United States of North America."

1858: 16 January, *Monmouthshire Beacon*, p. 4 (160 words).

President Buchannan is "doing his best to extirpate this noxious excrescence from the American Constitution."

1858: 16 January, *Usk Observer*, p. 2 (23 words).

> It is estimated that as many as twenty-seven thousand Mormons have emigrated from Europe to the United States within the past sixteen years.

1858: 23 January, *Cardiff and Merthyr Guardian*, p. 4 (32 words).

> With respect to the Mormons the House of Representatives have declared the State of Utah to be in rebellion, and it is proposed to expel Dr. Bernhisel, the delegate, from his seat.

1858: 30 January, *Cardiff and Merthyr Guardian*, p. 3 (225 words).

An update on the Utah expedition.

1858: 30 January, *Monmouthshire Beacon*, p. 3 (140 words).

News of the "fierce civil war raging in Kansas," plus an observation that "the Mormons are too strong to be easily put down."

1858: 30 January, *Caernarvon and Denbigh Herald*, p. 10 (34 words).

> Reinforcements were under orders for Utah, as the Mormons were determined on resisting to the utmost; a late telegram from St. Louis, however, says they were preparing to leave Utah for a British territory.

1858: 30 January, *Monmouthshire Beacon*, p. 4 (34 words).
The same article as in the *Caernarvon and Denbigh Herald* for 30 January 1858 (see previous entry).

1858: 30 January, *Monmouthshire Beacon*, p. 5 (315 words). "The Mormons."
Contains "further information respecting the Utah expedition."

1858: February, *Seren Gomer* (*Star of Gomer*), p. 93 (30 words).

> The House of Representatives, Washington, has indicated Utah as revolutionaries and has set up a committee to investigate the legality of their representative to take his seat in Congress.

1858: February, *Y Dysgedydd* (*Instructor*), p. 2 (105 words). "The Mormons."
A brief notice about "the war that has been started by the Mormons in Utah":

> The President of the United States has indicated in his latest proclamation that he is determined to put down the war that has been started by the Mormons in Utah: "This is the first war," he said, "that has begun in our midst, and mankind itself is asking us to put it down in such a manner that it will be the last. To take it lightly would be to encourage it and make it disastrous. We should go there with such great force as to convince this misled people that opposition would be vain, and by so doing to prevent the spilling of blood."

This armed confrontation between the settlers in Utah and the armed forces of the United States was known as the "Utah War." It lasted from May 1857 to July 1858, but there was no open conflict between the two sides.

1858: 6 February, *North Wales Chronicle*, p. 6 (1,125 words). "The American Expedition against the Mormons."
More details of the Utah expedition. A New York correspondent writes:

> I counted repeatedly five, and once seven horses, oxen, and mules lying dead from cold or starvation within the space of 100 yards. There has been such a prodigious loss of stock by theft, cold, and hunger, that since November 7th we have not advanced on the average two miles a day.

The writer also mentions a "stout, honest-faced Englishman" by the name of Wadsworth, who, alongside "an Englishwoman of forty-five" and "a pretty girl of seventeen," was converted to Mormonism in 1855 by a nephew of Brigham Young. The man then "set sail, with an adopted son, for the holy city in May 1856 with 3,000 dollars of gold in pocket." Before they crossed the Utah line, "every penny had disappeared before church assessments and the expenses of the journey."

1858: 6 February, *Cardiff and Merthyr Guardian*, p. 4 (1,125 words). "The Mormons."
The abbreviated version of the same article in the *North Wales Chronicle* for 6 February 1858 (see previous entry).

1858: 6 February, *Cardiff and Merthyr Guardian*, p. 7 (185 words). "Proposed Migration of Mormons to British Territory."
The article includes the following prediction:

> The United States' troops will, in all probability, find the Salt Lake City a desert, and all the Mormon rebels across the frontier, under the protection

of that British flag which they have threatened to hoist as a defiance to the Federal Government.

1858: 6 February, *North Wales Chronicle*, p. 7 (1,095 words). "The United States."

More details about the Utah War, with this closing statement:

> A subsequent arrival, however, from New York, brings rumors of an expected evacuation of the country. Brigham Young and his followers, it is said, contemplate retiring into the British territories. We do not believe, however, that they will take such a step without a struggle.

1858: 6 February, *Wrexham Advertiser*, p. 3 (490 words). "The Mormons' New Home."

Further discussion as to the future location of the Latter-day Saints with a prediction they will relocate to "the British territory along the Columbia."

1858: 6 February, *Caernarvon and Denbigh Herald*, p. 9 (180 words). "America."

The first half of the same article as in the *Wrexham Advertiser* for 6 February 1858 (see previous entry).

1858: 6 February, *Monmouthshire Beacon*, pp. 4–5 (185 words).

The report of a possible agreement between the Latter-day Saints and the Cheyenne and Comanche Indians to fight against the advancing United States troops.

1858: 13 February, *Monmouthshire Beacon*, p. 5 (540 words). "Mormon Newspapers."

The Latter-day Saints are now using Old Testament prophecies to describe their current situation. The writer makes the following prediction:

> It seems probable that Brigham Young will maintain a bold front until it becomes necessary to meet the troops in the field. If an irresistible force is brought against him, he may not improbably lead his followers in a second migration.

1858: 20 February, *Caernarvon and Denbigh Herald*, p. 9, item 1 (20 words). "America."

> It is reported that General Scott will certainly proceed to California, to organize an expedition against the Mormons.

1858: 20 February, *Caernarvon and Denbigh Herald*, p. 9, item 2 (51 words).

> Advices from California represent the feeling against the Mormons as very strong in all sections of the state, and thousands of volunteers are in readiness to march against the saints, as soon as a requisition should be made for troops by the President. A number of companies have already been formed.

1858: 20 February, *North Wales Chronicle*, p. 8 (125 words).

> There is some prospect of the dispute with the Mormons being accommodated. A Dr. Bernhisel is at Washington as the representative of Brigham Young; and he has offered, on the part of his principal, to relinquish the territory of the Salt Lake, and evacuate it with his people, "provided the Government of the United States will purchase, at a fair valuation, the Salt Lake City improvements." It is said, that President Buchanan has given a

> favorable reply to this proposition; and, if finally adopted, it is thought that the city will be made a grand military station, or depot, for the United States troops stationed in the "extreme west." The Mormons will move, it is thought, to the northwest, entering the British territories.

1858: 20 February, *Usk Observer*, p. 3 (140 words).

This article has information about the proposition made by Dr. Bernhisel for the United States to purchase "the Mormon property in Utah," as well as a report on the good condition of the troops, with new recruits and "an abundant supply of beef" recently obtained.

1858: 27 February, *Caernarvon and Denbigh Herald*, p. 20, item 1 (32 words).

> We know an old lady, who, when she alludes to the leader of the Mormons, always calls him—either unintentionally, or else by a curious jumble of ideas—'Mr. Bigamy Young.'—*Punch*.

1858: 27 February, *Caernarvon and Denbigh Herald*, p. 20, item 2 (135 words). "The Mormons."

> An official statement published this year by the United States government gives the following statistics of Mormonism: The Mormons have about ninety-five missionaries in Europe, and an equal number in Asia, Africa, and the Pacific Islands, besides large numbers of native elders in the various fields of labor, and a considerable number scattered throughout the United States and British America. They have one newspaper in Salt Lake City, issuing 4000 copies weekly; one in Liverpool issuing 22,000 weekly; one in Swansea, South Wales; one in Copenhagen, in the Danish language; one in Australia; one in India; and one in Switzerland, in the French language. The Book of Mormon has been translated and published in the Welsh, Danish, French, German, and Italian languages. The Mormons claim 280,000 members of their church scattered over the world.

1858: March, *Y Greal* (*Grail*), p. 72 (180 words). "The United States."

In his opening sentence, the writer states the current relationship between the United States government and The Church of Jesus Christ of Latter-day Saints:

> The United States intends to give a thrashing to the Mormons at the beginning of summer for their lawlessness and their impudence, and Brigham Young has decided to resist with all his might.

The writer then presents various statistics, such as the number of Latter-day Saint missionaries in various parts of the world, the circulation of their newspapers in Salt Lake City and Liverpool, and the translation of the Book of Mormon in various languages. He then gives his reason for presenting this information:

> We mention this for the purpose of putting our readers on their guard against this frightful plague.

1858: March, *Y Cyfaill o'r Hen Wlad yn America* (*Friend of the Old Country in America*), p. 106 (33 words). "Mormonism in Gloucester."

> It seems that Mormonism is doing frightful damage to the morals of some of the inhabitants. And so it does in several other places as well. It is too wicked to defend.

1858: 6 March, *Caernarvon and Denbigh Herald*, p. 6 (87 words). "Elopement of a Married Lady with a Mormon."

> Information has been received, that Mrs. Welch, hostess of the Rose and Crown Inn, at Ampthill, Bedfordshire, has eloped from her husband, taking with her considerable property, in company with a draper named Rogers, a Latter-day Saint, who, having converted Mrs. Welch to Mormonism had induced her to abandon her husband and fly with him to Utah. Mrs. Welch has left four children behind her, and Mr. Welch offers £30 to anyone who brings her back to Ampthill.

1858: 6 March, *North Wales Chronicle*, p. 5 (87 words). "Elopement of a Married Lady with a Mormon."

The same article as appears in the *Caernarvon and Denbigh Herald* for 6 March 1858 (see previous entry).

1858: 6 March, *North Wales Chronicle*, p. 6 (645 words). "The Mormon Expedition."

A letter from Colonel Johnston to a friend in Kentucky about his current circumstances. He reports that Brigham Young had sent him eight hundred pounds of salt as a present but that he had returned the salt to Brigham Young with the following message:

> That Brigham Young and his associates are in rebellion against the Government; that until they return to their allegiance and obey the laws, I will accept no favor or courtesy from them, nor hold any correspondence with them.

1858: 6 March, *Caernarvon and Denbigh Herald*, p. 9 (40 words).

> The Mormon news is interesting, but unreliable. There was a rumor of a battle between the United States troops and the saints, but it was not believed. A report that five American citizens had been killed by the Mormons.

1858: 6 March, *Usk Observer*, p. 2 (40 words).

The same article as in the *Caernarvon and Denbigh Herald* for 6 March 1858 (see previous entry).

1858: 6 March, *Merthyr Telegraph*, p. 3 (40 words).

The same article as in the *Caernarvon and Denbigh Herald* for 6 March 1858 (see previous entry).

1858: 6 March, *Usk Observer*, p. 4 (765 words).

A very negative report written by Lieutenant-Colonel Cook of the Utah Expedition. Among other things, he provides details about the impact of the cold temperatures and the loss of mules.

1858: 13 March, *Monmouthshire Beacon*, p. 5 (160 words).

More information about the troops of the Utah Expedition who were "earnestly wishing to make a decent on Salt Lake City."

1858: 20 March, *Caernarvon and Denbigh Herald*, p. 9 (220 words).

The latest news "from Salt Lake City, and from the camp." Regarding Brigham Young's message to the Utah Legislature, the writer reports:

> Having received no official notification of the intention of the Government to supersede him in the gubernatorial office, nor of the dispatch of troops to Utah, Young affects to regard the army at Fort Bridger and the civil authorities there as an organized mob, against which he has already fulminated a proclamation to disperse.

1858: 20 March, *Merthyr Telegraph*, p. 4 (220 words).

The same article as in the *Caernarvon and Denbigh Herald* for 20 March 1858 (see previous entry).

1858: 27 March, *Usk Observer*, p. 2 (660 words). "The War with the Mormons."

Additional details about the United States troops as they neared Salt Lake City for the conflict.

1858: 27 March, *Caernarvon and Denbigh Herald*, p. 10 (100 words).

> Our Washington dispatch states that Dr. Bernhisel, the Mormon delegate in Congress, has recently received letters from Brigham Young in which he predicts the annihilation of the United States troops now in Utah, unless they are recalled by the government. He also suggests the appointment of a commission to proceed to Utah, to inquire into the condition of affairs there. It is not in the least degree probable that the President will listen to overtures of this character, coming from persons in rebellion against the federal authorities, and against whom an indictment for treason is pending. *New York Herald.*

1858: 27 March, *Monmouthshire Beacon*, p. 8 (32 words).

> The Mormons under Brigham Young are preparing to fight to the last, and are said to have invented some infernal projectiles of the most deadly character to be thrown as hand grenades.

1858: April, *Y Cyfaill o'r Hen Wlad yn America* (*Friend of the Old Country in America*), p. 155 (170 words). "Utah."

This brief article begins with the following comment about the Utah War:

> The adulterous Mormons are clinging to their profession of faith, and they have decided not to bow to the laws of the Union, even if they are forced to lose their country or lose their lives in the battle for the Mormon faith.

The writer then quotes from a letter that a Latter-day Saint wrote from Utah to his brother in New York, explaining why he and his coreligionists were willing to stand up to the United States Army.

> Because we believe that Mormonism is the gospel of Jesus Christ, who shows the way to eternal life; and despite the trampling and persecution that it has suffered, it is more powerful and noble than ever.

1858: April, *Y Cyfaill o'r Hen Wlad yn America* (*Friend of the Old Country in America*), pp. 155–56 (120 words). "General Johnston."

After reporting on the numerous soldiers going toward Utah "with the intention of subduing the war of the Mormons," the writer concludes:

> The most obvious thing is that the Saints will retreat to some other place instead of fighting or surrendering.

1858: April, *Seren Gomer* (*Star of Gomer*), p. 187 (93 words).
A few lines to the effect that Brigham Young and others have been accused as "persons guilty of high treason."

1858: 3 April, *Caernarvon and Denbigh Herald*, p. 3 (125 words). A quote from a discussion of various religions:

> So with regard to Mormonism (which erroneous system is comparatively of recent date). What is it but a gigantic lie, an invention of falsehood? There is not a part of it that will bear the light of God's truth. It is from beginning to end a fabrication of falsehood and wickedness, framed for speculation, in order that its abominable and lewd leaders may feast on the spoil of their dupes. What is the Book of Mormon but a lie, a mixture of truth and nonsense, which has been presumptuously and blasphemously palmed off as a divine revelation to Joe Smith, a man utterly destitute of moral character, and addicted to almost every vice. The impostor's mark is legible in every page of this publication.

1858: 3 April, *Usk Observer*, p. 4 (33 words).

> The advices from Utah show the Mormons were as obstinate and rampant for war as ever. The Utah legislature had sent a petition to Congress, calling on that body to redress their wrongs.

1858: 10 April, *Monmouthshire Beacon*, p. 5 (255 words).

> The war with the Mormons is assuming serious proportions. . . . The address from the Legislative Assembly of the Mormons to the Senate at Washington, extracts from which we give in another part of our impression, is about the most arrant piece of bombast and impudence that can be conceived.

Regarding the beliefs of the Latter-day Saints, the writer declares:

> Mormonism in sooth lives in a sensual atmosphere of its own, it is a creature not of the feelings but the passions, and when these are let loose, men lose the attributes of humanity and become demons.

1858: 10 April, *Merthyr Telegraph*, p. 2 (123 words). "Mormons in British Territory."

> Advices from St. Louis state that Father Desmil, a Catholic missionary, who has spent many years among the Indian tribes, asserts that on another slope of the Rocky Mountains there is a perfectly practicable and easy route north from Salt Lake to the British possessions. Father Desmil states that he has traveled the route several times with light wagons. He gives it as his opinion that if the Mormons leave their present location, they will proceed northward to New Caledonia, British America, and settle at the base of the Portage Mountains, near the 48th parallel. The route is described in detail. The country and climate are stated to eminently superior in every respect to that of Utah. *Canadian News*.

1858: 10 April, *Caernarvon and Denbigh Herald*, p. 9 (70 words).

> We have later news from Utah. A mail from Fort Independence was three months in reaching the United States camp, and then half despoiled of its

contents. A Mormon prisoner had escaped, and it was feared that there were traitors in the camp. An express is said to have reached Leavenworth, from the camp of Colonel Johnston, requesting that supplies of ammunition and more men be sent him immediately.

1858: 17 April, *Caernarvon and Denbigh Herald*, pp. 8–9 (73 words).

Private letters from Colonel Johnston, at Camp Scott, to the 5th ult., have been received. He describes the Mormons as manifesting a decided intention to set up an independent government of their own, and expresses an earnest hope that supplies will be forwarded to him at as early a day as practicable. A large train with supplies, and two regiments of Infantry and two of Cavalry, have already left Fort Leavenworth for Utah.

1858: 17 April, *Monmouthshire Beacon*, p. 3 (75 words).

Private letters from Colonel Johnston, at Camp Scott, Utah, to the 5th of February, have been received. He describes the Mormons as manifesting a decided intention to set up an independent government of their own, and expresses an earnest hope that supplies will be forwarded to him at as early a day as possible. A large train with supplies, and two regiments of infantry and two of cavalry, have already left Fort Leavenworth for Utah.

1858: 24 April, *Caernarvon and Denbigh Herald*, pp. 3–4 (755 words). "Mormons."

A very negative letter dated 1 February 1858 from a young woman, Elizabeth Cotton. Cotton had left England with her grandmother, Mary Hutchinson, on the *Horizon* in 1856 and traveled to Utah as part of the Hunt Wagon Company. Her grandmother died at Martin's Cove, but Mary was rescued and arrived in Salt Lake City. In addition to the hardships of crossing the plains, Cotton also had very negative experiences in Utah. Her main complaint was about polygamy:

> On arriving at the Salt Lake, I was not a little surprised to see the men running after the women and asking them if they were married, but I have not got married yet, and I do not intend.

Cotton wrote this letter while on her way east after leaving Salt Lake City. She got as far as Putnam, Indiana, where she married William Secrest Eckels and had four children. She died in 1880 at age thirty-nine.

1858: 24 April, *Merthyr Telegraph*, p. 2 (320 words). "Mormon Trick."

The writer reports (in Welsh, though the *Telegraph* was an English publication) some bad behavior on the part of a Latter-day Saint who mistreated a shepherd he had in his employ. While the shepherd was in bed with smallpox, his employer insisted that he move some sheep right away. He obeyed and died soon after. The writer suggests that the employer had caused the shepherd's death. He ends his letter with a question:

> I would like to know from one of the Mormon clan whether behavior of that sort is in accordance with Christian principles.

He also explains in a postscript the reason he had submitted the letter in Welsh:

> The reason for writing these lines in Welsh is because I believe that there are as many subscribers to the *Telegraph* who are as proficient in Welsh as they are in English.

1858: May, *Seren Gomer* (*Star of Gomer*), p. 234 (14 words).

> The Mormons, it is reported, have decided to strive to establish their own government.

1858: May, *Y Drysorfa* (*Treasury*), p. 176 (120 words).

The same article as in the *Friend of the Old Country in America*, April 1858 (see previous entry).

1858: 1 May, *Merthyr Telegraph*, p. 4 (31 words).

> Private letters from officers of the army at Walla Walla, Columbia River, say that the Mormon settlements are being broken up in that region, and the Mormons leaving for Salt Lake.

1858: 1 May, *Wrexham Advertiser*, p. 3 (31 words).

The same article as in the *Merthyr Telegraph* for 1 May 1858 (see previous entry).

1858: 1 May, *North Wales Chronicle*, p. 6 (680 words). "The United States Expedition against the Mormons."

A letter dated March 1, 1856, from a soldier who was part of the Utah Expedition. He reports an improvement in the weather, the availability of beef for the troops, and assures the recipient of Colonel Johnston's determination to engage in battle to subdue the residents of Salt Lake City if necessary.

1858: 8 May, *Cardiff and Merthyr Guardian*, p. 7 (755 words). "A Picture of Life amongst the Mormons."

This is the same article as in the *Caernarvon and Denbigh Herald* for 24 April 1858 (see previous entry).

1858: 8 May, *Caernarvon and Denbigh Herald*, p. 9 (134 words).

The news from Salt Lake City as of 6 February was that the people there were preparing "to attack the United States forces and intercept their supplies." Plans were also underway to deliver a huge shipment of supplies to Salt Lake City for the troops.

1858: 15 May, *North Wales Chronicle*, p. 2 (585 words). "The Mormon Settlements."

A St. Louis correspondent of the *New York Herald* had recently visited Nauvoo. He reports:

> Nauvoo is a dull slumbering place, at present inhabited by an Icarian colony of Philosopher Greeley's pet friends, the French Fourierites. A more beggarly, God-forsaken place I have scarcely ever seen in this country.

He had met Joseph Smith's widow, along with "young Joe Smith [III], who should by right have been at the head of the Mormons." He added:

> I slept in the prophet's chamber, where he was often in the habit of receiving visits from supernatural strangers.

He also describes the current state of the temple:

> A portion of the ruins of the stately temple are still standing, ornamented with strange devices of men in the moon, rising suns and stars. It was built

said the prophet, from a plan furnished from above. Without intending irreverence, I should say that the celestial architects are a most tasteless set, or else humbugged Joseph.

Episode 15.1

Start: Several accounts are printed of Frederick Loba and his years with the Latter-day Saints

1858: 26 May, *Potter's Electric News*, p. 4 (1,070 words). "Mormon 'Experiences.'"

Taken from the 1 May 1858 issue of the *New York Times*, this article focuses on Frederick Loba, a Swiss convert to The Church of Jesus Christ of Latter-day Saints. Being "of a strong metaphysical turn of mind," Loba had felt some years earlier "rather uneasy with respect to sacred things and a future existence." Upon speaking with the Latter-day Saint missionaries, he was convinced that he had found the true religion. However, disillusionment began when he arrived in St. Louis with his family in December 1853. The feeling grew even stronger when Loba spent some time with Brigham Young, who he hoped would have "all the characteristics and virtues befitting a man of God." The writer describes Loba's "escape from Mormonism" following more than three years in Utah:

> On the 1st of April, 1857, he resolved to escape with his wife only, leaving his eight children in the care of his mother-in-law and her brother; and after many hardships, mountain adventures, and risks by flood and field the unhappy couple at length reached Green River, and were kindly received by the Snake Indians and some Canadian traders there encamped. Brigham Young had started 32 horsemen on Loba's track to recapture him, but after incredible exertions to do so they were forced to return. Loba arrived at Kickapoo last December, after several attacks of fever, in a state of perfect destitution. His relatives and children have rejoined him.

The writer quotes Loba's reflections on his time in Utah:

> This is a very brief outline of what I and mine have suffered from Mormonism. Every educated man will realize much more readily than I can describe it how keen has been my mental suffering amid the degraded, uncultivated, and besotted followers of Brigham Young. Could all that be obliterated from the pages of my memory, how lightly should I esteem the physical privations and sufferings of the last few years. But nothing remains to me but regret for the past, and joy that I have escaped the trammels of the Salt Lake, and that the remnant of my family are spared the contamination and ruin, which a life among "the Saints" would inevitably involve.

1858: 29 May, *Cardiff and Merthyr Guardian*, p. 7 (1,070 words). "Mormon 'Experiences.'"

The same article as in *Potter's Electric News* for 26 May 1858 (see previous entry).

1858: 29 May, *Monmouthshire Beacon*, p. 2 (1,070 words). "Mormon Moralities."

The same article as in *Potter's Electric News* for 26 May 1858 (see previous entry).

1859: July, *Y Dysgedydd* (*Instructor*), p. 270–72 (1,070 words). "Mormonism."

Just over a third of this article is devoted to the story of Frederick Loba, taken also from the *New York Times* (see previous entry).

End: Several accounts are printed of Frederick Loba and his years with the Latter-day Saints

1858: 29 May, *Cardiff and Merthyr Guardian*, p. 3 (530 words). "The Mormons in America."

The 20 February 1858 report of Lieutenant Colonel Reichenau about a conflict with the Utah army near Echo Canyon.

1858: 29 May, *Monmouthshire Beacon*, p. 4 (80 words).

> If any of our readers have not had enough exposure already of the gross immorality of the Mormon imposture, we beg to refer them to a paragraph on this subject in another column, giving a faithful history of the degrading mode of the inner life of Mormonism. It is written perhaps warmly by one who fortunately has escaped those horrors, but bears the impress of truth, and we inset it at once as a fearful revelation and an instructive warning.

1858: 29 May, *Monmouthshire Beacon*, p. 3 (31 words).

> Advices from St. Louis report the arrival of three men direct from Camp Scott. The Mormons were preparing to harass the troops. The weather and roads were unfavorable for their progress.

1858: June, *Y Cenhadwr Americanaidd* (*American Messenger*), p. 236 (230 words). "From Utah."

The writer reports:

> We have received the pleasing news from Utah that the Mormons have decided to put their weapons of rebellion down and to bow to the authority of the government of the United States.

He explains that the chief negotiator of peace was General Thomas L. Kane.

Episode 15.2

Start: Dr. Brindley of Leamington gives a lecture in the Wrexham Music Hall

1858: 5 June, *Wrexham Advertiser*, p. 1 (120 words).

> Music-Hall, Wrexham.
>
> Dr. Brindley, of Leamington, has accepted an invitation from a Committee of Gentlemen in Wrexham to deliver Two Lectures, In the Music Hall, Wrexham, as under:
>
> > Monday, June 21st, "Mormonism," its Follies, its Frauds, and its Vices, with a detailed account of doings at the Salt Lake, as related by those who have escaped therefrom.
> >
> > Tuesday, June 22nd, illustrated by a very large Map and Water-color Drawings, produced expressly for this Lecture—The Travels of St.

> Paul, with an account of the Countries and People amongst whom he traveled.
>
> Questions may be asked or Discussion entered into at the close of each Lecture. Admission, Front Seats 1s, Back Do. 6d. To commence at half-past 7 o'clock each evening.

1858: 12 June, *Wrexham Advertiser*, p. 1 (120 words).

The same advertisement as in the *Wrexham Advertiser* for 5 June 1858 (see previous entry).

1858: 19 June, *Wrexham Advertiser*, p. 1 (120 words).

The same advertisement as in the *Wrexham Advertiser* for 5 June 1858 (see previous entry).

1858: 26 June, *Wrexham Advertiser*, p. 4 (680 words). "Lecture on Mormonism."

The writer describes the welcome given to Dr. Brindley:

> The lecturer was received with loud cheers, and in an able and eloquent discourse, advanced a great deal of new and interesting information in connection with Mormonism. He gave a rapid but clear exposition of its follies, frauds, and vices, with a detailed account of the doings at Salt Lake, as related to the lecturer himself by persons escaped therefrom.

After speaking about the Book of Mormon and the practice of plural marriage, Brindley . . .

> gave the audience a specimen of the miracles with which their leaders sought to dupe the people, which excited a good deal of laughter. . . . He gave a striking outline of the dangers, privations, and difficulties they had to pass through in going to the Salt Lake. Out of the last batch which went out (2,000) only 230 arrived at their journey's end alive.

Brindley also predicted that "the American soldiers would soon displace them from the Salt Lake." The writer concludes:

> The lecturer was loudly cheered throughout, and concluded a very instructive though somewhat melancholy lecture, amid great applause. We are sorry to add, there were not many present.

End: Dr. Brindley of Leamington gives a lecture in the Wrexham Music Hall

1858: 5 June, *Caernarvon and Denbigh Herald*, p. 9 (710 words).

After presenting a brief analysis of the Utah War and an outline of the history of the Latter-day Saints, the writer concludes:

> As matters stand, our arms have acquired no new luster, and the Mormon leaders have derived fresh *eclat* for their imposture, from this new instance of Gentile persecution. It would be hard to devise a worse mode of extirpating a disgusting heresy than marching against it with a division of infantry.

1858: 5 June, *Monmouthshire Beacon*, p. 3 (31 words).

> From Utah we learn that the United States Commissioners had proceeded to Salt Lake City to confer with the Mormons who were apparently ready to receive them in a friendly spirit.

1858: 5 June, *Monmouthshire Beacon*, p. 4 (39 words).

> The Mormon campaign seems likely to come to a very strange and abrupt conclusion. We hear that Brigham Young has abdicated his ruling functions, fled from Utah, and that delegates have met General Cumming to arrange terms of peace.

1858: 12 June, *Merthyr Telegraph*, p. 3 (575 words). "End of the Mormon War."

In this article taken from the *New York Tribune*, the writer declares, "The Utah war is ended." He expresses his opinion as to what should be done at this point:

> If they are now willing to leave the country why should they be obstructed or harassed? If they are willing to leave, let them depart in peace.

He also credits Colonel Thomas L. Kane for facilitating this peaceful outcome:

> When the full truth becomes known we believe it will be found that great credit is due to Colonel Thomas L. Kane for this auspicious termination of the Mormon broil. He went out to Utah with the consent, indeed, of the President, but prompted by his own generous heart, animated by an earnest desire to prevent a needless, and therefore a highly culpable, effusion of human blood.

1858: 12 June, *Wrexham Advertiser*, p. 3 (575 words).

The same article as appeared in the *Merthyr Telegraph* for 12 June 1858 (see previous entry).

1858: 12 June, *Monmouthshire Beacon*, pp. 4–5 (180 words).

The writer theorizes about the future of the Utah residents:

> It is supposed that the Mormons will attempt to establish a settlement in the Mexican territory, where they will perhaps be able to set the weak government of that country at defiance.

He also expresses his sympathy for the women and children:

> In many points of view, it is melancholy to reflect on the hardships which must be incurred by the women and children in this flight from the country which they had so fertilized and improved to some place they know not whither.

1858: 12 June, *Wrexham Advertiser*, p. 2 (75 words).

> The widow of Joe Smith, the Mormon, still resides at Nauvoo, but she cares nothing for the saints, and has married a tavern keeper, who thinks all prophets humbugs. Young Joe, who should by right have been the head of the Mormons, is a stout gawky [young man] of 22, who hates Brigham Young and curses the Salt Lakers. Nauvoo was once a place of 20,000 inhabitants, but is now a place of ruins. *Washington Union.*

1858: 19 June, *Caernarvon and Denbigh Herald*, p. 10 (75 words).

The same article as appeared in the *Wrexham Advertiser* for 12 June 1858 (see previous entry).

1858: 19 June, *Caernarvon and Denbigh Herald*, p. 9 (39 words).

> Dates from Utah are to the 6th of May. The Mormons had expelled Governor Cumming, the regularly appointed executive officer of the territory, from the settlement, and had determined to resist the troops sent against them to the last.

1858: 19 June, *Monmouthshire Beacon*, p. 4 (230 words).

The writer is confused at the outcome of the Utah War:

> Mormonism seems likely to give more trouble than was expected in its repression. For the life of us we cannot make out from the last accounts whether, Brigham Young has fled from Utah or not, but one thing appears certain, that the Mormons are determined to make a stand now to the last, and that even by force of arms. . . . America is a great republic, it is true, but slavery and Mormonism are deadly diseases at its core.

1858: 26 June, *North Wales Chronicle*, p. 2 (26 words).

Governor Cumming had been installed as Governor of the Mormon Territory, and was well received. The settlements had been broken up, and the inhabitants moving south.

1858: 26 June, *Usk Observer*, p. 3 (47 words).

It is not officially confirmed that the Mormons expelled Governor Cumming, but it is said to be derived from unquestionable authority. It was expected the army would move towards the Salt Lake about the end of May. The troops were said to be living on mule meat.

1858: 26 June, *Monmouthshire Beacon*, p. 4 (162 words).

According to the *New York Daily Times*, "the telegraphic dispatches received from day to day, purporting to give us news from Utah, are of so contradictory a character as to render it impossible to fix upon anything as reliable."

1858: 26 June, *Cardiff and Merthyr Guardian*, p. 3 (85 words).

It was stated positively that Governor Cumming has not been driven from Salt Lake City, and that the intentions of the Mormons were not belligerent; but, on the contrary, that the Governor had been well received; that Brigham was perfectly willing to transfer all authority to him, and that the Mormons had given up all idea of fighting and had gone to work on their farms. The report that Captain Marcy's train had been cut off is contradicted, nothing whatever having been heard from him.

1858: July, *Y Cenhadwr Americanaidd* (*American Messenger*), p. 271 (290 words).

Three fairly brief paragraphs about "the Mormon war." The first, entitled "The Mormon War at an End," simply indicates that "this people had bowed to the authority of Governor Cumming," who had been sent by President Buchanan to establish peace and order once again in Utah.

The second paragraph, "Where Will They Go?" reports that the Latter-day Saints were "going toward the South by the thousands, taking their possessions with them." The *New York Herald* is cited as a reference for this plan:

> The plan in sight is to populate that country as soon as is possible and make it into a slave state and bring it into the Union. It is said that there is likely some agreement drawn up for doing so between the leaders of the slave masters and the Mormon elders.

And the third paragraph—"The Latest from Utah"—reports that the situation in Utah is normalizing and that "trade will soon be opened throughout the valley of the territory to supply the army."

1858: July, *Seren Gomer* (*Star of Gomer*), p. 324 (130 words).

Just a few lines to the effect that the news regarding the conflict between Utah and the United States government is "unclear."

1858: 3 July, *Caernarvon and Denbigh Herald*, p. 9 (88 words).

> Advice from Washington states that General Scott had received dispatches from Utah of five days' later day than those transmitted by Governor Cumming. They represent that the governor had been received by the Mormons; that after they had removed their women and children from Salt Lake City the men returned, strengthened their defensive positions, and assumed a threatening attitude. The news was regarded as reliable. The soldiers under General Johnston were on short allowance of food. Capt. Marcy was within six days of Camp Scott at last accounts.

1858: 3 July, *Merthyr Telegraph*, p. 2 (660 words). "Flight of the Mormons."

The writer reflects on the time when the Latter-day Saints constituted a significant presence in Merthyr Tydfil and the surrounding area:

> A few years ago, this town and the surrounding districts were the scene of Mormon labor. Here the converted tailor or shoemaker gathered a crowd around him in the evening, and on the Sabbath day; a crowd of workmen eager to learn a little of the mysteries of Mormonism, and be enlightened on the strange doctrines those strange and misguided men the Saints professed and practiced. On heaps of refuse, and by the banks of the slow rolling Taff, in outhouses, and on balks of timber, the apostles stood, and declaimed in strong language against existing beliefs, against the Christian faith, and the worthy ministers of our churches and chapels. Now and then the cudgels were taken up against them by a zealous Christian, knotty points would be argued, texts quoted, and strong truths hurled at them from the everlasting Word; but in despite of all the persuasion of speakers and writers, the drain from our places of worship continued, and daily, for a length of time, there was a continual secession from Christianity to Mormonism.

The writer describes this "continual secession:"

> The servant girl, ignorant of the world and the deception therein; the honest miner and collier, who for years had trudged to their humble chapels each day of rest—their wives and their daughters, led by the parent, and not from the force of reason; men of the lowest grade and men of property; with a sprinkling of individuals, ambitious to become elders and men of note, now swayed by belief in the inferiority of Mormon doctrines, forsook, one and all, the old creed, and became members of the worst society ever enrolled—forsook their homes, their friends, the scenes of their nativity, and traveled away with hopeful hearts to the promised land in far-away Utah.

The writer tells of the unfortunate consequences of some of the Welsh who left their native land to travel to the "promised land" in Utah:

> It was a sad sight to observe such delusion, and that too in the age of steam engines, and at a time when the Press disseminated knowledge broadly and cheaply over the land. They went. Many of our readers have friends or parents

> who left hither, and never reached their goal. Many more yet confess that relatives of their own still belong to the notorious confederacy against morality and religion; but few have need now to lament that the influence, the seduction of Mormonism, continues. It has become a dead letter. The eyes of our people are open to the deception, and however skillful the trap may be baited, there is no fear that Merthyr Tydfil will continue to supply frail and simple victims.

1858: 3 July, *Merthyr Telegraph*, p. 3 (73 words).

> The news from Utah is still conflicting. A dispatch from Washington states that General Scott had received dispatches from Utah of five days' later date than those transmitted by Governor Cumming. They represent that Governor Cumming had been deceived by the Mormons: that after they had removed their women and children from Salt Lake City, the men returned, strengthened their defensive position, and assumed a threatening attitude. This news was regarded as reliable.

1858: 3 July, *Cardiff and Merthyr Guardian*, p. 5 (630 words). "The Mormon Difficulty."

A description of the peaceful transition of power in Utah to Governor Cumming.

1858: 3 July, *North Wales Chronicle*, p. 3 (1,090 words). "Governor Cumming at the Great Salt Lake."

In a letter to General Cass, the Secretary of the United States, Governor Cumming details his peaceful reception in Utah.

1858: 3 July, *North Wales Chronicle*, p. 6 (180 words). "The Mormon Expedition—The Ruse of the 'Latter-day Saints'—The American Army Starving on Its Way."

According to the Washington correspondent of the *New York Times*, General Johnston has "conclusions directly opposite to those of Governor Cumming touching the intention of the Mormons, who, he says, are now arming and fortifying at every point."

> The administration is now fearful that Governor Cumming has been deceived. The next dispatches will be looked for with intense interest. Many gentlemen conversant with Utah affairs think the President acted prematurely in proclaiming peace. Private accounts from Salt Lake represent Governor Cumming as almost a prisoner, and the Mormon leaders are exercising full sway over the minds of the people.

1858: 3 July, *Usk Observer*, p. 2 (1,100 words). "The Mormon Exodus."

The same article as appeared in the *North Wales Chronicle* for 3 July 1858 (see previous entry).

1858: 7 July, *Potter's Electric News*, p. 1 (990 words). "Mormonism in Difficulties."

The writer satirizes the decision that Brigham Young now had to make as to whether his people would remain in Utah or whether he would lead them to a different location, perhaps further south to Sonora.

1858: 10 July, *North Wales Chronicle*, p. 2 (40 words).

> It appears that there are or were two parties—Peace and War parties—among the Mormons, and hence has arisen the difficulty with us to understand their

position. The Peace party appears to have triumphed. Brigham Young favored this party.

1858: 10 July, *Wrexham Advertiser*, p. 4 (455 words). "A Dreadful Prospect."

The writer speculates concerning the future of forty thousand Latter-day Saints who appear to have decided to flee southward.

1858: 10 July, *Usk Observer*, p. 3 (925 words). "The Mormons."

The minutes of a case tried in Thames Police Court having to do with the charges Mrs. Elizabeth Watson brought against Hannah Brown. The charges were that Brown, a Latter-day Saint with nine children, had assaulted Watson when she saw Watson kissing Mr. Brown. Watson claimed that the meeting was accidental and denied kissing Brown's husband. Watson also claimed that the elders had assigned Mr. Brown to convince Watson to rob her own husband and go off to Utah. The judge concluded the trial:

> Mrs. Watson had better not shake hands with Mr. Brown if she meets him again. As there was some aggravation I shall fine Mrs. Brown 1s. only, but if she molests Mrs. Watson again, I shall bind her over in heavy sureties to keep the peace.

1858: 10 July, *Monmouthshire Beacon*, p. 4 (133 words).

The writer is puzzled at "the two parties among the Mormons, one being for peace and the other for war." He concludes:

> The faithful history of this huge imposture has yet to be written, but its band of cohesion is evidently sensuality, acting on fanaticism.

1858: 10 July, *Monmouthshire Beacon*, p. 5 (68 words).

> President Buchanan is unwell, much upset, it is said, by the conflicting accounts from the Mormon territory. The Mormon abandonment of Salt Lake City is confirmed, but they intended to have set fire to it had they not been discovered in rendezvous at Provo City, and fortify it against the Government troops. General Johnston was expected to commence a forward movement. The Peace Commissioners had reached the camp.

1858: 10 July, *Cardiff and Merthyr Guardian*, p. 7, item 1 (925 words). "Mormonism in London. Disgusting Revelations."

The same article as in the *Usk Observer* for 10 July 1858 (see previous entry).

1858: 10 July, *Cardiff and Merthyr Guardian*, p. 7, item 2 (120 words). "The Mormons."

News that "70 Mormon families had come into Camp Scott and claimed protection." Also "extensive preparations had been made to set fire to the city" in case Johnston's forces invaded Salt Lake City.

1858: 10 July, *Caernarvon and Denbigh Herald*, p. 9, item 1 (38 words).

> It is said that the President is much perplexed at the contradictory nature of the dispatches from Utah, and expresses regret at what he now considers his premature message to Congress announcing the end of the Mormon rebellion.

1858: 10 July, *Caernarvon and Denbigh Herald,* p. 9, item 2 (57 words).
In Utah seventy Mormon families had come into Camp Scott to claim protection, which had been granted to them. When the great seal and records of the Mormons had been given to Governor Cumming, he was requested to put them in a fireproof safe. It was ascertained afterwards that arrangements had been made to fire the city.

1858: 10 July, *Caernarvon and Denbigh Herald,* p. 9, item 3 (20 words).
It has been rumored that the Mormons purpose concentrating and fortifying themselves at Provo, forty miles from Salt Lake City.

1858: 17 July, *Caernarvon and Denbigh Herald,* p. 9 (19 words).
One hundred and fifty Mormons from Salt Lake City have placed themselves under the protection of the United States.

1858: 21 July, *Potter's Electric News,* p. 3 (785 words).
Recently, an unnamed speaker returned from Salt Lake City and presented an "anti-Mormon discourse" at the Ebenezer Chapel in Tenby. He pointed out the evils of polygamy and "entered into many other details which clearly showed that in the Mormon Zion every bestiality which can tend to lower and degrade the human race is freely practiced."

1858: 24 July, *Cardiff and Merthyr Guardian,* p. 6 (56 words).
Advices from Camp Scott to the 12th ult., reported that Colonel Hoffman and Captain Marcy had reached the camp with supplies and reinforcements, and that the army, marching in columns, was to set out upon its march on the following day. Nothing was known of the ulterior designs of the Mormons, but the emigration southward continued.

1858: 24 July, *Cardiff and Merthyr Guardian,* p. 8 (460 words).
A shorter version of the account given in *Potter's Electric News* for 21 July 1858 (see previous entry).

1858: 31 July, *Monmouthshire Beacon,* p. 4 (195 words).
A report of peace in Utah and a description of "Mormonism":

> Brother Jonathan has made it all right with Brigham Young. The olive branch has conquered instead of the sword and the eventful Mormon rebellion is at an end. Mormonism is one of the most monstrous impostures that ever disgraced the face of God's fair earth, it is a revival of the obscene Pagan rites to Venus, an attempt to introduce the "social evil" into the sacred arena of every family fireside.

1858: 31 July, *Cardiff and Merthyr Guardian,* p. 3 (435 words). "The Mormons."
More news of the peaceful settlement between Brigham Young and Johnston's forces:

> The conditions agreed upon at the conference between Governor Cumming, the Peace Commissioners, and the heads of the Mormon Church, are, that the troops shall enter the city without opposition; that the civil officers shall be permitted to perform their duties without interruption; and that unconditional

obedience shall be paid to the laws of the land; while, on the other hand, past offences are to be forgiven, as was stated in the President's proclamation.

1858: 31 July, *North Wales Chronicle*, p. 3 (25 words).

The half-yearly Conference of the Mormons for London, Reading, Kent, and Essex was held on Sunday night, in St. George's Hall, St. George's Road, Southwark.

1858: 31 July, *North Wales Chronicle*, p. 6 (39 words).

The United States. According to a Washington telegram, the Utah peace commissioner reported in a dispatch to the Government that they had settled the difficulty between the United States Government and the Mormons. The dispatch substantially confirms previous accounts.

1858: 31 July, *Monmouthshire Beacon*, p. 5, item 1(110 words).

Reprinted from the *New York Herald.*

The peace commissioners had had a meeting, and it was reported that they had agreed upon conditions of settlement between the rebellious saints and the general government.

1858: 31 July, *Monmouthshire Beacon*, p. 5, item 2 (127 words).

The Utah correspondent of the *St. Louis Republican*, printing on June 18, says:

The conditions agreed upon at the conference between Governor Cumming, the peace commissioners, and the heads of the Mormon Church, are, that the troops shall enter the city without opposition, that the civil officers shall be permitted to perform their duties without interruption, and that unconditional obedience shall be paid to the laws of the land.

1858: 31 July, *Monmouthshire Beacon*, p. 5, item 3 (26 words).

Official advices from Utah give promise that the Indians in that territory might be relied on to remain neutral in case of hostilities with the Mormons.

1858: 31 July, *Monmouthshire Beacon*, p. 5, item 4 (34 words).

A Washington telegram says the Utah peace commissioner, in a dispatch to the government, states that they have settled the difficulty between the government and the Mormons. The dispatch substantially confirms the previous accounts.

1858: 31 July, *Monmouthshire Beacon*, p. 8 (76 words). "Important to Emigrant Mormonites."

A letter has been received by Mr. Watkin, Little London, Willenhall, from his brother Thomas, who some time ago emigrated with others of the Mormon faith, in which he expresses his regret that he had ever been led astray by the accursed Mormons, who, he states, are in an entirely different condition to that represented by their advocates in this country. Trade is also very bad, and the climate is very objectionable.

1858: August, *Y Dysgedydd* (*Instructor*), p. 324 (83 words). "The Widow of Joe Smith."

The widow of Joe Smith the Mormon continues to reside in Nauvoo, but she does not value anything in the "Saints." And she has married a tavern keeper, who considers every prophet as humbug. Joe the younger, who should rightfully be the head of the Mormons, is a strong twenty-two-year old lout who hates Brigham Young and curses the Salt Lakers. Nauvoo was at one time the residence of 20,000 inhabitants but is presently in ruins. *Washington Union*.

1858: August, *Yr Haul* (*Sun*), pp. 241–43 (1,430 words). "The Mormons."

In his opening paragraph, the writer describes this people as "the filthiest and most corrupt sect which has ever named itself under the name of Christianity." He then presents his thesis statement:

> But it is quite likely that the day of the success of Mormonism is about to end, and that its sun is about to set for all eternity.[4]

In the second paragraph the writer presents a depiction of "the fourth exodus of the Mormons" as they travel southward toward Mexico to avoid a conflict with the United States Army.

In the third paragraph the writer declares:

> It is noteworthy that Mormonism cannot exist or live near a Christian civilization, and that is the reason the Mormons retreat from among men and establish themselves on their own. They cannot live except in darkness with which their accursed system is covered. . . . What they have received from Joseph is nothing but an ungodly and sensual creed which shreds all societal relationships and lowers men to the same level as animals.[5]

In the fourth paragraph, the writer describes the arrival of Joseph Smith's followers in Illinois:

> In Illinois the Mormons were at first considered to be the targets of persecution by the slave traders, and they were treated kindly and gently; and new adepts enlisted under their banner.[6]

He then explains the development of Nauvoo—"a pool of corruption"—and the events that led to the death of Joseph Smith.

In the final paragraph, the writer places the blame for the failure of Brigham Young to dissolve the "corrupt traditions" he had received from Joseph Smith, his predecessor:

> Joseph Smith was nothing more than the representative of the most corrupt goods associated with human nature; and in its sum total Mormonism is nothing more than the representative of human nature in its entire corruption and squalor.[7]

1858: 7 August, *North Wales Chronicle*, p. 6 (28 words).

> Later news from Utah states that General Johnston entered Salt Lake City on the 26th June. The Mormons had been invited to return. Provo was still their headquarters.

1858: 14 August, *Monmouthshire Beacon*, p. 4, item 1 (121 words).

Here is the opening statement:

> From Utah we have news to the 23rd of June. Everything was quiet in the territory, and the Mormons were returning to their homes.

1858: 14 August, *Monmouthshire Beacon*, p. 4, item 2 (70 words).

By the last advices the Mormons were fast returning to their homes in Utah, and Brigham Young is to be tried for high treason, proffering the modest request, so characteristic of the man, that it shall be by a jury of Mormons only! Such a lame and impotent conclusion to a tirade of unsurpassed bluster and bravado, has rarely been recorded. What do the saints think of their Prophet now?

1858: 14 August, *North Wales Chronicle*, p. 6 (125 words). "The Mormons—Brigham Young's Idea of a Jury."

The dates from Salt Lake City, by way of Fort Leavenworth, are to the 30th of June. The army had marched from the capital to Cedar Valley, 40 miles below, and Brigham Young, his priests, his wives, and his people, are once more in their homes. No troops were in the city. The newly appointed Government officials were quietly entering upon the discharge of their duties. This news is all telegraphic. There is one other item which is so sublimely impudent that the wires must have made a mistake in transmitting the message—that "Brigham Young was anxious to be tried on the charge of treason, but insists that the jury should consist of Mormons only."

1858: 14 August, *North Wales Chronicle*, p. 8 (81 words).

These mails also bring accounts from the Salt Lake. The Mormons were returning to the Salt Lake City, and Brigham Young wanted to be tried for treason, but to have a Mormon jury. What his object was, does not appear; but we imagine it is to procure his acquittal of any charge made against him by the United States Government, on the ground of his resistance to its authority—and thus obtaining free leave and license to reside again in Utah.

Episode 15.3

Start: Chapters are printed from "Handy Helps to Useful Knowledge" about the Latter-day Saints

The 21 August 1858 issue of the *Cardiff and Merthyr Guardian* has the first chapter of a series entitled "Mormons." A new chapter appears in the following six issues for a total of seven. These are all taken from a source entitled "Handy Helps to Useful Knowledge."

1858: 21 August, *Cardiff and Merthyr Guardian*, p. 8 (1,475 words). "Mormons. Chapter I—Their Book, Prophets, and Mysteries."

1858: 28 August, *Cardiff and Merthyr Guardian*, p. 8 (1,350 words). "Mormons. Chapter II—The Prophet Joseph Smith."

1858: 4 September, *Cardiff and Merthyr Guardian*, p. 8 (2,100 words). "Mormons. Chapter III—The Golden Bible."

1858: 11 September, *Cardiff and Merthyr Guardian*, p. 8 (1,430 words). "Mormons. Chapter IV—The Church of the Latter-day Saints."

1858: 18 September, *Cardiff and Merthyr Guardian*, p. 8 (885 words). "Mormons. Chapter V—Building of Nauvoo—Death of the Prophet, Joe."

1858: 25 September, *Cardiff and Merthyr Guardian*, p. 8, item 1 (1,780 words). "Mormons. Chapter VI—The New Prophet—Exodus and Progress of the Saints."

1858: 2 October, *Cardiff and Merthyr Guardian*, p. 8 (1,345 words). "Mormons. Chapter VII—Mysteries and Present State of Mormonism."

End: Chapters are printed from "Handy Helps to Useful Knowledge" about the Latter-day Saints

1858: 21 August, *Merthyr Telegraph*, p. 4 (60 words). "Pigs in Harness."

> From the Mormon country, Governor Cummings testifies to having observed a wagon on the road from Salt Lake City to Provo, which was drawn by pigs harnessed to the tongue by an ingenious combination of straps and cords. In it was seated a fat man, who excited his team into a trot by the aid of a black snake whip.

1858: 21 August, *Monmouthshire Beacon*, p. 8 (57 words).

> Later news had been received from Utah. The territory was perfectly tranquil, and the general officers were in high favor with the Mormons. None of the soldiers of General Johnston's army were allowed to enter Salt Lake City, and strict orders had been issued, prohibiting any interference with the Mormons. The peace commissioners had left for Washington.

1858: 28 August, *Monmouthshire Beacon*, p. 3 (1,260 words). "The Mormons."

The *Morning Herald* provides considerable detail concerning the ending of the Utah War, then a very negative assessment of Brigham Young and his unlawful activities.

1858: 28 August, *Caernarvon and Denbigh Herald*, p. 10 (295 words). "Escape from the Mormons."

> Mr. J. D. Wilson, a very zealous disciple of the Mormon faith, who went out from Newcastle-upon-Tyne, with his wife and family, to the Salt Lake City, has found out his mistake and left the place.

The writer then quotes from a letter Wilson had written to his parents about his negative experience in Utah. Upon discovering that "Mormons preach one thing and practice another," he laid plans to leave:

> Brigham Young would have allowed me to leave Salt Lake in March last, but not my family. He would not allow me a horse, and if I had left, I should have had to carry on my back meat sufficient to serve me for 1,000 miles. If I had been mad enough to attempt it, they would have followed twenty or thirty miles and then killed me; they say, "Dead men tell no stories."

Wilson credits the coming of Governor Cumming for making it possible for his "escape."

1858: 3 September, *Cambrian*, (105 words).

A brief description of a mob attack incited by Andrew B. Hepburn in the London area:

> The Mormonites at Stepney have become objects of the popular indignation, and on Friday a discourse was delivered in the street outside their conventicle by Mr. Hepburn of Swansea notoriety which had the effect of inciting the mob to an attack upon the elders and their followers, who were at the time engaged in the mysteries of their worship. The affair became serious and the Mormons would have fared badly but for the protection of the police who had great difficulty in escorting them to a place of safety. The anti-Mormonite agitator and his lieutenant have been bound over to keep the peace.

1858: 3 September, *Cambrian* (1,450 words). "The Great Salt Lake City."

A lengthy description of Salt Lake City written by a "Utah Correspondent of the *New York Herald*." Much of the information is about the houses built for Brigham Young and other leaders. A somewhat longer version appeared in the *Patriot* for 18 September 1858 (see previous entry).

1858: 4 September, *Monmouthshire Beacon*, p. 3 (155 words).

The American Peace Commissioners arrived at Washington from Utah to work out an agreement.

1858: 4 September, *Usk Observer*, p. 2 (545 words). "Brigham Young in a Fix."

According to the Utah correspondent for the *New York Herald*, "Brigham Young, Esq., has really received a revelation from the Lord commanding him to hold his voice for a season." When asked when people could hear Brigham Young preach anew, two of his wives responded: "Brigham will not preach again, so long as you have a Gentile shorthand reporter here to take down his discourses."

1858: 4 September, *Monmouthshire Beacon*, p. 4 (137 words).

> We have a curious item of intelligence from Utah. The Peace Commissioners report to the Federal Government that no passage is to be found in the Book of Mormon authorizing polygamy or concubinage, so that Brigham Young in establishing the system of many wives in his community, has directly contravened an express command. This is a pretty exposure verily for the poor deluded women who have fallen in the power of his clutches, but happily they are now free if they please, and may live in something like comfort under the protection of the American Government. As for the arch fiend Young himself, it was expected he would be tried for treason and banished from the State, which will be a happy riddance for his followers, who complain of being worn down by his tyrannies and exactions.

1858: 10 September, *Cambrian* (945 words). "The Mormons."

A correspondent for the *London Times* "expresses his doubts that the peace patched up with the United States Government and the Mormons will be lasting and thinks that a reaction will follow worse than the original disease." The writer provides his impressions of visiting Salt Lake City just before the inhabitants returned from Provo:

> The houses were all closed, and windows and doors closed up with rough boards. Scarce a human being could be seen in the streets for in the entire city there were only two or three hundred men left to guard the property and to apply the torch if orders should come to do so.

He writes the following about Brigham Young:

> I should judge him to be shrewd in worldly affairs, a good business manager, a judge of human nature and capable of adapting it to his will. The cast of his mind, however, is evidently low and vulgar."

He writes the following about Heber C. Kimball:

> His reputation as a husband and father is bad, and many are the secretly whispered tales of his jealous cruelty to his wives, some of whom are younger than his firstborn child. He is certainly the most vulgar and blasphemous wretch it has been my misfortune to meet.

He writes the following about the women among the Saints:

> The women appear to be, as a class, discontented and unhappy, painfully conscious that their natural affections must ever be stifled, and the love they would share alone with a husband be divided with several female partners.

His final assessment is as follows:

> To all outward appearance the best order prevails; but it is evident that it is the good order of despotism.

1858: 11 September, *Usk Observer*, p. 2 (690 words). "Brigham Young and Kimball."

The writer of this article for the *Usk Observer* obviously draws from the writings of the correspondent for the *London Times*, as does the writer for the *Cambrian* for 10 September 1858, but this writer provides considerably more detail in his impressions about Brigham Young and Heber C. Kimball.

1858: 11 September, *Cardiff and Merthyr Guardian*, p. 3 (80 words).

> Later news from Utah was received by the arrival of the Salt Lake mail at Leavenworth. All the Mormons who were able had returned from Provo, and matters were apparently quiet. Brigham Young, fearing assassination, as was alleged, had shut himself up in his residence under a strong guard of his followers. General Johnston was making preparations for going into permanent quarters. Colonel Loring, with three companies of the 3rd Infantry and 100 riflemen, had departed for New Mexico.

1858: 11 September, *Cardiff and Merthyr Guardian*, p. 7 (2,120 words). "The Mormons at Utah."

The writer draws from the same letter of the *Times* correspondent as do the writers for similar articles in the *Cambrian* for 10 September 1858 and the *Usk Observer* for 11 September 1858, p. 2.

1858: 18 September, *Monmouthshire Beacon*, p. 5 (55 words).

> Letters from Salt Lake City, of July 30th, mention that preparations were going forward in Utah for the territorial elections, and those of the residents who were so disposed would have an opportunity to vote for candidates to fill the offices occupied by members of the Mormon priesthood. Brigham Young was residing at Utah.

1858: 18 September, *Usk Observer*, p. 4 (21 words). "Lives of the Latter-day Saints."

> The Mormons complain of persecution—but they have had no trials. Which of them has as yet been indicted for polygamy?

1858: 18 September, *Y Gwladgarwr* (*Patriot*), p. 2 (1,800 words). "Salt Lake City and the Mormons."

This is a longer version of the article that appeared in the 3 September 1858 issue of the *Cambrian*, the 11 September 1858 issue of the *Usk Observer*, and the 11 September 1858 issue of the *Cardiff and Merthyr Guardian* (see previous entries). All are taken from the *London Times* for 1 September 1858, p. 5.

Episode 15.4

Start: Henrietta Polydore is returned to her father in England

1858: 25 September, *Caernarvon and Denbigh Herald*, p. 10 (665 words). "An English Girl Rescued from the Mormons."

> An important law case (writes the Utah correspondent of the *New York Herald*) has just been disposed of by Judges Eckels and Sinclair, in which Henry Polydore, of Gloucester, England, was plaintiff, and Samuel W. Richards, a Mormon dignitary, and Jane Mayer, his fourth wife, were defendants. The nature of the case is fully explained in the subjoined letter of Mr. Polydore to the Earl of Malmesbury. It is dated Gloucester, March 26th, 1858:
>
> > My Lord, in 1854, my only daughter, Henrietta Polydore, then eight years of age, was abducted by her mother, without my consent and against my will, from the school at which I had placed her in Lincolnshire, and taken in a company of Mormons to America. At that time and whilst my wife and child were in the United States, I made strenuous endeavors to recover possession of the latter, and in my efforts I was aided by the Earl of Carendon, then her Majesty's Secretary of State for Foreign Affairs, who directed instructions to be sent out to the British consuls at New Orleans and Portland to aid me in recovering my daughter. However, all my attempts failed, and the child is still withheld from me. In 1855 the mother and child proceeded to the Mormons' settlement, Utah, and at the Salt Lake City was the child left on the mother coming to England in 1856. Mrs. Polydore long since returned to the United States, but it would seem she has not yet rejoined the child at the Salt Lake City. I should name that I have not seen either my wife or child since the latter's abduction in 1854, and that I have never been able to hold communication in any manner with my child. A few days since I received a letter from Mr. Hyde, an entire stranger to me, dated New Orleans, U. S. A., simply in which he apprised me, in mercy to the child, and in justice to myself, of the movements and intentions of the mother, and of the position of my child. Mr. Hyde, after informing me that he had been a Mormon, had a few days previously met Mrs. Polydore in that city (New Orleans), and that she desired to reach Salt Lake City this year, if possible, and to remove the child as soon as practicable; and, he added, your daughter Henrietta is now living under the assumed name of Lucy, with her aunt Jane Mayer (a sister of Mrs.

Polydore), who is the fourth wife of S. W. Richards, a Mormon dignitary, at Salt Lake City.

The government of Great Britain, through her representative, Lord Napier, as a matter of international courtesy, called upon the government of the United States to afford such assistance as might be in their power, with the view of securing the personal safety of the little girl, and her restoration to her father. Instructions were immediately given to General Johnston, commanding department at Utah, through the War Department, to adopt such measures as might seem to him advisable to bring about the release of the little girl from the Mormon community. But a different state of affairs existing here to what there was at the time the instructions were given, the General delivered over the papers to the civil authorities, whereupon the Attorney General, W. J. Cormack, prepared a petition, and brought the parties before Judges Eckels and Sinclair upon a writ of habeas corpus. A. G. Brown, Jr., assisted in the prosecution as attorney. The case was before the court for three consecutive days, and was finally disposed of by a judgment in favor of the plaintiff, Henry Polydore. The little girl is now in the custody of the United States Marshal, and will be sent on to the British Legation at Washington as soon as her wardrobe can be prepared for so long a journey, and a responsible person to take charge of her.

1858: 25 September, *Monmouthshire Beacon*, p. 4 (275 words).

An election has been held in Utah, in the Great Salt Lake City, when all the Mormon candidates were returned by large majorities. A proof, however, that there is a satisfactory return to something like order has been the giving up of a little girl to her English father, Mr. Henry Polydore of Gloucester. It appears that his wife left her husband and joined the Mormons; subsequently, in 1854, abducted their child, a girl eight years old, and carried her off to Utah. For a considerable time, all trace was lost, but intelligence being obtained, the intervention of the Foreign-office was sought, and the active assistance of Lord Napier was obtained. Instructions were immediately given to General Johnston, commanding department at Utah, through the War department, to adopt such measures as might seem to him advisable to bring about the release of the little girl from the Mormon community. The General delivered over the papers to the civil authorities, whereupon the Attorney General, W. J. Cormack, prepared a petition, and brought the parties before Judges Eckels and Sinclair upon a writ of *habeas corpus*. The case was before the Court for three consecutive days, and was finally disposed of by a judgment in favor of the plaintiff, Henry Polydore. The little girl is now in custody of the United States Marshal, and will be sent on to the British Legation at Washington as soon as her wardrobe can be prepared for so long a journey, and a responsible person to take charge of her. Another year, and the child would have been of age to be assigned to the harem of some Mormon.

1858: 4 December, *Cardiff and Merthyr Guardian*, p. 8 (70 words). "The Mormons."

> By the British and North American mail steamship America, which arrived at Liverpool on Monday, we have the following: "Judge Eckles, having in charge Henrietta Polidore, who had been rescued from the Mormons on a writ of *Habeas Corpus* at the request of the British Government, had arrived at St. Louis, *en route* for Washington. The girl was abducted from Gloucester, England, four years ago.

1859: 8 January, *Cardiff and Merthyr Guardian*, p. 3 (140 words). "Restitution of an English Girl by the Mormons."

> Among the passengers by the steamer *Africa*, for Liverpool, were a messenger of the British Government and the girl named Henrietta Polydore, who was brought from Utah by Judge Eckles, in obedience to instructions from our Government. Miss Polydore was some years since taken from England by her mother, who had embraced the faith of the Mormons, and her father applied to the British authorities for her restoration. After due investigation of the facts before the Federal Court at Great Salt Lake City it was decided to restore the girl to her father, and she was accordingly brought to Washington and delivered to the custody of Lord Napier, the British minister, who has dispatched her to England. It is said that the mother of the girl followed her to Washington.

End: Henrietta Polydore is returned to her father in England

1858: 25 September, *Cardiff and Merthyr Guardian*, p. 8, item 2 (21 words). "Lives of the Latter-day Saints."

The same article as in the *Usk Observer* for 18 September 1858 (see previous entry).

1858: October, *Seren Cymru* (*Star of Wales*), p. 456 (270 words). "Mormons Losing Ground."

The writer reports that many Latter-day Saints are now abandoning their faith. He quotes a paragraph from the *Jefferson Advertiser* to support his claim:

> With one voice, they condemned Brigham Young and the apostles, and his murder by the Mormons who remained in Fort Scott was talked about as a certainty. They all, without exception, loathe Mormonism, and have rejected it, and they demonstrate a resolve to do what they can from now on to try to oppose and eradicate Mormonism from the face of the earth.

1858: 2 October, *North Wales Chronicle*, p. 2 (155 words). "Mormon Blasphemy."

> A correspondent of the *New York Herald* writes—"I am told, *sub rosa*, by some of the Mormons of high standing, who are in the counsels of Brigham, that the prophet has a new Bible ready for the printer. Existing circumstances prevent its immediate publication. This Bible makes a god out of Brigham, and constitutes polygamy as the *summum bonum* of all religion. I am also informed by large numbers of persons that Brigham has heretofore been frequently called god in the Church. Speakers have thus addressed the audience—'Hero is our god' (pointing to Brigham); 'we worship a live god, and will have nothing to

do with dead gods.' The numbers of the persons, both apostates and saints, who have told me this, and their apparent sincerity, ought to be sufficient to gain credence for it. With any other people it would be beyond belief, but with this people all things (blasphemous) are possible.

1858: 2 October, *Monmouthshire Beacon*, p. 3 (80 words).

One week's later news from Salt Lake City has been received. The dates are to the 14th ult. There is little of importance from that quarter. The Indians were somewhat troublesome, and the murder of several Mormons was reported. On the arrival of the judges in the territory, the trials of Mormon leaders indicted for treason would be commenced. It will probably be merely an investigation, as the President's proclamation pardoning the rebels upon their submission will be honorably carried out.

1858: 2 October, *Caernarvon and Denbigh Herald*, p. 9 (29 words).

News from the Salt Lake is to the 14th of August, but there is nothing important. The Indians were somewhat troublesome, and the murder of several Mormons was reported.

1858: 9 October, *North Wales Chronicle*, p. 2 (180 words). "Three Hundred Mormons Renouncing the Faith."

A correspondent sends the following to the *Jefferson City Examiner*, under date Sept. 4: "I left Camp Scott on the 13th of June. The Mormon excitement had entirely abated. Several Mormon trains had passed Camp Scott on their way to the States. I came down with two Mormon trains from Camp Scott, numbering about 300 persons, who were chiefly English and Scotch; and the principal topic of their conversation throughout the absurdity of Mormonism and its principles. They were all unanimous in their denunciations of Brigham Young and his apostles, and talked of his assassination by the Mormons who remained at Fort Scott as a sure event. They have all (without exception) become disgusted with Mormonism, and have renounced it, and expressed their determination from henceforth to use all their efforts for the total annihilation of Mormonism. They all express their desire to return to their native countries, and would, if they had the means to do so, in order that they might be instrumental in saving others from the baneful influence of Mormonism."

1858: 9 October, *Cardiff and Merthyr Guardian*, p. 7 (24 words).

A Mormon preacher traveling about the country on a velocipede has been taken up at Bedford on suspicion of stealing that instrument of locomotion.

1858: 16 October, *Caernarvon and Denbigh Herald*, p. 2 (24 words).

The same article as in *Cardiff and Merthyr Guardian* for 9 October 1858 (see previous entry).

1858: 16 October, *Monmouthshire Beacon*, p. 2 (24 words).

The same article as in *Cardiff and Merthyr Guardian* for 9 October 1858 (see previous entry).

1858: 23 October, *North Wales Chronicle*, p. 2 (395 words). "Fight in the Streets of the Salt Lake City."

A detailed description of an altercation between Major General George D. Grant and Tom Williams. The latter had left Salt Lake City and the Church in 1856. The nature of their disagreement is not clear.

1858: 9 November, *Cardiff and Merthyr Guardian*, p. 7 (24 words).

The same article as in the *Cardiff and Merthyr Guardian* for 9 October 1858 (see previous entry).

1858: 13 November, *Caernarvon and Denbigh Herald*, p. 9 (110 words).

> Advices from St. Louis of the 26th say the Salt Lake mail, with dates of the 25th September, reached St. Joseph on the 17th. Business was very brisk at Salt Lake. Trains were constantly arriving from California with goods and provisions. There was good feeling between the Mormons and Gentiles. The former speak in high terms of Governor Cumming. General Johnston's command consists of 7000 to 8000 men, including troops and employees, all of whom were consolidated in one grand encampment, and would remain together during the winter. There were about 4000 troops at Fort Bridger under Colonel Cambrey. Colonel Morrison, of the 7th Infantry, had arrived at Camp Floyd.

1858: 13 November, *Cardiff and Merthyr Guardian*, p. 3 (120 words).

> The Salt Lake mail to the 25th of September reached St. Joseph's Mobile, on the 16th ult. Everything was quiet in the Territory, and a good feeling is reported to exist between the Mormons and the Gentiles. Business was brisk at Salt Lake City. Trains of goods and provisions were constantly arriving from California. The supply trains from the States were also arriving in good condition and great numbers. Sixty had passed Fort Bridger, and twenty were met on the Streetwater, and eight were north of the Platte. All the troops under General Johnston are consolidated in one encampment. His command, including employees, numbers 7000 or 8000. About 4000 men were also at Fort Bridger, under Colonel Cambrey.

1858: 24 December, *Cambrian* (620 words).

A detailed account of William Lewis, a policeman who was found hiding under the bed in a brothel in Swansea by a fellow policeman. Lewis was sentenced to ten days in prison with hard labor. Here is a note at the end of the article:

> The defendant is a married man and was for some time one of the chief members of those fanatics—the Latter-day Saints—in which capacity, so we are informed, he would sometimes be engaged preaching.

Episode 15.5

Start: The Instructor *prints seven long articles entitled "Mormonism"*

1858: December, *Y Dysgedydd* (*Instructor*), pp. 465–68 (2,910 words). "Mormonism."

This is the first in a series of seven articles by the title of "Mormonism." The writer declares his general intent in this opening paragraph:

> History is what I have foremost in my mind in writing this article, and history will be foremost in my mind as I write the articles I intend to publish thereafter. I do not intend to reason for or reason against. Mormonism, as a system of doctrine, is beneath our wasting time with such tasks. It deserves nothing but scorn and disgust. But as a demonstration of untamed religion in belief, and a composition of deceitful government in practice, it has a kind of majesty which calls for the attention of the statesman and the philosopher, the philanthropist and Christians.

In this lengthy essay, the writer touches on a number of points:

- The origin of the word "Mormon"
- The relationship of the Latter-day Saints over the past few months with the United States government
- The forced movement of the Latter-day Saints from Illinois to Utah
- The United States military expedition sent to Utah
- The peaceful agreement that was reached

The writer offers his general opinion about the Latter-day Saints:

> Whatever virtues may pertain to the Mormons, it appears that truthfulness and humility are not among them; and whatever they may lack, it cannot be said that they are lacking in effrontery.

He concludes with an expression of his feelings for his fellow Welshmen:

> We can do no less than feel genuine concern in the matter, since so many of our compatriots, yes, sons and daughters of Wales, have been beguiled by rascals, left the country of their birth, and have settled in a territory where God is dishonored, the Savior is blasphemed, and the principles of kindness, morality, and religion are shamefully scorned.

1859: January, *Y Dysgedydd* (*Instructor*), pp. 27–30 (3,130 words). "Mormonism," part two of seven.

The writer has borrowed heavily from English-language sources for this history of Joseph Smith's life and the rise of The Church of Jesus Christ of Latter-day Saints.

1859: February, *Y Dysgedydd* (*Instructor*), pp. 58–61 (2,515 words). "Mormonism," part 3 of 7.

1859: April, *Y Dysgedydd* (*Instructor*), pp. 146–50 (2,840 words). "Mormonism," part 4 of 7.

1859: June, *Y Dysgedydd* (*Instructor*), pp. 217–20 (2,760 words). "Mormonism," part 5 of 7.

In the January, February, and April issues of the *Instructor* for 1859, the writer focused on the history of The Church of Jesus Christ of Latter-day Saints, for which he borrowed from a variety of sources. In this issue, however, he declares:

> We are taking a look at a moral system that has been established in the depths of the desert—a system that denies our laws, our rites, our literature, and our God. A totally new invention, founded on new opinions, completely opposite to our beliefs, and perfectly contrary to all our family feelings. It is a system that is a mixture of Judaism, Catholicism, Mohammedanism, Paganism, and Socialism.

Regarding miracles, the writer declares:

> Time fails us to discuss what they claim about miracles. One does not really know how to feel upon hearing their stories, whether to laugh, to weep, or to wonder—laugh at the humor, weep at the deceit, or wonder at the impudence of the assertors and the stupidity of the believers.

The writer makes a few observations about Dan Jones and his brother, Reverend John Jones. Referring to the incident that took place on 31 December 1848 in Merthyr Tydfil, the writer tells of the experience Dan Jones had with casting out devils.[8]

1859: July, *Y Dysgedydd* (*Instructor*), pp. 270–72 (1,800 words). "Mormonism," part 6 of 7.

Taken from the *New York Times*, this article begins with information about the "Danites," also known as "The Destroying Angels." These men were reportedly "an armed group" who "had taken an oath the support the leaders of the 'Saints' in everything they did or said, whether it was good or evil." The writer then relates the story of Frederic Loba, a Swiss convert who became disaffected from the Church after going to Utah in 1854. Fearing for his life, Loba succeeding in "escaping" from Utah in 1857 and later told his story to a reporter of the *New York Times*.

1859: September, *Y Dysgedydd* (*Instructor*), pp. 337–39 (2,320 words). "Mormonism," part seven of seven.

The writer begins with an assessment of his previous words:

> The history given shows clearly the nonsense, the evil, and the arrogance of the Mormon family, and the lamentable surprise is that so many have fallen prey to it. In the latest statistics of this kingdom, their number in England and Wales is counted at thirty thousand. The Mormons themselves say that around four thousand of these are Welsh by birth and language. What explanation can be given for this?

But instead of offering an explanation, the writer concludes:

> Mormonism is so vile as a system that there is no use trying to analyze it. That would only be spending time analyzing filth. Some things are so extremely unreasonable that it is difficult to contradict them. It is very difficult to reason with men who have no abilities to present their own argument, or abilities to comprehend the argument of anyone else.

End: The Instructor *prints seven long articles entitled "Mormonism"*

Notes

1. *Zion's Trumpet*, December 1857, 408.
2. *Wrexham Advertiser*, 8 August 1857, 2.
3. *Wrexham Advertiser*, 26 June 1858, 4.
4. *The Sun*, August 1858, 241.
5. Ibid., 241–42.
6. Ibid., 242.
7. Ibid., 243.
8. See *Millennial Star*, 11:38–42.

Chapter 16

Episodes

16.1—Horace Greeley interviews Brigham Young on 13 July 1859

Salient Events

- **5 February 1859.** The writer for this brief article in the *Cardiff and Merthyr Guardian* quotes from a letter written by a Latter-day Saint "signing himself John Davies, of Merthyr":

> According to my promise to you at Cardiff, I now address you a few lines. Last Sunday I was at Swansea with President Evans and brother John. We had a very good conference there, and indeed have had in each of the conferences in the mission. We have endeavored to instill in the minds of the Saints the counsel and instructions we received from you at Cardiff, and my faith is, that a large amount will be added to the Emigration Fund the coming year from Wales. I have been traveling in the ministry nearly eight years, and I can truly say that I never saw so good a feeling generally as there is now. The whole Welsh mission, with but very few exceptions, is in good working order and healthy condition. President Evans, myself, and brother John are as one in mind and feelings, and so we have been. We are looking for a good time at Birmingham.[1]

The writer for the *Cardiff and Merthyr Guardian* observes that "the agents of Mormonism are making strenuous efforts to spread their debasing tenets throughout the Welsh district." He also remarks that the author of the letter "expresses himself confident of making great progress in Wales" and then adds the following comment: "For the sake, not only of true religion, but of common decency, we hope he will find himself thoroughly deceived."[2]

- **12 March 1859.** An article titled "Quarreling Mormons at Risca" is published in the *Cardiff Times*. Thomas Bullock, a Latter-day Saint, had pressed charges against Prudence Taylor for breaking the back door of his house and eight panes of glass. The questions posed to Bullock by a Mr. Owen, representing the defendant, suggest that Taylor had left her husband in order to go off to Salt Lake City with Joseph Thatcher, a Latter-day Saint, who was probably serving a mission in Wales at the time. Taylor "was ordered to pay 19s., the amount of damage, with costs, and told that she might reserve the right to sue Bullock for the assault."[3]
- **11 April 1859.** Elder Henry Harries and Mary Rees Harries sail from Liverpool on board the *William Tapscott*, along with 723 other Latter-day Saints. Only a small number of these emigrants were Welsh. Henry and Mary had married just four weeks earlier.[4] Nine years earlier, Henry's right arm and hand had been mangled in a mill accident. But without the use of his injured arm, Henry had managed to travel to Salt Lake City in 1854 and then to return to Wales on a mission in 1857. After returning to the United States in 1859, Henry and Mary settled in Salt Lake City and became the parents of fourteen children. Henry returned to Wales one more time in 1886 to receive his inheritance of about $3,000, an inheritance that his father, while living, had denied him as punishment for his conversion to The Church of Jesus Christ of Latter-day Saints.
- **9 September 1859.** An account of Horace Greeley's 13 July 1859 interview with Brigham Young is presented in this issue of the *Welshman*. The complete interview appeared the following day in the *North Wales Chronicle*. See Episode 16.1.
- **10 December 1859.** A 24 September 1859 letter from Daniel Daniels, writing from his home in Salt Lake City, appears in this issue of *Zion's Trumpet*. Daniels provides information on a number of the Welsh Saints then living in various parts of Utah, and he extends an invitation for the Latter-day Saints still in Wales to make haste in joining him in Zion.

(The five extant issues of the 1859 *Zion's Trumpet* offer sufficient pagination information to conclude that a complete, weekly volume was published during the year.)

Commentary

1859: 22 January, *Caernarvon and Denbigh Herald*, p. 9 (130 words).

We have papers and correspondence from Utah up to the 4th December. President Buchanan's proclamation of pardon to the Mormons was before the court of the third judicial district. Judge Sinclair claimed the right first to find out the guilty, pass sentence, and then apply the pardon. The prosecuting attorney for the United States supports the executive, commissioners, and new governor, and regards the course of the judge as unnecessarily tending to increase difficulties in that territory. . . . Accounts from Utah state that the service of a civil process upon Brigham Young had been resisted by his friends, and that trouble would perhaps grow out of it. There is, however, but little danger of serious difficulty in that region so long as General Johnston with his troops remains there.

1859: 5 February, *Caernarvon and Denbigh Herald*, p. 10 (175 words). "A Mormon Invitation."

Original punctuation and spelling have been maintained:

> A man of the name of Thomas Read,[5] who five years since deserted his wife and children to go to the Salt Lake City, has just written to Derby, asking his wife to come out to him. In a long letter, filled partly with "cant" and descriptions of his possessions, he states this strange inducement for his wife to join the Mormon sect: "I have Got A Nother wife and a Little Girl and Boy the Little Girl her name is Jane Elizabeth and the Little Boy is namd Thomas Robey Read the Little Girl is Just Lick my Little Jane and the Little Boy is Just Like my Thomas William and of them I am not ashamd Jane and Me Often talk abought you and wishes you ware all heare if you Can Make your Self comfortable a long with another woman or More as the Case may bee and Subject your Selvs to the law of Christ." Death has spared the poor woman, to whom this letter was addressed, the pain of perusing its atrocities.

1859: 5 February, *Cardiff and Merthyr Guardian*, p. 5 (240 words). "Mormonism in Wales."

> The agents of Mormonism are making strenuous efforts to spread their debasing tenets throughout the Welsh district. In a newspaper published by the fanatics, appears a letter from a man signing himself John Davies, of Merthyr, to President Calkin. He expresses himself confident of making great progress in Wales, but for the sake, not only of true religion, but of common decency, we hope he will find himself thoroughly deceived. Here is part of his epistle: "According to my promise to you at Cardiff, I now address you a few lines. Last Sunday I was at Swansea with President Evans and brother John. We had a very good conference there, and indeed have had in each of the conferences in the mission. We have endeavored to instill in the minds of the Saints the counsel and instructions we received from you at Cardiff, and my faith is, that a large amount will be added to the Emigration Fund the coming year from Wales. I have been traveling in the ministry nearly eight years, and I can truly say that I never saw so good a feeling generally as there is now. The whole Welsh mission, with but very few exceptions, is in good working order and healthy condition. President Evans, myself, and brother John are as one in mind and feelings, and so we have been. We are looking for a good time at Birmingham."

1859: March, *Y Dysgedydd* (*Instructor*), p. 124 (146 words). "Mormon Invitation."

The same article with some variation as appeared in the *Caernarvon and Denbigh Herald* for 5 February 1859 (see previous entry).

1859: 12 March, *Cardiff Times*, p. 4 (375 words). "Quarreling Mormons at Risca."

> Newport Police Intelligence. Saturday. (Before the Reverend T. Pope and J. Lewis, Esq.)
>
> Prudence Taylor was charged with breaking the windows of Thomas Bullock. Mr. Owen was for the defendant. Complainant said the defendant came to his house on Sunday week, and tried to force her way in, and in so doing broke the back door. He put her out, when she broke eight panes of glass. Mr. Owen (to complainant): I believe you had the misfortune to lodge in this woman's house at one time? Complainant: Yes. Mr. Owen: You are a Mormon; didn't you try to get her to the Salt Lake? Complainant: My religion teaches me to pray for the Queen upon her throne, her administration, and her subjects, from the highest to the lowest. I have always done so, but don't know whether you have or not—that's my religion, if you want to know anything about it. Mr. Owen: Did you tell her it would be a good thing if she would go to Salt Lake and become one of your wives? Complainant: No, I didn't. I did not strike her. I merely lifted her by the arms and put her out of the house. She did not break the window before I put her out. I never made any arrangement with her husband to go to Salt Lake. Their goods came to my house on a Monday morning, on which occasion her husband came to me at about six o'clock and said, "My wife is gone off again with that man (the man meant was Joseph Thatcher), and will you be kind enough to let me put my goods into your house, for I'm determined I will not live with her anymore." It is no difference whether Thatcher is of her or of my persuasion. Mr. Owen, addressing the bench, did not contend against the fact that the offence had been committed, but submitted that there had been much provocation. Mr. Pope said the complainant should not have taken the law into his own hands. The defendant was ordered to pay 19s., the amount of damage, with costs, and told that she might reserve the right to sue Bullock for the assault.

1859: 12 March, *Cardiff and Merthyr Guardian*, p. 3 (230 words). "Dissensions among the Latter-day Saints."

This article has similar content, though with fewer details, as the one in the *Cardiff Times* for 12 March 1859 (see previous entry).

1859: 18 March, *Cambrian*, (30 words). "Marriage."

This is the announcement of the marriage of Henry Harries, a Latter-day Saint missionary, to Mary Rees.

> On 15th inst. at Llanelly parish church (by license) Rev. D.M. Rees, curate, Mr Henry Harries President of the Latter-day Saint conference, to Miss Mary Rees of Meadow, Bedwellty, Mon.

Henry had gone to Utah in 1854 and three years later returned to Wales on a mission. His marriage to Mary Rees took place just a few days before they left Wales for Utah.

1859: 9 April, *Caernarvon and Denbigh Herald*, p. 10 (50 words).

> The steamship *L. N. Hvidt*, belonging to the Danish General Steam Navigation Company, is expected to arrive at Hull on Sunday next, from Copenhagen, with about 400 Mormon passengers, en route for the Salt Lake.

We understand there is a further lot of about 500 to follow. *Eastern Counties Herald*.

1859: 9 April, *Merthyr Telegraph*, p. 4 (100 words). "A Gentile and His Mormon Bride Separated in Utah."

A Gentile resident of Frogtown a short time ago went over to Provo after a young woman, who, it seems had taken a fancy to him, and who wished to leave Provo and come and live in Frogtown with her Gentile admirer. But a mob collected around the house where she and her lover were, and he was advised that he would find it conducive to his health to leave immediately, which he did. The young woman was then taken out and publicly whipped.—Utah Correspondent of the *New York Tribune*.

Frogtown has since been renamed Fairfield.

1859: 30 April, *Chepstow Weekly Advertiser*, p. 3 (195 words). "Latest about the Mormons."

Advices from Utah to the 9th of March had reached New York, from which it is evident that the citizens of that territory conclude that it is about time to again knock at the door of Congress and apply for admission into the Union as a sovereign State. From private sources we learn that the Mormons are satisfied that sending the army and new Federal officers to their territory, though at first it promised a collision, is turning to their advantage in a political point of view. Many of the charges against them have, in the course of investigation, been refuted, and consequently the prejudice of the Gentiles in the States is somewhat diminished. Every mail brings confirmation of a good understanding between the military and civil chief in the territory on Mormon matters. It is stated, however, but with what degree of truth we do not vouch, that Brigham Young is unpopular with the Mormons and that he has agents in the northern provinces of Mexico, and also in Central America, prospecting for a location to which he and his partisans may remove, and set up an independent hierarchy.

1859: 30 April, *Merthyr Telegraph*, p. 3 (195 words).

The same article as in the *Chepstow Weekly Advertiser* for 30 April 1859 (see previous entry).

1859: 30 April, *North Wales Chronicle*, p. 5 (195 words).

The same article as in the *Chepstow Weekly Advertiser* for 30 April 1859 (see previous entry).

1859: 14 May, *Caernarvon and Denbigh Herald*, p. 2 (45 words).

Accounts from Utah represent the condition of that territory to be deplorable. Irreconcilable dissentions exist among the United States officials. The Mormon Juries persist in refusing to return verdicts against Mormon prisoners, and a collision between the Mormons and the United States troops is apprehended.

1859: 28 May, *North Wales Chronicle*, p. 2 (110 words). "Arrival of English Mormons in America."

> On Wednesday morning a part of about one hundred and thirty Mormons came from the East by the Central Railroad and went to the west by the Canada route. They are destined for Utah, to join the colony of Brigham Young. This party was composed chiefly of females, many of whom were young and tolerably fair. They were from England and Wales, and were attended by Elders, who took good care none of the lambs strayed from the flock. The party were not disposed to hold conversation with the "Gentiles"—and had doubtless been advised to preserve the silence they maintained. *Washington Union.*

1859: 4 June, *Merthyr Telegraph*, p. 4 (155 words). "Reinforcement of Mormons."

> On Friday the ship *William Tapscott* arrived at New York, bringing seven hundred and twenty-six Mormon immigrants, including women and children. One half of them are from England, Scotland, Ireland, Wales; the other half from Norway, Sweden, Denmark. On Saturday about five hundred of them left for the West by the Albany steamer. President Brigham Young had sent positive instructions to his agents to push all immigrants forward towards Utah as rapidly as possible, and in thirty hours from the time they landed at Castle Garden, the main body were in motion up the Hudson. Verily, the Mormons have energy. The company had altogether 50,000 lbs. of baggage. It is said that not a person tarried behind who had the means to pursue his journey westward, but on the other hand, great numbers went on with the certainty that they must suffer toil and privation by reason of their poverty. *Boston Courier.*

1859: 4 June, *Wrexham Advertiser*, p. 2 (155 words).

The same article as in the *Merthyr Telegraph* for 4 June 1859 (see previous entry).

1859: 4 June, *North Wales Chronicle*, p. 3, item 1 (155 words).

The same article as in the *Merthyr Telegraph* for 4 June 1859 (see previous entry).

1859: 4 June, *North Wales Chronicle*, p. 3, item 2 (2,230 words). "A Religious Riot."

A very long article recounting Andrew Balfour Hepburn's arrest for creating a riot and disturbance at a lecture hall and assaulting James Portch, a police constable, in the execution of his duty.

1859: 11 June, *Caernarvon and Denbigh Herald*, p. 10 (265 words). "The Mormon Quarrel."

The writer reports that Judge Cradlebaugh, the federal judge for the district in Salt Lake City, believed that his life was in danger from uncooperative Latter-day Saints and called upon General Johnston for aid and protection. But Governor Cumming intervened and "openly took part with the Mormons." The writer concludes:

> What will be the end of it nobody knows, and to tell the truth, nobody cares. People are generally very tired of the Mormon imbroglio, and with a great war

raging in Europe are not disposed to spend much time in thinking of a little war on the shores of the Salt Lake.

1859: 25 June, *North Wales Chronicle*, p. 6 (125 words).

The latest advices from Utah represent that the people are in an excited and turbulent condition, bordering on rebellion. Governor Cumming had issued a proclamation ordering the Mormon militia, who had assembled for belligerent purposes, to disperse. These parties are a portion of the militia called out by the governor to resist the entrance of the Government troops during the session of the court at Salt Lake City. The Mormons are being monthly augmented by the arrival of foreign converts. The civil law having failed to answer its purpose, it is the opinion of intelligent Gentiles in the territory that peace can be preserved only by strong military rule, or bloodshed averted by favoring the removal of the Mormons beyond the jurisdiction of the United States.

1859: July, *Y Bedyddiwr* (*Baptist*), p. 211 (90 words). "Question."

The question is posed by someone who calls himself "Sentinel," possibly the editor himself:

I would like to know whether the account of the origin of the Book of Mormon was given in any volume of the *Baptist*? If it was, in which volume? If it was not, I believe that such an account would be very interesting to many of your readers. I have heard that the foundation of this book was a novel written by a minister to amuse himself during his illness. Information of the truth in this matter would be of particular pleasure to your obedient servant, "Sentinel."

1859: 27 August, *Cardiff Times*, p. 5 (70 words). "The Salt Lake."

We have advices from the Great Salt Lake to the 13th ultimo. A man named Brewer, had been arrested at Camp Floyd, for having in his possession 80,000 in counterfeit government cheques on the sub-treasury at St. Louis, most of which were ready for issue, excepting the signature. Horace Greely had arrived at Salt Lake City. The Indians were committing depredations in Humboldt county, and the Mormons were implicated.

1859: September, *Y Bedyddiwr* (*Baptist*), p. 274 (220 words). "Answer to the Question of 'Sentinel' in the July *Baptist*."

The answer presented to the question in the July 1859 issue (see previous entry) is that the Book of Mormon derived from the writings of one Solomon Spaulding.

1859: 3 September, *Usk Observer*, p. 4 (195 words). "Statistics of Mormon Population."

The *Valley Tan* copies the following statistics of Mormon population:

The population of Mormons in the United States and British dominions in 1856 was not less than 68,700—of which 38,000 were resident in Utah, 5,000 in New York State, 4,000 in California, 5,000 in Nova Scotia and the Canadas, and 9,000 in South America. In Europe there were 30,000; of which 22,000 were in Great Britain and Ireland, 5,000 in Scandinavia, 1,000 in Germany and Switzerland, and in France and the rest of Europe, 1,000; in Australia and Polynesia, 2,400; in Africa, 100; and on travel, 2,800. To these if we add the different schismatic branches, including Strangeites, Rigdonites, and Whiteites, and whole sect was not less than 126,000. In 1857 there appears to have been a decrease in the population of Utah—the number being only 31,022; of whom 9,000 were children, about 11,000 women, and 11,000 men capable of bearing arms. There are 388 men with 8 or more wives; of these 13 have more than 19 wives, 780 men with 5 wives, 1,100 with 4, and 2,400 with more than 1 wife. Recapitulation—4,617 men, with 16,500 wives.

Episode 16.1

Start: Horace Greeley interviews Brigham Young on 13 July 1859

1859: 9 September, *Welshman*, p. 6 (880 words). "A Visit to Brigham Young."

Mr. Horace Greeley, the editor of the *New York Tribune* gives an account in his paper of a visit he paid to Brigham Young, and of the conversation he held with him on the doctrines of the Mormons. When Brigham Young stated that none of the ministers or bishops received salaries, Mr. Greeley asked—"How then, do your ministers live?" Brigham Young replied—"By the labor of their own hands, like the first apostles. Every bishop, every elder, may be daily seen at work in the field or the shop, like his neighbors; every minister of the church has his proper calling, by which he earns the bread for his family."[6]

1859: 17 September, *Wrexham Advertiser*, p. 3 (880 words). "A Visit to Brigham Young."

The same article as in the *Welshman* for 9 September 1859 (see previous entry).

1859: 10 September, *North Wales Chronicle*, p. 6 (1,620 words). "Mormonism."

Here is the initial segment:

Mr. Horace Greeley, editor of the *New York Tribune*, records the following conversation with Brigham Young. It is valuable as the direct replies of the avowed leader of the Mormons to the searching questions of a clever man.

H. G.: Am I to regard Mormonism (so-called) as a new religion, or as simply a new development of Christianity?

B. Y.: We hold that there can be no true Christian Church without a priesthood directly commissioned by and in immediate communication with the Son of God and Savior of mankind. Such a church is that of the Latter-day Saints, called by their enemies Mormons; we know no other that even pretends to have present and direct revelations of God's will.

H. G.: Then I am to understand that you regard all other churches professing to be Christian as the Church of Rome regards all churches not in communion with itself—as schismatic, heretical, and out of the way of salvation?

B. Y.: Yes, substantially.

> H. G.: Apart from this, in what respect do your doctrines differ from those of our Orthodox Protestant Churches—the Baptist or Methodist, for example?
> B. Y.: We hold the doctrines of Christianity, as revealed in the Old and New Testaments—also in the Book of Mormon, which teaches the same cardinal truths, and those only.

1859: November, *Y Bedyddiwr* (*Baptist*), pp. 33–34 (1,720 words). "Two Hours with Brigham Young."

The first two paragraphs are as follows:

> On his recent visit to Salt Lake City the following conversation took place between Mr. Horace Greeley, the editor of the *New York Tribune*, and Brigham Young, the president of the Mormon church.
> After a few preliminary conversations (says Mr. G.) I said that I intended to ask some questions in order to get a broader understanding of the doctrines and organization of the Mormon church to which I would like to have direct answers, if there were no objections. President Young promised to give answers to all pertinent and polite questions.

The remainder of this article is identical to that of the *North Wales Chronicle* for 10 September 1859 (see previous entry).

End: Horace Greeley interviews Brigham Young on 13 July 1859

1859: 17 September, *Cardiff Times*, p. 3 (45 words). "A Disgraceful Scene."

> A Mormon preacher held forth on Thursday evening near the weighing machine Crockherbtown, and was met by Mr. Goodman, who controverted his dogmas. The crowd became excited at the Mormon who ultimately retreated, followed by a host who hooted him down Working Street.

Crockherbtown Street has since been renamed "Queen Street," the main thoroughfare in downtown Cardiff.

1859: October, *Yr Haul* (*Sun*), p. 318 (70 words). "The Middle of the way is what is best."

> Catholicism forbids their priests to marry; and Mormonism allows their priests to marry as many as they wish. Brigham Young gives a new explanation to the words, "A bishop then must be blameless, the *husband of one wife*." "Yes," says Brigham, in debating with Horace Greeley, "yes, the husband of one wife *at least*; but the more wives the better."

1859: 1 October, *Cardiff Times*, p. 5 (85 words). "To Correspondents."

> "G. Taylor" writes in reference to the paragraph headed "Disgraceful Scene," which appeared a fortnight ago [see previous entry], and gives a number of polemical questions and answers to show that it was not a disgraceful scene. We cannot insert such a report of the affair, neither is it necessary, as the writer admits there was a disturbance, and that was all which the paragraph in

question dealt with. We cannot be a party to disseminating Mormon dogmas by means of a side-wind, as the letter attempts.

1859: 8 October, *Usk Observer*, p. 3 (12 words).

Several assassinations have been reported by the Mormons at the Salt Lake.

1859: 15 October, *Chepstow Weekly Advertiser*, p. 3 (130 words). "It Is Time They Were Rooted Out."

The state of things in Utah (says an American correspondent of the *Morning Post*) continues to be most disgraceful to us. Polygamy is on the increase there. Old men *marry* (?) young women by the half-dozen; and cases are known in which mothers and daughters are the wives so-called of the same aged ruffians. One instance is mentioned in which a "venerable gentleman" has among his wives a mother and four daughters; and in another, a man has 10 wives, three of whom are sisters, and he is about to espouse their sister, who is about 13 years old. Of his other wives it is not stated they are relatives. Five thousand Mormons have arrived in Utah this season from Europe.

1859: 28 October, *Welshman*, p. 6 (33 words).

There are at present in the world about one hundred and twenty-one thousand Mormons. Eighty-three thousand live in Utah, of whom four thousand six hundred and seventeen have *sixteen thousand five hundred* wives.

1859: 29 October, *Caernarvon and Denbigh Herald*, p. 9 (33 words).

Same as the article in the *Welshman* for 28 October 1859 (see previous entry).

1859: 29 October, *Cardiff Times*, p. 5 (65 words). "Christianity versus Mormonism."

Last Sunday a gentleman from Bristol preached in the open air at the docks, his object being to check the progress of Mormon dogmas. We understand he is engaged in performing a similar work in a circuit of twenty miles round Bristol, and having heard that Cardiff was a place often visited by the Mormons he came hither to preach the gospel also.

1859: 5 November, *Monmouthshire Beacon*, p. 2 (33 words).

Same as the article in the *Welshman* for 28 October 1859.

1859: 19 November, *Cardiff Times*, p. 8 (100 words). "The Family of Joe Smith."

The *Boston Courier* says,

The family of the great Mormon prophet, Joe Smith, still dwell in Nauvoo. No persuasions can prevail on them to remove to Utah. His widow has married again, and with her husband keeps the Mansion house, the only house of entertainment that the city affords. The eldest son, who bears his father's name of Joseph, is a justice of the peace, and a useful and much respected citizen. Great inducements have been offered him to remove to Great Salt Lake City, but he steadily resists all such importunities.

1859: 18 November, *Welshman*, p. 2 (100 words).

The same article as in the *Cardiff Times* for 19 November 1859.

1859: 19 November, *North Wales Chronicle*, p. 6 (100 words).
The same article as in the *Cardiff Times* for 19 November 1859.

1859: 19 November, *Usk Observer*, p. 4 (100 words).
The same article as in the *Cardiff Times* for 19 November 1859.

1859: 26 November, *Monmouthshire Beacon*, p. 2 (100 words).
The same article as in the *Cardiff Times* for 19 November 1859.

1859: 3 December, *Cardiff and Merthyr Guardian*, p. 7 (27 words).

> The *Boston Courier* states that the family of Joe Smith, the great Mormon Prophet, still dwell at Nauvoo, and cannot be prevailed on to remove to Utah.

1859: 10 December, *Chepstow Weekly Advertiser*, p. 3 (100 words). "News from Utah."

> News has been received from the Great Salt Lake City to the 18th October. A man named Vincent was murdered on the night preceding, making the seventh murder since the commencement of Judge Sinclair's court in the latter part of July last! Vincent was a gambler by profession, and a man of most desperate character. Six of the murders were committed by Mormons, none of whom were brought to justice. Ferguson, the Gentile, who killed a shopkeeper at the close of a drunken spree, has been sentenced to be hanged. A pretty state of things, truly!

Notes

1. *Cardiff and Merthyr Guardian*, 5 February 1859, 5.
2. Ibid. See *Millennial Star*, 8 January 1859, 28.
3. *Cardiff Times*, 12 March 1859, 4.
4. *Cambrian*, 18 March 1859.
5. The personal identification number (PID) for Thomas Read on FamilySearch.org is KWJ4-MNF.
6. A full transcript of this interview is available online (JSTOR).

SECTION 2

Pamphlets

Contents

The complete facsimile translations of Pamphlets #1–4, #6–7, #10–12, and #14–16. These were originally published in Welsh and have a content focused primarily on the doctrine and teachings of The Church of Jesus Christ of Latter-day Saints.

The complete facsimile translation of Pamphlet #5. This was originally published in Welsh and has a brief segment entitled "Mormon Deceit." This segment is followed by three others: "The Judgments of God on False Prophets," "The Judgments of God on Blasphemers," and "The Judgments of God on the Breakers of the Sabbath." The only connection the author makes between the first section and the other three is that all are offensive in the eyes of God.

The complete facsimile translation of Pamphlet #8. This was first published in English in the form of two letters of warning from a minister to his flock. Several years later these letters were translated into Welsh and published as a pamphlet.

The facsimile translations of the introductory segments of Pamphlets #9 and #13. Only these segments have pronouncements regarding The Church of Jesus Christ of Latter-day Saints and its perceived false teachings.

The facsimile translation of the title page of the Welsh version of Pamphlet #17. The English version can be accessed at archive.org.

The facsimiles for the title pages of Pamphlets #18 and #19. These were published in Wales but in English only. These can be accessed at archive.org.

Contents

Pamphlet 1

Anonymous. ***Y Seintiau Diweddaf*** **(*****The Latter Saints*****). Merthyr: David Jones, 1846. 23 pages.**

The author states in his first chapter that "it is intended in this treatise to capture a brief account of the rise of the Mormon sect, or, as they call themselves, 'The Latter Saints.' This account shows an example of the religious deceit on the one hand and of idiotic gullibility on the other, the like of which is unprecedented in this century" (p. 5).

The content of this pamphlet is more focused on providing general information about The Church of Jesus Christ of Latter-day Saints than on attacking its beliefs. Compared to other writings in Wales about Joseph Smith and the Church he founded, this pamphlet is rather innocuous. No response from Dan Jones has been identified.

THE

LATTER SAINTS.

CONTENTS.

1. Foreword.
2. Original history of the Religious Denominations in the United States.
3. The testimony of JOSEPH SMITH, the Prophet of the Saints, about himself.
4. Origin and character of the Bible of the Saints.
5. Linguistic instruction of the Prophet.
6. The Saints being warned from the sky.
7. The new Temple of the Saints.
8. Missouri, Promised Land of the Saints—War—The Saints lose the day.
9. Commotion in Nauvoo—Imprisoning the Prophet—Hyrum his brother and he are killed.
10. Short history of the United States.
11. Reference to books about the history of the Saints.

MERTHYR:

PRINTED BY DAVID JONES, MAIN-STREET

1846.

FOREWORD.

It is clear that it is one thing to be deceivers, and another thing that all are deceivers. Unless there are false religions, it cannot be proven, and no perceptive person will say, that they are all false. Man tends to extremes in an outward show, and in public ungodliness; and he will go further without correct guidance. The power of false religion is imaginary communion with the Invisible; and the power of true religion is genuine communion with him. One must remember that true religion is quite varied in itself, and consequently as contradictory to false religion as it is to the obvious evil. The false is but *paint* on sin. We should avoid being deceived, and see the difference between Moses and Mohammed—between a servant of God and Joe Smith.

The skillful chemist solves and differentiates; so must we do in looking at the truth and a lie.

iv.

Some suppose that no notice should be taken of the sect which calls themselves The Latter Saints. Such should be asked on what should notice be taken. One says that too much spirit strikes on everything. True; and too much spirit leaves everything alone.

THE

LATTER SAINTS,

AND THEIR

PROPHET.

A short time ago the violent and dreadful death of Joseph Smith, the Mormon Prophet, was made known, the chicanery of whom has seduced thousands in Great Britain and America. It is intended in this treatise to capture a brief account of the rise of the Mormon sect, or as they call themselves "The Latter Saints." This account shows an example of the religious deceit on the one hand and of idiotic gullibility on the other, the like of which is unprecedented in this century.

The following quotation is from the history of Smith written by himself and from the fictitious revelations on which his prophetic authority is based.

About three years ago Mr. J. D. Rupp, from Lancaster, Pennsylvania, put together a history of the origins of the religious denominations of the United States, and in order to make the work as free as possible from complaints from each cause Mr. Rupp requested help from the ministers and the most well known lay members; many of

6

them immediately agreed to write or furnish the necessary articles. Among others, a request was sent to Joseph Smith; and he furnished the article from which we take the following account. Nothing can be more fair than to allow the prophet to tell his own story.

"I was born in the town of Sharon, Windsor county, Vermont, on the 23rd of December, 1805. When ten years old, my parents removed to Palmyra, New York, where we resided about four years, and from thence we removed to the town of Manchester, a distance of six miles.

My father was a farmer, and taught me the art of husbandry. When about fourteen years of age, I began to reflect upon the importance of being prepared for a future state; and upon inquiring the place of salvation, I found that there was a great clash in religious sentiment; if I went to one society they referred me to one place, and another to another; each one pointing to his own particular creed as the most perfect.

I retired to a secret place in a grove, and began to call upon the Lord. While praying, my mind was taken away from the objects with which I was surrounded, and I was enrapt in a heavenly vision, and saw two glorious personages, who exactly resembled each other in features and likeness, surrounded with a brilliant light, which eclipsed the sun at noonday. They told me that all the religious denominations were believing in incorrect doctrines, and that none of them was acknowledged of God as his church and kingdom; and I was expressly commanded to go not after them, and at the same time receiving a promise that the fulness of the gospel should at some future time be made known unto me.

On the evening of the 21st of September 1823, while I was praying unto God and endeavoring to exercise faith in the precious promises of the scripture, on a sudden a light like that of day, only of a far purer and more glorious appearance and brightness, burst into the room; indeed the first sight was as though the house was filled

7

with consuming fire. The appearance produced a shock that affected the whole body. In a moment a personage stood before me surrounded with a glory yet greater than that with which I was already surrounded. This messenger proclaimed himself to be an angel of God, sent to bring the joyful tidings that the covenant which God made with ancient Israel was at hand to be fulfilled; that the preparatory work for the second coming was speedily to commence; that the time was at hand for the gospel in all its fulness to be preached unto all nations that a people might be prepared for the millennial reign.

I was informed that I was chosen to be an instrument in the hand of God to bring about some of his purposes in this glorious dispensation. I was informed also concerning the aboriginal inhabitants of this country (America), who they were and from whence they came; their origin, progress, civilization, laws, governments, of their righteousness and iniquity, and the blessings of God being finally withdrawn from them as a people. I was also told where there was deposited some *plates*, on which was engraved an abridgment of the records of the ancient prophets that had existed on this continent. The angel appeared to me three times the same night and unfolded the same things. After having received many visits from the angels of God, unfolding the majesty and glory of the events that should transpire in the last days, on the morning of the 22nd of September 1827, the angel of the Lord delivered the records into my hands. These records were engraved on *plates* which had the appearance of gold. Each *plate* was six inches wide and eight inches long, and not quite so thick as common *tin*. They were filled with engravings in *Egyptian characters*, and bound together in a volume like a book, with three rings running through the whole. The volume was something near six inches in thickness, a part of which was sealed. The characters on the unsealed part were small and beautifully engraved.

The whole book exhibited marks of antiquity in its construction, and much skill in the art of engraving.

8

With the records was found a curious instrument which the ancients called Urim and Thummim, which consisted of two transparent stones set in the rim on a bow fastened to a breastplate. Through the medium of the Urim and Thummim, and by the gift and power of God I translated the record.

As soon as the news of this discovery was made known, false reports, misrepresentation and slander flew, as on the wings of the wind in every direction. My house was frequently beset by mobs, and evil designing persons; several times I was shot at, and very narrowly escaped, and every device was made use of to get the plates away from me; but the power and blessing of God attended me, and several began to believe my testimony. On the 6th April 1830, in the town of Manchester, Ontario County, State of New York, the Church of Jesus Christ of Latter-day Saints was organized. Some few were called and ordained by the Spirit of revelation and prophecy, and began to preach as the Spirit gave them utterance, and though weak, yet were they strengthened by the power of God; and many were brought to repentance, were immersed in the water, and were filled with the Holy Ghost by the laying on of hands. They saw visions and prophesied, devils were cast out, and the sick healed by the laying on of hands. From that time, the work rolled forth with astonishing rapidity, and churches were formed in the States of New York, Pennsylvania, Ohio, Indiana, Illinois, and Missouri; in the last named state a considerable settlement was formed in Jackson County; numbers joined the church, and we were increasing rapidly; our farms teemed with plenty, and peace and happiness were enjoyed in our domestic circle, and throughout our neighborhood; but we could not associate with our neighbors, who were, many of them, of the basest of men, and had fled from *civilized society* to the frontier country, to escape the hand of justice. In their midnight revels, their sabbath-breaking, horse-racing, and gambling, they commenced at first to

9

ridicule, then to persecute, and finally an organized mob assembled and burned our houses, tarred and feathered and whipped many of our brethren, and finally drove them from their habitations; these, houseless and homeless, contrary to law, justice, and humanity, had to wander on the bleak prairies, in November, till the children left the tracks of their blood on the prairie.

Here, in the fall of 1839, we commenced a city called Nauvoo, in Hancock county, which in December, 1840, received an act of incorporation from Illinois, and is endowed with as liberal powers as any city in the United States. Nauvoo, in every respect, connected with increase and prosperity, has exceeded the most sanguine expectations of thousands. It now contains near 1500 houses, and more than 15,000 inhabitants. The charter contains, among its important powers, privileges, or immunities, a grant for the University of Nauvoo, with the same liberal powers of the city, where all the arts and sciences will grow with the growth, and strengthen the strength of this beloved city of the saints of the last days. Since the organization of this church, its progress has been rapid, and its gain in numbers regular. Besides these United States, where nearly every place of notoriety has heard the glad tidings of the gospel of the Son of God, England, Ireland, and Scotland, have shared largely in the fulness of the everlasting gospel; and thousands have already gathered with their kindred saints, to this the cornerstone of Zion. Missionaries of this church have gone to the East Indies, to Australia, Germany, Constantinople, Egypt, Palestine, the Islands of the Pacific, and are now preparing to open the door in the extensive dominions of Russia. There are no correct data by which the exact number of this extensive and still extending Church of Jesus Christ of Latter-day Saints can be known. Should it be supposed at 150,000, it might still be short of the truth."

10

The Origin and Character of the Bible of the Saints.

One cannot help but feel angry upon reading these cold and careless lies, and the anger increases as one becomes more well acquainted with his history. Joseph Smith never shows the gold *plates* to anyone, and it is easy to know why; but for the purpose of winning the confidence of his disciples, he pretended to read their contents freely and openly to a man by the name of Harris, who served as a scribe for him, and after that to another by the name of Cowdery. This was done in a room separated by a blanket; on one side sat the "prophet," with his *mystic apparatus*, as he pretended; and on the other side sat the poor simpleton who was employed to write the English translation as spoken by Smith. Instead of translating the Egyptian characters, which he blasphemously pretended to do through the help of the divine oracle, he most likely read the fictitious account in a manuscript tale which had come into his possession in the following manner:—

In the year 1812, the Reverend Solomon Spaulding, of New Salem, wrote a fable to amuse himself and his friends: the basis of the fable was the supposition of the Hebraic origin of the Indian tribes. After this he moved to Pittsburg, and there he showed it to one Patterson, a printer, who wished to publish it on his press. Mr. Spaulding did not permit this; but since Patterson wished to borrow it, the manuscript was left in his possession over a long period of time, and eventually it was returned to its author. The gentleman died in 1816, and his widow kept the book in her care until 1834, when she was surprised to see the fruit of the creativity of her husband as a published volume, slightly modified as a new revelation from heaven, blasphemously proclaimed to be as much the word of God as the Bible itself. After extensive

11

research, it was determined that in the Printer's office in Pittsburg was a man by the name of Sidney Rigdon, a heretical preacher; and there is strong evidence to suggest that he copied this volume of Mr. Spaulding's manuscript, and that through him it came into the hand of Joseph Smith, whom he had befriended. And through his assistance, after three years, the "Mormon Bible" was finished and published, a twelve-fold volume consisting of nearly six hundred pages.

The book is divided into fifteen parts, each one signed as having been written by the author whose name is on it. They claim to give a history of two thousand years, from the time of Zedekiah, king of Judah, until 420 A.D. The entire work professes to be an abridgement prepared by one Moroni, the last of the Nephites, of the seed of Israel, from the writings of his people. Without troubling the reader with many of the details concerning this fictitious revelation from heaven, and concerning the greatest rascal of all, suffice it to say that he pretends to track the history of the original inhabitants of America, in their retrogressions, wanderings, tribulations, adventures, and their wars from the time of their departure from Jerusalem, during the reign of Zedekiah, under the leadership of onc Lchi, to their final misfortune, near the Hill Cumorah, in the state of New York, where Smith discovered the gold *plates*; and in this final conflict, according to the prophet Moroni, about 230,000 were killed in battle, and he alone survived to tell the tale.

The book itself, as the reader can see, is sufficient proof of its fictitious nature. It is full of grammatical, chronological, and philosophical errors. It says, for example, that Nephi was guided across the ocean by a compass, nearly two thousand years before that useful tool was invented, namely the mariner's *compass*.

12

Teaching of Joseph Smith—Account of an American Newspaper.

The reader sees, in the history of Smith, the prophet, that a university was founded in Nauvoo; how much education the Saints lacked can be inferred by the work of their leader: but the following account puts the matter beyond argument. "Some time ago, the Rev. Henry Caswall, Professor of Theology at Kemper College, near St. Louis, and a lay Episcopalian of renown, when he was about to leave America for England, he paid a visit to Smith, and the Saints, in order to better show to his compatriots Smith's deceit. The professor happened to have in his possession a very old copy of the Psalms in Greek, which, as an ancient relic, was an object of curiosity to everyone—but to some of the Saints who happened to see it, it was astonishing and wondrous. Supposing it to be as old as the Egyptian mummy belonging to the Prophet, and not knowing but what the professor had dug it out of the same hallowed hill in western New York, from whence the Holy Book of Mormon originated, they persuaded him to give brother Joseph a chance to translate it. The professor agreed to their idea, and with a number of the eager brethren, they all went to the house of the prophet and placed the wondrous book in his hand. Joe looked at it—he searched its worn pages, and turned its grey leaves. By now the expectation had gotten higher—the brethren looked now at each other, then at the book, and afterwards at the prophet. It was a rather remarkable scene!

In a short time, the spirit of prophecy grew within him, and he opened his mouth and spoke: "I pronounce this book," he said, "to be a Dictionary of ancient Egyptian *hieroglyphics*!" Then the brethren marveled greatly at this manifestation of the prophet's ability to reveal secret

13

things. After their jubilation subsided a bit, the professor said softly to them that their prophet was a contemptible fraud, for the book before them was nothing but *plain* Greek psalms. At this, Joe went outside.

The Saints receiving a sign from the sky.

When Dr. A. Reed was in the United States, he met with a number of these deceived fanatics on their way to the "far west." A gentleman asked one of them why they were leaving their own country? "O!" he said, "destruction is coming on it." "How do you know?" He said that it was revealed to him. "How was that revealed to you?" "I saw six letters in the sky." "Indeed. What were they?" "Famine," was the answer.

A New Temple of the Saints.

"Among the other wonders of Nauvoo, is the temple, about which Joe Smith was so shameless as to say the following—The temple of God, now in the course of erection, being already raised one story, and which is 120 feet by 80 feet, of stone with polished pilasters, of an entire new order of architecture. This will be a splendid house for the worship of God, as well as a unique wonder for the world, it being built by the direct revelation of Jesus Christ for the salvation of the living and the dead."

14

Promised land of the Saints, Missouri—War of the Saints—Killing and wounding on every side—Misunderstanding of the prophet.

Mr. Buckingham says of the Saints, as follows, "They took their resting place in the State of Missouri, where they purchased a considerable amount of land at the price of the government, namely, a *dollar* and a quarter per acre, and they began to form a settlement. Dissatisfied, however, at that which they could purchase, and exist on the yield that they could grow, they began to preach that Missouri was the land of promise secured by God for those who believed the Book of Mormon, and that their duty was, if they could not get it peacefully, to take it by the force of arms, and drive out the unbelievers there, as Moses did by driving away and destroying with the edge of the sword the Moabites and Ammonites who opposed his coming through their land; and as Joshua did by driving out the Jebusites and the Canaanites and others to possess their lands, which the Lord their God had given to them. From this example, and the declaration of direct inspiration of their prophet, this people supposed it not to be a sin, rather a unique virtue, to take possession of the promised land of Missouri as their own possession, as soon as their power was sufficient. However, the former inhabitants of Missouri, those who had purchased the land and improved it before Joe Smith or the Book of Mormon were known to them, did not acknowledge the heavenly covenant through which they were to be despoiled of their lawful possessions, and thus they forestalled the Mormons by taking up arms and driving them from the state.

This was not done without much hard effort, since all were armed, and many on both sides were killed and wounded. The conflict was the county sheriff, and the people of Missouri voted; and the outcome was for them to be driven across the river to Illinois, where they now

15

possess a small town named *Commerce*, close to twelve miles above Keokuk, on the other side of the Mississippi; and it is said that their number is more than five thousand people."

One could think, on reading the account the prophet gave, that the persecution the Saints received was entirely cruel and without cause: but this evidence presented by Mr. Buckingham puts the matter in a different light, and it shows how frightful the deceiver was in contorting the word of God. The authority of Moses over his laws, against the Moabites and the Ammonites, was proven by his possession of miraculous authority, which worked with the tribes in overthrowing their enemies. This authority from heaven was a sufficient base for revenge on the earth; but without any such warrant, the ambitious and cruel adventurer, by claiming divine authority, entangled all the territories in a frightful civil war, and when he was captured in retaliation, he complained because of the barbaric and unlawful behavior of the State of Missouri. After the Saints were driven out of Missouri, they received a safe haven for considerable time in the State of Illinois.

State of things in Nauvoo—State and ecclesiastical offices—Hyrum, brother of the prophet, and Church Patriarch—Conflict—The Government intervenes—Imprisonment of the prophet and his friends—His brother and he are killed.

Although Smith's report of his own condition, and that of his followers was so moderate, their circumstances in Nauvoo were already tumultuous. Among the other persons of great authority in their midst was General John C. Bennett, the Chief Captain of the Nauvoo Legion! The founder of the Nauvoo University!! The Mayor of the town of Nauvoo!!!

16

From these numerous and imposing offices, it seems to be clear that he was very well acquainted with the secret instructions of the great prophet and his brother Hyrum, patriarch of the church. These famous officials at some time disagreed with General Bennett, the Chief Leader of the army, the Chancellor of the University, and Mayor of the town of Nauvoo, who swore a public oath, in which he accused Smith of predicting the murder of *Ex-governor* Boggs, and afterwards, that he had used one of his sycophants to carry out the deadly predictions by killing his prey. Bennett threatened to prove the prophet guilty of another murder if the president intervened. Also, a wife of one of the elders declared under oath the exposure of Smith's shameful behavior toward her, and it is supposed that this drove her husband, elder Pratt, to kill himself. These things naturally caused opposition against the ministry of the prophet. A Newspaper was set up in Nauvoo in which his behavior toward his ignorant simpletons was fearlessly exposed. This their chief spiritual ruler did not allow; and he caused a mob of his most ardent followers to gather who then went to the Office of the *Expositor*,* attacked it, and brought it completely down immediately.

The Governor of Illinois, having heard of this assault, started, in June 1844, toward Carthage, eighteen miles from Nauvoo, and he found the people in this place greatly agitated against the "prophet" and his supporters, and he decided to go toward the blessed city of the Saints, in order to arrest him and all his city council, so that they would have to answer for this disturbance and other crimes. Before this, the governor sent emissaries to Nauvoo to summon Joe Smith and his friends to appear in Carthage to face the accusations that had been brought against them. The prophet, and his brother, the patriarch, and their co-conspirators were frightened, and they tried to escape from the city to avoid being put on trial; but the inhabitants saw that if they were not

*Name of the Newspaper.

17

secured, retribution would fall on the people, and the innocent would suffer for the guilty, and so they were not permitted to escape. Therefore, they all went toward Carthage, and they gave themselves up to the authority of the governor to arrest them, and they gave up all the arms of the Nauvoo Legion, which were the property of the state of Illinois. The prophet and his friends, after being bound to appear in the next court, were again arrested on the charge of crimes against the state of Illinois.

On this day they were delivered to prison, but their interrogation was postponed because of the military movements of the governor who left only one cadre of fifty men in Carthage, eight of whom were on duty in the jail, and the remainder were in a camp about a quarter of a mile away. Governor Ford and sixty of his cavalrymen started to Nauvoo, where he addressed the Saints, telling of the disturbance that was caused against them, and warning them of the dangerous situation they were in.

During this time in which the governor was absent from Carthage, an armed mob of about two hundred men in disguise attacked the jail on Thursday afternoon, June 27, and by overcoming the eight soldiers there on guard, they pushed their way to the room where the unfortunate deceivers were secured, and they fired on them. Hyrum Smith, after being struck with a bullet to his head, cried out, "I am a dead man." Joseph Smith received several shots in his body, and jumped toward the window, but escape was impossible, and he before the firing of his attackers, crying out, "O God," and he also died. Elder Taylor was seriously wounded in several places, and his condition was considered dangerous. The savage men who committed this frightful violence fled to the woods, but they were not followed since there was not sufficient force to apprehend them; and besides that, they were disguised, and their persons could not be recognized, but it is supposed that they were disaffected Saints.

18

It is said that throughout the land there is but one opinion concerning this dreadful work of deceit, namely that it is swift revenge coming down on those who deserve it. At the same time, no one can help but regret that this took place while they were prisoners and that they had a right to expect the defense of the government.

Now the Saints claim for their prophet the honor of being a *martyr*; had he been tried and found guilty he would have died the death of an evil doer, which, as it is supposed, he deserves in the most just manner.

When the news of this occurrence reached Nauvoo, the wife of the prophet and her children showed only a modicum of grief, and her *votaries* saw that she was very calm, despite the support of the town having been taken away by the inhabitants of the surrounding area, and their determination to not allow the Saints to remain as a body in that place. The governor issued a decree to call out the *militia* of ten Counties to keep the peace; 500 *Troops* of the United States were ordered to the area for the same purpose. It will be very fine if these measures forestall more bloodshed.

APPENDIX.

Topics of Faith of the Saints

As he reads the history of Joseph Smith, the Prophet, the reader will see better what is the religious creed of the Latter Saints. Perhaps it would not be unprofitable to note some things which are in this history; since their inspired Prophet gave the history, there is no need to ask, Do the Saints believe it.

19

1. That every religious denomination established before the Latter Saints is false, and that God commands not to join any of them.

2. That Joe Smith was called by God to bring the religious world to order.

3. That it is necessary, in order to bring this to pass, to have greater revelation from the mind of God, and that it is in the book or Bible of the Saints that it can be had.

4. That Joe Smith received visits from the angels of God, and that he learned the *Egyptian characters*, and that he received into his possession the Urim and Thummim, for the purpose of translating the new revelation.

5. That the Latter Saints is the only church of Christ on the earth.

6. That they have the Holy Ghost to reveal secret things, to prophesy, to cast out devils, to heal the sick, etc., etc.

7. That baptism should be by immersion, and that the Holy Ghost be given to them by the laying on of hands.

8. That the state of Missouri is the land of promise given to them by covenant from God.

9. That all the offices that were in the church in the time of the Apostles are occupied by the officers of the church of the Saints.

P. S. Apparently the Saints wish to raise up the offices that were in the Jewish church also, since they have some officers according to the order of Melchizedek, and others according to the order of Aaron.

A BRIEF HISTORY OF

THE UNITED STATES OF AMERICA.

The United States of America are famous for the extent of their territory, their sudden rise, and their free constitution. The majority of their inhabitants originated from England, and they were *colonies* dependent on her until 1775, when, as a consequence of the attempt to tax them against their will, they rebelled, and after a long struggle, they were recognized in 1783 as Independent States. Through a purchase from France and Spain, they obtained Florida, Louisiana, and thus, they possessed the right to the land on, and beyond the Mississippi, as far as the *Rocky Mountains*, and they claim the right to it as far as the Pacific Ocean. Consequently, this land is extremely wide, and it contains the Western part of extensive pieces of uncultivated land, and much of that can be obtained for a low price. There are many gatherings here from the eastern states, and from Europe. Because of this the population has increased more rapidly than in any other country. In 1791, the population was 3,900,000 (three million and nine hundred thousand). In 1840, it rose to 17,068,000 (seventeen million and sixty-eight thousand), of which number there are nearly 2,500,000

21

(two million and five hundred thousand) Negro slaves, which are a great shame and misfortune for the nation. The people are extremely diligent in increasing agriculture and commerce. They export a great deal of cotton, lumber, tobacco, grain, rice, bitumen, *potash* and hides. Their ships are seen in every part of the world. Their *imports* and their *exports* are worth close to £30,000,000 yearly. Besides this, they have extensive commerce on the Mississippi, the Ohio, and other great rivers. They are diligently increasing their canals, railways, and steam navigation; they were the first to bring forth these things to a large extent.

The republic of the United States is governed by a President, which is chosen every four years, and a senate every six years, and a House of Representatives every two years. The latter two make up the chief governing body, which is called the *Congress*.

The country is divided into Northern, Middle, and Southern States, twenty-six in number, and three subdivisions, which are called Territories.

The Northern States, and their Capitals, and their population in 1840, are as follows:—

States.	Population.	Capital-cities.	Population.
Maine.	501,793	Portland	15,218,
Vermont	291,948	Montpelier	3,725.
New Hampshire	284,5574	Concord.	4,897.
Massachusetts	737,699	Boston	93,383.
Connecticut	301,015	Newhaven	14,390.
Rhode Island	108,830	Providence	23,171.
MIDDLE STATES.			
New York	2,428,921	New York	312,710.
New Jersey	373,306	Newark	17,290.
Pennsylvania	1,724,033	Philadelphia	223,691.
Delaware.	78,035	Wilmington	8,367.
Ohio	1,519,467	Cincinnati	46,448.

22

Michigan	21,267	Detroit	9,102.
Indiana	685,866	Indianopolis	2,692.
Illinois	476,182	Chicago	4,470.
Missouri	383,702	St. Louis	16,469.
SOUTHERN STATES.			
Maryland	469,232	Baltimore	102,313.
Virginia	806,942	Richmond	20,153.
Carolina North	753,419	Wilmington	4,744.
———South	594,398	Charleston	29,261.
Georgia	691,392	Savannah	11,214.
Kentucky	779,828	Louisville	21,210.
Tennessee	829,210	Nashville	6,929.
Arkansas	97,574	Little Rock	a few.
Mississippi	375,651	Natchez	4,800.
Louisiana	352,411	New Orleans	102,193.
Alabama	590,756	Mobile	not noted.
TERRITORIES.			
Wisconsin	30,945	Madison	a few.
Iowa	43,111	Iowa	ditto.
Florida	54,477	St. Augustine	2,459.
Columbia	43,712	Washington	23,364.

New York is the largest town in the United States, and in all of America, and has more than 312,000 inhabitants. It is estimated that its commerce is larger than that of any town in the world, except for London. It has grown larger than Boston, which has 93,000 inhabitants, and it is famous for its enlightenment and teaching.

Philadelphia, which was settled by the Quakers, is an orderly city, organized, and of good construction, and it has 228,000 inhabitants. Baltimore has 102,000 inhabitants, and Charleston 29,000, and it is developing an abundant commerce. New Orleans was a poor and centralized place before the rise of the Western States. When it established its position at the mouth of the Mississippi

23

river, this town became a station of abundant and growing commerce. Its population is already 102,000, and no doubt it will increase rapidly. On a wild and wooded place along the Ohio river, in thirty years Cincinnati arose, a town with 46,000 souls, and steadily developing com-merce through *steam*. Towns and cities are rising almost every year, wherever the rivers and canals go.

Washington is the seat of the Government: it is in a lovely situation by the confluence of the two branches of the Potomac. The place was laid out so that it would be-come a large town, but it has not answered that expecta-tion; the population is no more than 23,000. Nevertheless, the *Capitol*, in which the *Congress* meets, is the most hand-some building in America.

The rivers of the United States are large and numerous. The Mississippi, Missouri, Chesapeake, Delaware, Hudson, and Ohio are the most outstanding ones. These rivers are joined together by splendid canals: the largest of them is 360 miles long, and joins the Hudson river and Lake Erie.

Guide to books which give the history of the Saints.

Rupp's Religious Denominations.
Baird's Religion in America.
Buckingham's Eastern and Western States of America.
Narrative of a Visit to the American Churches.
Congregational Magazine for 1844.
Chamber's Miscellany, Vol. II.

ERROR.

Page 12, line 11, in place of "lleyg," read *llen*.

Intended to be published soon,

CHURCH NONCONFORMITY

In its relationship with circumstances

The Nonconformist Churches of Llanelli, Brecknockshire, in Letters to the Pastor of that Denomination.

BY THE SAME,

VINEYARD OF THE CHRISTIAN:

CONTAINING

The Tempter in Paradise—Vocation and Religion of Cain and Abel.—Work of the Holy Spirit—The Christian as a traveler—Church and Pastor—Observations on Time—Election of Grace—Calumny—Slanderer—Hope of the Christian—The Lying Prophet, &c., &c.

THE

NATURAL, PHYSICAL, AND MORAL

HISTORY OF MERTHYR TYDVIL.

D. JONES, PRINTER, MERTHYR.

Pamphlet 2

David Williams. *Twyll y Seintiau Diweddaf yn cael ei ddynoethi, mewn nodiadau byr ar draethawd a ysgrifenwyd yn ddiweddar gan Capt. D. Jones, dan yr enw, "Traethawd ar Anghyfnewidioldeb Teyrnas Dduw," etc.* (*Deception of the Latter Saints Exposed in Brief Notes on a Treatise Written Recently by Capt. D. Jones, Under the Title, "Treatise Showing the Immutability of the Kingdom of God," etc.*). 2nd ed. Merthyr: D. Jones, 1846. 32 pages.

Williams was a railroad worker from Abercanaid, a town near Merthyr Tydfil. He declares in the preface:

> This pamphlet will not be restricted to one denomination in particular, nor will just one denomination of Christians be answerable for its content, only so far as they agree with what it contains (iv).

In polemic fashion typical of the age, Williams conducts a point-by-point analysis of the assertions and claims of the pamphlet which Dan Jones had published several months earlier in North Wales. Even though Jones had not made specific mention of the religion he represented and defended, Williams had no difficulty in identifying it and arguing against it. Toward the end of the pamphlet, Williams expresses particular shock at Jones's second publication, *Proclamation of the Twelve Apostles in The Church of Jesus Christ of Latter-day Saints*:

> By the time I had glanced over the above treatise on the kingdom of God, yet another one came to my attention, one so presumptuous as if it had been written by the fingers of the devil, who had dipped his pen in the venom of dragons, or in the fiery furnace itself, and had it printed in the gates of hell, and this under the name "*Proclamation of the Twelve Apostles—the Saints, etc., to all the kings of the earth, etc.*" Oh! for human nature to have sunk so low, and become so impudent as to assert such majestic things in a deceitful way. The above booklet, that is the Proclamation, has gone so far in its baseless assertions, that all [one] Welshman has to do is read it carefully to see its madness.

THE DECEPTION OF THE LATTER-DAY SAINTS

REVEALED,

IN

SHORT NOTES

ON

A TREATISE RECENTLY WRITTEN BY CAPT. D. JONES,

ENTITLED

"A Treatise on the Immutability of the Kingdom of God," &c.

BY DAVID WILLIAMS,

SILO, ABERCANNAID.

THE SECOND PRINTING.

MERTHYR:

PRINTED BY D. JONES, HEOL FAWR

—

1846.

TO THE READER.

DEAR COMPATRIOTS,

We have consulted together with regard to the following small Treatise before setting pen to paper: and it is because we judge that the mixture (not scheme) produced, and fostered and defended by those who falsely call themselves the Latter-day Saints is completely heretical. Therefore, we decided to write the following booklet which contains not abuse and hatred, but Short and Scriptural Notes on the fancies and superstition, and the heresies attempted to be spread through town and country in our midst, by those who call themselves the Saints, &c.

This booklet contains notes not only on the things generally claimed by them, but also on the main heretical things contained in a booklet called, "The Dead raised to Life, or the Old Religion anew, namely a Treatise on the Immutability of the Kingdom of God, by Capt. D. Jones."

iv

This booklet will not be restricted to one denomination in particular, nor will just one denomination of Christians be answerable for its content, only so far as they agree with what it contains.

As railway workers in Pentrebach, near Merthyr, we agreed as follows:—

1. That David Williams will compose the Notes.

2. That Mr. Edward James will be the treasurer—he will receive names, receive money, take care of every cost, and pay the publisher, &c.

3. That each of the subscribers will have a book; and if there happens to be a profit from it, this should go to a good cause.

Like this, brothers and colleagues, we offer it for your attention, wishing the truth every success—death to all heresy and eternal prevention to all deception, on behalf of all our friends we wish everyone to search daily as to whether these things are so.

EDWARD JAMES,
WILLIAM LEWIS, } *Baptists.*

STEPHEN WILLIAMS,
JOHN POWELL, } *Independents.*

FOREWORD.

As we begin to move ahead, we shall make a few Observations about the Captain's Foreword.

The first thing on which the Author focuses is an independent mind; he says that it is a heavenly gift to mankind and the most remarkable of all gifts; but he adds that only a few possess it; and the reason for his claim is that they do not know its worth. I ask in order to explain the matter, is it completely necessary for a man to know the worth of a gift before being a recipient of it? Did Abraham know the worth of the land of Canaan before God gave it to him; or the worth of the seed's promise before giving it in a promise to him; or did the world know the worth of a Savior before God gave his only Son? No, all common sense says that the gifts were far too valuable to have a price put on them.

But in boastful language, our author says that he is the only one of Gomer's descendants that he has seen asserting his right not only to believe, but also to reveal the doctrine set out in the Treatise published by him.

vi

Here there is an entanglement of inconsistencies; in one thing his manner of writing signifies that he alone has received this gift of Heaven, of all those he has seen; furthermore, he connects his statement with the content of his treatise; but for his claim that he is at God's right hand in the task, &c., let it be known to him, although he is a Captain, that I would not accept his assertion, any more than those of Mohammed or Johannah Southcott, &c. Many frauds have appeared, and we are determined to catch the foxes, large and small.

Next, the Captain advises us to compare his goods, or his things, with the law and the evidence, as to whether things are so. He says this is a very important question and should be answered not after, but before comparing them with the correct image. I say that it is after comparing them with the Correct Image that we prove if they are so, and that we have weighed them on the balance and found them wanting.

Next, our author ensures that his doctrine will be strange to no one in the next world, even if it is such.

Indeed, Sir, I am of the opinion that your doctrine has appeared before its time. It is an abortion, and you should have left it until the next world before mentioning it; but it does not matter much, because it will soon be written that it lasted for a night only, and that in that night it ended.

vii

I commend the Captain for his work in promising to take back his heresies if disproved; if he does this, all well and good, but if he does not, it would be better not to promise, rather than to promise and not pay up.

I do not know of the thousand and one false stories he mentions, nor do I care, because it is from your mouth and the mouths of your brothers that I take what I focus on in this work.

You can easily be excused for your language; and as for your principle, I do not wish to judge it. To your own Lord you stand or fall; and it is not intended to steal anything from you which you will miss; but rather I shall watch to see if at some time God will grant you forgiveness and return you to the truth, out of the devil's snare, so that you may be saved in the day of the Lord Jesus.

I am, the least of the nation,

The least worthy of its brothers,

And less than the least of God's true Saints,

DAVID WILLIAMS,

Silo, Abercanaid.

DECEIT OF THE SAINTS, &c.

The topic taken by the Captain on which to base his treatise may be seen in Matt. 6:33, "But seek ye first the kingdom of God," &c.

I beg the reader's attention to the Captain's first statement on the above important topic. After the author says that this is the definite commandment of the Son of God, he continues by claiming that the happiness and glory of all Adam's children, who have ever been, are now, or will ever be on earth, depends on their obedience to this commandment.

The Captain's false reasoning in the foregoing words becomes apparent in the following:—

1st. No definite commandment existed before it was given; therefore, 2nd. Thousands of years had passed, and generation upon generation taken to another world, before Christ gave this definite commandment; therefore, how could the happiness of such as these depend on what they had not heard? Will not the judge of all earth make judgment?

3rd. There are hosts of Adam's line, in different ages of the world, who since the time the commandment was given have not heard of it, and how can they believe something they have not heard? If I had not

9

come and spoken unto them, says Christ, they had not had sin: therefore, the reader sees that neither the happiness nor the unhappiness of such as these can be connected to the obedience or disobedience to a commandment of which they have never heard. Books will be opened by the Judge on the final day, and the dead will be judged by those things written in the books. I call upon the Captain, according to his promise, to call back his heresy, and may he remember that the Spirit of God leads no one but to the truth, and in the truth.

There is scarcely hope that the superstructure is safe when the main base and foundation is proved to be sand, and is blown away, and is exposed, and the sanctuary of lies is completely swept away.

Next, the Captain earnestly urges us to seek the Kingdom of God; this is good; but according to his method of reasoning, one might think it to be a wanderer that one might happen to notice in passing; but the truth is that the Kingdom of God will come only through waiting, as I will yet note.

The author urges us to give him our minds and senses to search for the kingdom. I say that we would be better to keep our minds and our senses than to give them to him or anyone else. What, do all your followers give their minds and their senses to you, Sir? If this is so, it is no wonder that many of them are so lacking in such precious things. Sir, let people keep that which God has given them, and urge them to search the scriptures, for they are the things which testify of salvation of the soul.

10

This author says that his search for the kingdom has cost him thousands. Thousands of what, I do not know; thousands of pounds, perhaps; if so, he has been trading in a very high and expensive market; it is quite likely that it was not the market of grace, for those precious things are to be obtained free of charge; it takes freely from the fountain of the water of life.

On page 6, the Captain tells us as Welsh people, that the heavens have blessed this age with privileges a thousand times better than our fathers had, and he has some sort of false reasoning to prove this. 1st. that this age need not seek the kingdom in vain; 2nd. Because the kingdom of God is among us today; 3rd. that we can be made subjects of it, if only we try, in fewer hours than he had been years seeking it, that is 18 or 19 years.

The reader should note the explanation of the deceit; 1st. the Captain's words say that our fathers sought the kingdom of God in vain; yet did not our Heavenly Father say that he who seeks shall find; 2nd. Is not the kingdom of God in whatever place the gospel is preached and believed? And did not our fathers in ages past have the gospel? And was it not from them that it was transmitted to us? But the Captain's gospel is a different one, about which our forefathers knew nothing; in fact, his is not actually a gospel; 3rd. As for making men subjects of the kingdom, only God can do this, and no one else; he who is created in Christ Jesus unto good works is a subject of the kingdom. It is God

11

who quickens those who are dead in transgressions and sins. It is He who brings men from the grasp of darkness to the kingdom of his dear Son; therefore, our forefathers did have the above privileges just as we do, and some found the kingdom nearer to home than does the Captain, and less expensive also; for the word is very nigh unto thee, in thy mouth, and in thy heart; that if thou shalt confess with thy mouth the Lord Jesus Christ, and shalt believe in thine heart that God hath raised him from the dead, thou shalt be saved.

It is true that this age has many privileges, but where are there a thousand better privileges, waiting to be experienced? Thou shalt not add unto his word.

The Captain asks, Oh Welshmen, who among you will venture to come with him out into the world to search for the kingdom of God?

What, is it between the mountains and hills of the world, or in the deserts or seas of the world, or in the exploits and games of the world that the kingdom is to be found? The kingdom of God is not food and drink, rather justice, peace, and joy in the Holy Spirit. The King and his kingdom are not of this world, nor are His subjects or His laws of this world, just as I am not of this world; therefore, I prefer to go to the scriptures to ask about it, rather than going with the Captain; for this, with the Lord's blessing, can make us wise unto salvation, and if any of you lack wisdom, let him ask, not of the Captain, but of God, that giveth to all men liberally, and upbraideth not; and it shall be given

12

him. In God's word we have the pure wheat; therefore, however full the sack of chaff of the Captain and his brethren may be, we can tell the chaff from the wheat. Many before now have worn raiment of camel's hair, and many false prophets and false teachers have risen and appeared like clouds without water and wandering stars, and many still exist; but they will soon go to their place: let the Captain tremble, lest he is one of these.

He also considers the sects and denominations of this age to be so different from the kingdom of God, that he considers it a wonder among those who take notice of them, that any Welshman could be so blind as to be mistaken in the matter.

Allow me to say, good man, that we do not think that all the different sects throughout the world have the gospel doctrine in its purity, nor do we hold the traditions exactly according to the plan of the early churches; and we freely admit that the best of us is open to failings, weaknesses and mistakes; but are you perfect, sir? Are you and your followers the kingdom of God? Did the King of Zion cease to reign from almost the end of the Apostolic age until J. Smith rose up in America? And you in Wales, was it not and is it not necessary for him to rule until his enemies become a footstool for his feet? and did he not take care of his bride when she was in the worst possible circumstances? What do the scriptures say that is needless? or were Christ and his kingdom vanquished—were the

13

devil and the great red dragon mightier than he? It is true that these make war with the Lamb, but the Lamb will vanquish them, for he is the King of kings, and the Lord of lords. I hope that you, sir, are not one of the chief captains who will ask the mountains and the rocks to hide them from his sight on the day to come.

God has those who have had the teaching of the New Testament in its purity before you were born, and have practiced its ordinances—possessing its spirit, and toiling with the things pertaining to the kingdom of God, and to the name of Jesus Christ. Do you pretend to convince us to believe that all those from bygone ages, from the first centuries until you rose up, are heretics, without any knowledge of the kingdom of God? Are you an Apostle of the nineteenth century, and have you seen the Lord and received your mission from him directly? If you are so brazen as to claim this to be true, we doubt you and consider you in danger for adding to His Word; and in our opinion, you are just one of those who make up the synagogue of Satan; and if you, or an angel from heaven, were to preach any other gospel unto us that was preached to us by the Apostles in their writings, let you be Anathema.

This author also claims that if anything is missing, or changed from what originally belonged to the true church, such a thing cannot be the kingdom of God, nor any part of it. I beg the reader's attention to the following in order to see the false reasoning of our author:—

14

1st. The Church in Corinth was a true church as we see in the Apostle's letter to it; despite that, there were terrible heresies suffered and upheld for a while, namely the following:—first, discipline with regard to adultery, as we see in 1st Cor. 6:1,2. Second, about the resurrection of the dead; see 1 Cor. 15:12. Third, about the supper of the Lord; see chap. 11 of the same letter. If Capt. D. Jones had been in Paul's place, confronted with the foregoing things, he probably would have asserted that the church in Corinth was not part of the kingdom of God; but whatever of the Capt., this is how Paul greeted them, 1 Cor. 1, 2, "Unto the church of God which is at Corinth, to them that are sanctified in Christ Jesus, called to be saints, with all that in every place call upon the name of Jesus Christ." 2nd. As proof of this, read Paul's letter to the churches of Galatia: these had been led astray by the false teachers, and they desired to justify themselves in the law—Paul greeted them as those who were mad, as those who did not obey the truth; but despite it all, the point is whether Paul considered them as part of God's kingdom, or his church, or as ones who had no part in the kingdom of Christ and God. Certainly, according to the Captain's opinion, they were not part of the kingdom; yet in the opinion of the great Apostle of the nations concerning them, they were children of the promise, and brothers, in the spiritual relationship, of Paul, and Paul wished for the grace of our Lord Jesus Christ to be with them all as brothers, &c. Paul did not expect perfection in

15

them, nor in himself, in the present situation, rather he endeavored to renew them in love, and educate them in the truth, and urge them to that perfection which they and he hoped to achieve. "Not as though I had already achieved it, or had already become perfect; rather I am following," &c., said he.

We could provide many such examples, such as the greater part of the seven churches in Asia, as we see in Rev. 1, our Lord reprimanded and chastised those he loved, but he did not say that they did not belong to His kingdom or that they were not part of it. So do we also admit that we are not perfect; yet we build on the foundation of the Apostles and the Prophets, with Jesus Christ himself the chief cornerstone.

The Captain considers everyone mistaken about the nature of the Kingdom, except for himself and his brethren apparently; and he says that the cause of the different opinions about the kingdom is that men spiritualize too much on the scriptures. And yes, supreme judge of the critics, is it not said that the words of Christ are spirit, and life, and that all the Scriptures have been given by the inspiration of God; and is it not proper for us to judge spiritual things according to spiritual things? What, should we spiritualize that which is already spiritual? I have never heard of such a feat, but I do know about the natural man, who does not receive or understand the things of God, for they are foolishness to him, and he cannot know of them, for they are spiritually discerned.

16

Then the Captain intends, he says, to cast away the rubbish, to have a look at the kingdom, it appears; but what is this rubbish but the different opinions of the judges? Rubbish, what is it but that nonsense which is mixed with the teaching of the truth, according to the Captain's opinion; but is he the judge of the judges?

Now I turn to you, the one who is called Capt. Dl. Jones, and desire to speak, not in anger, but out of zeal for the truth. The man I call an empty boaster, a deceiver of weak minds, like the false prophet, unless you can provide for us clear proofs of the following things and their like:—1st. Healing the sick of Merthyr and environs, and there will be great joy in the place. 2nd. Note when tongues cloven with fire have or will come upon each one or some of you who call yourselves Latter Saints. 3rd. Drink some deadly things, with no harm resulting. 4th. If the Holy Ghost leads you to all truth, are you able, you ungodly and foolish scoundrel, to convince us that it is he who leads you totally contrary to the Scriptures; if there is no prophecy of proper interpretation, and if you take, say you, the more sure word of prophets as the rule to search for the kingdom, then how can you portray the kingdom from things which have no proper interpretation. (Sir), It appears to me that you do not understand the scriptures or the power of God; do we not know that it is only in the scriptures that we have a portrayal of the nature of the kingdom of God—and its king, and its laws, and its privileges? And do we not have the same

17

right as you to judge it for ourselves? And if there is rubbish in it, it belongs to you as false teachers; therefore, physician, heal thyself. You and your brethren must take up your picks and your shovels and your brushes, and clean your own rubbish from your way; as for us, the sweet breezes of truth and sincerity keep the dust away, so that the picture of the kingdom is so clear that one running can read it; and we are determined to keep your rubbish and that of your like from invading our areas, despite the size of your ungodly and unreasonable claims; the meetings which you hold are a disgrace to a nation of brawlers, let alone to a nation of the Welsh.

As for your work in defining your ideas with regard to the kingdom of Christ, remember, we claim the right to it, and until now we understand its rules and its nature far better than you do; and you can keep the kingdom of the Latter Saints until its proper time to appear. It is an abortion now, having appeared before its time, and if its time ever comes, everyone will see in the light of the gospel that it is a fraud. I heard some say that you a brother of Mr. J. Jones; and others say that you are not related to him; some claim that you are neither a good angel nor a man, but that you are a small devil; but no matter how great the shame of men in general would be to claim a man such as you as a relative, yet I consider you to be some kind of man, but that you have been bedeviled to such an extent that a hellish odor rises up from your ungodly and deceitful assertions.

18

I advise you to renounce yourself and bow to the gospel of God, or take your person and your trash from out of its way, lest the stone should fall on you, and crush you to pieces.

We know very well that we belong to the kingdom of the living God, the king almighty and holy, just and merciful, rich and immortal, unchanging and everlasting; and that no one will ever be placed in office with him, or in his place, and that no one can overcome him, or turn him out of his office; and he will reign over his people forever and ever, and the sons of Zion will rejoice in their king, when the faces of all the deceivers of the world and their faces will be gathering soot; and we have the twelve Apostles of the Lamb, although dead, who continue to speak, and we can say Jesus we know, and his apostles we know, but who are you?

And laws pertain to this society, such that neither you nor anyone else can add to, or take away from; God will not permit you to do so, neither do the true subjects of the kingdom permit this; and neither you nor your boastful brethren are innocent of attempting to do so.

We know that there are subjects who belong to the kingdom of God who are not of this world, but who are called, chosen, and faithful, and you will have no place among these children except you repent and bear fruits fit for repentance, and believe the gospel, and confess your deceit, and truly come away from your current position to seek the Lord God of your fathers.

19

An unshakable kingdom is the one we claim, and not one that has died and come alive again, like the kingdom of the Captain and his brethren; the kingdom of the gospel is founded on the rock of ages, and neither the gates of hell (nor foxes, apes, or birds of the night) shall prevail against it.

What is necessary, apart from the miracles that were performed in the days of yore? Although these are no longer performed in the present day, we do not doubt the possibility of miracles being performed if the Almighty sees the necessity. We say that God, through miracles, first proved the divinity and the truths of the Christian faith, and there is no need for second proofs, for we have the full account in the Word, as well as the spirit of God that is leading the children of light to all truth.

The truth is that faking miracles has been a common practice of deceivers in every age, and thus these people insist that we believe that they, in fact, work miracles. But when they are asked to show proof, they excuse themselves with some fraudulent reasons, such as saying that one must have faith in the objects on which the miracle is performed. The reader should note, according to the foregoing statement, that the sea must have faith—the Jordan—the trees and mountains—and the dead, &c.

However, if there was faith in the mountain, or in the water, &c., was not what Christ said; rather, he told them, his disciples, when they asked why they could

20

not cast out the devil, that it was "Because of their unbelief: for verily I say unto you, if ye have faith as a grain of mustard seed, ye shall say unto this mountain, remove hence to yonder place; and it shall remove." Matt. 17:20. Thus, one sees here that it was doubt and lack of faith on the part of the workers of miracles, and that it had nothing to do with the objects; therefore, the reader sees that the deceitful saints dare not try putting forth our doubt as the reason for their failure to perform miracles. We call on them to prove their assertions, by showing the signs; but they say that the performance is secret. And I say that in the days of the establishment of Christianity the early miracles were public; and if our gospel is hidden, it is in the lost that it is hidden.

The Captain and his brethren make a great fuss about the signs that followed those who believed during the apostolic age. Note, however, that Paul proves that a religion of love surpasses all else: 1 Cor. 13:8, "Charity never faileth; but whether there be prophecies, they shall fail; whether there be tongues, they shall cease; whether there be knowledge, it shall vanish away;" but although they be thus, "Now abideth faith, hope, charity, these three; but the greatest of these is charity." See the 13th verse of the above chapter.

Once again, I say to those misnamed saints, in the words of the same Apostle, "Though you speak with the tongues of men and of angels, and have not charity, you are become as sounding brass, or a tinkling

21

cymbal. And though you have the gift of prophecy, and understand all mysteries, and all knowledge; and though you have all faith, so that you could remove mountains, and have not charity, you are nothing," 1 Cor. 13:1,2. But it appears to me that you have neither the thing about which you boast, nor the necessary thing.

On page 24 of his Treatise, the Captain asserts a barefaced lie by saying that eighty-two preachers were ordained by the King of Zion and sent out to preach the Gospel.

Behold the words of the saintly Captain as follows:—"But it is obvious," says he, "that not even the Apostles, although they had learned from the chief Scholar himself, dared to venture on the important task; not even those who had heard the King himself teaching the laws of His Kingdom in secret, and in public; and had seen his miracles before, and after his death," says he, "could Preach the gospel of His Kingdom, and not one of them dared to open his mouth so much as to say the Kingdom of Heaven was at hand; but they stayed in Jerusalem for the fulfillment of the *promise*."

Now I shall prove that he has asserted a lie, and I shall show this from the Holy Book.

1st. In Matthew 10:1–9, &c. In the first verse we see that Christ had called his twelve disciples to him, together with the authority that he gave them. In verses 2, 3, and 4, we have the names of the preachers; in

22

verses 5, 6, and 7, we have their sending out and the instructions they received: "These twelve Jesus sent forth, and commanded them, saying, Go not into the way of the Gentiles, and into any city of the Samaritans enter ye not: but go rather to the lost sheep of the house of Israel. And as ye go, preach, saying, The kingdom of heaven is at hand," &c. Read 6, 12, 13.

2nd. Let us read in the 10th chapter of Luke, the first part of the chapter, as follows:—ver. 1, "After these things the Lord appointed other seventy also," &c.; and in the 9th verse we see what their Divine master commanded them, namely, "And say unto them, The kingdom of God is come nigh unto you." Now, which one is to be believed, the Captain or the Bible? They are opposite to each other, and, therefore, they cannot both be true. I think that the majority of the Welsh would say with one voice, Let God be true and let the Captain be a liar, and so it is; a small sign from the Saints is that one of them opposes the Bible. The reader should remember that it was after Christ's resurrection to glory that the Father's promise was fulfilled, in the pouring out of the Holy Ghost on the day of Pentecost; and then those who were at the work were endowed with power from on high.

This is a sign that the Latter Saints, even their chief minister for Wales, have not received the Holy Ghost, nor one led by it; otherwise, they would walk in the truth and not in deceit and falsehood.

23

Matthew and Luke are strong men on the field of debate: the Latter Saints had better yield to the old Saints in time—and Mark also has his proof, chap. 6:12.

In his Treatise our author makes considerable mention of the conditions of adoption into the Kingdom.

Notice:—No such phrase exists in the order of the Gospel. We have heard of receiving the adoption, and of the spirit of adoption, through which the true saints cry, Abba Father. Concerning the conditions of adoption to the weak, unstable, and corrupt kingdom of those erroneously called Latter Saints, we know nothing of them, nor shall we have anything to do with them in their conditions; rather we shall leave them, the blind leaders of the blind; for as the blind leads the blind, they will both fall into the ditch.

The door of the Kingdom is baptism, says the Captain. I say that Christ is the door of his sheepfold, and nothing or no one else. John 10:7, "Verily, verily, I say unto you, I am the door of the sheep."

I exhort the errant saints not to place baptism, however excellent it may be, in the place of the Mediator himself; otherwise, you will be lost, and you will mislead others as well; consequently, sin will lie at your doors.

Baptism for the forgiveness of sins is extensively mentioned by our author. There is no doubt that the forgiveness has been connected with the true faith, along with repentance and forgiveness; yet men can be baptized, and then be lost—remember Simon Magus.

24

Baptism is not absolutely essential for salvation; if it were otherwise, the thief on the cross would not have been saved. Avoid putting baptism in place of the blood of Christ, which was shed for the forgiveness of sins—"In whom we have redemption through his blood, the forgiveness of sins, according to the riches of his grace." Without the spilling of this blood, there was no forgiveness: baptism can signify our cleansing, but it is the blood of Jesus Christ, his Son, which cleanses us from all sin.

Our arrogant author goes forward with shameless boldness, calling ministers of the New Testament preachers of another gospel, different from the one preached by the Apostles, and calling all to repentance, and receiving their baptism for the forgiveness of their sins. Aha! dear man, lower your ear for a minute, and I shall tell you that the ministers of the Baptists have been baptized once, and have done so according to the rule of the New Testament; and there is one God, one faith, and one baptism; therefore, you can put your song in your pocket. You are like Ishmael, the son of the slave girl, with your hand against everyone, and everyone's hand against you. I pity your immortal soul, and your lost condition: you are aiming at the bulging thickness of the shields of Heaven, and striking your rush arrows at the pupil of the eye of Deity: you wish to extinguish the lamps and the candles which God has kindled and lit, through your ungodly and arrogant blasphemies against the saintly people of the Highest.

25

I hope that at some time God will cause you and your weak-headed brethren to have contrition to recognize the truth, and bring you to the correct path out of the devil's snare in which you are restrained, according to his will.

But the greatest thing of all that our selfish author has, is something he calls a new lesson, &c.; namely, that the officials of the kingdom, it seems, have received their commission directly from the King. He mutters many contentious and irrelevant things on this matter, for the purpose, it seems, to attempt to prove two things: namely, 1st. That none of the ministers or preachers who belong to any one sect in the world have received their mission from God; and, 2nd. That he and his foolish brethren have received such a mission.

But let us focus on the first thing. I say once again, Captain, I come out as your opponent, for your way is heretical in my opinion. Now, I shall prove that God has a host of servants in the field who possess, by the grace of God, the authority and ability to proclaim the Gospel of Peace to the world, without ever having heard directly the voice of Jehovah, or without ever having seen an angel with their physical eyes; and this I will do as follows:—

1st. A command was given by the Head of the Church to his disciples to go and teach all the nations, and he promised to be with them always until the end of the world. Matt. 28:19–20, and Mark 16:15–16.

26

There are several important things contained in these excellent words, but at present I shall draw the reader's attention to only two things; first, a ministry is established here which is not to be changed by any other revelation, and a responsibility as widespread as all the nations, and so detailed as to include every creature, and the eleven could not have fulfilled this important mission without fellow workers and successors. Secondly, the promise connected by them and their successors to the end of the world contains the continuation of the proclamation of the same ministry.

2nd. God has endowed men and sent them to his work; for what does anyone have but that which he has received; each one has his own gift; and great is the company of those who preach it, "And how shall they preach except they be sent," says Paul. And though neither the fathers nor the prophets are alive now, and though all flesh is as grass, &c., yet the Word of our God will stand forever, yes, even though the Apostles and the preachers are dead, the Word of the Lord remains eternally—and this is the Word which was sent to you.

3rd. The success of the work linked with the preaching of the one worthy object to a lost world is proof of this. What did the Apostles of the Lamb have as the substance of all their sermons and writing but Jesus Christ and him crucified, and the unsearchable wealth in him; as for us, we shall never change our topic, even for the old, false Mormon oracles, or anything that Dl. Jones has, or any false prophets who

27

wear shirts of camel's hair to deceive; but we say with all our hearts that Jesus Christ is all things, and in all things. Preaching Christ, in this manner, has been God's power to many who are now alive, for salvation; and let the deceivers and false prophets remember, that it is now too light for them to come to us in their shirts of camel's hair—we can see through their old sackcloth and their shirts of camel's hair: therefore, it is in vain when they say, Lo, here is Christ, or there; for we have been warned, and we will not believe them.

This conceited and boastful author, before the end of what he calls a treatise, &c., makes frequent mention of offices and gifts in the church, &c. With this in mind I call the reader's attention to the following things:

1st. The church of the New Testament is the same from its beginning to its end, if, indeed, it has an end. God does not raise a new church with every age, rather he builds his church—he adds to it from the number of those who are saved. Therefore, 2nd. We refuse the apostles from America, and their chief minister for Wales, as well as those who pretend to be eternal high priests, &c.; for the true church has the same head as before, and the same apostles, the doctrine of which are the twelve stars on the head of the woman who has been clothed with the sun. We will accept no other foundation apart from the one placed in our church; and we will not accept twelve stones in place of the stones already placed, and we do not allow four

28

evangelists in place of those we have; but the entire building is properly interconnected, becoming a Holy Temple in the Lord; and we have those officers who serve honestly, faithfully, and diligently in the vineyard; and we would not exchange even the worst of them for the Captain of the Latter-day Saints. 3rd. Has anyone ever seen or heard mention in the new Testament of apostles who rose up after those twelve who were ordained by Christ, of which Paul was one? What, does every individual church, such as the church of Corinth or the church of Ephesus, have to have twelve apostles, four evangelists, and some prophets, &c., before it can be called God's church, or be part of His kingdom? No; the foolishness is obvious to all; for we have not only Moses and the Prophets, but also Christ and his Apostles, and his Evangelists, &c. And we will not take the Bible or the *plates* of the Mormons with or in place of the Word of our God; and they had better not add to His Word, or they will be found guilty.

I am confident that the reader will see from the notes which I have made in this book, that the chief minister for Wales (as he is called) is but a false teacher, and neither he nor his brethren are led by the Holy Ghost, or that they speak according to the Word of God.

By the time that I had glanced over the above Treatise on the Kingdom of God, yet another one came to my attention, one so presumptuous as if it had been written by the fingers of the devil, who had dipped his

29

pen in the venom of dragons, or in the fiery furnace itself, and had it printed in the gates of hell, and this under the name *Proclamation of the Twelve Apostles—the Saints, &c., to all the kings of the earth, &c.*" Oh! for human nature to have sunk so low, and become so impudent as to assert such majestic things in a deceitful way.

The above booklet, that is the Proclamation, has gone to so far in its baseless assertions, that all on Welshman has to do is read it carefully to see its madness.

It was pleasing, they say, that the great Elohim further spoke from heaven, and associated with man on earth through visions, and through the ministry of the Holy Missionaries; by means of these instruments, they say, the great eternal priesthood was restored or given to the world, according to the order of His Son, that is the Apostleship. This holds the keys to the kingdom of God, &c. I can say as Milton did, "Terrible is their rush, challenging the gates of heaven."

There is an incomparable mixture here, a mixture of priesthood and apostleship! and an attempt to convince us to add to his word. But whatever the scripture says about the priesthood and the high priesthood, the scriptures prove that Christ alone has the office. Read the following chapters, and the matter will be clear, namely Hebrews, chapters 4, 5, 6, 7, 8 and 9, &c. As for adding to his word, see Rev. 22, and verses 18 and 19: "For I testify unto every man that heareth the words

30

of prophecy of this book, if any man shall add unto these things, God shall add unto him the plagues that are written in this book," &c.

On hearing and seeing the foolishness of this deceitful address, someone said, "What, have old Magus and Simon his son risen from the dead; or have Sceva and his sons been released and possessed new bodies; or have the old satanical brother, Muhammed, and his old sister Johannah received some authority to move their persons to Wales at one time in the nineteenth century?" "No," said another who was nearby listening, "it is the twelve apostles of the Latter Saints who have come in the spirit and power of the old family, and if anything, the latter excel in boldness over their forebears."

"What," said another, "the false saints are also like Saul among the prophets; behold, according to their prophecies, the earth will soon tremble, let the Indians rejoice, for they will soon have a city and a holy temple in the middle of or on the American Continent, and they, the men of the long beards will soon rejoice—they will straighten their backs, put down their black boxes, and back with them to their old country, for their old city and their temple will be built for them in Palestine. You kings, &c., you need not worry, rather bring your gold, and your silver, &c., to the people of the Latter-day Saints, for you will be filled with the fullness of the deceitful blessings of the false saints.

31

Great are the cities, and the towns, and the temples, and the sanctuaries that are built by these poor people, if we could only believe them.

Let the earth shake, as the Mount of Olives is about to rend, and the storm and hail and plagues are near; and the new prophets have received knowledge about the time of the coming of the Lord, something no one has ever known before; not even the angels in heaven, but only the Father.

Who would not shout, "Great are the old oracles in America, because they make known all hidden things."

But listen and look, what is the proof that these and other similar things will be? O! only because the saints, and especially their false apostles say, "We know this!!!"

But who will believe them on their word? because it is too light at present for the birds of the night and the owls to appear. I do not consider their proclamation worth making critical notes on, for their foolishness is obvious to all who read it. Therefore, I shall hasten to the end, with an address, not from the Twelve Apostles of the Latter-day Saints, as they erroneously call themselves, but from the Apostles of the Lamb. The sum and substance of Paul's mission to the Corinthians is worth noting, 1 Cor. 2:2: "For I determined not to know any thing among you, save Jesus Christ, and him crucified."

If we were to have all other knowledge, but remained without this knowledge, it would do us no good; the true saints count all things as dung and loss

32

for the sake of the excellence of the knowledge of Jesus Christ, their Lord.

The false prophets and the false teachers have gone out, and it is essential for us to withstand them, close their mouths and salt the land around us, lest their odor have a harmful effect on others.

We must all wear the whole armor of God, so that we may stand against the intrigues of the Devil; and there is no sword like unto the sword of the spirit, which is the Word of God, to confront the battles and the power of darkness, and to bring down the children of the devil, &c.

Perhaps the Captain will be so kind as to take occasion to prepare another booklet, in order to make money; in view of this, especially if he has time before starting his journey to Nauvoo and Jerusalem; as for me, he is welcome to do so; but if his next writing does not far surpass that which has appeared before, I shall not consider it worth my notice.

Dear reader, take heart, pray to God, search his Holy Word with reverence, and keep your heart highly attentive, for it is from the heart that life comes. Now, I commend you to God, and to the word of his grace. May the grace of our Lord Jesus Christ be with us all. Amen.

D. JONES, PRINTER, MERTHYR.

Pamphlet 3

W. R. Davies. *Y Seintiau Diweddaf. Sylwedd Pregeth a Draddodwyd ar y Gwyrthiau, er mwyn Goleuo y Cyffredin, a Dangos Twyll y Creaduriaid a Alwant eu hunain yn Seintiau y Dyddiau Diweddaf* (*The Latter Saints: The Substance of a Sermon Which Was Delivered on the Miracles, to Enlighten the Public, and Show the Deceit of the Creatures Who Call Themselves the Latter-day Saints*). Merthyr Tydfil: David Jones, Heol Fawr, 1846. 20 pages.

In the years 1843–44, William Henshaw had baptized a small group of converts in the Merthyr Tydfil area. Two years prior to the publication of this pamphlet, the Reverend W. R. Davies began attacking Henshaw and his converts, preaching sermons from the pulpit of his Baptist chapel in Dowlais (a distance of two miles from Merthyr Tydfil) and publishing several articles against the Latter-day Saints in *Y Bedyddiwr* (*Baptist*) under a variety of pseudonyms.

Most of this pamphlet is focused on miracles as they are portrayed in the New Testament. In the preface, however, are a few lines directed at William Henshaw:

> This ignorant, unlearned, and characterless ENGLISHMAN from *Cornwall*, after recently being put in Cardiff jail by the Welsh for evil deeds, is he the one, together with a few ignorant and characterless creatures, who possesses the knowledge and secret of the kingdom of heaven (iii)?

Davies also tells of a visit that Henshaw had made to his home in Dowlais, when Davies asked Henshaw to speak to him in Welsh to demonstrate the gift of tongues: "But instead of speaking in tongues I heard (as I knew I would) *I can't speak Welsh, sir.*" Then Davies asked Henshaw to take some poison to demonstrate that "no deadly thing will harm you." Henshaw declined, and Davies concluded that what Henshaw was teaching was nonsense (17). Davies also disparages Dan Jones, mockingly calling him the "praiseworthy apostle" (16).

Dan Jones presented a thorough review of Davies's pamphlet in the December 1846 issue of *Prophwyd y Jubili* (*Prophet of the Jubilee*). His conclusion reads: "Having searched carefully through what you see fit to call 'The Substance of a Sermon,' we have failed to find any substance in it; and if this is an example of your sermons, one need not ask who sent you to preach them, for by your sermons shall ye be recognized" (159).

THE LATTER SAINTS.

THE SUBSTANCE OF A SERMON

WHICH WAS DELIVERED

ON THE MIRACLES,

TO ENLIGHTEN THE PUBLIC,

AND SHOW

THE DECEIT OF THE CREATURES WHO CALL THEMSELVES THE LATTER-DAY SAINTS.

BY W. R. DAVIES,

CAERSALEM, DOWLAIS.

MERTHYR TYDFIL:

PRINTED BY DAVID JONES, HEOL FAWR.

1846.

TO THE READER.

DEAR READER,

I call upon you in true respect for man, and in fear of God, to consider what you believe. I am truly worried that the Welsh people degrade themselves, to listen, especially to such unreasonable rubbish, and such obvious deceit.

The English degraded their character, by believing the false prophetess Johanna Southcott, and other frauds, but the Welsh stood as firm as a rock. They cast away the yoke of the beast of Rome, and they embraced the pure gospel of our great Lord. But Oh! my fellow nation, will you make a mockery of yourselves to all the nations of the earth, by upholding, and believing such a false Christian as this? This ignorant, unlearned, and characterless ENGLISHMAN from *Cornwall*, after recently being put in Cardiff jail by the Welsh for evil deeds, is he the one, together with a few ignorant and characterless creatures, who possess the knowledge and secret of the kingdom of heaven? It is surprising, and worrisome, that the hardworking people of Merthyr and Dowlais have not been wiser before now. How many times have you given the fruits of your hard labor and sweat to maintain wicked men? This rascal and his mad followers have boasted that they preach their foolishness for free, &c., while at the same time taking every opportunity to collect money from everyone they can. It is terrible that such ignorant lunatics presume to mock the administering of the sacraments of our Lord's gospel. I understand that they have now established a fund to help the apostle, &c., to go (so they say) to Jerusalem. Well, give them your money, as you will have plenty of time to regret, and suffer

iv

the mockery of your neighbors, when your deceiving deacons have escaped and left you in your shame, laughing at you, &c. In finishing, I hope that the *Satanists*, if these lines happen to come into their hands, will read them carefully and seriously, and compare them to the Word of Truth; and I am happy to inform you as I finish this time, that there is plenty of virtue in the blood of Jesus Christ, His Son, to cleanse you, however great your heavy and arrogant sins may be, and to return you repentant sinners to the way and order of God in an acceptable time.

I wish from my heart the blessing of God on these lines, to prevent, and forestall my fellow nation from sinking into the abyss of sins and presumption; and I earnestly entreat everyone not to give the name SAINTS to the filthy mob under consideration, rather give them their proper names, namely *Satanists* of the nineteenth century.

I am, &c.,

W. R. DAVIES,

Caersalem,

March, 1846.

DOWLAIS.

SERMON.

1 CORINTHIANS 12:28,

And God hath set some in the church, first apostles, secondarily prophets, thirdly teachers, after that miracles, then gifts of healings, helps, governments, diversities of tongues.

God has honored his people in every age, from the time when Israel was in Egypt until the time of the apostles, now and then, with miraculous powers, as we shall note going forward. We find that he blessed the Church of Corinth with these talents; but it seems that the members, either from lack of understanding, or carelessness and indifference, were guilty of not making proper use of them. All talent and grace flow from the same fountain. We find that wicked men cannot only profess Christianity, but accomplish (as instruments in God's hand) great things, which were done by those who were in possession of the true and saving grace. Matt. 7:22,23. "Many will say to me in that day, Lord, Lord, have we not prophesied in thy name? and in thy name have cast out devils? and in thy name done many wonderful works? And then will I profess unto them, I never knew you, &c." Here are men casting out devils from others, while at the same time being slaves of the devil and his sinful desires, and their hearts are nests to all filthy birds. We cannot judge for a moment, that their claims were not true; and the great Judge himself gives us no place to doubt them. The apostle mentions as many as ten different miraculous talents in this chapter; and he gives instructions so that the Corinthians should not be misled by strange spirits, and false teachers of the gentiles, who claim, and profess that they are under the influences of the Holy Ghost; and he explains to them, "No man speaking by the Spirit of God, calleth Jesus accursed," 1 Cor. 12:3.

6

The gentile, false teachers scorned and mocked Jesus Christ, and they called him "accursed;" yet they claimed that they were under the influence and direction of inspiration.

The apostle showed that this was impossible, and that it would have been no different from the Spirit of God divided against itself; because Jesus Christ was the holy person who was honored from Moses to Malachi by that Spirit, and was the soul of their prophecies; and because he continues to glorify them during the New Testament times through the most remarkable miracles; but mainly during his resurrection from the dead, as well as the great and powerful outpourings of the day of Pentecost, in the house of Cornelius, &c.; consequently, the apostle reasoned that it was impossible for anyone, whatever they do or say, if they have no true respect for Jesus Christ, to be under the direction or the influence of this Spirit. The writer goes on by teaching them of the great things which he accomplished for Christ, his people in particular, and his church in general. He mentions "diversities of gifts, differences of administrations, diversities of operations, all effects of the same Spirit;" and the aims, although different in their actions, were *the same*, namely the edification of the Church, verse 7. Our text mentions the officers of the apostolic church, as well as the different gifts given them to make them fully fit and suitable to carry out their important and excellent positions, such as declaring wisdom, for the apostles, declaring knowledge for the prophets; (see *Dr. Macknight*) for another, miraculous faith to suffer for the cause of the Savior, as well as complete readiness to withstand their enemies. Matt. 10:19, 20: "But when they deliver you up, take no thought how or what ye shall speak: for it shall be given you in that same hour what ye shall speak. For it is not ye that speak, but the Spirit of your Father which speaketh in you." See Luke 21:14, 15. To another, gifts of healing. This gift varied in its form, for which reason they are called *gifts*.

1. By the laying on of hands. Mark 16:18, They shall lay hands on the sick, and they shall recover.
2. By anointing with oil. James 5:14, 15, Is any sick among you? let him call for the elders of the church; and let them pray over him, anointing him with oil in the name of the Lord, &c.
3. Clothes, napkins, or aprons, &c. Paul: the shadow of Paul effected the same miracles. Acts 19:12, And God wrought

7

special miracles by the hands of Paul: so that from his body were brought unto the sick, handkerchiefs or aprons; and the diseases departed from them, and the evil spirits went out of them.

We find that miracles were clear, obvious, unhidden things; and the *Satanists* must be asked whether they did such things in Merthyr or Dowlais? That arrogant man they call a "*praise-worthy Apostle*" is here now—has his shadow, his clothes, or his body effected such powerful acts? It is answered negatively, no. Then we see that his claims and those of his followers are nothing but a nest of the most terrible and fearful lies claimed by wicked men, or the sons and daughters of hell, in any age of the world:—See the "Baptist" for last March.

Verse 5, "To another the working of miracles." The learned critics vary in their opinions with regard to these miracles. Their opinions are contained in the following:—one group believes that it means an enabling authority to give miraculous gifts to others, i.e., the spirit of the Lord would move the mind and feeling of such as this, to put his hands on the person, or persons, whom God intended, Acts 8:14, 17, "Then laid they their hands on them, and they received the Holy Ghost," &c. Others judge them to be gifts, or the power to strike the opponent with a judgment, or death, as it was with Ananias and Saphira; and others judge that the general miracles in the establishment of Christianity is what is meant, i.e., raising of the dead, giving sight to the blind, drinking poisonous and deadly things without harm; but the opinion of the most learned and knowledgeable critics is that the gift to cast out devils is what is meant, for the apostles had holy authority to cast them out of those possessed by them.

Verse 5, "And to another the gift of prophecy." The proper meaning of prophecy is the gift from God to predict things to come. See Acts 21:9, 10, 11; Acts 15:32, "Judas and Silas, being prophets also themselves."

Verse 6, "To another discerning of spirits," i.e., they possessed the gift of understanding which spirit moved the speakers, as well as the principle of those seeking religion and their suitability for office in the church, Chap. 14:24, 25; 1 John 4:1

Verse 7, "To another divers kinds of tongues," or *languages*. The possessor of this gift was enabled to preach the gospel in whatever country he visited, without going to the trouble of

8

learning the language of that country. Note here, for the purpose of deceiving the ignorant, the *Satanists* attempt to BABBLE some foolishness that is not a language, just as we hear children babbling, or attempting to imitate a foreign tongue by babbling *Horem, harem, hooram; Tyndram, Twmdram, &c.*, or something similar. In this, the children are but childlike and innocent, but the *Satanic* fiends do so to deceive unlearned women and children—it is devilish. After one of them has mumbled something like this, another gets up and with a holy look on his face informs the followers with such deceit, cunning, boldness and heresy, that the Holy Ghost in its miraculous talent has come upon the brother or sister, and that they have heard them speak a strange language, &c. Then another rises to his feet with infernal boldness and pretends to interpret the *gibberish, &c.* All those who study the New Testament will see that nothing could be more opposite to the talent of speaking in tongues than this method. If the false prophet *Henshaw*, an Englishman from Cornwall, or *Middleman*, an Irishman, were to speak in Welsh, Hebrew, &c.; and if A. Evans, a monoglot Welshman, were to speak in English, Irish, &c., they could profess the gift: the apostles did this as easily as breathing. While speaking with tongues, "And to another the interpretation of tongues," verse 8, (not everyone who could speak could interpret, &c.), the Word of the Lord spread like wildfire throughout the known world in the time of the Apostles; and despite how varied the gifts were, they were all given by the *same* spirit, and for the same purpose. Oh! my fellow nation, do not be deceived by such extremes of foolishness and madness: consider what speaking with tongues was, &c.

After the Apostle showed all these gifts, he put them into a unity of purpose, similar to how the limbs make up the human body. Note that God in the establishment of the Church organized and set in it several officers, with a view to the benefit and structure of the spiritual body of Christ, "which truly God has set."

1. Apostles. Apostle means a person sent by God; in this sense Christ is called the apostle of our profession. Heb. 3:1, "Wherefore, holy brethren, partakers of the heavenly calling, consider the Apostle and High Priest of our profession, Christ Jesus." But more generally, this character is given to the chief

9

officials of the New Testament. Eph. 4:11, "And he gave some apostles." We shall note the essential things, which they needed to have in order to be an apostle.

1. It was necessary for the apostles to have seen Christ after his resurrection with their own eyes. Acts 1:21, 22, "Wherefore of these men which have companied with us all the time that the Lord Jesus went in and out among us,—must one be ordained to be a witness with us of his resurrection;" as a result, they can bear personal witness as they were eye-witnesses of the things which they testify. 1 John 1:3, "That which we have seen and heard declare we unto you." The false prophets understood this matter and used it to blacken the character of the apostle Paul, and to try to convince the Church of Corinth that he was not an apostolic officer; to these he directs his words in 1 Cor. 9:1, "Am I not an apostle? have I not seen Jesus Christ our Lord?" 1 Cor. 15:8, "And last of all he was seen of me also." To make up for this lack, the aforementioned madmen claim that they too have seen Christ, that he is with them in person in the rooms of their special meetings, &c. I consider it unnecessary to spend time disproving or exposing this terrible boldness. Let every sensible man be afraid, and wonder at the patience and tolerance of God. What will evil men not do, yes, what will they not say?

2. The apostles had to be sent directly by Christ himself. John 20:21, "As my Father hath sent me, even so send I you." Acts 26:16, 17, "But rise, and stand upon thy feet: for I have appeared unto thee, to make thee a minister and a witness both of these things which thou hast seen, &c.

3. Each apostle was under the unfailing leadership of the Holy Ghost. John 16:13, "He will guide you into all truth." Gal. 1:12, "By the revelation of Jesus Christ."

4. They were endowed with miraculous gifts. 2 Cor. 12:12, "Truly the signs of an apostle were wrought among you, in signs, and wonders, and mighty deeds." Have any of these powerful signs been seen in Merthyr? No, *not one*.

5. The Holy Ghost was given by the laying on of hands of the Apostles. Acts 8:14–17. There were some visible manifestations accompanying the receiving of the Spirit, when the apostles laid their hands on them; so that it is said that Simon was "surprised to see the signs, and powers," &c.; he offered money to receive them himself.

10

6. Their ministry was not confined to one particular place, rather their field was the whole world. Matt. 28:19.

2. Prophets. Different things are understood by the phrase to prophesy, such as gift, ability to understand the prophecies of the Old Testament, and to explain Christ's Religion, for well-being and edification. 1 Cor. 14:3, "But he that prophesieth speaketh unto men to edification, and exhortation, and comfort." 1 Cor 11:4, "For every man praying or prophesying, having his head covered—every woman praying or prophesying," &c. The word in its original, common meaning signifies the foretelling of things to come. Acts 11:27, 28, "Such as Agabus, who signified by the Spirit that there should be great dearth throughout all the world, which came to pass."

3. Teachers, or preachers. Romans 12:7, "Or he that teacheth, on teaching."

4. Miracles.

5. Gifts to heal. We shall comment on this later.

6. Assistants. The opinions of the Commentators differ about these. Some regard them as persons who assisted the apostles during their travels; others say that they were ministers and that part of their work was to assist and strengthen the faith of the saints: others understand them to be men making generous gifts to help the poor, the widows, and the orphans.

7. Rulers; or men made worthy in wisdom, grace, and concern to be elders. 1 Tim. 5:17, "Let the elders that rule well," &c.

8. Diversity of tongues; those who speak various languages.

Having taken a brief look at the topic, in its context, we will now study the subject in more detail.

I. The nature of a miracle, or what is a miracle.

II. The purpose of miracles, or their necessity.

III. Their decline.

I. We ask what a miracle is. The original meaning of the word MIRACLE is something unusual; it is an action above the ordinary order of things, or above all natural law. A miracle is different from the ordinary order of nature, or an exception to the established laws of Nature. Earthquakes and commotions happened on land and sea, and yet were not miraculous; many strange happenings took place in the world that amazed and frightened its inhabitants, and at that time they were counted as miracles: but it was understood that they came about according to the order and laws of nature.

11

A miracle, or a sign, is an act above the laws of nature and not against them, for the purpose of authorizing some message and to give importance or a holy impression to this message, like Moses and Aaron before Pharaoh.—*Unusual things*; in this sense, can we consider everything beyond our ability to account for as a miracle? no, if we follow and trace these strange things to their origins, and understand their secrets, the miracle vanishes, although the ignorant and unintelligent may wonder and be surprised. What would the inhabitants at the equator, who enjoy sunlight for six months, think if they were moved to our location, and were to see it set in a few hours? Doubtless they would think that nature had been destroyed; as for us, if we were unknowingly moved to their location, we would think Joshua's miracle foolishness compared to what we would see there; but having understood how things are, the wonder disappears and Joshua's miracle would stand in its original glory. When it is said that a miracle is an act above or beyond the course of nature, it seems at first sight that this definition is not without opposition, and that it shows boldness or that we profess a perfect and complete understanding of the secrets of nature, &c. Before we can understand that such an act, or effects, are above them, and call it a miracle, we do not need to understand these things perfectly to be able to recognize a miracle. We know that the sun rises and sets at its appointed times, and that the moon keeps its seasons according to the laws established for them, and through this they show the greatness, power and wisdom of their Creator. Psalm 19:1,2. But if they should stand still, or go backwards, we have enough sense to understand that that would be a true miracle.

We take for granted the existence of God, his greatness, and his self-dependence, and, as a result, that he is the cause or source of existence, and that he has established laws to govern nature; this must be accepted as undeniably true, according to the evidence of reason and experience; like this, we see the causes and their effects working throughout the order so regular and straight, that we are led to the inevitable conclusion that they have their set, determined laws. The *Deist* and the Christian agree in this; but the former argues that God has bound himself to these laws so that he cannot change them at any time or for any reason. The latter, although acknowledging

12

the laws, believes that circumstances justify overruling them in order to perform a miracle. Miracles were performed in many ways. Sometimes by halting the laws of nature if we believe that the sun and moon stopped at Joshua's command; before the effect became obvious, he had to halt their progress. The same was done with the Red Sea, and the Jordan. At other times they were overruled; *Iron swimming*, the fire that was restricted from burning the lads, the lions prevented from killing Daniel, &c. Sometimes the same laws were extended, such as the multiplying of the loaves, giving sight to the blind, resurrecting the dead, &c. All these were above nature, not against its laws, and were, therefore, miracles.

Prophecy was a miracle. According to the law of nature, man is completely unable to foresee the future; yet, in spite of this, things which had not yet taken place were read and foretold in the clearest way; light was shed on the understanding of the prophets to serve a particular purpose; the eternal curtains were raised for them, and they looked forward to the time when there will be no time; when the curtains were lowered again, the future was as dark for them as it is for us: and if prophecy was above the laws of nature, it must have been a miracle.

Let us note the false miracles. By these I mean things done by the devil or through deceitful appearances by evil men. I must admit that I read about such deeds, and that I do not know how to account for them, except for the devil, (with God's tolerance); for example, the miracles of Egypt, the oracles of the gentiles, &c. In order to prove these statements more clearly, note

1. The existence of the devil must be admitted, or else deny the Bible. It is not unreasonable to judge that he can perform such things, and they appear to be miracles because they are beyond our understanding, since Satan is a strong and quick creature and invisible to us, but God allows him, as in Job's case, to perform a true and substantial miracle.

2. The truth confirms this opinion. Christ warned his disciples, telling them of evil men who would rise up, "and they shall show great signs and wonders; insomuch that, if it were *possible*, they shall deceive the very elect. Behold, I have told you before. Wherefore, if they shall say unto you, Behold, he is in the desert; go not forth; behold, he is in the secret chambers; believe it not." Many false prophets succeeded by promising

13

to show their followers signs and miracles; we read about one in particular from Egypt who bewitched many to follow him. Acts 21:38; the chief captain asked Paul by mistake, "Art not thou that Egyptian, which before these days madest an uproar, and leddest out into the wilderness four thousand men that were murderers?" These were captured and killed by Felix. Soon another rose up in the same way, and he and his followers were destroyed by Festus. Another named Jonathan, a Weaver, persuaded a great many to follow him into the dessert; he was captured and burned to death by Vespasian. Just as some attracted their followers to the desert, so others did to the rooms. Josephus mentions one who claimed that the Lord had given him a revelation in Jerusalem commanding the people to go to the temple where they would have a sign to save them; they went, men, women and children, but instead of being saved, the Romans set the place on fire and 6,000 of them were burned on the spot. We could note scores of similar ones who rose up in different ages of the world; but of all the fools ever seen, there has never been any similar in boldness and foolishness to the *Satanists*.

We read in Deut. 13 about false prophets, and dreamers, and the things they said coming true; this seems to be the difficulty, that is understanding the difference between a true and a false miracle. The tendency of every act which reveals its source is that if the fountain is bad, it must be, according to the nature of things, that the streams are also bad. The purpose of these men in Deuteronomy was to persuade their followers to worship false gods by promising them great things. The purpose of the deacons of the *Satanists* is to get money out of unlearned, foolish men, not to urge them to live in a godly way, but by promising them heaven and a blessed life in America, and by filling them with rubbish far below common sense.

3. The effect of what is called a miracle, has different names, such as *Wonder*. This name originated from the impression created on the onlookers, or the eye-witnesses. Who could not wonder at seeing the dead come back to life? Another time, *Sign*, a name which originated from the fact that the effect was a sign, or a proof of the truth of some testimony which was confirmed. Also *Strength*, a name signifying the cause of the effect, that is power, yes, godly power. *Miracle*, this is the name most used by us, although the others are more scriptural. This

14

name originates from what the effect is in itself, that is, an act or an effect beyond the laws of nature. Our Lord caused many of these effects; we have the history of forty, and reason to believe that there were a thousand; this proved the truth of its witness.

1. They fulfilled the prophecies. The prophets said that the Messiah would perform miracles; if he had not, he would not have answered them, but by performing them he proved who he was. Isaiah 35, "Then the eyes of the blind shall be opened," &c. "Go and tell John."

2. A miracle is proof in itself, by showing omnipotence. There is this difference: prophecy proves *Omniscience*; a miracle shows *Omnipotence*; and since a miracle shows *Omnipotence*, there was a connection between them and God, yes, God himself. No one but the Almighty could have turned the water into wine, healed the sick, given limbs to those who were without them, restored life to the dead—the Son of the widow from Nain, &c.

3. They are proven by their frequency—curing *every* disease and *every* illness, not just some.

4. By the direct way they were performed. Not using means, such as the hands of the apostles, and the prayers of the saints—just by saying the word, the sick would be healed, and the dead would be restored to life, &c.

5. By their publicity. We have already noted that our Lord warned his disciples, not to listen to, or believe anyone who tried to lead them to the rooms or to the desert. All the things of the gospel are public things, and we wish to draw your attention to this in particular. The evil men called Saints, try to *persuade* the ignorant, that the miracles are performed in the room, which they call a CHURCH, &c.: Note, *miracles never took place in the Church*, but out in the world, and in the most popular and public places, and claiming such a thing is no more than trying to make the blind blinder, and hiding deception. I wish the reader to note, yes to notice in detail, whether the following things were done in ROOMS, or in the CHURCHES?—

1. Turning the water into wine; not in the *church*, but in a MARRIAGE, in view of everyone, John 2:1–11. He taught and performed them in the Synagogues, so that he surprised them.

2. Casting out devils. Matt. 4:23, 24, "And Jesus went about all Galilee, teaching, healing all manner of sickness, and all

15

manner of disease, &c. See Luke 4:33, 37; and 9:37–43. Legion from the man in the Gadarenes.

3. Raising the dead. Daughter of Jairus. Luke 8:41–56. Here there was no faith in anyone, rather they were mockers. The son of the widow, from Nain—no one asked him for this; it was an unrequested favor. Lazarus, although rotting in his grave. "Then many of the Jews saw, and believed in Jesus."

4. Giving sight to the blind. See Matt. 8:22–26; Matt. 9:27–31; and John 9:1–7.

5. The lame. Matt. 15:29, 30.

6. Feeding the five thousand. Matt. 14:13–17. Every man will see, if he chooses to see, that the miracles were not performed in rooms, and that claiming such things is the deceit of evil men, for they are unable to perform them.

II. The purpose of miracles. God did nothing without a purpose.

1. Not to prove his existence. If some of the disbelievers were to ask for a miracle to prove this, they should be referred to a nature book. Psalm 19:1, 2, 3; Rom. 1.

2. Not to confirm moral commandments: reason and nature prove that getting drunk, committing adultery, killing, stealing are evil, &c.

3. In Egypt we have the first stories of miracles, and it seems that their purpose was to deliver the Jews from the idols of the place. Egypt had so many gods that when Moses, according to his Lord's command, asked Pharaoh for permission to worship them, he replied, "Who is the Lord? I know him not; i.e., I do not know the name of which of the gods you ask. Was it for the purpose of announcing himself and making his name glorious throughout the earth that the unforgettable miracles were performed?

4. Another purpose is to show and give proof to the world of the greatness and supremacy of the God of Israel over the idols of the gentiles—remember Elijah, and the prophets of Baal. NOTE. The prophet did not try to persuade Ahab, and others, to come to some room and believe; no, rather he took him to the top of the mountain; and however strong his enmity, and however deep his prejudice, he got him and the thousands of volunteers to believe before leaving the place; and if the men who claim miracles, can actually perform them, why do they not do so in the market place of Merthyr, or on the tops of the mountains, &c.; the men know better things.

16

5. The main purpose of a Miracle is to prove the truth of him who was sent, and that his teaching is from God. This was the intent in Egypt, on top of Carmel, and the purpose was answered everywhere; and this was how they answered in the time of the Son of God and his apostles; our Lord put all his testimony to rest on his miracles—"Though ye believe not me, believe the works," &c.

Our blessed Lord, when sending out his disciples in his great and glorious name, gave his holy seal to go with his testimony. Mark 16:17, "And these signs shall follow them," &c.; and it was not an empty, pretentious, or deceptive promise, but a substantial truth. The most deadly poison could not kill them, nor injure them, nor could the most dangerous snakes poison them, Acts 28:8; they cured the sick wherever they walked; they spoke whatever languages they chose—remember the day of Pentecost; is it enough, for brevity, to ask the inhabitants of Merthyr and its neighborhood, if such things were done here? Hands were laid upon T——s J——s, a woman in Pendarren, W——m H——s, and many more—were they healed? Yes, under medical treatment, but in no other way. For the purpose of trying to hide their shame regarding this, they put the blame on the faith of the one who had hands laid upon him, "that his, or her faith was too weak," &c. It is not IN the faith of the man that the miracle is contained, rather in the mighty name of Jesus of Nazareth—remember the lame man at the gate of the temple: that poor man expected nothing but money; and if faith is necessary, according to their own reasoning and admission, there must be few men of little faith under God's heaven, for they lay hands upon themselves. Does not *"dear little Maggie"* have faith? Did she get a strong hip instead of the withered one? I expect to see her without her crutch next time; but if I meet her in the same condition, I will not mention a miracle, for shame, on the praiseworthy apostle, namely *Cap. D——l J——s*, who was and is at present in Merthyr. No, no, the age of miracles has passed by: it is easy for an evil man, after being *satanized*, to take to his bed and pretend to be ill, and just as easy for a bold, ungodly, godless man to lay his hands on him, and for that man to pretend to be cured, &c. Things like this are no more than child's play in order to deceive ignorant and superstitious men on the one hand, although, on the other hand, it is bold, and the most

17

dreadful sin that mortal man can commit, namely to profess, or rather imitate the acts and miracles of the Spirit of the living God. The different sins of our corrupt nature are often great, loathsome, and perverse, but they do not deserve to be compared to the devilish presumption of these men: in a word, the conditions of the most wanton prostitutes and the most wicked thieves in the *Cellars of Pontystorehouse* are innocent; yes, even the hateful dealings of *Dic Tamer* and his sort, disappear from sight when they are compared with those of the *Satanists*, and they are not a thousandth part as purple and scarlet as those of the "praiseworthy apostle" and his brother, namely the prophet of hell. May the grace of God keep my fellow nation, the dear Welsh people, from being enchanted by such satanic deceivers. The false prophet of Pendarren called at my house some time ago, and began to claim and argue his miracles, &c.; that he and his brothers possess every power which the apostle possessed; I listened carefully for a while; but finally I grew tired of his boldness, and asked him to speak to me in the Gomeric tongue, since the Holy Spirit taught him to answer without worrying what he would say, Luke 21:14; but instead of speaking in tongues I heard (as I knew I would) *I can't speak Welsh, sir*. So, this is speaking in strange tongues after all the claims and the lies. Next, I asked him whether he could raise the dead. He was not sufficiently Satanic to answer me in the affirmative, but he did not admit that he could not; but he hurried to say that he had seen the raising of the dead with his own eyes; but he professed his miracles and enthusiastically argued for them, quoting the Scriptures relative to the subject, and, among others, "If you drink any deadly thing, it shall not hurt you;" at this point, I ordered him to stop and called one of my children; I gave her a few pennies, directing her to run to Mr. D. Lewis, the *Druggist*, and buy their worth of poison, reasoning with the prophet that there was no need to argue another word, that we had come to the *point*: the POISON would decide once and for all, and we would have proof as to whether "any deadly thing will harm you;" at this, he had had enough—his countenance changed; and I asked him, when I saw him pale, "Now, Sir, will you take the test? *Yes, or no?* The response I had was, *No, sir*. Then I gave him some advice, and away he went. The deceiver knew that his fate would be like

18

that of Muhammed. A woman named Zeenab, in the year 628, put poison for the Satanic Muhammed in a roast lamb in order to avenge the killing of her father. The poison did its proper work; and she said in self-defense, "I wanted to know, and I decided to find out whether the man's claims were true or false. You see, if he had been a prophet, he would have known that there was death in the lamb; and if he could perform the miracles he professed, it would not do him the least harm;" and she added, "Now his deceit has been revealed forever."

We will look at the ceasing of the *Miracles*.

1. Claiming the continuation of miracles proves the disbelief, hard-heartedness, and atheism of evil men, and, mercifully, this accusation only falls on a small number of the world's inhabitants. The Gospel has been proclaimed throughout Europe, and different parts of the world, and in every place where it has been made known; it is believed and embraced by myriads; consequently, miracles are not needed to confirm it. Thousands believed it between, and on top of, the hills of Wales, and they now sing of it in the Heaven of Heavens; and it will continue to be believed when the creed and deceit of Joe Smith are rotting in oblivion.

2. By claiming that miracles continue, they throw the greatest scorn on the miracles of our great Lord, and his apostles; if they are needed now, then they were not sufficient to prove and confirm Christianity; they left the system unfinished; but if they did everything to perfection, then they have proven Christianity, and there is no need for additional proofs—the kingdom is unshaken.

3. Claiming the continuation of the *miracles* spoils and destroys the miraculous proof forever, by making them ordinary things—*an uncommon deed* is a miracle; but if they are things to continue through every age and to be performed in every country, they are not uncommon things, rather they are constant, natural, and ordinary things; but if this is so, there is no reason to accept them as proof; they would be more likely to create unbelief than to remove it. If in every age, and country, we were taken up by their frequency, and not by their wonder: To ask why *miracles* did not happen daily, is to ask, why should miracles not cease to be miracles. Since eclipses of the sun and moon happen so frequently, they are not taken much notice

19

of: if they were to stand still in every age or every ten years, Joshua's miracle would be forgotten; and if the dead were raised, &c., everywhere there was preaching, the acts of Christ and his apostle would be no more miraculous and wonderful than seeing the earth produce plants year after year.

4. Claiming the continuation of miracles deposes faith, because it is God's will that we live by faith, and rest on the prophecies, God's testimony of his Son, and miracles before; for if there is a need for miracles, there is no need for faith—we remember Thomas.

5. Claiming the continuation of miracles is a characteristic of unchristian and evil men. See 2 Thes. 2:9, "Even him, whose coming is after the working of Satan with all power and signs and lying wonders; and with all deceivableness of unrighteousness in them that perish; because they received not the love of the truth." "Now the Spirit speaketh expressly, that in the latter times some shall depart from the faith, giving need to seducing spirits, and doctrines of devils," &c.

6. God never performs miracles where there are sufficient reasons to believe without them. Christ's enemies asked him, when he was on the cross, to come down, and then they would believe in him. If they had not had every opportunity before, he would probably have agreed to their request; but if he had come down, it would not have added anything to the things he did: what would this have been in comparison to raising the dead or darkening the sun, &c.?

7. No one except for the Catholics, Muslims, and the *Satanists*, claim their continuation. The Holy Ghost knew of their impudence, and for the purpose of giving a holy seal and impression on the gospel, he gave witness through signs and wonders, &c., and a challenge is given to the world, to evil men and devils, to show one thing which equals a miracle. When the Satanists are asked about it, they answer in the words of Christ, "An adulterous generation, &c., seeketh after a sign," &c., supposing that something like this answers the purpose. The Son of God showed several to them; as a result, he could not answer them in a more fitting way; but as for this group, they have not shown, and they do not show *a single one*. These are the extremes of insolence: a devil, despite all his cunning and craftiness, can never make a man more devilish and

20

infernal, than getting him to imitate miracles; and in my opinion, no man would do such a thing, unless his conscience had been seared with hot iron.

INSTRUCTION.

1. We see the glory of Christ's religion—no fault in it. God gave signs in the Old Testament, in order to shut out every false prophet; these glorious things were sent to ensure the gospel forever, and they will be like *walls* or foundations which evil men will never be able to climb or imitate. They pretend to heal the sick, and some evil men testify that they have received healing through them, but where is the blind who has received his sight, and the deaf his hearing, and the dead his life? Where is *Maggie* and her useless hip? It is humorous to see her carrying the *Proclamation of the Twelve Apostles* and promoting it about the place. It confirms their ability to perform miracles, but her poor hip proclaims its lie more loudly than her tongue. The "praiseworthy Apostle" can perform miracles, says Maggie and others with their tongues: "No, they cannot—it is all your infernal and satanic lies," says the withered hip. Which should we believe—their tongues or their hips?

2. The inexcusability of the Gospel's hearers. "How shall we escape, if we neglect so great salvation?" Heb. 2:3. If old, godly Morris Jones and benevolent Dafydd Saunders, strong their reasons, as well as many of the old ministers whom you have heard preach the gospel of God's grace in its purity, and not jabbering foolishness and madness, were to arise and be sent to address you from heaven and be allowed to tell you of the glorious sights of the land above, no doubt we would be filled with amazement; and also, what if the spirits of some evil and ungodly men were to appear from the flames, and tell of the terrors and the worm that does not die, &c., no doubt we would be frightened to an immeasurable degree, but it would be too weak to convince a single sinner—"If they do not believe Moses and the prophets, neither will they be persuaded, though one rose from the dead." Welshmen, do not believe every spirit; and remember, if thousands of deceivers, similar to the scoundrel Joe Smith, were to arise, or even if an angel from heaven, preach any other gospel unto you than has been preached to you, let him be accursed.

David Jones, Printer, Merthyr.

Pamphlet 4

Daniel Jones. ***Y Drych Cywir, lle y gellir canfod yn eglur Twyll Mormoniaid, neu "Seintiau y Dyddiau Diweddaf," mewn dull o Holiadau ac Atebion, rhwng Daniel a'i Gyfaill* (*The Correct Image, Wherein One Can Perceive Clearly the Deceit of the Mormons, or the "Latter-day Saints," in the Form of Questions and Answers, between Daniel and His Friend*). Carmarthen: J. T. Jones, 1847. 12 pages.**

Daniel Jones was a blind man who, after being baptized in July 1846, claimed to have his sight returned during his confirmation, but left the Church shortly thereafter (see Episode 4.2 for a more in-depth account).

Captain Jones's reaction to this pamphlet was an eight-page pamphlet of his own—*"Haman" Hanging from His Own Gallows!*—that contained his version of the details of the baptism, the momentary restoration of the blind man's sight, and the testimony of various witnesses. For the English translation of Dan Jones's pamphlet, see *Defending the Faith*, item J10.

THE

CORRECT IMAGE,

WHEREIN ONE CAN PERCEIVE CLEARLY

THE DECEIT OF THE MORMONS,

OR

"THE LATTER-DAY SAINTS;"

IN THE FORM OF QUESTIONS AND ANSWERS, BETWEEN DANIEL AND HIS FRIEND.

BY

DANIEL JONES, Penygraig.

"Beware of *False Prophets,* which come to you in sheep's clothing, but inwardly they are ravening wolves."

"For there shall arise false Christs, and *false prophets*, and shall shew great signs and wonders; inasmuch that, if it were possible, they shall deceive the very elect."

N. B. That which Daniel answers has taken place literally, as it is written.

CARMARTHEN:

PRINTED BY J. T. JONES, GREEN STREET.

1847.

TO THE WELSH PEOPLE.

DEAR FELLOW-COUNTRYMEN,—Such a leaflet as this, at first sight, may surprise you, and cause you to think that madness and foolishness were responsible for my making such a presentation to you; but I can assure you without hesitation that it was after sincere persuasion, having seriously conferred with religious brothers and friends of different denominations and my own careful considerations, that I ventured to the task, being completely convinced that it was my special duty. It is true that inability and ignorance like strong and high fortresses are before me as insuperable obstacles to overcome; but consider for a moment that deception and heresy are being spread around me, and through Wales generally, until some of my dear neighbors and many of my fellowmen are charmed to believe such heresy as is declared by the MORMONS, which causes me, despite all obstacles, to try to do my best against them, sincerely hoping and wishing that the following unworthy and disorganized lines will be a means, with the blessing of the GIVER of all blessings, to deliver some and prevent others more able and more suitable to withstand them wisely and bravely, so that enlightened Wales will not be darkened by deceivers, and many misled by false teachers as I was,

Is the wish of your unworthy servant,

DANIEL JONES.

THE CORRECT IMAGE, &C.

Some strange sound I hear
Everywhere I travel,
About the *Mormons* so great,
Or rather the Latter *Saints*.

They travel throughout Wales
And bitterly they announce,
That all are lost
Unless they join with them.

They say that the gifts
Are the same as in days of old,
Within the Church continuing,
To all those who believe.

So I too was deceived,
Their words I believed,
And with them I joined,
But behold my cry—I was
disappointed.

I believed in my Jesus,
That he was my Savior,
They told us that without fail
I would be blind no longer.

I believe now that Jesus,
Is as strong as before in his power,
That he can work great miracles
Should he now wish to do so.

But from some wise providence,
I believe that the miracles,
Are not to be found throughout the
wide world
And neither is there a need for them.

And now I must testify,
That the *Saints* only deceive,
If you buy this you will have the full
story,
Of the way I was charmed.

FRIEND.—Good day to you, dear Daniel; how have you been this long time?

DANIEL.—Good day to you. My mind has been very troubled for some time.

F. What causes you to be so?

D. I know you have heard of this new sect who call themselves The Latter-day Saints; or as they are commonly known, *The Mormons*.

F. Yes, many times; but what do you have to do with them?

D. I will tell you; they came to do what they call preaching in the neighborhood where I live; I went to listen to them, and when I heard their fancy talk, they charmed me into believing them, and into joining with them; but along came their deceit!

4

and after going with them I understood it, and I turned back from them afterwards.

F. For goodness sake, dear Daniel, what made you go to them? Were there not other denominations around you could have gone to? and as far as I can judge, there are godly men in these also; and why would these not do for you? But what happened? let me hear.

D. Well, I shall tell it from beginning to end. There had been something on my mind for some time, seeing so many different sects in the world, and so much condemning one of the other, that I was afraid that the spirit of Christianity was becoming lost from their midst. Also I had some idea that a new sect would arise, closer to the Bible; and when it came, it would swallow up all these different denominations into one body; and then, you see, my mind was ready to accept them. When they came to the neighborhood, I went to listen to them, and I heard them speak very strange things.

F. What did you hear from them that was like that?

D. Before I go further with my story, I shall tell you some of the things I heard: one strange thing they said was that the church had been sent to the wilderness twelve hundred and sixty years ago, and how they interpreted the prophecy in the Book of Revelation, 12. 6, and that God did not have a true church on earth during that time, and that an end had come to the appointed time recently through one called *Joseph Smith*, from America, having a supernatural revelation of the form and the order and the authority to restore them to their primitive privileges and gifts. Now, you see that this strikes very close to what I have told you.

F. Yes, indeed; but go ahead with your story.

D. They said also that miracles had been restored as in the time of the Apostles; that they could cast out devils; and if they ate something deadly it would do them no harm. They laid their hands on the sick, and they cured them, so that there was no need for anyone from their church to suffer any physical illness; they would, through the authority they received from Christ, and

5

the faith of the sufferer, directly remove the ailment. They said also that Jesus Christ will come to reign in twenty-five years' time in their midst on the earth for a thousand years, and that all the old godly ones would be resurrected to reign with them, and that every mountain and hill would be made flat by that time, according to how they explained Isaiah 40. 4, and before that time, they said that the godly who had died after the church had gone to the wilderness, would come back to them to ask some of them to be baptized in their place; and they proved this supposition from 1 Cor. 15. 29, and many other things too long to relate to you now. Strange, isn't it, friend!

F. Yes, indeed, very strange; but there was no need to be long before seeing whether some things they said were true or false, especially healing the lame, for there is plenty of opportunity for them in every district; and also, did you hear that they had healed anyone anywhere?

D. Yes, they said, far away from here.

F. Why did they need to go far away when there is plenty of opportunity here? You are the one who badly needs two eyes. I know of no other place in the world where they would have a better chance to show their miracles. Why didn't you seek this from them?

D. Oh dear, I did; and they promised, faithfully, that I would have my sight before joining them; but fair play to the Saints too, I don't wish to do them an injustice. You said one thing now that they did not profess or claim to do, that is to work miracles in order to be seen of men, but only for the sake of the church itself.

F. Let that be then; I don't know how they could have done more good for the church than by working miracles for the disbelievers to see, so they would believe, the same way that Jesus Christ did before. But go ahead as you have begun your story.

D. All right. After I heard these strange things from them, I began to think and meditate on the things they said; and after a while I began to consult with them and talk to them, when they told of the strange blessings they received the Spirit of the Lord,

6

and the clear testimonies they had that they were in the true church, and the certainty they had that they were the children of their heavenly Father, which things, they said, every man must have to be saved, and that I could possess them if I believed the Scriptures as they understood them, and submit to do as they wished; and they also added that there was no need for me to be without my precious sight, that the wise God had provided for the salvation of the body as well as the salvation of the soul for all his saints and his dear children on the earth; and they persuaded me not to be foolish and sell my comforts in this world, and my salvation for eternity, by being prejudiced against the truth they spoke. For my part, after serious consideration, I saw that I would be less than a reasonable creature if I were to disobey what they wanted. Then, in a meeting they held one evening, I decided to join them; and I revealed to them that I believed them completely, and that I wished to be baptized by them; after considering this we came to the decision that I would receive the ordinance they called baptism the following afternoon. And now, as you can understand, the news spread quickly around the neighborhood that the Saints were going to give sight to the blind that afternoon; and by the appointed hour, before the Saints and I had arrived at the place of baptism, a numerous crowd had gathered at the place in order to see the promised miracle. Then Capt. D. Jones, (one of the chief leaders of the Saints,) addressed the crowd at the start, relating those things they believed, and condemning anything different as false; and then another, authorized by them, carried out the task of immersing me, and by the time he raised me above the water, everyone's eyes were closely searching me to see if the blind had received his sight or not; and often I heard this question asked, "Does he see?" And great was the disappointment of many when they understood that Daniel, the Blind, was still blind! so that some were ready to say, From such deceivers, Save me, good Lord; for many like myself had been charmed to believe such deceit.

F. What were your feelings by then, when you realized you

7

could not see?

D. I was still strong in the faith, because I was not expecting much at the time, for they had said previously, Perhaps afterwards, by the laying on of hands, and anointing with oil, I would be made well.

F. When was that done to you, and in what way?

D. In the evening I went to a neighboring farmhouse where they usually held their worship, and on that night they held a service there, during which through their rituals I was to be received as a member of their church; and the manner and procedure they had in relation to me was as follows:—Capt. D. Jones put his hands on my head, pressing firmly, then poured some sort of oil on my head, until it wetted all my hair, and dripped across my clothes; also, at times, he rubbed my head with his hands while praying sincerely, as I thought, for a cure for me; then he said that I was a man who had received full forgiveness of all my sins, that he had received proof of this from above; then another whom they called a prophet joined (his real name was Abel Evans,) and he prophesied that I would surely regain my sight. Then Capt. D. Jones asked him how he knew this? To this he replied that he had seen a strange vision ensuring this; that is, he had seen the heavens open, and two bright stars appear there, and these were thrown down to earth, and that this showed that the blind man (that is, myself) would receive his sight; and he also added that it was not only the vision that ensured this, but that it always the practice of his heavenly Father to everyone in his church, and that what he himself felt also proved this to him, that is, he had received a direct and miraculous cure through it himself from a severe fever he had suffered earlier for three months and a week, and many other things also too long to relate here.

F. Indeed, my boy, they had some strange customs in their midst; but I fear sometimes I see where you went wrong.

D. Well, where is that?

F. Your faith was too *weak*, or your expectation was purely about your sight, and the *main* thing had taken second place, that

8

is, the salvation of your soul.

D. Oh, friend, you are mistaken; if I have ever known myself, I can *truly* assure you, that I have sincerely believed in Jesus Christ for years, that he is Savior enough to save my soul, and I have obeyed his laws as I understood them; but at that time I was in a strange state, and also believed that they had been sent as authorized *servants* by the Lord Jesus Christ, according to what they professed, and I felt very grateful that I had had the privilege of receiving the gospel in its purity, through its Ministers. It is true that I thought and believed I would regain my sight, indeed, I believed so strongly that at one time I thought I could see, and I shouted at them to continue, that I was beginning to see. My sight, although it is previous, is only second in my mind compared to my Salvation; I was very content for the great plan of the MOST HIGH, to do with me according to his wise will, but I expected to have a testimony like theirs that I *was* in the true Church.

F. I must be silent about that then; you previously mentioned that prophet; who showed him that vision?

D. Indeed, I don't know who, yet I heard him say it was through an angel I believe, for they all saw and often associated with such beings, but it could have been through some spirit, because they also often associated with them.

F. I don't know either, but I do know this, that it was some foolish angel or spirit, and he could not foresee much, because if it had been a wise spirit and knowledgeable of things to come, it would never have said that you would receive your sight, knowing that you would turn away from them to the other side; it was a terribly wicked trick he played on poor Abel, that is tricking him to prophesy that you would regain your sight, knowing that you would not, but that you would soon turn your back on them.

D. Fair play to every spirit and angel, I believe they were innocent that time, and that it was Abel's own wicked heart that wanted to trick innocent men to believe his deceit.

F. Doubtless that may well be, but you said they associated with

9

spirits; I would like to know how they did this.

D. Oh dear, that's too long a story for me to tell it all, and I cannot say in what way they received it, but I shall tell you some of the ways I heard them say it happened. The youngest of them received them only very weakly and infrequently at the start, and mostly when they received them, they felt something taking their breath away, until they gasped similar to how an animal sounds after much endeavor, and after the spirit had entered them they felt as if they had drunk a glass of *Gin*. I heard one of them telling a young lad who had just been accepted by them, that he had almost received the Spirit, because he said he had felt a shortening of breath, and the innocent boy, ignorant of their deceit, believed such a thing, because their leaders persuaded him that that is how it was at the beginning, because God was a wise and gentle Father, and he did not wish to give too much of this thing at first until they were strong enough and used to managing it, except for the older leaders, especially Abel Evans, the Prophet, as they called him; he could receive the Spirit for good or for evil whenever he wanted; sometimes the evil spirit, or the devil as they *more commonly* called him, tried to enter him; and once he did enter him, and as soon as he went among the saints, the *old boy* became restless in fear of them, and they said that he did not have *lodgings* there for long, because Captain D. Jones worked a miracle which amazed them all, that is, he cast the devil out of the prophet, and then when Dick had to leave his comfortable lodgings, surprising were the groans, the frowns, and the looks of poor Abel, an indication, he said, of the great torments he suffered, when the strong warrior resisted, unwilling to *yield* his dwelling place, but they said he had to *quit* in the end.

> Quite a difficult miracle was the trick,
> Changing the comfy lodgings of Dick;
> But too difficult was the alternative,
> That is, restoring sight to the blind.

Another time, *he* said, he was to receive the Spirit of the Lord in an

10

exceptionally powerful manner. One particular time I heard him mention that he was in a far away place, and he received the Spirit so abundantly that he prayed for it to cease, and the people praised and glorified God, and perceived him to be burning like a bright light, so powerfully did the Spirit descend on him.

F. How strange! I never heard such a thing, and reasonable men believed things like that as well.

D. Yes, it was true, and such things still continue as far as I know, and to my great shame I too was so foolish as to believe it as the pure truth.

F. You heard no more from them?

D. Yes, yes; before the end of their meeting, it was their custom for each one to stand up to testify that they had received the Spirit of the Lord, when they made some sort of speech, each one in similar in words, and then they sat down and sang a hymn; now the first meeting was over, and soon the leaders were leaving before another meeting that was to be held later; they gave a strict order that no one venture to open the meeting to receive the spirit in case they could not control it.

F. Regardless of that, let us hear how the second meeting went for you.

D. Despite all this, one rustic elder ventured to open the meeting, which he did as orderly as I had heard them, as far as I know, by singing and praying for the Spirit of the Lord to be poured on them; then we all waited quietly, for half an hour, earnestly waiting for the Spirit, and then as before, they stood up one after the other, testifying how they had received the Spirit, and everyone said, Amen, with each one, and so on until they came to me.

F. Well, what did you say to them?

D. I was not hypocritical with them, but I said that I was very happy to hear them say that they were able to testify to such things, and that I would be very glad if I could say the same, but that I had not received any more in their midst than I had received among other religious friends. To this the Elder replied,

11

saying, to begin to testify a little the first time, and I would improve the second time, like the old proverb, "A small lie the first time, bigger the second time;" but I must end now, for I'm going on too long, although there is still much untold.

F. Nevertheless, let us hear what made you turn back away from them.

D. One evening, while going with one of the strongest in the faith, in speaking at least, he told the whole neighborhood that he had felt strange things in their midst, and had had full assurance from God that he was his true child, yes, he had enjoyed, he said, more pleasure in one evening with the Saints than he had received in nine years with another respectable denomination. He was a leader in their midst, and he was testifying most eloquently in the presence of the Saints, that had received the gift of the Spirit, when I told him of my feelings as a brother in the faith at that time, and that I could not accept anything I heard them testify; and then I asked him seriously, had he received such things? To this he answered to my great surprise, *He had not*, but that he had decided to follow them for five years, and that if he had not received anything by then, he would become an Atheist, and that he would not believe there was any truth in Christianity.

F. That's the kind of faithful men the Saints are then.

D. Yes, indeed, and I said this in the hearing of a crowd of men in the presence of that man, and he did not deny it; another thing, I told them all before I turned back that I had not received anything in particular, and they replied that they were not receiving anything now, but that they hoped to receive something later when their leaders returned, and also the fulfillment of the prophecy of the old Prophet Abel that I would regain my sight; and my not regaining it discouraged me greatly, but the main thing that caused me to turn back was that when I began to search in detail each day, as the Bereans of old, I perceived clearly in the scripture that these things were not so, and if I had time now, I would tell you my reasons, and prove them in the Scripture, but I hope we will meet again soon.

12

F. What is your general opinion of the Saints? tell it again before leaving.

D. Well, my impartial opinion is that many of the most inexperienced group of them may believe all these things, and that they act with their cause out of good will, having been deceived by their leaders; but as for their leaders, I consider them to be lying deceivers.

F. Let us hear again, what do you say to the different religious sects in the world?

D. To do good and not be idle, for eventually you will reap, unless you become weary; the Latter-day Saints are here only for a short time to trouble us, because little by little their deceit will become obvious to the world, and then everyone will retreat from them. They are like many before now; it may be that they hinder the Gospel of the Kingdom from moving forward, and cause many of God's children to hang their heads because they make so much mockery of the Sacred Oracles of the Lord; but obstacles are bound to come; therefore, my dear brethren, be sure and steadfast in the Lord's work, and you know that your labors are not vain in the Lord.

Penygraig. BLIND DANIEL.

Pamphlet 5

Author Unknown. ***Llyfr Cronicl Prophwydi Mormonaidd. Ychydig o hanes Gweithredoedd Twyllodrus, rhai o'r "Seintiau y Dyddiau Diweddaf." Ynghyd a Melldithion Ofnadwy Duw, ar Gau Brophwydi a'r Rhyfygus*** **(*A Chronicle Book of the Mormon Prophets: Some of the Deceitful Deeds of Some of the "Latter-day Saints," Together with the Frightful Curses of God, on the False and Arrogant Prophets*). Llandovery: E. Morris, 1848. 12 pages.**

The first section of this pamphlet consists of just two pages (pp. 3 and 4) and is labeled "Mormon Deceit." The writer begins by expressing his disappointment that so many of the people in Wales have been deceived by the Latter-day Saints. He then presents a brief narrative of a failed attempt on the part of two of these "Mormon prophets" to restore life to the daughter of one of the members, who had died:

> The manner in which they attempted to do this was by filling her body with oil, and after that by blowing air into her through a tube!!!

But it was all in vain, "for they failed to breathe into this girl the breath of life, and the dead remained dead." The writer then tells of an old woman who testified that the two "Mormon prophets" had nearly destroyed her feet by anointing them with the oil used in their attempt to restore life to the girl who had died.

The third and final story is that of a Latter-day Saint shopkeeper who was about to travel to Bristol to purchase some shoes to sell in his shop. He was put in a quandary when he received a request to baptize some new disciples—should he respond to the request immediately or take care of his errand first? He knelt down and prayed for guidance, and when he arose, the box he planned to take to Bristol was full of shoes. "Thus, the prophet was able to go to baptize the disciples."

The other three sections of the pamphlet are entitled "The Judgments of God on False Prophets," the Judgments of God on Blasphemers," and "The Judgments of God on the Breakers of the Sabbath." None of the random examples presented in these three sections about false prophets, blasphemers, and breakers of the Sabbath bear even a remote connection with The Church of Jesus Christ of Latter-day Saints or its members. If Dan Jones was ever aware of this very strange pamphlet, he makes no mention of it in any issue of his monthly periodical or in any of his own pamphlets.

A CHRONICLE BOOK

OF THE

MORMON PROPHETS.

SOME OF THE HISTORY OF THE

DECEITFUL DEEDS,

OF SOME OF THE

"LATTER-DAY SAINTS."

TOGETHER WITH

THE FRIGHTFUL CURSES

OF GOD,

ON THE FALSE AND ARROGANT PROPHETS.

"Why hath Satan filled thine heart to lie to the Holy Ghost? Why hast thou conceived this thing in thine heart?"

"How is it that ye have agreed together to tempt the Spirit of the Lord?"—*Peter*.

LLANDOVERY.

PRINTED BY E. MORRIS, KING STREET.

MDCCCXLVIII.

MORMON DECEIT, &c.

It is a pity to think that so many of the people in Wales—noble Wales—a land so full of readers of the Bible,—are so deceived as to be led by fanatical men, to cultivate such shameful heresies as those of the Mormons, or those who call themselves "Latter-day Saints:" those who allege things so antithetical to common sense, to civility, and to the New Testament, as it has been understood and interpreted by the wisest and most godly Theologians, since the time of the Apostles until the present time. It would be thought that the common scriptural knowledge of our land would be a sufficient bulwark to every kind of false religions. But, despite it all, it is sad to think that it is not so, as you can conclude from the following examples.

In the eleventh year of the reign of Victoria, queen of Great Britain and Ireland, two men arose in south Wales, (the western principality of the kingdom), who said they were Prophets, according to the doctrine of one Joseph Smith, a deceiver from America; and they said they had received the spirit of working miracles, giving life to the dead, and many such things: and they acquired a great host of followers. And it happened in those days that a daughter of one of these Mormon prophets died; and the two of them came to the house where the body of the girl lay, in order to give life to her again, according to the great power they had received through the Mormon spirit; and the manner in which they attempted to do this was, by filling her body with oil, and after that by blowing air into her through a tube!!! From that we may conclude that the spirit with which they had filled her, shows more of the spirit of madness or pagan darkness than of anything else. It cannot be compared to any other spirit but the *Mormon Spirit*; but it can be said concerning this, that it was a *very ineffective* one, for they failed to breathe into this girl the breath of life, and the dead remained dead.

4

A man asked one of them, What kind of oil they used? And he answered by saying, If he became their disciple he could know, but not before that; and there would be a way of giving the spirit to him also; but an old woman lately testified that they nearly destroyed her feet by anointing them with the oil, in an attempt to heal them, and she had to leave them as soon as she could. And they thought that the best way was for her not to join with them lest when she was under the psalmic state, that the spirit would be like the gods of Baal, during the time of Elias of old—sleeping; and that they would have time to putrefy before being enlivened, so that the old woman could keep her feet.

A short time ago, a messenger was sent to another one of the inspired Mormon prophets, who was a shopkeeper, to request him to come immediately to baptize some of the new disciples; and it happened that when the messenger went in, that the prophet was talking with his wife about a box, which he had just prepared in order to go to Bristol, to request that it be filled with shoes, for the market. She was asking the prophet what to do—it was absolutely necessary for him to go to baptize—and also, he needed shoes for the market; and in this dilemma, it appears that he had forgotten the spirit; but here is his wife standing for the purpose of bringing back to his memory (as astute women are commonly able to adapt objects to circumstances), by telling him that the spirit usually gives to the "Latter-day Saints" whatever they request. Here is the saint immediately down on his knees, and he prayed earnestly, warmly, and also, I say, effectively,—for when he arose, behold, the box was full of shoes!!! Thus, the prophet was able to go to baptize the disciples also.

———ooo———

THE JUDGMENTS OF GOD ON FALSE PROPHETS.

MANES, or Manieheus, the heretic, denied the Old Testament, by calling himself the Holy Ghost, and bragging that he had authority to work miracles; because why had the king of Persia

5

sent for him to heal his son who was sick; but when he could not cause any healing to the child, who died under his hand, the king commanded that he be put to death, and his skin was filled with husks, and he was put up in front of the city gates.

Cerinthus, the heretic, was in the bath-house in Ephesus, when he saw the apostle John, who said to those who were with him, let us flee, lest this house, wherein is the enemy of the Lord, falls on us. As soon as the apostle turned his back, the house fell on Cerinthus and his friends, and it killed them.

Simon Magus, after being scolded by Peter, went to Rome, and there he taught his loathsome heresies to many, saying that he was the true God, that he had created the world with angels, that Christ had not come in the flesh, and that he had not suffered anything; he also denied the resurrection; he tried to show his power to the people by flying in the air, but he fell down and broke his thigh, and suffered a pitiful death.

In the year 1653, there was in Kendal, in Westmoreland, in England, a man named John Gilpin, who went to one of the meetings of the Quakers, or the Shakers; and the speaker that day was Charles Atkinson: the purpose of his speech was to pull down the ordinances and the ministry of the gospel, and he counseled the people to wait for the light from within, which, he said, lies beneath the earth, namely the old man who is from the earth having the nature of earth. Gilpin received this doctrine cheerfully, he remained faithful to the Shakers, he was afraid to read any good books, and he did not listen to a single godly preacher; he also tried to forget all the truths that he had learned earlier from the scriptures, for they told him that such knowledge was carnal, and depended on the tree of knowledge, and cursed is everyone who depends on this tree. In the next meeting he heard many things about the light within, about which he had never had any experience as yet, and was sad about that and wished to be able to shake, hoping through that by doing so he would receive wondrous revelations from God. After a few days, as he was walking around in his room he began to shake terribly, so that he could not stand on his feet, but upon falling on the bed he wept and cried out

6

in a dreadful and atrocious way, but he was not afraid, for he supposed that he was now among the weavers of the second birth. Within half an hour he ceased to shake and bleed, and then he rejoiced that he could now testify against the Ministers of England, as false prophets and priests of Baal. That night he had frightful dreams about his sins, and when he awoke he felt something going down his neck, and giving him hard blows, once, twice, thrice, and a fourth time, each one lighter than the other, until it descended half down his back, then he felt something going into his body; satan gave him to suppose that it was the spirit in the form of a dove; he heard a voice from within himself say, It is day; adding it twice more, As sure as it is day; Christ will give you light. Two or three days after that, as he was waiting for more light, he lay down with his face toward the earth, his right hand began to shake terribly, then he became very happy looking at this as a sign of the spiritual marriage, and his unity with Christ. After this his sins came to his memory, he struck his hand against the floor, for every particular sin, and he heard a voice saying, Now such sin is dead. He now believed that all his sins instantly died, and he heard a voice saying, Ask what you wish in my name, and it will be given to you. Gilpin said, What shall I ask? He received an answer, Ask for wisdom in the first place. Then he wished for such things as would glorify God, and benefit others; the voice answered, Grant unto him his request, and give him the gift of prophecy, and of singing praise to God. In another meeting while John Audland was speaking, Gilpin was taken out of the chair by the devil within him, and was thrown to the ground, where he lay that night.

During the entire time that his body and his members were agitated, he turned at times on his back, at times on his stomach, and he made crosses by throwing his legs across each other, and writing on the floor with his fingers. The voice said to him, That that writing on the earth was written signs of the law on his heart; then his hands were moved to his head, and he heard a voice saying, Christ in God, and God in Christ, and

7

Christ in you; he sang out these words in a strange way, and with an unusual voice. He sang also many of the scriptures that satan had put in his head. After that he was lifted up by the devil on his feet, who then commanded him to be humble, and he set him on his knees again, and said to him, Lift up your cross and follow me. After that the devil led him through the street to the door of the fiddler. Then his two friends followed him, and they asked him, Where are you going? this is the fiddler's house. He then answered, Whoever's house this is, Christ has led me here, and I must go in here. He knocked at the door, and the voice commanded him shouting, Behold, Christ stands at the door and knocks. The fiddler opened the door, and Gilpin went in, and took the fiddle in his hand, and he played it, dancing joyfully. Then he felt doubt within himself; what spirit had put him to work. The voice answered, This is not because I love music, but to show you the happiness that is in heaven about your conversion and the spiritual happiness you will have according to this. After returning home, a stone rose from the floor, and the voice said to him, That Christ has taken that stone out of his heart, and has given him a heart of flesh. Then he showed the stone to those who were present, and said, unless you see signs and wonders, do not believe anything; and while throwing the stone in their midst, he said, Behold, this is my heart of stone. Then he fell on his face, and the voice said, You shall have two angels to guard you: and soon two smiling beings came down through the chimney, and sat on the table near him. At that, he shouted out, My angels, my angels; that night an evil spirit incited him to take a knife in his hand, and to put it at his throat. The voice said to him, Open a hole there, and I shall give you eternal life. But he threw away the knife, deciding that the devil had possessed him; he cried out in the morning with a loud voice, Now the devil has gone out of me. The family heard the commotion at that time, but the neighbors heard nothing. After that Satan came again, and said, That the devil was deceiving him, and had used him for his work until then, but now Christ came to cast out Satan, and he also said, That just as he had served

8

satan the day before in his clothes, that he must undo everything in his shirt in obedience to Christ. At that he arose from his bed and ran in his shirt through the street, and when some tried to restrain him, satan said in him, That four women must bring him in, lest he be turned into a column of salt as was Lot's wife. Then he was taken to his bed between four women; and satan said to him, Yesterday angels of the devil served you, but now the angels of Christ will fortify you round about. Then he saw two flies in the window; he swallowed one and put the other on his throat, and the voice said to him, You will go in there, for nothing is impossible to him who believes.

At this he began to understand that satan had beguiled him again, and in great fear he shouted out, Lord, what will you have me do? The devil answered, It is too late for you now to cry unto the Lord, for a judgment has been given against you already; you served me and blasphemed God this whole time, and now it is too late for you to repent. After this he fell into hopelessness for a time, yet it pleased God to give him true repentance, and peace of conscience, and the Lord delivered him completely from the snare of the devil, so that he went no more among the Shakers. He wrote a treatise of this matter himself, and he printed it. The truth of these things were witnessed under the hands of the mayor of Kendal, the Minister, the schoolmaster, and others.

In the same year some Quakers came from the North to Wales in the area of Wrexham, and they beguiled one William Spenser, who followed them and shook several times. It happened at night when he was in the bed with one of them, and he could not sleep, having heard something whispering and speaking like voracious wasps around the head of the Quaker, who was greatly fearful; so he tried to get up: but the Quaker wanted him to lie still, and suddenly a very tempestuous wind arose, to the point of shaking the house they were in; this added to his terror, so he tried to get up again, but the Quaker compelled him a second time to lie still, and shake for the virtue of the spirit to come; at that he heard again the very same voice he heard before, and he became all the more fearful, so that he made every effort to try to get up; then the Quaker placed his head on the shoulder of Spenser, and he blew like a goose several times in his face, saying, Receive the Holy Ghost. This made

9

him jump out of the bed in great surprise. After this he completely left the Quakers, and he testified to this in the presence of the Quaker, in the presence of many witnesses.

———ooo———

THE JUDGMENTS OF GOD ON BLASPHEMERS.

Bishop Ridley in a sermon relates a story about a young gentleman from Cornwall, in the time of king Edward VI. The young gentleman was riding horses with some other gentlemen when he swore some terrible oaths; some of his friends rebuked him, but then he swore some even more atrocious oaths. A godly church man said to him that he would have to give an account some day for those oaths, and that it was best for him to repent, for death gives no warning. At this the gentleman became angry, and while swearing great oaths he told him, Do not worry about me; so he continued forward until he came to a bridge, and the young man spurred his horse to cause it to jump with his rider over the bridge into the water. As he fell, he shouted, The horse and the rider, to the devil with them all.

In the year 1649 a soldier went to Ware to bathe in a river, but the water was not deep enough. The soldier asked whether there was a sufficiently deep place to swim in. Some told him that a very deep pool was near there but that one could not go in it without danger. He answered, God damn me that I shall be lost, even if it be as deep as hell I shall swim in it; and so he went, but he immediately sank to the bottom in that placc, and he never came up.

In Tubing in Germany there was a boy who used his imagination to utter new and unusual oaths; but God sent to him a wild crab which destroyed his tongue, so that it rotted out of his mouth.

There was a fisherman in Suffolk who sold Mackerel to the people. Because they were delicious to them, they pressed him to sell them, and some of them against his will went into the boat; the fisherman took a rock in his hand and swore in the name of God that he would make them stand back, but just as soon as the oath came out of his mouth, he fell down and died.

10

King Louis of France severed the lips of a great man in his court with a hot iron because he blasphemed the name of God.

When Julian, the emperor, offered sacrifice to the goddess Fortuna, Maris, the Bishop of Chalcedon, rebuked him and called him an ungodly man, &c., the emperor shouted to the Bishop, You blind fool, your Galilean God will not heal your sight. Maris replied, I thank God for making me blind and depriving me of the power of beholding your face.

In March in the age of Christ 1632, Albertus Pericoscius, an honorable man, lived in the vicinity of Moscow where he worked as a tax collector. His practice was (when the poor people were unable to pay the tax) to confiscate their cattle and drive the animals to his own land. It happened that when this powerful man was away from home, he lost his unjust profit in one night; all the cattle that he possessed died suddenly. When he returned home, his wife and his servant told him what a terrible judgment from God had befallen him; at this, this ungodly man became enraged and blasphemed and shot his gun against the heavens, breaking out in blasphemous words, such as, May he who killed my cattle eat them himself, since you did not allow me to eat them, eat them yourself. At this rage of barking against God, drops of blood fell and turned this unfortunate man into a black dog, and while barking he ran to the dead cattle and began to eat them; and for all I know (says the author who wrote this account at that time), he is still eating them. The author admits that he obtained this story from some who were eyewitnesses. *Cluver, in Beard.*

It happened that some soldier was traveling through Marchia in Saxony. When he came to an inn he gave some money to the lady of the house to hold a room for him; a while later he came back for the room, but the woman had counseled with her husband and denied having received the money; the soldier was infuriated and said that she was a deceitful and cunning woman. At this the man of the house came to the place, and, siding with his wife, he pushed the soldier out of the house. The soldier became enraged, took out his sword and ran toward the door. The man of the house cried out, Thief, trying to come into my house by force. Because of that the soldier was arrested and thrown into jail; the man of the house prosecuted him, and he was found guilty of murder. But before the man was condemned, Satan came in the

11

form of a man to the jail, and counseled him to petition the judge to give permission to a man in a blue cap to plead his case. The jailer appeared before the judge and requested that he allow the man in the blue cap, who was present, to plead his case (the man in the blue cap was the devil); the judge gave him permission to speak. Satan began to plead his case, showing clearly that the soldier was wronged; on the other hand, the innkeeper denied everything, and he wished for the devil to take him away, if he had the money. Then the lawyer in the blue cap gained the advantage by taking hold of the innkeeper and dragging him from the courthouse, and threw him up into the air in the sight of everyone, so that he was never seen again. In this manner the soldier was saved from tyranny in a wondrous manner, and it happened to the innkeeper because of his blasphemy and his reward.

———*000*———

THE JUDGMENTS OF GOD ON THE BREAKERS OF THE SABBATH.

God commands us to remember the Sabbath, to think about him before his coming, so that we may prepare our hearts, and put aside our earthly concerns, to keep holy the day of Sabbath. If the deeds of our vocations are unlawful on that day, how much more unlawful are the pleasures of the flesh and worthless games. St. Austin says, It is better to plow than to dance on the Sabbath.

The Lord commanded to stone the man who was found gathering sticks on the Sabbath day. Num. xv. 32, 36.

One of the sins of the Jews was breaking the Sabbath, and on that day the Romans burned Jerusalem.

One time there were three Jews on their journey together, when it became night, and the Sabbath was approaching. One said to the other, What shall we do? the way is very dangerous, because of thieves and wild animals; we had better continue on our way, and not stay here to keep the Sabbath, in danger of losing our lives. The third responded, I shall go no further until the Sabbath ends, for he who commanded me to keep the Sabbath holy will protect me in the midst of this forest. The first two began on their journey, and the third alone remained;

12

as he pronounced a blessing on his food on Friday evening, (for Saturday is the Sabbath of the Jews, and they begin the Sabbath at sunset the previous night) a wild boar, of enormous size, lay by his side as if he were hungry; in great fright the Jew tossed it some bread, but he understood that God was all he needed to defend him as long as he pleased him. The wild boar ate the bread and lay quietly; after finishing supper the Jew gave thanks and lay down on the ground, and since he entrusted himself to the Lord, he slept comfortably that night. When he awoke in the morning, he found the wild boar lying beside him; then he blessed the name of the Lord who had kept him from harm, and he spent the Sabbath in meditation and prayers. After the Sabbath was over, he traveled the night after that with the wild boar following him throughout that night. His friends had fallen among thieves that night, and they were robbed of everything they had. Finally, he caught up with his friends, and when the wild boar saw them it charged them and mangled them to death. When he saw the fate of his two friends he feared greatly, expecting the same violent death. After he went a little further, the thieves crossed paths with him and asked him who he was and from where he had come. He answered that he was a Jew and that he had come there from the king's court. They further inquired of him where he had gotten the frightful wild boar. The Jew said that the king had given it to him to send him through this forest. Then one of the thieves said that the Jew must be a good friend of the king since the king had ordered him to be accompanied by this wild boar. The other said, "Let us give him all our money, and let us accompany him out of the forest lest he reveal us." So they gave him all their riches, and they accompanied him the greater part of the way. When the Jew had come through the forest the wild boar returned to the forest, and the Jew went home in safety.

In the year 1680, Brookes from Nantwich, a sawyer by trade, went with others on the day of the Lord to a wooded slope to cut a birch tree before May-day eve, having beforehand made an agreement with the singer to sing as he set up the tree. But after the sawyer had struck the tree two or three times with his axe, he fell down dead in that moment without saying another word. This account was obtained from a famous churchman from that neighborhood.

E MORRIS, PRINTER, LLANDOVERY.

Pamphlet 6

David Evans. *Saint y Dyddiau Diweddaf a Doniau Gwyrthiol. Sef Pregeth a draddodwyd, Dydd Sul y 27ain Awst, 1848, yn Eglwys Sant Dewi, Caerfyrddin, gan y Parch. David Evans, Curad yr Eglwys Hono* (*The Latter-day Saints and Spiritual Gifts. Namely a Sermon Delivered, Sunday the 27th of August, 1848, at the Church of Saint David, Carmarthen, by Rev. David Evans, the Curate of that Church*). Carmarthen: William-Spurrell, 1848. 20 pages.

This pamphlet lacks the vicious language that other antagonists were then using whenever they mentioned The Church of Jesus Christ of Latter-day Saints. Evans does, however, severely criticize the defense that the Church offered for a continuation of miracles from the time of Jesus Christ. He presents his ideas in a gentlemanly fashion and concludes that the members of the Church are false prophets and heretics.

John S. Davis published his response to David Evans's pamphlet in *Prophet of the Jubilee*, December 1848, pp. 176–83, in an article entitled "Observations on a Sermon about 'The Latter-day Saints and Miraculous Gifts.'" He writes,

> I thought when I gave my sixpence for this ten-page sermon that I was buying an original product, and one worthy of the order of priesthood; but when I saw that the most particular materials of the product had been in the skull of W. R. Davies, Dowlais, (Baptist) and a host of other heretics in the eyes of the Pure Church, I was tremendously disappointed.

Davis defends the idea that miracles continue to occur in modern times, especially in the Church of Jesus Christ of Latter-day Saints. He concludes with an invitation to anyone who wishes to have evidence of modern-day miracles to go to Newport and talk with Reuben Brinkworth, a young man who had been deaf and dumb for several years because of the effects of an electric storm while at sea, but who, following his baptism as a Latter-day Saint, had had his speech and hearing restored. See Episode 5.11.

THE LATTER-DAY SAINTS AND SPIRITUAL GIFTS.

NAMELY

A SERMON

DELIVERED, SUNDAY THE 27TH OF AUGUST, 1848, AT THE CHURCH OF SAINT DAVID, CARMARTHEN,

BY THE REV. DAVID EVANS,

THE CURATE OF THAT CHURCH.

"And the evil spirit answered and said, Jesus I know, and Paul I know; but who are ye?"—ACTS xix, 15.

PRINTED AT THE REQUEST OF THOSE WHO HEARD IT.

CARMARTHEN:

PRINTED BY WILLIAM-SPURRELL, KING STREET.

1848.

PRICE TWO PENCE.

THE LATTER-DAY SAINTS AND SPIRITUAL GIFTS.

NAMELY

A SERMON

DELIVERED, SUNDAY THE 27TH OF AUGUST, 1848, AT THE CHURCH OF SAINT DAVID, CARMARTHEN,

BY THE REV. DAVID EVANS,

THE CURATE OF THAT CHURCH.

"And the evil spirit answered and said, Jesus I know, and Paul I know; but who are ye?"—ACTS xix, 15.

PRINTED AT THE REQUEST OF THOSE WHO HEARD IT.

CARMARTHEN:
PRINTED BY WILLIAM-SPURRELL, KING STREET.

1848.

THE LATTER-DAY SAINTS AND SPIRITUAL GIFTS.

MARK XVI. 17, 18.

And these signs shall follow them that believe; In my name shall they cast out devils; they shall speak with new tongues; they shall take up serpents; and if they drink any deadly thing, it shall not hurt them; they shall lay hands on the sick, and they shall recover.

As it was before the destruction of the holy city of Jerusalem, many false-Christians and false-prophets, rose up, showing such great signs and wonders, deceiving, if it were possible, the very elect of God; so it is in these latter days, "before the destruction of the whole world," many destructive heresies abound and many false prophets are rising up, speaking of Christ, Behold he is in the wilderness,—namely, over with the Mormons, in the wilderness of America; or behold, he is here with us in the secret rooms, and not in the churches and chapels of the country.

Among the thousands of heresies and schisms which have sprung to life from the womb of the carnal spirit, and crept into the church of God, there is a small number of people in our country lately who have formed

4

themselves into a religious sect, and who call themselves the "Latter-day Saints."

These men separate themselves from the church of God, as well as from all the other religions of the age, and as such are a kind of *double Non-Conformists*. They believe that they are unique objects of the race and spirit of God, having received light and wisdom from the heavens, and that the world in general knows nothing about them, and that all who do not belong to their secret association are "unlearned and without the Spirit."

But what the wise man said is true, "there is nothing new under the sun." Despite how great the commotion of these people, and their ignorant zeal as they strive to proselytize the populace to their beliefs, they do nothing more than spell out the old *Shibboleth*. The heresies that are now being personified by the "Saints" in Wales, have appeared on the stage many times before; not only in the persons of Edward Irving and his followers in England, and Joseph Smith and his followers in America, but as early as the *second century* of the era of Christ.*

The "History of the Church" mentions one *Montanus*, who in the second century caused a sizeable division in the church, by his heretical tenets. Even though this person was orthodox in basic religious doctrines, he went to the extremes of believing that he had been inspired by God, and that God had given to him and his followers some uncommon light, and gifts of the Holy Ghost, so

*Also they are not unlike the Ana-Baptists or the Double-dippers in the time of Cranmer.—See "History of the Life of Cranmer," by Todd, chap. xii.

5

that they could understand the scriptures and the secret things of the gospel, better than anyone else. They called themselves Spiritual beings and Saints; and they proclaimed that all who doubted their tenets were devoid of the Spirit, and un-reborn.*

Is there not some similarity, dear listeners, between these Montanites of the second century, and the sect that exists in our days, prolonging the schisms in the church under the name Latter-day Saints?

Perhaps some will judge it to be foolishness on my part to take such public note of a sect so inconsequential as this one, and tending to give weight to insignificance by preaching against them. Obviously, I do not think this way; and if I am wrong, my intentions are good. Part of the work of the ministry, I believe, is to rebuke *heresies*. A minister of the gospel is a *shepherd*; and as such, he must raise his rod and his staff against anything that tends to harm his flock. He is a *watchman* on the wall in Zion; and as such, he must keep a close watch, and give prompt warning to the people if there is danger nearby, so that he may be "free from their blood." Therefore, since the minds of men are open to be agitated, and their souls to be entrapped by the heretical beliefs of the "Latter Saints," it is appropriate to warn the people in the language of Christ, "go not forth" (into the desert, or to the tops of the roads, or to the secret chambers) "after them, and do not believe them."

*See "History of the Church," by Burton.—Second century.

6

There are several oddities of the faith of this people; but *at present* I intend to take notice of just one article in their creed (the one on which they base the words of their argument), namely, that the Author of the Christian religion has promised in these words, that the spiritual gifts would remain continually in the church until the end of the world, that the only reason they would cease is the lack of faith in the church, and that they expect the restoration of these gifts in their system. Let us now thoughtfully look into the meaning of these words,—words referred to by the "Saints," as the main column of their faith.

I. Let us examine the promise in the text.

The Lord promises here that he would bear witness to the gospel through miracles; and he made this promise in the first century of the church. The Author of nature promises here to go against the established rules of nature, or impede the natural operation of cause and effect. Such a miraculous gift as this was necessary to enable the apostles and others in the infancy of the church of Christ, to cast out devils—to speak fluently in tongues they had never learned—to take up serpents, and drink any deadly thing without being hurt—and to heal the sick without using the medicine of men.

Think of the situation in which the apostles found themselves when they received a commission of their Lord to go into all the world to preach the gospel. Except for Paul, all the apostles were unlearned men; also the topic of their sermons was *new* to the world; their faith was tested continually by bitter trials; and their freedom

7

and their lives were continually in danger. Without the power to work miracles, who was likely to receive the testimony of "the foolish things of the world," as the apostles were perceived to be? who would receive such strange doctrines as those they were preaching, unless they had miracles as God's letters of recommendation for them to show to the world? And in the face of the false accusations of enemies, the miraculous power sustained the apostles, and gave comfort and encouragement to them—knowing "that the hand of the Lord was working with them."

And if it was necessary to show the Jews that the old dispensation had ended—that the veil of the temple had rent—that there was no need for the blood of sacrifice to run, nor the altars to emit smoke—how was it likely that the prejudiced Jews would believe this, without signs and wonders? And since the old dispensation had been established through miracles, so also it was necessary to confirm the new dispensation in the same way.

And how was it possible to overthrow the polytheism and paganism of the world by preaching the cross without miracles? The worship of idols and false gods had taken root in the world a long time before. Is it likely that all the idols would fall, and all the false gods would disappear before the man of Nazareth? And will all the Greek and Roman teachings bow before these illiterate Galileans? No attention would have been given them; they were considered piteous lunatics, unless the miracles had been performed and stirred up the attention of the world, and crying out *Behold the finger of God!*

8

Furthermore, since God intended that the success of the gospel happen quickly, he endowed the first preachers of it with miraculous gifts. Godly wisdom did not deem it best to use human teaching*, or a gradual manner in order to shake the foundations of paganism; rather it was miraculous power, in order to show that the hand of God was working with the apostles, much as it did with Israel in Egypt, and with Joshua in the land of Canaan.

And as for the miracles of the apostles, they bore all the aspects of true miracles: there was ample evidence that they were divine—the power of God was perceived in them. They bore no resemblance to those which were worked by the conjuration or witchcraft of the pagan priests. The observers could see that the wonders and miracles of the apostles were far beyond all human power, and were obliged to confess "that indeed a notable miracle hath been done by them, and we cannot deny it."—Acts 4:16. There was no falsification or deceit that pertained to those miracles. There was no secret inside the curtain; and the apostles showed no sign of hiding anything, for they had nothing to hide. Everything was open to the eyes of the observers, and

*If illiterate and unlearned men were the first preachers of the gospel, that is not any reason against the need for human learning now. Unlearned preachers must prove possession of a miraculous gift before showing aptness equivalent to that of the Apostles to preach the gospel. Without that, they need to have been in the best *college* for years—namely at the feet of Jesus. See Acts 4:13.

9

no hidden instruments or secret manner of operating employed.

Notice also with what kind of authority the apostles worked miracles: for example, Peter says to the lame man at the gate of the temple, “silver and gold have I none; but such as I have give I thee: in the name of Jesus Christ of Nazareth, rise up and walk.”

Yet, they were endowed with miraculous gifts to substantiate the gospel they preached. True miracles are worked not to substantiate deceit, rather scriptural truth, if it is not thought that miracles are worked under the influence of satan. But the apostles were appealing to the scriptures of the Old Testament for a confirmation to the doctrines they were preaching. It is clear, then, that the miracles which were worked by the apostles were not an illusion; rather they were great signs and wonders through the finger of God.

The men who denied these miracles were few in number; satan has not been trying to work these miracles in the world, rather to *imitate* them. He tried to degrade and undo the miracles of Moses in Egypt, through the wizardry of his servants; and Christ himself forewarned his disciples about these; see Mark 13:22. The wicked sons of Sceva the Jew, imitated the true apostles of our Lord; Acts 19:13. “And no marvel, for Satan himself is transformed into an angel of light.” The power to work miracles is as strong a proof of the presence of God, as is the Catholic church and the idol worship of Rome, striving to uphold its unscriptural system by referring to its miracles; and also the “Latter Saints,” about which is now our primary focus, and they pretend to have the same

10

power. Are these not the ones about whom the Scriptures speak, whose "coming is after the working of Satan, with all power, and signs, and lying wonders."—2 Thes. 2:9. This leads us to,

II. To show that Christ, upon giving the promise in the text, did not intend for the miraculous gifts to continue in his church until the end of the world. It is admitted, even by those who claim the right to the miraculous powers in these days, that the end of the true miracles took place in the church more than fifteen hundred years ago; and they ended based on the accusation of the lack of faith in the church generally. Here is the reasoning:—Christ promised power to work miracles to those who believed; there is no power by the church now to work miracles; consequently, there is no faith in the church. But let us take a more detailed look at the topic.

We do not deny that the age of miracles ended a long time ago. How, then, are the words of Christ in the text true? The power was promised unconditionally to be given those who believed. He who made the promise is the "faithful and true witness," who is the author of the faith of his people, and the source from which the miraculous power originates. If Christ, on giving this promise, intended for miracles to continue in his church, and if they were indispensably necessary for the success of his kingdom in the world, how is it that he allowed them to disappear for many centuries in this manner?

We do not find a single account that the "excellent oath of the martyrs," those who sealed the miracles with their blood, ever worked any miracles; and consequently, we must make the same gloomy conclusion, (and we

11

must make it according to the doctrine of the "Saints,") that they have died without having faith in the gospel! If Christ intended for his church to practice these miraculous gifts continually, how is it, when he had so many faithful servants in the world, that those who possessed an abundant degree of his Spirit, did not work a single miracle and did not give a single external proof that they were servants of God, and that they spoke the words of God?

Again, the principles of the correct interpretation of the word of God teach us, that we must understand the word *believe* in the words of the text according to the same meaning that is used in the previous verse. There it is said, "He that *believeth* and is baptized shall be saved; but he that believeth not shall be damned." And then the following words, "And these signs shall follow them that *believe*," &c. Now, in the first verse, *believe* is linked with *salvation*, and in the second with *miracles*. Are we to believe, therefore, that saving faith has not been in the world for more than fifteen hundred years, since no miracles have been worked by those who profess the religion of Christ during that period of time? Was the whole world condemned during so much time? Have diligent and useful men who labored so hard in the name of Jesus in those centuries fallen to eternal damnation? God forbid us from drawing such a frightful conclusion! And yet, if we are to understand the words in the broad meaning in which the "Saints" understand them, this is the *only conclusion* that can be drawn from the lack of miraculous faith in the church. If these kinds of conclusions are unreasonable and ungodly, we must

12

understand the promise in the stricter meaning than do the "Latter Saints."

This promise does not say that these signs will follow *every faithful person*, and it does not say that they will continue until the *end of the world*. The only thing, then, that can be concluded from these words is this: that there would be sufficient godly evidence to be provided for the ministry of the Apostles, and their co-workers, and their successors, *as long as that would be necessary*.

Furthermore, whatever we may think on our own is nothing, unless we have a foundation to build on. If the Scriptures do not say definitively that these miracles would cease, the apostle in the thirteenth chapter of the First Epistle to the Corinthians, gives a rather obvious hint that they would cease. Having mentioned in the previous chapter about the desire of the Corinthians to have the miraculous gifts that were in the church at that time, he shows the superiority of charity* over them all. This is the effect of being born again; but one may have the miraculous power, like Judas, without being qualified for the grace of God. In the eighth verse it says, "Charity never faileth: but whether there be prophecies, they *shall*

*Some of the "Saints" need to read with greater *attention* the characteristics of the Christian grace of charity—"Which *vaunteth* not itself, is not *puffed up*, is not easily provoked, thinketh no *evil*." Then they will see how unchristian it is to judge others as having no part at all in the Salvation; and they will learn that the power to speak with the tongues of heaven and earth, without this charity, is no better than the vain sounds "of sounding brass, or a tinkling cymbal."—1 Cor. xiii. 1, &c.

13

fail; whether there be tongues, they *shall cease*; whether there be knowledge, it shall *vanish away*." The power (as the apostle would say) to foresee future things, or to explain the words of God under spiritual influence will *cease*. The power to speak in strange tongues in order to convince the faithless will *fail*. The knowledge of the secrets of the Spirit will *vanish*. But it is charity that is more excellent grace than all these gifts. But it is charity that *never faileth*. Yes, faith, and hope, and charity remain after the spiritual gifts cease. In this manner these graces are more excellent than they. But even though faith and hope will remain in the church until the end of the world, and thus are better than the miraculous gifts, still, since the time will come when faith will become sight, and hope will become enjoyment, charity will be more excellent than *they*. For this grace, as the poet says—

"And it will become highly pure
In the land of glory a second time."

Instead of being useful, divine wisdom saw, no doubt, that the continuation of miracles in the church would be harmful; since they would *shut out* the *practice of faith "in the things that are not seen*," and would create continued belief dependent on *sensory* proofs. It is said that signs to the *unbelievers* were the gift of speaking in strange tongues, &c. Consequently, when Christianity had spread universally throughout the known world, and when the convincing of its divine origin was nearly as common, there was no need for such signs any longer.

Also, the holy standard, namely the Scriptures, were complete when miracles ceased in the church. Belief in

14

the miracles of the apostles was established, and this belief confirmed the truth of the doctrines of the gospel. And the prophecies contained in the Scriptures, *some already* fulfilled, and *some* yet to be fulfilled, provided additional and continual confirmation to the world, that Almighty God was the author of the Bible. The Scriptures, then, (and such proofs as these which they contained of their divinity) show that they needed no further proofs, and they proclaim to the unbelieving world in the language of Abraham to the rich man in hell, "If they hear not Moses and the prophets, (and Christ and his apostles,) neither will they be persuaded, though one rose from the dead."—Luke xvi. 31.

If the holy Scriptures of the Old and the New Testaments are a sufficient standard for our faith and our practices, I would fear falling underneath the judgment of God by claiming the right to such new revelations of his will, such as men are doing in these days, "For I testify unto every man that heareth the words of the prophecy of this book, If any man shall add unto these things, God shall add unto him the plagues that are written in this book," &c.—Rev. xxii. 18.

And since *wonders* are miracles, their daily occurrence would nullify the effect they were meant to have, and render them ineffective in answering the intended purposes in their fulfillment. Instead of constituting exceptions to the general rule of nature, because of their commonness they would become the rule.

Giving eyes to the blind every day, raising the sick at every hour, and raising the dead as frequently as men are born to the world, would be to expect them as a matter of course; and the wonders would be for them not to happen.

15

Furthermore, have the "Saints" given a single proof to the world that they possess the miraculous gifts, those which they claim should "follow the believers?" Are not the "false miracles," such as the ones which the Roman church boast of having, the best of their wonders? Perhaps the illnesses and sickness that arise from weak spirits, or some obstacle in the body's system, are transformed by acting on men's imagination; perhaps bodily strength overcomes such fevers and sicknesses without the use of drugs and medicines;* but where are such miracles as those of the apostles being worked in our days? Where are the lame that have been healed such as the man who was healed by Peter and John? Bring forth the deaf, whose hearing has been restored through the power of the "Saints." Who among them has loosed the bands of the mute's tongue, causing him to speak praises unto

*See "Paley on the Truths of the Christian Religion," the second part, chapter ii. Some *imaginary* wonders such as these in one or two examples, happened in Oxford some years ago, when the Rev. H. Bulteel (a minister who separated from the church of England) and his followers were zealous in support of *Irvingism*. We know a gentle and virtuous lady, in the above city, who arose from her sick bed (where she had lain for years), through, it is supposed, the prayers of Mr. B. and his friends; but since it was not a particular illness, rather a lowness of spirit that had risen from the disorder of the corporeal system pertaining to that woman, there is no doubt that the zeal and enthusiasm that had worked on her imagination, were what caused commotion throughout her entire body, to the point of enabling her to accomplish that which she had not the disposition to do previously.

16

God? Where is the blind man who has received his sight through the miraculous gifts of these Latter Saints? And if there are some of them like Irving, who think they have the gift of the Spirit to speak in tongues they have never learned, let them show which language it is, and which men on the earth speak it. If they cannot do this, all their ranting is nothing but sound without substance—

"Vox et praeterea nihil."

and prattle worse than the confusion of Babel!*

And lastly, what is the purpose of this miraculous power they claim? We already have sufficient proofs that the Scriptures are the word of God, and that God is the protector of his word. If there is no need for further confirmations of any scriptural truth, one must believe that not all things that are called miracles are anything other than human deceit, since the Lord never makes manifest his power to confirm a lie, and "no man speaking by the Spirit of God calleth Jesus accursed."—1 Cor. xii. 3.

We see, then, that the miracles of the "Saints" and others are not authentic in the face of the standard of true miracles; consequently, one must believe that miracles have not been in the church of Christ for more than fifteen hundred years.†

* The Christian world around Merthyr Tydfil, Carmarthen, and other places, has received quite curious examples of the miraculous gift of the "Saints" to raise the dead, and heal the sick! And we must conclude that the "Elders" did not have faith, since the signs failed to follow! or else, "God did not do his work."

† The disciples in the Bulteel congregation made a sound like doves, &c.

17

III. But even though God for centuries has failed to bear witness of the truths of the gospel through miracles, there is other evidence that continues in the church, and will continue until the end of the world, namely the *conversion of sinners*. To some degree this evidence can be considered miraculous, even though the *soul* is the object that is affected here, and *not the body*. This evidence does not address the eyes and ears of men, rather "justice, peace, and joy in the Holy Ghost" are sufficient proofs to the attributes of a born-again soul, that the divine power works together with the truth. Upon giving the commission to his apostles to preach the gospel, he promised that he would be with them until the end of the world. And he showed that he was present with them through the extraordinary success that accompanied the preaching of the gospel. "A great many turned to the Lord," throughout Judea and Samaria, and came from the gentiles throughout all the countries, until the gospel overcame the imperial throne of Rome; and the pagan temples and the mute idols fell before the name of Jesus, "as Dagon was fallen before the ark of the Lord."

The Lord continues to work through and with his gospel. Now *conversion*, and not *miracles*, is the lasting proof of the divine gifts in the church of Christ. It is not by working miracles that rebirth and the imparting of the privileges of the gospel are perfected, rather through the Holy Ghost, in whose hand is the word, which like a "two-edged sword, pierces even to the dividing asunder of soul and spirit, and of the joints and marrow, and is a discerner of the thoughts and intents of the heart." Miracles do not provide

18

a single benefit unless one experiences the conversion of the spirit.

Many saw miracles during the age of the apostles without believing: but if there is no need for the miraculous power now, yet the cooperation of God and the truth are indispensable for salvation. The conversion of the sinner shows, as clearly as do miracles, that the word preached is from God; yes, as clearly as the opening of the eyes of the blind and the ears of the deaf.

The miraculous power casting out savage devils from the bodies of men is no longer seen; but devils equally as cruel and detestable are continually cast out of the souls of sinners, for the Spirit of God upholds his word. The devil of pride and drunkenness, adultery, injustice, and every wicked deed, are driven from the heart, where they nest; and the sinner becomes a lowly, humble, sober, chaste, just, saintly, and godly Christian. Is this not a miracle from the grace of heaven? and one that bears witness that God is still with the church? The corporeal eyes of the blind-from-birth do not come to see in our days; but the eyes of the minds of many a blind sinner who does not see his wretchedness, his danger, or his duty, now come to see the miracle of the soul, and the worth of Jesus as Savior. And does not this show the *"finger of God?"*

No one now possesses the power to give feet to the lame, and ears to the mute, or to raise the dead in a temporal sense; but there are thousands of the mute who come to hear the voice of the Son of God, and live; thousands of the lame who receive strength to jump to their feet to praise the grace of heaven! and thousands of those

19

who died in transgressions and sins, who come out of their unclean graves having received life to their souls! Are not these miraculous proofs of the presence of God in his church? The fangs of that old serpent satan yet again fail to harm those who believe in the one who was lifted up on the cross. The fiery darts of the evil one will be quenched by the shield of faith of the gospel, and the bitter waters of Mara will be sweetened by the enshrining wood of the cross!

This is not figurative language to describe that which will never take place. Do we not have around us sufficient examples of the deeds of divine grace? Have we not seen those who earlier were like the Corinthians, "Fornicators, adulterers, effeminate, thieves, covetous, drunkards, revilers, extortioners, washed, sanctified, justified in the name of the Lord Jesus, and by the Spirit of our God?"—1 Cor. vi. 9—11.

Do not the saints in our days possess so many comforts of religion as to cause them to rejoice in the midst of tribulations, and to sing when their heart and their flesh weaken, and the hour of their release has come? What is it that administers such comfort as this to men who have never learned the *philosophy* of this world, and yet are made far more valiant than Socrates the wise, as they face the "final enemy"? It is the grace of God which works these *miracles*. A new heart is given through conversion—a tender heart of flesh, causing the cruel to become sensitive—the miser to become generous—the deceptive to become as innocent as a child—and he was as frightful as the wolf to become as gentle as the lamb! These visible changes which are put into effect by the Spirit of God, are sufficient proofs, without seeking any additional signs, that God through miracles of his grace still bears witness to the truth of his holy word. See 2 Cor. i. 12.*

Thus, instead of dreaming of enjoying the miraculous gifts that followed the believers in the age of the apostles, let us all strive to obtain the witness within ourselves, that we have gone across "from death to life." Without so doing, it would not be of any benefit for us to possess all the miraculous gifts; for Christ says in this manner: "Many will say to me in that day, Lord, Lord, have we not prophesied in thy name? and in thy name have cast out devils? and in thy name done many wonderful works? And then I will profess unto them, I never knew you: depart from me, ye that work iniquity." Matt. vii., 22, 23.

*See some quite remarkable examples of the effects of the grace of God in the conversion of sinners, in a book published lately under the title "Philosophy of the plan of Salvation," chap. xix.

PRINTED BY W. SPURRELL, KING STREET, CARMARTHEN.

Pamphlet 7

Edward Roberts. *Twyll Mormoniaeth. Darlith a draddodwyd gan y Parch E. Roberts, Gweinidog y Bedyddwyr, Rhymney* (*Deceit of Mormonism. A Lecture Delivered by the Rev. E. Roberts, Minister of the Baptists, Rhymney*). Merthyr Tydfil: David Jones, 1848. 23 pages.

[In order to make the print size more readable, the English translation consists of 48 pages.]

On 2 September 1847, Baptist minister Edward Roberts presented a two-hour lecture in Dowlais against the teachings and doctrine of the Latter-day Saints. Dan Jones sat near the front and took notes during this lecture, planning to give a rebuttal the following evening.

It was not until February 1848 that Roberts's lecture found its way into print. Entitled *Deceit of Mormonism*, its contents are basically a Welsh translation of materials taken from the writings of Eber D. Howe, John C. Bennett, and Henry Caswall. See Episode 4.6.

Jones also published a 42-page pamphlet reviewing Roberts's lecture (see *Defending the Faith*, item J13). In this preface, Jones declares how opposition serves as a catalyst for the work to move forward:

> The bulls and the anathemas of the Pope, and the conspiracies of the papist friars regarding the life of Luther, were better for the spreading of his reformation than all the previous peace and sufferance. And the blasphemies and unfounded claims of Mr. Davies of Dowlais, and Mr. Roberts of Rhymney; yes, the public blasphemies on the streets made by their followers are better for the spread of Mormonism than the stillness to be found in some other places; and while persecution and shame, although falling on myself and my brethren, are a means of spreading the truth in my dear country—welcome persecution! Welcome pain! Welcome shame! Behold the bodies, the characters and the feelings that suffer them are happy, even though they flow from men who should know better (p. [2]).

One direct result of the attacks on Dan Jones and the Church he represented and defended is the conversion of William Howells, a lay Baptist minister in Aberdare. Howells would later write, "I can testify boldly in the day of judgment that it was the Review of brother Capt. D. Jones, on the Lecture of Roberts from Rhymney, that was the means of convincing me of the deceit of the religion that I professed" (*Zion's Trumpet*, April 1849, p. 93.).

PRICE SIXPENCE.

DECEIT OF MORMONISM.

A LECTURE

DELIVERED BY

THE REV. E ROBERTS,

A BAPTIST MINISTER, RHYMNEY

MERTHYR TYDFIL:

PRINTED AND PUBLISHED BY D. JONES.

1848.

DECEIT OF MORMONISM.

A LECTURE

DELIVERED BY

THE REV. E ROBERTS,

A BAPTIST MINISTER, RHYMNEY

MERTHYR TYDFIL:

PRINTED AND PUBLISHED BY D. JONES.

1848.

Dear Fellow Countrymen,

At the earnest and unceasing wish of a number of those who heard this Lecture delivered, it is sent out to you through the Press. Many of my friends judged that publishing it would not be any hindrance to the intended book of Roberts, from Blaenau, as he will be taking a different plan; the certainty of this caused me to change my decision about publishing it. Hoping with God's blessing, it will enlighten many of my fellow-men about the Mormon superstition,

I remain, yours,

Most sincerely,

IORWERTH GLAN ALED.

Rhymney, February 4, 1848.

LECTURE.

Religion in general is denoted as an order of faith and worship; and in this depiction the Patriarchal, the Mosaic, and the Christian areas are represented.

Superstition is denoted as an order of will-worship; and this represents all the variations scattered through the history pages in the Pagan and Muslim areas, and their like. The only Holy religion to be practiced in the world for over 1800 years is the Christian one, with strong and clear principles which are contained in the New Testament. It is based upon undeniable facts, which have been immortalized by divine proofs; while many of the enchantments conceived in empty dreams, and which depend on unfounded opinions, have been shattered, and thrown beyond the shadows of scorn; this religion is like a high-pinnacled mountain, strong and clear; its author is Almighty God—its center point is Christ—its early defenders are heaven-sent apostles and its subjects are willing carriers of the truth.

In the face of the simplicity and holiness of this religion, we have observed, to our worry, various attempts to confuse it and its traditions, to undermine its authority and add to its content, by many who claim the right to a share of the authority of heaven,—while in truth they are nothing but awful deceivers, attacking the weak in order to claim them to everlasting damnation. All extremes are dangerous; but of all extremes, those religious in name are the most dangerous. In the last one thousand years we have heard of about twenty false-christs and false-prophets, almost more than can be counted. These accursed deceivers have charmed many men of superstitious tendency—and have been a means to damn thousands and millions of eternal souls!

6

In every nation and in every age, we have some men who will follow anything under the *name* of religion; and to our shame, we have examples among Welshmen in the nineteenth century of the corruption of the human mind reducing its subjects to kneel before the most terrible religious deception and oppression ever offered by the devil's servants to mankind! This lecture is given for the sake of those weak in knowledge in our nation; as for the strong and cautious, you have not the least fear. It is clear by now, that the more unreasonable and ungodly the superstition, to that degree is the beastly and rude check of its followers; the support of ignorant people is the most difficult in the world to deal with; they do not hold forth for a minute—and they are not politely ashamed in the face of the exposure of their deceit. They carry on in their enchanting stubbornness, taking malicious ignorance and blind prejudice as their main leaders. Among the various deceiving traditions offered under the name of religion in recent times, there is not one more shameful, in its moral character and ignorance of its followers—as well as the weakness of the self-betrayal of its principles—as that called MORMONISM; it seems to be the fruit of fancies and the oppression of a crazy enchanter—intended to attract men to make fools of themselves in this world, and to give themselves over as lost lunatics in the spiritual world!

Atheists can reason somewhat on the principles of Nature; and the Pagans can have some excuse for reasoning in favor of their gods in view of the examples of their forefathers—if they do not have reason and spiritual revelation in their favor, at least theirs is a feeling of belonging; but as for the deceiving hotheads which rise up one after the other to throw scorn on the common sense of mankind, they have neither law nor feeling and are in a more inferior class than the reptiles of the earth; they push themselves with the most bold impudence to the shadow of confused dreams—the fruit of minds tormented by the devils of sleep; they claim discourses with self-created angels—and to

7

crown the deception by enthroning it on the highest pinnacle of madness, they boast of performing miracles—and to their permanent shame, the world from fallen *Nauvoo* to the mountainous nooks of Wales is ready to throw the lie back in their faces! THEY HAVE NEVER PERFORMED A SINGLE MIRACLE; and they have never tried to prove that they have accomplished such, only by making *assertions*: yet base claims are poor things to offer as evidence of a religion which claims to be divine, to inquisitive lads of the nineteenth century.

It could have been thought that the deception and enchantment of MUNZER and BOCKHOLT in the year 1525 in Germany, in the midst of the fuss of the revival, with their prophecies and alleged miracles, as well as the state's obligation to destroy them in order to protect the civil peace of the inhabitants—would have been enough to open the eyes of future ages, and to keep them on their guard against their sort; but this was not so; in the year 1790 one RICHARD BROTHERS rose up claiming that "*his mind had been enlightened and that he had foreseen that he would be a great man in the future.*" He began to announce things under the name of prophecies; and among these he claimed that the town of London would be destroyed in the year 1791; but, did that take place? In order to correct his foolishness, he then said that it was he who had saved it from such a disaster! and as a fitting end to his journey, the British Parliament was forced to commit him to prison as a maniacal wretch.

Then we are told of Women of this tendency: one by the name of ANNE LEE began her activities in the year 1776, in the state of New York. She pretended to be under the influence of epileptic convulsions: and when like this, she claimed that she had visions and revelations from heaven; and that she was the woman mentioned the Book of Revelation, "*And a strange thing was seen in the heavens, a woman clothed in the sun,*" &c. Among her claims, she said that she would never die—but that she would be taken up to heaven in the blinking of an eye. But in a short

8

time after that, death proved stronger than the prophecy of ANNE LEE. She ended, like her predecessors, in self-proven deception. There arose one called Jemima Wilkinson who excited the land about her visions around the year 1775; she was similar in her claims to the others. She claimed that she could heal illnesses—reveal the secrets of every heart—that she would live for a thousand years, at which point she would be moved to heaven without dying. But when she went to offer proof on illnesses, she failed *every time*; despite claiming that she would walk on water without sinking, but when she tried to do so, she failed in the presence of witnesses; and despite saying she could raise a dead body to repossess life, when a corpse in a coffin was brought before her, she failed despite all her efforts! And this enchantress, like others similar to her, blamed her failures on weakness and lack of faith! This was, and still is, a very necessary sanctuary for the deceiving crowd. We could mention MRS. BUCHAN, who appeared in Glasgow, *Scotland*, and JOHANNA SOUTHCOTT who claimed that she was pregnant by the Holy Spirit, &c., &c., but these names are quite well-known, as well as the false religious claims connected with them.

In the list of this species, and in the lowest class of all, we can conscientiously put the deceiver Joe Smith, and his Mormon Bible, &c. He began in self-explained deception—the ignorance of his followers was his starting power, and their shameful superstition was the main defense to his claims. By now, this new wanderer in the atmosphere of religion is coming to his end, and the true weight and attraction of his ideas are bound to pull him down to his proper *level, namely scorn*. The *main* aim of this lecture is to make observations about the deception as a *warning* to the weak in the future; as for *exposing* it, its warmest friends save me from doing that, making the task very simple. We could not fulfill our task better, than by giving a true story, public facts that cannot be refuted—those which give a clear explanation of this sect of religious madness.

9

1. WE SHALL BEGIN WITH THE FOUNDER OF THIS ENCHANTMENT—namely, JOSEPH SMITH, OR JOE SMITH:—The beginning of that which is called MORMONISM, took place around the year 1830. The founder was Joseph Smith, Jr., who claimed he was a Priest, a Prophet, and an Apostle; called and set apart spiritually, as it were, through a direct revelation from God. He was the son of one named Joseph Smith who moved from the town of Royalton in the State of Vermont, around the year 1820, —and Joseph, the son, was 16 years old at the time. They lived in the town of Manchester, Ontario County, until the year 1830. This town was the main place of his early activities. As for his appear-ance, (it is said by someone, who visited him with the pur-pose of obtaining correct information about Mormonism), "He had a rustic, boorish appearance, and his face showed a strange mixture of the scoundrel and the ignorant. His hands were big and fat, and on one of his fingers he wore a heavy, gold ring with something engraved on it. His clothes were coarse; his hat was white—bound in black *crepe* as a sign of mourning for a dead brother by the name of Don Carlos Smith, who had been the editor of a Newspaper called '*The Times and Seasons*.' His age at that time was about 35 years. I tried (says the historian) to see his eyes, but I failed in my attempt, because he was completely bereft of the open and honest look belonging to a sincere man." Another true historian wrote as follows about his family and his upbringing in the world:

"All who became intimate with the family of the pre-tended prophet during this period, judged them to be lazy —ignorant—and exceptionally superstitious; believing in devils and sorcerers, as well as fortune telling; pretending to believe that the earth was filled with hidden treasurers. Such an upbringing had its expected effect on Joseph, the son, and in time he too had become very expert in the arts of necromancy, i.e., one who pretends to raise the Spirits of the dead; juggling, the use of the diving rod, and looking into what they termed a peep-

10

hat and when he put his face in it, enabled him to find the places of hidden treasure.

In time he collected about him a crowd of young men—those who were too lazy to work in an honest way for their living, and they worked by digging into the hills and mountains and lonely places, in a search of gold. They opened many pits in the locality, which were then pointed out by them as the place from whence the "golden plates" were obtained. When the deceiver began to spread his revelations around, little attention was paid to his foolish enchantments; but when they began to influence the belief of the most ignorant and superstitious group, the respectable inhabitants of Palmyra and Manchester, (where the Smiths lived) considered it their duty to give public notice of their true character as a family. A public oath was drawn up by 50 gentlemen of different occupations and religious denominations, in order to reveal this without the shadow of doubt; see this which follows:

Palmyra, December 4th, 1833.

"We, the undersigned, have been acquainted with the Smith family, for a number of years, while they resided near this place, and we have no hesitation in saying, that we consider them destitute of that moral character, which ought to entitle them to the confidence of any community. They were particularly famous for visionary projects, spent much of their time in digging for money which they pretended was hid in the earth; and to this day, large excavations may be seen in the earth, not far from their residence, where they used to spend their time in digging for hidden treasures. Joseph Smith, Senior, and his son Joseph, were in particular, considered entirely destitute of moral character, and addicted to vicious habits.

Martin Harris was a man who had acquired a handsome property, and in matters of business his word was considered good; but on moral and religious subjects, he was perfectly visionary—sometimes advocating one sentiment, and sometimes another. And in reference to all with whom we

11

were acquainted, that have embraced *Mormonism* from this neighborhood, we are compelled to say, were very visionary, and most of them destitute of moral character, and without influence in this community; and this may account as to why they were permitted to go on with their impositions undisturbed. It was not supposed that any of them were possessed of sufficient character or influence to make any one believe their book or their sentiments, and we know not of a single individual in this vicinity that puts the least confidence in their pretended revelations."

Following this notice are 50 signatures—see *Rise, Progress, and Causes of Mormonism, by Professor J.B. Turner, New York,* 1844.

Further on this subject we have the evidence of another respected historian—which confirms the previous ones. "Smith belonged to a very unstable family, near to Palmyra. They lived a wandering life—and they were mainly known as diggers of silver. From his childhood, Joe seemed to be a rascal completely bereft of talent; but his father claimed that he (the son) could see down into the earth and find valuable treasures which were hidden there. Far back, before thinking of the *Golden Bible (!),* Joe was the leader of the gang searching for hidden treasures; he would place a stone in his hat through which he pretended to see, to find the places in which they should dig. It was generally at night that they would do this work. After one of these nights, Martin Harris said that the leader had had a strange dream while in bed. An angel of God appeared to be approaching him, surrounded in a holy brightness. This holy messenger informed Smith that he had been set aside by the Lord to be a prophet for Almighty God—to bring to light hidden things, which would turn out to be of exceptional good to the world. Then the angel informed him of the existence of the *Golden Bible,* and the place where it was hidden; at the same time it warned Joe to follow the holy leadership carefully, or he would bring the terrible wrath of heaven upon himself. Neither did he have the freedom to look for the

12

golden plates for three years. First, he had to go on a journey to Pennsylvania, and there between the mountains, he would meet a very beautiful woman who belonged to a very responsible family—and he was to take her as his wife. As soon as he saw the woman, he would fall in love with her; and although he was a stranger to her, and she belonged to a much higher social circle than he in the world, yet she would agree to marry him there and then, and to follow him to the ends of the earth. After their marriage, they were to return to his original home and live there peacefully until the birth of their first child. When this child reached two years of age, then Joe could venture to the hill where the chest and plates were hidden—and take it out and announce his findings to the world. After this dream, Joe awoke and did as the angel had told him; and according to Harris' testimony everything came to pass. But we are informed, that Joe was not careful enough in his obedience, because he told the secrets to his father and his family. The old digging spirit arose in the father, and he insisted on going to search for the chest *straight away*, to be satisfied about it. They went to the place at night, and after working for awhile, the chest began to appear to them—but soon moved out of sight. After consulting further with Joe, they worked again and discovered its size. But when they pushed forward to have a look at it, the thunder of the Almighty roared until the earth shook; and bright sheets of lightning went across the side of the hill until the area around the site of the dig was burned,—and after this, with a rumbling noise the chest moved from their sight again. They were all afraid, and hurried home. Joe had gone alone, and on the way, in the middle of some trees, an angel of the Lord appeared to him very angry. This angel chastised Joe sharply in fearful language, because he had not kept the secret to himself.

Poor Joe went home very shakily under the effects of this lesson! but in a while he came to himself, and he had another revelation instructing him to go himself and raise the chest from the earth, and then hide it secretly under

13

the hearthstone of his house, and not to look at it on any account. Harris said that Joe possessed two shining stones by which he could interpret the carvings on the golden plates, *at that time*; but how he got them before opening the chest he did not know!"

It would be beneficial for us here to have Joe's history from one who had frequent and honest opportunities to know him as a person, and his enchanting customs as a deceiver,—this witness was his FATHER-IN-LAW.

The historian who handed over the following evidence of Joe's father-in-law says, "When I was in Palmyra I met a respectable minister belonging to the Diocesan Church, who previously belonged to the union of Methodists. This man was very familiar with Mr. Hale, Joe's father-in-law. He informed me that Mr. Hale lived near Great Bend in Pennsylvania, and that he was quite a skillful hunter. He professed the religion of the Methodist union. To this Mr. Hale signed his name on an essay explaining Joe and his deceiving tricks, confirming that it contained thorough and honest truths —and he did this before Charles Dimon, J.P., and in addition to this, a letter belonging to William Thomson and Davis Dimock, judges in the Court of Common Pleas, in the county of Susquehanna—testified that they had been very familiar with Isaac Hale, of Harmony Township, for many a year, and that he was a man of exceptionally good character—the sort on whose evidence one could confidently depend.

The letter containing Mr. Hale's evidence is as follows—"I became familiar with Joseph Smith, junior, in the month of November 1825; at that time he worked with other persons digging into the earth in a search for silver; his main task was looking, or pretending to look through a stone which he put in his hat. In this way he pretended to find minerals and hidden treasures.

At this time he seemed to be a worthless young man, quite ignorant, and bitter, and very nasty to his father.

Smith, his father, and a number of other miners, boarded in my house when they were digging in an old mine, which

14

they thought the Spaniards had opened and worked years ago. At the beginning, Smith, junior, lively encouraged the workers; but when they got close to the place in which he had prophesied the valuable treasure was hidden, he told them *that the magic was so strong that he could not see it!* Then they gave up the task, and dispersed. After this time, Smith, junior, often visited my house, and finally he asked for my permission to marry my daughter Emma. I refused, giving him reasons why I did so; some of these reasons were that he was a stranger to me, and doing work of which I did not approve. After this he left the place; but before long he returned; and when I was away from home he took my daughter away to the state of New York, where they married against my will. When they reached Palmyra, New York, Emma wrote to me, wishing to have her belongings, that is her clothes, &c. I wrote back to her, informing her that her belongings were safe and that she could have them when she saw fit. Eventually they both returned, bringing with them one named Peter Ingersol, and at last they decided to establish themselves close to my home.

At this time Smith informed me that he had given up the work of *looking through the stone*, and that he was keen to work hard and honestly for his living. A short time after this, I was informed that they had brought some strange Book of plates with them. They showed me the chest in which they said this book was to be found. They allowed me to feel the weight of the chest but not to look in it.

I asked Joseph Smith who would be the first to look into the chest and see the Book of plates? He replied *that it would be a small child.*

After this, I became uncomfortable, and told him that if there were such a thing in my house, which I could not see, that he would have to take it away. Following this, it was said that the plates were hidden in the trees. About this time, Martin Harris made his appearance; and Smith began the work of interpreting the signs which were carved on the plates, while Harris wrote his interpretations down. It is

15

said that Harris wrote 116 pages, and then lost them. Soon after this, Harris said that he wanted stronger evidence than he had—and that he had spoken to Joe about this; but Joe informed him that he could not and dared not show the plates to him, but that he would go to the woods to the place where the book of plates was hidden—and when he had returned, Harris could follow his footprints in the snow, and find the Book, and judge for himself.

Harris later told me that he had done according to Smith's instruction, and that he could not find the plates—and that he was still very dissatisfied.

The next day after this happened, I went to the house where Joseph Smith, junior, was living, and where he and Harris were working at translating the Book. Each one of them had a written piece of paper which they composed—and some of the words on them were as follows, "*My servant seeks more evidence, but more evidence I cannot give him.*" There was also something about "*three were to see the thing*"—meaning, I suppose, the Book of plates; and also, "*if the three did not closely follow the commands it would be taken from them.*" I asked whose words they were, and I was told by Joseph or Emma that they were the words of Jesus Christ. I told them at the time, that I considered it all a fraud, and I advised them to put it all aside. The method Joe used to read and interpret the plates, was the same as he used when digging for silver, that is with the stone in his hat, and he would stare at it, *while the book of plates was at the same time hidden in the trees!* About this time, Martin Harris left, and Oliver Cowdery came to write for Smith, while he interpreted what was depicted. This was the same Oliver Cowdery as the one named in the Book of Mormon. This man remained as Smith's secretary until the Book of Mormon was finished, as I understood. Joseph Smith, junior, lived near me for some time after this, and I had a fair opportunity to get to know him and his friends: and I sincerely believe, from the facts I noted, as well as other various occasions not necessary to note at present,

16

that the whole Book of Mormon is a foolish collection of lies and wickedness, mainly intended to charm and fool superstitious and careless men, so that its creators might live on those robbed people who swallowed the deception!"

ISAAC HALE.

2. WE REFER AGAIN TO THE BOOK OF MORMON:—

When Joe Smith was up to his tricks digging for silver, he says according to his own story, that he received several revelations from heaven, in relation to different groups of religions. On the first occasion of this sort, he had gone to a grove, and there he asked for heavenly help to inform him which of the religious sects existing at that time he should follow; and he said that a bright light appeared above his head, and that he was taken up into it; there he saw two angels who told him that all his sins were forgiven, that the whole world was astray with regard to religious matters, and that the truth would be revealed to him at a suitable time. The second revelation of a similar nature, which Smith noted, was that the American Indians were the remnants of the children of Israel, and that prophets and inspired men had once existed among them, and who hid heavenly documents in a safe place—to keep them from the grasp of sinful hands. Another revelation Smith had, on the morning of the 22nd of September, 1823, was that these remains were in a cave on a big hill to the east of the main road of Palmyra, County of Wayne, in the state of New York.

Joe made a search in this place; and he said that he found a stone chest, containing plates similar to gold, about seven to eight inches in length and width and not as thick as common tin plates. On these plates the contents of the Book of Mormon were engraved. It was believed that Mormon wrote these and hid them securely in this place. Smith was not allowed to take these gold plates away, until he had learned Egyptian, in which language, or recent dialect of it, the Engraved Book was composed.

In September 1827, Smith was considered prepared to receive the gold plates; and he translated them into

17

English, publishing the translation in one Book in the year 1830. This book had quite an effect on the lower class in the United States—and a *Sect* of them was formed, and they called themselves the "LATTER-DAY SAINTS." The Book of Mormon is almost the same size and length as the Old Testament; and it contains, according to the ordinary way of speaking, two different stories. In it there is the history of the Nephites, a part of the tribe of Joseph, who it is thought had emigrated from Jerusalem under a prophet by the name of Nephi, and were miraculously led to America. In the book is the history of the Nephites, a branch of the tribe of Joseph, which is it supposed had left Jerusalem under a prophet by the name of Nephi, and had been miraculously guided to America. It is said that the Nephites were the root of the Indian nation. A number of years after their establishment, it is said that they found the records of the Jaredites, an extinct nation which came to America about the time of the building of the tower of Babel. Things such as this, belonging to different imaginary prophets among the Jaredites and the Nephites, and alleged contributions in relation "TO MY SERVANT JOSEPH SMITH," the *Sect*'s apostle—are what make up that which is called the Book of Mormon! Smith used a strange method to bring out his translations and his manuscripts with Harris. Although they were in the same room, there was a thick curtain like a *Blanket* separating them, with Smith hiding behind it, pretending to look through the clear stones, and writing or saying what he perceived—and when he spoke aloud, Harris, who sat on the other side of the curtain, wrote it down. Harris was made to understand beforehand, that if he dared to come close to the sacred chest, or look at Smith while he was translating the engravings, he would incur the most terrible wrath of Jehovah against him! In order to bring the finished translation through the Press, Harris mortgaged his land.

3. AFTER THIS BEGINNING WE NEXT REFER TO SOME OF THE ACTS OF THE MORMONS:—

18

After setting the aforementioned Book down as a foundation, they started to build on it. Smith and Cowdery set out to carry forth their divine authority; they baptized each other: they won some unlearned followers and baptized them—and together with these converts, they professed to impart the forgiveness of sins, and the working of miracles, &c.

In September 1830, Smith had a revelation that Cowdery, Pratt, Patterson and Whitmer, were to go among the Indians whom they called the *Lamanites*, to preach the Gospel to them. It should be remembered here, that the Book of Mormon claimed to give the history of the American Indians, showing that they were the ten scattered tribes of Israel. The first converts were sent to these people to preach—"*raising a pillar as testimony in the place where God's temple was built in the new and glorious Jerusalem.*"

In October of the same year they started out; and as they went along the way, they tried preaching to several tribes, but without success! Then they turned their attention and their persons to the Missouri, and when near to the eastern boundary of that state, they stayed for some days to inquire about the Indians further to the west. They feared that their infallible leader was unable to lead them further, and they began to appeal for help from men. After they reached the western boundary of Missouri, they went to the territory of the Indians, where they had not been long, when they received a notice from the Overseer of the United States, that they had to cross the border, or stay in the garrison 40 miles up the Arkansas River. As they were bound to do one of these two things, they chose the first, and they never again had the courage to venture over the boundary and visit the Indians, those whom they had once considered to be God's Chosen People! After this, they lived in the village of Independence over the winter, about 12 miles from the state boundary. In June the prophet held an assembly of his followers, in which he said that wondrous things were about to take place. All the leaders and elders were ordered to leave immediately for the western part of Missouri; only

19

two were to go together, and in pairs they were taken to different routes, preaching as they travelled. The Prophet promised that they would receive the land of their inheritance in the land of Missouri; that it was there that Christ would come again, and there that the Temple of God and city of Zion would be built! In this place there was to be a sanctuary from the wrath and storms which would be poured out upon the earth, and which would sweep away all those who would not accept and bow to the Book of Mormon! Since there is nothing more appropriate and effective to reassure the minds of men about such nonsense as this, as genuine, simple, honest facts, especially from those who had a fair chance to get to know these deeds, we shall quote the evidence of a sensible eye-witness, (and taking into account that he had bowed to the Mormon idol) but honest, *nevertheless*, having awoken from his superstitious dream;—our witness, namely one by the name of Ezra Booth, was one of those who was assigned to travel on foot; only the leaders had the honor of traveling at the society's expense, and go in a way more worthy of their greatness.

Ezra Booth says as follows—

"I was one of those chosen to make the journey across country; and since I was not used to travelling on foot, I was somewhat hesitant; but believing that this was God's will, I decided to bow to the decision; and on the 15th of June, 1836, in the company of the one selected to go with me, I headed towards Missouri. I preached three times in Ohio—three times in Indiana, once in Illinois, and once in Missouri. We were commanded to preach according to how we received the influence of the spirit; and the impressions on my mind were, that I would enjoy more of this influence as we neared the west; but although I travelled *a thousand* miles, my expectations in this field were completely unfulfilled. I thought that the spirit would direct me to preach with exceptional degrees of freedom, sometime in the future; at that time it never came; now, I honestly hope that the spirit will direct my pen while I attempt to depict the heresies, and

20

the foolishness which belong to the order I defended. When we reached the place to which we were intended to go, we found to our worry that disappointment had arrived there before us. When we began our journey to Missouri, we had expected to have an open door to proclaim the new order there, and that those endowed with the talent to speak with tongues, would have a full opportunity to show their supernatural talent, by preaching to the Indians in their own dialect. But for a fortnight after arriving there, the elders stood against preaching. We had expected to meet a great church, about which we had been informed by Smith that he had seen in a vision, which had been established there by Cowdery. This great church contained *four women*! We had expected to be witnesses of the miraculous gifts with which persons in Ohio had been ordained. But the lack of faith in the people always prevented this! We had expected to see the foundation of the temple laid down; we did see this, but it was not worth going to the Missouri to witness it. The honor of consecrating the land given to Rigdon; and the commandment regarding it was as follows—"*let my servant Sidney set apart and consecrate the land, and the place to build the temple.*" Furthermore, "*I give a commandment to my servant Sidney, that he write a description of the land of Zion, and an account of God's will, as it will be made known to him through the Spirit; and that a collection be made through the Churches to obtain money to purchase lands as an inheritance for the children of God, for, behold it is the will of the Lord that the disciples, and children of men, open their hearts to purchase all the surrounding land, lest they have an inheritance only through the spilling of blood.*"

The prophet received a sign, (he said) from God, that he had chosen this spot, that is the state of Missouri, as a place of sanctuary, and safety, and everlasting inheritance for the Mormons.

The following account about the setting down of the foundation of the city and the temple was written by a

21

truthful witness who was there at the time,—

"The laying down of the foundation of Zion was followed by much pomp, and proud displays of talents, by Rigdon and Cowdery. Rigdon consecrated the land, first, in a speech to the God worshipped by the Mormons; after that, he made some comments on the purpose of our gathering together—and he swore an oath of faithfulness to those who were to receive the eternal inheritance in the city.

He pointed out to them especially the importance of our duty to obey all Smith's commands; and he urged them to give many thanks to the Lord for the free gift given to them through him, although that *free gift* had at the same time cost them a great sum of money!

At the end of this, an oak tree was cut, about ten inches thick at the trunk, the best available at that time; and twelve men corresponding to the number of the twelve apostles, carried it to its place on wooden staves. Cowdery took for himself the honor of placing the corner stone; when the stone had been laid the oak tree was planted upon it. The following day, the land on which the Temple was to be built was consecrated; and Smith himself claimed the honor of laying the corner stone; and if one were to go half a mile from the town to a small piece of raised land not far from the southern side of the road—the place can be seen, with a tree on it, different to the other trees because the bark has been cut away on the northern and eastern sides. On the southern side can be seen the letter T, which stands for Temple; and on the eastern side can be seen *Zom*, for *Zomas*, which, said Smith, is the original word for Zion. Near to the bottom of the tree can be seen a small stone, hidden with thorns cut for the purpose—that is the corner stone of the temple. There one has the privilege and the joy of seeing the capable work completed by 30 men who left their homes—and who travelled a thousand miles—the great majority of them on foot, and who bore the cost of a thousand *dollars* in money!! (Oh Mormonism! Behold the integrity of your Prophet! It is an incomparable integrity!!!) After this the poor souls set

22

about returning to their homes as disappointed creatures. They came on water for part of the way; but they quarreled dreadfully there, and the prophet and the elders could not keep order; so they were forced to disperse across the land,—but Smith and his chief friends insisted on money from the others,—three of them to the cost of a hundred *dollars*; and by the time they reached Cincinnati they had no money, and they had to mortgage their *Box* to get help to reach home! Behold such a peaceful religion! Behold a Prophet second to none!! and behold everlasting proof of Joe Smith's miraculous talents!!!

After these feats, we have stories of their disturbances and riots, against the peaceful inhabitants of the environs, with all sorts of weapons, until the civil powers were forced to use their authority to send them away from the borders. On the 20th of July 1833, a meeting was held in Independence, when between 400 and 500 of the citizens volunteered; their purpose was to decide on measures to get rid of this disturbing and riotous crowd. A message was announced to the people explaining the purpose of the meeting—and this purpose was set out as follows—

"We consider ourselves bound, on every account of self-defense, good society, public morality, together with every pleasant aspect we wish this young land to possess—to announce at once,

1.From now on that no Mormon will be able to move to or stay in this country.

2.That those who are here now, if they give definite assurance of their intention to move from here within a reasonable time, shall be permitted to stay unoppressed until they can sell their belongings and close up their business without loss.

3.That the editor of their Star (*the name of their newspaper*) must close its office immediately, and cease printing in this county; and as for any storerooms or businesses belonging to the *Sect*, their owners must completely agree to these

23

terms; for if they do not, effective methods will be used to carry this out.

4.That the Mormon leaders must use their influence to prevent more of their distant brothers from moving into this county; and advise and urge all of their brothers to agree to the above terms.

5.That those who do not agree to these statements, should appeal to their brothers who have the gifts of prophecy, for an explanation of what will happen to them if they disobey."

At first, the Mormons promised to agree to these easy and reasonable terms; but they did not keep their promise: because of this, ways were taken to force them—and these people of pitiful strength, prepared to meet the state defenders—bringing rifles, pistols, rusty swords, meat cleavers, and all sorts of similar things, proving publicly to the world and church, *that the weapons of their warfare were of the flesh*,—and that there was no shadow of similarity between them and Christians, no more than there is between a rusty steel sword—and the sword of the Holy Ghost! As a result of this riotous foolishness of theirs, they were forced to flee for their lives, some to Illinois, and some to Nauvoo, and others to places they were fortunate to reach.

With regard to Nauvoo, there has been much mention of it—and the boasts of the Mormons with respect to its marvels and privileges have been so numerous and false that it is difficult to refrain from refuting them, however foolish and degrading they may be; it is quite a comedown to observe such a collection of ignorance, carnality, immorality and barbarism, which are the peculiarities of that excommunicated part of the world; on hearing of some of the acts that were practiced there, even by arrogant minor prophets, and the daring chief-prophet—and that under the cloak of Christianity, we think that our flesh is jumping off our bones inch by inch; but without going over such things, and offending the feelings of our fellow-men by revealing them, we shall keep within the boundary of what is suitable to be written, although we cannot do this without sometimes

24

venturing to raise the curtain higher than we would wish. We have quite a concise story that occurred in a small area of that place, from an impartial author who visited the place in order to get knowledge of the inhabitants' customs. This story is as good an example as any we could choose from the great number, to answer our purposes at the moment—because it is simple, polite and sincere. We quote this story: —"Monday, April 18, 1842, I took an old Greek textbook of the Psalms which was in my possession, and I hurried to the river to cross over. The boatman was employed to take an emigrating family to Nauvoo. The family soon came on board. The husband seemed to be an American simpleton, and with him was his wife and several children. They also had two bulls, two cows, a calf, beds, tables, chairs and a wooden clock. When we were about to start a traveler on horseback came onboard, and I understood that he was from one of the 'gentiles,' driven by curiosity to visit the Zion of the West. After rowing much further than Nauvoo, (because the tide was strong) the boatman and his men hurried to cross the river. As I was in a hurry to cross over, I was allowed to go in the company of the immigrant. I conversed with him a little on the way and discovered that he was completely taken with the enchantment. I reached the city and hurried along quite a wide, uneven street. I came to a business place, which was quite tidy in appearance—I went in, and began to converse with the businessman. I told him that I had been informed that Mr. Smith possessed several Egyptian wonders, which I wanted to see; and that if I could do this I would show him a strange book which I had recently acquired. The businessman informed me that Mr. Smith was away from the city, having gone to Carthage that morning—but that he would be back by 9 o'clock that evening. He promised to clear the way for me to see the wonders, earnestly wishing at the same time to have a look at my strange book. I unfolded the various things which I had wrapped around it in his presence, and that of various other persons who had gathered there. Having brought its

25

covers and letters into view they were all amazed; and one of them, wiser than the others, said 'that he knew it was a revelation from God and that it was quite likely to be one of the lost books of the Bible restored through the order of fate. He told me that I had brought it to the right place to be translated—that there was no one on earth who could explain it but the prophet of the Lord.' They were all very eager for me to stay in the city until the prophet returned—but I refused this because my time was short. However, I promised to go there the following morning if they would bring a boat to Montrose to fetch me: thus it was decided. Then the businessman went about fulfilling the promise made to me—that is having a look at the wonders. He led me to a room behind his place of business, and on the door was written, "*The office of Joseph Smith, the president of the Church of Latter-Day Saints.*" Having entered this holiest of holies with several Mormons, he locked the door behind him and went to a small chest; out of it he took some *slides* similar to picture frames, holding sheets of papyrus, with Egyptian symbols and pictures on them. They were claimed to have been taken from four *mummies* and bought by the prophet for 2400 *dollars*; the businessman informed me that Smith had discovered, through some incomprehensible method, that these sheets contained the writings of Abraham, and that they had been written by his own hand when he was in Egypt. He referred to a picture of a man who was lying on the table, and said, 'That's a picture of Abraham about to be sacrificed. That man standing beside him, with a knife in his hand, was an idol-worshipping priest in Egypt. Abraham prayed to God and he released the bindings on his hands, and saved him.' After this, he referred to another symbolic picture, and one of the Mormons said, "Mr. Smith tells us that this picture signifies the redemption. Do you see those four small *figures*? They are the four quarters of the world. Do you see that big dog looking at them? That's the old devil. Do you see that person keeping the dog back? That's Jesus Christ keeping the devil from destroying the world. Look

26

here; that *figure* near to the side is Jacob, and those are his two wives next to him. Do you see those lines?" "What," I said, "those lines across the dress of one of his wives?" "Yes," he said; "that's Jacob's ladder." "*Strange*," I said "*Jacob's ladder with one end on the ground and the other end no higher than his wife's waist*!"

From here I was invited to the house of one of the elders and I was followed there by several of the Mormons; they were amazed at my Greek textbook; but I told them what it really was: yet despite this, they still said that no one could explain it but their prophet. Then one of them began to teach me about the proofs of their religion; he assured me that America had been noted by the prophet Isaiah; I asked him to show me the chapter and verse,—he referred to something, but I called for a *map* to show him his mistake; but the defense he took was, that he had never used a *map* to study the Bible.

I went back to the businessman because he had promised that I could see the *mummies*. I was led to a small house where the prophet's mother lived. After entering I greeted her—and she welcomed me to the holy city, saying that I would see there the great things done by the Lord for his people. She said, "My son Joseph has had revelations from God since he was a child; and he is a great prophet of Jehovah. An angel of the Lord appeared to him fifteen years ago, showing him the cave where the golden plates were hidden. He also showed him the Urim and the Thummim through which he could understand the printings on the plates,—and he also showed him the golden breast-plate of the high priesthood. My son received these valuable talents and explained the holy notes and now there are a hundred thousand believers in these revelations." The old woman seemed quite cautious when she spoke—she did not once look into my eyes; and she seemed to me to be not only enchanted by her son's deception, but also a great help to him as a deceiver. I showed her my book; and as she inspected it, she said that the Lord was bringing some secrets into the light; that my book was some revelation from God and that it was supposed to be made known to the world now through her son Joseph. Then she directed me upstairs, and followed me; she showed me a pitiful looking chest, in which there were four bare *mummies*, horribly mutilated, and in truth the remains were too terrible in the claws of death for any moral man to look upon! She said that one was a king in Egypt and two of the others were his wives—and that the other was a daughter of another king. I went from there to the printing house; and I met several Mormons there: one wished to see my book; when he looked at it he said 'that it was the strangest thing he ever saw.'

The following morning one of them came with a boat to Montrose to fetch me; and I returned with him to Nauvoo. I met the prophet near his home. He led me into the house and a great number of elders, bishops, preachers, and other ordinary Mormons followed us. After entering, chairs were given to the prophet and myself to sit on and the others stood nearby. I put the book in his hand asking him to explain it. He asked me if I had any idea of its content? I replied that I thought it was a Greek Psalm, but that I would like his opinion. "No," he said, "apart from the odd word here and there, it is not Greek. What is not Greek is Egyptian, and what is not Egyptian is Greek. This book is very valuable. *It is a dictionary of Egyptian symbols*." Referring to the capital letters at the beginning of the chapters, he said, "Those figures are Egyptian *symbols*; and those which follow are an explanation of the symbols, written in reformed Egyptian: those notes are similar to the ones engraved on the golden plates." At this, behold the surrounding Mormons congratulated me on the explanation I had received. And they said, "we told you that our prophet would satisfy you: there is no one but our prophet who can explain these secrets." Then the prophet turned to me and said, "This book is of no use to you, as you do not understand it." "Oh yes," I said, "it is of use; if I needed money I could sell it, and maybe have enough from it to sustain me for a year."

28

He and the elders asked how much would I take for it? I answered them, that my price was higher than they would want to pay. They asked how much it was? I answered, "I will not tell you, but if you were to offer me now nine hundred *dollars* in gold, you would not have it from me." They earnestly asked to borrow it, until their prophet had time to translate it, promising me security for its return; but I refused all their offers. When I kept the book, they all seemed very disappointed. Then I asked the prophet to show me the symbols, and explain them to me himself, as the one I had received was only second hand. He came with me to the office and the crowds followed us. He showed the *slides* to me, but he was in no hurry to explain the signs; I referred to one sign in particular but no answer came,—and when I raised my head, behold! the prophet was no longer there, rather he had slipped away stealthily! His followers said that maybe he would come back in a while; having waited awhile, but without his return, I went down to the road when I heard the noise of wheels, and behold! the prophet in his carriage with his whip in his hand, escaping in clouds of dust, as quickly as two strong horses could carry him!! I left Nauvoo having had a good opportunity to turn a new page in the great book of human nature." We do not offer any explanation of the above story; the weakest in comprehension need only look at its content, and we venture to swear that afterwards he will not dare to think that such a mixture of ignorance, boldness, and foolishness belongs within a thousand generations to *common sense*, not to mention DIVINE RELIGION! What will some men not dare to do under the influence of pride and the corruption of their hearts?

With regard to the moral character of Joe Smith and the inhabitants of Nauvoo, Mr. Caswell, who visited the city to find out the truth, says, "that their story was too loathsome to repeat—that he would have to refer to shameful facts—filthy scenes of corruption, which if noted, would only scorn the listeners and readers. A weaver from Lancashire who was enchanted with Nauvoo says: "The Mormon preachers

29

in England described Nauvoo to me, as a land flowing with milk and honey, and the place where Jehovah ordered the building of a temple which would be a sanctuary for mankind. "But this poor weaver was deceived and charmed there, and he made it clear afterwards that he had been dreadfully treated—and it was not only to his disappointment, but to his great concern and pain! The witnesses we could note, to confirm the above stories, are too numerous for our present limits to allow.

4. THE DECEIT WHICH IS THROUGHOUT THE BODY OF THAT WHICH IS CALLED "MORMONISM":—The unassuming story, and the genuine bare facts, already noted about the *founder* of this enchantment, are sufficient for any perceptive mind to see that he was quite an untrustworthy creature in ordinary matters, without mentioning religious matters. There is the imprint of laziness—deception, and superstition on his life history, before the mention of Mormonism. He had been brought up in a family with that tendency—and made good use of the examples of corruption set before him, until he reached the heights of a champion as a defender of deceit! One who knew him and his family well, says—"*They lived a sort of vagrant life; Joe from a boy appeared dull and utterly destitute of genius; but his father claimed for him a sort of second sight*." Under the influence of this *second sight*, the feats of digging for hidden treasures were carried out, pretending to look through a stone in his hat,—and a "second printing" of that stone divided in two, was had by his mother in Nauvoo when she called them *Urim and Thummim!!* It could be expected that all the disappointments had, when following this scoundrel in the search for hidden metals, would be enough to destroy any trust in him forever; but the weak ones who followed him are just an additional example of the corruption of the heart of man. Joe stood in exactly the same repute when digging for the *golden plates*—as when searching for imagined treasures: Was the man not brought up in that way? And the golden plates are just as imaginary as the other treasures!

30

Because he could give no proof of them and nobody else dared to offer proof—only a mass of the weakest claims ever put before men. Their work *at night* does not strike the wise ear as very strong and honest; why did they have to hide under the cloak of darkness, if their work was honest? This, no more than the baptism at night in our country, does nothing but confirm that they are birds of the night. The circumstances of the revelation of the plates is unbelievable: it is said that an angel visited Joe, revealing to him their existence as well as their location; who claims this? Joe himself, without a shadow of proof that that is true anymore than his previous claims! He does not mention a word about the nature of those associations; no example is given of as many as one of them; we have the first *phantom example* when the plates are mentioned—but how much better are we for that, for we have only imagination to confirm imagination. Supposing that an angel or angels visited Joe, if the *circumstances* of this cannot be proven, should not the proof be shown in the *results*? proof must be obtained from somewhere; but the deceiver falls into a trap even about the ministry of angels; take the story he gives about the angel's instructions with regard to his wife and his wedding, and his child; but by the time we have the story of these circumstances from Isaac Hale, his father-in-law, the most blatant contradictions have taken place! The angel, instructing him as a *prophet*, and he, following the instructions as a *thief*! Deception is bound to reveal itself everywhere; according to Joe's story we find his angel very detailed about *small things*—yet quite careless about *important things*: the angel described to Joe in detail the woman, the way of obtaining her, the birth of the child, and the results; he goes on with this almost mechanically; but he was not informed in such detail about the chest and the plates, which was so necessary; for we have Joe, according to the story of one of his followers, acting with such irregularity—as to invoke the thunder and lightning of the Almighty to frighten him from his attempt! More detailed instructions should have been

31

given about this important matter in order to prevent Joe and his angel from colliding head on! The deceiver, so he says, was instructed to move the chest from its original hiding place, after the trouble with himself and his father—and to where? *under the hearthstone of his own house!* How much safer was it there than in its holy hiding place? one could think that it would have been safer in the bowels of a mountain, in the midst of the strength of the aged rocks, under the protection of an angel, than under a moveable hearthstone supervised by Joe Smith! Yes, says the Mormon, that may be—but others had come to know of it in its original place; what difference? it is said that it moved completely out of sight, eventually, when Joe and his father went to see it the first time; if it was frightened away before the eyes of its friends—how much more would it be frightened away if the corrupted eyes of thieving enemies were to fall on it? The story of the clear stones is very muddled; it seems that these stones were as sacred as the plates, and that they were together in the chest; it was impossible for Joe to get the plates from the chest before opening it—but according to Harris, the same Joe had got the clear stones from the same chest before opening it! For what purpose was he permitted to get the stones before getting the plates? We are given to understand that the stones were to interpret the engravings on the plates; but behold the stones in Joe's possession, while the plates were quite safe in the chest! Was it not perhaps the *witch* stone that the deceiver had when searching the depths of the old Spanish works, which was called clear stones? Some Mormon reasoning causes us to believe *this*.

The translation of these plates is still in the same line of deceit, without wavering at all; we are given to understand that Joe had witnesses to the plates, and also the divine help to translate them; it was good for him to have such, as one who was confronting human belief with secret and divine things: but he had a very strange way of confirming the minds of his witnesses; they must have seemed exceptional

32

creatures to all who heard mention of them in the human environment.

Harris was the original witness,—the main one as it were, according to all expectations; but when he explained the circumstances of his testimony there were strange doubts about it; remember the story he himself gave about the plates hidden in the woods,—Smith preceding him through the snow, promising that his footprints would be directions for Harris to the plates so that he could see them; but after that escapade he came back extremely disappointed! When Harris asked his master for surer proof than he had, did he have this? No, or he would have said so. The translation was not undertaken in a very honest way; for what purpose was that partition between them in the same room? and what was the purpose of the threat of thunder and the wrath of God against poor Harris if he dared to approach Joe's most holy place? It would have been just the thing for Harris if the partition had been taken down so that he had the freedom to approach Joe and see the secret, because he was supposed to be *a witness*. But it suited Joe better to be otherwise, because he intended to *deceive* the poor fellow. It would have done Harris no harm to be near Joe, and see the plates at that time; but it would have been very harmful to the world, for Harris's opinion of him would have changed immediately, and he would have called him a deceiver without any hesitation! In order to excuse such *tricks*, Joe said that no man could look at the plates and live: but men had to look at them in order to be *witnesses*: that threat was enough while the Book of Mormon was in their presence—to get Harris and Cowdery to continue working as deceived men to complete their writings; but once the book was completed—new *tricks* had to be found to keep the witnesses apart. Here we can be directed to the testimony of Oliver Cowdery, David Whitmer and Martin Harris—to supplant our reasoning; all right; that testimony is printed and we quote it here—"an angel of God came down from heaven, and he brought and laid before our eyes, that we beheld

33

and saw the plates, and the engravings thereon." Joe had the plates, so he himself says, but here an angel brings them from heaven in front of these men; it is necessary to have witnesses to them as well, in order to be sure that their befuddled brains were not having a confused dream; well, mercifully, we have a witness, one who gave his testimony in cold blood, as follows:—

"I had the opportunity to investigate the command given to these witnesses, before they saw the plates. They were informed that they would see and hear *through faith*—then they could testify to the world, as if they had seen and heard, as I see a man or hear his voice: but after all it amounts to this—that it was through faith or supposition that they saw the angel and the plates." EZRA BOOTH

There we are! through faith is it! is this how testimonies should be offered to reasonable beings? Was it through faith that Christ's disciples saw him after his resurrection? Was it through faith that Thomas saw the marks of the nails in his feet and his hands, and the spear in his side? No! Christ did not depend upon the shadows of befuddled minds for the certainty of his revelations; rather it was in the full light of day; respecting mankind as it is, and not as Joe Smith insists that it is!

We need not be sparse about exposing this deception; we have yet another witness—"Martin Harris and his wife were in my house together. In a conversation about Mormonism she made the following comments:—"that she wished her husband to leave them as a *sect*—and that she believed that it was all a lie." To this Harris replied,—"what if it is a lie; if you leave me be, I shall make money from it." The witness said about this, "I am telling the truth as God is my witness"—ABIGAIL HARRIS.

Harris's wife confirmed this afterwards. In that testimony the secret was found out! the money was and is the point! if this were taken from the system, it would all collapse like a body without breath; this was the point in America—and is again the main point in Wales with Harris'

34

imitators. *These people* talk of the respectable ministers of Christ's Gospel plundering churches! – and it is not just *talk* —they assert untruthful examples; they would throw the claimants into prison without a care, except that some actually wish to suffer wrong, in order to "*love their enemies*." These fools that are all over the country should be stopped, as well as the money they contribute under the shadow of this deceit, and surely they won't be troubled so much with less talk of apostles (?) and prophets (?)! Men who cannot read or write ten words correctly in their mother tongue, boasting in the gift of "*speaking with tongues*!" Their public addresses are too incorrect in language, apart from images, for the lowest of the low to understand; were the true apostles like this? No! although they were the ignorant of the world as men, they were the wisest of heaven as apostles. Are *these their* counterparts? Let them blush! If they are *conscientious*, as they claim, they ought to go as pilgrims to lick the dust of destroyed Nauvoo for the rest of their lives, as an atonement to their imaginary God whom they worship in deceit, for the dreadful outrages of their leader! Let the poor Welsh care for their families in their homes, lest there be there some poor children with empty stomachs—while some of them contribute to this enchantment. If they live a few more months, perhaps they will see this sack of plunder carried over the waves, to a place beyond recall and the law.

Let this serve as a warning in passing. We refer again to things which prove our point;—if we consider the deception of the pages Harris lost, there is some strange weakness in that occurrence, especially when it was considered as being connected with such high claims. The *numbers* were too great to accept as a failure of divine revelation: if one word were lost it would be an impardonable mistake in inspiration; but here, behold 116 pages lost! This is a terrible betrayal of the system! In the name of all common sense, why did the prophet not use his official rights to get hold of them? If the plates were of importance, we suppose that

35

the engravings were of importance,—unless the *metal* was more valuable in Joe's eyes, than the engravings on it. Some intolerable contradictions arise from this circumstance. Behold the plates and the chest have been defended for a long time as a miracle—they were revealed through a miracle—they were retrieved from there by permission from the God of miracles—and in the end behold 116 pages of the translation become lost, and neither a miracle nor a spell could get them back!! But who needed a *miracle*? Did not Joe have the plates and the *witch* stone as before; why did he not translate them again? Because in all sense, it was neither fair nor divine for so much revelation to be lost, after all the trouble over it from the time of Mormon to the day of Joe Smith. But the point is—IT WAS DECEIT! The failing was discovered by the honesty of the *system* towards itself; it did not want to lose its good name at any cost. If Smith had tried a *second* translation, he would have been making things worse for himself, than had he done nothing; for the original work still existed, although Smith, while calling himself a prophet, did not know where it was. The original work would have differed in some way from the second, and then the infallibility of the translation would have been lost. The way these pages were lost was as follows:—Harris took them home with him and locked them up, thinking that they were quite safe; but his wife, who never was nor had been a member of the deceivers, used the opportunity, when he was out, to take the work from its place and place it into the care of neighbors; when Harris discovered that the work was missing, he immediately suspected his wife,—but she refused to say anything about it,—and she answered him like this—"*If this is a divine revelation, then the being who revealed it to you can easily restore it.*" Mrs. Harris thought that it was all a dreadful deception—and she undertook a plan to prove the deceit in the following manner:—she took it for granted that they would try to reproduce the work she had, and that they could not do this exactly word-for-word; so she would keep the work until the Book was published;

36

and then she would place the work in the hands of some-one who was able to show their discrepancies. But she was dealing with *deceivers*—and they did not dare! Harris felt very angry towards his wife, and went into dreadful rages at times; it is said that he badly beat her with a rod on one of these occasions. But she remained steadfast, and did not give up the work. In order to keep his witnesses around him, Joe used many tricks and lies; once he assured Martin Harris that he would definitely possess the golden plates himself, and that it would be quite legal to show them in public. Because of that promise, poor Martin mortgaged a great sum of money on his land to aid the Book through the press; and before this he had lent Joe about 25 *dollars* for the privilege of sharing with him in the secrets. But in a while, (while Harris was becoming uncomfortable about the fulfillment of the promise) Joe said that he had had a new revelation from heaven, that he was to show the plates to only 3 persons, those who helped in the continuation of the work. Somehow, however, from one lie to the other, he got Harris to testify that he had seen the plates; but whether it was true or not should be carefully judged in the light of the following:—There was a gentleman living in Palmyra who had been brought up as a solicitor—and he professed religion; his character was of the highest degree; he once asked Harris, "Did you see the plates?" He answered that he had. Again, the man asked, *"Did you see the plates and the engravings on them with your own eyes?"* He replied, "Yes, I saw them with my eyes, they were shown to me through the power of God, and not that of man." More importantly the man asked, *"But did you see them with your natural and physical eyes as you see this pen in my hand now?"* The reply to this was, "I did not see them as I see that pen but I saw them with the eyes of faith; I saw them almost as clearly as anything around me—*but that they were clothed in cloth at the same time.*" That is as far as the original witness himself got! he who had been so laboriously helping the deceiver by writing—and so kind in raising money on his land—that

37

was the highest assurance he had of the main foundation of Mormonism, in the reign of the never-to-be-forgotten Joe Smith, the arch-prophet in the world of superstitions!

The Book of Mormon *as it is*, is a strange mixture; it's not like the lineage of *one Father*—but it seems to have more than one: the style is not unique—but there is *internal evidence* in it to show it worthy of suffering on the same gallows as its false father. The style of the language of the scriptures was borrowed, but in some places that betrays itself; its language is full to overflowing with shameful mistakes—in it there are misrepresentations, mistakes, and obvious things which contradict true history,—that we can say it is a collection of foolish lies. In it, *it is claimed* that the American Indians are the remnants of the children of Israel; when the color of their skin is mentioned to oppose such a claim, it is claimed that it was changed through a miracle! It would be quite reasonable to expect some sort of assurance about that miracle; where was it accomplished? When? Who are or were the witnesses? Does Joe Smith in his assertions, get to be an exception to the chief officers which God has had through all time? Changing the color of skin of a nation famous as God's chosen people is a very important thing in the history of the world and religion; and doubtless if there were such a God as this, he would not have left himself without a witness.

Considering our present restrictions, *at the present time* it would be too long a task to note all the things in the Book of Mormon which prove to be lies; but when time and peace from really important duties permit, it is intended to give *an explanation of it*,—because, if it is intended to give an explanation of it,—because, if it is a Bible, it should surely have an Explanation of it,—because, if it is a Bible, it should surely have an Explanation at its side.

In any event, it appears to be beyond all doubt that this Book has been patched together from bits and pieces—and that these came into the hands of Joe Smith. Whatever the minor Mormons in our country say about Mr. Spaulding's

38

writing—the *evidence* for this thinking is stronger than their imitative logic. It is obvious to every critic that Joe Smith and his friends never had enough knowledge and talent to compose even the Book of Mormon, however poor it is; the history given about Joe in his youth—in middle age—and especially when claiming that the Greek letters were Egyptian characters—proves to every unbiased man that he was a creature of the lowest degree of knowledge, as we see these deceivers usually are. Only quite general knowledge at best was required to compose the Book of Mormon; and it seems to me that Spaulding, who was the true author of the original, as it will be later proved, had only very general knowledge; but by the time that work came into the hands of Joe Smith, and he took away from it, and added to it, and mixed and fragmented it, what was to be finally expected? There are unforgivable mistakes in the book, which betray any author as one quite foreign to understanding and judgment. All the *anachronisms* in it betray its truth—and the grammatical errors condemn it as the fruit of ignorance. The following clearly proves that most of it was taken from Mr. Spaulding's essay,—the story given by Mrs. Davidson, who had been Spaulding's wife. The notice was published in the *Boston Recorder*, to the editors of which it was sent by the Rev. John Storms, the Congregational minister in Hollistown; as well as a testimonial from two very respectable Church men named Mr. Austin and Mr. Ely, from the place where Mrs. Davidson now lives. The letter from the Church ministers assures that Mrs. Davidson, the teller of the story, was previously the Rev. Solomon Spaulding's wife, and that after his death she remarried to another man by the name of Davidson, and that she was a woman of good character and a humble Christian; and that the fullest trust may be placed in her testimony,—and that testimony is as follows; "Since the Book of Mormon, or the "Golden Bible," has drawn the attention of some people, and has been placed by some new *sect* in place of the holy scriptures, I consider it my duty for the sake of the public, to say what I know

39

about its source, that its claims of divine origin are completely baseless, there is no need for proof of this for anyone who has not been charmed by this most deceptive trickery. Having understood recently that Mormonism has worked its way to a church in Massachusetts, and has caused the excommunication of those who had embraced it—I have decided not to delay any longer form pulling the mask from its face and opening this pit of horrors.

The Rev. Solomon Spaulding, to whom I was married early in my life, was ordained in Dartmouth College; he had a very lively imagination—and a strong inclination to history. During our marriage he lived in Cherry Valley, New York.

From this place we moved to New Salem, the county of Ashtabula, Ohio. Soon after moving there, his health began to fail and he withdrew from his usual work. In the town of New Salem there are several mounds and forts, which are considered by some to belong to some destroyed nation. These ancient remains attracted the attention of the new inhabitants, and they became the objects of the research of the curious. In them were found several machines, and other things which displayed considerable skill in the arts. Since Mr. Spaulding was so keen on history, he paid great attention to these old finds; and in order to spend his spare time more enjoyably, and have material for his vivid imagination, he decided to collect the history of this extinct nation. His age inclined him to write in the oldest style, and since the Old Testament was the oldest book in the world, he imitated it as closely as he could.

His main purpose in writing this historical tale, was to entertain himself and his neighbors. This took place around the year 1812. As he wrote on, some of the neighbors would come in now and then to hear parts being read, and they took quite an interest in the work.

It was intended to be as if it were written by one of the nation, having been reclaimed from the earth; and the proper name for it was "THE MANUSCRIPT FOUND." The

40

neighbors often asked how Mr. Spaulding was getting on with interpreting the original; and when he had a section prepared he would inform them and they would gather around him to listen to it. Apart from a knowledge of the *classics* and ancient history, he was able to bring in many peculiar names which were noted in detail by the people so that they would recognize them again. Solomon Spaulding had a brother by the name of John Spaulding, living there at that time, who was quite familiar with the work, having heard it being read many times.

We moved from New Salem to Pittsburg; and there Mr. Spaulding met a friend in the person of Mr. Patterson who was the editor of a Newspaper. He showed the work to Mr. Patterson who was very pleased with it and who borrowed it. He kept it for a long time, and he told Mr. Spaulding that if he drew up a title page for it and composed a preface—that he would publish it, and that it could turn out to be profitable. Mr. Spaulding refused to do this, for what reason I do not know. Sidney Rigdon, who is much mentioned in the circumstances of the Book of Mormon, had some connection with Mr. Patterson's Press at that time, as is well known in that district—and as Rigdon has himself said numerous times. Here he had the opportunity to become familiar with Mr. Spaulding's writing, and copy it also if he wished. After a while the work was returned to the author; and soon after that we moved to Amity, in the county of Washington, where Mr. Spaulding died in the year 1816. The book came into my possession after that, and was carefully kept. My daughter, Mrs. M. Kenstry, from Monson, with whom I now live, often looked over it, and it was also looked over by several other people. After the Book of Mormon came off the Press, a copy of it was taken to New Salem, where Mr. Spaulding wrote his book. Some women called a meeting there; in the meeting she read several excerpts from it to the gathering. The historical parts were immediately recognized by the oldest inhabitants there, and they were sure that it was Mr. Spaulding's work.

41

Mr. John Spaulding was there at the time; he is a very godly man; he too recognized the work. He was surprised and greatly troubled that his brother's work had been used for such an accursed purpose. He stood up, and he testified to the audience of his worry that his dead brother's writing had been used for such a purpose.

The happening created much attention in New Salem; so much so, that the inhabitants called a meeting; in this meeting they chose Dr. Philastus Hurlbut to come to this place, to ask me for the original book for the purpose of comparing it with the Book of Mormon, and to satisfy their minds, as well as to prevent their friends from being charmed into such deception. This took place in the year 1834. Dr. Hurlbut brought a written request for the book with him, signed by Misters Henry Lake, Aaron Wright, and others whom I knew because they were my neighbors when I lived in New Salem. I am sure that nothing would trouble my husband more, if he were alive now, than the deceitful use which has been made of his book. Doubtless that the ancient style used in its composition, created the original idea to use it for such a purpose. This is how an historical tale, with additional phrases and excerpts from the holy scriptures, was turned into a *new Bible*, deceptively put forward as a divine one for the belief and defense of a few poor religious maniacs! I have given the above short history, so that this work of deception and wickedness may be searched to its foundation, and the author laid open to the disgrace and infamy which he truly deserves.

MATILDA DAVIDSON.

When we turn from the circumstantial and external facts which belong to Mormonism, and go into what Joe called a *church*, there are several deceptive claims doomed because of their boldness. Some of these claims are set out as follows:—

"The relationship Smith claims with the Church is that of prophet, seer and translator; when he speaks through the spirit, or when he claims to receive some revelation from

42

the spirit, these are to be accepted as direct from the mouth of the Lord.

These contributions are to be accepted in the church as inspired; they are to be called *The Lord's Commandments*, and they are to be considered as *secrets of the kingdom*; announcing these to the world is considered as throwing pearls before pigs.

When these revelations and the scriptures disagree, it is claimed that the scriptures have not been correctly translated; and Smith, although completely ignorant of the original languages, can easily bring them to agreement! Everything in the church is done by commandment; yet, it is claimed that everything is carried out according to the voice of the church! For example—Smith receives a commandment that he is to be considered the *head of the church*—or that he is to *rule by conference*—or that the church is to *build him an excellent house*—and endow him with a 1000 *Dollars*; church members must vote for these things or they will be judged guilty of breaking the *commandments of the Lord.*

That is how things are carried out under the wing of Mormonism!! Recently we are quite accustomed to hearing of our failing, not to oppose Mormonism *from the scriptures;* this originated from those who embrace the enchantment. Beware everybody! *Scriptures* for or against MORMONISM; why are scriptures not mentioned directly to shatter the imaginations of "Ferdinand Count Fathom" or similar tales! The Book of Mormon is nothing but a dry and artless tale of the same sort—except that it hides under the cloak of religion, rather than brazen out on the dance floor of the playhouse. We do not degrade our senses for a moment, by appealing to the holy book with regard to the order; true, we could look for very suitable features of the charmed followers; but listening to a series of these would not be music to their ears! Their claims are too self-asserted to reason anything about them: there is need to do that; it is easy for everyone to hear the lie of the *claim* in the echo of the *assertion*. What are their claims?

43

1.That Joe Smith is a prophet. By prophet, we understand one who explains and teaches principles—or one able to foretell the future. We are given to understand that Joe Smith's claim is mainly in the latter sense. We would like to know of as many as *one* circumstance which happened according to Joe's prediction, which gives him the weakest credit as a prophet. Where was the prophetic talent at the time of the losing of the pages? Why had he not prophesied the destruction of Nauvoo in order to save such trouble and cost to the charmed ones? We are told that he had foretold his death: but did he note the way, the time and the circumstances? It was quite natural for him to make up his mind to die; for the riots and civil troubles caused by his rebellious statements ensured his death. The pistols and the swords, and the angels were able to prophesy that. Saying this is the same as it would be for a sentenced scoundrel in Newgate, to foretell his hanging! Joe had decided his fate clearly enough. In his life with his religious revelations and merciless deception as a prophet, we remember him sending some madmen to preach to the Indians, as the chosen ones of heaven—ordaining them as possessors of some *strange talents*; but the question is, was there one example of the plan succeeding? Did any Indians receive the message? Was there any proof of receiving gifts apart from deceit and madness? Were the apostles (?) faithful to their inspiration, by turning away from the chosen because of lack of success? Was it not a definite prophecy of Smith's, that there was a great church in Missouri? Having gone there, behold a great church of *four women!!* This has been testified by one who was present there: the evidence is true. Others, apart from Smith, claimed the gift of prophecy; we have an example at hand,—Martin Harris wrote to a friend as follows: —"*Within four years from September, 1832, there will not be one ungodly person left in the United States: the just will gather to Zion, that is Missouri, and there will be no Governor of the United States at that time.*"—MARTIN HARRIS.

44

Again,—"*I testify that within four years from today, every sectarian and religious sect throughout the United States will be broken down—and every Christian will gather to the Mormons, and the rest of the human race will die. If these things do not take place, I swear my willingness to have my hand cut from my body*!"—MARTIN HARRIS.

The writer of the above claims that he was endowed *with the spirit of prophecy*; but how did things turn out? Sixteen years have passed since the prophecy was written, and to our great surprise there is still a Governor of the United States—and there is strong evidence to suggest that there are thousands of ungodly people—there are several religious *sects*; and mercifully there are thousands and thousands who conscientiously judge that Mormonism is the most foolish and ignorant deceit of all the world's superstitions.

Now, if we must appeal to the Holy Scripture in the face of such circumstances as these—what is said there about prophets like the above? "When a prophet speaketh in the name of the Lord, if the thing follow not, nor come to pass, that is the thing which the Lord hath not spoken, but the prophet hath spoken it presumptuously: thou shalt not be afraid of him."—Deut. 18:22. There is no relationship between such things and the Spirit of the Lord, no more than there is in *witchcraft*, and common dreams. If anything, all the claims and assertions of this superstitious bunch are in this category. Talking about angels, and golden plates, and the tribes of Israel, is complete foolishness: the angels and the plates sprang from the heat of Joe's brain; and the story about them gives an impression of their origin.

2. *Miracles*. On no account would I touch this subject, if it weren't that their one claim confirmed the foolishness of the other.

We know what miracles are, and what they should be, from their explanation and confirmation in the New Testament. We are not such strangers to the things of Christ and his apostles to be deceived in haste about such things.

45

The claim of miracles by the Mormons is a collection of such boldness and ignorance, that it betrays the deceit straight away. If they claim that they can perform miracles, it is right for us to have an example, or we are bound by conscience to condemn the order as a terrible fraud. They boast in this; it is too public a fact now, for even the most unprincipled Mormon to deny.

I am sure that many of them would have been glad if they could have disassociated themselves from this side of the deceit before now. Failure in this is *mathematical proof* that it is all superstition. Well, Welshmen! did these people in your midst give you *a single* example of the miraculous talent? There was not as much as one example in America; are they no more fortunate on this side of the ocean? The sad answer we have from all parts is—NO, THEY ARE NOT! Alas! Not *a single* example has been shown.

In some Welsh Pamphlet we have recently read, *we almost* caught hold of a miracle; in it we are told of quail raining down on the Mormons on the banks of the Mississippi, near Nauvoo—when they were starving. We quote the story:—"They had nothing on which to live there, nor anything to start them on their journey. When they were in this predicament, they turned to the Lord, and he sent a great many *quail* which descended into their midst, on their resting places, and at their feet, until the sick and everyone caught them in their hands until they were filled: so their tables were spread with meat morning and night."

That's *clear proof* of what we call the miraculous care of the Mormon God when they were starving: but was this true? Not only do we *doubt* its truth, but the author and the Book cause us to disbelieve the happening when we consider it in light of other circumstances that are noted. They were in other predicaments and facing starvation, without anyone caring for them. That is not God's custom. Listen to the same storyteller going forward,—"The government should invite the Mormons back to their homes, and ensure them a defense against all attack. They are now dying from

46

starvation and cold in the desert, or are prey to the savages and beasts.! And listen again,—"Hosts of them are now lying on the ground on the banks of the Mississippi, set aside for the city which they had built through endeavor, and now seeing it all in the possession of the worst sort of thieves."

Where is the God who saved them from starvation before with the quail on the banks of the Mississippi? The God of heaven is the same in all his people's predicaments; but here there is a change—and more than a *shadow* of a transformation; and rather than prove that our good Lord is one of these, we prefer to take the final declaration in order to prove the first one worthy of its source—*namely a lie*.

Not only do these people testify that God performs miracles in their midst, but that they can transmit the miraculous gift to each other! They say that all those who believe in Mormonism, receive one, or several of the miraculous gifts; we have at hand the testimony of one who was caught in this trap,—he received the laying on of hands by some; and they spoke with him about a month later. He was asked which of the gifts he received? He answered, "I have had no sign of any YET, but many of the Mormons have told me that they discovered nothing during the first weeks—but I expect to have a sign sometime!" This is a constant support for the miraculous gifts! One would expect, between their prophecies and their miracles, that between them they could defend themselves more favorably. One of their elders who had been in the fight in Missouri, gives the story of his escape in the following evangelical way—"I escaped by hitting the jailor on the head, and while he was stunned by the blow, I got away." Remember that these are the people who claim a religious relationship with Paul and Silas, and of course they must prove their similarity in their spirit; does the similarity hold good in the above example!!

When they fail to achieve miracles despite trying, the defensive retreat is *lack of faith in the subjects*; this was the retreat of Jemima Wilkinson earlier, and is open space for the Mormons after her; it seems that she left this for Joe

47

Smith in her religious-communion letter! However, the poor things are glad to have it! The question is, is faith on the part of the recipients necessary to perform miracles on them? No—if we believe in the Miracles of Christ. Listen;—"And he could do no miracles there, *save* that he laid his hands upon a few sick folk, and healed them. And he marveled because of their unbelief," Mark 6:5,6.

What faith did the 5000 apart from women and children have, those who were fed with bread and fish? What faith was there in Lazarus' dead body? We could cite many examples, to conclude this argument.

Then it is claimed that the miracles are in the church, out of sight of the world:—yes, what a powerful argument! *miracles in the church*?! For what purpose are they there? The purpose of miracles is not answered in that way; miracles are performed for the conviction of the truth of principles or facts: do the Mormons in the Church live in continual doubt? The poor things, did not their father Joe leave them the infallibility of revelations? But the question is on what thing, or things *in the* church are miracles performed? If by *the church*, a congregation of Mormons is meant, we can be sure that miracles are not performed on *their persons*, especially their bodies! They have their lame and their half-blind; why are these not cured? If lack of faith causes this failure, where can one expect to have faith, if not in the dear "Saints!" Indeed! It is not faith that is needed; plenty of *cash* on the table, and magic, and the different enchanting tricks will be done, and this will do as "signs and wonders" for the Mormons! Instead of going to the trouble of composing a *peroration* for our Lecture, we shall leave these imitative "Saints" to converse with the old, talented Welshman, who is called TWM O'R NANT—

> *"There is nothing but deceit and cunning,*
> *Going on in this business,*
> *Because of the questioning and searching to*
> *understand the squares,*

48

So tell everyone through flattery
What you think pleases their nature:
If you please the women all over the world,
You will have wonderful favor.
Walk in fairness to the neighbors' houses,
Teach superstition and interpreting dreams,
You will make a living I assure you,
And sleep and be lazy enough."

We could imagine hearing an apostle speaking to Joe—

"Good health to you for teaching me,
I shall be the best fortune teller in Wales,
I read the mists great and small,
And I try at the fireside to draw the eye.
I now have, upon my word,
A good and comfortable living without fail.
Telling the occasional friend's fortune
Is more enjoyable than going begging.
I have really become excited,
And gone wild about my success;
Where I get a hearing I can roar easily
And I can tell a good lie.
And if a lie follows me
It's easy to make an excuse before it falls on me,
And throw off all the trouble
Happily on to someone else's back."

Well, good night tonight, remember that I urged you
To think of the end of this lazy enchanter—
Who travels the world and who, out of laziness, will remain
A jaunty fortune teller."

D. JONES, PRINTER, MERTHYR.

Pamphlet 8

W. J. Morrish. ***Cyfeiliornadau a Dichellion Saint y Dyddiau Diweddaf a Llyfr Mormon, yn cael eu dynoethi, gan y Parch W. J. Morrish, Ledbury*** **(*Heresies and Stratagems of the Latter-day Saints and the Book of Mormon, Exposed by the Rev. W. J. Morrish, Ledbury*), translated by David Roberts. Caernarvon: H. Humphreys, 1849. 24 pages.**

The title of this twenty-four-page pamphlet was modified from the two "letters" which Rev. W. J. Morrish had published in English several years earlier in Ledbury. (The first letter was entitled "The Latter-day Saints and the Book of Mormon. A Few Words of Warning from a Minister to His Flock," and the second letter was entitled "The Latter-day Saints and the Book of Mormon. A Second Warning from a Minister to His Flock.") The contents, however, are unaltered in the pamphlet's Welsh translation. In the first letter, Morrish focuses mainly on the Book of Mormon and the theory that it was written by Solomon Spaulding, declaring that Joseph Smith simply forged Spaulding's manuscript into the content for a book whose origin Smith claimed to be some plates of gold given him by an angel. In the second letter, Morrish writes the following:

> Now I say *you do not know the doctrines these people really teach*, because they are too cunning to let you know the whole depth of the wickedness at once, lest you should be afraid to join them.

He then provides numerous quotes from the Book of Mormon and the Doctrine and Covenants and explains what he judges to be the heresy in the doctrine contained in them. He assures his readers that no new revelation is needed for them to be saved.

Unlike other critics of The Church of Jesus Christ of Latter-day Saints, Morrish shows evidence of having read and researched the Book of Mormon and Doctrine and Covenants in his critique of the teachings of the Latter-day Saints. But upon receiving a copy of this pamphlet, John S. Davis stated his reason for not writing a response to it: "The booklet in question is not worth reviewing, for it contains nothing that has not already been answered" (*Zion's Trumpet*, September 1849, wrapper, p. 2).

Heresies and Stratagems

OF THE LATTER-DAY SAINTS AND THE BOOK OF MORMON,

EXPOSED.

BY THE REV. W. J. MORRISH,
LEDBURY.

TRANSLATED, WITH PERMISSION OF THE AUTHOR,
BY DAVID ROBERTS.

CAERNARVON:
PRINTED AND PUBLISHED
BY H. HUMPHREYS

Price Three Pence.

HERESIES AND STRATAGEMS

OF THE

THE LATTER-DAY SAINTS

And the Book of Mormon,

EXPOSED.

BYTHEREV.W.J.MORRISH,
LEDBURY.

TRANSLATED, WITH PERMISSION OF THE AUTHOR,
BY DAVID ROBERTS.

**CAERNARVON:
PRINTED AND PUBLISHED BY
H. HUMPHREYS.**

1849.

THE LATTER-DAY SAINTS AND THE BOOK OF MORMON,

A WARNING FROM A MINISTER TO HIS FLOCK.

My dear Friends,

One of the duties which I solemnly engaged to perform when I was ordained a Minister of God by the hands of a Christian Bishop was, that, "the Lord being my helper, I would be ready with all faithful diligence, to banish and drive away all erroneous and strange doctrines, contrary to God's word:"– to lift up my voice in warning, against all errors calculated to injure the souls committed to my charge. It is in discharge of this duty that I address these few pages to you. I have seen with great regret, that for several months past, a set of men calling themselves Latter-day Saints or Mormonites have been going

4

up and down among you, unsettling the minds of many pious Christians, and teaching you doctrines contrary to the Gospel of Jesus Christ.

And as you of course cannot know any thing about these men, who come to you pretending to be Ministers of God, I have made inquiries into their origin, progress and doctrines, and I do believe a more infamous deception was never practiced upon man than that which they are practicing upon you.

They pretend that they are in possession of a book which they say was dug out of the earth, where it had lain for many hundreds of years: this book was written upon plates of gold, in an unknown language, which the man who discovered it was enabled to translate by means of a certain stone. They call this book the "Book of Mormon," or the "Golden Bible;" and they tell you it was hidden in the earth by God himself, and the place of its concealment was revealed by an angel. Now God has mercifully allowed the falsehood of this statement to be *proved*. The wife of the very *man* who *wrote* the Book of Mormon was *living* in 1840 in Monson, Massachusetts, America, and *she has borne witness that the whole scheme is a most*

5

infamous deception. The Book of Mormon which these people pretend was written by God himself was produced in the following manner: –

In the year 1812 there lived at New Salem, Ashtabula County, Ohio, in America, a Minister of the Gospel whose name was the Rev. Solomon Spaulding, who, from ill health, had been obliged to give up all active duties. Near his residence were a great many mounds and fortifications, and many relics and implements were discovered there which had evidently belonged to some race of men then extinct. Mr. Spaulding, by way of employing his time, merely for the amusement of himself and his neighbours, undertook to write an imaginary history of the ancient people; and because he wished to write it in the most ancient language, he copied, as nearly as he could, the language of the Bible. He called his work the "Manuscript Found": and pretended that it was written by one of *the lost nation* and *buried in the earth*. This book was read to his brother and to many of his neighbours, who were much amused by it.

Soon after this, Mr. Solomon Spaulding removed from

6

Salem to Pittsburg, Pa., where he became acquainted with Mr. Patterson, the editor of a Newspaper. To this Gentleman the work was lent *for a considerable time*, and he wished to print it, but Mr. Spaulding would not allow him. The work was well known to all the people who worked in the Printing-Office of Mr. Patterson, and among these was *a man by the name of Sidney Rigdon, who was afterwards connected with the first beginning of the Mormonites*.

In 1816, Mr. Spaulding died at Amity, Washington County, and the Manuscript work was left to his widow. Some time after the publication of the "Book of Mormon," when the delusion began to spread, a Preacher belonging to this new sect went to New Salem and held a meeting, during which many passages were read from the Book of Mormon. All the older inhabitants were surprised, for they immediately knew that what they heard was part of the very *Tale* which they had heard read so often by their old friend, Mr. Solomon Spaulding. His brother, Mr. John Spaulding, an eminently pious man, was present, and *knew perfectly* the work of his brother. He was amazed and afflicted that it should have been turned to so wicked a purpose. He burst into tears, and rising at once expressed to the meeting his sorrow that the writing of his

7

sainted brother should have been used for so vile and shocking a purpose. Great excitement arose among the people at New Salem, and Dr. Philastus Hurlbut, with other respectable people, was sent to the widow of Mr. Solomon Spaulding to compare the "Book of Mormon" with his work. He did so, and immediately found that the "Book of Mormon" *instead of being a revelation from God*, was nothing more or less than *Mr. Solomon Spaulding's Tale* with a passage from Isaiah in one place, a passage from the Revelations in another, and a little of our Lord's Sermon on the Mount in another, with a sprinkling here and there of doctrines and precepts calculated to support the deep deception and wickedness of the new sect.

Such is the origin of the Book of Mormon as given by the wife of the very man who wrote it. Since his death she has married a second husband named Davidson. She now resides at Monson, Massachusetts, is a woman of irreproachable character and an humble Christian; and A. Ely, D. D., Pastor of the Congregational Church in Monson, and D. R. Austin, Principal of Monson Academy, both men of eminent piety and great learning, have borne witness that her testimony is *worthy of full confidence.*

8

Now, my dear Friends, I do beseech you to consider well this plain statement of truth, and thank God who has been pleased to discover such gross deception. If men begin by practicing so infamous a cheat; if they come to you pretending to be ministers of God, telling you of dreams and revelations and visions of angels, and bringing with them a Book which they pretend was written *by the finger of God* and given to them *by an Angel*, while you are *sure, upon good testimony*, that the same was written by a poor weak mortal like yourselves, *of course you know how little credit is due to them on any other point*. What they tell you is *founded* upon a lie, and therefore cannot be true. Whether or not all of those who go about teaching these mad doctrines are aware of the sinful deception, or whether they too are some of them deceived, I cannot pretend to say. I hope they have done these things in ignorance. I hope the knowledge of the fraud practiced is confined only to the leaders. But however this may be, your duty is plain, to "come out from these wicked people and be separate." I have not said any thing to you about the doctrines taught in their books, because, when we know that the very

9

book from which these doctrines are taken is a deception, we can but expect that the doctrines themselves are contrary to the Gospel. And so they are; though they have been too cunning to commit themselves by teaching a lie without some mixture of the truth as it is in Jesus.

Another strange thing which they teach you, is that you must leave this country and go to America, there to reign with Jesus Christ until this wicked part of the world is destroyed: and I am sorry to hear that many persons have been induced to sell their little property under this idea. Now why this deception has been attempted I cannot certainly say; but there are reasons that almost lead me to suppose that there is some *more worldly scheme* than appears outwardly. I find that mention is made of some Land that has been bought on the shores of the Mississippi River in America; and, they tell you, "that 119,000 acres more *may be purchased by a united effort of the Saints*." They tell you too "that Jesus Christ has declared that whosoever gives food or clothing or *money* to the Latter-day Saints, shall be rewarded; and that he has commanded

10

such money to be sent to *the Bishop in America*, that it may be *consecrated for the establishment of Zion.*" Now 119,000 acres cannot be cultivated without hands; and it is more to the advantage of those who possess them to persuade poor people to sell their little all, under a *religious delusion*, and so *pay for their own* passage, than to be obliged to *give a free passage* to labourers from England, that they may go to America to cultivate their otherwise useless acres.

My dear Friends, I trust the plain truths I have put before you may have their due effect. If you know the Gospel you will not be surprised that such warnings should be necessary. St. Peter has declared that "false prophets shall arise who through covetousness with feigned words shall make merchandise of you; despising government; presumptuous, self-willed, not afraid to speak evil of dignities; speaking great swelling words of vanity." And St. Paul warns us to expect those who "desiring to be teachers of the Law, understand neither what they say or whereof they affirm; speaking lies in hypocrisy; creeping into houses and leading captive silly women;" he has prophesied, that the time will come when "men will not endure sound doctrine, but will heap to themselves teachers, having itching ears." Knowing therefore that those things are but the confirmation

11

of Scripture, go to Scripture for aid and direction. "Seeing ye know these things before, beware lest ye also, being led away by the error of the wicked, fall from your own steadfastness." "Believe not every spirit; but try the spirits, whether they are of God, because many false Prophets are gone out into the world." "Be not carried about with divers and strange doctrines; for it is a good thing that the heart be established with grace."

May that God who is the giver of all wisdom grant you grace to "continue in the faith grounded and settled and not to be moved away" by the gross delusions of religious impostors "from the hope of the Gospel which ye have heard," is the fervent prayer of

Your affectionate Pastor and Friend,

W. J. MORRISH

Ledbury.

A SECOND WARNING FROM A MINISTER TO HIS FLOCK.

~~~~~

My Dear Friends,

I addressed a letter to you, some time ago, warning you of the deception practiced upon you by a set of men calling themselves "Latter-day Saints:" and it is with much pain, therefore, that I see many of you still led away by these false teachers: and the only reason I can assign for it is, *that you do not really know the doctrines they teach*.

I am well aware of the manner in which you are led astray. Many of you, I believe, are simple-minded Christians, really anxious about the salvation of your souls, but at the same
~~~~~

13

time you are not sufficiently "grounded in the faith;" – you are unstable and wavering, and therefore you run after these men, desiring "to hear every new thing." Well – you attend one of their meetings, and some one of their preachers gets up–takes a text from your own Bible to cover his designs, and pours forth for half an hour a torrent of words, - text after text, - passage after passage, - talks a little about baptism, - a little about Christ's second coming, - and (if there is no one present likely to contradict his statements) a little about New Jerusalem and America; he utters all this so rapidly that you are not able to hear, much less to understand, one half; but you do know that *a great deal of it is taken out of the Bible*, and therefore you go away quite satisfied that *all must be true because it is Scripture*.

I say to you again that which I said before, *you do not know the doctrines these people really teach*, because they are too cunning to let you know the whole depth of the wickedness at once, lest you should be afraid to join them. I have told you before, *how* the Book of Mormon *was forged*, I intend now to show you what it *contains*, that you may judge for yourselves

14

whether it is *a revelation from God*, as they pretend, or *a vile forgery*, as I have shown you.

You must not expect to learn the real doctrines of these people from their preachers; because they can teach one thing today and another tomorrow, to suit circumstances. Their real doctrines are to be found in two books, one called the "Book of Mormon," and the other, "The Book of Doctrine and Covenants," containing directions for their preachers. From both of these books I shall now give you some extracts.

First, let us examine the Book of Mormon. This professes to be,

> "An account written by the hand of Mormon, taken from the plates of Nephi . . . written by way of commandment and also by spirit of prophecy and revelation . . . to come forth by the gift and power of God unto the interpretation thereof."

We have the following account of the translator:

> "Be it known unto all nations, kindreds, tongues, and people unto whom this book shall come, that we, through the grace of God the Father and his son Jesus Christ, have seen the plates which contain this record . . . and also know that they have been translated by the power and gift of God, for his voice hath declared it unto us . . . and we also declare *with words of soberness* that an angel of God came down from heaven, and he brought and laid before our eyes the plates and engravings thereon."

This is the testimony of the Book of Mormon to its own

15

truth; and in the "Book of Doctrines and Covenants" we are told, in Section 2, Page 2,

"That the Book of Mormon contains the record of a fallen people and *the fulness of the Gospel of Jesus Christ* . . . confirmed by ministration of angels."

Again it is called (Section 4, Page 8)

"*God's new covenant* with the children of Zion."

Again the elders are commanded (Section 13, Page 5)

"To teach the principles of the gospel of Jesus Christ which are in the Bible, and in the *Book of Mormon in the which is the fulness of the gospel.*"

In Section 1, Pages 5 and 8, I find these words:–

"Behold, I am God, and these my commandments were given unto my servants, that they might have power to lay *the foundation of this church . . . the only true and living church upon the face of the earth.*"

Again, in the Book of Mormon, page 123, we read as follows:

"Many of the Gentiles shall say, *a Bible, a Bible, we have got a Bible*–O fools! Because I have spoken one word, ye need not suppose that I cannot speak another. *Ye need not suppose that it contains all my words.*

You see that these people pretend to be apostles and prophets of the Church of the Latter-day Saints, the only true and living Church on the face of the earth; and, as such, they tell you that God *has not revealed in the Bible all that is*

16

sufficient to salvation, but that they are commissioned to declare to you a *new revelation* wherein is the *fulness of the Gospel*. Now the simple question is, Is this according to Scripture, or is it not? You are told (Romans xvi. 25,) that "the gospel and the preaching of Jesus Christ, according to the *revelation* of the mystery, which *was* kept secret since the world began, but NOW is made manifest, and by the scriptures of the prophets, is made known to all nations for the obedience of faith." You read (Col. i. 14,) "that "the dispensation" to the apostle Paul was to be made "a minister to fulfill (or *fully* to preach) the word of God, even the mystery which had been *hid* from ages and from generations, but is *now* made manifest." And the same apostle could say of his ministry that he had kept back nothing that was profitable unto his hearers, that he had "not shunned to declare unto them all the counsel of God." More than this Jesus Christ himself declares (John xv. 15) "all things that I have heard of my Father I have made known unto you," and he promises (chap. xvi) to send the Holy Ghost to "guide them into *all* truth, to bring all things to remembrance; and according to this promise, you will find St. John (1 John ii. 20) writing to "babes in Christ" in these words, "ye have an unction from the Holy One, and ye *know all things*. I have not

17

written unto you because *ye know not the truth*, but because *ye know it*."

Now, my dear friends, here is a very plain case.—Inspired apostles tell you—yes, Jesus Christ himself tells you—that the *whole* counsel of God has been revealed to you in your Bible, and that the way of salvation is so plain that even "a babe in Christ" may know the truth. These men tell you, a new revelation is necessary—it has been made—we are the people appointed to bring it, and unless you believe it, *you must be damned*. Now the simple question is, Which will you believe? St. Paul and St. John, or Joseph Smith?—Jesus Christ, or these mad deceivers?

These things, you see, are contrary to God's word; I could give to you numberless other instances in which these contradict the Bible; but what do you think of the matter when I tell you that they not only contradict the Bible, *but also deny that it is the pure word of God, and do away with it altogether*? Read their own words, (Section 47, Page 1,)

> "Behold, I say unto you that *all old covenants* have I caused *to be done away in this thing*, and this is *a new and everlasting covenant*."

18

Now, my dear friends, you read (Heb. 13. 20) that the new covenant, which Jesus Christ sealed with his blood, was an "everlasting covenant;" – his priesthood is said to be "forever," and "after the power of an endless life." The Spirit through whom he offered himself is said (vii. 16v.) to be *eternal*; the redemption he secured is called "everlasting;" the perfectness of the worshiper, as to conscience, was continual;" the cleansing was "once for all." Then what is this *new and everlasting* covenant that is now brought in by the setting up of *this thing*–this New Church? The truth is, the Bible stood in the way of these deceivers, and therefore they were obliged to deny it at any hazard, or they could not have taught the false-hoods they now teach you. I bring no charge against these men which I am not able to prove from their own writings. Read the following passage, and judge for yourselves (Page 33,)

> "And the angel of the Lord said unto me *it* (that is the Bible) contained the plainness of the gospel of the Lord . . . wherefore these things go forth from the Jews *in purity*, but after they go forth by the hand of the twelve apostles of the Lamb, thou seest the foundation of an abominable church, more abominable than other churches, for behold they have *taken away* from the gospel many parts which are plain and most precious; nevertheless . . . I will manifest myself unto thy seed that they shall write many things that I shall minister unto them . . . and in them shall be written *my Gospel*," that is the Book of Mormon.

19

Now my Friends, after these men have taken away your Bible and told you that it is so corrupt that it is no longer God's word, perhaps you would like to know what doctrines they teach you in place of these corrupt doctrines of the Bible. It would be a hateful and a useless task to go through all the folly and blasphemy that is put forth in their books in the shape of doctrine, but I will give you a few specimens. Of faith they say:--(Section 1, Page 16,)

> "Faith is the principle by which Jehovah works. Take away this principle and *he would cease to exist*. God spake, and worlds came into order *by reason of the faith that was in him*."

So God could not have created the world if he had not had faith. FAITH IN WHOM? St. Paul, if you recollect, says, "faith cometh by hearing," and that it is "the gift of God;" but the Latter-day Saints tell you Faith is to be acquired "by the sacrifice of all things," and by "the knowledge of doing what is well-pleasing to God." So the Bible tells you "good works are the fruits of faith;" – the Latter-day Saint says, No, faith is the fruit of good works and mortification!

Again, The apostle's answer to the question "What must I do to be saved?" was "Believe on the Lord Jesus Christ and thou shalt be saved;" but these lying records teach very different doctrine; they say:–(Section 7, Page 9,)

20

> "If we can find a saved being, we shall understand what all others must be to be saved. Now Christ is a *saved being*. How is he saved? *Because he is just and holy*."

Now if this blasphemy means anything it must mean that Jesus Christ *was saved by his good works*, and that every man must be saved by "works of righteousness which he has done:" and in fact the whole doctrine of the Book of Mormon virtually does away with the Atonement made by the blood of Christ, and sets up sundry sayings and declarations, and our own good deeds, as our Saviors. Take but a few examples: (Page 619,)

> "Be perfected in Christ and deny yourselves of all ungodliness; and if you do this and love God with all your hearts, etc., THEN is his grace sufficient for you."

That is, unless you first save yourselves, God is not able to save you. Again (Page 614,)

> "The fulfilling the commandments bringeth remission of sins." (Page 160,) "Continue in fasting and prayer, and endure unto the end, and ye shall be saved."

It would be idle to place before you more of the folly which these deceivers teach in the shape of doctrine; but, after what you have seen, you will not be surprised to find both

21

disloyalty and *inhumanity* in their books. You, my friends, have been taught to think "Fear God, honor the king." "Let every one be subject unto higher powers," part of the revealed will of God; but, if you follow this new delusion, you must learn a very different doctrine. The Book of Mormon tells you, (Chapter 13, Page 230,)

> "Because all men are not just; it is not expedient that ye should have kings to rule over you." "Ye cannot dethrone an iniquitous king, save through much contention and bloodshed." I desire that this irregularity (between kings and subjects) should be no more in the land, and this land to be a land of liberty."

Now would you believe that these men who thus preach *Treason* under the cloak of religion, can uphold *Slavery* too, when it suits their purpose? Book of Revelations, (Section 102, Page, 12,)

> "We do not believe it right to interfere with bond-servants, neither preach the gospel to, nor baptize them, contrary to the will and wish of their masters . . . Such interference, we believe unlawful; and unjust, and dangerous to the peace of every government, allowing human beings to be held in servitude."

22

So, here are these heaven-sent prophets, whom you have just seen preaching opposition to all lawful authority, and denying the right of kings to govern, and with the next breath, stating that Jesus Christ will not have the way of salvation declared to a poor black man, unless his master wishes it–in fact upholding *slavery* in all its abominations!

Dear Friends, WHEN WILL YOUR EYES BE OPENED? I have now discharged what I conceived to be my duty towards you, and I pray God that what I have said may have its due effect. You see what these men *really* teach you in their books.

They contradict your Bible, they reject it altogether, they consign to eternal damnation all other sects or denominations, they teach false doctrines, they preach disloyalty, they uphold slavery. Can such men be prophets of God? Can such things be written by the Spirit of God? There is no doubt the deception will soon work its own cure; and your eyes will be opened to see the infamous cheat that is being practiced upon you. But at the same time life is uncertain; and many of you may be called into eternity depending for salvation upon this awful delusion, and then, Oh! what will become of your souls!

23

It is this thought that has induced me to address these plain words of warning to you, and not to wait till the error discovers itself. The whole is doubtless a delusion of the Great Enemy to draw you off from the exercise of repentance, faith, and holiness, to dependence upon outward forms. The Evil One knows that to inquire what shall be hereafter; to speculate on the second coming of Christ; to talk of the New Jerusalem and the latter-day glory; and to assume a position in which we can say to our neighbor, "Stand off, I am holier than thou,"–is much more agreeable to the natural man, much more flattering to our pride than the diligent examination of our lives and hearts by the law of God; daily communing with God in fervent prayer; and a constant endeavor after increased conformity to his will. But, my dear friends, your duty may be summed up in a few words: pray to God to enable you to know the truth and to experience the truth; keep close to the word of God; try all by that standard; seek earnestly for divine grace; avoid those who are given to change; and, holding fast "the faith once delivered to the Saints," seek that pardoning mercy which is freely offered to all who ask it by fervent prayer through the merits and the intercession of the Lord Jesus Christ. Do this, and you need no *new* Revelation, no *new* Covenant; "*the kingdom of God is within you*," verily "YE SHALL BE SAVED."

Your affectionate Pastor and Friend,

W. J. MORRISH.

Ledbury.

PRINTED BY H. HUMPHREYS, CAERNARVON.

Pamphlet 9

Evan Lewis. *Hanes Chwech o Benboethiaid Crefyddol. Sef, Joseph Smith, Mahomet, Richard Brothers, Jemimah Wilson, Ann Lee, and Joanna Southcotte* (*History of Six Religious Fanatics. Namely, Joseph Smith, Muhammed, Richard Brothers, Jemimah Wilson, Ann Lee, and Joanna Southcott*). Merthyr Tydfil: Rees Lewis, 1849. 24 pages.

In the foreword to this pamphlet, author Evan Lewis declares,

> Since the deceitful Mormons suppose their honorable prophet to be someone great, I have put him alongside his brothers and sisters, so that they and all who read the book can see the similarity between the one and the other.

Only the first five pages of this pamphlet are focused on Joseph Smith, and these are simply quoted from Joseph Smith's account of his first vision and the initial spread of the Church he founded.

Since the remainder of the pamphlet has nothing to do with The Church of Jesus Christ of Latter-day Saints, only the foreword and the first five pages are translated in this volume. No printed reaction from John S. Davis has been identified.

HISTORY OF SIX

RELIGIOUS FANATICS

NAMELY,

JOSEPH SMITH,

MUHAMMAD,

RICHARD BROTHERS,

JEMIMAH WILSON,

ANN LEE,

AND JOANNA SOUTHCOTTE.

BY EVAN LEWIS.

MERTHYR TYDFIL:

PRINTED BY REES LEWIS, MAIN STREET.

1849.

FOREWORD.

At the request of some of my friends, I present to your attention this small booklet which contains the History of Religious Fanatics, or even irreligious. Since the deceitful Mormons suppose their honorable prophet to be someone great, I have put him alongside his brothers and sisters, so that they and all who read the book can see the similarity between the one and the other. Hoping that it will have the blessing of the most high, to cause my fellow countrymen to completely reject the false Prophets, together with their false beliefs, and trust Jesus Christ, the only savior of sinners, for eternal life, is the wish of your obedient servant and opponent of all wicked lies.

EVAN LEWIS.

July 16, 1849

STORY OF JOSEPH SMITH.

The following quote is from the history of Smith about himself, and from the fake revelations on which his prophetic authority is based. About three years ago, Mr. I. D. Rupp, of Lancaster, Pennsylvania, composed an original history of the religious denominations in the United States, and so that the work would be as free as possible from angry complaints, Mr. Rupp sent to the Ministers and most famous lay members of the various denominations for help; many of them promptly agreed to write, or request the necessary articles. Among others, a request was sent to Joseph Smith; the article was offered, and from this article I take the following account. Nothing can be more fair than for the prophet to relate his own history.—I was born in the town of Sharon, Windsor County, Vermont, on the 23rd of December, A. D. 1805. When ten years old, my parents removed to Palmyra, New York, where we resided about four years, and from thence we removed to the town of Manchester, a distance of six miles. My father was a farmer, and taught me the art of husbandry. When about fourteen years of age, I began to reflect upon the importance of being prepared for a future state; and upon inquiring the place of salvation, I found that there was a great clash in religious sentiment; if I went to one society they referred me to one place, and another to another; each one pointing to his particular creed as having the most of perfection.

I retired to a secret place in a grove, and began to call upon the Lord. While engaged in supplication, my mind was taken away from the objects with which I was surrounded, and I was enrapt in a heavenly vision, and

4

saw two glorious personages, who exactly resembled each other in features and likeness, surrounded with a brilliant light, brighter than the sun at noonday. They told me that all the religious denominations were erroneous, and that none of them was acknowledged of God as His Church and Kingdom. And I was expressly commanded to go not after them, at the same time receiving a promise that the fullness of the gospel should at some future time be made known unto me.

On the evening of the 21st September, 1823, while I was praying unto God and endeavoring to exercise faith in the precious promises of scripture, on a sudden a light like that of day, only of a far purer and more glorious appearance and brightness, burst into the room; indeed the first sight was as though the house was filled with consuming fire. The appearance produced a shock that affected the whole body. In a moment a personage stood before me surrounded with a glory yet greater than that with which I was already surrounded.

This messenger proclaimed himself to be an angel of God, sent to bring the joyful tidings, that the covenant which God made with ancient Israel was at hand to be fulfilled; that the preparatory work for the second coming of the Messiah was speedily to commence; that the time was at hand for the gospel in all its fullness to be preached, unto all nations, that a people might be prepared for the millennial reign. I was informed that I was chosen to be an instrument in the hands of God to bring about some of his purposes in this glorious dispensation.

I was informed also concerning the aboriginal inhabitants of this country, (America) and shown who they were, and from whence they came; a brief sketch of their origin, progress, civilization, laws, governments,

5

of their righteousness and iniquity, and the blessings of God being finally withdrawn from them as a people, was made known unto me.

I was also told where there were deposited some plates, on which was engraved an abridgment of the records of the ancient prophets that had existed on this continent. The angel appeared to me three times the same night and unfolded the same things. After having received many visits from the angels of God, unfolding the majesty and glory of the events that should transpire in the last days, on the morning of the 22nd of September A.D. 1827, the angel of the Lord delivered the records into my hands. These records were engraved on plates which had the appearance of gold; each plate was six inches wide and eight inches long, and not quite so thick as common tin. They were filled with engravings in Egyptian characters, and bound together in a volume, as the leaves of a book, with three rings running through the whole. The volume was something near six inches in thickness, a part of which was sealed. The characters on the unsealed part were small and beautifully engraved. The whole book exhibited many marks of antiquity in its construction and much skill in the art of engraving. With the records was found a curious instrument which the ancients called "Urim and Thummim," which consisted of two transparent stones set in the rim on a bow fastened to a breastplate. Through the medium of the Urim and Thummim I translated the record, by the gift and power of God. As soon as the news of this discovery was made known, false reports, misrepresentation and slander flew, as on the wings of the wind, in every direction.

My house was frequently beset by mobs, and evil designing persons; several times I was shot at, and very

6

narrowly escaped, and every device was made use of to get the plates away from me but the power and blessing of God attended me, and several began to believe my testimony. On the 6th of April, 1830, the "Church of Jesus Christ of Latter-day Saints," was first organized in the town of Manchester, Ontario County, state of New York. Some few were called and ordained by the spirit of revelation and prophecy, and began to preach as the spirit gave them utterance, and though weak, yet were they strengthened by the power of God; and many were brought to repentance, were immersed in the water and were filled with the Holy Ghost by the laying on of hands. They saw visions and prophesied, devils were cast out, and the sick healed by the laying on of hands. From that time work rolled forth with astonishing rapidity, and churches were soon formed in the states of New York, Pennsylvania, Ohio, Indiana, Illinois, and Missouri; in the last named state a considerable settlement was formed in Jackson County; numbers joined the Church and we were increasing rapidly; our farms teamed with plenty, and peace and happiness were enjoyed in our domestic circle and throughout our neighborhood; but as we could not associate with our neighbors, who were, many of them, of the basest of men, and had fled from the face of civilized society to the frontier country to escape the hand of justice in their midnight revels, their sabbath-breaking, horse-racing, and gambling, they commenced at first to ridicule, then to persecute, and finally an organized mob assembled and burned our houses, tarred and feathered and whipped many of our brethren, and finally drove them from their habitations. These, houseless and homeless contrary to law, justice, and humanity, had to wander on the bleak prairies, in the month of November, till the children left

7

the tracks of their blood on the prairie. Then, toward the end of the year 1839, we began to build a city called Nauvoo, in Hancock County, which in December, 1840, received an Act of Incorporation from Illinois, and is endowed with as liberal powers as any city in the United States. With respect to increase and prosperity, Nauvoo has exceeded the most sanguine expectations of thousands. Nauvoo now contains near 1,500 houses, and more than 15,000 inhabitants. The charter contains, amongst its important powers and privileges, a grant for the University of Nauvoo, with the same liberal powers of the city, where all the arts and sciences will grow the growth, and strengthen the strength of this beloved city of the Latter-day Saints. Since the organization of this church its progress has been rapid, and its gain in numbers regular. Besides these United States, where nearly every place of notoriety has heard the glad tidings of the gospel of the Son of God, England, Ireland, and Scotland, have shared largely in the fullness of the everlasting gospel, and thousands have already gathered with their kindred Saints, to this the cornerstone of Zion. Missionaries of this Church have gone to the East Indies, to Australia, Germany, Constantinople, Egypt, Palestine, the Islands of the Pacific, and are now preparing to open the door in the extensive dominions of Russia. There are no correct data by which the exact number of members composing this now extensive, and still extending, Church of Jesus Christ of Latter-day Saints can be known. Should it be supposed at 150,000, it might still be short of the truth.

Pamphlet 10

William Jones. *Egwyddorion Saint y Dyddiau Diweddaf yn cael eu pwyso yn nghlorianau rhesymau ac ysgrythyrau* (*Principles of the Latter-day Saints Weighed on the Scales of Reasons and Scriptures*). Bethesda: R. Jones, 1851. 24 pages.

William Jones begins with this statement concerning the opinions of the Latter-day Saints:

> The remarks made in these pages are intended to review only a few of the weak-headed opinions of the Mormons, who call themselves Latter-day Saints, for they are too numerous, and too full of inconsistency.

With respect to their doctrines, he adds:

> Their doctrines are an interwoven mixture of reckless, destructive heresies, if one looks at them in the simplicity of the gospel.

He presents a list of eight of the Latter-day Saint beliefs with which he takes issue:

1. They believe that the true church left the earth following the apostolic age.
2. They believe God revealed the gospel to Joseph Smith and authorized him to reestablish the Christian church on earth.
3. They claim that they have the same commission that the apostles received from Jesus Christ.
4. They claim to have the same qualifications to make a Bible as the apostles and the holy prophets had.
5. They believe that there is to be a trial situation after death, and that all who were in the world from the apostolic age to the time the gospel was revealed to Joseph Smith will be subject to it, and that salvation will be offered to them, through the preaching of the gospel in paradise.
6. They believe that the day of judgment will last a thousand years.
7. They believe there are two heavens, quite apart from the firmament and the starry heavens.
8. They believe, after they have gone to California, that Jesus Christ will come to meet them, and that they shall reign with him for 1,000 years, when everyone else will be destroyed.

Jones then presents numerous scriptures along with his own explanations in refuting the beliefs of the Latter-day Saints. See Episode 8.5.

PRINCIPLES

OF THE LATTER-DAY SAINTS

WEIGHED

ON THE SCALES OF REASONS AND SCRIPTURES.

~~~~~~~~~~~~~~~~~~~~~~

BY WILLIAM JONES, BETHESDA.

~~~~~~~~~~~~~~~~~~~~~~

"Tekel, You have been weighed on the scales and found wanting."

BETHESDA:

PRINTED ON BEHALF OF THE AUTHOR, BY R. JONES.

—

1851.

PRINCIPLES, &c.

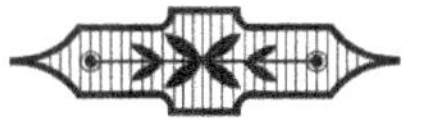

The remarks made in these pages are intended to review only a few of the weak-headed opinions of the Mormons, who call themselves Latter-day Saints, for they are too numerous, and too full of inconsistency; and if they were not so, they would not bear the image of their relations, which are Catholicism, Islam, and Puseyism. Their doctrines are an interwoven mixture of reckless, destructive heresies, if one looks at them in the simplicity of the gospel: if they cannot find sufficient material to satisfy their aims in connection with their doctrines in spiritual things, they insist that there is some particular interference with the elements of the material creation, and that it is to have a strong influence on the sinner, before, and whilst he is created anew in Christ Jesus. Material things comprise the Muslim religion. The poor creatures who profess this *system* are so blinded that they do not see a gleam of light; in time they lean on the material to sustain them, they rejoice in the material as their hope, and they respect the material more than the fruit of their womb, for many of them have given their children as willing sacrifices under the wheels of the Juggernaut for the material, and after the end of time, they expect only the material to constitute their glory in the world of the spirits. O! poor things, when they expect to receive their inheritance according to their present opinion, the materials will melt in true heat, and their hopes will die like the crackling of thorns. The Catholics also, believe they may obtain forgiveness of their sins for money, not only those they have committed, but for those they commit henceforth; and they put shoes and a stick with a corpse in the grave, so that they can be of some further use to him. Puseyism too, says that a baby is born again when water is poured on his forehead through the fingers of the

4

Priest,–and that the bread and the wine in the Sacrament turns into the true body and blood of our Lord Jesus Christ.

Is there any similarity in the Mormons or in Mormonism to what has been said about the others? Yes, for that is what made me mention them; those are Mormonism's family. Do the Mormons–who call themselves saints–say that an immortal soul needs matter in order to be suitable for the spiritual world? Yes, the main points in their belief are that they can heal the body by anointing it with oil, and if one of their ministers is immersed in water, his soul will receive salvation. St. Paul foresaw these doctrines, and their harmful influence on God's Church, and said; "Now the Spirit speaketh expressly, that in the latter times some shall depart from the faith, giving heed to seducing spirits, and doctrines of devils." And in order to be able to withstand their enchantments, "It is good for our hearts to be strengthened by grace." The Mormons mantle their deceit with their attractions. St Peter says, "False prophets shall rise, and through covetousness shall they with feigned words make merchandise of you." I do not think the deceit is so hidden that all who understand the Bible cannot clearly discover it. St Paul foresaw their aim and their influence, along with those most in danger of being deceived by them, "Some desire to be teachers of the law; understanding neither what they say, nor whereof they affirm, speaking lies in hypocrisy, creeping into houses, and leading captive silly women laden with sins." Silly women here means the most ignorant class in the land of the gospel; ones like this and their ilk are in the same danger, of being seduced by the Mormons. It can properly be said that these silly women refer to two classes. The 1st, those who are voluntarily ignorant of the truth of the doctrine of the gospel, who have spent the most advantageous season of their life in order to gain knowledge in trivial things, and in idleness and laziness, saying, "Tomorrow will be as today, and very much better." On Sundays, they are on the squares speaking of the celestial signs, and the produce of nature; and in the evenings, they sit in the corners slandering their neighbors; and if there is a Bible in the

5

house, there will be half an inch of dust on its cover, and its precious pages will be covered in mildew. Those are one class of the silly ignorant women, who are not much of a problem for the Mormon teachers to lead into bondage; let those (silly) women take advice not to get too close to the snares, lest they be captured by them. The 2nd class which is in great danger of being enticed by the Mormons are the hopeful youth of Wales: it is of great import whether it is the principles of Christianity or else the heresies of these false prophets that are spread among them; the youthful mind is uncultivated ground that has not been sown, and it is important, not only to itself, but also to the age and the nation, whether it is tares or wheat that is sown in it at present, if the tares are put there first, they have the greatest advantage to possess and overfill the land, and when one goes to sow the wheat grain, there is nothing to be expected but thorns and briers. A man's mental, moral and intellectual powers begin in his youth to open up to receive impressions, and of every period in his life, that is the most advantageous time to imprint truths on it; as the first impression is easily put on white paper–clear to see, and difficult to erase, so too is the youthful mind; it is very easy to influence it; the fruit of the influence is very obvious, as it is natural, and whether it be good or bad–it is very difficult to change it. "Train up a child in the way he should go: and when he is old, he will not depart from it." So, I would advise my fellow young people to listen to the gospel in its simplicity, as it is preached in our age, and was preached in the age of our fathers for their salvation, rather than go to listen to peerless fables, and mad and superstitious imaginings. But lest I go on at length in this manner, I shall attempt to look in more detail at their doctrinal subjects, by showing their inconsistency with themselves, and their inconsistency with the truth of the New Testament. Here are some of the Mormons' opinions:–

1. They believe that the true church, or the Christian church, and the gospel of the Son of God, along with the influence of the Holy Spirit, left the earth following the apostolic age–and that it has dwelt in oppression, with no one to uphold in truth remembrance of the Lord for 1600 years.

6

2. They believe that God through the agency of an Angel of light revealed the gospel to one Joseph Smith, and that he authorized him to reestablish the Christian church on earth by preaching the gospel himself, together with the authority to ordain others to the work.

3. They claim that they have the same commission as the Apostles received from Jesus Christ,–that they are to establish the church in the same manner, on the same conditions, and possessing the same authority as the Apostles.

4. They claim to have the same qualifications to make a Bible as the Apostles and the holy Prophets had, and that they do not know how soon they will be commanded to do so.

5. They believe that there is to be a trial situation after death, and that all who were in the world from the apostolic age to the time the gospel was revealed to Joseph Smith will be subject to it, and that salvation will be offered to them, through the preaching of the gospel in Paradise, (or, as the Pope calls the place, Purgatory).

6. They believe the day of judgment will last a thousand years.

7. They believe there are two heavens, quite apart from the firmament and the starry heavens.

8. They believe, after they have gone to California, that Jesus Christ will come to meet them, and that they shall reign with him for 1000 years, when everyone else will be destroyed, &c.

I shall not comment on the deceit of the Book of Mormon; its fate to my mind is like the Mohamed's Koran. Humanity should blush because of it, and deny its relationship with it; let it be buried in the land of its birth, and let its memory go to a vortex of perdition.

1. They assert that the world has for 1600 years been without a church of God in it. It is hard for philanthropic feeling, let alone Christian experience, to tolerate such a presumptuous assertion;–let heaven wonder, and the earth be shaken that humanity is so blinded that one of those who were created only a little lower than the angels should believe such a thing. Reader, meditate on the principles that derive naturally from the awful doctrine noted; you will see that it is unworthy of a God rich in mercy, who wishes that every man be saved. If the gospel left the earth, the main instrumental means of the Atonement of Grace to save the world, left the world, so, consequently, however much the gnawing of conscience, the fear of dying, and the terrors of the devil might achieve,

7

there was no relief to be had; however bitterly repentance worked on the sinner, even though he saw his affliction to be great, the balm of Gilead had finished; even though he saw the avenger upon him, the city of refuge was closed – the tempest rough and turbulent, and he without a shelter and shore in hope, looking about him, and with only despair printed on every side; if he looked up, he saw the wrath of God resting on him; if he looked down, hell opened up willingly to receive him. That is one of the principles that arises from the assertion. Reader, is it consistent with the mercy of the Father, who loved you, and the sacrifice of the Son, who bought you, and the visitations of the Spirit, who convinces you? I can answer without fear; no it is not, for your consciences and the word of God testify to that.

2. That the church has ended on earth. The first assertion certifies this; as every building stands when the tools are removed; so too, since the treasure was put in clay vessels, that is the power of God was the tool which was bought through the blood of the Intercessor to destroy the corners of Moab, and to build the walls of Jerusalem – and that this tool was removed, and left the stones not hewn from the rock; the result was that the spiritual edifice necessarily stood. And when the stones that were in Jerusalem down below were perfected, (that is St. Paul, St. Peter, and St. John, &c.), they were taken up to the Jerusalem, that is above, to the unveiled presence of their Redeemer, to sound the harps of victory. What is the conclusion from that assertion? Only that the foundation laid in Zion has no building on it.

The principle that arises naturally from that consideration is 1. the perdition of babies. Jesus Christ said, "Let the little children come unto me, and do not hinder them, for theirs is the kingdom of heaven." If the heaven of glory is meant, they cannot possess it, without first being made fitting through the sanctifying influence of the Holy Spirit, and there was no way for them to have been thus sanctified, since the Spirit had ceased to have influence on earth, hundreds of years ago. But if an earthly church is meant, that had been taken away following the apostolic age, therefore, Christ and the

8

Mormons–God's book and the book of Mormon are at odds with each other, God's book saying that the kingdom of heaven belongs to babies, and the book of Mormon asserting that it was not accessible to them. The conclusion is, that all the babies who died from the time of the Apostles till Joseph Smith, are lost. Readers, especially fathers and mothers, what are your feelings when confronted with such an awful doctrine? We are greatly obliged to be grateful for a better light on the present situation of our departed babies,–that they do not "pave the depths of hell," but that their strings are taut, their gowns are white, and their songs melodic as they sing the praises of their Redeemer, on the branches of the Tree of Life.

Next, that all the Christians from the age of the Apostles to the time of Joseph Smith are unacceptable in matters of faith–that their doctrines were nothing but heresies–their labor merely vain and useless–and that they are mantled in darkness as a dark fog covers the top of a hill,–that they do not have a Christian doctrine,–a Christian experience, nor Christian influence, and that their situation in another world is no better than the situation of the most idolatrous pagans, and however much work and effort is made by the various religious denominations of this age to do good, the Mormons say their labor is only vain, and will be of no benefit to them–nor to the world, nor to the glory of God; and that they cannot be saved, without being baptized by one of the Mormons; and the condition is come as you are, whatever your state of mind, that is of little importance; but the only condition is for you to be baptized by complete immersion in water, and you will come out having been forgiven for all your sins, without wetting your cheeks with tears, nor afflicting your spirit with sighs; and only if one of the sanctimonious Mormons puts his hands on your head – will you receive the gift of the Holy Spirit. They say that water and the hand of a Mormon are indispensable tools for qualifying an immortal soul for the glory of the immortal world. I once asked one of the Mormons, what was his opinion with regard to the present situation of the famous old reformers,–Luther, Calvin, Wesley, Elias of Anglesey, Williams, from the Wern, Christmas Evans, and Jones, Bathafarn,–who in God's hand, were like the smelter's fire, and like the launderers' soap, cleaning out the paganism of Europe; and like lamps of light reflecting the wealth of the glory of

9

God, and his generosity to men, in Christ Jesus, who sacrificed their lives to do good; they traveled often, and in danger of floodwaters, in danger of robbers, always in toil and weariness: have these famous and hard-working men gone to Canaan, after traveling such a solitary wilderness? Have they received a pearly crown instead of grievous crosses–palms instead of the sword, is heaven their home, are the Lamb, the angels, and the saints their companions, is there a song on their lips –are there harps in their hands, to sing praise for their redemption and salvation through the sacrifice of the cross? The answer I received comprised what follows, essentially;–that the famous men mentioned know nothing of such happiness, nor anyone from whom they took their names, because the ways of these teachers are entirely at odds with the gospel, and therefore unacceptable to God, and that their present situation is only a situation of trial;–that the gospel is preached to them, and unless they repent and believe, their perdition will be inevitable, and that their fate will be in the lake burning with fire and brimstone; likewise do they judge the godly martyrs, who willingly accepted torture by stakes, with faggots, and barrels of *pitch*, in the most unbearable manner for bodies in which souls reside, for the word of God and the testimony of Jesus Christ; the Mormons' answer about these is, that neither their service, their profession, nor their sufferings for religion were sufficient virtues to merit the attention of heaven,–and that preaching the gospel to them is as essential as it is to pagans. But the word of God says that those who suffer with Christ will also be glorified with him. And the poet sets out their transformation in striking terms:

> "They escaped from a bonfire of faggots, their lighting was the beginning of their song;
> They flew from the night to their Redeemer, to the day on wings of fire."

But mercifully, knowledge of the gospel is too widespread in Wales for such aforementioned assertions to receive hardly any acceptance: it is a valuable truth for humanity, that no generation went to the grave in terms of their bodies, nor to God in terms of their spirits, without receiving a bright and adequate revelation, through one dispensation or the other, that God through the Intercessor is ready and willing to welcome them into his favor.

10

Theologians regard God's general governance of our world in three parts, which are creation, providence, and grace; they also divide God's gracious governance into three parts, namely that from Adam's fall to John the Baptist, the Father ruled; from John the Baptist till the Pentecost, the Son ruled, and from the Pentecost to the end of the world, the Holy Spirit rules. This means that there is a particular dispensation related to the three eras mentioned, namely the Mosaic stewardship, the stewardship of John the Baptist, and the stewardship of the Holy Spirit, which is also called the dispensation of God's Grace, the dispensation of the fullness of time. When the Father ruled, the people's minds are directed to a superior dispensation; although Jesus Christ was set out in the shadows, and the prophecies, under the old dispensation, yet the preparatory dispensation of John the Baptist was to take place according to God's immutable purpose, and to have a favorable effect on the success of the gospel; for it was like a candle being lit in a dark place, until the Sun rose. And here is the promise about John, together with the consequent blessings. *"Behold, I will send to you Elijah the prophet, before the coming of the great and dreadful day of the Lord, and he shall turn the heart of the fathers to the children, and the heart of the children to the fathers, lest I come and smite the earth with a curse."* And after the coming of John the Baptist according to the predictions; the main aim of his preaching was to attempt to convince, and teach people that his ministry was nothing more than an introduction to a superior, better dispensation. *"This is he who was spoken of by the prophet Isaiah, saying, the voice of one crying in the wilderness, prepare the way of the Lord, make his paths straight. Every valley shall be exalted, and every mountain and hill shall be made low, and the crooked shall be made straight, and the rough places plain; and all flesh shall see the salvation of God."* That is the dispensation that has operated from the time it was established, and is to operate as long as God's mercy and the sinner are together. Under the Mosaic dispensation, God spoke on earth through his angels; under John the Baptist's stewardship, God spoke on earth in the flesh, but under the present dispensation, God speaks on earth through his Spirit; and the ministry of the Spirit is

11

called the latter days. *"But this is that which was spoken by the prophet Joel; And it shall come to pass in the last days, saith God, I will pour out my Spirit upon all flesh: and your sons and your daughters shall prophesy, and your young men shall see visions, and your old men shall dream dreams: And on my servants and on my handmaidens I will pour out in those days of my Spirit; and they shall prophesy."* Was it on the day of the Pentecost, 1800 years ago, or in the time of Joseph Smith, 23 years ago, that the dispensation of the last days began? The Mormons say that it was Joseph Smith who received information through revelation of the last days, and that he was the Elijah that Malachi prophesied about, that it was for him that an angel flew in the middle of heaven, with the eternal gospel,–and that it was about his days that the prophet Joel prophesied. In relation to the pouring of the Holy Spirit, are Mormons or St. Peter to be believed? Let the reader choose. The prophecy referred to the Pentecost according to St. Peter; but the Mormons say that it refers to the days of Joseph Smith. The exciting influence that occurred on the day of the Pentecost, let alone the inspiration, through which the Apostle spoke, was enough to convince every heedful mind, that Joel's prophecy was being fulfilled at that time, and that everything related to the Pentecost corresponded consistently to the prophecy, it is therefore but blasphemy and arrogance to say that it was in the days of Joseph Smith that Joel's prophecy was fulfilled.

The Mormons say that Joseph Smith was the first of the latter-day saints, and that no one is such except his followers. I believe St. Peter, that the 3000 who willingly accepted his word on the day of the Pentecost, are latter-day saints; and that the Spirit that convinced the 3000 that day remains in the world in terms of its influence, up until today; and that the salvation whose strength was certified sufficient at that time, is in force in every age and generation; and in the face of that, the great folly is to say that the gospel and the church were taken from the earth! What a dreadful thought; after a merciful God gave his Son to die for sinners,–that he left the world, for which his Son suffered agony and pains all over on the cross, in

12

blindness, despair, and misery, with no hope, and no God in the world for 1600 years. God had redeemed the world, but it was out of reach; a well opened to wash sinners, but it was closed; yes, all the provisions of Redemptive love were taken away, the merciful God having kept his mercy for the ages to come; are thoughts such as these worthy of the one who loved us? No they are not, rather they are dreadful blasphemy and arrogance, and as a comfort to us, they are not the truth.

The stability of the Christian stewardship mantled previous dispensations in shame, and dressed itself in glory; whatever weaknesses and changes take place in earthly kingdoms and empires, Christianity stands upright like Joseph's sheaf, stable in the midst of storms; it met with the cruellest opposition, and the fiercest persecutions; Hume in Scotland, and Voltaire in France, and Joseph in America strove and prophesied about its fall and destruction, but their prophecies were false, and their objectives in vain, and their names are rotting; but God's strong foundation stands. *"Upon this rock I will build my church; and the gates of hell shall not prevail against it."* It stands in the face of all the attacks of men and devils; and when the fiery flow, accumulated for thousands of years breaks over everything;–then the refuge of lies will be swept away, when the book of Mormon will receive its share of the conflagration, with the hay, the straw and the stubble; but the truth will be proclaimed publicly in the worlds, and the saints of every generation and age will be invited to the endless bliss; that is the first time the church will be removed from the earth, let the Mormons say what they want.

Next, they claim that they have the same commission received from Joseph Smith as the Apostles received from Jesus Christ, namely that they are to establish the church on earth in the same manner, on the same conditions, and through the same authority,–and that some of them are Apostles, some Prophets, some Teachers, and that some of them have healing powers, others the gift of speaking in foreign tongues, others the gift of translation, and others the ability to perform miracles. Now I shall attempt to prove through the light of reason and scriptural revelation, that they do not have apostolic authority. Firstly, those who call themselves latter-day apostles do not match the characteristics of an Apostle, although they say they have received the apostolic order, and that they can perform powerful and miraculous acts like Christ and his apostles. But who among their followers, or from the world can answer that from the same experience and testimony as the man born blind? *"Whether he be a sinner or no, I know not: one thing I know, that, whereas I was blind, now I see."* The Mormons have a lot of excuses for not performing miracles, which Christ and his Apostles knew nothing about; one reason they have is that they cannot in order to satisfy men; secondly, that they cannot without faith on the part of the one who asks; thirdly, that they cannot without belief on the part of the one on whom the miracle is performed believing. Now if I may prove through scriptural facts that Christ and his apostles performed miracles outside of the conditions the Mormons require before they can perform them. It is incontrovertible that they do not have the apostolic authority; they are like the ones St. Peter spoke of. *"Which have forsaken the right way, and are gone astray, following the way of Balaam the son of Bosor, who loved the wages of unrighteousness; these are wells without water, clouds that are carried with a tempest; to whom the mist of darkness is reserved for ever."* Jesus Christ performed miracles to satisfy men. Christ did not mention the mind of the director of the feast before turning the water into wine, but he did it without the director's knowledge. John II. 9, 10: also Christ performed a miracle to satisfy strangers, yes, his enemies. St. Matthew XVII. 26, 27.

If the Mormons have this authority, why do they not operate by the same rule as did Christ and his Apostles; if their doctrine is the truth, let them prove it, by their defendants doing what they say, to the world entrusted to them for them to operate. It is reasonable to ask for the proofs they have of their authority, in order to establish the standard of their doctrines according to the truth of the Scriptures, if it is so. Also, Christ and his Apostles performed miracles without the faith of the one who asked them. When Christ said that the girl was not dead, but sleeping, some mocked him; therefore they did not believe, nevertheless

14

he woke the lass from the sleep of death. Was it because the one possessed by a devil had no faith that the disciples failed to cast out the devil? No, because if they had waited for that, he would have been possessed until the day of his death. When the lame man, who stood every day by the temple door, saw Peter and John about to go in, he asked for something from them, and after receiving a command from Peter, he paid attention, hoping to get alms from them as from others who went in; and Peter, seeing his misunderstanding, said to him, *"Silver and gold have I none; but such as I have I give thee: In the name of Jesus Christ of Nazareth get up and walk."* When Eutychus fell from the window, while Paul was discoursing at length, he was taken up dead. Acts xx. 10. The fact that the lame man was begging, and that Eutychus was dead proves that they were not asking for nor thinking about the things they received through the Apostles: consequently the miracles noted must have been performed without faith in those the miracles were performed upon. Now, which of those who call themselves latter-day apostles, has given such evidence of their divine mission; if they possess apostolic authority of every manner to heal the sick, perform miracles, &c.; before they can prove that, they must perform some, and of the same nature as the Apostles; the Apostles proved their divine mission, by casting out devils, healing the sick, calming the storm, rocking the foundations of the prison, and raising the dead. Christ and his Apostles performed miracles in the most public way, in the houses and the villages, the towns and the cities, the temple and the synagogues, in the presence of a host of men of every station and character, on all sorts of men,–enemies and friends. Also their miracles brought with them in the most obvious way their vast difference from any trickery, falseness, and deceit; they drew the attention of their enemies and friends to them, in the presence of those they were being performed on at that time, as incontrovertible and direct proofs of the divinity of their mission; they bore with them such convincing clarity, that their enemies had to admit, and say of Christ, *"This man doeth many miracles; if we let him thus alone, all men will believe on him:*

15

lo, the world is gone after him." The same testimony is given about St. Paul, and the other Apostles too. "And after the High Priests beheld the man which was healed standing with them, they could say nothing against it. But when they had commanded them to go aside out of the council, they conferred among themselves, saying, What shall we do to these men, for that indeed a notable miracle has been done by them is manifest to all them that dwell in Jerusalem; and we cannot deny it." If the powerful deeds performed by them were not so known, especially in Jerusalem, we would deny it, for the name of the man in whose name they act is undesirable to our nation, and especially so to our sect; and they say that high priests are no longer needed, for they say that the Jesus they preach is an eternal Priest, after the order of Melchizedek, and that he entered into the sanctuary through his own blood; but whatever the consequence will be for us and our religion, we cannot deny this remarkable sign: and their desire was that they did not instruct any more in this man's name. There are a few of the Apostles' rules, and of the Apostles' miracles, with their exciting effect on their enemies. Now, I ask you where those who call themselves latter-day saints made a sign so obvious that it cannot be denied, or that it can be believed; it is said all over this area that a remarkable miracle was performed in Machynlleth; there they say that the thing happened in Carmarthen, and in Carmarthen, they say that it was in Merthyr Tydfil that a blind man regained his sight; there they said further that they heard one of the apostles had subdued the storm on the voyage to California; so, consequently, it is difficult to find the sign that cannot be denied; they cloak their deceit and their tricks so much, that they are as difficult to catch as the robber Turpin, even though the trickery of the one is as obvious as the other's; and I would find it easier to believe that a blind man could make a rope out of sand, than that the Mormons could give him sight.

Next, the Mormons say that a church to God cannot exist without having 12 Apostles associated with it. When Judas went to his own place, Mathias was chosen instead of him; following that, the apostles died, one after another, most of them through martyrdom; it is considered that all of them met

16

death in that way, apart from the Apostle John; but we have no account of 12 other Apostles being ordained in their place. If the latter-day saints have an account of that, we would wish to know who they were by name;–and before their testimony will stand it will have to come from God's Book, and not from the book of Mormon. Now, since the latter-day saints argue that a church of God cannot exist without having 12 Apostles in it, and since the first 12 ordained have been called from the earth, through the ordinance of the Head of the church–and as there is no proof that others have been called to that office, therefore it must be that if no church could be without 12 apostles, and God had called the twelve ordained to himself, and had not chosen 12 others in their place, that the church has been annulled according to the will and design of God, or else that he wishes to carry on his work outside the apostolic order. Which of the two postulations is more consistent with the Word of God? Let the reader decide; the opinion of theologians throughout the ages is that only 12 Apostles were ordained, although a few changes were made, in the apostolic age the office of apostle was particular and unique;–an Apostle was one who had seen the Lord Jesus in the flesh, and was a witness to his resurrection. Every one of the Apostles was to receive his knowledge of Christian doctrine–not from men, but from the Son of God himself, through whose Spirit they were led to all truths. St. Paul's expression proves that he could not have been an Apostle, had he not seen Christ in the flesh, and if he had waited a while, it would have been too late for him. "And last of all was he seen of me also, as of one born out of due time;" and from then on the Apostle says, "For I neither received it of man, neither was I taught it, but by the revelation of Jesus Christ; and Christ said to him; for this is why I appeared to you, to make you a minister and a witness of the things you have seen, and of the things in which I shall appear to you." This proves that no one could be an Apostle without seeing Christ, and being taught by him personally. The Apostles had Christ's thought directly, and they were authorized commentators on his gospel,–endowed with several spiritual gifts; they were inspired men, in the widest sense of the phrase; "And the church is built

17

on the foundation of the Apostles, and the Prophets, Jesus Christ himself being the chief cornerstone;" this is what our Lord told them about, in a meaning that was not appropriate for anyone else. Did I not choose the twelve for you, and that they should sit on twelve thrones, judging the twelve tribes of Israel. St. John saw, in the Revelation, the New Jerusalem descending from heaven from God; and the city wall had twelve foundations, and in them were the names of the twelve Apostles of the Lamb. From this, it appears beyond dispute, that only one apostolic age was ordained; and it was while God saw fit that he allowed Apostles to remain in the church; the highest Archbishop is as far from being equal to the Apostles as is the lowest of the traveling evangelists. The Apostles received their education from Christ personally, and were led by the complete inspiration of the Holy Ghost; and from that time on, it is pointless to expect any higher assistance than the natural influence of the Holy Ghost; and although there is no apostolic office in the church in these times, the ministry is still constantly in force, and will be so until the end of the world. *"Lo, I am with you always, even until the end of the world."* Is the evangelical, apostolic, and Christian ministry preached by the Calvinistic Methodists, the Congregationalists, the Baptists, and the Wesleyans, &c., in previous ages, and in the present age, or is it that which is now preached by the Mormons? Let the reader reply after receiving an accurate summary of the two ministries; part of the content of the Mormons' ministry is this,– they must believe that twelve Apostles belong to the church, and that they are, or have been, called in a supernatural way–that they are to perform miracles–heal the sick, &c. They believe, and argue for the divinity of the book of Mormon–the divinity of Joseph Smith's sending, and that no one from the time of the Apostles to the days of Joseph Smith went to heaven, and that no one from his time to end of the world will go, apart from the Mormons. They believe that the most essential things to qualify a man for glory, are immersion in water, anointing with oil, the laying on of hands, &c.; they believe that, because the rites noted were not performed, by the religious denominations of ages gone by, their situation while they were in this world, was no different from the situation of the pagans, and that their present situation in the realm of the spirits is not

18

any better, and that the gospel is to be preached to them again by the Mormons! What foolishness, that cannot be described; the strongest reasoning can only wonder at it. If it is appropriate to call Catholicism a Beast, it would also be appropriate to call Mormonism an excommunicated Monster. The stench of the stinking carcass rises up to heaven: speed the time that the rays of the Sun of Righteousness through the gospel chase away the utter darkness of Mohammedanism, Catholicism, and Mormonism over the banks of time into eternal oblivion; and it is just as certain that these beasts arose out of a sea of pride, superstition, and fanaticism, that they will fall into a sea of disgrace and shame, as St. Paul announced the fate of all false teachers. 2 Tim. iii. 8,9. *"Now as Jannes and Jambres withstood Moses, so do these also resist the truth: men of corrupt minds, reprobate concerning the faith. But they shall proceed no further: for their folly shall be manifest unto all men, as theirs also was."* Is it some fetid mixture like that that is preached from the Nonconformists' pulpits? No, otherwise it could be said of the churches that broken wells without water; but like Jerusalem and the mountains surrounding it, so too has there been defense of God's church, also, *"God among you is powerful."* And although the apostolic office has been lost, the ministry is in force, that is apostolic truth, and apostolic success; we believe our forefathers stood in this succession, namely Calvin, Wesley, Whitfield, &c. And the same truths were preached in Wild Wales, for the salvation of thousands, by Elias of Anglesey, Williams of Wern, Jones of Bathafarn, &c.; and the ministers of the present age are in the same succession insofar as they are stirred by the same Spirit, and walk in the same paths as they,–but no further, the laying on of hands, anointing with oil, &c., whether by Bishops, Presbyterians, or Mormons, can never constitute a true ministerial nature, where there is no evangelical knowledge and personal godliness, and high-principled motivation for the work. Mormons, can you muster enough boldness to answer the following questions negatively, about the state and qualifications of the famous men mentioned? Did they know

19

God as a forgiving God? Did they have the love of God residing in them? Was their conduct holy? Did they have goodness and grace for the work? Did they have a correct comprehension of justification through faith? Were some people truly convinced of their sin and returned to God through their sermons? Is their present situation blessed? If these things were asked of the damned and the demons, they would answer in the affirmative, but a Mormon answered me them all negatively; and is it not a dreadful thing that mankind is more heretical and arrogant than devils; but my thinking is that it is the devil who is blinding them, and that he will mock them when he draws the curtain, before long. The deceit of the book of Mormon–the superstitions and dreams of Joseph Smith, falls to pieces, and is like straw and combustible stubble when compared to the truths of the gospel, which has been preached throughout the ages, and will be preached until the end of time. *"For proper ministers of the New Testament do not preach themselves, (like the Mormons) but Jesus Christ and him crucified."* And their sermons do not contain anything that is superficial, uncertain and imaginary; they proclaim about the Divinity and Humanity of Christ;–they say his death was a sacrifice of divine arrangement for the sin of the world, and indispensably necessary for the justification and salvation of sinners; with his death they link his intercession for transgressors against God's law, and they call on every man, everywhere, to repent and to believe in him, on pain of eternal punishment; they preach Christ, not only having died for men, but also living in them through his Spirit, enlivening them to a new state of morality, and making them partake of the godly nature; for Christ they call for service and heartfelt dedication, together with the consecration of all human abilities, body and soul to him, considering that men do not belong to themselves, but to Christ, through redemption, as they have been redeemed through his blood, they show every spiritual blessing as being transferred to men through the intercession of Christ, who is the only point of entry to the Father. They teach every religious duty in Christ's name, and they urge the same with his authority; it is to him that they ascribe the victory over death enjoyed by the believers, and it is his presence that

20

they portray as comprising the happiness of the blessed in their heavenly situation; they assert that he has complete and general supremacy throughout all the generations,–that it is through his powerful action that the dead will be raised, and the living will be changed, that he will judge all the nations in perfect justice and rightness, *"For he will come again a second time in all his Father's greatness and glory, taking vengeance on them that know not God, and that obey not the gospel; and giving eternal life to those who by continuing to do good seek honor and purity."* We find in this ministry a steadfast attachment to the principle adopted by St. Paul as guidance for himself. *"For I determined not to know anything among you, save Jesus Christ, and him crucified. And whoever takes it upon himself to preach a gospel other than this, let him be anathema maranatha."* This is the ministry preached by teachers of Christianity for hundreds of years. Was it an evangelical ministry? No, say the Mormons! Were some of the preachers, and some of the listeners saved to eternal life? No, say the Mormons. Faced with the heresies which were to arise at that time, Timothy advised *"To preach the word earnestly, in season, out of season; for the time will come when they will not endure sound doctrine; but after their own lusts shall they heap to themselves teachers for themselves, having itching ears; and they will turn away their ears from the truth, and shall be turned unto fables."* The proper way to characterize the Mormons is as people who have turned away from the truth towards fables; they encircle the sea and the land to make one proselyte, and after they have succeeded in their attempt, they fill the poor convert with such whimsical new fables as to make him into a son of hell, twice as bad as themselves. What else but a made-up baseless fable is it to say that the book of Mormon is from God, and that Joseph Smith received in a revelation from an angel the right to establish God's church on earth. For my part, I would believe Mohammed as willingly as Joseph Smith, and the Koran as willingly as the book of Mormon; and it would be just as easy for me to give credence to the mad, crazy claims of Joanna Southcott, or to some of the religious tricksters who arose before him, or after him, as it would to his claims. Also, it would be

21

as credible to me that all the angels of heaven be seen in the flesh, as that Jesus Christ be seen going to and fro in the Salt Lake Valley, with the Mormons.

They say "we have in our church apostles and prophets." I proved that they do not have apostles, and I shall prove also that they do not have prophets. They say that Joseph Smith is some great prophet, like Saul in Israel, with broader shoulders than anyone else; they say it is to him that that prophecy refers;–"*I will raise up unto thee a Prophet from the midst of thee, of thy bretheren, like unto me.*" They say that he was the sun of righteousness that Malachi prophesied about; therefore he is their Christ, because those prophecies referred to Christ. Now, I ask the Mormons, about what event which took place did Joseph Smith prophesy, or is there proven fact that he, or any other of the Mormon prophets, foretold a particular event, and that this event took place in the same manner, and at the same time as they said it would? No, no, silence has to ensue, and because of this, it would be just as easy for me to believe the prophets of Baal as to believe the prophets of the book of Mormon. It is certain that the holy prophets could not have foretold anything that was to come, except as they received revelation from God: mysteries belong to the Lord, and nothing is more mysterious than foretelling things to come. God offers part of his own throne to whoever can foretell things in the future; "*Shew the things that are to come hereafter, that we may know that ye are gods.*" And if the Mormons receive revelations from the Lord like the old prophets, before this age can believe this, it needs the same manifestation as past ages–that a prophecy has been fulfilled, or that there are signs of its happening. Nahum prophesied that Nineveh would be a lake of water, and this is what is has been for ages; Babylon has belonged to the bittern for hundreds of years, according to the prophecy of Isaiah; Tyre is a place for spreading nets in the middle of the sea, according to the prophecy of Ezekiel. I have heard some of the Mormons' prophecies,–they say I will meet with damnation for writing against the saints. If I thought I was doing that, I would expect nothing

22

else. They also prophesy the end of all the religious denominations apart from the Mormons! What a pitiful state for the inhabitants of the earth, if that is fulfilled; they prophesy there will be some great destruction in this country, and that they will be safe and happy in Salt Lake Valley! They can wait in vain for better company than themselves. They prophesy that Christ will come there to meet them. The first meeting they and we will have with Christ will be when he meets us on the cloud, and everyone is whisked into the sky to meet him. See how great is the Mormons' opinion of themselves, since they expect him who resides among the Cherubs in the heaven of heavens to come to meet them in Salt Lake Valley. Is heaven to be empty of Emmanuel? Yes, say the Mormons! for he is the one they expect on earth, who is in the middle of the throne, like a newly slaughtered Lamb. Is heaven to go dark? Yes! say the Mormons; its light is the Lamb, and they say the Lamb will come to meet them in Salt Lake Valley! They are building a costly city, and a splendid temple; and thousands of the brethren have gone, and thousands more are preparing to go to meet him there! What folly that they believe Christ would come from the city which has foundations, to Salt Lake Valley, and from the temple which contains the holy of holies, to a temple that has been designed by nothing but deceit – deceit maintaining it, yes, and folly, even if their city were more beautiful than Jerusalem, and their temple finer than Solomon's temple. Its deceit will be made clear when all false doctrines are published publicly throughout the world. If there was a lull in heaven during half an hour when the Son of God was on the cross, and joy when he ascended into glory, there would be just as much reason for grief and a lull, if the King of heaven were seen taking off his pearly crown, and leaving the redeemed family and descending to the deserted wilderness of earth; if their songs were more melodious than the "sound of the music of a brave writer from Italy," when the gate opened to let in the King of glory; if he were seen going outside the gates, their grief would be greater than Rachel's grief for her children. If Christ said he was going to leave heaven, the Archangel would come to him straight away, and would tell him that the trumpet needed to be prepared; for he said that he would come the

23

second time with the cry of the Archangel and with God's trumpet; and Enoch would argue for the saints to follow him, because he foretold through him that he would come the second time with a myriad of his saints to dispense justice on the earth The Bible says that Christ will appear for the second time on the cloud; but the Mormons assert that it is in Salt Lake Valley;–the Bible says that he will come with a myriad of his saints to judge the world; but the Mormons say he will come to them to their society, in order to comfort them, for a thousand years! O poor things, they are sure to meet him at the same time by staying at home, and their welcome will be just as great; let them persuade themselves that Christ will not come down to meet them, but that they will be snatched up to meet him, from Salt Lake Valley, the same as from anywhere else. It is surprising that rational beings pay heed to such childish and foolish assertions. The false prophets always take advantage of the gospel to establish their opinions; they arise in the same country where the gospel is preached, in order to take advantage of the gospel to deceive. The Jews whitewashed their graves; they boasted a great deal about the robes of the Mosaic dispensation; but they were careless about the root of the matter, and because of that the Lord said to Israel, *"I will not reprove thee for thy sacrifices or thy burnt offerings, to have been continually before me."* Thus the false prophets are very careful about the most trivial things–external things; they take the clothes of the gospel to hide their deceit. The mother always takes more care of the child than of the child's clothes, but the Mormons are more concerned about the external clothes of the gospel than about the gospel itself; if they can have the clothes of the gospel to hide their fanaticism and their superstition, let the gospel go where it will. Let these people try to remember the rebuke made to their ilk by Jesus Christ when he said, *"For the kingdom of God is not meat and drink; but righteousness, and peace, and joy in the Holy Ghost."*

All the religious tricksters who have arisen bear a considerable resemblance to each other; they always claim some particular superiority for themselves. America is a country where a large crop of religious tricksters has grown. One of the American false prophets was Mathews; he said he had received a revelation from heaven through an Angel, that

24

Albany would be destroyed, unless people believed in him. He laid great importance on anointing with oil. When the wife of one of his disciples died, he thought she would rise from the dead; a large crowd gathered around him while he was anointing the body, and praying over it; but after every effort, the body had to be buried out of sight. He claimed to have had the plan of the New Jerusalem, and that he was to build it–that it was to surpass Greece and Rome in its splendor, and that it was to stand on the west side of New York. That wretch's deceit has now been revealed, and his disciples have scattered in shame and disgrace.

The beginning and the increase in superstition of Mormonism are the same as Mathews,' and those of other religious cheats. Hasten the days when all false doctrines speed from the world, through the influence of the Holy Ghost, so that everyone comes to embrace the truth, as it is in Jesus.

May Catholicism and Mormonism
Go over the parapets of the big wide world;
Let no one be so foolish as to impede them,
When they are on their journey.
    Let us sound, let us sound
    The Hallelujah after this.

Let there be no memorial to them
Here on earth in any place;
Let there be no burial for them
In any mount or churchyard.
    Let us sound, &c.

Let the ones who have been blinded,
Come to the light under heaven;
Let them not be fools,
Is now my wish, Amen.
    Let us sound, &c.

PRINTED BY R. JONES, BETHESDA.

Pamphlet 11

Hugh Jones. *Dirgelion Saint y Dyddiau Diweddaf, yn cael eu Dinoethi* (*Mysteries of the Saints of the Latter Days, Exposed*). Caernarvon: Thomas Jones Evans, 1852. 24 pages.

Hugh Jones, author of this pamphlet, had been with The Church of Jesus Christ of Latter-day Saints for two years before leaving. In his preface, dated 6 November 1852, Hugh Jones explains the reason behind his 24-page pamphlet:

> My conscience compelled me, to the extent possible, to undo whatever damage I was enabled to do by defending such an organization; and I have no way to do that except through the press.

Jones also expresses his wish for all who may read of his experience:

> I can only hope that the reading of the following pages will be a means of keeping those who may be as little children, from being led to such foolishness, and I am confident that it will be a means of opening the eyes of every honest person who may be among them, so that they may be able to flee from such a mortal sin.

Jones provides numerous details regarding his conversion and his two-year journey in his new faith. Over time, he wearied of the constant monetary collections imposed on him—for tithing, fast offerings, emigrating funds, temple funds, and the support of the district president. He had doubts about the Book of Mormon and the Doctrine and Covenants. He also questioned the comportment of some of the leaders. But it was the whisperings of the practice of polygamy in Utah that appear to have prompted him to leave the Church. For "the sake of fair play," Jones includes in his pamphlet a copy of the entire letter written by William Phillips to the editor of the *Times* and printed in the 15 October 1851 issue. In his letter Phillips states categorically,

> The polygamy of the Saints is an old story, and everyone can know that it is a lie just like its devil father.

Hugh Jones writes that "Mr. Phillips is concealing the truth in order to preserve his own character." And he concludes by saying that his two-year journey with The Church of Jesus Christ of Latter-day Saints was a "departure from the [true] path" and one that he regrets.

The only mention of the name of Hugh Jones in any Latter-day Saint publication is one in the 1852 volume of *Zion's Trumpet* for 16 October, just three weeks before the preface date of *Mysteries of the Saints*:

> President Simms, of the Anglesey Conference, wishes it to be known that Hugh Jones, a seller of varnish, etc., has been cut off from the Church, together with his wife.

MYSTERIES OF THE SAINTS

OF THE

LATTER DAYS,

EXPOSED.

BY HUGH JONES.

ONE WHO WAS A TEACHER IN THEIR MIDST FOR TWO YEARS.

CAERNARVON:

PRINTED BY THOMAS JONES EVANS,

1852

PREFACE.

DEAR COMPATRIOTS,

From serious consideration of the Apostolic counsel "When thou are converted, strengthen thy brethren," I wish to present this booklet to your attention.

I have been professing Mormonism, and I went to them with a sincere purpose; I had a desire to "go about pleasing God," and no sacrifice was too great for me to make to obtain the approval of the Infinite. But after living according to the most exact religious order as a Mormon, (or according to their own forename as a Latter-day Saint), I had the opportunity to become acquainted with their various procedures, with their deceit and their ungodliness, so that my conscience compelled me, to the extent possible, to undo whatever damage I was enabled to do by defending such an organization; and I have no way to do that except through the Press.

For years my whole soul was with the Mormons, and I could not help but consider it my obligation and duty to come out against them.

I have come to understand that at present I have been reproved by them: but I received a certificate of release from the Church (as they call it) in Liverpool, to the Church in Caernarvon, where I wished to come to be released, since it was there where I joined.

I can only hope that the reading of the following pages will be a means of keeping those who may be as little children, from being led to such foolishness, and I am confident that it will be a means of opening the eyes of every honest person who may be among them, so that they may be able to flee from such a mortal sin.

Sincerely yours,
HUGH JONES.

Caernarvon, November 6th, 1852.

SECRETS OF THE SAINTS, &c.

It is pleasant for the seaman to arrive at some port after being in peril in the midst of storms out on the fierce and tempestuous sea, even though he had been comforted in his prayer, and bore signs of hardship in his entire demeanor; nevertheless, since he is in port there is hope as he regathers his strength, and as he removes completely all the signs of hardship, and before long he will be as courageous as ever to undertake another voyage. That is to some extent a small portrayal of my own difficulties after being in the dangers of the doctrines and principles of the LATTER-DAY SAINTS,—it was a shipwreck of my Saintly faith. But through great mercy I have come to land safely, and I can do no less than kneel down on the beach of their deceitful secrets to thank God for my deliverance. If the seaman had lost his life in the storms he found himself in, the salvation of his soul would be safe notwithstanding, but for me my salvation was in danger, for I was in the storms of *false religious doctrines*. But since I have reached

6

the shore, I am confident of the mercy of the inhabitants who have brought me to some house, and have succored me, despite how pitiful I am. I have been greatly soiled, and everything I owned, except only my life, has been lost; and if I can but have a place at the hearth of some generous-hearted person, I shall sit by the fire to relate to the whole dear family the circumstances of this religious voyage.

A few years ago the "Saints," as they are called, came to the neighborhood where I was living, and great was the rush to listen to them, and in their midst I went; and because I had been a devout member for many years, and considered myself as being quite eager for knowledge, I supposed that it was necessary to have a change regarding several things that seemed inconsistent to me. And when the Saints came, and mentioned the same things that were in conflict in my mind, I said immediately, there they are—there are the people who preach the correct Gospel. And so for a time I reflected on this new teaching, since it was contrary to the teaching that I had received previously; and on every count I found it to be far superior; and at every opportunity I conversed with these strange preachers, until, in spite of myself, I had nearly devoured the teaching and was willing to sacrifice nearly everything I had on its altars. These preachers told me that they had received the Holy Ghost in its exceptional gifts—that they had been sent by it to preach—had been authorized to work miracles, and that whoever received their message—and believed their doctrines, and

7

conformed to all their customs, would receive the same, in the same way as they had; and that all the other sects, including the Nonconformist and the Established, were nothing but deceitful and unauthorized claimants; and to prove the truth of their assertions they showed me how contradictory to one another were all the religious denominations, and thus it was not possible for them to be of the truth, and have the Spirit, "For God is not the *author* of confusion, but of peace." And had I understood a particle of *logic* at that time, I would have immediately perceived that they were worse than *all the other sects* together, for they had started later and were opposed to them all!!

And thus they themselves were not of the truth, nor did they have the Spirit. They also told me that if the spiritual gifts were necessary at the beginning of the gospel they were just as necessary still, and that all who received *their* witness, and believed firmly *their* divine mission, would receive them, after being baptized by *them*, by the laying on of *their hands*. But, it does me no good to remain silent, to them I went. Upon perceiving the sameness of their doctrines with the scriptures, according to my judgment at that time, I believed that they were the true and only Church of God in this world, yes, I believed so strongly in their divine mission as the restorers of Christianity, that I was completely willing to deal with every reproach in my support for them. Then I was baptized (even though I had been baptized before. May the Lord forgive me for such mockery of his holy ordinance), and there I was in the true

8

Church of God, according to their assertions and my own opinion.

Having set my feet on the holy ground, I shall now make known what my eyes saw and what my hands felt, and what my ears heard about the secrets of the Saints of the Mormon religion, so that the reader can judge for himself about the customs of this dangerous class of believers.

Now we shall go to a gathering, or as it is commonly said a religious meeting of the Latter-day Saints. Everyone looks very devout, taking their seats in a mannerly and organized fashion, everyone quiet, soberly awaiting the President to enter; for every branch of the church has its President, who has the authority and wondrous influence over all the members. He possesses all inspiration,—every word he says is completely *infallible*, for he is under the direct leadership of the Holy Ghost. But here is another secret, much greater; this President is subject to another President, namely the Conference President, as he is called; namely a number of church branches gathered in a determined place; if the two Presidents cannot agree regarding each thing, the branch President *yields* to the opinion of the Conference President. Both Presidents are as spiritual as the other: and, consequently, as infallible: and when they happen to disagree with one another, and the junior President yields to the greater one, then it must of necessity be the infallible Spirit which has led the junior President astray!! After the President comes in, everyone appears to be remarkably happy; then some kind of hymn is sung and a

9

prayer is given; after that the President would stand up for a moment to instruct the Saints concerning their principles, and then the meeting was opened by the President in the name of Jesus Christ, i.e., taking hold of the authority which Jesus Christ gives to the Saints about everything. Then the evil spirits are commanded to go out of them. And now, since there are none there but true disciples under the guidance and direction, and influence of the Holy Ghost in all his gifts, the President declares that freedom is given to all who wish to prophesy, speak in strange tongues, interpret, sing, &c. And if no one is ready to take hold of this task within a minute, they begin to pray for the gifts. Someone prays for the gift of prophecy, and immediately it is given to him; another prays for the diversity of tongues, it is heard being spoken, and if there is no one there to interpret, that person must pray again for the gift of interpreting his tongues.

And now, reader, I know that many will be surprised when I tell you in total awareness that I myself have been under the influences of the above strange influences, yes, I prophesied, I spoke in diverse tongues, and also interpreted them: but I shall not reveal to you at the present time where the mystery is in this,—make your best guess, and if you fail to decide on it, I shall reveal it to you before you finish reading this booklet.

And after having reviewed all the achievements mentioned, there is one other very important and interesting thing to be brought forth, namely to prove and weigh how much religion everyone has—to

10

what degree their feelings extend for the gospel of Christ, and the criterion or *standard* that is used concerning the COLLECTIONS. They have a great number of different kinds of collections. One collection is made to support the Conference President, who is a kind of steward under the Holy Ghost, and is also a connection throughout the church branches, to determine whether they are firm in the faith, and to inform them of all the instructions that are received from the Salt Valley. The Conference Presidents are to be supported by the branches of the church which make up the *Conference* over which they preside.

They have another collection which is called the Emigrating fund. The purpose of this collection is to assist the poor members of the Saints to go to New Salem, in America, because they think that is where all natural and religious happiness come together,—the paradise of the Saints will be there, along with the imperial throne of Jesus Christ over a thousand years, when the most awful judgments will come down on Babylon, namely all the other parts of the world, for refusing the mission of heaven through means of the ministry of the Saints. Many of the Saints in Wales and England are intoxicated with the imaginings they have for happiness and the privileges of Mount Zion—this is the main focus of practically all of their *prophesying*—this is commonly the substance of their utterances with the strange tongues, if in fact the interpretation is accurate.

Another collection they have is for the building of the splendid and magnificent Temple in the place

11

of happiness they speak of. They expect the Son of God will come to this temple during the Millennium, and that his imperial throne will be placed therein. They considered themselves fortunate to have the privilege of contributing to the building of such a splendid work, although it is a topic to be doubted as to whether or not this collection is going to swim to distant America. (?)

There is another collection they have, namely the Fast. This is a monthly collection, and the way to receive it is as follows:—They refrain from lunch once a month, and they bring the worth of this meal that is missed in this way to the meeting, putting it at the feet of the Apostles, as it were: and according to the present signs an effort will be made to have this fast *weekly*, if not *daily* also before long. Besides this abstention from the lunch, they also abstain from intoxicating drinks, and from *tea* and *tobacco* and *snuff*, and they do so like this:—They calculate that this or that amount of drink is used weekly, and this or that amount of *tea* and *tobacco* and *snuff*; well, one must abstain from it, and bring the *full* worth of that which they used to consume of each one of them to the meeting, and take care not to deceive them whatever they might have been. This law caused much concern, especially because it was necessary for the older sisters to turn away their beloved cup of tea. Indeed, there is a very *whimsical* look on the occasional old and holy sister in the afternoons—her eyes red—her lips loose, and it is sometimes feared that her saintliness has almost changed her nature. I know of one, at least, who decided to put the Salt

12

Valley, and the splendid Temple, together with all her Saintliness at the same time in the *teapot,* as it is said in the North, and I can ascertain that the sister looks much more *hearty* in drinking water than I ever saw her when she was drinking the foolishness of the Saints. My dear reader will empathize with me, when I tell you that in the fervency of my fanatical zeal, I, myself, prepared a mound of gorse, near Cemaes, in Anglesey, as an altar on which, rather into which I offered up my chaw of tobacco and as much as was in it, and for about nine months I was ruled by complete abstinence.

They have another device for getting money, which is to sell a likeness of the President of Wales, as he is called, who is the general president over all the churches of the Saints in Wales. It is not believed that a blessing of any success will ever be in the houses of any of the Saints in Wales unless there is a likeness of this President there, as a watchman for them, to keep all the evil spirits away; for as the shadow of Peter gave healing to the sick, so it is that the likeness of this President keeps away pestilence, plagues, and devils. And besides all this, there are many incidental collections to pay for a visit with the Saints occasionally, and also there are rumors about *collecting tithing*, if the churches were to become more numerous, for that is already the procedure in the Valley. I can confirm that one must get from half a crown to a crown each week before he can come up with all these collections, and unless an effort is made to come up with them, such a one will not be a responsible and respectable Saint. And

13

besides all this there are so many wandering creatures under the names of preachers who come by so often, and unless you fill their empty spaces with tender mercies, you will not be a Saint worth a needle in their estimation. They claim to have authority from God to insist on receiving the belongings of the members. My wife told me that Mr. Phillips, under his title of the President of Wales, came to Caernarvon when I was not at home, and that he said that he had come to seek their *hearts and also their wealth*, and that he had authority from God to seek their wealth!! I suppose that had I been at home, I would have asked to see his *warrant*, or to have some proof of his authority. Poor man, had he taken all that was in our possession as a branch of the church he would not have been much better off. Would it not have been more suitable and appropriate for a man like him to have come more like a minister of Christ through this part of his presidency, than the way he came? He looked more like a secular *tyrant* than a Christian minister; he was adorned with beautiful chains, and rode in a splendid carriage, and he was sufficiently rude to demand the possessions of poor creatures who were barely able to get bread for their little children!!!

But after all this, one can hear the SAINTS boasting arrogantly as they preach that they preach Christ for free! There you have, fellow countrymen, their generosity. Now the secret has come to light for you, yes, there you have the secret for free, but it is expensive to me, heaven help me.

14

Now we must reveal something of the secret about their instruction and their doctrines. They do not recognize that the Bible is sufficient and suited for our circumstances in this age. There is a continual need for revelations from heaven, and to respond to this they profess to have such, and among other things they have books, which are suitable for the present age; one of them is the one they call the Book of Mormon. They pretend that this Book has been revealed to one Joseph Smith through the ministering of angels: but there are large parts of the book that have not yet been revealed, and they say that they will be revealed only when God sees fit to clarify them to his ministers, namely the Saints! The book "Doctrine and Covenants," as they call it, does not possess much less authority, which book contains all their rules of discipline. But this is a secret that cannot be perfectly deciphered, no doubt, until all secrets are revealed in the light of the great judgment, namely, that they are united concerning their disciplinary rules, they say, using discipline on *some*, and leaving others unpunished, even though they may have committed the same wicked deeds. Yes, I say *wicked*, and I know that the reader will agree with the phraseology, when I reveal to him the secret in this. They set forth in their own midst the necessity of calling on every male Saint to search for a female Saint to be his *holy wife*, before they go to the Valley and the holy Temple in America; they say it is lawful for them to search for her, and covenant with her before beginning their journey to there, whether they already have a lawful wife or not: and if they have a lawful

15

wife, she will be a *servant* to the holy wife after they have gone to the dwelling place of their saintliness beyond the Atlantic Ocean. And they permit every bed-associated practice to be carried on by the holy couple before they leave from their country, but to be careful that no one except the Saints knows about that. Concordant with this arrangement, a District President known to me acted in this holy manner as an infallible example for the group to which he belonged, and that was in Caernarvon, under her name; and whosoever feels in his heart a desire for additional affirmation in this regard, need only direct himself to me, in secret or in public, and he shall be satisfied, for *proven facts* are the burden of my witness, and not some cantankerous old wives' tales; for my primary purpose in writing these notes is to be of some help to others who are attracted to them, to reject them, as I am doing, through the great mercy of heaven. The aforementioned District President, after experiencing the graciousness of the holy woman, was so wise and evangelical as to acquaint another District President with the pleasures he had experienced, wishing for his infallible brother to have the same privileges, who, because of his great *interest* in the first President, who acted in the same manner as had his brother. And permit me to clarify the secret according to my motto; this is the person who revealed the truth to me of the things I now declare, the proper name of whom, out of kindness, I shall keep to myself for the time being, until such time as someone manifests disbelief in the truth of my declaration. Nevertheless, the lascivious acts of the first District

16

President I noted became public; and because of that they became sinful, and it was decided to excommunicate the brother, and so it was. But since the same acts of the other President have not become public, they are not a sin, and thus no discipline has been administered to him. The reader must understand, it is not that the Saints know things like these *about each other* that they are considered a *public* thing, but after the children of Babylon, namely everyone except for themselves, come to know of the matter, is it considered *public*, and thus it is necessary to turn the pages of the book of their confession, and administer discipline. In fact, how is it that the knowledge of *the world* about transgressions make them a sin, when the knowledge of the Saints themselves about the same thing does not make them a sin? The answer is instant,—that is the secret. They persuade the poor women that it will be the highest honor to bear children to populate the lovely Paradise in the *Salt Lake* after they go there, and that in that place there is now a host of *holy* women possessing the same blessed master. I have heard many times that the climate affects the moods, and causes the Saintly polygamy, so it must be that the tale has become *fact*; for when there are only *two* women in that land are of the same mind to make happy the same loving person, they will have the same moods which characterize the fateful region, so that they cannot deal with the thought of living together more than as phantoms, and if they happen to meet one another someplace, the Grammar of the Devil will be wielded by them with incomparable dexterity; but by the time

17

they go to California, all the surliness will suddenly be lost, so that dozens of them will consider it to be an honor to be jointly subjected to the same male master, jointly striving to sow Paradise with Saintly seeds, &c.

Not all laws, rules and practices of Mount Zion, passing traditionally from one official to the other, are written; and new rules in that land are always arriving, and among them came the rule of polygamy; and it is fitting for me to acknowledge that I receive every new rule, fully believing that they bring printed marks of divinity, without the least impulse of guilt, since I am until now a *conscientious Saint*. But when the unworthy behavior of the President which I noted came to my awareness, and when I heard that it was completely true, a spark of doubt ran through my mind, and it soon grew larger and larger until I became completely wretched in my feelings. I feared—I wondered—I questioned. What, I thought, has God changed, He who said, "Thou shalt not commit adultery?" or Jesus Christ, He who said, "Whosoever looketh on a woman to lust after her hath committed adultery with her already in his heart." How is Jesus Christ consistent with himself when he permitted different things for the Latter-day Saints than he permitted for the Saints of the former days? Instead of peace I felt bitter anger, unable to sleep, eat, or console myself in any way; I saw that I had sold my good name, and the wholesome principles I professed previously for erroneous stupidity; and I had only *one* position where I could find comfort, namely my hope that the corrupt

18

practice I have noted was not the *established rule* in the Valley, but what had happened to the President was a fall into impurity, and I did not know how in the world I could find out the truth. Now, in my affliction, I went to visit various counties of the North, and not one man on the face of the earth knew anything of the turmoil that was in my mind; and I had made a vow that I would *insist* on having the truth about the matter, and if the President had slipped into sin I was determined to disclaim him, and adhere to my faith, but if that was the rule in the Valley, I had already determined their fate, namely that their entire religion was nothing but deceitful fiction, and that I would withdraw from them, and that I would proclaim their fraud to the world.

Now, on the journey that I had dreamed about, I visited the President of the District closest to the one in which I knew that, in my opinion, its President had fallen, but I did not reveal to him anything of my predicament; rather I pretended to be a thorough Saint, willing to receive all of the traditions that would be taught to me by the Inspired Presidents. And very fortunately because of my errand, he explained that the aforementioned President had *started to use* the light of the dispensation of love, supposing that I knew nothing; and he explained that he himself had also acted in the same manner, declaring that the other had blessed him with the blessed light on this new *science.* But if it was bad at first, it got worse,—by this time I was so uncomfortable in my feelings that at times I was afraid to fall into other extremes, namely to deny that not *every kind* of religious inspiration

19

was nothing but madness, and that there was no worse animal than man, &c. I went on my way again, and I visited Liverpool; and there I quickly went to visit some brethren with whom I was acquainted. And on one morning as I was pondering on the strange teaching that was on my mind, although I had not yet revealed any doubt about its divinity, I met with a church official, i.e., the church of the Saints, and this one had a good name, since he had served at that time for twenty years, and he was completely acquainted with all the rules of the Valley, and in whatever he said he was an oracle for the whole church; and knowing all these things, now I seized the opportunity, as if I could in some way grab hold of the chief objective to which I referred through all things, namely the Truth. Now we went for a walk along the *Docks*; and I failed to understand how to lead up to the topic that was on my mind; I was afraid to show him my doubt, lest he hide the secrets from me; however, in no time at all, after beginning our walk, he asked me what I thought of the "*holy wife.*" Now, since everything had become *noble*, I said that I did not know for sure, but that I was willing to receive everything that was received from the Valley, and from them, the Officials—and I asked whether that was the rule in the Valley. Then he assured me that it was. And furthermore, he told me that I could, quite within the rules, make a covenant with any woman before going to Mount Zion, namely the Salt Valley, in California. And he explained to me that I would need to keep this secret to myself. And he asked me what I thought with respect to such and such a woman. I said that I

20

considered her to be virtuous. After this conversation I went home while pondering over the matter, and I loathed such detestable behavior in a man who was one of the Elders of the Church of God, (but my reader will forgive me, the Church of the devil I should have said), and he arranged for a room for her in the same town where he lived, namely Liverpool, although he had a wife at the time; and he adopted one of her children (for she was a widow) for himself, and he took it to his own home.

I saw a letter in the 'Times,' for October 15th, 1851, from Mr. W. Phillips, the President of Wales, attempting to defend the Saintly system; and I include it in this treatise for the sake of fair play to all to judge for themselves, but at the same time I bear witness that polygamy is taught generally in the Valley. Here is the letter:—

Mr. Editor—Be so honest as to receive a defense as well as accusations relating to the Latter-day Saints, by providing space for the following:—At present some of the publications of the country are making quite a commotion about the polygamy of the Mormons. They claim to have received a letter from someone who discovered that President Brigham Young has about twenty-five wives; and some say that Capt. D. Jones also has the same number, while others testify that he has two, and that one of them is a "spiritual wife," which he took from Carmarthenshire. The person who says this is an eye witness, say the publications; but they are afraid to give his name. The polygamy of the Saints is an old story, and everyone can know that it is a lie just like its devil father. We think that the "spiritual wife" is Mrs. Lewis, formerly from Kidwelly, who emigrated at the same time as Capt. Jones, leaving her husband and her sister behind to settle some legal matters, which were still unfinished at the time of the emigration; and since Mrs. Lewis had arranged for space on a ship for her family, and to prepare everything, her husband and her sister agreed to remain behind until the next emigration, in order to receive some other money that was coming to them. Her husband and her sister ended up emigrating with the first ship after her; and we understand that they have joined with the family in the Valley. This is not the first lie about Brigham Young and

21

Capt. Jones, neither will it be the last. Those who wish to know with certainty in relation to the truth, let them read the following from the "Doctrine and Covenants," page 300—"Inasmuch as the church of Christ has been shamed as being guilty of the transgression of adultery and polygamy, we proclaim that we believe that one man should have but one wife, and one woman but one husband, except in the case of death, when the one and the other are at liberty to marry a second time." Read also Doctrine and Covenants, page 115—"Thou shalt love thy wife with all thy heart, and shalt cleave unto her and none else; and he that looketh upon a woman to lust after her shall deny the faith, and shall not have the Spirit; and if he repents not he shall be cast out. Thou shalt not commit adultery; and he that committeth adultery, and repenteth not, shall be cast out; but he that has committed adultery and repents with all his heart, and forsaketh it, and doeth it no more, thou shalt forgive; but if he doeth it again, he shall not be forgiven, but shall be cast out." Read also, page 300—"Marriage should be performed with prayer and thanksgiving; and in the performance, the persons who are to be married are to stand side by side to one another, the man on the right hand, and the woman on the left, and an address will be given by the one performing the marriage as he is directed by the Holy Ghost; and if there are no lawful objections, he can say, calling each one by name, 'You two agree to be friends with one another, as husband and wife, respecting the lawful rights of this condition; that is, to keep yourself entirely for one another, and away from all others, throughout your lives." And after they answer, "We do," they can be proclaimed husband and wife, (and not, husband and wives) in the name of the Lord Jesus Christ, and through the power of the laws of the land and the authority that he possesses; may God increase his blessings and keep you to fulfill your covenants from now on and through eternity. Amen." Polygamy is something that is not tolerated in the church, and neither the president nor anyone else is to practice it. It is contrary to the confession of our faith. I have been in this church for eight years, and I have never heard such a teaching, and it is a pity that we are wrongly treated, and we are determined not to suffer more. We have respect for you and your publication, as long as it contains truth, but the lies that are in it are repugnant to us, and we counsel you to prevent such writings of your correspondents lest you yourself receive grief because of them.

Yours sincerely,
WILLIAM PHILLIPS,

14, Castle Street, Merthyr Tydfil.

22

Now, reader, with respect to the foregoing letter, I testify that I have been a member with the Mormons as has Mr. Phillips, but that he is the President of Wales, and I am a Teacher in their midst, and that Mr. Phillips is concealing the truth in order to preserve his own character. But I can confirm that *adultery* is being practiced secretly in their midst, and

> "He who denies this, so be it,
> "Will deny that the sun is risen."

The aforementioned authority requests that "we believe all spirits unless we test the spirits." The Saints claim the above authority. You claim that you are the only authorized teachers, and that you have received revelations from God! That only yours is the Apostolic Church, and that you, the ministers of this Church, only, possess the only authority from God,—that all others are Babylonians. I tested the spirit that supposedly was bestowed on me and which was to give me such spirituality as this,—I searched earnestly for your spirituality—your assertions did not work for me—I did not want "the speech of them which are puffed up, but their power." The apostle Paul showed *signs of his apostleship* in powerful works and wonders; I failed to ever have proof of your succession. The Savior proved his authority to forgive sins, by saying to the lame man suffering from paralysis, "rise and walk" in the presence of eyewitnesses. But I was with you several times visiting with the sick, and I myself was near death, and even though five Elders placed their hands on me and anointed me with oil, I finally had to

23

proclaim that you were deceitful spirits, and false teachers.

I told you, my reader, that I had been under strange influences, namely prophesying, &c., and that I have to inform you that I had made every effort to obtain the Spirit in its several gifts. But finally, they began to overwhelm me, after understanding through their teaching how to begin. One person told me to just begin speaking, whatever came to my mind at the time, if only "*Rock and hole*," and I was in considerable confusion because of that, how to reconcile such *chaos* that the Saints were demanding that I engage in; in truth I was in the same circumstance as was the Doctor when he told his assistant, "Imagination heals and imagination kills." So, my reader, I must say that imagination is everything that relates to the miraculous or spiritual gifts that are in practice among the Saints. I know that many famous, responsible, and truthful men, have imagined many foolish things about themselves; such as the famous Irving, he who supposed himself able to speak in an exotic tongue—and that he could interpret it for others—and also you will remember the venerable Doctor Watts, when once he imagined that he had swallowed a Cobbler—and there was nothing that would persuade him to desist from this strange belief, until one afternoon the doctor went to an old shoemaker who was working near his home, and the shoemaker said that the Doctor believed that he had swallowed him, and he asked the Cobbler if he would be so kind as to come with him to his room, and secure himself under the Doctor's bed that night, and to be sure to put his apron in front of him; and when the doctor

24

said that he would give an *emetic* to the sick person so he would throw up, he instructed the Shoemaker to be ready to come out from under the bed, and crawl across the room toward the door, and thus it happened, when the Doctor cried out, "There he is!! There he is!!" And he was perfectly sound from that minute on. Thus it was with me, reader, it was all my imagination. "I departed from the path"—I left the true doctrine taught to me by my Fathers, and I completely disavowed their teachings, "and I did my best in every way, to cause many others to transgress the law," to turn from the truth, to old wives' tales, the Mormons.

The wisdom and conscience of the country has awakened against Mormonism—the church and the clergy are like the rich man in the parable, dressing in purple and fine linen and having the good life in daily abundance, at the expense of the hard-working misfortunates, and who have always been more of a stumbling-block on the way of the temporal and spiritual well-being of the people than anything else—the church and the teachers who at the present time are doing all they can to bind the nation by the feet and hands, and transfer it to the possession and authority of the darkness and superstitions of Mormonism. Just as sure as you are deceitful pretenders, and that the principles you attempt to teach to the people through your sermons, and through the mouths of the two disasters —'Star of the Saints'—and the 'Deseret News,' are the "doctrines of devils" as sure as this, I saw, the day of visitation of your church is at the door.

THOMAS JONES EVANS, PRINTER, CAERNARVON.

Pamphlet 12

Thomas Hughes. *Darlithiau ar Dwyll Mormoniaeth: Darlith I* (*Lectures on the Deceit of Mormonism: Lecture 1*). Rhuthin: Isaac Clarke, 1852. 16 pages.

This pamphlet is the printing of the first lecture given by Thomas Hughes (using the nom de plume "T. ab Gwilym") at the Rhuthin town hall on 3 September 1852. His intent was to present a total of six lectures on the following topics:

1. Exposing the deceit of the beginning of Mormonism
2. The opinion of the Saints about God, angels, and the souls of man
3. The Spiritual Gifts—the belief and claims of the Saints about them
4. The belief of the Saints about preaching to the spirits in prison and baptism for the dead
5. The Bible is the only standard of faith and conduct of man, and there is no basis to expect new revelation.
6. The primary objective of the prophet Joseph Smith and his apostles through this deceit was to establish an earthly kingdom in America for their own benefit and worldly glory.

Hughes declared at the outset:

> After delivering the stated lectures, I am confident that I will have painted a very accurate picture of the monstrousness of Mormonism; and it is not impossible that a clear look at the corrupt system may perhaps give fright to a few saints to come to the point of shouting, "Who will deliver me from this society of suffering?"

In this first lecture, Hughes quotes substantially from the writings of Orson Pratt and then explains why Pratt is mistaken in his assertions. Hughes also borrows heavily from a 70-page booklet by John Bowes entitled *Mormonism Exposed*.

In addition to the printing of his first lecture, only the pamphlet that resulted from Hughes's second lecture has been identified. See Pamphlet 15. Also see Episode 9.8.

LECTURES

ON THE

DECEIT OF MORMONISM.

LECTURE I.

On the deceit of the Beginning of Mormonism:

Which was delivered in the RUTHIN TOWN HALL, September 3rd, 1852,

By THOMAS HUGHES, (T. ab Gwilym.)

R. EDWARDS, ESQ., SOLICITOR, IN THE CHAIR.

"Prove all things: hold fast that which is good."

Mr. CHAIRMAN, &c.

At the request of a number of respectable men, and after the promise that we made, I stand up now to address you with respect to the "new teaching" that is called Mormonism, which is upheld by the men who erroneously call themselves "Latter-day Saints."

Since I am unable to trace this deceitful sect in all its component parts in one lecture, I intend to deliver six lectures on the various topics which this sect appears to be divided into by nature. The first lecture, namely the one that will be delivered tonight, contains chiefly *The exposure of the deceit of the beginning of Mormonism.*

The 2nd, *On the opinion of the Saints about God, angels, and the soul of man.*

The 3rd, *On the Miraculous Gifts,—the opinion and claims of the Saints pertaining to them.*

The 4th, *On the opinion of the Saints about Preaching to the spirits in prison, and baptism for the dead.*

Lecture I, Price 2c.—I. Clarke, Agraffydd, Rhuthin.

2

The 5th, *That the Bible is the only standard of faith and way of life of man, and that the world has no base for expecting new revelation.*

The 6th, *That the chief objective of the prophet Smith and his apostles for this deceit, was to establish an earthly kingdom in America, for personal gain and worldly glory.*

After delivering the stated lectures, I am confident that I will have painted a very accurate picture of the monstrousness of Mormonism; and it is not impossible that a clear look at the corrupt system may perhaps give fright to a few saints to come to the point of shouting, "Who will deliver me from this society of suffering."

Since I am but a lay person, having never been in a church order, perhaps there may be some ready to ask, "What is your reason for writing about my religious practices?" I shall answer, because it is the duty of every man to read, seek, and defend the truth. Religiousness, any more than irreligiousness, is not the base for his duty; but his relationship with his Creator as a *creature*, and the natural aptitude that is in him to perform his duty, together with his possessing sufficient means to acknowledge his duty. Beelzebub, the father of lies, has as much duty to defend the truth, as does Gabriel the archangel. Thus, the irreligious is on the same ground with respect to *duty* as is the religious. Therefore, it is not appropriate for the saints to condemn me for doing this part of my duty, namely, defending that which I believe to be true, against the deceit of Mormonism. The saints insist that the various Ministers of the Christian world have no divine authority to minister; that they have come to the inhabitants of the world as "prophets of Ahab, with lies in their mouths, to deceive them, to devour them, and to destroy them." Orson Pratt, one of their apostles, says, "O ye Ministers of the Christian world—ye enemies of new revelation! How can ye escape the damnation of hell! How many millions of good, honest-hearted people you have deceived by your cunning craftiness, and lying hypocrisies! How many millions would have called upon God, in faith, for revelations, prophecies, visions, and the ministry of angels, and received these precious blessings, had it not been for the wicked, most abominable, and soul-destroying lies, which you have instilled into their ears by telling them that these things were repealed and done away."* Since that is the characteristic of all the respected and

*See "*To expect more Revelation is not unreasonable*," by Orson Pratt, page 16.

3

godly Ministers of the entire Christian world, are not they and I, in the view of the saints, on the same irreligious ground? We are all hypocrites, with the curse of God hanging above our heads; and we have only some horrible expectation of the damnation of hell with one another in the end!

In this manner, everyone sees the unreasonableness of the saints in refusing to defend their doctrines when they are attacked by lay persons, under the pretext that they are not in church orders, when at the same time they believe that all the Ministers of the various religious denominations of the world are as far removed from the church order as is the devil himself. When such disrespect and insult are thrown on all the nations of the world, and especially on the entire Christian and religious world, for refusing the heretical doctrines of Mormonism, is it not time for all of us, as reasonable creatures, to make the mightiest effort to expose the false doctrines, to keep the poisonous tares from being sown in the fields of Christianity! All the powerful machines of the press and the pulpit should be ignited more widely on the castles of these false prophets, so that neither Balak nor Balaam can build altars to blaspheme and curse Israel.

To expose Mormonism, so that all may see it in its own shape and color, is my objective through the Lectures which I shall deliver in your hearing, if I have life and health; and I am confident that all will listen attentively, ponder seriously on what is said, and judge for themselves, whether Mormonism is based on the truth.

Now to the point. The founders of this sect were a man by the name of Joseph Smith, son of a farmer by the same name, in Palmyra, state of New York, America, and one by the name of Sidney Rigdon, a printer, who was also a lay preacher. We have a printed affidavit,* signed by 51 names of respectable and reputable men, who knew Smith and his parents over a period of several years, who jointly testify that there was no family more disreputable, immoral, and wicked, in the neighborhood where they lived, than the family of the false prophet Smith, especially his father and himself;—that they were superstitious dreamers;—that they spent the greatest part of their time searching for buried treasure;—and that many of the excavations in that neighborhood were seen as signs of the weakness of their minds. Although there was not one sign in the character of Smith that anyone would suppose him to be a prophet, or the son of a prophet, rather a son of the devil; yet

*"*Mormonism exposed,*" by Bowes.

4

he could stand resolutely before the world, although the sign of the beast was on his forehead, and claim that he was a prophet of God! and, surprisingly, he won over thousands to believe his presumptuous assertions, and to follow him through fame and disrepute, respect and disrespect, yes, even to death! But listen to the story which Smith gives about himself—his conversion—his call to the exalted office as prophet of the latter days—and obtaining the Book of Mormon in mount Cumorah.

When he was about fourteen or fifteen years old, (according to his own account to his followers,) he was in doubt with respect to his soul, and wanted to be qualified to face the other world; and since religious opinions of the world were contradictory with each other, he could not know which path he should take. In that quandary, the only thing that seemed reasonable to him was to read the Scriptures, and strive to follow their direction. And when he was reading the Bible in this manner, he found that verse,—"If any of you lack wisdom, let him ask of God, that giveth to all men liberally, and upbraideth not; and it shall be given him." James i. 5. He felt such happiness on reading the aforementioned verse, thinking that if he asked God he would have certainty as to which church and which doctrines were from God. He retreated to a secret place in a grove near his father's house, and he began to pray earnestly, earnestly, and while he was calling on the name of the Lord, and wishing eagerly for an answer from God, he saw a very bright light that appeared above him; and as he continued in prayer, that light descended gradually, until Smith feared the grove would ignite the minute it touched the tops of the trees; but when he saw that that effect would not take place, he was heartened to think that he could withstand its presence. That brilliant light continued to descend gradually until it reached the ground, and Smith enveloped in its midst. Some strange feeling went through him, and he fell into a vision. While in that vision, he saw two glorious beings standing face to face with him, who said to him that his sins were forgiven,—that none of the religious denominations of the world were of God,—that they all preached erroneous doctrine, and he was commanded to join none of them—that the true doctrine, the gospel in its fulness would be made known to him at some future time. It is said that he had several such visits from time to time, until at length he had the aforementioned visit from an angel of God, in his bedroom, telling him that the Indians in America were the remnant of Israel,—that they were

5

an educated, magnificent people, with many privileges, when they first went to America—that their priests and their governors kept records of their history and their teachings; but since they had fallen away from the faith into great wickedness, that the biggest part of them had been destroyed, but not before a prophet by the name of Mormon had prepared an abridgment of their political history and their religious beliefs. Smith was told that that abridgement still existed, buried in the earth, and that he was the instrument chosen by God to retrieve it from the earth, and to preach its contents to the world. It was also made known to him that that Abridgement contained several prophecies pertaining "to these latter days," and instructions for "gathering the saints together" into a temporal and spiritual kingdom, as advance preparation for the second coming of the Messiah, which was soon to take place. After several visions, wherein he received numerous instructions the previous night, an angel appeared to him on the morning of the 22nd of September, 1823, when he was at work, and commanded him to go to the hill Cumorah to see the *plates*. After digging for a while, and retrieving a closed stone chest with a light lever, he had a look at the carved volume which Moroni, the son of Mormon, had hidden 1400 years earlier in the bosom of the hill! As he gazed and marveled in wonder at the gold plates, behold, an angel of the Lord stood before him, and he was filled with the Holy Ghost,—the heavens opened, and the glory of the Lord shone around him and rested on him. When he stood, gazing and wondering, the angel said to him, 'Look!' and immediately he saw the prince of darkness surrounded by a numberless host of devilish escorts. The angel said that the evil and the good—the glory of God and the force of darkness, were being shown to him, so that he would henceforth recognize the two forces, and that he would not be influenced or overcome by the evil one.

Smith was not to receive the hidden volume at that time, but in four years from that same morning, on the 22nd of September 1827, was when he received the *plates* from the hand of the angel, together with two transparent stones, that were called the ancient "*Urim and Thummin,*" which were hidden together with the *plates* in the hill, through the instrumentality of which, by divine inspiration, Smith was to translate into the English language the Egyptian *hieroglyphics* that were carved on the *plates*, which were held together as a book with three rings.

6

That is a brief account, according to the tale of Smith and his followers, of the conversion of the prophet and the circumstances surrounding them until the coming forth of the Book of Mormon from the closed chest in the hill Cumorah.

Now for the *grand secret!* Whether or not the smooth-tongued tale you have just heard is the truth or whether it is deceit? I shall tell you, in contrast to Smith's tale, a fact that the saints cannot disprove, which is as clear as the light of the sun, that the deceit of Mormonism is a "lying secret."

In the year 1809, there was a man by the name of Solomon Spaulding living in Cherry Vale, the state of New York. He was an educated man, having been trained in a University, and a notable man with respect to his taste for history, well known in the *classics*, which was a particular advantage for him to select strange names. He took a great interest in all things ancient, and he was a man of very lively *imagination*. This man went to live in New Salem, Ashtabula County, Ohio. There were in that town several bare mounds with ancient fortresses in ruins; and many supposed that they were old dwelling places that belonged to an old and primitive nation which at that time had perished. From the ground many instruments and weapons were discovered that exhibited great skill in workmanship. This caused a remarkable interest among the settlers, and investigations into the histories of the periods, and heated debates as to the identity of the skilled nation who had created them. Many believed that the Indians of North America were the descendants of the ten lost tribes of Israel. That common opinion had a strong influence on the mind of Mr. Spaulding, that the belief among the people would make a good foundation for a *Romance*. Since his health was weak, and to amuse himself during the hours of his retirement, he threw himself into the work of writing an imaginary history of the lost tribes. He took three years to write it, and he called the composition "*The Manuscript Found*." This tale professed to give a detailed account of the journey of the ten tribes of Jerusalem, on land and on sea, until they landed in America, under the leadership of Nephi and Lehi. Mr. Spaulding wrote his tale as closely as he could according to the *style* of the Bible.

Mormon, and Moroni his son, names of great importance throughout the Book of Mormon, are two of the personifications used by Mr. Spaulding in his imaginary tale.

7

As the writer went forward with this tale, his neighbors used to come to his house to listen to readings of the various parts he wrote. His wife, his brother, his neighbors, and various other friends, as they heard him from time to time in reading his tale, became well acquainted with its contents and with the strange names he used in it.

Sometime after finishing his tale, Mr. Spaulding and his family moved to Pittsburg, Pennsylvania, where he became acquainted with an old friend by the name of Patterson, who was a printer and bookseller there, and also the editor of a newspaper. Mr. Spaulding presented his tale to the attention of his friend, who greatly praised it, and told the author that if he could write a foreword and the *title page*, he would print it. Mr. Spaulding declined to do that, for he did not ever wish to see that which he had written by way of an imaginary history in print.

The aforementioned manuscript was in the possession of Patterson the printer for a long period of time. In the meanwhile Sidney Rigdon (the man I noted as the associate of Smith in the work of establishing Mormonism,) who was at the time working as a printer in the printing business of Patterson, became familiar with the manuscript, and according to the acknowledgement of Rigdon himself, he made a copy of it. Sometime after this, the manuscript was returned to its author, who, after moving to Amity, Washington county, died there in the year 1816. Consequently, the manuscript came into possession of his wife, who carefully kept it.

After the Book of Mormon was printed, a woman came to New Salem to preach about it. (As you heard, it was in New Salem that Mr. Spaulding had previously lived, and it was there also where he wrote his imaginary tale.) As that missionary read and related large parts of the Book of Mormon, many of the old inhabitants who were in that meeting were surprised that the revelation, or the new Bible of the Mormons, about which there had been so much talk, was in the historical part of it none other than the *imaginary tale of their old friend Mr. Solomon Spaulding!!* Mr. John Spaulding was present, and he recognized the work of his brother immediately. He stood on his feet in grief and sadness, weeping copious tears, upon thinking that the writings of his deceased brother had been used to such an evil purpose, and he explained the execrable deceit to the meeting. New Salem was disturbed throughout; a meeting was called by the inhabitants,

8

and Dr. Philastus Hurlbut was appointed to compare the Book of Mormon with the imaginary tale of Mr. Spaulding, who without delay brought the deceit to light.

At one time Dr. Hurlbut was a follower of Smith, and a member of the church of the saints; but as he says about himself, "he left them when his eyes were opened to see the deceit and the allurement to which he had once fallen victim."*

Mrs. Spaulding testified in a long letter, which has been printed, to the truth of all this. And Mr. John Spaulding took an oath to confirm the truth of the same thing.

Now, friends, you can see clearly from this, that the Book of Mormon is a deceitful stratagem, fashioned between Smith and Rigdon, on the foundation of Spaulding's imaginary tale, in order to benefit and promote themselves! These fanatics were the columns on which the Mormon system was raised up. These are the *Architects* who devised the plan to make a new Bible from Spaulding's tale, by mixing the Scriptures from the Old Testament and the New, together with their own foolish imaginings!!

After composing the Book of Mormon according to their whims, it was necessary to design and play a trick before opening the Mormon *Exhibition* to the world. It appears that the trick was for Smith to play the part of Muhammed. Just as Muhammed claimed to have received the Koran from the hand of an angel in a cave, so the impostor Smith claimed to have received the Book of Mormon secretly on mount Cumorah! It was in a cave that Muhammed was anointed as prophet for the world; in a secret corner of a shady grove the American Muhammed was anointed as prophet of "these latter days!" The Asian Muhammed says he was taken up through some seven heavens, and that he saw in one night, under the guidance of the angel Gabriel, all the wonders of the heavenly borders; so the American Muhammed saw all the heavens opening above him,—angels ascending and descending to him,—that he had witnessed inexpressible things—that the Lord himself had left his throne and come down to him to speak with him face to face, as some emperor speaks with his prime minister! That he had seen legions of hellish demons at the same time, a larger army than that of Napoleon when he first went to Russia.

See "*The Mormons*," pages 31 and 33.

9

No doubt it was the account of the Asian Muhammed which motivated Smith or Rigdon with the idea to play this bungling trick.

You have heard that "*The Manuscript Found*," was the name that Spaulding gave to his tale; you see the use the prophet Smith made of that by adopting the same idea,—"*The Plates Found*," after being buried in the hill for 1400 years!

The saints claim that Smith's translation of the found *plates* is the Book of Mormon; but when they are called on to show them to the world, so that we can have proof of the truthfulness of the alleged translation by seeing the original engravings of Mormon, this is what their impudent response is to us,—"no one can see them and live!" Moses showed the engraved tablets of the first law to the Israelites—the world and the church were able to see the original writings of the Evangelists and the Apostles; but the deceitful cause of the saints cannot tolerate scrutiny, because Smith did not have the alleged *plates* to show; this is clear from the proof I gave of the manner in which the Book of Mormon was composed. Therefore, it is obvious that part of the trick which Smith deemed necessary to play on the world before printing his accursed book is the claim that it was a translation of the *plates* found, combined with the threat of death for those who attempted to see the *plates* in order to have proof of their existence. It is true that eleven names are associated with the Book of Mormon, despite the death threat, as witnesses who had seen the *plates*. Three of these witnesses were Smith's father and two brothers, and five of his neighbors by the name of Whitmer. It is a notable fact that the more part of these witnesses had turned their backs on the Mormon church, and that in the year 1849 not so much as *one* of them still belonged to the saints! What, therefore, do you think of the testimony of such men, when they say that God had given to them sure knowledge that the Book of Mormon had been translated through the divine spirit and that they knew it was true? There is no need to waste time with further scrutiny concerning the characters of these witnesses,—the proof already given of the fraud of Mormonism, together with proofs that will yet be brought forward, is sufficient to show that the men who participated in the same *plot* were bound to fall amid the ruin of the Book of Mormon as did the Philistines of old when they were buried in the ruins of that house, when Samson leaned against its columns.

10

Some old Welsh proverbs say—"One who tells lies must have a good memory;"—"the guiltless will have the truth." No wonder, then, that Smith says of himself, with the first printing of the Book of Mormon in the year 1830—"THE AUTHOR AND PROPRIETOR!!" In doing this, Smith *forgot* about the tale of the *Plates* found, and he was *guiltless* enough to let the "cat out of the bag." If he was the *Author* of the book, how could he say that the engraved *plates* of Mormon were a *translation*? Some of the apostles of the saints, in seeing the weakness and foolishness of their prophet, tell the truth so bare to the world, after leaving out "*The Author and Proprietor*" from the following printings!! Nevertheless, they cannot ever delete the influence of the fraud from the mind of every man of wisdom and judgment.

It is not impossible that Smith had some engraved plates prepared to show to the superstitious fools,—that is quite likely, as the following fact will make plain.

Martin Harris, one of the first followers of the prophet, a man who possessed considerable wealth, felt the great need to see the *plates* found; but Smith told him that he "was not sufficiently pure of heart to see such treasures," but that he would give him a *transcript* of one of them to satisfy him! Martin Harris took that transcript from Palmyra to New York to Professor Anthon, a man renowned in all scholarship, and very well known as such in Europe and America, to obtain the opinion of the learned Professor about it before selling his possessions, which was his intention to do, to enable the prophet to print the Book of Mormon. Here is the opinion of Professor Anthon about that transcript:—"It is obvious that it has been prepared by some person who had before him a book containing various alphabets of various languages. The Greek and Hebrew letters, crosses and flourishes, Roman letters inverted or placed sideways, were arranged in perpendicular columns, and the whole ended in a rude delineation of a circle divided into various compartments, decked with various strange marks, and evidently copied after the Mexican Calendar given by Humboldt, but copied in such a way as not to betray the source whence it was derived."*

In light of all these clear proofs, who but those to whom was given "solid error so they would believe a lie," would not see the Mormon fraud through it! But despite how clear the fraud appears in the manifestation of the proofs I have noted, and despite

* "*The Mormons*," page 28.

11

how great is the contempt the saints show for the Bible in their sermons, their conversations, and their writings, they challenge the world to prove that Mormonism is fraud by "the word and the witness." Although I do not believe that they have any true respect for the Bible, nor any belief in it as the word of God, yet, since they appeal to the Bible, it is to the Bible they have to go, "and if they speak not according to this word, it is because there is no light in them."

Now I take it for granted, and give that advantage to the saints, that they, like us, believe that the Bible is truth. Thus, here we have a standard or an infallible law agreed on, to prove further and more definitely the fraud of Mormonism in this court.

Everyone admits that the truth is ONE; consequently, if the Book of Mormon and the Bible are at odds with each other with respect to their doctrines, it must be, according to all reason, that one of the two is untrue; or it must be that God contradicts himself by saying one thing through a series of Prophets and Apostles in Asia,—that which is contained in the Bible; and saying contrary to that through a number of prophets and apostles in America, that which is contained in the Book of Mormon, and the revelations of Smith and the Latter-day Saints.

Our first investigation can be, What does the truth say about God. This is what the Bible says, "God is a Spirit." John iv. 24. A being without any of the attributes of material essential to him; and with respect to his immortal attributes, omniscient, omnipresent, almighty, and eternal; without a "shadow of turning with him;" "the same yesterday, today, and forever." But the Book of Mormon, the prophet Smith, and the apostles of the saints are perfectly contrary to this. The Book of Mormon says that God is *substance* with respect to his essence; that he has a body "of flesh and blood!"* although Christ says clearly that "a *spirit* hath not flesh and bones, as ye see me have." What is God? asks the prophet Smith, in the *Millennial Star*, volume vi, and then he answers,—"An intelligent being, organized, and useful, having a body and parts. He is in the form of a man, and, in fact, he is of the same species as man. This being cannot be in two different places at the same time; therefore, he cannot be omnipresent." The apostle Orson Pratt says,—"When we speak of the spirit of God, extending through all space, we do not mean that it absolutely fills every minute portion of space, for if this were the case, there would be no room for any other matter. Therefore, the Spirit exists in different parts of

*"*Book of Mormon*," page 521.

12

space in greater or less degrees of density, like heat, light, or *electricity.** I suppose that this is sufficient to convince every reasonable creature that the Mormon doctrines are perfectly contrary to the clear teachings of the Bible about God, and thus bound to be untruth and deceit.

The Bible says with respect to the Creation, that God has *created* everything "through the word of his power." But Mormonism says that all the elements of matter exist like God himself for all eternity; that to say that God has created everything from nothing is nonsense. If the opinions of the saints are true, the witnesses of the Bible are bound to be untrue. But if it is the Bible that is true, the contrary witnesses of the saints about the creation are baseless assertions, and thus are complete deception. The saints and the chief atheists of the world are of the same mind on this topic. Voltaire and Mirabeau believed, as well as all the atheists of the various ages of the world, in the eternal existence of matter. Should not the saints be ashamed that they have no other foundation for their opinions than atheism!

With respect to the position of man's probation, the Bible says that "*now* is the accepted time,"—that "*now* is the day of salvation." That the season of life is the limits of man's hope for salvation: "Where the tree falls, there it will remain." But Mormonism teaches the opposite of this,—"that forgiveness is to be given in the world to come;" that "all must hear the gospel either in this world or in the world to come;" that "it is clear that Christ, while his body lay in the grave, went to the world of the spirits to proclaim freedom to the captives and open the prison for those who were bound;" "we who are on the earth must be baptized for the dead who believe from time to time in the world of the spirits;" "that God reveals those in the other world who believe, and has appointed places of baptism in his temple for administering the ordinance of baptism for them on the earth;" that "those who are baptized for the dead can be considered *saviors* for those dead, since they *release them on the earth from their sins!*" That "some pay their debt earlier than others, and therefore, the opening of the prison cannot be proclaimed at the same time;" "'those who were once disobedient,' (namely, the antediluvians,) were all imprisoned at the same time, and for the same transgression; and in the days of the crucifixion of Jesus Christ it appears that they had paid the 'last farthing,' otherwise Jesus would not have gone to them to preach liberty and the opening of the prison." That

*"*Absurdities of Immaterialism,*" page 25.

13

"many spirits are in prison still, and within many days (perhaps) they will be visited." And here is the honey which the fanatical saints extract from these "devilish doctrines,"—"O, how lovely is the thought that our revered forefathers, those who died without hearing the gospel, are in so much hope of yet being saved, as if they were on the earth now."*

In this manner, you will see clearly that Mormonism is contrary to the Bible about the essential nature of the Godhead—about his work of creation—about the probationary state of man, and statements of the intercessory order. Therefore, I appeal to all of you, as just jurors, must not Mormonism be *deceit*? I am confident that your unanimous verdict is,—"*Let God be truthful, and every man a liar*."

I wish to call your further attention to the harmony that exists between *Mormonism* and *Catholicism*. The Pope is the head of the Roman church, and the ruler of the state institution. So was the prophet Smith, and is Brigham Young, his successor, on the church and the state institution of the saints in Deseret. The Pope claims infallibility; so do the saints—they speak as moved on by the Holy Spirit: *they cannot* err. The Pope and his cardinals say there is no true church in existence except for the papal church,—that all who are not within their system are heretics! So say the 'Latter-day Saints,' that they are the only church with its foundation on "the rock of ages," and that eternal woe will be part of all who do not receive the Holy Spirit by baptism and the laying on of hands of the apostles and elders of this church,—that the day of their retribution and their burning is at the door, and they will not escape anything! The Catholics say that the Bible in and of itself is a sufficient rule of faith, without the traditions of the fathers; so say the saints, that it is necessary to have the Book of Mormon—the revelations of Smith, Brigham Young, Orson Pratt, Orson Spencer, Taylor, Moffat, and some hosts of other fanatics, to make up the "gospel in its fulness!" "Fools" is what the Book of Mormon† calls everyone who acknowledges the Bible as the only rule of faith and conduct, and who refuse the claimed revelations of the saints. The Pope and his priests make every effort to keep the Bible out of the hands of the common people; not "Bible to all the people of the world," but the *Book of Mormon*† is the cry of the saints. Here is what Orson Pratt, one of the chief apostles, says,—"After they are baptized in this manner into the kingdom of God, they should make every effort to translate the Book of

* See the pamphlet called "Preaching to spirits in prison, and baptism

14

Mormon into all the written languages of the earth, and to send it out by the thousands of copies to every nation, and to refrain from giving up their efforts until all the people have heard the good news."* Thus, you see that the Bible is not to be in the hands of anyone except as a balance for the Book of Mormon to refer to. If the saints were to succeed in putting the Book of Mormon in the hands of the world, instead of the Bible, they will have answered the purpose of keeping the Bible, like the Catholics, from the hands of everyone. The Catholics claim that baptism is a rebirth; so claim the saints, as their writings on baptism testify! The saints and the Catholics jointly reason in favor of some *middle position* which is called by the one "prison," but by the other "purgatory," to which the souls of the dead go, and from which position they are released, according to the opinion of the saints through baptism which is fulfilled for them on the earth; and according to the opinion of the Catholics through prayers, the recitation of mass, and the payment of money to the priests. It is quite soon in the future for the saints, as it once was with the Catholics, to begin selling letters of forgiveness to free the dead from their prison; but I fully believe that some prophet will rise up in their midst before long and claim that he has received a revelation from God to change *baptism* to *tax for the dead!!*

We see clearly from this, that Mormonism is a mixture of Atheism, Mohammedanism, Catholicism, and a *form* of Christianity! And this is the system that Smith said that John the Baptist, under the direction of Peter, James, and John, have come in a chariot of light on a mission from heaven to ordain him and Oliver Cowdery to preach to the world. The saints also have twelve apostles, sent out into the world, to proclaim the deceitful teachings that have been mentioned. In a small newspaper pertaining to the saints, called the "*New York Prophet*," the names and titles of the Apostles are reported by W. W. Phelps. The Writer says the following,—"I know the twelve, and they know me. Their names are,—

Brigham Young, the Lion of the Lord.
Heber C. Kimball, the Herald of Grace.
Parley P. Pratt, the Archer of Paradise.
Orson Hyde, the Olive Branch of Israel.
Willard Richards, the Keeper of the Rolls.
John Taylor, the Champion of Right.
William Smith, the Patriarchal Staff of Jacob.
Wilford Woodruff, the Banner of the Gospel.

*"*To expect more Revelation, &c.*" page 2.

15

George A. Smith, the Entablature of Truth.
Orson Pratt, the Gauge of Philosophy.
John E. Page, the Sun Dial.
Lyman White, the Wild Ram of the Mountains!!

They are good men,—the best ones the Lord could get. They will do the will of God, and the saints know that." But despite how high their titles and how good their lives, according to the report of W. W. Phelps; even though the belief of the saints is that the Bible is *out of date*, and that the Book of Mormon is the gospel in its fulness; yet, it is from the Bible they take their subjects to preach about, and it is the Bible they refer to, through its perversion, to try to prove their assertions. Since they believe that the Book of Mormon is divine revelation, more complete than the Bible, and that the 'Latter-day Saints' are the chosen of the Lord to preach him to the world, why do they use the lantern of the Bible, which gives off a weaker light than that of the Book of Mormon, to enlighten those "who sit in the valley and the shadow of death?" The saints are not heard a single time taking their topics out of the fifteenth chapter of the second book of Nephi, or quoting proofs for their assertions out of any chapters in the books of Alma, Omni, Mosiah, or Helaman.* It is said in the 11th chapter of the book of Nephi, that the day will dawn in which the sealed book, namely the Book of Mormon, will be read from the housetops; behold those days have come, say the saints, but it appears to be clear that they are ashamed to read it on the corners of the streets, without mentioning from the housetops. What can be the reason for this? No doubt it is because they know they must use deceitful means to defend deceit, and because of that, they cover the Book of Mormon with the truths of the Bible! And in this manner the devil can transform himself into the form of an angel of light.

It appears from the *statistics* of the saints in January 1851, that this deceitful stratagem throughout the United Kingdom has been effective in seducing 30,747 into their system. And it is lamentable to think that 4,848 of that number are being counted in Wales! That during the last fourteen years more than 50,000 have been baptized in England, and that 17,000 have emigrated to the American Zion. What wonder, in reason, when we consider that they had at that time, according to the same statistics, 12 High Priests, 1,761 elders, 1,590 priests, 1,226 teachers, 682 deacons, with all employing the same cunning stratagem to attract those thousands to embrace the Mormon deceit.

The saints assert that all who do not humble themselves to embrace this deceit, are living in Great Babylon, and that their destruction is as sure as that of the inhabitants of Sodom and Gomorrah of old. It is a lamentable fact that according to the report of the saints in Zion, that they are marshalling armies under weapons of war. The prophet Smith, earlier in Nauvoo, was *General* of the army, before he was killed in Carthage jail. The army of the saints was called by the name of "destroying angels!" We have testimonies of Thos. B. Marsh, who was once chairman of the twelve apostles, and Orson Hyde also, who was one of the twelve, to the effect that the objective of the prophet Smith in forming the aforementioned army was to destroy the opponents of the saints. So we see that the saints like the Pope and Muhammed wanted to defend their false religion with the sword! The

*Names of some prophets of the Book of Mormon.

16

slogan of Muhammed was, “the Koran or the sword;” “Catholicism or the sword,” says the Pope; “the Book of Mormon or the sword,” says the impostor Smith and his followers. But here is what Christ and his Apostles say,—“Glory in the highest to God, and on earth peace and good will to men.” No matter what the peaceful principles of the Bible are, the saints confident that their *destroying angels* will completely destroy all the nations who oppose them. You know of the destruction that *one* destroying angel inflicted earlier in Egypt! What will the destroying legions of the saints do, when they come out against their opposing enemies? They will make every Alexander tremble,—every Napoleon faint, every Wellington flee!! But what about America,—the earthly Canaan and Zion of the saints? (For they believe that it is they as Mormons who will inhabit that entire continent very soon.) The sound of Hallelujah will resound there throughout all its borders, from the distant borders of Greenland to the extreme frontiers of Cape Horn, when the inhabitants of Great Babylon, namely, Europe, Asia, and Africa,—those who are not under the sign of blood of Mormon, falling in a heap of dead bodies before this destroying angel!

Our comfort in the face of such awful threats is that they are the belches of the false prophet Smith and his deceitful followers! Many an attempt has been made, since the time of Christ and his Apostles, by ungodly, demented, impudent, and brazen-faced men, to set themselves up as prophets of God, who proclaim the most severe curses against all who do not humble themselves to embrace their foolish imaginings. But where are they now? They are prisoners of death until the morning of the judgment. Their names are a malediction and a curse, and the systematized idols they form will have been crushed under the wheels of the chariot of the Gospel. “This gospel of the kingdom shall be preached in all the world,” in spite of the Paganism, Atheism, Catholicism, Mohammedanism, and Mormonism of the age. Since the “sun of justice” has arisen, all the gloomy clouds of the heresies of the world must vanish like shadows: they shall not be able to stand before the splendor of its bright rays.

Now, I shall finish, by saying, “All Scripture is given by inspiration of God, and is profitable for doctrine, for reproof, for correction, for instruction in righteousness: that the man of God may be perfect, thoroughly furnished unto all good works.” (2 Tim. iii. 16, 17.) And although the Mormons “withstand the truth,” just as Jannes and Jambres withstood Moses, “but they shall proceed no further, for their folly shall be manifest unto all men, as theirs also was.” (2 Tim. iii. 8, 9.)

[*It is intended to publish the six Lectures referred to on the first page, in the same form as this Lecture, so that they may be bound together.*]

RHUTHIN:
PRINTED AND FOR SALE BY ISAAC CLARKE.

Pamphlet 13

John Davies. ***Y Doniau Gwyrthiol fel eu Darlunir yn yr Ysgrythyrau Sanctaidd, gyda Sylwadau ar Bynciau Eraill Cysylltiedig a Gwyrthiau (The Spiritual Gifts as They Are Portrayed in the Holy Scriptures, with Observations on Other Topics Related to Miracles)*. Brynmawr: John Davies, 1852. 60 pages.**

The pamphlet has eight chapters, the last of which—pages 55–60—is entitled "The Growth and Deceit of the Latter-day Saints."

The contents of this final chapter consist mainly of information taken from English-language sources about the history of Joseph Smith and the origins of the Book of Mormon. Davies ends the pamphlet with a caution for his fellow Welsh:

> Who in Wales will be so foolish and insult his intelligence and damage his temporal and eternal well-being by joining with and supporting this kind of deceit! The latest letters published from Salt Lake, as well as the reports of the United States delegates, prove the existence there of violence and oppression, sin and corruption of the most loathsome kind. No doubt if Salt Lake were closer to us and the delivery of letters were more convenient, we would have hundreds of letters revealing the repentance from those who spent their money for that which was not bread and gave their labor for that which does not satisfy.

John S. Davis reviewed this pamphlet in connection with his review of the Reverend J. Jones's lectures on miracles. See Episode 9.3.

THE

SPIRITUAL GIFTS

AS THEY ARE PORTRAYED

IN THE

HOLY SCRIPTURES,

WITH

OBSERVATIONS ON OTHER TOPICS

CONNECTED WITH MIRACLES.

BY

JOHN DAVIES, LLANELLY,

BRECONSHIRE.

Second Printing, enlarged.

BRYNMAWR:

PRINTED BY JOHN DAVIES, KING STREET.

—

MDCCCLII.

FOREWORD.

I DELIVERED the substance of the following observations, in the form of a Sermon, in the chapel where I minister. Completely unknown to me, in an evening meeting the same day, it was proposed by one of the listeners, and seconded by another listener,—That the sermon be printed, and all manifested their desire for that; and so I agreed, in hopes that it would be, under the blessing of God, of benefit to turn some sinner from the error of his ways. Soon after this, I received encouragement to reprint it, and divide it into short chapters, for the benefit of the reader. We did so and added a little more to some parts of it.

The chapter entitled "Account of men claiming to work miracles" shows that it is nothing new to claim having miraculous powers,—It is a common thing among the Catholics, and it is seen that many small sects have arisen, the one after the other, through the ages, pretending to work miracles; but they have nearly all disappeared. There is no danger of a protracted existence for any sect that claims the power of working miracles, when it fails to show as much as even one miracle.

There is no doubt, according to the account seen in Chapter VIII., signed by the father-in-law of Joseph Smith and Mrs. Davidson, that the founders of Mormonism are intentional deceivers; but there are no doubt many unlearned men with the Saints who believe it all, and are being led to temporal and spiritual destruction. To some extent the fault in this lies at the doors of the churches of our country, for the men who never came to a place of worship constitute the greater part of them, and if we were to go out to the "highways and hedges," as well as laboring in the chapels, there would be hundreds of followers of the Saints become splendid members in our churches.—They are with the Saints, not because Saintism is true, but because the Saints went to them to offer some religion to them. With a sincere prayer for a missionary spirit and a spirit to combat sin prevail in the churches, I offer the following observations as a blessing for the Head of the church.

CONTENTS.

55

CHAPTER VIII.

RISE AND DECEIT OF MORMONISM.

SEVERAL persons cooperated to form and establish Mormonism. Joseph Smith, Sidney Rigdon, and Martin Harris were the main priests, although a few others belonged to the work. Sidney Rigdon did the planning, Joseph Smith published the plans, by pretending to have received them from God, and Martin Harris gave the necessary money for the expenses. The calling of Joseph Smith was to indicate places in the earth where silver and treasures were buried. He pretended to do that by putting some small stone in his "*hat*," and then placing his "*hat*" over his eyes and looking into it, and thus he saw, says he, the place where the buried treasures lay.

Sidney Rigdon spent much of his time in a printing establishment in Pittsburg, America, with a man by the name of Mr. Patterson. Martin Harris owned a plot of land, which he mortgaged to have money to proclaim and establish Mormonism. It appears that Martin Harris was a respectable businessman, but was quite lacking in ability to weigh and judge religious matters. Money was promised to him, with great interest after getting the new religious machine to work well.

The way that the arrogant deceit called Mormonism was invented, was as follows. In America there are very many old mines, and remnants and ruins of towns and cities; since a variety of opinions exist concerning their beginning, and the reason for their destruction, a learned and famous man by the name of Mr. Spaulding composed a kind of fictitious history about them. He imagined how things could have taken place, and he wrote those imaginings

56

according to the writing style of the authors of the Old Testament. He read his manuscript many times to his friends in New Salem, Ashtabula County, the State of Ohio. They greatly loved the manuscript, as it was entertaining and cleverly written, and they came frequently to his house to listen to him reading it. After some time Mr. Spaulding moved to Pittsburgh, where he became a great friend to Mr. Patterson, a newspaper editor. Spaulding showed Patterson the imaginary story he had composed; Mr. Patterson found it to be exceptional and offered to publish it; all that lacked was for Mr. Spaulding to prepare an introduction for it. Mr. Spaulding refused to give his permission to print it, since it was all an imaginary tale. Hearing this, Mr. Patterson requested the loan of the manuscript so that he could read it at his own leisure, and to this Mr. Spaulding agreed. Mr. Patterson had the manuscript for some time, and eventually Sidney Rigdon made a copy of it. Soon afterwards Mr. Spaulding died, and the manuscript was returned to Mrs. Spaulding. About this time Sidney Rigdon took the copy which he had made of the manuscript to Joseph Smith, in order to plan and counsel together what they should do. They agreed not to show the manuscript directly to everyone; but instead they decided to noise it abroad to awaken interest in it from the world. And also to strive to prove its divinity,—one evening while on his journey, telling of his search for silver buried in the earth, Joe pretended to have had a vision, in which he was told by an angel that he was to be a prophet of the Most High, and to reveal a Golden Bible which was hidden in the earth and written on golden plates. The angel showed him where they were, but told him not to take it from there or to show it to anyone.—It was to remain there until Joe had married and until after his firstborn had appeared; when his child was two years old, at that point he could dig for the Golden Bible. As proof that the angel had told him the truth, he revealed to Joe that he needed to go on a journey toward the mountains of Pennsylvania where he would find a young woman, who was to become his wife. He

57

did not need an angel to show him about this young woman, since he had been staying for some time in her house and had asked her father for her hand in marriage. He had replied that he was not agreeable to that, since he did not like Joseph's vocation or his manner of living; but despite her father's opposition, the girl agreed to the marriage;—Smith departed promising to return after a while, and so he did, making known in the area where he was at the time, that an angel had directed him to a girl he had never seen before. During this time Sidney Rigdon was busy changing and adding to Mr. Spaulding's imaginary tale, so that it would be ready to be lifted from the earth and revealed at the time Joe Smith indicated. He said that it was written on golden plates, and that it was in a stone box, and he pretended to have two magic stones which enabled him to read the plates without opening the box. Before long, the Golden Bible was published in the form of the Book of Mormon, without any credible person having seen the golden plates or the stone box that contained them.

As proof of the foregoing account, we note the testimony of Joseph Smith's father-in-law, and that of the widow of Mr. Spaulding. "I first became acquainted with Joseph Smith in November, 1825. He was at that time in the employ of a set of men who were called "Money Diggers;" and his occupation was that of seeing, or pretending to see by means of a stone placed in his hat, and his hat closed over his face. In this way he pretended to discover minerals and hidden treasure. His appearance at this time, was that of a careless young man, not very well educated, and very saucy and insolent to his father. Smith and his father, with several other money diggers boarded at my house for a while . . . . . . Smith gave the money diggers great encouragement at first; but when they had arrived in digging to near the place where he had stated an immense treasure would be found, he said the enchantment was so powerful that he could not see. The diggers then became discouraged, and soon after dispersed. After these occurrences, Smith made several visits at my house, and at length asked my consent to his marrying my daughter Emma. This I refused, and gave my reasons for so doing, that he was a stranger, and followed a business that I could not approve. He then left the place. Not long after this, he returned, and while I was absent from home, carried off my daughter, into the state of New York, where they married without my approbation or consent. In a short time they returned, bringing with them a Peter Ingersol . . . . . . Soon after this, I was informed they had brought a wonderful book of plates down with them. I was shown a box, in which it is said they were contained, which had to all appearances, been used as a glass box, about the size of the common window glass. I was allowed to feel the weight of the box, but I was not allowed to look into it . . . . . . After this, I became dissatisfied, and informed him that if there was anything in my house without my knowing what it was: and that if he had any such thing he must take it away; if he did not, I was determined to see it. After that, he said that the plates were hidden in the woods. About this time Martin Harris arrived there. . . . . . .The manner that Smith pretended to read and translate the writings to Martin Harris, was the same way as when he looked on behalf of the money diggers, with the stone in his hat, and his hat over his eyes, while the plates were still hidden in the woods . . . . . . I conscientiously believe from the facts I have detailed, and from many other circumstances, that the Book of Mormon is a silly fabrication of falsehood and wickedness, and was made with a design to profit, to dupe the credulous and unwary, in order that its fabricators may live upon the spoils of those who swallow the deception." Isaac Hale, father-in-law of Joseph Smith.

This is the testimony of Smith's father-in-law,—now we shall note the testimony of Mrs. Spaulding, (presently Mrs. Davidson,) having remarried. She portrays the manner in which her first husband composed his imaginary story about the old American remnants, and the great pleasure his neighbors received from listening to him reading it. She said they came New Salem to Pittsburgh, and that Mr.

59

Patterson, accompanied by Sidney Rigdon, borrowed the manuscript. Mrs. Davidson continues as follows:—As is well known in that neighborhood, and as Rigdon has admitted many times, he came to be acquainted with the manuscript of Mr. Spaulding, and he copied it . . . . . . After the Book of Mormon came out, a copy of it was taken to New Salem, the former residence of Mr. Spaulding . . . . A woman preacher appointed a meeting there, and read and repeated copious extracts of the Book of Mormon. The historical parts were immediately recognized by the older inhabitants as the work of Mr. Spaulding . . . . . . Mr. John Spaulding was present and recognized perfectly the work of his brother. He was amazed and afflicted that it should have been perverted to so wicked a purpose. He broke out in tears, and he arose on the spot, and expressed to the meeting his sorrow—that the writings of his deceased brother should be used for a purpose so vile and shocking. I am sure that nothing would grieve my husband more, were he living, than the use which has been made of his work." Matilda Davidson.

It is impossible to have more fitting witnesses, and testimonies more clear and appropriate.—The father-in-law of the founder of Mormonism,—"I conscientiously believe from the facts I have detailed, and from many other circumstances, that the thing called the Book of Mormon was *fabricated through falsehood and wickedness,—made with the intent to profit*, by duping the credulous and unwary, in order that its fabricators might LIVE UPON THE SPOILS OF THOSE WHO SWALLOWED THE DECEPTION." No benefit or profit could proceed to the father-in-law of Joseph Smith from his accusation, and it must be love for the truth and hate for deceit that cause him to bear his testimony in the foregoing manner. Second, we have Mrs. Davidson, the widow of Mr. Spaulding, as well as John Spaulding, his brother, fervently testifying that the tale composed by Mr. Spaulding constitutes the greatest part of the Book of Mormon.—These are persons who had a chance to know, and here they are testifying fearlessly to the world—that

60

the imaginary tale composed by Mr. Spaulding is the Book of Mormon. Who in Wales will be so foolish as to offend his own senses, and cause harm to his own temporal and eternal welfare by joining with, and supporting deceit such as this!!

The latest letters published from Salt Lake, together with the reports of representatives of the UNITED STATES, prove that tyranny and oppression, and sin and corruption of the most disgusting kind exist there. If Salt Lake were nearer to us, and if the carrying of letters were more convenient, we would no doubt have hundreds of letters expressing repentance by some who have spent their money for that which is not bread, and their labor for that which satisfieth not.

For several years, some of the infallible preachers of the Latter-day Saints have been heard taking their text from the seventeenth chapter of the "Gospel of John the Baptist," and while preaching in English, they say that "*All damnations* are in the wrong," and that all preach for money except for them.—That they preach for free; but that the spirit has commanded their leaders to collect *tithing* from all the Saints.

Pamphlet 14

William Rowlands. ***Twyll Mormoniaeth: yn nghyd a hanes bywyd a marwolaeth Joseph Smith, o America, Prophwyd Santyddol y Dyddiau Diweddaf*** **(*****Deceit of Mormonism: Together with the History of the Life and Death of Joseph Smith, from America, the Hallowed Prophet of the Latter Days*****). Merthyr Tydfil: D. Jones, 1852. 16 pages.**

This entire pamphlet by William Rowlands consists of a series of questions and answers. Most of the questions are about Joseph Smith and the church he founded. The answers come from a variety of publications listed on the final page. Here are some examples:

> Q. What did Joe have in mind by putting verses from the Bible in his own book, to mix truth and untruth together?
>
> A. Only to make the fly similar to the color of the water, in order to hook men.
>
> Q. Are men so ignorant as to believe such foolishness as this?
>
> A. Yes, and to our great surprise, the Welsh believe it.

Instead of responding to Rowlands's criticisms point by point, John S. Davis wrote an article published in *Zion's Trumpet*. See Episode 9.8.

DECEIT OF

MORMONISM;

TOGETHER WITH THE

HISTORY OF THE LIFE AND DEATH OF

JOSEPH SMITH,

FROM AMERICA,

The Hallowed Prophet of the Latter Days.

BY THE

REV. WILLIAM ROWLANDS,

CURATE, MERTHYR.

Deut. 18. 22, "When a prophet speaketh in the name of the LORD, if the thing follow not, nor come to pass, that is the thing which the LORD hath not spoken, but the prophet hath spoken it presumptuously: thou shalt not be afraid of him."

MERTHYR TYDFIL:

PRINTED BY D. JONES, MAIN STREET.

1852.

TRACT ON MORMONISM, &c.

QUESTIONER. Where was Joseph Smith born, the Founder of the false religion of the Latter Days, false prophet of the nineteenth century?

ANSWERER. In Palmyra, Illinois, America.

Q. When was he born?

A. On the twenty-third of December, 1805.

Q. When he was young, were there any signs that he would increase in favor with God?

A. No, not in the least.

Q. What did he do when he was young?

A. He went around the country saying that he had seen some light, so that he could know where there was a gold mine; is it from the Holy Spirit that one is likely to have a glimpse of corrupt things, such as silver and gold? Yes, says Joe.

Q. Did he begin to deceive men in his youth?

A. Yes, when he was seventeen years old.

Q. How did he do that?

A. By putting a hat with a stone in it over his eyes, and going around in this manner, testifying that he could see a great light when he was close to the gold, at times too strong for him to see anything because of the power of the light.

Q. There was probably no one so weak in the head to believe him.

4

A. Yes, quite a lot.

Q. Were there any so foolish as to give money to him for such deceit?

A. There were.

Q. What did Joe do after getting hold of the money?

A. Very easy to understand,—he went away, leaving the fools to do what they could about the gold that was in the earth, while he tended to the gold that was in his possession.

Q. Didn't the lad Joe become a prophet after a while?

A. Yes, and he also saw angels.

Q. Did anyone else see them when they were on a *visit* to Joe?

A. There was no one else, and we can only hope that he was honest and truthful, and a very holy man; otherwise, he will be terribly sober in the end, with the men who put their trust in him.

Q. Well, did not Jesus Christ say that by their fruits ye shall know men?

A. Yes.

Q. What kind of fruits did Joe have in order to discover the life of a prophet in him?

A. Some that were plenty vile at best.

Q. Hopefully there not many with black spots on them.

A. Yes, there were, and some also that were completely black; but I shall give an account of his life, and you can judge.

Q. Did the prophet receive visions from heaven?

A. Yes, some of them quite remarkable, he said.

Q. What was one of them?

A. The most singular revelation was on the 21 of September, 1823, when the lad was 18 years old, when he saw that all the sects were heretical, and abominable in the sight of the Lord; this was the beginning of the religious life of the holy sect of the

5

latter days. Until then Joe deceived with gold, and it is not unlikely that he saw the color of gold in his religion and his visions after that.

A. But what was the vision that showed the color of gold in it?

Q. The great prophet of the west said, The Lord spoke to me in this manner, I command my saints to build a house for my servant Joseph Smith, and to keep in it food and raiment, and whatsoever thing he needeth. (Might there not perhaps be the color of gold in all this?) And also my servant Sidney Rigdon, his fellow prophet, to have everything that seemeth him good: *very genteel indeed—noble*, is it not?

"It is meet that my servant Joseph Smith, should have a house built, in which to live and translate, and for his seed forever, together with food and raiment, and whatsoever thing he needeth; and also, it is meet that my servant, Sidney Rigdon, should live as it seemeth him good."

Q. Now, what should one think about the deceit and cunning associated with taking in money like this?

A. Indeed, there is reason to fear that he was an evil man, for not one of the prophets of the Lord ever received a vision of that nature, as far as I know.

Q. What should be made of discussing the Lord's prophets in connection with the deceiver?

A. It should not be done, it's true.

Q. What color was on the life of the prophet?

A. Very black, indeed. One can hardly mention a single sin of which Joseph Smith has not been charged and found guilty in the courts of the land.

Q. How is he shown guilty of any public and shameful sin?

6

A. By his taking the wives of other men for himself, under the guise that the Lord had permitted him the blessing of Jacob, so that he could have however many wives of other men he chose for himself, which he called *Ladies of the white veil.*

Q. "*Ladies of the white veil!*" there was something in that similar to the Catholics.

A. Yes, and so it was with his followers also, for they believe in purgatory—baptism as a second birth—miracles—the laying on of hands for granting the Holy Spirit—the anointing of oil for the health of the body.

Q. Where can one obtain an account of the tricks of Smith as named?

A. One can obtain the entire account by Mr. Bennett, *Mayor* of Nauvoo, who says (in the *Boston Herald*) that Joseph Smith was guilty of the blackest and most corrupt sins. ("*The life of Joseph Smith is of the blackest turpitude, spent in villainy, profligacy, seductions, and robberies.*")

Q. Did not Smith deceive the saints with regard to the Temple of Nauvoo?

A. Yes, the poor things, and by the time a hundred were deceived and left him, it was not long before gathering in their place another hundred, much more faithful.

Q. What ever became of the Temple, the one which was to be of pure gold, and the glory of the entire earth, the one which was the object of prophecy?

A. Yes, remembered as the object of Smith's prophecy, for it has today been turned into an old mill to grind wheat for the bread of the people.

Q. Did the prophet ever have a bank?

A. Yes, by the name of "*The Bank of safety,*" but *safety* for himself, it appears.

Q. Were *Bank Notes* ever given out by the prophet?

7

A. Yes, many of the saints took 20,000 dollars' worth of his papers from the gentiles, and some 40,000, which were delivered to Joe and the *Bank*.

Q. How was he able to carry the *Bank* forward.

A. Extremely well, until word got out that the *Bank* was about to fail. At that time, Joe took 200 rather large boxes, and he filled them with some rubbish, but he filled one with gold, and he wrote on the outside of each one of them 1000 *Dollars*.

Q. What did the saints do then?

A. What else, but to run as fast as they could to the *Bank*.

Q. Yes, yes, but what did he do about money for them, is the question?

A. He did as he usually did, confusing them and deceiving them. When some came to the prophet, he turned the *box* with the gold on the *counter*, top down, and showed 200 minus one of some other, saying, This is enough, isn't it?

Q. Were the saints satisfied with only that?

A. Oh, it did the trick very easily, to the point that there was great rejoicing in the camp of the saints, and much more additional money was collected for the *Bank* after that, money that was not in it at the time.

Q. What became of the *Bank*?

A. It disappeared just like the Biblical Jonah, and the prophet fled with the civil officials after him, because of the persecution of the saints against the deceiver, until he went across the state's borders; he sent word to the saints, chastising them severely for their lack of faith, and calling them apostates, and saying that they were like Korah, Dathan, and Abiram.

Q. Where do we find the prophet next?

A. Retreating as Captain of the army of the Saints, arming them with swords and rifles, intending to

8

have their own way, as did many before them.

Q. Did they have their own way?

A. Oh no, even though they were in the land of great freedom, Americans.

Q. What were the names of the *Generals* who went to arrest him on the fourth of May, 1834?

A. *General* Lucas and *General* Clarke, when they took thirty of them as prisoners to the Richmond *jail*.

Q. What was the crime the prophet was accused of by them?

A. High treason.

Q. What were the reactions of the poor saints at the time, under the guidance of their leader?

A. A strident cry and shouting "that it was necessary to do with all the sects as the Apostles did with Judas Iscariot of old, namely to trample his body under their feet, until his bowels spilled out, and to smite them as Peter did with Ananias and Saphira."

Q. Well, here is the brother of the old Pope at last, in spirit.

A. There are many other pairs of brothers that are not half as bad.

Q. Was Joe hanged for his high treason?

A. He escaped from jail before the day of his trial.

Q. How is it that he was not caught?

A. Because he fled for his life to the state of Illinois.

Q. Did the false prophet receive any wondrous revelation while in exile?

A. Yes, he saw in it that the *Mayor* of Missouri would die that year; now we can see how much truth are in the words of the prophet.

Q. It would be quite remarkable had Joe not tried to assist in the fulfillment of the prophecy.

A. This is what he could do, and that is what he did. He promised 500 *dollars* to any of the *Danite Band*, who would take the life of the *Mayor*, so that Joe would remain a prophet.

9

Q. Did one of them try to do that for him?

A. Yes, and he came back, and testified to Joe that he had killed the *Mayor of Missouri*, according to the agreement.

Q. Did Joe pay the 500 *dollars* as promised?

A. Fair play to Joe, he paid every farthing, and he proclaimed that the prophecy had been fulfilled: but the truth was something Joe did not know, namely, that the *Mayor* had not been killed, despite all the effort.

Q. I hope no one came to know the secret?

A. Yes, the entire plot, and there was poor Joe, facing the warrant of the *Mayor of Illinois*, by order of the *Mayor of Missouri*, in the lock-up.

Q. By then, it is likely that things went dark for Joe, especially if there were witnesses against him?

A. Yes, Mr. Bennett, the Mayor of Nauvoo, came out against him, and woe was Joe.

Q. What was done to him?

A. He was found guilty of an attempt on the life of the *Mayor* of Missouri, and he was thrown in the Carthage jail, and these things were the beginning of the afflictions of the Saints and their prophet.

Q. Was he hanged?

A. No, he was shot.

Q. What happened when the Saints shot the keeper of the jail where Joe was held?

A. Joe did the same as the others inside, namely they fired shots.

Q. How did the conflict end?

A. When Joe was at the window trying to escape, he was finally shot by the soldiers, and he died on the spot; this is the end of that wicked man, namely the prophet of the Mormons.

Q. Was this not dissimilar to the fate of Muhammed?

A. No, it was not; it was sometimes said that he was to this era what Muhammed was to his era,

10

and that he proclaimed the faith by the power of the sword.

Q. What was the opinion of the false prophet about the Bible?

A. That it was the Word of God.

Q. What about the Book of Mormon?

A. That it was also the Word of God, as well as every other good book.

Q. Where, and how, did the prophet obtain this book?

A. In the hill Cumorah, written in the language of the Egyptians, on gold plates.

Q. Could he understand the language of Egypt?

A. Not a word.

Q. How did he know that it was the language of Egypt?

A. I don't know—let the Latter-day Saints judge.

Q. Is there any way to believe that a man is a prophet, if he ever once fails in his prophecy?

A. No, there isn't; if he speaks through the inspiration of God, he cannot be in error.

Q. It is obvious that Smith failed when he said that he would return to raise the second Testament from the dust of the hill.

A. Yes, and just as obvious that Joseph Smith was an impostor is it that the second Testament will be in the hill until the morning of the resurrection, for his part, if in fact he is there.

Q. What does the Book of Mormon say about the nation of Israel?

A. Almost everything contrary to the Bible: let us put the two side by side:

Bible. The ten tribes went to the country of Assyria in captivity.

J. S. To the country of America.

Bible. The scepter shall not depart from Judah, (the secular government in the tribe of Judah) until Shiloh come.

11

J. S. The tribe of Joseph reigned in Jerusalem before the coming of Christ.

Bible. The priesthood was established by the Lord in the Tribe of Levi.

J. S. In the tribe of Joseph: strange how fond he was of the name Joseph; perhaps he is from the same *family*.

Bible. Christ ascended from the Mount of Olives.

J. S. In America.

Bible. "The disciples were first called Christians in Antioch," in the year 41. Acts 11:26.

J. S. In America hundreds of years by that name before the birth of any of the Apostles.

Bible. The Twelve Apostles live in Jerusalem.

J. S. No, in California.

Bible. Ephesians 3. 4, 5, "The mystery of Christ, which in other ages was not made known unto the sons of men, as it is now revealed unto his holy Apostles and Prophets by the Holy Spirit."

J. S. That Christ was preached, together with baptism for the remission of sins, in America, hundreds of years before the birth of Christ in Bethlehem.

Q. Are not verses 17, 19, and 23 of the 11th chapter in the Epistle of Paul the Apostle to the Romans, given by Smith in his Book in the mouth of some Nephi, about 500 years before the birth of the Apostle?

A. Well, what is the wonder, the man was no doubt a fraud.

Q. There is a huge difference, isn't there?

A. Yes, and no wonder, since it was not through the same Spirit they were speaking.

Q. Is not the god of the Book of Mormon, and of all the sainthood together, the same as the God about which the Bible presents an account?

A. No, nothing similar.

Q. *Bible.* God is a Spirit.

J. S. The god of the Latter-day Saints has a body:

12

one cannot know anything unless an angel indicates what is going on.

Bible. He is omnipresent and omniscient. "Whither shall I go from thy spirit? or whither shall I flee from thy presence? if I ascend up into heaven, thou are there; if I make my bed in hell, behold, thou are there: if I take the wings of the morning, and dwell in the uttermost parts of the sea, even there shall thy hand lead me." Psalm 139.

Q. Is that not sufficient?

A. Yes, forever: it is sufficiently obvious for eternity that the two do not have the same God.

Q. What additional such frightful and dreadful differences are named?

A. Imagination is the god of the Latter-day Saints, and it is measured and unknown.

Q. It is quite likely that that is the reason they are so bold with him, and testify that they speak with him.

A. Very likely, because if they believed that he knew of all the lies about the miracles, they would not behave so arrogantly.

Q. I wonder if they believe all they say?

A. Perhaps they do, because they do not understand anything about the one who says, "I have listened attentively, but they do not say what is right."

Q. Is it possible to find out what the Book of Mormon is, because it is quite certain that Smith was not able to produce any such thing?

A. Yes, there is evidence that a man by the name of Spaulding, in America, wrote all of it, except for some of the Bible verses that are in it; this has been proven by the sworn oaths of Mr. Spaulding's wife, and his brother, and many of the neighbors who used to be called by the aforementioned man, to hear him read it for amusement.

13

Q. What did Joe have in mind by putting verses from the Bible in his own book, to mix truth and untruth together?

A. Only to make the fly similar to the color of the water, in order to hook men.

Q. Are men so ignorant as to believe such foolishness as this?

A. Yes, and to our great surprise, the Welsh believe it.

Q. What is the reason that men have such feelings, seriously?

A. There is reason to fear that many have become tired of the old teachings of the Gospel to the point of having a yearning for something new, and that the Lord has given them up to solid error to believe a lie.

Q. What is likely to have created in the minds of men when the Word of God, and all other good books, have been brought down to such a low state with the Book of Mormon?

A. No doubt it is atheism that has created such a state.

Q. Is it not possible, as in times of old, to chronicle and set forth the revelations of the Bible?

A. No, it is not possible.

Q. Why not?

A. Because the Book of Revelation of Jesus Christ to John in his prophecies extends to the end of time; and there is a commandment not to add to it, or to take anything away from it.

Q. Yes, to the prophecy of that Book, but would it perhaps be permissible to add to the Bible, despite that?

A. No, it would absolutely not be permissible, since the Book of Revelation is the last book of the Bible, and it was written, *Woe unto anyone who adds to it*.

Q. What does the Revelation of Jesus Christ to John say about this?

14

A. "If any man shall add unto these things, (namely the words of this prophecy) God shall add unto him the plagues that are written in this book," Rev. 22, 18, 19. It might be thought that might be sufficient to any man who treasures the salvation of his soul more than the hypocritical whim and sinful pride of his corrupt heart.

Q. Are there men in Wales these days who can be so arrogant as to proclaim themselves as preachers, not of the Gospel of the New Testament, but of some gospel they themselves invent each day?

A. Yes, there are many such men to be had, unfortunately.

Q. What do they say?

A. That the Gospel is not to be had in the New Testament.

Q. Pray, what is the Gospel?

A. The Gospel is good news, and that has been proclaimed by Jesus Christ, and four of the Gospel writers have chronicled it; and that gospel shall stand when California, in America, is in ashes, the stuff burned by the genuine heat that melts.

Q. Has not Jesus Christ mentioned something about "this Gospel of the kingdom?"

A. He has, namely the one that he himself preached, and his apostles after, "Jesus Christ came into the world to save sinners."

Q. Did he not mention that we should "search the scriptures, for in them ye think ye have eternal life, and they are they which testify of me;" and is this not what Timothy taught also, "which are able to make thee wise unto salvation?"

A. Yes, without doubt, and if there were more searching of them, there would be fewer Mormons, and followers of Joseph Smith in the world.

Q. Joe's bible cannot be the Word of God.

A. No, it cannot, since Smith's bible claims its existence in the dirt of the mountain 600 years before

15

Christ, and in 1823 after that. Thus it must have been there at the time that Jesus Christ was preaching, and frequently refers to that which was written about him by Isaiah, Jeremiah, &c., and there is never any mention about *Joe* and his bible; thus it must be that his book was not worth remembering; but it is quite likely that *Joe's hieroglyphics*, as well as he himself, were not in existence at that time.

Q. Is the Bible sufficient divine revelation for man?

A. Yes, "that the man of God may be perfect, thoroughly furnished unto all good works," 2 Tim. 3. 17.

Q. If miracles were performed by men to reinforce their gospel, and if light from heaven were to descend to illuminate the place where baptisms were taking place, would that be sufficient?

A. No, it would not, for the devil can take the form of an angel of light, and cast wondrous light, that would be of no worth, since the apostle Paul says in writing to the Galatians, 1. 8, "But though we, or an angel from heaven, preach any other gospel unto you than that which we have preached unto you, let him be accursed."

Q. Are there not some who dare to say that there is no power in a gospel written on paper with *ink*?

A. Yes, there are, but what significance is there in an assertion of foolish men, blinded by zeal without knowledge, and prejudice without a particle of understanding.

Q. Is there power unto the salvation of a soul in the written Bible?

A. Yes; the writings of the Bible under the influences of the Holy Spirit are able to convince: "The law of the Lord is perfect, converting the soul." "And that from a child thou hast known the holy scriptures, which are able to make thee wise unto salvation through faith which is in Christ Jesus," 2 Tim. 3, 15.

16

Q. Is it possible to have revelations from Heaven now, as the Latter-day Saints claim?

A. No, it is not, because until all came together in a unity of faith, the inspired writers were to be given revelations by the Lord, which were received as the gift of the holy volume, to make it possible for all in every country to come together in a unity of faith and knowledge of the Son of God, through the Holy Scriptures. Eph. 4. 13, "Till we all come in the unity of the faith, and of the knowledge of the Son of God, unto a perfect man, unto the measure of the stature of the fulness of Christ."

Q. Is it not to the day of judgment that this refers?

A. No, so the men will be no more children, and carried about by every wind of doctrine, after the morning of the resurrection. Eph. 4. 14, "That we henceforth be no more children, tossed to and fro, and carried about with every wind of doctrine, by the sleight of men, and cunning craftiness, whereby they lie in wait to deceive."

Q. If so, will there be but one Divine revelation?

A. Just the entire scripture that has been given through the inspiration of God, &c.

See "Boston Herald," "Bennett and Joseph Smith," "Louisville Journal," "Congressional Documents, 1841," "Gleanings by the Way, Rev. J. A. Clark, D. D., Philadelphia, 1842." "Mormonism Portrayed, by W. Harris, Warsaw, Illinois," "Tracts on Mormonism, by the Rev. Edmund Clay, B. A., Leamington," "Mormonism, by the Rev. F. B. Ashley, Vicar of Wooburn, Bucks."

D. JONES, PRINTER, MERTHYR.

Pamphlet 15

Thomas Hughes. *Darlithiau ar Dwyll Mormoniaeth: Darlith II: Ar Farn y Saint am Dduw, Angylion, ac Enaid Dyn. A draddodwyd yn Neuadd Tref Rhuthyn, Chwefror 25ain, 1853* (*Lectures on the Deceit of Mormonism: Lecture 2: On the View of the Saints about God, Angels, and the Soul of Man*). Rhuthin: I. Clarke, 1853. 16 pages.

This is the printing of the second lecture given by Thomas Hughes (T. ab Gwilym) at the Rhuthin town hall on 25 February 1853. The topic for this second lecture was "the opinion of the Saints about God, angels, and the souls of man." As in the first, Hughes borrows heavily from the writings of Orson Pratt and refutes them with a great deal of sarcasm.

In the final paragraph of the pamphlet, Hughes expresses his satisfaction at having exposed the truth about the Latter-day Saints:

> Now, in light of the exposure we have made of the opinion of the saints about God, angels, and the soul of man, I appeal to every impartial man, is it not obvious that the claims of the Mormons, that they speak under divine inspiration concerning these beings, are nothing but a collection of the assertions of pagan philosophers and atheists of various ages? (p. 15)

Despite the plans Thomas Hughes stated at the outset, this second pamphlet appears to have been his final one. See Episode 9.8.

LECTURES

ON THE

DECEIT OF MORMONISM.

LECTURE II.

On the Opinion of the Saints about God, Angels, and the Soul of Man.

Which was delivered in the RUTHIN TOWN HALL, February 25th, 1853.

By THOMAS HUGHES, (T. ab Gwilym.)

R. EDWARDS, ESQ., SOLICITOR, IN THE CHAIR.

"To the law and to the testimony: if they speak not according to this word, it is because there is no light in them." Isaiah viii.20.

MR. CHAIRMAN, &C.

The title of our lecture tonight, as announced, is, *The Opinion of the Saints about God, Angels, and the Soul of Man.* The opinion that is held by these men with respect to the aforementioned spiritual beings, is based on the Book of Mormon, delusional visions and

Lecture II, Price 2c.—I. Clarke, Printer, Rhuthin.

revelations of the false prophet Smith, and their apostles exalted in their knowledge and their titles! and, thus, as truth, "yea and amen" in the hearts of all the saints.

Lest I make a mistake regarding their views as Mormons, and in order to have the advantage of meeting them fairly on their own ground, I shall allow one of their apostles to present before us now the doctrines they teach on these topics; thus we shall find out the true views of the saints so they will be a clear explanation of the Book of Mormon with regard to God, angels, and the soul of man. But to which one of their apostles shall we present this important task? Shall it be to "*The Sun Dial?*" No, I cannot do anything with the *dial* at this time of night, for the sun has already set. Indeed, I have no faith in their *dial* even "in the face of the sun and the eye of the light." Shall it be to the "*Wild ram of the mountains?*" No, it is better to leave the *mountaineer* alone also in his pasture. By permission of "*The Keeper of the Rolls*," we shall dissect their opinion as Mormons from out of the epistles of the apostle Orson Pratt, "*The Gauge of Philosophy*."* For this man is the great apostle of the saints, and their debating Tertullus. He is the chief oracle of the saints, and the great gospel trumpet of Mormon. But I suspect that never have tambourines descended on the ears of Christians sounded more difficult than those of this trumpet. Listen to its sound. I shall present to you now a fair translation of his words:—

"The Godhood," says he, "consists of the Father, the Son, and the Holy Spirit. The Father is a *material* being. The substance of which he is composed is *wholly material*. It is a substance widely different in some respects from the various substances with which we are more immediately acquainted. In other respects it is precisely like all other materials. The substance of his person occupies space the same as other matter. The *elementary materials of his body* are not susceptible of occupying, at the same time, the same identical space with other matter. The substance of his person, like other matter, cannot be in two places at the same instant. It also requires time for him to transport himself from place to place. It differs from other matter in the superiority of its powers, being *intelligent*, *all-wise*, and possessing the power of *self-motion* to a far greater extent than the coarser materials of nature. 'God is a spirit.' But that does not make him an immaterial being—a being that has no properties in common with matter. A spirit is as much matter as oxygen or hydrogen.† It has many properties in common with all other

*Titles of the apostles of the saints: see the first lecture, page 14.
†A kind of *Gases*.

3

matter. He is not a being '*without parts*,' as modern idolaters teach; for every whole is made up of innumerable parts. There must also be, to a certain degree, a freedom of motion among these parts, which is an essential condition to the movement of his *limbs*, without which he could only move as a whole."

"All the foregoing statements in relation to the person of the Father, are equally applicable to the person of the Son."

Then he says further:—

"The Holy Spirit being one part of the Godhead, is also a *material substance*, of the same nature and properties in many respects, as the spirits of the Father and the Son. It exists in vast immeasurable quantities in connection with all material worlds. This is called God in the scriptures, as well as the Father and Son. God the Father and God the Son cannot be everywhere present; indeed they cannot be even in two places at the same instant: but God the Holy Spirit is omnipresent—it extends through all space, intermingling with all other matter, yet no one atom of the Holy Spirit can be in two places at the same instant, which in all cases is an absolute impossibility. All the innumerable phenomena of universal nature are produced in their origin by the actual presence of this intelligent, all-wise, and all-powerful material substance called the Holy Spirit. It is the most active matter in the universe, producing all its operations according to fixed and definite laws enacted by itself, in conjunction with the Father and Son. What are called the laws of nature are nothing more nor less than the fixed method by which this spiritual matter operates. Each *atom* of the Holy Spirit is intelligent, and like all other matter has *solidity*, form, and size, and occupies space. Two atoms of this spirit cannot occupy the same space at the same time, neither can one atom, as before stated, occupy two separate spaces at the same time. In all these respects it does not differ in the least from all other matter. Its distinguishing characteristics from other matter are its almighty powers and infinite wisdom, and many other glorious attributes which other materials do not possess. If several of the atoms of this Spirit should unite themselves together into the *form of a person*, then this person of the Holy Spirit would be subject to the same *necessity* as the other two persons of the Godhead, that is, it could not be everywhere present. No finite number of atoms can be omnipresent; an infinite number of atoms is requisite to be *everywhere* in infinite space. Two persons receiving the gift of the Holy Spirit, do not each receive at the same time the same identical particles, though they each receive a substance exactly similar in kind. It would be as impossible for each to receive the same identical atoms at the same instant, as it would be for two men at the same time to drink the same identical pint of water."—*The Kingdom of God*, by Orson Pratt, page 4.

4

Orson Pratt says in another one of his pamphlets:—

> "The Father and the Son govern the immensity of creation, not by their own actual presence, but by the actual presence of the Spirit. The union of the three does not give any additional wisdom and knowledge to either, but by the union, they are able to carry on certain works which could not be carried on by one singly. By the *union of the three*, each is *able* to act in all places through the *assistance* of the others."—*Absurdities of Immaterialism*, by O. P. page 30.

In light of this opinion of the Mormons about God, we can see clearly that the saints consider the Father, the Son, and the Holy Spirit to be *three separate Beings;* there is no *spiritual* matter, according to the definition that every Christian philosopher gives of *spirit*, that exists; and that *matter* is everything that is in existence. We see also that they believe being able to *think* is essential to *matter*. It is true that the Scriptures say that "*Three* bear record in heaven; the Father, the Word, and the Holy Ghost;" 1 John v. 7. But it is just as true "that there is *one God*," Mark xii. 32, and that "God is a Spirit," John iv. 24. Since there "is *one* God," *one immortal substance* is what exists. For it is said, "and these three are *one*." How the *trinity of persons* in *one spirit substance* remains a mystery to the world. The two aforementioned facts are just as clear with each other as they are expressed in the Scripture; and even though we are not able, because of the finite nature of our powers of comprehension of this mystery, we are obliged to believe the clear witnesses of the Bible.

God, as a spiritual and immortal Being, of necessity fills every space at the same time. He is a Being whose center is everywhere, and a *circumference* for him does not exist in any place. And as such the *unity* of his essence is an undeniable proof that there cannot be *parts* that belong to him.

If the doctrine is true that omnipresence is a natural attribute of God, then "God must be a *Spirit*," and such a doctrine in the meaning that is viewed by the religious world as an orthodox view; namely, that substance is not to him one of the attributes of *matter* that is essential to him. For it is eternally impossible for one material body to be present in the place where there is another material body at the same time. Thus, if God is omnipresent, his substantive essence of necessity must be completely different

5

from *substance*; if otherwise, the existence of a material creation is undeniable proof that the *material god* of the Mormons cannot be omnipresent. And since he is not omnipresent, he is an imperfect being. And an imperfect being cannot be God.

The apostle Orson Pratt admits, as you heard, that the Father and the Son are not omnipresent, but he insists that this attribute is essential for the Holy Spirit. He also insists that the Holy Spirit, although a *being of matter*, is *immortal, omnipotent*, and *all-wise*. But what contemplative mind, having heard that which I quoted from the epistles of this apostle, does not see the foolishness of the assertion. Is he not telling us that the Holy Spirit has a *form* like all other matter? If so, the Holy Spirit must have limits; for anything that has no limits has no *form*. There are specific limits for a thing that causes a specific *form* for that thing. Therefore, seeing that the Holy Spirit, according to the opinion of the saints, has a *form*, one can challenge them to prove that he is an *infinite* Spirit. What *form* can an *infinite being* have? Let the saints answer. Also, since the Holy Spirit is composed of particles of matter, and since that Spirit cannot, any more than the Father and the Son, fill the void that is taken up by all the particles of matter of creation, I ask again, how can they prove his Infiniteness? Since the material Holy Spirit of the saints occupies space as does all other matter, the existence of other matters of necessity links the god of the saints within the circle of finiteness.

Every finite being is not *Omnipotent*. Neither is the god of the "Latter-day Saints!" You have already heard their opinion that "Through the *unity of the three* the one is *enabled* to act in every place through the *assistance* of the others." If so, it is an obvious fact that the deeds of "that one," according to the admission of the apostle Pratt, "*could not* be brought forward *on one's own!*"

The various *parts* of the Godhood, say the Mormons, are the Father, the Son, and the Holy Spirit! Since omnipotence is not an essential attribute of the *individual parts* that compose the god of the saints, how can omnipotence be essential to their god, since that attribute is not essential to *one part* which composes it? Is the whole body able to possess that which does not pertain to *one part* of that? And if omnipotence is essential to the different parts, namely, the Father, the Son, and the Holy Spirit, are independent from each other, what need do they have of the *assistance of one another* to accomplish the "various deeds" referred to? The more one deals with the opinion of the Mormons about God, the more the immensity of the foolishness connected with that opinion comes to light!

The opinion of the Mormons about God is nothing other than the atheistic system of *Spinosa*, dressed with deceit! *Spinosa* and his followers taught that the great *Universe*, together with the perfections seen in it, such as power, wisdom, knowledge, goodness, &c., is God. They believed that one kind of substance is in existence,—and that that substance is in existence for eternity,—and by nature contains in itself the power of bringing around all nature in its various manifestations! The effect of substance working according to the principles that are essential to itself, is that all things are this!! Now, hear the opinion of the saints contrasting with the opinion of *Spinosa* the atheist, as it is set out in the epistles of their chief apostle; and you may judge as to whether the apostle Pratt is worthy of the lofty title given to him, namely, the "*Gauge of Philosophy*." Here you have a translation of his statements:—

> "As there is no evidence whatever in favor of the *creation* of any substance, we are justified in believing that the elements of every substance *existed eternally*. We can trace back the history of the earth for about six thousand years, or to the period of its formation. During this time countless millions of organizations, both vegetable and animal, have been constantly taking place. But in every case which has come under observation, the beings organized have been made out of pre-existing elements.—*Great First Cause*, by Orson Pratt, page 3.

He says also:—

> "All the ancient Schools of philosophy conceived every substance to be eternal; and it was not until modern times, that men conjectured otherwise."—*Ibid.* page 2.

We see clearly from this that Mormons believe that all the particles of matter have existed eternally. But since they assert that all things that now exist "have been made out of pre-existing elements," it is well for us to come to know the foundations of this belief. Therefore, listen. The Saints believe that every *particle of matter*, is not only eternal in its nature, but, also, possesses

7

understanding, knowledge, wisdom, consciousness, will, and *self-motion.* And since all the things mentioned are essential to matter, all things that are in existence are nothing more than the *self-formed* result of these substantive elements, and through the stated qualifications, they are different substances! Here are the words of apostle Pratt:—

"All these self-moving *materials* must be possessed of a high degree of *intelligence,* in order to obey with such perfect and undeviating exactness the innumerable laws which obtain in the universe."—"It is evident that each particle must have not only *perceived* the utility of such laws, but must have mutually consented to *obey* them in the most strict and invariable manner."—"If ever there were a period when the *wisdom and knowledge of the materials of the universe* were more imperfect than what they are under the present law, they would be unqualified to act under this law, and therefore they would act under an inferior law, such as they could *understand.*"

He says also:—

"If we assume that some of the materials of nature have been eternally *all-wise and all-intelligent,* then they could have eternally acted according to the best laws, so far as their own substances were concerned; but if we assume that many of the materials, instead of possessing great *wisdom and knowledge,* only possessed the *capacities for receiving intelligence,* and had to be *taught and instructed by experience,* then the laws devised for their rule of action would be at first extremely simple, and as *they advanced in experience,* these laws would be changed for those of a higher order, proportioned to their increased *wisdom and knowledge*; and as countless ages rolled along they would at length attain to all that *fulness of wisdom and intelligence* which characterizes all their present operation."

We are told by this apostle, that

"One of the first and most simple things which *material particles had to learn,* as we may suppose, was simply to exercise the force of cohesion, so that their infinitely small parts might be bound together in union." "The next thing," says this apostle, "in the great school of experience would be for one portion to form itself into an immense number of atoms of the same size and form, and for another portion to form itself into a vast number of atoms of another size and form, and in this way all the elementary atoms of nature could be formed out of the same substance; their difference of quality would depend, not upon the difference of the original substance, but upon the difference of their magnitude and form, and upon the difference of their hardness, depending upon the intensity of the cohesion of their parts. After substance has learned by experience all operations, they would be qualified

8

to act according to systematic laws, or those laws that are generally called chemical laws. And in like manner, after sufficient experience, they could learn to act according to the law of universal gravitation, that is, each particle could learn to move itself towards every other particle with a force varying according to the inverse square of the distance."—*Great First Cause*, pages 10, 14, 15.

Now, what is the positive conclusion that can be taken from these atheistic doctrines? Here it is in the words of the chief apostle of the saints:—

"All the organizations of worlds, of minerals, of vegetables, of animals, of men, of angels, of spirits, and of the spiritual personages of the Father, of the Son, and of the Holy Ghost, must, if organized at all, have been the result of the self-combinations and unions of the pre-existent, intelligent, powerful, and eternal particles of substance. These eternal forces and powers are the Great First Cause of all things and events that have had a beginning!!" *Great First Cause*, page 16.

We see clearly from this that the Mormons believe that all the elements of matter have existed for eternity. That every particle that forms any material body, is an *intellectual* particle. That every material has knowledge, consciousness, self-will and self-movement independent of each other. Because they are intellectual, they can gather together to form all things that are seen in the universe! But this is the *climax* of the blasphemous opinion of the saints, that the effect of self-gathering of what they call the intellectual particles of nature is angelic beings, and men, and the persons of the Father, the Son, and the Holy Spirit!! What do you think, friends, of this opinion of the saints? Is it not pure atheism? If "the madman who says in his heart that there is no God," the madmen who erroneously call themselves "Latter-day Saints," deny him in thought, word, and deed! Even though "The heavens declare the glory of God; and the firmament sheweth his handiwork;" even though "day unto day uttereth speech, and night unto night sheweth knowledge;" even though "there is no speech nor language, where their voice is not heard;" and even though "their line is gone out through all the earth, and their words to the end of the world;"—*Psalm* xix. 1, 2, 3, 4. about the eternal, Almighty, and absolute Creator; yet, these atheists of "the latter days" assert publicly and in print that God is nothing more than self-gathered *material particles in the form of a man!* If so, the persons of the

9

Father and the Son must not be eternal. There must be a time when the material particles that now, according to the opinion of the saints, form those persons were in a state of separation: every particle different from the other, similar to the state all of you were in before gathering together in this Hall to form the congregation. If otherwise, it is foolishness to talk about intelligent particles having *self-gathered in the form of persons*. For how could *eternal persons*, which as such of *necessity* possessed a personal form, be the effect of self-gathered particles? This could not be any more than inconsistency in words.

According to the opinion of the saints we are to look at different elements of material as schoolchildren in the school of nature. And we are from the same mass of material substance that everything in existence formed itself from the dust that we trample, up to Deity himself!! The only difference between the particles which gathered themselves into the form of God, an angel, and the soul of man, is the *difference of the degrees of their understanding!*

> "All the powers of the universe," says 'Orson Pratt,' "from the almighty powers of Jehovah down to the weakest powers which act are the powers of the particles of substance."

In another place he says:—

> "The chief forces, the chief powers, and understanding, are *synonymous words* when referring to particles."
>
> "Substances without understanding cannot have forces, powers, or attributes of any kind; neither can they draw near to, retreat from, join together, or obey any other fixed law."

Is there anyone here who can believe that such unscriptural and unreasonable blasphemy was spoken by divine inspiration?

Chemists say that there are 54 different material elements. And naturalists offer proof that all the bodies of matter of creation, which they recognize, are composed of some number of those elements, much like all the words of our language are composed of a particular number of letters of the alphabet. Since the saints assert that *matter* is the substance of God, angels, and the soul of man, we would like to know from them of what number of elements of nature those substances are composed. If from *one* element, which one is that? If from a number of elements, which

10

ones are they? If they are not from any of the elements which are now recognized by chemists, on what basis do they know that? And if they have no knowledge of this, it is wondrous in our sight; those who converse face to face with God, and angels, and receive so many direct revelations from them. Whatever of that, the saints have a surety of knowledge that they are *matter*! If so, we can say that we are certain that such matter as that is bound to be one or more of the elements of nature. And since the material Holy Ghost of the saints is mixed together with all the other matter matters of creation, the diggers of the world should remember, that when they are digging their mountains, they must dig through the Holy Spirit of the saints! And that strikers of the rocks should crush them into a thousand pieces! And it is a great comfort to the sick of the world to think that they are receiving the Holy Spirit mixed together with the medicines of the doctors! No wonder that some foolish saint said once to his friend, when he heard rumbling in his bowels, as he was listening to some saintly prophet speaking,—"Do you know what, Peter, I heard myself receiving the Holy Spirit." "You don't say, Rhys!" "Yes, indeed!" "Well, how did you hear it?" "It went inside me while rumbling!" If that saint had had his lunch, I am certain that he would not have had there an audible sign of receiving the Holy Spirit. This is the way that the blasphemous opinion of the saints degrades the title of the Godhood. The title of the Highest Being is too sacred to use in sarcasm, to expose the extremes of the absurdity of their opinion.

Now, in order for all to see how baseless is the opinion of the saints about God, angels, and the soul of man, I shall endeavor to show and prove that there are *two kinds of substance in existence*, namely, the *material* substance, and the *spiritual* substance.

When giving the definition of *substance*, Dr. Watts says,—"Substance is the entity that exists on its own, independent of all other created entities. The notion of existing on its own is what gives cause to the *Logicians* to call it an entity." Locke also observes, "that the word *substance*, when it is used to set out *spiritual* entities, is used only to clarify that nameless something, in which the attributes we perceive exist, and that it is used in this manner, for lack of words more explanatory." Thus we see

11

that the word *substance* of necessity is not restricted to *substance only*, but it may, with the same appropriateness, be used to set out anything that contains in its nature the concept of self-existence, even though that would not bear any natural relationship with a body of substance.

All the knowledge that we have about the existence of substance depends entirely on the essential attributes that pertain to substance, in every age, and under every circumstance. Among the attributes that are necessary for the existence of substance, are *solidity*, size, and form. Without these distinctive attributes, we cannot form any understanding of anything that is substance; and in whatever object we find the stated attributes, from that discovery we call that substance "material substance." The aforementioned attributes are as essential to the smallest *atom* as they are to the largest planetary orb. There is an *extension*, also, in the essential attribute for substance. Every body of substance must be extended according to its size. For if the concept of *extension* is taken away from any material substance, the concepts of solidity, size, and form are destroyed, and we will have in our mind only complete non-existence. The saints acknowledge all this with respect to *matter*, but they deny the existence of *spiritual* substance according to the common definition that is accepted by the religious world.

When we say that "God is Spirit,"—that "ministering spirits" are angels,—and that there is "a spirit in man," we mean that that *spirit substance* is perfectly separate from substance in its nature; that is to say, there is no solidity, size, form, or extension, that pertain to a *spirit* being, and there is not a relationship between him and *space*, as pertaining to substance; but the certainty that we have of the existence of spirit depends entirely on the existence pertaining to those *spiritual attributes* that we know about. The nature of *physical* and *spirit substance* is as completely unknown to the philosopher as it is to the pagan. But the certainty of the existence of the one substance and the other is proved through their various attributes. Wherever *certainty*, *consciousness*, and *will* exist, they show clearly the existence of some *principle* in which they are intrinsically adherent, and from this they are in this manner inseparable. The greatest absurdity is to admit the

12

existence of *certainty*, *consciousness*, and *will*, and at the same time deny the existence of the *principle* that constitutes certainty, consciousness, and, also, will. When we believe in the existence of the concepts that we have of certainty, consciousness, and will, the understanding of the need is carried back to some substance in which these attributes exist. Since the attributes of these are completely different from the attributes of *matter*, and, thus, of a *spiritual* nature, the principle on which they exist must be *of the same spiritual nature*. No substance can be of a nature that is different from the nature of the attributes essential to its existence; if otherwise, it would be necessary that that substance is different from itself. And that would prove clearly that the presumed attributes are not essential to that substance, and, consequently, there would be no relationship between them. It would be entirely impossible to form a concept for a substance or a spirit separate from their essential attributes. Take away, in your mind, from matter its essential attributes, namely, solidity, size, form, and extension, and I ask, what mental image do you now have of matter? Are you able, despite trying, to grasp it? No, you cannot; for only from its essential attributes can you recognize and name the substance. Thus, in the same manner, it is only by the *spiritual powers* of the mind, which are entirely different from those of matter, can one recognize and name the mental principle in the soul, or the "spirit in man."

The entire course of the Scriptures undeniably proves the existence of *spiritual matter*, and not one of the attributes of substance pertains to spiritual matter. It is clearly stated that "God is a *Spirit*." Good and bad angels are seen as *spirits*. "Who maketh his angels *spirits*." Psalm civ. 4. Mark i, 27. Eccl. xii. And the soul of Christ is seen in this manner, John xix. 50; for that seen by God is "the God of the spirits of all flesh," Num. xxvii. 16; and *spirit* and *flesh* are contrasted, Isaiah xxxi. 3. "The Egyptians and their horses are *flesh* and not *spirit*." And Christ himself says,—"A Spirit hath not flesh and bones as ye see me have." Since "God is a *Spirit*," and since *spirits* are angels and the souls of men, angels and men are called on to give *spiritual worship* to God. These views are supported by all the Prophets—by Christ and his Apostles—and by all the learned Theologians through the ages. Therefore, in light

13

of this, it is obvious to every unbiased mind, that the baseless and atheistic assertions of the Mormons that God, angels, and human souls are material substance, are all vain conjectures!

It is grievous to contemplate the cunning means that are used by the Mormons to defend their heretical opinion. There is no doubt that it was for a deceitful purpose that Smith and Rigdon composed the Book of Mormon,—and the purpose of the apostles of the saints in their writings, by teaching the doctrine of the material nature of God, angels, and the souls of men, was to satisfy the carnal imaginings of man about these beings! Consistent with the same purpose, they explain the figures of the Bible *literally*. Since the Scriptures say that God has appeared to Abraham and Jacob in the *form* of a person—that angels have appeared in the form of persons to Lot, &c., and that Moses and Elias have appeared to Peter, James, and John in ancient times on the mount—the saints say, consequently, that God, angels, and the souls of men must be *beings in the form and according to the size of common man*!! If we were to follow the rule of the saints of explaining figures of the Bible literally, we would be led to the extremes of foolishness. "If we were to suppose," says Charnock, "that God has a body like that of man, because he describes himself as thus, we would have to imagine that he is like a bird, because mention is made of him with wings. Psalm 36.7. Or like a lion, or a leopard, because he likens himself to them in deeds of wrath. Hosea 13. 7, 8. He is called a rock, a horn, fire, to show his strength and his anger; and if anyone is so obtuse as to suppose that God is truly like such things, they will make him not only a man, but worse than a monster." Thus, we see clearly that the purpose of figures in the Bible is to lead the mind through them to moral and spiritual truths. "We are not capable of comprehending spirit," as one learned author observes, "without some kind of comparison beneath it; or understanding the workings of the spirit, without considering the workings of the human body in its various members. Just as the glory of the other world is conveyed to us through the pleasures of this world, so it is with the nature of God, through condescending humility to our capabilities, being presented to us through the parable that we can understand. The more familiar we are with the things God uses for this purpose, the more appropriate they

14

are to teach us in the things that are intended through them.—— Such signs are to show the works of God, in order to bring some familiarity to those that are accomplished by us through those members which he ascribes to himself. So are those members who are attributed to him and show his external works to us, instead of his unseen nature; by showing that God does some works similar to those of men through the aid of those members of our bodies. Thus, the wisdom of God is called his *eyes*, because with his mind he knows that which we see with our eyes. The power of God is called his *arm* and his *hand*; because as we act with our hands, so God does with his power. The divine abundance is shown as follows:—by his eyes and his ears, we understand his omniscience; by his face, the manifestations of his favor; by his mouth, the revelations of his will; by his nostrils, the acceptance of our prayers; by his bowels, the tenderness of his sympathy; by his heart, the sincerity of his affections; by his hand, the strength of his power; by his feet, his constant presence. And for that which he intends as guidance and joy:—through his eyes he shows his care for us; through his ears, his willingness to listen to the cry of the oppressed, Psalm xxxvi. 15; through his arm, his power,—an arm to destroy his enemies, and to defend his people. Isaiah li. 9. All with which God is endowed to show his divine works, are done by him without corporeal instruments, like the ones we have."

In perfect consistency with the foregoing, we can say that the kind of aspects with which God, angels, and the souls of men are endowed—are not to show their *spiritual essentials*, but to give a *manifestation of their presence* to the eyes of flesh. In ancient times, when the bush was burning without being consumed, the truth pertaining to the essence of God was the same:—"The *unseen* God." "No one has ever seen God." But the fiery figure gave *evidence* to men of his *presence*. Since those manifestations were supernatural, it is foolishness in man to attempt to explain the figurative appearances according to the principles of nature.

Since the atheistic speculations of the false prophet Smith and his apostles are the same as those of Hume, Voltaire, Mirabeau, and Robert Owen, the *Socialist*, it would just as reasonable for a man to believe the aforementioned atheists if they were to claim that they are prophets of God; or to believe Payne and Volney if they were to claim to be apostles of Christ, as it would be to believe the claims of Smith and his apostles. Can any thoughtful man believe that the Lord gives continuous revelations to atheists who deny him and disrespect his Word? I believe, and do so on the basis of the Bible, that the claims of the Mormons, that they see God and angels, and converse with them, are as foolish and baseless as are those of the fearful who see every hillock as a spirit.

If Smith and his apostles possessed the *Ventriloquism* of the "*Great Wizard of the North*," the number of converts to the Mormon faith would be thousands more. The saints would have a continual Pentecost. If Smith and his apostles possessed that gift, they would but need to raise their voice to heaven, and every time they inquired of the God, the listeners would get to hear the answer immediately in a voice as if descending from the clouds. And if they were to rebuke Satan and his angels, the deceived, to their surprise, would hear the demons with a frightful cry as they flee through the bowels of the earth to their bottomless pit below!

Now, in light of the exposure we have made of the opinion of the saints about God, angels, and the soul of man, I appeal to every impartial man, is it not obvious that the claims of the Mormons, that they speak under divine inspiration concerning these beings, are nothing but a *collection* of the assertions of pagan philosophers and atheists of various ages? Who, also, does not see clearly that the Book of Mormon, and others of their books, have been adorned with phrases of the Bible in order to trick their listeners and their readers into believing those assertions? If what the apostle Orson Pratt declares is true, that elements of substance have been in existence during all eternity; that those elements have *self-formed* into various substances; and, that God, angels, and the souls of men have *self-formed*; it must consequently be that scriptures are used through the Book of Mormon to set God out as an eternal and unchangeable being—that he is called the Creator of all things—and that the universe is the creation of God! In this manner you see that deceit is the principle that runs through Mormonism. The false prophet Smith knew, and the apostles of the saints have the same knowledge, that the more similar the *counterfeit* is to the *real coin*, the more likely it is to be

16

accepted by the world. Therefore, I leave the opinion of the saints about God, angels, and the soul of man, exposed and wide open before you, and end by saying—"Beloved, believe not every spirit, but try the spirits whether they are of God: because many false prophets are gone out into the world." (1 John iv. 1.) "Ye therefore, beloved, seeing ye know these things before, beware lest ye also, being led away with the error of the wicked, fall from your own stedfastness." (2 Peter iii. 17.)

P.S. We intend to publish the series of six Lectures in the same form, so that they may be bound together. We wish to announce that they can be obtained wholesale on the most reasonable terms.

RHUTHIN;

PRINTED AND FOR SALE BY I. CLARKE.

Pamphlet 16

The Levite. *Dynoethiad Mormoniaeth; yn cynwys Hanes Joseph Smith, Saith Gradd y Deml, Gwreigiaeth Ysbrydol, yn nghyda'r Seremoniau a arferir ar Dderbyniad i'r Urdd hono. O Enau Tystion Profedig* (*Exposure of Mormonism; Containing the History of Joseph Smith, Seven Degrees of the Temple, Spiritual Wifery, Together with the Ceremonies That Are Used on Acceptance into That Order. From the Mouths of Proven Witnesses*). Swansea: Joseph Rosser, 1853. 44 pages.

In his foreword, dated November 1853, "The Levite" gives his place of residence as Ystradgynlais (though no other identifying information) and describes his motive for producing this pamphlet:

> The current situation of our compatriots in their relationship with Mormonism is sufficient reason for calling attention to the subject. No matter how stupid and foolish this religion is, how senseless its followers are, and how low and contemptuous are the one and the other in the opinion of the best men of the world, since there are souls being enticed by them, it is good to try to do something to head off the calamity. And we cannot think of anything better than to present an open description of the life and religion of the Mormons before our friends, from the mouths of credible witnesses, and allow them to judge for themselves. We have selected that which is seen on the following pages from several English-language books published in America, with a wide circulation—read by a host of Mormons, who dare not refute their veracity. We have made extensive use of a critical article in the *British and Foreign Evangelical Review* of one of the books referred to above.

The historical information about Joseph Smith contained in pages 5–17 appears to have been borrowed from the writings of Eber D. Howe and a variety of other sources. Publications by John Van Dusen, an excommunicated Latter-day Saint, are the source for pages 17–35. He and his wife had participated in the ceremonies performed in the Nauvoo Temple during its brief use in late 1845 and early 1846. They published their recollections, along with some possible embellishments of their experience, and sold them for a substantial amount of money in New York. The commentary in pages 35–41 is inserted to answer the question "What are the religious tenets of the Mormons?" Several passages from the Doctrine and Covenants are used to provide information about Latter-day Saint teachings. Pages 41–44 contain the oft-used tale of the missionary who pretended to be dead after spending the night at the home of a kind family. The next morning, two of his colleagues claimed they could raise him from the dead, at which point the head of the house raised the missionary from his bed by threatening to cut off the missionary's head with a knife.

EXPOSURE OF MORMONISM;

CONTAINING

THE HISTORY OF JOSEPH SMITH,

SEVEN DEGREES OF THE TEMPLE,

SPIRITUAL WIFERY,

TOGETHER WITH THE

Ceremonies that are used on Acceptance into that Order.

FROM THE MOUTHS OF PROVEN WITNESSES.

GATHERED BY THE LEVITE.

SWANSEA:

PRINTED BY JOSEPH ROSSER, HEOL FAWR.

1853.

FOREWORD.

Dear Reader,

Will you read a word of introduction, if I were to write it? Confident that you will, I shall spend a pen-full or two of ink for the task.

The current situation of our compatriots in their relationship with Mormonism is sufficient reason for calling attention to the subject. No matter how stupid and foolish this religion is, how senseless its followers are, and how low and contemptuous are the one and the other in the opinion of the best men of the world, since there are souls being enticed by them, it is good to try to do something to head off the calamity. And we cannot think of anything better than to present an open description of the life and religion of the Mormons before our friends, from the mouths of credible witnesses, and allow them to judge for themselves. We have selected that which is seen on the following pages from several English-language books published in America, with a wide circulation—read by a host of Mormons, who dare iv

not refute their veracity. We have made extensive use of a critical article in the *British and Foreign Evangelical Review* of one of the books referred to above.

Well, reader, make haste over these pages, look at Mormonism in its founder and its leaders—in its greatest perfection—in its Temple and its Sanctuary; and after that if you can ever again look at it with a joyful eye and a kindly heart, do not blame us for saying resolutely that only license and indecency will be the reason.

Yours respectfully.

THE LEVITE.

YSTRADGYNLAIS, NOVEMBER, 1853.

HISTORY OF JOSEPH SMITH.

THE name Joseph Smith is remarkable among the religious deceivers of the world. It appears that the chief claim this man has to notoriety exists in his lack of mental and physical qualifications. He set about, although bereft of faith, character, education, genius, and even enthusiasm, to establish a religious sect on very peculiar principles, a sect which has greatly increased and is likely to continue on for a considerable time, and from which respect will result from its memory, perhaps, for a long season. There was one thing pertaining to his character which accounts for his success in his adventuresome undertaking; namely *steadfastness of purpose:* he had the *will to accomplish.* Once he decided, he plotted every stratagem, he carried out every means toward fulfilling that decision. And in this lies the secret of his success.

Very little, comparatively speaking, is available from his early history—his beginning was low, and very infrequently would he himself speak about that period; he chose (not without good reason, perhaps) to keep that under the curtain out of sight.

It is said that Joe Smith was born in Sharon, Windsor County, Vermont, in North America, on the 23rd of December, 1805; but judging from his appearance at the time of his death, one could think that he was years older. His parents, who were in low circumstances, moved to Palmyra, state of *New York*, when he was ten years old. At that time Joe was a cunning, wicked, lazy, and imperious boy; and his entire character was destitute of all desirable things. It is said that he was such a rogue, that everything his fingers touched would adhere to them; that he was so disposed to tell lies that he never spoke the truth, even by accident; and that he had the most vindictive temperament ever before seen in a child. As proof of the last characteristic we shall give the following quotations.

When he was very young he was beaten by an old woman by the name of Tracey for stealing eggs from her; and the following night her chickencoop was set on fire, and Joe was found

6

guilty. When he was thirteen years old he stole some clothes from a hedge, and he exchanged them with a peddler for *cosmetics*, and within three days he testified having seen one James Bradshaw steal them. One day his father took a switch to punish him, and to spite his father he poisoned the big dog he had to guard the house. Another time, when he had a grudge against one of his family members, he put some elixir in the *coffeepot* which made all of them sick. After being beaten by a boy who was bigger than he, he watched constantly for an opportunity for revenge and one day found him bathing in the river; he took his clothes away and scattered them here and there across the surface of the water so that not one shred of them was ever found.

In school there was never a bigger *blockhead* than Joe; his favorite activity was to steal, beat the children, and tell lies: and he was totally destitute of any abilities for working; he never took hold of any tool except against his will, and when he did, he was determined to do as much damage as he could by making things wrong, breaking the tool, and such things. Everyone considered Joe the most abominable and wicked lad throughout the entire neighborhood of Palmyra.

It is quite likely that the boy observed and learned all of this from his father, who contributed generously to his wickedness and cunning and caused him to take the path he took. His father was a low class, disreputable farmer, having the same name as he had; he had devoted himself to sorcery, searching for buried treasure, revealing secrets, telling wild and imaginary tales, deceiving and telling lies. Joseph was his father's favorite child; he possessed his entire character, with a great enhancement of the same elements. In the witness of Mr. Peter Ingersoll, under oath in 1833, he said that he "was a neighbor to Smith the elder from 1822 to 1830. The usual occupation of the family was digging for money. I went with him sometimes, when I saw him performing many strange ceremonies; but I never saw him find anything. He said to me on one occasion, that the best time to dig for money was in the midst of the heat of the summer, when the heat of the sun caused the coffers to rise near the surface of the earth. 'Look at this stone,' he said; 'we call them stones, and they have that appearance; but in fact they are coffers of money having been raised up by the heat of the sun.'"

7

The truth of the foregoing testimony is confirmed by the Rev. John A. Clark. He says the following:—

"Joe Smith, who after that was the Mormon prophet, belonged to a worthless family near Palmyra. They lived a nomadic life and were known chiefly as money diggers. Joe was a dull, talentless boy; but his father claimed that he could see through the whole depths of the earth, and that he could discern all the hidden treasures that were in it. In their wanderings for money, Joe was normally the leader; he would carry with him a special stone in his hat, through which he would look and determine where to begin digging."

In the following quotations is a description of the Smith family by eye and ear witnesses. William Stafford says: "I first became acquainted with Joseph, Senior, and his family in the year 1820. They lived, at that time, in Palmyra, about one mile and a half from my residence. A great part of their time was devoted to digging for money; especially in the night time, when they said the money could be most easily obtained. I have heard them tell marvelous tales, respecting the discoveries they had made.

They said that Joseph, Junior, by placing a stone of singular appearance in his hat, could see all things within and under the earth, that he could see vessels of gold and of silver of every description, and large coffers and barrels full of treasure, together with the spirits in whose charge these treasures were. At certain times, these treasures could be obtained very easily; at others, it would be a remarkably difficult task. The facility of approaching them depended in a great measure on the state of the moon. If I remember correctly, new moon and Good Friday were regarded as the most favorable times for digging for money. * * * *

Joseph, Senior, came to me one night, and told me that Joseph, Junior, had been looking in his glass, and had seen two or three kegs of gold and silver, not many rods from his house, some feet under the surface of the earth; and that none others but the elder Joseph and myself could get them. I consented to go with him; and early in the evening we arrived at the place. Joseph, Senior, first made a circle, twelve or fourteen feet in diameter, and he said that the treasure was within that circle; then he stuck in the ground a row of witch hazel sticks around the circle, for the purpose of keeping off the evil spirits.

Within this circle he made another of about eight or ten feet in diameter. He walked around between the two, saying something

8

I could not understand. He next stuck a steel rod in the center of the circles, and then enjoined profound silence upon us, lest we should arouse the spirit who had the charge of these treasures. After we had dug a trench about five feet in depth around the rod, Smith asked by motions leave of absence and went to the house to inquire of young Joseph the cause of our disappointment. He soon returned, and said that Joseph had remained all this time looking in his stone and watching the motions of the spirit, and had seen the spirit come up to the ring and as soon as it beheld the cone which we had formed around the rod, it caused the money to sink. We then went into the house, and old Joseph observed that we had made a mistake in the commencement of the operation; if it had not been for that, we should have got the money.

"At another time, they devised a scheme, by which they might satiate their hunger with the mutton of one of my sheep. They had seen in my flock of sheep, a large, fat black wether. Old Joseph and one of the boys came to me one day, and said that Joseph, his son, had discovered some valuable treasures, which could be procured only in one way; that way was as follows: That a black sheep was required; after cutting his throat, it should be led around a circle while bleeding, making a circle of its blood; this was to be done to appease the wrath of the evil spirit; the treasures could then be obtained, and my share of them was to be four fold. To satisfy my curiosity I let them have the sheep; but some mistake was made in the process this time also, and it did not have the desired effect. This, I believe, is the only time they ever made money-digging a profitable business. They, however, had around them constantly a worthless gang, whose employment it was to dig money at night, and who, during the day, had more to do with mutton than money."

When they found that the people of this vicinity would no longer put any faith in their schemes for digging money, they then pretended to find a gold Bible, of which, they said, the book of Mormon was only an introduction. Another man by the name of Barton Stafford said, that—

"Joseph, Senior, was a noted drunkard, and most of the family followed his example, especially Joseph Junior, who was very much addicted to intemperance, even when he professed to be inspired to translate the book of Mormon. One day while at work in my father's field, he drank until he was quite drunk. Finding his legs to refuse their office, he leaned upon the fence and hung

9

for some time; at length he got up and began to argue with one of the workers, and it became a scuffle between them, and Joe had his shirt nearly torn off from him. His wife happened to be at our house at the time, and she appeared very much grieved at his conduct; and to protect his bare back from the rays of the sun, she took off her *shawl* and threw it over him, and in that plight she escorted him home."

The reader sees from the foregoing testimonies that the Mormonism of Joseph Smith rises to some extent from its evil tendencies to deceive and tell lies, together with the practices that were taught him by his father and his family. Joe eventually proved that he had the appropriate character to deal with the mysteries, to have conversations with good and evil spirits, and to receive revelations and the like.

When he was about fifteen years old, he had a very serious religious craze, but it lasted only for about a month, and then he fell into his corrupt inclinations which were far worse than anything else. He would wander from one place to the other, leading the most disgraceful life, doing so with the greatest impudence imaginable. During the years following this, he was accused of sins that are sufficient to cause the walls of the prisons to quake, and to make the *Newgate* records blush. On the list of his transgressions are assaults, casting of spells, robberies, minting counterfeit money, etc.; indeed, even murder is suggested. He was remarkably successful in avoiding state punishments, although one of his biographers maintains that he spent two years in a Massachusetts prison under an assumed name for stealing horses. It is quite likely that many stories are put forth about him; but his closest friends admit "that equally evil temptations were just as powerful for him until he yielded himself completely to their influence during the season of his youth." And it is a well-known fact that honesty and morality were insignificant things in his view, even during his more mature years. Indeed, they are completely absent from the virtues taught by his religion.

During this period of his life he visited the chief cities of the United States, under various names and occupations. He lived for a season in Boston, passing counterfeit money in connection with some Englishman by the name of Miles Anderson, who had taken Joe into his confidence. It is said that he learned to engrave from this man, and that that is the origin of the *hieroglyphics* on the plates of the Book of Mormon. For, even though the *hieroglyphics*

10

bear some resemblance of antiquity, it is quite clear that they were engraved with modern instruments.

At this time, Joe was practicing every wicked deed; a heavy drinker, a bold fighter, and associating with all kinds of dissolute and bad company; he sang all the ribald and drinking songs; he had a penchant for playing cards; and only infrequently did he end a sentence without embellishing it with an oath, or a frightful curse. Sometimes he would try to show himself as being highly devout by connecting the word "reverend" with his name, and by looking through religious publications, and it is quite likely that the various, unusual temperaments he dealt with in these associations are what prompted him to take the step by which his name became so well-known.

Now we lose our focus on Joe and his history for several years; we know nothing about him until we see him suddenly appear as the founder of Mormonism about the year 1830; of all the religions, this is the wildest and the most foolish. Among its leaders there are childish wanderers, with no talent or character. All its rules and commandments are the opposite of good morals. It not only permits, but also supports adultery, theft, and other abhorrent evils; and yet it has taken root and spread greatly. At first sight this was not surprising. Sinners, men and women, rushed in throngs to it, happy to have such a way to go to heaven—one so different from all the others, and one that is in complete harmony with their corrupt dispositions and appetites.

The first task of Smith in his office as prophet was to translate the Book of Mormon. The account of the "Golden Bible" in Smith's own words by Mr. Peter Ingersoll, is an explanation of its evil character, its predilection for deceiving and telling lies, and its perfect agreement with the previous stories about it. Mr. Ingersoll says:

"Joseph Smith came to me one day, and he greeted me with a cheerful countenance. After I asked him the reason for his unusual cheerfulness, he answered me in the following words: 'As I was passing through the woods yesterday, after a heavy shower of rain, I saw in a cave some lovely white sand washed up by the water. I took off my *frock*, and in it I secured several quarts of the sand, and I took it home. I found the family at the table eating dinner. They were all desirous of knowing what I had. At the moment I remembered an old story told in Canada which was called the 'Golden Bible,' and I told them very solemnly that what I had was the Golden Bible. To my great surprise, I found them all to be sufficiently gullible to believe that. And then I said that I was commanded not to let anyone see it; 'because,' said I,

11

'no one can see it with the naked eye and live. Nevertheless, I promised to take the book out and show it to them; but they refused, and they went out of the room.' In spite of that, he told me that he did not have such a book, and that he did not believe that he ever had; yet he went to Willard Chase to try to get him to make a chest in which to keep the Golden Bible. But since Chase failed to do so, he made one himself, and put it in a *pillow case* and allowed people to heft it and feel it."

The story of the acquisition of the Golden Bible is told by Joe and his father. The stories differ greatly one from the other; and needless to say that the two of them differ in their accounts of the above story which was told by Joe to Ingersoll. Mr. Chase says that Joe came to his house one day, and told him the following story. That he arose one morning, the 22nd of September, and that he and his wife went to the hill where he obtained the book. That he left his wife in the wagon alongside the road and went himself some two hundred yards from her; and that he then took the book out of the earth and hid it at the foot of a tree, and returned home.

The account given by Smith Senior, of the acquisition of the treasure, is very different. In the summer of 1827, according to the testimony of Mr. Chase, the father said that a spirit appeared to his son Joseph several years ago in a vision, and told him that a record on gold plates was in some particular place, hidden, and that he was the person that should obtain it, and that he had to do the following: That he had to go to the place on September 22, after dressing in black clothing, riding a black horse with a tail that reached to the ground, and request the book in the name of someone. And after he obtained it, he was supposed to take it away immediately, without putting it down or looking back. After putting the clothing on him (doubtless the chief purpose of the vision) and making everything ready, Joe went away toward the place, and he requested the book, which was in a box of stone so close to the surface of the earth that he could see one end of it; and he took it. But fearing that someone might find out the place where he obtained it, he put it down so he could replace the stone; and upon turning to take hold of the Bible, to his great surprise, it was missing. He opened the box a second time, and he saw the book in it; and he attempted to take it, but he was prevented from doing so. He saw something in the box similar to a toad, which soon took on the form of a man, and which struck him

12

on the side of his face. Joe, not one to be discouraged by small things, bent down and tried again to get the book, and the spirit struck him a second time with such force that he was thrown about twenty yards away, and he was seriously injured. The spirit commanded him to come back a year from then; he did so, and received the same command again. He came there a third time, and he saw the book and the pair of stones with which he afterwards translated the Book of Mormon. The old man leaves the story at that point; but of course, it is for us to understand that he obtained the book at that time, despite the fist and the toad.

The origin of the Book of Mormon is a clear and undisputed matter, and it can be explained in a few words. The way in which Joe obtained it has been proven satisfactorily. A priest by the name of Solomon Spaulding, a graduate of Dartmouth College, after a few years gave up preaching. In 1809 he moved to Conneaut, Ohio. In that place he spent his leisure hours writing a fictitious account of the old inhabitants of that area, a work that required his labor of several years. Since he intended the origin of the work to be fictitious as well as the story, he decided to bring it before the public as a volume that he found in a cave; and to give an ancient appearance to the book, he wrote it in the manner of the scriptures. He finished his work in about 1812 or 1813; and he announced in the newspapers of the time that the Book of Mormon, recently discovered, contained an account of the lost tribes. For some reason its publication was delayed; and within fifteen years, through a fortuitous accident, the book came into the possession of Joe, and he said that he had found it on plates of gold, and that he was committed to translating it from the strange language in which it was written. He added some things to it that pertained to himself.

The foregoing account has been verified by eight witnesses, to whom the book was read on various occasions. Mr. Spaulding died in 1816. His widow confirmed the foregoing testimony, and she said that the book was left in the office of Patterson and Lambdin, printers in Pittsburg, where her husband stayed two years between finishing the book and his death. Dr. Bennett says that the Mormons themselves told him that the book was taken from the above office by the famous Mormon Divine (Sidney Rigdon), and that it was presented to Smith in order for him to publish it.

13

Joe Smith began his career as a prophet in Fayette, in the western part of New York, in the year 1830. His church there contained six persons—Sidney Rigdon, who was the most talented of them; Martin Harris, the only one who had a penny to his name; and Joe and two or three of his brothers. After gaining some proselytes, he moved to Kirtland, in Ohio, which place soon became famous as the home of the prophet. He received a revelation "that he was a seer, translator, prophet and apostle of Jesus Christ, and the elder of the church." It was revealed to him that the entire government of the church was in his hands—that he had the authority to make rules, choose officials, appoint followers, set taxes, and a hundred similar things. And that the church was to receive his commandment according to his choice, to provide food and clothing for him, and whatever else he would call for to move the work forward, with frightful threats for disobedience. Whatever whim might occur in Joe's head, whatever wish arose in his heart, he had a commandment handy to put it into force.

After being for a few years in this place, according to a revelation (?) a large number of them moved to *Far West*, in the state of Missouri. Joe had met with success far beyond any expectation. This adventure turned out to be a thousand times better than digging for money in Palmyra. Proselytes flooded from every part of the world as a strong and steady stream, until the church was filled, which was nothing but a congregation of abomination. Indeed, the corruption of the Mormons at that time had gone beyond description; they had already infected everything with blasphemy, dishonesty, and promiscuity. Their society was like hell unleashed; and the older it became and the more it increased in number, the worse everything became.

But the evil was too insolent to survive long. In the beginning, rational men looked at the matter with feelings of curiosity and wonder; but after a while, after the newness had worn off, and after the bare ugliness of Mormonism became apparent to them, their wonder turned to indignation, and they proclaimed they could no longer stay in their midst. By this time the Mormons were so numerous and strong that they raised an army, and they raised their banner to defy whoever stood against them. At that, the people of Missouri arose, under the leadership of Governor Boggs, to oppose them. After several fierce attacks, and much spilt blood, they succeeded in driving them out to the state of Illinois, where they were received with

14

open arms on the supposition that the oppressed were fleeing from oppression.

This is the reason for the terrible anger that Joe showed after than toward Governor Boggs. His ferocity was so great that he hired a vicious rascal for several months to seek out the opportunity to kill him; this person succeeded as far in his venture that he was able to shoot the Governor in his own home, and he severely wounded him. And after that, he made so many threats and attempts at the life of Mr. Boggs, that he was forced to emigrate to California, from which place he soon returned, most likely because the attraction of the Mormons was so great to that direction.

After Smith and his people found their way to Illinois, he purchased a plot of land in Hancock County; he designed the layout for the city of Nauvoo, and he laid the foundation for his magnificent temple, the cost of which is estimated to be a million dollars.

By then, Joe had reached the highest pinnacle of his glory and his success. His name had become a worldwide surprise. He made laws, he established taxes, he purchased cannons, and he raised up an army. He had proselytes in every nation under the name of *"Latter-day Saints."* His city became a magnet for immigrants, and it increased in population and wealth. He was at the same time king, leader, and prophet, and a threat to become a Muhammed of the New World.

And yet, through it all, he was but a small and ordinary man, and the perfect opposite to the gentleman and the saint; because he was of a worldly mind, dissolute, carnal, and vain: he told the most laughable tales; he swore like a trooper; he fell out with his neighbors; and he was extremely fond of brandy, especially when others paid for it.

But woe! to the virtue of mankind. No fanaticism of any false religion could ever reach the depths of Mormonism; but his strength was that he provided freedom to the wicked; feasting to the licentious; sanctuary to the fugitive thief; school to young criminals; safety to deceivers; respect and rewards to every kind of evil doers; and this is what accounted for his success. Smith maintained his supremacy only by means of his invincible desire; and the way he showed the most talent was through his efforts to transform free thinking and dishonesty into virtues; and by doing so he guaranteed followers to himself.

15

But as the Mormons increased even further here, they became more and more churlish and obstinate; and they caused the state of Illinois to understand before long, that it had received a viper in its breast. They published misleading *bills*, and they produced their own counterfeit money before the eyes of the public. Their throngs of burglars, highway robbers, and horse thieves preyed upon the country before them with such precision that it all worked like a machine. Adultery and the most shameless lasciviousness, under the aegis of "Spiritual Wifery," were one of the leading matters of their religion. They won the secular leadership of Hancock County, and every important situation was under their influence. And not one man was safe among them, with regard to his person and possessions, unless he was a Mormon. The county courts and court officials were Mormons; the jurors were Mormons; and it did not matter what mischief a Mormon committed against others; he was rarely tried, and never condemned. And they threatened other counties with revenge if they interfered in their business. They sent out their secret murderers to frighten them, and they left nothing undone to broaden their power and their gain, and they strengthened their government of fear across the country.

But the day of their reward came to an end. The judgment of the public came out against them, and they gave them warning to leave. But they refused to obey; and then the second Mormon war began, the details of which were published in the newspapers of the time.

This effort came to an end with the death of Smith, for directly after his death the Mormons gave up, and the greater part of them migrated further to the west, with the intent to settle in California.

The death of Joe Smith, as one could expect, was bloody. He was in the jail of Carthage, Illinois, under several accusations, when word got out that he was to be freed without punishment, by virtue of his influence and wealth. With this news a mob of armed citizens broke into the prison and shot the prisoner dead, when he was in the act of escaping through a window. It is not known what became of his body. Some say that he was buried secretly in Nauvoo; others say that the Mormons embalmed it, and took it away with them in a silver coffin; and still others say that it was thrown into a ditch and that the pigs

16

ate it.

Biographers friendly to Smith knew that his "natural life" was but an unimportant one, and they had little to say about it; but they are considerably long-winded about his "spiritual existence."

They say that when he was fifteen years old he was deeply impressed with the importance of religion and requested the Lord to guide him to choose the correct religion, and that he was told by the angel who had appeared to him on several occasions, that all the denominations were false, and that it was his task to establish the only one capable of leading to salvation. But soon afterward Smith lost his religious fervor, and he continued to sin as much as he could until the year 1830, at which time he had repented so effectively that the angel returned to him, and he put him to the task to which he had been appointed "since the foundation of the world." The angel told him that there was no commandment of Christ about preaching the gospel relating to anyone of their successors, only to them; therefore, there was no true church in the world any later than one hundred and fifteen years after that; but Smith was told that the time had come when it was necessary to establish one. He was told also that the common translation of the Bible was full of errors, but that the North American Indians, who were once a powerful and learned people, had buried a stereotype of the *true Bible* in a hill in Manchester, near Palmyra, where he could obtain it, and that by doing so he would bring all of mankind to a knowledge of the true faith. The plates were obtained, as said, in a stone box, full of engravings, which, although he was quite unlearned, Joe translated readily and eloquently.

There is nothing clearer than the fact that Mormonism in its entirety was established on a foundation mixed with dishonesty and lust. The deceit and lasciviousness that came together under its banners were not only perfectly shameless, but also the impression was conveyed that when the children of men are inclined to believe that when anything is in agreement with their inclinations—that they are complying with the will of heaven. The immediate increase, and the riches of Nauvoo, together with its splendid temple, are attributable to the endless deceit and pillaging of the Mormons, who plundered the land for over a hundred miles around them. And their "*spiritual wifery*" was nothing more than the most brazen and shameless adultery that

17

mankind has ever before heard of; for according to this practice a man could take any number of "spiritual wives" that he wanted, although from three to six was the most common number; and there was the same freedom, although not as public, for women to have a number of spiritual husbands. In the account of "*Degrees of the Temple*," which we shall give below, we have confirmation of this loathsome doctrine. The account was written by an apostate from Mormonism by the name of Thomas White; and since it agrees with others we have seen and heard, and has been proven before court judges of the state of Illinois by several responsible witnesses, there is no room to doubt its truthfulness. The Nauvoo Temple is a splendid edifice built in order to give prestige and permanence to Mormonism. It is supposed that it originated from a head superior to that of Joe Smith, and its cost, as was said, was a million dollars, not to mention the inside organization, the design of which has been kept as secret as possible, in order to give a supernatural aura to its admission.

We give here the "*Degrees of the Temple*," in the words of Mr. White, in his account, except for some portions which we were obliged to leave out, for the sake of modesty and decency. The reader must remember that it is necessary for the Mormons to undergo a year's probation before being fully received into the order, through the ceremonies of the Temple: and even then, none are permitted unless their reputations are irreproachable, according to the principles of Mormonism.

THE FIRST DEGREE OF THE TEMPLE.

After going through the time of our probation, my wife and I, along with about fifty other persons, men and women, proceeded to the temple by invitation to be fully received into the bosom of the church.

We prepared for the ceremony by wearing very strange clothing, as if it were intended to take our picture in it; and Smith led us in his half military attire. It was late evening when we went in to the vestibule, with everything still and dark; but soon we heard the sound of trumpets, and through a faint, shining light we saw a large gate that led to a narrow, crooked, and rugged path, full of loose stones and brambles, behind which a gigantic-looking man stood with a club in his hand.

"Children of the darkness," he said, "what has brought you here?"

18

"They are in darkness," said Joe, who stood in front of us; "but they are in quest of light."

"Are they fit to receive it?" asked the giant.

"Their spirits are willing, and their flesh is strong," said Smith.

"Let me have proof, then," said the giant.

Then we were ordered to open the gate, which we strove to do for several minutes, while the giant smiled scoffingly at us, shaking his club.

"Fools," he said at length, "trying to break down the barrier of the giant Error, who has swayed the destiny of all mankind for sixteen hundred years."

"Not of *all*," said Smith.

"Of all but one," said the giant, "and those who see by his light."

"Who is that one?" asked Smith.

"I dare not say his name, lest my barrier fall."

"Is it Moses?"

"A greater than he."

"Is it Christ?"

"One gifted with his power."

"Is it Muhammad?"

"One mightier still."

"Is it Joseph Smith?"

"Thou hast said." With the last word he opened the gate wide, and the giant fled howling; and several voices sang melodiously some distance from us—

"Fit for the Kingdom of Heresy
Before such a name he takes his flight,
He has scattered Jew, Turk, and Pagan,
He has made Rome tremble, poor thing,
He let in light on the Sectarians
They failed daily and saw together;
Now admit what was said,
That God is God—and Smith is his Prophet."

We now entered the narrow path, when the gate closed on us, and we were left in darkness; but still, from time to time, the occasional weak ray of light shone before us. We stumbled over stones, and tore ourselves with briers and thorns as we advanced. We heard verses being sung, and we understood that the words urged us to go forward. At length our spokesman exclaimed:

Smith. Friends, avaunt! in vain you fight.

Spirits. Who are you, so strong and bright?"

19

Smith. One whom God is ever with.
Spirits. Say his name. "Joseph Smith."
Spirits. So we feared; for none beside
Could thus subdue our strength and pride.
Perish, Error—Earth, farewell!
For here may we no longer dwell.

The spirits vanished, and we arrived at a point of the road where the path divided into two: the left path was wide and smooth, and full of people; and the other was narrow, rugged, and lonely. A handsome man stood on the crossroad before us, and greeted us with a smile—"Welcome, welcome, good people; this way, this way. It is a good road, you see; plenty of company, and a religion that suits the taste and imagination of everyone. Here there are Jews and Greeks, Protestants, Catholics, Quakers, Baptists, Universalists, and Presbyterians. Walk in, walk in! There is no doubt that you will be satisfied; and all of you will be sure to obtain close and warm quarters at the end of your journey."

"And what of the road on the right?" asked Smith.

"I don't know," said the man; "for none have ever traveled it.

"But where does it lead?"

"Pooh, pooh, does it matter where?" said the man: "use your eyes instead of your doubts; and if you are people of taste, let your feet and your hearts soon be on this path with the rest of the world."

"And be damned for our pain?" said our friend.

"It is not the preachers who say that," said the man; "ask them, and they will say different."

"But what is the fact?" asked Smith.

"Excuse me, I am the Prince of Prejudice; and I don't deal in facts," said the man smiling.

"The father of lies, we know that all right," said our hero, stretching forth his hand; "but behold, I am answered."

And instantly the portly personage became a hideous devil; while on the left was seen a pool of liquid fire, from which proceeded gnashing of teeth; and on the right, and apparently at a great distance, a small white light of intense brilliancy, surmounted with a scroll containing these words:

"THE WAY IS DANGEROUS, BUT THE REWARD IS HEAVEN."

Then we hastened toward this light, which several times escaped us; but at length we reached it by ascending an inclined

20

plane, which led to another story of the building. But before we could examine its nature, a loud voice exclaimed:

"Prostrate yourselves, oh, blessed among mortals, for you are in the presence of the *holy of holies!*"

And thus ended the first degree.

THE SECOND DEGREE OF THE TEMPLE.

As we lay prostrate, we heard a choir of sweet voices, accompanied by a musical instrument, singing the following words:—

"Rejoice, ye dust of the ground,
  For ye are close to the rapture-giver,
He can drive out all sin,
  And glorify you eternally.
Your release from your captivity,
  Although it pains society,
It will win the great prize as you submit;
  Oh, make haste for your salvation."

On arising, we saw a bright flame which issued from a silver urn placed upon a gorgeous throne; and in the midst of the flame, and altogether uninjured by the fire—if fire it was—lay a richly bound copy of the Mormon Bible, open at the Revelations, and printed in letters alternately of red and gold.

On a yet higher throne, and surrounded by clouds which rendered them nearly invisible, sat three beings in shining robes, who were intended to represent "the Father, the Son, and the Holy Ghost;" the first of these greeted us in the following words:

"O, valiant children, you have now worked your way
To the lovely parts of the eternal day;
The place, if you maintain your faith forward boldly,
Your honor, will be as splendid kings and queens forever,
From your loins will come royal seed;
You will be blessed with *fruit and increase*;
And this will be but the first fruits at the base
Of your honor and your bliss in the great heavens.
But woe—eternal woe—will be yours
If you fail to be as unshakable as the beacon above
In the rights of your faith, and all the secrets you will receive,
Which you will affirm on the Book that you make!
Up with your hands; and oh! remember that
Your faithfulness is in heaven—your failure an endless woe!"

21

Then, down on our knees before the throne, the Bible above us, and with our right hand up, we swore the following oath, reciting it word by word:—

> "By the Holy Trinity now,
> Which reigns in heaven and on earth,
> And here, before the true Book,
> (It is all completely the true word of God)
> We swear an oath;—whether it may be good or bad,
> That we will keep the Mormon faith,
> To do everything it requires of us,
> However difficult it may be for us;
> And on our life we shall never
> Reveal its secrets that we receive.
> If we keep this oath, come what may;
> Or if we weaken and break our word,
> Oh God! reward us with joys eternal,
> Or tortures in the nest of hell!"

The last word was followed by vivid flashes of lightning, and terrific claps of thunder; it became silence and darkness for several minutes, and the following lines were spoken by the deep voice which had addressed us before:

> "I take your pledge, remember ye today
> That I shall judge you by it when ye die!
> And now go forth, and ye shall receive the earth,
> Its honors, its mirth, and its wealth ye shall enjoy;
> For whosoever may lose, it is yours to win;
> *And come what may, I hold you free from sin;*
> *Let Nature be your guide in all you do,*
> Save in the voice of heaven, when it comes in force,
> For the work of Nature is my voice, and cannot err;
> You worship her—you will worship God."

And the lightning and the thunder were renewed; and we were all wondering at the impact of the words we had heard, when the floor opened beneath us, and we were precipitated into the depth below.

THIRD DEGREE OF THE TEMPLE.

On recovering from our astonishment, we perceived that we were in an ample bath of tepid water, sunk in the floor of a room. Our dress being loose and of linen, we suffered but little inconvenience from the water, but otherwise our situation was sufficiently awkward, not to say indelicate. Since we possessed the

22

presence of mind, having received the fall and the unexpected immersion, our guide, who hovered over us in a moving cloud, attired as a winged angel, cried aloud—

"Children of the promise, you are now in the *waters of oblivion*, which shall wash your souls as white as snow, and leave no trace of sin behind. Now you are on the threshold of your reward for your souls have been purified; and so long as you live in the bosom of the church, those things which are considered sinful in others shall not be sinful in you; for you are clean, but behold, the waters are departing."

And such was the fact; and in a few minutes there was scarcely a drop in the basin. And then, on a signal, we all left it, and were baptized with new scripture names (my name was Jacob), and we were dressed with peculiar dresses of various fashions, but loose trousers formed a portion of each, and were supplied to the males and females indifferently. When we were all equipped, the apartment was filled with light, and the place was filled with a delicious odor; and soon six priests appeared in sacerdotal robes; they poured oil on our heads, and they anointed us kings and queens in time and eternity! And when this ceremony was finished, a mighty angel ascended through the floor of the bath in a chariot of clouds, and he spoke the following words:—

"Mormons, by the will of Heaven,
All your sins are now forgiven;
And henceforth you are free to rove
Through all the wiles of wealth and love,
Still taking Nature for your guide
In choice of bridegroom or of bride.
You are free, and no conflict
Can bind you with human laws;
And whatsoever you win now,
Will be with you in the great heavens:
And you can sin never again,
Unless against the Mormon bible!"

And when the angel had ceased speaking, there was a crash of brazen trumpets, followed by a seraphic melody. And then there were several minutes of profound stillness and darkness. And so ended the *third degree*.

FOURTH DEGREE OF THE TEMPLE.

I now, by an arrangement, found myself in a kind of dark hole like a cave, and a vision appeared to me which was designed

23

to represent the first creation of man. Someone beside me said, "Lo, I have made you in my own image, and now I will tell you a mystery. One of thy ribs have I taken to make unto thee a wife in the flesh; *but thou art also permitted to have as many wives in the spirit as thou hast ribs remaining; for the people of thy kingdom in the world to come must be of thy own posterity; so that according to their number shall be thy greatness*. And this, thou wilt readily perceive, is the evident solution of the mystery involved in the formation of the first among women; but still I have hidden it from the world for six thousand years, to reveal it unto the Mormon church, which is alone the true one. But go thy ways; for she who was thy rib awaits thee, and has matter to communicate which it imports thee to learn."

And on withdrawing a curtain at the entrance of the cave, I recognized my wife outside, seated on a stone; and she appeared to be buried in reflection, and not without good reason, as I came to understand when she revealed her thoughts to me, which was to this effect:—A man in another cave, who had just assumed to have made her out of a rib, had informed her of the male privilege of having wives and ribs of equal number, which she thought unfair, for not having the same privilege; but he told her that she was now divorced; and although a woman could have no more than one husband, she was at liberty to choose her partner. "And this has caused me to think," said my wife very coolly, "that there are perhaps other men in Nauvoo whom I would prefer to yourself." "I trust not," said I; "but" (being then a faithful Mormon, and not much averse to the spiritual wife system, I said,) "let all things be done according to the rules of the church."

FIFTH DEGREE OF THE TEMPLE.

While we were yet speaking, a wall before us separated like a scene in a theater, and to our astonishment, we beheld a large garden before us; its size appeared quite extensive because of the mirrors surrounding us. It was full of plants, flowers, and fruit trees; in it was a fountain of living water, with two fruit trees in the center, the first of which, as we were subsequently told, was the *tree of knowledge*, and the other was *the tree of life*. There were hosts of angels soaring about and singing under the evening atmosphere above us. The place seemed to be charming beyond description.

24

There is no need to inform the reader that this was the garden of Eden. It differed from the original one in at least one way; that there were now some twenty Adams and Eves in it. And, indelicate as it may be to the feelings of the reader, we were all within a point of being in a state of nudity, which, however, was partially atoned for by the faintness of the light and the shade of the trees. And now we wandered here and there, plucking and eating the fruit, avoiding those that were forbidden. As we were pondering the drama, we saw a large serpent which enfolded the tree of knowledge. The old "temptation" was imitated when all the women accepted of the fruit and gave it to their husbands. The question and the confession were reenacted, and we were driven out; a shower of lightning and thunder came down; and the cherubs came with flaming swords to oversee the garden.

And now an epoch was supposed to have passed, when a person representing Moses came forth to obtain fruit from the tree of life; but he was baffled by the flaming swords. And then came in succession Zoroaster, Wodin, and Muhammad, with the same result. And after this, Lucifer perched himself upon the topmost branch, like a king upon a throne. After a lengthy period of time had elapsed, others came forth to represent all the religious denominations of the world, trying to obtain the fruit; but they could not. Each one insisted to the others that the tree was his; and they tried with all their might to keep each other from partaking of the fruit. And all this while, the devil kept addressing them thuswise:—

"That's it, my worthy friends—fight it out! Well done, Quakers! Well done, Shakers! Blaze away, Protestants, Catholics, and all! A lusty set of fellows you, no doubt! And by the grace of your creeds, hell will never be empty! Let me have such saints when I'm in want of sinners! And whenever there's a dearth of lies in the market, only inoculate me with one of your books, and I'll put truth to the blush for a month of Sundays! You are the people, boys, to keep up the value of brimstone, and to save us devils from overworking ourselves in the way of temptations; for you damn people so fast that you leave us nothing to do but to make additions to hell and heat the ovens!"

And his Satanic majesty concluded his harangue with a hearty laugh, and was at the commencement of another jocular address, when the sky opened and an angel descended with a book in his right hand, which checked his mirth; for when Lucifer beheld the book, he trembled and fell prostrate on the earth, exclaiming,—"My reign is over!" And then the sectarians vanished. And the flaming swords ceased waving around the tree of life, and the angel gathered the fruit, and we (the Mormons) entered the garden and ate thereof, having ascertained beforehand that the conquering angel was Joseph Smith, and the book, by means of which he had performed such a miracle, was the Book of Mormon.

SIXTH DEGREE OF THE TEMPLE.

Everything in the Temple seemed to work by machinery. As we sat in a circle eating the fruit, the light died out, and, by a sudden inclination of the floor, we were lowered into a dark and gloomy apartment, devoid of furniture, and with an earthy smell. For a time, we thought it was unoccupied except by ourselves; but in a few minutes, when our eyes had accommodated themselves to the darkness, we perceived a number of human skeletons hanging in chains; we heard the rattling of their bones in the afflictions and the pangs of death. And yet further to increase our dismay, a sudden opening in a distant wall disclosed a lake of liquid fire surrounded by an iron grating; and therein were a number of persons in chains and in an extremity of torture. And by and by, there was a rushing sound, succeeded by a hollow voice, which spoke in a threatening tone as follows:—

"Mormons, though you have eaten of the bread of life, you are still liable not only to the natural, but to an eternal death. But such can only befall you through faithlessness to your oath of initiation; for otherwise you are superior to all mortal sin! Betray that oath, and you hang for all time and burn for all eternity; for in such case, no power can shield you from the vengeance of the brotherhood and the punishment of hell! *But honor it to the end, and no crimes which you may commit can deprive you of an everlasting reward in heaven!* Look on those skeletons! They are the bones of faithless Mormons. Behold those captives in that burning lake! They are their tortured souls. And assuredly such shall be your reward, if such shall be your provocation! But be faithful and fear not! Be true to Mormonism, and no species of falsehood can affect you! Against a Mormon must you never fight! Against a Mormon you must never swear! Your words must comfort them, and your money must succor them!

26

As judges, you must deliver them! As jurymen, acquit them! As brothers and sisters, live and die for them! You must exalt them into all offices which they covet! You must abandon clan and kin and country for their sake! And, in fine, you must make Mormonism the great object of your life! And now go forth upon your mission, and be this your motto:—

"An oath I have given,
Let me honor it well;
For to KEEP, *it is heaven,*
And to BREAK, *it is hell!"*

And with the last word, the skeleton and the burning lake vanished; and by some new method we were transported into another apartment, where the women were taken from us, and the men were placed standing in a row. By and by the females returned, with a thick veil across their faces, through which it was impossible to distinguish their features, *and one by one they chose us for husbands, until every woman was mated.* And then there was a grand chorus by invisible vocalists; and presently, a curtain being withdrawn, a high priest appeared at an altar and solemnized our nuptials in these words:—

"By the rib from Adam taken,
By the Mormon faith given,
Valiant brother and fair sister,
Here I wed you to each other,
To abide together forever,
Unless you choose yourselves to sever!
All previous bonds were broken duly;
Now alone you're wedded truly—
Whether in the same connection
Or to a present first affection.
Now, wife, throw off the screen that hides you!
Now, husband, take what Heaven provides you!"

And on the last word, off went the veils, when it was perceived that the majority of the husbands had their former wives; but several of them had new ones; and among the latter fell my fate. I received a rather good-looking lady, who was a perfect stranger to me, whose husband who had met with a fate similar to mine. We were not surprised by such a change; but truly, I must confess that I felt some jealous throbs upon seeing my wife leaning her chin lovingly on the shoulder of

27

a tall Mormon, who appeared to be highly pleased with his bargain. I tried to make my mind humble and agreeable to the arrangements of the church in this also; and I had every assistance for that from the incomparable affection of my new wife.

SEVENTH DEGREE OF THE TEMPLE.

An hour of inaction (with no good end in view) in a darkened room well-furnished with couches, succeeded our nuptials; and this was followed by a grand chorus of many voices, in some other place, singing the following stanzas:—

"You have left the center of the world,
Full of darkness and blatant lies,
In the hand of the servant of Heaven himself;
Enter, enter, Mormons wise!

And with the fiends you've striven,
You have driven Satan, old and strong
Away back to his infernal den;
Enter, enter, Mormons bold.

At the oath you never trembled,
You made a promise to hold your ground,
Without casting a doubtful glance;
Enter, enter, Mormons true.

You need not be alarmed henceforth,
But honor the oath of your faith still;
Sin no more has power to harm you:
Enter, enter, and be blessed."

On the conclusion of the song, immense doors were thrown open, and behold a splendid great hall, in a style of grandeur, opened before us. The whole place glittered with gold, silver, mirrors, silks, and every kind of pictures and adornments, showing the rise and progress of Mormonism; the carpet was like a beautiful prairie in full blossom; and the lofty vault painted to represent the summer, the clouds in motion, and the sun in the center. At one extremity of the hall there was a magnificent throne (seated on which was the arch prophet) of gold and scarlet, supported on the backs of four winged lions; at the other end was spread a delicious banquet. The spacious place was filled with the most lovely aromas, and we heard occasional strains of such pleasant music as though they were proceeding from angels' harps. The whole scene and all its circumstances were beautiful and

28

exciting beyond description; and it left such a vivid picture on my memory which the hand of time can never efface.

This hall was crowded with a gay and sparkling company, whom the uninitiated would have never supposed to be the grave and cynical Mormons as seen in their everyday life. Their dresses were of the loose Turkish fashion, highly becoming, and inflamed the passions, for which they were doubtlessly intended. We all were furnished with the same costumes, and we were received into their midst. And on the whole, the women were handsome, and the men more than passable; but there appeared to be no moral beauty in the one or the other. And how could such a thing be expected, when we consider that all those persons were accepted saints and chosen pillars of the church, and that immorality is the cornerstone of the Mormon faith? The freedom of their conduct, however, even exceeded the bounds which the warmest imagination might ascribe to it, and exhibited the *spiritual wife system* in a light altogether too glaring for exposure to the public eye. Suffice it to say, that they indulged in the license afforded them by their matrimonial laws up to its most extreme extent; yes, and even above it as Joe Smith himself proves, who had *sixty* wives—spiritual and otherwise—instead of limiting himself to one for each of his ribs. And the females also, almost without exception, had changed the law in their own favor, on this subject. And thus the entire Mormon population, or at least that portion of it which had taken the *seven degrees*, was so mixed up in matrimonial cross-quarterings, that there was probably not so much as one of them who could say what relationship he or she had to the others.

But here I must pause; for I find that I cannot write on so dangerous a subject without running the risk of giving offense. In fact, I dare not describe a tithe of the mysteries of the *seventh degree*. I will merely add, that they had lowered themselves to feasting and carousing and exceeded all limits in speech and behavior, and since there were male and female, there was such a scene there that was probably never paralleled outside the walls of the great Mormon Temple.

In connection with the foregoing description of the *Degrees of the Temple* by Mr. White, we shall place here the strange ceremonies of the reception into the order of the system called *Spiritual Wifery*, as it was administered to over twelve thousand men and women in the Nauvoo Temple, in the year of 1846, which

29

testimony is given by a man and wife by the name of John and Maria Van Dusen, who were brought up in the State of *New York;* they accepted the Mormon religion; they went to Nauvoo, and lived there for three years. They were received into the secrets of the Temple. They left the Mormons because of a strong conviction and a troubled conscience, upon perceiving the wickedness of the elders of this sect. They published the following testimony in order to warn their fellow men of this frightful danger.

The reader will see that we have had to limit the boundaries of taste and modesty in the following pages: this is not an easy task for us; but we cannot desist from doing justice to the topic.

SPIRITUAL WIFERY.

RECEIVING MALES AND FEMALES INTO THE ORDER,

In which is concealed a conspiracy against the liberties of this country.

The order of initiation is as follows:—A gentleman and lady pass through a narrow hall in the attic of the Temple, at the opposite end of which is a man stationed, whose duty it is to guard the door, and admit proper persons only. Then they are separated; he passes the gentleman through a door to the right, and the doorman leads the lady through a door to the left, to an unfurnished room, with the exception of a few chairs. There another conductor meets her, and questions her to know who she is, where she came from, &c.; then she is divested of all her outside apparel, and taken to a rather small room, a considerable distance from there, and she is presented to yet another conductor, who is to administer the strange ceremonies of the initiation, who divests her of the remainder of her clothing, until she is completely naked. The conductor takes her into a bath of water, and washes her from head to foot, reciting the following purposes going forward:—I wash your eyes, that you may behold the glory of God; your mouth, that you may speak forth his praise; your breasts, that you may give suck to a numerous posterity; your bowels, that you may bring forth spiritual sons and daughters; your * * * * * * * and so down to the feet, that you may be swift to run the race set before you.

She is now pronounced clean, and is taken out of the water, and a hornful of perfumed oil is poured on the top of her head, and the conductor anoints her with his hand over her entire body. Then she is seated, and ordained to be a queen from this

30

time forth and forever. Then she is presented with a kind of light undergarment, in one piece, similar to a chemise and drawers in one, which forms a tight fit on her. There were two particular marks cut on the garment, one on the breast and the other on the knee: the first to represent protection, I think, and the other to signify willingness to bow to the Lord. She is told that this garment represents the *white stone* spoken of in the scripture, in which was a new name given, which no man knew but him which received it. Then the conductor whispers a name in her ear, which she was never to reveal, except to a certain individual (B. Young), on a particular occasion. The meaning of this will be revealed to her by Brigham when he meets her at the Veil, as it is called. After being furnished with white stockings and a nightgown, she is conducted to another part of the Temple, where she is left on her own for a short time, to have the opportunity to reflect on the scenes she has just passed through. She had been there for two hours already, with her mind under so much excitement that she doubted whether the whole thing had been a dream; but after a little rest she comes to the conclusion that it was reality; and she has only now to wait the final result of this strange procedure.

The object of this unheard of initiation, and the woman's being left here alone, in this peculiar dress and situation, will be fully realized by the reader after knowing about the initiation of the gentleman who was separated from her. He was taken by another conductor, questioned, and divested of his outside clothes, and taken to another conductor, who removed the remainder of his clothing from him, which left him perfectly naked, and he washed him in a bath of water, performing on him ceremonies similar to those of the woman, with some exceptions. After being rolled and tumbled about in the bath, he is pronounced clean, taken out of the water, and the perfumed oil is poured on his head, and he is anointed in detail over his entire body. Then he is seated on a chair and proclaimed to be a king for time and eternity. In this his pride is pampered. After this he is clothed with a lightweight garment which is a tight fit, over which is put a common shirt. In this fix he is conducted into another apartment, and after being placed in a certain position on the floor, he is left alone. Here now are the man and the woman in separate apartments, unbeknown to each other, and having passed through the similar, strange ceremonies. All is now silent, and a perfect silence pervades the whole Temple. The silence is broken

31

by a commotion in a distant part of the building, and afterwards voices are heard speaking of the propriety of organizing matter, worlds, &c., when Brigham Young commences, in a grave tone of voice, first by speaking the world into existence; after that darkness prevails, and he says, "Let there be light; let the light be divided from the darkness; let there be a firmament in the midst of the waters; let the firmament be called heaven; let the waters under the firmament be gathered together into one place, and let the dry land appear; let the dry land be called earth, and the gathering together of the waters seas; let the earth bring forth grass, the herb yielding seed, and the fruit tree yielding fruit after its kind, whose seed is in itself upon the earth; let the earth bring forth the living creature after his kind." He then adds, "All things which I have now made are very good; but there is not a man to till the ground, or to have dominion over all that we have made, which walks and moves on the face of the earth. Now let us make man in our image, after our likeness."

While he is uttering these words, he goes in the room to the man, puts his hands on him, pretending to form him from the dust, and breathes into his nostrils the breath of life, and man became a living soul. Next Brigham puts the man into a feigned sleep, and acts out this scripture—"And the Lord God caused a deep sleep to fall upon Adam, and he slept; and he took one of his ribs, and he closed up the flesh instead thereof; and the rib the Lord God had taken from man, made he a woman, and he brought her unto the man."

After going through a ceremony as if in the act of taking the rib, he goes to the apartment where the woman was, and he forms her from it. The particular manner in which this is done I will not explain; in any event, it is not very long before he returns with the woman by the hand to the man who was in a profound feigned sleep. Then Brigham calls out, "Adam, here is thy companion that I give to thee; what wilt thou call her?"

The man arose and saluted the woman, saying, "This is bone of my bone, and flesh of my flesh; she shall be called woman, because she was taken out of man."

Brigham next orders his Adam and his Eve to follow him to a large room, all nicely decorated with flowers, plants, and fruit trees, with a lovely path through them, which characterized the Garden of Eden; in it also were the tree of life, the tree of knowledge of good and evil, the flaming sword, &c. In all this Brigham

32

assumes to personate the Lord. He leads them around, showing them the beauties of his creation: "This is a beautiful place," he says, "everything to delight the eye, the ear, and the taste. Of all these things you may freely partake; but of the tree of knowledge of good and evil (pointing to it), of this you may not partake, for in the day you eat of it, you shall surely die."

After giving strict charge of all the particulars of the garden, Brigham leaves his Adam and his Eve alone in the garden, to amuse themselves as seemeth them good.

Now, the serpent, who was Orson Hyde (who acted the part of the devil in this ceremony, which part was well sustained, he being more than half devil himself,) who was more cunning than all the creatures which Brigham made, came to the garden, and disturbed the happiness of the blessed couple, saying, "Did not the Lord (Brigham) say, You may not eat from every tree of the garden?" And the woman said to the devil (Orson Hyde), "Of the fruit of every tree in the garden we could eat; but of the fruit of the tree in the middle of the garden, the Lord (Brigham) said we should not eat, or touch it, lest we die." And the devil said to the woman, "You shall not surely die!" (for he knows that Brigham Young will succeed in the day you eat of that tree in causing you to believe that the strange plan that he and his accomplices have concocted is a revelation from God, and that he has received a commandment to make you in this manner, and that it is a reward from God for building this temple: and then you will be incapable of judging between God's truth and Brigham's lies. After that he can easily make you believe that God has given you to him and his accomplices as a spiritual wife, to populate the Mormon city, in the Salt Lake Valley, California, for the purpose of fulfilling his evil designs). The devil (Orson Hyde) succeeded in getting the woman to partake of the fruit, and he had her give it to her husband, and they did eat. Soon thereafter the voice of Brigham was heard coming to the garden, and they hid themselves. After looking around him, he called out, "Adam, where art thou?" Adam answered, "I heard thy voice, and I was afraid; for I was naked, and I hid myself." And Brigham said, "Who told thee that thou wast naked? Hast thou eaten of the tree, whereof I commanded thee that thou shouldst not eat?" And the man said, "The woman thou gavest to be with me, she gave me of the tree, and I did eat." And Brigham said to the woman, "What is this that thou hast done?" And the woman answered, "The serpent (Orson Hyde) beguiled me, and I did eat."

33

And Brigham said to the devil, "Because thou hast done this, thou art cursed above all cattle, and above every beast of the field, and upon thy belly shalt thou go, and dust shalt thou eat all the days of thy life." (After Orson received the curse from Brigham, he fell on his belly on the floor, and crawled on the floor for a while, and thus he exited.) "I will put enmity between thee and the woman, and between thy seed and her seed." Unto the woman he said, "I will greatly multiply thy sorrow; thou shalt bring forth children, and thy desire shall be to thy (spiritual) husband, and he shall rule over thee." And to the man he said, "Because thou hast hearkened unto the voice of thy wife," &c., "cursed is the ground for thy sake, in sorrow shalt thou eat of it all the days of thy life," &c. (And you shall not have a wife, for I choose to take her for myself, spiritually, for I see that she is young, fair, and desirable.)

Now Brigham Young turns to his accomplices, Parley Pratt, Orson Pratt, Heber C. Kimble, Orson Hyde, Wilford Woodruff, and several elders who are involved in this great scheme. "Behold! through our clever designs we have succeeded in deceiving the people. And now, lest any of them go out and reveal the secret, and expose us and destroy our scheme, let us administer a solemn oath, and let us connect it to the most cruel punishment." The man and the woman are placed to kneel before the altar, on which is the Bible. They place their hands on the Bible while the following oath is administered.

THE OATH.

You do solemnly swear, in the presence of Almighty God, his holy angels, and these witnesses, that you will avenge the blood of Joseph Smith on this nation, and teach the same to your children; and that you will, from this time henceforth and forever, begin and carry out hostilities against the nation, and to keep the same intent a profound secret, now and forever. So help you God.

They are here instructed in a variety of signs and tokens that they are to use among themselves. All are here told—that the killing of Joseph Smith in Illinois is a national offense, that it has angered God, and that God has ordered this secret organization to overthrow the whole nation.

After a great variety of similar instruction, they are conducted to another part of the Temple, where the present world

34

is represented, especially in a religious capacity, where the leaders of all the churches are brought to view and mocked. Orson Hyde here also acts the part of the devil; he enters in caricature fixings and cries out, "Good morning, brethren, the Methodists, the Presbyterians, the Universalists, the Quakers, the Baptists, the Catholics, we have done well this winter; we have had good revivals—the world is nearly prepared for the millennium; but now this Joe Smith's doctrine is making rapid progress in the world, and we must be on the lookout; otherwise, they will over-throw us in our long-established plans." After a long and laughable conversation between the devil (Orson) and all the sects, represented by several of the leaders of the Mormons, the devil fellowships with them all. Brigham Young next comes in as the Lord, and commands the devil to let the deceived sects alone, for the time has come when they are all to be converted to the true faith (Mormonism); and in token of this, those who have represented them are dressed in white clothing; and then they are conducted into another room, which represents the future time between the present condition of man and his final rest, or the kingdom of heaven. On the center of this floor is an altar, where the man and the woman are requested to kneel, and enter into the most solemn covenant with their hands on the Bible, that they will carry out Brigham's purposes in the future, right or wrong.

After a variety of ceremonies, a female conductor takes the man and leads him to what is called the veil, which separates the holy from the most holy place. There were several marks on the veil (which consisted of thin cloth) which were explained by Young who stood on the other side of it: after that the man is conducted through a door to the left, to the most holy place. Brigham next explains the marks on the veil to the woman, and he tells her she must have corresponding marks in some special place of her under garment, and that it is his duty to make them. After doing so, she is taken through the door after her husband, who takes her to the celestial kingdom, where they are crowned king and queen. Here also Brigham Young reveals to them all the mysteries of the kingdom—the plurality of wives system, and the like; when the women are seduced and led into all manner of abominable and licentious practices; in short, everything which is of such a character that it cannot be made public, is here taught and practiced. And this is the

35

object, no doubt, of this wonderful initiation, to restrain the mind from revealing them—which it has a tendency to do, so that, in case those abominable principles should be disbelieved by some, no one can affirm them, or tell them, by reason of the penalty.

Although strange and foolish as this procedure may appear, the greater part of those who go into it under the circumstances described, believe that it is a revelation from God. And we, having providentially our eyes opened, and having escaped the dire consequences of following these designing leaders, feel anxious to prevent others from going after them; which important object we shall no doubt accomplish, to a greater or lesser extent, by an extensive circulation of this work, which will be read by many foreign nations as well as this; and we hope that all who love truth, and hate religious imposition, will assist in its circulation.

JOHN VAN DUSEN, and MARIA
VAN DUSEN, his wife.

NEW YORK.

The above couple gives the names of several respected persons in *New York* at the end of the pamphlet as REFERENCES.

Perhaps some are ready to ask, What are the religious tenets of the Mormons? This is a question much easier to ask than it is to offer a correct and satisfactory answer. Neither Smith, the founder of the church, if it is not blasphemy to call such an organization a church, nor the five members that were with him in the beginning in Fayette, had the same idea about a specific religious faith, or the competence to explain it, had it been formed, with the possible exception of Rigdon. It was not their intention, in any way in the world, to establish any faith, or to form any profession. Smith was a prophet in hiding. He was sufficiently careful to keep his Golden Bible out of sight, for the direct mortal danger to whoever might look at it. One could suppose that the doctrinal topics and the articles of faith held by the prophet had the same bright and deadly clarity as those of the Golden Bible; for we believe it to be a fact, that the one and the other, until the present time are unknown to the sight and feeling of man. The few things that are established as a creed and guidance for the church, are revelations that

36

Smith received from time to time to answer his intentions at the moment. He did not have a set purpose in this way, or any established points for his faith. For the most part, his revelations are directive, and are chiefly connected with the purse. Church members are commanded to give their money to the Lord; to steal it from the gentiles, in the name of the Lord, and assist Smith. For the most part, these commandments and their like make up the body of the revelations. Some others were to confirm the inspiration of Smith's books and his saintly character, whom they were to obey in all things, as a revealer of God's will. Miraculous inspiration and power are given also to the Saints, as the following revelation shows:—

"And as I said unto mine apostles, even so I say unto you, for you are mine apostles; therefore, as I said unto mine apostles I say unto you again, that every soul who believeth on your words, and is baptized by water for the remission of sins, shall receive the Holy Ghost. In my name they shall cast out devils, heal the sick, open the eyes of the blind, and unstop the ears of the deaf; and if they drink anything deadly it shall not hurt them."—*Book of the Doctrine and the Covenants, page* 92.

I found a series of revelations also that are connected with the future political power of the Mormon Church. In this category are the following:—

"Verily I say unto you that in that time ye shall have no king nor ruler; for I will be your king and watch over you; and you shall be a free people; and ye shall have no laws but my laws when I come."—*Doc.* and *Cov.* Page 119.

Again, page 194:—

"Ye shall assemble yourselves together to rejoice upon the land of Missouri, which is the land of your inheritance, which is now in the hands of your enemies."

Again, page 232:—

"Therefore, get ye straightway unto my land; break down the walls of mine enemies; throw down their tower, and scatter their watchmen; avenge me of mine enemies, that I may inherit the land."

The body of doctrine and faith of the Mormons, their theology and their morality, can be summed up as follows—*That which is received from time to time through revelation.*

The book of covenants, which contains the greatest part of the things they believe, is but a small part of the revelations

37

which have been given to Smith. There is a large volume of revelations received, but unpublished, about which we can say nothing until the appropriate time. The few topics of their faith that can be named are, first, about the nature of faith, which is treated by him extensively in the Book of the Commandments, and it is confirmed that he relies on human testimony. Next, about the nature of God. They profess to believe in the Trinity: and it is said in the last chapter on faith, that the only way for a man to know of his acceptance by God is to sacrifice all his earthly belongings. In this last topic there is the most perfect and detailed consistency and agreement throughout. It is the great topic of the faith, without which there is no acceptance.

A large part of the converts of the Mormon church have been brought from England, and chiefly from the poorest people in the working class. And those who are acquainted with such know that they, with respect to their mental condition, are remarkably low and obscure. It appears that their acute ignorance is beyond that of their fellow subjects in the Green Island. Several of their English converts also are men of learning, as well as many of the American members of the church. With regard to possessions, the article of faith mentioned above, that they cannot know of their acceptance by God except by the sacrifice of all their earthly things, is a sufficient explanation of their condition. Smith's objective was not only to "exploit the Gentiles," but the saints as well; consequently, those who had money or some other possessions customarily gave it up to the pastor upon coming into the fold; and if some more money were found, it would likely be directed to the same hands. Some who emigrated from England to the holy city refused to pay tithing from their possessions to the wealth of the church; but afterwards they had to sacrifice everything they owned.

While in Missouri, during the time of their journey in that state, through Smith's incitements, revelations, and threats, the members of the church were organized into several companies, for the purpose of robbing the gentiles around them. They were called the Danites, and they numbered, according to the sworn testimony of one of their number, from eight hundred to a thousand. The witness said that they built *blockhouses*, and if the crops that were raised could not sustain them, they would

38

take from other townspeople. The army took an oath that they would assist Smith against the authorities of the state, and that they would flog whoever said a word against him. They had another small army which they called the "destroying angel," the duty of which, according to the testimony of Bennet, was to kill those who happened to fall under the displeasure of the church or its leader. This army, according to the above witness, visited the Indians and compelled them to unite with Smith against the people of Missouri. This testimony was given in September, 1838; the following month the counties of Caldwell and Davies were invaded and plundered by their armies, the inhabitants of nearly all the neighboring counties were persecuted, the houses, the farms, and the storehouses were plundered, and some of the buildings were set on fire. Some of the members of Smith's church had to leave the church and the place, and separate themselves from this army and were forced to cooperate with them. Among them were Cowdery and the two Whitmers, who were the foremost witnesses of the truth of the Book of Mormon, and the first was a professed scribe, lawyer, and an early and zealous participant of Smith's deceit, who traveled two or three hundred miles to see him, and who was the means of compelling the move of the church from Fayette to Kirtland, the place of his own residence.

It is said in the testimony of another one of the apostates, who had been president of the twelve apostles and the president of the church in *Far West*, that a company had been sent out to steal fat pigs, animals, and honey; and at the same time that another company, containing eighty men under the charge of a captain, had gone to Gallatin, and, according to his own witness, they had confronted about twenty or thirty men, and set Gallatin on fire. They robbed the *postmaster* and plundered the neighborhood. The same witness says,—"The plan of Smith the prophet is to take this State (Missouri), and tell his people that he intends to take the United States, and finally the whole world." This testimony is confirmed by Orson Hyde, one of the twelve apostles, who left the church because of his conviction of their immorality and their ungodliness. "I know," he said, "that the greatest part of the above things is true, and I believe that the other things are true also." No great importance is to be given to Hyde's testimony. He has returned to the Mormons again. But the foregoing things are confirmed by plenty of other witnesses.

39

As a consequence of this intolerable trail of plundering and ravaging the country, the citizens gathered together in a large number, and they drove them out of the state. They went to Illinois, and settled in Nauvoo, as was said previously.

It should be noted that the time of the move from Missouri to Illinois was a season of great success in the purposes of the prophet; for it appears that this was the time that he began methodically to work out his intention of setting up political power in addition to his episcopate; and also to greatly expand the privileges pertaining to the priestly office, especially the establishment of spiritual wifery. From this time to his death, a little more than three years later, was the period of the greatest success and the most brilliant day in Smith's life. He could have with a single nod two thousand votes, and as easily as that an equal number of bayonets for war if there were need; the politician recognized his influence, and the city and the country felt and feared his power. After making public the revelation which he received from God commanding polygamy as a Christian duty, it was fitting for the prophet to set a good example before his people by being obedient to the commandment himself; and if he could be measured by the number of his friends, Mohammed himself could not boast in holiness any more than Joseph Smith.

His growth from the beginning until now causes one to think about a *banker* beginning his career in the world by selling apples and cakes valued at halfpennies, and ending by loaning a hundred million to kings in order to prop up their thrones. Smith began not having anything but the materials of a common liar; and gradually as his materials increased, and the trust in him became larger and larger, he expanded his business until he made himself a prophet, whose word, albeit blasphemous and corrupt, was gospel, truth, and law to ten thousand souls who had put their hopes in him,—the political master and ruler, through whom political and societal matters of all his people were treated and steered, and the people themselves were governed by completely dictatorial power. He had never foreseen or thought of the great things that were to come out of his shameless workmanship of lies. He used them at the time for amusement and to win the moment, and they became of unexpected worth and importance through the gullibility of those who received them; and the money digger obtained such a ready

40

and winning market for the sale of his wonders, that he was motivated to broaden the limits, until finally through continual growth he found himself in possession of souls, bodies, and the possession of his ten thousand people—and of ecclesiastical and dictatorial power, great political influence, together with an abundance of wealth.

The Book of Commandments put an end to the authority of the Bible, and it set up the revelations made through Smith in their place. "Behold, I say unto you that all old covenants have I caused to be done away in this thing; and this is a new and everlasting covenant." (*Book of the Covenants*, page 178). And after turning away the Gospel in this manner, the next objective was to turn away all the laws except for the ones Smith supported. As was quoted previously:—"Verily, I say unto you that in time ye shall have no king nor ruler, for I will be your king and watch over you; and you shall be a free people, and ye shall have no laws but my laws when I come." (*Doctrine and Covenants*, page 119.) Another section tells of a complete temporal as well as a spiritual government of the Mormon president. In this manner we have shown the blossoming of the Mormon flowers. The season of the church after the move to Illinois was mid-summer; the fruit was ripening quickly as well as the prophet himself, while making a good business in the "Nauvoo House," creating great political influence, and holding the ambitious leaders of the people in his left hand, as he held his Mormons in his right hand: he put his more cunning mind to work and used his most serious moments to establish military power, the leader of which was himself, as in all other things; to publish new revelations as an augmentation of his priestly honors, especially in the abundance of wives and to elevate the church by building the great Temple.

Soon after settling in Nauvoo, Smith obtained authorization from the State to be the Adjutant General of the Nauvoo militia, and he raised up the military might to two or three thousand men, which he put under good discipline; and he was quickly preparing to fulfill the prophecy, according to which he was to govern the whole earth. He was a little more careful concerning his command "to assume the name of the Lord" in this State than he had been in Missouri. He learned the lesson which they received in that State for them to be a little more secretive in this part of their religious duty. Yet they had discharged their duty to such

41

an extent as to load themselves with other means, and to stir up the animosity of the people who lived around them. Finally the people tired of suffering, their patience ran out, and they rose up against them; Smith was arrested and imprisoned, and in the prison his life was ended, as well as that of his brother Hyrum, as was previously said. After this his people were scattered here and there; some went to Iowa, but the greatest part of them went to the shore of the Salt Lake, in the valley between Nevada and the Rocky Mountains. As of today, many have found their way to the latter place, and there are several thousand Mormons there.

After the United States government made this area its own territory, the appropriate officials were appointed to carry forth the pattern of the government. Unfortunately, the one appointed was Brigham Young, the English Mormon, who had been in that country but a few years, and whose only merit was the inheritance of the spiritual greatness and offices of Smith, whose mantel he assumed—this man was appointed governor of the territory. Some other important offices were given to Mormons. It was a great defect and folly to put the administration of the main offices of government into the hands of men who had previously distinguished themselves in the greatest crimes. The consequence of this could not be good. Two judges and the scribe, who did not belong to the Mormon church, were turned out of office by Brigham and his allies. It was revealed that Young took the entire government to himself, seizing all the money, proclaiming that no law would be administered except through himself, and that no authority could succeed in the territory but that of the church. This is nothing but the carrying out of the command of the revelation given by Smith, who attempted to accomplish this in Missouri and Illinois; and since it was consistent with the religious duty of the faithful, there was nothing else that could be expected.

Made known also were several incidents of their cruelty toward those who opposed them, and their very faithful obedience to the revelation of polygamy.

Before ending, since we have not mentioned the claims of this sect regarding their power to work miracles, we present the account of a remarkable miracle (?), which is related by Mr. Tucker, who gives the account of the circumstance connected with the printing of the Book of Mormon. The account is related in the volume published by Dr. Bennett as follows:—

42

"Towards the close of a fine summer's day, a farmer, in one of the States, found a respectable-looking man at his gate, who requested permission to pass the night under his roof. The hospitable farmer readily complied: the stranger was invited into the house, and a warm and substantial supper set before him.

"After he had eaten, the farmer, who appeared to be a jovial, warm-hearted, humorous, and withal shrewd old man, passed several hours in pleasant conversation with his guest, who seemed to be very ill at ease, both in body and mind, yet, as if desirous of pleasing his entertainer, replied courteously and agreeable to whatever was said to him. Finally, he pleaded fatigue and illness as an excuse for retiring to rest, and was conducted by the farmer to an upper chamber, where he went to bed.

"About the middle of the night, the farmer and his family were awakened by the most dreadful groans, which they soon ascertained proceeded from the chamber of the traveler. On going to investigate the matter, they found that the stranger was dreadfully ill, suffering the most acute pains and uttering the most doleful cries, apparently without any consciousness of what was passing around him. Everything that kindness and experience could suggest, was done to relieve the sick man; but all efforts were in vain, and to the consternation of the farmer and his family, their guest expired in the course of a few hours.

"In the midst of their trouble and anxiety, at an early hour in the morning, two travelers came to the gate, and requested entertainment. The farmer told them that he would willingly offer them hospitality, but that just now his household was in the greatest confusion on account of the death of the stranger, the particulars of which he proceeded to relate to them. They appeared to be much surprised and grieved at the poor man's calamity, and politely requested permission to see the corpse. This of course the farmer readily granted, and conducted them to the chamber in which lay the dead body. They looked at it for a few minutes in silence, and then the oldest of the pair gravely told the farmer, that they were Elders of the Church of Jesus Christ of Latter-day Saints, and were empowered by God to perform miracles, even to the extent of raising the dead; and that they felt quite assured they could bring to life the dead man before them!

"The farmer was of course pretty considerably astonished by the quality and powers of the persons who addressed him, and

43

rather incredulously asked if they were quite sure that they could perform all they professed to.

"O certainly! Not a doubt of it. The Lord has commissioned us expressly to work miracles, in order to prove the truth of the Prophet Joseph Smith, and the inspiration of the books and doctrines revealed to him. Send for all your neighbors, that, in the presence of a multitude, we may bring the dead man to life, and that the Lord and his Church may be glorified to all men."

"The farmer, after a little consideration, agreed to let the miracle-workers proceed, and, as they desired, sent his children to his neighbors, who, attracted by the expectation of a miracle, flocked to the house in considerable numbers.

"The Mormon Elders commenced their task by kneeling and praying before the body with uplifted hands and eyes, and with most stentorian lungs. Before they had proceeded far with their prayer, a sudden idea struck the farmer, who quietly quitted the house for a few minutes, and then returned, and waited patiently by the bedside until the prayer was finished, and the Elders ready to perform their miracle. Before they began, he respectfully said to them, that, with their permission, he wished to ask them a few questions upon the subject of this miracle. They replied that they had no objection. The farmer then asked, 'You are quite certain that you can bring this man to life again?' 'We are.' 'How do you know that you can?' 'We have just received a revelation from the Lord, informing us that we can.' 'Are you quite sure that the revelation was from the Lord?' 'Yes; we cannot be mistaken about it.' 'Does your power to raise this man to life again depend upon the particular nature of his disease? or could you now bring any dead man to life?' 'It makes no difference to us: we could bring any corpse to life.' 'Well, if this man had been killed, and one of his arms cut off, could you bring him to life, and also restore to him his arm?' 'Certainly—there is no limit to the power given us by the Lord. It would make no difference, even if both his arms and his legs were cut off.' 'Could you restore him if his head had been cut off?' 'Certainly, we could.' 'Well,' said the farmer, with a quiet smile upon his features, 'I do not doubt the truth of what such holy men assert, but I am desirous that my neighbors here should be fully converted by having the miracle performed in the completest manner possible. So, by your leave, if it makes no difference whatever, I will proceed

44

Accordingly, he produced a huge and well-sharpened broad axe from beneath his coat, which he swung above his head, and was apparently about to bring it down upon the neck of the corpse, when, lo and behold! to the amazement of all present, the dead man started up in great agitation, and swore he would not have his head cut off for any consideration whatever! The company immediately seized the Mormons, and soon made them confess that the pretended dead man was also a Mormon Elder, and that they had sent him to the farmer's house, with directions to die there at a particular hour, when they would drop in, as if by accident, and perform a miracle that would astonish everybody. The farmer, after giving the impostors a severe chastisement, let them depart to practice their humbuggery in some other quarter."

J. ROSSER, PRINTER, HIGH STREET, SWANSEA.

Pamphlet 17

F. B. Ashley. *Mormoniaeth, neu Draethawd ar y Sect a Elwir "Seintiau y Dyddiau Diweddaf"* (*Mormonism: Or a Treatise on the Sect Called "The Latter-day Saints"*), translated into Welsh by G. C. F. Harries. Merthyr Tydfil: M. W. White, 1853. 34 pages.

Editor's Note: Since the original English pamphlet can be accessed on archive.org, only the title page is included herein.

The English pamphlet was published in 1851 in London, and the Welsh translation made its appearance in 1853 in Merthyr Tydfil. The following headings appear in the table of contents:

- Joe Smith
- The Golden Plates
- The Book of Mormon—Its Origin
- The Book of Mormon—Its Nature
- Mormon Doctrine
- Mormon Attractions
- The Experience of a Mormon in America

A review of the Welsh translation of this pamphlet appeared in the June 1853 issue of the *Sun*. The writer of the review gives his name as "Hywel," but his real identity is most likely David Owen, the one-time Baptist who had become an Anglican vicar and editor of the *Sun*. In his review, Hywel praises Harries for his work in providing this "inexpensive treatise on Mormonism in the Welsh language." Hywell also recommends that Anglican vicars and "others who wish the good of their parishioners" purchase a few hundred copies of the treatise for distribution.

No review from either John S. Davis or Dan Jones has been identified.

MORMONISM:

OR

A TREATISE

ABOUT THE SECT KNOWN AS

"THE LATTER-DAY SAINTS,"

BY THE REV. F. B. ASHLEY.

TRANSLATED INTO WELSH

BY THE REV. G. C. F. HARRIES, A. C.,

A Scholar of Jesus College, Oxford; and a Curate

Merthyr -Tydfil, Glamorgan.

A PENNY AND A HALF PENNY.

MERTHYR TYDFIL: PRINTED BY M. W. WHITE.

Pamphlet 18

Andrew Balfour Hepburn. *Mormonism Exploded: Or, the Religion of the Latter-day Saints Proved to Be a System of Imposture, Blasphemy, and Immorality; with the Autobiography and Portrait of the Author.* London: Simpkin, Marshall, & Co., 1855. 48 pages.

Editor's Note: Since the original English pamphlet can be accessed on archive.org, only the title page is included herein.

The author, Andrew Balfour Hepburn, was a weaver by trade and had converted to The Church of Jesus Christ of Latter-day Saints in 1844 while living in Biggar, a small town located twenty-seven miles southwest of Edinburgh. Ten months after his baptism, he began presenting lectures against the Church. He claims in his autobiography that he had convinced many to leave the Church. In 1850, he went to England to continue his lectures, and in 1854, he was in Merthyr Tydfil, where he claims to have been "the means of rescuing six of the Mormon 'saints' from the errors of the church." In Swansea, he was assisted by the Reverend Charles Short of the Mount Pleasant Baptist chapel in preparing and publishing this 48-page pamphlet. Hepburn's autobiography is dated May 1855.

Hepburn is mentioned in the 9 February 1855 issue of the *Cardiff and Merthyr Guardian* as having presented a series of lectures at the Temperance Hall "Upon the Horrid Doctrines of the so-called Latter-day Saints." Dan Jones responded to Hepburn's points in *Zion's Trumpet,* but he does so in a new and uncharacteristic manner as compared with his previous combative manner, acting "according to the counsel of our head President in the matter" (*Zion's Trumpet,* 14 April 1855, p. 114). See Episode 12.2.

MORMONISM EXPLODED;

No 3

OR,

THE RELIGION OF THE LATTER-DAY SAINTS

PROVED TO BE A SYSTEM OF

IMPOSTURE, BLASPHEMY, AND IMMORALITY;

WITH THE

AUTOBIOGRAPHY AND PORTRAIT OF THE AUTHOR.

IN TWO PARTS.—PART I.

BY A. B. HEPBURN,

ANTI-MORMON LECTURER.

EDITED BY THE REV. CHARLES SHORT, A.M.

PRICE SIXPENCE.

LONDON:
SIMPKIN, MARSHALL, & CO., STATIONERS' HALL COURT.
SWANSEA:
E. PEARSE, 15, WIND STREET.
1855.

Pamphlet 19

John E. Davis. *Mormonism Unveiled; or a Peep into the Principles & Practices of the Latter-day Saints*. Bristol: C. T. Jefferies, 1856. 48 pages.

Since the original English can be accessed on archive.org, only the title page is included herein.

On 5 February 1853, sixty-two-year-old John E. Davis, a convert from Cardiff, sailed on the *Jersey* as part of a group of 314 Latter-day Saints going to New Orleans and then to Salt Lake City. In this pamphlet, Davis provides considerable detail of the disillusionment he experienced during his time with the other immigrants and then with the community of Latter-day Saints in Salt Lake City. One of his main disappointments had to do with his failing eyesight:

> When I first arrived in Utah, being partially blind, I was in hopes that my eye sight would be restored to me, by some means, and those with whom I conversed persuaded me that our leaders had the power to heal me (36).

After a blessing from the bishop of the tenth ward failed to have any effect, Davis approached Brigham Young. But the President "sent someone else, that it might not be said, that he had laid his hands on me and failed to render me any benefit."

No printed response from any of the Latter-day Saints has been identified. See Episode 12.1.

MORMONISM UNVEILED;

OR,

A PEEP INTO THE

Principles & Practices of the Latter-day Saints,

BY

JOHN E. DAVIS,

(Formerly of No. 12, Herbert Street, Cardiff,)

A DELUDED BROTHER OF THE SECT, WHO HAS HAD THE HAPPINESS OF RECOVERING FROM HIS INFATUATION BY DISCOVERING THE INIQUITOUS PROCEEDINGS OF THE LEADERS, DURING NINE MONTHS' RESIDENCE AMONG THEM.

GIVING AN ACCOUNT OF HIS JOURNEYINGS TO UTAH, THE SO-CALLED CITY OF ZION, IN THE VALLEY OF THE SALT LAKE, IN COMPANY WITH UPWARDS OF THREE HUNDRED OF THE INFATUATED VICTIMS OF THE DELUDERS. ALSO HIS OBSERVATIONS ON THEIR CONDUCT AND PRACTICES DURING HIS SOJOURN AMONG THEM, AND HIS HAPPY ESCAPE FROM THE THRALDOM OF THE SELF-INTERESTED DECEIVERS, AND SAFE RETURN TO OLD ENGLAND.

A WARNING TO THE CREDULOUS.

Second Edition,

REVISED AND ENLARGED.

TO WHICH IS ADDED

A DISSERTATION ON "POLYGAMY AND THE BIBLE"

WITH NUMEROUS SCRIPTURE REFERENCES AND PROOFS, FURNISHED BY A GENTLEMAN WELL VERSED IN SUCH RESEARCHES.

BRISTOL:

PRINTED BY C. T. JEFFERIES, CANYNGE HOUSE, 97, REDCLIFT STREET.

1856.

SECTION 3

Poems

Contents

Nonpoetic English translations for twenty-two oppositional poems published in Wales from 1846 to 1854 which appeared in various Welsh-language periodicals—nine in *Star of Gomer* and thirteen in nine other periodicals—#1 through #22.

Nonpoetic English translations for four undated oppositional poems, each of which was bound separately with other unrelated items—#23, #24, #25, and #26.

The facsimile of the only identified English-language oppositional poem in Wales—#27 which appeared as a separate publication in 1851 in Llandovery.

Contents

The Latter-day Saints†

"You, Latter-day Saints,
I shall follow while I live,
If you can perform the miracles
Which our Lord's Apostles did,
But this,—if you cannot—if you are deceivers,
If you are men without ability for the work,
I will not come one inch to follow you,
For hell will be the end of your journey.

In Wales you were heard preaching:
But yet not one miracle was seen;
According to every omen and sign,
Your name will fall to scorn:
The same thing that happened to Southcott and Courtney,
To Martha and Mary of the White Shawl,
Will happen to you, I believe,
Your "Latter Days" will come to an end."

CLWYDFARDD.

† *Yr Amserau* (*Times*), 19 November 1846, p. 2; *Seren Gomer* (*Star of Gomer*), January 1847, pp. 7–8.

Proclamation of the Latter-day Saints to Their Compatriots†

We the fervent Mormons,
Who are men proficient in signs,
And who know black Necromancy,
For we possess the means;
We perform a miracle that is lively.
If we have sufficient alcohol and steam.

We have oil as well—
We can make a flexible Saint in a moment,
To believe he is of orthodox faith.
And he goes throughout the whole world,
Bewitching every unstable person,
To evolve into our image and our spirit.

If we see a shameless man,
In very unhappy passions,
And who deserves no respect where'er he may be,
We approach him with the true faith;
And we swear him in on every side,
And then he converts from the false faith.

A Saint, a Saint will he be now,
He won't swim in unhealthy water,
Now he will judge everyone who is,
Who was, and who will be, as rubbish;
And the holy army, which now is,
Has had a better dawn.

Our path is to scandalize
All men of religion who have hitherto been,
Until the time of Joe Smith, a good man,
Who deserves to be remembered;

---

† *Seren Gomer* (*Star of Gomer*), November 1847, p. 341.

And the great Captain who fills his place,
A quick man is he, we will testify.

It was placed in hiding,
The Word which is blessed,
Until Joe's time, when a dawn broke,
Between the great seas of America;
This he left behind him,
Blessed as a father.

Joe Smith received the book,
Through highly wondrous means,
Where the arrangements are all superb,
To improve the world completely;
Not as it was for a long time,
Before receiving the exceptional language.

We have apostles,
And faithful high priests,
And great hosts of lower officials,
That no longer exist, say fools;
But Joe, truly wise, says they do,
All to be set in harmony.

We baptize some previously baptized,
But we fear not,
To say boldly that it was not valid,
From men who were not sent;
There was no truth in its authority,
Until, enlightened, we came.

Misers come to us,
And they become generous,
Their houses and money they give to us,
To serve us without complaints;
But this we do secretly, secretly,
To be just and faithful.

We hide from sight,
From the scowling enemy,
Certain things in our organization,
Lest our honor come into view;
The yellow gold, and the white metal,—
These lead to great evil.

We have secrets,
Which no one knows but Saints,
Of the most expert in our midst,
Where fake miracles are wrought,
So that we may exploit the innocent,
And eliminate further dispute.

We can deceive the populace
To become an army,
And work for us everywhere,
And unite the weak novices;
So that they'll happily follow our leader,
For the sake of the grand prize.

There's but a short time,
Until we cross the depths,
Where we shall have heaven on earth,
And meet together in numbers;
And California is the place,
We shall go aloft our banner.

One Who Wishes to See Every Man and Woman a Saint.

Address to the Mormons, or Satanists, Who Misname Themselves *Latter-day Saints*†

PART I

How once, Satanists,—would you dare,
In order to please wicked Joe,
To rise up as faction shouting together,
And declaim a foolish mistaken idea?

The villain took care—of money,
He fought elegantly;
A great moneylender with narrow eyes,
To look after his body.

He won and in holes deceived—many,
With his oaths and his poses;
His guideline was a false plan,
In darkness under cloaks.

One who injures foolish men—a two-mouthed
Wicked wretch;
When a host heard his prattle,
Afterwards, they left God.

Certain foolish, faithless men—would follow
The influence of his false faith;
The word of Joseph, and his Nephi,* and his perversion,
Was stronger than the old religion.

With Joe was all the go—money
The madman got easily:
And we see the respect of the world's ignorant
Which now rises to the hollow opinion.

Gifts upon gifts, for him—they give
Endlessly to please him:
These rise up to keep Jo
Above care, and remember him well.

Treasure upon treasure for the *ungodliness*—of Jo Smith,

† *Seren Gomer* (*Star of Gomer*), June 1848, p. 180.

* One of the names that is in the Joe's play book, which he claims to have received from an angel in a Book to worship him properly.

They make the Judas comfortable;
You become as if you are servant of Satan,
From a multitude of graceless men.

Stupid men from regions—afar,
With not a bit of sense,
Rose in a host with a shout,
To maintain him, yes, hundreds.

An idle man, with a filthy talent—and dishonorable,
Would be thought the worst;
The man spent, said good men**
A foolish contract for a devil here.

An arrogant, sorcerous family—always
At some work for darkness,
From them Jo is sprung—
Sore their appearance as a host will testify.

The most extreme and the worst of the army—issued
From them a wicked host;
Jo is the one with his harsh cry
Who arose as missionary for Satan.

A missionary for the devil, he was—mendacious
Shameful to the peoples,
To his mouth, in hosts,
A thick-skinned man, they listened.

His boys spread, swarmed—to Wales
From crooked rule doubtless,
Over hell with the false devil-host,
Running with nets.

PART II

Satanists, how will you unite—your bitterness
And love of true peace?
You will be scandalizing a hundred, a mass of greed,
And pleasing Satan.

** Namely, scores of responsible people in a state court, who under oath testified that neither Joe, nor his family, nor his relatives were worthy of any trust for any kind of virtue.

O! the gibberish which you make known to the—country,
From some place below,
Which makes the girls
Silly, as they should not be.

An insult against voice is to speak—awkward nonsense,
From a taste for empty praise;
Satan is, till he hits shallows,
A Mormon, a careful man.

Mormons, do not *boil*—to praise
So much the darkness;
Bewitched swarm, in filth and dust,
It's a pity, why do you stay?

Come, Saints, to the fine, pure light—leave
The throng who are with Satan:
Come out completely,
To have peace and virtue on your side.

Every *trickster*, everyone you see—of the babbling
Mob, do not believe;
When these speak with the sense of a sow,
Do not believe, but retreat away.

Flee and run from the offensive—swarm,
They do not know the value of a soul;
Since they are a stupid sort, they must be left,
And their credo, with vagabonds.

Saints, if you are about to leave—your impure country,
On an adventure,
To see life in a pure land,
Let Mormon be your whispering forever.

If whispering about Mormon rubbish—chaff,
Before the faithful word,
Do not *mention*, with your spells,
God's Book and its loud tune.

If you have adventure in you, Saints—to go
To a place over the waves,
Watch the bright *Captain*,
Over there closely, lest he prove deceitful.

The Quack has Quick talents—to deceive
In darkness an empty shallow many
And bewitch every vagrant,
With his skilled learning, Oh! what a filthy man.

Yes, a Captain who understands Coptic—a mild man
Who also knows Egyptian,
The truth is with him, as every language knows,
In the same way that he is a filthy beast.

JOE'S ADDRESS TO HIS PUPPETS AND HIS HALF-WITS
In his greed, yes, truly,
Jo spoke long, with his beautiful Book:
"I got this, the mark is well remembered,
In the earth, and fine sand,
In golden plates, it's worthy of
Our grasp and being rightly remembered.
By an angel it was all hidden,
I assert that in the earth
It was for hundreds of ages, I know,
Without decaying at all as I could see;
To me as an honor, despite the amount there was
Of darkness blinding,
Was given the red-gold Book,
And gold plates will stay the same.
I am a firm prophet,
An Apostle with a single zeal,
I am not sick, I will light the world,
I will win the gold of the whole world;
The Book of Mormon will whisper
With a great shout louder than the Book of the Lord."

A WELL-WISHER TO THE SAINTS.

An Interpretation of the Dream of T. Hughes, Rhuthin.†

Many objects were seen,
Flying through the heavens,
But few of them answered
The notes on the curtain;
John the angel was seen
With the Gospel in his hand,
Which he hid in an old cave
On the land of distant America,
And there it would be kept hidden
Through the ages of the world forever,
Had it not been for the *true godliness*
Of the great Prophet Joe Smith!
But Joe lost parts
Of it, in a fever and trembling,
Nevertheless, there is still plenty
For the Saints who are in the world!
Other objects were seen
By many in our country;
One very strange one was perceived by
The lucky inventor
After reading the notes of the object,
And serious and skillful reflection
I thought at last
That it was fierce Sky Rocket.
In success and happiness,
T. Hughes perceived this,
Shooting and spreading
Its bright sparks, happily.

Abercarn. Little Davy.

† *Seren Gomer* (*Star of Gomer*), August 1848, p. 238.

Llandovery versus Mormonism†

Mormonism is trying
To extend its dwelling place;
To Llandovery it now has gone,—
But it will find no succor there.

For there is no need there
For any of its miracles;
The magic there will thrash its foolish
And strange, empty assertions.

If its missionaries speak
One of the deep languages
Given to the seed of the men of the ark,
The Arch-deacon will know it.

No miraculous help is needed
For any human tongue;
With the power of learning, it's an easy task
To deal with a foreign language.

If they try to come near
A sick man at the brink of his vigil,
They will be driven far away,
And Doctor Thomas sent for.

He is there regularly
Passing among the sick:—
At sending sickness away from its cell,
He's much better than a Mormon.

If they boastfully claim,
They can overcome deadly poison,—
Annihilate serpents, trample the den
Of the lethal scorpions,—

† *Sun*, November 1848, pp. 354–55.

Nearby is Brutus once more,
Killing evil vipers,
Of every color, and every kind,
And he will kill Mormonism.

Therefore I shall end now,
Shouting to the utmost,—
Of every trick that has come to the world,
Mormonism is the meanest.

Glan Bran. ANTI-MORMON.

Invitation to California†

Oh, come to California,
Dear Welshmen, dear Welshmen
Stand here no longer,
Dear Welshmen;
There are heavens for us there,
We shall have land without rent or taxes,
Prepare to come without delay,
Dear Welshmen, dear Welshmen,
Do not tarry here except for that,
Dear Welshmen.

We can get corn without sowing or harrowing,
Everyone believe, etc.,
And bread without baking it,
Everyone believe,
Houses will grow for us from the earth,
Lovely and attractive palaces,
Oh, this is an alluring place,
Everyone believe, etc.,
A place where pain or sorrow will not come,
Everyone believe.

There are geese by the thousands,
Come quickly, etc.,
Running through the streets,
Come quickly,
And those after being roasted
Are ready by lunch,
Who would not go there?
Come quickly, etc.,
With the feast prepared for him,
Come quickly.

There are fat oxen there,
This is heaven, etc.,
And thousands of fat pigs,
This is heaven,
Are waiting by the doors

† *Seren Gomer* (*Star of Gomer*), December 1848, p. 373–74.

With the knives in their throats,
Ready, morning and night,
            This is heaven, etc.,
There is no one with a sparse table,
    This is heaven.

Soon vehicles will run,
            Listen, etc.,
By themselves without horses,
            Listen;
We shall not have to have servants
To serve us, or maids,
There are no problems there,
            Listen, etc.,
To trouble the family of Zion,
    Listen.

Clothes come from the clouds,
            Become Saints, etc.,
Like hail in showers,
            Become Saints;
The cow milks herself,
The milk soon turns to cheese,
The butter comes without effort,
            Become Saints, etc.,
'Tis a sin for you to doze,
    Become Saints.

Give love to the things of the earth,
            Venture forth, etc.,
Some are extremely attractive,
            Venture forth;
Joseph Smith is calling,
A very famous man was he,
There is strength in his name,
            Venture forth, etc.,
Although he had to die,
    Venture forth.

You wealthy farmers,
            Hasten to come, etc.,
Provide work for the splendid auctioneers,
            Hasten to come;

Oh, sell your possessions,
Before the heavy judgments come,
And consume you with the plagues,
  Hasten to come, etc.,
To gain refuge for your souls,
 Hasten to come.

The man of Glantren is about to get under way,
  A great prophet, etc.,
He is zeal from his feet to the crown of his head,
  A great prophet;
He has sold his things,
Already for the journey,
May a fair wind call him to begin,
  Great prophet, etc.,
Until he reaches the land of the Saints,
 Great prophet.

Near Bogeyman's Hole
A Little Wren

Greeting to the Doctor of Madness†

Good day to you today, excellent Doctor of Madness,
Where have you been living these days?
There are many worrying here now, down this way;
Give the people a tonic, they are almost going mad.

The disease is infectious, it consumes like cancer,
It is troubling poor multitudes of the people of Llanybydder;
Some Captain of a Herring Boat brought it here;
For the sake of the weak, put a stop to it.

It swells their throats so they will not swallow reason,
It affects weak headedness; it puts them down terribly;
No Priest or Pope can raise them;
Joe Smith, with his poison, has caused it.

Wil of Over the Hill cannot cure them,
He cursed them, the disease goes on;
John James, the Tinker, gave them two *pills*;
We must confess, his pills did not do the trick.

The signs of the Madness are believing the Book of Mormon,
Going with a false teacher, having a dunk in some river,
And speaking, like geese, quite a multitude of languages,
And performing false miracles to deceive the people.

Under the influence of the Madness is *Will from the Valley of Pride*
Making his faces, to the concern of many;
and *Tom of Laziness Palace* with his oil, anointing
The backsides of wenches, incapable of being ashamed.

Ann Push, Destitute Village, who pulled out her teeth,
Under the influence of madness. Oh! that is a strange thing!
Now her tongue is free to deliver.
In foreign languages, mountains of nonsense.

The ones most tending towards the Madness are children,
Perverse apostates, sin-laden women,

† *Seren Gomer* (*Star of Gomer*), January 1849, p. 17.

Those soft in the head, and senseless little people,
The refuse of humanity, and *arch-adulterers*.

Please, Doctor of Madness, give the people a tonic,
You will be paid for your trouble from the taxes of the poor.
You will be thanked by many, and you will get a song from me,
If you pull the Madness from the Saints' cloaks.

If there must be some *pit* in which to sink them,
Before you can pull the madness from their heads,
The *pit* is ready near the Cave of the *Boogeyman*,
And you are welcome to sink them in there.

A Small Druid.

Beware of False Teachers[†]

O, Zion, awake to your work,
And leave your drowsiness now;
Your adversary openly
Wants to put you down.

His servants, he sends them out,
To bewitch those who are weak;
But he can only get, however great his lust,
The chaff on his side.

God's wheat is too pure
To be cast into the land of briers;
And the pearls of the cross are too highly honored
To be trodden down by these.

They would deceive the true chosen
Children of Heaven, were there a way;
But those ones shout with a louder cry
"Heaven delights us."

When they fail in their deception
In rash enchantment and sickness,
They welcome the refuse of the world,
And call them all "Saints."

They make apostles of these,
Asserting to the extreme
That they alone
Have the great commission of Heaven.

And that they would be received by the angel of God
In some secret place;
And that they alone have the responsibility
Of inhabiting the world to come.

They say that since the days
Of the Apostles before there was no work done
By God in the wide world,
But now is the time it came.

† *Seren Gomer* (*Star of Gomer*), April 1849, p. 116.

Farewell to the Saints[†]

Farewell to the *Smithites*, or the Saints,
Ones great in gifts, and learning, and honor;
May you have success and clear weather,
Until you reach the land of California.

You were useful in our country,
To spread your ideas freely;
In Wales you dealt with the matters of the Word,
But your minds turned to the gold.

Before leaving the soil of your country,
It was gold you thought about undeniably;
And when asleep you would think that now
You were inside the big mine.

It was the gold fever that charmed you,
To leave Wales of great renown;
And a band of men of no grace,
That you would call cruel cheats.

But of what value are dear souls,
That are in this section of the world?
"Let them go to misery," says your word,
"It will not be good for us to lose the gold."

Farewell to your dreadful deceit,
Your people have gone over the sea,
According to your wish; your desire is great,
To collect poor earthly wealth.

T. ab Ieuan

† *Y Drysorfa Gynulleidfaol* (*Congregationalist Treasury*), June 1849, p. 181.

Verses†

Through the mirror, I shall examine the Saints,
The latest chaff of the scoundrel* *Joe Smith*
Their contemptible beliefs I declare
To be a great darkness in our Lord's world.

They boast and they shout in their bondage that it is men
With plentiful talents
That the revelations are now feeding,
They say, in the land of their upbringing.

I do not believe the mighty words,
They are false to my heart
The Saints are surely announcing them abroad
To foster dark practices.

That the miracles of the days of God for the second time alive
Are in good shape.

Was the Mormon and his miracles viewed
In America from Wales
Giving succor to scores
Of sick in a foul-weather summer?

No. Everyone confesses
That not one was cured of his fault.

A fool realizes it is witchcraft that bewitches
Our wretched Saints
And remember that it is being superior
That earns censure as a payment for its style.

The wretched of the world and the more wretched
Of the noble and pure church, are the trash;
And also from an unhealthy terrain
Of despicable drunkards is their lineage.

Carnal and magical works they employ
To create the government.
Wretched Satan has done
In great Eden a change.

---

† *Y Cenhadwr Americanaidd* (*American Messenger*), July 1849, p. 212.

A great surprise it is to me that the emigration
Of good, dear men, more's the pity.
Are enticed to join the mobs;
On the weak, their influence will be worse.

See the good impression they give that they are the light-weight
Sons of Sceva* come again. *See Acts 19:14
To deceive them and to bear them away wounded
To a fine, enlightened country.

Reject them; the good, dear,
Genuine people of God are invaluable;
And the unbelievers, were they to survive
Would be beloved beauty without equal.

From my heart I desire – that you should not go
Dear ones, to join
The saints of sins, while there is
In you a soul uniting.

Minersville. EIDDIL.

More Verses to the Latter-day Saints†

I sing, I offer to give advice—to the saints
To pause a while;
And my prayer today to God:
Open the eyes of the unbelievers.

Oh! Astonishment that is strange it is to mention – and to think
Of the prattle of the men.
Ah! Pointless their pondering,
He does not love heaven who does not love true.

They challenge but do not prove any facts – and pale
From our sight instantly;
Man, forget thy unbelief;
Ah! Hell will be a long-lasting furnace.

They say they can work miracles, – by means of their God,
They try sometimes;
With strange dialects –
Who will believe the false unbelievers.

Minersville.
Dewi Mynwy. [David from Monmouth.]

† *Y Cenhadwr Americanaidd* (*American Messenger*), July 1849, p. 212.

Verses to Mormonism†

Of all people, and of all pains,—I never saw
A worse one than Saintism;
Mormonism is a wall of peat,
Dung of the age, it has gone to nothing.

Remarkable speakers and claim-makers,—that they can
Speak an unknown tongue;
Oh! Joe Smith, it is a curse that
One county bears your dross.

Oh disgrace, we do not believe,—his funny
Religion we do not want;
False doctrine; its worse I know
Will never be brought out of hell!

They claim they can without fail,—wondrously,
Perform miracles without number;
And the Saint can, they tell me,
Do what you want on the spot!

Let him give if he can, to the blindman on his way,—his sight,
That he may see perfectly;
Let him give speech to a dumb person,
And then indeed his work will be very fine.

Or if he can, with no tinge of loss,—bring from the grave
A man to the world—they will rise
Up, to rightful enjoyment,
Then, Sir, I will become a Saint too.

Composed by the late J. W. Hughes (Edeyrn of Anglesey)

† *Y Drysorfa Gynulleidfaol* (*Congregationalist Treasury*), November 1849, p. 340.

Untitled†

What are the saints of the Mormon religion?
If not a gutter for the vomit of the world,
A dunghill of the dregs of the churches.
The cattle gnats of the Pharoah all together;
A family curse, the plague of the neighborhood,
A tribe cursing the people of God,
The servants of slander, abominable deists,
The chaff of society, living maggots.

Biting fleas, gadflies,
Friends of the heart to suck blood;
Dogs barking at the man in the moon,
Murderers of love, in the image of their father;
A wretched company to forge lies,
Flies from hell, halfpenny a quart,
A hornet's club, a bustle of riff-raff,
A shop of idiots—that's smart.

† Y Diwygiwr (Revivalist), February 1850, p. 68.

Verse to the Mormons[†]

Wolves and wanderers full of faults—fools,
Failing to work miracles;
There's no sense in the false guides,
Nor truth in their words.

OWAIN ARAN

† *Y Dysgedydd* (*Instructor*), April 1850, p. 120.

A Remarkable Story†

Let everyone who has ears listen
To these lines,
You may hear a true story,
Which is famous and surprising,
About a faction of a new religion
Which is beginning in our country,
Curing every disease,
And giving their work cheaply.

A man came from the town of Carmarthen
To live in the town of Llandovery,
And this was the chief Satan,
In all humanity;
He gives the spirit
In measure to them,
And speaks foreign tongues,
Ba le! Ba la! Ba loo!

You only need to believe
All these people's rule,
The pox and the itching get better,
The cough and the ague:
Benny Bwt went with his bottle
To work in his house,
He intended to cast the devil
From Nanny, Cwmsarnddu.

There he did his best,
Calling "*Sam-ba-la!*"
With the devil in Nanny
Laughing, *Wah! Wah! Wah!*
Nanny went into great passions,
Swearing on the floor,
"If you were going to work miracles,
Why don't you do it now?"

† *Seren Gomer* (*Star of Gomer*), May 1850, p. 149.

"Miracles!" said Benny,
"Yes, many times before this,
I have caused men to be surprised,
While faith is in power;
I have the keys
To the whole wide kingdom of heaven,
And it is an apostolic religion
That we have on our journey.

"Blissful are those who believe us,
That is the faithful servants of the Lord,
They may go to California,
Where they will be without pain;
All the Saints will gather
From the four corners of the earth,
That is, everyone of an honest heart,
They may occupy the sheltering kingdom."

"To work miracles,
You silly, nasty Satan,
You tell frightful lies,
For the sake of getting hearty food;
Oh! may the morning dawn,
When the gospel of God
Will chase away all Satanists
Who are now in the land of the living.

"Oh, shut up about miracles,
I won't believe for the life of me,
Leave alone your telling of lies
While you're in earshot of me?"
At this Benny cried
"Oh! Oh! Oh, dear me!
Now I have to yield
To Nanny, Cwmsarnddu."

Siencyn

The Latter-day Saints[†]

It is readily seen that a putrid plague,
Is the spirit of the wandering Saints;
It is the followers of *Smith*, the son of the black devil,
Who seek to deceive our dear nation.

Futile and foolish they boastfully declare
Their power to work miracles as did Paul;
To give a foot to one, and a hand to the other,
And eyes to the poor blind!!

They subdue the power of the devil,
And raise up the dead to life;
Move mountains, extinguish fire,
And work a myriad of small miracles.

Their principles are filled
With the stench of hell, that is their gift;
If they cannot truly repent,
Before long their place will be hell.

Holyhead
Dafydd Williams

† *Yr Amserau* (*Times*), 17 December 1851, p. 1.

Impromptu Verses to the Mormons†

This I have to say without delay—
A plaintive and serious task—
A pity we have to cross
Anyone of our own kind.

Behold ungifted black magicians—all
Wanting to trick each soul,
And some dark hideous swarm—lowly minstrels,
The old Mormons we wish they were dead.

They utter without mercy—lies
Shamefully strange,
With a distracted, ravenous air
They claim great vengeance.

They promise truly,—as a joke,
That they can work miracles;
But a brittle selfish boast
Comes empty from their mouths.

Disrespectful, distrustful dragons,—furthermore,
Shockingly irrational,
Therefore, what contentious throng
But these are the chaff.

Pushed, without a second threat,—they were
Before apologetic talk;
And their retreat was orderly
Clearly every soul from our land.

All after being thoroughly chased,—a weak troop,
From England and Wales,
Roughly they go despite plague troublesome
And fierce to California.

Now after their vigor,—imprudent course,
And their deserved disappointment,
Dully the great wonder
What worse they will do next.

† *Y Dysgedydd* (*Instructor*), April 1852, p. 119.

The Mormons†

Who are the wandering strangers,
Of devilish, poisonous tongue,
Who swear on some frightful whim
That God has called them to the work?
They are doubtless Joe Smith's followers,
Maintaining lies throughout the land;
The old tricksters of hell are easily known,
They are the spitting image of their father.

The most wretched dregs of society
Are these wanderers, fool-headed priests;
They roar great webs of lies,
All reason is left behind:
They turn the heads of the foolish rabble,
And immerse them at night in a frenzy;
Brainless, weak-headed gad-flies,
Are the swarm who are caught in their net.

A fine religion to the taste of mortals,
It gives the comforts of the here and now;
Their hope is in the things of this world,
Their faith in the California gold!
They perform wondrous false miracles,
They make the blind more blind,
They teach hard workers to be idle,
And send their children on the parish.

Holyhead
Clwydfardd

† *Y Drysorfa Wesleyaidd* (*Wesleyan Treasury*), June 1852, p. 207.

The Fall of the Anti-Christ†

An array of wonders
At times filled my mind,
Upon perceiving the folly
And the emptiness in the world,
The angels are surprised
That men beneath the heaven
Refuse the true doctrine
Of the Man who was on the cross.

I perceive a throng of people
Who profess to be
Second to the apostles,
But far from accomplishing their objective,
They prefer to be known
As "saints" here and there,
But I know that they will not be known
As such in the days to come.

It is said that the Mormons
Are wicked and wild people
And that they can work miracles
As in the days of old,
Namely to cause the blind to see,
And the lame to walk freely,
And the mute to speak
If he has the faith.

The wicked Mormon says
That it is appropriate for man
To have a great number of wives
All to himself;
But reason and the scripture
Clearly forbids it,
For Adam had only
Eve in the garden.

† *Y Cenhadwr Americanaidd* (*American Messenger*), August 1852, p. 253.

The Holy Bible speaks
Truth to us that
No one will go to the heavenly kingdom
Unless he has accepted it,
It says, to the adulterer,
In a rather agitated voice,
That the fiery pit of the devil
Will be part of his cup.

I understand that several thousand
People are under heaven
Serving the beast
From now until they accomplish their objective,
Among which are seen
Evil heathens of their kind
Who dare to say that emptiness
Is all the book of God amounts to.

The deceit of Mormonism will end,
Catholicism will have the same fate,
Before the Archangel is heard
Above the world shouting
That all the kingdoms of the earth
Henceforth belong to our Lord,
At that time no one will believe
That which they assert.

The Pope will say boldly
To flawless men
That it is he who has authority
To forgive all sin,
We prefer to believe the scripture
Which clearly confirms
That it is to one who lives eternally
That the pardon of faults belongs.

The Pope will say again
In order to go to the pit of hell
He can make the transfer
From distress to happiness above,
Because he is a learned man
Like some wise ruler

He has the money
To take them from fiery purgatory.

The poor Catholics will come,
Those who reverence the wooden cross
More than the man who was on it
Suffering pain and agony,
To say in a special manner
There is beneath the heavens
Only Jesus Christ
Throughout the world to rule.

Although the uncivilized papist,
While on our earth,
Moved about in honor
And revered greatness and prestige,
I see that Catholicism,
Despite its ostentation and power,
According to the language of prophecy,
Is bound to come to nothing.

The Father himself presents
To the Son as a gift,
The furthest extremes of the earth
That is uncivilized mankind,
He shall have all the nations
As hosts to heal,
The truth will hunt out
And destroy every false religion.

May the lovely and blessed morning come,
According to the truthful promise,
May the stone that Daniel saw
Roll across the earth,
May it completely crush
The evil idol and its like,
And may the world come to reverence
The truth and the living God.

O Lord, strengthen thy servants
To yet deliver to the field
For the benefit of the damned soul
The everlasting wealth of grace,
And the waters of Salvation
To wash away its stain,
Until the whole world becomes completely
In possession of worthy Jesus.

William Watkins
Llewelyn, Pa., May 13, 1852

Verses[†]

To the Latter-day Saints

Latter-day Saints—there is a miracle,
If I follow true power,
I shall flee from the disgrace of lies,
To better men, if I find deceit.

The value of miraculous gifts is very good—if they are
Based in reality;
If an invention learned from a devil,
The Lord will throw it back to the devil.

The fruit of the tree of Eden, and its passions rule
Many sham saints;
The spirit of the devil, miraculously false,
Promised—they would be gods.

Saints, and their days will end—there is no value
In a miracle from deceit, only disappointment–
With the same deceit with which they deceive,
In the hand of truth, they will be deceived.

lolo Gwyddolwern

† *Seren Gomer* (*Star of Gomer*), June 1853, p. 278.

Mormons Leaving Abergele Last Year[†]

Fleeing from Abergele—flew,
Some swam in the guise of saints,
Who can say after they have moved further
That they will not sail after them?

Crowding together, a large foolish herd—vainly
To the heaven of the mad,
A poor heaven for the ungodly,
Despite speaking and crossing the sea.

They are frightful and harmful weeds—they grow
Along the fields of the devil;
Or a swarm of men who enchant
All around the country speaking nonsense.

A Welshman

† *Gwron Cymreig* (*Welsh Hero*), 3 August 1854.

Song†

In the manner of a conversation between Mother and Son on the day of the Son's departure to the Salt Valley, he being one of the Latter-day Saints.

THE MOTHER
Oh! David why do you now leave
Your Mother to grieve for you so;
Who studied your dearest face,
Who nursed you upon her lap?
Oh, don't break my aching heart,
Don't load so my spirit with grief;
Why not be content to stay home
As always in times hitherto?

THE SON
Sweet mother, is this the last time
I'll ever behold your face?
Such a thought is just like a spear
Piercing my very heart;
But I must set forth whatever the pain—
So farewell, farewell my mother;
You'll never be far from my mind—
I'll always retain you there.

THE MOTHER
Oh, don't leave the land of your birth
In order to seek out the Valley;
To search for a treasure which will,
No doubt, only disappoint;
Seek wealth of eternal duration,
By the ordinance of God in One,
He'll keep you in death and in judgment
When the kindness of others is done.

THE SON
From sight of my native land,
I'll speed to the Valley to live
For joy and repose without end
And the greatest of any wealth;

---

† *Y Tywysydd a'r Gymraes* (*The Guide and the Welsh Woman*), September 1854, p. 182.

In death it's as strong as a rock,
Will never retreat with the tide;
If will be my mate and my friend—
Mormon, Mormon—that's him!

THE MOTHER
Oh! David, why do you not keep
But break this essential command
Laid down by the Prince of our lives,
Creator of heaven and earth:
Obedience to parents who bore you
And the fifth command of the Word,
Both promise a lengthy existence—
An extension to these your days?

THE SON
Leaving my dearest friendships
Now heavily lies on my breast;
My heart is also now breaking
At leaving my parents' embrace;
But go I must, with moistened cheek
Though resolute of step,
And saying as my journey starts,
Farewell, farewell, my mother.

THE MOTHER
Oh! child, who can share such sorrow
As that in your mother's heart
In seeing the jaws of the ocean
Awaiting to swallow you whole?
Those furious salt waves are arising
And climbing the sides of your ship;
Your prospect is not of the Valley
But a grave in the ocean deep.

THE SON
Mother, this is a high calling—
To travel despite all constraints:
Here soon there will be hard dealings
Of fire, green brimstone and all;
Ours is a happy voyage, led by a worthy Guide.
He'll steer our ship ever-onward;
All will go smoothly, don't worry—
Farewell, farewell my mother.

THE MOTHER
Oh! David, consider the ocean
And see how the vessels all weave
Over its green-surfaced surging,
The weary affliction you'll know;
The fearful, storm-driven thunder
Will open such fear in your heart,
While you, so forlorn and so helpless,
Will roll on the swell of the waves.

THE SON
Not fearing the wind or sea-rage
Boldly, I shall press on,
To the distant Valley beyond the tides,
Where friends are gathered now;
There'll be a feast like none before
There, where I'll keenly tread,
Declaring as I travel forth,
"Farewell, farewell" my mother.

THE MOTHER
There is no need of a Vale of Salt
Nor California land
For a Latter-day Saint,
To voyage forth
To gain a fuller share
Of all salvation's joy—
For Jesus who was crucified
Encompasses the world.

THE SON
Perfect joy abides but there
Where sickness is not known;
Within the Valley's happy bounds
No winter, only Summer comes;
And there our dear prophet* lives,
His loving spirit stays,
With *Book of Mormon* close at hand—
My parents both, farewell!

* Joseph Smith

Achddu—W. R.

The Mormons†

The "Saints of the Latter days,"—blindly,
Are deceivers of the utmost;
Bold enemies of the Lord God
Is the appearance, of the worst kind.

They profess, shouting with words—seemingly,
They are able to perform miracles;
But the false bandits are wolves,
They cherish telling lies.

They are hidden wizards—intentions
They have as of vipers;
Followers of Endor are they,
That is the truth about them.

Faulty, indecent magicians—infected,
Beyond old Simon;
Promised seed of wicked enchanters
Greedy from the root.

They seek for themselves—tradition
To pierce such as crying;
The worst college of Rome,
Under a curse, is the guise of these.

Woe to those men that give credence—to their fierce
Hellish teaching;
Could a devil, of ugly enchantment,
Full of complaint, design worse?

Let every man care for his heart—not ever believe,
Such horrible lies;
Away with faithless rigmarole
Like mist before breezes.

---

† No publication date. Bound with other items.

A New Song, Setting Out†

Journey of the Saints to California, together with their wish to return back to the land of their birth, namely Wales.

On the wave—Railway Speed

Now friends come and listen,
To the Bard picturing truly,
The scene he had here,
That sent him into a fainting fit.
That was so great in the world
That was so great in the world
Magnifying Dan and Josi,
For preparing such a comfortable country.

On my journey I went to Merthyr,
On a Saturday when idle,
To get a view of the crowd
That were going to California.
That was so great etc.

There were some singing,
And others preaching,
And the women prophesying
Of the delicacies after going there.
That was so great etc.

There were some there feasting,
On their faith in California,
Where they will have eternal life,
Without more oppression nor enemy.
That was so great etc.

There were some through the morning
Intending to perform miracles,
To heal some worthy Collier.
On his journey to Mount Zion.
That was so great etc.

I saw Hawker Tea raising,

† No publication date. Bound with other items.

His grey wings aloft,
And shouting, "O My Father."
With his hands upon the head of the Collier.
  That was so great etc.

After understanding and considering,
The brother was mortified,
Without a hope of being healed,
While the days of his life lasted.
  That was so great etc.

2

Then Captain Jones, Llangollen,
Rose up like a snail,
To speak with the people,
California is heaven.
  That was so great etc.

After singing and praying,
I heard Dan blessing them,
A Book of Mormon in his hands,
Oh such deceit was in the fox
  That was etc.

They all started from Merthyr,
After receiving such comfort,
On their journey to California –
Mount Zion, City of Refuge.
  That was etc.

Leaving loving Father and Mother,
Leaving dear old friends,
Leaving brothers and sisters,
In order to follow Dan and his religion.
  That was etc.

Leaving the amiable Independents.
Leaving the gentle Weslyans;
Leaving the Methodists too,
Leaving the Baptists, buying adversity.
  That was etc.

Leaving Merthyr, leaving Hirwain
Leaving Nation, and Waunhelygain,

Leaving Britain and Blaenafon,
Nantyglo, and Aberafon.
 That was etc.

Leaving Cyffin, leaving Llwyni,
Also leaving the Rhymni Valley.

3

Leaving Dowlais and Sirhowy,
Abersychan, and Llanelli,
 That was etc.

Leaving Aberdare and Onllwyn,
Without fear of meeting an enemy
Penycae and Victoria town.
I will go to California.
 That was etc.

Having reached California,
Land of the Saints and City of Refuge,
They were forced to sleep there,
On the ground without a bed.
  Oh how grey is their appearance,
  Oh how grey is their appearance,
  Without either savior or religion
 But looking in fear to the grave.

Having woken in the morning,
There were here no places,
Or any hope of getting bread,
Over on the hills of California.
 Oh how grey etc.

There everyone together,
Began to leap to the president,
And asking him at once,
Of the country named mount Zion.
 Oh how grey etc.

After this everyone doted,
In their wrath towards Dan and Josi;
We would be blessed to be in Wales,
Instead of listening to the sharp dog.
 Oh how grey etc.

None of the Saints thought
That Zion was such torture,
But now we are like an owl,
Having believed D-n Llangollen.
 Oh how grey etc.

To what place went the Prophet,
And the old Captain that was crowned,
To lead them to glory,
As he formerly related so forcefully.
 Oh how grey etc.

4

I read in the "Star," [*Star of Gomer*]
That the Captain has seven wives,
And these are spiritual,
The Saints told the people.
 Oh how grey etc.

One Monday night, one Wednesday night,
One Tuesday night, one Friday night;
One Thursday night, one Saturday night,
And the seventh Sunday night I suppose.
 Oh how grey etc.

There are also twenty-five,
With the President for himself,
To be like Solomon and David,
Say the Saints, are Dan and the President.
 Oh how grey etc.

Richard Jones sent a letter,
To Llanelli quite correctly,
Of the hunger and the poverty,
Come to meet with the happy family.
 Oh how grey etc.

Having read there the letter,
No one received any comfort,
After hearing of the hanging,
That came upon the family of Josi.
O how grey etc.

Some in California ,
Had no pardon for their sins,
They were condemned to death,
For transgressing the law of Holiness.
Oh how grey etc.

In finishing this song,
I hope you have heard;
Our sure wish here
Is to come back from California.
Oh if we had not come,
Oh if we had not come,
All the host over the sea,
Then we would sing sweet praise.

Ieuan Cadfan (Breece, Evan)
J. T. Jones, Publisher, Carmarthen.

Amusing Song†

Giving a little of the story of Twm the Tailor, from Cardiff, having left his craft of tailoring to preach with the Latter-day Saints!!

1

Every quite noisy Welshman, that is listening to this song,
You must not laugh, in case of preventing going on;
Everyone listen quietly, you will hear every detail,
Namely of some wondrous event that was in the world;
Namely the story of Twm the Tailor, without sense became a Saint,
Who was accursed, although of small stature:
He was shouting like an ass, and reeling drunk,
From drinking to excess without observing a Sunday!

(Chorus)
He was shouting like an ass, and was reeling drunk,
From drinking to excess without observing a Sunday!

2

A meeting had been arranged to take place in a church.
The tailor promised to come to say his piece;
A chair was placed in the middle, upon this he stood erect,
His skull was spotted with pleading to them;
But the chair fell without warning,
And threw the amiable tailor gently on his backside,
Everyone was of ugly appearance, laughing at him now,
He was found after the fall, like a young animal on the ground.
He was shouting like an ass etc.

3

Some Saints, their privilege and fame obvious,
Bringing Will the Barber's barrow to carry Twm to the house;
And finding himself there, Twm said—
"I'm sure my collar-bone is out of place."
The doctor came pleasantly and a good physician to Twm,
He asked the friends, "What caused such a heavy fall:"
But the fool fell and scraped his behind,
And the words in his mouth were of the Apostle Paul.
He was shouting like an ass etc.

† No publication date. Bound with other items.

4

Another doctor came next day, to see little Thomas,
As it was generally seen that the man wasn't well;
After reaching the bed, he could hear perfectly,
"That Thomas the Reverend was 'a little better.'
He made a mustard plaster to place on his breast,
Saying in English- "My man I've done my best,
So now you must take care when in the open air,
Preaching to the people, and standing on a chair."
He was shouting like an ass etc.

5

After a little time we heard the tailor shouting in anger,
That the mustard plaster was drawing like fire;
He was tied fast by his feet and hands to the bed posts,
Because the mustard plaster was not half to his taste.
Twm was shouting "Murder," to get the plaster off,
And the doctor said, "That it was better not to meet him.
Such a racket was never heard on land or sea,"
And the doctor said, "His head must be shaved I'm sure."
He was shouting like an ass etc.

6

Again they began to treat his shoulder,
After much boxing, they pictured their place;
Two were holding Thomas, and two pulling the arm,
And Twm was groaning, like a pig under its load;
And he was begging hard for them to be gentle,
He would leave preaching, and stick to his work.
There was never such a turn, in town, or hill, or district,
I'm sure if I have health to live to remember him.
He was shouting like an ass etc.

7

This gives a warning to every gentle clothier
Not to become a preacher, but stick to his work,
It is better to work with cabbages, than do something worse,
Like Twm telling lies, fashioning by the yard,
He is an earnest topic through all the area,
And some are for sending the ram away from the world;
But he was thrown in one lump by falling on his rump,
The healthy man will remember his fall excellently.
He was shouting like an ass etc.

By Evan Davies (Ieuan ap Job), Penydarran.

A New Song†

Namely a Self-reflection of the Dream of the Mormons, those who call themselves Latter-day Saints, on their journey to California.

What is the great noise I hear?
What do I see?
Like an armed host, fine and flashing,
Or some bannered throng,
So unassailable, traveling bravely
Toward the Western land,
By the great promises of the Book of Mormon
They will find Zion and its blessings;
They all are from great to small with their fine tuneful song,
All brothers of true heart,
Deny the Pure Scriptures:
And all the birds of the woods,
And the fish of the vast seas,
Sweetly sing that they wish them
Success on their journey;
They cure, says Kitti Pugh, all types of sickness,
The destructive pox and the fatal cholera
Which ravage mankind,
They are able to cure Dropsy,
And the Itch which is so terrible,
Yellow Fever, Swelling, and Glands,
And burning by the fiery element.

They make the deaf hear clearly
And the blind see daylight;
From old prisons the Saints set
The captive free of their chains:
The Tertian Ague too, and the Feverish Cold,
And every tiresome ailment,
And Indigestion which always wastes
Man's whole constitution;
The man with the wooden legs has at last become,
Through the power of Sion Dyfed and Dewi Elfed
As healthy as ever;
And Great was the suffering of Guto the Grinder,

† No publication date. Bound with other items.

And Ned the little Collier,
From Erysipelas and nasty Boils,
They now are quite well;
Farewell to tiresome pains which destroy man's nature,
The lunatic and the possessed are healed,
The doctor is awake:
They cure Chilblains, and Corns on Big toes,
And painful Warts,
And Red Eyes, and Running Noses
For the weak at no cost.

They are the subjects of the king of Babel,
And Jezebel and her seed,
And the old priests of Pharaoh Necho,
Who are set on deceiving the country;
These are the angry worshippers of Dagon,
And old Balzephon,
Who now support the army of Pluto,
And pray to the wind;
They swear undeniably that they have permission,
Through the faultless rule of Joe and Hiram,
And Balaam full of treachery;
That they can raise the dead
To the shore in the name of Joe,
The ones who are in death's clutches,
Are safe and sound on the shingle;
Therefore gather nearer, the faith is at its hottest
By the Salt Lake with the Captain,
The men with the brass forehead;
On the banks of the Sacramento river,
Where Fantago dwells,
A Devil was bound by a powerful chain –
Mankind's old enemy.

They choose some of the wise ones,
To go to mount Zion,
In California, to the sons of Sceva,
To fill the office of the Lake,
Where their Captain from Llangollen
Tames the fiery element,
In the name of great Cowdry and Josi,

The pure old prophets;
The Saints strong and weak, come from Babylon to the shore,
After they have stopped chewing tobacco,
Or smoking anywhere;
The brethren speak in a foreign tongue,
Through this the gift is shown,
Of the Saints each day so the countries believe,
That they have the proper faith
After they have paid the tax and the tithe without fail,
The Saints despite grief gain wealth
By taking the odd thing;
And Tea and Coffee must be sacrificed,
And Snuff and Whiskey completely,
The wise means of the Saints
Will shed light in the evening.

The great President of the countries
Gives his warning to everyone,
While taking the great crowd from Britania
To the lair of California,
Where now hundreds who went from Wales
Are clearly under hardship's sway,
Captives over in a foreign land,
The words are true enough.
This memory came to mind about little Jonny Blacksmith,
Who made his escape to California,
His story here I'll tell;
He was sacrificed on the altar of indolence,
And carried by the wind
Toward the Salt Lake to the Captain's company,
With his four score pounds;
He is quickly called as an official in their court,
And Thomas Gilbert and old Will Herbert,
And Nedi Robert Rhys
And Shon Llewelyn and Dafydd Siencyn,
And a nephew of Robin Hood,
And Nathaniel's wife, whose grip is strong
For fairing Daniel Good.

And before I end I could name

A host of this family,
Who are with Hiram Smith and Josi
All around the lake;
Some Lady went, once from Kidwelly
Her name I need not tell,
The strength of her love for some Mormon
Filled her joyful gaze;
She ventured over the water, ignoring scorn and fuss,
In her passion she went after the Saints,
Because of the weakness of loving her husband;
And Ifor Ivan and Meurig Morgan,
And some old Nathan Llwyd,
Like Bili's wife Sian went to the same company,
So as to tame the passion;
Many were seen selling land and houses,
Going singing and rejoicing
After false prophets,
They today are under enemies' feet,
Amidst the black people,
Saying out loud, The slaves of Babel
Were more at ease than we.

Thomas Murray (Highway Saint) who sings it.

Saints of a Latter-Day: A Rhyme

SAINTS OF A LATTER-DAY:

A RHYME

FOR THE

PRINCIPALITY OF WALES.

BY J. H. MARSHALL.

"IF MEN CANNOT BE REASONED OUT OF THEIR FOLLY, THEY SHOULD BE RIDICULED OUT OF IT."—*Lavater*.

PRINTED FOR THE AUTHOR.

PREFACE.

MANY readers will doubtless object to the manner in which the Author has handled certain portions of his subject; but he thinks their censures will be considerably mitigated when they take into consideration the numberless absurdities which these people run into. This trifle was composed for those readers amongst whose ranks the designing find their dupes and fanaticism its victims, and should any object that there are passages of a somewhat indecent character in the following pages, the Latter-day Saints are the proper parties with whom to settle their objections.

For did they breathe a Christian spirit,
Naught should we say to their discredit.

LLANDOVERY, MAY 8th, 1851.

SAINTS OF A LATTER-DAY.

"If men cannot be reasoned out of their folly, they should be ridiculed out of it."—LAVATER.

A class of men there is on earth,
Whose judgment is of little worth;
Poor wretches, who to us appear
Like asses, though of shorter ear;
From fools like these great rogues prevail,
To get their bread by some strange tale;
No matter how absurd the story,
To disbelieve they would be sorry;
They are not prone to contradiction,
But love to swallow every fiction,
And he who starts the grossest fable,
To earn success is surest able.

Hail, superstition, mighty power,
Thy reign is great this present hour;
Not only in the distant east,
Where men bow down to block or beast,
Nor far beyond the Atlantic's roar,
But even at our neighbour's door,

4

Thou holds't firm sway and seeks't to bind
With iron grasp the human mind.
Though o'er vast regions thou dost roam,
America's thy fitting home.
'Twas there Joe Smith besought thy aid
To drive a snug fanatic trade;
For worldly trouble, toil, and care,
Were more than he would meanly bear;
The soil around him wanted tilling,
But then, alas! he was not willing;
His frame by labour had been tired,
So he resolved to be inspired.
This wily knave the world has told,
That certain angels did unfold (1)
To him, in vision, trance, or dream—
Their robes were white without a seam—
Where Mormon's (2) book did lay concealed,
And unto him it was revealed;
It was not of an earthly mould,
Its letters all were heav'nly gold,
And God had chosen his frail spirit
To propagate its secret merit;
They pointed out to him the place
Where he should found a chosen race
Of people, free from spot or taint,
And christen each Latter-day Saint.
Their sins already were forgiven,
And none but they could enter heaven,
With God to dwell, by angels nursed,
When all mankind beside were cursed;
It was ordained he should be king,
Or great high priest, or some such thing,

5

To lead this people all to glory,
Such is a part of his strange story.

This tale took well, for people ran
To dwell with this most godly man;
They were to have all things in common,
Naught excepted, only woman;
Nor even that when 'twas her study
To serve the cravings of her body;
Her king could grant her absolution,
Should she be caught in prostitution.
The farmer sold his ploughs and chattels,
To furnish Joe with cloth and victuals;
The blacksmith gave up forge and bellows,
To swell the treasure of these fellows;
The painter left his oils and paints,
To add one fool more to the saints;
The tinker timely notice gave us,
That naught on earth but they could save us.
The labourer threw down his hod,
To join the chosen of his God;
But he who had no goods in store,
Could find no entrance at that door.

Time rolled on, and sweetly too,
At least it proved such to Joe;
His house, his furniture and cloak,
Were all derived from other folk.
He said it was 'mongst God's decrees (3)
That he should keep all their monies.
(We think we hear a voice exclaim,
"That was the beauty of the game.")

A3

6.

He further said 'twas God's commands (4)
That he should not work with his hands;
But they must toil and till the ground,
Whilst he did study and propound
All mysteries which to them were given,
For which he was ordained by heaven.
But disaffection will creep in,
'Mongst saints as well as sons of sin;
We often find that worldly joy
Is tinged with some base alloy;
That disappointment is our doom,
Whilst journeying this side the tomb.
A farmer (5) who had gone from Kent,
To see the book was firmly bent;
To gaze upon this golden prize,
He thought would much enrich his eyes.
The king and elders said this notion
Would militate against devotion;
And thought to vanquish all his fears,
By telling him to mind his prayers.
The farmer quickly took occasion
To call this conduct mere evasion;
The films from his weak eyes did fall;
He saw they had no book at all,
At least that they had not a gold one.
But one they had which was an old one,
Which he who held the highest station,
Declared was its true translation.
The farmer deemed this delusion,
Which brought about a strange confusion;
His hardy frame was so much heated,
That he did swear he had been cheated;

7

His voice assum'd its harsher tones,
He said the elders all were drones,
Who had, with Smith, this plan contrived,
To plunder those whom they had hived;
That all their deeds were fraught with evil,
As if they were saints of the devil.
His footsteps thence he quickly bent,
To find the gainest way to Kent.

The farmer's tale spread far and wide,
"What fools!" "What rogues," too, many cried.
The storm near Smith arose still higher,
For he was called shameless liar;
And round him rose such bitter strife,
That 'mongst it Joseph lost his life,
Of which he made a goodly barter,
For "knave" was exchanged for "martyr."

The elders mourned, their king being dead,
For by his aid they got their bread;
But as he'd taught them how to thrive,
They swore to keep the game alive;
To propagate their vile contagion,
To every far and distant region.
From England, where it droops and fails,
It was imported into Wales;
And here its doings to rehearse,
Will somewhat soil our feeble verse.

At Merthyr Tydvil, we have heard,
Which story we tell word for word,
A sister of this sect or craft,
Of human life became bereft.

8

The brethren could not afford
" To give this sister to the Lord ;"
She'd earned more than absolution,
By paying well her contribution ;
She'd scraped all for her dear friends,
Aye, even to her candles' ends.
For this to life they would restore her,
For never better came before her ;
And to astound both lay and clerical,
They would perform a lasting miracle.
They could restore lost sight 'twas said,
Then why not try to raise the dead.
One of these crazy hair-brain'd fellows,
Implor'd a blessing on a bellows,
Which he filled with wind in vain,
Eor bringing her to life again.
This being done, a few did bend
Around their much lamented friend ;
All high in hope and expectation
Of witnessing her resurrection ;
At length a noise or crack was heard,
And some one said " her foot had stirr'd !"
Which made them shout—so runs the story,
" She lives ! she lives ! Oh, Glory ! Glory ! !"
But soon they find the noise or crack,
Was merely wind a coming back.
And 'twas declared by Brother Sutton,
That she remain'd as dead as mutton ;
Which they confess'd with crimson'd face,
Then altogether left the place,
Suspecting themselves only fools,
At saving or restoring souls.

9.

Romantic Neath, in thy sweet vale,
This pestilence now swells the gale;
The idle oft in Wind-street prowl,
To catch its melancholy howl.
There in a room they often find,
One blind man leading many blind;
Delightful task, in pulpit leaning,
Explaining that which hath no meaning;
Confounding all with mystic fable,
Until the place appears a Babel.
Telling strange tales in voice of thunder,
That fill the moonstruck with such wonder;
That after their departure thence,
They understand not common sense.
The rogues with such strange phantoms tease them,
That naught but miracles will please them
And to convince us they are holy,
Right overhead they plunge in folly,
Or something worse, as we shall show,
As longer this our tale doth grow.
They ask at every house they reach,
If they may be allow'd to preach;
One of them called at a dwelling,
Where one poor girl was sick and ailing;
He saw the creature somewhat faint,
And told her that he was a saint,
That if he laid his hands upon her,
She would be whole, upon his honour,
And as she was a poor lost sinner,
He must create new life within her,
That when her soul in bliss had shared,
Her body soon would be repaired!

Her parents looked with mistrust,
Upon this piece of saintly dust;
But as the daughter was intent,
To try her luck they gave consent.
The man began with his grimaces,
He pray'd, and groan'd, and made wry faces,
And worked with such saintly skill,
The maid forgot that she was ill;
And often did he go that way,
With her to sit, and watch, and pray,
To guard her from all earthly evil,
And chase the promptings of the devil;
And by his aid good health was brought her,
For daily she was growing stouter;
Until at length—unlucky morn,
A baby to this maid was born!
This saint, therefore, deserves his due,
For what he said had proved true:
He must awaken this poor sinner,
By creating "new life within her."

We here conclude, in hope that Wales
Will purge itself of idle tales;
There are no saints in this our day,
No matter what thick-heads may say;
And few good men, who here have striven,
By virtue's path to enter heaven.
But fanatics abound to loathing,
Who prowl amongst us in false clothing;
Should one upon you call to preach,
And imposition wish to teach,

To California bid him sail,
Where scoundrels will his coming hail:
But as for you, your spirit fails,
To think of leaving Christ and Wales.

NOTES TO LATTER-DAY SAINTS.

(1). "That certain Angels did unfold to him."

Immediately he was enwrapped in a heavenly vision and saw two glorious personages dressed in white garments, which were seamless. They informed him that his sins were forgiven, that all other denominations were believing in incorrect doctrines, &c. &c. &c.—*Extracted from a Pamphlet published by* Mister *Pratt, who styles himself one of the twelve apostles of the Church of Latter-day Saints, aud who is their Emigrational Agent in Liverpool.*

(2). "Where Mormon's book did lay concealed."

People have often wondered what the word "Mormon" meant. It is easily explained: Mormi or Mormon, is the Greek for humbug, or hobgoblin, and paraphrastically for delusion or counterfeit. Little did that crafty impostor, Joe Smith, with all his craftiness, suspect the close fitting cap he was making for his own imposture, when he gave his statute book the name of "the Book of Mormon," literally meaning the "Book of Humbug."—*Welshman, Sept.* 27, 1850.

(3). "He said it was 'mongst God's decrees."

Hearken unto me, saith the Lord your God, for it is not wisdom in me that any one should be entrusted with the Commandments and the monies which are to go into the land of Zion, but my servant Joseph Smith, who is true and faithful.—*A Revelation of Dec.* 1830.—*News of the World.*

(4). "He further said, 'twas God's commands,
He should not labour with his hands."

A revelation given in February, 1831, says—"If ye desire the mysteries of my kingdom, provide Joseph Smith, Jun., food and raiment and whatsoever thing he needeth." "In temporal matters," says another revelation of July, 1831, "Thou shalt not have strength, for that is not thy calling. Attend to thy calling, and thou shalt have wherewithal to magnify thine office and expound all scripture." —*News of the World, Aug.* 4, 1850.

(5). "A farmer who had gone from Kent,
To see the book was firmly bent."

From a letter which was sent to England by this man, in 1833, and which was published in the London weekly papers, we learn that there was no such thing to be seen as a golden book, for he had frequently asked permission to look at it, and had always been put off with some paltry excuse, and that he had discovered that he had been imposed upon.

(6). "But one they had which was an old one."

It was at length discovered that the leading ideas of Mormonism were taken from a manuscript romance which had got into the hands of the parties.—*News of the World, Aug.* 4, 1850.

PRINTED AT THE TIMES OFFICE, WIDEMARSH-STREET, HEREFORD.

Index

M

Q

R

S

T

Y

Z